KERUX COMMENTARIES

GENESIS

KERUX COMMENTARIES

GENESIS

A Commentary for Biblical Preaching and Teaching

JOHN M. SODEN

RANDAL EMERY PELTON

Genesis: A Commentary for Biblical Preaching and Teaching

Published by Kregel Ministry, an imprint of Kregel Publications, 2450 Oak Industrial Dr. NE, Grand Rapids, MI 49505-6020.

Italics in Scripture quotations indicate emphasis added by the authors.

The Hebrew font, NewJerusalemU, and the Greek font, GraecaU, are available from www.linguistsoftware.com/lgku.htm, +1-425-775-1130.

Cataloging-in-Publication Data is available from the Library of Congress.

ISBN 978-0-8254-2550-9

Printed in China

25 26 27 28 29 / 5 4 3 2 1

Contents

PUBLISHER'S PREFACE TO THE SERIES

Since words were first uttered, people have struggled to understand one another and to know the main meaning in any verbal exchange.

The answer to what God is talking about must be understood in every context and generation; that is why Kerux (KAY-rukes) emphasizes text-based truths and bridges from the context of the original hearers and readers to the twenty-first-century world. Kerux values the message of the text, thus its name taken from the Greek *kērux*, a messenger or herald who announced the proclamations of a ruler or magistrate.

Biblical authors trumpeted all kinds of important messages in very specific situations, but a big biblical idea, grasped in its original setting and place, can transcend time. This specific, big biblical idea taken from the biblical passage embodies a single concept that transcends time and bridges the gap between the author's contemporary context and the reader's world. How do the prophets perceive the writings of Moses? How does the writer of Hebrews make sense of the Old Testament? How does Clement in his second epistle, which may be the earliest sermon known outside the New Testament, adapt verses from Isaiah and also ones from the Gospels? Or what about Luther's bold use of Romans 1:17? How does Jonathan Edwards allude to Genesis 19? Who can forget Martin Luther King Jr.'s "I Have a Dream" speech and his appropriation of Amos 5:24: "No, no, we are not satisfied, and we will not be satisfied until 'justice rolls down like waters, and righteousness like a mighty stream'"? How does a preacher in your local church today apply the words of Hosea in a meaningful and life-transforming way?

WHAT IS PRIME IN GOD'S MIND, AND HOW IS THAT EXPRESSED TO A GIVEN GENERATION IN THE UNITS OF THOUGHT THROUGHOUT THE BIBLE?

Answering those questions is what Kerux authors do. Based on the popular "big idea" preaching model, Kerux commentaries uniquely combine the insights of experienced Bible exegetes (trained in interpretation) and homileticians (trained in preaching). Their collaboration provides for every Bible book:

- A detailed introduction and outline
- A summary of all preaching sections with their primary exegetical, theological, and preaching ideas
- Preaching pointers that join the original context with the contemporary one
- Insights from the Hebrew and Greek text
- A thorough exposition of the text
- Sidebars of pertinent information for further background
- Appropriate charts and photographs
- A theological focus to passages

- A contemporary big idea for every preaching unit
- Present-day meaning, validity, and application of a main idea
- Creative presentations for each primary idea
- Key questions about the text for study groups

Many thanks to Jim Weaver, Kregel's former acquisitions editor, who conceived of this commentary series and further developed it with the team of Jeffrey D. Arthurs, Robert B. Chisholm, David M. Howard Jr., Darrell L. Bock, Roy E. Ciampa, and Michael J. Wilkins. We also recognize with gratitude the significant contributions of Dennis Hillman, Fred Mabie, Paul Hillman, Herbert W. Bateman IV, and Shawn Vander Lugt who have been instrumental in the development of the series. Finally, gratitude is extended to the two authors for each Kerux volume; the outside reviewers, editors, and proofreaders; and Kregel staff who suggested numerous improvements.

—*Kregel Publications*

PREFACE TO GENESIS

Genesis narrates captivating stories, mesmerizing the youngest readers yet appealing to the most erudite with subtle and complex characters, plotlines, and theology. We may initially and appropriately consider Genesis as a primer of beginnings. This is where it all started with God's good creation of his universe and all its inhabitants. Alas, humanity's sin introduces estrangement from God and burgeoning corruption that requires God's judgment. Yet God initiates new hope from the beginning and declares his intent with new covenants and promises. With further reflection, however, we see more subtle yet crucial implications, providing the necessary foundations for our worldview.

As an initial statement of reality, Genesis structures our understanding of the transcendent, the creation, the correlations, and life itself. Beginning with a good God who defines how our world works, we find purpose, meaning, connection, and real value. The reality of God's singular transcendence, originating all creation, requires a paradigm shift for ancient and modern audiences alike. The resulting necessary theological reality entails essential practices for all humanity to thrive and enjoy the blessing of relationship and life with their Creator, both now and into eternity.

Though it was written thousands of years ago in a very different world to a budding nation, it continues to provide timely perspective and necessary expectations for all times and to all of God's renewed people from all ethnicities. Genesis helps us to understand and appropriate truth, rooted in a sovereign yet accessible God through his revelation. We can appreciate beauty in his character, actions, and creation. And we can evaluate goodness based on his perfect reality, necessary for both temporal and ultimate flourishing. In short, Genesis teaches us how we need to see and respond to God. We learn our roles and responsibilities before him as his people, in his program, providing our hope for blessing and life in a sin-cursed world. Genesis furnishes the initial steps that will lead us to Jesus as God's final word of revelation as well as the foundational realities that ground his life, death, and resurrection in eternal significance for God's redemptive plan.

Genesis calls every person to take his or her place as God's image, bowing in worship and representing him in holy service to show his character and extend his blessing to his lost and dying world. We must respond to God in faith as we wait for evil to be crushed and God's rule to be fully realized over all his creation.

EXEGETICAL AUTHOR'S ACKNOWLEDGMENTS

To my wife Janet, God's gracious blessing to me,
my sunshine and my joy, who consistently refocuses me in dependence on our Lord.
And to my adult children who cheer me on and support me in innumerable ways.

I am honored to have been asked to contribute to the Kerux series with the incredibly rich book of Genesis. I have learned and grown greatly from the process of study, teaching, and writing the profound truths of Genesis. I pray that God will use this in the lives of the readers of this volume by focusing their attention on the eternal truths of God's word that I can only feebly express. May our worldview be shaped by God's evaluation as we walk with him to see and live his justice and righteousness and yearn for his final consummation of all things.

Thank you to Herb Bateman IV for entrusting this endeavor to me and to Shawn Vander Lugt and the rest of the editorial staff who have enriched the writing and production of this volume to make it a reality. I deeply appreciate your patience through unplanned and unavoidable life changes.

I am grateful for the support and encouragement of many colleagues and friends. I must start early in my training with the incredible input and exciting motivation of my early teaching in Hebrew and Hebrew Bible, Alan Ross and Don Glenn at Dallas Seminary. Both had a profound impact, instilling a love for the language, the theology in the text, and most of all the desire to walk with Yahweh, the giver of life and revelation. More recently, numerous colleagues have encouraged scholarship, discussed points of grammar, context, interpretation, application, and general theology, especially Doug Finkbeiner, Dan Carver, and Tony Shetter. I am also grateful for the sabbatical that Sam Harbin and Phil Dearborn supported to get this endeavor off the ground, and the many students who interacted with me over the text of Genesis. My Adult Bible Fellowship at Calvary Church in Lancaster, PA deserve mention as well as they put up with numerous lessons from Genesis and discussions on God's program and working in human history.

Thank you to Randal Pelton for his encouragement, consistently helpful feedback, and time meeting to discuss preaching portions. I grew from his partnership in the writing process as he questioned and crafted the preaching helps.

Special thanks to my daughter Anna Deckert who read large portions of the manuscript and made invaluable editorial suggestions, to K. Lawson Younger and his private conversations on the structure and specific aspects of the text, and to Training Leaders International, who have given me time to write as part of my responsibilities to strengthen the church around the world.

My wife Janet deserves my unending gratitude for her sacrifice, support, and encouragement through the years of study, writing, and physical setbacks. Without her love and sacrifice, this would never have become a reality. You are truly an excellent wife!

Finally, and most obviously, I want to give glory to my Lord and Savior Jesus Christ, who strengthens me and gives me the grace to serve him in this small way. May my life reflect his life in me and may he use my work to bring him glory, blessing to his world, and promote his kingdom by building his church.

—John Soden

PREACHING AUTHOR'S ACKNOWLEDGMENTS

To my dear wife, Michele, God's best gift to me, who continually supports my extra-church teaching, research, and writing with constant prayer and proofreading.

When John Soden asked me to join him in writing this Genesis volume, I was both delighted and humbled. Joining John made my part relatively easy because he moves so well from exegesis to theological expression. In virtually every pericope John's skill taught me more about the meaning of Genesis. Readers will note that he did the lion's share of the work and was a model of faithful endurance. The time spent with him made me want to preach through Genesis again!

The congregation of Calvary Bible Church from 2003 to the present continues to be a constant source of encouragement to me. From the beginning of our relationship the leadership has understood and supported my teaching and writing. Every Sunday provides a kind of Kerux experience as we read and study Scripture together with the goal of worshipping our God.

I want to thank others who have contributed in major ways to this project. The Evangelical Homiletics Society provided wonderful friends who excel in interpreting Scripture in a way that functions for the church. I can't overestimate the impact EHS has had on my life and ministry. Many years ago, Dr. Jeffrey Arthurs graciously invited me to teach Doctor of Ministry cohorts with him. My time with him, including interacting with great ministry colleagues in the classroom continues to refine my own method and preaching. The same goes for twenty years of teaching in an adjunct capacity at Lancaster Bible College | Capital Seminary & Graduate School. One of the privileges of teaching is the opportunity to keep learning.

Finally, thank you to Kregel's staff, especially Shawn Vander Lugt, for working with us on this massive volume. Years ago, in private conversations at the Evangelical Homiletics Society meetings, I heard of Kregel's plan for Kerux and was hoping it would appear. Thank you for making this volume attractive and readable.

After all this, I desperately want our Lord to receive glory in the church and in Christ Jesus (Eph. 3:21) because of the Kerux volume possibly contributing to the preaching of God's word on Sundays. He alone deserves all the praise. What a privilege to have a small part to play in his kingdom!

—Randal Emery Pelton

OVERVIEW OF ALL PREACHING PASSAGES

Genesis 1:1–2:3

EXEGETICAL IDEA
The Sovereign King showcased both his sole transcendent power and imminent goodness, ordering and filling his very good creation and crowning it with his regal representative, humanity, culminating in the realization of his holy rest.

THEOLOGICAL FOCUS
The sole sovereign, transcendent creator crowned his good universe with humankind to serve him with his blessing and enter his rest.

PREACHING IDEA
Our sovereign Creator calls on his images to submit to him and extend his rule in exclusive worship.

PREACHING POINTERS
The original hearers of Genesis 1:1–2:3 were living in a world where numerous other creation stories and gods existed. God's people needed to understand how different their worldview should be in societies full of idols that were all part of creation. Here they heard of the sole, sovereign, transcendent God who created heaven and earth and all that is in it. The author starts "In the beginning," presuming that God already existed, by describing the condition of "the earth" before creation began (1:2), and the active presence of "the Spirit of God . . . hovering over the face of the waters" (1:1–2). Then in verses 3–27 God begins to speak everything into existence day after day, including God's crowning creation, "man in our image, after our likeness" (v. 26). Everything in God's world is portrayed as "good" (vv. 10, 12, 18, 21, 25) and even "very good" (v. 31). When everything is complete, God stops creating his world and rests, blessing the seventh day (vv. 2:1–3). It is near the end of the creation process that human beings receive the blessing of God and their marching orders to represent God in his world (vv. 26–30), cared for by him rather than having to care for the gods.

Today we live in a world in which creation stories are considered fables and God's existence as sovereign king is challenged, or multiple gods may be worshipped, as in Egypt. Humanity is confused as to their purpose on Earth and their relationship to the rest of creation. We face competing worldviews that produce dramatically different responses in our world. Genesis 1 presents a corrective to idolatry, whether polytheism, animism, hedonism, or self-worship. Anyone who hears this creation account and believes it are themselves new creatures who worship and serve the transcendent creator in a world full of idols, representing him in his world.

Genesis 2:4–25

EXEGETICAL IDEA
Their generous personal creator established and prepared humankind with all life-giving resources to lead creation as his king-priests in worship, so that all creation could flourish through their obedient faith in purposeful unity.

THEOLOGICAL FOCUS
God generously prepared humankind to lead his creation in worship to flourish through obedient faith and unity.

PREACHING IDEA
God's images lead creation in the worship of God by keeping his world and word.

PREACHING POINTERS
Genesis 2:4–25 continues with more detailed information about the climax of God's creation. Special attention is given to the formation of man and woman and the work that each of them would have in a well-watered garden in Eden. Human origins, including the family, and human purpose in God's world are clearly present. Within the context of working in God's world, God gave man a command and a terrible promise: "but of the tree of the knowledge of good and evil you shall not eat, for in the day that you eat of it you shall surely die." They have the choice of life or death, based on their response of faith to their King. It was up to the newly created man and woman to function in God's world according to God's rules.

Today we still function according to this original plan. Occupations and technology have dramatically changed the way much work is done, but the responsibilities of God's people have not changed. In a world where our Creator is rejected or ignored, we must understand our purpose. Through faith in Christ and the power of his Spirit, we fight hard against our world's understanding of life to thrive in obedient faithful service and direct worship to our Creator.

Genesis 3:1–24

EXEGETICAL IDEA
When the human couple, prompted by the crafty snake, rebelled in unbelief against the command of Yahweh, his response showed both the awful consequences of sin, bringing conflict and pain to humanity and creation, and his redemptive grace, providing hope for life and ultimate victory over the adversary.

THEOLOGICAL FOCUS
Humanity's unbelieving rebellion confirms the decreed death sentence, propagating conflict, pain, and frustration, yet revealing God's redemptive grace with its promise of blessing and victory.

PREACHING IDEA
Our fight for fidelity to God is won because of his gracious provision of life instead of death.

PREACHING POINTERS
It is easy to be excited about the prospect of preaching or teaching the tragic, telling narrative of Genesis 3. The wonderful life of the man and wife described at the end of chapter 2 is soon to be ruined.

What is commonly referred to as "the fall" began with the entrance onto the world's stage of a crafty serpent that could communicate. We are reading foundations for a theology of Satan and temptation. In 3:1–5 dialogue between the serpent and Eve takes place aimed at enticing the woman to disobey God's direct command to not eat from the tree of life that was in the middle of the garden. The serpent exploited her doubts and misunderstanding of God's command and contradicted him claiming that God was withholding something good from the woman. Our sin results in tragic consequences in our relationship with God!

Thankfully, in verses 9–13 God graciously reached out to his deceived and disobedient creatures to provide an opportunity for confession. The infamous blame game began. Then, our Lord pronounced judgments that affected all three participants. In verse 15 we learn that a battle is brewing between the serpent "and the woman" but also "between your offspring and her offspring . . ." It appears that her offspring gets the upper hand! However, pain entered the home and the field. The section closes in verses 20–24 with hope as the wife is named Eve, the Lord graciously provides a more adequate covering for Adam and Eve, and God allows the couple to continue worshipping him and working for him outside the garden. Do not forget that wonderful first announcement of the gospel in verse 15!

Genesis 4:1–26

EXEGETICAL IDEA
When Cain spurned God's promise reflected in procreation and worship, rejected Yahweh and his grace, choosing sin over God's presence, he spawned a line beset with homicide, self-promotion, even self-worship, but hope reawakened through Seth's line with genuine worship.

THEOLOGICAL FOCUS
Profane worship and spurning God threaten his images, bring alienation and judgment from God, and deepen self-protection and self-worship, but God's grace preserves promise for life through genuine worship.

PREACHING IDEA
By God's grace his people bury Cain-like tendencies at work and worship as God keeps his promise of life alive in a broken world.

PREACHING POINTERS
In Genesis 4 God provides the first glimpses of how Adam and Eve's rebellion or lack of fidelity

to God's will affects their children. It is striking that the first recorded sin after the initial fall is murdering one's brother ("Cain rose up . . . and killed him"; v. 8). And this happened all because of the contrast between genuine worship and religious activity devoid of a real heart for and trust in God. Both Cain and his brother, Abel, bring offerings to the Lord. Cain and his offering are rejected, while Abel and his offering are accepted. Cain, therefore, kills his brother.

Before Cain commits murder, his interaction with the Lord instructs us with respect to what sin attempts to do to us. Chapter 4 shows God being extremely gracious to the murderer, even though Cain moves "away from the presence of the Lord" (v. 16). Cain represents all who give the appearance of worshipping God, all who offer something to God with their hands, but without a heart for him. Remember, an "offering from the fruit of the ground" was not the problem; the lack of any designation such as "firstborn" or "fat portions" was the issue (vv. 3, 4).

Listeners will appreciate how God presents cultural advances in the ancient world within the context of Cain's life away from the presence of God (vv. 17–22). Lamech, one of Cain's grandsons, highlights how sin continued to show itself in the exaltation of self and the resulting ravage of God's good world with violence (vv. 23–24). Finally, we can let out a sigh of relief with the hope for humanity found in Adam and Eve's son Seth and the key sentence with which chapter 4 ends, "At that time people began to call upon the name of the Lord" (v. 26).

Genesis 5:1–6:8

EXEGETICAL IDEA
God's blessed images, inheriting death through Adam, used God's gracious empowerment to further their domination and destruction of his good creation, leading to judgment though God graciously extended life and relief to those who would walk with him.

THEOLOGICAL FOCUS
God's blessed images, inheriting death through Adam, use God's empowering to deepen their destructiveness, leading to judgment, but God graciously extends life and relief to those who walk with him.

PREACHING IDEA
Following Enoch and Noah, God's people walk with him, finding favor and avoiding his judgment on our wicked world.

PREACHING POINTERS
It doesn't take long in chapter 5 before we see opportunities to transition from the original audience of Genesis to our listeners. Verse 1 provides a reminder that God created man "in the likeness of God," and verse 3 includes the concept of Adam fathering "a son in his own likeness, after his image." Everyone sitting in your sanctuary or classroom is also made in both images. But let's be honest: no one, including you, will think that the repetition of names and ages is exciting, except for the huge lifespans. The repetition of "and he died" throughout the chapter certainly shows that disobedience to the Lord's commands results in death (cf. 2:17). So, you will probably want to pick your spots carefully while covering this section. I

suggest picking up on the hope tucked away in all that death. Important places to pause are verse 24 and the description of Enoch walking with God before disappearing and at verse 29 with Noah's important name. Then in 6:1–8 you can describe for your listeners the depth of human depravity. This is certainly humankind at its worst, according to the Lord's assessment in 6:5. On top of that is the opportunity to show that the Lord judges human wickedness because of what it does to his good creation. Finally, every listener will be relieved to find Noah finding "favor in the eyes of the Lord" (v. 8). And you will look forward to making sure each of them is in the same boat.

Genesis 6:9–8:19

EXEGETICAL IDEA

Faithful to his promises, God fully judged the verified evil of all flesh in his world, reducing his creation back to watery disorder yet sparing righteous Noah, who endured in obedience, with his family and representative animals, bringing them out into a renewed world with renewed blessing.

THEOLOGICAL FOCUS

In appropriate justice and suitable grace, God judges his world, bringing the consequences of sin fully to bear, and yet delivering the righteous remnant to a new world, according to his promise, for renewed blessing.

PREACHING IDEA

Like Noah, the righteous in God's eyes enjoy his salvation in a world under judgment.

PREACHING POINTERS

The mood of the sermon should match the mood of the message. In this case, the mood is a mixture of great sorrow due to the devastating flood but also great relief and hope due to Noah and his family being saved. As you begin to move from Noah and the flood to your listeners, keep two general categories of judgment and salvation (or, if you prefer, rescue or deliverance) in mind. The holiness and justice of God require judgment on human rebellion just like we saw in Genesis 3, although often delayed (cf. Psalm 73 and the prosperity of the wicked during the interim); the grace and faithfulness of God *require* salvation of those he has promised to deliver. Both God's ability to rescue the godly and punish the ungodly are mentioned by Peter in 2 Peter 2:9 to encourage faithful living during our exile. God will keep his promise, including the complete defeat of all evil (cf. Gen. 3:15); he will have a people who bear his image and display his glory in creation, even if it is in a new creation.

Noah provides an example of how genuine faith works in obedience to God in the middle of a culture that does not believe. This kind of countercultural righteousness is required by all who would enjoy LifePlus. I am using this term as a substitute for the more familiar, eternal life. LifePlus emphasizes the quality of the life God provides for those who trust Him. Those are the kind of people God saves. Listeners will enjoy seeing all the parallels-in-reverse between the de-creation occurring at the flood and the original creation story of Genesis 1–2 as pointed out in the exposition of our passage. Our God will not let sin go but, as he promised, he will have a people who represent him well in his new world. You should urge your listeners to be confident in their own faith-based righteousness and to enjoy God now while also having hope of ultimate deliverance at the return of Christ.

Genesis 8:20–9:17

EXEGETICAL IDEA

Responding to Noah's genuine worship, Yahweh established his covenant, promising never again to destroy all life with flood and to provide blessing and boundaries so that his fully depraved yet valuable images could thrive.

THEOLOGICAL FOCUS

Yahweh responds to genuine worship with covenant promise, valuing his depraved images with boundaries and gracious protection for their blessing.

PREACHING IDEA

Remember the rainbow: God remembers his covenant to all life and commands us to honor life made in his image.

PREACHING POINTERS

We can only imagine the anticipation, excitement, and wonder Noah felt as he and his family stepped off the ark onto the dry ground of a freshly cleansed world. Earliest readers or hearers of this narrative would immediately recognize it as a new start for humanity led by the righteous character Noah. How does a person respond when the Lord has been so gracious to them? Answer: genuine worship that recognizes the value of relationship with God and his salvation—especially since human nature has not changed (cf. 8:21b)! The Lord accepted Noah and his sacrifice and makes vows (cf. "I will never again. . . . Neither will I ever again," 8:21). We are still living our Christian lives within the context of God's promises to Noah. And Noah leads the way for us to conduct our own genuine worship. All Christians follow his example (Noah is human; he will also provide a "go and do otherwise" example later in chapter 9!). We're also still living in the context of God's blessing on "Noah and his sons" (9:1). God's blessing contains instruction that includes how God's people are to honor life. This includes what to do whenever a life is taken, whether an animal for food ("you shall not eat flesh with its life, that is, its blood," 9:4) or of a human being ("Whoever sheds the blood of man, by man shall his blood be shed," 9:6; consider the implications this has on issues such as abortion, euthanasia, and violent crimes committed by individuals against individuals). Finally, God's people can live confidently knowing that he will keep his promise not to repeat the judgment of the flood ("I will see [the bow] and remember the everlasting covenant," 9:16). God's people who worship him receive grace, not judgment.

Genesis 9:18–29

EXEGETICAL IDEA

After the flood, Noah and his sons, the progenitors of all humanity, expose the human heart, receiving cursing and conflict or blessing and grace based on honor or dishonor to Yahweh and his authority structure.

THEOLOGICAL FOCUS

Human response to Yahweh's authority structures exposes the state of the human heart, portending future cursing and conflict or blessing and grace for submissive honor to Yahweh.

PREACHING IDEA

Our spiritual heritage reveals both the dangers of cursed sin and the possibility of salvation blessing—which will we choose?

PREACHING POINTERS

Remember our broad options for teaching and preaching this section: the "go and do otherwise" angles from Noah ("drunkenness" in v. 21) and Ham ("saw the nakedness of his father and told his two brothers" in v. 22) and the incentive of blessing on Shem and Japheth for all listeners to find their place in their lineage. The first readers/hearers of this narrative couldn't believe what they were seeing. This is not what anyone expected to happen in Noah's family, but this reminds us of the condition of the human heart after the flood. When we have a saint who falls and is in a compromising situation (surprise?), how do we react? What should we expect from those we hold highly in the Lord? We may be less surprised to see the youngest act foolishly and suffer, but we must see the possibility in any of us to fall. The entire human race, starting from Noah's three sons (v. 19), exists within the curse and blessing announced by Noah. The implications of the repetition, "a servant of servants" (v. 25), "his servant" (v. 26), and "his servant" (v. 27), creates the response of, "That's not the life I want! I want to be free!"

Genesis 10:1–11:9

EXEGETICAL IDEA

The family history of the sons of Noah presents the dispersed nations with their responsibilities and hope from Yahweh's judgment, reversing human aspirations and exposing their false pursuit of security as folly, preparing Israel for their purpose and place in God's program to spread blessing.

THEOLOGICAL FOCUS

The spread of the nations conveys both human responsibility and hope in God's redemptive purpose for all peoples stemming from his gracious judgment on human folly, preparing for his choice of Israel to spread his blessing.

PREACHING IDEA
Our Lord is watching whether his people are making a name for themselves or for him, and directs history to spread his fame.

PREACHING POINTERS
Part of the excitement of reaching this section is that we finally get to continue the story. Chapter 5 ended with verse 32: "After Noah was 500 years old, Noah fathered Shem, Ham, and Japheth." Then comes the painful parenthesis in 6:1–9:29 that describes terrible wickedness, the awful judgment of God, and yet hope for God's world.

We are working our way from Adam to Noah to Noah's three sons. God's blessing is continuing in what might be considered a restart (9:1, "God blessed Noah and his sons"). And, if you want to stay excited about this pericope, we suggest you move very quickly through chapter 10: "Sons were born to them after the flood" (v. 1). Prepare listeners for what's coming with a look at the human condition (vv. 8–9), significant places such as Babel and Shinar (v. 10), and significant kingdoms and cities such as Assyria and Nineveh (v. 11). Of course, you might also point out references to the Canaanites and Sodom and Gomorrah (v. 19).

Redemptive history is wrapped up in this genealogy: "From these the nations spread abroad on the earth after the flood" (v. 32). The list of seventy nations teaches us we're all a part of the same family. But as almost all modern readers sense the story really gets going in 11:1–9 and the incident surrounding the Tower of Babel. What is God's explanation for the plethora of languages that exist in the world today? As we anticipated from the end of chapter 9, human hearts are not all bent on enhancing God's fame, but their own *name*. God simply cannot let that happen. Humanity could not image God Instead, it would destroy his images when he desires to bless them. God's people have always been called to live out their faith in a world that rejects his rule.

Genesis 11:10–12:9

EXEGETICAL IDEA
After scattering the peoples from Babel, Yahweh extended grace and called Abram to follow in faith at great personal cost, promising to bless greatly and establish a nation despite human impossibilities, to bless all peoples through relationship with Yahweh in true worship.

THEOLOGICAL FOCUS
God continues to extend grace and promise through his chosen servants, whom he calls to follow him, trusting him for the impossible, at great cost, for great blessing, and to bless his world in relationship with him.

PREACHING IDEA
God is graciously calling you to follow him in order to bless you to be a blessing to those around you.

PREACHING POINTERS

After some pretty severe—to say the least—judgment narratives, listeners will sigh in relief as God shifts our attention to the descendants of Shem and Terah, especially Abram. God is continuing to extend his grace and fulfill his promises, and it all begins "in Ur of the Chaldeans" (11:28). He will do the work; miracles must be a part of the plan in this badly broken, yet blessed world (cf. 11:30, "Now Sarai was barren" and, in case we didn't get the point, "she had no child"), which requires radical faith. Out of the blue the Lord commands Abram to leave everything he knows and loves and travel to an unknown land that he would reveal later (12:1). You can quickly see how this command, often referred to as a call, mirrors the path of faith and what it means to be a Christ-follower. If listeners need any incentive, it's found in the promises (12:2–3). If they need any grand purpose in life—and every human being does—it's found in being a conduit of blessing to the whole earth (vv. 2–3). God is the one who does this for the one he commands to follow him (note all the "I wills"). Abraham's obedience (v. 4, "So Abram went") is exemplary. Apart from the Lord, Abram is the major character in the narrative. His journey will in many ways be our journey of faith. His repeated action of building altars to the Lord leads the way for our own worship.

Genesis 12:10–20

EXEGETICAL IDEA

Facing fear when tested with famine, Abram trusted in deception for his welfare rather than Yahweh's promise, endangering Sarai and the promise, as well as bringing God's curse on Pharaoh, gaining rebuke and expulsion rather than being a blessing.

THEOLOGICAL FOCUS

Acting from fear during testing leads to compromise, danger, and loss, both for the God-fearer and those in his circle of influence, instead of blessing through faith.

PREACHING IDEA

Forsake fear for faith and find your place as a recipient and conduit of God's blessing.

PREACHING POINTERS

Abram's understanding of the cultural mores, his cleverness in devising a plan for self-preservation, and the Lord's surprising reaction provided the original audience with a "go and do otherwise" narrative. What makes the transition to listeners easier are all those circumstances in life that create the same kind of fear in us that Abram experienced. As you can see, entrance into Egypt posed a threat. Let the scheming begin: "I know I trusted you a little earlier, Lord, but all my instincts are telling me I'd better come up with a plan or else you can kiss all the promises goodbye!" Enter the curse.

It is tragic when others pay the price for our own disbelief. God is determined that his plan for us will succeed, but that doesn't mean that we cannot trust him. Pharaoh is helpless against the Lord's attack. The narrative leaves me wanting to ask Abram, "So, did you learn your lesson?" Abram fails the test and shows believers the consequences. A lack of faith coincides with a lot of fear, and the results are devastating for the soul.

We do not want to send the signal that this narrative shows that God will always bail out his servants when they take matters into their own hands. We do want to disclose God's mercy to his own throughout their lives so that they are able to experience the fulfillment of his promises to them. Abram's poor example helps us learn that we extend God's blessing to his world only when we trust him.

Genesis 13:1–18

EXEGETICAL IDEA

When Abram returned to the land, publicly identified with Yahweh in worship, and demonstrated faith by separating from Lot (who chose wicked associations for expected profit to his detriment), Yahweh certified and expanded his promise to Abram.

THEOLOGICAL FOCUS

God, as sovereign king, rewards those who walk by faith in dependent worship, which shows in generosity and grace, while those who selfishly choose personal gain and associate with evil will suffer loss.

PREACHING IDEA

God's promised blessings are only for those who are righteous by faith, while those who walk by sight suffer the consequences.

PREACHING POINTERS

Many listeners can relate to being blessed by God with many things, especially in the time and part of the world in which we are living. The opening verses, then, can easily describe many of us, including the dangers in verse 7 of sharing neighborhoods and workspaces with non-Christians. The contrast between Abram and Lot presents listeners with their daily choice for living life in God's kingdom. Abram is certainly one of those blessed "peacemakers" Jesus referred to.

Lot is too much like his maternal ancestor, Eve, who takes what looks right to the eyes. Some of our listeners walk by faith, others by sight. One question for us all to ask is whether the good stuff we see is part of the promise or out of bounds. Lot's choice was clearly out of bounds as he "journeyed east" (v. 11). Better to stay with God in Canaan, synonymous at least with worshipping him and walking with him, the source of LifePlus. The opposite life is to move one's "tent as far as Sodom" (v. 12) and experience the wrath of God against "wicked, great sinners" (v. 13). And our gracious God gives yet more assurance that walking with him by faith is the way to go as he recounts his promises to us throughout Scripture.

Genesis 14:1–24

EXEGETICAL IDEA

When Lot was caught up in retribution against his neighbors, Abram exhibited faith, rescuing Lot and his neighbors with their goods, giving public glory to Yahweh and valuing God's promise over immediate gain that could tarnish God's greatness.

THEOLOGICAL FOCUS
Loving my brother at personal expense, honoring God with necessary praise and sacrificial worship, and guarding his glory while expecting his promised outcomes embodies loyal faith.

PREACHING IDEA
Faith in God empowers you to love your brothers and sisters at great personal cost for God's sole glory.

PREACHING POINTERS
You can see from the theological focus that Genesis 14 functions for the church as one of those "go and do likewise" narratives. Abram's reaction to Lot's dilemma—his love for his brother—is the fruit of faith in God. Abram leads the way for us in our faith journey. We are writing this commentary in a time of great social unrest in our country. It's a great time to be preaching about loving God and neighbor. When is it ever a bad time to preach the Great Commandment? So all the historical data about the kings listed in Genesis 14:1–12 provides the context for Abram to flex his faith muscles (v. 1 begins with, "In the days of [multiple kings making war]"). Listeners have an opportunity to see faith in action in verses 13–16 as Abram unhesitatingly rescues Lot. Although not listed yet in the narrative, God is powerfully at work because there is no way Abram should have conquered these enemies to rescue Lot.

If anyone is wondering if it's worth it to follow Abram's example, give them a good look at verses 17–20 where God's blessing is once again emphasized ("Blessed be Abram by God . . . and blessed be God"). Finally, Abram's loyalty to the Lord is clearly displayed when he refuses the offer made by the king of Sodom. His confession, "I have lifted my hand [in an oath] to the Lord, God Most High" (v. 22), is yet another example to follow (cf. vv. 18, 19, 20 for the repeated title).

Genesis 15:1–21

EXEGETICAL IDEA
Acknowledging Abram's righteousness by faith, Yahweh assured Abram of security and reward, including innumerable descendants, and confirmed through covenant his promise of descendants and land, clarifying their extended painful waiting with subsequent justice for all.

THEOLOGICAL FOCUS
Based on his righteous and just control over history and nations, and his servants' faith, Yahweh secures his promises for his righteous people, despite struggle, through his covenant.

PREACHING IDEA
God said it, I believe it, he guarantees it, and I have to accept the suffering part.

PREACHING POINTERS
While Genesis 15:6 gets the most press—certainly warranted—the prophetic vision that opens the chapter is enough to let you know that this pericope will preach: "Fear not, Abram, I am

your shield; your reward shall be very great" (v. 1). Like your listeners, Abram has been repeatedly faced with the decision: "Will I believe God or not?" So much depends on what Abram believes about God. For instance, if Abram doesn't think much of God's abilities, then God being his shield doesn't amount to much. That is like my son when he was very young saying that he would protect *me*.

The original audience was greatly encouraged to hear God make this promise, to see Abram ask for clarification without being chastised for asking, to hear the omniscient narrator announce Abram's faith and reception of righteousness, and to witness God's elaborate covenant ceremony that gave Abram assurance. Many of those details explain the Christian's faith journey. In fact, just like us, his faith is not yet mature and complete. He has and will continue to stumble. Yet God considered him righteous! So much boils down to whether or not we believe God each day as we walk with him. One reason that faith is necessary is because the promise remains in the distance (cf. v. 13, and Israel's sojourner status matches ours). Besides that, by the time God announced this promise to Abram, only God could do it. Despite all the oppression of living in exile, God will keep his promise to those who trust and obey.

Genesis 16:1–16

EXEGETICAL IDEA

When Sarai pursued God's promise in the flesh from unbelief, breeding pain, conflict, and alienation, Yahweh rescued Hagar with promised blessing, rewarding her faith with a son and giving Abram and Sarai a lesson in faith to God's glory.

THEOLOGICAL FOCUS

Teaching faith and endurance for blessing through the pain of unbelief, God honors any who trust him, mitigating loss from faithlessness, fulfilling his promises, and lifting the humble to the praise of his glory.

PREACHING IDEA

It pays to patiently wait for the Lord's blessing rather than working out our own "blessing."

PREACHING POINTERS

Chapter 16 provides another opportunity for us to see how our sinful tendencies surface during lapses of faith. There is comfort knowing that we struggle in our faith journey just like God's finest did way back then. This time it is Sarai that finds herself in a most difficult situation for an Old Testament matriarch: she's barren. But she is resourceful and devises a plan to "obtain children by" Hagar, her Egyptian servant (16:1–2). We know that "ten years" had passed before we read those two fateful verbs again: "took" and "gave . . . to . . . her husband" (v. 3). "And Abram listened to the voice of Sarai" (v. 2); he didn't learn Adam's lesson back in Genesis 3:17.

The narrative shows how sin destroys relationships: Hagar turned on Sarai (v. 4), Sarai turned on Abram (v. 5), Abram abdicated any responsibility to do good by Hagar (v. 6), and Sarai "dealt harshly with" Hagar (v. 6). This is what happens whenever God's people take matters into their own hands. But in verses 7–14 what the angel of the Lord does and says to Hagar demonstrates God's mercy and intention to bless all who believe. His instructions to Hagar show how difficult obedience can be and how obeying goes against all our instincts (v. 9). Of all the people in the story, Hagar is the good example of a faith that works itself out in obedience. Even though the prophecy about Ishmael isn't all roses (v. 12), the narrative shows us that our God hears us and sees us when we're in pain (vv. 11, 13).

Genesis 17:1–27

EXEGETICAL IDEA

Yahweh appeared to Abram in his old age to pledge his covenant through Sarah and Isaac, eternally establishing relation with them as Sovereign with expanded promises requiring loyalty from Abram and his descendants, as evidenced by their new names and circumcision.

THEOLOGICAL FOCUS

Yahweh remains faithful to his promise, offering increasing blessing in relationship with him for greater loyalty and faith, and extending grace and hope to his struggling servants, despite deepening human obstacles, to his glory.

PREACHING IDEA

The only right response to Almighty God's promises is unhesitating faithfulness that leads to full benefit.

PREACHING POINTERS

When the original audience read Genesis 17 their faith was bolstered to see God revealing himself to Abram and challenging him to "walk before me and be blameless" (v. 1). All that was so that God might confirm the covenant agreement he made with Abram back in chapter 15, and now Sarah and Isaac too. Listeners with ears to hear will be just as encouraged when they read and believe that what God said to Abram is at work in their lives. The narrative is one of those classic places in the Old Testament where God's work and our response of obedient faith somehow work together in the salvation package. For instance, the former occurs in all God's "I will's" (vv. 6–8), and the latter is spelled out in verse 9 when "God said to Abraham, 'As for you, you shall keep my covenant.'"

More encouragement comes from seeing the faithful as part of Abraham's huge family tree. Those hearing this for the first time must put themselves into this narrative and assess whether or not they are putting their faith to work like Abraham did when he made sure Ishmael and everyone in his household were circumcised.

This is an excellent time for us to urge listeners to evaluate their attitude toward God in every area of their lives. Like Abraham, we must be faithful to the Lord with our motives (loving God and his reputation above all things), time (making sure we serve him as part of the body of Christ), and money (using our money to further his agenda in the world of making disciples). This is the only way to enjoy all the privileges and blessings that come from being in a covenant relationship with our Creator/Redeemer. And this is a foretaste of eternity for all who display a faith that works.

Genesis 18:1–15

EXEGETICAL IDEA
Yahweh, sharing covenant fellowship in theophany through Abraham's hospitality, confirmed his promise of descendants by confronting Sarah's unbelief; revealing his presence, omniscience, and omnipotence; and challenging them to trust him for his promise.

THEOLOGICAL FOCUS
With deepening relationship and through consciousness of our own inability, Yahweh confronts unbelief in his covenant people, challenging them to trust in his presence and power to accomplish his promise.

PREACHING IDEA
Faith is no laughing matter: how our faith grows each time we learn that nothing is too hard for God!

PREACHING POINTERS
There are times in every parishioner's faith journey where they need to hear the Lord say to them: "Is anything too hard for the Lord?" (v. 14). Abraham and Sarah, both "advanced in years" (v. 11), certainly needed to hear it in light of the Lord's unbelievable prophecy. Our struggles to believe require the same assurance of the Lord's powerful ability to remain faithful to deliver us in a badly broken world.

As we've seen throughout these narratives, Abraham shows us the kind of person to whom God gives his precious promises. His reception of the "three men" (v. 2) was remarkable. Just as remarkable is seeing God spend that kind of quality time with his own. Readers must see themselves in this story, reacting in the same way for the same reasons: lavish hospitality is a fruit of faith.

And, of course, since the human heart doesn't change with respect to its natural response to God's revelation, Sarah's laugh (v. 12) shows that faith indeed is required for our walk with God. Our tendency is to judge God's ability to deliver us in terms of our own capacity. Ridiculous, I know! We can probably all identify with Sarah's fearful attempt to cover her tracks: when she denied her incredulity, the Lord graciously corrected her. He handles our unbelief very well. Thankfully, he takes it within the context of an overall stance of faith.

Genesis 18:16–19:38

EXEGETICAL IDEA
God chose Abraham to be a blessing, teaching righteousness and justice, interceding for his world in the face of God's paradigmatic judgment, justly condemning the wicked, and graciously delivering Lot and his family despite their costly infection by the world.

THEOLOGICAL FOCUS
God teaches humanity his character and expectations of righteousness and justice through his loyal followers and his actions, justly judging the wicked and graciously delivering the righteous, despite serious compromise and loss.

PREACHING IDEA
Make sure we are "the righteous" ones not swept away by the judgment of God and able to bring blessing to others.

PREACHING POINTERS
One of the most exciting things about preaching through Genesis is the opportunity to communicate the justice of God in a way that will elicit worship in church. That is especially true in a climate when more and more listeners are breathing the air where modern sensibilities are offended by such doctrine. In this pericope, the original audience comes face to face with the justice and judgment of God. Critical, however, is seeing that God's pronouncement of impending judgment on wicked citizens occurs within the context of God's previous promises made to righteous-by-faith Abraham. The move from those readers to our listeners is straightforward: the patience of God will run out at some point. As the Judge of all the earth he will certainly judge rightly (separating the righteous from the wicked), he will tolerate much wickedness to exist ("For the sake of ten I will not destroy it," 18:32), and judgment will fall on the wicked.

Abraham's intercession frames the story and becomes crucial to the point. The Christian needs to see the privilege he has both in declaring God's character (his justice and righteousness) and interceding for the wicked and the righteous among them. We are called to bless our world. We cannot do that if we become like it. We can only do it by living out God's character and teaching his goodness to our world.

Two other things to consider as we think about moving from the original audience to our listeners: (1) Lot's wife shows a different level of wickedness and also experiences a different judgment; and (2) the situation that occurs after the destruction of Sodom and Gomorrah between Lot and his two daughters shows the ongoing effects of sin's spread—more incentive for us and our listeners to be righteous by faith and obedience.

Genesis 20:1–18

EXEGETICAL IDEA
When Abraham lied about Sarah, precipitating her abduction, God intervened to preserve his promise, endangering Abimelech and revealing Abraham's status and responsibility to intercede for the innocent Abimelech to bring blessing instead of cursing.

THEOLOGICAL FOCUS
The failings of God's people may endanger God's redemptive plan and threaten cursing on God's world, but God faithfully works to accomplish his good purposes, developing his servants in their faith to bring blessing.

PREACHING IDEA
Praise God for times when our unbelief is overturned by the faithfulness of God and we are back on track to bring blessing.

PREACHING POINTERS
One of the goals of these homiletical sections is to continue to explore how meaning is made in the narrative. In this case first readers and current readers have a hard time comprehending that Abraham would lie again, saying about "Sarah, his wife, 'She is my sister'" (v. 2). Not this again! Yes. This is another "go and do otherwise" narrative, at least from the perspective of Abraham's actions. Many listeners are familiar with the concept of a besetting sin. Whether the cause is rationalizing it, downgrading it, or simply enjoying it too much, the besetting sin repeats itself in the Christian life along with its damaging effect.

As you can see, though, in the Theological Focus, Abraham is not the main character of this narrative; God is. So, while we are all appalled at Abraham's fear and lack of faith, our own faith is also bolstered as we watch our God continue to make sure his promises remain. If we spend just a moment with Abraham's actions, we are reminded again how it is possible for one intended to be a conduit of blessing to end up becoming a curse-causer. Poor Abimelech does not know what hit him in this narrative when he hears in a dream, "Behold, you are a dead man because of the woman" (v. 3). Certainly, our God will not "kill an innocent people" (v. 4). Unfortunately, because of what God tells us in his word about birth-sin, none are innocent. If we move back to God for a moment, listeners may gain confidence in God's faithfulness as they hear God tell Abimelech, "it was I who kept you from sinning against me. Therefore I did not let you touch her" (v. 6).

Genesis 21:1–34

EXEGETICAL IDEA
God began fulfilling his covenant promises to Abraham by providing and protecting a son through Sarah, delivering and blessing Ishmael, extending blessing to Abimelech, and giving Abraham a foothold in the land through the faith and faithful action of his servants, to the praise of his name among the nations.

THEOLOGICAL FOCUS
God faithfully honors his promises, blessing believing responses to his word in difficult conditions, to his praise among the nations.

PREACHING IDEA
God will be faithful to his promise to bless, and we will be faith-filled to be a blessing.

PREACHING POINTERS
The narrative confronts its initial audience and its modern audience alike with the faithfulness of God to fulfill his promises to us. No one can miss the emphasis on the impossibility of this fulfillment: "a son in his old age. . . . Abraham was a hundred years old when his son Isaac was born to him" (21:2, 5, 7). We should all laugh with Sarah! But Hagar the Egyptian's son soon

interrupts the celebration of the promise fulfilled. God makes it clear, contrary to Abraham's feelings, that his inheritance is not for the "children of the slave" (Gal. 4:30–31). Human effort cannot secure the blessing of God; it is only by faith in his miraculous promises that God works personally in and for us.

The mercy of God is on display in the way he promised to make another nation from Ishmael. We see Abraham's obedience, and he functions as an example of faith in action. The middle of the chapter shows an even greater display of God's mercy (vv. 15–21) as God rescues Hagar and her son and restates his promises in response to the boy's prayer.

This chapter closes as chapter 20 began, reminding us of the kind of influence God's people are to have in the world as they function as conduits of his blessing. It is also a great comfort to know that God can redeem even poor testimonies when his people respond humbly to him. Abraham gets off to a poor spiritual start, but through God's intervention and Abraham's humble cooperation, God accomplishes his will.

Genesis 22:1–19 (20–24)

EXEGETICAL IDEA
Abraham passed God's extreme test in faith, offering his beloved son of promise and receiving God's ratification of the extended promises of his covenant as God's loyal vassal, guaranteeing blessing to all nations.

THEOLOGICAL FOCUS
A believer's faithful obedience, choosing loyalty to God over every competitor, allows God's greatest blessing in his life and his world.

PREACHING IDEA
God blesses his people and all nations through the tested obedient faith of his servants.

PREACHING POINTERS
First readers of this "test" narrative watch in horror as God asks Abraham to do the unthinkable. It is the ultimate test of faith, and readers have been watching his faith grow as he gets up there in years. As you begin to transition to your listeners, begin by noting that this is another of those "go and do likewise" stories. Abraham is now functioning as a positive exemplar. His unhesitating obedience sets the stage for all future sons and daughters of Abraham to take their own place in redemptive history.

On his part, God ratifies his covenant promises to Abraham in response to or in conjunction with Abraham's obedience. This is nothing new since all along in Genesis we have seen God be faithful to those who are also faithful to him. God creates this kind of faith in his children; his children exhibit this loyal faith just like Abraham did. Early and later readers should all be made aware of what makes this test so radical. God called Abraham to give up his most loved person, the son he had waited for twenty-five years for. God asked Abraham to choose God over all that he valued most.

Does all faith in all ages look like this? By definition, the answer is "yes." God tests Abraham's faith because ultimately faith, like the fear of the Lord, obeys. God's tailor-made test examined whether or not Abraham would believe God or his own reasoning ("God is asking me to do something that destroys his promise?"). Well, you know how the story goes: Abraham passes the test; God delivers just in the nick of time and ratifies his covenant promises to Abraham so the blessing might continue.

Genesis 23:1–20

EXEGETICAL IDEA

When Sarah died, Abraham negotiated and purchased a heritable tomb in the land of Canaan for her burial, in faith securing a portent of God's promise and impetus for his descendants to follow his anticipation of God's fidelity, despite the immediate cost.

THEOLOGICAL FOCUS

The righteous respond to death with faith, looking beyond this world to follow God's unfailing promises and prepare future generations to embrace God's ultimate plan and working, regardless of cost.

PREACHING IDEA

The faithful trust God and provide a foundation for a legacy of faith for future generations of the faithful.

PREACHING POINTERS

One way to begin the move from the original audience to current listeners is with the opening reference in verses 2 and 19 to "the land of Canaan." That location translates into our Christian experience. Listeners are currently exercising their faith in the promises of God in this world. Our ultimate home and full realization of the promise exist in the future new heaven and earth. Abraham continues to function for us because his faith, which drives his purchase, continues to inform our faith and the prospect of God's favor. For anyone wanting some kind of New Testament validation of our likeness to Abraham's situation, they might benefit from the description of Abraham saying, "I am a sojourner and foreigner among you" (v. 4). We Christians are also considered "elect exiles" (1 Peter 1:1). One day this will not be the case, but now we strive to be faithful to God until he returns.

As noted in many of our homiletical discussions, this narrative is one of those "go and do likewise" exemplars. Abraham's faith, his reputation (cf. v. 6, "you are a prince of God among us"), and his wise dealings during the entire transaction are exemplary; all of this leads the way for us. This is all being accomplished among outsiders of the covenant (cf. vv. 3, 5, 7, "Hittites"). Abraham's faith in the promise of God meant that he purchased property for his family long into the future. This is the kind of faith in the promises of God that allows Christians to flourish in their walk with God, even though they are exiles. First, we believe strongly in the promises of God now, and that faith translates into faithfulness to God. Like Abraham, we will not turn back into slavery to sin. And like Abraham, our faith and obedience will ensure that our families and future generations continue to experience the blessing of God as they follow our example.

Genesis 24:1–25:11

EXEGETICAL IDEA

Abraham secured Isaac's promised future by sending his godly servant to find Yahweh's choice of a wife for Isaac, Rebekah, and by protecting Isaac's status, sending his other sons away with gifts.

THEOLOGICAL FOCUS

God's faithful servants walk confidently in God's loyal love, expecting his faithful working to accomplish his promises, taking each necessary step to pursue his priorities and prepare for his intended future, according to the light given.

PREACHING IDEA

The faithful trust their Father's blessing as they follow him each step on the way.

PREACHING POINTERS

To read the narrative of Abraham making arrangements with his servant to locate a suitable wife for Isaac is to gain confidence in the Lord's sovereign control in the lives of his faithful. Abraham makes it clear that the promises of God must go forward; a wife from the old life will not do, but a wife there must be. Everything about this plan is so important that a serious oath is taken.

Abraham's servant shares Abraham's faith, as can be seen in the servant's prayer. Twice the servant refers to God's steadfast love for Abraham. God's loyal love will have to answer this prayer very specifically—and he does. When the servant speaks to Laban about Abraham, he reminds us about the kind of kingdom we inhabit by faith: truly we are blessed with every spiritual blessing.

It is very encouraging to listeners to see themselves in this same redemptive history and with the challenge to follow the example of Abraham's servant. Add to that the encouragement of watching God provide the perfect wife for Isaac, someone who matches Abraham's character. Rebekah's family announces this in their blessing on her as she departs with the servant. The promise will continue. Abraham made sure of that at the end of his life as readers enter chapter 25: he is generous to all his children, but the promise would go through Isaac. God showed his steadfast love to Abraham, and he continues to show that to his own today.

Genesis 25:19–34

EXEGETICAL IDEA

God revealed his plan to fulfill his covenant promises to Abraham through Isaac's line, responding to prayer, with his unexpected choice of the younger Jacob despite his obvious flaws, and rejecting Esau who despised his birthright.

THEOLOGICAL FOCUS

God's sovereign work, realized through prayer, will be accomplished through flawed faith, rejecting one who despises his promise.

PREACHING IDEA
"It's not for sale!": What Esau should have said and how faith feels about the blessing of God.

PREACHING POINTERS
When the Lord graciously allows Rebekah to conceive twins, their struggles within the womb culminate in the reversal of cultural norms seen so often in redemptive history (the prophecy in v. 23). God often chooses the unlikely for carrying out his work to remind us that it is his work, not ours alone. Another unexpected—or maybe better, unwanted—element is that God's plan for his people includes what appear to be long delays. According to verse 26 it took twenty years for the couple to conceive. That is a long time for a child of God to wait for the promises of God to come true! That is a long time to keep praying to God. That is a lot of patient waiting in hope.

Finally, God presents to us two sons representing two nations that could not be more different. God chose the younger, Jacob, to be the conduit of blessing. Jacob is far from perfect, but the Lord will see to it that he is being perfected along the way. Esau's profane nature is on display in the way he treats his birthright (see v. 34's summary statement: "Thus Esau despised his birthright"), what should be his most prized possession because all the promises of God and his plan are wrapped up in that gift. Jacob, on the other hand, wants that birthright for himself more than anything. Readers find themselves in the story: some, like Esau, treasuring the temporal things of this world, and others, like Jacob, with a new nature desiring the best God can give.

Genesis 26:1–33

EXEGETICAL IDEA
When Isaac received the covenant promises from Yahweh, his fear and deception brought conflict despite initial obedience, endangering God's purpose of blessing the nations, but his subsequent worship and faith in God's reassurance brought peace and blessing for the nations.

THEOLOGICAL FOCUS
The servant of God must respond to the presence and promise of God with faith, in true worship, to bring blessing and peace to his world, rather than fearfully, creating conflict and loss.

PREACHING IDEA
It takes faith, not fear, to both receive God's blessing and be a blessing to others.

PREACHING POINTERS
One way to transition from the original audience to current audiences is to focus on the Lord's commands to his chosen conduit of blessing, Isaac. Begin with the negative command in verse 2, "Do not go down to Egypt," and continue to the positive side of that same command: "dwell in the land of which I shall tell you. Sojourn in this land" (vv. 2–3). The famine provided the pull or push to return to Egypt, but the promises of God are enjoyed alongside the challenges related to trusting him for life. The promises of his presence, blessing, and being a conduit of universal blessing continue to drive our faith journey. And we cannot miss that all of this is explained by Abraham's obedience (v. 5), which is to be passed down to Isaac and on down the line.

However, readers are caught off guard as another "go and do otherwise" series of scenes occur as fear takes center stage instead of faith (vv. 6–11). As the saying goes, the apple didn't fall far from the tree. Yet, the blessing of God causes Isaac to be a most successful farmer (vv. 12–16). Isaac is still the conduit of blessing, warts and all. There is a great deal of comfort knowing the promises of God are not dependent only on our fickle faith. However, there is just as great a warning from watching all the conflict that occurs from Isaac's lack of faith (vv. 17–22).

When the Lord appears to Isaac a second time, his first command is "Fear not" (v. 24), especially appropriate after Isaac's reaction recorded in verse 7. Isaac is now in a position to be a blessing to others. He leads the way to genuine worship and trust and a testimony of the powerful presence of God (see especially v. 28). Fellowship replaces friction as the narrative closes.

Genesis 26:34–28:9

EXEGETICAL IDEA

Isaac's blind and self-centered leadership in attempting to subvert God's revealed will by advancing his disqualified son, though thwarted by deception, precipitated foolish responses and unnecessary conflict leading to sin and division, before conveying the appropriate Abrahamic blessing to his divinely chosen son.

THEOLOGICAL FOCUS

Poor leadership by God's chosen leaders produces dysfunction and conflict and engenders foolish choices by those under their lead, creating greater pain, even when rectified by God's providence.

PREACHING IDEA

God's people learn from this messed-up family to lead the way to be a blessing in their world.

PREACHING POINTERS

Forty-year-old Esau's action of taking wives forms the outer rim or bookends of this preaching portion and the first potential preaching point: he continues to function as a "go and do otherwise" character who does not share values associated with the promises and blessing of God. However, Isaac, Rebekah, and Jacob quickly join Esau and show God's chosen vessels to be a complete mess. They are all poor examples! Yet, this is God's chosen family, and he will continue to work his plan through Jacob.

God will accomplish his plan, and that includes directing the affairs of those with little or no faith. Esau's father, Isaac, had spiritual sight that matched his physical sight, as he intended to bless Esau. Isaac appears to value his favorite meal more than the plan of God. And then the parade of bad examples continues in this family as Rebekah and Jacob devise a plan to secure the blessing. Jacob's only concern is that their actions might bring a curse on himself "and not a blessing" (27:12). When Isaac delivers the blessing, its contents barely resemble the blessing promised to Abraham, another sign that Isaac's faith is immature at best. If any of our congregants questioned all the fuss about this family blessing, they learn from the father and son's reaction about what just happened. Both react with extreme emotion. And the anti-blessing or curse Esau receives makes it clear: to be blessed is far better. If Esau gets his way, another Cain-like murder will occur in Genesis due to the hatred Jacob's ruse created. Despite all her scheming, Rebekah does know how important it is that the son of promise marry in such a way that the promise and blessing might continue. Imagine a God powerful enough to move his purposes along with such ungodly means!

Genesis 28:10–22

EXEGETICAL IDEA

Appearing to Jacob as he fled, God granted him the Abrahamic promises of the land, innumerable offspring, and blessing to all people, with necessary personal protection and provision, prompting Jacob to consecrate the place as a worship center with vows of personal devotion.

THEOLOGICAL FOCUS

Never out of God's purview nor separated from his promises, God's people must recognize their role through committed devotion for his glory.

PREACHING IDEA

The dream of God's powerful presence comes true as we awake to worship him.

PREACHING POINTERS

Once again, the original audience hears theology through the adventures of Jacob. He is now the carrier of the promises of God and is on his way to secure a wife (see 27:46b–28:2). On this trip Jacob encounters the Lord in a spectacular dream. In that dream the original audience and our audiences experience their own review of God's promises to his people. One of the most comforting and stabilizing of all the promises of God is found in verse 15, "Behold, I am with you and will keep you wherever you go." Each generation of God's children hears him speak to them and has an opportunity to affirm that they believe God's promise. In this way God's people on earth are always at that "awesome . . . place" and "house of God" and "gate of heaven" (v. 17). Christians have been and continue to be encouraged by Jacob's dream throughout their own faith journeys. Early and later readers follow Jacob's example and respond to God's promises with their own: "then the Lord shall be my God. . . . And of all that you give me I will give a full tenth to you" (vv. 21–22).

Genesis 29:1–30

EXEGETICAL IDEA

Jacob's arrival in Haran revealed God's provision for Jacob's progeny and necessary lessons in deception and self-will, even as Jacob's pursuit of his own agenda ended in frustration and fitting consequences.

THEOLOGICAL FOCUS
Even when he is not obvious, God delivers on his promises, teaching his self-willed images the consequences of their folly and their need to walk with him for blessing.

PREACHING IDEA
We are all sons and daughters learning to endure the discipline of God to bring his blessing to the world.

PREACHING POINTERS
If you're preaching through this section of Genesis, by now your listeners know what kind of person Jacob is. He's God's chosen blessing-bearer, but Jacob has shown himself to be anything but godly. God has some work to do in him, in us, to accomplish his purposes in the world.

Enter the character of Laban. This explains why God would put Jacob through this long ordeal with his soon to be father-in-law. Jacob is about to come face-to-face with someone who plays by his own rules. God is about to refine Jacob's character through another character who does to him what Jacob did to his own father in order to secure the blessing. Jacob's patience will be tested through Laban's deception.

More importantly, instead of being served (one element of Isaac's blessing), Jacob ends up serving Laban. And all of this is God's way of training his chosen one to receive God's blessing so that he can be a blessing in the world. God is teaching Jacob how much he needs God's guidance and transforming power. Jacob's lack of wisdom and arrogance simply will not do. The way God disciplines and molds Jacob is a picture of what God is doing to each of his own children.

Genesis 29:31–30:43

EXEGETICAL IDEA
God humbled Rachel and Jacob and graciously provided children and flocks to his hurting, imperfect servants, fulfilling his promises and answering their desperate cries even as they experienced the consequences of their self-interest and foolish manipulations through conflict and broken relationships.

THEOLOGICAL FOCUS
God graciously fulfills his promises, helping the hurting, humbling the proud, and providing protection and provision for his chosen servants while allowing them to experience the consequences of their folly.

PREACHING IDEA
We receive hope and help from watching God keep his promise to a most dysfunctional family.

PREACHING POINTERS
The narrative portrays the faithfulness of God to bless Jacob despite the utter dysfunction of his family life. The original audience has a front row seat to watch the Lord spring into action

to build Jacob's family tree, a big part of the promise. God first responds to unloved Leah (29:31–35), then uses Rachel's servant (30:1–8), Leah's servant (30:9–13), and bizarre bargaining for Jacob (30:14–20)—and finally remembers Rachel (30:22–24). God is gracious to both Leah and Rachel in the middle of ancient Near Eastern family dynamics. God promised Jacob a huge family and God delivered, regardless of all the conflict (28:14). The Lord sees Leah and the Lord remembers Rachel, but there is no record yet in the narrative of Jacob interacting with the Lord on any of these family matters. Jacob does take initiative in 30:25–43 with respect to returning to his own country. What is clear through these pastoral scenes is that the Lord is causing Jacob to prosper: "Thus the man increased greatly" (v. 43).

What is amazing to readers is how the Lord grants his grace to Jacob and his family despite all the ungodly actions and motives of all members! And, again, we learn of God's intention not only to grant blessing but also to extend it through the ones he blesses (v. 30, "and the Lord has blessed you wherever I turned"). Finally, all readers should realize how much damage is done when God's people act selfishly instead of gladly submitting to his will in their lives.

Genesis 31:1–55 (HB 32:1)

EXEGETICAL IDEA

In escalating conflict, God directed Jacob to return to the promised land to fulfill his vow, teaching him God's authority over people and deities to protect, endow, and establish boundaries for his servants, despite their fearful and foolish reactions.

THEOLOGICAL FOCUS

God protects his servants, drawing them to faith and loyalty, keeping their promises, and trusting him to provide and protect even through foolish reactions and conflicts that only he can resolve.

PREACHING IDEA

Look at what God does to secure the blessing for and extend the blessing through his struggling, growing chosen ones!

PREACHING POINTERS

The original audience must have been encouraged to hear the record of how God protected Jacob through the Laban years. If any listeners are doubting God's ability to cause them to flourish in his will and in their relationship with him, their faith will be strengthened by seeing all that God does to bless Jacob despite Laban. God's wonderful promise, "and I will be with you," provides courage for his people just as it did for Jacob (v. 3). What congregant who is facing gross injustices isn't encouraged by overhearing "the angel of God" say to Jacob, "I have seen all that Laban is doing to you" (vv. 11–12)? Modern listeners will join early readers in seeing that God indeed has the desire and capacity to deliver on his wonderful promises to bless his faithful ones.

And what listener wouldn't be encouraged by reading about a helpless god being stolen? The so-called household gods (v. 35) are no match for Yahweh's power. Nothing can stop God from keeping his promises to bless his children so they can be a blessing. Laban's benefiting from

Jacob's presence and work shows how the blessing of God extends to others through his faithful ones (v. 38), but it also shows how God ultimately used Laban to provide for Jacob (v. 43).

Genesis 32:1–32 (HB 32:2–33)

EXEGETICAL IDEA
God's presence, verified by his angels, guaranteed Jacob's security and future blessing, despite Esau's threat and Jacob's self-reliance, ironically, by incapacitating him so that he might cling to Yahweh and receive blessing, commemorated by a new name.

THEOLOGICAL FOCUS
God's presence guarantees the security and blessing of his servants who turn to him in prayer, requiring humble dependence, graciously fostered through confrontation with their inability to secure it on their own.

PREACHING IDEA
God's training camp is where his children receive his blessing in his presence through trials, prayer, and humble dependence.

PREACHING POINTERS
The original audience learns theology that functions for the church through following Jacob's experiences as he journeys back to the promised land. His character functions both as a "go and do likewise" and a "go and do otherwise" exemplar. The pathway to transition for listeners occurs through encouraging them not to follow Jacob's example of fear and distress. Readers can see that Jacob only trusts God to a point, but that faith does not overcome his fears with respect to Esau's reaction. That explains why Jacob prepares for Esau's attack.

We can also encourage listeners to emulate Jacob as he prays to the Lord. His prayer is packed with instructions on how to address the Lord. The prayer also shows Jacob confessing his unworthiness to be on the receiving end of God's love and faithfulness. Jacob is honest with God about his fear of his brother, Esau. And, for his own sake, Jacob reminds God of the promise God made him.

One of the highlights of the section is Jacob wrestling with God at night. Jacob's bout shows his tenacity in desiring to receive God's blessing. His experience results in the kind of dependence that every true child of God must grow into. God changes Jacob's name to Israel, the meaning of which marks every true Christian because of Christ's work. God fought for his own and continues to fight in the person of Christ. And by faith we, like Jacob, cling to Christ and receive the blessing, the result of our wrestling with God.

Genesis 33:1–20

EXEGETICAL IDEA
Meeting Esau relieved Jacob's fears and revealed God's work in Esau bringing reconciliation and prompting Jacob to extend blessing and part in peace with public worship.

THEOLOGICAL FOCUS
God's working in hearts provides hope for reconciliation, blessing, and opportunity to extend blessing to others, exposes false hope in manipulation of relationships and circumstances, and leads to appropriate public worship.

PREACHING IDEA
Trust the Lord to fulfill his promise to bless you and make you a blessing—easier said than done in difficult relationships.

PREACHING POINTERS
Readers of Jacob's encounter with Esau are anxious to know how the meeting will go for Jacob. More specifically, listeners will be encouraged to see how the Lord fulfilled his promises to bless Jacob and make him a blessing when the situation with his brother was so tense. As the scenes proceed, the Lord clearly has been working in Jacob's and Esau's lives. With respect to Jacob's faith journey, the narrative shows his desire and capacity to bless his brother. Jacob can present Esau with an extravagant gift because the Lord has given Jacob so much.

The way Jacob reacts to Esau shows that he is not sure whether the Lord will protect him from his brother's rage (Jacob bows down to Esau, instead of the other way around, according to Isaac's oracle). There is no guarantee that God will give healing and peace in all difficult relationships. One way the Lord carries out his promise to Jacob is to change Esau's heart and allow reconciliation to take place. Jacob's worship at his arrival in Shechem shows his heart for the Lord. God had revealed his faithfulness to Jacob in this encounter with Esau, and now Jacob will move toward greater faithfulness to the Lord.

Genesis 34:1–31

EXEGETICAL IDEA
When Shechem raped Dinah, Jacob abdicated leadership to his sons, who deceptively risked their blessing and threatened assimilation for vengeance and profit, killing and plundering an entire Canaanite city instead of doing righteousness and justice and extending blessing from Yahweh.

THEOLOGICAL FOCUS
God's people must respond to evil in faith, according to God's character, by doing righteousness and justice to experience and extend blessing to their world rather than cursing from self-interest or vengeance.

PREACHING IDEA
Overcoming "evil with good" is the only way to be a blessing in God's world.

PREACHING POINTERS
The original audience would have been appalled to read what Shechem did to Dinah (v. 2). Even the tenderness recorded by the narrator in verse 3 would not be enough. The transition to modern listeners begins with this unfolding plot of Shechem trying to marry

Dinah after what he had done to her. What a test for Jacob's family! According to Jacob's mission, they have a job to do in the world: bring God's blessing by the way they live and reveal Yahweh (see Gen. 28:14). In Genesis 18:19 the Lord had said, "For I have chosen him, that he may command his children and his household after him to keep the way of the LORD by doing righteousness and justice, so that the LORD may bring to Abraham what he has promised him."

Jacob's sons are furious because they recognize the injustice; all the while, their father is silent (34:5, 7). And early readers recognize the spiritual danger in Shechem's father's request: "Make marriages with us" (vv. 9–10). Will anyone trust the Lord in this narrative? Evidently not, as Jacob's sons act the way he used to ("deceitfully" in v. 13). So much for doing righteousness and justice.

The Hivites fall for it and suffer because of it. And so does God's plan for his people, at least temporarily, because of Jacob's inactivity. The narrative concludes with the question, "Should he treat our sister like a prostitute?" (v. 31). The answer is, "No." Preachers might conclude with another question, "Should God's people act in the place of God and act vengefully?" The answer is also, "No."

Genesis 35:1–29

EXEGETICAL IDEA
At God's prompting, Jacob purified his camp and traveled to Bethel to fulfill his vow, where he worshipped, received God's extended covenant promises and challenge for God's future program, and continued in the land, burying the past with its human failures and struggles and erecting monuments to God's faithful working.

THEOLOGICAL FOCUS
God moves his servant to faithful service and worship, putting away self-effort and fruitless struggle, centering on God's faithfulness, and trusting God's promise for future blessing and fulfillment of God's good purposes.

PREACHING IDEA
Worship, purify, and trust: three responses to God's promised blessing in a curse-contaminated world.

PREACHING POINTERS
God's command to Jacob in 35:1 provides ancient and postmodern audiences with an opportunity to learn or review one of the most basic aspects of the life of faith: true worship of Yahweh alone. God graciously nudges Jacob to fulfill the vow he promised earlier about going to Bethel. A vital part of worshipping the Lord is putting away the foreign gods (v. 2), anything that competes with God for supremacy in our lives.

Jacob's instruction to his own household and those traveling with him signifies the need for all of God's people to continually allow the Spirit of God to transform them into righteous pilgrims. True worship includes being changed into a person that reflects God's holiness. As we've seen so many times before in Genesis, God continues to protect his children so they can experience his blessing (v. 5).

Experiencing the blessing, however, is always in the context of suffering the results of the curse. The narrative shows this by recording multiple deaths of significant people (vv. 8, 19, 29). And there is still the presence of sin (v. 22 on Reuben's immorality and Israel's hearing but doing nothing). However, God also reinforces his promise to bless Jacob. The blessing includes a name change, which teaches us about the importance of growing into the kind of person who represents God well in his world. Another name-changing event occurs around the death of Rachel as she gave birth to Benjamin (v. 18). There is hope for God's children in the future even though they are badly flawed and live in a badly broken world.

Genesis 36:1–37:1

EXEGETICAL IDEA

From his Canaanite wives Esau produced a large family with powerful clans, which he moved to Seir, establishing a national identity and fulfilling God's word, while Jacob sojourned in Canaan waiting for God's promise.

THEOLOGICAL FOCUS

God can always be trusted to keep his word, even to profane people, but his purposes in his chosen servants are often only realized over extended time through testing and trials.

PREACHING IDEA

God will do what he says, moving his people out into his promised rule, but we may have to wait, enduring testing, to experience his best.

PREACHING POINTERS

While few preaching venues will allow the time to devote to this section, it provides fertile ground for reflection and instruction for the people of God. Though few modern western listeners enjoy a genealogy, reflection on the implications of this genealogy in the context of God's promises to his people shows God's working. He works not only in Israel's life, but also in the lives of the nations around them. He keeps the promises not only to Abraham, Isaac, and Jacob, but also to their other offspring. In fact, here we see the promises to Esau bearing fruit while Jacob seems to be in a waiting state. Our chapter, then, focuses on Esau's family tree (36:1).

The fact that Esau takes "wives from the Canaanites" is a bad sign (v. 2). This means that "the sons of Esau who were born to him in the land of Canaan" (v. 5) will be Jacob's neighboring nations. You can see that God's blessing is on Esau's family along with Jacob's family, so much so that they must separate in the land (vv. 7–8). You may want to do some cross-referencing to find more about the Edomites, "the sons of Esau (that is, Edom)" (v. 19). Esau's family tree includes numerous kings and kingdoms (v. 31). And this is all before Israel had any king. Later in redemptive history, the fact that all the nations have kings drives Israel's request for a king, to be like them. We learn from 37:1 that "Jacob lived in the land of his father's sojournings, in the land of Canaan." The two brothers may have reconciled, but we must wonder how these families will get along as neighbors.

Genesis 37:2–36

EXEGETICAL IDEA

Joseph's favored status and future role in God's program deepen his brothers' animosity, supplying their excuse to eliminate him by selling him into slavery and covering it up, devastating Jacob yet advancing God's plan for his chosen family.

THEOLOGICAL FOCUS

Though human failings and even God's favor may induce desperate evil actions that cause grievous human suffering, God will quietly orchestrate circumstances to accomplish his purposes.

PREACHING IDEA

Make no doubt about it: no forms of evil in or around us can stop God's purpose for us.

PREACHING POINTERS

This is not the first time the original audience becomes engrossed in redemptive history featuring an unlikely pathway to God keeping his covenant promises to royal families (the families God chooses to receive and extend His blessing). No one expects Joseph to ascend to power the way he does! The boy Joseph is featured and favored but gets into immediate trouble that threatens his life. Sibling rivalry once again threatens the promise. And, as God's people have seen before, this promising youngster has a lot of growing up to do. He is chosen by God to lead his people, but God will mature him along the way. Because of the dreams, readers know what is in store for Joseph and his brothers.

Our audience can be assured that their God will also keep his promises to them despite the ups and downs experienced through life. Some of the bumps are self-caused, as in Joseph's case; it is no wonder his brothers loathe him! Other bumps are caused by others, as is also Joseph's case. Either way, God will not abandon his own. It may feel like God's people are "wandering" about through life (v. 15), but everything is moving according to God's plan. That is true even when God's plan includes our pain.

If not for the prophecy of Genesis 15:13, first readers and modern readers might think all is lost as they read the end of chapter 37: "They took Joseph to Egypt" (v. 28). Joseph's dream will come true after all; he will rule over his family, and God's purposes will be established. It was true then and is just as true now.

Genesis 38:1–30

EXEGETICAL IDEA

God prepared the line of Judah for his promise, judging evil and blessing Tamar's righteous actions, granting her children to prepare for greater blessing while exposing Judah's heart to initiate heart change.

THEOLOGICAL FOCUS
God achieves his promises and program both directly by judging sin and indirectly by rewarding the righteous acts of all who value his promises and standards and disciplining his people who stray.

PREACHING IDEA
Neither blatant sin nor borderline righteousness will keep God from fulfilling his promises for the sake of his reputation.

PREACHING POINTERS
While the original audience is left wondering what will happen to the main character, Joseph, they learn about the character of his brother, Judah. Our audience will once again find themselves in this narrative through the examples of Judah and his daughter-in-law Tamar. Judah and his sons provide several "go and do otherwise" examples. Although Judah is clearly in the line of the Messiah, his actions help all listeners by urging us to reflect God's character and remain faithful to him.

Tamar, on the other hand, is more in tune with God's plan and purposes. She is a widow that suffers from Judah's injustice and takes matters into her own hands. While, from our cultural perspective, it is difficult to applaud her methods, she does emerge as the more righteous one. Original and contemporary audiences all get a glimpse of God's judgment as he shows his displeasure with Judah's sons.

If listeners have been traveling with us through this Genesis journey, the way God's promise is carried in Judah's family is another example of God working his plan through unlikely events. He will not be thwarted with respect to fulfilling his promise to bless a people and to bless the nations through that people. His people are not always godly, but God is always working his plan to perfection through imperfect people.

Genesis 39:1–23

EXEGETICAL IDEA
Yahweh's presence brought Joseph spectacular success both in Potiphar's service as his personal attendant and in prison after being falsely accused when he righteously resisted Potiphar's wife's advances.

THEOLOGICAL FOCUS
While God's presence provides success, righteous living in the face of temptation may include suffering and loss to accomplish God's purposes within his faithful care.

PREACHING IDEA
Success, severe setback, temptation: expect it all with heavy doses of God's powerful presence and loyal love for the faithful.

PREACHING POINTERS

The original audience sees that things are not going well for Joseph, and they have no idea how the Lord is going to fulfill his promises to bless him so he can be a blessing to the nations. Nothing about the opening verse is promising. That is, until we read: "The Lord was with Joseph, and he became a successful man" (v. 2). Very quickly readers begin to see some hope as his master sees God's blessing on Joseph, gives him almost total control over his affairs, and experiences the blessing of God "on all that he had, in house and field" (vv. 3–6). Listeners are encouraged as they learn that the same Lord is with them in a powerful way as they walk with him each day. Their success may vary, depending on what the Lord has gifted them to do, but they will be able to accomplish his will in their sphere of influence.

But, just as quickly, everything appears to come unglued due to a tragic injustice done to Joseph by Potiphar's wife. God puts Joseph to the test, and he passes it with flying colors (v. 9). But God does not spare Joseph from tremendous heartache. Listeners must see that the life of faith, the powerful presence of God, and the ability to perform his will also include hardship. Great comfort comes with belief that, as the Lord did to Joseph, he will also continue to show "his steadfast love and . . . favor" (v. 21). For listeners who value God's kingdom, great encouragement comes from knowing that the Lord's presence guarantees our success in accomplishing his will. This is especially important when we face circumstances like Joseph's, those times when we have no idea of how things will work together for good.

Genesis 40:1–41:57

EXEGETICAL IDEA

God clarified Joseph's perspective and provided for his world by moving Joseph to prominence in Egypt, beginning with his dream interpretation for Pharaoh's officials, and culminating in his interpretation and advice for Pharaoh.

THEOLOGICAL FOCUS

Working behind the scenes, God orchestrates events to use his people to accomplish his blessing in his world in his time, while growing their faith and perspective in his service.

PREACHING IDEA

Even when you feel forgotten by God, he is working his purposes and accomplishing his will.

PREACHING POINTERS

For any listeners whose experiences seem to contradict what God has promised them, this segment of the Joseph story is a welcomed tonic. Chapter 39 ended with the hope-filled "And whatever he did, the Lord made it succeed" (v. 23). But at the beginning of chapter 40, Joseph is still in prison unjustly. God is continuing to give success by arranging to have two dreamy prisoners assigned to Joseph's prison. Both original and contemporary audiences see what's happening: God is moving Joseph into position so he can accomplish God's will to experience and extend his blessing to the world.

The vehicle of success in Joseph's case is his God-given ability to interpret dreams. And this ability gets him that much closer to realizing his own dream. The fact that Joseph is forgotten (40:23) only delays Joseph's rise to prominence because in chapter 41 Pharaoh dreams too. We already know who is able to interpret the dream. The cupbearer who forgot about Joseph now "remember[s]" his offenses before Pharaoh and tells him about Joseph's abilities (vv. 9–13). Amazing series of circumstances, don't you think?

Numerous times in the narrative Joseph testifies that his God gets the credit for his interpretative skills (41:16, 25, 28, 32) and even Pharaoh buys this explanation (41:38, 39). In the end, Joseph names his two sons, and listeners can receive hope as they accomplish God's will in a badly broken world. Like Joseph, they too can be an instrument for carrying out God's desire to bless the nations.

Genesis 42:1–44:34

EXEGETICAL IDEA
Two trips to Egypt with ongoing testing during God's designed famine revealed God's work in Joseph's brothers, bringing them to repentance and unity to save Benjamin through Judah's self-sacrifice.

THEOLOGICAL FOCUS
God uses testing and life circumstances to awaken the consciences of his people and lead them to repentance, prompting them to choose brother-love and self-sacrifice over self-love.

PREACHING IDEA
Our sovereign God, in his perfect timing, transforms us all by testing our faith so we can represent him in the world.

PREACHING POINTERS
The original audience has been watching Joseph's rise to power, albeit with some ups and downs along the way. They know the dreams are coming true. So when chapter 41 concludes with "all the earth [coming] to Egypt to Joseph to buy grain" (v. 57), all that's left is for Joseph's whole family to arrive (chapters 42–44). The first part of the dream comes true in 42:6. Now it is time for Joseph's brothers to come face-to-face with their sins (quite the opposite of their own estimation: "We are honest men" in 42:11, 31, 33, 34).

Joseph crafts the perfect set of circumstances to test their integrity (42:15, "By this you will be tested") and lead them to repentance. Trying to convince his father, Israel, to allow "the boy" to join his brothers, a transformed Judah promises to protect him (43:9). Joseph constructs the visit in a way that highlights how the brothers will treat their youngest brother, Benjamin. Full confession follows in 44:20. This part of the narrative unfolds with Judah leading the way to making sure he and his brothers do not repeat the sins of their past. Their dialogue is replete with confession and genuine guilt for the way in which they treated their brother Joseph. The test works.

Genesis 45:1–28

EXEGETICAL IDEA

Revealing his identity, Joseph declared God's sovereign oversight of history to accomplish his purposes of preserving life and fulfilling his promises, prompting Joseph's forgiveness and reconciliation of their relationships, and the blessing and restoration for the family in Egypt.

THEOLOGICAL FOCUS

God's sovereign working in human history grounds his faithfulness to his promises and the necessary human responses of forgiveness, reconciliation, and restoration to experience his blessing.

PREACHING IDEA

Trust God's sovereignty and be freed to forgive, reconcile relationships, and experience his blessings.

PREACHING POINTERS

Joseph's actions towards and dialogue with his brothers teaches the original audience and modern listeners. In the opening scene Joseph tells his brothers not to "be distressed or angry with" themselves because they sold him into slavery (v. 5). Clearly God has done a strong work in Joseph's heart for him to arrive at this place. Most of us can think of situations far less extreme than Joseph's when yet it was very hard to extend forgiveness.

At last, all the friction in this family is healed; Joseph stops the intense testing of his brothers, and a reunion is about to take place. In that same verse, Joseph explains his perspective: "for God sent me before you to preserve life" (v. 5). In verses 7 and 8 the announcement of God's sovereignty continues with more detail. This is one of those rare chapters in Genesis that provides a clear doctrine for us to preach. In verses 16–20 Pharaoh announces to Joseph: "the best of all the land of Egypt is yours" (v. 20). Pharaoh's words show that God's promise to Abraham, which we learned about in Genesis 15 is coming true. This is in large part due to Joseph's belief in and faithfulness to God as Joseph's dream finally came true (45:26, "he is ruler over all the land of Egypt").

Genesis 46:1–47:31

EXEGETICAL IDEA

God honored Israel's worshipful obedience, richly blessing his family through Pharaoh, increasing them, and blessing Pharaoh and all Egypt for honoring his chosen family.

THEOLOGICAL FOCUS

God moves his plan forward, going with his worshippers into difficult times to accomplish his purpose: blessing his faithful people, those who bless them, and his world.

PREACHING IDEA
God's faithful resist their fears by resting in his presence to experience God's blessing and extend his blessing to others.

PREACHING POINTERS
One of the most exciting features of this narrative section is the way in which it shows God's people experiencing many of the promises of the covenant he made with Abraham. God is showing himself faithful to his covenant; his people are being blessed and extending the blessing to others even though the process has been filled with troubling circumstances. Original and current audiences gain confidence in God's ability to fulfill his promises to them in a badly broken world.

Just think about all that God has put Joseph through en route to ruling in Egypt. Just think about all the emotional agony Israel has experienced concerning Joseph. Just think about all the years that have gone by with all those ups and downs. The narrative begins with Israel worshipping at Beersheba (46:1) and God speaking to him about not being afraid to go to Egypt, where God would make Israel a great nation and accompany him (46:3–4). When Joseph's father and brothers are reunited in Egypt and presented to Pharaoh, they hear evidence of the blessing: "Settle your father and your brothers in the best of the land" (47:6, 11). Then, the narrator makes it clear: "Jacob blessed Pharaoh" (47:7, 10). And then, from verses 13–31 Joseph continues to bless everyone, especially the Egyptians, as he works his wise plan for saving lives through the terrible famine. God is faithful and his faithful can count on experiencing what he promises: "they . . . were fruitful and multiplied greatly" (47:27).

Genesis 48:1–22

EXEGETICAL IDEA
Reflecting on God's promises and faithful shepherding throughout his life, Jacob blessed Joseph with the birthright, elevating Joseph's sons and passing the covenant promises on to the next generation for the future blessing of the burgeoning nation, through God's ongoing presence and care.

THEOLOGICAL FOCUS
God's promises and faithful care for his people ground their loyalty and faith, passing on their legacy and pursuit of his future blessing to the next generation as God carries out his redemptive plan.

PREACHING IDEA
Trust in God's promise to bless you and to make you a blessing to the next generation of disciple-makers.

PREACHING POINTERS
Our God has been blessing his creation since the beginning of Genesis. In 1:28 we read, "And God blessed them. And God said to them, 'Be fruitful and multiply.'" And now in chapter 48 we read Jacob telling Joseph: "God . . . blessed me, and said to me, 'Behold, I will make you

fruitful and multiply you'" (vv. 3–4). The original audience must have been encouraged to see God's continued faithfulness to his people. As we read of Jacob blessing Joseph and his two sons, we receive encouragement from knowing that our Lord wants to bless us and wants us to extend his blessing to others around us.

Jacob's blessing to Joseph includes a rehearsal of God's faithful care. We take great comfort in his words, "the God who has been my shepherd all my life long to this day" (v. 15b). We too must look for God's faithful care in our past to ground our anticipation and preparation for God's working in future generations.

And, of course, the challenge is for us to make sure we are also characterized as those who walk with God (v. 15a). In the blessing of Joseph's younger son, there is a strong reminder to us that the blessing of God does not move according to conventional standards of the day. It is solely based on his grace and mercy. Finally, Israel teaches us that the blessing of God goes along with his powerful, ongoing presence (v. 21, "but God will be with you").

Genesis 49:1–28

EXEGETICAL IDEA

Jacob declared God's blessing for the future tribes of Israel as they would loyally follow him: disqualifying the eldest for unrighteousness and injustice, elevating Judah to lead the tribes and nations, prospering Joseph with God's abundance and fulfilled promises, and reminding all that deliverance only comes from Yahweh.

THEOLOGICAL FOCUS

God's people experience his discipline for unrighteousness and injustice but enjoy his blessing as they loyally follow him, leading his work, experiencing his fulfilled promises, and understanding that deliverance only comes from Yahweh.

PREACHING IDEA

God's people believe in and faithfully follow "the Almighty who will bless you with blessings of heaven above" (49:25) while suffering loss for unfaithfulness.

PREACHING POINTERS

We know from the final verse in our preaching portion that the things Jacob tells his sons that "shall happen to" them (v. 1) are the "blessing" (v. 28). God has promised blessing on his people from the beginning of the Genesis narrative. We preach this section to people who profess to know God through faith in Christ. Primarily, this Scripture reminds them of the spiritual blessings they have in Christ and his Spirit, both now and forever. While the details pertaining to each son are not relevant for modern listeners, the idea of blessing is.

More specifically, the non-blessing on the first three sons and extra blessings on Judah (vv. 8–12) and Joseph (vv. 22–26) do provide glimpses into how God continues to work with his people of faith. Concerning the first three boys, this non-blessing shows that unbelief and disobedience have consequences. It is because of our relationship as children of God that he lovingly disciplines us when we sin against him. His discipline is designed to add righteousness.

The blessing on Judah reminds us of our Savior's rule and our obedience of faith, the combination that results in LifePlus now and complete blessings upon his return. The blessed life, mentioned six times, is described in the Joseph section. We may have attendees overhearing our worship, and this text does show that God is the source of blessing (vv. 18, 24–25), a blessing they can receive only by faith and experience now through obedience.

Genesis 49:29–50:26

EXEGETICAL IDEA
Because Jacob and Joseph recognized God's good oversight and expected his promises beyond their last days, God could greatly bless them, and Joseph could respond with grace and forgiveness to his brothers' evil.

THEOLOGICAL FOCUS
Faith in God's current and future working to accomplish his good purposes gains God's blessing and shapes the believer's response to death and life.

PREACHING IDEA
Faith in God's faithfulness and powerful sovereignty inevitably shapes the way believers respond to both death and life.

PREACHING POINTERS
Modern listeners, like the original audience, worship by trusting God like Jacob as he neared death. After blessing his sons, he commanded them to bury him back in Canaan—where God's people ultimately belong (49:29–32). The way that the Egyptians responded to Jacob's death teaches us how God's people can be salt and light in their world (50:11, "a grievous mourning"). Jacob fulfilled his calling of blessing others with the blessing he received from the Lord.

Jacob's faith is not the only faith on display in this section. Joseph also shows us how faith in the promises of God leads to godliness in the form of forgiveness. Joseph's brothers relayed a message from their father, "Please forgive," and Joseph responded with genuine tears and faith, refusing to take God's place by being vengeful (50:17, 19). Joseph also provides one of the clearest statements about the sovereign power and purposes of God: "As for you, you meant evil against me, but God meant it for good, to bring it about that many people should be kept alive" (50:20). It is one of those statements of theological reality that provides stability for believers living in a badly broken world where evil can and does happen.

ABBREVIATIONS

GENERAL ABBREVIATIONS

AD	*anno Domini* (in the year of our Lord)
BC	Before Christ
HB	Hebrew Bible
LXX	Septuagint
MT	Masoretic Text
NT	New Testament
OT	Old Testament
SP	Samaritan Pentateuch
TO	Targum Onkelos

TECHNICAL ABBREVIATIONS

ca.	circa
cf.	*confer* (compare)
ch(s).	chapter(s)
col(s).	column(s)
ed.	edition
e.g.	for example
esp.	especially
et al.	*et alii* (and others)
etc.	*et cetera* (and so forth, and the rest)
fn.	footnote
Hi	*Hiphil*
i.e.	*id est* (that is)
inf.	infinitive
lit.	literally
n(n).	note(s)
p(p).	page(s)
Pi	*Piel*
s.v.	*sub verbo* (under the word)
trans.	translation
txt.	text
v(v).	verse(s)
vol(s).	volume(s)

BIBLICAL SOURCES

Old Testament

Gen.	Genesis
Exod.	Exodus
Lev.	Leviticus
Num.	Numbers
Deut.	Deuteronomy
Josh.	Joshua
Judg.	Judges
Ruth	Ruth
1 Sam.	1 Samuel
2 Sam.	2 Samuel
1 Kings	1 Kings
2 Kings	2 Kings
1 Chron.	1 Chronicles
2 Chron.	2 Chronicles
Ezra	Ezra
Neh.	Nehemiah
Esther	Esther
Job	Job
Ps./Pss.	Psalm(s)
Prov.	Proverbs
Eccl.	Ecclesiastes
Song	Song of Songs
Isa.	Isaiah
Jer.	Jeremiah
Lam.	Lamentations
Ezek.	Ezekiel
Dan.	Daniel
Hos.	Hosea
Joel	Joel
Amos	Amos
Obad.	Obadiah
Jonah	Jonah
Micah	Micah
Nah.	Nahum

Old Testament (continued)

Hab.	Habakkuk
Zeph.	Zephaniah
Hag.	Haggai
Zech.	Zechariah
Malachi	Malachi

New Testament

Matt.	Matthew
Mark	Mark
Luke	Luke
John	John
Acts	Acts
Rom.	Romans
1 Cor.	1 Corinthians
2 Cor.	2 Corinthians
Gal.	Galatians
Eph.	Ephesians
Phil.	Philippians
Col.	Colossians
1 Thess.	1 Thessalonians
2 Thess.	2 Thessalonians
1 Tim.	1 Timothy
2 Tim.	2 Timothy
Titus	Titus
Philem.	Philemon
Heb.	Hebrews
James	James
1 Peter	1 Peter
2 Peter	2 Peter
1 John	1 John
2 John	2 John
3 John	3 John
Jude	Jude
Rev.	Revelation

REFERENCES

ABD	Freedman, D. N., ed. 1992. *Anchor Bible Dictionary*. 6 vols. New York: Doubleday.
ANET	Pritchard, James B. 1969. *Ancient Near Eastern Texts Relating to The Old Testament*. 3rd ed. Princeton, NJ.: Princeton University Press.
BDB	Brown, Francis, Samuel Rolles Driver, and Charles Augustus Briggs. 1977. *Enhanced Brown-Driver-Briggs Hebrew and English Lexicon*. Oxford: Clarendon Press.
CAD	Gelb, Ignace J., Michael P. Streck, and Oriental Institute University of Chicago. 1956–2010. *Assyrian Dictionary*. 23 vols. Chicago: University of Chicago Press.
CoS	Hallo, William W., and K. Lawson Younger. 1997–2017. *Context of Scripture*. 4 vols. Leiden; Boston: Brill.
DOTP	Alexander, T. Desmond, and David W. Baker. 2003. *Dictionary of the Old Testament: Pentateuch*. IVP Bible Dictionary Series 1. Downers Grove, IL: InterVarsity Press.
HALOT	Köhler, Ludwig, and Walter Baumgartner. 2000. *The Hebrew and Aramaic Lexicon of the Old Testament*. Edited by Johann Jakob Stamm. Translated by M. E. J. Richardson. Leiden: Brill.
GKC	Gesenius, Wilhelm, E. Kautzsch, and A. E. Cowley. 1910. *Gesenius' Hebrew Grammar*. 2nd English ed. Oxford: Clarendon.
JM	Joüon, Paul, and T. Muraoka. 1993. *A Grammar of Biblical Hebrew*. Subsidia Biblica 14. 2 vols. Rome: Editrice Pontificio Istituto Biblico.
NBD	Wood, D. R. W., and I. Howard Marshall. *New Bible Dictionary*. Leicester, England; Downers Grove, IL: InterVarsity Press, 1996.
NIDOTTE	VanGemeren, W. A., ed. 1997. *New International Dictionary of Old Testament Theology*. 5 vols. Grand Rapids: Zondervan.
OEAE	Redford, Donald B. 2001. *The Oxford Encyclopedia of Ancient Egypt*. 3 vols. Oxford: Oxford University Press.
TDOT	Botterweck, G. J., H. Ringgren, and H.-J. Fabry, eds. 1974–2006. *Theological Dictionary of the Old Testament*. Trans. J. T. Willis et al. 17 vols. Grand Rapids: Eerdmans.
TLOT	Jenni, Ernst, and Claus Westermann. 1997. *Theological Lexicon of the Old Testament*. Peabody, MA: Hendrickson.
TWOT	Harris, R. Laird, Gleason Leonard Archer, and Bruce K. Waltke, eds. 1980. *Theological Wordbook of the Old Testament*. 2 vols. Chicago: Moody Press.
WOC	Waltke, Bruce K., and Michael Patrick O'Connor. 1990. *An Introduction to Biblical Hebrew Syntax*. Winona Lake, IN: Eisenbrauns.

BIBLE TRANSLATIONS

ERV	English Revised Version
ESV	English Standard Version
HCSB	Holman Christian Standard Bible
JPS	Jewish Publication Society, 1917
NASB	New American Standard Bible
NCV	New Century Version
NET	New English Translation
NIV	New International Version
NJPS	Jewish Publication Society, 1985
NKJV	New King James Version
NLT	New Living Translation
NRSV	New Revised Standard Version
RSV	Revised Standard Version

INTRODUCTION TO GENESIS

OVERVIEW OF GENESIS

Author: Moses with some later inspired editing

Place of Writing: Wilderness journey after leaving Egypt

Original Readers: Israel coming out of Egypt

Date: Early to mid-thirteenth century BC

Historical Setting: Wilderness wanderings after Israel's exodus from Egypt

Occasion: Giving of the Mosaic Covenant to Israel as they are being commissioned in their role as God's chosen people to represent him and mediate true worship to his world (Exod. 19:4–6)

Literary Genre: Narrative (with some genealogy, oracle, and poetry).

Theological Emphasis: Yahweh, the sovereign creator of the universe, chose the descendants of Abraham to bring blessing out of cursing to all humanity by representing him and leading humanity to true worship, in the face of humanity's persistent rebellion.

NAME

The book of Genesis, or "Beginning," appropriately begins both the Jewish and Christian Scriptures because it provides the necessary foundation for the overall metanarrative and the theology of both. It takes its English name from the title of the Greek translation (Septuagint or LXX—Γενεσις Κοσμου, "The Genesis of the Cosmos"), which is also the Greek term used to translate the Hebrew term *toledot* (תּוֹלְדוֹת), the main structural marker for the Hebrew narrative (see below). The Greek term means "beginning," particularly in the sense of birth, as well as lineage or history (Louw and Nida 1989, 2:50).

The idea of beginnings is especially suitable because of the many ways that Genesis sets the stage for the purpose and plan of God, including the goal for the nation of Israel and the foundation of the covenantal promises. Theologically, Genesis, beginning with the creation account, contends for a unique understanding of Israel's God in the ancient world. Yahweh is transcendent, good, and purposeful in his relationship with humankind, and humankind has a unique purpose and place in the world before God, as God's images. Not only do we learn about the initiation of history, but we come to understand the necessary theological context for the historical development up to Israel's time of coming out of Egypt, including their place on the world stage. That being said, it provides for Israel a dramatically different worldview along with the necessary backdrop to God's working in history up to the New Testament and the long-awaited consummation of the age.

Genesis then, envisions the completion of God's plan throughout history. Genesis 1 presents God's creation of the universe, with special reference to the centrality of humanity as God's vice regent. Genesis 2 places humankind in the sacred precinct of the garden with assigned responsibilities, which include leading in worship of the Creator. Genesis 3 relates the fall of humankind, with the resultant damage, danger, and hope in God. The outworking of that fall is dark (Gen. 4–11) until God moves to bring hope through a covenant with Abraham, looking forward to bringing blessing to all the families of the earth (12:1–3). The themes of the garden and the role of humanity as both king and priest will culminate in Christ fulfilling God's covenant with Abraham and accomplishing God's promised blessing by restoring mankind to their position and role before God (Rev. 20:6). Ultimately, these themes culminate in the New Jerusalem as the fruition of what began in the garden (Rev. 22:1–5).

AUTHORSHIP OF GENESIS

Taking the later Scripture at face value, the Pentateuch is basically the work of Moses, Israel's chosen leader as God brought them out of Egypt. While the Pentateuch itself refers to Moses writing some of the content (Exod. 17:14; 24:4; 34:27; Num. 33:2; Deut. 31:9, 24), later Old Testament books cite Moses as the author of the "book of the law" (Josh. 1:7–8; Ezra 6:18; etc.), and the New Testament appears to unanimously refer to the whole Pentateuch in the name of Moses (Luke 16:29; 24:27; Acts 26:22). None of this requires Moses to have written every word, nor does the New Testament name the books, but the traditions clearly view Moses as the basic source.

Critical scholarship has questioned Moses as the source of Genesis since the middle of the nineteenth century. While there are clear cases in which some later inspired editing must have occurred (Dan, for example, was not "Dan" until the period of the Judges—Gen. 14:14; cf. Judg. 18:29, see Grisanti 2001), the names, style, customs, settings, and numerous details fit a much earlier period than the critical dates permit (Kitchen 2003, 313–52), allowing Moses to compile the main materials. For additional reading on this issue, see Collins (2006, 221–35), Hess (2007, 46–59), and Sarna (1989, xiii–xiv). If we accept a general Mosaic origin, we also, then, must recognize the implications for the setting and audience of the narrative, which in turn impacts our understanding of the message and theology.

DATE AND PLACE OF WRITING

Assuming Moses provided most of the Pentateuch, then we must ask, "When?" For those who accept a historical exodus and a historical Moses, there are generally two main positions. The traditional setting for the exodus is in the mid-fifteenth century BC because 1 Kings 6:1 places the beginning of the temple of Solomon in his fourth year and 480 years after the exodus from Egypt. Solomon's fourth year would have been about 967–66 BC, giving a date of the Exodus at about 1447–46 BC On the other hand, the naming of the city of Raamses in Exodus 1:11 suggests a later date, to correspond with the Egyptian Pharaohs of that name (Hoffmeier 1997, 116–19). Many scholars also see a greater coherence with the archaeological record with a date in the early thirteenth century (ca. 1290–50 BC) instead of the mid-fifteenth century BC In that case, the number 480 in 1 Kings 6:1 would be understood as generational or symbolic.[1] In our estimation, the later date better fits the evidence as a whole.

---

1 For discussion from a late date perspective, see Hoffmeier (1997; 2007). For discussion from an early date perspective, see Wood (2007).

Regardless of which date one accepts, the Egyptian setting of the exodus will significantly aid in understanding the message of the Genesis narratives. It puts the writing of the book in the wilderness soon after the exodus. Some was likely written early in the wilderness wanderings (Sinai and soon after, as Exodus was), and Deuteronomy clearly represents the end of Moses's life in the plains of Moab before they enter the land.

Prominent Egyptian gods (out of almost 1,500 known gods and goddesses [Wilkinson 2003, 6])	
Amun	• deity of Thebes • self-created creator deity, god of wind or breath • sometimes merged with Re as Amun-Re and connected with the sun; creator of man
Aten/ Aton	• sun disc • creator and giver of life • later became the focus of Akhenaten's attempt to force worship of only one god in Egypt (fourteenth century BC)
Atum	• deity of Heliopolis who was connected with Re as Atum-Re • sun god and self-created creator, making gods, plants, animals, and man (from his tears)
Geb	• deity of Heliopolis • god of earth • married to Nut, the sky goddess
Hekat	• deity of Elephantine • goddess of fertility • wife of Khnum • animated man with her breath
Khnum	• deity of Elephantine • god who was the source of the Nile • creator of humankind on a potter's wheel from clay
Nun	• deity of Hermopolis • god of the primordial waters • the source of all that becomes creation
Nut	• deity of Heliopolis • goddess of the sky and heavenly bodies • wife of Geb
Ptah	• deity of Memphis and connected to the primordial mound • creator who called the world into being • patron of artists
Re/Ra	• deity of Heliopolis • sun god and creator who created man as his image and animated man with his breath
Shu	• deity of Heliopolis • a personification of air who held his daughter (Nut, the sky goddess) and separated her from his son (Geb, earth god)

OCCASION FOR WRITING

With Genesis being written to an Israel coming out of Egypt, we need to read it considering that audience and their concerns and needs (or God's concerns for them!). After four hundred or so years in Egypt, they had assimilated significantly to the culture and worship of the Egyptians, which God would address. In fact, Joshua stated that they were still carrying around Egyptian gods at the end of Joshua's life (Josh. 24:14, 23), and centuries later God still reminded them through Ezekiel of their infatuation with the gods of Egypt from the time of their exodus (Ezek. 20:7–8, 24) as he continued to discipline Israel for the same sorts of idolatry. In Genesis, God would provide a worldview reset, with a renewed understanding of Yahweh, humanity's role before him, and Israel's national identity and role before him as his chosen and covenant people. These messages are still appropriate today as we struggle with assimilation into the culture with its prevailing worldview and our role before God as his chosen new covenant people.

INITIAL RECIPIENTS

The oppressed Israelites leaving Egypt needed to understand their future in a new land that Yahweh was promising them, along with a new role in his world. The worldview that they had adopted shaped their understanding of their origins, life's meaning, right and wrong (is the source of morality in God or the gods?), and their future destiny. Genesis presented a radically different worldview. Their origin begins with a single, all-powerful, uncreated Creator who is outside of creation and on whom all creation depends. In addition, their national origin presented a transformational perspective as God chose them and orchestrated their history. He even moved them from slavery to a kingdom of priests in his service to bring blessing to the world. Yahweh, the sole, sovereign creator, is the source of meaning and morality, which he codified in the Mosaic covenant in Exodus (chs. 20–24), Leviticus, and Deuteronomy. Right and wrong, then, was based in the character of Yahweh and defined by their holy God. Their future destiny was grounded in him as creator, requiring walking with him in sustained relationship. Of course, all this radically challenged their Egyptianized worldview. As the reader begins to realize, it was much easier to take Israel out of Egypt than to remove Egypt from Israel.

While they had digested much of the worldview of Egypt, as evidenced by their worship, it is hard to say how much they remembered of their own history and divine purpose. Because they were an oral culture, there must have been some oral traditions recalling Abraham and before. While oral cultures preserve traditions very effectively, not only had Egyptian culture clouded Israel's thinking, but other non-Israelites had come with them, bringing their beliefs (Exod. 12:38; Num. 11:4). Israel needed to understand God's perspective as well as his place and purpose for them. They must represent God (Gen. 1:26–27), and then, as God's chosen nation, show the world his glories and bring blessing to the families of the earth through their role in the land of Canaan (Gen. 12:3; 18:18; 22:18; 26:4; 28:14; Exod. 19:4–6). They were no longer slaves of Egypt but vassals of and priests to the Creator of the universe. The book of Genesis, as the introduction to the Pentateuch, addressed the incipient nation of Israel to establish their perspective on their purpose and place in the world.

THEOLOGICAL EMPHASES OF THE BOOK

Doctrinal

Genesis provides the introduction to the Pentateuch and the rest of God's revelation. It is not only the initial book by position, but its message introduces the metanarrative of God's work in his fallen world. Here we find the good creation, the fall of humanity, and God's initial revelation of his coming redemption. Moses wanted Israel to know that Yahweh, the sovereign creator of the universe, had chosen the descendants of Abraham to bring blessing out of cursing to all humanity by representing him and leading humanity to true worship, in the face of humanity's persistent rebellion.

Moses presented an alternate worldview to the ancient Near Eastern beliefs around Israel. Israel needed to understand their place in God's world and their purpose under his rule. God's role in creation profoundly diverges from contemporary creation accounts prevalent in the ancient world (Miller and Soden 2012). God's sovereign goodness contrasts with the pain and frustration resulting from the rebellion of humanity against God's good and lifegiving word of command. Moses offered a high view of humankind from their creation as God's images. He highlighted the need for people to find relief from the struggle induced by sin by walking with God in obedience, worship, and relationship. God's redemptive plan would bring blessing out of cursing, reaching out to humanity and revealing his promise of life within the outworking of death. The book of Genesis pulls numerous threads of theology together to present an intricate and rich tapestry of reflection on Israel's requisite view of their world, beginning with the sole deity and creator, Israel's God, and their role in God's universe.

The Theology of Narrative

We do not often think of narrative in general as teaching theology. The exception, perhaps, is the account of the creation and fall in Genesis 1–3. The rest of Scripture often refers to these chapters in theological ways, and we resonate with those theological reflections even though we still may elevate the historical over the theological intent. However, for most of the rest of the narrative in the Old Testament, we tend to think of them more historically and as story, rather than as theology. Unfortunately, when we do so, we miss the main points that the authors intended. Paul makes this clear when he refers to the Old Testament both as intending "instruction" for us to learn how to deal with temptation (1 Cor. 10:11, speaking of the wilderness narratives), and to have hope (Rom. 15:4). Paul elevated it all "for teaching, for reproof, for correction and for training in righteousness" (2 Tim. 3:16, referring to "all Scripture," which is contextually the Old Testament learned in Timothy's childhood [v. 15], and dealing with how to live righteously before a holy God). While narrative is historical, it is primarily intended to teach theology, and we need to recognize the narrative claims about God, humanity, and the relationship between God and humanity.

To understand the theology of the narratives, we need to understand the ways the Hebrew narrator communicates his rhetorical message and develops the underlying theological themes. We need to pay careful attention to several tools that the narrator uses to communicate his message: the typical flow of narrative with the standard and nonstandard verbal forms in narrative, including disjunctive statements; patterns and repetitions on all levels; word choice and plays on words or theologically freighted words; dialogue, especially if God speaks; and places where the narrator evaluates, summarizes, or expresses motives or thoughts, among other things. Of course, all of this will enhance the flow of the narrative, but one should not expect Hebrew narrative to mirror modern norms for narrative or history writing. Numerous helpful works have been written to help decipher Hebrew narrative discourse. Some valuable works to consider include Alter (1981); Berlin (1983); Collins (2006), who has a brief, helpful summary (chapter 2: "A Discourse-Oriented Literary Approach"); and Mathewson (2021), who applies it to preaching, walking the reader through the process.

God's Sovereignty

Yahweh, as the sovereign creator of the universe, has authority to order this world. Moses initiates the creation account with "In the beginning God," announcing God as preexistent and independent of all creation (Gen. 1:1). As uncaused and outside of creation, he was distinguished from all the other gods of the ancient world. All of creation exists as the expression of his will, showing graphically his sovereign and ultimate control (he spoke ten times in Gen. 1 with immediate results). In contrast to other ancient Near Eastern creation accounts, there was no conflict, nor any other preexisting power. Yahweh created all things by his will, without peer or threat, exercising absolute and effortless control. This expression of his sovereign rule echoes repeatedly through the rest of Genesis as God judges humanity (chs. 3, 6, 11), pronounces and offers blessings to obedient subjects (1:22, 28; 2:3; 5:2; 9:1, 26; 12:2; and the many extensions to the line of promise and reverberations throughout Genesis), and makes covenants with people who trust him (6:18; 9:8–17; 15:17–21; 17:1–14, 19–21; with the promises reiterated to the succeeding generations). He climaxes the account, accomplishing his good plan from the evil intentions of his fallen images (45:5–9; 50:19–20).

The role of God as sovereign creator controls the logic of chapters 1–11 within the broad issues of humankind's sin, judgment, and hope for blessing. God is moving his creation toward his purpose. The narrative then narrows focus as Yahweh calls, blesses, and uses Abram and his family to bring about that hope of blessing in chapters 12–50, revealing the imminent nature of God's sovereign working (though in progressively less obvious ways). It concludes with Joseph's statement that God brought good through the evil purposes of wicked men (50:20). This movement toward the called individual and his descendants stresses God's sovereign working even before birth and the resulting people who will receive the promise (Isaac and Jacob, along with their descendants—12:2, 7; 15:4–6, 18; 17:2–8, 19, 21; 18:10, 14; 25:23).

God's Goodness

The God who created everything good and brought blessing out of cursing must necessarily be good. The creation account states seven times that God saw his creation and evaluated it as "good" (טוֹב), concluding that all he had made was "very good" (1:31—טוֹב מְאֹד). While humankind had not yet corrupted God's world, the emphasis on the goodness of creation deals initially with God's assessment of his creation and its suitability to accomplish his good purposes. Significantly, the goodness of God is viewed in contrast to the desolate, dark, and empty world with which he began. Yet considering the ensuing threat of sin and evil, it is recalled and underlined by the statement of Joseph in 50:20 that God sovereignly used even the evil purposes of Joseph's brothers for good (לְטֹבָה), framing the book with God's goodness and underlining his good plan of redemption, beginning with the initial sin (Gen. 3:15).

In between a very good creation and Joseph's good view of God, we see the goodness of God in his grace to humankind: they do not physically die in the day they eat but have hope for blessing (ch. 3); he pronounced judgment on the snake (3:15); he clothed them with skins (3:21); he did not take Cain's life for murder (4:11–12); he gave opportunity to find relief from the curse in walking with him (5:22–24); he delivered righteous Noah and his family (chs. 6–9); he would never again judge all men with a flood (9:11); he scattered all men (11:1–9); and he then chose one man to bring blessing to all the families of the earth (12:1–3). God then demonstrated his goodness as he worked to put a dysfunctional family into position to bring about his good purposes (blessing), working miraculously in the lives of Joseph, Judah, and their brothers, even as he used their evil to bring his good (50:20). God's goodness is clear in both the express purposes of the Creator and the outcomes of his effective word and working.

Word of God

In presenting the sovereign rule of God, Genesis 1 also shows the significance of his word. Reflecting the great king he is, when God speaks, it happens! In distinction from Egyptian accounts, God does not make any magical use of some outside power when he speaks (Hasel 1974, 90). He alone guarantees the outcome. The anthropomorphic description of God speaking, instead of willing or some other way of stating God's creative acts, sets the stage for the importance of whatever God says. It is paradigmatic. When God blesses, you can expect it to happen. When God commands, you had better pay attention. After the repetition of God's word happening just as he spoke it in chapter 1, the command to Adam in Genesis 2:16–17 takes on new importance. Even though Adam was not there to witness the commands, the reader knows the significance of God's word. God's pronouncements of cursing in chapter 3; individual and universal judgments in chapters 4, 6, and 11; and promise of blessing throughout Genesis convey similar certainty. In fact, the recurring purpose of blessing for all humanity communicates the sure outcome from God's proclamation. Expanding our view to the whole of the Pentateuch, God's ten words of command in chapter 1 (see above) prepare for his ten words of command in the law (Exod. 20:1–17; Deut. 5:6–21; cf. Exod. 34:28; Deut. 4:13; 10:4). God's word gives life or death, defining the outcome for every response to God's word, whether faith or rebellion, from God's images (Deut. 30:15–20).

Faith

Trusting God's word, the essential response, provides the foundation of true worship. Faith offers the only hope for a cursed world. Even though it is not named until Genesis 15:6,[2] faith presents a major theological theme, beginning with the fall. The command of warning (2:16) expects a response of faith, but, of course, the absence of faith initiates the first sin (3:1–6).

After that first rebellion against the command of God, faith becomes the basis for salvation and relationship with God. Immediately Adam declares his faith in God's word of blessing to them when he named Eve (3:20). Abel offered an acceptable sacrifice (4:3–5). Enoch walked with God and did not die because God took him (5:24). The suggestion of walking with God by faith comes from comparing Noah (6:9) and Abram (15:6; 17:1). Noah was righteous, the mark of faith (6:9; 15:6) demonstrated by taking God at his word and acting on it (6:22). For Noah, not only does faith result in salvation from the flood but in covenant or relationship with God (6:28; 9:8–17). Abraham has the same experience as God immediately follows the announcement of Abram's faith (15:6, initially exhibited as he left Ur) with the enacting of the covenant (15:7–21).

The rest of the patriarchal narratives present the working of God in the lives of the patriarchs until they come to recognize the reliability of God's word. Even the conniving scoundrel Jacob matures into one who can bless Pharaoh (47:7, 10) and dies with the request to be buried in the land of promise (49:29–30). Genesis ends with Joseph's faith in God's promise to return the nation to the promised land, seen in his final request to his brothers (50:24–25). Faith instigates the necessary obedience to the command of God (2:16–17) and grows through the ongoing testing and working of God (22:1; 28:15; 45:5–8; 50:19–20).

Genesis reveals faith as the basis for proper worship, beginning in Genesis 2. When God placed humanity in the garden, God did not just charge them with gardening but with worship.

2 The verb translated by the ESV "believed" (וְהֶאֱמִן) describes Abram's previous acts of "faith" (the noun) clarified in the NET translation, "Abram believed the Lord, and the Lord credited it as righteousness to him."

The impact of the charge for humankind to serve and keep the garden was for them to be God's priest and priestess in his temple precinct. Humankind was to lead creation in their worship of Yahweh. Worship, then, results from faith in God's word/promise leading to blessing, from Abel (4:4) and Adam's unnamed progeny (4:26), to Noah (8:20), Abram (12:7–8; 13:17–18; 22:1–14), Isaac (26:24–25), and Jacob (28:18–22; 35:3, 7, 9–15). Also, however, discipline from God results from the lack of faith (3:1–19; 4:1–7).

Worship

As sovereign, God's authority is complete, and so all must bow. The creation account unmasks all other contenders worshipped by the surrounding cultures as merely God's effortless creations. He alone is deity. All must bow to him alone.

Because he is good, worship is not only necessary, but it is deserved. Because he is imminent and not just transcendent, he offers a relationship with himself as the source of goodness and life. Worship describes at least part of the responsibility of God's images in their new environment (Gen. 2). That worship describes the effect of hope amid rebellion and judgment (as seen above, 4:26; 12:8) and goes hand in hand with walking with God, providing life in the midst of death (5:24; 6:9; 17:1). It offers opportunities for the world to see the hope and light in the darkness. Worship permeates Genesis. Worship was the expectation of Adam (ch. 2), the hope and renewal of people at the time of apostasy (4:26), the reality of life (5:24), the catalyst for hope and promise (8:20–22), the testimony of the righteous (12:8), the expression of faith (ch. 22), the necessary response to promises fulfilled (8:20–22; 35:1–15; 47:31), and much more.

In contrast to Israel's neighbors, worship requires submission and obedient service. Humanity cannot care for a god or provide for his needs. Yahweh has no needs, and humanity's obedient service results in the enhancing and blessing of humankind rather than benefit to God. God's priests, Adam and Eve, picture the possibility, caring for his sacred garden while God abundantly cares for them.

Blessing

Blessing both precedes and follows true worship. In the initial narrative we see God pronouncing blessing three times (ברך). When God created the living things on the fifth day (1:22) and man on the sixth day (1:28), he blessed them all with fertility and fruitfulness. Finally, he blessed the seventh day (2:3). The idea of blessing here carries the idea of empowering someone or something or being "filled with the potency of life" (Waltke and Fredricks 2001, 63). In this case, it is for the task that God has given them to do. Blessing is God's empowering to accomplish his will. The creatures will fill God's world with life, and humanity will also fill the world and rule over God's creation. The main value and core provision of blessing, however, is in relationship with the Creator, often linked to walking with God (3:8; 5:22–24; 6:9; 17:1) or God's presence (26:3, 28; 28:15, 20; 31:3, 5, 42; 35:3; 39:2, 21; 48:21; cf. Clines 2001, 36, 50). The seventh-day rest shows God has completed his creation and taken control of his universe to run it and bring blessing to all of it.

Immediately after the fall of humanity in Genesis 3, however, we see God working to bring them back to a place of rest, service, and blessing. Hope for blessing is declared in true worship, as people began to call on the name of the Lord (4:26), and experienced in walking with God, as Enoch escapes death (5:24). God would begin anew with Noah after his judgment on humanity, with promise for life, blessing, and good (8:21–9:17). The judgement after the Tower of Babel left humankind scattered and in tension (ch. 10), yet God promised hope in his new beginning through Abram, bringing blessing to all the families of the earth (12:3).

Blessing, then, becomes a major theme in Genesis 12–50, with the root being used only six times in Genesis 1–11 and sixty-six times in Genesis 12–50. As God begins bringing blessing to his world after sin, he directly blessed Abraham as a result of his faith (12:1–3; 14:19; 22:17; 24:1), extended blessing to the descendants of Abraham (25:11; 26:24; 27:33; 28:3; 47:7; 49), and then, through Abraham and his descendants, continued the blessing to all the families of the earth (12:3; 17:20; 18:18; 20:17; 22:18; 26:4; 28:14; 30:27; 39:5). God revealed his plan to bring blessing out of cursing to all who would walk before him by faith in humble obedience. The ultimate blessing, as developed through Genesis, is knowing God, being his, and living joyfully in that relationship with Yahweh, the source of life and blessing. The life that leads to and enjoys blessing describes true worship.

Humanity as God's Images

In Genesis 1:26–27, God created humankind "in his own image." Not only does Genesis 1 highlight a new and necessary understanding (and response) to a sovereign and transcendent creator, but it also describes a significantly unique view and role of humankind in this world, compared to Israel's neighbors. Several similar ideas to the creation of humanity in God's image appear in ancient literature, both in Egypt and Mesopotamia. In almost every case, however, the rest of the ancient world only sees the king as the image of the god. In a unique Egyptian passage in "The Instruction Addressed to King Merikare," however, all of humankind was made in the image of the sun god (Lichtheim, 1973, I:106). The point in this passage is that humankind is the "god's cattle" (106, l. 131) and exists for the sustenance for the god, so the king needs to care for them. Otherwise, in Egypt only the pharaoh is made in the image of the god, which pictures his authority and responsibility to protect the land for the good of his subjects.

Mesopotamia has several contexts in which the idea of "image" may relate to this passage. Walton (2009a, 21) summarizes them helpfully as contexts in which the king is the image of the god, an idol is the god's image, or the image of the king is set up in territories he has conquered. This shows that the point of the image is not physical likeness but that "the image of god did the god's work on the earth."

Genesis reverses this imagery, showing that God provides fully for his images. God does not need them, but they exhibit his ruling glory. All of humanity is in God's image so that no one is above the others or solely representing God.

What it means to be in the image of God has been explained in various ways, but Genesis 1 focuses on the purpose of humanity as the ruler in God's world, representing him (1:26, 28). Humankind's creation in God's image allows that representational role. Humanity in Genesis was to reflect God and carry out his rule as he blessed and cared for them. It is their identity. They are his images (see exposition on 1:26–27, p. 88). The nations around Israel, however, saw their role as working for and caring for the gods. Genesis 2 adds another dimension to human responsibilities, showing the placement of the image of God into God's garden for the service of worship.

The Image of God

The meaning of humanity being "in the image of God" has been understood in many ways: as dominion, human relationship, the human soul, or mind, body, virtue, existence, or a general idea of capacity. In our (the authors) estimation, however, it is best defined as "the common identity shared by all particular human beings" (Peterson 2016, 65; cf. Imes, 2023).

From Dust

Yahweh Elohim fashions humankind from dust (Gen. 2:7). This depiction of humanity's origin also has a rich heritage in the ancient world, in which many different accounts relate something similar to the creation of humankind from dust (Soden 2015). The implication in the text highlights the dependence of humankind on God for life (breathed in), the care and concern with which God has placed humanity into his carefully crafted world (both chapters 1 and 2), and the frailty of human life (3:19), even in their role of service to the Creator.

Mankind's rebellion would obviously make both these purposes difficult, but it did not negate the special place and purpose of humanity as God's images. In fact, Genesis 5:1–3 carefully notes the initial creation of people in God's image (both male and female) and the passing of the image of Adam to his son. The implication, in the context of each generation dying, is both that the purpose of humanity as God's images continued (though difficult to see!) and the consequence of the sin in the garden continued. God's covenant with Noah recognized the value and purpose of human life as God's images (9:6).

Humanity and Kingship

Identified with God as images, humanity was created to represent God in his rule and authority in his world (1:26–28). Through humankind's rebellion we could no longer function in that capacity, but we retained his identity (9:6). God's promise to destroy the snake and so evil (3:15) through the descendants of the woman points to the restoration of humanity to their created role. Humankind had submitted to the creature in their rebellion. Humanity required restoration to God to act as his representative and, wielding his authority, to crush the snake and redeem God's creation. The book of Genesis, then, follows the line of the woman with royal genealogies (chs. 4–5), choosing Seth (ch. 5), then Noah (6:8–9) and his line (ch. 10), until God declared his purpose to bless all of humanity through Abram (12:1–3). That purpose would be carried out with the promise of kings through Abraham (17:6), Sarah (Gen. 17:16), and Jacob (35:11), culminating in Jacob's oracle of rule for the descendants of Judah (49:10). In the progress of revelation, God provided his perfect image and representative in the incarnation of God the Son to finally restore humanity to rule and crush evil and Satan for all time. Humankind would finally be able to fully function as God's kings and priests (Rev. 20:6).

Sin

Of course, humanity's rebellion, beginning in Genesis 3, provides the tension in the narrative of God's working to bring blessing. While God made his creation good and perfectly formed to sustain life, it does not always appear so good to humanity. The second *toledot* (2:4–4:26) highlights what happened to the heavens and the earth. Humankind, placed in the garden to serve and guard it, failed to keep faith with God and exercise dominion, but instead allowed the snake to deceive and kill when humanity rebelled. The snake cast doubt on the spoken word of the Creator, but God's word proved true. When Adam and Eve ate the forbidden fruit, they were separated from God and their physical death was assured (3:8–10, 22–24; 5). In addition, the struggle for life would drive humankind to see their need for help only found in God (e.g., 5:29). The ongoing basis for death for humanity as rebellion against God stands alone among known ancient creation accounts.

Cursing

God responded to sin and the rebellion of his creatures with cursing. Cursing removed God's empowering blessing, imposing a barrier to human ability. Even in his cursing, God gave grace and opportunity for blessing for his wayward images. God cursed the snake with humiliation and eventual death, with destruction by the seed of the woman (3:14–15). He cursed the ground and pronounced his oracles against the woman and the man to provide them both with pain and frustration as they would attempt to experience his pronounced blessing of fruitfulness, dominion, and even life itself (3:16–19). He does not curse the couple directly, however. Pointedly, God's curse would preserve their ability to find blessing by allowing immediate (though short-term) life. Through pain and frustration, it would show their need for help from God. He even graciously provided the clothing for their nakedness through the life of an animal, while he expelled them from the garden so they would not live forever in this fallen state (3:21–24).

Genesis 5 shows the continuing consequences of Adam's rebellion, as each generation died. Then the cursing continued as judgment on rebellious humanity, both in the flood (chs. 6–9) and in the dispersion from the tower of Babel (11:1–9). In Genesis 12–50, as blessing comes to the foreground, cursing recedes in prominence, though any who would curse Abram would be cursed (12:3), and God did bring judgment on evil in Sodom and Gomorrah (ch. 19). Even Joseph's ten brothers suggest that God's judgment is at the root of their seeming misfortune in Egypt (42:21; 44:16). With the cursing progressively retreating to the background, the development of the book itself suggests that God is moving to swallow up cursing with his blessing.

Good versus Evil

While we have considered the contrast and intended comparison between good and evil briefly with relation to the goodness of God, the battle highlights God's good purpose to bring blessing. It comes up consistently in Genesis, from the declarations of good in Genesis 1 (and the contrast, not good for man to be alone, 2:18), to "the tree of the knowledge of good and evil" in the middle of the garden (2:9), to the statement of Joseph that his brothers meant it for evil, "but God meant it for good" (50:20). Genesis initiates the cosmic battle between good and evil or God and Satan (as we later see it), as the snake tempts Eve with the tree of the knowledge of good and evil (3:14–15). While Genesis does not identify the snake as Satan, the challenge to the good rule of God is clear, and the ancient context makes it clear that this is a cosmic battle (Averbeck 2004). The focus in Genesis, however, is not directly placed on the cosmic battle. Rather, Genesis focuses on the consequences of humankind's rebellion and God's working to bring blessing and good to people, even through cursing and evil.

The terms good (טוֹב) or evil (רַע) certainly deal with moral issues (6:1–8), but Genesis fuses the morality with the outcomes (beneficence vs. calamity). From Genesis 1 where God's evaluation of creation is good (טוֹב), implying both well done and functioning well, to Joseph's words that while his brothers meant evil against him (calamity or destruction), God meant it for good or to preserve many alive (50:20), morality and outcomes are conjoined. The theology of good and evil clearly shows specific and practical actions bringing physical consequences of benefit or calamity in the human experience. Rather than denying the eternal consequences, they illustrate tangibly the timeless truths.

Good versus Evil

Genesis 41 highlights this contrast between good and evil, or beneficence and calamity, with the repeated reference to the "bad-looking" (רַע) cows and "fine-looking" (טוֹב) cows (and ears of corn). Even Genesis 6 highlights the wickedness of humanity destroying God's creation (vv. 11–12) so that in talionic justice, they are also destroyed (v. 13). In the larger context of the Pentateuch, Moses drew this together in his final challenge to Israel in Deuteronomy 30:15–20. "Look! I have set before you today life and prosperity [טוֹב] on the one hand, and death and disaster [רַע] on the other" (Deut. 30:15 NET). Moses emphasized life as living in the land based on obedience (v. 16) and death as dying early (not necessarily spiritually—v. 18), but both concepts will present tangible illustrations of the intangible spiritual truth of blessing and cursing before God. Sin and rebellion certainly are moral (obedience to God's word), but the focus is on the consequences, especially in the outworking of human history. The inner or spiritual aspect shows more clearly in the emphasis on "rest" and "walking with God."

Rest

The goal of creation is rest (day 7), and the fallen person longs for that rest or relief from the toil God imposed (5:29), looking for it in all the wrong places (ch. 4). The Sabbath rest on the seventh day emphasized the cessation of God's creative work yet declared that God was taking control of his new world to manage the affairs of his kingdom (see Exposition 2:1–3, p. 90). Rest would become a major theme for Israel's daily life, but in Genesis, rest pictures enjoying the working of God as he gives blessing, and the hope of humankind amid their struggles. Rest is only found in the sovereign management of God in his world. The theme of walking with God suggests the practical expression of entering God's rest (3:8; 5:22, 24; 6:9; 17:1) and pictures the submission to that rule and authority of God.

Together, Moses has intertwined these theological themes into his overarching message: Yahweh, the sole and sovereign Creator has chosen Israel to represent him, lead the nations in worship, provide hope from the curse, and bring blessing to all the families of the earth.

PRACTICAL APPLICATIONS

Of course, all of this presents numerous opportunities to see it working in everyday living.

Worship

God's transcendent, sovereign position, as well as his goodness and consistent working to bring blessing, should produce both humble submission and heartfelt worship. The significance of "walking with God" in the lives of Enoch, Noah, and Abraham (5:22; 6:8; 17:1) illustrates this pursuit of submissive worship, as does the concluding story of the heart of Joseph, growing throughout his life. Such worship is shown in the daily work of service—a life of honoring the sovereign king (*soli deo gloria*!), rather than merely isolated acts, which we must consistently choose in the trenches of daily living.

Faith

God's control and goodness allows us to trust him when we encounter darkness. Faith can rest in the clear character of God, shown in obedience and resulting in rest. Abram is the explicit example of such faith (15:6), which grows through his life. However, faith is equally evident in the actions of Enoch, Noah, Joseph, and anyone who will act on God's word without the benefit of hindsight. In fact, many of us will identify more with Jacob. God must graciously convince us to trust and worship him even while experiencing the consequences of our own struggle in faith.

Obedience

Our view of God's word should be heavily influenced by the creation narrative. If God said it, it will happen! We must, then, believe God and act in accord with what he says is true, even when we do not yet see the outcome. Such obedience, of course, is the evidence of faith (Noah building the boat, Abram leaving Ur, Joseph refusing to take vengeance into his own hands). Eve and Adam present the archetypal rejection of God's word as they believe the snake and plunge God's good creation into judgment with their disobedience.

Holiness

We exist to reflect and glorify the King through holy living, service, and faith. The lives of the patriarchs again flesh this out, showing a positive reflection of Yahweh in their obedience, as noted above, bringing honor to God in his blessing to those around them, such as Abram's blessing from Melchizedek (14:19–20), Potiphar's evaluation of Joseph (39:3), the keeper of the prison's view of Joseph (39:23), Pharoah's view of Joseph (41:38–39), and Joseph's own declaration of God's working through him (45:5–8). Conversely, they damage their world in their disobedience, such as Abram's lack of faith in the two "she is my sister" episodes (12:13; 20:2) with resulting dishonor to God's name (20:9).

Human Value

If humankind is truly in the image of God, then all people have value before God and deserve respect. In the wake of the flood, God will legislate this value (9:5–6). Cain and Lamech have gained notoriety (and God's judgment) for not valuing life (4:8–12, 23–24), whereas God values even the child of the flesh, Ishmael (16:10–12; 25:12–18). We must see our own value based on God's value for humanity. We must not only treat all people with that respect, but we should stand for that value in the marketplace.

Blessing

Our desires and expectations from God should focus on our need to know and walk with him, rather than on the physical benefits we might gain. We must see blessing as God's empowering to serve him, even if that means hardship and testing. We must see knowing and walking with God as the highest good (Ps. 16:11). While Joseph certainly ended with material wealth, he viewed the process as part of God's working as well (45:5–8; 50:19–20). We must look for blessing in the presence of God rather than in the things of this world.

Spiritual Warfare

We should expect to encounter temptation, conflict, deception, and warfare when we choose to walk with God. God, however, will work through those challenges to accomplish his good ends. While perhaps less explicit in Genesis, the conflict initiated in the garden with the snake and declared between his seed and the woman's seed continues throughout Genesis, from Cain and Abel to Joseph's life. Just as the promised seed of the woman moves through the genealogies to the promised seed of Abraham, so the conflict that follows must be seen in terms of the initiated spiritual warfare from the tempter (3:15).

Sin

Our sin starts with unbelief in the goodness and word of God. The sin planted in the garden continues to blossom, bear fruit, and spread throughout the book of Genesis. The two obvious nadirs of human history in Genesis—at the flood and the tower of Babel—form the prelude to God's redemptive plan through Abraham, and yet the struggle with sin continues.

Grace

While we see the stark consequences of sin in Genesis, we also see the grace of God in calling for repentance. He offers hope with true repentance (4:6–7). It is on display in the rehabilitation of characters that sinned against their brothers deeply (Jacob, the brothers of Joseph). We must learn to respond to conviction quickly, repenting genuinely from sin to maintain close relation with our creator.

STRUCTURE OF GENESIS

The author has structured the book of Genesis with a recurring clause in Hebrew, usually translated as "these are the generations" (ESV) or "this is the account" (NET; 2:4; 5:1; 6:9; 10:1; 11:10; 11:27; 25:12; 25:19; 36:1; 36:9; 37:2). The Hebrew term translated "generations" or "account" is the term mentioned above in discussing the title: *toledot* (תּוֹלְדוֹת). Typically, each section beginning with this phrase carries the action forward, telling what resulted from the major or climactic player in the previous section (usually a person). It comes from the root "bear a child" (ילד) and usually refers to the generations following a "family history" (Wenham 1987, xxii). Of course, the first use in Genesis is the *toledot* of the heavens and the earth, referring to what happened to God's good creation. The eleven following sections that begin with the *toledot* divide the book into twelve sections. Each subsequent section tells the reader what happened next, especially narrowing and following the key individuals (after the second section) and their family outworking.[3]

On the larger scale, the emphasis of Genesis shifts after chapter 11, with the last six sections. Genesis 1–11 (the first six sections) develops the broad strokes of the world and all peoples on it in two parallel movements. In the first, God spoke his good creation out of a watery mass, blessed humankind, and placed them in a fresh new world, only to have growing rebellion require judgment (1:1–6:8). In the second, God recreated the world through a watery mass, blessed humankind, and placed them in a renewed world, only to see continued rebellion, again requiring judgment (6:9–11:26). The second movement reverses the genealogy and the judgment, highlighting the transition to a third new beginning for the remainder of Genesis with Abram (from Terah) to bring blessing to all the families of the earth instead of judgment (Rendsburg 2014, 7–25).

The second six *toledot* sections develop the way God will work through his new beginning to bring about his desired blessing. It presents the history of a single family with three major sets of narratives, working out the promise of God to their patriarch, Abraham (11:27–50:26). Rendsburg (2014, 27–97) demonstrates that these three main sets of narratives parallel each other as well, in very similar chiastic constructions. These constructions show the overarching concerns of the author as each one begins with the oracle from God, centers around the main concern, and climaxes at the end with the resolution to the threats and the clarifying of the working and promise of God to the family (and the world). These narratives also present a progression of God's working and promise. God offers and confirms the promise to Abraham, emphasizing Abram's growing faith (11:27–25:11). He wrestles with Jacob to bring him to submission and the place of blessing, emphasizing the requirements for experiencing blessing (25:19–35:29). Finally, he brings blessing out of calamity for Joseph and his brothers, illustrating the opportunity to be a blessing and the faith and character required (37:2–50:26).

Chiasm

Chiasm (or chiasmus) is a narrative device in which the narrator mirrors words, motifs, concepts, or major sections to show development and continuity and emphasize key ideas and progressions. In chiasm, the second panel of elements mirrors the initial panel (a b c / c' b' a'). This pattern in the text signals units, flow and progression, and elements to compare. Sometimes the elements are odd, so that the middle element stands by itself as an emphatic position. In the Hebrew Bible, chiasm is often done in single verses:

Genesis 2:4—"This is the account of

a the heavens and the earth
  b when they were created
  b' when the LORD God made
a' the earth and heavens."

Notice that even "heaven" and "earth" are reversed between a and a'. This chiasm is significant in the discussion regarding the relationship of the verse and its parts to the structure of the larger whole. It shows that it cannot be divided into two parts, according to the author's device. It is also significant in understanding the way the writer transitions from the initial account to what follows, tying them together and showing their complementarity rather than pitting them against each other as competing creation accounts. For a very helpful overview of the more common patterns in ancient literature and their significance, see Parunak (1981).

3 The exceptions to the general flow are in the patriarchal narratives where the author includes *toledots* to record God's fulfilled promises to Hagar and to Rebekah regarding Ishmael and Esau.

Figure 0.1 Primeval History (Rendsburg 2014, 7–25)	
A Creation, God's Words to Adam (1:1–3:24) B Adam's Sons (4:1–16) C Technological Development of Humankind (4:17–26) D Ten Generations from Adam to Noah (5:1–32) E Downfall: The Nephilim (6:1–8)	A' Flood, God's Words to Noah (6:9–9:17) B' Noah's Sons (9:18–29) C' Ethnic Development of Humankind (10:1–32) E' Downfall: Tower of Babel (11:1–9) D' Ten Generations of Noah to Terah (11:10–26)

Figure 0.2 Patriarchal Narratives (Rendsburg 2014, 27–97, with some modification suggested by K. Lawson Younger)		
Abraham Stories (11:27–25:11)	**Jacob Stories (25:19–35:29)**	**Joseph Stories (37:2–50:26)**
A Genealogy of Terah (11:27–32) B Start of Abram's spiritual odyssey (12:1–9) C Sarai in foreign palace; ordeal ends in peace and success; Abram and Lot part (12:10–13:18) D Abram comes to the rescue of Sodom and Lot (14:1–24) E Covenant with Abram; annunciation of Ishmael (15:1–16:16) E' Covenant with Abraham; annunciation of Isaac (17:1–18:15) D' Abraham comes to the rescue of Sodom and Lot (18:16–19:38) C' Sarah in foreign palace; ordeal ends in peace and success; Abraham and Ishmael part (20:1–21:34) B' Climax of Abraham's spiritual odyssey (22:1–19) A' Genealogy of Nahor (22:20–24)	A Oracle sought, struggle in childbirth, Jacob born (25:19–34) B Interlude: Rebekah in foreign palace, pact with foreigners (26:1–34) C Jacob fears Esau and flees (27:1–28:9) D Messengers (28:10–22) E Arrival at Haran (29:1–30) F Jacob's wives are fertile (29:31–30:24) F' Jacob's flocks are fertile (30:25–43) E' Flight from Haran (31:1–54) D' Messengers (32:1–32) C' Jacob returns and fears Esau (33:1–20) B' Interlude: Dinah in foreign palace, pact with foreigners (34:1–31) A' Oracle fulfilled, struggle in childbirth, Jacob becomes Israel (35:1–18)	A Joseph and his brothers, Jacob and Joseph part (37:1–36) B Interlude: Joseph not present (38:1–30) C Reversal: Joseph guilty, Potiphar's wife innocent (39:1–23) D Joseph, hero of Egypt (40:1–41:57) E Two trips to Egypt (42:1–43:34) F Final test (44:1–34) F' Conclusion of test (45:1–28) E' Two tellings of the migration to Egypt (46:1–47:12) D' Joseph, hero of Egypt (47:13–27) C' Reversal: Ephraim firstborn, Manasseh secondborn (47:28–48:22) B' Interlude: Joseph nominally present (49:1–28) A' Joseph and his brothers, Jacob and Joseph part (49:29–50:26)

Figure 0.2 Patriarchal Narratives (Rendsburg 2014, 27–97, with some modification suggested by K. Lawson Younger)		
Abraham Stories (11:27–25:11)	**Jacob Stories (25:19–35:29)**	**Joseph Stories (37:2–50:26)**
Epilogue: A Death and burial of Sarah (23:1–20). B Marriage of Isaac (24:1–67). C Abraham's sons (25:1–6). D Death and burial of Abraham (25:7–11). E Ishmael's sons (25:12–18).	Epilogue: A' Death of Rachel (35:19–21). B' Illegitimate marriage of Reuben (35:22). C' Jacob's sons (35:23–26). D' Death and burial of Isaac (35:27–29). E' Esau's sons (36:6–43).	Epilogue: C" Joseph's sons and grandsons (50:22–23). D" Death and requested burial of Joseph (50:24–26)

Finally, Genesis presents a general progression of the interaction between God and humans. It begins with God at the center, telling the story from God's perspective exclusively (ch. 1), and then with his images at the center yet still from God's perspective (chs. 2–11). As we move into the patriarchal narratives, we see more of the human viewpoint, and God seems to move farther into the background. In the beginning, his interaction with humanity was direct, focused on the corporate nature and the dramatic major turning points. Beginning with Abraham, it is still direct but also personal. And as we read the Jacob stories, God becomes less direct as we see the character of Jacob more clearly. God recedes even farther into the background in the stories of Joseph and his brothers as the storyteller paints the character and struggles of the sons of Jacob more vividly. Yet, even here, God clearly controls the outcomes as evidenced by the dreams and Joseph's final proclamation that "God intended it for good" (50:20). God has not gone away, but the narrative presents the human-divine interaction in increasingly more relatable terms. Genesis moves the reader progressively from the divine viewpoint and the necessary worldview to how that worldview should inform the reader's view of circumstances in their ordinary world in which God is not as clearly seen.

NARRATIVE STRUCTURE OF GENESIS (*TOLEDOT* DIVISIONS)[4]

Primeval Narratives (1–11)

I. **The Sovereign King showcased both his sole transcendent power and imminent goodness, ordering and filling his very good creation and crowning it with his regal representative, humanity, culminating in the realization of his holy rest (1:1–2:3).**
   A. The transcendent uncreated creator created the universe (1:1).
   B. The story of God's creation began with a desolate, empty, and dark watery mass (1:2).

4 While this outline follows the most obvious structural markers of the narrative with the *toledot* sections, there are simultaneous narrative structures that we will point out as we proceed through the exposition. For the general overall structure as two parallel movements through the primeval narratives that operate in conjunction with the *toledot* sections, see the Introduction to the Primeval Narratives, p. 75.

- B'. Revealing his transcendent power and goodness, God fashioned and filled his universe, setting up his images to represent him (1:3–31).
- A'. On day seven, having finished his creative work, God rested and pronounced blessing, entering his sanctuary to administrate his kingdom (2:1–3).

II. Toledot 1: God's good creation, led by his blessed king-priests, descended into rebellion and the resulting judgment, even as God provided hope (2:4–4:26).

- A. Introduction: The story of God's created universe required his featured images (2:4–6).
- B. God's commissioned, completed king-priests rebelled, receiving God's appropriate yet gracious judgment, offering hope in true worship (2:7–3:24).
- C. Humankind's sin intensified in willful rebellion and self-worship, even as hope was declared in Yahweh (4:1–26).

III. Toledot 2: Adam, as God's image, fathered descendants in his own image who experienced the consequences of increasing rebellion and deserved judgment, in contrast to the grace found in walking with God (5:1–6:8).

- A. Introduction: God created and blessed his images (5:1–2).
- B. Humanity grew through blessing amidst cursing, with hope (5:3–32).
- A'. God declared coming judgment with grace on his rebellious images (6:1–8).

IV. Toledot 3: Though God delivers righteous Noah, resetting humanity in worship and covenant relationship, humanity will still rebel and require judgment (6:9–9:29).

- A. Introduction: Righteous Noah walked with God and had three sons (6:9–10).
- B. God appropriately judged his rebellious images but delivered a righteous Noah to reset humanity in true worship and covenant relationship on a purified earth (6:11–9:17).
- A'. Noah and his sons expose the unchanged human heart, heralding coming conflict (9:18–29).

V. Toledot 4: Humankind's spread across the earth in various ethnicities and kingdoms resulted from God's judgment on their prideful rebellion (10:1–11:9).

- A. Introduction: The sons of Noah started the spread of humanity anew (10:1).
- B. All the ethnicities and kingdoms around Israel originated from the sons of Noah (10:2–32).
- C. Humankind's spread was forced by God's gracious judgment on the prideful rebellion of humanity (11:1–9).

VI. Toledot 5: The line of descents from Shem leads to hope in Abram (11:10–26).

The Patriarchal Narratives (12–50)[5]

I. Toledot 6: God chose, matured, established in covenant, and blessed Abraham to bring blessing to all the families of the world (11:27–25:11).

- A Terah, with Abram and the family, moved toward Canaan, stopping in Haran (11:27–32).
- B When God called Abram to follow him

5 The Patriarchal Narratives outline generally follows Gary Rendsburg (2014, 27–97), with some private communication and influence from K. Lawson Younger. The significance of the chiastic structures will be explored with the summary of each patriarchal narrative section and the exposition.

for blessing and to extend blessing to all families of the earth, Abram followed with worship and proclamation (12:1–9).

C God delivered Abram and Sarai from Abram's foolish lie in Egypt and blessed him with renewed promise when he trusted God for the land (12:10–13:18).

D Abram delivered Lot and Sodom, declaring his exclusive worship of Yahweh (14:1–24).

E Yahweh established his covenant with believing Abram, who tried to achieve the promise through his wife's handmaiden (15:1–16:16).

E' God renewed his covenant with Abram, calling him to loyalty, marked by his name change and sign of the covenant, clarifying the promised descendant would be through barren Sarah (17:1–18:15).

D' Abraham embodied blessing, promoting justice and righteousness as he interceded for Sodom and Lot, securing Lot's deliverance (18:16–19:38).

C' God delivered Sarah again, providing the promised son in security and prosperity (20:1–21:34).

B' God rewarded Abraham's extreme loyalty when Abraham chose faith in God over Isaac, ratifying his expanded covenant promises (22:1–19).

A' The family remaining in Haran were prospering, producing Rebekah (22:20–24).

Epilogue to Toledot 6: Abraham safeguarded God's promise, preparing his descendants to thrive in the promised land in blessing after his death.

1. Abraham prepared his descendants to pursue the promise with a new homeland by faith, securing a foothold in the land of promise for the burial of Sarah (23:1–20).
2. Abraham pursued an appropriate wife for Isaac to nurture, through God's providence, the promised line and to continue the promised blessing (24:1–67).
3. Abraham protected the promised blessing though Isaac, generously releasing subsequent sons (25:1–6).
4. Abraham's death and burial launched the new homeland as blessing passed to Isaac (25:7–11).

II. Toledot 7: God honored his word, fulfilling his promise to Hagar with the descendants of Ishmael (25:12–18).

III. Toledot 8: God passed his promise of blessing through Isaac to Jacob, refining his character and renewing the covenant (25:19–35:29).

A God would fulfill his covenant promises to Abraham through Isaac's line, by prayer, with his unexpected choice of the younger Jacob (25:19–34).

B Isaac's fearful deception endangered God's promised blessing and threatened his neighbors with judgment, but his faith brought blessing (26:1–34).

C Jacob, taking the blessing by deception, feared Esau and fled to Haran for a wife (27:1–28:9).

D God, with his angels, confronted Jacob's fear with promise and blessing, prompting Jacob to vow exclusive worship (28:10–22).

E Arriving in Haran, Jacob received two wives through Laban's deception (29:1–30).

F Amid conflict within the family, God blessed Jacob with children (29:31–30:24).

F' Amid conflict in the extended family, God blessed Jacob with flocks (30:25–43).

E' Leaving Haran, Jacob fled with his family, deceiving Laban (31:1–55).

D' God, with his angels, confronted Jacob's fear through conflict, promising blessing with Jacob's submission (32:1–32).

C' Jacob, giving blessing, reconciled with Esau when he returned from Haran (33:1–20).

B' Jacob's sons used deception to destroy their Canaanite neighbors, avenging the rape of Dinah (34:1–31).

A' Jacob fulfilled his vow to Yahweh in purified worship, who renewed and extended his covenant promises to Jacob (35:1–18).

Epilogue to Toledot 8: Jacob strengthened ties to the homeland, siring the progenitors of the nation.

1'. Jacob buried Rachel with a special marker, adding a foothold in the land (35:19–20).

2'. Reuben's affair with Bilhah would redirect the promised blessing (35:21–22a).

3'. The twelve sons of Jacob, mainly born in Paddan-Aram, showing God's promised fruitfulness and would advance God's purposes despite their conflicts (35:22b–26).

4'. When Isaac died, Jacob and Esau buried him in Hebron, further establishing the homeland (35:27–29).

III. Toledot 9: God blessed Esau with children and a land (36:1–8).

IV. Toledot 10: Esau's line grew and prospered in Seir (36:9–37:1).

V. Toledot 11: God passed his promise of blessing through Jacob to his sons, blessing their world, refining their character, and giving the birthright to Joseph and blessing to Judah (37:2–50:26).

A Announcing God's choice of him, Joseph alienated his brothers, who sold him to Egypt and deceived Jacob (37:2–36).

B God judged Judah's evil sons, blessing Tamar and exposing Judah's character, initiating heart change in Judah (38:1–30).

C Joseph is blessed by God with his presence and given success despite his unjust accusation and unexpected imprisonment (39:1–23).

D God raised Joseph to power in Egypt to save lives (40:1–41:57).

E Joseph's brothers traveled to Egypt twice to save their families, bringing them to repentance and unity (42:1–43:34).

F Joseph tested his brothers, revealing Judah's changed heart (44:1–34).

F' Joseph revealed his heart to his brothers, declaring God's work and prompting restoration for the family (45:1–28).

E' With God's promise, Jacob took all his family to Egypt to save them, expressing blessing to Pharaoh (46:1–47:12).

D' Joseph saved lives, enriching the Pharaoh and prospering the family of Israel (47:13–31).

C' Based on God's presence and care, Jacob blessed Joseph with the birthright, elevating Joseph's sons (48:1–22).

B' Jacob blessed his sons, elevating Judah to leadership and prospering Joseph with God's abundance (49:1–28).

A' Jacob and Joseph demonstrated their faith, with Jacob requesting burial in Canaan and Joseph reconciling fully with his brothers (49:29–50:21).

Epilogue to Toledot 11: With God's blessing, Joseph directed the growing nation's attention back to God's promise and future in Canaan.

3" God blessed Joseph in Egypt with great-grandchildren (50:22–23).

4" Joseph, dying, requested in faith to be buried in Canaan (50:24–26).

OUTLINE

These twelve units can be preached in forty-five messages.

PRIMEVAL HISTORY (1:1–11:26)

PROLOGUE: GOD CREATED THE HEAVENS AND EARTH (1:1–2:3)

- Creation and Rest: God's Good Universe Under His Image's Dominion (1:1–2:3)

TOLEDOT 1: CREATION IN REBELLION: JUDGMENT AND HOPE (2:4–4:26)

- Priesthood of Humanity: Created to Lead Worship (2:4–25)
- Rebellion: Death and Hope (3:1–24)
- Worship and Self-Worship: Life and Death (4:1–26)

TOLEDOT 2: DEATH AND JUDGMENT EXCEPT BY WALKING WITH GOD (5:1–6:8)

- Way of Life Choices: Death or Life (5:1–6:8)

TOLEDOT 3: CREATION RESET WITHOUT HEART CHANGE (6:9–9:29)

- The Flood: The Righteous Rise as Judgment Falls (6:9–8:19)
- Extending Grace: Blessing and Boundaries (8:20–9:17)
- Noah's Line: Exposing Heart Issues (9:18–29)

TOLEDOT 4: HUMANITY SCATTERED IN JUDGMENT (10:1–11:9)

- Making a Name: God's Grace in Judging Human Pride (10:1–11:9)

TOLEDOT 5: FROM SHEM TO ABRAM (11:10–26)

THE PATRIARCHAL NARRATIVES (11:27–50:26)

TOLEDOT 6: ABRAM: CHOSEN TO BLESS HUMANITY (11:27–25:11)

- Called to Bless: Opportunity and Responsibility (11:10–12:9)
- Fear or Faith: Thriving (or Not) Under Testing (12:10–20)
- Promise Renewed: Faith Rewarded (13:1–18)
- Loyal Faith: Costly Brotherly Love (14:1–24)
- Promise and Faith: God's Guarantee (15:1–21)
- Faith and Faithless: Learning in God's Classroom (16:1–16)
- Rewarded Loyalty: Obedience Through Growing Obstacles (17:1–27)
- Impossible Promises: No Laughing Matter (18:1–15)
- Justice and Grace: Living Brightly in a Dark World (18:16–19:38)
- Faith or Consequences: Responsibility in God's World (20:1–18)
- Laughing Last: Promises Secured (21:1–34)
- Complete Loyalty: Expressing Extreme Worship (22:1–24)

- Looking Ahead: Faith and Preparation (23:1–20)
- Faithful Following: Planning a Godly Future (24:1–25:11)

TOLEDOT 7: ISHMAEL: GOD HONORED HIS WORD (25:12–18)

TOLEDOT 8: JACOB: REFINING CHARACTER AND RENEWING COVENANT (25:19–35:29)

- Usefulness: Valuing God's Gifts (25:19–34)
- Fearful Faith: Compromised Blessing (26:1–33)
- Leading Blind: Hunting for Blessing (26:34–28:9)
- Jacob's Dream: Awed by God (28:10–22)
- Blessing: Learning God's Best (29:1–30)
- Jacob's Blessing: Hope in the Trenches (29:31–30:43)
- Vow Called: Lessons in Security (31:1–54)
- Blessed Disability: Limping into Trust (32:1–32)
- Reconciliation: God's Work in Human Hearts (33:1–20)
- Shechem's Fall: The Curse of Vengeance (34:1–31)
- Burying the Past: Anticipate the Promise (35:1–29)

TOLEDOT 9: ESAU: BLESSED WITH CHILDREN AND A LAND (36:1–8)

TOLEDOT 10: EDOM: PROSPERITY IN SEIR (36:9–37:1)

- Where's the Blessing? Waiting for God's Best (36:1–37:1)

TOLEDOT 11: THE TWELVE BROTHERS: GROWING INTO THEIR PURPOSE TO BE A BLESSING (37:2–50:26)

- Favoritism and Fratricide: God's Hidden Work Amid Desperate Evil (37:2–36)
- Judah's Backstory: How Tamar Salvaged the Promise (38:1–30)
- Yahweh's Blessing: Painful Righteousness and Unexpected Outcomes (39:1–23)
- Joseph's Rise: God's Surprising Work (40:1–41:57)
- Transformation: God's Heart Work (42:1–44:34)
- Joseph's Reveal: Shock and Awe at God's Work (45:1–28)
- Blessed with God's Presence: Living and Giving God's Best (46:1–47:31)
- Birthright: Passing on God's Blessing (48:1–22)
- Blessing: Possibility and Purpose (49:1–28)
- In Good Faith: Seeing God's Goodness in Death and Life (49:29–50:26)

INTRODUCTION TO THE PRIMEVAL NARRATIVES (GENESIS 1:1–11:9)

The history of humanity from creation to Abram's choice, refining God's plan for redemption, presents the foundational worldview on which appropriate worship must be built. These narratives present a transcendent Creator building his creation for his glory and setting his images in his holy temple. These images, identified with God to rule over his realm as his representatives, revolted against their sovereign, forfeiting life itself. The rebellion of those images, instigated by the enemy of the Creator, provides the opportunity for the reader to understand the gracious character of God and his plan to bring redemption to his creation and restore his images, crushing the snake.

The problem of the revolt expands as the narrative depicts the rapid movement of humanity away from God and blessing in self-will and tyrannical insurrection. All humanity inherits not only God's likeness but also the likeness of Adam, revealing heart disease that drives them away from God. They use their gift of dominion for self-exaltation and tyranny rather than representing their good creator, corrupting his creation. Yet simultaneously, we recognize hope in walking with God and in true worship that provides life amidst death and grace through judgment.

While showing the desperate needs of humanity in judgment, God extended grace and the promise of blessing even to his corrupted creatures. He would have to change hearts, and he would accomplish it without such complete destruction again. Instead, he would provide the needed pain and frustration to show humanity their deficits. In frustrating their plans and scattering humanity, God would show their trivial pursuits for what they are, destructive folly. In contrast, he would dissemble humanity's foolish union and point to a new paradigm with his choice of Abram.

LITERARY STRUCTURE AND THEMES

The *toledot* structure clearly shows the linear development of the promise and plan of God to give blessing and bring a seed of the woman to crush evil (See Narrative Structure of Genesis, p. 68). Rendsburg (2014, 8–26), however, has developed Sasson's (1980) initial observations, showing how the development of the narratives and genealogies simultaneously work together to prove the multiple reboots to God's world that we notice in the exposition:

A Creation, God's Words to Adam (1:1–3:24)
  B Adam's Sons (4:1–16)
    C Technological Development of Humankind (4:17–26)
      D Ten Generations from Adam to Noah (5:1–32)
        E Downfall: The Nephilim (6:1–8)
A' Flood and Recreation, God's Words to Noah (6:9–9:17)
  B' Noah's Sons (9:18–29)
    C' Ethnic Development of Humankind (10:1–32)
        E' Downfall: Tower of Babel (11:1–9)
      D' Ten Generations from Noah to Terah (11:10–26) (Rendsburg 2014, 8)

God's promise and plan through Adam appeared to be progressing toward a meltdown in human violence when God brought appropriate justice and restarted with Noah. The congenital heart problems of humanity resurfaced, however, driving humankind away from God again in a pride and power scheme when God again brought judgment. The final genealogy, breaking the parallel order intentionally, transitions the reader to the means by which God will establish the needed heart change for humanity and real blessing in walking with God through relationship with Yahweh.

In this analysis, the linear development of the narrative up to the announcement of judgment on humanity is matched by the development of the new world after the flood until the judgment on Babel. The significant difference is the genealogy of Shem, which is relocated to lead the reader to Abram and the program of God to bring the promised blessing. God renewed his creation, beginning afresh with Noah and drawing many parallels from his initial beginning with Adam, adding an explicit covenant with repeated promises. He finally rebooted a second time with Abram, who will also get a covenant with promises.

Theologically, this structure shows the foundational nature of these narratives to prepare for what will follow in the patriarchal narratives and the choice of Abram and, ultimately, Israel. These introductory narratives show the larger purpose and plan of Yahweh to provide blessing and to end evil and rebellion. They highlight the sovereign working of God and his justice, yet they also demonstrate God's grace and compassion to Noah, humanity at Babel, and Abram.

The linear structure moves the reader directly ahead, showing the logical progression and the consequential outworking of human evil. The impact of moving from creation to recreation to Abram builds expectations in the reader of a new beginning with Abram (a third Adam). Through Abram, God will work to bring about his good plan (covenant), which is confirmed both in its sovereign outworking and in its goodness at the end of Genesis (50:20). The evil human heart (6:5; 8:21) cannot stand in the way of the good working of God. Joseph's paradigmatic explanation, "you meant evil against me, but God meant it for good" (50:20), highlights God's purposeful salvation of his chosen family and blessing to the world in the form of food and life, despite and even using evil people's evil choices. As introduction to the Pentateuch and all that follows, Genesis will effectively illustrate the flourishing life offered by Yahweh as he brings his people out of Egypt to establish them as a kingdom of priests and a holy nation (Exod. 19:5–6) and to bring about blessing to all peoples through changed hearts and lives in obedience to Yahweh (Deut. 30).

PREACHING SUGGESTIONS

We have designed the Exposition to cover the section in nine messages. You can easily take longer in several of these foundational passages that present archetypal events and worldview concepts. Genesis 1, for example, could provide a message on the character of God with a separate message on humanity as God's images and God's purpose for them, among other possible teachings from the passage. Alternatively, sets of passages can be combined, such as we suggest for chapters 2 and 3 or even 2–4 (the first *toledot* section) or 6:9–9:29 (the third *toledot*), providing opportunity to do a shorter series.

However you structure your series, these narratives need to clearly expose the foundational truths about God, humanity, and how humanity must relate to him to flourish. The paradigmatic nature of these opening stories offers wonderful opportunities for theological reflection and exposition of basic, crucial concepts, such as human nature, marriage, purpose, temptation, sin, grace, sacrifice, responsibility, pride, rebellion, and many more. These key themes form a needed background to contemporary and age-old discussions, from our view of and response to God to our view of ourselves and our responsibilities to others and to our world itself. We encourage you to take time to clarify and work through the implications of these crucial passages for the benefit of the church of Jesus Christ.

Genesis 1:1–2:3

EXEGETICAL IDEA
The Sovereign King showcased both his sole transcendent power and imminent goodness, ordering and filling his very good creation and crowning it with his regal representative, humanity, culminating in the realization of his holy rest.

THEOLOGICAL FOCUS
The sole sovereign, transcendent creator crowned his good universe with humankind to serve him with his blessing and enter his rest.

PREACHING IDEA
Our sovereign Creator calls on his images to submit to him and extend his rule in exclusive worship.

PREACHING POINTERS
The original hearers of Genesis 1:1–2:3 were living in a world where numerous other creation stories and gods existed. God's people needed to understand how different their worldview should be in societies full of idols that were all part of creation. Here they heard of the sole, sovereign, transcendent God who created heaven and earth and all that is in it. The author starts "In the beginning," presuming that God already existed, by describing the condition of "the earth" before creation began (1:2), and the active presence of "the Spirit of God . . . hovering over the face of the waters" (1:1–2). Then in verses 3–27 God begins to speak everything into existence day after day, including God's crowning creation, "man in our image, after our likeness" (v. 26). Everything in God's world is portrayed as "good" (vv. 10, 12, 18, 21, 25) and even "very good" (v. 31). When everything is complete, God stops creating his world and rests, blessing the seventh day (vv. 2:1–3). It is near the end of the creation process that human beings receive the blessing of God and their marching orders to represent God in his world (vv. 26–30), cared for by him rather than having to care for the gods.

Today we live in a world in which creation stories are considered fables and God's existence as sovereign king is challenged, or multiple gods may be worshipped, as in Egypt. Humanity is confused as to their purpose on Earth and their relationship to the rest of creation. We face competing worldviews that produce dramatically different responses in our world. Genesis 1 presents a corrective to idolatry, whether polytheism, animism, hedonism, or self-worship. Anyone who hears this creation account and believes it are themselves new creatures who worship and serve the transcendent creator in a world full of idols, representing him in his world.

CREATION AND REST: GOD'S GOOD UNIVERSE UNDER HIS IMAGE'S DOMINION (1:1–2:3)

LITERARY STRUCTURE AND THEMES

Genesis 1:1–2:3 offers a highly stylized and tightly structured account of the Creator and his work. Moses begins with a summary statement, heralding God's actions (1:1). Day seven (2:1–3) reflects the opening statement, providing the frame for the narrative and highlighting the theological impact. God's work creating (ברא in 1:1; 2:3) the universe (הַשָּׁמַיִם וְהָאָרֶץ in 1:1; 2:1), summarized in 1:1, is completed in 2:1–3 (כלה in 2:1, 2) so that God rests (שׁבת in 2:2, 3) from all his work that he had done (אֲשֶׁר עָשָׂהוּ מְלַאכְתּוֹ, occurring three times in 2:2–3). The frame then, drives home God's creativity, God's sole authority, and God's transcendence over his creation.

The initial conditions (1:2) follow the general statement (1:1), which will be remedied by the creative activity of the transcendent Creator to bring about God's good creation: the desolate Earth is uninhabitable and uninhabited. Yet, despite the pervasive darkness and water, hope overspreads the elements with the hovering Spirit of God. The text focuses on the Earth as the arena of activity and place for humanity. The first three days of creation, then, will make the habitat fit for life, and days four through six will fill that habitat with life. Filling the Earth with the inhabitants in days four to six parallels constructing the environment (days one to three), highlighting three pairs of days, with progressive development, leading up to the culmination on the seventh day. Day seven supplies the goal of creation as God rests and his work is complete.

The passage, then, presents the creation account that initially states the conditions to be overcome (1:2), progressively corrected with creation (1:3–31) and framed with the statement of God's creation and completion (1:1; 2:1–3).

A. The transcendent uncreated creator created the universe (1:1).
  B. The story of God's creation began with a desolate, empty, and dark watery mass (1:2).
  B'. Revealing his transcendent power and goodness, God fashioned and filled his universe, setting up his images to represent him (1:3–31).
    1. In the first three days, God spoke, creating a good, ordered, productive habitat out of the dark, desolate world (1:3–13).
    2. In days four through six God filled his empty world, speaking into it life, purpose, and blessing, culminating with humanity, which he pronounced very good.
A'. On day seven, having finished his creative work, God rested and pronounced blessing, entering his sanctuary to administrate his kingdom.

The many repetitions in the account repay careful attention, revealing both the structure of the account and the intended lessons. Each day moves predictably from God's creative command to the accomplishment of the command, concluding with God's evaluation and naming or blessing. Various terms and constructions are repeated three or seven or ten times. One cannot miss the goodness of the creation (seven times) and, by extension, the goodness of the Creator. God spoke ten times (וַיֹּאמֶר אֱלֹהִים), suggesting the ten commands (see "Word of God," p. 59). The length of the description of day six, along with the several significant repetitions, draws attention to the climax of God's creative activity, crowned with the image of God himself in humankind. The narrator emphasizes the seventh day, repeating the day three times, crowning it with blessing, sanctity, and his rest. The narrative concludes that the creation is complete (2:1, 2), actualizing the initial summary statement in 1:1 with emphasis on the Creator who had finished and rested from all the work he had done (three times). The final blessing and sanctification of that seventh day because of God's rest on it (2:3) punctuates the significance of the entire creation event.

- ***God Created from Desolation (1:1–2)***
- ***God Fashioned and Filled His Universe (1:3–31)***
- ***God Rested, Pronouncing Blessing (2:1–3)***

EXPOSITION

Genesis 1 introduces not only Genesis, but all of Scripture. The creation account grounds Israel's theology and therefore, also, the theology of the church and the believer. The writers of Scripture often look back to Genesis 1 to support their theological conclusions. Based on a date of initial composition for Israel after approximately four hundred years in bondage in Egypt, and now starting life as a nation under Yahweh, we must look for God's message for his people coming out of Egypt before we try to answer our own questions or make application to the modern world.

The Exodus account describes God purposefully declaring to them his nature, distinguishing himself from the gods of Egypt in which they have been immersed. The nature of God forms the root of the second objection by Moses to leading the nation (Exod. 3:13–17) and the core of the objectives for the plagues against Egypt, revealing Yahweh to Israel, Egypt, and the world (Exod. 6:1–10; 7:3–5; 9:14–16; 10:1–2). God significantly highlights his role in creation at this crucial historical moment.

The creation account provides a worldview for the new nation of Israel that dramatically changes their absorbed Egyptian background, teaching them a radically distinct perspective of God, their role, and their responsibility before him. Genesis 1 supports the theological concerns of the exodus and provides the necessary background and cohesion to the claims of Yahweh as sovereign over all the gods of Egypt, all nations, and the entire world. It provides the apologetic for Israel to bow before him alone and, at the same time, understand their role and responsibility as a representative nation, a kingdom of priests (Exod. 19:5–6). It provides a new nation with its charter as God's promised people and a homeland prepared for it as their Creator apportioned his world to his people for an inheritance (Deut. 32:8). Genesis 1 instructs God's people in his worldview, exposing the lie in the claims of all false gods, the powerless creation of one Creator. The sovereign King, then, showcases both his sole transcendent power and his imminent goodness, ordering and filling his very good creation and crowning it with his regal representative, humanity, culminating in the realization of his holy rest.

God Created from Desolation (1:1–2)

God created the universe out of desolation and emptiness.

God Created the Universe (1:1)

The transcendent, uncreated Creator created the universe.

1:1. The narrative opens with a comprehensive statement about the Creator. God appears as the creator of all things, without introduction, "in the beginning." He existed without explanation or defense before anything existed. Unlike Israel's pagan neighbors, God does not need an explanation of origin because he is eternal (Ps. 90:2). He is preexistent and transcendent.

TRANSLATION ANALYSIS 1:1a
Most modern versions translate the initial phrase, "In the beginning" (בְּרֵאשִׁית), as an independent clause. A few, however, translate this as a temporal clause, like the NRSV, "In the beginning when God created," or NJPS, "When God began to create." There is an additional issue here as these two versions take the main clause in different places. The NRSV understands verse 2 as the main clause ("the earth was a formless void" when God began to create), and the NJPS translation understands verse 3 as the main clause, with verse 2 being parenthetical ("When God began to create . . . God said"). The traditional understanding of "In the beginning" (בְּרֵאשִׁית) as an independent clause is preferable and most natural (Mathews 1996, 138–40).

TRANSLATION ANALYSIS 1:1b
The plural form for "God" (אֱלֹהִים) emphasizes his majesty (or possibly an intensive). It does not refer to number, as we can easily see, since the plural could be used of a single pagan god as well (e.g., 1 Kings 11:5).

The statement that God created the heavens and the earth describes the creation of the whole universe (merism). All that has come into being is his creation under his effortless control, without conflict, and does not include other deities. It is best not to view this statement as the initial creation of everything, followed by what happened next, 1:2–2:3, because of the structure of the verses. Instead, verse 1 presents an introductory umbrella statement of the whole creation account.

The Creation of Everything

Traditionally, verse 1 has been understood as the initial creation of everything after which the rest of the chapter follows chronologically. Reading verse 1 as the prelude to the action here has been challenged on several grounds. Each following section of Genesis begins with the *toledot*, which functions as a title. The structure of each of the next two *toledot* sections follows Genesis 1:1–2 even more closely. After the introductory statement or title to the section, each new section includes disjunctive clauses that provide (or remind of) background information that is necessary for the ensuing action (no *wayyiqtol* forms). In Genesis 2, the *toledot* is followed by clauses giving the initial conditions as necessary background, into which God will place humankind and commission them (vv. 5–6). In chapter 5, the status and blessing of humankind is important for the fertility that will follow, but also for establishing the ongoing image in man and expectation of God's plan and working (vv. 1b–2). Not only does chapter 1 follow this pattern (most closely to 2:4–6 [Excursus 1.1]), but day seven declares God's creation of the heavens and earth "finished" (repeated twice, 2:1–2) framing the narrative with 1:1 and suggesting the accomplishment of the creation declared in 1:1. Genesis 1:1, then best summarizes the section, with initial conditions recorded in verse 2, and recapitulated in 2:1–2, rather than as a precursor to the action in the section. In other words, verse 1 provides an overall statement, which will then be fleshed out in the rest of chapter 1 (Waltke 1975, 1976).

Having presented God as the Creator of all that is, the narrator steps back and says, "Let's start with a little background, then I will pick up the story with what you need to know about God's creation." Significantly, the account includes much that parallels ancient accounts, particularly Egyptian accounts (Israel's world), and yet radically challenges their prevailing view of the gods.

Excursus 1.1	
Genesis 1:1–3a	**Genesis 2:4–7a**
1 בְּרֵאשִׁית בָּרָא אֱלֹהִים אֵת הַשָּׁמַיִם וְאֵת הָאָרֶץ׃ 2 וְהָאָרֶץ הָיְתָה תֹהוּ וָבֹהוּ וְחֹשֶׁךְ עַל־פְּנֵי תְהוֹם וְרוּחַ אֱלֹהִים מְרַחֶפֶת עַל־פְּנֵי הַמָּיִם׃ 3 וַיֹּאמֶר אֱלֹהִים	4 אֵלֶּה תוֹלְדוֹת הַשָּׁמַיִם וְהָאָרֶץ בְּהִבָּרְאָם בְּיוֹם עֲשׂוֹת יְהוָה אֱלֹהִים אֶרֶץ וְשָׁמָיִם׃ 5 וְכֹל שִׂיחַ הַשָּׂדֶה טֶרֶם יִהְיֶה בָאָרֶץ וְכָל־עֵשֶׂב הַשָּׂדֶה טֶרֶם יִצְמָח כִּי לֹא הִמְטִיר יְהוָה אֱלֹהִים עַל־הָאָרֶץ וְאָדָם אַיִן לַעֲבֹד אֶת־הָאֲדָמָה׃ 6 וְאֵד יַעֲלֶה מִן־הָאָרֶץ וְהִשְׁקָה אֶת־כָּל־פְּנֵי־הָאֲדָמָה׃ 7 וַיִּיצֶר יְהוָה אֱלֹהִים אֶת־הָאָדָם עָפָר מִן־הָאֲדָמָה
Each section begins with an initial clause (1:1; 2:4) followed by a series of disjunctives (*waw* on a non-verb at the beginning of the clause) and finally with the *waw* consecutive on the preterite marking the beginning of the main narrative (1:3a; 2:7a).	

God Began with Desolation (1:2)

The story of God's creation began with a desolate, empty, and dark watery mass.

1:2. The background to the creation of the universe surprises modern ears. Moses begins the story of God's creative acts in an uninhabitable and uninhabited place, described as "without form and void" (תֹהוּ וָבֹהוּ) and with "darkness" (חֹשֶׁךְ) over "the deep" (תְהוֹם). These four ideas sound like the beginning of a typical Egyptian account of creation (Miller and Soden 2012, 83, n. 20). Here, however, the narrator is not agreeing with the Egyptian accounts, but he will use language they understand to highlight the fundamental differences between the true God and the Egyptian deities; the other "deities" are merely part of God's effortless creation (polemic). In other ways, he will use seemingly familiar concepts for Israel to draw brand new paradigms and perceptions of God.[1]

TRANSLATION ANALYSIS 1:2a

The relation of verse 2 to verses 1 and 3 has provoked long discussions. Do these verses present an unbroken train of logical thought, or does verse 2 stand outside the flow of thought? The problem is foregrounded by the two translations viewing verse 1 as relative (NJPS, NRSV), as well as a few translations that begin verse 2 with "now" (HCSB, NET, NIV) instead of "and" (KJV) or merely leaving out any connector (ESV, NASB95, NLT). At issue here is the syntax of the Hebrew and how the initial *waw* plus a non-verb at the beginning of the clause should be understood in verse 2. Since the main Hebrew narrative flow uses the *wayyiqtol* form, and these clauses do not have *wayyiqtol* forms, verse 2 presents information that is background, not part of the normal narrative flow. Instead, verse 2 begins with a typical disjunctive *waw* construction, which supplies information critical to the narrative (Joüon 1993, §159f; Waltke and O'Connor 1990, §39.2.3). In this case, the parallels in the next two *toledot* sections support the parenthetical use. In this analysis of the clause, the verse does not provide the next step after verse 1; it provides information that is not in chronological order but is necessary backdrop for the narrative that follows. In addition, each creative day begins with "And God said" (וַיֹּאמֶר אֱלֹהִים; vv. 3, 6, 9,

1 For an extended treatment of the relationship of Gen. 1 to the ancient cosmologies around Israel, see Miller and Soden (2012).

14, 20, 24), adding support to the argument that day one begins with verse 3.

"Without form," or desolation, and "void" will be the starting point of God's creative work. Days one through three will make the inhospitable world ("without form") ready to welcome and sustain life. Days four through six will fill that "void" but now hospitable world. In the ancient context and in much of the Old Testament, "darkness" and "deep" would have mythical connotations, foreboding and with undercurrents of tense cosmic battle, but here God will effortlessly speak light into darkness and bring habitation out of the watery deep without combat or opposition. Bringing good out of darkness and disarray becomes paradigmatic for Israel's God (Gen. 15:12; 50:20).

Amid what may feel dark and foreboding, the "Spirit of God" hovers. The ancient context, both in Egypt and Mesopotamia, would have suggested that "Spirit" (רוּחַ) here be understood as "wind." However, in the context of Genesis and the Old Testament, reference to the Spirit of God seems too clear to miss. Moses seems to use this term with intentional ambiguity to relate their expectation of the pagan creative presence (wind—רוּחַ) to the working of God, and it will parallel the wind (רוּחַ) of God in 8:1 as God brings his creation again out of the watery mass after the flood. With the Spirit of God at work, hope permeates the narrative, and the initial foreboding of the primal conditions evaporates in the light of a coming new dawn.

God Fashioned and Filled His Universe (1:3–31)

Revealing his transcendent power and goodness, God fashioned and filled his universe, setting up his images to represent him.

God Fashioned the Habitat (1:3–13)

In the first three days, God spoke, creating a good, ordered, productive habitat out of a dark, desolate world.

1:3–5. Creation began with God's command, "God said." God's spoken word highlights his ultimate and effortless control. He is the king who speaks, and it will happen. Each day presents the progressive outworking of his will, with no difficulty or opposition. God is completely in charge.

The first day began with the creation of light. The actual commands and resulting phenomena seem strange or impossible to the modern perspective, but again, they were right at home for Israel. For example, how can you separate light from dark as if they were commodities? How can you have light before any luminaries to produce light (day four)? In Israel's context, however, both propositions made sense. Light was commonly considered an entity that did not require any source in the ancient world, and, in fact, in both the Egyptian and Mesopotamian accounts light appeared before the luminaries because it was an attribute of the creators who came into being before the rest of the creation (Miller and Soden 2012, 88–89, 120). The process of the creator god in Egypt coming into being would parallel the biblical creation of light, with the dramatic difference that light is not pictured here as a deity or even the characteristic of the deity. Light was the creation of God and only a means to differentiate between the day and the night. Then, when God created the sun on day four, he did not even mention the name, avoiding reference to a deity across the ancient world.

Genesis 1 presents a stark contrast to the worldview of the polytheistic environs of Israel. God was not speaking to a modern scientific culture but to Israel, in language they understood. What he said is true. He created light and day and night. He did not explain what that meant astronomically or physically, but phenomenally (speaking in ways that describe what people appear to see). He communicated according to their way of speaking about their world, based on their observations.

God appraised his work and called it "good" (טוֹב—see Theological Emphases of the Book,

God's Goodness and Good versus Evil, p. 58 and p. 63). God's evaluation of his work, occurring six more times, does not speak to morality directly but shows that it is exactly what he desired, and it will accomplish his purposes. It also reveals his nature, producing good. When he finished, at the end of day six, he would pronounce it "very good" (טוֹב מְאֹד). God had accomplished his work that would showcase his glory (Ps. 19:1), with his images demonstrating his goodness and experiencing his blessing.

Day one ends with the familiar formula that "there was evening, and there was morning, the first day." A more grammatically consistent translation would be "one day" rather than "the first day" (יוֹם אֶחָד). While it does not make sense to us, this unusual way to say "the first day" had great significance in an Egyptian context. For Egypt, creation was done in a single day, and every day after that was a recreation or re-enacting of creation. The initial act of creation was called the "first time" (Morenz 1992, 166). The Egyptians had a cyclical view of history and seem to have believed that there would come a day when the sun would no longer rise from the primeval ocean, and time would cease. All "creation" would go back to the chaotic, watery, and dark initial conditions.

TRANSLATION ANALYSIS 1:5

The differing translations of the numbered days is important because the Hebrew is unusual for a numbered sequence. The construction for "first day" (יוֹם אֶחָד) would normally be translated "one day," as in the NASB (cf. "one place," מָקוֹם אֶחָד, v. 9). While the cardinal can be occasionally translated as an ordinal (e.g., Gen. 8:5), it is unusual, especially in this sort of a sequence. However, since it is clearly in a numbered sequence of days, most translations translate it as "the first day," which logically makes sense (so KJV, ESV, HCSB, NET, NIV, NLT, NRSV) but misses the theological significance of the unusual form. The Jewish Publication Society tries to show both ideas ("a first day," JPS). The Hebrew lacks the definite article on any of the first five numbered days until the sixth day, reflected in the JPS, NASB, and NET ("a second day," etc.) but added in most other translations.

In contrast, the biblical account began with "one day" (יוֹם אֶחָד). That one day was followed by a second day, a third day, and so on, until it reached its climactic creation in "the sixth day" and its goal of rest in "the seventh day" (repeated three times). Moses provides a corrective for Israel. The biblical view of history is teleological, under God's exclusive and sovereign control. It is not random, chaotic, nor cyclical, but it is moving in sequence toward God's ultimate rest.

1:6–8. Day two presents a similar challenge. What does it mean that God separated the waters to create "heaven?" This statement is difficult to visualize in our world, but it made complete sense in ancient Israel's world. Consistently, in the ancient world, they talked about the universe as if there were cosmic waters above the sky, as well as below the Earth (Allen 1988, 18–19, 24; Tsumura 2005, 36–53). Again, this language is phenomenal, describing what it looked like.

In Egyptian cosmology, the initial creation was also out of water, but it was not what we usually picture when we read Genesis 1:2. Egyptian writings described precreation conditions as continual, unending water (no surface or top, just water!). In the midst of the water the initial creator separated the waters to make a bubble of light and order (Allen 1988, 7). While this is very different from our understanding of reality, it was a common ancient way to describe their world. This likely would be what Israel understood when this description was read. Moses does not endorse a particular "science" but uses the phenomenal language of their world to describe God's working. God made the atmosphere, keeping back the waters from inundating the earth.

The Egyptian creation account, most completely expressed on the Shabaka stone, provides the closest parallels to the biblical account (see Soden and Miller, *In the Beginning, We Misunderstood*).
Photo by James Hoffmeier

TRANSLATION ANALYSIS 1:6–8

The barrier between the waters above and the waters below (רָקִיעַ) is variously translated as firmament (JPS, KJV), expanse (ESV, HCSB, NASB, NET), vault (NIV), dome (NRSV), or space (NLT). The referent presents the difficulty here. Is this term referring to the atmosphere or something else? While we naturally think of the atmosphere as the most obvious referent, the ancient conception of the cosmos included a barrier that held back cosmic waters above that atmosphere and below which the sun, moon, and stars tracked as they crossed the night sky. While it is difficult to know exactly how the ancient peoples around and including Israel really conceived of the makeup and functioning of the universe (how much did they understand was figurative?), this term parallels accounts across the ancient world that consistently present the picture of a solid barrier. The verbal form of the noun is used of beating out metal sheets, such as in Exodus 39:3 or Numbers 16:39 (HB, 17:4), and in Job 37:18 Elihu asks Job, "Can you, like him, spread out the skies, hard as a cast metal mirror?" (ESV). The verb translated "spread out" is the same Hebrew root (רקע).

1:9–13. On day three, God again separated to create, but this time he separated the waters from the land. Again, the words do not fit our world picture, as the waters are gathered into one place (מָקוֹם אֶחָד), but it fits the way Israel would have described their world (Clifford 1994, 105–6). On the newly exposed land, God brought forth vegetation, highlighting the seed and fruit-bearers, which would provide food for the coming creatures. Twice on day three God declared his creation good—the separating of the land and seas and the filling of the land with vegetation.

On the first three days, God provided the necessary light, space, and sustenance for life, highlighting them by naming (day and night, heaven, land, and sea) and repetition (six times using the same root: two times for the verb "sow" and four times the noun "seed" [both from זרע]; and three times "fruit" [פְּרִי]). When he named each element he created, he underscored his sovereign creative control and the reality of the things that he had spoken into existence. Israel's God is sovereign over day and night (all of time is under his control; Ps. 139:11–12) and all the universe (no place is out of his purview and control; Ps. 139:7–10).

God Filled His Habitat (1:14–31)

In days four through six God filled his empty world, speaking into it life, purpose, and blessing, which he pronounced very good.

1:14–19. The second three creative days parallel the first three as God filled the new heaven with luminaries (day four), the seas and atmosphere with fish and birds (day five), and the land with animals and, climactically, humanity (the sixth day). Day four describes God's creation of the lights in the expanse that he had created in day one. Here God declared the lights to separate day from night (reflecting God's creation of the light in 1:3–5), to be signs marking the seasons or festivals, and to give light on the earth (vv. 14–15).

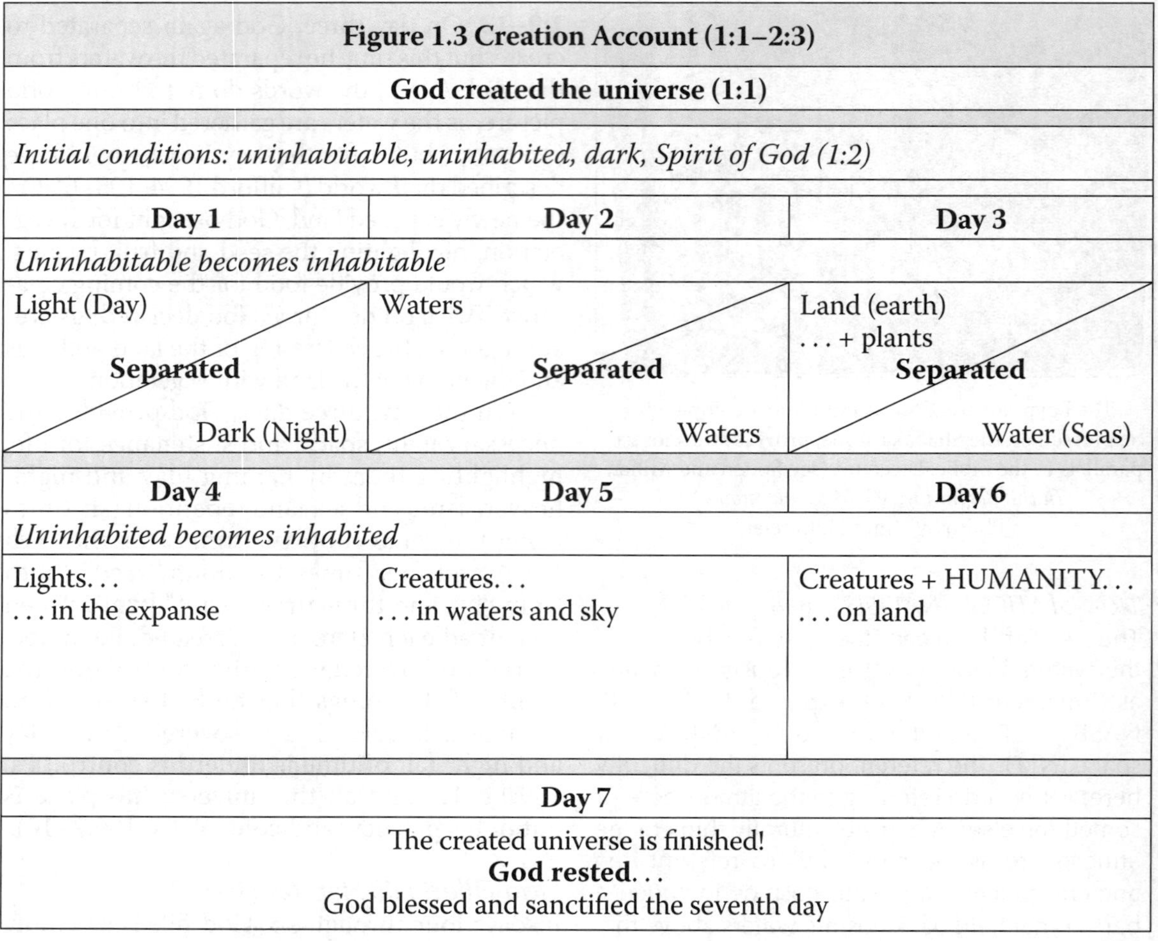

Figure 1.3 Creation Account (1:1–2:3)		
God created the universe (1:1)		
Initial conditions: uninhabitable, uninhabited, dark, Spirit of God (1:2)		
Day 1	**Day 2**	**Day 3**
Uninhabitable becomes inhabitable		
Light (Day) **Separated** Dark (Night)	Waters **Separated** Waters	Land (earth) . . . + plants **Separated** Water (Seas)
Day 4	**Day 5**	**Day 6**
Uninhabited becomes inhabited		
Lights. . . . . . in the expanse	Creatures. . . . . . in waters and sky	Creatures + HUMANITY. . . . . . on land
Day 7		
The created universe is finished! **God rested. . .** God blessed and sanctified the seventh day		

TRANSLATION ANALYSIS 1:14

The NIV translates "seasons" (מוֹעֲדִים), as "sacred times," and HCSB translates it as "festivals." The term is often used of festivals in the Old Testament, as well as the appointed time for the meeting or festivity or even the place for the meeting. Because the festivals and religious occasions were typically related to the lunar calendar in the ancient world, it would be appropriate to think of the moon as the regulator of such convocations, signifying more than we would normally think of with "seasons." Two of these three functions are repeated in reverse order in verses 17–18, framing the "two great lights" in verse 16, which he made to rule day and night. The separating of day from night (v. 14a) in verse 18b reflects the day one creation with "to separate the light from the darkness." The giving of light (v. 15b) is shortened to merely shining on the Earth (v. 17b). The marking of festivals in verse 14, however, is replaced in verse 18 by repeating the rule of the great lights, emphasizing their role in the regulation of the seasons and festivals. Significantly, the sun and moon are not named as such, possibly because naming them would also name ancient deities, so here they are merely the greater and lesser lights, emphasizing their created status. Their role of ruling (using both the verb and nominal forms of the root משל, vv. 16, 18) stresses their

Lights		
Notice the frame, highlighting the role of the two great lights to mark special occasions:		
1:14–15	**1:16**	**1:17–18**
"'Let there be lights. . . a "to separate the day from the night.	"And God made the two great lights—	c' "And God set them in the expanse of the heavens "to give light on the earth,
b "And let them be for signs and for seasons, and for days and years,	"the greater light to rule the day and the lesser light to rule the night—	b' "to rule over the day and over the night,
c "and let them be lights in the expanse of the heavens to give light upon the earth.'"	"and the stars also."	a' "and to separate the light from the darkness."

prominence over the day and night as well as the seasons and festivals. It adds to the polemic against the pagan gods by suggesting that their "rule" is merely prominence and functional but without any power since they are simply God's creations. Using the same verb as in verse 4 (בדל), the narrator also ties the work of the sun and moon into the initial creative work of God, maintaining the distinction between day and night. God declared it good (v. 18).

TRANSLATION ANALYSIS 1:16

The role (מֶמְשָׁלָה) of the two great lights is variously translated "rule" (ESV, KJV, JPS, NET, NRSV), "govern" (NASB, NIV, NLT), or "have dominion" (HCSB). While this last seems formally comparable to man's job description in verses 26 and 28, it is from a different root and merely speaks of the prominence of these lights and their role in marking social and religious occasions.

1:20–23. On day five, God filled the waters with living creatures and created birds to fly before the expanse (created on day two). Here, the narrator pointedly goes back to the term for the "waters" (הַמַּיִם) from day two, highlighting the relation with day two rather than what God named them in day three, "seas" (יַמִּים). Moses is drawing the attention of the reader to the patterning and symmetry of the account. For the first time, we hear the blessing of God, given as a command to the birds and fish to be "fruitful and multiply and fill" the waters and the Earth (v. 22). It is God's creative word that gives blessing by command or, better, by empowering them to carry out his desire, asserting his creative will. Creating both the creatures of the waters and the birds, God declared them "good" (v. 25).

TRANSLATION ANALYSIS 1:21

The term that is translated "whales" (KJV), "sea creatures" (ESV, HCSB, NET, NIV, NLT) or "sea monsters" (JPS, NASB; הַתַּנִּינִם) is related to the term in the Ugaritic Baal Myth describing the sea serpent adversary of Baal (see similar descriptions in Ps. 74:13–14 and Isa. 27:1). Here, however, the great creatures of the sea are not primordial enemies of Yahweh but his creations and under his care. There is no mythology here, but rather polemic against the pagan beliefs. Those super or deified powers in pagan belief are simply creatures under the control and care of Yahweh.

1:24–31. Day six presents the climax of creation, which the author shows in multiple ways. The narrator devotes approximately twice as much space to day six than to any of the other days. God spoke four times (אמר—used only once on most days, but twice on day three). He not only declared his creation good (v. 25), but he evaluated "everything that he had made" and pronounced it "very good" (v. 31), the seventh time he has pronounced the goodness of his creation. Three times Moses describes God's activity with "made" (עשׂה—also used three times on day seven) and three times with "created" (ברא—all referring to humankind). For each of the first five days of creation he did not use the definite article in the concluding formula, but on day six, for the first time, it was "*the* sixth day" (יוֹם הַשִּׁשִּׁי).

TRANSLATION ANALYSIS 1:24–25
The categories of beasts listed here refer to domesticated "livestock" (בְּהֵמָה), small creatures near the ground or "creeping things" (רֶמֶשׂ), and wild "beasts of the earth" (וְחַיְתוֹ־אֶרֶץ).

The spotlight on the sixth day emphasizes God's crowning creation, humanity (over half of the Hebrew text relates to human creation). God was drawing Israel's attention to humankind's role in his program (which would be passed on to Israel), distinguishing their role from all other views of humankind in the ancient world. Israel needed to understand a vastly different perspective on their significance before their God. They were royal, representing the Sovereign of the universe.

The creation of humankind completed God's creation. In contrast to the creatures of the sea, air, and land that were created "according to their kinds" (seven times in vv. 21, 24–25), God created humanity as his image (three times in vv. 26–27) and likeness. Explicitly, male and female both represent God and carry out his mandate to rule over his creation (vv. 27–28; see the Introduction on "Humanity as God's Images," p. 61). In this passage, the dominant impact of the image of God is the representation of him over his creation. Humankind functions as the vice-regent of God in his world, with responsibility over the Earth, the fish, the birds, and every living thing (v. 28). Such a theology radically opposes the typical ancient teaching in which humanity was created to slave for the gods, working and providing for them. Here God provides for man! The snake will be the immediate challenge, however, to human authority and responsibility in chapter 3.

TRANSLATION ANALYSIS 1:26–27a
Three times in these two verses Moses tells the reader that man was created "in (God's) image" (בְּצַלְמֵנוּ, בְּצַלְמוֹ, בְּצֶלֶם אֱלֹהִים). In each instance, the preposition בְּ provides helpful corroboration. We have argued that God is placing his images into his creation (cosmic temple) analogous to the image of a common deity in the ancient world. Man is then identified with God as his image. The preposition בְּ fits that picture as the בְּ of essence (Ross 1988, 112, Imes 2023, 4–6; *HALOT*, s.v. בְּ 3. "expressing the quality or nature embodied in the noun," though *HALOT* takes it as "according to" because it alternates with כְּ, 104, which would mean "after the pattern of," Wenham 1987, 28). "Image" (צֶלֶם) is used elsewhere in the Hebrew Bible for the images of the gods (e.g., Num. 33:52; Ezek. 7:20; Amos 5:26). Humanity, then, is God's image. We were created to represent him as our identity, not with something added on to be like him.

TRANSLATION ANALYSIS 1:26–27b
While "humankind" (NET, NRSV; אָדָם) is translated both as "man" (ESV, HCSB, JPS, KJV, NASB) and as "humankind" (NIV), it clearly refers generically to the whole human race, male and female, and not merely males (note 1:27).

"Let Us Make"

The unexpected plural for the divine speech, "let us make," expresses the original text well, as reflected in the consistent translation. The problem here is the plural for God in an Old Testament context that consistently asserts his sole claim to deity (Deut. 4:39). For many New Testament believers, it has been tempting to claim explicit evidence for the Trinity here. However, the fact that the Trinity was not suggested until the New Testament era makes this impossible to prove, though it allows for the Trinity. Instead, while it could simply be the "'we' of self-address" (Collins 2006, 59–61), as Walton (2001, 128) notes, it is not consistent in biblical Hebrew, and in this ancient context it would more likely have been understood as the "divine counsel" or heavenly court (E. Theodore Mullen, Jr., "Divine Assembly," *ABD* 2:214–17). The idea of a heavenly court is prominent across the ancient world. In their context, it was made up of the realm of the various gods and goddesses. In biblical thinking, it was supernatural beings that God used to administrate his kingdom (Heiser 2015, 28–37; cf. 1 Kings 22:19–22; Job 1:6; 2:1). That is not to say that any heavenly beings helped in the creation of humanity. Genesis 1:27 makes it clear that it was God alone. Rather, 1:26 was more of a royal address to his court asserting that he would create another class of beings to represent him (his images) in his new creation (cf. Heiser 2015, 38–43).

Numerous issues deserve special attention in this passage. For discussion regarding the image of God, including the meaning and purpose of being in God's image, see the Introduction ("Humanity as God's Images," p. 61). The blessing of being fruitful and filling the Earth seems clear enough, but the idea of dominion implies responsibility and privilege. Clearly, man stands in God's place in the world, ruling. Clearly, also, God is good and to represent him requires a good and benevolent rule that cares for his creation with the same good purpose.

Subdue the Earth

The first term used may be the most freighted (כבשׁ) because it describes a forcible subjugation and is even used of rape later (Esth. 7:8). In its earlier usage, however, it may not have had the same destructive overtones as in later time, even though it is never used in the Old Testament of a willing or easy subject (e.g., the Canaanites [Num. 32:22, 29; Josh. 18:1; 1 Chron. 22:18], enemies [2 Sam. 8:11; Zech. 9:15], or slaves [Jer. 34:11, 16]). Of course, in a very good world with humanity representing well the sovereign and good God, even a forcible rule would be benevolent. It will be with humanity's rebellion that malevolence enters the picture and dominion becomes destruction. Perhaps here we see a hint of the coming conflict and man's need for watchfulness.

Finally, God highlighted his bountiful care for his creatures, declaring the purpose of the plants he created on day three (vv. 29–30). Seven times he used "all" in two verses (כֹּל), emphasizing the complete provision of God, giving humankind *every* plant in *all* the Earth and *every* tree with fruit. In addition, he provided for *every* beast, *every* bird and *every*thing with the breath of life, giving them *every* green plant. Israel's good God cared generously for his good creation.

The daily pattern for days four through six continued from days one through three, with a few exceptions. As we already noted, God saved the naming of the creatures for man to exercise his reflected authority (2:19–20). Each day would continue to flow from the creative word of God and be judged good (twice on day three and twice on the sixth day), with the final seventh judgment after the creation of humanity, pronouncing all that he had made "very good" (1:31). The seventh emphatic proclamation of the goodness of his creation highlighted the work of God (and so his character) and set up the contrast with the result of sin, beginning with the initial sin in the garden with the tree of the knowledge of good and evil (2:17; 3:5, 22) and crystalizing in the pronouncement of God that man's evil actions are a result of their evil heart (6:5).

God Rested, Pronouncing Blessing (2:1–3)

On day seven, having finished his creative work, God rested and pronounced blessing, entering his sanctuary to administrate his kingdom.

2:1–3. Though God's creative activity climaxed on day six, day seven pictures the goal of creation and the perspective of what God's goodness means in his good, ordered world. God blessed and sanctified the seventh day, doing what a god in the ancient world was expected to do at the end of his creation. He declared his satisfaction with his very good creation by resting from his work. In Egypt, Ptah rested after creating and setting things in order "in satisfaction of a job well done" (Atwell 2000, 464; for the text, see Allen, "From the Memphite Theology," CoS, 1:23, cols. 58–61). In Mesopotamia, the creator gods rest in the temples that they have built (Walton 2009b, chapters 1–9). While the ancient parallels reveal temple imagery in Genesis 1, which we may not see from our culture, it is clearly presented in other parts of Scripture, where all creation is God's temple (Ps. 11:4; Isa. 66:1) in which he rests (2 Chron. 6:41–42; Ps. 132:7–8). God's rest in his creation is not inactivity, however. While he has ceased the creative activity, he is now overseeing his kingdom (Walton 2009a, 23).

Moses acknowledges day seven as the completion and goal of creation in several ways. As we already noted, these three verses form an *inclusio* with 1:1. As his conclusion, he initially summarized: "The heavens and the earth were completed with everything that was in them" (2:1 NET). He then repeated three times that God "finished" or "ceased" "all the work that he had been doing" (vv. 2–3), also repeating "the seventh day" three times (vv. 2, 3). God's very good creation is complete. His "work" (in creating) is done. Rest became the expected and necessary goal of creation now that it was completed and functioning as designed ("very good"). If humankind is to reflect their king, one would expect that they, too, would find rest as the necessary and providential goal in service to him (so, Heb. 4:1–13).

> *TRANSLATION ANALYSIS 2:2*
> The logical difficulty of God having done all his work by the end of day six and yet finishing his work on day seven is solved in some translations that appropriately translate the verb as a pluperfect ("had finished," NIV, NLT) or by making it all relative ("by the seventh day," HCSB, NASB, NET).

When God blessed and sanctified the seventh day, he underlined the goodness of his creation, empowering it and setting it apart to his purpose. As the goal of creation, the seventh day presents a window into what God desires his creation to experience. When he is at rest, all of creation is at rest, suggesting his "peace" (*shalom*, שָׁלוֹם) or "well-being" (Nel, שָׁלוֹם, *NIDOTTE* 4:131). On the other hand, the following narrative will highlight the destructive frustrations and struggle for survival, not to mention the struggle for God's blessing, following man's sin and God's paradigmatic oracles.

The groans of humankind and their striving to find rest will permeate the pages and be punctuated both by humanity's own statements and actions, as well as God's. For example, at the end of Cain's genealogy, Lamech from Cain seeks to establish his own security (Gen. 4:23–24), and at the end of Seth's genealogy, Lamech from Seth is looking to Noah for "relief" from the curse (from נחם in a word play on Noah, נֹחַ and נוח, a synonym for "rest," 5:29). At the same time, the reader understands that God offers relief from the curse through obedience and walking with him (4:7; 5:24).

The sole transcendent deity has created the universe, revealing his character in his words, work, and even an image. He has spoken into the empty darkness of desolation and disorder to bring light and order, teeming with life. All that was worshipped and feared in Israel's day (and ours) falls under God's effortless command to do his bidding and accomplish his will. Humankind, far from the slaves of the gods, are the images of the sole God, representing him in rule and authority over his creation. God does not need man to provide for God but chooses man and cares for man. God rests in his elegant universe, administrating his good creation through his blessed representatives.

THEOLOGICAL FOCUS

The sole, sovereign, transcendent Creator of the universe has created humankind to exhibit his image, enjoy his blessing, and enter his rest.

The book of Genesis provides the biblical foundation for the working of God throughout human history, setting the trajectory of his good and sovereign response to humanity's rebellion and explaining the goal of creation: the satisfaction of God's rest. In many ways it becomes paradigmatic. Genesis 1 initiates the plan of God, setting the benchmark from which humankind falls and beyond which all of creation must pass, through his redemptive work, to ascend to his ultimate purpose. The rich theology of God's initiation of his story centers on the nature and working of God, climaxing his creating with his representative rulers. It concludes with the goal that humanity intuitively pursues: rest.

As we have already seen, the many theological themes of the initial creation account infuse the following narratives throughout Genesis. The character of God must take center stage here. Clearly, we see his sovereignty, transcendence, creativity, and goodness, as well as his distinction from all the deities of the peoples around Israel, both in his person and in his claim to absolute control and authority over all that claim deity. As pointed as they may appear, polemics against the other gods is not the main point. The narrative focuses on positively characterizing God in bold relief. He is Sovereign. His word produces immediate and absolute results. He is good. He brings good and order out of disorder. He fills emptiness with good and blessed creations that will show his creativity and goodness. He blesses, empowering his creation to fruitfulness and fecundity. He draws his creation into his rest.

On the other hand, the climax of creation shows the nature and purpose of humankind. Humanity, male and female, were created to reflect their creator in rule over his world as his images. They are not slaves to make life easier for the gods. They are kings, enacting God's beneficent rule over the earthly realm, under the authority of the Sovereign they represent, with all the value and prestige endowed by their creator. Their identity is rooted in God. They are empowered to accomplish the work of the Sovereign, blessed by his enabling command to bring all of God's creatures on Earth into submission to their good creator. As God's images, they reflect his value. Humankind is not equal with the other creatures. They are clearly set above and, as the next narrative will point out, animated by his breath (2:7).

We also recognize in the creation account that the purpose of God will not be thwarted. As sovereign over all, the God who effortlessly brought it into existence drives his creation toward his rest (2:1–3). He will not easily be frustrated by his creation's rebellion. Not only does humankind continue to have value as his images (9:7), but humanity will appropriately look for that rest and good from the hand of the one who is good and creates good (3:15; 4:26; 5:22–24, 29; 6:8–9; 12:3; 17:1–2; 50:20).

While the narrative focuses on the sovereign creator, the necessarily resulting worldview must see the character and working of God and the created supporting role of humankind, with its implications for God's people (beginning with Israel) and all peoples, in every age. Dramatically different from the worldview of any nation surrounding Israel, the initial narrative promotes a positive picture of the God that they will serve and the way they must view the universe and all competing voices for authority, as well as their own place in creation and purpose before the Creator. This view of creation affects every decision and perspective of life. Those who serve and worship this Creator expect to find good and purpose when they encounter darkness and desolation in life, even when the good is not clear or the pain lasts seemingly long periods of time (e.g., Joseph). They must respond to God's word in faith and obedience because his word is the source of all life, the authoritative statement of all that is. Humankind itself finds value in the Creator as his images, serving and representing him. Each person must value all people and realize their responsibility before God as King, the source of blessing and hope for rest.

PREACHING AND TEACHING STRATEGIES

Exegetical and Theological Synthesis

At the beginning of recorded redemptive history our Lord created the heavens and the earth. In the first three days, God made the Earth inhabitable. In the next three days, he filled his newly created world with life. Finally, everything culminated in a day of rest, the goal of all creation.

In doing so, he separated himself from all god-substitutes, those in ancient Egypt and the sophisticated idols of our day. Our Lord presented himself as sole creator and sovereign over all he had created, especially human beings, his crowning creation that bears his image. We are created beings; we did not create ourselves. And God is "good." His good character immediately emerges through the repetition of his pronouncing his creation as "good."

These opening lines of Genesis provide a worldview for God's people that is distinct from the one believed by most of the world's population throughout history. We learn that (1) there is a sole creator/God, (2) all humans are created beings made in his image, and (3) humanity is charged with a responsibility and privilege in God's world to represent him well.

Preaching Idea

Our sovereign Creator calls on his images to submit to him and extend his rule in exclusive worship.

Contemporary Connections

What does it mean?

In the beginning of God's Word, God introduced himself to us. In doing so he taught us a distinctly theological worldview, one that is not shared by those who do not believe his Word. He presented himself as eternal. He alone is the Creator of all that is. He alone oversees his world, including his crowning creation, us. Indirectly, he told us repeatedly that he is good through the good that he creates and the rest that follows all his creative work.

Since we are created beings, we are not our own creators. God placed humankind into his world for the purpose of representing God. We do not set the agenda; God does. Everything about humankind finds its meaning and significance in relationship to our Creator. We do not worship this world or ourselves; we worship our Creator. Our Creator alone is the source of our lives and every good thing we can enjoy. We consider him worth our affection, adoration, and service.

Is it true?

Some preachers may want to spend time doing expository apologetics—arguing for the existence of God. Such an argument is appropriate in our world, but in the biblical world, there were no atheists. Genesis 1 assumes that God exists. In addition, Scripture is clear that such belief is ultimately an act of faith, not empirical proof. Hebrews 11:3 (NET) reads, "By faith we understand that the worlds were set in order at God's command, so that the visible has its origin in the invisible." When a person begins to understand and trust this Creator-God, sincere worship follows. With this faith comes a new worldview. The believer begins to interpret everything about his life—who he is and why he exists—in light of his relationship to his creator.

Now what?

Many have argued that idolatry is the source of all sins. The Ten Commandments begin the way they do for a reason. It's important that the church knows its God. It's important that any non-Christians overhearing our worship on a given Sunday know their creator. Once we answer the question of who or what we worship, everything else falls in line. LifePlus, thriving in life now and forever, awaits all those who exclusively worship the sovereign Creator. Anything else is idolatry and leads to a different kind of life. According to the apostle Paul, rejecting God as creator is the reason for all the moral mess we experience in God's world (Rom. 1:18–32). When creatures worship his creation, including themselves, rather than their Creator, God gives them over to that thinking with all its dehumanizing results. So, when you preach this section, you are laying the foundation of who God is, where we come from, and what it means to be human. Pretty important topics!

In Genesis 1:1–2:3, God states realities about his world. This theological information is designed to move God's people to worship-filled attitudes and actions in the church and in the world. Sermons on creation are designed to highlight the Creator. It won't be until Genesis 3 that we see the first record of humankind's response to their Creator. Will they worship their Creator or a creature? We are currently experiencing the results of their choice. God's original creation has suffered severe damage.

One of the decisions expositors must make when preaching Genesis 1:1–2:3 is how much time to spend restating and explaining the detailed information of what God created each day. Even a minimal amount of attention to those details will consume many message minutes. The main preaching point of the chapter is not the length of creation or the timing of creation, but the worldview the creation account generates: recognizing the Creator, his power to speak everything into existence with a word, his intention in creating everything "good," his relationship to his images, and the intended response on the part of his crowning creation to carry out his mission in the world as his representatives.

For those who want to interpret and apply Genesis 1:1–2:3 within the context of the canon, remember:

- Genesis 1:1–2:3 does not present the only significant creation account in Scripture. Sixty-five books later God will reveal himself as the Creator of a new heavens and earth (Rev. 21:1). Throughout the story are many examples of people becoming new creations through faith in the Lord Jesus Christ (2 Cor. 5:17). He is our Creator (John 1:1–3). God graciously provides his Son to accomplish the recreation of what his creatures originally and continually de-create.

- God spoke creation into being. His word has unbelievable power: "And God said . . . and there was." God continues to speak his powerful word through his Word, and it continues to fulfill his purposes in his world (Heb. 4:11–13). Resting in his Word is the only way for humankind to experience God's eternal rest.

Creativity in Presentation

Genesis 1:1–2:3 provides opportunities for God's people to think about the vast world God has created. YouTube videos abound, such as Louie Giglio's, "How Great Is Our God." God has created a marvelous universe!

Then again, you may find it helpful to take the opposite approach and quote those who deny the existence of God and who believe that humankind's only hope is science and technology.

Encourage your congregation by reminding them that there is not any hard evidence for the various proposed anti-creation theories. It is easy for Christians to be intimidated by all these findings.

At the time of writing this commentary, humankind's understanding of gender and sexuality is rapidly changing. The morality—or immorality—Paul presents as the result of God's anger is now being presented to the world and church as lifestyle choices to embrace. Such philosophies present a major way in which the rejection of our Creator/God evidences itself in society's thinking and practice.

What a time to encourage a faith-family to reaffirm its faith in our sovereign God who created and controls his world. What a time to recommit ourselves to genuine, life-altering worship. You might want to show a list of American idols similar to Timothy Keller's list in *Counterfeit Gods*.

After all, all new creations in Christ worship their Creator, not the creature, and experience the rest only he can give. Ancient Augustine was right when he said to our Creator: "Thou hast made us for thyself, O Lord, and our heart is restless until it finds its rest in thee" (*Confessions*, 1, 1.5).

You may wish to present your message as the characters unfold, focusing on God, his character, and humanity's role:

- God alone exists outside of creation as creator (1:1).
- God shows his goodness and holiness, bringing all things into being (1:2–31).
- Humanity represents him as his images in his temple to his glory (1:26–29).
- God rules over all with blessing (2:1–3).

DISCUSSION QUESTIONS

1. List the attributes you see of God in the opening chapter of Genesis. Which one currently challenges your thinking and living most deeply? Why?
2. What does it mean to worship something or someone?
3. How has society changed recently because of not acknowledging God as creator?
4. Can you list the idols that often capture your affections? How do they relate to Genesis 1?
5. What is my responsibility as God's image before him in his creation?
6. How does the fact that every human is created in his image impact my view of myself and those around me?

Genesis 2:4–25

EXEGETICAL IDEA

Their generous personal creator established and prepared humankind with all life-giving resources to lead creation as his king-priests in worship, so that all creation could flourish through their obedient faith in purposeful unity.

THEOLOGICAL FOCUS

God generously prepared humankind to lead his creation in worship to flourish through obedient faith and unity.

PREACHING IDEA

God's images lead creation in the worship of God by keeping his world and word.

PREACHING POINTERS

Genesis 2:4–25 continues with more detailed information about the climax of God's creation. Special attention is given to the formation of man and woman and the work that each of them would have in a well-watered garden in Eden. Human origins, including the family, and human purpose in God's world are clearly present. Within the context of working in God's world, God gave man a command and a terrible promise: "but of the tree of the knowledge of good and evil you shall not eat, for in the day that you eat of it you shall surely die." They have the choice of life or death, based on their response of faith to their King. It was up to the newly created man and woman to function in God's world according to God's rules.

Today we still function according to this original plan. Occupations and technology have dramatically changed the way much work is done, but the responsibilities of God's people have not changed. In a world where our Creator is rejected or ignored, we must understand our purpose. Through faith in Christ and the power of his Spirit, we fight hard against our world's understanding of life to thrive in obedient faithful service and direct worship to our Creator.

THE PRIESTHOOD OF HUMANITY: CREATED TO LEAD WORSHIP (2:4–25)

LITERARY STRUCTURE AND THEMES

After the elevated style of Genesis 1, the rest of Genesis, beginning in chapter 2, reads much more like the Hebrew narrative we find in the rest of the Old Testament. With less patterning and repetition, the author still shows great care and artistry with how he expresses his story and carefully selects his words, both for impact and his intended theology. He uses a high degree of wordplays and archetypal language, especially in chapters 2 through 11, as well as many reminders of the initial account of creation, displaying the damage to God's good creation. After the eloquent focus on God's preparation of his good creation, the narrator focuses our attention on how God's generous provision for his images in their workplace goes tragically wrong through their rebellion (chs. 2–3) and what that meant for the human family (ch. 4).

Following the first *toledot* statement of Genesis, or transitional title (2:4, summarizing the initial account and shifting attention to what will follow) and preliminary conditions (vv. 5–6), Genesis 2:7–25 establishes humanity in their new role, as God set up his images in their new world to represent him. The initial narrative emphasizes the generosity of God's provision in the garden for their life, as well as humankind's necessary unity for service in his temple realm. At the end of chapter 2, humankind is fully cared for and in harmony. This idyllic scene contains the seeds of tension, however, that will bear the dreadful fruit of death and curse in the rest of the *toledot*.

At first glance, the completion of united humanity in honorable innocence appears to be a self-contained unit. Though not immediately apparent to the modern English reader, it is deeply connected with what follows and forms the complex introduction to the larger narration of the reversal of God's good creation in a well-crafted chiasm in Genesis 2–3.[1]

I. God's universe required his images (2:4–6).
II. God's formed and generously provisioned images rebelled, suffering gracious judgment (2:7–3:24).
  - A. God formed and placed his priest for service (2:7–17).
    - B. God provided man's needed complement (2:18–25).
      - C. The snake challenged God's goodness (3:1–5).
        - D. Humanity rebelled in unbelief (3:6–8).
      - C' God confronted rebellion (3:9–13).
    - B' God graciously sentenced rebellion (3:14–21).
  - A' God confirmed his judgment with exile (3:22–24).

We will explore the form and significance of this chiastic structure in Genesis 3, the third preaching unit. For the immediate narrative we need to recognize the initial emphases and concerns that will bear fruit in what follows.

---

1 The current outline is based on the work of Walsh (1977), supported by Wenham (1987, 50–51). See also Ouro's (2002) modifications and Kuruvilla's (2014, 55) helpful summary.

The pericope in chapter 2 flows with two main movements to address a need raised in the introduction. Transitioning from a universal focus to an earthly focus (v. 4), it begins with notice of a deficit that cannot allow creation to flourish (v. 5). God addressed the need, creating the man and situating him in a place of generously endowed service. Man, however, was still deficient (v. 18), and God completed him with woman to accomplish their commission before God. The final statement leaves man and woman at peace and rest in his world (v. 25). God's "very good" assessment in 1:31 has been fleshed out in the creation of man and woman in harmony.

The major themes of this section, then, include the role of humankind as God's images, set up in his sacred space in authority to lead in worship; the immanence of God in his creation, in contrast to the transcendence of chapter 1; the necessary dependence of humankind on God and his word in order to thrive in his realm; the necessary interdependence of man and woman in order to accomplish their commission before God in his world; and the goodness of God in his provision for his world to function in peace, harmony, and innocence before him. These themes resonate in many ways with our modern sense of order and God's purposes, but they were in distinct contrast to much of the ancient world in which humanity was an afterthought to care for the needs of the gods. Instead, the single supreme God of the universe and Creator of all provides for his creation in all ways. He is the one that holds all things accountable to his word and so to his will. He is the one that gives life and flourishing or deterioration and death.

- ***God's Universe Required His Images (2:4–6)***
- ***God Formed and Placed His Priest for Service (2:7–17)***
- ***God Provided Man's Needed Complement (2:18–25)***

EXPOSITION

God revealed his sovereign control over the universe in creation and placed humankind as his representative over his creatures. The necessary worldview for humanity centers around this transcendent creator God and their role before him. That role, however, needs further definition and development, especially in the context of the fallen world in which modern readers find themselves. The first *toledot,* as the narrator develops the rationale for their existence and purpose, focuses on humanity's ideal responsibilities in worship and how their rebellion led to cursing, destruction, and yet hope in restored worship (2:4–4:26). This first movement of the broader pericope (2:4–25) sets the stage for the rebellion by presenting the gracious provision of God, now seen in his imminence as Yahweh Elohim,[2] for humankind to experience life and rest in service as they choose to trust and obey his word, the source of life.

The first verse transitions from the creation account to the outworking of that creation. The title statement recaps the creation account (v. 4a) and what will happen to that creation (*toledot*), moving the focus to the Earth and the covenant God, Yahweh, who will establish human relations (v. 4b, see below). Proceeding from the very good creation, this section will initially highlight the provision of God for his creation in two movements, the remedy for the needs of creation with the creation and placement of man and the remedy for the "not good" state of man with the creation of woman. Their generous personal creator established and prepared humankind in unity to lead creation as his king-priests in worship through obedient faith in purposeful unity. The good provision of God preparing humankind to accomplish their mandate highlights the heinous nature of their subsequent rebellion and its disastrous consequences.

2 See v. 4 for the significance of this change in name, as well as the discussion in ch. 3.

God's Universe Required His Images (2:4–6)

The story of God's created universe reveals the need for his featured images.

What Became of God's Created Universe (2:4)

The history of God's created universe reveals the omnipotent Creator as the covenant keeping God of Israel.

2:4. Verse 4 shifts the attention of the reader from the overall creation account to the initial history of humankind. It describes what happened to God's good creation. Presenting the first of the eleven *toledot* sections, the narrator carefully crafts this chiastic title, connecting Yahweh as the explicit creator. The initial "the heavens and the earth" (recalling 1:1) mirrors the final "the earth and heavens" (foregrounding the changing focus from all creation to the Earth). "When they were created" mirrors "in the day the LORD God made" (using both ברא and עשׂה from ch. 1). The creative working of God in the center of the chiasm draws attention to the Creator himself, noted here as Yahweh Elohim, the "LORD God."

TRANSLATION ANALYSIS 2:4

As with each section after the introduction (see Narrative Structure of Genesis, p. 68), Genesis 2:4 begins a new section with the use of toledot (תּוֹלְדוֹת). The term comes from the root "give birth, to beget" (*HALOT* s.v. "ילד" 411–12) and generally refers to "descendants" or "successors" or sometimes something like a "family history" (*HALOT* s.v. "תּוֹלְדוֹת" 1699–1700). "This is the account" fits the context well (NASB95, NET, NIV, NLT), as the narrative shows what happened to the initial creation that was "very good" to produce what came after, which we know is no longer "very good"! In effect he is initiating the "history" (NKJV) of the created heavens and earth (or as NCV and JPS translate, "story"), but it will be a human history, as clarified by the notice of verse 5 and beginning with creation of man, verse 7. This structural device of succeeding *toledot* sections will trace the ongoing human history through the chosen family lines, bringing fulfillment of promise to humanity through the working of God. The family line is particularly significant as we see the royal focus from human creation and the search for a king to fulfill the mandate and quell rebellious evil in the kingdom, beginning with 3:15, the seed of the woman. Genealogy, then, forms the backbone of Genesis and will trace God's working to the hope of his promises.

Yahweh Elohim

The changing of the name here from Elohim (ch. 1) to Yahweh Elohim (ch. 2) has been used, in conjunction with other factors in the recounting of the creation of man and his environs, to suggest that an editor has combined two different stories that did not originally belong together. The Documentary Hypothesis, or source criticism, uses these sorts of details in the narrative to separate what are assumed to be originally distinct documents or narratives. Chapter 1 is typically placed with what is known as the priestly editor (or P), and the use of Yahweh signals the use of the Yahwistic editor (or J) in chapter 2. Regardless of the origins of the narratives, source criticism misses the theological implications of the change and assumes that the changes are evidence of a redactor rather than clues to a significant theological message. While there is no inherent objection to seeing two originally different stories put together for a purpose, the assumption generally is that they are contradictory and poorly edited together. In addition, they are expected to come from a later period than a historical Moses would warrant.

If, on the other hand, we recognize significant artistry in the whole account, especially in the significance of both accounts for the first eleven chapters of Genesis and the structure and message of the whole book, the possibility of separating the different original stories out and assigning different time periods and different editors becomes less secure. So Kikawada and Quinn (1985) argue that the literary unity of Genesis 1–11 (and, by implication, the rest of the book of Genesis) provides a more satisfactory and effective answer to the questions raised by documentary scholars, suggesting a single united editing of the book. While Kikawada and Quinn develop the literary artistry of Genesis 1–11, Gary Rendsburg (2014) exposes the intricate unity of all of Genesis, with special focus on the patriarchal narratives in Genesis 12–50. Specifically, here, verse 4 ties the two narratives together. The explicit chiasm of verse 4 in the Hebrew ties together the previous section ("the heavens and the earth when they were created" [הַשָּׁמַיִם וְהָאָרֶץ בְּהִבָּרְאָם]) with the following narrative ("in the day that the LORD God made the earth and the heavens" [בְּיוֹם עֲשׂוֹת יְהוָה אֱלֹהִים אֶרֶץ וְשָׁמָיִם]). Notice the unusual switch of the order to "earth and heaven" in the latter phrase, focusing attention from the cosmos to the earthly realm and tying this in with the creation of man and the garden narrative. It also adds Yahweh (LORD), which will be used throughout the following narrative (see Wenham 1987, 55). With a clear and artistic design in the narratives, we can expect to find a coherent and unified message shining through the challenging details and unexpected expressions of those narratives.

The narrator significantly combines the personal name Yahweh ("LORD") with the divine name Elohim ("God"), suggesting a significant shift in perspective. Of only thirty-seven times that the two names for God are used together in the entire Hebrew Bible, the writer paired them twenty times in 2:4–3:23. They are only used one other time together in the rest of the Pentateuch (Exod. 9:30, which emphasizes the God of Israel as sovereign Creator). Together they emphasize that the omnipotent Creator (Elohim, 1:1–2:3) is the covenant-keeping God of Israel (Yahweh, Exod. 3:14–17; 6:6–8) and connect the responsibilities for his new images with Israel's responsibilities. For what follows, Israel needs to see how their covenant-keeping God will deal with his representatives, both in provisioning and preparing them to succeed, as well as his gracious response to their rebellion. Israel, too, will be his special representatives (Exod. 19:5–6) with his mandate (Mosaic covenant), including the choice for life and death, a blessing or a curse, based on their choice for obedience (Deut. 30:15–20).

The significance of the combination becomes apparent in chapter 3, the temptation narrative between the snake and the woman, who both speak only of Elohim ("God"—Gen. 3:2–7). It is as if the snake steers the conversation away from God as faithful, imminent, and covenant-keeping. The woman follows his lead, believing his insinuations and overlooking the faithful character of her king. Rebellion seems easier and more reasonable from a harsh, distant, unreasonable despot than from a faithful, loyal, gracious, reliable king.

The chiastic structure of verse 4 also supports the unity of the verse as the hinge or transition, rather than suggesting it should be divided between the two narratives. This independent sentence foregrounds the coming narrative. Verses 5–6 will present the initial deficits, much like 1:2, after which God will work to make it good.

God's Creation Needed Humankind to Thrive (2:5–6)

Humankind took center stage as the necessary keeper for God's new world to thrive, serving God's abundant creation.

2:5. After the title statement, Moses presents initial conditions that do not follow the narrative flow (no *wayyiqtol* forms but initiated with a *waw* disjunctive). Instead, these verses present background material that sets up the coming narrative. The structure of 2:4–6 mirrors the structure of the first two verses in Genesis 1, showing the same flow of title, deficit conditions (stated negatively here, but also using the *waw* disjunctive), hope, then story line. As the narrator goes back chronologically before the creation of man, he again presents negative conditions (no bush or small plant; no rain or man) followed by a hopeful observation ("springs would well up" to water the land) before God steps in with his action (v. 7).

From a modern western perspective, these verses do not easily fit together with the initial creation account in chapter 1. Not only do they go back in time to before the creation of man (and perhaps plants, animals, etc.), but the narrator orders the events differently, presenting the most obvious challenge. Genesis 1 records the creation of plants on the third day (v. 12), birds on the fifth day (vv. 20–21), and animals, then man and woman, on the sixth day (vv. 24–27). Genesis 2:5, however, seems to place the creation of plants after man, an impression reinforced by the planting of the garden (v. 8) after the creation of man (v. 7). The statement that God created the beasts and then the birds follows both events in chapter 2 (v. 19—see the Translation Analysis for 2:19, p. 109). In thinking through this issue, it is helpful to consider that Hebrew narrative does not require or expect a strictly chronological presentation. Obviously, there is already a somewhat non-chronological approach here, with the writer going back and beginning again in 2:5 before the creation of man or plants (in some respect).

Genesis 1 vs. Genesis 2

Numerous ways of relating Genesis 1 to Genesis 2 have been suggested. Often Genesis 2:4–25 is related to day six, since the creation of man is the focus and Genesis 1 places man's creation on day six. Collins (2006, 111, 121), then, suggests that the terms for *land* should be understood locally, so that the place is somewhere in the Levant, the rains are the fall rains, and the vegetation refers to what springs up in the fall from that rain. This is that fall just before Adam was created, referring to a specific location and time, not the general creation of all vegetation. Alternatively, it could be combining days three and six with emphasis on the vegetation and the role of man, non-chronologically leading up to the main tension in the next few chapters (Futato 1998). Others relate these terms to the very similar wording for the two types of vegetation in the curse (3:18), so that the plants referenced in 2:5 refer to the thorns, thistles, and cultivated grains that did not exist before man's fall, and the introduction is looking ahead to the tensions and judgement sin will bring (Cassuto 1978, 101–3; and more recently, Mathews 1996, 192–94, among others). see, however, the sidebar "Literary Convention" for a contextual solution.

Rather than trying to fit the chronologies together in a strict sense, however, Genesis 2:5 may present more of a general literary statement, tracing a specific issue under the overall umbrella of Genesis 1. The wording reverberates in the curse (see exposition on 3:18, p. 130). The initial setting reflects the structure of Genesis 1:2 with the negative conditions (no bush, small plant, rain, or man), and yet the hopeful "springs" were welling up to water the land (structurally like the Spirit of God in 1:2). Out of this deficit, God will bring his good creation, starting, in this case, with man. While the rains will grant the fertility to allow the bush (but also the destruction of the flood) and the man will allow the cultivation of grains (but also enable the thorny weeds), Yahweh Elohim alone, again, brings good out of emptiness and desolation. In God's good working, the themes and interrelationship of of plant life, water, and humankind will dominate this initial narrative: absence of plants, water, and man (v. 5); followed by the rising of springs (v. 6), creation of man (v. 7), and the resulting viability of the garden (vv. 8–9); then the extended abundance of water with the four rivers allowing the garden and surrounding areas to thrive (vv. 10–14), the placement of man in the garden (v. 15) implying the garden can flourish (v. 5), with extended description of the requirements allowing man to prosper (vv. 16–17); concluding with the completion of man to fulfill his mandate (vv. 18–25).

To focus on humankind, then, the writer uses a common literary convention for his time (see sidebar, "Literary Convention." He begins with necessary missing conditions (uncultivated and cultivated plants requiring rain and man) to highlight the significance of humanity in the story. The deficiency would be rectified in the following narrative and, in the process, show the good provision of God and the centrality of man. Moses moves man to center stage, showing another aspect of man's responsibilities and expanding the cryptic comment that humankind in the image of God is male and female (1:27). Humanity is the necessary ingredient, allowing God's creation to flourish and caring for that creation. Highlighting the vegetation also directs attention to humanity, both with the initial positive opportunity and the final negative reality. It is not, then, attempting to give a chronology of the events.

Literary Convention

Sumerian and Akkadian cosmologies occasionally began by describing a time before certain things existed or had begun. For example, one text (NBC 11108) begins when the earth is in darkness, no water flowed to the earth, no crops were produced, and there was no priest (among other things, Clifford 1994, 28). The Babylonian Creation Account begins similarly when "no cane brake was intertwined nor thicket matted close. When no gods at all had been brought forth.... Then were the gods formed..." (Foster, "Epic of Creation (1.111)" CoS, 1:390, ll. 1:6–9). In another, the introduction to the disputation *Ewe and Wheat* begins (logically!) when neither existed, nor the benefits of them (Vanstiphout, "The Disputation Between Ewe and Wheat (1.180)" CoS, I:575). Though not all cosmologies had this sort of beginning, it is particulary helpful for the narrative purpose here. Stordalen (1992, 9) concludes that it was a narrative technique, usually "in stories of primaeval times" with a fixed literary function, to define "certain deficiencies (problems) that are going to be filled (solved)," giving "specific information about direction and theme in the following narrative." The author of Genesis 2:5, then, used an understood literary introduction to draw attention to the importance of key elements in what will follow. In this case it is the work of God to provide the necessary ingredients for his creation to thrive, especially showing the central role of humankind in his kingdom.

The significant narrative point here relates to the role of man in creation. In Genesis 1 the creation of man is the climax, drawing attention to the image of God, who represents the rule of God. In Genesis 2, the emphasis shifts, starting the narrative with a focus on the man and his necessary role in the blossoming of God's good creation. Without man's benevolent representation of God in authority, the creation cannot reach its full potential (and so will groan with man's sin, Rom. 8:19–23). Genesis 2, then, develops more fully man's intended role. God prepared for his creation. The rains would bring the conditions necessary for the "bush of the field" (שִׂיחַ הַשָּׂדֶה), and the man would allow for the cultivated grains (עֵשֶׂב הַשָּׂדֶה), which they would eat in the future. Man, however, is the central concern of the section. Therefore, the narrator highlights humanity's role and develops all the aspects of creation for humankind to tend around them. The centrality of humankind here will prepare the reader for the significance of the temptation and fall in chapter 3, as well as demonstrate how much man lost because of sin, apart from the gracious redemptive purpose of God.

Moses starts his narrative with the absence of two members of the plant kingdom, the "bush" and "small plants" of the field. The "bush" (שִׂיחַ) only occurs four times in the Hebrew Bible but seems to refer to the shrubs or plants of the "desert or steppe" (uncultivated areas) that grow with the fall rains (*HALOT* s.v. "שִׂיחַ" 1320–21). The "small plants" (עֵשֶׂב) here refer to cultivated plants that require man's assistance (most likely grains; cf. 3:18), though they can refer to other grasses when not referring to food for man (Deut. 11:15). God will provide the rain and humankind to yield a productive creation. The following narrative will draw together God's provision of humankind, the plant kingdom (though it will be the trees in particular), and the abundant rivers flowing out of Eden. The rain will only become prominent in Genesis 6–9.

The wording here suggests a double entendre as the narrator introduces the entire *toledot*. "Plant of the field" (עֵשֶׂב הַשָּׂדֶה, 2:5) will be used again (translated "grain of the field" in 3:18 [עֵשֶׂב הַשָּׂדֶה]), and the bush of the field (שִׂיחַ הַשָּׂדֶה) may include smaller plants, like the thorny weeds in 3:18 (Cassuto 1978, 101–3). The initial statement, highlighting the central role of man in creation, will also reverberate in the rebellion, reminding the reader through God's oracle that the coming of man led to reversal. What was to bring blessing brought the struggle that we now find ourselves in through sin. What promised the blessing of growth in 2:5, the rain (מטר), also becomes a reminder of how damaging sin is as it recurs for only the second time in Genesis (7:4) to announce the coming judgment of the flood.

2:6. Finally, God had already provided the resources to bring fertility. The springs, however, require the anticipated humanity to produce maximum fruitfulness through irrigation. The term used (אֵד) is unusual and may reflect a common word picture and language of Moses's day, a "cosmic river," but any mythical implications from pagan literature are absent in Genesis (Wenham 1987, 58).

TRANSLATION ANALYSIS 2:6

The term "springs" (אֵד, NET, NLT) only occurs twice in the Hebrew Old Testament and has been difficult to define clearly. Comparing the other use in Job 36:27, it is sometimes translated "mist" (ESV, JPS, KJV, NASB). In this creation context, however, in comparison with similar terminology in other accounts, a reference to subterranean waters fits better (Mathews 1996, 194–95; Wenham 1987, 58).

God Formed and Placed His Priest for Service (2:7–17)

God formed the man and endowed him generously to serve effectively as his priest, placing him in his sacred garden.

God Formed, Animated, and Established Man in His Sanctuary (2:7–8)

God formed the man from dust, infused him with life, and established him in God's delightful garden sanctuary as his priest.

2:7. Verses 7–8 introduce this section, summarizing the context of the man's creation and placement in the garden. The *inclusio* of God forming (יצר) the man brackets the introduction (initial term in v. 7 and final term in v. 8). By starting with the creation of the man, the narrator foregrounds and places him at the center of this pericope. In contrast to the initial creation account, in which the man is the climax of God's good creation, now the man becomes the center. Everything else described in creation in this chapter is subordinated to humanity and their role. Genesis 1 situated the man in God's creation, and Genesis 2 will elaborate on his role and the means to accomplish it. The order of presentation, then, is theological.

God "formed" (יצר) the man from dust. The verb focuses on the shaping of the object and the care involved (Konkel, יָצַר, *NIDOTTE* 2:504). While the verb can refer to a potter (Isa. 29:16, a figure used for the formation of man by the gods in other ancient accounts as well), the "soil" or "dust" (עָפָר) is not the typical word for clay (usually חֹמֶר). Instead, the word choice prepares us for the end of the man after the fall (Gen. 3:19), showing his frailty—he will return to the dust. As the narrative will highlight, the man is fully dependent on his Creator and, apart from God, he is completely vulnerable. The ancient backgrounds are filled with similar accounts of the gods creating humans from dust or clay. Although the biblical account differs from all of them in significant ways, the similarities are helpful. Outside of the Bible, the creation accounts become paradigmatic or archetypal for every person. As we notice the ways that the rest of Scripture reflects on this creation account, it also consistently shows up as "a paradigm for the source and fragility of every human life" (Soden 2015, 60). Viewing the description as intentionally archetypal does not mean it is not historical. It can be both a real event and a description in terms that present a paradigm for all humankind.

The breath of life that animates the man also shows that his life is sourced in God, and it differentiates him from the creatures and their creation described in 1:19. The beasts and birds also are "formed" out of the "ground," but man will rule. Humankind alone has the very breath (נְשָׁמָה) of God and reflects the Creator.

2:8. Verse 8 summarizes the ideal environment into which the LORD God placed the man. God planted a garden in Eden, a name which means something like "bliss, luxurious or delight" (Tsumura 1989, 136). The garden planted by God may be conceived of as an "orchard" (NET), since all that is mentioned are the trees. However, perhaps it should be conceived more like a "royal park" or walled garden (Wenham 1987, 61). This garden was planted "in Eden, in the east" but is not Eden itself. It later takes the name Eden (Isa. 51:3) and is called the garden of God (Ezek. 28:13). The title "garden of God" suggests a sanctuary where God dwells. The garden, then, adjoins Eden on the east as the Holy Place adjoins the Holy of Holies in the temple. The imagery is completely at home in both the ancient world and the rest of the Bible, describing the temple area in which the priests serve their God, which also often included sacred parks (Beale 2004, 66–80). The garden was the sacred park adjoining the dwelling of God, part of the royal or temple precinct. The narrator fills out this initial summary of the bounty of the garden in Genesis 2:9–14 before returning to the role of the man in verse 15.

TRANSLATION ANALYSIS 2:8

The Hebrew for God planting (וַיִּטַּע) can indicate a simple past (God "planted," so most translations) or a pluperfect ("had planted," NIV). Given the clear pluperfect in the final relative clause ("had formed"), God most likely planted the garden after creating the man and especially for the man, rather than having already planted it. That also, however, would suggest a quick maturation to provide for the man.

Eden as a Temple

Beale (2004, 66, n. 87) correlates and summarizes a variety of evidence for the view of Eden as a temple, following several scholars before him (See chapters 2–3, and especially pp. 66–80. He presents a more concise description in his more popular work, 2014). Not only does the river flow from Eden, much like the temple of Ezekiel or Revelation, but this is the place of God's unique presence (where he walks with Adam, 3:8). The tree of life may well be behind the model of the lampstand in the tabernacle/temple later, with its branches, buds, and flowers (Exod. 25:31–36) and the rest of the garden imagery of the temple (1 Kings 6–7). Of course, Ezekiel calls Eden the "garden of God" (Ezek. 28:13) in which was a guardian cherub (28:14, 16) and which was also the "holy mountain of God" (28:14, 16, the ancient designation for the sanctuary of the god—compare Mount Zion). Beale (2004, 77–79) also cites early Jewish sources presenting Eden as a temple and Adam as a priest.

God Provided Generously for His Images (2:9–14)

God provided generously for the immediate and future thriving of his images, both aesthetically and physically.

2:9. Verses 9–14 describe the richness of the garden (v. 9) and the sustenance of that abundance through the profuse water supply (vv. 10–14). Syntactically, the string of disjunctives and offline clauses place verses 9–14 in the background. The main narrative resumes with God placing man in the garden (v. 15, cf. 8).

In verse 9, God's generous provision for man ("every tree") included both the aesthetics ("pleasing to look at," NET) as well as the necessary and desirable ("good") sustenance. The narrator draws attention to two trees out of the whole orchard. Taking center stage in the garden is the tree of life and, close by, the tree of the knowledge of good and evil. Their significance only becomes clear with the resumption of the narrative in verses 15–17. The tree of life sustained life so that by eating it, humanity may not die (3:22). It seems intended to extend life rather than grant eternal life (comparing Prov. 3:16–18 with Gen. 3:22; Walton 2001, 170). In contrast with the tree of the knowledge of good and evil and its parallels in Proverbs (note 3:18), it indicates quality or kind of life as well (see Exposition on 2:17 below). Significantly, it shows up again in the new heavens and new earth, beside the river flowing from the throne of God, and provides healing for the nations (Rev. 22:2). Based on the parallel construction of the two names of the trees, the tree of the knowledge of good and evil will in some way produce knowledge (see Exposition of 2:17 below).

2:10–14. Verses 10–14 describe the water supply, which comes from Eden, just as the river flows from the throne of God (Ezek. 47; Rev. 21:1–2) and goes on to water four major areas of the known world. The obvious implication in the ancient world of such a prodigious source of water is the steady prosperity and growth available. Two of the four rivers it produces are uncertain, though the descriptions show an emphasis on the richness of the regions (gold and precious stones) connected by the rivers to their source in the garden of God. By giving this brief description of the generous provision of God for Adam in the garden and what flowed from it, the narrative foregrounds the goodness of God and implies that the man will have all needs met and his future secured as humankind fills the earth (Gen. 1:28).

God Put the Man in His Sanctuary for Service (2:15–17)

God placed the man in his sanctuary, commanding his careful service, providing generously for his needs, but warning of the death effect of autonomy.

2:15. In verse 15, the narrative returns to the man in the garden, focusing now on his role or purpose in God's new economy. Initially, God had "placed" (וַיָּשֶׂם) the man in the garden (2:8). Now in verse 15, the narrator changes the verb, though appropriately still translated "place" or "put" (וַיַּנִּחֵהוּ). While this new verb is often used as it is here in 2:15, it is also used in Exodus 20:11 for God resting on the seventh day, and the root (נוח) is behind Noah's name, when his father, Lamech, cries out for relief from the curse (Gen. 5:29). It refers to God's promised rest for his people in the promised land, which he withdrew from the wilderness generation in Psalm 95:11. Considering the other allusions in the text and the description of the garden as sacred space in the temple precinct, the author chose a verb that also suggests (by double entendre) that the man will be able to experience rest in his assigned role in the garden. This possibility is strengthened by the other allusions and significant terms used for the man's service in this garden temple.

The job description given for the man's placement in the garden continues the impression that he is not merely God's gardener. While "to care for it and maintain it" (NET) may best translate the terms presented, given the garden context, they also suggest overtones of service to God in the temple. The first infinitive, "to care for it" (לְעָבְדָהּ, "to work it," ESV) appropriately expresses agricultural work (Gen. 4:2). However, it also, often in the Pentateuch, describes priestly service. The second term, "to maintain it" (וּלְשָׁמְרָהּ, "to keep it," ESV) recurs in Genesis 3:24 with the angel guarding the garden from the man and woman returning. It is commonly used in the Pentateuch of keeping the law and service to God. This job description both impacts the immediate command (maintaining or keeping the garden must include keeping it in God's express way) and implies danger or threats from which to keep it (realized with the challenge of the snake in ch. 3).

TRANSLATION ANALYSIS 2:15

The terms God uses for the role of the man in the garden present some interesting possibilities. The first term (עבד) occasionally denotes farming the ground and so is appropriately translated "dress it" (JPS, KJV), "work it" (ESV, HCSB, NIV), "till it" (NRSV), "tend it" (NLT), or "cultivate it" (NASB95). In the near context, Cain is one who works or tills the ground (Gen. 4:2, 12). The second word (שמר) is commonly used (over four hundred times), but not of working the ground. In fact, even here it would seem to have more of a protective sense, being generally translated as "keep it" (ESV, JPS, KJV, NASB95, NRSV,), "take care of it" (NIV), or "watch over it" (HCSB, NLT). In the near context, that is exactly how it is used in Genesis 3:24 where the cherubim "guard" the way to the garden. Together, however, these two terms are often used in the Pentateuch for priestly service, so this presents yet another double entendre, reflecting the role of Adam (and Eve) here as more than mere gardeners, but rather serving in God's garden as his priests. See the commentary for this.

Keeping as Service

The Hebrew verbal root translated here by the ESV as "to work" (עבד) occurs often (289 times in the Old Testament and 113 times in the Pentateuch) with a range of meaning including "serve," "work," or "do." It frequently refers to service to God as well as others. The verbal root for "keep" (שמר) occurs 148 times in 139 verses in the Pentateuch alone. Of these, only twenty do not directly relate to keeping law or service to God and fourteen relate directly to priestly service. Beale has noticed that whenever these two roots (in either verbal or nominal forms) occur together (within fifteen words) in the rest of the Old Testament, "they refer either to Israelites 'serving' God and 'guarding [keeping]' God's word (approximately 10 times) or to priests who 'keep' the 'service' (or 'charge') of the tabernacle (see Num. 3:7–8; 8:25–26; 18:5–6; 1 Chr. 23:32; Ezek. 44:14)" (Beale 2004, 67).

The maintenance, then, of the garden as a sacred garden or temple precinct includes more than trimming trees. God placed humankind in his royal park to serve God as his priests and carry out the rule of God in this sacred space. Together with the role of humanity in Genesis 1:26–27 of ruling, we recognize the common ancient perspective of the king, who also would function as a priest in service to his god (for an Old Testament parallel, consider Melchizedek, Gen. 14:18–20). Of course, for Israel later, the priesthood is distinct from the kingship until we get to the Messiah (Ps. 110; Zech. 6:9–15). The last Adam will unify both offices in his rule, and believers will fulfill God's original plan in their participation with him (Rev. 20:6).

2:16–17. Immediately, God charged his king-priest with maintaining his order. In verse 16, he gave the man freedom to eat from his abundant provision from all the trees. However, in verse 17, he gave a single restriction. God commanded him not to eat of the tree of the knowledge of good and evil on pain of certain death. If the tree of knowledge of good and evil imparts knowledge, what is that knowledge and what does it mean? How is it like God?

> *TRANSLATION ANALYSIS 2:16*
> The translational question in verses 16 and 17 is how to faithfully represent the use of the infinitive absolute with the related verb. According to Waltke and O'Connor (1990, 584, §35.3.1.b), this use of the infinitive absolute should emphasize the "sense of irreality" in the verb. In verse 16, the verb is probably giving permission ("you may eat"), so the emphasis is appropriately the freedom of the permission or complete permission: "freely eat" (JPS, KJV, NASB, NLT, NRSV) or "free to eat" (HCSB, NIV), with the idea of as much and as often as you wish. The ESV translation is less clear, emphasizing certainty or permission with "surely eat." In verse 17, the emphasis of the verb is on their resultant death, so the infinitive absolute emphasizes the certainty, which is generally translated with "surely" or "certainly," though the NRSV simply says "you shall die." These emphases become particularly important in the dialog between the woman and the snake in chapter 3.

The knowledge of good and evil offers a form of wisdom. Of course, it cannot refer to all knowledge without qualification, but in Deuteronomy 1:39 the use of "good and evil" with the verb to "know" refers to children who do not yet have the capacity to discern and so choose the right over the wrong (לֹא־יָדְעוּ . . . טוֹב וָרָע and cf. Isa. 7:16; 8:4; Jonah 4:11). Similarly, in the arena of aesthetics, 2 Samuel 19:35 uses these terms to refer to age that deprives the senses of the ability to distinguish good and bad (in eating, drinking, or music). Choosing what is right and wrong, however, without the fear of the Lord, no longer submits to the Creator of wisdom. Instead, it becomes a secular, self-serving autonomy leading to death. To put it another way, to take the knowledge of good and evil for oneself, rebelling against the word of the Lord and choosing one's own standards rather than accepting it from the mouth of the Lord (Prov. 2:6) puts oneself over God, which is idolatry. Within this context of wisdom, then, the tree of life must include more than mere physical living. It implies the life of wisdom (Prov. 3:16–18), which is thriving in all ways (not just length of days) and surely includes the spiritual life ("fear of the Lord"). Rebellion will disqualify the rebel from representing the King, removing one from God's presence and therefore from the source of life and the ability to thrive.

Tree of Knowledge

Several main suggestions have been given for this knowledge, including experiential knowledge, moral discernment, sexual knowledge, and even omniscience. Certainly, there is an aspect of experiential knowledge, but that does not explain how they are like God (Gen. 3:5, 22) since God never sins. Sexual knowledge does not fit this context in which the blessing is to be fruitful and multiply (nor does the expression used fit the OT usage for sexual experience), and clearly the man and woman do not achieve omniscience. Moral discernment as a mere choice of obedience does not fit the context since they were already expected to choose obedience over rebellion. Moral discernment, however, as the outworking of wisdom and maturity and being able to make appropriately discerning decisions as befits wisdom, suits the similar usage in the Old Testament. Solomon admits to his youthfulness (1 Kings 3:7) and so his need for God to give him "a discerning mind so he can make judicial decisions for your people and distinguish right from wrong" (NET, giving the same idea with a slightly different verb and the same adjectives: לְהָבִין בֵּין־טוֹב לְרָע, 1 Kings 3:9). Such knowledge would certainly be wisdom (Gen. 3:6). For a helpful summary and explanation of the major positions, see Wenham (1987, 62–64). Since this discernment is not evil in itself but is necessary for the mature and for kings, Walton (2001, 205) argues that the prohibition was because it was not yet in God's timing but would come with maturity, comparing it to a five-year-old driving a car (see also Wilder 2006, 56). Such discernment and the ability to truly thrive will be needed for the representative rulers, but it can only be acquired through submission to the word of God (Deut. 30:15–20; Ps. 19:7–11) and grows with maturity.

Life or Death, Consequences of Wisdom
The wisdom literature clearly portrays this dichotomy. The introduction to Proverbs, chapters 1–9, is bracketed by the assertion that the fear of the Lord is the beginning of knowledge (1:7) and wisdom (9:10). True wisdom gives life (3:16, 18, 22; 4:13, 22; 8:35; 9:11), but false wisdom (Dame Folly) brings only death (5:5–6; 7:23, 25–27; 8:36; 9:18). True wisdom is a "tree of life to those who obtain her" (3:16–18). The contrast in the garden, then, mirrors the contrast in Proverbs 9. Lady Wisdom is a tree of life, but Dame Folly offers deadly autonomous choices. Ezekiel 28 supports this understanding. God condemns the Prince of Tyre because he makes himself a god, and his heart is proud, "like the heart of a god" (v. 2, 6). The text affirms his self-serving "wisdom" (three times in vv. 3–5) and in verse 17, the King of Tyre's heart is proud and he "corrupted [his] wisdom" and so he is thrown out of Eden (v. 16).

To eat of the tree spurns God's authority (and God's process or means to attain humankind's role), shows no fear of God, and enters a path of autonomy in which one becomes one's own god or master. Choosing one's own good and evil ironically opens a person's eyes to the reality of the consequences, the need (and impossibility) to self-protect and play god, and the difficulties of one's own way. To obey, abstaining from this forbidden fruit, submits to God's authority in godly fear, learning the true meaning of wisdom, allowing one to better image him and thrive in the life that follows. Godly wisdom based in the fear of the Lord obeys and lives, while secular wisdom that seeks one's own proud desires dies in its arrogance. What this death will mean becomes clearer in the following narrative.

TRANSLATION ANALYSIS 2:17
The typical translation of "in the day" (בְּיוֹם, so most translations) does not intend to refer to a twenty-four-hour period but is the normal Hebrew expression for "when" (NIV), though as Wenham (1987, 68) notes, it is expected to be prompt. The problem here, of course, is that they did not physically die on the day that they ate (see Gen. 3:6–24) leading us to understand a more figurative intent.

God Provided the Man's Needed Complement (2:18–25)

God provided the man's complement necessary to fulfill humanity's purpose.

God Established the Man's Need (2:18–20)

God noted the man's deficiency by himself and then established that need in the mind of the man through the naming of the animals.

2:18. The narrative now shifts focus. It moves from the role of the man in the sacred garden to the need for help to accomplish his task. God declared the problem, which, after chapter 1 and the seven assurances of the goodness of God's creation, sounds jarring: "It is not good for the man to be alone" (2:18 NIV). This statement helps us to process the recurring declaration in Genesis 1 that each aspect of God's creation was "good" (see Theological Emphases of the Book: God's Goodness, p. 58; and Exposition on 1:4, p. 83). God evaluation was not a moral evaluation. Man's aloneness was not suitable to accomplish God's intended purpose.

Instead, the man needed "a helper fit for him." The man needed another in community with him to complement him. The problem was presented in the context of the man's job description. God placed him in the garden with purpose and resources and then said, "not good—we need one more thing. . ." The man could not fulfill his mission alone.

TRANSLATION ANALYSIS 2:18, 20

The KJV translation "help meet" is more clearly rendered in modern thought as "helper fit" (ESV), or "helper suitable" (NASB, NIV), or even "a companion for him who corresponds to him" (NET). The phrase includes the noun from the common word for "help" (עזר) and the compound preposition on the pronoun. The noun simply refers to someone who provides the needed help or assistance without reference to relative status, though mainly the noun refers to God as the one who helps. The NET "companion" misses the idea of the help that the man needs, though it does avoid the unwarranted connotation (in the English) of a subordinate role. The compound preposition (כְּנֶגְדּוֹ), made of the common prepositions "like," "according to," (כְּ) and "opposite," "in front of," "before" (נֶגֶד), suggests the essential equivalence between the man and God's new creation—"like [what is] before him." She will correspond to him precisely and be what he needs.

With the immediate context of man's job description (2:15) and the clear statement in Genesis 1:27 that it was male and female together in God's image that were to represent him in his rule, the statement that he needed a helper explained the man's deficit. He needed help to fulfill the role God had given him, and God would provide that needed help by creating another of his images, corresponding to Adam.

2:19–20. The man's need for this suitable partner frames the naming of the animals (2:18, 20b) and precedes the creation of the woman, showing the purpose for the naming. God declared his need, the narrator reminds the reader of the creation of the creatures that God brought to the man to name, and Adam got the point (v. 20b). Adam's reaction will expose his growing realization in verse 23, "This one at last!"

TRANSLATION ANALYSIS 2:19

The problem in verse 19 centers around chronology. If this refers to initial creation, then chapter 1 has already placed the creatures before man on day six and the birds on day five. The Hebrew shows the normal narrative flow with the *wayyiqtol*, normally suggesting sequence, so most translations simply translate "the LORD God formed" (HCSB, JPS, KJV, NASB95, NET, NLT, NRSV). It could refer to a new creation of garden animals, or Collins (1995) argues for past perfect (or pluperfect) as in the NIV and ESV translation, "the LORD God had formed." While the past perfect fits, the narrator, putting this together with chapter 1, clearly wanted the reader to notice and wrestle with the order of creation to highlight the emphasis on the man.

TRANSLATION ANALYSIS 2:20

For the first time, the word ʾadam (אָדָם) does not have the article in the Hebrew. Usually without the article, it is understood as the personal name "Adam" (so ESV, KJV, NASB, NET, NIV), but with the article, it is generally understood as "the man." Because of the use of the attached preposition here (וּלְאָדָם), the only difference is the pointing, which was added by the Masoretes much later, so some argue that it should be "the man" rather than "Adam" (HCSB, NRSV).

The narrative here gives sparse details. Regardless of the debate over whether God created more animals for naming or if these are the animals he had already created, Adam began to accomplish his initial task of ruling by showing his authority in naming the animals. He also began to see his need. Whether it is the fact that none of them really match him, or whether he saw them in complementary male and female pairs, he recognized his deficit: "no companion who corresponded to him was found" (2:20 NET). Man is now ready for woman.

God Satisfied the Man's Need (2:21–25)

God completed his images with the complement that would allow the man to fulfill his purpose in unity of relationship and innocent harmony.

2:21–22. Moses describes the first surgery under general anesthesia as God took from the man's side to build his partner and complete the man's service to God. The term usually translated "rib" (צֵלָע) typically refers to the side of something (like a hill [2 Sam. 16:13], building [Exod. 26:20], or altar [Exod. 27:7]). Here God symbolically chose "part of the man's side" (NET; rather than "one of his ribs," ESV) to help capture the role of woman as man's complement and equal sharer in the task of representing God as priest-kings.

2:23. The man saw the implication immediately as he exclaimed, "this one at last!" or "finally!" He expressed the frustration he had discovered in naming the animals and having no partner like himself. He described her as being of the same bone and flesh, made of the same stuff, both recognizing the source and the significance of the unity and complementarity of his new companion and fellow servant to Yahweh Elohim. He understood the implications of God's actions and highlighted their unity in his declaration. The narrator emphasizes the point by using a word play on what she would be called. She was woman (אִשָּׁה, *ʾisha*) because she was taken from man (אִישׁ, *ʾish*). The two Hebrew words are not actually related, though they sound like they are. The similarity of sound, as in English (man and woman), emphasizes their natural and intended interconnection. Adam does not use the typical naming formula but simply notes that she is of the same kind as he is—the woman is human and not like the other creatures. He now has the companion he could not find among the animals.

2:24. In verse 24, Moses applies the narrative to his readers, connecting the unique unity that a married couple has and must maintain (leaving father and mother). He related the oneness that Adam proclaimed from their physical connection to the family relationship. He was not just talking about sexual union because the "new family" (NET) anticipates the way later Scripture will use the idea of "flesh" and "bone" (Gen. 29:14; Judg. 9:2; 2 Sam. 5:1; 19:13–14; 1 Chron. 11:1). Here, however, the new family supersedes the parental relationship and is closer than just "kin." Marriage forms the foundation of society with bonds that are as close as if they were the same organism, made of the same materials. The married reader still has opportunity to live in the unity and priority of the marriage relationship, even over the parental bonds.

2:25. The final verse of the chapter summarizes the resulting condition of the first humans, symbolizing their innocence and their harmony. They are at rest together, in peace and harmony, without concern for exploitation. The literal nakedness shows much more than mere lack of clothing, as chapter 3, beginning with verse 1, will illustrate. It provides the transition and significance of the unique quality of the snake that, in the next scene, will successfully ensnare humanity. Humankind in their innocence is vulnerable if they do not carefully know and keep the word of command.

Nakedness

In the Old Testament, nakedness can indicate poverty (e.g., Job 24:7–10) or humiliation such as captivity (e.g., Isa. 20:2–4). The only time it does not imply shame seems to be in a newborn (Job 1:21; Eccl. 5:15). Some have seen a similar idea with a very young child who does not yet understand this public consciousness of "shame" (Walton 2001, 179; Wenham 1987, 71). There is another implication in the ancient world, however. In a similar setting to Genesis 2, the old Babylonian "Disputation between Ewe and Wheat" begins at the beginning of creation and describes early humans at a time when humankind went about naked. Here the nakedness of early humanity indicated uncivilized, primitive culture when people did not yet know how to make bread or cloth but ate grass and drank from the ditches "like sheep" (Vanstiphout "The Disputation Between Ewe and Wheat" (1.180) CoS, I:575. ll. 20–25). While the setting for Genesis is similar (no progress yet in culture, as witnessed in Gen. 4), the implication is not primitive but innocent, as the character and role of the snake in 3:1 will illustrate.

Humanity has responsibility but no need to fear or self-protect. God has blessed them and given them all that they need to thrive and experience the richness of their new world. Man and woman, infused with God's life, enjoy his abundant provision and personal presence (see also ch. 3), to serve their Creator as his king-priests. They are positioned to begin learning to effectively lead creation with God's authority, to his glory.

THEOLOGICAL FOCUS

God generously prepared humankind to lead his creation in worship, in obedient faith, and in purposeful unity.

Genesis 2 returns to the creation of humankind, narrowing the focus of the narrative to humanity and the roles in which his images would function. Genesis 2 highlights a deeply personal Creator crafting and animating man with his breath then generously providing for man's fruitfulness, preparing the reader for the terrible loss through disobedience. Beginning his selective history of God's good creation, Moses characterizes the Creator as providing all things good to enjoy and uniting man and woman in harmony and purpose. The conflict in relationship that follows the fall (3:16; 4:1–8) does not result from creation, but from rebellion. The struggle that follows the fall for survival and blessing (3:16–19) was not God's intended design. Humankind's disfunction and death can trace its source to sin alone.

The pain in relationship in Genesis 3 will only emphasize what God already has highlighted by the creation account. Woman and marriage are God's special gifts to humanity to allow us to fulfill his design for us. Woman was given and intended as God's special gift to complete what was not good apart from her. Man must treasure both woman and the special one-flesh relationship created for his good and God's glory. This foundational gift for human flourishing is strongly emphasized in the text and must be appreciated for humanity to thrive. To denigrate the differences of the sexes or the role of marriage is to reject and corrupt God's good and necessary gifts and, ultimately, to reject the ability to live out his plan and flourish.

This pericope highlights the central role of the man in God's plan and the goodness of God in providing for his ultimate success in service. God showcased his goodness, carefully crafting the man and placing him in his sanctuary garden to serve, with all the provisions he needed to thrive. God graciously prepared the man see his need for the woman to fulfill his task, understanding their unique unity in representing God together in their worship and service. This needed unity has implications both for marriage and society. For marriage, Moses declares the necessary outworking of that unity, placing the union of marriage even over the bonds of parenthood. The union of marriage must take priority as the starting point for a family's service to God. The family, beginning with marriage, becomes the foundation for society and social structure.

God created humanity to serve in his garden sanctuary as his king-priests, leading creation in worship of the Creator and guarding the sanctity of his sanctuary. God's purpose for the man will continue after the fall, even though sin will threaten it. Worship and walking with God will be a central theme of Genesis, and the rest of God's narrative, but it is especially crucial in the role of specific individuals (especially the patriarchs—Gen. 12:7–8; 26:25; 35:1–7), the nation of Israel (Exod. 19:5–6), and the New Testament believer (1 Peter 2:4–10). God will fulfill his initial plan in Christ (Rev. 20:6).

In the garden, God presented the choice for humanity to thrive in life or certainly die, depending on their response to his word. As God's priest-kings, not only is obedience necessary to reflect him and lead in worship, but it grounds wisdom in the fear of God, the prerequisite for appropriate rule/worship (expressed in wisdom literature, especially Prov. 1–9). Looking for wisdom contrary to God's command disqualifies one from his presence and the resulting life itself.

This choice for the first man, fleshed out in Genesis 3, is paradigmatic for Israel and all humanity, and it brackets the whole of the Pentateuch with the Mosaic covenant and especially Deuteronomy 30:15–20. It will become more explicit, starting with Abraham, that obedience springs from faith in the word of God (Gen. 15:6). The choice to obey by faith for life and blessing or die in rebellion becomes a model repeated continually throughout the Scriptures, certainly in Genesis (from Cain and Abel to Noah and the flood to Abram and the patriarchs), Israel (and individuals) under the Mosaic covenant throughout the Old Testament (Josh. 1:8–9; Prov. 19:16; etc.), and of course for the believer under the new covenant as well (John 3:36).

All of this comes together as we recognize that God's gracious gifts for humanity's flourishing include not only the physical aspects of food, environment, responsibility, and purpose, but also his word of command requiring obedience, responsibility, and growing faith in the fear of God. Even the marriage relationship that can bring pain and frustration (because of the fall in chapter 3) is God's gift to allow humankind to accomplish God's work. All these share God's design, intended to lead to human benefit and success and, ultimately, to his glory. He provided all that humanity needed to thrive and enjoy the fullness of God's designed life finding its culmination and final realization in Christ.

PREACHING AND TEACHING STRATEGIES

Exegetical and Theological Synthesis

It is clear in Genesis 2:4–25 that God created humankind—man and woman—and put them to work in a beautiful environment that he also created. It is also clear that obedience to one stipulation was mandatory and that disobedience paid a terrible price: "you shall surely die" (2:17). This response of keeping God's world and word allows believers to lead in the worship of our Creator God. When God's people hear this second summary of original creation, they realize how different this story is from the stories they hear all around them. They realize that their God is different from all the god-substitutes of the nations. They realize how different they are from most human beings in the world. Unlike most, God's people recognize that they are created to relate to him through their work in God's world. Believers lead others into that same worship of God only as they fulfill their function. They realize that being male and female matters to God and that the union of one man and one woman forms a very important part of society in God's world. They realize that loving obedience is the right response to such a gracious Creator and the ticket to LifePlus.

Preaching Idea

God's images lead creation in the worship of God by keeping his world and word.

Contemporary Connections

What does it mean?

Like Genesis 1:1–2:3, Genesis 2:4–25 continues to describe God's version of the creation of the heavens and the earth. The result is that God's people are given a distinctly theological worldview. Humankind did not just happen to exist; God "formed the man of dust from the ground" and "took one of his ribs" and "made [it] into a woman" (2:7, 21–22). Incredible, right? This means that we do not dictate our own existence in our world. It is not our world; it is his world. We must gladly accept our rightful place and function according to his ways. We hear and heed the stern warning in the middle of the chapter. He has given us so much good. He is protecting us from so much evil.

Is it true?

Well, it is certainly true that most of the world's population does not believe in the creation accounts of Genesis 1 and 2. This is not just a debate about whether the days of creation are literal days. The world operates on the belief that humankind is in control of its own destiny. The best and brightest minds on earth are working day and night to heal this good world of its brokenness. Technology, not theology, provides hope for a new heaven and a new earth—and humans believe they have the right to do as they please. Nothing exemplifies this belief more during the writing of this commentary than the gender issue that rages in society. Rather than acknowledge God as Creator of man and woman, many men and women today believe they can reassign their gender. In fact, in general humankind continues to operate on the belief that there are no absolutes to govern thinking and acting in the world.

God's people live in this world, but according to a different worldview. Probably the best thing we can do for our listeners is to remind them that we are people of faith. We acknowledge that we are created in the image of God to hold a special place among all other created creatures. We choose life through obedience to our Creator. We believe the record in Scripture of our origins, when they are properly understood. According to Romans 1 the visible things of creation make our invisible God visible to those who have eyes to see. That does not mean there is no room for some commonly used arguments for the existence of God or the purpose of man. It does mean that we remind each other in church that we believe this story.

Now what?

Nothing is more relevant than knowing the answers to the biggest questions of life. How did we get here? Who is in charge? What is my purpose for being here? As Christians listen to all the conversations around them each day, they realize how different their worldview is. Our unbelieving contemporaries do not want to relinquish control of their world. Yet, the world is experiencing the terrible effects of having disobeyed its Creator. The death our Creator promised in the middle of Genesis 2 is evident continually every day. God's people bring a unique perspective to their world. Their loving allegiance to their Creator shows the way to real LifePlus.

This creation account provides a wonderful opportunity for God's people to worship him in societies that have rejected his offer of life. The Christian life revolves around the worship and service of our Creator. This implies, of course, that we know him and his will for our lives. We are applying a biblical narrative. Sermons on this Genesis narrative and the ones to follow usher God's people into his world. All new creatures in Christ acknowledge God as Creator and Ruler of their lives and live accordingly, fulfilling their purpose in his world.

Creativity in Presentation

One of the most difficult concepts for Christians to understand is how the major part of their week—their work—can be performed as an act of worship. Present a handful of occupations so listeners can see themselves in this creation narrative. It is also important to provide an illustration that explains why disobedience to God results in death. Discuss why breaking the law of gravity, for example, can have such damaging effects. Human beings are not built to withstand the impact of disobedience.

Then you may want to spend some time presenting our society's plan to heal the broken world. Congregations gain confidence in their God when they see society doing everything possible to escape the reality of the curse. It reminds them that God is in control of his world and its redemption.

Another helpful illustration in this sermon is to present some ways in which society preaches about what it means to be human, especially male and female. Your congregants will quickly see how different God's original design is from current understanding.

Finally, one of the most helpful points for the church is helping them know what it means to work for God in his world. Help parishioners heading to work on Monday morning to know what it means to do their jobs as an act of worship to their Creator. That mindset is radically different from going to work to earn a paycheck. Teach them that God created them to work in his world and lead others to worship him. You might include testimonies demonstrating worship in the workplace.

- God's good world (2:4–6, 9–14)
- Our assignment in it (2:7–8, 15–25)
- How we carry it out

That final point provides an opportunity for you to explain that our work for God in the world stems from our own recreated heart. It is impossible to do justice to Genesis 2 without a brief reference to Genesis 3 and the tragic decision of the first couple to believe another message, another worldview. That fatal decision created the need for humanity to be recreated. From that moment onward, God sets out to redeem his world through his Messiah, the obedient God-Man, who becomes a curse for us. Through him, the stage is set for the new creation described in Revelation. So, we believe this creation account and the resulting worldview because we first believed that God provided new life in Christ.

Another option would be to preach the flow of the text, showing God's design for his images in his world and focusing on his good provision and human responsibility as it develops:

- God created the man with a mission (2:4–6).
- God lavishly provided for the man to fulfill it (2:7–17).
- The success of humanity's mission requires marriage (2:18–25).[3]

All the way through we must emphasize the goodness of God in his provision and intentional preparation for his purpose and humanity's flourishing. We must also emphasize the value of the differences between the sexes and the need we both have for the other. If you decide this chapter requires more than one sermon, one option would be developing a sermon on the theology of work and worship. You certainly could devote a sermon to what it means to be male and female in this world, God's ideal for marriage and family, and how the family unit ultimately points to the relationship between Christ and the church (cf. Eph. 5).

3 The importance of marriage in God's created order does not diminish the value of single people, either as they pursue God and serve him before eventual marriage (or between marriage, i.e., Ruth), or as fulfilling unique and indispensable roles in committed singleness (e.g., Jeremiah, Jer. 16:2, and Paul, 1 Cor. 7:6–8). Rather marriage was created as the foundation of God's society to accomplish humanity's mission and to illustrate our relationship to God (Eph. 5:22–33).

DISCUSSION QUESTIONS

1. Can you list the ways in which the worship of God transforms the way in which Christians go about their tasks at work each day?

2. Why do you think our culture has begun to explore the gender issue so vigorously?

3. Can you explain the kind of death God promised would be the result of disobeying his command in verse 17? What does it look like to "die" while staying alive?

4. Why is the reason God created the first woman potentially offensive to contemporary society? What did God envision? What happens to God's plan if her role is removed?

5. Why is work so important to being human?

Genesis 3:1–24

EXEGETICAL IDEA

When the human couple, prompted by the crafty snake, rebelled in unbelief against the command of Yahweh, his response showed both the awful consequences of sin, bringing conflict and pain to humanity and creation, and his redemptive grace, providing hope for life and ultimate victory over the adversary.

THEOLOGICAL FOCUS

Humanity's unbelieving rebellion confirms the decreed death sentence, propagating conflict, pain, and frustration, yet revealing God's redemptive grace with its promise of blessing and victory.

PREACHING IDEA

Our fight for fidelity to God is won because of his gracious provision of life instead of death.

PREACHING POINTERS

It is easy to be excited about the prospect of preaching or teaching the tragic, telling narrative of Genesis 3. The wonderful life of the man and wife described at the end of chapter 2 is soon to be ruined.

What is commonly referred to as "the fall" began with the entrance onto the world's stage of a crafty serpent that could communicate. We are reading foundations for a theology of Satan and temptation. In 3:1–5 dialogue between the serpent and Eve takes place aimed at enticing the woman to disobey God's direct command to not eat from the tree of life that was in the middle of the garden. The serpent exploited her doubts and misunderstanding of God's command and contradicted him claiming that God was withholding something good from the woman. Our sin results in tragic consequences in our relationship with God!

Thankfully, in verses 9–13 God graciously reached out to his deceived and disobedient creatures to provide an opportunity for confession. The infamous blame game began. Then, our Lord pronounced judgments that affected all three participants. In verse 15 we learn that a battle is brewing between the serpent "and the woman" but also "between your offspring and her offspring. . ." It appears that her offspring gets the upper hand! However, pain entered the home and the field. The section closes in verses 20–24 with hope as the wife is named Eve, the Lord graciously provides a more adequate covering for Adam and Eve, and God allows the couple to continue worshipping him and working for him outside the garden. Do not forget that wonderful first announcement of the gospel in verse 15!

REBELLION: DEATH AND HOPE (3:1–24)

LITERARY STRUCTURE AND THEMES

Genesis 2:4 begins to tell the human story after the introduction, moving from the big picture of universal creation to the earth and the place of humankind. Genesis 3 narrates humanity's unbelief that leads to rebellion, with the resulting declaration of pain and death. The imminence of Yahweh Elohim in chapter 2 intensifies the tragedy of humanity's insurrection. The second movement of the *toledot*, Genesis 4, will follow the tragic outworking for the human family as their worship turned from God, yet it concludes with hope in true worship. Genesis 2–3, then, explains how the very good creation of chapter 1 became the deeply flawed creation in which humanity dwells, rebels, and seeks relief (ch. 4). The narrator's multiple frames for Genesis 2–3 draw attention to the crisis of rebellion and their consequences for humanity and God's good creation.[1] The account begins with God giving life to the man and placing him in the garden to thrive (2:5–17) and concludes with God removing man and woman from the garden so that they would not live on in this state (3:22–24). At the center of the section lies the succinct turning point of rebellion (3:6–8):

The first half of the unit, A–C (2:5–3:5) emphasizes the goodness of God in providing everything for humanity to thrive in his service (and humanity's necessary dependence on such), including the prohibition that is immediately challenged when the snake questioned God's gifts and command. The turning point, of course, was the couple's unbelieving disobedience to the command and rejection of God's good authority (3:6–8). The second half emphasizes God's gracious authority over the pair and the resulting consequences, confirming their eventual death (3:9–24). Overall, the pericope begins and ends outside the garden. God alone put them into his sacred space, and God put them out. The center of the narrative isolates the couple physically in their insubordination, highlighting their autonomy and demonstrating their alienation from God.

A. God formed and placed his priest for service (2:7–17).
  B. God provided the man's needed complement (2:18–25).
    C. The snake challenged God's goodness (3:1–5).
      D. Humanity rebelled in unbelief (3:6–8).
    C' God confronted rebellion (3:9–13).
  B' God graciously sentenced rebellion (3:14–21).
A' God confirmed his judgment with exile (3:22–24).

While Genesis 2–3 could all be preached as a single message, we suggest using it as two preaching passages because of the density of important teaching points and because the natural flow of the passage breaks logically between chapters 2 and 3. Chapter 2 provides the positive purpose and goodness of God, placing humankind in the sacred garden, and chapter 3 provides the temptation and sin with the concluding consequences.

---

1 Articulated by Walsh (1977) and supported by Wenham (1987, 50–51). See also Ouro's (2002) modifications and Kuruvilla's (2014, 55) helpful summary.

Multiple Frames: Impact of the Chiasm

Numerous key words and themes draw the connections between the sections, as well as the interplay between the narrative and the dialogue. It is helpful to compare the two halves of each frame to see how the narrator highlights the consequences of the rebellion in the movement of the narrative.

Comparing A and A': Initially, the man was placed into the garden to serve the King in his sacred space "to care for it and to maintain it" (Gen. 2:5, 15 NET) with the hope of life. In the end, however, the man was expelled from sacred space because he had failed to maintain it and himself, bringing disaster—conflict, pain, and death. The job of guarding was given to the cherubim (3:24). Man must still cultivate the ground (3:23), but outside of the sacred space and without the same blessing of productivity.

A. God formed, furnished and placed the man to serve in the sacred garden, offering life (2:5–17)	A'. God banished humankind to serve outside the garden, confirming their death (3:22–24)
"the tree of the knowledge of good and evil" (2:9) (וְעֵץ הַדַּעַת טוֹב וָרָע) "but of the tree of the knowledge of good and evil" (2:17) (וּמֵעֵץ הַדַּעַת טוֹב וָרָע)	"knowing good and evil" (3:22) (לָדַעַת טוֹב וָרָע)
"the tree of life" (2:9) (וְעֵץ הַחַיִּים)	"also of the tree of life" (3:22) (גַּם מֵעֵץ הַחַיִּים)
"a garden in Eden, in the east; and there he put the man" (2:8) (גַּן־בְּעֵדֶן מִקֶּדֶם וַיָּשֶׂם שָׁם אֶת־הָאָדָם) "The LORD God took the man and put him in the garden of Eden" (2:15) (אֱלֹהִים יְהוָה וַיִּקַּח אֶת־הָאָדָם וַיַּנִּחֵהוּ בְגַן־עֵדֶן)	"Therefore the LORD God sent him out from the garden of Eden" (3:23) (וַיְשַׁלְּחֵהוּ יְהוָה אֱלֹהִים מִגַּן־עֵדֶן) "and at the east of the garden of Eden he placed. . ." (3:24) (וַיַּשְׁכֵּן מִקֶּדֶם לְגַן־עֵדֶן)
"to work the ground" (2:5) (לַעֲבֹד אֶת־הָאֲדָמָה) "to work it" (2:15) (לְעָבְדָהּ)	"to work the ground" (3:23) (לַעֲבֹד אֶת־הָאֲדָמָה)
"and keep it" (2:15) (וּלְשָׁמְרָהּ)	"to guard the way to the tree of life" (3:24) (לִשְׁמֹר אֶת־דֶּרֶךְ עֵץ הַחַיִּים)

Comparing B and B': The man's relationship with the woman was placed at the core of their service to God, providing a united, innocent basis for maintaining sacred space. Sin brought conflict and loss of innocence, compromising humankind's reflected authority and ability to serve and requiring God's gracious intervention.

B. God completed humanity in unity to fulfill their purpose (2:18–25)	B' God declared humankind's consequences bringing conflict and struggle to their purpose (3:14–21)
"she shall be called Woman, because she was taken out of Man." (2:23) (לְזֹאת יִקָּרֵא אִשָּׁה כִּי מֵאִישׁ לֻקֳחָה־זֹּאת)	"The man called his wife's name Eve, because she was the mother of all living." (3:20) (וַיִּקְרָא הָאָדָם שֵׁם אִשְׁתּוֹ חַוָּה כִּי הִוא הָיְתָה אֵם כָּל־חָי)
"Then the LORD God said, 'It is not good that the man should be alone. I will make him a helper fit for him'" (2:18). (וַיֹּאמֶר יְהוָה אֱלֹהִים לֹא־טוֹב הֱיוֹת הָאָדָם לְבַדּוֹ אֶעֱשֶׂה־לּוֹ עֵזֶר כְּנֶגְדּוֹ) "and hold fast to his wife, and they shall become one flesh" (2:24). (וְדָבַק בְּאִשְׁתּוֹ וְהָיוּ לְבָשָׂר אֶחָד)	"Your desire shall be for your husband, and he shall rule over you." (3:16 NRSV) (וְאֶל־אִישֵׁךְ תְּשׁוּקָתֵךְ וְהוּא יִמְשָׁל־בָּךְ)
"And the man and his wife were both naked and were not ashamed" (2:25). (וַיִּהְיוּ שְׁנֵיהֶם עֲרוּמִּים הָאָדָם וְאִשְׁתּוֹ וְלֹא יִתְבֹּשָׁשׁוּ)	"The LORD God made for Adam and for his wife garments of skins and clothed them." (3:21) (וַיַּעַשׂ יְהוָה אֱלֹהִים לְאָדָם וּלְאִשְׁתּוֹ כָּתְנוֹת עוֹר וַיַּלְבִּשֵׁם)
Authority/rule over the creatures (naming—2:19–20)	Enmity between the snake and people (3:15)

Comparing C and C': The deception by the snake, in challenging God's word of command, focused on twisting the consequences, but the bottom line was really obedience. The snake addressed the woman alone, bypassing the one God had addressed with the command, and using partial truth to entice her. Contrary to his claim, only obedience will allow life and thriving, while disobedience will separate from God, our only source of life. When God addressed the man, he clarified the nature of the command and so the sin.

C. The snake questioned God's good word to the woman (3:1–5)	**C' God questioned the man and woman about their actions (3:9–13)**
"Did God actually say, 'You shall not eat of any tree in the garden'?" (3:1) (אַף כִּי־אָמַר אֱלֹהִים לֹא תֹאכְלוּ מִכֹּל עֵץ הַגָּן) "God said, 'You shall not eat of [it]'" (3:3) (אָמַר אֱלֹהִים לֹא תֹאכְלוּ מִמֶּנּוּ)	"Have you eaten of the tree of which I commanded you not to eat?" (3:11) (הֲמִן־הָעֵץ אֲשֶׁר צִוִּיתִיךָ לְבִלְתִּי אֲכָל־מִמֶּנּוּ אָכָלְתָּ)
The snake casts doubt and half-truths (3:1–5)	"The serpent deceived me" (3:13) (הַנָּחָשׁ הִשִּׁיאַנִי)
The snake discovered what they knew and believed.	God discovered what they had done.
The conversation included three statements (one question, one answer, one assertion).	The conversation included three questions and answers.

The major themes that this structure stresses include those that we already highlighted in Genesis 2:4–25: humanity's role and interdependence, their necessary dependence on God, God's goodness, imminence and provision for humankind, and the function of God's word in providing the parameters for blessing (or cursing). The movement in the structure of the continuing section draws attention to God's character and God's word. The snake's challenge to God's goodness initially seemed (naively) to prove accurate when the man and woman did not immediately physically die. However, the outworking through the judgment of God not only verified God's word (and character), demonstrating the faulty expectation, but also enhanced his goodness through his gracious provision for the man and woman.

This section also emphasizes the consequences of sin. Here the unity of the human family (Gen. 2) is broken, but that conflict will extend beyond the marital relation of the man and woman (3:16) to all relationships. There will be conflict between humanity and God himself (3:8–13), humanity and the natural world (here represented by the snake [3:15], and later the rest of the animals [9:2–3] and the ground [3:17–19]), as well as spiritual conflict (the power behind the snake, see below, 3:15). Man's purpose has been compromised, both formally (no longer "keeping" the garden, 3:24) and globally, as the ability of man to rule in God's realm is turned on its head. Instead of ruling over their kingdom as representatives of the great King, they accept the leadership of an insubordinate snake, rebel against their sovereign, and find themselves exiled from his sacred space. While they are still in the image and likeness of God (9:6), they will not be able to fulfill their calling apart from the divine intervention that will follow, beginning here and continuing throughout the rest of God's redemptive story.

- ***The Snake Challenged God's Goodness (3:1–5)***
- ***Humanity Rebelled in Unbelief (3:6–8)***
- ***God Confronted Rebellion (3:9–13)***
- ***God Graciously Sentenced Rebellion (3:14–21)***
- ***God Confirmed His Judgment with Exile (3:22–24)***

EXPOSITION

Genesis 3 reveals what happened to God's good creation. The mood shifts abruptly from the good, extravagant provision of God, as a mutinous conspirator challenged the goodness of the Creator and his stated consequences. Testing the woman's knowledge and understanding of God's commands, the snake deceived her, and she not only rebelled but took her husband with her. In a surprising twist, the snake seems initially vindicated as God graciously drew out his creatures in confession, without the pain of immediate physical death. The implications of the promised death sharpened as God announced the consequences to each antagonist, proclaiming subjugation, conflict, pain, frustration, and ultimate death, yet hope for continued, temporary life and the ultimate destruction of the snake. The scene closes with the expectation of provisional ongoing life with divine covering. When the human couple, prompted by the crafty snake, rebelled in unbelief against the command of Yahweh, his response showed both the awful consequences of sin, bringing conflict and pain to humanity and creation, and his redemptive grace, providing hope for life and ultimate victory over the adversary.

The Snake Challenged God's Goodness (3:1–5)

The snake challenged God's goodness, tempting humanity with the claim of a greater good while denying the consequences of rebellion.

3:1. The idyllic scene of man and woman in peace and security was unexpectedly jarred by the sudden appearance of a talking snake. The immediate characterization of the snake as "more 'crafty' (*ʿārûm*, עָרוּם) than any other beast of the field" draws the reader's attention through wordplay to the innocence of humanity in Genesis 2:25, in which "the man and his wife were both naked" (*ʿărûmîm*, עֲרוּמִּים). The unrelated words sound very similar in this form, but the impact of this characterization of the snake is not immediately clear. As noted, it can describe either clever wisdom (Prov. 12:16, 23) or shrewd and unscrupulous cunning (Job 5:12; 15:5). Here, the narrative reveals it to be the latter. The ominous nature of this snake, and the impending conflict, become apparent as he surprisingly speaks.

TRANSLATION ANALYSIS 3:1

"Shrewd" (NET, NLT) or "crafty" (ESV, NASB, NIV, NRSV) translates a word that is significant both for its sound as well as its meaning. The term "crafty" (*ʿārûm*, עָרוּם) sounds like the unrelated term used in Genesis 2:25 to describe the "naked" couple (*ʿărûmîm*, עֲרוּמִּים from עָרוֹם). The narrator chose the homonym to draw attention to the coming attack on their innocence. The word itself can be either positive or negative. Of the eleven times the adjective is used in the Old Testament, eight of them occur in Proverbs in a positive sense, in contrast to the fool or the simple. In Proverbs 14:8, for example, it can be translated "prudent" (ESV, NIV, NKJV, NLT), "shrewd" (NET), "clever" (NRSV), or "sensible" (NASB): "the wisdom of the shrewd person is to discern his way, but the folly of fools is deception" (NET). The other two uses in the Old Testament outside of Genesis, however, are clearly negative. In Job 5:12 Eliphaz praises God who brings justice, frustrating "the devices of the crafty," and in 15:5 he accuses Job of being "crafty," with his mouth taught by "iniquity" (עָוֹן). The related verb is used only five times and, outside of the two positive uses in Proverbs, it is also negative, much like the adjective. The significance of this usage lies in both the ambiguity it creates (why is the snake being characterized this way?) and in the expectation from the series of statements that at first glance appear positive, but on further examination (and in hindsight) will be demonstrated to be very negative. Perhaps the most obvious immediate clue is the questioning of the command of God.

In the ancient context, creation usually included a battle, and in the Egyptian theology, the creator (and sun god) was attacked by the snake Apophis, both as he completed his creative day, and entered the Duat to travel to the beginning of the next day, and just before emerging on the new day. Photo by Leon Petrosyan, from the tomb of Ramses I

The Serpent

The fact that the snake speaks is certainly unusual in Scripture, where Balaam's donkey is the only other creature to speak (Num. 22:28–30). Israel coming out of Egypt, however, would not necessarily have been surprised. "A distinguishing feature of animals in Egyptian literature (especially the fables) is their ability to speak, hear, and comprehend human (and divine) instruction, and to display intuition about human behavior" (Teeter 2002, 253–54). The speaking animal, however, presumes magic or supernatural activity (Heiser 2015, 73–74). This would not have been perceived as any ordinary snake. The gods were often seen in animal form in Egyptian literature (Teeter 2002, 252), and the only other speaking animal in the Hebrew Bible, Balaam's donkey, is clearly enabled by God (Num. 22:28). In Egyptian literature the snake can show up either as evil or as a protector, giving either death or wisdom (for a helpful summary of the role of snakes in the ancient literature, see Walton 2009a, 33–34). In this narrative, the character of this snake will be determined shortly.

In specific relation to Genesis 3, ancient creation accounts sometimes included a challenge by a powerful snake, either to the creator or to the hope of eternal life for humanity. In Egyptian accounts, the enemy of the creator was Apophis, pictured as a powerful serpent who attacks the creator to return creation to a primeval chaos (Morenz 1992, 168). Regarding eternal life, the Mesopotamian Gilgamesh Epic records the travels of Gilgamesh, king of Uruk, who gained a plant from the bottom of the ocean that he was told would restore one's youth. Unfortunately, on the way home a snake stole the plant, and he lost the hope of eternal life (George 2000, 98–99, especially lines XI.305–6). For a helpful summary of the thinking and imagery of snakes in Mesopotamia, Egypt, and Canaan, see Fabry (נָחָשׁ, *TDOT* IX:361–62).

These images from Israel's cognitive environment impact the original audience's understanding of the narrative, yet even in the Old Testament canon, the snake presents negative connotations. As Wenham (1987, 73) notes, in the Old Testament, "the snake must count as an archetypal unclean animal" and "an obvious candidate for an anti-God symbol, notwithstanding its creation by God." While there was none of the open conflict in the biblical creation accounts in Genesis 1–2 that we see in ancient creation accounts around Israel, that underlying conception in Israel's world, along with the supernatural and evil connotations of snakes that were heightened by the snake speaking, supplies the inference here of danger and opposition to the Creator's good design. This negative inference is borne out by the following narrative.

The Egyptian motif of wisdom associated with the snake also shows up here, but it becomes a misleading wisdom that draws the human pair away from true wisdom, destroying their ultimate purpose and potential. The curse in the latter part of the narrative crushes any divine implications here or suggestions from the cognitive environment of the power of the snake. It is introduced as a creature (Gen. 3:1), and even if there is power behind the snake, they are both impotent before the omnipotent Creator (while Sarna does not see any demonic activity here, his observation on the absolute authority of Yahweh Elohim is critical; Sarna 1989, 24).

He immediately challenged the goodness of his Creator with his question that the woman seems to have taken as innocent. In addition, he referred to God as merely "Elohim," starkly contrasting the narrator's consistent reference in Genesis 2–3 to "Yahweh Elohim" (see discussion above under 2:4, p. 99). It is as if he was distancing himself and their conversation from the imminent and faithful character of Yahweh. The woman followed suit, losing her grounding in God's character. The snake downplayed God's "command" (2:16—צוה), instead asking what God had "said" (אמר). She would follow suit again (v. 3). The reader now recognizes the word play as ominous, highlighting the attack of the snake on the vulnerability of the innocent couple (2:25), centered in her carelessness with or ignorance of truth.

God had commanded, "You may freely eat fruit from every tree of the orchard" (2:16 NET) except, of course, the tree of the knowledge of good and evil. The snake erased God's generosity (the freedom indicated by the infinitive absolute) and reversed God's gift, turning God's generous provision of "every" tree into an absolute prohibition of all trees ("you shall not eat of any tree. . . ?"), questioning God's good bounty toward them.

Ironically, the snake was one of the beasts of the field. Genesis 1 had emphasized that humanity was to rule over every living thing on the Earth (repeated twice: 1:26, 28), and in chapter 2 God brought "every beast of the field" to the first man to name, exercising dominion (v. 19). The point here is that the created and commanded order was reversed. To anticipate the outcome, humankind would believe and bow to the word of the beast instead of the command of the creator of the beasts and would be ruled by sin instead of ruling over the beasts and sin (see the similar choice presented to Cain in 4:7). It is a matter of failed leadership. Though Eve was deceived (3:13), the man was not. Rather than believe God, taking his King's word in submission, he accepted the insubordination of his new wife. Rather than lead in his rule on behalf of God, he acquiesced to Eve's lead in rebellion. Rather than exercise dominion over the beasts, he bowed to the will and words of the beast rather than the will and words of their Creator.

3:2–3. Possibly trying to defend God's goodness, the woman answered that they could eat, but she quoted God inaccurately. Her misquote downplayed God's generosity, not only leaving out the emphatic freedom but also leaving out the breadth of "all" of the trees. Instead, when she related the prohibition, she added not touching it. Her faulty report also indicated uncertainty in the consequences, missing the certainty of the infinitive absolute ("surely die," 2:17), and she followed the snake's lead by changing God's command to merely a speech report (אמר). With her deviation from God's word, showing either her inattention to detail or her ignorance of it, the snake now showed his true agenda.

3:4. God had stated with certainty that when "you eat of it you shall surely die" (2:17). The snake now flatly contradicted God's statement and truthfulness. Where the woman missed the certainty (leaving out the infinitive absolute), the snake included it with the negative assertion ("You will not surely die," 3:4). The reader now can see that not only is the snake unscrupulously cunning rather than wise, but he was in opposition to God and had known all along what God had said. He had been testing the woman.[2] The trouble is that he was right—or so it naively appears. They did not physically die on the day that they ate.

The impact of the snake's deception turns on the ambiguity of the command or, perhaps more to the point, the naive understanding of

2 The snake used the plural verb here ("you [pl.] will die") where God had used the singular, addressing Adam alone before the woman was created (2:17). Cassuto (1978, 144) infers, then, that the snake was not flatly contradicting God, since that statement is too remote in the context, but rather is responding to the woman, who used the plural verb in her recollection of God's words (3:3). However, both the snake and the woman used the plural in the command not to eat, perhaps because both naturally included the woman in the command. It is natural for the same reason for both to include the plural here as well. The use of the infinitive absolute to show the certainty (here in negation) strongly suggests that the snake was indeed directly contradicting the original penalty. The snake already knew the prohibition, since the woman did not use the infinitive absolute. Using the woman's modification to apply to both humans, he rejected the word of his Creator, challenging the truthfulness of God as well as his goodness. The larger context and the chiastic structuring of the two chapters strengthens the impression of rebellion against the command of the Lord. The snake's curse, humiliation, and ultimate destruction emphasize his culpability.

"death" (along with the claims to be like God and to have their eyes opened). Certainly, the reader is expected to make this assumption, but so, apparently, did the woman. The narrative will go on to play with that expectation, developing the intentional gap in the reader's understanding until further revelation and the developing narrative will clear it up. As noted, however, for the deception to work, it must also be the naive expectation of the woman (and the man) that it is speaking of physical death (as well as being "like God" in a simplistic sense). This insight impacts the significance of her response as well (3:6).

3:5. In contradicting God's express command, the snake also challenged the goodness of God, implying that God was withholding a greater good from them. "For God knows" also claimed knowledge for the snake. He provided a clear choice for the woman. It was a decision of who to believe. His claim matched God's declaration that the tree would provide knowledge, however, he added a partial truth that he implied God had withheld from them: they would be "like God." Ironically, of course, they were already "like God," his very images, in the intended sense of reflecting him and representing him in rule and authority (1:26–28). While presented as desirable, the ironic truth is that becoming "like God" in autonomy (see comments and "Keeping as Service" sidebar on 2:15, p. 106) devastated their ability to fulfill God's purpose for them to be "like God" in their created roles as his images, as well as their ability to thrive—really *live*. Without recognizing or evaluating the claim, the woman was left to choose God or the snake, based on her limited observations.

Humanity Rebelled in Unbelief (3:6–8)

In unbelieving rebellion, the woman ate and gave to the man, exposing their folly.

3:6. The woman evaluated the snake's contention by her own perceptions. Her actions here already mimic God's but show her developing autonomy. Seven times in Genesis 1 God "saw" (ראה) his creation and called it "good." She now evaluates the snake's claim by what she "sees" (ראה). Her first two observations are already declared by the narrator in 2:9 and are fully expected. All of the trees were "good for food" (טוֹב לְמַאֲכָל [2:9]; טוֹב ... לְמַאֲכָל [3:6]), and all of them were "pleasing to look at" (נֶחְמָד לְמַרְאֶה [2:9], synonymous to תַאֲוָה ... לָעֵינַיִם [3:6]). Raising tension, observation suggested that the snake was right. If indeed the tree is good for food (as created by God!), then it certainly would not kill her. Her evaluation, along with her experience with the rest of the trees that are "good for food," appeared to contradict God's warning. This fruit must be harmless. Of course, this assumes she understood death in a physical sense. The temptation required that she would not have thought of death in a more sophisticated sense of the loss of the abundant life, including spiritual death or separation from God. It also raises the first conflict between sight and faith. Would she believe her experience and observations or God's word?

Granted, the first couple should have merely obeyed the command of God. God had given them reason to obey, but the snake shifted their focus to doubting God and so doubting the need to obey. The temptation, then, tested her understanding of and faith in God's word in the face of experiential and visual clues that seemed to contradict his warning. She substituted her limited evaluation for God's stated consequence, usurping God's role. Her next thought expressed a strong attraction to the fruit, feeding her craving. Her focus on the fruit confused her ability to evaluate the danger.

Her final appraisal is also expected, with her naive interpretation again presenting the problem. She concluded it was "desired to make one wise" (3:6). God had called it "the tree of the knowledge of good and evil," suggesting the idea. There is wisdom involved here, but the prohibition and so the choice, as discussed above in 2:16–17 (p. 106), involves choosing the fear of the Lord—leading to obedience, his wisdom, and life—or choosing one's own good and evil, which is secular, self-serving autonomy (self-centered idolatry), leading to death. It is trying to gain God's good plan by human means apart from submission to him—a deadly deceptive shortcut to qualities needed for leadership.[3] God calls humanity to obey him, believing his declaration that one can only thrive in submission and that autonomy in choosing one's own standards always leads to death. The snake questioned the penalty and offered a mirage of a greater good. Unbelief chooses the appearance of benefits over the clearly expressed (but unexperienced) consequences, so Eve and Adam rebelled. There is clear progress in the temptation. When the woman ruled out physical death because the tree was "good for food" (3:6), felt the attraction, and saw what she believed to be a greater benefit, she felt free to rebel, leading to death (James 1:14–15).

In another way, her evaluation itself is reminiscent of God's creation account and his evaluations of his creation. Seven times in Genesis 1 God appraised his creation (וַיַּרְא) and assessed it as good (טוֹב, 1:4, 10, 12, 18, 21, 25, 31). Now Eve appraised God's creation (וַתֵּרֶא) and assessed it as "good" (טוֹב), "pleasing," or "desirable." Tragically, however, she used her expected conclusion to discount God's stated consequence rather than reinforce his word. The reader already feels her usurping God's role, even as she moves toward rebellion.

When we believe the benefits outweigh any possible penalty, portraying God as withholding from us and challenging his goodness, the way is cleared to reject God's word. The woman not only ate but gave to her husband and he ate. There is no narration of struggle or temptation for the man. He simply eats. The narrative is silent on how much of the temptation he heard or understood, though it says he was "with her." Had he listened to the whole conversation without intervening? We do not know, but we suspect he did. Even under God's cross examination, he will not admit to anything more than "The woman . . . gave" (3:12). He accepts her assumptions and offer rather than Yahweh Elohim's command (emphasized in v. 11 and reiterated in v. 17) without struggle or question. The man's rebellion was his clear choice.

3:7. The consequences are immediate but unexpected. The snake initially appeared to be vindicated. Their eyes were opened just as the snake promised (v. 5). The promise of "opened eyes" was a promise of new perception (e.g., Gen. 21:19; 2 Kings 6:17) or greater knowledge (the expectation from the tree "of the knowledge of good and evil"). The only divine knowledge they gained was their own vulnerabilities—their nakedness. The wordplay in Genesis 2:25 and 3:1 reminds the reader that the sneaky snake has struck. Their innocence and openness now had become a liability since they removed themselves from the protective authority of Yahweh Elohim, to be their own gods. They now understood the significance of what had been said, and they began to see the consequences.

They recognized their own vulnerability, and they tried to self-protect. Their good beauty under God's protection became disturbing and dangerous when left to themselves. In 2:25 there was no shame in nakedness. They were innocent and had no fear of exploitation or exposure. With the rebellion, however, nakedness was immediately recognized as a danger that must be covered and protected. The fig leaves seem laughable, but God validated their pathetic attempt to cover themselves by covering them in 3:21. In terms of wisdom language (see Exposition of

3 For the position that the tree would be appropriate at some point in the future but was not proper or available yet in the plan and timing of God, see Walton (2001, 205–6) and Wilder (2006).

2:16–17), they could no longer thrive. They could not experience life as God intended. They could not live in open, joyful communion with him. Immediately they would feel their separation from God himself.

3:8. The narrator closes this scene with the realization of God's presence and the fear it produced. By not introducing God's entrance directly, he accentuates the concern for hiding and covering through the perception of the pair. "They heard the sound of the LORD God walking in the garden." By addressing God as Yahweh Elohim, he returns to the theme of chapter 2 and emphasizes the nearness and imminent nature of God that was missing in the woman's conversation. The couple, however, did not feel comfort at his approach, but hiding, fear, and blame-sharing, which becomes so typical of human failing. It is perhaps ironic that the wording of their hiding "among the trees of the orchard" (NET; בְּתוֹךְ עֵץ הַגָּן) so closely recalls the placement of the trees of life and knowledge "in the midst of the garden" (בְּתוֹךְ הַגָּן, 2:9; 3:3), drawing attention to the impossibility of hiding from their rebellious choice.

> *TRANSLATION ANALYSIS 3:8*
> The NET Bible removes the possible anthropomorphism usually translated as God "walking" in the orchard (ESV, NASB, NIV, NKJV, NLT, NRSV) with "moving." While it is a good translation for this context of the Hebrew verb (הלך), the NET Bible loses the natural connection to the later righteous ones who "walked" with God (Enoch [5:22, 24], Noah [6:12], Abram [17:1]) and even the command to Abram to follow in faith ([12:1]).

God Confronted Rebellion (3:9–13)

God graciously called his rebellious images to confession and repentance.

3:9–13. While the snake had reversed the order of creation—assuming authority, questioning the Creator, and addressing the woman rather than the man—God returned to the order of creation by questioning the man first and then the woman, before addressing the snake. When God addressed the man, he focused attention on the rejected divine command. His initial questions called the man to confession. Their nakedness and how they understood the shame of their nakedness took center stage. They must recognize, admit, and expose their shame before God before they could find grace and help. Though their nakedness is repeated, the emphasis is really on their rebellion. Adam focused on the consequence, but God's questions became more pointed, asking for confession of the cause. The exposed nakedness is the symptom of their violation of the divine command. God called Adam to account for breaking the command, pointedly adding it in both the questioning and sentencing phases of his confrontation with the man (vv. 11 and 17). Ironically, while God had given the command to Adam explicitly, the man had remained deafeningly silent when the woman gave him the fruit. Even in his confession he reported no struggle or question, but only listening to his wife, not his God.

While the man did not answer God's question directly, he inferred that receiving the gift from the woman was a natural result of receiving her from God. God did not respond to this implied accusation but turned to the woman, who pled deception. God did not repeat the accusation of breaking his command but merely asked what she had done. Her response was brief and to the point. She was tricked! She left out her studied evaluation of the fruit based on what she perceived and what she knew about God's creation already, in contrast to her understanding of God's command. She had believed the snake's spin rather than God's clear command.

God Graciously Sentenced Rebellion (3:14–21)

God declared the resulting pain, conflict, and frustration for humanity in creation, yet with grace and hope.

3:14–15. After the woman's complaint, God directly cursed the snake, validating the woman's accusation. The curse brims with talionic justice, beginning with the snake's role in the animal realm. It reinforces the previous observation of the order of creation being turned upside down, moving the snake from his attempt to usurp authority to the lowest of the beasts (literally and figuratively!). The snake had attempted to destroy God's creation from dust by tempting them to eat in rebellion, and so he will eat dust, both symbolizing his humiliation (Lam. 3:29; as also crawling in the dust, Ps. 44:26; Isa. 47:1) and recognizing the appropriateness of him being humiliated by being forced to eat the decomposed substance of his target (cf. Gen. 2:7; 3:19). In addition, however, the tempter will become the casualty of the woman's offspring. Ironically, just as the human couple did not immediately physically die, he would ultimately be destroyed. Their ongoing struggle for life would produce an offspring that would end the snake's struggle for supremacy and life.

TRANSLATION ANALYSIS 3:14

The snake was initially introduced as more "crafty" than any "beast of the field" (חַיַּת הַשָּׂדֶה) in 3:1. Here the same phrase is paired with the common word for cattle (בְּהֵמָה—translated "livestock" by ESV). While the term for "cattle" can refer to animals in general, the pairing of the terms suggests that the narrator puts the cursed snake beneath all animals, whether domestic or wild.

Verse 15 has occasioned significant discussion of the initial intended meaning, with positions ranging from a clear prediction of a promised redeemer to a simple statement that there will be conflict between humans and snakes.[4] While the veiled nature of the curse only becomes clear over time, the immediate context suggests more than just a conflict between humans and snakes. As mentioned above, the consistent ancient Near Eastern picture of the malevolent snake in similar contexts supports a more cosmic conflict here. The hostile stance of the snake toward God, deceiving God's creatures and fomenting rebellion (3:1–5), bolsters the perception of a malevolent presence beyond (and behind) the devious beast of the field in opposition to Yahweh Elohim. The battle between good and evil or, more appropriately, between the Creator and evil forces was expected in creation accounts in the ancient world (see "Cosmic Conflict" sidebar), but the clear identification of the personal evil one, Satan, will await the progress of revelation (Rom. 16:20; Rev. 12:9).

Cosmic Conflict

We see examples of this sort of cosmic conflict across the ancient world in relation to initial creation and the possibility of eternal life, including snakes (see sidebar and Excursus, "The Serpent," above). With Apophis attacking the creator in Egypt, Marduk slaying the dragon Tiamat in *Enuma Elish* (the watery basis for the earth and heavens), and a snake stealing the flower of life from Gilgamesh in the Gilgamesh epic, cosmic conflict would have been expected in a creation account. One big difference occurs in the very peaceful and effortless creation of all things in Genesis 1, even though that is where the battle occurs in many myths. In Genesis the battle does not occur until chapter 3, and it is not a direct attack on Yahweh, but indirectly through his images (Tsumura 2005). This passage recognizes both the insidious nature of the attack and the eventual utter failure (for a helpful discussion of the relationship of Genesis 1–3 and the ancient mythology, see Averbeck 2004).

4 Collins (1997) argues from the grammar for a single future deliverer while, on the other end of the spectrum, Westermann (1994, 259) argues that it refers to the line of descendants and merely refers to "humans and the serpent continually (the imperfect in 15b* is to be understood iteratively) trying to kill each other."

The three-tiered universe is clearly depicted on this kudurru, or boundary stone, with the heavens, the earth, and the waters under the earth (with Marduk represented as the horned snake). Photo by Rama, courtesy The Louvre

The promise that the offspring (or "seed," זֶרַע) of the woman would attack the snake's head, which would likely be fatal, suggests the crushing of the opposition to God's chosen representatives. The pronoun for the woman's seed that will attack the snake's head is singular (הוּא, v. 15), and the referent for "your head" (יְשׁוּפְךָ רֹאשׁ, again singular, v. 15) is certainly the snake, suggesting an ongoing cosmic battle between the power behind the snake and a future descendant of the woman (Collins 1997). Corporate solidarity could suggest that it refers to the defeat of the snake through the crushing of his offspring (representing him) by her offspring. Though used by Westermann (1994, 259–60) to support the physical snakes view, it more likely points toward the ongoing cosmic battle, otherwise missing from the creation account in Genesis 1–2 but still lurking in the background and finally culminating in that singular offspring.[5] It fits both the ongoing struggle of humanity with evil (Cain and sin crouching, Gen. 4:7) and the struggle between those who would pursue God and those who would not (Cain and Abel in ch. 4), which both have the same genesis. The crushing of the snake, however, also reminds the reader strongly of the sovereign rule of the Creator who assigns appropriate judgment for any creature who challenges his good administration.

TRANSLATION ANALYSIS 3:15a

The noun translated "offspring" (ESV, NET, NIV, NLT, NRSV) or "seed" (NASB, NKJV) is a common noun (used 229 times in the Hebrew Bible). It can refer literally to the seeds of plants (Gen. 1:11–12, 29) or figuratively to people, as here. When it is used of people, it may indicate an individual descendant (1 Sam. 1:11), or it can designate multiple descendants as a collective for the entire group (Gen. 9:9). Part of the interpretive challenge here is whether it is intended collectively, individually, or perhaps even as a double entendre (Kidner 1967, 75; Waltke and Fredricks 2001,

5 See sidebar, "Cosmic Conflict." Here the snake is presented as one of the creatures that was to be under the authority of humankind (3:1). Not only do we have the reversal of intended authority as it questioned the word of God, but we also see that there is power behind the snake that presents the cosmic conflict referenced above. The ongoing battle receives greater clarity in the New Testament, as the writers define more clearly that the real enemy is spiritual and personal (Eph. 6:10–20; Rev. 12:9). John sees the ongoing battle with evil among humanity as an ongoing outworking of this cosmic battle that will only be finally resolved in Christ (John 8:44; 1 John 3:8–12).

93). As Mathews (1996, 246) points out, the term is crucial in Genesis (used largely in the patriarchal narratives in the context of God's promise to Abram) and so has added significance here.

TRANSLATION ANALYSIS 3:15b
The verb that the ESV translates "bruise" (שׁוּף) occurs only four times in the Old Testament, and two of them are here. Though the meaning is not completely clear, the context indicates struggle or even open warfare. The effect of the heal striking, attacking, or bruising the head of the snake is devastating, while the effect of the snake on the heal would be painful or even crippling, but not deadly.

The ultimate referents in the initial context, then, are not clear. The ambiguity of this promised seed heightens the significance of perpetuating the line of the woman through the genealogies, looking for the fulfillment of the promise, which will become the backbone of the progress of Genesis. Each succeeding genealogy will lead the reader to new hope and new questions regarding the outworking of the plan and promise of God.

3:16. While the snake would be destroyed by the life coming from the woman he tried to destroy, the woman would only realize this vindication through increased pain in reproducing that life. The initial blessing for humanity (reproduction, 1:28) continued in their hope for deliverance (descendants, 3:15) but would only be realized through pain (v. 16). Life, then, was still possible and in fact promised through that pain (as Adam's naming of Eve in 3:20 highlights). Every childbirth with its pain for every woman will now both signal the hope and blessing of life that God had promised, as well as the eventual defeat of the enemy of humanity (as suggested by Ps. 8:2 in context). It would also remind them, however, of the consequences of sin and the role woman had in that rebellion.

Just as the snake would be at enmity with the woman whom he deceived, fomenting rebellion yet being ultimately defeated, so the woman would struggle with her husband, whom she led into rebellion. As with the snake, her attempt to take the lead would be turned on its head. In contrast to the man's passive acceptance of the rebellion, in which there was no reply to the woman either in the initial account (3:6) or in the man's report of the account (v. 12), the man must take the lead. While this has been used for inappropriate male dominance, the pattern in the narrative is for the man to take the expected leadership. Twice Yahweh Elohim reminded the man that he had not obeyed the command that he had given him (vv. 11, 17), though he did not mention the infraction to the woman. The implication reveals the responsibility of the man for the rebellion, with the necessary responsibility to lead in obedience moving forward.

TRANSLATION ANALYSIS 3:16
The Hebrew behind the term translated "want to control" (NET, תְּשׁוּקָתֵךְ, or "your desire," ESV, NASB, NIV, NKJV, NRSV) only occurs in the Hebrew Bible three times, with two in this context. In Song of Songs 7:11 it refers to sexual longing, so a variety of views have been suggested here, including such things as making her dependent for sexual satisfaction on the husband or still being willing to reproduce despite the pain (noted by Sarna 1989, 28). It is also used, however, in Genesis 4:7 of sin's desire to master Cain. In that context, it is collocated with "subdue" (משׁל), which is also translated "rule" in this context. The two sets of clauses are nearly identical yet adjusted for the different subjects. In this context, the best overall approach, represented in the NET, would understand the use of both clauses in a way parallel to Genesis 4: the woman's "desire is to contend with him for leadership" resulting from her sin, but the man must exercise his role as head, though certainly not in any abusive way (Foh 1975, 383). Human sinfulness will equally effect the men, however, leading to domination and abuse rather than godly leadership (Eph. 5:25–33)

3:17–19. Several narrative clues point to the greater responsibility of the man in the whole incident. While the snake was directly cursed as the instigator and would be destroyed (3:14–15), the woman received painful consequences, though no mention of "curse" (v. 16). The man, though not directly cursed, was responsible for cursing rather than blessing on the ground that was under his care (2:5, 15), and he experienced the consequences personally as well. In addition, God did not mention to the woman his initial command, presumably since she did not directly receive it and was deceived, but he emphasized the disobeyed command twice to the man (3:11, 17). He specifically based man's judgment on man's obedience to the woman rather than his own command not to eat from the tree, highlighting man's culpability. God addressed the man last as the climax of the judgment oracles. Human sinfulness will equally effect the men, however, leading to domination and abuse rather than godly leadership (Eph. 5:25–33).

> *TRANSLATION ANALYSIS 3:17*
> The NET translation "obey" (שׁמע) makes explicit the implied nuance of the verb usually translated "hear" or "listen to" (ESV, NASB, NIV, NLT, NRSV), often intending more than hearing, but actual obedience (Deut. 6:4).

It is clear that the consequence of sin is conflict (snake→←woman; woman→←man; and man→←ground) and "pain" (עִצָּבוֹן, for both man and woman, vv. 16–17). "Your . . . pains" (עִצְּבוֹנֵךְ, v. 16), which increased for the woman during the event of childbirth (which also extends life!), similarly describes the experience of the man in trying to sustain life from the ground "in painful toil" (בְּעִצָּבוֹן, v. 17). For the man and woman, the pain will be precisely in the areas of expectation for blessing (multiplying and caring for the ground, both blessed responsibilities before the sin and necessary for life and hope). Both will also, however, remind the man and woman of their failure to secure life by obedience, instead securing death. Ironically, the rebellious choice to eat will make eating involve more pain, less satisfaction, and eventually death, proving the lie of the snake.

The outcome for the man, returning to dust, suggests that the description of his creation as a vessel in the Potter's hand was also drawing attention to the man's dependence on God for his existence, highlighting his fragile and vulnerable life (Soden 2015, 46–48). He was dust and would certainly return to dust. Of course, it also pointed to the promise of death for eating the fruit. God's stated consequences would end in physical death as well as the shriveling loss of God's presence and the opportunity to thrive.

Just as the consequences for the snake and the woman mirrored their infractions, the man's pain in eating reflected his rebellious eating. He could still eat, but now there was added difficulty, frustration, and futility.

3:20–21. Verses 20 and 21 highlight hope and grace amid the cursing and pain. In a surprising sequence, Adam responded to the cursing and consequences of the rebellion by trusting God's promise and expectantly naming his wife "Eve" (חַוָּה), as the mother of the living (אֵם כָּל־חָי). Here, as the painful realization of the resulting death from the disobedience begin to sink in, we have the hopeful statement of life and continuation of the initial blessing of being fruitful and multiplying to fill the earth. This naming formula also reminds the reader of the oracle that he must rule over her (v. 16). As with the frequent naming formulas in Genesis, the man demonstrates authority here by naming.

Tacitly affirming the insufficiency of the man and woman's solution to their nakedness, God clothed his representatives as he prepared to send them out of his temple precinct. Without comment, he took the life of an animal to prepare sturdy garments of skins for them, replacing the fragile loincloths they had made. The life of the animal or animals foreshadows the sacrifices that will be used to atone for sin, with which the reader would be very familiar. While the text does not relate how much explanation they received, they clearly understood sacrifice in chapter 4. The clothing may also suggest their greater need as they leave the protected garden.

God Confirmed His Judgment with Exile (3:22–24)

God banished humankind to serve outside the garden, confirming their death.

Once again Yahweh spoke reflectively, affirming the autonomous consequences of the human actions. Partly confirming the lie of the snake, humankind is now like God—ironically not so much as they had been or thought they would be, but inappropriately like God by their choice to decide for themselves what is right or wrong, good or evil. This power grab only produced distress and dysfunction. God now limited the effects of their sin by limiting their lives. While he had graciously allowed ongoing life in procreation, he also graciously limited the individual lifespan so that humanity was not locked into this sin-tainted body. They would never eat from the tree of life. They would not live forever in these bodies.

The LORD God now sent them out of the garden to fulfill their original mandate yet reminded them of their origin. The narrator's description links the initial purpose of the man (2:5, 15) with the origin of the man (2:7). The purpose of humankind frames the pericope, showing it is still intact and, in fact, necessary, while the creation reflection reminds the reader of the fragile and temporary nature of man. He will still fulfill his role, even though it is briefly accomplished in pain and conflict. His service to the ground, however, is now menial, maddening, and momentary, for he will die. He will not, however, fulfill the fulness of the role originally offered to him (2:15). While he will serve the ground, he will not keep the garden. That job was reassigned to the cherubim, barring humankind from reentry. Humankind was expelled so that they could not live forever by eating from the tree of life. God confirmed his penalty: their death.

Cherubim

Cherubim, composite creatures in the angelic realm, are commonly associated in the Old Testament with the presence of God, depicted in the tabernacle (Exod. 25) and temple (1 Kings 6), and described by Ezekiel in his visions (Ezek. 1:4–21; 10:1–22). The cherubim guard sacred space and appear to be in various forms both in the Old Testament and in the ancient Near East. Though they are not clearly described, they sometimes seem to be four-legged creatures (Ps. 18:10 = 2 Sam. 22:11), although Ezekiel 1:5–11 describes them as two legged ("In their appearance they had human form" v. 5, cf. 10:22). They sometimes seem to have two wings and two faces (as per the cherubim in the tabernacle, Exod. 25:19–20) and at other times have four wings and four faces (Ezek. 1:6; 10:20–22). The four faces in Ezekiel are human, lion, ox and eagle (1:10), though in 10:14 the face of a "cherub" (הַכְּרֻבִים) replaces the face of the ox. They also have humanlike arms and hands (1:8). The form, then, may not be fixed, or it may be more symbolic than concrete in description.

In all cases they are closely connected to the presence of God, and in Genesis 3:24 we see their role in guarding the sacred space from the unholy. Their appearance here removes any possibility of humanity gaining access to the garden and the tree of life, guaranteeing humankind's eventual death. Their placement in the tabernacle suggests the same guardian function, and their role in Ezekiel, accompanying the presence of God, seems to confirm the conclusion. For a very helpful and exhaustive look at the biblical passages, the etymological evidence in comparative Semitics, and the archaeological evidence for similar creatures outside of Israel, see Alice Wood (2008). She suggests that the images in the ancient world portray similar spiritual creatures with the same function of guarding sacred space and the sacred presence (pp. 157–204).

THEOLOGICAL FOCUS

Humanity's unbelieving rebellion confirmed the decreed death; initiated conflict, pain, and frustration to humankind and creation; and yet revealed God's redemptive grace with its promise of blessing and victory.

Genesis 3 completes the pericope begun with Genesis 2:4 and presents several archetypal events. Humanity's rebellious reaction to the initial test of their faith, cultivated from the snake's challenge to the character of God through his word, presents a paradigm of temptation and sin. The woman doubted the word of the Creator while the man failed to challenge the false narrative and temptation. Instead, he passively accepted and ate the fruit at the woman's suggestion, in his own response of unbelief. The pattern for rebellion is birthed through a willful misperception of the outcomes and skepticism of the consequences, leading to disobedience to the command of God.

The outcome of sin is death. The penalties for sin follow the clear command of God, with separation from life itself (initially in relation to the Creator and then his provision for life), dysfunction, conflict, frustration, and finally death. By God's grace, death is not immediate, but the consequences clearly fit the crime; humankind will suffer in the very arenas that have the greatest hope for the future and bear the greatest relation to their core lives. Humanity will experience only limited success pursuing their purpose as God created them and receiving God's intended blessing. Though they will reproduce life through pain, they will only briefly maintain that life through laborious struggle. The tranquility and mutual aid of the family unit is now a battleground for control. The consequences of sin add a new arena to the ongoing cosmic battle, initiating a struggle in marriage for dominance and adding frustration in toiling for a temporary existence.

The conflict initiated by the snake has presented the common ancient image of the cosmic battle between the forces of good and evil in the creation narratives. Genesis 3 provides but a brief acknowledgment of the greater powers behind the struggle humankind faces in this world. While a clear theology of evil is not presented here, there is an assumption of a greater spiritual world that underlies the challenges to God's authority but that will eventually be crushed. God will assert his authority and show his rule over all rebellious creatures.

And yet, God is revealed as gracious and loving as he offers humankind the opportunity to confess and repent. Rather than the expected immediate physical death, yet distinct from the snake's suspicious accusation, God draws out confession and offers consequences with hope. The struggle with the snake will end in victory over him. The woman will bear children, and the man will live and exercise dominion, however badly, serving the ground. God will clothe humankind with sturdy relief from nakedness and propel them into his world to preserve them from perpetual enslavement in their judged state while allowing ongoing relationship with their Creator. While much of this will await further revelation from God and ultimate fulfillment in Christ, the exodus generation and those to follow will begin to understand the benevolent provision of a judging God.

These consequences and the outworking of the curse reinforce the clear and absolute supremacy of the Creator over his creation. Yahweh Elohim does not lose control of his wayward creatures, nor is his purpose thwarted. Rather, he further demonstrates and declares his effective rule and generous superintendence of humanity and history toward his desired end. He will bring about the end of sin and death finally seen in the death, burial, and resurrection of the ultimate seed of the woman. Jesus Christ will then offer that life to all who will follow him in faith, fulfilling his purpose for humanity, fully transformed into his image and ruling with him as his king-priests. Humanity will again be able to fully walk with God and find thriving life in his presence.

At the same time, no rebellious creature is outside of his purview and justice. No insubordination is without cost. Yet, every punishment fits the crime and reveals his gracious reign.

Of course, Genesis 3 presents the reasons for the pain and struggle in human experience. It also reveals the backstory to the transitory nature of life and the propensity of humanity toward rebellion, hiding, and conflict. The unbelief of Genesis 3 initiates the rampant degeneration in the following narratives that require persistent intervention by God to deliver humankind from their sin and its consequences.

PREACHING AND TEACHING STRATEGIES

Exegetical and Theological Synthesis

The Hebrew wordplay in Genesis 2:25 and 3:1 with "naked" and "crafty" prepares the reader for the disruption of the idyllic condition of the created couple. The narrative in chapter 3 describes the fall of humanity from God's good creation. Theology is conveyed through the narrative, and everything begins with "the serpent" (3:1). The fall of humanity occurred because the serpent deceived the first created couple into disbelieving and disobeying God's one commandment concerning "the tree" (v. 3). You will want to develop the beginnings of a theology of Satan that describe the spiritual warfare that God's people experience each day.

Part of this conflict involves an understanding of how temptation works, including those times when it succeeds and we fail. The narrative also provides a glimpse into what happens every time we believe a lie and disbelieve what God said. We end up deciding for ourselves what is right and good for us. However, we are not God and the "good" presented to us by the lie never delivers but always disappoints (overpromises and underdelivers). As you can see in the story, the couple's relationship with themselves, with God, with the serpent, and with their respective tasks is badly marred.

This analysis explains why we experience more brokenness than blessing so often in our lives. The curse is not good, but fortunately it is not the last word in Genesis 3. The kind of death described in this chapter that is the result of disbelieving God's word also includes glimpses of God's grace to his fallen creatures. Here is a list: (1) the wonderful first announcement of the gospel in 3:15; (2) Eve is named with respect to life, not death; (3) our Lord graciously provides a new and better covering for the couple's nakedness; (4) God allows the couple to move outside the garden to continue their relationship with him; and finally (5) he protects them from reentry to where they would live forever in their brokenness.

Preaching Idea

Our fight for fidelity to our God is won because of his gracious provision of life instead of death.

Contemporary Connections

What does it mean?

Genesis 3 shows that the condition of our broken world is the result of God's creatures disbelieving his word. The narrative presents a theological, supernatural explanation for the human condition. This includes the existence of Satan, who is attempting to move human beings away from God and LifePlus. This means that the tempter and temptation are powerful and deadly. Humankind is portrayed as susceptible to spiritual attack; we are prone to disbelief and disobedience. We need not only to know what God commands, but also to trust that he knows what is best. The original sin stemming from deciding to become autonomous with respect to right and wrong has cosmic consequences for God's creatures living in his world.

An expositor will want to spend time explaining the meaning and significance of the multifaceted announcement of the curse. The curse affects the serpent, its severely strained relationship with the woman and her family, the woman with respect to childbearing and her husband, and Adam with respect to the ground he works. Finally, this cursed context also includes glimpses of God's grace. Verse 16 looks forward to the seed of the woman who will bruise the head of the serpent! Eve is the mother of the living, not the dead; the Lord provides better covering for the couple; and he sends them out of the garden to continue to worship and serve as his representatives in his world. God will not let his creation slip further into rebellion and take from the tree of life like they did from the tree in the middle of the garden.

Is it true?

You can imagine that some listeners will struggle to believe in a talking serpent. Of course, many of our listeners will simply accept it due to their familiarity with the story. Either way, we are talking about supernatural phenomenon. You will have to decide how many message minutes need to be devoted to expository apologetics. The entire narrative is at odds with a society that believes the human condition has nothing to do with its relationship with the Creator. The real world presented in this story includes a powerful enemy bent on disrupting and derailing faith in God's word. It also provides us with answers to life's most important questions about our identity, purpose, and responsibility to our Creator God.

Some listeners may wonder if disobeying God is really that bad. This is prime time to communicate how God's laws work, leading to life through obedience and death through disobedience for his creatures (cf. Deut. 30:15–20 where Moses preaches that message, closing the Pentateuch the way it started). You will want to address questions such as, "Is it true that God alone enjoys the privilege of 'knowing good and evil?'" and "Do the results of Adam and Eve's disobedience, including the announced curses, adequately explain the brokenness in our world?" Notice in the preaching idea that we win because God graciously provides life for us instead of the pronounced death sentence for disobedience. God is the one who adequately covers the couple and provides for life outside of Eden.

Now what?

Nothing is more relevant than providing our listeners with the theological explanation of our current existence in a badly broken world. A huge part of living the Christian life involves facing, fighting, and conquering temptation by the grace of God and in the power of his Spirit within us. The anatomy of temptation provided in Genesis 3 helps prepare believers for this daily fight. The description of the curse helps them know what they are up against and helps explain many of their struggles (e.g., trouble with the enemy of our souls, at home, and at work). A large part of the relevance of this sermon hinges on the angle of not recreating the same sinful pattern as our spiritual parents. While the next chapter shows how humankind handled temptation, it is important to stress that even though we are no longer living in Eden, we still have access to our powerful God who delivers us from temptation.

Creativity in Presentation

One way to structure a message on Genesis 3—winning the fight for fidelity to our God when tempted—is to follow the storyline.

- Set the context of the original temptation in paradise (Gen. 1–2).
- The tempter ("the serpent was more crafty") (3:1)
- The temptation ("Did God actually say . . .") (3:2–5)
- The fall and its consequences ("the woman saw . . . took . . . ate") (3:6–19)

- Our hope ("the mother of all living") (3:15, 20–24)

Notice that the fall, including the resulting curse, covers most of the verses in the pericope. While we are presenting this section as a unit, you might decide to spend more sermon/lesson time on it because of its importance. If so, consider the following structure:

- The tempter and temptation
- The curse versus blessing
- The hope for living life outside of Eden

It is important to help our listeners feel the push and pull of temptation. You may need to lead them to identify the temptations that are strongest for them. The same things do not tempt everyone equally. You must be careful not to lose credibility, but a story from your own life is usually compelling. Or you might choose to communicate an episode in the life of someone you know about or have read about.

You will want to spend some time making sure everyone can feel the devastation of losing fellowship with God (cf. Gen. 3:10 "and I hid myself"). As noted above, much biblical real estate in this section is devoted to the results of the rebellion, including God's announcement of the various ways in which the curse will be felt. This is the time to help everyone believe that sin cannot produce in us what it promises to deliver. You could present a contrast between an ideal, Eden-like world and its current, broken expression. Show an image of a beautiful garden. Not far from where I live in Pennsylvania is an attraction called Longwood Gardens. Contrast such beauty with the uglier side of life. While it may be true that a picture is worth a thousand words, it is helpful to present statistics that show how broken the world is. The curse is real, including the pressures it puts on marriages. Our listeners should respond with a renewed sense of trusting God through faith in Christ and the power of his Spirit to fight for fidelity. Finally, you may want to let everyone know how our Savior has made it possible for believers to remain faithful to God and enjoy his good life.

DISCUSSION QUESTIONS

1. How does a possessed-by-Satan serpent change the way you think about fighting against temptation?
2. What does Eve's surrender to temptation teach us about resisting temptation?
3. How can we cultivate a more accurate understanding of truth to prepare for future temptation?
4. When we do not understand what God has said or done or how it fits with what we experience, what assumptions should we make? How can we remember our limited perception in the moment?
5. How should an appropriate response to sin show, as evidenced by God's questions to Adam?
6. How should we view a God who judges sin, and how does that impact our response to him as sinners?

Genesis 4:1–26

EXEGETICAL IDEA
When Cain spurned God's promise reflected in procreation and worship, rejected Yahweh and his grace, choosing sin over God's presence, he spawned a line beset with homicide, self-promotion, even self-worship, but hope reawakened through Seth's line with genuine worship.

THEOLOGICAL FOCUS
Profane worship and spurning God threaten his images, bring alienation and judgment from God, and deepen self-protection and self-worship, but God's grace preserves promise for life through genuine worship.

PREACHING IDEA
By God's grace his people bury Cain-like tendencies at work and worship as God keeps his promise of life alive in a broken world.

PREACHING POINTERS
In Genesis 4 God provides the first glimpses of how Adam and Eve's rebellion or lack of fidelity to God's will affects their children. It is striking that the first recorded sin after the initial fall is murdering one's brother ("Cain rose up . . . and killed him"; v. 8). And this happened all because of the contrast between genuine worship and religious activity devoid of a real heart for and trust in God. Both Cain and his brother, Abel, bring offerings to the Lord. Cain and his offering are rejected, while Abel and his offering are accepted. Cain, therefore, kills his brother.

Before Cain commits murder, his interaction with the Lord instructs us with respect to what sin attempts to do to us. Chapter 4 shows God being extremely gracious to the murderer, even though Cain moves "away from the presence of the Lord" (v. 16). Cain represents all who give the appearance of worshipping God, all who offer something to God with their hands, but without a heart for him. Remember, an "offering from the fruit of the ground" was not the problem; the lack of any designation such as "firstborn" or "fat portions" was the issue (vv. 3, 4).

Listeners will appreciate how God presents cultural advances in the ancient world within the context of Cain's life away from the presence of God (vv. 17–22). Lamech, one of Cain's grandsons, highlights how sin continued to show itself in the exaltation of self and the resulting ravage of God's good world with violence (vv. 23–24). Finally, we can let out a sigh of relief with the hope for humanity found in Adam and Eve's son Seth and the key sentence with which chapter 4 ends, "At that time people began to call upon the name of the Lord" (v. 26).

WORSHIP AND SELF-WORSHIP: LIFE AND DEATH (4:1–26)

LITERARY STRUCTURE AND THEMES

Genesis 4 brings closure to the initial *toledot* section begun in 2:4. Though it ends with hope, it generally portrays a dismal reality for humankind. As we have seen, 2:7–3:25 forms a complex unity, showing how the very good creation (ch. 1) became the deeply flawed creation that we experience today through the rebellion of Adam and Eve. Genesis 4 concludes the section by drawing out the historical outworking of the consequences of their rebellion. It records the first physical death because of sin and demonstrates that the account of chapter 3 was paradigmatic for human sin that will continue to spiral farther and farther away from God's created ideal.

Genesis 4 records the initial genealogy of humanity, but it includes several additions that provide a narrative commentary on the progressive condition of humankind. The genealogy begins with the birth of Eve's first child, Cain, and her hopeful exclamation. It ends with a third birth to Eve and a second hopeful exclamation, both seeming to draw attention to God's promises from chapters 2–3. After the birth of the first two boys, Moses reports the first acts of sacrificial worship. The account of the third birth at the end of the chapter likewise concludes with proclamation of worship. This frame of birth, hope, and worship sits in stark contrast to the intervening genealogy and the interpolations of selfishness, pride, and murder.

Structurally, the genealogy is divided into three segments, with the notice that "the man had marital relations with his wife Eve" at the beginning (וְהָאָדָם יָדַע אֶת־חַוָּה אִשְׁתּוֹ, 4:1 NET) and concluding with "And Adam had marital relations with his wife again" (וַיֵּדַע אָדָם עוֹד אֶת־אִשְׁתּוֹ, v. 25 NET), with the parallel phrase resuming the genealogy through Cain in verse 17 ("Cain had marital relations with his wife," NET, וַיֵּדַע קַיִן אֶת־אִשְׁתּוֹ). Between these genealogical notices the two interpolations form an additional inner frame, paralleling the murderous act of Cain with the murderous boast of Lamech. The center section of the genealogy describes Cain fathering sons and building a city, followed by the sons of Lamech and their achievements. The genealogy, then, forms a chiastic whole:

A. Announcing the fulfillment of blessing, Eve bore two sons who offered worship (4:1–5).
  B. God graciously warned and judged murderous Cain (4:6–16).
    C. Cain fathered heirs, building a city in his son's name (4:17–18).
    C'. Lamech fathered sons from two wives, establishing technology in his sons' names (4:19–22).
  B' Lamech celebrated taking another's life without consequences and declared his own protection (4:23–24).
A' Announcing hope, Eve again bore sons, leading to genuine worship (4:25–26).

The outer frame of this structure develops the birth, promise, and theme of worship in parallel sections. In each case, we read of the birth, the explanation for the name, and the progeny establishing worship. We will explore the significant differences in the Exposition. In the secondary frame, the main theme is murder and its rightful punishment. While the text draws specific attention to the comparison of these acts, the differences provide clear indication of the theme as Lamech boldly declared his own autonomous authority. The center of the chiasm focuses on the achievements of man, yet they are apart from Yahweh. The Exposition will explore the significance of this as the rebellion of man escalates and culture seems to provide relief from the curse and distance from the consequences of sin.

The developing themes in chapter 4 focus on the outworking and implications of both the sin of chapter 3 and the gracious response of Yahweh in judgment and promise. The initial impression of the genealogy may tend to focus the reader on the murder of Abel and, perhaps, the devolution to Lamech's murderous boast, as we see sin burgeoning. God's grace, however, remains constant, both in warning and in judgment with limits. In the development of humankind from the first humans, and within the context of growing evil, the narrative notes various advancements of technology throwing such achievements into dubious relief.

Framing the troubling genealogy of man's blossoming murderous rebellion, expectation of the fulfillment of God's promise shines through Eve's two birth announcements. In addition, worship in sacrifice and proclamation connects the optimistic frame, drawing attention to the means of hope for God's working. The appropriate initial response of worship, introduced by Cain and Abel, degenerates into false worship, murder, and finally idolatry. Yet in the concluding frame a remnant projects hope in the name of Yahweh, reminding the reader again of his promise. These themes of growing rebellion, necessary judgment with attendant grace, hope of the fulfillment of promise especially found in true worship, and the dangers of civilization apart from submission to God will be clarified and focused through the rest of Genesis to show the working of God as he progressively reveals his purpose to bring redemption and blessing to his sin-cursed world.

- ***Announcing the Fulfillment of Blessing, Eve Bore Two Sons Who Offered Worship (4:1–5)***
- ***God Graciously Warned and Judged Murderous Cain (4:6–16)***
- ***Cain Fathered Sons, Building a City in His Son's Name (4:17–18)***
- ***Lamech Fathered Sons from Two Wives, Establishing Technology in His Sons' Names (4:19–22)***
- ***Lamech Celebrated Taking Another's Life Without Consequences and Declared His Own Protection (4:23–24)***
- ***Announcing Hope, Eve Again Bore Sons, Leading to Genuine Worship (4:25–26)***

EXPOSITION

The larger section (2:4–4:26) began with hope, narrating God's provision for creation's need and establishing humanity with his blessing to oversee his physical realm. This expectant preamble, however, quickly turned to the reason creation is not experiencing God's blessed intentions through the rebellion of his curators. The desire of humankind to be autonomous resulted in pain, frustration, and alienation from each other, creation, and God himself. God's grace was clear in his response, but this resulting genealogy presents the cascading effects of their sin, almost overshadowing the hope in the promised victory.

The initial and final focus on worship keeps that hope alive, but the central emphasis clearly reveals the increasingly disastrous outworking of the initial sin in the garden. Cain's offering was not only unacceptable, but he failed to respond to God's gracious warning, murdering his brother and complaining about God's generous judgment.

Humanity deteriorated still farther, shown by Lamech's boast of his murder and his hubris, usurping God's role and declaring his own justice. Framed by this increasing independence from God, the initiation of civilization with its arts and achievements rings hollow. The achievements of humanity will only grow darker in later narratives. The concluding notice of progress in man's relationship with Yahweh on the heels of the reminder of God's provision of another "offspring" (זֶרַע, 4:25), however, provides an optimistic ending to a dismal portrayal of developing humanity. Despite God's promise reflected in procreation and worship, even with specific grace, Cain spurned Yahweh, yielded to sin, and left God's presence, leading to fratricide and reproducing self-protection, self-promotion, and even self-worship. However, hope continued in new births and genuine worship.

Announcing the Fulfillment of Blessing, Eve Bore Two Sons Who Offered Worship (4:1–5)

The growing family of Adam and Eve produced hope that God was fulfilling his promised blessing for humanity to be fruitful and multiply, the necessary foundation for the promised victory over the snake, both in the new man-child and in the new worship, but hope was short-lived.

The immediate outworking from the sin and God's judgment begins with the first human birth and Eve's reaction of excitement. It then moves immediately to a second birth and the two resulting occupations, glossing over the growing up years (4:1–2). Immediately the narrative transitions to recount their worship and God's response, focusing on Cain and his initial reaction to rejection. These two sections both obviously frame Abel's birth and occupation with Cain's (vv. 1–2) and Abel's offering and God's response with Cain's (vv. 3–5):

A: Cain's birth and naming (v. 1b)
  B: Abel's birth (v. 2a)
  B: Abel's occupation caring for herds (v. 2b)
A: Cain's occupation cultivating the ground (v. 2c)

A: Cain brought an offering from the ground (v. 3)
  B: Abel brought an offering from the flock (v. 4a)
  B: Abel and his offering were accepted (v. 4b)
A: Cain and his offering were not accepted (v. 5)

The structure initially offers hope in Cain (Eve's exclamation), carrying on the cultivation of the ground from Genesis 2 and initiating worship ("at the designated time," 3:3 NET). In an unexpected twist, Yahweh rejected Cain's sacrifice, and Cain reacted in anger. Abel, then, becomes the foil to Cain's response and the necessary background for what will follow as the reader sees the effects of sin in the first family and the resulting alienation from God.

4:1–2. Appropriately introducing the genealogy, Adam's cohabitation draws attention to the initial command of blessing, "be fruitful and multiply" (1:28). The first son born was named "Cain" in a word play on the verb translated to "create."[1] In Eve's exclamation, nearly every word has difficulties that challenge the translation. The verb "I have created" can also be translated "I have gotten" (see Translation Analysis). The semantic range allows both ideas and some ambiguity. The singular use of "man" (the only use of אִישׁ for a baby in the Hebrew Bible) referencing the new birth suggests that she was thinking of either the fulfillment of God's blessing to multiply (1:28) or the reversal of 2:23 as now man comes from woman (Sailhamer 1990, 62–63). Perhaps a double entendre was intended as she saw God's blessing continuing the line of her husband. In addition, the use of her exclamation

1 The terms sound similar but are not lexically related, and the meaning of Cain's name is uncertain.

by the narrator provides another connection to the concluding frame in 4:26, since the last son born in the chapter was named "Enosh" (אֱנוֹשׁ), also meaning "man." The defiling consequences of sin in the intervening verses heighten the importance of humanity's continuation and hope in God's promise.

TRANSLATION ANALYSIS 4:1a
The clause initial waw on the noun ("Now Adam," וְהָאָדָם) signals a new episode in the narrative, providing the opportunity to compare Genesis 4 with Genesis 3 (see below).

TRANSLATION ANALYSIS 4:1b
The translation of the verb is disputed; Eve's use of "man" (אִישׁ) for a newborn is unusual, and whether to take the Hebrew אֶת as a particle (the untranslated marker for the definite direct object) or as a preposition, meaning "with," is also disputed, along with the significance of either. The verb translated "gotten" (ESV, NASB) or "acquired" (NKJV) can also be translated "created" (NET), "brought forth" (NIV), or "produced" (NLT, NRSV). The two main ideas of "create" or "acquire" are both within the semantic range and usage of the Hebrew verb (קנה), and *HALOT* concludes it is impossible to decide between them in this context (p. 1113). Given the context, the distinction need not be too significant, as discussed in the Exposition. The particle (אֶת) can be taken either as the sign of the definite direct object (Kaiser 1978, 79) or as the preposition, translated "with (the help of)" (ESV, NASB, NIV, NLT, NRSV), "from" (NKJV), or "just as" (NET). If it were the sign of the definite direct object, it could suggest that she was connecting this birth to the promised seed that she was already viewing as the promised Messiah and connecting with Yahweh. The construction, however, should be understood as the common preposition "with." The meaning is often understood as "with the help of" the Lord (as ESV, NASB, NIV, NLT). The translation "just as the LORD did" (NET) takes the preposition in the sense of "along with" or "like." The two ideas are not far apart, but if she is thinking of the command of blessing, "with the help of" fits more closely.

Eve celebrated the help of Yahweh in her fulfillment of blessing. Her exclamation presents optimism and excitement in the face of the curse and initiates the genealogy with an expectation of life and fulfilled promise. Her expectation continues with a second birth. This child she named Abel, without explanation, though the name is the common noun for "vapor" or "mist" and is often translated figuratively as "vanity" (used 38 times in Ecclesiastes). Moses immediately informs the reader of the occupations of the boys. Abel was a shepherd (v. 2) while Cain cultivated the ground (v. 3). Though establishing the basis for their offerings, one cannot miss that Cain was doing precisely what Yahweh created humankind to do (2:5) and which was the focus of frustration and painful toil (3:17–19). Fulfilling man's commission, Cain's occupation, then, would seem to add anticipation.

4:3–5. Sometime later, Cain brought some of his produce from the ground as an offering to Yahweh in worship. Abel also brought an offering from his flock. With little discussion, the text records that "the LORD was pleased with Abel and his offering, but with Cain and his offering he was not pleased" (vv. 4–5 NET). Various explanations have been given for God's rejection of Cain and pleasure with Abel.[2] How did the author to the Hebrews know it was not

2 Wenham (1987, 104) summarizes five main explanations for why Cain was rejected: God prefers shepherds, animal sacrifice was more acceptable, it is a mystery of divine election, different motives are known only to God, and a different approach to worship was shown in the quality of their gifts. The first explanation does not fit

of faith (other than revelation—Heb. 11:4)? Because the offering is specified as a *minchah* (מִנְחָה), Israel would expect the sort of offering described in the law as a *minchah*, which appropriately referred to a gift (Gen. 34:14, 19, 21–22) or an offering. When given to God, it commonly referred to fine flour, unleavened bread, or the roasted first fruits of the grain (e.g., Lev. 2:1–16; 5:11–13). For that reason, and because there are no instructions in the context, the issue appears to be the heart of the giver (faith), not animal (or blood) rather than vegetable.

TRANSLATION ANALYSIS 4:3a
"In the course of time" (ESV) is taken more specifically by NET, "At the designated time" (מִקֵּץ יָמִים), literally, "at the end of days." When a specific number is added before "days" in this formula it refers to the end of that specified period (e.g., Gen. 8:6; 41:1; Num. 13:25). Without any indicators in the context and no specific number of days given, it most likely is referring to an unspecified passing of time, as in ESV (cf. NASB, NIV, *Tanakh*) or even the NCV ("later").

Several observations in the immediate context impact the discussion. First, the narrator includes the resulting response of Cain, both in his reaction to God's displeasure with anger (4:5), which he acted out in murder (v. 8), but also in his refusal to respond to God's initial questioning (and do what is right) or to God's later questioning (with honest confession and repentance, vv. 6–8, 9). Clearly the narrator has given the reader a window into Cain's heart, which shows rebellion and self-protecting rather than any faith or humility before God.

Second, Moses carefully describes the offering of Abel as "some of the firstborn of his flock—even the fattest of them" (v. 4, NET). The clear statement that Abel brought the very best (which God expected of Israel in the law) exposes the simple statement that "Cain brought some of the fruit of the ground" (NET) as lacking the intentional excellence that Abel brought. It suggests that Cain was not fully invested in his worship, which the following reaction, both to God's challenge and to his brother, confirms.

TRANSLATION ANALYSIS 4:4a
Two prepositional phrases are joined in the Hebrew Bible: "from the firstborn of his flock" and "from the fat of them." The NET Bible translation reflects taking the second prepositional phrase as grammatically modifying the first and pointing to the best of the best (similarly in the *Tanakh*, "the choicest of the firstlings of his flock"). They could also refer to the firstborn, clarifying that he included their fat portions (so the ESV, "the firstborn of his flock—and of their fat portions"). Or the second phrase could be narrowing the gift to the fat portions of the sacrificial sheep as in the NIV (the "fat portions from some of the firstborn of his flock," compare the NASB, NKJV, NLT).

Finally, God indicated divine pleasure with Abel and with his sacrifice, but not with Cain and his sacrifice. The word order and emphasis on the two men before their offerings is important. By listing the men first in each case, Moses highlights God's pleasure with the individual and their heart, from which the resulting sacrifice is determined acceptable or not. The

the context, since the purpose of man was to care for the ground, as Cain did, a positive even though frustrating activity. As discussed in the exposition, the use of the term *minchah* for the offering puts it into the realm of the grain offering in the law, which was perfectly acceptable. While divine election may be a mystery and motives are only fully known to God, the narrator in the Old Testament often gives insight into those motives, and this text does provide evidence cited in the exposition for understanding the point of the narrative. For more on the reasons for God's rejection, see Waltke (1986).

verb to "gaze" or "look at" (שׁעה), figuratively indicating his pleasure by gazing with favor, does not indicate the actual means by which they understood the outcome of their offering. For Moses's purpose it does not matter. The focus was on Cain and his response. While Genesis does not explain how they knew what was expected any more than how they knew of God's acceptance and rejection, the point of both would have been clear to Israel. They would have immediately related the expectations to the law and understood that God's favor or disfavor could have easily been immediately clear, whether by outward sign (fire from heaven?) or by inward understanding.

Cain clearly understood and reacted with anger. Cain's intense anger, expressed strongly by the common Hebrew idiom "burn" (חרה) plus the adverb "very" (מְאֹד), is outwardly demonstrated when "his face fell" (וַיִּפְּלוּ פָּנָיו), exposing his reaction. Anger, rather than sorrow, revealed his selfish agenda, not pleasing God.

God Graciously Warned and Judged Murderous Cain (4:6–16)

After Cain ignored Yahweh's warning and killed Abel, Yahweh graciously pronounced his judgment, including divine protection.

The scene shifts to Cain and his reaction, focusing on the downward plunge of humanity in sin. Verses 6–16 form a unit as God addressed Cain with warning and judgment, interrupted only for the actual crime (v. 8).

4:6–7. Just as the narrative emphasized that God did not accept Cain and his offering, God's initial questions to Cain addressed the heart first ("why are you angry") and then his appearance. Either Cain did not respond, or God did not wait for a response as he warned against compounding the sin, offering opportunity for a renewal and restoration of relationship. While not defining what was expected, Yahweh stated Cain's opportunity. If Cain would do "well," he would "be accepted." "Be accepted" translates the simple substantive "uplifting" (שְׂאֵת, from נשׂא), referring to lifting or raising the face (Job 11:15) or acceptance with God (cf. 32:20 [HB 32:21]). The following statement more clearly defines the issue. God was not merely looking for a better sacrifice.

TRANSLATION ANALYSIS 4:7a

Hamilton (1990, 225) calls this "one of the hardest verses in Genesis to translate and to understand." The main concerns begin with the noun (or infinitive construct) meaning "uplifting" and typically translated "accepted" (ESV, NIV, NKJV, NLT, NRSV), but in NET Bible "you will be fine." The verb (from נשׂא) can be used for acceptance or forgiveness (Job 10:15; 11:15), assuming "head" as the object. Second, the word for "sin" is feminine (חַטָּאת), but the participle is masculine ("crouching," רֹבֵץ). This term is often related to a Mesopotamian demon that could be either benevolent or malevolent (Speiser 1964). The connection is plausible and fits the cognitive environment of Israel. It would be personifying sin in a form familiar to the audience.

In verse 7b, God voiced his concern that Cain would fall victim to sin, pictured as a destroying demon (see the Translation Analysis). Cain was at a decisive juncture. He must "rule over" the temptation to sin, or he would be destroyed by it. His responsibility is clearly emphasized. Rather than being conquered by sin, resistance to sin with a righteous response would allow victorious living and acceptance with God. The issue, then, was the heart of the worshipper, revealed in the sacrifice and again in Cain's response to the rejection of the sacrifice. In fact, in a disturbing omission, no response from Cain is recorded.

TRANSLATION ANALYSIS 4:7b

The phrases here are nearly identical to 3:16 (see Translation Analysis there) and have similar connotations. The phrase "you must rule over it" can be translated as most translations do (command or strong wish) or as invitation, "you may master it," or even as simple future, perhaps implying promise, "you shall master it," (Hamilton 1990, 228). The first two are most likely, and the clause initial disjunctive with the 2ms pronoun emphasizes Cain and his responsibility.

4:8. Instead, Cain addressed Abel, his brother, as if that was his response to Yahweh. The narrative stresses the crime against a brother, using "brother" six times in the next four verses, including three times without naming Abel. Crimes against a brother will take center stage in Genesis, gaining attention until the climax in the Joseph narratives. At the same time, the motif of revenge against a brother will find resolution in the Joseph narratives in the final chapter as Joseph submits to God's authority (50:19–20). This was not simply murder. It was fratricide.

Failing to understand that God was aware of Cain's heart, emotions, and motivations, Cain rejected God's warning. Instead, he invited Abel out to the field. Cain's reply to Yahweh in verse 9 revealed his presumption that Abel's murder was secret. Rather than rule over the temptation, he had assaulted his brother, thinking he could keep it hidden. His reply also suggests premeditation to the murder, inviting Abel into the field where he was vulnerable.

TRANSLATION ANALYSIS 4:8a

The actual words that Cain spoke are not preserved in the Hebrew text. The request, "Let's go out to the field," used in the NET Bible and the ESV note is taken from the ancient translations (Samaritan Pentateuch, LXX, Vulgate, Syriac, and some Targums). Some modern translations leave the disputed phrase out (e.g., ESV, NASB, NKJV), but this would be the only place in the Hebrew Bible where the verb "to speak" would not have an actual object (Sailhamer 1990, 64). Hamilton (1990, 230) retranslates the verb to mean that Cain was "looking" for Abel, though it is not attested in that way. It is likely that the phrase is missing by copy error. If the invitation is original, it merely spells out what is implied in the otherwise cryptic "Cain said to his brother Abel" without the content. If the invitation was not original, then perhaps the narrator is shortening the dialogue, with the obvious omission, to draw attention to the crime and heighten the implication that Cain's response to God's warning was the assault.

4:9–16. The narrative moves immediately to Yahweh's confrontation with Cain for his fratricide and the ensuing judgment. Justice is swift but surprisingly gracious. The penalty in the law for homicide is consistently death (Exod. 21:12, 14; Num. 35:16–21; Deut. 27:24). The Genesis narrative will arrive at that penalty later, within the context of the Noahic covenant, citing the value of a human life made in God's image (Gen. 9:5–6). With the first murder, however, God not only does not demand his life but protects Cain against blood vengeance (4:15) even while sending Cain into exile.

4:9. God's address to Cain follows a similar pattern to his address to Adam and then Eve after their sin in the garden (also cf. 4:6–7). In both cases he presented questions designed to elicit a response of confession and repentance, but in neither case did he get the desired result. His question clearly does not reflect ignorance, even though Cain naively took it that way. Rather, Cain deceptively pled ignorance and absence of responsibility, even accusing God of failing.

The irony of Cain's response lies in the term he used to deny his responsibility. "Guardian" (NET) provides a much better translation for the term also translated "keeper" (שֹׁמֵר, so ESV, NASB, NIV, NRSV, etc.) and has occurred already in the narrative as man's failed responsibility in the garden (see Translation Analysis at 2:15). Riemann (1970) points out that this is not a social responsibility that we see anywhere in the Old Testament. The appropriate answer to Cain's question was, "Of course not!" Riemann's conclusion, however, that Cain was claiming a tender conscience (p. 491), misses a much more insidious implication. God is called the keeper of man, while no man ever is (e.g., Ps. 121 and the Aaronic prayer in which blessing is to have God "keep" you, Num. 6:24). Cain was, in effect, saying, "Why are you asking me? That is your responsibility!" Of course, this does not deny Cain's responsibility as a murderer, but he is lying, deflecting, and, much as Adam pushed the blame for his sin back on God as the giver of the woman who led him, Cain seems to be saying that if anything has happened to Abel, it must be God's fault, since God is the only one who can "keep" him.

4:10–12. Reminding the reader of his confrontation with Eve, God bluntly responded to Cain. His indirect offer for confession becomes a direct confrontation of guilt with his rhetorical question. Cain would now realize that God did indeed know all about this all along, and his ploy was the foolish attempt of a toddler caught in the act to hide in plain view from a parent. When Yahweh revealed his full knowledge, his words were freighted with significance for Israel. Abel's blood is personified, testifying against Cain for the crime committed. Because blood is the life of the man, it is sacred (Lev. 17:11), pollutes the ground so that it is unfit for God's presence, and must be atoned for (Num. 35:30–34; cf. Ps. 106:38). In this case, God is the judge to whom the blood appeals for justice, which he will mete out.

Cain's punishment fits the crime, as the ground that accepted the polluting blood would then refuse to return its fruit ("best" or, literally, "strength," כֹּחַ) for Cain's labor. The curse on the ground because of Adam's sin made survival painful and frustrating. The curse on Cain because of his sin made living by his skill with the soil impossible. Instead, he would now be "banished," unable to live off the land and so a "fugitive and a wanderer" (Gen 4:12).

TRANSLATION ANALYSIS 4:11

The verb often translated as "cursed" (ESV, NASB, NKJV, NRSV; ארר), both here and in most of its uses, is translated by the NET Bible as "banished" (the NET Bible translates the root as "curse" in the other eight occurrences in Genesis). The term is used in curse formulas frequently in the Old Testament as a means of calling for privation, suffering, or servitude as the opposite of blessing (בְּרָכָה, see Deut. 27–28). Some versions translate the phrase with both the idea of curse and the idea of banishment (NIV, "under a curse and driven from the ground," or NLT, "cursed and banished from the ground"). The problem of translation reflects the interpretive problem of the preposition *min* (מִן) that is included before "ground." The preposition could indicate movement away from, suggesting banishment, or it could indicate the cause or the originator, in which the ground refuses to be fruitful for Cain. Both consequences follow specifically in the narrative, and both work together against Cain. Genesis 4:14 uses the same preposition (in conjunction with a second) with "ground" in which he clearly complains that God has driven him from the ground, supporting the translation of "banished."

TRANSLATION ANALYSIS 4:12

The NET Bible's smoother translation, "homeless wanderer," takes the two participles together as a single idea (*hendiadys*) with one modifying the other, rather than two different, complementary ideas. Other translations similarly try to express this single idea (NIV, "restless wanderer"; *Tanakh*, "ceaseless wanderer").

4:13–14. Cain's reaction now moved from evasion to fear. He stated that his "punishment is greater than I can bear." He was driven from the land and must now hide from the presence of Yahweh (v. 14). Cain echoed Adam and Eve's experience, as God drove him away (cf. 3:24) and he hid from God's presence. In Cain's response to Yahweh, he reiterated the two consequences stated by God (driven from the land and a homeless wanderer) and two consequences that are new to the narrative (hiding from the Lord and fear for his life). Since the second, unstated consequence is Cain's fear for his life, clearly not decreed by Yahweh but a conceivable outcome, it is likely that hiding from Yahweh's presence is also Cain's fear. Certainly, he will feel farther from the presence of God the farther he goes from Eden, since that has been identified as God's sanctuary. Yahweh responded to Cain's fear of retaliation with protection, but he did not respond to his fear of God's presence. Comparing human experience in chapter 3 suggests that Cain did not have to "be hidden" (or fear being hidden) if he would turn in confession and repentance.

TRANSLATION ANALYSIS 4:13

The traditional translation represented in the Exposition has been challenged by John Sailhamer. The noun translated "punishment" (עָוֹן) has a primary meaning of "sin" or "iniquity" but by metonymy can be used of "guilt" (Exod. 20:5) or "punishment" (Jer. 51:6). The verb translated "endure" (נשׂא) can also be used in various ways. When used with sin and guilt it can be understood as to "bear" or "forgive." Sailhamer (1990, 65–66) has argued that Cain was repentant and was stating that his "iniquity is too great to forgive." Given the immediate context—of punishment (v. 12), consequences that he seemed to be concerned about (v. 14), and God's response of protection (v. 15)—the traditional understanding is preferred. Leviticus 5:1, 17 shows a very similar meaning of these two terms together, supporting the traditional sense here.

Cain's concern for blood vengeance has raised questions through the centuries regarding the possible antagonists. The narrative has not mentioned any other offspring of Adam and Eve yet, nor has it given any indication of the amount of time that had passed or how old Cain was at this point. While it is not explicit, the traditional explanation seems to be most likely, that the narrative envisions other offspring of Adam and Eve that will be a possible threat to Cain, as well as providing a woman to marry (4:17).

4:15–16. God's response to Cain's fear included grace, declaring divine protection on the murderer "seven times." Yahweh's use of "seven times" for the vengeance provided complete justice or perhaps divine justice, since seven was often used in the ancient world and in the Old Testament figuratively for completeness (cf. Ps. 79:12; Prov. 6:31). As a guarantee of his word, God put a "special mark on Cain" (v. 15 NET) that would guarantee Cain's divine protection. With this guarantee, Cain left the presence of Yahweh. The narrative sounds an ominous note with the movement east, away from God's presence. This geographical and relational separation continues the movement from the garden (3:24) and the deepening of the consequences of humanity's rebellion.

TRANSLATION ANALYSIS 4:15

Literally, the "mark" is a "sign" (אוֹת), perhaps like Ezekiel 9:4, 6. Given the broad use of "sign" in the Hebrew Bible, it is also possible that God showed Cain some clear and convincing evidence that God would carry out his word, though the purpose clause seems to indicate the physical mark.

The many parallels between Cain's sin and judgment and the initial rebellion in Genesis 3 show the prototypical nature of the initial sins of humanity. The rebellion of Adam and Eve in the garden are being used by Moses as a paradigm of humanity's continuing rebellion.[3] This

3 Hauser (1980) summarizes eight significant parallels between Genesis 2–3 and Genesis 4:1–16, in addition to numerous thematic and linguistic links. While he clearly demonstrates the unity of the overall narrative from

expansion of this genealogy, as well as the last one (4:23–24), focuses on the deadly consequences both among humanity and between humanity and their God.

Cain Fathered Sons, Building a City in His Son's Name (4:17–18)

Far from a homeless wanderer, Cain established a dynasty and built a city in the name of his son, mitigating the curse.

4:17–18. Resuming the genealogy after the long excursus describing Cain's sin and consequences, the notice that Cain "knew his wife" (ידע) parallels the initial notice for Adam in 4:1. Paired with the concluding notice of the line of Seth in 4:25, these frame the account. This notice signals the center of the chiasm and initiates the cultural accomplishments of Cain, from building a city with his first son followed by four generations to Lamech, whose sons establish the arts and technologies.

The section easily divides into two segments. Verses 17–18 present the first five individuals from Cain by name, recording the establishing of a city in the name of the son. Verses 19–22 name six more individuals (two wives, three sons of Lamech, and one daughter) with the cultural achievements connected to the sons. Both the city and the cultural achievements of the descendants summarize the advancement of humanity on the world stage, showing the origins of the advances particularly significant for Israel.

The first section adds the building of the first city to the genealogical framework of Cain. City-building was a common theme in protohistoric accounts in Mesopotamia.[4] The first city in the Sumerian King List came with kingship as a gift of the gods.[5] Yahweh had already given rule to all humanity, but if Cain's genealogy is intended to comment on civilization, including city-building and technology, Cain may be establishing a dynasty as well as a city in opposition to God's established rule. That intent impacts the boast of Lamech as he extended his power. The building of the city also mitigated the judgment of God to be a homeless wanderer, making life more bearable, and establishing Cain's power. Cain would rule, but not over sin (4:7), nor as a functioning representative of God.

Lamech Fathered Sons from Two Wives, Establishing Technology in His Sons' Names (4:19–22)

Lamech extended the benefits of the dynasty, establishing technology through his sons and providing the tainted gifts of culture and civilization to humanity.

4:19–22. The innovation of the cultural achievements by the sons of Lamech appears in the context of blatant disregard for human life and self-exaltation. The achievements add

---

2:4 to 4:26, the many parallels also support the paradigmatic nature of the text, both with the original sin and with the decline of man away from Yahweh, which will continue to the end of the line of Cain. After examining the function of similar accounts across the ancient world, Lowery (2013, 233–35) concludes that these accounts are consistently intended to be archetypal.

4 In the Sumerian King List, the first city where the gods established kingship was Eridu, which is very similar to Irad, Enoch's son in v. 18 (Pritchard 1969, 265). Some scholars have proposed emending the text to say that Enoch built the city and named it after his son, Irad, which would parallel the Mesopotamian tradition (e.g., Cassuto 1978, 230).

5 For a helpful discussion of the background texts and cognitive environment in Mesopotamia surrounding cities and kingship as the gift of the gods, see Lowery (2013, 137–58). The gifts of cities and kingship were considered the beginning of real history because they were the beginning of civilization. In contrast, the biblical narrative presents cities, technology, and kingship as primarily a human endeavor, though God had established humankind to rule his creation.

to the impression that humanity was finding relief from the curse through its own achievements rather than returning to the source of life in Yahweh. The things that made life easier also made independence from God easier (rather than the dependence required in Gen. 2), leading to self-exaltation (Lamech's boast). On the other hand, the sons of Lamech who establish the great cultural achievements are also presented as the end of the line of Cain. They do not have children recorded, and they will perish in the great flood. The line of Cain boasts, and dies, in its independence.

As the structural midpoint of the chapter, we find humankind thriving culturally. However, in the flow of the narrative, the accomplishments are in tension with the pronounced curse and the unresolved sin. The context of rebellion and curse reveals the shallow nature of humanity's triumphs. They are far from the presence of Yahweh and remain under his curse. The cultural successes, then, emerge as humanity's attempts to block the pain of the curse intended to drive humanity back to Yahweh.

Lamech Celebrated Taking Another's Life Without Consequences and Declared His Own Protection (4:23–24)

Lamech publicly celebrated both his excessive revenge, and his role usurped from God, pronouncing absolute vengeance on any attacker.

4:23–24. The narrator inserts a poem into the genealogy, providing a parallel to the initial interpolation in the genealogy in 4:6–16. Not only does the murder of Abel in the initial account form an obvious parallel here but the intrusive use of poetry indicates a significant shift in the heart of the descendants of Cain. The genealogy moves from the sobering account and accountability before Yahweh (with judgement) of Cain for Abel's murder to the concluding self-celebration of Lamech's power and seeming invulnerable status. The loss of human life has moved from a crime and crying out to Yahweh for justice to being applauded and commemorated in song. This is all in the immediate context of Lamech's sons developing the technological advances that provide humanity with such benefits. Humankind has descended steeply into the deadly effects of sin, running from their creator, and their divine creativity has only reinforced their blindness to their need for God.

Lamech's song calls for his two wives, drawing attention again to his polygamy, to share with him in his moment of glory. Lamech's tune revels in exacting overwhelming vengeance against someone who hurt him. Lamech initially referred to his antagonist as a "man" (אִישׁ). Reminding the reader of Eve's proclamation and hope (4:1), the only other use of "man" in this chapter, Moses highlights the degeneration of that hope.

In parallel lines, Lamech pronounced his judgment against "a young man." The crime against him that justified his action included "wounding" and "hurting" (פֶּצַע and חַבּוּרָה) him, two terms that appear in Exodus 21:25 together for appropriate talionic justice. In the law, justice required "wound for wound, bruise for bruise" (פֶּצַע תַּחַת פָּצַע חַבּוּרָה תַּחַת חַבּוּרָה). Here, Lamech has killed a man for these offenses. As Israel understands God's law for them, they would understand an obvious violation of appropriate justice. Whereas God's judgment was gracious to Cain when he murdered Abel, Lamech's vengeance is harsh, excessive, and culpable.

> *TRANSLATION ANALYSIS 4:23*
> The other term, "young man" (יֶלֶד), also translated "boy" (NASB) or "lad" (Tanakh), may not refer to a child (in parallel with אִישׁ). Rather the term may suggest that it was in a formal conflict, perhaps even a "young warrior" (1 Kings 12:8, cf. Hamilton, יָלַד, *NIDOTTE* 2:457). On the other hand, Hamilton (1990, 241) argues in his commentary that these are not intended to be a word pair and that the boast of Lamech is not what he has already done, but what he would do if provoked. He would kill a man or even a

> child if provoked. If this last suggestion is accurate, Lamech's song reveals even more heinous depravity (p. 241).

Lamech added his exclamation point to the obvious violation of justice with his pronouncement of impunity. His hyperbole underscored his seeming immunity. It may express a faulty reasoning that if murder out of jealousy is protected, then vengeance for a tangible offense, even if excessive, warrants far greater protection. What he missed was the value of human life, created in the image of God (9:6). It also suggests that he was in a position of authority to be able to make such a pronouncement, adding to the impression that Cain's genealogy records kings of human civilization and revealing the injustice of humanity as they abandon their commissioning to represent God in their rule (1:26–28).

In the flow of the narrative, however, the fact that he announced his own judgment contrasts with God's pronouncement on Cain (4:11–15) and suggests that he was taking the place of God in his own experience. He was making himself a god, extending the original sin of self-determination of both right and wrong and deciding his own justice (see Exposition on 2:16–17). He was attempting to be like God (3:5, 22), revealing how far his pride and self-justification was from the reality of God's transcendent power and grace. In just seven generations, humanity has moved from dependence to boastful independence, from submission to unapologetic autonomy, from worship as defined by Yahweh (4:3, 5) to self-determined self-worship. Ironically, however, his self-determination is short lived. Lamech is the end of the genealogy of Cain.[6] This is the last to be heard from the line of Cain, with God's judgment destroying all but the four descendants of Seth.

Announcing Hope, Eve Again Bore Sons Leading to Genuine Worship (4:25–26)

Eve bore another son, reigniting hope in God's promise, initiating a new line, replacing what was lost with Abel, and restoring genuine worship.

4:25–26. The concluding section moves from the genealogy of Cain to a new line from Adam in Seth. There are several points of contact with the initial scene in this pericope. Both begin with the nearly identical phrase, "Adam knew his wife" (4:1, 25). While 4:1 specifies Eve, verse 25 adds "again," clearly drawing the attention back to the beginning of the narrative. In both cases Moses records Eve's significant explanation of her optimism, and again, the second statement of Eve in verse 25 also points back to the initial birth of Abel and the subsequent murder. Both sections record the birth of two boys, and in both cases the second birth leads to the expression of acceptable worship (vv. 4, 26). One last detail that connects them is the use of "man" by Eve (אִישׁ in v. 1) and the naming of the last son, Enosh (אֱנוֹשׁ), meaning "man" (v. 26), perhaps adding to the growing return of optimism in God's promise.

The many parallels between the two sections invite comparison and contrast within the flow of the story. In 4:1, Eve was celebrating the birth of a man, but in verse 25 she celebrated the birth of another "child" (זֶרַע or "seed"), drawing attention back not only to the restoration of the lost son, but also suggesting the hope of the promise from 3:15 in which an "offspring" (זֶרַע or "seed") would destroy the snake (see Exposition on 3:15). This last statement seems to have clearer focus on the promise (seed) rather than the general offer of blessing and procreation, including the movement of hope to a line other

6 Hess (1991, 22) suggests that the repetition of the number seven and seventy-seven, along with Lamech's position of seventh in the genealogy and the many references back to Cain here imply what will become obvious in the flood: "the line of Cain comes to an end with this figure."

than the firstborn. Focusing that promise, Eve chose the name Seth, explaining it with the statement that God had "appointed" (שָׁת) another "offspring" (זֶרַע or "seed") in place of Abel. She used a verb that sounds like "Seth," but it is also the verb that God used in 3:15 to express that he would "put" enmity between her seed and the snake's seed. Her words remind the reader of both the enmity, provoked by reference to Abel, and the promise, encapsulated in the new seed.

The pericope concludes with a return to appropriate public "worship" (NET, lit., "to call on the name of Yahweh," לִקְרֹא בְּשֵׁם יְהוָה). This phrase will be used throughout the patriarchal narratives to record the patriarchs' worship of God (12:8; 13:4; 21:33; 26:25), which at times includes sacrifice (correlated with building an altar, 12:8; 21:33; 26:25), prayer (cf. 1 Kings 18:24–26; 2 Kings 5:11; Ps. 116:4; Joel 3:5), and proclamation (cf. Exod. 33:19; 34:5; Ps. 116:13, 17).[7] As public proclamation and worship, it indicates identification or commitment to Yahweh (Isa. 44:5). In drawing attention to the "name" of Yahweh, worship (and hope) must be based in the eternal character of the Creator who made all things good, commanded blessing, and promised hope. His promise will be fulfilled despite the decadence of humankind.

The narrative in Genesis 4, then, has depicted the decline of man away from God, from Cain's rejected worship and jealous murder to Lamech's unrestrained and self-exalting vengeance. Amid this precipitous fall into ruin, humanity established what seemed to be the redeeming qualities of civilization but which only serve to enable their rebellion and self-exaltation. In contrast, real hope (and redemption) finds its initial place in the true worship of Yahweh, the ultimate king.

THEOLOGICAL FOCUS

Profane worship and spurning God threaten his images, bring alienation and judgment from God, and deepen self-protection and self-worship, but God's grace preserves the promise for life through submissive worship.

Hope in God's promise of a conquering descendant frames the deepening catastrophic rebellion of humanity, highlighting their false sense of security and providing a counterfeit relief from the curse in Genesis 4. The initial hope of Eve and her exultation at new birth focused on the general promise of blessing and new life despite death. The very child bringing promise, however, became exhibit A of the power of sin to control and destroy.

If we analyze Cain's profane worship as unwillingness to honor God first and foremost, then it reveals idolatry. He exalts himself over God, planting the seeds of self-worship that come to full flower in Lamech's murder and taunt song. Idolatry and self-worship in both cases devalue and destroy God's images. The longer sin festers, the more grievous it grows. Cain murdered Abel, thus rejecting God's gracious warning, lamenting only his loss of prosperity and security, and giving further evidence to his self-focus. Humanity's unwillingness to listen to God's warnings endangered its future. Not only did Cain allow sin to dominate and destroy without repentance, but in his movement away from God he built a dynasty using his God-given creative abilities to initiate civilization. Beginning with a city and kingship, his line provided technological advances that insulated humanity from the struggle of the curse and their need for God, further empowering their autonomy. Humanity immediately prostituted their God-given blessing and purpose of dominion for their own ends.

---

7 Psalm 116 uses the phrase parallel both to the cry for help (v. 4) and the proclamation of praise (vv. 13, 17), showing the public cultic context (v. 17) and demonstrating the broad implications of the phrase. See also the exposition of Gen. 12:8.

The destructive power unleashed by Eve and Adam's rebellion was only beginning to be seen in the growing distance from Eden, God, and appropriate worship. Human rebellion degenerated from unacceptable worship to blatant self-worship, with humanity usurping God's role as judge over life and declaring their own consequences for sin. That independence would be short lived as the fathers of technology are the last of Cain's line and human achievement ends with judgment.

However, God's grace shines brightly through the narrative, contrasting the downward slide of man away from God. Rather than the expected eye for an eye (as Lamech's song reminds the reader), he warned Cain against the power of sin and then provided gracious consequences, including unexpected protection. Though gracious, his judgment is clearly talionic, so that the ground that drank up Abel's blood refused to support the killer, narrowing the already thin line of survival from the man's initial commission (and Cain's occupation) of serving the ground. The narrative continues to show the longsuffering and faithful nature of God. He allowed humanity to prosper in his rebellion and did not intervene with the proud and autonomous Lamech yet reignited expectation in his promise as Eve continued to bear sons. The expectation now shifts to the promise of the seed of the woman's victory over the snake.

The new child, and Eve's explanation, reminds the reader that God's promise still waits. The expectation crystalized in the actions of the descendants. The hope of the fulfilled promise can only come through relationship with the giver of the promise. Humanity, then, would only find the benefit of the promise through genuine reliance on Yahweh, expressed elegantly in humanity beginning dependent worship based in the character of Yahweh. That worship will only come to full flower through the expected seed as Jesus both fully reveals the Father and the provides the means to walk with him in full communion, blessing, and acceptance.

PREACHING AND TEACHING STRATEGIES

Exegetical and Theological Synthesis

Preparation for a sermon or lesson in Genesis 4 begins with the move from the description of how Abel and Cain worshipped to our own worship. Our worship is conducted within the context of humankind continuing to exist in the aftermath of the initial rebellion. By the grace of God, faith in Christ, and the power of his Spirit, we worship like Abel while fighting against the Cain-like tendencies within us.

Genesis 4:2–5a shows that both men, along with their occupations, could worship God appropriately. More importantly, the verses show us what God considers to be appropriate worship ("Abel also brought of the firstborn of his flock and of their fat portions"). Cain's response to God reveals his heart toward God. God's reply to Cain teaches us about the fight we all have (v. 7, "sin is lurking at the door. Its desire is for you" [my translation]). There is, of course, an organic connection between wrongheaded worship and committing sin.

The narrative highlights a heinous sin and God's unexpected response: "Cain rose up against his brother Abel and killed him" (v. 8). Verses 9–16 display the Lord's grace toward sinners ("And the Lord put a mark on Cain," v. 15) in the midst of another announced curse (v. 11, "you are cursed from the ground": we are all, after all, living "east of Eden"; cf. also 3:24). Here you will want to analyze the direct consequences of sin (compare Cain's original occupation with the cursed situation).

One of the interesting pieces of this narrative is the way in which the development of culture is presented from Cain's family tree. What is a person to do, living life "away from the presence of the LORD" (v. 16)? Part of the answer might be to self-medicate or anesthetize through all our activities, like we see with the accomplishments of Cain's sons. Of course, the family tree also produces the badly bent branch, Lamech, who shows us the natural progression of rebellion against God. His speech to his wives shows how sin and the curse continue to infect humanity (vv. 23–24). Lamech functions as a "go and do otherwise" kind of character in the narrative. Finally, the pericope ends with proper worship occurring as a result of Adam and Eve's son Seth and grandson Enosh (vv. 25–26).

Preaching Idea

By God's grace his people bury Cain-like tendencies at work and worship as God keeps his promise of life alive in a broken world.

Contemporary Connections

What does it mean?

Your listeners will want to know, "What was wrong with Cain and his offering (v. 5)?" Be sure to clear up the confusion with something like, "Cain didn't give God the first and best like Abel did." Explanation is also required at verse 7 and the deadly intent of sin "crouching at the door." You may also want to explain the significance of God's approach to Cain in verse 9, "Where is Abel your brother?" God knew but gave Cain an opportunity to confess and repent. As noted above, you may want to explain the connection between the consequence of sin ("cursed from the ground," v. 11) and Cain's original occupation. Your listeners will also ask the meaning of God's "mark on Cain" (v. 15) and the tragic implications of him choosing to go "away from the presence of the LORD . . . east of Eden" (v. 16).

The section in verses 17–22 provides a fascinating look at the development of human culture, all in the context of Cain's family existing apart from the worship of God. Life goes on, doesn't it? As noted above, we have enough ingenuity to provide our own temporary relief from the curse. It's difficult—impossible even—to feel any need for God and his LifePlus when we are not only seemingly self-sufficient but also seemingly flourishing. The recorded speech of Lamech in verses 23–24 puzzles our listeners, but it's a sign of how sin continues to escalate on earth because of the original rebellion. Finally, your exposition will want to include the meaning and hope contained in verse 26, "At that time people began to call upon the name of the LORD."

Is it true?

One of the places in Genesis 4 that requires some proof is in verse 7. Many of our listeners may not realize how dangerous sin is. Someone once said that sin will always take you further than you are willing to go, keep you longer than you intended to stay, and cost you more than you were willing to pay. True? Help your folks *believe* that sin wants to kill them. Cain killing his brother is prime time for us to attempt to prove that the human heart is this bad. At the time of our contributing to Kerux, the belief on the street is that human beings are inherently good. It might take some work convincing our listeners that Cain-like intent lurks potentially within all of us. It was M'Cheyne (1813–1843) who wrote concerning original or birth sin: "the seeds of all sins are in my heart" (*A Puritan Theology*, 210). Cain and Lamech are proof.

Now what?

You may have a difficult time showing the relevance of worship for living life. Here's where a strong dose of explanation combines with the relevance of "So what?" Everybody worships something or someone, and whether a person worships the God revealed in Genesis is life and death. You've heard it said, "You are what you eat." Well, Scripture is also clear in revealing that we are what we worship (cf. Pss. 115:4–8; 135:15–18). Then, if it's true that "sin is crouching at the door" of everyone's house, nothing can be more relevant than preparing oneself for intense encounters.

Since we want to help our listeners *believe* that sin wants to kill them, we also want to help them *want to* avoid sin at all costs. Surely, we "must rule over it" (v. 7). During the writing of this section of Kerux, I drove to downtown Manhattan in New York City, arriving just before 5:00 p.m. For approximately one hour the streets teemed with fast-paced pedestrians headed for their rides to get back home. Like Cain's son, Enoch, and his family, many of them were enjoying city life and all their created culture with no apparent sense of loss from being away from the presence of God. Finally, the action of calling "upon the name of the LORD" (v. 26) needs to be adopted by all who gather for worship.

Creativity in Presentation

Our homiletical idea for this pericope is: by God's grace his people bury Cain-like tendencies at work and worship, keeping the promise of life alive in a broken world.

You might consider the following elements or thought-blocks in the sermon:

- Two kinds of worshippers (Cain and Abel): what is acceptable to God in worship and what is not
- The results of not worshipping well (God's announcement to Cain about sin's intention)
- Making sure we worship well (fleshing out how to follow Abel and the Sethites' example, including possibly exploring New Testament references to both men's spiritual condition)

To achieve this end following the flow of the narrative, consider introducing the story with the problem of understanding our own hearts and evaluating our own worship for what is acceptable to God. Then follow the narrative tension regarding worship:

- New life, new worship, new hope (vv. 1–4a)! Eve's expectation, Cain's occupation, and the immediate worship provides hope God is soon going to accomplish his promises and destroy evil.
- Warning, conflict, and death: the heart of the matter (vv. 4b–16). God's response shows his grace amid serious trouble, while Cain's response and the clues from the previous section show the real issue: the empty heart claiming worship.
- Cities, technology, and kingship: the medicated death spiral (vv. 17–24). Humanity tries to solve their problems by easing the pain and providing alternatives to God's blessing and presence, only taking them farther from him. The progression here shows Cain and his line's movement from false worship to self-protection to self-promotion to self-worship. All this ends in death.
- New life, new worship, real hope (vv. 25–26). Worship frames the narrative, providing hope and the real solution. Between, humanity spirals out of control apart from God. Verse 24 is the end of the line of Cain (think flood). Life is only found in submission to God, appropriately proclaimed in public worship.

If you decide to preach the chapter in two sermons, the second sermon could highlight the contrast between Cain's family and what it produces and Seth's family (Abel's replacement in the line of the "seed of the woman," vv. 17–26). As is often the case, the narrative invites your congregants or students to find themselves in one of these two categories.

As I mentioned above in the "Now what?" section, some illustrations or images and sounds of the hustle and bustle of city life will help bring the middle section of chapter 4 alive. All this cultural activity works like anesthesia to deaden the effects of the curse. The section on verses 23–24 and Lamech's speech to his wives is a good opportunity to use statistics of violence and war in our world. There are more Lamechs in our world than we realize!

Finally, this sermon/lesson contains a strong dose of the grace of God, from his approach to and treatment of Cain to his allowing Seth and his grandson to be born and giving people faith to begin to call upon him for help. We see also the faithfulness of God in keeping his promise alive in the line of Seth (Eve's statement). If you're interested in reading Genesis 4 in light of its canonical context, you will enjoy reminding your listeners how God provided victory over sin through the sacrifice of his Son, the Lord Jesus Christ, and the provision of his Holy Spirit to all who believe.

DISCUSSION QUESTIONS

1. Why does humankind naturally include worship as a part of life?
2. What is it about the nature of God that requires worship from his creatures?
3. What makes worship acceptable to God, and what makes it unacceptable?
4. On a scale of one to five, take a moment to rate your current Christian experience ruling over the sins that plague you most often (one being very successful and five being mostly failure).
5. What do we use to deaden our need for God in our lives?
6. How can we expose the idolatry in our hearts and restore a thirst for real blessing and the presence of God?

Genesis 5:1–6:8

EXEGETICAL IDEA

God's blessed images, inheriting death through Adam, used God's gracious empowerment to further their domination and destruction of his good creation, leading to judgment though God graciously extended life and relief to those who would walk with him.

THEOLOGICAL FOCUS

God's blessed images, inheriting death through Adam, use God's empowering to deepen their destructiveness, leading to judgment, but God graciously extends life and relief to those who walk with him.

PREACHING IDEA

Following Enoch and Noah, God's people walk with him, finding favor and avoiding his judgment on our wicked world.

PREACHING POINTERS

It doesn't take long in chapter 5 before we see opportunities to transition from the original audience of Genesis to our listeners. Verse 1 provides a reminder that God created man "in the likeness of God," and verse 3 includes the concept of Adam fathering "a son in his own likeness, after his image." Everyone sitting in your sanctuary or classroom is also made in both images. But let's be honest: no one, including you, will think that the repetition of names and ages is exciting, except for the huge lifespans. The repetition of "and he died" throughout the chapter certainly shows that disobedience to the Lord's commands results in death (cf. 2:17). So, you will probably want to pick your spots carefully while covering this section. I suggest picking up on the hope tucked away in all that death. Important places to pause are verse 24 and the description of Enoch walking with God before disappearing and at verse 29 with Noah's important name. Then in 6:1–8 you can describe for your listeners the depth of human depravity. This is certainly humankind at its worst, according to the Lord's assessment in 6:5. On top of that is the opportunity to show that the Lord judges human wickedness because of what it does to his good creation. Finally, every listener will be relieved to find Noah finding "favor in the eyes of the Lord" (v. 8). And you will look forward to making sure each of them is in the same boat.

WAY OF LIFE CHOICES: DEATH OR LIFE (5:1–6:8)

LITERARY STRUCTURE AND THEMES

Genesis 5:1–6:8 forms the third section of Genesis, following the introduction (1:1–2:3) and the first *toledot* section (2:4–3:24, see introductory *Structure of Genesis*). While it has become common to treat the genealogy in chapter 5 and the difficult narrative in 6:1–8 as independent sections, and they can be profitably preached that way, they function in the book as a unity, and we have chosen to keep them together to see the message of the whole.

The *toledot* begins with an introduction that rehearses the initial creation of humankind and begins a new genealogy (5:1–2). It then fleshes out the genealogy previewed at the end of chapter 4, adding the express outworking of the stated blessing (repeated, "other sons and daughters") and the curse (repeated, "and he died"), along with two statements of hope in Enoch (5:21–24) and Lamech (5:28–31). The *toledot* concludes with growing violence and devastation (6:1–2, 5; cf. 6:11–12), bringing God's announcement of coming calamity yet grace (6:7–8). God's creation of humanity (5:1–2) and judgment on his creation (6:1–8) frames the narrative, underlining the unity and connecting Genesis 1–4 with the judgment to follow.

A. God created and blessed his images (5:1–2).
   B. Humanity grew through blessing amidst cursing, with hope (5:3–32).
A'. God declared coming judgment with grace on his rebellious images (6:1–8).

As we might expect with a parallel genealogy to Genesis 4, the themes also parallel the previous *toledot*. God's blessing works out in the background with the fruitful multiplication of humankind, yet corruption grows. The curse punctuates each generation with death, emphasized with its steady repetition, yet hope is clearly highlighted in the life of Enoch and the words of Noah's father Lamech. Their experience and proclamation illustrate the means for finding relief from death in the presence of God, fleshing out the hint of hope at the end of Genesis 4. While noting the creation of humanity and alluding to the sin in the garden, the narrative concludes with the deepening decadence of humankind requiring God's intervention. Grace shines brightly against the backdrop of (nearly) universal death and the announcement of God's (almost) total judgment.

- ***God Created and Blessed His Images (5:1–2)***
- ***Humanity Grew Through Blessing Amidst Cursing, Yet with Hope (5:3–32)***
- ***God Declared Coming Judgment with Grace on His Rebellious Images (6:1–8)***

EXPOSITION

Genesis 5 reiterates and expands Seth's preview in chapter 4 and requires further comparison with Cain's genealogy (4:1–24). The similarities of the initial two *toledot* sections, however, go beyond the genealogical comparison to the entire flow. Both sections:

- begin with a look back at creation and give specific mention of the creation of man (2:4–6; 5:1–2);
- recap a climactic scene from the previous pericope (creation of man and

woman, 2:7, 22; birth of Seth and his son, 5:3–8);
- use a genealogy to show the outworking of the tension between blessing and the consequences of sin (deepening rebellion yet blessed with procreation and creative technology, 4:1–24; image of God and fruitfulness yet experiencing death, 5:3–32);
- include a summary statement of the intensified rebellion and evil that cries out for judgment (Lamech's boast, 4:23–24; and the sons of God and daughters of men, 6:1–4);
- conclude with chronological regression to the beginning of the immediately preceding genealogy (4:25–26; 6:1–4); and
- close with hope based on faithfully pursuing God (4:26; 6:8).

Both the relation to the creation account and the comparison with Cain's genealogy impact the message that Moses was intending for the reader. The reference to initial creation raises the expectations for God's images, reminding the reader of their responsibility to represent God well in their rule over creation (see Exposition on image of God in 1:26–27, p. 88), yet with the added consequences of sin in consistent death. The contrast with Cain's genealogy will highlight the source of hope in walking with God and in his gracious promise, as well as intensify the devastation and violence God sees growing in humanity.

The observations on the flow of the narrative underline the unity of the passage and the need to treat it together with one cohesive message. The unity of the pericope is reinforced by significant repetition of key words throughout 5:1–6:8, and the incomplete nature of the narrative at 5:32 (Wenham 1987, 121, 136). When 6:1 returns to the beginning of the expansion of humankind (5:3–32) it is not a surprise, but it encapsulates the need for the coming judgment on the growing destruction despite blessing and hope. God's blessed images, inheriting death through Adam, typically used God's gracious empowerment to further their domination and destruction of his good creation, leadng to judgment. God, however, graciously extended life and relief to those who would walk with him.

God Created and Blessed His Images (5:1–2)

The family history of humanity begins with God producing his blessed likeness.

5:1a. Genesis 5 begins with a variation on the *toledot* formula, identifying the beginning of a new section. As with the initial *toledot* section (2:4–4:26), Moses returns to the creation of man. This history (or "book of the generations," *sepher toledot*, 5:1) initiates the family history of all humanity to follow, as God's images. Genesis 5 anticipates the outcome of the pericope and the following *toledot*, that all future humanity will trace its lineage back to Adam through Seth because all other lines end in the flood.

TRANSLATION ANALYSIS 5:1

The text adds "book" (ESV, NASB, NKJV) to the typical toledot formula (also translated "record" [NET], "written account" [NIV, NLT], or "list" [NRSV]). The generally assumed reason for the addition, as reflected in the translations, is that this was a written genealogy used by the editor in the writing of Genesis. It may suggest the presence of other written accounts as well.

TRANSLATION ANALYSIS 5:1–2

The same Hebrew term (אָדָם) can be used as the proper name for Adam or as the general noun translated "man," "human," "humankind," and the like. Usually, it is understood generically when it has the definite article (so most of the occurrences in Gen. 1) and as the proper name when it is used without the article (e.g., 4:25; 5:3, 4, 5). In Genesis 5:1–2, however, it occurs three times without the article, and yet in verse 2 it is clearly intended to be generic, referring to both "male and female." In the following verses it is just as clearly referring to the specific human, Adam. Modern translations, then, have a variety of wordings but translate it specifically in the first use as the family line or generations of "Adam" (5:1a) but generically in the other two uses of 5:1b–2. The impact of the ambiguity relates the creation and image of God to all humans, whether male or female, and traces them all back to God through Adam.

5:1b–2. Referring to the initial creation, Moses now describes God as the progenitor of his human creation. Moses inserts God into Adam's genealogy. Just as Adam fathers a son in his image and names him, so God has fathered a son and daughter in his image and named them. The transmission, then, of the image of Adam (including death) to each descendant also transmits the image of God (stressing man's responsibility to represent God well in their rule over his creation, 1:26–27). Both will be significant in the following narratives. Just as each son and daughter carries the image of his or her father (and mother), so all humanity (men and women) carries the images of their earthly parents and their heavenly father, implying value and responsibility but also resulting in consistent death. People benefit from God's blessing on the human family (God's empowering to accomplish his purpose, here as bearing sons and daughters), yet each generation dies. Both images have tragic and ironic implications for the destructive actions of humanity in chapter 6 and the pain humankind's rebellion caused to their Creator father as humanity exploits their opportunity for evil purposes.

The family history of Adam, however, will describe the results of the catastrophe of Genesis 3–4. As this genealogy (and narrative) traces the results of blessing and cursing (procreation and death), the reader will see the pervasive destructive effects of humanity until God must step in and stop the madness. Yet there is still hope, as God's grace toward Noah will narrow the promise of the seed from 3:15 to one of the descendants of Noah.

Humanity Grew Through Blessing Amidst Cursing, Yet with Hope (5:3–32)

Humankind reproduced their likeness experiencing blessing (multiplying generations) amidst cursing (inexorable death), finding hope for relief in walking with God.

5:3–5. God's created image procreated his own son "in his own likeness, according to his image" echoing the wording of Genesis 1:26. What God initiated, man reproduced by God's enabling blessing, with multiple copies! The careful wording of Adam's offspring imitating the wording of 1:26–27 ("in his own likeness, after his image") points the reader to the image of God being passed down but now including the fallenness of Adam. Each succeeding generation continued to reproduce their own copies. Just as God named his images, so Adam named his image. God had, however, also pronounced the judgment on sin even before the act ("you will surely die," 2:17). Humankind consistently experienced the effects of that sin as each generation died. Genesis 5 reflects the outworking of God's effective blessing and cursing in both fruitful multiplication and certain death.

Genesis 5 records ten generations with a nearly consistent pattern of six clauses in three sets of two:

A lived X years and he fathered B.
A lived Y more years and he had other sons and daughters.
A lived a total of (X+Y) years and he died.

Of the ten generations from Adam to Noah, four of them deviate from the pattern: Adam, Enoch, Lamech, and Noah. Adam deviates significantly only in the second and third clauses of the first set, though there are minor deviations in both the second and third sets. In the first set, the narrative recalls the creation account as Adam bore a son "in his own likeness, according to his image" and imitated the work of God in verse 2 when he named his son Seth (v. 3). These significant deviations tie the ongoing proliferation of man to the initial work of God in creating and blessing man in his likeness. Noah, of course, is the final generation, although the final two sets of clauses to complete Noah's generation are not in Genesis 5; they are in Genesis 9:28–29 after the narrative of the flood. The two variant generations in between Adam and Noah, Enoch and Lamech, are curiously both duplicate names from Cain's genealogy and both very significant for the message of the genealogy. Not only does the extended description for each of them distinguish them from Cain's descendants, but they also provide much of the point of the genealogy.

5:6–20. Each of the second through sixth generations after Adam follows the pattern precisely. The only variations are the numbers of years and the names of the individuals. The long lifespans of the antediluvian ancestors have produced a lot of speculation, but the interpretation of the large numbers is uncertain. While we cannot deal with all the specific arguments[1] here, some basic observations provide important implications.

Long Ages

The views on the long ages generally take one of three main approaches: an idealization of some ancient time, straightforwardly literal, or representative of whole family units in which the span of the whole clan is listed rather than the individual (Sailhamer 1990, 72). Other generally figurative positions have been suggested, such as seeing the numbers as representing a sexagesimal system or some system or significance lost in history to us.

The long lifespans of this line would have reminded an ancient audience of the Sumerian King List (SKL)[2] or one of the other similar lists. Often compared to Genesis 5, the SKL presents eight kings (some other lists have ten), ruling in five cities from the time "kingship was lowered from heaven" to a great flood (Pritchard 1969, 265). The length of those reigns is significantly longer than the ages in Genesis 5, ranging from 18,600 years to 43,200 years. While the specifics are substantially different, the general flow of the SKL includes a listing of long-lived kings, a flood, and more kings following. The similarities suggest that the early audience may have assumed that the genealogy of Seth was a royal lineage as well. If so, the implications will become apparent as we consider Genesis 6.

1 It is hard to be too dogmatic on the specific numbers since the MT, the Samaritan Pentateuch, and the Septuagint vary widely on the numbers reported. Even beyond that, there are indications that they are not intended literally. The parallel but astronomically large numbers of the Sumerian King List (and others) for the antediluvian kings would have set a precedent for how to understand these. Lowery (2013, 183) has noted that "most would agree" that the large numbers in the ancient antediluvian king lists were not intended literally even though the purpose is not clear. The common literary device of recording ten generations, even when some must be left out to do so, suggests other purposes (also evident in Genesis 11). Even if these individuals are intended as a specific line of descent, they most likely allow gaps in the genealogy (Steinmann 2017).

2 Both the Cain and the Seth genealogies present some similar constructions and conceptual parallels to the SKL. See Preaching Unit 4, Genesis 4:17–22 and notes 4–5 (p. 146). The purpose for the SKL was to defend the legitimacy of Utu-hegal, king of Uruk, by presenting the gift of kingship from the gods and tracing the movement of legitimate kingship (Pritchard 1969, 265). Hess (1989, 250) notes the significant differences in form and function of the ANE lists compared to the biblical lists, leading to caution with conclusions for Genesis from them.

5:21–24. The seventh generation records the second individual named Enoch. Distinguishing this Enoch from the son of Cain (4:17), the narrator includes significant descriptive material. This additional material deviates from the pattern in both the second set of clauses and the third set of clauses, which work together to frame the message. In 5:22, instead of saying he "lived" (וַיְחִי, repeated in eight of the ten generations) for three hundred years, as the pattern would expect, Enoch "walked with God" for three hundred years. In 5:24, instead of simply dying, as the pattern predicts, the text repeats that "Enoch walked with God" and then states that "he was not, for God took him." In a genealogy dominated by the death of each descendant, experiencing the consequence of sin (2:17), Enoch is unique. Both his walking with God (repeated twice) in contrast to merely "living" like everyone else and his connection to God who "took him" suggest a far more significant end to life and consequence of a life of faithful fellowship with God. Life and hope for humanity from the curse of death and pain is not found in merely "living" but in walking with God.

TRANSLATION ANALYSIS 5:24

The translations are consistent in understanding Enoch's fate to be one of God taking him into eternity, with the implication that he did not have to die. The Hebrew text is cryptic, with the simple negative usually indicating non-existence (אַיִן) and the 3ms pronominal suffix "he was not" (ESV, NASB, NKJV) or "he was no more" (NIV, NRSV). The idea that someone "is no more" (אַיִן) can mean death (Gen. 42:13, 32, 36), though it is a circumlocution since the idea is probably not being present (Gen. 42:36, referring to Simeon). "God took" a person can be used of simply relocating that person (Gen. 2:15; 24:7) or specifically of relocating him to heaven (2 Kings 2:3 [cf. 2:1, 9–11]). The implication that Enoch disappeared and was translated bodily apart from death makes the best sense of this structural and theological contrast in the genealogy.

The idea of walking with God was behind the scenes already in the garden but will stand out boldly with both Enoch and Noah. Noah, who "walked with God" (6:9), found grace when all humanity was judged, supporting the significance, already illustrated with Enoch, of life instead of death. With Enoch, then, walking with God led to relief from death. With Noah, walking with God led to grace and life instead of judgment and death. With Abraham, the promise of walking with God was the blessing God had been holding out to him and, through him, to humanity.

All this centers in the presence of God. His presence brings blessing, and his absence means cursing. People had been driven from the garden, the sacred space and God's dwelling (and Cain from God himself, 4:14, 16) but hope regained traction in real worship of Yahweh as humankind called on the name of the Lord (4:26). Hope is now displayed as rooted in walking with God. The meaning of walking with God is not explained, even though it is a deeply significant phrase in Genesis. The main idea, however, is clear. As with two people who walk together, it implies accompaniment, presence, and often aid or companionship. It intimates communion and fellowship and common direction and purpose, as well as relationship—enjoying and thriving in the presence of God. The implication of "God took him" includes the movement of Enoch from this world into the presence of God. God bypassed the normal rule of death based on (as seen in the repetition) Enoch's life of living in fellowship and pleasing disposition with God. Of course, as Genesis develops, that will only be done by faith.

To Walk With

While "walk with" someone (הלך + אֵת) occurs forty-six times in the Old Testament, it occurs these three times of Enoch and Noah with God, suggesting a unique relationship and underlining the opportunity for hope and life. It occurs once more of God's expectations that all the priests would walk with God in "peace and integrity" (Mal. 2:6) and once with the preposition *'im* (עִם) for God's expectations for all people to "live obediently before" him (Mic. 6:8). Similarly, however, Abraham is called to "walk before" God and be blameless (Gen. 17:1, using the same verb but the compound preposition לִפְנֵי), which he does (Gen. 24:40; 48:15). The general use of this combination typically indicates the idea of living in the view, presence, or sight of someone and is used consistently of faithfulness before Yahweh (1 Kings 2:4) or living under his favor (1 Sam. 2:30). The implication is one of loyalty to his king (Sarna 1989, 123). While the two phrases are similar and prominent in Genesis, the initial phrase here seems to focus more on the intimacy while the second highlights their accountability. Enoch was clearly a godly saint, embodying the ideal intimacy with God. His short life (365 years!) perhaps highlights the pain of living (Gen. 5:29) and the preference for the presence of God (Phil. 1:22–24). The significance of the specific number is uncertain.

It is difficult to miss the direct contrast with the seventh generation from Adam through Cain. Lamech was a god unto himself, reminding the reader of Adam and Eve's sin in the garden. He attempted to declare his own security, but ironically, he and his line did not go beyond his sons being swallowed up in the flood. In contrast, the seventh from Adam through Seth moved from this troubled world into the presence of God.

5:25–32. The eighth generation, Methuselah (well known for his length of life), follows the script of the genealogy, but the ninth, Lamech, does not, deviating in the first set of clauses (5:28). As with Enoch, the genealogy of Cain also names a Lamech (the seventh and extended generation from Adam, 4:19–24). As with Lamech in Genesis 4, this Lamech also speaks. In Cain's genealogy, Lamech was the apex of hubris, independence, and self-worship. The Lamech of Seth's genealogy, however, articulates hope in the working of Yahweh to bring relief from the curse on the ground with Noah. Here the hope is for relief from God's pronouncement in 3:17–19, referring both to the curse on the ground (הָאֲדָמָה אֲשֶׁר אֵרְרָהּ יְהוָה) and to the pain as a result (וּמֵעִצְּבוֹן).

Noah's name (נֹחַ), though possibly not related, sounds like the Hebrew noun for rest (נוֹחַ, used only a few times late in the Hebrew Bible) and the common verbal root (נוח), which is used of "rest" among other translations (e.g., Deut. 3:20). Moses does not connect the two here, however, but rather connects it with the root *nhm* (נחם). With the same first two consonants, this becomes prominent in Genesis 6 where, rather than "relief" (5:29), it indicates the pain and grief in the heart of God caused by humanity's sin (6:6–7). It becomes an ironic twist to the hopes of Lamech that the "relief" experienced is really the judgment on the evil-doers and the deliverance of the righteous into a new world.

The tenth generation (Noah) only begins the pattern of Genesis 5, finishing the pattern in the next *toledot* in 9:28–29 with Noah's longevity and death. On the other hand, the genealogy concludes with three sons, paralleling the genealogies of Genesis 4 and Genesis 11. Genesis 10 follows each of the three lines of Noah's sons after the narrative of the flood and its aftermath, anchoring this genealogy in the greater flow and message of the larger narrative. The sin of humanity in 6:1–8 and the judgment of the flood, with its resolution in the Noahic covenant (ch. 9), are not independent stories but part of the larger tapestry, weaving together the necessary background for God's overarching plan to redeem his damaged creation.

Up to this point, then, the genealogy has drawn intentional comparisons with the genealogy of Cain, contrasting the development of pride and rebellion with dependence, faith, and hope in Yahweh's working. Each generation strongly highlights the certainty of death so that Enoch's surprising life shines brilliantly in the darkness. The futile technological achievements of three descendants in Cain's line contrast with the faith and resulting life of three in Seth's line. It seems as if all is going well, and humankind is on the verge of a breakthrough to life in God's presence. The three in Genesis 5, however, turn out to be exceptions rather than examples of a growing norm. Genesis 6:1–8 restores reality, succinctly describing the ruined state of humanity and the coming and necessary cleansing of the earth.

God Declared Coming Judgment with Grace on His Rebellious Images (6:1–8)

When the burgeoning human population only destroyed God's good creation, God sorrowfully declared their destruction, while Noah found grace.

The final section of this *toledot* forms the bridge to the flood narrative, but it also draws the reader's attention back to the beginning of creation and the previous genealogies in several ways. The unity of these eight verses is undercut by their difficulty in interpretation, but these verses are important for understanding the message of the whole pericope.[3] Without these verses, the reader would have no clear reason for the flood narrative that follows and how it flows from the previous narratives. Humanity seemed to be redeeming their freefall away from God through the positive actions of some of Seth's descendants.

Limits for Growing Oppression (6:1–4)

The growing population empowered increasing oppression by human rulers, requiring God to limit man in his evil.

6:1. "When man began to multiply . . . and daughters were born to them" immediately draws the reader back to the initial blessing on humanity to multiply (1:28) and the recapitulation at the beginning of the genealogy (5:2). God's blessing of multiplication grows with each succeeding generation that "had other sons and daughters" (5:4, 7, 10, 13, 16, 19, 22, 26, 30), the first mention of "daughters" in Genesis. Genesis 6:1 sets the context for the subsequent comments on the moral state of humankind through Genesis 5, moving from what had seemed hopeful in the tension between blessing and cursing and hope in faith to the tragic multiplication of rebellious humans. To understand the much-debated questions of who the sons of God and daughters of men are we need to notice that Moses reached back to the beginning of human procreation. The outworking of God's blessing leads to the crisis of evil. Genesis 6 is not subsequent to Genesis 5 but goes back to the beginning, again.

6:2. Who were the "sons of God" and the "daughters of man," and what did they do that was so heinous? The terse nature of the text and level of ambiguity make the interpretation uncertain, but the general thrust is clear. Beginning with the immediate context, and recognizing Genesis 6:1–8 as the conclusion to the *toledot* begun in 5:1 rather than the introduction to the flood narrative (though it certainly bridges to what is coming), the narrative appears in a new light. The narrator has constructed the genealogy with God as the initial Creator and forebear (5:1–2), casting the whole line as "sons of God." As well, noting that "daughters" do not appear in Genesis until 5:4 and that "daughters of men" is not only a natural way to refer to them, including the reference in 6:1, but a common way of saying "human daughters," it would seem straightforward to see this as a reference to the taking of wives for these men, the normal course of events.

---

3 Fockner (2008) strongly supports the unity of the section and its place in the context, arguing for the need for understanding this context to understand the identity and role of the sons of God and daughters of men in the pericope. He notes the cohesion and helpfully shows general parallels between 1–4 and 5–9, as well as the *inclusio* binding it together ("on the face of the land," vv. 1, 7, עַל־פְּנֵי הָאֲדָמָה).

The Sons of God

There are three main views that have been prominent over the centuries. 1. Taking clues from the preceding two genealogies, some have argued for the sons of God being the (more) godly line of Seth, descending from God (5:1–2), and the daughters of man being the fleshly humans from Cain (Gen. 4), with the sin being intermixing of faith with unbelievers, strongly defended by Fockner (2008), among others. 2. Others have noted the usage of "sons of God" in passages like Job 1:6 and 2:1 to refer to angels and, correlating that with 1 Enoch and the possible references in Jude 6 or 2 Peter 2:4, they interpret these to be angels, gods, or demigods intermarrying with human women. This is often also correlated with ancient mythical notions of deities cohabiting with women to produce hero offspring. Westermann (1994, 371) considers the conversation "closed" and the identity as non-human certain and only challenged with preconceived bias (cf. Heiser 2015, 101–9). 3. Still others see the sons of God as human rulers, taking the phrase from the common ancient Near Eastern designation of kings as sons of the god and seeing parallels with the Sumerian King List, as well as the Davidic covenant in which the Davidic king is the son of God (2 Sam. 7:14; Pss 2:7; 89:26–27; cf. Walton, "Sons of God, Daughters of Man," *DOTP* 793–98). We will argue for a variation on the third view.

The view tentatively held here relies on the context, both in the immediate text and in the ancient world. Despite the widespread support among many scholars and the lexical support from Job, the angel or divine counsel view seems less likely for several reasons. The judgment is solely on humanity with no mention of judgment on other-worldly beings. As with God's judgment on the snake (see Gen. 3), the reader may expect judgment on all involved in the evil. While there are later myths of intermarriage between gods and humans, to this point Akkadian and Northwest Semitic literature give no examples of such activity (Walton 2009a, 43–44). The main reason for the angel view historically seems to be the cryptic mention in Jude 6 and 2 Peter 2:4, along with the intertestamental literature, including Enoch. The lines of Cain and Abel or intermarriage of believers and unbelievers view is also possible but less likely because the section is particularly concluding the *toledot* of Adam. The mixing of believers and unbelievers would certainly be relevant to the original audience, but it is not clear in the text or immediate context. As noted in the exegesis, the beginning of the genealogy (5:1–3) suggests "sons of God" may even be immediately referring to this genealogy, and the language of the Old Testament can refer to kings as such (especially the Davidic covenant). Divine descent of kings as a rhetorical device for legitimization of the king is common in the ancient world, even though they do not typically refer to "sons of God" as a group (Walton, "Sons of God, Daughters of Man," *DOTP*, 797). Walton provides a helpful overview of the views, evidence in the literature and ancient world, and problems of clear identification (pp. 793–98). If it is intending human despots, as we think likely, the references in Jude and 2 Peter may be referring to another incident, or they may be seeing this as an outworking of the cosmic battle begun in Genesis 3, as these despots are demonized and enabled by demonic forces to defy God's boundaries (Ross 2008, 68). Though some do not see this as an evil act at all (Sailhamer 1990, 77), the question of their identification remains.

If the implication of the comparison with the Sumerian King List is accurate, these are royal and powerful figures. While these may not actually be "kings" per se (or at least the text does not present them as such), they are "royal" since they are of the line of Adam, who has been commissioned to rule over God's creation (Gen. 1:26, 28).[4] This implication is buttressed by the use of the epithet for kings in the ancient world and the later relation of the Davidic king to Yahweh (2 Sam. 7:14; Ps. 89:24–26).[5] The characterization of the men as "sons of God" by the narrator may emphasize the power of these men, providing a clue to the nature of the crime. Drawing attention to the women as daughters of men indicates both their general human status and perhaps shows their vulnerability to powerful men. The result is growing power for the offspring, as 6:4 indicates, both with the shadowy reference to the Nephilim and by describing the offspring of these unions as "mighty heroes" (הַגִּבֹּרִים) and "famous men" (אַנְשֵׁי הַשֵּׁם, 6:4). As such, these men were neither supernatural nor God's gifts to humanity but supernaturally empowered oppressors of God's images.[6]

The wording in verse 2 suggests trouble. These men "saw (וַיִּרְאוּ) that the daughters of humankind were beautiful (טֹבֹת)" (NET), reminding the reader both of God's evaluation of his creation (1:4, 10, 12, 18, 21, 25, 31) and of the woman's temptation (3:6). When the narrative adds that "they took (וַיִּקְחוּ) wives for themselves," the attention shifts to the woman who also took (וַתִּקַּח) from the fruit in rebellion. Perhaps the comparison with Pharaoh taking Sarah is helpful here as well. The princes of Pharoah saw her beauty (12:15), and Pharoah took her into his house so that God judged him because she was Abraham's wife (v. 12:17). The final relative clause seems to record the problem, but it is ambiguous, qualifying their procuring "from any they chose" (6:2 NET). Did they create harems with multiple wives or oppress unwilling women by taking the best for themselves without concern for the people involved? The framing of these powerful men as "sons of God" adds to the impression of their overwhelming power, which is being wielded destructively. The stated purpose of humanity as God's images to rule as his representatives makes this particularly heinous (1:26–28). The specific implications are far from clear, but God's response indicates a growing rebellion and evil that must be addressed.

6:3. God's response presents numerous challenges, but the overall message is generally clear. Yahweh reflects on the actions of humanity and concludes that he must put limits on their lives. This deliberation is similar to Yahweh's reflection after the sin in the garden when he removed humanity from the garden (cf. Westermann 1994, 374). Here, Yahweh declares that his "spirit will not remain in humankind indefinitely" (NET). The translation and the intent to end human life in judgment (6:5–7) fit the context of God's subsequent actions. Humankind is "mortal" or "flesh" (בָּשָׂר), requiring God's sustaining (Ps. 78:39). He would remove that sustenance so humanity would die.

TRANSLATION ANALYSIS 6:3a

The main problem in verse 3 is identifying Yahweh's threat that his spirit would not "abide (יָדוֹן) in man forever." The Hebrew verbal form is unique in the Hebrew Old Testament. Some versions interpret the root to be from the common

4 Hess (1989) helpfully warns against making too close of a comparison with the king lists without realizing the differences, and Alexander (1993) notes that these genealogies are not intending to deal with kings overtly as much as they are to present the lineage for what will become Israel's royal promise and heritage.

5 See also McDowell's (2015, 131–37) evaluation of 5:1–3, reinforcing the royal sonship of Adam (and his descendants) in this context with Gen. 1:26–27, the broader Old Testament context, and the ancient Near Eastern context. She argues that this makes all of humanity in some sense God's royal offspring.

6 The polemic against the ancient worldview, then, is not merely that they are evil rather than noble (Heiser 2015, 101–9), but that they are rebellious humans, supernaturally empowered rather than semi-divine.

verb "judge" or "contend" (דִּין) and translate it "contend" (NIV) or "strive" (NASB95, NKJV). The intention would be to declare the frustration of Yahweh with their evil, which is either understood to result in God imposing a limit on human lifespan or bringing judgment on all people. The main problem with this view is that the form of the verb is not what is expected for this root. Others regard this as a *hapax legomenon*, translating it "remain" (NET) or "abide" (ESV, NRSV) following the Old Greek and possibly an Arabic cognate (Westermann 1994, 375). The intention in this case would be similar except that the removal of God's spirit would be to declare the end of humanity (understanding the "spirit" here as God's life-giving spirit, Ps. 104:30).

God then decrees that humankind will be limited to 120 years. While some have taken this to refer to the subsequent lifespan of people, the context does not support this, nor does experience. It is more likely that Yahweh refers to the time until the flood will bring the end of rebellious humanity.

TRANSLATION ANALYSIS 6:3b
The translation of the NET makes this position clear: "They will remain for 120 more years." The NLT takes the reference as to human lifespan ("their normal lifespan will be no more than 120 years," which requires special explanation for the patriarchs). Most translations leave the interpretation ambiguous in keeping with the Hebrew, translating "their days will be 120 years" (ESV, NASB95, NIV, NKJV, NRSV).

Typically, these verses have been understood as the state of humanity at the end of the genealogy. As we have seen, however, these verses go all the way back to the beginning of humanity's multiplication. The problem here is that Yahweh's judgment occurs at the end. If, however, we understand that verses 1–2 characterize the whole period from the beginning, it grows throughout this period. God's judgment finally falls after a long period of patience with humanity, which builds consistently from the genealogy of Cain and the decline into self-worship.

6:4. Verse 4 returns to the consequences of the procreation of the powerful. The relationship of these verses is not clearly expressed so the associations are not certain, but it appears to be connecting the Nephilim with the offspring, who are also described as mighty men with great fame. Often, the "mighty heroes" (הַגִּבֹּרִים) in the rest of the Old Testament refer to military champions (1 Sam. 17:51). This characterization fits with their broad fame. The outgrowth of the powerful and their self-interest was even greater power and fame.

TRANSLATION ANALYSIS 6:4
"Nephilim" is merely a transliteration of the Hebrew letters into English since the meaning is uncertain. It only appears here and in Numbers 13:33 where the spies understand "Nephilim" to be giants. The translation "giants" (NKJV) or "giant Nephilites" (NLT), then, comes from that correlation and perhaps from the LXX, which translates it as γίγαντες or "giants." Heiser (2015, 107) relates the Hebrew as an interpolation of later scribes to an Aramaic root meaning "giant" to "villainize the giant offspring." If we are right, they are not large in stature but in power.

Certain Judgment Includes Grace (6:5–8)

Because of the painful, pervasive nature of evil, Yahweh must judge all humanity, yet he extended grace to Noah.

6:5. The narrative turns now to Yahweh's stark evaluation of the actions of his creatures and the root cause. The narrator uses the divine appraisal of the previous two genealogies to crystallize the reader's perceptions. Emphasizing the degeneration of humanity, Yahweh evaluated the outcomes of humankind. In contrast to his initial creation, which he "saw" as "very good" (1:31), he now "saw" that human wickedness "was great in the earth." The problem, however, is internal. Describing a perspective that only Yahweh can "see," "every intention of the thoughts of his heart was only evil continually." The reason humanity continued to slide into increasing rebellion was that their heart was fully corrupted by evil. The narrator's description leaves no space undamaged. "Every intention," referring to the purposes of the individual (8:21; Deut. 31:21; 1 Chron. 28:9; 29:18), qualifies the "thoughts" (מַחְשְׁבֹת) of their "heart" (or "mind," לֵב). These deepest purposes are fully corrupted. The writer emphasizes "*every* intention," "*only* evil," and "*continually*." No doubt is left concerning the cause of man's continued and increasing rebellion.

TRANSLATION ANALYSIS 6:5

The Hebrew term (לֵב) may refer to the "heart" literally, but it is figuratively used often for one's "inclination" or desires, "will," "intention," or "mind in general" (e.g., Gen. 8:21; *HALOT* s.v. "לֵב" 513–15).

While this passage emphasizes the root cause of humanity's rebellion and resulting judgment, the next passage will demonstrate the outcomes and the appropriate justice of Yahweh. As we will see in the next portion, Genesis 6:11–13 draws a careful picture of the violence and destruction that humanity has wreaked on God's world. God's response will bring that very destruction on humanity, as emphasized by the repeated use of the same terms for man's actions in God's reaction (שׁחת).

6:6. Again, several terms draw our attention in verse 6. Yahweh "regretted" that he had made humanity, and "it broke his heart" (NLT). God feels pain from human sin, reminding the reader of both the pain inflicted on man for his sin (3:17, from the same root), as well as Lamech's naming of Noah. The narrative characterizes the rebellion of humanity toward Yahweh with his appropriate outrage. The specific terms used, invoking the words of Lamech from 5:29, underline the irony of what man wants, needs, and receives. Lamech was longing for "relief" (יְנַחֲמֵנוּ) from our "work" (מַעֲשֶׂה) and from the "painful toil" (עִצָּבוֹן) of our hands," (reflecting on 3:17). "Regretted" (נחם) in 6:6 and repeated in verse 7 ("sorry") uses the same verb translated "relief" (5:29) but with its other major meaning. The report that God "made" humankind (עשׂה) reflects man's "labor" (from the same root, also repeated in v. 7). Finally, God's offense, pain, or grief (וַיִּתְעַצֵּב) reflects man's toil (again using the same Hebrew root). The ironic connection exposes the thrust of the overall passage. Comfort will ultimately require judgment on evil and, so, on humanity since evil is a heart issue. The faith and faithfulness of people who walk with God provide the only real relief from sin and its consequences (Enoch and Noah). Of course, mere judgment on evil will not solve the problem, precisely because it is a heart issue, but that will be for the next section to clarify.

TRANSLATION ANALYSIS 6:6a

The Hebrew term translated "regretted" (from נחם, ESV, NET, NIV) or "was sorry" (NASB95, NKJV, NLT, NRSV) in verse 6, and repeated in verse 7, is complex in its varied usage but seems to stem from two main ideas. It is clearly used often of comfort for some pain or loss, as we have seen in 5:29, adding irony to this use. It is also, as here, used of feeling pain ("sorrow") or "regret," which may show in "relenting" or deviating from a stated course based on the new circumstances or God's compassion (anthropomorphically related as to "change one's mind"). Here, man's sin causes God (anthropomorphically) sorrow or pain, which is intolerable with his character, bringing the necessary judgment on their sin rather than the blessing he had pronounced (1:28; 5:2). The text is not suggesting God wishes he had done differently. It is affirming the pain that sin causes God himself and the necessary response. This is one of a few places where God's "regret" causes a change from something positive that was promised (blessing, 1:28; 5:2) rather than relenting of disaster (Jonah 4:2), but it is not out of character. Rather, most of God's pronouncements of future actions should be read as conditioned upon the continued future actions of the human participants (Jer. 18:5–10; for a helpful discussion, see Chisholm 1995).

TRANSLATION ANALYSIS 6:6b
NET Bible's "highly offended" paraphrases the more literal "it grieved him to his heart" (ESV, NRSV or similarly NASB95, NKJV). Less dramatically, the NLT translates, "It broke his heart," and NIV, "his heart was deeply troubled." The verb can refer to various sorts of distress, pain, or grief, and it can be either physical or emotional. It can be intense and provoke a reaction, moving beyond merely suffering with pain to an offense that requires response (Isa. 63:10). With intense irony, God deeply anguishes in his "heart" over the wickedness of humanity's "heart."

6:7. Yahweh's solution, then, will require a complete makeover. All creation needs to be wiped clean to begin again. Yahweh's proclamation is comprehensive. He will "blot out" all living things from the face of the earth, from "man" to "animals and creeping things and birds." His sorrow (see Translation Analysis, 6:6a) drives him to action, emphasizing the intolerable and pervasive nature of human sin.

Both the reminder at the end of verse 7 that Yahweh had "created" or "made" them and the extent of the destruction stated in verse 7 remind the reader again of the initial creation account and tie this conclusion with both the creation and the beginning of the pericope in 5:1–2, even as it prepares for the next section and the flood. The author unites the role of Yahweh as creator with his resulting response as judge even as he highlights that he is "a God merciful and gracious," giving ongoing blessing to his wayward creation, and yet he will "by no means clear the guilty" (Exod. 34:6–7).

6:8. In contrast to Yahweh's observation of humanity's wickedness resulting in judgment (6:5), Noah "found favor in the eyes of the Lord" (6:8), which would result in Noah's salvation. Lamech's longing for relief (5:29) and Yahweh's oracle of the conquering seed (3:15) both find ongoing expectation in the exception provided for Noah. The reason for this grace in Yahweh's eyes awaits the subsequent narrative. As with the previous *toledot,* the descent of humanity away from Yahweh into rebellious self-glorification that will end in destruction concludes with a flash of hope in the continued working of Yahweh within his images and his ongoing redemptive purpose.

The connections already noted between Genesis 6:1–8 and the genealogy of Seth serve to raise the tension between the persistence of the image of God in humanity and their corruption, requiring judgment. The notice that the evil has been from the beginning (6:1) highlights the ongoing grace of Yahweh to allow this longevity and provide hope for life amid such growing evil (v. 5). Not only does this narrative, then, show the means for life and hope amid corruption as walking with God (see also v. 9), but it underlines the certainty of the judgment (vv. 5–8) and the necessity to take advantage of the offer of God's presence.

THEOLOGICAL FOCUS

God's blessed images, inheriting death through Adam, use God's empowering to deepen their destructiveness, leading to judgment, but God graciously extends life and relief to those who walk with him.

Genesis 5 begins by reminding the reader that God created humanity as his likeness to represent him. Initiating the genealogy and mimicking the form of Adam's generation, reminding humanity of their identity ("likeness"), relates humankind to God, requiring both responsibility (reflecting Gen. 1) and privilege (citing his blessing). God is good and has given man all that he needs to thrive, and the outworking of that blessing shows in continuing generations, including sons and daughters. Humankind, however, also experiences the outworking of the fall as each generation died, in monotonous repetition.

The ongoing blessing of new life, limited and in tension with the expected judgment of death, is interrupted by the unexpected hope of one who walks with God and does not experience death. Hope of living springs, surprisingly, from walking with God instead of "living." The reader must realize that Cain's complaint was not the last word. Humankind was driven from the garden but still has access to the presence of God. Humanity can walk with God apart from the sacred space and among the secular and profane in the world and find life.

The bright hope of Enoch echoes in the words of Lamech, which ironically will demonstrate that hope and comfort for the godly will finally require the judgment of God on his creation. The character of man is illustrated again, as 6:1–4 captures the depravity of humanity in the oppression by powerful rulers of their world. That depravity is characterized by Yahweh as the complete corruption of the heart of man so that every purpose, intention, and action is always evil, contrary to their holy Father/Creator and requires his necessary and appropriate judgment. What God had offered as blessing, to rule and multiply, is twisted so that authority is perverted in self-serving power, and reproducing merely adds more wickedness, degenerating into darkness.

The final verse, with the foundational statement of God's grace and favor toward the faith of Noah begins to clarify the hope offered. Humanity does not find hope in actions that work but in the grace of God toward faith that works (described and illustrated in the following section). The God who blesses also judges, yet he is longsuffering and gracious. Oppression and evil have been going on for generations (6:1–4), but God withholds judgment until necessary. Even then, God preserves the righteous (v. 9) and will use blessing, patience, grace, and judgment to instruct the people of God in his character.

God's preservation of Noah also preserves the promise, both of God's purpose for his images and of the specific defeat of the snake. God's pledge to crush evil holds forth with the gracious working of Yahweh, but the heart of man will need to be radically changed. Humanity is fully exposed, revealing the effects of sin. It has fully involved all men to their core. Humankind's helplessness underscores the challenge and raises new questions as to how God will work to use one of these descendants to crush evil. God's intent to change hearts and crush evil will only be understood in the New Covenant through the work of Christ by the Holy Spirit. Yet as long as humanity lives, God's purpose remains, and the opportunity for humanity to turn to him in faith for what he would certainly do.

PREACHING AND TEACHING STRATEGIES

Exegetical and Theological Synthesis

As noted above, the process of preparing a sermon or lesson on this section begins with the theologically significant mentions of the "likeness of God" (5:1) and "in his own likeness, after his image" (with reference to Adam in v. 3). The blessing of God continues as the human population explodes in the narrative. Though Adam's gene pool is polluted, Enoch is a relatively clean spot in the Seth-pool. Verses 22 and 24 have theological and homiletical significance: we will urge every listener to enjoy that same communion with God, without promising, of course, that the Lord will take them up and out. God must have seen something in Enoch he liked. God must have done something special in Enoch's heart and mind. This is our only hope as genuine worshippers walking in this world where the curse and death are alive and well.

Noah's name—the wordplay with the Hebrew for "relief"—also brings us hope in a badly broken world. Noah will once again prove instrumental in the narrative in 6:8. But before then verses 1–7 provide critical information about the condition of the human heart. Even if we can't be sure about the identity of "the sons of God," thanks to the narrator we can be sure they are committing a string of sins similar to Genesis 3 (cf. the sequence of verbs, "saw . . . took"). And, of course, the Lord's reaction to human actions settles it. An important part of being saved is receiving a new heart. Anyone who has not received God's gracious deliverance is destined for his judgment, exemplified in the flood. As mentioned with Enoch, the narrative doesn't yet tell us how Noah "found favor in the eyes of the LORD" (6:8). You probably won't want to wait until the next section to tell them how he found it and how your listeners can find it too.

Preaching Idea

Following Enoch and Noah, God's people walk with him, finding favor and avoiding his judgment on our wicked world.

Contemporary Connections

What does it mean?

It is impossible to restate enough the meaning of being "made . . . in the likeness of God" (5:1; cf. the definition provided in the first unit). You will also want to explain the theological implications of Adam fathering "a son in his own likeness, after his image" (v. 3). This involves an understanding of original sin, or birth-sin. Your listeners will demand an attempt to explain humanity living so long, including Methuselah's record 969 years, especially since 120 years was mentioned in 6:3. As mentioned above, our text offers no answer for why Enoch alone is singled out as one who "walked with God" (5:24). You will want to provide theological options, citing reasons from God's perspective and Noah's positive response. Make sure you explain the significance of Noah's name in verse 29. Your explanation will have to include what kind of "relief" is intended "from our work and from the painful toil of our hands" (v. 29). This doesn't mean that the curse would be erased through Noah's life or the flood. It does mean that the Lord would continue to keep his promises to his own who trust and obey him in the soon-to-be-inhabited post-flood world. Don't let too much speculation about the identity of the "sons of God" distract your listeners from the escalating sinful condition of humanity in 6:1–5. Adam's likeness/image reaches its lowest forms. This is a wonderful opportunity to explain how the holiness and justice of God demands judgment on sinful humanity. Finally, we have the delight of explaining what it means to find favor with God and how to find it through a faith that works.

Is it true?

Genesis 5:1–6:8 is filled with truths of which some listeners will demand, "Is it true?" You can start with the gender issue, a very important topic at the time of the writing of this commentary. Some listeners might struggle with the opening of 5:2: "Male and female he created them." And what about all these long lives? At least be ready to address the issue using options from the earlier analysis. As the exegetical section taught us, this certainly shows how patient our Lord was with those generations who were mostly wicked in the eyes of the Lord. Those unfamiliar with the miracles of God in Scripture will demand some proof about Enoch's sudden disappearance. You might decide to mention how the hope surrounding the prophecy concerning Noah's name provides opportunities for us to talk about the Lord's ability to rule history. Another issue requiring proof is the depth of human depravity: "every intention of the thoughts of his heart was only evil continually" (6:5). Can it get that bad? Finally, you will want to let everyone know that it is true that the Lord must judge all rebellion that threatens his good world.

Now what?
If it's true that humankind is made in the image of God and in the image of Adam, nothing is more relevant than this understanding of human origins. If humanity understood their identity as God's images, it would revolutionize their worldview and our world! Imagine what happens to creatures who refuse to admit their origins. No one can refuse to admit that death is a part of life as we know it. The best and brightest minds on the planet are working day and night to erase the effects of the curse. If it's true that Enoch and Noah provide hope in this dismal death march, then nothing is more important than following their example. Also, pundits in society have their reasons for the condition of humankind worldwide. Virtually no one will allow God the right to judge humanity. The Scriptures are most relevant because they present God's estimate of the cause of wickedness and his decision to judge all rebellion against his rule.

Creativity in Presentation
Our preaching idea for this section is: following Enoch and Noah's example, Christians walk and find favor with God, avoiding his judgment on our wicked world. One way to keep such a large section of Scripture from fragmenting in the minds of our listeners is to keep the idea of rescue in mind. A key concept in this pericope is that Enoch and Noah are singled out as different in their generations. So, you could frame your message/lesson along the lines of:

- Humankind is created in two likenesses.
- Faces two kinds of lifestyles and destinies.
- And is given two spiritual role models.

Children reflecting both sets of parents can illustrate the two likenesses. You know how a child can look like one parent in some ways but also look like the other in other ways: "She's got my chin but has your eyes."

The second section contrasts the righteous and the wicked. Encourage your listeners to imagine what it would be like if a gang infiltrated your neighborhood. How would your daily life change if violence and law-breaking were the norm? Any righteous person would plead with the authorities to restore law and order so that life could resume.

The final section urges our listeners to follow the examples set by Enoch in chapter 5 and Noah in chapter 6. Those who have received Christ walk with God like Enoch did. At least that's the ideal. The reality is that every Sunday we preach to some believers who are in fellowship with God and some who need to adjust their walk. The faithful enjoy regular communion with him and with other faith-family members. Like Noah, they have also found favor with God through faith. They have escaped the judgment on sin. And their lives show that they are different from the rest of society. If we're going to be "men of renown" (6:4), we should be famous for our love for God and neighbor, the opposite of the infamous Nephilim.

DISCUSSION QUESTIONS

1. Compare and contrast the two likenesses in 5:1–3 (likeness of God and Adam). How does the image of God show in my life? How does the image of Adam show in my life?

2. What are the evidences that you walk with God in your home, at work, and during leisure?

3. How does reading about the Lord's sorrow and grief in 6:6–7 fuel your desire to live righteously?

4. Why do many today find it hard to believe that the human heart is full of corrupt intentions? How do we verify this to be true?

5. What about the concept of the Lord judging human sin/sinners is so repulsive to human beings? Why was it necessary and defensible?

GENESIS 6:9—9:29

OVERVIEW

Because of the clear unity of the overall section, it would be effective as a single message, and we will give some suggestions to that end. However, due to the theological density of this section, we will present the *toledot* as we would communicate this section as a mini-series of three messages (6:9–8:19; 8:20–9:17; 9:18–29). It may be that the preacher would even want to overview the whole passage as a single message and then go back and tackle each preaching unit to work through the significant issues involved.

EXEGETICAL IDEA

God judged human evil, and delivered Noah and his family to reform his creation with blessing and covenant promise.

THEOLOGICAL FOCUS

God appropriately judges human evil while faithfully delivering the righteous and fostering his promised redemption through blessing, covenant promise, and boundaries to restore his depraved images.

PREACHING IDEA

With full justice, God judges those who refuse him, yet offers grace and blessing to all his depraved images who will humbly walk with him.

PREACHING POINTERS

To tackle the entire unit in one sermon/lesson, consider the following structure:

- First, remind your listeners that they are functioning in the world just as Noah did (he was "blameless in his generation" says 6:9). The narrative places Noah in an "earth [that] was corrupt in God's sight, and. . . filled with violence" (6:11).
- Second, by faith our righteousness saves us in a world that is already under the condemnation of our righteous God.
- Third, because of God's salvation we worship him as Noah did (8:20). This includes following his instructions concerning the value of human life and living within his covenant with us and his world—which he will remember every time he sees the rainbow.
- Finally, we humbly walk with God knowing that temptations to sin abound and choosing the blessing that comes with obedience (contra Ham and following Shem and Japheth).

This section and what follows should resonate deeply with our culture: our world needs true justice and righteousness. All humans are composed from the same stuff and we all suffer from the same broken heritage. So no one is superior or should be exalted over others. All ethnicities draw from the same corrupted heart and yet all also have the same image of God within. We all have the same propensity for evil and the same offer of grace and blessing from Yahweh. Though oppression follows from our evil, God offers freedom, hope, and life in following him.

LITERARY STRUCTURE AND THEMES

The *toledot* of Adam ended with a preview of what was coming, exposing the overwhelming decline of mankind from the likeness of God (5:1) to their virulent wickedness (6:5), requiring God's painful justice (6:6–7) yet with his gracious exception (6:8). The *toledot* of Noah describes the outworking of God's judgment and grace, exposing both the justice and mercy of God's character. Noah's character and progeny frame the *toledot* and prepare for the subsequent spread of humanity. The final verses also formally close the genealogical entry of Noah opened in 5:32 in the pattern from Genesis 5 (9:28–29). All of this shows the continuity of the message Moses is weaving, that God is at work to accomplish his overarching plan of rescue for his planet by his grace through the faith of his damaged images.

The flood narrative has been tightly woven together by Moses to present a highly structured, theologically significant account. Numerous scholars have demonstrated symmetry in the many repetitions of terms, phrases, numbers, and ideas. The symmetry is natural, since it does record Noah's preparations for and the inundation of the great flood, followed by the receding of the waters and the activities of Noah immediately after. However, Wenham shows the clear structuring of the writer as well, drawing attention to the theological implications.[1] In addition to recognizing the many repeating terms, phrases, and ideas, it is helpful to see the overall flow of the scenes, which generally follows the four major discourses of God (6:13–21; 7:1–4; 8:15–17; 8:21–9:17).

A. Righteous Noah walked with God and had three sons (6:9–10).
   Themes/terms: Noah's righteous character; 3 sons; genealogy revisited

   B. Because the earth was totally corrupt in God's sight, God declared his intent to destroy all life, instructing Noah to build an ark so that he could establish his covenant, preserving the lives of an obedient Noah, his family and representative life from the earth (6:11–22).
      Themes/terms: corruption brings destruction; destroy all flesh (three times); God's covenant (divine speech #1)

      C. Reiterating his intent to destroy all life through flood, and by Noah's obedience to deliver his righteous follower and his creatures to a lasting covenant, God closed them safely in the ark (7:1–16).
         Themes/terms: flood begins; Noah, sons, wives and all the classes of animals enter the ark at God's command (divine speech #2)

1 Wenham has offered several ways to see the symmetry, showing the chiasm, or as he says, "palestrophe on a grand scale" with fifteen repeating, interlocking details from Genesis 6:10–9:19 and with "God remembered Noah" (8:1) at the center (1978, 22–23). Particularly significant to show the intent of Moses in the story are the parallels between the pre-flood and post-flood scenes. That is not to say that the event is contrived, but that the record of it is carefully constructed to draw attention to aspects that will demonstrate the desired point. Here, of course, the biggest point will include the faithful saving intervention of God to deliver Noah (340).

D. The flood lifted the ark safely so that only Noah and those with him lived (7:17–24).

Themes/terms: ark rose, waters prevailed, mountains covered, 150 days, 40 days

E. "God remembered Noah" (8:1a).

D′. God ended his flood as he had promised, settling the ark safely on a drying world (8:1b–12).

Themes/terms: ark rested, waters receded, mountains appeared, 150 days, 40 days

C′. God brought Noah and all saved life out of the ark for fruitful blessing (8:13–19).

Themes/terms: "the waters had subsided"; Noah, sons, wives and all the classes of animals leave the ark at God's command (divine speech #3)

B′. Pleased with Noah's worship, God established his lasting covenant, despite the continued evil of the human heart, to never again destroy all life by flood (8:20–9:17).

Themes/terms: not again destroy all flesh (three times) in spite of heart evil; God's covenant (seven times—divine speech #4)

A′. Noah and his sons expose the unchanged human heart, heralding coming conflict (9:18–29).

Themes/terms: Noah's questionable conduct; 3 sons; genealogy completed

The structure highlights the central theme of God's grace amid his talionic justice, beginning with the righteous character of Noah, his obedience, the promise of the covenant and finally centering on "But God remembered Noah." Noah responds with acceptable worship to God's act of salvation and receives God's covenant promise that "never again" will he cut off all flesh with a flood (9:11), even though man's heart is still wicked (8:21). God begins again with a renewed earth, starting with a new Adam and a renewed blessing and promise despite the remaining human depravity. Man is still in his image with blessing and promise, though the evil heart will continue to bring cursing and pain. God's justice, highlighted in 6:11–22, emphasizes his grace to save any, especially considering the unchanged heart of all humanity (even Noah, 8:21) punctuated by his covenant promise in 8:20–9:17.

Genesis 6:9–8:19

EXEGETICAL IDEA

Faithful to his promises, God fully judged the verified evil of all flesh in his world, reducing his creation back to watery disorder yet sparing righteous Noah, who endured in obedience, with his family and representative animals, bringing them out into a renewed world with renewed blessing.

THEOLOGICAL FOCUS

In appropriate justice and suitable grace, God judges his world, bringing the consequences of sin fully to bear, and yet delivering the righteous remnant to a new world, according to his promise, for renewed blessing.

PREACHING IDEA

Like Noah, the righteous in God's eyes enjoy his salvation in a world under judgment.

PREACHING POINTERS

The mood of the sermon should match the mood of the message. In this case, the mood is a mixture of great sorrow due to the devastating flood but also great relief and hope due to Noah and his family being saved. As you begin to move from Noah and the flood to your listeners, keep two general categories of judgment and salvation (or, if you prefer, rescue or deliverance) in mind. The holiness and justice of God require judgment on human rebellion just like we saw in Genesis 3, although often delayed (cf. Psalm 73 and the prosperity of the wicked during the interim); the grace and faithfulness of God *require* salvation of those he has promised to deliver. Both God's ability to rescue the godly and punish the ungodly are mentioned by Peter in 2 Peter 2:9 to encourage faithful living during our exile. God will keep his promise, including the complete defeat of all evil (cf. Gen. 3:15); he will have a people who bear his image and display his glory in creation, even if it is in a new creation.

Noah provides an example of how genuine faith works in obedience to God in the middle of a culture that does not believe. This kind of countercultural righteousness is required by all who would enjoy LifePlus. I am using this term as a substitute for the more familiar, eternal life. LifePlus emphasizes the quality of the life God provides for those who trust Him. Those are the kind of people God saves. Listeners will enjoy seeing all the parallels-in-reverse between the de-creation occurring at the flood and the original creation story of Genesis 1–2 as pointed out in the exposition of our passage. Our God will not let sin go but, as he promised, he will have a people who represent him well in his new world. You should urge your listeners to be confident in their own faith-based righteousness and to enjoy God now while also having hope of ultimate deliverance at the return of Christ.

THE FLOOD: THE RIGHTEOUS RISE AS JUDGMENT FALLS (6:9–8:19)

LITERARY STRUCTURE AND THEMES

The *toledot* of Noah describes the outworking of God's judgment and grace, exposing both the justice and mercy of God's character. Noah's character and progeny frame the *toledot* and prepare for the subsequent spread of humanity. The final verses also formally close the genealogical entry of Noah opened in 5:32 in the pattern from Genesis 5 (9:28–29). All of this shows the continuity of the message Moses is weaving, through the use of the continuing genealogy. God is at work to accomplish his overarching plan of rescue for his planet by his grace through the faith of his damaged images.

The flood narrative has been tightly woven together by Moses to present a highly structured, theologically significant account. Numerous scholars have demonstrated symmetry in the many repetitions of terms, phrases, numbers, and ideas. The symmetry is natural, since it does record Noah's preparations for and the inundation of the great flood, followed by the receding of the waters and the activities of Noah immediately after. However, Wenham shows the clear structuring from the writer as well, drawing attention to the theological implications.[1] That is not to say that the event is contrived, but that the record of it is carefully constructed to draw attention to aspects that will demonstrate the desired point. Here, of course, the biggest point will include the faithful saving intervention of God to deliver Noah (Wenham 1978, 340).

While the full *toledot* is an important unit to understand and explain, we suggest preaching the first two chapters as a smaller unit to focus on the justice of God and highlight his grace during judgment. The following section (8:20–9:17) will focus on the Noahic covenant and the important themes of the sanctity of human life in the image of God and the continuing promise of blessing, in ongoing tension with the depravity of the human heart. The final section (9:18–29) will allow us to see the tensions beginning to show with the actions of both righteous Noah and his son, preparing for the spread and degeneration of humanity after the flood.

In the chiastic structure of the *toledot*, we are dealing with seven of the nine sections. This section, then, begins with righteous Noah and God's plan to judge human rebellion and deliver his righteous follower (6:9–7:16) and ends with God's fulfilled promise as Noah enters a newly cleansed world (8:13–19). In between, the judgment falls, but God remembers and delivers Noah as the chaos retreats.

A. Righteous Noah walked with God and had three sons (6:9–10).
   B. God announced judgment, while providing salvation (6:11–22).
      C. Amid judgment, the obedient family found safety (7:1–16).

1 Wenham has offered several ways to see the symmetry, showing the chiasm, or as he says, "palestrophe on a grand scale" with fifteen repeating, interlocking details from Genesis 6:10–9:19 and with "God remembered Noah" (8:1) at the center (1978, 337–38). Particularly significant to show the intent of Moses in the story are the parallels between the pre-flood and post-flood scenes.

D. God destroyed life by flood while Noah floated (7:17–24).
E. "God remembered Noah" (8:1a).
D'. God dried up the flood (8:1b–12).
C'. God repopulated his world for fruitful living (8:13–19).
B'. God established his covenant, despite lingering evil, to guarantee life (8:20–9:17).
A'. Noah and his sons expose the unchanged human heart, heralding coming conflict (9:18–29).

The flood itself details God's evaluation of humankind and his response, bringing their actions back on their own heads. God's justice fits humanity's crime. The narrative also illustrates the righteous obedience of one who walks with God, clarifying further the opportunity humanity has for deliverance from the judgement on evil. Creation is undone with the flood, reminding the reader that God brought this world into being and he can reverse (and redo) his creation as he wills. The narrative builds as God blots out all life but remembers Noah. As a new Adam, Noah and those with him are delivered into a new world with renewed blessing.

- ***Righteous Noah Walked with God and Had Three Sons (6:9–10)***
- ***God Announced Judgment, While Providing Salvation (6:11–22)***
- ***Amid Judgment, the Obedient Family Found Safety (7:1–16)***
- ***God Destroyed Life by Flood While Noah Floated (7:17–24)***
- ***God Remembered Noah (8:1a)***
- ***God Dried Up the Flood (8:1b–12)***
- ***God Repopulated His World for Fruitful Living (8:13–19)***

EXPOSITION

Righteous Noah presents a stark contrast with the wicked populous who are destroying creation. God announced his intent to destroy all life and yet deliver Noah, his family, and representative animals and establish a covenant. God's judgment reversed creation, but he did not neglect his promise, delivering his faithful remnant into a new world with renewed blessing. God has been gracious to Noah and his progeny, giving them life and new hope in his promise even as he has cleansed the earth from the pervasive wickedness of humanity. Both God's justice and grace are presented in tension. Faithful to his promises, God fully judged the verified evil of all flesh in his world, reducing his creation back to watery disorder yet sparing righteous Noah, who endured in obedience with his family and representative animals, bringing them out into a renewed world with renewed blessing.

Righteous Noah Walked with God and Had Three Sons (6:9–10)

The story of righteous Noah, who walked with God, and his sons will highlight the tensions of God's announced judgment on humanity while carrying forward the likeness of God and image of Adam.

6:9. The standard *toledot* introduction to the section does not introduce a genealogy or stories about the descendants, as most of Genesis will, but more like Genesis 2:4 it introduces the family story of Noah (Cf. above on 2:4, p. 99, and Schwartz 2016). This account will complete the genealogy of Noah begun in 5:32 with the addition of the flood account and the ensuing covenant as Moses reveals the redemptive program of God. As with the previous two *toledot* sections, Moses established the crucial context for what would follow with three highlighted clauses set apart from the narrative. We learn that the one who found "favor" (6:8) was "a righteous man, blameless in his generation. Noah walked with God" (v. 9).

What may sound presumptuous to modern ears designates a significant consideration to the ancient world. "Righteous" (צַדִּיק) does not describe perfection, but rather someone who conforms to the expected standard, especially in the context of relationship (Reimer, צֶדֶק, *NIDOTTE* 3:744–69). Here, Noah was a pious man who served God rather than all the other competing priorities in his world (Mal. 3:18). He is also one who has integrity ("blameless," תָּמִים, cf. Olivier, תָּמַם, *NIDOTTE* 4:306–8). It is often used for acceptable sacrifices that are without blemish (Lev. 1:3, 10). In Joshua 24:14 it is translated "sincerity" and paired with "faithfulness" (אֱמֶת) to indicate loyal service to Yahweh.

The distinction with "righteous" focuses on the consistency in living. Later, Abram will be declared righteous by his faith (15:6) but then called to live his life in integrity and faithfulness before Yahweh and so be "blameless" (17:1). Again, however, it is not perfection, but it is a life of integrity that recognizes and responds to God's prompting in open repentance (Ps. 18:21; cf. 139:23–24). In a culture of evil and self-serving rebellion, Noah believed God and served him faithfully. He "walked with God" (see on Gen. 5:22, 24 above, p. 159). Noah is significantly designated as "righteous" because God will enter covenant relation with him (6:18).

The notice compares Noah to the rest of his generation not as an afterthought, but as a clear contrast to all the rest of humanity. Of all those currently alive, Noah was the only one to live up to God's standard, following him. As will be apparent at the end of the pericope and as is explained throughout God's revelation, God is not looking for perfection, but rather Noah lived in integrity and faithful obedience to Yahweh (see 6:22–7:1 below).

6:10. The continuity that this section provides with the previous section by reviewing Noah's genealogy (5:32, 6:8) includes the tensions of the previous section as well. Noah is righteous and has found favor with God, but the mention of his sons also reminds of the spread of humanity and evil with them that the following verses will highlight. The passing on of God's image and Adam's sinfulness (5:1–3) has continued so that God's observation after the flood (8:21; 9:6) that humanity has not changed fundamentally should be of no surprise. While the main tension will fall between those inside and those outside the ark, there is a nagging suspicion that the seeds of this tension will be carried with Noah in the ark, yet necessarily so to also maintain the promise (3:15).

God Announced Judgment While Providing Salvation (6:11–22)

Based on firsthand evidence of pervasive human rebellion against God's commission by destroying his good earth that they were to care for, God announced full judgment yet offered life to his obedient follower for a new beginning.

The section begins with God's firsthand evaluation of human evil (vv. 11–12) and then alternates between his justice for humanity (vv. 13, 17) and his grace for his righteous companion (vv. 14–16, 18–21). It concludes with the expected notice of Noah's full obedience (v. 22), contrasting the introduction to the section. The contrast and alternation underline the tension between judgment and grace, between humankind and Noah, as well as the promise available to those who will obey the righteous King.

6:11–12. Verses 11–12 remind the reader of Genesis 1. Seven times in Genesis 1 God evaluated his creation and "saw" that it was good. Verse 11 summarizes God's evaluation, while verse 12 rehearses the basis in God's careful evaluation. Described anthropomorphically, God's observation of human evil was already recorded in 6:5, and the same image will be used consistently through Genesis to show God's scrutiny and accurate evaluation of human evil (or righteousness) before responding appropriately (cf. 7:1; 11:5; 18:21; 29:31–32; 31:12, 42). God is not judging from afar or on hearsay but is personally involved and familiar with the human condition. His response will be just.

In these two verses, the earth is "corrupt" (שׁחת) and full of "violence" (חָמָס, repeated in v. 13). The verb "corrupt" (שׁחת) appears seven times in this narrative, including three times here for what humanity had done to God's creation. It describes things ruined or destroyed by the noted actions (Gen. 18:28; Jer. 13:7). In verse 13 God would "destroy" (שׁחת) his creation—he would bring on them the full effects of what they were doing, accomplished by the flood (v. 17, again translated "destroy"). Theologically, humanity, far from ruling over the earth as God's representatives (1:26, 28) and bringing good as God did, have spoiled his creation.

Humanity had ruined God's good creation by filling it with violence (adding color to the evaluation and cryptic statement of evil in 6:1–8), so God would ruin humanity (שׁחת). Humanity was intended (and commissioned) to fill the earth with God's likenesses (1:28), but instead they filled the earth with violence. "Violence" (חָמָס) can refer to all sorts of violent injustice, from bloodshed (49:5) to hyperbolically described dishonor (16:5) to all sorts of social injustice (Jer. 22:3; Joel 4:19; Mic. 6:12, and throughout the prophets). God's resulting evaluation can no longer be "good" but requires remedial attention to bring good.

6:13. God announced coming judgment to Noah, using the terms of his observations in the previous two verses. The repetition here emphasizes that God would hold humankind accountable for their responsibilities, bringing on their own heads the appropriate consequences of their actions. God's justice is appropriate and carefully evaluated. He would destroy "all flesh" (vv. 13, 17) when he destroyed the earth they had ruined because "all flesh" was corrupted (v. 12). God's hyperbole emphasized the extent of man's sin and necessary judgment. At the same time, he was making plans to deliver Noah and his family.

Parallel Flood Narratives

The parallel flood accounts in the ancient world have been widely studied and discussed. The closest parallels occur in the Gilgamesh Epic (Foster, CoS, I:458–60), Atrahasis (Foster, CoS, I:450–53), and Eridu Genesis (Jacobsen 2003). In each case the general similarities are obvious as the gods attempt to destroy humanity with a flood, but the specific details diverge significantly. Eridu Genesis presents parallels to the first nine chapters of Genesis, beginning by populating the earth with humanity and animals and instituting city-building and kingship. Then the gods decide to destroy humanity with a flood because of the noise of humanity, but one god, Enki, warns the king, Ziusudra, to build a boat and save animals along with his own family. Atrahasis similarly records the creation of humanity to do the work for the gods and then a flood to destroy humanity because of their noise. In this case the god Ea warned Atrahasis, who saved humanity from extermination. In the Gilgamesh Epic, Gilgamesh is looking for eternal life and hears the story of the great deluge from the flood hero, Utnapishtim (or other names in other versions). Each of them has similarities to the biblical account, as well as significant divergences. While some authors argue that the biblical author borrowed the story from another ancient account, the picture is far from clear. Longman, Walton, and Moshier (2018) give a helpful summary of the ancient accounts and describe both similarities and differences. They conclude that the best explanation, given the many striking similarities and distinctive differences, is that they were writing from a common perspective with shared understanding of basic themes, concepts, and common language, without borrowing or direct influence on the story (see propositions 7–8).

6:14–16. God's recorded instructions to Noah provide only a brief snapshot of Noah's massive project in building the ark. The narrative includes several rare or unusual terms in addition to the "ark." The type of wood used ("gopher" is transliterated from the Hebrew) and the "pitch" used to waterproof it both occur only here. The type of wood is uncertain, but the pitch is related to a common Akkadian term used in the Gilgamesh epic. The term generally translated here as "rooms" (קִנִּים) is consistently translated "nest" in the other twelve Old Testament uses. Some scholars repoint the text to mean "reeds" (קָנִים) and relate it to the use of reeds in the Gilgamesh epic, perhaps using the reeds for caulking (Wenham 1987, 173, REB). Overall, the shape and design of the ark is not defined, though the term "ark" may suggest more of a barge-like box. The text gives only enough details to understand that the project is massive, especially for one family in the ancient world (approximately 450 feet long, 75 feet wide, and 60 feet tall), suggesting to some that these numbers may be hyperbole.[2]

TRANSLATION ANALYSIS 6:14
The word typically translated "ark" (תֵּבָה) is certainly to be understood as a large boat of some sort (NLT), but the exact shape and design is not explained. The term occurs only here (Gen. 6:14–9:18) and in the narrative of Moses's infancy (Exod. 2:3, 5). It generally is understood as an Egyptian loanword meaning "chest" or perhaps "sarcophagus" (Wenham 1987, 172).

6:17. God emphasized to Noah the complete destruction of all flesh. Repeating his intent to destroy all life under heaven, God's justice will be absolute. The judgment is emphatic (disjunctive marked clause beginning with וַאֲנִי) and imminent (הִנְנִי with the participle). His instructions to Noah are grim.

The Extent of the Flood

The extent of the flood has occasioned a longstanding debate. The pervasive nature of the language, as we note repeatedly, sounds like universal destruction (e.g., "all flesh" and "everything on earth shall die," 6:17; cf. 7:21–22; and "all the high mountains under the whole heaven were covered," 7:19). For a defense of a universal flood, see Mathews (1996, 365). Others, however, have argued for a flood that was only over the known world, regional, or even local. There is clearly some hyperbole in the passage already. It was not literally "all flesh" since Noah and his passengers did not die. Hyperbole was commonly used in much of the Old Testament narrative, such as the extent of destruction in battle. In Joshua 11:23, "Joshua took the whole land, according to all that the LORD had spoken to Moses . . . . And the land had rest from war" (see also 21:44; cf. Num. 34:2–12; Deut. 7:2; 20:17). Yet it was not total (Josh. 13:1, "there remains yet very much land to possess"), and in many battles that followed, Israel was unable to fully win. We also see this hyperbole in the extent of the famine in the time of Joseph (Gen. 41:57) or the extent of the knowledge and fear of Israel (Deut. 2:25). Walton has argued that the ancient understanding of the cosmic geography and the terms used to describe their world would use universal language for what, in their perception, would be worldwide; although it would not cover a globe (they did not perceive of a globe), it was still an extremely devastating flood (*DOTP* "Flood," 315–26; see also Longman, Walton, and Moshier 2018, 91–99). Of course, even if the judgment was less than global, all humanity could have been killed in judgment, other than Noah and his family.

2 See Longman, Walton, and Mosier (2018, 38–40), who list the largest wooden boats known from antiquity, including one depicted in Old Kingdom Egypt (about 2500 BC) that is perhaps up to 170 feet long and the Isis in the first couple of centuries ad that was 180 feet long.

6:18–21. In tension with his absolute dictate, God foregrounds his covenant to Noah, fleshing out the grace already declared (6:8). The focus of the promise is Noah. The second person pronoun is repeated six times in addition to the verb, which includes the second person subject. The righteous one will enter the ark with his wife, sons, and sons' wives. God's promise is channeled through Noah, his blameless companion, who would be God's means to save a remnant of humanity and animals for his new world. God's promise to establish (using the verb קום) the covenant, in the structure of the passage, refers to the promised agreement he would establish after the flood (see the chiasm above and compare 9:9). Since it is not the normal verb for establishing a new covenant (כרת), however, it may refer to the formalizing of a covenant already in place with Noah (Wenham 1987, 175). Noah and his passengers would be the only exceptions to the complete destruction of life in God's world.

The Noahic Covenant

The Noahic covenant is understood by some, because of the terminology, to be a reconfirmation of an unexpressed Adamic covenant otherwise only hinted at in Genesis 1–3 (e.g., Gentry and Wellum 2018, chs. 5–6). Wenham (1987, 175) allows for a previously unexpressed covenant already with Noah, which will be ratified or confirmed in chapter 9, and others would suggest 6:18 merely looks forward to a new covenant with Noah and all life (e.g., Mathews 1996, 366–67). The view accepted does not materially affect the message of this passage.

Noah would stock the ark with everything required to "keep them alive" (repeated), including matching pairs of every sort of creature and the food that all of them would need to eat. The reference to birds, animals, and creeping things (6:20 and repeated two more times in 7:8, 13) reminds the reader of his catalog of created things (1:20–25) and summary of beasts, birds, and creeping things for which he had provided food (1:30). God was beginning again. He was again providing all that was needed for his creations to thrive in his (re) created world.

6:22. Noah's obedience is not only notable for the brevity of the statement, emphasized by repetition, but for the completeness. Noah did not reply. He merely did what God said. In fact, he did all that God commanded. Noah's full obedience starkly contrasts the violence and corruption of the humanity around him (6:11–12) and illustrates his characterization. In fact, the next verse will show that the same scrutiny condemning all life instead offers life to Noah, the one who shows his righteousness in obedience (7:1). God offers life to those who will walk with him in obedience.

Amid Judgment, the Obedient Family Found Safety (7:1–16)

Noah demonstrated his righteousness, fully obeying God and finding safety in God's provision as the cosmic flood inundated his world.

7:1–5. Yahweh's second address initiates a new section. With the construction completed (6:22), God invited Noah to take refuge because he was righteous (see 6:9 above). While the pericope began with the narrator declaring Noah righteous (6:9), Noah's obedience has demonstrated the appropriate nature of God's evaluation. God now declared to Noah and his family that his righteousness formed the basis for his deliverance (כִּי). As in 6:9, the comparison with "this generation" highlights the contrast between Noah and the rest of humanity. Consistently throughout the pericope Moses reminds the reader of the tension between God's judgment and grace and the means to experience that grace. The foundation for righteousness—faith (15:6)—works out in obedience, becoming evident to all.

In his first address, God described the construction job and how it would deliver Noah, his family, and the animals. Now he specified the details for loading the ark. Noah must include seven pairs of clean animals, as well as seven pairs of birds.[3] Both are necessary to make sure they all survive after the flood (7:3), especially for birds who may be lost (8:6–12) and animals that must be offered to God (8:20).[4]

This address marks Noah's seven-day warning (7:4). God specified that the deluge would actively occur for forty days, a much more reasonably disastrous time frame than the seven days of Gilgamesh (Foster, CoS, I:458–60). Again, God emphasized the total destruction from this flood. He would cleanse his earth. The narrative specifically views God's planned annihilation (v. 4) as accomplished in 7:22–23, repeating the phrase (and the verb twice).

TRANSLATION ANALYSIS 7:4

The verb to "blot out" can literally refer to "wiping clean" such things as the mouth (Prov. 30:20) or a basin (2 Kings 21:13). Metaphorically, then, the annihilation of all life is a similar, complete removal or even, perhaps, "cleansing" of God's earth.

A second time, Noah did all that Yahweh commanded (Gen. 7:5). Even though Noah has yet to speak, Noah's complete obedience speaks volumes. God honors the one that honors God with his obedience.

7:6–16. The final two segments of this section develop in remarkable parallel, showing the safe entry of Noah and all his charges, just as God commanded:[5]

A. Noah's age when the flood came (7:6).
  B. Noah, his family and all the creatures entered the ark (7:7–9a).
    C. "As God had commanded Noah" (7:9b).
      D. After seven days the flood came (7:10).

A'. Noah's age to the day when the cosmic sources inundated the earth, raining forty days (7:11–12).
  B'. "On the very same day" Noah, his family, and all the creatures according to their kind entered the ark (7:13–16a).
    C'. "As God had commanded him" (7:16b).
      E'. "And the LORD shut him in" (7:16c).

The repetition of these panels draws attention again to the obedience of Noah. It is not just the refrain "as God had commanded him," but it is the repetition of the loading of the ark with family and animals that had been stated (6:18–20), commanded (7:1–3), and then recorded two times here with mounting detail the second time. Noah fully carried out every detail.

On the other hand, the reader cannot miss the frame to each of these panels. The flood came on the earth on the very day that God

3 The reference to clean animals here, long before the law of Moses, assumes that even Noah, a righteous man who walked with God, knew which animals were appropriate for sacrifice and which were not.

4 There has been much discussion on the repetition in these verses and the case for multiple sources (Documentary Hypothesis) based on things like God's instructions to have pairs (6:19–20) or seven pairs (7:2–3), as if they are redundant or contradictory. However, 6:19–20 is merely describing in general what Noah will do. Genesis 7:2–3 is the actual command for what he must do. Of course, it assumes in chapter 7 that the rest of the animals will be in pairs as described in chapter 6 and described again in 7:9, 15, where they enter in pairs, not commenting on how many pairs!

5 Similarly, Wenham (1987, 177) shows parallels between these verses.

had promised (7:6, 10, 11–12). God's word was true and right on time. The frame in the first panel is the coming flood, and the beginning of the second repeats the frame with added cosmic intensity. However, in verse 16, when you expect the grand finale intense deluge, the reader is surprised by Yahweh shutting the door. The surprise both arrests attention and points to the grace of God to Noah and his charges. Amid the rising waters of the terrible flood, God secures their refuge from the storm. Not only has the flood come as God promised, but their safety was secured according to promise. God was not late in either case, again raising the tension of his justice and mercy.

Verse 11 records the opening of "the fountains of the great deep" and the "windows of the heavens." This terminology is very much part of the cosmic geography of the ancient world (Walton 2009a, 49–51). Scholars differ on how literally or figuratively the ancient world understood these descriptions, but certainly they reflect the perspective of observation. The waters are pictured as being held back by the sky and the ground. This language again reflects the creation account (the separation of waters in 1:6–7) with God undoing creation, returning it to the pervasive "deep" (תְּהוֹם, the same word in 1:2 and 7:11), and reversing it to reorder creation in 8:2 by again restoring the boundaries to the cosmic waters.[6]

Again, as noted above, the lists of animals add to the image of undoing and recreating, reminding the reader of the categories of creatures in creation (1:26, 28). Noah was given authority over these creatures, caring for them fully (cf. 6:21), again reminding the reader of the expected disposition of the responsibilities of humanity in contrast to their recorded violence (1:26, 28; 6:5, 11–13).

God Destroyed Life by Flood While Noah Floated (7:17–24)

God's judgment with his flood blotted out all life, leaving only Noah and those with him alive.

7:17–20. The narrative carefully builds the coming flood in the reader's mind even as he imagines the waters rising. The initial statement confirms God's promise of rain for forty days and nights (7:4). The bare statement confirms God's word, but what follows builds the flood and the floating ark as the earth is covered. The Hebrew here is dramatic. The clauses progressively lengthen as the words for the growing water gain intensity. The coming flood begins with two words in the Hebrew, "the waters increased," (וַיִּרְבּוּ הַמַּיִם), lifting the ark over the earth (v. 17). Then come two clauses of two words and four words, adding intensity, as the "waters prevailed and increased greatly on the earth," again bearing the ark over "the face of the waters" (v. 18). Verse 19 again adds intensity with six words as "the waters prevailed so mightily on the earth" that they covered "all the high mountains under the whole heaven." Finally, repeating and specifying that the waters rose to fifteen cubits above the mountains, the flood reaches its dramatic peak (v. 20). The impact is extraordinary. Not only will the ark not touch any soil (assuming it would draft less than fifteen feet), but there is no place that any life could survive. God's dreadful judgment is complete, which the following verses confirm.

7:21–24. Again, repetition serves the narrator as the awful toll is reviewed. Twice these verses

6 There are verbal parallels that might suggest ancient creation accounts to the ancient audience, such as the splitting of the deep, which sounds very similar to how Marduk created the heavens and the earth in *Enuma Elish*. Here, however, it is the undoing of creation, and it is not in cosmic battle but in complete control. The reversal of the motifs highlights the sovereign control of Yahweh over his creation. Hamilton (1990a, especially 292–93) specifically notes helpful parallels to the ancient Near Eastern accounts throughout the flood narrative.

document the death of all classifications of living creatures in addition to all humankind (vv. 21–22). The repetition graphically portrays the toll of the flood. In the Hebrew, verse 21 begins with the death of all flesh, which is described in the familiar categories he has been using. Verse 22 then summarizes the extent of everything with "the breath of life" which "died" (last word). The *inclusio* frames all of God's creatures with death. As if that is not clear, in verse 23 God twice accepts the agency, blotting out every living thing of all creatures, including man (see on 7:4 above). God has fully kept his word, vividly and emphatically depicted in the description. God reversed his good creation, removing all the good life he had created but which was now corrupted (note "all flesh" in 6:12 showing the impact of human sin on all of God's realm). He has returned his ordered realm to the disorder of 1:2 with nothing but watery deep.

It is not quite a return to the beginning, however. Rather than begin with life new and fresh, he has kept alive the seeds for his new world. In stark contrast to the desolation, "only Noah was left, and those who were with him in the ark" (7:23c). The favored one was alive with his family and remnant of creatures, though left floating far above the carnage for about five months (v. 24).[7]

God Remembered Noah (8:1a)

God would accomplish his promised salvation.

8:1a. The center of the pericope strategically focuses on God's grace amid destruction and death. The key statement that "God remembered Noah" presents another anthropomorphism that highlights the action of God in salvation. Only God's intervention assures Noah's survival. Of course, the point of God remembering is not merely recall but the action that God will do based on acknowledging the situation. In the human realm, remembering may lead to more than mere reflection, such as a change of perspective (Ps. 77:11) or obedience (Deut. 8:2, 18). When used of God, remembering leads to answered prayer (1 Sam. 1:11), fulfillment of promise (Exod. 32:13), salvation (Ps. 106:4–5), or judgment (Jer. 14:10). The point is not whether God might forget, but rather the poignant expression of God's conscious intervention based on his character or promises. It will be revisited in his promise with the Noahic covenant (Gen. 9:14–16).

Here the central point is God's gracious deliverance, accomplishing his promise to Noah amid total destruction. While the drama of the passage is the flood and the complete devastation, the passage centers and focuses on God's rescue of Noah and the life with him in the ark. Just as the narrative begins with the righteous character of Noah, it turns on God's gracious intervention for the righteous from the consequences of the evil around them.

God Dried Up the Flood (8:1b–12)

God reversed the disorder, drying up the waters for a new order.

8:1b–5. With an echo from Genesis 1:2, God caused a "wind" (רוּחַ)[8] to "blow over the earth" (8:1), and the waters began to recede. In an explicit reversal from 7:11–12, God intervenes, fleshing out the impact of "remembering," closing "the fountains of the deep and the windows of the heavens," and

7 Wenham (1978) carefully works out the timeline, which is meticulously documented and repeated strategically throughout the flood narrative (with chiastic precision), showing the coherence and careful attention to detail (see especially p. 343). The consistent references to the time frame, including the age of Noah (7:6, 11; 8:13), provide a credible aura of reality to what otherwise feels surreal.

8 רוּחַ is the same word used in Gen. 1:2 for the "Spirit" of God and here most likely denotes a drying wind. In both cases the impact will be bringing definition and order out of the watery disorder.

restraining the rain (8:2). The resulting recession of the waters completed the 150 days (7:24; 8:3) until the ark came to rest (8:4). The ESV correctly translates the "mountains of Ararat" (v. 4). These are not a single peak but a range of mountains in the region of Eastern Turkey, Russia, and Iran. The location has been identified with a variety of peaks, but the text does not identify it. Emphasizing the extent of the flooding, the peaks are not visible until the tenth month (v. 5).

TRANSLATION ANALYSIS 8:4
The term "Ararat" (אֲרָרָט) refers to the ancient kingdom of Urartu, which was to the north of Syria. Cassuto (1974, 103–5) discusses the various traditional identifications for the ark's landing but notes that the text is not specific.

8:6–12. In 7:17–20 the water built up dramatically and quickly to cover the mountains and destroy all life. Here, however, the narrative slows down the reversal. In the first five verses, only the tops of the mountains become visible. Then another seven verses pass before the water is finally dried up. The pace of the narrative seems to call the reader to empathize with Noah and his passengers as they wait impatiently for the day that they can disembark.

Verses 6–12 describe the process of determining the status of the outside, suggesting both that whatever opening they had easily available did not allow much visibility and that God was not giving them specific updates! In verse 6, Noah opened a "window" to send out a raven (v. 7) though he could not see clearly from it (v. 13). The purpose for the raven is not stated, although the assumption is logical that it was the same as the dove, which is stated. The outcome of the raven, however, was not helpful. Since it lives on the carrion, it apparently had food and did not help Noah's concern. It flew "to and fro" (v. 7) until the waters dried up.

How long Noah waited before trying the dove is not stated, but the progression of sending out the birds highlights the monotonous waiting. Sending out the dove three times shows the recession of the flood and perhaps the impatience of the occupants. It is not, however, until God gives them permission that they leave the ark.

God Repopulated His World for Fruitful Living (8:13–19)

With the earth dry, God sent Noah and all the preserved life out to multiply in the earth by their families.

8:13–14. The dates recorded indicate that Noah had been on the ark ten and a half months when he first removes the covering and sees the earth is dry.[9] It is almost two months later, however, one year and ten days, when God finally allows them off. Three times the narrative notes the land is dry, twice after ten and a half months, then again after twelve months and ten days. For almost two months Noah waited, knowing the ground was dry before God spoke. The subtle message again underlines Noah's submission to God and quiet obedience.

8:15–17. Finally, God allowed them to leave the ark. In his third discourse, paralleling his command to enter the ark (7:1–4), God commanded Noah to bring out all his family and all the animals, "that they may swarm on the earth, and be fruitful and multiply on the earth" (v. 17). Again, paralleling the creation account, God began his renewed world with his command of blessing that the creatures would be fruitful and multiply. As we will see in what follows, the narrative presents this as a new start in a renewed

9 The numbers in the account are clearly important following the overall chiastic structure and are repeated frequently at significant times (Wenham 1978). The specific significance, however, is difficult to determine in the ancient context, especially since we no longer know what calendar the ancient world used.

world with a second Adam. Some things will be the same, however, bringing tensions into the new world.

8:18–19. Noah disembarked as God commanded. The reader again appropriately sees Noah's obedience in both the patient waiting and action, and yet, to this point, Noah is a flat character. The narrative has not recorded any verbal response. He has acted in consistent righteousness and compliance, in complete contrast to the generation in which he lived. Significantly, Noah will remain flat until the final scene, when the narrative will illustrate the tension in the following section.

THEOLOGICAL FOCUS

In appropriate justice and suitable grace, God judges his world, bringing the consequences of sin fully to bear and yet delivering the righteous remnant to a new world, according to his promise, for renewed blessing.

The flood highlights God's righteousness and grace as he returns his damaged world to watery disorder in judgment and then recreates it to re-establish life and blessing for his righteous remnant. The righteous and blameless person who walks with God contrasts deeply with his world, characterized as corrupt, violent, and evil. Though it is not always obvious to mortal eyes, that conflict will remain until God brings his judgment, destroying evil and restoring his creation with his righteous remnant. As with all of Genesis so far, the narrative is typical of human action, God's expectations, and God's response.

Clearly in this narrative God's judgment is appropriate to the crime, showing the justice of God's response and emphasizing its necessarily pervasive nature to counter the overwhelming damage from humanity's widespread and deeply rooted evil. Humanity's sin slides precipitously toward the destruction of God's good creation, ruining all the good that God has brought about. Far from innocent, humanity presses their rebellion to corrupt God's purposes, presenting unmitigated disaster apart from divine intervention. The completely corrupted heart (6:5) leads to completely corrupted life, infecting the entire sphere of influence. Only radical surgery can provide hope before all is lost.

At the same time, faith, shown in obedience and thereby validating God's characterization of righteousness, provides hope in God's gracious response. Faith, revealed in quiet submission to God's commands, describes walking with God and provides hope in God's gracious salvation from impending disaster. Such countercultural "righteousness" listens to God and experiences his pleasure and provision.

That is not to say that any human deserves his deliverance. God's response to faith is clearly "favor" (6:8, חֵן), or undeserved grace, which must rest in the character and purpose of God (Exod. 33:19; 34:6). God is consistent and will act fully in concert with his character, bringing complete justice and yet extending grace and promise to the submissive, delivering his righteous companions. The structure argues for seeing both the clear understanding of God's righteous judgment as well as his consistent grace in establishing his covenant promise in tension. Both are true and necessary expressions of the nature of God. Both must be fully embraced in a biblical worldview, taking seriously the commands of the Creator King.

Humanity, then, must choose to bow or be destroyed. God will reduce his creation back to disorder to restore the full potential for blessing. The one who lives in integrity with God, responding in faithful obedience, will enjoy the favor of God's presence and the resulting life and promise of his approval. As the next scene will remind the reader, however, it is all rooted in the heart. Just as the evil was a result of the heart (8:21; see 6:5 above, p. 164), so the key to walking with God will be from the heart (therefore, "faith," 15:6 NET).

In this narrative, righteous character shows in active obedience (6:22; 7:5, 9, 16; 8:18–19).

It also shows, however, in patient waiting for God's direction (8:6–14). Both reveal faith, receive reward from God, and flow from walking with God (5:22, 24; 6:9).

PREACHING AND TEACHING STRATEGIES

Exegetical and Theological Synthesis

This narrative speaks to our situation every Sunday because of how this new start entered human history—with an act of worship. First, we are watching our Creator rule his creation. Second, God views the vast majority of humankind just as he did in Noah's generation (cf. 6:11, "Now the earth was corrupt in God's sight"). Third, God has created a people who, like Noah, are "righteous . . . blameless" (cf. 6:9). Fourth, God will always judge sin and sinners. He will not allow his name and his good creation to be destroyed forever. Fifth and finally, our Lord will give his LifePlus to all who trust and obey him.

Those five concepts are not exhaustive but do represent major motifs in the section that move us from the historical context to our day. Note that they include references to our fallen condition, but also to God's gracious provision. Our listeners who know the Lord like Noah did are enjoying their relationship to God within this same history; they sincerely worship the Lord and their life reflects that. Others in church on Sunday profess to know the Lord but are not walking with God like Noah. All of us need to be challenged to live out our faith each day with the same kind of faith/Spirit-driven spiritual integrity. And, like Noah, we must wait patiently and confidently for God's promises to come completely true. One day our Lord will again create a new start with a new heaven and new earth where only the righteous will dwell (cf. 2 Peter 3:13). And if, while we wait, we ever wonder if God has forgotten, we can take comfort in Genesis 8:1: "But God remembered Noah." And we should also remember that this section is a wonderful opportunity to highlight God's enormous power demonstrated in judgment and salvation.

Preaching Idea

Like Noah, the righteous in God's eyes enjoy his salvation in a world under judgment.

Contemporary Connections

What does it mean?

It is crucial to explain the connection between Genesis 6:8 ("Noah found favor") and 6:9 ("Noah was a righteous man, blameless"). It is easy to read that to mean that Noah had inherent righteousness that God rewarded (Noah's righteousness earned God's favor) versus that Noah's righteousness and blamelessness were the result of a relationship he had with God, which God graciously gave him. You can point listeners to 15:6 ("And he [Abram] believed the Lord, and he counted it to him as righteousness."). If you plan on teaching or preaching this section in one session, you will want to fight the temptation to answer all the "what does it mean" questions surrounding the details of the ark and flood (cf. 6:14–7:24). The details are endless. We suggest you stick with the theological implications. Genesis 8:1 is strategically placed in the narrative and provides an opportunity to carefully explain the action of God in remembering Noah. Its importance far outweighs the space given in the narrative. It is important to provide explanation, as pointed out earlier, concerning the mention of God's earliest command: "be fruitful and multiply" (8:17; see also 1:22; 6:1).

Is it true?

As is so often the case in Old Testament narratives, God's record confronts readers with miracle upon miracle. The flood is one of the granddaddies of all miracles. It's possible that on any given Sunday there are listeners who stop listening because the miracle offends their sensibilities. You may decide to either (1) announce that you are aware of the problem and address it as part of your overall understanding of God's power, or (2) do your best to present evidences for the veracity of the flood (including whether it was universal or more local/regional).

In a day when virtually everyone believes in the inherent goodness of the human heart, you may have to reestablish the truthfulness and reality of the human condition from God's perspective (see 6:11–13; the total corruption of the human heart will be the focus of 8:21 and 9:18–29, so you will have time to develop it more as you proceed through Genesis). If you're teaching or preaching through Genesis, or at least this section of Genesis, you will be able to borrow, repeat, and restate some of the proofs you communicated from the previous section (see 6:5).

Now what?

If we're not careful in our presentation, we can easily teach and preach from the stance of a historian. Our listeners can very quickly hear us describe ancient events that may not relate to their lives. This is a great time for us to show that God's kingdom continues to operate on the basis of (1) his assessment of his creatures, not their self-assessment; (2) his standard of righteousness, which Noah possessed in contrast to the rest of society; (3) his right to judge all who do not meet his standard; (4) his graciousness to create and deliver all who do meet his standard by faith; and (5) his faithfulness to those he promises to deliver.

Since we know the rest of the story, we know that although the Lord promises never to flood the earth again, he will judge the world and deliver his own at the end of history. Peter, for instance, mentions the judgment and deliverance of the flood in a list of other similar occurrences in redemptive history and reasons that "the Lord knows how to rescue the godly from trials, and to keep the unrighteous under punishment until the day of judgment" (2 Peter 2:4–10, quoting from v. 9). The ancient flood teaches us about our Christian existence now. It is an important time for all who profess Christ to affirm or confirm their "godly" status by lives that match our profession.

Creativity in Presentation

Let me begin this section with some ideas for anyone deciding to give proof for the flood miracle, both the deluge and the ark of deliverance. At the time of our writing, several ministries focus on the early chapters of Genesis, including creation and the age of the earth. Our caution is that some provide answers that Genesis was not designed to answer. However, some will provide enough apologetic material to fill critical message minutes. Also, this week while writing this section, I received information in the mail from the Westminster Conference on Science and Faith. The conference title was "Design & Designer: The Convergence of Science & Theology." This is the kind of information that may help you show the reasonableness of early Genesis narratives such as the great flood.

When it comes time to create your sermon/lesson form, keep the following broad themes in mind:

- God's righteous requirement,
- humankind's inability to meet that requirement,
- God's right to judge unrighteousness, and
- God's grace in saving some who do meet his righteous requirement.

Alternatively, you can touch on these as you walk through the passage:

- The righteous must live by faith in a corrupt world (6:9–22).
- God will preserve his righteous saints through his judgment (7:1–8:1a; cf. 2 Peter 2:9).

- God will deliver his righteous saints into his new world (8:1b–19).

As noted above, I suggest you save time near the end of the sermon/lesson to take your listeners from the ancient world of the flood to the future judgment described in 2 Peter 3 (I remember learning an old song based on the flood narrative that also included the future judgment: "It's gonna rain. It's gonna rain" and then, "no more water but fire next time"). Peter mentions the flood and then proceeds to the future judgment. As he brings his letter to a close, he urges all people "who have obtained a faith . . . by the righteousness of our God and Savior Jesus Christ" (2 Peter 1:1), "Since all these things are thus to be dissolved, what sort of people ought you to be in lives of holiness and godliness" (2 Peter 3:11). Notice how this aligns with our preaching idea: like Noah, the righteous in God's eyes enjoy his salvation in a world under judgment.

If your listeners are living in comfortable surroundings, it is difficult for them to feel the urgency in this call to holiness. You may need to help them feel this with the stories of people who hear from a physician that they have a terminal illness and how that news changes the way they live. The same is true for a person who experiences an unexpected full recovery from a devastating illness. Their brush with death changes the way they look at life. They get a fresh start, sort of like humanity in Genesis 6–8.

DISCUSSION QUESTIONS

1. Discuss how "Noah found favor in the eyes of the Lord" (6:8) relates to the description of Noah in 6:9: "a righteous man, blameless in his generation. Noah walked with God." Take note of Noah's condition in light of the rest of Scripture's presentation of how a person becomes righteous.

2. What is the distinction between "righteous" and "blameless," and what does that imply for our ongoing walk with God?

3. How does our world continue to believe in the inherent goodness of the human condition despite all the evidence? (Cf. 6:11, "Now the earth was corrupt in God's sight, and the earth was filled with violence.") How does our world believe the human condition can be changed for the better? What is their answer to all the violence and corruption?

4. What does it communicate to us to hear "God remembered" when we know he could not really forget? Why did Moses use that anthropomorphism?

5. Why do you think the account does not reflect on the opposition Noah must have experienced, while it does rehearse Noah's obedience several times (6:22; 7:5, 9, 16)?

6. Why do you think that Moses's description of the flood makes so many connections with the original creation story? What are the implications for Israel, and for us as we read it?

Genesis 8:20–9:17

EXEGETICAL IDEA

Responding to Noah's genuine worship, Yahweh established his covenant, promising never again to destroy all life with flood and to provide blessing and boundaries so that his fully depraved yet valuable images could thrive.

THEOLOGICAL FOCUS

Yahweh responds to genuine worship with covenant promise, valuing his depraved images with boundaries and gracious protection for their blessing.

PREACHING IDEA

Remember the rainbow: God remembers his covenant to all life and commands us to honor life made in his image.

PREACHING POINTERS

We can only imagine the anticipation, excitement, and wonder Noah felt as he and his family stepped off the ark onto the dry ground of a freshly cleansed world. Earliest readers or hearers of this narrative would immediately recognize it as a new start for humanity led by the righteous character Noah. How does a person respond when the Lord has been so gracious to them? Answer: genuine worship that recognizes the value of relationship with God and his salvation—especially since human nature has not changed (cf. 8:21b)! The Lord accepted Noah and his sacrifice and makes vows (cf. "I will never again. . . . Neither will I ever again," 8:21). We are still living our Christian lives within the context of God's promises to Noah. And Noah leads the way for us to conduct our own genuine worship. All Christians follow his example (Noah is human; he will also provide a "go and do otherwise" example later in chapter 9!). We're also still living in the context of God's blessing on "Noah and his sons" (9:1). God's blessing contains instruction that includes how God's people are to honor life. This includes what to do whenever a life is taken, whether an animal for food ("you shall not eat flesh with its life, that is, its blood," 9:4) or of a human being ("Whoever sheds the blood of man, by man shall his blood be shed," 9:6; consider the implications this has on issues such as abortion, euthanasia, and violent crimes committed by individuals against individuals). Finally, God's people can live confidently knowing that he will keep his promise not to repeat the judgment of the flood ("I will see [the bow] and remember the everlasting covenant," 9:16). God's people who worship him receive grace, not judgment.

EXTENDING GRACE: BLESSING AND BOUNDARIES (8:20–9:17)

LITERARY STRUCTURE AND THEMES

As the rescued family disembarks, Noah marked his salvation with grateful worship, and God responded with acceptance of Noah's offering and God's self-determination to avoid this destruction in the future, introducing the coming covenant (8:20–22). The covenant explanation that follows consists of three speeches from Yahweh that define the parameters and blessing of the covenant (9:1–7), followed by the sign of the covenant (9:8–16) summarized in verse 17.

A. Yahweh responded to Noah's worship with promised grace to all life (8:20–22).
  B. God declared his covenant with blessing (9:1–7).
A'. God established his covenant promise of grace to all flesh with a sign (9:8–17).

God's promise to preserve life frames his commands for man to honor life. In 8:20–22, God vowed to "never . . . again strike down every living creature" as he had just done (v. 21). In 9:8–17 he established his covenant with the sign of the rainbow that he would never again use a flood to destroy all life (9:11 [2x], 15, using "all" twelve times in these nine verses). In between he blesses humanity but requires that human beings honor life by honoring the blood of all creatures and especially protecting the lives of all people (9:1–7). The structure demonstrates the connection between God's promise of grace and his expectation for man to remediate the recurrence of violence previously witnessed (6:11–13).

- ***Yahweh Responded to Noah's Worship with Promised Grace to All Life (8:20–22)***
- ***God Declared His Covenant with Blessing (9:1–7)***
- ***God Established His Covenant Promise with a Sign (9:8–17)***

EXPOSITION

Genesis 8:20–9:17 parallels 6:11–22 in the chiastic structure of the *toledot*, highlighting the movement of the narrative from the promise to destroy all flesh (כָּל־בָּשָׂר, three times) in chapter 6 to God's pledge in 8:20–9:17 to preserve all flesh (כָּל־בָּשָׂר, five times) or every living thing (כָּל־נֶפֶשׁ חַיָּה, four times; and כָּל־חַי, two times). God's covenant with Noah and his family formalizes the promise. Instead of complete destruction because man was destroying his earth (שַׁחֵת, five times, 6:11, 12, 13, 17), God promised lasting regularity and restraint from watery destruction (שַׁחֵת, two times, 9:11, 15). With the promise of the Noahic covenant in this section, and in tension with the judgment justly brought in chapters 6–7, God underlined his grace, recognizing the incorrigibility of man's heart (8:21).

The Noahic covenant also presents numerous parallels with Genesis 1–4, drawing attention to a new beginning with Noah as a new Adam with new boundaries. These parallels highlight God's faithful persistence in fulfilling his promises and accomplishing his redemption despite pervasive and enduring evil in humanity. It also draws attention to the continuing value of humanity as God's good creation in his image, man's responsibility for God's other creatures, and the hope that humankind has before their gracious covenant-keeping Creator. Responding to Noah's genuine worship, Yahweh established his covenant, promising never again to destroy all life with flood and providing blessing and boundaries so that his fully depraved yet valuable images could thrive.

New Beginning with Noah

Genesis 9:1–7 parallels Genesis 1–4 with specific terminology and general ideas:

"God blessed . . . and said to them, 'Be fruitful and multiply and fill the earth'"	1:28	9:1, 7
Man will rule	1:26, 28	9:2
God provides food	1:29	9:3
Man is created in God's image	1:26–27	9:6
Man must account for man's blood	4:10–12	9:5–6

Yahweh Responded to Noah's Worship with Promised Grace to All Life (8:20–22)

In response to Noah's acceptable worship, Yahweh purposed never again to curse the ground, destroying every living creature as he had done.

8:20. As his first recorded act after disembarking from the ark, Noah built an altar to Yahweh and offered burnt offerings. This is the first explicit reference to the burnt offering. The text does not explain how Noah knew what was acceptable to offer and what was not nor the significance of the burnt offering, but the ancient reader would have related both to the law, assuming a similar understanding and significance for appropriate worship to Yahweh. The narrative explicitly relates the appropriate nature of the sacrifice, both by Noah's use of "clean" (טָהֹר) beasts and birds as well as by Yahweh's response (8:21), smelling the pleasing aroma (רֵיחַ הַנִּיחֹחַ) and guaranteeing ongoing stability with blessing.

The Burnt Offering

The burnt offering was used in appropriate worship outside of the sanctuary worship (both before a tabernacle or temple were built, as here or in Gen. 22, or after being built, as in Exod. 24:5; 2 Sam. 6:17–18) as well as in unacceptable worship (Exod. 32:6; 2 Kings 10:24). It was appropriate as a gift to God that could be offered to please God and assure his attention to one's prayers (Num. 23:3; 1 Sam. 7:9–10) or to fulfill a vow or offer a freewill offering with thanksgiving (Lev. 22:17–25; Num. 15:1–11), which would be particularly appropriate here (see *NIDOTTE* 3:405–15; Averbeck, "Sacrifices and Offerings," *DOTP* 712–13).

Noah's initial act after leaving the ark again confirmed his righteous character, modeling the appropriate response of those who walk with God, when God acts in favor toward them. Noah offered his gift to God in worship and thanksgiving, responding with spontaneity and generosity. He offered something from all the clean beasts and birds, also an act of faith. When one's supply is limited, generosity becomes more conspicuous and costly. The survival of each sort of creature, as with humanity itself, was fully under God's control and had already been demonstrated dramatically in the flood. Noah's actions again verify God's assessment (6:9; 7:1). Noah's worship, however, precipitated God's gracious covenant promise for all life.

Covenants

The covenant was a common means both in the Bible and in the ancient Near East to define relationships of all sorts requiring oaths. It was used in individual relationships (Gen. 31:44; 1 Sam. 18:3), including marriages (Mal. 2:14), between clans or tribes (Gen. 21:27), between nations

(1 Kings 5:26), and between God and humanity (as here and in the Abrahamic, Mosaic, Davidic, and New covenants). Current debate questions whether any covenants were ever without any expectation for the recipient. In the ancient world, the closest possibility was the land grant treaties, though some argue that there are also conditions or expectations there (see discussion on the Abrahamic covenant, particularly in Gen. 15, p. 298). Other treaties or covenants, however, would make clear requirements of both parties so that both sides would take an oath to abide by the stipulations, with both penalties for violating them and benefits for keeping them (in the ancient world, the Suzerain Vassal Treaties were such treaties that were very similar in form to the Mosaic covenant). While we do not see any oath formula for Noah, we do see responsibilities, which we will argue are part of the covenant. (Cf. Hahn, "Covenant," LBD; McConville, בְּרִית, *NIDOTTE* 1:747–55.)

God's covenant with Noah and "all flesh" is the first covenant mentioned in Scripture and forms the foundation for God's ongoing relationship with humanity. Through Noah, God effectively deals with all humanity, and God will increasingly define his program with humanity through his covenant with Abram (Gen. 15, 17, 22), envisioning his blessing of and relationship with humanity and clarifying the expectations for humankind in the Mosaic covenant at Sinai (Exod. 20–24). He will continue to build and delineate his future working through the Davidic covenant (1 Sam. 7) and finally the new covenant (Jer. 31).

8:21–22. God's response to Noah's sacrifice in verse 21 pictures, with anthropomorphic vividness, Yahweh's pleasure in Noah's worship and reminder of Lamech's desire (5:29). Just as God's reaction of judgment (6:6) plays on the sounds and terms of Lamech's dedication in naming Noah, so God's pleasure and promise (8:21) plays on the name of Noah. Yahweh smells the "pleasing aroma" (נִיחֹחַ), a word derived from "rest" or "get relief from" (נוּחַ; cf. Oswalt, נוּחַ, *NIDOTTE* 3:56–59) and which sounds like "Noah" (נֹחַ). After necessary judgment, humankind will indeed find some relief from God's wrath through Noah's righteous worship. Appropriate sacrifice provides the atonement necessary for humankind to enjoy God's blessing and promise, which Yahweh will formalize in a covenant (Averbeck, עֹלָה, *NIDOTTE* 3:405–15).

Not only does the word choice recall Lamech's desire (5:29) and God's initial proclamation of judgment (6:5–6), but Yahweh's stated reason for staying future judgment recalls his reason for bringing judgment. God's response conveys a nearly opposite interplay between human action and his stated intent. Both comment on the state of the human heart, and both relate the reaction in the heart of God (see translation analysis, 6:5–6, p. 165). Here, however, a nearly identical statement about the intransigence of the human heart leads to grace whereas previously it precipitated judgment. The narrative draws attention to the discrepancy, inviting reflection on why God would destroy life and, for the same reason, not destroy life again.

God spoke to himself, anthropomorphically letting the reader see the reaction of God to appropriate worship, both in his pleasure in worship and his intention to refrain from future similar judgment. His decision not to "curse" (from קלל) the "ground" (אֲדָמָה) reminds the reader, however, not only of the judgment of the flood but also of the judgment in the garden (3:17) when God "cursed" (from ארר) the "ground" (אֲדָמָה) for the first time on account of humanity. While a different verbal root is used for the "curse," showing distinction, that distinction cannot be pushed too far since they can be used in parallel with little difference (Exod. 22:28 [HB 27]). God is not intending to reverse the initial curse (contrary to Frankena 1972, 122). He is reminding the reader that he is starting over with a new Adam, only here the original curse is still in effect and does not need to be repeated. Rather, God will never again destroy the world in flood as the following declarations make clear.

God's Pleasure in Worship

This response of God contrasts with the gods of Mesopotamia in the Gilgamesh Epic who swarm around the sacrifice of Utnapishtim like flies after the flood because they are hungry and need to be cared for (Foster, "Gilgamesh (1.132)," *CoS*, I:458–60). Yahweh appears in direct contrast to the gods of the ancient world. He displays his holy character and sovereign control, judging out of righteous justice rather than unreasoning irritation at not getting sleep. He spared righteous Noah with purpose to carry out promise, rather than in angry surprise discovering too late that another god spared humans against his will, yet easily pacified by reason. He responded in pleased and principled grace to Noah's loyal offering, rather than starved greed. Yahweh not only is solely sovereign, but he is seen to be holy and righteous and good, in complete distinction from the ancient gods made in man's image.

The reason for God's decision, however, provides a dramatic lesson for the post-flood world. God responded with his vow of clemency because ("for") humanity's heart had not changed! It seems completely counterintuitive. The conjunction "for" (כִּי) presents the last thing we would expect as a reason for God's kindness. Before the flood, God declared judgment on a sin-obsessed world (6:5–6). Now he uses nearly the same assessment to announce grace. His previous grace now also shows even more clearly since the corrupt human hearts include "righteous" Noah. His righteousness was not objective perfection but God's characterization based on his faith (Gen. 15:6) shown in specific obedience (Gen. 6:22; 7:5, 9, 16). The two clauses are nearly identical, but not quite:

TRANSLATION ANALYSIS 8:21a

The main ways to understand the conjunction (כִּי) are reflected in the translations. It can be understood with its more common causal force, "because" (NJB), or explanatory, "for" (ESV, NASB95, NRSV), or less commonly as concessive, "even though" (NET, NIV, NLT), or "although" (NKJV). The interpretations from this tension vary greatly. The causal force suggests to some that the flood could never change man, but it changed God, giving him new resolve to "stay with" his rebellious creation through the pain he feels (Brueggemann 1982, 81). On the other hand, the concessive sense has suggested to others that though the flood failed to allow the changes in man God was hoping for, he accepted Noah's sacrifice to change his mind and not destroy his world this way again (Williams 2004, 106–7). Either way, the emphasis is on the unchanged heart of humanity, though the implications must be clarified. We will note a subtle shift of emphasis in the text. As we argue in the Exposition, the better sense is to see that the flood exhibited the justice of God, which humanity needed to see, understand, and remember, while the surprising response of Yahweh to Noah will trumpet the grace of God for humanity, developing his character in unambiguous contrast to the recalcitrant humans.

6:5	8:21
and that every *intention* (יֵצֶר) of the thoughts of *his heart* (לִבּוֹ) was only *evil* (רַע) continually	for the *intention* (יֵצֶר) of man's *heart* (לֵב) is *evil* (רַע) from his youth

Righteousness
The tension in this narrative serves to highlight the theological truth that righteousness before God was never a matter of perfection or a blameless heart. This passage, by declaring the decadence of the human heart when it can only apply to Noah and his family, shows that Noah's righteousness must also be seen in the same category as Abraham later (Gen. 15:6): a product of faith.

In Genesis 6:5, the judgment of God came on humanity because their sin was pervasive in all their thoughts, continuously ("every inclination . . . all the time," NET, repeating כָּל twice). The pervasive emphasis matched the pervasive judgment (כָּל is used thirty-seven times in Genesis 6–7, speaking mostly of the extent of God's judgment). Genesis 8:21 emphasizes the lack of change in the human heart. "All" is absent and "all the time" becomes "from childhood" (NET). God's focus shifts to the unchanging nature of the heart. The issue here is not that what he tried did not work. Rather, we see the character of God on display. The judgment was necessary to show the outcome of evil. It did not fix the problem, which was not a surprise. Rather, it highlighted the need for mercy and grace, which God will now show as his means to accomplish his promise from the beginning (3:15). The character of Yahweh that requires both justice and extends compassion and grace is most clearly declared in Exodus 34:6–7, and in that very context the same tension exists. In Exodus 32:9 God declared judgment because Israel was "stiff-necked." In Exodus 34:9 Moses, understanding God's self-revelation in verses 6–7, prayed for God's favor precisely because they were "stiff-necked." In comparing the same construction Moberly (1983, 90) concludes in both cases that "God will show mercy, a mercy experienced supremely in his accompanying presence, because it lies within the character of God not only to inflict judgment but also to show mercy—even to a continuingly sinful people" (cf. p. 92).

TRANSLATION ANALYSIS 8:21b
The term usually translated "youth" (נְעוּרִים, ESV, NASB95, NKJV, NRSV) can also be used for an infant (Ezek. 16:22, and in parallel to "from my mother's womb," Job 31:18) and is better translated "from childhood" (NET, NIV, NLT). The passage is acknowledging sin from the beginning.

The purpose of the flood, then, is both immediate justice and a declaration of God's right to judge the pervasive evil of humanity that will destroy God's good creation. It also, however, graphically demonstrates the merciful character of Yahweh, who will continue to bless and work to bring about his redemptive purpose despite man's unchanged heart. Never again will God judge "every living creature" (Gen. 8:21) as he had done here. The promise of God's internal vow will resonate with the audience of any age. It will also serve as a warning to humanity, as the Noahic covenant will suggest.

Yahweh's final statement again returns to his creation, not just the creatures. For the benefit of the creatures, and especially humankind (the only ones bringing in a harvest), he ensures the regular rhythm of life each year. Rather than something that is controlled by the warring of the gods and the dying and rising of the storm god (following the theology of the Baal Epic and Canaanite mythology), God guarantees that he will keep the seasons on time, headlined by planting and harvest. That is not to say that he is not free to use famine and drought to discipline his people (Lev. 26:19; Deut. 28:23–24). Humanity can depend on the ongoing regularity of God's creation because Yahweh is trustworthy. The millennia of reliable yearly cycles have repeatedly demonstrated that reality.

God Declared His Covenant with Blessing (9:1–7)

God blessed humanity with fruitfulness and boundaries for his images to thrive.

9:1. For the second time since Noah disembarked, recalling his initial blessing on all living things (Gen. 1:22, 28), God pronounced blessing on his creatures in his renewed world. In Genesis 8:17 God blessed the animals with fertility (recalling 1:22), and now he blessed humanity with the same (recalling 1:28). God was starting fresh after the flood with renewed promise. Noah, the new Adam, would have all the empowering that he needed to accomplish the task and thrive in God's new world. Of course, the flood did not come from overpopulation (contra Gilgamesh Epic). God had wanted humanity to fill up his world before the flood, and he wanted the same again.

This blessing will be repeated one more time, framing the covenant (9:7). The *inclusio* sets the parameters for the covenant. Within the context of blessed numerical growth with the problems that will entail, humankind must be restrained in their treatment of the animals and other people. Or conversely, for humanity to enjoy the blessing, they must respect life, including how they treat anything and anyone that they can exercise power over. Humankind may eat animals, but only within the boundary of appropriate draining of the blood. And the life of God's images must be honored, requiring the life of any that take human life lightly.

God's full blessing can only be realized in the context of appropriate administration:

A Blessing: be fruitful and multiply (9:1)

  B Administrate your authority well over animal life (9:2–4)

  B' Administrate your authority well over human life (9:5–6)

A' (Blessing:) be fruitful and multiply (9:7)

9:2–4. Humanity's relation to the beasts, previously described in terms of ruling as God's representative (1:26, 28) would now be marked by tension. God built in self-protection ("fear") for the animal kingdom, introducing tension in the relationship. Yet that fear may also bring danger to humanity. God, then, reinforced people's power over the animals. Humankind's job description has not been changed. The command to rule appropriately as God's images was still valid (they are still God's images under his rule, as 9:6 will show), highlighting man's authority by the metonymy of God giving them "into your hand" (v. 2).

Holy War

Numerous scholars note the similarities of this language with holy war language and the language of conflict with Israel's enemies. God puts the fear and dread of Israel on the enemies and then gives the enemies into their hand. This language and its implications are summarized well by Mason (2007, 186–91) and related to the implications in Genesis 9: these human-animal relations describe the relation at Noah's time, prefigure Israel's relation with their enemies later, and present common covenant ideas, which he argues are part of the Noahic covenant. The significance here shows the responsibility man has as part of the Noahic covenant to rule and subdue (1:28) his world, maintaining the original mandate for humanity.

In verse 3, God gave humanity generous authorization to eat animals (9:3), just as he gave them generous permission to eat from every plant or tree (1:29). The first word of the first clause and the last word of the second clause, "all" (כֹּל), frames the verse, showing by *inclusio* the emphasis on God's generous gift. He also referenced the initial permission to eat plants (1:29), which emphasized the lavish opportunity. The permission to eat plants in Genesis 1 did not preclude animals but focused on the liberal grant. Verse 3, then, is not necessarily a reversal of a taboo, but the conferring of new freedom. It may also be that part of the sin before the flood was the abuse of animal life, consonant with the following instruction concerning the value of human life.

Though humankind has new freedom to eat animals, they must still respect animal life by not consuming the blood (9:4). For the Israelite hearing the law, this would be obvious, since the blood is the symbol of the life of the animals ("its life, that is, its blood," בְּנַפְשׁוֹ דָמוֹ; cf. Lev. 17:11, 14) and would be used for atonement and must be honored (Lev. 17:10–14). Significantly, however, as with the following injunction regarding human life, God expected all humanity to maintain these restrictions. The law clarifies for us how that would be carried out (Lev. 17:13; Deut. 12:16, 24; 15:23).

9:5–6. If the blood of the animal, representing its life, is sacrosanct, then how much more is the blood of the image of God? Verse 5 declares, again connecting humankind's blood (דִּמְכֶם) with his life (נַפְשֹׁתֵיכֶם), the inviolable nature of that blood. God himself will bring justice, requiring satisfaction from any offender, whether man or beast. Three times God repeats that he will "require" it (אֶדְרֹשׁ) or "exact punishment" (NET), emphasizing his oversight and judgment. The final sentence specifies that not only are beasts culpable, but people also must answer to God for taking human life. This presents a clear expression of God's standard, underlining God's grace to Cain (4:11–12) and Lamech's overweening pride in his self-assertion (4:24).

In comparison with the antediluvian narrative, however, it also implies that the rationale for this new parameter may be precisely in this area. The narrative of Genesis 6 was not clear on the specific crimes of humanity that demonstrated the "evil" intent of the heart (רַע, 6:5), "corrupting" the earth (שׁחת, 6:11–12) and showing such "violence" (חָמָס). The need for these parameters at this juncture, along with the overall structure (this section is parallel in the chiastic structure of the narrative to the statement of the cause, judgment, and promise of covenant, 6:11–22), suggests that at least part of the destruction of God's good creation was taking human life (and perhaps animal life) lightly. The progression from Cain to Lamech leading up to this judgment would indicate the same violation of God's representative images. The use of "brother" (אָח) in verse 5 (NKJV, NASB) highlights this comparison, suggesting a regulation for what has been a problem throughout human history.

TRANSLATION ANALYSIS 9:5

The Hebrew is difficult to render into good English and retain the allusion to Cain. Literally, the Hebrew reads, "from the hand of a man, his brother," showing the family relationship all humanity shares. NASB95 translates "from every man's brother," and NKJV "from the hand of every man's brother." NET Bible adds a clause at the end, "since the man was his relative." Other versions simply paraphrase "fellow" man (ESV, NLT) or "another" (NIV, NRSV).

Verse 6 declares the general principle and the rationale for that principle. "Whoever" (including humans or beasts) takes the life of another human will forfeit his life. God lays the responsibility of enforcing that penalty at the feet of humanity. The penalty has already been declared as God's justice, and the structure of the initial clause of verse 6 visually communicates the just nature of the penalty. Many translations mirror the Hebrew, showing the chiastic construction and framing the clause with the verb "shed," then "blood" and "man" in the center: "Whoever sheds the blood of man, by man shall his blood be shed" (שֹׁפֵךְ דַּם הָאָדָם בָּאָדָם דָּמוֹ יִשָּׁפֵךְ). Humanity must appropriately redress the injustice perpetrated against humanity so that talionic justice is accomplished. While God will never again destroy all life by flood, justice must still be served by God's representatives. God not only gave them the mandate but the authority. God appropriately delegated his responsibility and right to judge (9:5) to his images to carry out (v. 6), functioning within their originally mandated responsibility to represent God in their rule over his world (1:26, 28).[1]

TRANSLATION ANALYSIS 9:6
The preposition "by" (בְּ, instrumental use, so most translations) can be translated alternatively as substitution, "for" (REB). The latter understands the murderer to be the substitute for the victim in his death, leaving the responsibility up to God to carry out. Since the normal sense of the preposition would indicate instrument (substitution is unusual) and verse 5 has already assigned responsibility to God, the traditional interpretation fits best here (for a helpful overview, see Mathews 1996, 404–5).

God did not specify the means for carrying out justice. But he did identify the reason. The causal clause "for" (כִּי) provides the basis for the command. Generally, we have understood this to state that human life is inviolable because it is in God's image (see Exposition on 1:26–27, p. 88). That is certainly true, but as we have argued, more significantly, human must rightly guard the life of human because he or she rules as God's representative image and must maintain appropriate order. God's declaration not only showed the value of human life but declared that even the rampant sin because of Adam and Eve's rebellion had not removed the image of God and the inseparable responsibility of his creation. While humankind bears the mark of his ancestry through Adam and so bears the effects of sin (5:3), he still also bears the image and likeness of God (1:26–27; 5:1). Humankind, then, holds immense obligation in God's world.[2] Ruinous violence against humanity, including the most vulnerable and least able to care for themselves, must be opposed, as the prophets often reminded Israel and Judah (e.g., Amos 5:10–15; Mic. 2; Zech. 7:8–14).

9:7. As we saw in verse 1, God framed the boundaries for his new world with his blessing of fertility. While tasking humanity with the responsibility to care for creation by maintaining the rule of law and the value of life, God provided the boundaries that allow people to fill the earth and be fruitful in it. Verse 7 shifts attention from the general command, which will be largely future for all humanity in contrast to the preflood deterioration of humanity, to the specific immediate responsibility and blessing on Noah and his family, "But as for you" (NET). The emphasis here on Noah and his family will contrast with God's own responsibility declared in verse 9, "As for me" (NKJV, see Translation Analysis 9:9 below).

TRANSLATION ANALYSIS 9:7
The *waw* on the non-verb at the beginning of the clause is the classic disjunction (WOC, 39.2.3, 650–52), validating the NET translation and the similar "As for you" (NASB95, NIV). Another common translation, "And you" (ESV, NRSV), loses the focus on the immediate concern instead of the previous general prohibition. See Mason (2007, 184–86) on the use in covenant formularies (especially 185, n. 23).

The restatement of the blessing also shifts slightly from the initial reminder in 9:1. In verse 1, God repeated verbatim the initial part of the blessing from 1:28. Here he began the same, but instead of "fill the earth" (וּמִלְאוּ אֶת־הָאָרֶץ), he emphasized the outcome with

1 For helpful discussions on man's responsibility representing Yahweh in carrying out God's justice, see Mason (2007, 191–94) or Wilson (2017). For discussion on capital punishment in human society, see Waltke and Fredricks (2001, 157–58) or Walton (2001, 354–55).

2 Mathews's (1996, 405–6) discussion is helpful, especially n. 129 on the abortion debate, including other resources. The issue, however, is broader than abortion alone and needs to include discussions on social justice and protection for all the powerless and disadvantaged in society.

"increase greatly" and repeated "and multiply in it." His repetition of the blessing emphasized the focus on his gracious blessing of humanity, even as he established their boundaries. The subtle shift of the blessing in 9:7 adds to the impact of that gracious blessing. God graciously gave humanity the ability to thrive, even with corrupted hearts, both by his blessing and by his limitations.

God Established His Covenant Promise with a Sign (9:8–17)

God established his covenant promise that he would never again destroy all life on earth through flood, with the sign of the rainbow.

God concluded his dialogue with Noah with his declaration of the sign of the covenant, providing ongoing confirmation of his vow in 8:20–22 that he would never again destroy all life with a flood. Moses laid out three formal addresses from God: an initial statement of promise, the confirming sign of the covenant, and a final summary (vv. 8–11, 12–16, 17, each introduced by וַיֹּאמֶר אֱלֹהִים). These work together chiastically (similarly, Wenham 1987, 194):

- A. God established his covenant with "every living creature" (9:8–11).
  - B. "This is the sign of the covenant" between Noah and "every living creature" to "all future generations" (9:12).
    - C. He set his "bow in the cloud" (9:13a).
      - D. The bow will remind God that he will never again destroy all flesh with a flood (9:13b–15).
    - C'. The sign comes with the storm, "when the bow is in the clouds" (9:16a).
  - B'. God will remember the "everlasting covenant" with "every living creature" (9:16b).
- A'. "This is the sign of the covenant . . . established . . . (with) all flesh" (9:17).

The structure outlined here focuses attention on the establishing of the covenant (vv. 9, 11, 17) and its sign (vv. 12, 13, 17), the bow (vv. 13, 14, 16). It visibly confirms, when the rainbow appears, that God will remember and never again destroy all flesh by flood (stated two times in v. 11 and again in verse 15).

9:8–11. God's first address summarizes his covenant promise that he was establishing (vv. 9, 11) with Noah and his sons (v. 8), which would affect all of Noah's future descendants (v. 9) and every animal that came off the ark and lives on the earth (v. 10). Having delineated human responsibilities, God established his covenant responsibilities to all life. Yahweh's responsibility is reinforced by the repetition of "my" covenant (four times, 6:18; 9:9, 11, 15) and the repetition that it is for God to see and remember (9:15, 16). God emphasized the inclusion of all life (two statements and all categories listed in v. 10) and his commitment never to use a flood like this (repeated twice in v. 11) to bring their destruction or to destroy the earth (by metonymy, reinforcing all life on the earth). When we connect 9:1–7 with 9:8–17, God's covenant with Noah includes responsibilities for both parties, yet God's promise not to destroy with a flood is not directly conditioned on people keeping their responsibility.[3] God's destruction of life will not be repeated (Kreider 2014).

> *TRANSLATION ANALYSIS 9:9*
> Another disjunctive clause (see translation analysis 9:7, וַאֲנִי) now emphasizes Yahweh's personal role in this. He declares his own role in this covenant: "I Myself" (NASB95), "as for Me" (NKJV, NRSV).

9:12–16. God's second address introduces the rainbow as the sign of the covenant, making explicit the lasting nature of the covenant ("for all future generations," v. 12; "everlasting covenant,"

3 Williamson makes this helpful distinction ("Covenant," *DOTP* 140).

v. 16) and as a reminder of the promise (vv. 15–16). The "sign" (אוֹת) of the covenant is largely mnemonic (Kruger, *NIDOTTE* 1:331–33). Here, the sign is focused on God (he will remember), but the impact is still for humanity, who need to know that God remembers (see below). In chapter 17, circumcision will be instituted as the sign for the Abrahamic covenant, providing the visual symbol for the nation of Israel of their inclusion in the covenant (17:14), though it would certainly include a reminder of the promised procreation as well (17:2, 4, 6–8).

Numerous words and phrases are repeated chiastically here. The frame in verses 12 and 16b describes the covenant as for "all future generations" (לְדֹרֹת עוֹלָם, v. 12) and so "everlasting" (עוֹלָם, v. 16b). The covenant is between God, Noah and his family, and every living creature (vv. 12, 16b). The frame provides the point of the section as initially God established the sign (v. 12) and then declared his faithfulness to the covenant when he sees it (v. 16b).

The secondary frame (vv. 13a, 16a) identifies God's bow as the sign in the clouds.[4] The "bow" (קֶשֶׁת) can refer to either a hunting weapon (27:3) or a weapon of war (48:22), supporting the common opinion that, visually and metaphorically, God was identifying the rainbow hanging up in the clouds with his cessation of hostilities against the earth, at least in this way. One problem appears obvious, since it does not represent the cessation of all judgment but only total judgment through flood. Other scholars have noted several difficulties with this identification (Hamilton 1990, 317–18; Wenham 1987, 196). Turner (1993) gives the best suggestion, saying that it represents the firmament holding back the waters from flooding again, relating it to Ezekiel 1:22–28 (cf. Gen. 7:11; 8:2). It provides a very visual illustration for humanity because it appears with the storm and graphically portrays the promise.

The center of the chiasm summarizes the placement of the bow as God's reminder to himself that he will never again destroy all people with a flood. The irony is that the human population needs to know and accept God's promise. God, however, assured humanity with a visual reminder that he would remember and withhold his judgment (see Exposition on 8:1a, p. 183). When the rainbow appears (ראה, 9:14), he himself will "see" (ראה, v. 16) the rainbow and will "remember" (זכר, vv. 15, 16) the covenant. As with God remembering Noah in 8:1, the anthropomorphism does not declare that God might forget, but it emphasizes the assurance to humanity that God would continue to be faithful to his promise as long as rainbows occur. That also reminds humanity that they must be faithful to this covenant (live as his images in his creation) because he does remember his covenant. They have responsibilities to which he will hold them accountable.

9:17. God's final address recaps God's promise, establishing his covenant and providing a sign. People can be confident that God will not forget. They can live without the fear of total destruction through the many storms that will occur in their experience. God will keep his covenant, including the blessing that man can be fruitful and fill the earth.

THEOLOGICAL FOCUS

Yahweh responds to genuine worship with covenant promise, valuing his depraved images with boundaries and gracious protection for their blessing.

4 When God established the rainbow as the sign of the Noahic covenant, some have assumed that there was never a rainbow before this. However, establishing a sign does not require a new phenomenon. When Yahweh would establish circumcision, it was already a well-known custom among ancient peoples at and before the time of Abraham (Williamson, "Circumcision," *DOTP* 122–25). God, however, chose to use this as an appropriate reminder and symbol of the new relationship he was establishing and humanity's participation in that covenant.

Yahweh's response to Noah's worship highlights Yahweh's grace that has already been on display in Genesis, most recently in delivering righteous Noah. Here, however, the tension with his justice comes into sharp relief when he affirms that every human heart (including Noah's!) is corrupt from their beginning. While humanity will continue to deserve full judgment, God will graciously withhold justice, at least in this world, simply because it is his character. This also provides the ability for God to fulfill his promise, crushing evil (3:16) and giving the blessing he consistently holds out to humanity (9:1, 7).

Yahweh is a God of order and guarantees the regularity of the seasons, which allows humanity to thrive and grow. He declares blessing on his creatures, reiterating his purpose from the beginning (9:1, 7; cf. 1:28). He gives generous gifts, including a lavish food supply (9:3) and the ability to access it (9:2). He also provides safety for his images by declaring their sanctity (9:6). When God does declare judgment on violators, it is appropriate (9:6a–b), bringing commensurate justice to any person who takes the life of his brother (9:5), because all human beings are in God's image (9:6). It is God's appropriate justice to mete out (9:5), but he delegates the responsibility to humanity (9:6).

In establishing his covenant, God both declares and demonstrates his faithfulness to his promise. The regularity of the seasons will demonstrate it, but the recurring rainbow in the clouds will illustrate with every passing storm that God will remember his promise (9:15–17). Thousands of years have repeatedly confirmed the promise of God.

Humanity suffers from incurable heart disease and is hopelessly corrupt from birth. Even a righteous Noah is not judged righteous by his meritorious heart but through faith that works in obedient submission to God. All people, then, need God's grace. His grace culminates in Christ where he finally provides the means to counter the heart disease and provide the final means to righteousness imputed through faith.

Noah demonstrated the appropriate response of humankind to God's grace, by presenting an offering acceptable to God (8:20–21). Not only does God offer a means to please him by faith resulting in obedience, but he accepts the gifts of that righteous person, even though his heart is still replete with evil (8:21). Such grace is still active, waiting for the complete dissolution of evil and glorification of his people in the return of Christ. We are reminded that human privilege and blessing begins with worship (ch. 2) lived out by honoring God and valuing his images (9:6).

The human heart presents the real problem that must be corrected. God extends grace, working to bring blessing despite the enduring corruption of the human heart. His plan for redemption, however, will deal with this core corruption in Christ. Human heart damage requires remedial safeguards to keep the resulting destruction of his world to a minimum so that God will be able to bring about his plan of redemption (crush the snake). Specifically, for humankind to image God they must have safeguards to value life and promote justice, including both the animal kingdom (9:4) and humankind (9:5–6). As God's images, humanity must be honored so that they can multiply and experience God's blessing, indicating their qualitative difference from the rest of the animal kingdom.

PREACHING AND TEACHING STRATEGIES

Exegetical and Theological Synthesis

Begin preparation for the sermon/lesson by focusing on Noah's first recorded action upon leaving the ark: "Noah built an altar . . . and offered burnt offerings" (8:20). While their worship will look different, many of your listeners will be following Noah's example; others will need to evaluate whether the moniker "worshipper" fits. The narrative describes how God and worshipper relate. It is this act of worship that the Lord accepts, and he responds with more grace, even though the heart condition of humankind has not changed since the pre-flood days (cf. 6:1–7).

Next, you'll want to focus on the instruction the Lord gives concerning the value of animal and human life. This instruction is intended to create a new world where violence and brutality are no more. God has the right to take the lives of those he has created. He also has the right to dictate how human beings treat the lives he has created. All this is in the context of the commandment, "be fruitful and multiply, increase greatly on the earth and multiply in it" (9:7; also similar in v. 1).

One thread that holds this unit together is the taking of a life. We see this in the final description of God's covenant to Noah and his sons (9:8–17). God promises to "never again" cut off all flesh by flood (v. 11). And he graciously provides a visible "sign of the covenant": "I have set my bow in the cloud" (vv. 12–13). Our listeners live their Christian existence within this same "everlasting covenant" (v. 16). More precisely, we could say that Christians experience their new covenant existence under the umbrella of the Noahic covenant.

Preaching Idea

Remember the rainbow: God remembers his covenant to all life and commands us to honor life made in his image.

What does it mean?

As pointed out in the exegetical section, listeners will want an explanation for the fact that the evil in the heart of humankind functions differently in this section than it did in Genesis 6. The heart condition of humanity has not changed—we'll see an illustration of this next section—which is why the Lord devised a plan in eternity past that allowed him to be both "just and the justifier of the one who has faith in Jesus" (Rom. 3:26). In this day and age, the value of a life is low. A simple reading of this section will cause listeners to reflect on God's estimate of the life he creates, especially human life made in the image of God. If a canonical reading is part of your repertoire, you may want to compare God's covenant with Noah, his family, and all creatures on earth with the judgment that is described in 2 Peter 3:1–10. One day God will destroy "the ungodly" (3:7). That judgment will not be by water, but by fire. The rainbow does show us that we are still living under God's gracious provision of life. He is still being patient with us. The rainbow reminds God of his promise; it should remind us of his grace.

Is it true?

Congregations and classes that know their Bibles well may still need a refresher course in God's feelings about our worship. In Genesis 8:21 we read, "And when the Lord smelled the pleasing aroma, the Lord said in his heart . . ." Is that true? Does God react like that? It's an opportunity for us to show the meaning of such anthropomorphisms. It is true, isn't it, that the Lord is worthy of our worship? Next, some listeners might not know how to read the dietary freedom in this section. Maybe more critical is spending a few moments in the message about the sanctity of human life made in the image of God. It's one thing to argue for a Creator/God; it's quite another thing to argue for a Creator/God who creates humankind in his image. Amid all the meteorological explanations for the phenomenon of a rainbow, listeners will appreciate hearing how God infuses it with theological meaning. Some of our listeners might wonder if God's explanation is true. You can decide how many message minutes deal with the relationship between the scientific and the theological. The mixture in the sky of dark clouds, rain, and sunshine capture the elements of judgment and grace operating in God's kingdom.

Now what?

The "now what?" or "so what?" in this section begins with the importance of worshipping the

Lord alone as the gracious giver and sustainer of life, both physical and spiritual (8:20). We express our gratitude to God for the rhythms and seasons of life we enjoy (8:22). God's instructions direct the way in which we interact with our world, especially with respect to the way in which we treat other living beings (9:3–6). As stated earlier, violence against individuals, the unborn, the elderly, and the powerless occur in virtually every part of God's world. Finally, there is a kind of calmness or comfort that comes from believing that the Lord will keep his covenant, of which the rainbow serves as a sign. We do not live in fear that the Lord will send another flood. Our listeners from Noah's line can be assured that they will experience the Lord's deliverance in this world and for all eternity when he once again begins with a clean new world.

Creativity in Presentation

Imagination can be such a powerful tool for exposition of Scripture, and the scene in Genesis 8:19–20 is a great place to help your listeners use their sanctified imagination. Can you imagine what it must have been like for Noah and his family to exit the ark and look at their "new" world? For instance, do you picture a pristine vista or a world littered with debris? A person's experience of the realization of God's grace will be different depending on the view. You may also want to paint a picture of the human condition in all its ugliness. In a day when everyone believes in the inherent goodness of the human heart—think Pink's song "What About Us" that preaches, "We are billions of beautiful hearts"—we can never restate the reality of human depravity too much, especially when it's wrapped in the context of the saving grace of God.

Concerning the overall structure of this unit, I suggest keeping a message/lesson unified around the subject of the sanctity of human life created by God in his image. This will keep the session from fragmenting in the minds of your listeners. In this section of Genesis God spares Noah and his family's life, honors life with a dietary restriction ("you shall not eat flesh with its life, that is, its blood" in 9:4), protects life with the death penalty (9:6), and finally promises never again to end all life by means of another flood. When you arrive at this final section of God's covenant with Noah and all living creatures, you will want to display or paint a picture of a rainbow. The mixture of sun and rain that creates the bow is a wonderful picture of hope in a world where brokenness can overshadow blessing.

You might consider the following movement for your message:

- God values life.
- Humanity made in the image of God must also value life.
- Remember that God remembers his covenant promise to preserve life for the final judgment.

To follow the layout of the passage, you could structure it something like this:

- God extends grace, giving life to his undeserving creatures (8:20–22).
- God provides boundaries so that all life can thrive (9:1–7).
- God guarantees his promise (9:8–17).

DISCUSSION QUESTIONS

1. What in our worship provides a pleasing aroma to God? What makes it pleasing? How can we cultivate that practice?

2. What characteristic(s) or attribute(s) of God is (are) involved in his decision to never again judge all the earth with a flood?

3. What responsibilities does being in God's image require of us, especially as believers being made into the image of Christ?

4. Genesis 9:6 reads like justification for the death penalty. Spend some time thinking about whether it's possible to do justice to humankind being created in God's image if the death penalty is rejected. Can a person argue against the death penalty based on moral or humanitarian grounds and still honor the fact that "God made man in his own image"?

5. How can we explain the promise of the rainbow to our children so that they both see God's grace and God's justice?

6. What actions can we take to promote a higher value for all life in our communities, states, and nation?

Genesis 9:18–29

EXEGETICAL IDEA

After the flood, Noah and his sons, the progenitors of all humanity, expose the human heart, receiving cursing and conflict or blessing and grace based on honor or dishonor to Yahweh and his authority structure.

THEOLOGICAL FOCUS

Human response to Yahweh's authority structures exposes the state of the human heart, portending future cursing and conflict or blessing and grace for submissive honor to Yahweh.

PREACHING IDEA

Our spiritual heritage reveals both the dangers of cursed sin and the possibility of salvation blessing—which will we choose?

PREACHING POINTERS

Remember our broad options for teaching and preaching this section: the "go and do otherwise" angles from Noah ("drunkenness" in v. 21) and Ham ("saw the nakedness of his father and told his two brothers" in v. 22) and the incentive of blessing on Shem and Japheth for all listeners to find their place in their lineage. The first readers/hearers of this narrative couldn't believe what they were seeing. This is not what anyone expected to happen in Noah's family, but this reminds us of the condition of the human heart after the flood. When we have a saint who falls and is in a compromising situation (surprise?), how do we react? What should we expect from those we hold highly in the Lord? We may be less surprised to see the youngest act foolishly and suffer, but we must see the possibility in any of us to fall. The entire human race, starting from Noah's three sons (v. 19), exists within the curse and blessing announced by Noah. The implications of the repetition, "a servant of servants" (v. 25), "his servant" (v. 26), and "his servant" (v. 27), creates the response of, "That's not the life I want! I want to be free!"

NOAH'S LINE: EXPOSING HEART ISSUES (9:18–29)

LITERARY STRUCTURE AND THEMES

The concluding segment of the *toledot* of Noah bridges the Sethite genealogy (Gen. 5) to the table of nations (ch. 10). This short section is framed with notes that situate the narrative and its theological impact in the larger story of God's working through human history. The working and purposes of God continue as he teaches his images the consequences of evil and the blessings of obedient worship. The flood forms a parenthetical theological statement in the plan of God, showing the consequences of human sin, but now the narrator concludes the Seth genealogy (9:29). The overarching unity stresses God's sovereign design to bless despite human failure and frailty, moving toward the completion of God's promised goal.

The first two verses transition from Noah's family leaving the ark (8:18) to fulfilling God's blessing by spreading across the whole earth (ch. 10). The final two verses conclude the genealogy of Noah begun in 5:32, ending the genealogy of Seth. In between, Moses relates a vignette that would show Israel the dangers and opportunities of their world as they come out of Egypt. It anticipates the choice of and blessing on Shem (highlighted by the choice of Abram and so Israel, 12:1–3) through identification with Yahweh, as well as the coming and necessary judgment on the Canaanites for their perversions (and the Egyptians, 15:16–21; Lev. 18; 20:22–25).

A. The sons of Noah would fill the earth (9:18–19).
B. Noah and his sons reflect humanity, connecting heart, actions, and consequences (9:20–27).
C. Noah completed the Seth genealogy (9:28–29).

The passage, then, continues the theme of blessing, both in multiplying humanity (9:1, 7), and in alluding to God's blessing on Shem (v. 26). It also extends the idea of cursing through Canaan, reflecting both the curse on the ground and Cain. Both themes sharpen the reader's perspective on God's working in the world and the role of his images as Noah pronounces cursing and blessing. Both carry forward the promise of God (narrowing the expectation from 3:15) and anticipate God's choice of Abram and his judgment on the Canaanites. Themes of honoring or dishonoring parents, drunkenness and the resulting disgrace, and sexual perversions also stand behind the blessing and cursing.

- ***The Sons of Noah Would Fill the Earth (9:18–19)***
- ***Noah and His Sons Reflect Humanity, Connecting Heart, Actions, and Consequences (9:20–27)***
- ***Noah Completed the Seth Genealogy (9:28–29)***

EXPOSITION

As noted in the introduction to Genesis 6:9–8:19, this section returns the reader's attention to 6:9–10 and the introduction of the *toledot*, framing the flood account with attention to the character and offspring of Noah. While the majority of the *toledot* declares and demonstrates the righteous and blameless character of Noah, the final scene presents a shocking contrast, drawing out the implication of God's evaluation in 8:21, along with his blessing in 9:1, 7 to his only surviving images. Conflict will renew and deepen, bringing renewed cursing even among hopeful blessings. After the flood, Noah and his sons, the progenitors of all humanity, expose the human heart, receiving cursing and conflict or blessing and grace based on honor or dishonor to Yahweh and his authority structure.

The Sons of Noah Would Fill the Earth (9:18–19).

In the new post-flood era, Shem, Ham, and Japheth will father the inhabitants filling the earth.

9:18. While Noah will figure prominently and his genealogy will conclude the section, the focus now shifts primarily to the three sons. Shem, Ham, and Japheth disembarking links the previous narrative (6:9; 7:13) and the coming genealogy (ch. 10). As verse 19 will note, they are the progenitors of the world. Oddly, Canaan the son of Ham also appears in the narrative. The proleptic remark introduces a new character, preparing the reader for the curse that will follow. In fact, Canaan will appear five times in this narrative and two more in the following section, drawing attention to the ancestor of the Canaanites in the world of the Israelite recipients (10:15–19).

9:19. The attention now centers on fulfilling the blessing God gave when they disembarked. After the note on Canaan, the narrative returns to the three sons to underline that "from these the people of the whole earth were dispersed." The foregrounding of the results seen in chapter 10 also significantly impacts our understanding of the vignette that immediately follows. The attention moves from the personal story of Noah to the source of the nations and international relations. Noah's viniculture, drunkenness, and ensuing curse provide the relational backdrop to the global connections surrounding the nation of Israel heading to their land of promise. These characterizations will persist in the progeny, informing Israel's world. The following narrative, then, is not intended to merely document individuals, but to characterize the dangers, conflicts, and source of blessing for the human family as it grows.

Noah and His Sons Reflect Humanity, Connecting Heart, Actions, and Consequences (9:20–27).

The progenitors of all humanity expose the human heart, resulting in cursing and conflict when dishonoring authority, yet receiving blessing and grace in obedient service to Yahweh when honoring authority.

9:20–21. Noah now briefly returns to the fore as he plants a vineyard and enjoys the fruit. Wenham (1987, 198) suggests that labeling Noah the "man of the soil" (הָאֲדָמָה) may be an ironic reference to Noah's birth, since Lamech looked for relief through Noah from the work in the "ground" or soil (5:29, הָאֲדָמָה), and the result was certainly a "mixed blessing" at best. This irony is heightened by the additional parallels with the creation and fall narratives and may provide a double entendre with Adam's occupation on the one hand (2:5, 15) and Cain's curse on the other (4:11).

TRANSLATION ANALYSIS 9:20

The ESV note shows one of the tensions in this verse. Should the sense be understood as beginning something new for him or as being the first to do something? What has begun? Did he begin "to be a man of the soil" (ESV, cf. NASB95, NKJV, NLT) or did he begin "to plant a vineyard" (NET, cf. NIV)? The Hebrew construction is unusual since the initial verb ("begin") does not have a complementary infinitive to say what was begun (cf. Gen. 4:26; 6:1; 10:8; 11:6), so the nominal phrase (literally "man of the ground," אִישׁ הָאֲדָמָה) or the following verb ("plant") provide the options. In addition, the initial verb could imply being "the first" if it is beginning something new, which here would more likely be to plant a vineyard (ESV note, NET note, NRSV,

JPS), since people had been working the ground since Adam (contr. REB, RSV).

We have already seen that the flood was presented as an undoing of creation that allowed for a re-creation with Noah as a new Adam, fathering humanity with blessing and authority as God's images. Now he drank too freely of the wine he made and uncovered himself in his tent. In contrast to Adam and Eve, who recognized their shame and attempted to cover their own nakedness (3:7) which God did for them (3:21), Noah exposed himself. Ham did nothing to cover his shame but further revealed his shame, leaving Shem and Japheth to cover him appropriately.

TRANSLATION ANALYSIS 9:21

Many translations do not reflect the clarity of the Hebrew here. The *hithpael* gives the reflexive sense that he "uncovered himself" (9:21 NASB95, NET, JPS). The common translation that he "lay uncovered" (ESV, NIV, NRSV, RSV) implies his own responsibility, but the text is explicit that he exposed his own shame (cf. 2:25; 3:7, 10; Hab. 2:15–16).

The text is silent on Noah's culpability for his drunkenness. If he is the first to plant a vineyard and produce wine, he may be excused for not knowing the effects. The Old Testament praises wine as a gift of the Lord (Gen. 27:28, 37; Deut. 7:13; Ps. 104:15) that was appropriate for celebrating before the Lord (Deut. 14:22–26). Yet, the Old Testament also clearly warns against the dangers of drunkenness (Lev. 10:9; Prov. 20:1; 23:29–35), which brings shame (Jer. 48:26; Lam. 4:21; Hab. 2:16). In addition, public exposure was shameful (Gen. 3:7, 10; Exod. 20:26). Significantly, the text explicitly places Noah inside his tent (Gen. 9:21), out of public view, shielding Noah and amplifying Ham's offense.

The degree to which Noah sinned is debated. As the new Adam, the parallels with the first sin in the garden (eating and exposing himself, with the inability to cover his own nakedness) present a decidedly negative portrait. At the least, Noah's actions are foolish (extending the wisdom motif we saw in 2:17) and provide the occasion for Ham's shameful behavior. The focus of the text, however, is clearly on Ham's response rather than Noah's conduct, as we will see below. Regardless, the introduction of wine into human society brings pain and trouble. "Cursing and slavery, rather than festive joy, proceed from its introduction into the world" (Ross 1980a, 228). At the same time, the contrast with the beginning of the *toledot* is crucial to note.

In Genesis 6:9–10 Noah is "a righteous man, blameless" and "walked with God." In 8:21, we hear God declare that even the intention of the human (including Noah's and each of the sons') "heart is [still] evil from his youth." We now see his folly, and the growing infection in his sons, even though preserved from the flood, will again produce cursing, conflict, and pain among brothers. This final vignette of the *toledot* highlights the ongoing heart disease that must be redeemed and is the main point to declare to God's people from this passage. Even the best of humanity, those who choose to walk with God, require the grace that God just declared when he refrained from such universal destruction by flood again. It also sets the stage for the coming international conflicts, the world Israel will be living in, and the need for a new means to bring blessing to all the families of the earth (12:3).

9:22–23. While wine itself is good, abusing wine to look on another's nakedness characterizes wickedness leading to God's judgment (Hab. 2:15). Of course, Ham did not cause Noah to expose himself, so the initial question here is, what did Ham do that brought the curse upon Canaan (and why Canaan?)? Foreshadowing that question, the text significantly spotlights Canaan, repeating the identification of Ham as the "father of Canaan" (Gen. 9:18, see below).

The text itself appears to be straightforward. Ham "saw" (ראה) Noah's "nakedness" (עֶרְוָה) and reported it to his brothers outside. Given the strength of Noah's curse (vv. 25–27) and the fact that he cursed Canaan and not Ham, various suggestions have been made, supposing this to be a euphemism for something much worse to a modern sensibility.[1] The wording as it stands, however, does not fit any of the euphemistic interpretations, as numerous commentators note, leading to excising the following verse by assumed editorial activity in order to make a more serious offense fit (Bassett 1971, 232, 237). The received text supports the obvious, simple intent.[2]

The Sins of Ham

Suggestions for the sin committed include 1) maternal incest of Ham with his mother, producing Canaan as the illegitimate offspring (Bassett 1971; Bergsma and Hahn 2005); 2) the castration of Noah, either by Ham or by Canaan (Midrashim cited by Bergsma and Hahn 2005, 27–28); 3) paternal incest (sodomy) by Ham (Bergsma and Hahn 2005, 28–34); or 4) seeing Noah naked and then perhaps his own sexual pleasures (voyeurism) or, more likely, his response of revealing it to his brothers (Embry 2011). As noted in the Exposition, the text as it stands argues strongly for the last position, though there is no hint in the text of personal sexual interest (Odhiambo 2013).

So how can just seeing Noah's nakedness bring a curse? As noted, nakedness displayed the shame of the fall (3:7, 10, 21). Ham not only neglected, or worse, refused to cover his father's shame (contra Adam and Eve [3:7] and God [Gen. 3:21]) but rather exposed Noah's dishonor to his brothers, disgracing his father (Exod. 20:12; Deut. 5:16). Such disgrace would indeed bring a curse under Israel's law (Deut. 27:16) because it reflected a rejection of the authority structure placed by God. It included the possibility of capital punishment, such as cursing a parent or general incorrigibility (Exod. 21:17; Deut. 21:18–21). So the offense was not merely the passive and (possibly) accidental viewing but the public exposure of his father (notice the emphasis on "father" [four times] in vv. 22–23), a serious transgression in the ancient world and in Israel in particular (Mathews 2005, 417–20).

When Ham reported his observations about his father, verse 23 laboriously reports the actions of Shem and Japheth as they walk backward without looking to cover Noah's nakedness, drawing out the account to stress the righteous response (Wenham 1987, 200). It also, however, emphasizes the antithesis to the offense, highlighting the folly of Ham in dishonoring Noah. If the appropriate response and necessary remedy for the problem was to cover him discretely, the offense was not one of incest, sodomy, castration, or some other undescribed sexual nature.

9:24–27. Without explanation, Noah knew Ham's offense against him and pronounced a curse, again paralleling Genesis 3 in which Adam knew his nakedness, resulting in cursing. Ham's curse, however, was not directly on the offender. The parallels draw attention to this scene as an outgrowth of human sin beginning with Adam. Rather than name Ham as the narrative has done to this point (three times in this scene), he is called the "youngest son" (v. 24). The emphasis

1 Bergsma and Hahn's (2005, 27) complaint with regard to Ham merely "seeing" summarizes the dilemma well: "The strength of this position is its conservatism: it refuses to see anything in the text that is not explicit. Yet, in a sense, voyeurism is a nonexplanation, since it fails to elucidate either the gravity of Ham's offense or the reason for the curse of Canaan. It also requires the interpreter to assume the existence of a taboo against the accidental sight of a naked parent that is otherwise unattested in biblical or ancient Near Eastern literature".

2 See Mathews and Embry for a helpful defense of the most direct meaning (Mathews 2005, 418–20; Embry 2011).

by variation will suggest part of the reasoning for the curse on Canaan, his youngest son.

Noah's curse (ארר) reminds the reader of Yahweh's curse on the serpent (3:14), the ground (3:17), and Cain (4:11). Repeated three times, he emphasized Canaan's low servant status. In 9:25 Canaan would be the lowest of slaves. In verse 26 he will be Shem's slave, and in verse 27 he will be Japheth's slave. The term "servant" or slave (עֶבֶד) can refer to anything from the lowest permanent slave, to a temporary "servant" that has no inferiority or obligations, and even to a noble term for a representative of Yahweh (Naudė, "Servant, Slave," *NIDOTTE* 4:1183–99). The superlative, however (see Translation Analysis 9:24), indicates the lowest possible status before his "brothers" (אָח). Reminiscent of the initial narratives, there will be conflict among brothers, though here the expression is figurative (see below).[3] The flood has not changed the human heart, so human relations will continue to struggle with ongoing class conflicts. Noah consigned Canaan to the bottom rank in the human family.

> *TRANSLATION ANALYSIS 9:25*
> One way to express the comparative superlative in Hebrew is to use the singular noun in construct with the definite plural of the same noun, such as "king of kings," or the highest king (WOC, 270, §14.5d). Here, the "servant of servants" (ESV, NASB95, NKJV) is better understood as the "lowest of slaves" (JPS, NET, NIV, NRSV, cf. NCV, NLT).

Verse 26 continues the oracle with Noah's blessing for Shem. The blessing, however, does not follow the normal form of blessing on an individual. In fact, Noah's words follow a typical praise formula: "Blessed be the Lord, the God of Shem" (e.g., 24:27; 1 Sam. 25:32). The blessing here for Shem results from the clear statement that he is (and his line will be) a Yahweh-worshipper, which will certainly bring blessing. He has identified himself with Yahweh as his God. The unexpected statement within the context and flow of Genesis provides "the first intimation that the line of God's election blessing is going through Shem" (Wenham 1987, 202). It also connects the actions of honoring the parent with the Yahweh-worshipper. To honor Yahweh is to honor one's father, the immediate authority in one's life (Exod. 20:12; Lev. 19:3; Deut. 5:16). That action brings praise to Yahweh and so will also bring blessing to the worshipper. The greatest blessing goes to Shem as the chosen line.

Noah continued by blessing Japheth (v. 27), though the significance is uncertain. The verb "enlarge" plays on the name Japheth (the same root, פתה). The idea here suggests prosperity and expansion, which may well indicate a future sharing of territory with Shem ("let him dwell in the tents of Shem").

> *TRANSLATION ANALYSIS 9:26*
> The subject of the verb ("let him dwell in the tents of Shem," 9:27) is ambiguous in the text. It could refer to either God or Japheth, though the presence of God with Shem hardly seems to be a blessing on Japheth, and the plural "tents" seems to fit human inhabitants more than God (Wenham 1987, 202–3). Some translations (NCV, NIV, NLT) clarify, repeating "Japheth."

Both verses 26 and 27 end with the same phrase: "let Canaan be his servant." The repetition of the curse three times, alone and following each of the blessings, magnifies the severity and clarifies the phrase "to his brothers" in verse 25. The question raised, however, has vexed commentators from the earliest traditions. Why is Canaan cursed when Ham committed the offense? The received text does not allow for any

3 As we will argue, this is not intended literally but will look ahead to future national interests. Sarna (1989, 67), however, suggests that in conventional cursing it indicates "comprehensiveness."

of the more creative explanations, either in the specific wording or because of the inclusion of verse 23, but it does provide clues to the answer.

First, Moses frames the narrative by noting that from these three men, "the people of the whole earth were dispersed" (v. 19) and concluding with this oracle on the future of the progeny. These pronouncements are future and national, not merely immediate and personal. In other words, the oracles reflect the later descendants of Canaan rather than merely the individual Canaan himself. Similarly, Genesis will record Isaac's "blessings" (ch. 27) and Jacob's pronouncements (ch. 49), which may include both curse and blessing (27:39; 49:3–7). Jacob makes it clear he is not looking at immediate outcomes but future events when he says, "that I may tell you what shall happen to you in days to come" (49:1). These deal with the future clans. Similarly, chapter 9 magnifies the distant future perspective since Noah will father the entire human race. What follows (ch. 10) will not be an individual history but will reflect the political and national realities of the world of Israel at the time of Moses.

Second, the focus on Canaan has already been foregrounded with the notes on his relation to Ham (9:18, 22). The filial relationships have been emphasized (repeating "father" five times [vv. 18, 22–23], even when a personal name might be expected, stressing the relational aspect of both offense and remediation), suggesting that talionic justice may be served. Just as Noah's youngest son has dishonored him (v. 24), so Ham will be dishonored by his youngest, or at least by the descendants that will come from Canaan (10:6, 15–20).

Third, since these patriarchal oracles are not prophetic pronouncements, per se, they are not declarations of what God will necessarily do (Walton 2001, 349–50). Rather, they reflect the perspective of the one cursing or blessing, and his curses and blessings are still subject to the working of God as God sees appropriate (Num. 23:8; Deut. 23:5; 2 Sam. 16:12; Prov. 26:2). We may also realize that as patriarchal pronouncements, there may be much more backstory to the declarations than is expressed in this short vignette. Ross (1980a, 233) suggests that Noah saw in Canaan the same propensities as Ham exhibited since Torah shows that later generations are only judged for sins they also exhibit. Of course, the same will be true of future generations and people groups, who are judged by their sins and not an ancestor's sin (Deut. 24:16; Jer. 18:1–11).

Finally, we should remember that in 9:19 Moses is consciously preparing the reader to understand the spread of the nations in chapter 10, particularly the relation of the nations as Israel will enter into and live among the nations in Canaan (see the Exposition of Gen. 10, p. 218). On the one hand, he may not have recorded all that Noah declared in his oracle but rather recorded what was of particular interest to Israel and Moses's agenda. On the other hand, these men "embody and personify the character of their descendants" (Wenham 1987, 201). Israel, then, would be particularly interested in their blessing as descendants of Shem, the curse on Canaan for causes that would appear to prefigure the much more serious sexual immorality of the Canaanites, his distant descendants (Lev. 18, 20), and the relation to (the descendants of) Japheth, which is less clear today.

Noah Completed the Seth Genealogy (9:28–29).

Noah's death brought an era to an end.

9:28–29. The postscript to the episode closes the immediate scene but also formally closes Seth's genealogy (5:32).[4] On one level, the flood narrative intrudes into the

4 In Gen. 5, we noted that the genealogical formula repeated three clauses, concluding with the final two: "A lived Y more years and he had other sons and daughters. A lived a total of (X+Y) years and he died." For Noah,

genealogy and the movement of God's promised blessing. It added God's good blessing on another righteous man. Much like Enoch, Noah walked with God (5:22–24; 9:9) and was spared the judgment on sin, demonstrating the real hope from cursing and judgment in the presence of God. On another level, however, the flood narrative explains the appropriate justice for the human condition in tension with Yahweh's ongoing patience with humanity when evil is rampant. It also relates the resulting and ongoing pervasive evil in the human heart after the flood.

In the structure of Genesis, the flood becomes a line in human existence dividing the pre-history, with little detail and a few significant and archetypal narratives, from the more immediate history, directly impacting Israel's existence and near future. The end of Noah's life closes one era and opens a new one. Now the text will move to narrow the focus from the whole earth (9:19; 11:1, 4, 8, 9) to the descendants of Abraham, Isaac, and Jacob (chs.12–50), through whom he will bless all the families of the earth (12:3; 18:18; 22:18; 26:4; 28:14).

THEOLOGICAL FOCUS

Human response to Yahweh's authority structures exposes the state of the human heart, portending future cursing and conflict or blessing and grace for submissive honor to Yahweh.

The concluding narrative of the Noah *toledot* exposes the corrupted hearts of the human family through reactions to God's authority structures. These archetypal actions and consequences foreshadow humanity's future, through both God's blessing (9:1, 7, 19) and cursing (11:8–9), and lead to the fractured and conflict-ridden world scene into which Israel will emerge (ch. 10). God does not directly act here, though we see Noah's words indicating God's perspective (9:25–27).

Even the most righteous of humanity are corrupt at the core. The most righteous and obedient worshipper is deeply infected (8:21). The paradigm of humanity declares that salvation is always a result of God's grace (6:8, חֵן) and clearly not performance-based through some ongoing valor or honor. Rather, God declares people righteous by faith (15:6). Consequently, we all have hope, since no reader who truly understands God's character can identify themself as righteous and blameless apart from God's gift through faith (Rom. 3:20–26). And still God offers blessing (Gen. 9:1, 7), which is fleshed out in the ongoing generations to proceed from these few.

God's warning also correlates the ongoing strife in this world with the heart condition and the tension between God's blessing and the consequences of sin. Noah's conflict and resulting pronouncements provide the theological underpinnings for the interaction of the nations and mission of Israel. Blessing (more than numerical growth!) is still available. Yahweh will bless those who will identify with and submit to him (9:26), worked out in honoring his authority structures (Gen. 9:23, 26–27; Exod. 20:12; Deut. 5:16). That blessing was already pictured in walking with God. In contrast, Yahweh will curse those showing allegiance to their own lusts, dishonoring the authority structures God has placed (Gen. 9:22, 25; Exod. 20:12; 21:17; Deut. 5:16). Israel's mission will be to bring blessing to all families of the earth (Gen. 12:3; 18:18; 29:18; etc.). Such blessing is found in the true worship exhibited in Enoch, Noah, and Shem's identification with Yahweh, and later Abram, Isaac, and Jacob (12:7–8; 13:4, 18; 26:25; 33:20; 35:7) and ultimately in one's response to Christ.

God's character takes shape as his promise bears fruit. Humankind will fill the earth (9:19; cf. 9:1, 7) without fear of flood (9:8–17). The

---

the second phrase is modified because it has already described both his age at the flood and the three boys he fathered. It concludes with the precise final clause of the Genesis 5 formula.

succeeding history of humanity will confirm God's promise and character, showing both blessing and cursing, but never as he did with the flood. He will be faithful to his covenant promises regardless of human circumstances, reaching out to humanity in new and significant ways, leading his images to his final image, Christ.

PREACHING AND TEACHING STRATEGIES

Exegetical and Theological Synthesis

The narrative begins with the mention of Noah's three sons. The author prepares us for what's about to happen by expanding only on one son, Ham (cf. "Ham was the father of Canaan"—whose descendants would become the enemies of Israel). Every listener will soon identify with Noah's three sons, particularly whether they are living in the curse or in blessing. Very quickly, however, we're surprised by what happens to Noah. In Genesis 6:9 he's "a righteous man, blameless in his generation" and a man who "walked with God." Now we see him like this: "drunk and . . . uncovered in his tent" (9:29). Even if we can't say for sure that he's unrighteous, he certainly is undignified. And, even if we can't be sure of what Ham did, we know from Noah's reaction that it was pretty bad ("Cursed be Canaan," Ham's son, v. 25; see v. 18). The author of Genesis wants us to get yet another look at the human condition through the eyes of God. The new start begins with old tendencies. Humankind, redeemed through the flood, still retains elements in need of God's redemption. Thankfully our Lord blesses two of the three sons. God's indirect blessing on Shem (note that v. 26 reads, "Blessed be the Lord, the God of Shem") and the direct blessing on Japheth linked to Shem ("and let him dwell in the tents of Shem," v. 27) become the realm in which God works in the world to proclaim his fame and name.

Preaching Idea

Our spiritual heritage reveals both the dangers of cursed sin and the possibility of salvation blessing—which will we choose?

What does it mean?

It is important to explain that Noah's three sons form the family tree for "the whole earth" (v. 19). Scripture states this clearly, but our listeners might miss the connection with the announced curse and blessing (vv. 25–27). The population of humankind explodes from these three, and their lives in some way relate to the blessing or the cursing. This will be restated below in the "Now what?" section.

The heaviest burden of explanation in this pericope has to do with Noah's and Ham's actions. Noah's drunken condition is unexpected after such glowing reports in chapter 6. Whatever Ham did was reprehensible enough to warrant Noah's curse. Even though it is impossible to know, we still owe it to our listeners to entertain an explanation for how Noah "knew what his youngest son had done to him" (9:24). God may have given Noah inside information so he could speak accurately to his three sons about their futures. It's important in this section to carefully explain the meaning of both curses and blessings with respect to Noah's sons. The oracles look ahead to God's working in the nations' futures, showing the outworking of these sorts of heart responses to God. God will subjugate and humiliate those that do not bow before him, both nationally and personally. Those that bow in submission will be raised in honor.

Is it true?

Some quick, sociohistorical research will help your listeners believe that humanity does have a start in one part of the world. Books that explore the origins of humanity address such issues. Hollywood evidently has no trouble writing apocalyptic scripts that include restarting the world's population after total destruction. Our society may not allow God the prerogative to destroy the world in a flood, let's say, but it embraces the concept of humankind destroying itself and needing to begin again. Another concept in our pericope that might need some proof is that ancient curses and blessings do work. I (Randal) currently serve in the eastern side of the United States, where most of us have a hard time believing in such things. Either we never encounter curses and blessings or are unaware that we have. Not so in many places in the world today. This might be a good time to take your listeners forward into the Old Testament story to see how things played out for Canaan, for instance.

Now what?

Speaking of curses and blessings, I stated above that Noah's announcement to his sons has profound implications on each of our lives. If you asked your listeners, "Which life sounds least appealing?" everyone in the house would say, "Canaan's!" If we've been effective in explaining the meaning of "cursed" and "blessed" then that should provide incentive for everyone to find his or her place in the Shem/Japheth branches of the family tree. This is not the first time in Genesis, nor will it be the last, when a character's actions reveal their relationship with their Creator/God, specifically, whether they, like Noah, have "found favor" (6:8). We also need to consider the fall of godly people. It is possible for anyone to fall. All believers must be vigilant, dependent on God in prayer, and seeking support and accountability from God's people. Finally, we can also point more specifically to imitating Christ in our world as the people around us act foolishly, wickedly, or pressure the believer to follow suit. We all face unexpected or surprising temptations and opportunities to exercise love and loyalty or selfish ambition.

Creativity in Presentation

Part of the presentation of this pericope should involve images and imagination of humanity's new start. You might create a family tree with Noah and his three sons. Because of the narrator's parenthetical sentence at the end of verse 18, you will want to include Canaan somehow. I suggest distinguishing him somehow from the other brothers since the narrative repeats his future servanthood three times. It is helpful to clearly differentiate the cursing and blessing sides of the tree. From there, consider structuring the narrative sermon this way:

- Noah's enjoyment of the fruits of his labor creates the test of Ham's character (vv. 20–21). Part of what makes this section special is not allowing listeners to vilify Noah too quickly for his drunkenness. This sets the stage for all three sons to prove their spiritual mettle.

- Ham provides an example of unrighteousness (v. 22), while the other two sons display the opposite (v. 23). We're writing in the United States, so most of our listeners are removed from an honor-and-shame society. Plus, our morality with respect to "nakedness" is pretty much nonexistent. All that to say that Shem and Japheth's actions should cause us to pause and reflect on how the Spirit of holiness works in us.

- Cursing and blessing become the two options for life on earth.

- Whether considered a fourth point or part of the conclusion, it's important to make sure everyone knows how to be on the blessing branch of the family tree and that the outcome is not merely salvation or damnation. God offers flourishing to all who will walk with him, though our rebellion leads to shriveling. Our response to God and temptation defines the outcome. And when we fall, the believer confesses, repents, and replaces unrighteousness with Holy Spirit-driven righteousness.

DISCUSSION QUESTIONS

1. Do we expect perfection of the righteous? How should we view someone who sins?

2. How do we respond to God when we recognize sin in our lives or roots of flesh in our own hearts?

3. Considering Shem and Japheth going to extreme lengths to protect their father and avoid any impropriety, how should believers today view their responsibility to avoid evil in either act or appearance?

4. Define carefully what it means to be cursed or blessed.

5. What does it mean in practical ways to call Jesus your God and Savior? If I identify with him, what expectation does that require of me for my actions and for my heart response to him?

6. How does my honoring of authority in my life bring honor to Christ? What authority structures do I need to honor, and what will that look like?

Genesis 10:1–11:9

EXEGETICAL IDEA

The family history of the sons of Noah presents the dispersed nations with their responsibilities and hope from Yahweh's judgment, reversing human aspirations and exposing their false pursuit of security as folly, preparing Israel for their purpose and place in God's program to spread blessing.

THEOLOGICAL FOCUS

The spread of the nations conveys both human responsibility and hope in God's redemptive purpose for all peoples stemming from his gracious judgment on human folly, preparing for his choice of Israel to spread his blessing.

PREACHING IDEA

Our Lord is watching whether his people are making a name for themselves or for him, and directs history to spread his fame.

PREACHING POINTERS

Part of the excitement of reaching this section is that we finally get to continue the story. Chapter 5 ended with verse 32: "After Noah was 500 years old, Noah fathered Shem, Ham, and Japheth." Then comes the painful parenthesis in 6:1–9:29 that describes terrible wickedness, the awful judgment of God, and yet hope for God's world.

We are working our way from Adam to Noah to Noah's three sons. God's blessing is continuing in what might be considered a restart (9:1, "God blessed Noah and his sons"). And, if you want to stay excited about this pericope, we suggest you move very quickly through chapter 10: "Sons were born to them after the flood" (v. 1). Prepare listeners for what's coming with a look at the human condition (vv. 8–9), significant places such as Babel and Shinar (v. 10), and significant kingdoms and cities such as Assyria and Nineveh (v. 11). Of course, you might also point out references to the Canaanites and Sodom and Gomorrah (v. 19).

Redemptive history is wrapped up in this genealogy: "from these the nations spread abroad on the earth after the flood" (v. 32). The list of seventy nations teaches us we're all a part of the same family. But as almost all modern readers sense, the story really gets going in 11:1–9 and the incident surrounding the Tower of Babel. What is God's explanation for the plethora of languages that exist in the world today? As we anticipated from the end of chapter 9, human hearts are not all bent on enhancing God's fame, but their own *name*. God simply cannot let that happen. Humanity could not image God. Instead, it would destroy his images when he desires to bless them. God's people have always been called to live out their faith in a world that rejects his rule.

MAKING A NAME: GOD'S GRACE IN JUDGING HUMAN PRIDE (10:1–11:9)

LITERARY STRUCTURE AND THEMES

Following the flood, the fourth *toledot* situates Israel among the nations in the resulting spread of humanity. Genesis 10 shows Israel how she relates to all the nations around her, while Genesis 11:1–9 describes why they spread out as distinct nationalities. Moses reminds the reader of the continuing heart problem of human arrogance and God's enduring interventions, setting up his redemptive plan for blessing through Abram.

I. One Humanity in Many Nations (10:1–32)
   A. What became of Noah's Sons after the flood (10:1)
   B. The line of Japheth on distant shores (10:2–5)
   C. The line of Ham in tense proximity (10:6–20)
   D. The line of Shem, the ancestor of Eber's descendants (10:21–31)
   E. Diversity from unity (10:32)

II. Scattered by Grace (11:1–9)
   A. People were united in language and direction (11:1–2)
      B. Humanity proudly plotted for a name and unity (11:3–4)
         C. Yahweh condescended to judge human arrogance (11:5)
      B'. Yahweh pronounced their fractured future (11:6–7)
   A'. God dispersed humanity with confused language (11:8–9)

Genesis 10 follows the lines of the three sons of Noah to describe Israel's then-current political realities in terms of family relations. All nations are part of one extended human family. Like both previous genealogies, chapter 10 begins with the most geographically distant and theologically insignificant relations (sons of Japheth) moving to the more immediate and adversarial neighbors (the line of Ham) before the chosen line of Seth and those nations most closely related to Israel. Historically, these relations reflect the much later period of Israel's entry into the land, long after Babel (vv. 5, 20, 31–32).

Genesis 11:1–9 presents a tightly woven narrative providing the theological reason for human divisions by language group (ch.10) because of their failed attempt to erect their own legacy and security. The intricate chiastic structure (with interwoven parallel development) emphasizes the transcendent rule of Yahweh, who stoops to see humanity's puny efforts and block their attempts to thwart his desired blessing on them. The vast chasm between humanity's assessment and God's perspective emphasizes the chasm between what people desire and what will ultimately bring them blessing. God's desire to bless requires immediate frustration and confusion so that humankind will be able to learn true worship, walk with God, and truly flourish.

- ***One Humanity in Many Nations (10:1–32)***
- ***Scattered by Grace (11:1–9)***

EXPOSITION

God's promise of blessing, endangered by human folly, evil, and violence, emerged from

God's judgment in the flood, bringing renewed expectation in the completion of the promise for the end of the tempter and evil (Gen. 3:15). The conflict between God's promise and human sin, however, stayed in focus when God acknowledged the ongoing evil bent of the human heart (8:21), even as he offered a new covenant and blessing to his twisted images. Noah's overindulgence exposed the evils that would infect international relations through the coming dispersion (9:18) via the descendants of the three sons of Noah. Genesis 9:18–27 anticipates the divisions and relations that chapter 10 implies for Israel's world. All of humanity spread from these three, and the heart issues unfolded with them. Genesis 11:1–9 then backtracks and explains why humanity spread so effectively and why one family ended with so many nationalities and language groups. The family history of the sons of Noah presents the dispersed nations with their responsibilities and hope from Yahweh's judgment, reversing human aspirations and exposing their false pursuit of security as folly, preparing Israel for their purpose and place in God's program to effect blessing.

One Humanity in Many Nations (10:1–32)

The family history of the sons of Noah situates Israel among the nations, near and far, friend and foe, and prepares for God's working in the following narratives and Israel's yet-future history.

The "table of nations" in Genesis 10 develops the relationship of the nations as they spread after the flood (10:5, 20, 31–32). The national and geographic emphasis shows strongly in the names used, which are "not primarily personal names" but largely gentilics and place names (Hess 2009, 73; although the names in the line of Shem seem to include more individuals, at least as presented in ch. 11). Family terminology was used in ancient times to reflect treaty relationships, suggesting political and geographical relations rather than strictly genealogical ones (Wenham 1987, 215). That is not to diminish the point of a single human family, but rather to draw the boundaries of relationship along more contemporary lines to Israel.[1] The resulting table makes the theological point that all "the nations" (הַגּוֹיִם) are descended from Noah (each segment ends with "nations," vv. 5, 20, 31, as does the conclusion, v. 32, twice).

What Became of Noah's Sons After the Flood (10:1)

These are the descendants of Noah's sons.

10:1. The introduction to the *toledot* and 10:32 frame the genealogy. Verse 1 introduces the "generations" (תּוֹלְדֹת) of the three sons of Noah "after the flood" (אַחַר הַמַּבּוּל), and verse 32 repeats these phrases, summarizing the account by "their genealogies" (תּוֹלְדֹתָם) from which "the nations spread abroad on the earth after the flood" (אַחַר הַמַּבּוּל). The frame draws attention to the point of the genealogy, that all the nations spread from the one family (exhibiting God's blessing, 9:1, 7, even through judgment, 11:1–9) so that all humanity is related and responsible to each other (Noahic covenant, 9:1–17).

> *TRANSLATION ANALYSIS 10:1*
> See 2:4 on *toledot* (p. 99). Here, the "generations" (ESV, RSV) clearly intend to relate the national "descendants" (NRSV), "family history" (NCV), or "lines" (JPS) of Noah's sons.

The Line of Japheth on Distant Shores (10:2–5)

The most distant peoples from Israel are fully related.

10:2–4. Of the seventy total names in the table, only fourteen are listed for Japheth, in

1 For a helpful discussion of the terms used and significance for both the political relationships and the structure of the table, see Ross (1980b).

two groups of seven each—seven sons and seven grandsons—so the emphasis clearly lies with Ham and Shem. With none listed for five of the sons, the author makes a symbolic point of completeness for the distant nations. The genealogy does not attempt to list all nations that exist but represents all nations, showing that all of them, originating in the line of Noah, are one common family (Sailhamer 1990, 99–100; cf. Sarna 1989, 69). He will make this point in several ways, including the symbolic total (seventy), colophons (10:5, 20, 31), and frame (10:1, 32).

The list of names connected to Japheth represents the countries more distant from Israel, from the north (Asia Minor—Gomer [and "sons"], Magog, Javan) and northeast (Madai, Tubal, Meshech) to the islands and territories near the Mediterranean (Tiras, Elisha, Tarshish, Kittim, Dodanim).[2] These nations form the swath of northern to western nations on the periphery of Israel's experience.

10:5. The peoples are distinguished according to their geography, languages, clans, and nationalities. While not all of these peoples appear, from our current perspective, to be island-dwellers or coastland peoples, it was "from these the coastland peoples spread," representing the farthest nations (10:5). This short and most distant segment of the genealogy differs slightly in its colophon from the other two by foregrounding the "coastland" nations, emphasizing the distance and probably the seafaring role of some who will intersect with Israel later (JPS, NIV, NLT).

TRANSLATION ANALYSIS 10:5

The Hebrew translated "coastlands" (אִי) reflects the most distant parts of the world, especially to the west (HALOT s.v. "אִי" 38), and so may be used figuratively for the farthest removed.

The Line of Ham in Tense Proximity (10:6–20)

The line of Ham situates Israel's most contentious neighbors, bridging the history from Noah and the curse on Canaan (Ham) through Babel, the patriarchal narratives, and Israel's entry into the land.

10:6–7. The descendants of Ham include thirty nations that form a closer proximity to Israel (and greater conflict), particularly including Egypt, the Canaanites, and Mesopotamia. Moses lists the direct descendants of Ham as Cush (African tribes south of Egypt), Egypt, Put (probably Libya), and Canaan. These "sons" lay out the geographical sweep from North Africa through Canaan to Syria. Cush, presumably the firstborn, was the "ancestor" of the nations, stretching from upper Egypt (possibly Seba, though it also could be in Arabia) through the Arabian Peninsula (the rest listed from Cush, though not all are certain). When we recognize this fertility as God's blessing, we also realize that God is blessing Ham (and Canaan) despite the curse of Noah (Kuruvilla 2014, 136; Mathews 1996, 429).

10:8–12. The shift in formula in verse 8 draws attention to Nimrod, the only name in Japheth's or Ham's genealogies that is clearly personal (Hess 2009, 73). Moses draws attention to Nimrod with five verses (over a third of the Ham genealogy by word count), foreshadowing the Babel narrative in 11:1–9. Nimrod's name as it is vocalized in the MT would likely have been understood by its Hebrew readers as "we will rebel" (Hess 2009, 74). He is presented as the first "mighty man" (10:8, גִּבֹּר) in the earth, which often refers to military champion but clearly here is a powerful and tyrannical king (v. 10; cf. 6:4, Westermann 1994, 516). This tyranny, however, is not anything new but returns to the oppression that brought the judgment of

2 See Ross (2008, 85–87) for a concise analysis of the various nations listed in the table.

the flood (cf.. 6:4; Osborne, "Table of Nations," *DOTP* 594).

> *TRANSLATION ANALYSIS 10:8*
> Instead of "the sons of x: y, . . ." (without a verb, 10:2, 3, 4, 6, 7, 22, 23), this entry includes the verb "bear" (ילד). "Cush fathered" reflects the genealogies of Genesis 4–5 (also used of Egypt [10:13], Canaan [10:15], and similarly in the line of Shem [10:21, 24, 25, 26]). The difference between "son of" (no verb) and "bore" (verb) may allow for "generational gaps" or skipping generations (Ross 2008, 86). "The former [בְּנֵי] emphasizes the beginning; the latter [ילד] the continuing results" (Ross 1980b, 347).

The repeated description of Nimrod as a "mighty hunter before the LORD" (10:9) portrays the strength of his rule, which reflects the ancient kings' boasting about their hunting from Assyria to Egypt.[3] Connecting his prowess to Yahweh suggests a play on Mesopotamian ideology, recognizing Yahweh as "the true king of the world" (Hom 2010, 68). His empire began in Babylon and the surrounding cities and extended to the founding of some of the great Assyrian cities, apparently uniting northern and southern Mesopotamia.

Attempts to identify Nimrod and his rule have been unconvincing, but Moses seems more intent on connecting this descendant of Ham with the rebellion of Babel and perhaps connecting the building of cities and human despots with humanity's independence from Yahweh (see Exposition of Gen. 4:17–22, p. 146, and 6:1–4 above, p. 161). He becomes "the prototype of rebellion" (Hamilton 1990, 338), supported by the interconnected terms and themes in 11:1–9 (Hom 2010). In fact, his cities will later emerge as major enemies of Israel, and Babel will become a symbol of opposition to Yahweh.

10:13–14. Egypt, the second son of Ham, fathered seven tribes that appear to cover northern Africa and Crete (Hamilton 1990b, 340–41). Verse 14 also introduces the Philistines, significant for Israel entering the land.

> *TRANSLATION ANALYSIS 10:14*
> The MT places the origin of the Philistines from the Casluhim, an unknown people group (ESV, NASB95, NKJV, RSV), also translated Casluhites (NET, NIV). However, based on Amos 9:7 and Jeremiah 47:4, some have assumed the clause should be related to the Caphtorim (JPS, NLT, NRSV), which could be translated as "people of Crete" (Caphtor was Crete; NCV). There is, however, no reason to doubt an origin from the unknown Casluhim, which may have then migrated through Caphtor and which may even be a different group than in the later narratives (Ross 1981, 27).

10:15–19. The last son of Ham connects Noah's curse on Canaan from Genesis 9:25–27 to the era of Israel's conquest, delineating the peoples in the land of Canaan. The listing of peoples includes the dispersal (v. 18b) through the territory into which God will bring Israel (v. 19). It provides context for the narratives that follow with Abraham, his heirs, and God's promises to them, as well as for the nation leaving Egypt for the land that God intended them to live in, fulfilling Noah's oracle (15:18–21).

Each of the three sons listed from Ham includes a note providing points of contact with Israel in their history, from Babylon to the Philistines to the territory of the Canaanites. The following segment of the table will incorporate similar insertions pointing ahead to what will follow in the narrative and connecting God's intention of blessing to the spread of the nations and to his necessary choice of Abram.

3 Westermann (1994, 516) explains the origin and celebration of this pastime from the king's original need to secure his kingdom from predators.

10:20. Verse 20 concludes the line of Ham with a similar refrain to verse 5 for the line of Japheth. It uses the same four main terms, though in a different order. As with verse 5, it ends with "and their nations," emphasizing the overall impact of the table as describing nations, delineated by their family relations, languages, and geographic boundaries (see also the Exposition on 10:31).

The Line of Shem, the Ancestor of Eber's Descendants (10:21–31)

The line of Shem and Eber situates Israel among the tribes most closely connected to them and prepares them for their choice through Abraham, Isaac, and Jacob.

10:21. While each of the segments (Japheth, Ham, and Shem) begins with "The sons of x: y, . . ." (vv. 2, 6, 22), the final section for Shem inserts an additional note (with the verb; see Translation Analysis on 10:8) highlighting Eber (ancestor of Abraham) and the birth order. These three segments, then, are not being presented in the birth order but in the order of importance to the narrative, with the most important last, in line with the consistent practice of Moses in Genesis (Cain, then Seth [chs. 4, 5]; Ishmael, then Isaac [25:12–18; 25:19–35:29]; Esau, then Jacob [chs. 36, 37–50]). The focus on the children of Eber looks ahead to the following genealogy in chapter 11, leading up to Abram. With this insertion, Eber will be mentioned seven times in the two chapters, highlighting God's narrowing of the seed of promise to the family of Abram, Isaac, and Jacob (11:10–26), along with several people groups closely connected with Israel.

> *TRANSLATION ANALYSIS 10:20*
> Some translations follow the LXX and many medieval Jewish interpreters in connecting the adjective with Japheth (e.g., "whose older brother was Japheth," NIV; cf. KJV, NKJV). In Biblical Hebrew, however, "an adjective does not usually modify a proper name," so Shem would be "the elder brother of Japheth" (Sarna 1989, 78; ESV, NASB95, NCV, NET, NJPS, NLT, NRSV, RSV).

10:22–25. Of the five sons of Shem, Moses will trace only two: Aram (the last) and Arpachshad. As with the line of Ham, the line of Shem is also interrupted with a historical note. The son of Eber, of the line of Arpachshad, is named Peleg (פֶּלֶג), "for in his days the earth was divided [נִפְלְגָה]" (10:25). The wordplay draws attention to an event that is traditionally related to 11:1–9 and the division of languages. Sarna (1989, 79) objects that the verb here (פלג) is not used either in the tower narrative nor in the notes on dispersal (9:19; 10:32; 11:1–9). The reference is certainly cryptic, with many possible referents. The overall structure, however, as we will see supports the traditional interpretation.

10:26–30. The birth of the two sons not only offers a window into the timing of the division of languages, but it shows the selective nature of the genealogy. Peleg's line pauses here until Genesis 11 picks it up again, but his brother Joktan's line continues with thirteen descendants. Resuming Peleg's genealogy after Babel, suggests both that Moses pauses the genealogy to connect it to Babel, and that Babel provides crucial background to the choice of Abram. With the sons of Joktan, however, Moses also includes a geographical note, placing these tribes east of Israel in the Arabian Peninsula, in proximity to the future Israel.

The structure of the line of Shem mirrors the line of Ham, including an initial genealogical list (10:6–8a; 21–25b), an historical comment (vv. 8b–12; 25c), further genealogical listing (vv. 13–18a; 25d–30), and a final geographical description (vv. 18b–19; 30) before the concluding refrain (vv. 20; 31). Both historical comments draw attention to the Babel narrative, with the first pointing to a cause based in power and rebellion (vv. 8–12) and the second pointing to the outcome of division (v. 25). The two geographical notes locate the respective tribes relevant to the patriarchal narratives and with which Israel will have significant contact, both in the conquest and in the following years.

10:31. The colophon of Shem's genealogy mirrors that of Ham's almost exactly, linking these two segments in distinction from Japheth's much shorter segment. These two emphasize the tribal relations by putting them first (לְמִשְׁפְּחֹתָם, vv. 20, 31) instead of Japheth's geographical or linguistic emphasis (Ross 1980b, 349). Together the three accentuate the international boundaries of the ethnic, linguistic, and geographical distinctions within the single family of humanity. The stress in the three colophons is on breadth and diversity, with all three concluding with "their nations" (לְגוֹיֵהֶם, vv. 5, 20, 31). The frame will tie them all together from the same ancestor.

Diversity from Unity (10:32)
The spread and diversity of all nations is rooted in the single family of Noah.

10:32. The concluding verse, framing the genealogy begun with 10:1, reminds the reader that the nations after the flood stem from the clans and family structure of Noah's descendants, so all are related. The connection of the whole human family, precarious because of the national identities (בְּגוֹיֵהֶם) as seen in their clans, languages, and geographic differentiation (10:5, 20, 31), find their affiliation "according to their genealogies" (תּוֹלְדוֹת) as "sons of Noah" (בְּנֵי־נֹחַ). As such, they fulfill the blessing of Yahweh in 9:1, 7 (Hamilton 1990, 347), despite the coming description of his curse.

Moses, then, underscores the overall unity of humankind. He has included seventy nations, which in the biblical world was symbolic of the totality (Fensham 1977). Moses represents all nations of the earth and clearly states that they are all part of the same human family. Considering what follows, the table of nations begins with essential unity, which would allow humankind to challenge God's good rule, and delineates the outcome of that rebellion in the resulting fracturing by language and region. It also, however, shows the responsibility of the whole human family for God's covenant with Noah and the hope they all have in the initial promises (blessing, no more flood, and crushing of the snake). In doing so, it prepares for Israel's role among those nations, to provide the path to blessing, redemption, and the only lasting unity.

The Table of Nations

The table lists seventy-one names. It is likely, however, that the ancient reader would have counted seventy and understood the common ancient convention indicating totality, since this is clearly a selected list of nations (for a helpful brief explanation, see Sarna 1989, 69). Scholars differ on which name should not be regarded as intended by Moses. Some would discount Nimrod from the total because he is the only individual in Japheth's or Ham's line (e.g., Cassuto 1974, 177; Sarna 1989, 69), while others would more likely eliminate the Philistines since they are not connected by genealogical link, only geographically (e.g., Sailhamer 1990, 99; Wenham 1987, 213).

Scattered by Grace (11:1–9)
Reversing human unity and aspirations of legacy and security, Yahweh exposes their false security as confused folly, giving opportunity for blessing.

Genesis 10 tracks the scattering of the nations, ending with them being spread abroad on the earth (10:32), which was the expected result of blessing and the fulfillment of God's command (9:1, 7). Genesis 11, however, regresses chronologically to relate why people scattered. Humanity did not disperse from obedient concern for God's blessing. God spread humanity to prepare for his blessing, which will gain clarity with Abram in chapter 12.

Genesis 11 weaves a very tightly structured narrative portraying the talionic justice of Yahweh on his rebellious and self-absorbed people. On the one hand, the narrative develops along parallel lines, building human pride in their project (vv. 1–4) that Yahweh mimicked in his deconstruction (vv. 6–9).

THE STRUCTURE OF GENESIS 11:1–9

Fokkelman and Kikawada provide a similar description of the dual interlocking structure of Genesis 11:1–9 (with some variation) (Fokkelman 2004, ch. 1; Kikawada 1974). Kikawada not only notes the terms in chiasm but the sections as well, presenting the repeated terms and motifs to define five scenes in three episodes:

Episode 1:	A. Indirect discourse (11:1–2)
	B. Predominantly direct discourse (11:3–4)
Episode 2:	C. Indirect discourse (11:5)
Episode 3:	B'. Predominantly direct discourse (11:6–7)
	A'. Indirect discourse (11:8–9)

He also effectively shows the intricacies of the structure, with interlocking patterns and introversions indicating a high degree of artistic working.

Both authors expose the significant Hebrew terms in the narrative that present the structure (here from the simpler presentation of Fokkelman 2004, 20, 22):

11:1–4 about the men
A "one language and the same words" (שָׂפָה אֶחָת וּדְבָרִים אֲחָדִים)
B "Come, . . ." (הָבָה [2x] coh.)
C "Let us build" (נִבְנֶה)
D "Let us make a name for ourselves" (וְנַעֲשֶׂה שֵׁם)
E "Lest we be dispersed over the face of the whole earth" (פֶּן־נָפוּץ עַל־פְּנֵי כָל־הָאָרֶץ)

11:5–9 about Yahweh
A' "one people, and . . . one language" (עַם אֶחָד וְשָׂפָה אַחַת)
B' "Come, . . . " (הָבָה coh.)
C' "and they left off building" (וַיַּחְדְּלוּ לִבְנֹת)
E' "So [he] dispersed them . . . over the face of all the earth" (וַיָּפֶץ אֹתָם עַל־פְּנֵי כָל־הָאָרֶץ)
D' "its name . . . Babel" (שְׁמָהּ בָּבֶל)
E' "[he] dispersed them over the face of all the earth" (הֱפִיצָם עַל־פְּנֵי כָּל־הָאָרֶץ)

And:
11:1–4 about the men

A "the whole earth had one language" (כָל־הָאָרֶץ שָׂפָה אֶחָת)
B "there" (שָׁם)
C "to one another" (אִישׁ אֶל־רֵעֵהוּ)
D "Come, let us make bricks" (הָבָה נִלְבְּנָה לְבֵנִים)
E "let us build ourselves" (נִבְנֶה־לָּנוּ)
F "a city and a tower" (עִיר וּמִגְדָּל)

11:5–9 about Yahweh

X "And the LORD came down to see" (וַיֵּרֶד יְהוָה לִרְאֹת)
F' "the city and the tower" (אֶת־הָעִיר וְאֶת־הַמִּגְדָּל)
E' "which the children of man had built" (אֲשֶׁר בָּנוּ בְּנֵי הָאָדָם)
D' "Come, let us . . . confuse" (הָבָה וְנָבְלָה)
C' "one another's speech" (אִישׁ שְׂפַת רֵעֵהוּ)
B' "from there" (מִשָּׁם)
A' "the language of all the earth" (שְׂפַת כָּל־הָאָרֶץ)

A. "the whole earth had one language and the same words" (11:1)
B. They settled "there" (11:2)
C. "they said to one another" (11:3)
D. "Let us build ourselves a city and a tower" (11:4)
E. "let us make a name for ourselves" (11:4)
X. "the Lord came down" (11:5)
A'. "they are one people, and they have all one language" (11:6)
B'. "there" confuse (11:7)
C'. "so that they may not understand one another's speech" (11:7)
D'. "they left off building the city" (11:8)
E'. "its name was called Babel" (11:9)

In the center, Yahweh condescends to view man's achievement (v. 5). The parallels reveal the irony and talionic justice of Yahweh's response. They stress the triviality of humankind's activity in God's view and rule, as well as the futility of their rebellion.

Simultaneously, Moses weaves an elegant chiasm as Yahweh nullifies the goal of humankind. Yahweh, stooping to see man's achievement, centers the chiasm (v. 5).[4] The structure highlights God's sovereign reversal of human unity and rebellion, re-emphasizing the talionic justice as well as the proportion of God's justice (Fokkelman 2004, 29–43). What we know (3:15; 9:1–17) and yet will rediscover is that God is moving humankind toward his blessing, even in judgment (ch. 12).

4 Kikawada (1974, 71–74) details and defends the intermingling of parallel and chiastic structuring with intricate detail (cf. Kikawada and Quinn 1985), while Fokkelman (2004, 11–45) defends the intentionality and theological significance of both aspects of the interlocking narrative. The chiasm functions both on the scene level as described in the next paragraph, as well as the word and phrase level as detailed by both Fokkelman and Kikawada.

God blessed humanity, united for fame, with fractured infamy in their folly so that he could refocus them on true blessing through Abram (12:1–2).

A. People were united in language and direction (11:1–2).
   B. Humanity proudly plotted for a name and unity (11:3–4).
      C. Yahweh condescended to judge human arrogance (11:5).
   B'. Yahweh pronounced their fractured future (11:6–7).
A'. God dispersed humanity with confused language (11:8–9).

People Were United in Language and Direction (11:1–2)

A growing family finds a fertile plain on which to establish their unified kingdom.

11:1. Verse 1 introduces the narrative: all humanity is united. The narrator returns to an early stage of human migration after the flood, toward the beginning of the table of nations in chapter 10. Humanity, rather than being divided by their clans, languages, lands, and nations (10:5, 20, 31–32), are united in one "language" (שָׂפָה). The emphasis on a single language (used five times in nine verses and restated here as "the same words") highlights both their intrinsic unity and the point of weakness that Yahweh will sovereignly exploit to frustrate their plans.

11:2. People migrate eastward (or southeastward) from the mountains of Ararat (8:4). They settle in Shinar, drawing the reader's attention back to the note in chapter 10 on Nimrod (vv. 9–10). Moses does not claim that every person has migrated here but rather presents Shinar as the power center of a growing family. Though scattering is on the horizon, great kingdoms and human tyranny commence from here in opposition to the rule of Yahweh, reminding the reader again of Genesis 6.

TRANSLATION ANALYSIS 11:2

Translations are somewhat divided over whether to take the Hebrew as "from the east," translating the parts literally (מִקֶּדֶם, ESV, JPS, NCV, NKJV, NRSV, RSV), or idiomatically, as "eastward" (NASB95, NET, NIV). Wenham (1987, 238) notes that "elsewhere in Genesis מקדם, when used adverbially and not as a preposition, means 'in the east' (2:8; 12:8; cf. Isa 9:11 [12])," supporting the idea of "eastward." Reinforcing this translation, Genesis 13:11 requires something like "eastward."

Humanity Proudly Plotted for a Name and Unity (11:3–4)

In pride, people built a monument to entice God down and ensure their legacy and security.

11:3. Using the common building materials of Babylon, where mud was abundant and rocks were scarce, the narrative reminds the reader of the Babylonian creation account (*Enuma Elish*) and the building of the temple to Marduk in Babylon (Foster, "Epic of Creation (1.111)." CoS, I:401, tablet VI, lines 57–64). Here, however, the narrative presents a derogatory polemic against the cosmopolitan power structures of Babylon, the region from which Abram will migrate to initiate God's plan of blessing. In contrast to the Babylonian creation account, it is not the gods building the temple, but rebellious people; it is not commanded by the high god, but contrary to the only God, and it is not lauded by the deity as a great work but viewed as miniscule and judged.

11:4. The first audience would have clearly recognized the main structures of Babylon in the building project, even if the city had not been named (v. 9). The tower was likely describing a ziggurat, which was a man-made mountain connected to a temple complex, allowing the gods easier access to earth and their temple, a means of communication and assurance of

The Babylonian Creation account contains similarities with Genesis 1, and many differences that show a very different worldview and conception of god/the gods than Genesis teaches.

divine attention.[5] The description of "its top in the heavens" was "a cliché in Mesopotamian building inscriptions" for the ziggurat (Sarna 1989, 82).

TRANSLATION ANALYSIS 11:4
Some translations render this as "a tower that reaches to the heavens" (NIV, cf. NASB95, NCV, NLT) rather than "a tower with its top in the heavens" (ESV, NET, NRSV; cf. JPS, NKJV, RSV). The latter, more literal translation better shows the focus on the place, not the height of the tower (despite our modern western impression). Rather, the heavens represent the dwelling of the gods, leading to the expected descent of the gods to man.

The purpose of the builders was to make a "name" (שֵׁם) for themselves, with the expected consequence of not being scattered "over the face of the whole earth." In the first two lines of the Babylonian creation account, having a name determines existence and "not to have a name, or to have the name cut off, was to cease to exist" (Ross, שֵׁם, *NIDOTTE* 4:147). The fear of being scattered relates to the loss of name and so existence. They will lose their "immortality" (the pagan concept of continuing in the afterlife by remembrance) and so security. Of course, the filling of the earth was the blessing of God (1:28; 9:1, 7), suggesting that opposing the scattering was an affront to God's authority and the only source of true blessing (contrary to Enoch and Noah!).

The Sin of Babel
The exact nature of the sin has long been debated. The concluding note that they "left off building the city" suggests to some their sin was trying to gain their security in city-building (Hamilton 1990, 356). The search for a "name" without permission from the gods, especially in Mesopotamian building traditions, suggests human pride (Giorgetti 2014, 10–13). Their intent to make a name "lest we be dispersed" suggests rebellion against God's command to fill the earth by unifying (Ross 2008, 90–91). The making of "a name" for themselves in conjunction with the

5 See Walton (2009a, 60–63) for an overview of the ziggurat and the connections to this passage. He concludes that "in the earliest stages of urbanization, the city was not designed for the private sector.... Consequently, the city was, in effect, a temple complex" (p. 61). On the other hand, Giorgetti (2014, 13–14) maintains that this could identify some other structure, though a ziggurat is likely.

purpose and function of the ziggurat, the Mesopotamian cognitive environment, and the context of Genesis 1–11 suggest they were pursuing their own security and future with a pagan view of God rather than exalting him as the supreme King (Walton 2001, 374–77; cf. Longman, Walton, and Moshier 2018, 130–33). The sin may be multifaceted, creating layers of culpability in the hearts and plans of humanity.

Ziggurat Dūr Untash. By Alireza.heydear

The importance of "name" has already been seen in Genesis 6:4 in connection with powerful tyrants ("men of renown" are literally "the men of name"), also reminiscent of Nimrod (10:8–12). It will resurface again with God's promise to Abram to "make your name great" (12:2), suggesting that they are usurping the prerogative of God in their quest for immortality. Lasting honor can only come from God, not at the expense of his reputation, but only as it honors him. The comparison with royal Mesopotamian ideology suggests a backdrop of powerful kings seeking to guarantee their own immortality while usurping divine prerogative (Giorgetti 2014, 14–16). As with Lamech (4:24), they are trying to guarantee for themselves what only God can provide, and only through true worship. They are trying to reverse the curse and regain what was lost in the garden. But they are missing the true immortality (and human flourishing) of walking with God in life and security, as we have seen with Enoch and Noah, and as Abram will learn.

A "Name"

Moses emphasized the quest for a "name" (shēm) with the use of similar sounds throughout the narrative, from Shem (mentioned 10x in chs. 9–11) to them settling "there" (sham), from God confusing them "there" (sham) to even the "heavens" (shamayim). This emphasis on "name" highlights both their purpose and God's reversal, showing their folly. Numerous alliterations, paronomasias, other wordplays, and repetitions of similar words enhance this short narrative (Cassuto 1974, 232–34). In contrast, God will give a great name to the one he chooses and who follows him in faith (Gen. 12:2).

Building the ziggurat promoted their agenda because it opened a way to commune with the divine and ensure his approval and blessing. The ziggurat was the realm of the god, not the human, and was how the god would come to participate in their worship. Human religion was about serving the god so that the god would then benefit the worshipper in co-dependence. If they could co-opt God's presence, which humankind lost through their rebellion, they might be able to regain the blessing on their own terms and gain from him renown, so continuing their existence. In the Babylonian creation account the gods were credited with construction of the temple and ziggurat to honor Marduk, and they proceeded to exalt him above all the gods. Here, in ironic contrast, it is not worthy to be called divine, and God must come down to even see it. In the Mesopotamian monuments, the king would exalt himself and pray for his own immortality while ostensibly honoring the gods (Giorgetti 2014, 15–16). These people are also exalting themselves, which, as the narrative clarifies, dishonors Yahweh. He will view their grand accomplishment very differently.

Yahweh Condescended to Judge Human Arrogance (11:5)

Yahweh condescends to evaluate the grand project for righteous judgment.

11:5. In ironic distinction, Yahweh does indeed come down (as they apparently desired), but in sharp contrast to their expectation and all the gods of the ancient world. In sarcastic humor and anthropomorphism, the condescension of Yahweh to see the great tower spotlights the insignificance of their achievement. This is not an honor to him, but an abomination. This narrative turns the Babylonian creation account upside down (Sarna 1989, 83). The tower was not worthy of deity but so trivial Yahweh must stoop (11:5). Their attempt to use Yahweh and create their own sacred space dishonored him and reeks of idolatry, the historic purpose of the ziggurat. Mesopotamian worship aimed to care for the needs of the god so that he would care for their needs. Yahweh cares for his images and has no needs. The human quest for legacy and blessing is completely wrong-headed and anthropocentric. Rather than the desired unity, fame, and blessing, they receive infamy and dispersal. In further irony, however, his judgment will allow Yahweh to eventually bring them true blessing in true relationship and worship.

Yahweh Pronounced Their Fractured Future (11:6–7)

Noting human unity, Yahweh pronounced his imminent disruption of their purpose by confusing their language.

11:6. Yahweh declared his conclusion to his evaluation as the basis for his judgment (11:7). Yahweh's declaration (vv. 6–7) directly counters the plan and desire of his human population (vv. 3–4). Pointedly, his conclusion did not mention the project, further reducing its significance, but instead addressed the underlying condition. Human unity from their heritage and language presents a formidable obstacle to their well-being. It is not merely that they will be able to accomplish great feats but that they will be able to succeed in their self-destructive pursuit of a devastating agenda and false worship. They will feel significant and secure apart from their very real need to know and walk with God. They will have nothing to challenge their misperception and their false sense of security in their own abilities. If we are correct in our assessment of this city as a power center for tyranny as well, then there will be no natural check to inhibit the violence and oppression for which God had judged the world in the flood (6:11–12).

11:7. In humorous irony, Moses shows the judgment as well as tells it. Yahweh's speech mimics the speech of the builders. His "Come, let us go down and there confuse their language" imitates the sounds and forms of the call of the builders to make bricks and to build (11:3–4). Moses shows and tells that God will directly respond to their arrogance and self-determination by reversing their plans to provide for his declared outcome, destroying evil and providing blessing. Yahweh will disrupt their unity, rooted in their language (v. 1), immediately arresting their cooperation but providing long term distinctions and tensions that are implicit in the resulting table of nations in Genesis 10. Reading through the table, the initial audience would immediately feel the distrust, intrigue, alliances, and hostilities along with the resulting warfare, oppression, and destruction resulting from Yahweh's action. He leaves humankind with pain and frustration reminiscent of God's initial judgments after the fall in chapter 3, which stress humanity's need for God. True blessing and peace can only be experienced in walking with God.

TRANSLATION ANALYSIS 11:7

The plural ("let us") reflects the literal Hebrew and is consistently translated so. For the plural with Yahweh, see the sidebar on 1:26 (p. 88). Here, however, there is a further element to consider. The use of the royal address also allows Moses to cast Yahweh's speech in more direct and ironic parallel with the call of the workers to make bricks and build (11:3–4). The direct parallel emphasizes the reversal of their plans and Yahweh's talionic justice.

Meaning in the Artistic Language

The cohortative ("Come") is identical, leading to the question of the plurality ("Let us"—see Translation Analysis 11:7). The verb beautifully plays on the sounds, reversing the consonants from their plan to make bricks (לבן, l-b-n, and very similar sounds in "let us build," נִבְנֶה־לָּנוּ, n-b-n-l-n), to Yahweh's declaration to confuse (נָבְלָה, n-b-l) illustrating that his action will reverse their plans and scatter them (Fokkelman 2004, 15–16). He will confuse them "there" (שָׁם), reminding of where they settled (v. 2, שָׁם), and from where (מִשָּׁם) they would be scattered (v. 8), but also that it was their desire for a "name" (שֵׁם) that caused it.

God Dispersed Humanity with Confused Language (11:8–9)

God fractured human unity in language and geography, removing legacy and security and exposing it as confused folly apart from Yahweh, preparing for his planned future.

11:8. Verse 8 describes the outcome, reversing the migration of people in verse 2. They had settled "there" (שָׁם), but Yahweh dispersed them from "there" (מִשָּׁם, repeated in v. 9). He directly countered the misguided goal of the people (v. 4), strewing them "over the face of all the earth." Yahweh's solution both advanced his original blessing ("be fruitful and multiply and fill the earth," 1:28, 9:1, 7) and curbed the ability of people to unite in rebellion. As the concluding narrative of the primeval history, it frames the history with Genesis 1, highlighting the purpose of Yahweh to fill his earth and bless (Kikawada and Quinn 1985, 74–79). Their building stopped.

11:9. Framing the narrative with 11:1, Moses finally identifies the city as "Babel." The "gate of god" (to the Babylonians) is really a monument to "confusion" (using the similar Hebrew sounds b-l-l instead of b-b-l). Human search for a "name" (שֵׁם, v. 4) ends with the "name" (שֵׁם, v. 9) "confusion." The Hebrew word play caps the satire on the great monument to human pride and idolatry of Babel as merely babble. The great building projects and cosmopolitan society with the many languages only reminds the reader of the futility of usurping God's prerogatives and trying to build one's own legacy apart from Yahweh.

Verse 9 draws together the themes of the narrative. The pursuit of fame and security (שֵׁם, vv. 4, 9) has only precipitated confusion, infamy, and insecurity. Their proud unity is shattered. Again, the initial unity of "the whole earth" (v. 1) is reversed as "all the earth" (2x, vv. 8–9) will reflect the necessary outcomes of Yahweh's grace in both dispersion and confusion. While he did not bring the complete ruin of the flood (fulfilling his promise of 9:8–17), his judgment was both devastating and compassionate. He has prepared his images for a new stage in his plan to crush the head of the snake and bring humankind his blessing. That new stage will see a fresh start with Abram and the promise to Abram to produce descendants and bring blessing to all the families of the earth (12:1–3). It prepares, then, for the place of the nation of Israel in God's program as he clarifies his promise for blessing.

THEOLOGICAL FOCUS

The spread of the nations reveals both human responsibilities and hope in God's redemptive purpose for all peoples from his gracious judgment on human folly, preparing for his choice of Israel to accomplish his blessing.

God showed his sovereign grace in bringing justice that both effectively halted human offense and honored his promise and blessing, even to a rebellious and cursed humanity (9:25–27). Yahweh condescended his transcendent splendor to inspect the grandiose project of human pride. He graciously taught his foolish images that their attempts at immortality and security would always fail apart from him. God graciously puts humanity into the position to learn that ambition apart from him will only destroy. It is only in knowing, serving, and walking with God that humanity can flourish. The lesson of walking with God (Enoch, Noah) will be revisited by Yahweh in his covenant with Abram and developed in his progressive covenants through Noah, Abraham, and Moses, and continued through David and Jesus. God patiently teaches and prepares his creations for his blessing the sole result of submission and loyalty to his rule and experienced in his presence. It is received as a gift, not wrested by human wisdom or power

Simultaneous with his grace, Yahweh's justice is entirely appropriate for the crime and his faithfulness to his promise to not judge as he did in the flood. He balances his promises of blessing and redemption (3:15) with needed judgment (1:26; 9:1, 7). The spread and relations of the nations show his authority to bring appropriate future justice as the nations line up to fulfill the oracle of Noah for Shem, Ham, and Japheth (9:25–27). Yahweh consistently frustrates rebellion and assures blessing, even though it may often only be seen from the vantage of history.

Humanity, however, reveals their obliviousness to the realities of lasting significance and security. Failing to learn the lessons of past generations, the evil bent of every heart (8:21) blossoms into tyranny and rebellion, pursuing a fully self-focused agenda with no understanding of a transcendent God. The egocentric human heart searches for stability and security in its autonomy. People feel the need to guarantee their future and their power, whether corporately or individually. Here the corporate push (11:3) seems to be backed or perhaps driven by individual tyranny (10:8–12). Humankind uses their ability and innovation together with an inherent unity, endowed by their creator as his images, to pursue their own agenda and rebellion against him.

Failure to learn the lessons of previous generations further limits their perspective but not their responsibility. Humankind is accountable to their heritage, with its revelation and requirements (e.g., Noahic covenant), even if it is not remembered or acknowledged. Without it, humankind must grope in their own blindness, unable to see the true heights of the dwelling of God or the realities of true life, walking with him.

Humankind is, therefore, also unable to appreciate the futility of our own pride and foolishness. What people believe to be grand is feeble. What we expect to be solid is flimsy. What we see as brilliant is folly. The limited perspective of humanity skews our perception of reality and directs our attention to empty mirages.

The sovereign working of God to accomplish his eternal plan provides the sole hope. The narrative confirms that despite the human heart, Yahweh will accomplish his good and planned goals. His judgment will bring pain, frustration, suffering, and the possibility for redemption.

PREACHING AND TEACHING STRATEGIES

Exegetical and Theological Synthesis

Chapter 10 begins to speak to us and our listeners by a detailed reminder about our historical roots in redemptive history. As pointed out in the exegesis of chapter 10, the list of seventy nations is symbolic of the unity of the entire human race. Chapter 9 ended with one curse and two blessings aimed at Noah's three sons. If Hess (1989) is right about readers understanding Nimrod's name to mean "we will rebel," then we immediately see how God assesses our human condition with respect to his rule and authority (10:8–9). Another clue concerning the kind of people God is dealing with throughout history is in 11:2, "And as people migrated from the east" (cf. 4:16 and Cain moving away from the Lord and settling "east of Eden"). Humanity naturally follows the path of Cain!

But we know that our gracious God has made promises to us by blessing Noah and his three sons. So, the question is, how is God going to make good on his promises to bless a people that are bound and determined to rebel against him? Well, the first part of that answer is in the incident surrounding the Tower of Babel. Later we will see the Lord graciously creating a people to shine brightly in his world as his representatives. But in our text God's creatures are attempting to make a name for themselves apart from worshipping and serving him. This describes humanity's endless attempts to secure the good life on their own. What is ironic is that their attempt to connect with God ("let us build ourselves a city and a tower with its top in the heavens" in 11:4) does in fact bring him down (cf. v. 5, "And the LORD came down"). Somehow the inhabitants have forgotten their history and the flood!

God does announce impressive human capability (v. 6, "nothing that they propose to do will now be impossible"), but their inspiring monuments are only grand sinkholes. God somehow messed with their brains and ended their ability to succeed. The Hebrew wordplay in verse 9 summarizes the event. It is enough to convince me not to attempt to succeed in life without God! You? God will not allow his plan to be thwarted! Better for us to allow him to place us within his plan.

Preaching Idea

Our Lord is watching whether his people are making a name for themselves or for him, and directs history to spread his fame.

Contemporary Connections

What does it mean?

"So, this is how we got more than seven thousand languages?!" We begin to see meaning emerge in chapter 10 with an early reference to "each with his own language" in verse 5. You will see it again in verses 20, 31, and in 11:1, 6, 7, and 9. The Shinarians explain the reason for their plan: "let us build ourselves a city and a tower . . . and let us make a name for ourselves, lest we be dispersed over the face of the whole earth" (11:4). The concept of "the whole earth" is also a key to meaning. The repeated phrase in chapter 11 (vv. 1, 4, 8, and twice in v. 9) takes us back to 9:19 ("and from these [three sons of Noah] the people of the whole earth were dispersed"). God has a reason for talking in "whole earth" terms: he wants his fame to extend throughout his world. The people have a reason for collecting in a city: they want to make a name for themselves (11:4). This may be society's signature sin. A human race that speaks one language is a powerful force against God's agenda in the world (cf. v. 6, "nothing . . . will now be impossible for them"). God will make a name for himself, which means he will not allow humanity to continue in their rebellion for long. At some point in history, he will come down (cf. v. 5), take a look, and act in his best interest. What's fascinating is that the Lord mercifully keeps his covenant promise by not destroying people, but instead simply destroys their ability to work together against him. Instead, they must see their impotence without him.

Is it true?

Is it true that humanity possesses so much ability that it can pose a threat to the Almighty? The narrative says "yes" (11:6, "nothing . . . will now be impossible for them"). Our Lord does not downplay humanity's potential power to rule on earth. However, there are times in history when he sees attempts to thwart his rule, and he steps into "our" times so he can continue his plan of spreading his fame to every nation.

You might spend a moment explaining what goes into a miracle such as confusing someone's language. Our Lord changes the wiring in a person's brain, erasing their memory and learning and replacing it with new vocabulary, grammar, and syntax. Incredible stuff. This section also provides insight into the religious experiences of human beings. Verse 4 explains their worldview: they can make a name for themselves by building a sprawling city and high tower. Is it true that these things are important to human beings? Look around the next time you're in the big city.

Now what?

During the writing of this commentary there has been a surge of interest in a person's heritage. Numerous ads for such sites as ancestry.com appear on popular networks. This is an excellent time to be talking about Noah's three sons being the foundation for all post-flood humanity. Also, we're living in a society that desperately wants harmony for all. Language and cultural barriers are huge, and our text teaches us that our Lord will not allow too much global teamwork to occur except on his terms and for his purposes.

While Nimrod's kingdom is highlighted in chapter 10, it is clearly God's kingdom that oversees human history after the flood, just as the flood narrative proved. The Lord will continue to do what he wants with the nations so that ultimately his will is done on earth as it is in heaven. This is tremendous comfort to God's people. But this also provides a corrective for us today. All too often I am tempted to pursue my own agenda for my own sake. And that pursuit destroys the relationships around me. I exist to make a name for God. Wherever it occurs, our disciple-making mission occurs in the context of the table of nations provided in the pericope.

Creativity in Presentation

Consider the following progression for this section:

- Society's signature sin of self-exalting pride (especially seen in 10:8–12 and 11:1–4)
- Our Lord's response to that sin (11:5–9). Recall our preaching idea for this section: our Lord is watching whether his people are making a name for themselves or for him and directs history to spread his fame.
- Our mission in God's world. Looking ahead . . .

Even though the list of nations in chapter 10 is tedious for most of us modern readers, there is an interest these days in websites such as ancestry.com. People want to get in touch with their roots, and this section certainly does that. If you have ever wondered how we got so many languages and cultures, here is God's explanation. I often think, "It would be so much better if everyone spoke the same language. I wish I could understand so and so." Former U.S. president Barack Obama was once asked what superpower he would choose. Without hesitation he replied that he wished he could speak every language in the world. What a classic answer, especially considering what God did to humanity in the Tower of Babel narrative! God feels otherwise right now, for his stated reasons in the pericope.

Consider displaying the ethnic breakdown of your congregation: Where do they fit into the world's population? As stated in the final point suggested above in the outline, God is calling his people to live the life of faith among the nations. Matthew's gospel ends with our Lord saying, "make disciples of all nations" (28:19). It's possible that in Luke 10 the Lord selects seventy to match the number of nations recorded in our

Genesis pericope. Here is another indicator of how God's people carry out their mission in God's world. Although clearly in the minority, God's people represent his kingdom among the powerful kingdoms of the world.

DISCUSSION QUESTIONS

1. In the table of nations, God provides two amplifications, one surrounding Nimrod (10:8–13) and another brief explanation at Eber (10:24–25). What is the theological significance of both expansions? You may need to look at 11:10–26 to answer the second one.

2. In chapter 10 God repeats, restates, and emphasizes the concept of humanity spreading across the land and numerous nations. What does this say about his kingdom and plan?

3. Can you think of how you are tempted to make a name for yourself instead of for God (11:4)?

4. What is the greatest ambition that you see represented in popular movies? How does that lead to either a fool's errand or eternal greatness?

5. Why was making a name for themselves so offensive to God?

6. How does our society underestimate God? How do we tend to underestimate God? How can we see him for who he is?

INTRODUCTION TO THE ABRAHAM NARRATIVES (GENESIS 11:10–25:11)

The flow of Genesis dramatically shifts with the introduction of Abraham. The first six sections of Genesis (introduction and first five *toledots*, 1:1–11:26) focus on all humanity and outline their precipitous decline, with God's promise lingering in the shadows of human violence, oppression, and self-promotion. In the final six *toledots* (11:27–50:26), however, God introduces his plan to reverse the curse, progressively clarifying his promises of life for humankind and death to the snake, through a single family. That promised life will be a blessing for all humanity through the line of Abraham, Isaac, and Jacob, which will be worked out in the rest of the Pentateuch and the history of the nation. The promises to Abraham in 12:1–3 introduce this shift and provide the focal point for the message of Genesis. The first eleven chapters have exposed humanity's growing need for divine intervention. They must know God and enjoy the relationship with him for which his images were created by walking with God, beautifully illustrated with the anthropomorphism in the garden (Gen. 3:8), stated in the notes on Enoch (5:22–24) and Noah (6:9), and explained in God's promised blessing (Lev. 26:11–12). The Abraham narratives provide that world-changing opportunity, as God initiates his program.

God intervened in human history to choose a single man through whom to reach his images with his redemption. Calling Abram to follow him, God offered him promises, intending to provide blessing for all people. To an obedient and loyal Abraham, God would reveal his covenant, drawing all nations to walk with him, the source of all blessing (22:18). The rest of Genesis builds out God's program, beginning with blessing Abraham and his family and providing a glimpse of God's plans to bless all his images.

Abraham, then, provides a new beginning, much as with Noah, furnishing a new Adam to accomplish the plan of God. As such, the royal theme continues. Through Abraham (17:6) and Sarah (17:16) God would bring kings to his troubled world. The promise of kingship would extend through Jacob (35:11), culminating in Judah (49:10) as God's promise for the defeat of the snake and the extension of his rule through his blessed images takes shape. Yahweh, the sovereign creator of the universe, chose the descendants of Abraham to bring blessing out of cursing through true worship, extending his rule to a world continually turning away from him in rebellion.

LITERARY STRUCTURE AND THEMES

The Abraham narratives provide a tightly structured set of accounts that systematically develop God's purposes from his initial promise to Abraham. The promises themselves grow: the land gains specificity, from uncertain (12:1) to general (12:7), then delineated geographically and ethnographically (15:18–21), climaxing as an "everlasting possession" (17:8); the promise of a great nation (12:2) becomes innumerable (as dust, 13:16; as stars, 15:5; or stars and sand, 22:17) as a multitude of nations (17:4–5) with kings (17:6); and the promise to bless all the families of the earth in Abraham (12:3), or all the nations of the earth (18:18), will occur through his offspring (22:18). Throughout, God validated his promise as he blessed Abram (12:2; cf. 24:1, 35–36) and demonstrated that those who blessed him were blessed and the one who dishonored him would be cursed (12:3; e.g., Pharaoh, Abimelech).

The promise to bring blessing to all humanity appears in seed form throughout the stories as Abraham is tasked with bringing blessing to his world (12:2) in his obedient faith. God's promise to bless those who bless Abram and curse anyone who dishonors him follows Abraham's faithful actions with blessing accompanying Abraham's intercession for Sodom (and Lot, 18:22–19:29) and Abimelech (20:17–18), and treaty with Abimelech (21:22–34). Abraham's faithless actions, however, brought cursing reflected in the two "she is my sister" narratives (12:10–20 and 20:1–18).

The actual outworking of the land and seed promises forms the main tensions of these narratives. The covenant ceremony guaranteed the defined land to the descendants of Abraham (15:7–8, 18–21), even though none yet existed. The final ratification added God's oath to fulfill all the promises and expansions, specifically noting the number of Abraham's descendants, their power over their enemies, and God's blessing through them to all nations (22:16–18). All of this with the only promised descendant, Isaac, yet in view, and precipitously delivered from God's requested offering. The trajectory of the growing promise and commitment of God to his irrevocable promises follows the growth of Abram in faith and loyal service to his king, providing tangible and poignant illustrations of responsibilities and expectations that accompany the invitation to all people to walk with God for blessing. The tight structure enhances and carries the message.

Toledot 6: God chose, matured, established in covenant, and blessed Abraham to bring blessing to all the families of the world (11:27–25:11).[1]

- A. Terah, with Abram and the family, moved toward Canaan, stopping in Haran (11:27–32).
  - B. When God called Abram to follow him for blessing and to extend blessing to all families of the earth, Abram followed with worship and proclamation (12:1–9).
    - C. God delivered Abram and Sarai from Abram's foolish lie in Egypt and blessed him with renewed promise when he trusted God for the land (12:10–13:18).
      - D. Abram delivered Lot and Sodom, declaring his exclusive worship of Yahweh (14:1–24).
        - E. Yahweh established his covenant with believing Abram, who tried to achieve the promise through his handmaiden (15:1–16:16).
        - E' God renewed his covenant with Abram, calling him to loyalty, marked by his name change, and sign of the covenant, clarifying the promised descendant would be through barren Sarah (17:1–18:15).
      - D' Abraham embodied blessing, promoting justice and righteousness as he interceded for Sodom and Lot, securing Lot's deliverance (18:16–19:38).
    - C' God delivered Sarah again, providing the promised son in security and prosperity (20:1–21:34).
  - B' God rewarded Abraham's extreme loyalty when Abraham chose faith in God over Isaac, ratifying his expanded covenant promises (22:1–19).
- A' The family remaining in Haran were prospering, producing Rebekah (22:20–24).

---

1 The Patriarchal Narratives structure, both here for the Abraham narratives, as well as the Jacob and Joseph narratives, generally follows Gary Rendsburg (2014, 27–97), with some private communication and influence from K. Lawson Younger and personal modifications.

Epilogue to the toledot: Abraham prepared for Isaac and his line to remain invested with God's promise after he died.

1. Abraham prepared his descendants to pursue the promise with a new homeland by faith, securing a foothold in the land of promise for the burial of Sarah (23:1–20).
2. Abraham pursued an appropriate wife for Isaac to nurture, through God's providence, the promised line, to continue the promised blessing (24:1–67).
3. Abraham protected the promised blessing though Isaac, generously releasing subsequent sons (25:1–6).
4. Abraham's death and burial launched the new homeland, as blessing passed to Isaac (25:7–11).

God's promised redemption through the coming descendant to crush the head of the snake frames the Abraham stories through the narrowing genealogies. The genealogy in 11:10–26 guides the reader to Abram. While Genesis 11:27–32 describes Abram's family and their move to Haran, the main Abraham stories close with the family in Haran growing, pointing to Rebekah and the next stage of the promise (22:20–24; fleshed out in the epilogue, ch. 24). Between the genealogical bookends, Yahweh calls Abram to leave with the promise of blessing to bring blessing to all families (12:1–9), which climaxes in the ratification of the covenant and full promise by God's oath after Abraham demonstrated his unconditional loyalty to Yahweh (22:1–19).

Between the promise and the ratification, the narrative builds the tensions of unrealized promise in both land and descendants. The first major movement of the Abraham stories, beginning with the two imperatives for Abram to go and be a blessing, advances these tensions, with the covenant ceremony in 15:1–21 at the center of the structure recognizing both Abram's faith (15:6) and God's guarantee of both land and seed (15:18–21). The second half of the Abraham stories reverses course with two additional imperatives calling Abram to absolute loyalty (17:1; see below), reiterating the covenant promises, and giving of the sign of the covenant (17:2–27). Abraham's foolish attempt to realize the promise in Hagar (16:1–16) was corrected by God's declaration of the fulfillment through Sarah (17:15–18:15). While God guaranteed both land and descendants by covenant (15:1–21), each would be endangered and scarcely initiated (water rights and one son) before God called Abraham to put his limited fulfillment of the promise, Isaac, on the altar to declare God's priority and the ultimate source of blessing. Abraham's offering satisfies God's demand for Abraham's loyalty (17:1–2), which the angel proclaims fulfilled (22:12). Abraham has grown into a worthy vassal to receive the full intent of God's gracious gifts and bring blessing through his offspring to all the nations of the earth (22:16–18).

The epilogue provides Abraham's appropriate response to the promise as he prepared his family to pursue the implications of the promise (cf. 18:19) by staying in the land and expecting the final outworking as God promised: he established a burial plot for the family (23:1–20), a wife for Isaac (24:1–67), and sent away all other sons (25:1–6) before dying and being gathered to his people in the land (25:7–11), showing faith in the promise.

In his writing of Genesis, Moses effectively demonstrated the gracious and purposeful character of God, as well as his sovereign intervention in human affairs, guaranteeing his promise despite periodic unbelief or disobedience. God will show his world his character and draw all families in all nations to walk with him and find blessing. We see both his loyal love and faithfulness as he inexorably accomplishes his purpose, as well as his righteousness and justice, whether in necessary immediate judgment (ch. 19) or gracious announcement of future judgment (15:16). For all humanity, his expectations are clear and righteous, providing both hope and warning, grace and justice.

COVENANT GROWTH, CLARIFICATION, AND IMPACT

The growth of the promise from 12:1–3 to ratification of the covenant in chapter 22 draws the reader into the import of the narratives. God's promise of a descendant to an aged couple by miraculous intervention sets the stage, provides the tension, and prepares for the cumulative test. Additional developing promises add conflict and growth for Abraham and Sarah, both in faith and understanding of Yahweh. The growing tensions and responses to them by Abraham and Sarah provide exemplars for every generation to emulate, or resist. They show the responses of the believer in faith or unbelief. They demonstrate the possibility of bringing blessing to our world or of causing pain and cursing. They challenge the reader to walk in the ways of the Lord in loyalty to experience and bring good and to illustrate the deception and disaster of walking by sight in the allurements of the world.

They also teach us valuable insights into the character, plan, and working of God. He is good and sovereign, working his purpose and plan through both the faith and failures of his chosen images. He desires blessing for all people and is moving his plan forward to accomplish good for all. He uses human failings and painful waiting to teach and grow his servants into useful conduits of blessing and sharers in his promised future. Abram provides a window into God's working even as God declares and expands his promised purposes for his good redemptive program.

This growing covenant may be pictured in the following chart, which generally coincides with the key sections of the structure (B, E, E', B' above):[2]

Covenant Development Through the Abraham Narratives				
	Promise initiated and reiterated (Gen. 12–13) with two commands (לֶךְ and וֶהְיֵה בְּרָכָה)	**Covenant cut (Gen. 15)**	**Promise extended (Gen. 17–18) with two commands (הִתְהַלֵּךְ לְפָנַי and וֶהְיֵה תָמִים)**	**Covenant ratified (Gen. 22)**
Land promise	To Abram and his descendants (12:7; 13:15) delineated (12:1, 7; 13:14, 17)	Delineated geographically and ethnographically (15:18–21) with timing (15:13, 16, 18)	Named ("Canaan") as everlasting possession (17:8)	No mention

2 Our understanding of the development of the covenant with Abraham here is deeply indebted to Bob Chisholm (1992, 2007) and Tony Shetter (2019). See exposition for clarification on God's expectations for Abraham and his development of the covenant promises.

Covenant Development Through the Abraham Narratives				
Seed promise	Great nation (12:2), innumerable as dust (13:16)	Innumerable as the stars (15:5)	Multiply greatly (17:2), multitude of nations (17:4, 5), nations and kings (17: 6; 16)	Multiply offspring like the stars and sand (22:17)
Blessing promise	"In you all the families of the earth shall be blessed" (12:3)	No mention	Yahweh will be God to you and to your offspring (17:7–8); "All the nations of the earth" blessed in Abraham (18:18)	"In your offspring shall all the nations of the earth be blessed" (22:18)
Covenant prog-ress and formal oath	Promises made (12:2–3)	Formal covenant cut (15:18): land and de-scendants (15:6, 16).	Condition (sign) of everlasting covenant (17:6, 13) given for relationship (17:9–14) to Isaac (17:19, 21)	Formal oath: mul-tiplied offspring, power over ene-mies, and blessing to all nations (22:16–18).
Condi-tion ex-pected	Obedience (12:1)	Faith credited as righteousness (15:6, 16)	Loyalty / obe-dience (17:1, 9–14), righ-teousness and justice (18:19)	Because of loyalty (22:12); "because you have obeyed my voice" (22:18)

Notice that these four sections work as two parallel sets and chiastic sets. Chiastically, the initial promise (12:1–3) is clearly and precisely paralleled in numerous ways to the testing and ratification (22:1–19; see exegesis). The cutting of the covenant and Abram's attempt to realize it (15:1–16:16) parallels and contrasts with God's expansion and sign of the covenant, and affirmation of Sarah as the source (17:1–18:15).

In addition, the second half (chs. 17–22) parallels the first half (chs. 12–16). The narrative begins with two commands, implicitly requiring faith from Abram ("go" and "be a blessing," showing God's desire 12:1–2). God then certified his faith in obedience to the task, immediately before the covenant ceremony (15:6; see exposition). Abraham, the man of faith, received the covenant by ceremonial oath.

The reversal of the chiasm also begins with two commands requiring Abram's loyalty ("walk before me and be blameless," 17:1) as ground for the realizing of the covenant (17:2). The two commands formally mirror chapter 12 using the same two roots (הלך and היה) though semantically diverse, drawing attention to both the parallel and growth. At the end of the narratives God declared Abraham's loyalty evidenced by his obedience (22:12) before he swore to the covenant ratification (22:15–18).[3] So, in both major movements of the stories there is both parallel progress and evaluation of the expected requirement (12:1–2 >> 15:6; 17:1 >> 22:12), and invited chiastic comparison (12:1–9||22:1–19; 15:1–16:16||17:1–18:15).

PREACHING SUGGESTIONS

God's faithful pursuit of his redemptive plan to counter man's disastrous rebellion shines through in his choice and shaping of Abraham, both in timely interventions and in growing expectations and challenges to loyal faith. His expectations for Abraham to live in faith and loyalty before him provide a template for every loyal subject, but also challenge future generations to live in the way of the Lord, practicing righteousness and justice and teaching future generations to carry on the character of God so that God will fulfill the breadth of his promises to Abraham (18:18–19). The preacher, then, has opportunity to challenge his audience with the responsibility of living the faith of Abraham in righteousness and justice, but also of passing along the necessary training to produce ongoing generations of loyal followers of Yahweh. God will use each generation to bring blessing to all the families of the earth culminating in the work of Christ, the final and ultimate child of promise, lived out in the faith of his followers.

The Abrahamic narratives can be preached as a standalone series, which would allow more focus on the covenant and the promises. A message summarizing the need from the first eleven chapters would set up the series with the basic problem of human rebellion and God's redemptive purpose. The final narrative of Abraham's protection of Isaac's status, death, and burial (25:1–11) could be used as a conclusion to summarize the sweep of the whole narratives, rather than in concert with chapter 24. The preacher could use it to show the overall growth of the promise, the satisfaction and blessing of Abraham, and the passing of the blessing to Isaac.

If you are considering an abbreviated miniseries on Abraham, we would suggest focusing on 12:1–9; 15; 17; and 22. The births of Ishmael and Isaac (16, 21) and the resulting tensions for the promise could be added as time allows, as well as God's clarification to the promise (13, 18:1–15). These could be used in a larger series on the whole of Genesis to see the larger sweep of the book without dealing with every chapter.

---

3 This structure provides background for the supposed tension between Paul and James. In the first movement of the chiasm, Yahweh declared Abraham righteous by his faith, as Paul notes (Gen. 15:6; cf. Rom. 4:1–3). In the second movement, Yahweh declared Abraham loyal, proven by his actions (demonstrating his righteousness), as James appropriately notes (James 2:21–24; cf. Gen. 22:12, 18; McCartney 2009, 162–72, 272–79). As noted by Paul, God evaluates the heart (15:6), which bears full fruit in living (22:12), as explained by James.

Genesis 11:10–12:9

EXEGETICAL IDEA

After scattering the peoples from Babel, Yahweh extended grace and called Abram to follow in faith at great personal cost, promising to bless greatly and establish a nation despite human impossibilities, to bless all peoples through relationship with Yahweh in true worship.

THEOLOGICAL FOCUS

God continues to extend grace and promise through his chosen servants, whom he calls to follow him, trusting him for the impossible, at great cost, for great blessing, and to bless his world in relationship with him.

PREACHING IDEA

God is graciously calling you to follow him in order to bless you to be a blessing to those around you.

PREACHING POINTERS

After some pretty severe—to say the least—judgment narratives, listeners will sigh in relief as God shifts our attention to the descendants of Shem and Terah, especially Abram. God is continuing to extend his grace and fulfill his promises, and it all begins "in Ur of the Chaldeans" (11:28). He will do the work; miracles must be a part of the plan in this badly broken, yet blessed world (cf. 11:30, "Now Sarai was barren" and, in case we didn't get the point, "she had no child"), which requires radical faith. Out of the blue the Lord commands Abram to leave everything he knows and loves and travel to an unknown land that he would reveal later (12:1). You can quickly see how this command, often referred to as a call, mirrors the path of faith and what it means to be a Christ-follower. If listeners need any incentive, it's found in the promises (12:2–3). If they need any grand purpose in life—and every human being does—it's found in being a conduit of blessing to the whole earth (vv. 2–3). God is the one who does this for the one he commands to follow him (note all the "I wills"). Abraham's obedience (v. 4, "So Abram went") is exemplary. Apart from the Lord, Abram is the major character in the narrative. His journey will in many ways be our journey of faith. His repeated action of building altars to the Lord leads the way for our own worship.

CALLED TO BLESS: OPPORTUNITY AND RESPONSIBILITY (11:10–12:9)

LITERARY STRUCTURE AND THEMES

We have included the transitional *toledot* genealogy of Shem (11:10–26) in this preaching unit, which literarily finishes the primeval narratives leading up to the Abram stories. The genealogy of Shem (vv. 10–26) along with the genealogy of Seth, which it mirrors (5:1–32), connects Adam to Abram, the continuity of the promise of God for blessing (1:28; 9:1, 7), and a seed to crush the serpent's head (3:15). The *toledot* of Shem also explicitly bridges from the flood (9:18–19), through Yahweh's judgment at the tower of Babel (11:1–9), to his plan to bless all people through Abram (12:1–3) (see Exposition below). The genealogical introduction continues in Terah's *toledot* with Abram's family background (11:27–32), introducing the characters that will be significant in the following stories. When God called Abram, promising him blessing and a legacy in God's redemptive program, Abram responded in obedience and worship, proclaiming God's character even as God clarified his promise.

- A. Shem's genealogy leads to Abram (11:10–26).
  - B. God called Abram (11:27–12:9).
    1. Terah's family clarifies Abram's challenges (11:27–32).
    2. God called, and Abram answered (12:1–9).
       - a. God called Abram to go to bless (12:1–3).
       - b. Abram went as God commanded (12:4–9).

This unit emphasizes God's growing promise through his call of Abram and Abram's response. God's promise to Abram marks a turning point, beginning to delineate his plan to bless humanity, which God will work out through the rest of history. Here Moses highlights that the gracious and sovereign purpose of God is to accomplish blessing for his rebellious images despite their heart damage. It stresses God's continuous work from the beginning of creation, the preparation in the primeval narratives for this plan, and his sovereign accomplishing of his strategy. He moves from all humanity to specifying one family to help all families. Abram will illustrate the journey of faith, learning to walk with God, even as he is the focal point of god's purpose. Reminiscent of Enoch and Noah, his faith will benefit all humanity.

Finally, the one who alone determines fame, security, and fruitfulness will lay the foundation for the Abrahamic covenant, the basis for his formal future relationship with humanity and the redemption of his images. People's response to God's working through his chosen representatives will shape their experience of his blessing or cursing.

- ***Shem's Genealogy Leads to Abram (11:10–26)***
- ***God Called Abram (11:27–12:9)***

EXPOSITION

After the disaster for human unity and security at the tower of Babel, the *toledot* of Shem reminds the reader of God's promise. They bear fruit and multiply! Humanity still has hope for life and a future despite the continual and progressive human indifference and opposition. Terah and his family set the stage for the immediate narrative. They will raise tensions that will dominate the following stories, defining the opportunities of faith and the clear intervention of God. After scattering the peoples from Babel, Yahweh extended grace and called Abram to follow in faith at great personal cost, promising to bless him greatly and establish a nation through him despite human impossibilities to bring all peoples into the blessing of relationship with God in true worship.

Shem's Genealogy Leads to Abram (11:10–26)

Shem's genealogy anticipates the hope for humanity that is missing from the judgment at Babel, leading the reader to Abram.

11:10a. The *toledot* of Shem links the primeval history with the stories of Abram and his family. It will present the descendants of Shem, bridging the survivors of the flood (9:18) to Abram (11:26). As the fifth *toledot* (sixth panel), it brings us to the rhetorical midpoint of the book (twelve panels).[1] It also transitions from thousands of years of human history dealing with all humanity (in eleven chapters) to a few hundred years of the single family history of Abram (in thirty-nine chapters). Theologically, it moves towards God's more sharply focused plan.

11:10b–11. Verse 10 returns the reader to the immediate aftermath of the flood with the birth of Arpachshad. It restarts Shem's genealogy but presents it linearly, tracing the promise from Shem (established as the recipient of blessing in 9:26) through a single line to Abram (11:26) rather than the segmented genealogy in chapter 10 (the same first five generations were listed in chapter 10 as part of the spread of the nations, vv. 21–25). The text now moves from the broader genealogy including the "sons of Shem" (10:31) to the specific line of descent from Shem to Abram ("the generations of Shem," 11:10). The linear format establishes the claim of promise. The human pride and resultant scattering from Babel did not thwart God's promise for the coming seed of the woman or his purpose to bless humanity.

Up to this point, each new phase, including the judgments of God, had concluded with a hopeful anticipation of those promises. The judgment in the garden ended in hope (3:20–21); men calling on the name of the Lord contrasts the travesties of Cain's genealogy (4:25); God's declaration of judgment on humanity after the sons of God rebellion culminates with Noah finding grace (6:8); and the covenant with Noah (9:1–17) caps the flood account. Even the cursing of Canaan includes the blessing on Shem and Japheth (9:26–27). The tower of Babel, however, ends in judgment with no explicitly hopeful anticipation. Shem's genealogy provides that expectation of fulfilled promise, pointing to the blessing through Abram that will occupy the rest of the book of Genesis. The Abram narratives answer the tensions between promise and judgment as they allude to the initial narratives and provide "partial resolution" from the Babel episode (Awabdy 2010). We finally move out of the steady deluge of human depravity into the brightening promise of God's intervening work.

11:12–25. The genealogy follows the pattern of the genealogy of Seth in Genesis 5 (see Exposition on 5:3–5, p. 157).[2] However, Moses leaves

1 Or eleven panels with ten *toledots*, if you count the two *toledot* formulas for Esau as a single panel (36:1, 9).

2 On the large numbers for the ages, see the exposition on 5:6–20, p. 158. Here the numbers drop quickly but still are much longer than expected for this time (from archaeology and history). See Mathews (1996, 493–96) for a discussion of the numerical problems of the ages here.

out the final two clauses of the Genesis 5 pattern (total years lived and the notice that "he died"). Theologically, chapter 5 stressed the death consequence for humanity, with the noted exception of Enoch. The differences here move the genealogy more quickly and give the impression of new life rather than death. The rapid transition looks toward God's future promise to Abram, the hope of life instead of death, of coming descendants of promise. Blessing comes into focus.

11:26. Like Genesis 5, this genealogy concludes with three sons from the final ancestor, giving ten generations. Between chapters 5 and 10, Genesis presents twenty generations from Adam to Abram with Noah as the tenth and Abram as the twentieth, both significant points. Each character presents a new beginning for humanity in the plan of God. Expectations grow for the following narratives.

God Called Abram (11:27–12:9)

Yahweh extended grace and called Abram to follow in faith at great personal cost, promising to bless him greatly and establish a nation through him, despite human impossibilities, to bring all peoples into the blessing of relationship with God in true worship.

Terah's Family Clarifies Abram's Challenges (11:27–32)

Terah's family and their migration from Ur to Haran introduces Abram and the impediments to God's call in his life.

11:27a. The *toledot* of Terah (11:27–25:11) introduces Abram with his call, covenant, and life, announcing the working of God to bring blessing to all families of the earth through Abram's descendants. Each of the main patriarchal narratives has a similar structure (see "Structure of Genesis," p. 65, and "Narrative Structure of Genesis," p. 68, for an overview, as well as the above "Introduction to the Abraham Narratives," p. 236 and each following introduction). These narratives will initiate God's program, forming the basis for the rest of history. Yahweh will build the Mosaic Covenant and the Davidic Covenant on these promises, culminating all three in the New Covenant.

11:27b–30. The opening annotated genealogy introduces the family of Terah. Abram immediately becomes prominent, listed first of the sons even though he may not have been the firstborn[3] and mentioned five times in 11:27–32, just one less than Terah. Each character (except Iscah) will reappear in the following narratives. The annotations preview some special challenges for what will follow. The note that "Haran fathered Lot," for example, along with the following annotation of Haran's death and Sarah's barrenness, indicates that Lot became the presumed heir of Abram (11:31; Silberman 1983, 19).

Sarai and the daughters of Haran also stand out, not only because they are the only daughters specifically noted in the genealogies so far, but because they are the only women named so far in Genesis other than Eve. Their names may indicate something of the pagan background that God called Abram out of (Josh. 24:2), as well as why they stopped over in Haran. Sarai in Hebrew would mean "princess," but if it originated in Akkadian, as we would expect from Ur, it meant "queen," a title of the wife of the moon-god Sin, main god of Ur (Westermann 1995, 138). Similarly, Milcah is another name for "queen" and was used of Ishtar, the daughter of Sin, called the "Queen of Heaven" (Sarna 1989, 87). As verse 31 declares, they settled in Haran even though they were headed to Canaan, perhaps partly because Haran was also known for its worship of the moon-god.

3 Wenham (1987, 272) suggests that Haran is firstborn because he died in Ur and Nahor married Haran's daughter.

Ur of the Chaldeans

The location of "Ur of the Chaldeans" (11:31) has occasioned significant scholarly debate. Because of the trade routes and the anachronism of the name "Chaldeans," some have defended a northern location (e.g., Hamilton 1990, 364–65; Westermann 1994, 139–40). The earliest and still widely accepted view, however, identifies the reference with Ur, south of Babel, which is supported by many scholars (e.g., Walton 2009c, 65–67; Wenham 1987, 272). In this case the identification as "Chaldeans" would be a later gloss to explain which Ur.

Not only does the family, with its pagan background (cf. Josh. 24:2), appear to be unlikely candidates for following Yahweh fully by faith, but Sarai is declared to be barren. While the modern reader may not yet understand the significance of either the names or the barrenness, the nation of Israel would have immediately heard the importance of both. To anticipate 12:1–3, God called pagans to follow him, believing in promises that get less and less plausible the more we understand.

11:31–32. Terah and his family moved out of Ur, leaving the land of Shinar to go to Canaan. In the narrative flow, this appears either as the reverse of 11:2 or perhaps an outgrowth of 11:8–9. We find out in 12:1, correlated with 15:7, that God is directly at work here, orchestrating this family move to bring blessing rather than cursing. So far, the patriarch, Terah, was leading Abram and the family. Their purpose was to go to Canaan. The narrative does not explain why, nor does it explain why they stopped in Haran. Rather, it merely observes that they settled there. And there Terah would die.

Terah

The age of Terah at his death in the MT is 205. The SP, however, lists it at 145. The difference is significant because of the chronology of the passage. If Abram was born when Terah was seventy (11:26), then Terah lived another sixty years in Haran after Abram left (12:4), according to the MT. But according to the SP, Abram left when Terah died. The ages in the genealogies in Genesis 5 and 11 vary significantly between the MT, the LXX, and the SP. Generally, the MT preserves the harder reading, which is usually considered better. If, of course, Abram is not the eldest, all of this is less clear since we do not know precisely when Abram was born, but the general issue would still stand. Terah would have already died according to the SP, but he was probably still alive according to the MT.

God Called and Abram Answered (12:1–9)

When God called Abram to leave his own security to follow God's promise of land, descendants, and blessing, and be a blessing, Abram went despite costly impossible obstacles, proclaiming Yahweh in his public worship.

God Called Abram to Go to Bless (12:1–3). God called Abram to leave his own security, to father a great nation in a new land with great blessing for himself, and to bring blessing to all humankind.

12:1. God called Abram to leave his own country, kindred, and father's house. He must leave his security and significance, with only God's promise of a greater security and significance. It was costly for Abram to go. While it may have seemed impossible at first, it only got worse as he followed.

The call appears to come while Abram is settled at Haran, if we are following the narrative flow. In Genesis 15:7, however, Yahweh states that he brought Abram "out from Ur of the Chaldeans." Yahweh's claim in 15:7 could mean that he gave this specific call in Ur but it was only reported in 12:1–3, or he could have spoken a second time in Haran. Either way, God was at work in the entire move with his own purpose of giving this land to Abram to bring blessing, ultimately reversing the curse.

12:2. God's call of Abram, connected by genealogy to the Tower of Babel, presents the promise of blessing to the scattered nations (ch. 10).[4] In Genesis 10, the nations (הַגּוֹיִם) that spread out were defined by "their clans (לְמִשְׁפְּחֹתָם), their languages (לִלְשֹׁנֹתָם), [and] their lands (בְּאַרְצֹתָם)" (vv. 20, 31; cf. v. 5). In chapter 12, God promised to place a new nation (גּוֹי, v. 2) among them to accomplish the promised blessing. Abram must leave his "country" or "land" (אֶרֶץ) to go to a new land (אֶרֶץ) that God would give him (v. 7). Then God would make him a great nation (גּוֹי, v. 2) and bring blessing through him to all the "families" (מִשְׁפָּחָה, v. 3, translated "clans" in 10:5, 20, 31) of the earth. The descendants of Abram would take their place before God among the nations as God's source of blessing.

For Abram to leave his land, kindred, and father's house was to leave his identity, inheritance, much of his potential wealth (land holdings), and family connections. He must trust God, who promised to replace all Abram left in verse 1 with a much greater return. The promises of God, using three cohortatives in verse 2, were conditioned on the obedience of Abram. Because he went (v. 4), he could expect God to keep his promises, replacing what he left. God promised to replace the former land with another land (vv. 1, 7) and his extended family ties with his own extended family growing into a great nation (v. 2). Anything he left, materially or socially, God's blessing, including Abram's great reputation, would replace.

Volitive Sequence

The cohortative states the express will of the speaker (WOC, §34.5). Only the third one is clearly marked in the MT as a cohortative, but because they follow an imperative and are not preceded by the subject or a negative particle, they should all be understood as cohortatives (WOC, §34.6). More than one cohortative in sequence or in sequence with an imperative can indicate sequence of will, simultaneous desires, or purpose/result.

TRANSLATION ANALYSIS 12:2a

Both the progression of verbs and the context of the Abraham narratives indicate that the command for Abram to go formed the initial basis for the following promises from God, but it does not always show clearly in the translations. Some are more explicit with "Then I will make" (NET) or implied with "And I will make" (ESV, NASB95, RSV). The more debated issues arise with whether there are more conditions attached and how the following command to "be a blessing" should be understood. The following narratives will suggest additional conditions as the promise is progressively revealed (see Exposition at Gen. 17–18, 22, pp. 323, 339, and 389). The imperative following the cohortative can indicate sequence, "then be a blessing," purpose or result, "so that you will be a blessing," or another simultaneous command, "and be a blessing" (Baden 2010). Many translations indicate purpose explicitly, "so that you will be a blessing" (ESV, NRSV, RSV, cf. NASB95), but some leave it implied as a result without clear volition ("and you will be a blessing," NCV, NIV, NLT, cf. NJPS, NKJV). Only a few older translations include a clear imperative (ASV and ERV "be thou a blessing," and in the note of the HCSB), which help preserve the double intent.

While purpose finds some support in context, especially with the following cohortatives expecting blessing to all families (Shetter 2019, 154–57), purpose alone would more clearly be stated with the preposition לְ and infintive construct (or לְמַעַן and a finite verb, WOC, §36.2.3d). In the context, Abram appears to have obligation both toward those

4 In fact, the call of Abram is the "key to the primary history" of Genesis (Waltke and Fredricks 2001, 45–54).

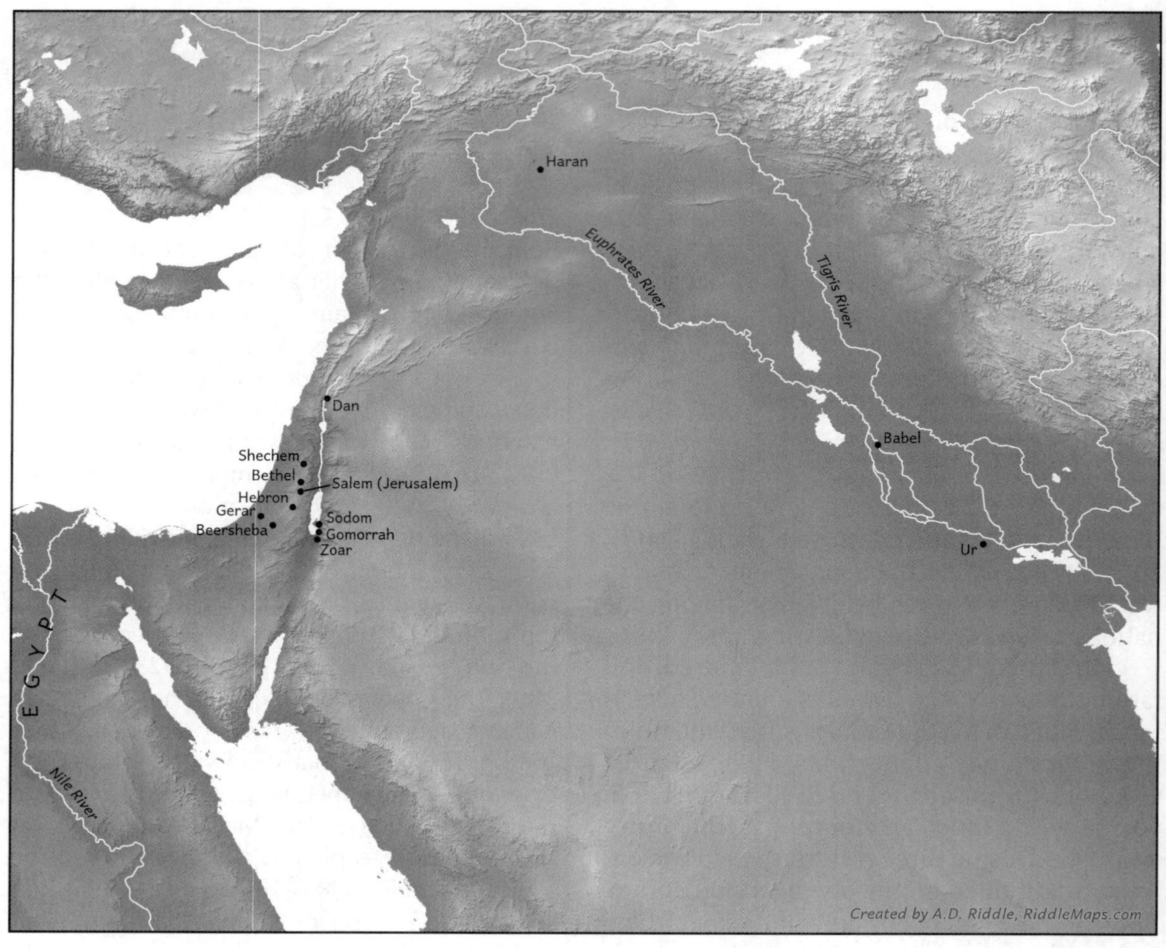

Map of Journeys of Abraham. By A.D. Riddle, used by permission

he encounters, and toward his descendants, to represent Yahweh rightly. In the two "she is my sister" narratives, he is held accountable for his actions that endanger the king of the land (12:18–20; 20:9–18), and God declares Abraham's responsibility to teach his heirs the way of Yahweh (18:18–19). Together with Moses's portrayal in Genesis of blessing arising from God's presence in obedient faith, the imperative appropriately declares Abraham's expected responsibility (which is of course, also God's desired purpose for him). Abraham's response will be a growing, but mixed obedience.

God's promise to bless links the new Adam (Abram) with the first Adam and second Adam (Noah). In all three cases there would be fruitfulness and many offspring. Blessing, however, is not merely children or wealth, though that may be expected for the Old Testament saint; ultimately blessing is empowerment to accomplish one's God given purpose (Introduction: Theological Emphases: Blessing, p. 60) and is found in relationship with God himself (K. Richards, "Bless/Blessing," *ABD* 1:754; Clines 2001, 36, 50). No one gains God's favor apart from relationship with him. Abram must be walking with God (Gen. 17:1), and for Israel, it would mean keeping his commands (Deut. 28:1–14; 30:16). To be a blessing, then, would include showing and telling the character of God (see 12:8) and the means to know and walk with Him.

God promised Abram a "great name," immediately recalling the goal of the builders in 11:4. The fame that the builders sought so futilely could only be given by God through the faith of the recipient. Abram must go as God commanded. God, then, in calling Abram and blessing him, would provide opportunity for blessing to all the scattered families of the earth (10:5, 20, 21, מִשְׁפָּחֹת) who had sought their own good at Babel and so were scattered (Awabdy 2010, 17–18).

God called Abram to "be a blessing." Abram would be the conduit for God's working. God's desire to bless counters the necessary cursing previously (ארר, used five times [3:14, 17; 4:11; 5:29; 9:25] followed by the five uses of the root "bless" in these verses, ברך), recalls his promises to bless, and evokes the promise of the seed to crush the snake. This promised blessing will ultimately restore the relationship with Yahweh, lost in the garden but afterward seen in those walking with him.

TRANSLATION ANALYSIS 12:2b

While most translations take the passive idea, "you will be a blessing" (e.g., ESV, NASB95, NIV, NLT), the NET Bible translates it "you will exemplify divine blessing," and REB translates, "make your name so great that it will be used in blessings." These translations are wrestling with what it means to be a blessing and are understanding this in terms of the reflexive nuance possible for the similar statement in 12:3. We will argue below that the passive is the better option, and the idea is that Abram and his descendants will be the conduit of divine blessing as they lead the nations to real relationship with the eternal creator (see Translation Analysis 12:3).

Abram would progressively learn that this blessing, rooted in his relationship with Yahweh, requires his ongoing response. Abram must continue to walk with God in faith.[5]

12:3. Verse 3 expands and explains the purpose of this call to Abram (the imperative to be a blessing). Yahweh would actively bless all who bless him, but the one who dishonors him Yahweh promised to curse. Blessing will finally come to all families through him.

God again shows his intent to bless despite human failings. The cohortative expresses his intent to bless those who would bless (plural) Abram. Yahweh would reward all who enrich his servant, allowing them to share in his benefits toward Abram and his family. God used the plural for those who bless Abram, indicating his generosity and desire to bless all who qualify. Repeating the verb, God affirmed that he would repay appropriately. It would pay to deal carefully with Abram! Abram would be the means for his world to find that ultimate empowerment and enrichment in Yahweh.

God would also reward the one (singular) who "dishonored" Abram (קלל), declaring him "insignificant or contemptible" (*HALOT* s.v. "קלל" 1103–05, *Piel*). God's response brings direct and individual intervention. If anyone would declare or treat Abram as insignificant, God would curse them (ארר). Strongly contrasting blessing, God would restrict this enemy from fertility and fruitfulness (V. Hamilton, אָרַר, *TWOT* 75–76). Instead of enabling, he will disable. In contrast to God's blessing on all who bless Abram (plural participle), he singles out for retribution any individual who dishonors Abram (singular participle).

5 The presence or absence of ongoing conditions for what will become the Abrahamic Covenant has been discussed widely. The narratives will expand and delineate the promises, and they will also show God's ongoing expectations for his friend, Abram (Shetter 2019, ch. 4).

The final clause summarizes the core of God's program. In Abram, "all the families of the earth shall be blessed." This statement expands God's stated purpose for Abram in verse 2 and, in turn, will be expanded progressively through the Abraham narratives. God's desire to bless, traced through the background of the primeval narratives, now takes center stage, repeated five times with either the verb or noun in these three verses. Of course, this will work out in tangible expressions of God's favor for Abram, those around him, and his descendants (24:35–36; Deut. 28:1–15), recognized by their surrounding culture as God's presence (e.g., Gen. 21:22; 26:28; Num. 23:21). All good things come from God, and "the presence of God walking among his people is the highest of his blessings" (Wenham 1987, 275).

TRANSLATION ANALYSIS 12:3

This clause parallels the imperative in 12:2, providing the explanation of God's purpose. The verb in the *niphal* is often understood as a passive: "in you all the families of the earth shall be blessed" (ESV, NASB95, NKJV, NRSV, cf. NCV, NIV, NLT). However, the *niphal* can also be taken as a middle, "find blessing" (Wenham 1987, 277–78), or reflexive, "all the families of the earth shall bless themselves by you" (JPS, cf. REB, RSV); this is more fully spelled out by NET, "all the families of the earth will bless one another by your name." The decision is not clear cut, especially since the verb form changes among the various repetitions of the promise, being used twice in the *hithpael*, which is often reflexive (22:18; 26:4). However, the *hithpael* can also be passive, the *qal* passive is used in Gen. 27:29, and Moses expresses the reflexive sense differently in 48:20 where he explicitly says, "by you Israel will pronounce blessings." Here, it is best to understand the passive meaning in the sense of seeing Abram and his descendants as the chosen channel for God to bring blessing (cf. Hamilton 1990, 374–75). Abram as the means or instrument of blessing and cursing helps the reader to better understand both the patriarchs' folly and God's response when both Abraham and Isaac endanger their wives with their claim to be siblings (Biddle 1990).

The promises to Abram have often been summarized in the terms "land, seed and blessing." God promised Abram a place to raise a nation (the implication in the call is formally promised in 12:7), a great nation, and not only that he would be blessed (great name and divine protection) but that he would be a divine channel of blessing to the whole human family. Each of these promises will become more clearly defined and expanded throughout God's continuing interaction with him. God promised land to Abram in 12:7, reiterated to his offspring forever in 13:15. He then gave the boundaries (15:18–19), revealing that they would not receive it for over five hundred years. The descendants, which would be a great nation (12:2), would be like the dust of the earth (13:16) and the stars of the sky (15:5–6). They would include a multitude of nations and kings (17:4–6) through Sarai (17:16). All the while, God reiterated his blessing to Abram, Isaac, Jacob, and all nations through the descendants of Abraham (12:1–3; 14:19; 17:20; 18:17–18; 20:17; 22:18; 24:1; 25:11; 26:4, 24; 27:33; 28:3, 14; 30:27; 39:5; 47:7; 49). This promise of blessing specifically works out in relationship with Yahweh, as Abraham would be his loyal vassal (17:1) and Yahweh promised his presence (26:3, 28; 28:15, 20; 31:3, 5, 42; 35:3; 39:2, 21; 48:21; cf. Clines 2001, 36, 50).

This central passage provides the turning point of the book (see the "Introduction to the Abraham Narratives," p. 236). From the decline of humanity, with God's promise in the background to the judgments, God began with Abram to bring clarity to his purpose. God began to explain his plan, introduce this change, and focus the message of Genesis toward God's blessing. The first eleven chapters have introduced why God must intervene, and they provide a means by which humanity can know him and enjoy the relationship with God for which humanity was originally created. Moses now can develop the hope that Yahweh, the sovereign creator of the universe, has chosen the descendants of Abraham to bring blessing out of cursing through true worship, to a world continually turning away from him in rebellion.

Abram Went as God Commanded (12:4–9). Abram went as God commanded despite human obstacles, responding in consistent public worship and being a blessing.

12:4–6. God commanded Abram to go (12:1) and he went, repeated three times and emphasized with "as the Lord had told him" (v. 4). Abram began the odyssey, initiating God's promises that would define the program of God for the rest of history. As we will explore throughout the Abraham stories, Abraham still has some obligations to experience the full impact of God's promises for him, but from here on, these promises will govern the narratives and Abram's experience. Moses will show Abram being a blessing and bringing cursing. He now has tremendous responsibility regarding those around him, and he learns the impact of that in daily encounters.

The promises, however, are clearly in jeopardy from a human perspective. Sarai has already been announced to be barren (11:30). Here Abram is noted to be seventy-five years old (12:4), not the expected age to sire a nation. This and later notes on the age of Abram (16:3, 16; 17:1, 24; 21:5) will build the tension, challenge Abram's faith, and magnify the working of God to accomplish his promise. The very impossibility of achieving God's blessing underscores the ironic pursuit of human pride apart from God, which achieves its goal only to find it fully empty (11:6).

Abram appears already to have a large entourage as he moves to the land of Canaan, including his nephew Lot (possibly a legal dependent with the death of Lot's father, 11:27–28).[6] The unusual expression translated "people they had acquired" (12:5, וְאֶת־הַנֶּפֶשׁ אֲשֶׁר־עָשׂוּ) does not generally describe servants and cannot be children. It may refer to proselytes Abram influenced to come with him in pursuing God's promise (Ross 2008, 97). However, when he entered Canaan, a second aside informs the reader that "at that time the Canaanites were in the land" (v. 6). The land was not available! Again, the promise appears to be in jeopardy.

12:7–9. Yahweh, however, appeared to him and immediately reaffirmed and clarified the promise of the land. What was implicit in the call to go now becomes explicit as Yahweh promised the land to Abram's offspring. The extent of the land is not yet defined, nor the timing of the grant, but the promise is becoming clearer. The appearance of Yahweh (rather than just speaking, 12:1) heightens the expectation, adding weight to the growing clarity of the promises to Abram. The land will not be for Abram, and the assured offspring seem impossible given Abram's age and wife, but God promised, and Abram responded in worship, building an altar.

From Shechem (v. 6) he moved south through the hill country to near Bethel and again built an altar. Abram began fulfilling his purpose to be a blessing as he offered consistent and public worship to Yahweh. Here, he "called

6 Moses highlights Lot's presence (12:4, 5). The question often raised here regards Abram's obedience. Should he have allowed Lot to join him? If Lot is the presumed family heir (Silberman 1983, 19), how does that impact the promise to Abram? The affirmation of Abram's obedience (12:4) dismisses a problem with Lot, but Lot certainly adds tension and becomes a significant part of the story and so must be noted here. Lot will provide opportunity for Abram to show faith both in chapter 13 and chapter 14, as well as illustrate God's judgment and grace in chapters 18–19. The tension will not overtly surround his status as possible heir, though perhaps it is an intended implication, but rather his wealth and relationship to Abram (and so responsibility and opportunity to extend blessing).

upon the name of the LORD" (v. 8), recalling the worship of the line of Seth in 4:25 (see Exposition on 4:25, p. 148). One implication of Abram's worship is proclamation of the character of Yahweh in this land (cf. Exod. 33:19; 34:5–7; Ps. 116:13, 17; Ross 2008, 97–98), especially since Yahweh later described Abraham as his prophet (Gen. 20:7). Abram publicly identifies with Yahweh in worship, in Canaan. Such public expression would make a statement to the peoples around him. Abram was being a blessing.

In verse 9 Abram continued his journey to the south. Abram's constant moving indicates another challenge to his faith in God's promise. There is not always enough pasturage for another large family settlement with herds and flocks. The Canaanites have already taken all the good land, and Abram must keep moving to find the feed he needs for his group. All these challenges set the stage both for Abram's responses and for God's actions. The following narratives need to be measured by the expectations that God's promises put on Abram and on God himself to deliver what he has promised.

THEOLOGICAL FOCUS

God continues to extend grace and promise through his chosen servants, whom he calls to follow and trust him, at great cost, for the impossible, for great blessing, and to bless God's world in relationship with him.

God consistently displays grace even through judgement, promising the real blessing that humankind needs rather than the self-promotion they desire, responding to humanity by calling Abram after the Babel event. Contrary to dull human perception, God is always working. He scattered the nations so that they would experience their need for him and accomplish his purpose for humankind. As with Abram, God consistently chooses unlikely people with unlikely heritage and many obstacles to accomplish his purpose, to his glory (1 Cor. 1:18–31). God must help humanity see that he alone can make a name for people as they follow him in faith, walk with him in true worship, and find the ultimate blessing that humanity was created to experience in that relationship with him. We can only flourish with him, and we can only perish without him.

God calls all people with all sorts of baggage to respond to him in faith. That call may require leaving things of great perceived value for the promise of true and eternal value. The choice of faith is ultimately between relationship with God and the affairs of this world. The power, prestige, and possessions of life militate against the uncertain and less-tangible promise of God's life and blessing. The reality, however, is not what seems obvious in this world.

God, then, honors and develops that response of faith. On the one hand, he shows his faithfulness to his promise as he reiterates and clarifies the implications in response to obedience. He may not be quick to fully validate faith. Rather, he provides ongoing and increasing obstacles to faith and obedience, implicitly testing and stretching faith. The promise ultimately cannot be humanly possible or reasonable but is solely dependent on the supernatural working of a sovereign Creator to accomplish. God, however, does not leave his servant without any encouragement; he provides indications along the way that he is still offering and prompting, despite the barriers to that faith. God asks humanity, then, to trust him, responding in obedience to his call to experience the outworking of his promises.

The outworking of God's promises in the lives of his servants brings hope and blessing to all of God's world, offering relationship with the creator to humanity through his provision. As the follower of Yahweh hears the confirmation of Yahweh's promise and reaffirmation of his presence, he must appropriately respond in worship. His worship demonstrates his identification with Yahweh as his God and provides the evidence and opportunity for his world to also connect with Yahweh, forming the basis for them to also experience blessing. The promised nation would reveal the character and way to appropriate relationship with God (Exod. 19:5–6, Mosaic covenant), which is still the purpose of the people of God (1 Peter 2:9–10). It would also, however, produce the ultimate seed of Abraham, Jesus, who reveals the father (John 14:9; Gal. 3:16; Heb. 1:3), giving humanity eternal relationship with their creator (Gal. 3:8–9).

God's blessing on those who walk with him by faith is crystalized in that relationship with him. The immediate benefits may be tangible for quality of life, especially for Abram and Old Testament Israel. The underlying reality and goal, however, is the abundance of life, both now and eternally (see Exposition on Gen. 2:17 and the tree of life, p. 106). God's plan will return his images to his intended purpose. Even for Israel, material prosperity is not the final goal, and it is an ongoing danger (Deut. 8). The goal has always been knowing and walking with God.

Finally, God will guard his program, accomplishing his stated promise against all opposition. His curse against the enemies of Abram guarantees his desired outcome. That does not preclude pain or struggle for his servants, however. He may allow bad things to happen to his chosen people, but he will always bring about his purposes, even through evil actions (Gen. 50:20).

PREACHING AND TEACHING STRATEGIES

Exegetical and Theological Synthesis

As you may have caught in the exegesis, one of the ways to begin the process of moving toward preaching and teaching this narrative is by noting how the genealogies continue the story that began with Adam. Severe judgments of the flood and confusing the languages at Babel interrupt the march of God fulfilling his promises to bless his world through his people. While most of us struggle with the long list of names in the family tree, ultimately, people of faith find their place in the line. As was pointed out, the lineage leading us to Abram is focused on life, not death. When the first death is recorded (11:28, "Haran died"), only two sons remain, one of which is Abram. Our faith journey in this world in many ways reflects his. For instance, we anticipate the need for God's supernatural assistance in our badly broken world (11:30, "Now Sarai was barren"). Our decision to obey the Lord's command to follow him always involves submitting all other allegiances and affections to our loyalty to him, trusting in the promises of God to bless us for the sake of his glory, gladly accepting the small, costly part we can play in his global mission, and worshipping him at every turn. You might spend some extra time unpacking the incredible promises of God in 12:1–3. That will include carefully defining God's blessing as enabling us to successfully carry out God's mission, explaining how to pass that blessing on to others, and describing the expected honor from the Lord ("I will . . . make your name great," v. 2).

Preaching Idea

God is graciously calling you to follow him so he can bless you to be a blessing to those around you.

Contemporary Connections

What does it mean?

Part of the burdensome joy of preaching and teaching this section of Genesis is explaining the theological significance of the genealogy that leads us to Abram. Take some minutes to show God continuing to work his plan to bless in history through families: Noah to Shem to Terah to Abram/Abraham, "the father of us all" (Rom. 4:16). Here's where our own faith journey begins in history. Sarai's barrenness is emphasized because everything about God's plan to redeem his world requires his power (Gen. 11:30). Human methods alone will not do. In our evangelical circle, most listeners are too familiar with the word "blessing." It is too often associated with American, middle- or upper-class creature comforts. God's blessing is his enduement of special powers that make it possible for believers to carry out his work in his world so that his blessing can be conferred on others. Our faith journey is supernatural; God provides the enablement for us to do his will. The phrase "all the families of the earth" must be explained in light of the end of the story and the "new song . . . by your blood you ransomed people for God from every tribe and language and people and nation" (Rev. 5:9). One of the most difficult aspects to explain is the difference between how God's promise worked itself out for Israel in the land versus how it continues to be worked out in the lives of Christians. Both the Old and New Testament talk about the spiritual nature of the promises, but the former includes a heavy dose of land and temporal blessings that morph into primarily spiritual ones in our day. That changes, for instance, how the promise to curse Abram's enemies applies today to God's enemies and the enemies of his church.

Is it true?

One thing that screams out from listening to the Lord's promise to Abram is: "Is this promised blessing really true for me? It doesn't feel that way!" This is one reason why it's critical to explain God's blessing. It's not true that a Christian can disbelieve and disobey and expect the blessing of God. According to the definition above, that's impossible. One can't disobey God's ways and accomplish God's plan at the same time. So, while the promises are true, in the context of God's revelation conditions of faith and obedience are attached to our relationship with him. The content of that blessing may look different in our new covenant world. God's enabling for his purposes does not require prosperity but may require suffering. In a world where Christians are certainly in the minority and with no voice in government, if the promise of God to curse those who dishonor Abram is true, it needs to be nuanced according to the program and purpose of God. Otherwise, the promises of Genesis 12:2–3 will not ring true at all.

Now what?

As the covenants between God and his people in the Old Testament continue to mount—from Noah, to Abram, to Moses, to David, to the promised new covenant—an understanding of our own relationship with our redeemer develops. In Genesis 1–11 we've seen God's dogged determination to bless his images, despite major rebellion. As Paul makes clear in Romans 4, for instance, Abraham's life is critical for understanding our own walk with God by faith.

In some sense, it's difficult to overstate the relevance of the call of Abram to the Christian life and the entire plan of redemption. Try framing the concept of eternal life or salvation in terms of the promised blessing as explained above. God desires to give more than a future hope, but human flourishing now and forever, available to all. How many of our listeners need to be reminded that our God's intention is to bless his people for the sake of his reputation? His blessing that brings him glory in the church and in Christ Jesus (Eph. 3:21) is for our good too. How important for our listeners to find the part they play in God's plan to extend his blessing to "all the families of the earth" (Gen. 12:3)!

Creativity in Presentation

A suggested framework is:

- God's work requires a miracle from start to finish (keying on Gen. 11:30 and Sarai's barrenness); it's possible your listeners are confronted with some "impossibles." Better for them to know this from the start of their Christian experience so they're ready for the feeling of helplessness and dependence that God honors. God chooses to accomplish his plan through unlikely means to his glory. To be unlikely or undesirable in this world is not a barrier to God.

- God's work involves his gracious choice of his servants (the Lord's choice of Abram in 12:1a); what a time to praise God for his choice of each professing Christian! And, if you asked them if God had a reason for choosing them, do you know how they would answer?

- God's work calls for our obedient faith and sacrifice (12:1b, 4–9); it's clear in the Old and New Testament that being a Christ-follower involves great sacrifice, total trust, and absolute loyalty that puts all our affections in proper perspective. As Bavinck says in the opening of *The Wonderful Works of God*: "God, and God alone, is man's highest good" (p. 1).

- God's work includes our receiving and extending his blessing (12:2–3); God makes promises that involve both curse and blessing as well as an intention to carry the blessing to the ends of the earth.

Following the flow of the text you could structure it:

- God is at work, choosing the unlikely and stressed (11:10–32).

- God calls the unlikely to bring blessing to his world with his empowering (12:1–3).

- God honors the response of faith (12:4–9).

Also consider an angle such as God's commission and promise and our mission and worship. All listeners can be urged to find their place in this story. Several listeners will experience a rude awakening as they admit that key elements are missing. If we're on a mission to eliminate any surprises at the judgment for those entrusted to our care, the Abram narrative is our friend. All the language of exile, pilgrimage, refugee, and journey fit the call of Abram and our Christian experience. I'm currently reading *On the Road with St. Augustine*, by James K. A. Smith. Images of packing up all your belongings and heading off to a new, known destination is one thing; an unknown destination is another. It's all about *answering God's gracious call for us to receive his blessing and to bless those around us.*

DISCUSSION QUESTIONS

1. Discuss how the church worldwide continues to operate within these promises to Abram. This might include discussing the similarities and differences between God's mission for Israel in the Old Testament and his mission for the church.

2. If blessing is God's empowering to accomplish one's God given purpose in life (Introduction to Genesis: Blessing, p. 60), what does that include in our current lives, and what would that exclude? Can the same thing be blessing for one and not for another?

3. What does it mean to be a source of blessing to those around us in our world? A source of cursing?

4. What do you see as impenetrable obstacles to God accomplishing his promised purpose through you that he will have to miraculously remove for his glory?

5. How do ou show my gratitude and worship to his world, publicly identifying with Christ, for his working and promise in your life?

Genesis 12:10–20

EXEGETICAL IDEA

Facing fear when tested with famine, Abram trusted in deception for his welfare rather than Yahweh's promise, endangering Sarai and the promise, as well as bringing God's curse on Pharaoh, gaining rebuke and expulsion rather than being a blessing.

THEOLOGICAL FOCUS

Acting from fear during testing leads to compromise, danger, and loss, both for the God-fearer and those in his circle of influence, instead of blessing through faith.

PREACHING IDEA

Forsake fear for faith and find your place as a recipient and conduit of God's blessing.

PREACHING POINTERS

Abram's understanding of the cultural mores, his cleverness in devising a plan for self-preservation, and the Lord's surprising reaction provided the original audience with a "go and do otherwise" narrative. What makes the transition to listeners easier are all those circumstances in life that create the same kind of fear in us that Abram experienced. As you can see, entrance into Egypt posed a threat. Let the scheming begin: "I know I trusted you a little earlier, Lord, but all my instincts are telling me I'd better come up with a plan or else you can kiss all the promises goodbye!" Enter the curse.

It is tragic when others pay the price for our own disbelief. God is determined that his plan for us will succeed, but that doesn't mean that we cannot trust him. Pharaoh is helpless against the Lord's attack. The narrative leaves me wanting to ask Abram, "So, did you learn your lesson?" Abram fails the test and shows believers the consequences. A lack of faith coincides with a lot of fear, and the results are devastating for the soul.

We do not want to send the signal that this narrative shows that God will always bail out his servants when they take matters into their own hands. We do want to disclose God's mercy to his own throughout their lives so that they are able to experience the fulfillment of his promises to them. Abram's poor example helps us learn that we extend God's blessing to his world only when we trust him.

FEAR OR FAITH: THRIVING (OR NOT) UNDER TESTING (12:10–20)

LITERARY STRUCTURE AND THEMES

As soon as Yahweh announced hope and blessing through his chosen servant, the skies darkened again, jeopardizing the promise of God both physically and spiritually. Severe famine overtook his chosen family in the new land of promise (12:10). Surprisingly, God was silent in the face of danger after his call to Abram to relocate with generous promises. Without direction from God or faith in God's promise, Abram went to Egypt to care for his family and flocks. His abbreviated sojourn in Egypt also presented a dramatic departure from the picture of Abram so far and the hope for him and his family.

The narrative flows chiastically, centering on the consequences for Abram, Sarai, and the Pharaoh from Abram's ruse:

A. Introduction: Abram migrated to Egypt (12:10).
  B. Abraham planned for security (12:11–13).
    C. Abram succeeded at Sarah's expense (12:14–16).
    C'. Yahweh intervened at Pharaoh's expense (12:17).
  B'. Pharaoh rebuked Abram and his plan (12:18–19).
A'. Conclusion: Pharaoh expelled Abram from Egypt (12:20).[1]

Narrative Boundaries

The boundaries of this narrative vary significantly between commentators. Some will include it with 12:1–9 (Pickering 2014) or end it with 13:4 (Sailhamer 1990, 115–18) or 13:1 (Mathews 2005, 126). We locate the boundaries here because it presents a decided scene change from 12:1–9, beginning the narrative outworking of the promise, and while it is closely connected both with what precedes and what follows, 13:1 reintroduces Abram along with Lot, forming a fitting introduction to the following narrative (Wenham 1987, 286).

This story raises numerous questions that it only begins to answer or answers indirectly. Considering some of the questions helps us begin to see the theological impact of this vignette on the larger narrative: Why doesn't Yahweh give Abram clear direction like he would for Isaac (26:2) or Jacob (46:2–4)? Why did Abram plan to deceive? How does this relate to the promises just given? What is the function of this unflattering story in the larger Abram complex? These questions and more direct our attention to the character (and characterization) of Abram, God's working with Abram to nurture his faith, God's larger oversight in Abram's life, the role (and meaning) of the promises for Abram, the implications of Abram's life (and his descendants') for those around him, and the ongoing darkness in the hearts of God's images. It will show God's faithfulness despite human faithlessness, honoring his promise yet using failure to build a ground for faith and initiate growth.

- ***Abram Migrated to Egypt (12:10)***
- ***Abram Planned for Security (12:11–13)***

1 Cp. Wenham (1987, 286) and Mathews (2005, 126).

- ***Abram Succeeded at Sarah's Expense (12:14–16)***
- ***Yahweh Intervened at Pharaoh's Expense (12:17)***
- ***Pharaoh Rebuked Abram and His Plan (12:18–19)***
- ***Pharaoh Expelled Abram (12:20)***

EXPOSITION

Abram's call established him as the channel of God's blessing to all humankind and the eventual antidote to the heart disease keeping humans from thriving in the life God had planned and offered to them. This sequel will now raise tensions that must be resolved to fulfill those promises. Abram speaks for the first time, raising doubts for the reader regarding the viability of God's plan and putting the promise in extreme peril. His self-centered plotting required divine intervention and brought a rebuke from a pagan Pharaoh. On one level, the reader may be asking if God made the right choice. On another level we need to be asking what Moses wants the ancient or modern reader to learn from this disappointing and disturbing story.

This short story also presents clear, purposeful parallels to the later Egyptian bondage and exodus narratives.[2] The lessons here include much larger purposes than merely a record of an ancestor's failing or even God's protection and provision through such a time. The Abram stories are paradigmatic, with Abram exemplifying the making of a man of faith, the father and exemplar from whom the nation (and people of faith of all times) must learn. Facing fear when tested with famine, Abram trusted in deception for his welfare rather than Yahweh's promise. He endangered Sarai, the promise, and brought God's curse on Pharaoh, gaining rebuke and expulsion rather than opportunity for blessing.

Abram Migrated to Egypt (12:10)

In the face of severe famine, Abram took his family to Egypt for survival.

12:10. Following the clear evidence of faith from Abram and his public identification with Yahweh as his God in open worship, verse 10 tersely relates the first real challenge to that faith. God had promised to make him a great nation with a great name and blessing. That sort of security should be comforting in any tense situation. The arrival of a severe famine, however, provided the first opportunity to see how Abram would respond under pressure to his new status and promise.

Famine was not surprising in the Negev,[3] but unexpectedly, Abram did not receive any instruction from God, since God had led him there, promised the land to his descendants, and later, in a similar situation, would give Isaac clear instruction to stay in the land (26:2). God's silence here increases the tension and heightens the perception that the incident presents a test to Abram. The immediate proximity to the promise narrative and the direct relevance to the promises reinforce that conclusion. Abram chose to leave the land God had promised. God's promises of blessing, progeny, and a great name all require him to stay alive, have children (though he would struggle with that one later as well, 15:2), and prosper. In the face of the severe famine, Abram's choice was logical. The consistent inundation of the Nile

2 "There was a famine in the land (12:10; 47:13); they went down to sojourn in Egypt (12:10; cf. 47:27); there was an attempt to kill the males and save the females (12:12; cf. Exod 1:22); God plagued Egypt (12:17; cf. Exod 7:14–11:10); they spoiled Egypt (12:16; cf. Exod 12:35–36); they were expelled from Egypt (12:20; cf. Exod 14, 15, where the same verb is used: *shalakh* [TH7971, ZH8938]); and they escaped to the Negev (13:1; cf. Num 13:17, 22)" (Ross 2008, 99–100).

3 The subsistence farming in the Negev is fragile. Rainfall is four to twelve inches per year, allowing a yield of wheat or barley only one year out of every three or four (Walton 2009c, 73).

provided prosperity in Egypt even when there was drought in Canaan. He would "sojourn" there, a term describing a foreigner living by the hospitality of the host country without the rights of the citizen and dependent on them for protection (Spencer, "Sojourner," *ABD* 6:103–4). His concern was what that "hospitality" might mean in Egypt.

Abram Planned for Security (12:11–13)

In fear, Abram planned his own welfare through deception rather than trusting the promise of God.

12:11–12. Abram left the land of promise to which God had specifically brought him. But God had not said he must remain continuously nor that he would personally take possession, but that it would be for his offspring. So, the propriety of this choice is ambiguous. When Abram was going to Egypt, however, he raised more obvious concerns. Here we learn not only his fears, but that he believes he must take responsibility for staying alive so that God can carry out his promise. He does not trust God's unaided provision.

This is the first time that Abram has spoken, and his words dramatically adjust his characterization. Up to now he has appeared obedient, submissive, and pious before Yahweh. He has been courageous enough to leave his own security and travel to a new land with only the promise of God leading him. He has openly declared his loyalties to Yahweh in worship in a very pagan land (12:6–8; cf. 13:13). Now he reveals suspicion, fear, and willingness to endanger his wife for his own skin.

Considering Sarai's beauty, he was concerned that she would be coveted by the Egyptians (validated by 12:14–15), and he could be in danger. Sarai was sixty-five years old at this point (17:17, cf. 12:4), raising the question of how they evaluated "beautiful in appearance" (and the cultural gap from our perspective).[4] While he is right that Sarai's beauty would be noticed, there was no indication that he was accurate in his assessment of the danger he would be in. Pharaoh clearly regarded taking another man's wife as offensive (12:18–19), but it is not clear how much of his reaction was driven by the plague he was under and whether he would have felt the same had he not felt the power of Abram's God. Whether Abram's assessment was right or not, however, he clearly failed to account for the promise of God and God's ability to protect them all from any hostility.

12:13. Abram's belief that his life was in danger because of Sarai's beauty assumed someone in Egypt would stoop to murder to get her. What he intended to do by calling her his sister, however, is not clear. If they would murder to take her, how would he protect her as her brother? Or did he plan to protect her? Would he let her be taken simply so that he could live (prosper?)? Would he use her as some sort of bargaining chip to promote his own safety and prosperity (Hoffmeier 1992)? Assuming the best, did he plan on the current social custom that required the brother to arrange a marriage for his sister in the absence of a father, giving him time to get away (Cassuto 1974, 350)? If so, he did not reckon on the power of Pharaoh to take what he wanted. Whatever he intended, he was not trusting God or God's promise. Rather, he feared for his life. He seemed to feel the need to help God out (as when he took Hagar later as a surrogate for Sarai, 16:2).

His request in 12:13 may have been innocent of designs to gain wealth. His desire that it "go well with me" may have entailed

4 Walton (2009a, 74. n. 300) notes the similar description of Penelope in Homer's Odyssey, who may be up to fifty-five years old and yet had suitors lining up for her hand. Since she bore a son at ninety (though clearly miraculously) and died at 127 (23:1) she was in mid-life!

nothing more than what he clarified with the desire to spare his life. The outworking in the text, however, will present tension between God's promise to bless him and the abundance of prosperity he received from his deception of Pharaoh "for her sake" (v. 16). It highlights the question of his intentions, however, for both going well and sparing his life are "because of you" and "for your sake" (v. 13). Does he simply mean that he will be spared because she is willing to play along in the ruse for him? The ambiguity will cause the repetition of the phrase and the enumeration of his rewards to stand out in stark contrast to Sarah's fate and the Pharaoh's judgment.

Sarai's silence is not surprising. While she certainly goes along with the plan (Hamilton 1990, 382), her complicity is not the point. There is little dialogue in these initial narratives and no responses. Abram did not respond to Yahweh in 12:1–9 or to the Pharaoh in verse 20 (unlike 20:12–13 where he defended himself). Only the crucial statements are included here. Sarai's role and feelings are not considered. The narrative is not concerned with her involvement but Abram's responsibility and lack of faith. With this revealing request, the narrative moves quickly to the climax.

Abram Succeeded at Sarah's Expense (12:14–16)

Abram's plan worked personally but failed to account for the exceptional power of Pharaoh, who endangered Sarai.

12:14–15. Abram was right about Sarai's stunning appeal. He had observed that she was "a woman beautiful in appearance" (אִשָּׁה יְפַת־מַרְאֶה, 12:11), and the Egyptians immediately saw that "the woman was very beautiful" (כִּי־יָפָה הִוא מְאֹד, v. 14). The text emphasizes her beauty (מְאֹד), but she is not named. Sarai had become "the woman." Abram's plot had relegated his wife to a prop. She was an object of value to be traded—or taken—without regard for her feelings, will, or status. This lack of standing is emphasized again in verse 15 where the description of the "princes" (שָׂרֵי, cognate to Sarai's name) underlines her un-named status as Pharaoh took "the woman."

In quick succession, the Egyptians saw her beauty, their princes saw her and praised her to Pharaoh, and "the woman was taken into Pharaoh's house" (12:15). The concluding passive both depersonalizes the act and adds immediate finality with the unanticipated power of Pharaoh. The action occurs without recorded objection or reference to the turmoil and concerns that we would expect from either Abram or Sarai. The compressed action emphasizes the outcome. The ruse has accomplished all that Abram asked for, but God's promise was in much more certain danger than Abram had imagined.

12:16. Abram had asked Sarai to lie "that it may go well with me because of you" (יִיטַב־לִי בַעֲבוּרֵךְ). In verse 16 we read that "for her sake [Pharaoh] dealt well with Abram" (וּלְאַבְרָם הֵיטִיב בַּעֲבוּרָהּ). Abram's plan worked! In fact, it worked exceptionally well. The long list of animals and servants stands in contrast to the brevity of the report so far. Now we see that "going well" for Abram was not just surviving, but it included tremendous financial gain, whether that was his intent or not. She was truly valuable!

This list also stands in contrast, however, to what Abram had lost. By his scheming, even if without his intent, he had just traded the promised blessing of God, descendants, and the means God would use to bring great blessing to all humanity, for the treasures of Egypt. With God's character and plan for redemption on the line, God would not allow the trade to stand. Abram had jeopardized God's promise greatly.

This accounting of Abram's profit, structurally, also stands in contrast to Pharaoh's loss. Up to this point Yahweh had been silent and absent from view. Abram had been the focus, but now Abram moved into the shadow and Pharaoh (and Yahweh) took the attention. Pharaoh lost far more than the price of a new wife. And as the Pharaoh would note, Abram did it to him (12:18).

Yahweh Intervened at Pharaoh's Expense (12:17)

Yahweh intervened with cursing on Pharaoh as the result of Abram's deception.

12:17. After Abram's stated fears and the elaborate enumeration of Abram's bounty, Yahweh's judgment on Pharaoh abruptly intervenes with "great plagues" (נְגָעִים גְּדֹלִים). "But the LORD" sharply redirects the narrative "because of Sarai, Abram's wife." Yahweh elevated Sarai both personally (explicitly named) and in her role as Abram's wife. What Abram feared, Yahweh covered, publicly revealing and censuring Abram's private fears.

The significance of the contrast, then, goes beyond what Abram won and Pharaoh lost. It introduces Yahweh's intervention to maintain his promise of descendants, and it reflects the wider promise. If Abram would go, God had said that he would bring blessing on all who blessed Abram and cursing on anyone who dishonored him (12:3). Abram went as Yahweh had said (v. 4). Pharaoh dishonored Abram (unintentionally) by taking his wife. Yahweh noted that dishonor by acting "because of Sarai, Abram's wife" (v. 17). Abram had great opportunity to bring blessing, but here he was responsible for Pharaoh's plague.

As with many other things in this brief narrative, much is left unsaid. The reader does not know how long Abram was in Egypt, how long Sarai was in Pharaoh's house, exactly what that meant for Sarai, or how quickly Yahweh acted. We also do not know the nature of the great plagues upon Pharaoh and his entire house, nor how he knew it was Yahweh or that it was because of Sarai and that she was Abram's wife. All these details take a back seat to Yahweh's intervention, highlighting Abram's responsibility.

Pharaoh Rebuked Abram and His Plan (12:18–19)

Pharaoh restored Sarai, rebuking Abram for his deception and the resulting devastation.

12:18–19. Immediately, Pharaoh called Abram and rebuked him. His initial statement laid the blame for his plagues squarely on Abram. It was not the only time God would rebuke his servant through the words of a pagan (20:9–10; 26:9–11; cf. 2 Chron. 35:22; Jonah). Pharaoh directly rebuked Abram because he had misled Pharaoh with the sister story. The rebuke echoes God's rebuke of Adam and Eve in the garden (Gen. 3:13, "What is this that you have done?") and Cain (4:10, "What have you done?"), highlighting Abram's culpability. The Pharaoh appears to have a better moral compass than Abram (Hamilton 1990, 385).

The questions Pharaoh posed to Abram in his rebuke highlight gaps in the narrative. What happened to Sarai at the hand of Pharaoh because of Abram's fear? What did God plague him with? Why was Abram silent here when he defended himself to Abimelech later (20:11–13)? Why didn't Pharaoh demand his goods back?

The brevity of the narrative produces ambiguity. Pharaoh says that he took Sarai for his wife (12:19, וָאֶקַּח אֹתָהּ לִי לְאִשָּׁה). Did he merely take her into his harem, or did he commit adultery with her? The phrase does not require the consummation of the relationship but seems to focus on the status (so Boaz took Ruth as wife, then he went in to her, Ruth 4:13), leaving it ambiguous. The plagues and the way they are described may indicate actual adultery (Peleg 2006, 203–5), but the narrative emphasizes Abram's guilt, underlined by his silence. No defense is possible. His lack of faith and resulting guilt is the point.

Since adultery was generally regarded as worthy of death in the ancient world, Wenham concludes that Pharaoh's dismissal of Abram acknowledges Yahweh's protection (Wenham 1987, 290). Abram's education in Yahweh's faithfulness to his promises comes at Pharaoh's expense. He walked away with great wealth, but it was not blessing. It did not promote relationship with Yahweh or accomplish God's purpose for him, but rather brought cursing on those around him and pain in his family.

Pharaoh's order to take her and go tersely communicates both his authority and anger yet powerlessness to do what he might choose. Abram left with the added baggage that would bring strife with Lot (13:5–7) and Sarai through the Egyptian servant, Hagar (16; 21:8–21).

Pharaoh Expelled Abram (12:20)

Pharaoh expelled Abram from Egypt, forfeiting any opportunity for blessing through him.

12:20. The conclusion is abrupt. The idea is extremely clear. When Pharaoh "commanded men concerning him" (lit., וַיְצַו עָלָיו פַּרְעֹה אֲנָשִׁים), he "expelled" Abram (NET), or "escorted him" to the border (NASB95). Pharaoh would take no chance of further damage to his country by this powerfully connected deceiver. Unfortunately, he would also lose any opportunity for blessing from Abram and his good God. Explicitly, he sent him away with "all that he had," which included the profit from his deception. Abram would have to learn that "bread gained by deceit is sweet to a man, but afterward his mouth will be full of gravel" (Prov. 20:17). While deceit would be an ongoing problem for Abram, Isaac and Jacob, the narrative will document his growth in the underlying cause of his deception, his lack of faith.

THEOLOGICAL FOCUS

Acting from fear during testing leads to compromise, danger, and loss, both for the God-fearer and those in his circle of influence, instead of promised blessing through faith.

God's silence does not indicate absence. As in this narrative, he is in full control and complete awareness, with authority over all powers of this world. Allusions to the later Egyptian sojourn and exodus narratives magnify the sovereign working of Yahweh and the impotence of the threat to Sarai and to God's promise. Not only does Yahweh keep his promises, but he also guards them. No one will interfere, whether a human potentate or a God-fearer. Yahweh will follow through with his defense of his people and his plan against any who would dishonor him. We can expect that blessing will also follow suit to all who bless God's people and plan.

On the other hand, when God's promise is clear, God's silence announces testing. As in Job, untested faith is ambiguous and uncertain. The times when God is silent provide opportunities to reveal the believer's motives, object of faith, and extent of faith. These revelations provide opportunities and incentives for growth. They also remind the reader that Yahweh's promises must be trusted even when he is not clearly present. Of course, the righteous person will struggle at times. Even the great heroes of the faith occasionally struggled in their faith.

Fear, the antithesis to faith, focuses on self (my abilities or weaknesses, my needs or wants) through a limited perspective, rather than on God, his promises, and his perspective. His chosen people must follow in faith, both for their own good and for the good of those around them. Likewise, Yahweh's followers can share blessing by trusting and representing Yahweh well as his image. Israel, and the people of God of all generations, will share that opportunity and responsibility (Exod. 19:5–6; 1 Peter 2:9–10).

As we see here, however, Yahweh does not abandon his servants, even in his failure. God still honors his promise and his worshippers. The faithless follower may incur rebuke and censure, even with deliverance, leading to opportunity to grow in his journey with God.

Neither sins of ignorance nor fear are excused, but neither are all sins immediately judged. God did not immediately or overtly judge Abram's obvious sin, though it would bring consequences. On the other hand, some sin, such as Pharaoh's sin of ignorance, is necessarily judged immediately for the sake of God's promise.

One of the recurring themes of the Abram stories will be the need to continue to trust God for the yet unfulfilled promises. The promises of land and descendants will dominate the next thirteen chapters. The promise of a son will not be fulfilled until chapter 21, and even after that, it will be endangered along with the building of the "great nation" promise (Exodus and beyond). The land promise will not be fulfilled until Joshua. God consistently presents his servants with the opportunity to wait, sometimes for long periods, before he fulfills his promises. Waiting for the fulfillment of God's promise provides ongoing testing of faith for God's people and opportunities to see God at work.

Yahweh exhibits an ongoing pattern of deliberate delay and incremental revelation, producing growth and greater clarity regarding the nature of blessing in the growing relationship rather than merely the fulfillment of promise or the attaining of objectives. Producing character, faith, and loyalty appears more significant than tangible benefits and specific events, requiring time, personal choices, and struggle. The line of growth will not be straight but will include successes and failures or faltering, as with Abram in Egypt. Yet God will guard his word and grow his servant.

PREACHING AND TEACHING STRATEGIES

Exegetical and Theological Synthesis

There is a marked change in the way theology is presented as we enter Genesis 12. As we experienced in 12:1–9, our text continues the narrative. Abram's action of going "down to Egypt" (v. 10) and his lie (v. 13) drive the story. As noted above, Abram provides an example for people characterized by faith to avoid. A couple of tests of faith threaten life: "a famine in the land" and Sarai's beauty ("they will kill me" in v. 12). All of this happens in the context of God's promises to Abram and Abram's stellar initial response of faith (cf. 12:1–9). Clearly, Abram fails the test of faith. Fear gets the best of him. God cannot be trusted; self-preservation instincts take over. Abram's fear was not far-fetched. He called it right from the start.

We forget that God must keep his promises to us because he's the one who called us into this relationship. His reputation is on the line. Anyone who sees the Lord react like he did against Pharaoh should gain confidence in him for their own lives. We can expect that our faith will grow as God sends tests our way. We should not, however, put him to the test through our unbelief. That's our human tendency and this narrative helps us fight hard for faith. It also reminds us that unbelief can spill over into our relationships in this world and cause us to lose tremendous opportunities to be a conduit for blessing.

Preaching Idea

Forsake fear for faith and find your place as a recipient and conduit of God's blessing.

Contemporary Connections

What does it mean?

Since the narrator does not pass judgment on Abram's decision to go "down to Egypt to sojourn there, for the famine was severe in the land" (12:10), it will be difficult to assess the morality of that choice. However, the decision does create the opportunity for his faith to be tested. You will want to explain how the culture and morality of Abram's day in the ancient Near East meant that he had reason to fear for his life. Egypt was not modern-day America! When our listeners read, "And the woman was taken into Pharaoh's house" (v. 15), they may not understand the possible ramifications of what that meant for Sarai, especially when she has been repeatedly described in terms of her beauty (vv. 11, 14). It's also tempting to see verse 16 as a positive for Abram: "Look at how much stuff he received from Pharaoh because of Sarai!" As shown in the exegetical section, that's not the case; it's a poor tradeoff. Since the narrative is silent about how Pharaoh knew Abram lied, we want to be clear that God was at work protecting his own promise.

Is it true?

Some listeners might clue in to the fact that Sarai is quite old by this time. Yet she is still described as "a woman beautiful in appearance" (v. 11) and desirable to the point of killing Abram. You may need to crunch some numbers from what we know in Genesis about how old she might have been with respect to how long she lived. Because of my (Randal's) current age and the beauty of my wife, who is slightly younger than I, I can see Sarai being a mature, desirable woman. Sarai is aging very gracefully and could easily be seen modeling certain products in the ancient Egyptian advertising world. And then we might wonder, "Is it true that the Pharaoh had such power that he could take whatever woman he wanted?" We don't have to take our readers back very far in Genesis to see powerful men seeing attractive women and taking any wife they chose (cf. 6:2). Finally, you can prepare your listeners for what's coming in the exodus by highlighting that God is just warning us with the "great plagues" with which he "afflicted Pharaoh" (v. 17). He's got the power!

Now what?

Nothing is more relevant than knowing that "the trying of your faith" does unbelievable good in the life of a believer (cf. James 1). In God's kingdom, faith grows through testing, and mature faith is the goal of God for each of his children. That means there is no such thing as walking with God without opportunities for spiritual growth. This narrative is a great time to take inventory of your own fears.

It's healthy considering Abram's situation to ask myself about key areas where I am more susceptible to letting fear derail my faith. The connection between unbelief and disobedience is critical to living the Christian life well. I learned this from The God of Promise and the Life of Faith by Scott Hafemann, where he wrote something like, every act of disobedience is first and foremost an act of unbelief (this concept first appears on pages 56–57). So, to attack any specific disobedience, we must first attack unbelief. It's when we fail to believe God's precious promises that we walk in disobedience.

Creativity in Presentation

Let's begin with an angle on illustrations. You could explore a list of top phobias to prepare for a discussion on our fears. Our goal, remember, is to urge listeners to forsake fear for faith and find their place as a recipient and conduit of God's blessing. In a world where there is often more brokenness than blessing, fears will come; faith will be tested. You can decide on where that illustration fits into the following framework:

- The immediate context is God's call of and promises to Abram plus Abram's initial response of obedience (12:1–9); especially important is to highlight receiving and extending God's blessing, plus Abram's obedience.

- The test and the unbelief pose a threat to God's promise (12:10–16). Over the years I've heard numerous people ask me, "What is God trying to teach me in this?" The "this" is a trial or test. My answer has always been the same: "God is saying, 'Will you trust me in this? Let me put your faith under the load to strengthen it.'" Nothing beats a good personal story of faith being tested. A similar-to-Abram's failing grade won't hurt this sermon/lesson, although at some point it might be good to celebrate an actual or hypothetical victory.

Both our planning and our reactions to trauma, hardship, and expected trouble reveal our maturity and degree of faith (or not). If my plan for my security fails to plan for trusting and obeying God, it will fail, even if it works.

- God puts an end to that threat; he will not see his purposes thwarted (12:17–20). God has immense, unlimited power to rule our world. He's dead serious about his promises. My world will reflect the folly or wisdom of my choices in their experience of God's glory and/or justice.
- One of the most wonderful aspects of the gospel is that God can keep his promises to us despite our lapses into unbelief. (This involves such theology as God's sovereignty, eternal security, and perseverance of the saints. God does finish what he started in us. Cf. Rom. 8:28–30; Phil. 1:6).

Ultimately, this narrative calls for a sermon/lesson that uses Abram as a negative exemplar. His actions take a back seat, however, as the Lord flexes his muscles in history to keep his promises intact, despite unbelief in his children. It also challenges our perception of "blessing" and how we decide if our choices were good or not.

DISCUSSION QUESTIONS

1. God's people often encounter famines in Scripture (cf. also Gen. 41–44). Discuss the similarities and differences in the narratives, including the implications of these experiences for people of faith.
2. Discuss what it is about the nature of fear that is so detrimental to being a Christ-follower.
3. Discuss why, although the Lord bailed Abram out this time, the narrative does not guarantee that he will always do that for us.
4. Discuss those times in your life when you look back and know that the Lord protected you so his plan for you could continue. You know that you could have easily been derailed unless he came to your aid and did not allow you to suffer the consequences of your disbelief or disobedience.
5. How are those around us experiencing God's blessing and being drawn to him? Or how might they be suffering when we are not living in faith?

Genesis 13:1–18

EXEGETICAL IDEA

When Abram returned to the land, publicly identified with Yahweh in worship, and demonstrated faith by separating from Lot (who chose wicked associations for expected profit to his detriment), Yahweh certified and expanded his promise to Abram.

THEOLOGICAL FOCUS

God, as sovereign king, rewards those who walk by faith in dependent worship, which shows in generosity and grace, while those who selfishly choose personal gain and associate with evil will suffer loss.

PREACHING IDEA

God's promised blessings are only for those who are righteous by faith, while those who walk by sight suffer the consequences.

PREACHING POINTERS

Many listeners can relate to being blessed by God with many things, especially in the time and part of the world in which we are living. The opening verses, then, can easily describe many of us, including the dangers in verse 7 of sharing neighborhoods and workspaces with non-Christians. The contrast between Abram and Lot presents listeners with their daily choice for living life in God's kingdom. Abram is certainly one of those blessed "peacemakers" Jesus referred to.

Lot is too much like his maternal ancestor, Eve, who takes what looks right to the eyes. Some of our listeners walk by faith, others by sight. One question for us all to ask is whether the good stuff we see is part of the promise or out of bounds. Lot's choice was clearly out of bounds as he "journeyed east" (v. 11). Better to stay with God in Canaan, synonymous at least with worshipping him and walking with him, the source of LifePlus. The opposite life is to move one's "tent as far as Sodom" (v. 12) and experience the wrath of God against "wicked, great sinners" (v. 13). And our gracious God gives yet more assurance that walking with him by faith is the way to go as he recounts his promises to us throughout Scripture.

PROMISE RENEWED: FAITH REWARDED (13:1–18)

LITERARY STRUCTURE AND THEMES

Abram returned to the land with renewed confidence in God's provision and restored purpose in public, consistent worship. What may have appeared as "blessing" in Egypt has become the root for conflict and a threat to the peace and the promise. Instead of fear and scheming, however, Abram offered generosity, separated from his nephew, and was rewarded by Yahweh with expanded and clarified promise. This conflict reveals Abram's faith, which graciously promotes peace and is rewarded with extended promise.

A. Abram returned to the land with worship (13:1–4).
  B. Conflict confronted Abram (13:5–7).
  B'. Abram generously resolved the conflict (13:8–13).
A'. God rewarded his generous worshipper with a clarified land promise (13:14–18).

Abram's return to the land and worship introduces this section, and God's renewed promise of the land with Abram's response of worship completes the frame. His faith takes center stage as his prosperity brings about a crisis of resources, and he chooses faith over prosperity. Abram and Lot's combined wealth threatened the fragile ecosystem and their relationship, setting up the test (13:5–7) and allowing him to rebound from the previous test. Abram's generous offer and Lot's response (vv. 8–9, 10–13) parallel God's generous offer to Abram and Abram's response (vv. 14–17, 18). Abram's liberality, obedience, and worship contrast with the previous narrative and Abram's self-preservation and fear. It also prepares for God's renewal and expansion of his promise to his growing protégé.

The section, then, not only restores Abram to his role before the Lord in faith and appropriate worship but moves him forward in faith to a new stage in his growth in full obedience. It also highlights an appropriate response of faith in testing, in contrast to the sojourn in Egypt, and so offering blessing rather than cursing to those around him. Of course, it simultaneously contrasts Lot's foolish choice based on appearances with Abram's walk of faith, warning of the dangers of walking by sight and highlighting the blessing of faith.

- ***Abram Returned to the Land with Worship (13:1–4)***
- ***Conflict Confronted Abram (13:5–7)***
- ***Abram Generously Gave Lot His Choice (13:8–13)***
- ***God Rewarded His Generous Worshipper with a Clarified Land Promise (13:14–18)***

EXPOSITION

After setting up the conflict and threat to the promise (13:1–7), that threat will be resolved in two distinct and parallel movements that will draw out the theology of the passage (13:8–13; 14–18). The significant contrasts are both internal between the parallel sections and external, with the episode in Egypt. Abram's characterization grows in complexity, even if somewhat tarnished, as he returns to true worship, his generous obedient faith contrasting his previous reactionary fear. When Abram returned to the land, publicly identified with Yahweh in worship, and demonstrated faith by separating from Lot, who chose wicked associations for expected profit to his detriment, Yahweh certified and expanded his promise to Abram.

Abram Returned to the Land with Worship (13:1–4)

Abram returned in prosperity to the land of promise and his public worship.

13:1–2. The new scene opens with a reminder that Abram had been in Egypt, the abundance he had acquired, and the presence of Lot, in preparation for the coming tension. Verse 2 highlights Abram's abundance with a disjunctive offline comment that will become significant in the later narrative. For the first time, Abram's financial resources are mentioned. Abram's considerable wealth is not just in animals but in silver and gold. Abram is becoming a force to be reckoned with. It is not clear if the silver or gold was part of the settlement with Pharaoh as it was with Abimelech later (20:16, Mathews 2005, 133), but it does seem to foreshadow the exodus and Israel plundering the Egyptians (Exod. 3:22; 11:2–3; 12:35–36). As such, this verse provides a mixed message. God had promised personal blessing, and Abram was coming to worship Yahweh (Gen. 13:3–4). However, it will also be the basis for the conflict that will force the separation with Lot.

For Israel reading this later, the imagery of the exodus will underline the danger of Lot's later choice to associate with Sodom, highlighted in 13:13 and building on the curse on Canaan (9:25–27). It will also provide opportunity to reflect on the need for obedience and faith in God's promise to receive confirmation and fulfillment of that promise (13:14–17). In contrast to the previous episode, Abram responded in faith and obedience to Yahweh.

13:3–4. Abram proceeded back to the site of the climax of his initial narrative (12:8), where he offered public identification with Yahweh in worship near Bethel. Genesis 13:3 pictures the orderly but considerable movement of his camp "by stages" (JPS). Abram brought an imposing presence. He was moving back to his source of faith. Wenham (1987, 296) notes the repetitive itinerary, suggesting that the narrator intends to present Abram recapturing his "previous experience with God." Yahweh was initially absent from the Egyptian sojourn narrative until he afflicted Pharaoh with the plagues, and Abram did not acknowledge him in the narrative; Abram now returned to his place of worship and public identification with Yahweh, calling on the name of Yahweh (see Exposition on 12:8, p. 251). Abram appropriately recognized his deliverance with loyal worship.

TRANSLATION ANALYSIS 13:1

The term reflected in the ESV merely as "journeyed on" (מַסַּע) and translated "by stages" (JPS, NLT, NRSV), "on his journeys" (NASB95, NKJV), or "from place to place" (NET, NIV) occurs only eleven other times, all in Exodus (17:1; 40:36, 38), Numbers (10:2, 6, 12, 28, 33:1–2), and Deuteronomy (10:11). Each other occurrence refers to the travels of the Israelites in the wilderness, suggesting the breaking of camps or daily march (*HALOT* s.v. "מַסַּע" 607). The use here may imply the size and orderly movement of Abram's herds and camp as well as adding to the parallels with the exodus from Egypt and the implications for the nation reading this to act in faith as Abram would.

Conflict Confronted Abram (13:5–7)

The combined prosperity of Lot and Abram overwhelmed the land already inhabited by the Canaanites, bringing strife.

13:5–6. Lot returns to the forefront, already noted in verse 1, to draw attention to his wealth. The disjunctive again interjects information into the narrative, drawing attention to Lot and preparing for what will follow. Lot's wealth, added to Abram's, overwhelmed the available pasture. Lot's spread, including flocks and "tents" (v. 5), highlights the number of people and animals each man has in his entourage so that they cannot "dwell together" (v. 6, twice). As nomads, they had to follow the pasturage, but with such large groups of people and animals they were overgrazing what was available.

13:7. What may have appeared to be God's blessing had brought strife. The herdsmen fighting over the grazing land jeopardized the promise. Ironically, it was not conflict with the neighboring Canaanites but among brothers.

As noted, the land was not empty. With the Canaanites already laying claim to the best grazing, Abram and Lot would have to forage, raising tensions between those charged with keeping the flocks thriving. The presence of the Canaanites and Perizzites reminds the reader of the threat to the promise noted in 12:6 and God's promise to give the land to Abram, testing Abram's trust in God.

Parallels between the final two sections emphasize the contrast between Lot and Abram: sight and faith. Each section begins with a direct address (Abram addressed Lot [vv. 8–9]; Yahweh addressed Abram [vv. 14–17]), followed by their respective response (Lot chose and moved [vv. 10–13]; Abram believed and traveled through the land [v. 18]). The two sections are explicitly tied together (v. 14) and include numerous verbal parallels, contrasting Lot's choice according to the land's appearance (in contrast to its spiritual evaluation) leading into wickedness, with Abram's choice according to faith in the promise of Yahweh leading to worship. The obvious implication for Israel and readers of every age promotes faith that may have to wait over prosperity and immediate gratification.

Abram Generously Gave Lot His Choice (13:8–13)

Abram generously granted Lot his choice of the pasturage, which Lot took without regard for the wicked spiritual heritage, removing another obstacle to God's promise.

13:8–9. Abram responded to the fighting between the herdsmen with generosity to Lot. It was Abram's by God's promise, and he had the right as the patriarch to tell Lot his place, but he did not cling to it. Rather, he offered Lot his choice of land. Abram's concern to avoid the "strife" (v. 8) prompted him to his generous offer. "Strife," as it is used here, only occurs one other time, in Numbers 27:14, where it refers to Israel quarreling with Moses over their lack of water, prompting God to bring it out of the rock for them (Num. 20:2–13), giving it the name "Meribah." Water rights may have been involved here also, especially given the emphasis on Lot's choice being "well watered" (13:10).

Abram's concern against quarreling particularly arose out of the relationship they had. He called them "kinsmen" (v. 8). By drawing attention to the relationship, he provided a righteous alternative to the conflict that led to murder in Genesis 4 (see Translation Analysis 13:8). Lot's presence provided an additional tension, however. Lot is likely the heir apparent, but here the character of Lot will show clearly in contrast to Abram. Lot's enchantment with the wealth of the plain over the promise of Yahweh reveals the necessity of parting ways. It was more than just the grazing rights. The promise was in jeopardy because a potential heir, not in the plan of Yahweh and, as he will show, not of the character necessary to carry the hope of blessing, was positioned to claim the promise. Whether Abram understood the dangers or not, he graciously parted ways for the good of the relationship.

TRANSLATION ANALYSIS 13:8

"Kinsmen" here translates the term that has often come up in Genesis for "brother" (אָח, so "brothers" [NASB95, NKJV, NCV]). The significance here is in the allusion to Genesis 4 and the strife between Cain and Abel, though the term for "strife" is not used there.

While the text does not clearly declare his motivation here other than to preserve the relationship, there is also a clear trajectory with chapters 14 and 15 that leads the reader to see Abram's faith. In 14:22–24 Abram declares his vow to Yahweh that he would not take anything from Sodom that would compromise God's glory in making Abram wealthy. Here we see a marked contrast with Lot's pursuit of wealth, right after Abram's declaration of faith through worship (13:4). God rewarded Abram's action by extending the promise, declaring his approval, and implying Abram's faith. Abram immediately validated his faith by establishing a new worship center in Hebron. That faith is explicitly declared in 15:6, which, as we shall see, does not declare something new but summarizes what Abram has shown. While we do not wish to overstate his intention, his faith is clearly growing.

Faith has the privilege of generosity and blessing based on Yahweh's promise. Abram offered Lot a free choice without restriction. He offered "the whole land" (13:9), probably referring to the land of promise, for Lot to choose from. He could go left (north, in an ancient Near Eastern orientation) or right (south). Tragically, Lot chose neither but saw the greener pasture ahead (east) and chose both to move out of the land of promise and to move toward what would become the epitome of wickedness, based solely on seeming benefit.

13:10–13. Abram had offered Lot any part of the land, and Moses slows the narrative to describe Lot's careful survey of the land, emphasizing the appearance. Lot observed the "well watered" and so productive character of the land, very significant in a semi-arid country. The added descriptions of its appearance, "like the garden of the Lord, like the land of Egypt, in the direction of Zoar" (v. 10) emphasize the appearance but also subtly draw attention to the temptation narrative (ch. 3), the immediately preceding narrative (12:10–20), and the reason for the conflict. In both narratives, foolish choices based on appearance led to compromise and judgement, even if God rescued Sarai and Abram from their folly. The narrative goes on to explain why it was so lush. "This was before the Lord destroyed Sodom and Gomorrah" (v. 10). The explanation also does double duty in this narrative. It not only explains the obvious lushness of the plain, but it provides another subtle warning of the dangers that Lot was missing in his survey. What he saw was neither lasting nor indicative of future benefits for those living there.

Reminiscent of Genesis 3, Lot saw and chose the most appealing to the eye. While there are some terms in common dealing with their visual perception, the first thematic parallel is what arrests the attention. Just as Eve chose what appealed to her eyes while disregarding God's clear perspective and the warning of danger, so Lot chose what appealed to his eyes without regard for God's perspective (whether known or not) and the resulting danger. His concern, clearly for immediate and material prosperity, would contrast with Abram's concern and pursuit of God's promise. Lot would have a temporary gain but lose it all in the end. Abram would have a temporary testing and struggle but gain promise and blessing for his posterity and the peoples of the earth.

Lot's choice, based on the outward beauty, took him east. The idea of moving eastward reminds the reader also of Adam and Even driven from the garden (3:23–24), Cain running from family eastward (4:16), and humanity after the flood moving toward Shinar (11:2). In fact, movement eastward in Genesis seems to consistently be away from blessing and promise and even "suggests divine judgment" (Wenham 1987, 298). Practically speaking, it provided the necessary separation (13:11b). Verse 12, however, seems to indicate an additional result: Lot moved completely out of the land of promise.

Abram offered blessing (part of the land), but his offer had not anticipated Lot leaving the land. "The whole land" (v. 9) seems to anticipate that they will partition the land. However, the contrast in verse 12 places Abram "in the land of Canaan" and Lot "among the cities of the valley," declaring that Lot has moved away from the land of promise. The Jordan is the boundary of the promised land (Num. 34:12), although Yahweh would give the eastern part to the two and a half tribes at their request (Num. 32; Deut. 3:12–17). The cities mentioned appear to lie outside of the promise, so that Lot not only leaves the hope of God's promise but is no longer a possible heir for Abram (Helyer 1983, 79–80; cf. Hamilton 1990, 393).[1]

For Lot, then, his separation from Abram was far more significant than merely putting some distance between them. He had broken with the source of blessing by separating from Abram, and he had moved away from open worship (Gen. 13:4) and into companionship with very wicked sinners against Yahweh (v. 14, cf. Coats 1985, 115–18). A nomad and pastoralist had moved to the evil city. He was leaving the divine promise and source of his wealth for what he expected to be a greater or more immediate promise.

The final verse of this section adds the ominous conclusion to Lot's choice. In preparation for what will come and as a second harbinger of the coming judgment (cf. 13:10), The narrative emphasizes the great wickedness of these cities. Again, setting the note off with a disjunctive and piling up terms, Moses describes their extreme wickedness. This profound evil is against Yahweh and of course will be judged. However, the immediate implication is the folly of Lot's choice. He chose what he could evaluate with his eyes from a distance. Even when he got close and saw the sin, he would not leave until forced to go, after his loss of everything except his daughters (ch. 19).

TRANSLATION ANALYSIS 13:13

Two adjectives describe the character of the men of Sodom: "wicked" (רַע) and "sinners" (חַטָּא). Rather than giving two different descriptions in parallel (as perhaps understood from translations like the NIV, "wicked and were sinning greatly"), these adjectives form a hendiadys (so the NET Bible, "extremely wicked"), emphasizing their depth of offense to God. They are the worst kind of sinners—wicked sinners! Such sin is against Yahweh (לַיהוָה), but then the text piles on the emphatic "very" (מְאֹד). The result is a very emphatic denunciation of the moral character of the residents of Sodom.

God Rewarded His Generous Worshipper with a Clarified Land Promise (13:14–18)

Yahweh expanded and clarified his promise of the whole land to Abram's innumerable descendants forever, drawing Abram's appropriate response of worship.

13:14–17. Yahweh now reviewed his promise to Abram, including all the land that Abram had graciously released. God directed his gaze. All the land he could see would be bequeathed to his descendants. The promise expands on the promise in chapter 12 in several ways. First, the land is more clearly and expansively designated as "all the land that you see" (v. 15). In addition, the offer is "forever" (עַד־עוֹלָם, v. 15).

Abrahamic Covenant, Treaty, and Conditions

Abram is also included as a recipient, though he will not receive any of the land personally (v. 15) because Yahweh is using language of the royal grant treaty (Sarna 1989, 100). The similarities with the royal grant have been documented and discussed widely, including debate on the assumption of obligation on the part of the recipient. Weinfeld argued for the Abrahamic Covenant as a promissory covenant based on the loyalty

1 The ambiguity around the location of the cities suggests that they are at least on the periphery of the land of promise, if not fully outside (Wenham 1987, 299).

of the vassal without further obligation of the vassal (Weinfeld 1970). McCarthy noted, however, a more flexible structure and continuum between treaties and grants that often included obligations which Knoppers supported with relation to the Davidic Covenant (McCarthy 1981; Knoppers 1996). We shall see the obligations for Abraham that are both explicit and implicit in the text (see Shetter 2019).

Finally, the emphasis is centered on the offspring rather than the land. These offspring will be innumerable (v. 16), which is the center of an explicit chiasm. "I will give [the land] to you" (vv. 15, 17) frames the reference to Abram's "offspring" (vv. 15, 16) with "dust of the earth" repeated in the center (v. 16). This focus on the offspring and renewing of that promise from 12:2 adds significance to Lot leaving both the land and consideration as the possible heir of the old and barren couple (Helyer 1983). While Yahweh does not explicitly say "from Abram's body" as he will in chapter 15, the implication is certainly there as God emphasized Abram's "offspring" (זַרְעֲךָ, three times in 13:15–16).

God's command to Abram was to get up and walk through the land, perhaps symbolically taking possession (Sarna 1989, 99–100; Wenham 1987, 298) but also anticipating and enjoying the promise—"a kind of enacted declaration of faith in God's promise" (Goldingay 2010, 157). Again God repeated the promise to give this land to Abram, which would come to fruition through his posterity. God's renewal of his promise, emphasized by reiteration, served both to reward Abram's faith and to clarify Abram's expectations.

TRANSLATION ANALYSIS 13:17

The verb to "walk" (הִתְהַלֵּךְ) occurs here in the hithpael stem, which indicates walking "to and fro" or to "walk about" in the land (HALOT s.v. "הלך" 246–49). The use suggests going back and forth and covering the whole land. The translations indicate this with various adverbs, such as "walk through" (ESV, NCV, NIV, NKJV, NLT, NRSV, RSV), "walk about" (JPS), or both (NASB95).

God's renewal of promise to Abram closely follows Abram's offer to Lot. Abram offered "the whole land" (כָּל־הָאָרֶץ, 13:9), either to the north or south. God offered Abram "all the land" (כָּל־הָאָרֶץ, v. 15) to the north, south, east, and west (v. 14). In response to Abram, "Lot lifted up his eyes and saw" (וַיִּשָּׂא־לוֹט אֶת־עֵינָיו וַיַּרְא, v. 10) the lush plain. God told Abram to "lift up your eyes and look" (שָׂא נָא עֵינֶיךָ וּרְאֵה, v. 14) at the land he was promised. In response to Abram's offer, Lot "settled" (יָשַׁב) among the cities and "moved his tent [וַיֶּאֱהַל] as far as Sodom" (v. 12). Lot found himself in opposition to Yahweh (v. 13), where all he had would be destroyed (v. 10), and he would have nothing to give his descendants (19:30–38). Abram, however, in response to God's promise, "moved his tent" (וַיֶּאֱהַל) and "settled" (וַיֵּשֶׁב) near the oaks of Mamre where he established a new worship center, trusting God's promised gift of all the land he could see "to [his] offspring forever" (13:15).

The numerous parallels draw attention to the connection between Lot's foolish choice and God's response to Abram. Lot removed himself and a possible competitor to God's miraculous intervention from Abram's consideration. Abram must fully trust God's promise. Yahweh would now reiterate and expand the promise.

The parallels also draw attention to the significant differences in the two scenes. The basic frame of the stories match, but the motivation (faith or sight) and the outcomes (promised hope with true worship and impending doom in opposition to Yahweh) differ dramatically. Lot pursued folly and loss based on his inability to see beyond the lush grass and physical prosperity, valuing immediate gratification rather than a pursuit of Yahweh. In contrast, Abram's faith in God's promise, founded in appropriate worship, resulted in enduring promise to his innumerable offspring forever (and blessing to all the families of the earth!).

13:18. Abram responded to God's renewed promise by moving his camp south to the area of Hebron and establishing a new worship center with an altar. This final verse completes the section and parallels with the Lot account, contrasting Lot's opposition to Yahweh by association (vv. 10–13; see exposition on 13:14–17). It also provides an *inclusio* with the initial section where Abram entered the land, traveled to his altar between Bethel and Ai, and worshipped, calling on the name of Yahweh (v. 4).

Worship initiates and culminates the narrative, establishing true worship as the necessary grid through which to view the characters' actions and Yahweh's response. Abram's renewed hope and expectation of promise is based in his worship or, as we have seen already and will see again, walking with God. On the other hand, expectation of judgment and loss arise from materialistic self-interest, neglecting concern for righteousness and the necessarily primary pursuit of Yahweh.

Irony abounds here. The blessing of wealth becomes a cursing of strife; the prosperity of the plain becomes a cursing of sin and final destruction. Releasing the land in the pursuit of God in faith and waiting on him provided clearer and enhanced promise.

This narrative also contrasts with the previous narrative of Abram and Sarai's sojourn in Egypt. Worship was not mentioned in 12:10–18, and Yahweh only appeared when he must judge Pharaoh because of Abram and Sarai's lie. Again, the contrast is clear and instructive for the reader. Deceptive self-protection may bring destruction to one's world and presumes on God's providence, precluding his blessing, and it is far from his presence. Yet worship evidencing generous faith can offer blessing, experiencing the fullness of God's promise in his presence.

THEOLOGICAL FOCUS

God, as sovereign king, rewards those who walk by faith in dependent worship, which shows in generosity and grace, while those who selfishly choose personal gain and associate with evil will suffer loss.

As in the previous narrative, Yahweh righteously judges the wicked and evil (13:10, 13). Here he also comes with blessing and renewed promise in response to faith, validating loyalty and worship (vv. 4, 18). The context of Genesis emphasizes his faithfulness to his promises, rewarding faith and enhancing his promise. He will fulfill his promise and bless his loyal worshipper.

Yahweh exercises his divine rule, bequeathing territory to his faithful vassal and offering an enduring legacy in his posterity. He is the true owner of the land, not the Canaanites and Perizzites, nor Abram (Rickett 2011, 40–41).[2] God still creates mystery and opportunity for continued growth in faith by extending the promise without any immediate concrete realization of that promise. The walk of faith will necessarily live in the tension of promise without clear or immediate outworking. Though God continually repeats and validates his promises, proving his faithfulness and integrity, the fulfillment will only necessarily be partial until the final consummation of his redemptive program. That does not detract from his sovereign

2 Rickett's argument that Yahweh is the true owner of the land is appropriate and crucial for the argument of Genesis. His assumption, however, that this is the place (and apparently the only place) where Yahweh dwells is missing the point (Rickett 2011, 39–40). He will choose to dwell there (Exod. 15:17; Num. 35:34). He is not bound by geography, but as Creator, he is over all and is not limited to any land. It is his to give to any and all nations (Deut. 32:8). In fact, the exodus will billboard that sovereignty (Exod. 12:12), which this narrative and the previous allude to, as Yahweh brings judgment on Egypt and takes Abram out with great wealth to a land occupied by the Canaanites.

oversight but only from the human ability to see it and our necessity to live in faith.

The underlying themes also reflect the responsibilities of humanity before this holy and righteous Judge of all the earth. Abram shows the right attitude in worship and public identification with Yahweh, which leads to generous faith. Faith does not cling to the promise or, better, to one's expectation of how God will accomplish the promise. Faith can give generously and allow God to deal with his promise in his time and his way.

This sort of faith is in direct contrast to the drive to establish one's own wellbeing by taking the best for oneself. The faith also must be able to evaluate what is good based on the righteousness it produces, promotes, or associates with. Faith, then, values God's promise over immediate benefit and righteousness over personal profit. The implications here include the continued tension between our perceptions, our experience, and our faith, exposing our values. Lot exposed his values and his lack of discernment when he moved into Sodom. Abram exposed his values when he freely offered the land to maintain the peace of the relationship and when he offered public worship, establishing worship centers throughout the land.

Abram's restoration after floundering in Egypt and failing to trust shows the complexities of his character. He encourages every believer to see that the walk of faith is not a straight line upward, but that God faithfully works in the lives of his saints. One failure does not disqualify but provides opportunities to learn, grow, and move forward to be a blessing in the next time of testing.

Lot's move into Sodom also provides a significant lesson that not only are appearances deceiving, but one who has followed Abram to share in the promise can be seduced by the appearance of immediate profit. He who would be rescued by God nevertheless showed his weak values and, by desiring immediate gain, faced ultimate loss.

PREACHING AND TEACHING STRATEGIES

Exegetical and Theological Synthesis

The sermon/lesson begins with the relationship between Abram and Lot. While both have been the recipients of God's blessing (see 13:2 and 5), only the former is described as a worshipper (v. 4). The presence of the "altar" at the beginning and end of the narrative (v. 18) sends a strong signal that Abram is the one to emulate. He seems to have recovered nicely from his faith fiasco in Egypt in the previous chapter, and that's good news for any of us who struggle with an inconsistent faith. Living the Christian life in a badly broken world includes being in the presence of those who do not share our faith (v. 7). We need to be prepared to fight against their destructive influence. Abram displays his righteousness by the way he treats his "brother" (translated "kinsmen" by the ESV; v. 8). It takes quite a bit of selflessness to let the pick of the litter go to Lot.

These characters speak theology through the narrative by the way in which they act. The problem with walking by sight is that our sight is severely less than 20/20 with respect to evaluating what's best for us. How many "Jordan Valleys" present themselves to us every day! What's not to like in verse 10, "like the garden of the LORD"? The narrator shows us what's not to like in the rest of the verse! Better to be in Canaan than near Sodom, especially for those of us who know the rest of the story. It's impossible for a person not to worship God and still not worship another god; idolators are sadly characterized as "the men of Sodom" (v. 13). Far better for us to walk with God and believe his promises to be best.

Preaching Idea

God's promised blessings are only for those who are righteous by faith, while those who walk by sight suffer the consequences.

Contemporary Connections

What does it mean?

Like so many places in Genesis, and in the Old Testament for that matter, this is a good place to explain the significance of building an altar and worshipping the Lord. The narrative begins and ends with reference to this action and describes Abram in these terms. My favorite sources on the subject of worship and idolatry are Scott Hafemann's *The God of Promise and the Life of Faith* (my favorite section is "The Nature of Idolatry," on pages 35–39, and Timothy Keller's *Counterfeit Gods* (see his Introduction through page 21). On page 36 Hafemann suggests that a believer can identify their idol(s) by completing this statement, "I would be happy if only I had Jesus and ________." Whatever you put in the blank has achieved idol status in your life. Everything in our life flows out of our worship beliefs and practices. So before going much further on urging our listeners to be like Abram and not like Lot, let's be clear on what it means to worship God and not an idol.

It is also a good place to help listeners be clear about what it means to walk by sight and why that is so destructive. We walk by sight when we allow our senses to override our ability to evaluate options in life based upon our worship of God. In terms of a purely human perspective, Lot made the right choice of where to take his "flocks and herds" (v. 5). It was a no-brainer. Since there is no indication that he was evaluating his options with God's wisdom, his was the natural choice. However, not worshipping the Lord puts us in league with "the men of Sodom [who] were wicked, great sinners against the Lord" (v. 13).

Is it true?

In the climate in which we're currently writing, some listeners will always give a puzzled look when they hear God's estimate of sinners: "Now the men of Sodom were wicked, great sinners against the Lord" (v. 13). We can't assume anymore that all attendees believe in birth-sin or that God is holy and judges sin/sinners. You may want to spend a moment on God's right to judge, and his criteria or basis for judging humankind.

It is true that Lot is placing himself in extreme spiritual danger due to his decision to walk by sight and not by faith. It is also true that Abram is secure—secure enough in his walk with the Lord to trust that he will not be selfish (no looking out for #1) or driven by greed. It is true that a person cannot do both: they cannot walk by sight and by faith in the same decision. It is true that a person who walks by faith will often choose an option that does not look right to an unregenerate person. In the case of Lot, what is true is that he chose where to live without any guidance from his Creator.

Now what?

I cannot think of anything more relevant than the pathway suggested by these two characters, Abram and Lot. These two set the priorities and trajectory of every human being. We worship the God revealed in Scripture or we worship idols. We walk with God or else we live according to human ingenuity and resourcefulness of all kinds. God promises to give us LifePlus. God's presence offers the highest good and greatest value we can have. Yet everything inside us screams that there is more to life outside the promise of God. We suffer from the same vision problems as Lot and walk by sight, not by faith. Better to follow Abram's example of calling on the name of the Lord in worship, adoration, and glad submission to his will. Better to trust that his promises are better than anything the world, flesh, and the devil can offer us.

Creativity in Presentation

Let's begin with a possible structure that places listeners into this narrative:

- First, there is this concept of worship in verses 4 and 18. Here is the place to provide a list of common American idols.

Our preaching idea from above is that God's promised blessings are only for those who are righteous by faith while those who walk only by sight suffer the consequences. Righteousness that God acknowledges is possessed only by those who worship him in spirit and in truth. In fact, true worship is the frame for a faith-filled life of making choices dependent on God rather than on what I perceive in my flesh.

- Second, out of this foundation of worship comes a righteousness that makes peace as much as possible (v. 7). Abram's statement to Lot, "Let there be no strife between you and me" (v. 8), seems like a relatively trivial matter until you see how important harmony is in Scripture. But his peacemaking is surely a sign that he is one of the blessed. At the time of this writing, I (Randal) have never witnessed more unrest and disunity in our country. It's hard to find a peacemaker.

- And then, Lot's character is linked to so many negative locations, such as Egypt (v. 10), an easterly direction (v. 11), and close to Sodom (v. 12) with its "wicked, great sinners against the Lord" (v. 13). You will want to help your listeners identify those times when they make decisions based on sight, not faith. For instance, lots of parents and their young adult children are deciding what to do about college. On what basis are they deciding what and where to study? Do they even know about the fine line between choosing based on potential for remuneration or kingdom-of-God potential? The worshipping life values God's priorities over fleshly priorities.

- Third, the Lord invites us to look over all that he has promised for those who trust him (vv. 14–17). He promises us good all the days of our lives. Every spiritual blessing is promised to us; what more could we want?! Can you imagine Abram's trek through every piece of property? And with every aspect of spiritual blessing we say, "God has given this to *me*!" The Christian life can be summarized as an ongoing relationship with God where we continually learn, believe, and live life according to God's gracious promises. Temptations are strong because sin makes appealing promises too. The question since the beginning of redemptive history is which promise we will believe.

Can we say that as we walk in faith with God the opportunity for greater benefit grows? In choosing faith, we grow closer to God and experience his promises more deeply. We don't gain greater promise (like Abram did), but we gain deeper appreciation for and experience of his great and magnificent promises.

DISCUSSION QUESTIONS

1. Compile a list of idols you tend to worship, such as good health, comfort, relationships, and so forth.
2. While we don't want to excuse our lapses into unbelief, we do want to take comfort in Abram reemerging as a person of faith. Discuss the encouragement that comes from God's decision to allow us to see all the spiritual warts of his finest.
3. How close is your proximity to "Sodom" and such? How hard are you attempting the mortification of sin? (This a reference to John Owen's famous title *Of the Mortification of Sin in Believers*; an excellent resource for this is *Overcoming Sin & Temptation: Three Classic Works by John Owen*, edited by Kapic and Taylor.)
4. Whether we are talking about Eve, Lot, or us, what is the connection between our birth-sin and our tendency to walk by sight and not by faith?
5. How do we stay focused on eternity when the glitter of immediate benefit shines brightly?
6. How do I evaluate my current worship, and how does it show to my world? How can I build deeper worship patterns into my daily living?

Genesis 14:1–24

EXEGETICAL IDEA
When Lot was caught up in retribution against his neighbors, Abram exhibited faith, rescuing Lot and his neighbors with their goods, giving public glory to Yahweh and valuing God's promise over immediate gain that could tarnish God's greatness.

THEOLOGICAL FOCUS
Loving my brother at personal expense, honoring God with necessary praise and sacrificial worship, and guarding his glory while expecting his promised outcomes embodies loyal faith.

PREACHING IDEA
Faith in God empowers you to love your brothers and sisters at great personal cost for God's sole glory.

PREACHING POINTERS
You can see from the theological focus that Genesis 14 functions for the church as one of those "go and do likewise" narratives. Abram's reaction to Lot's dilemma—his love for his brother—is the fruit of faith in God. Abram leads the way for us in our faith journey. We are writing this commentary in a time of great social unrest in our country. It's a great time to be preaching about loving God and neighbor. When is it ever a bad time to preach the Great Commandment? So all the historical data about the kings listed in Genesis 14:1–12 provides the context for Abram to flex his faith muscles (v. 1 begins with, "In the days of [multiple kings making war]"). Listeners have an opportunity to see faith in action in verses 13–16 as Abram unhesitatingly rescues Lot. Although not listed yet in the narrative, God is powerfully at work because there is no way Abram should have conquered these enemies to rescue Lot.

If anyone is wondering if it's worth it to follow Abram's example, give them a good look at verses 17–20 where God's blessing is once again emphasized ("Blessed be Abram by God . . . and blessed be God"). Finally, Abram's loyalty to the Lord is clearly displayed when he refuses the offer made by the king of Sodom. His confession, "I have lifted my hand [in an oath] to the Lord, God Most High" (v. 22), is yet another example to follow (cf. vv. 18, 19, 20 for the repeated title).

LOYAL FAITH: COSTLY BROTHERLY LOVE (14:1–24)

LITERARY STRUCTURE AND THEMES

Abram's faith received another immediate test as he stepped in to rescue his nephew from the consequences of Lot's new associations. Lot's capture prompted Abram's intervention and demonstration of faith in Yahweh (vv. 1–16). The extended campaign report highlights Abram's achievement in defeating the coalition and prepares for Abram's second test facing the two kings (vv. 17–24). Initially he trusted Yahweh for physical safety and the rescue of Lot but subsequently for his wealth, refusing the king of Sodom's offer of the spoils of war. Instead, he accepted the king of Salem's blessing, offering public praise in worship of Yahweh.

I. The battle reports reveal Abram's faith (14:1–16).
   A. The Dead Sea kings rebelled against their Mesopotamian overlords (14:1–4).
   B. The Mesopotamian kings brought retribution and defeat (14:5–12).
   C. Abram rescued all the captives and property (14:13–16).

II. Abram declared his allegiance (14:17–24).
   A. The king of Sodom met Abram (14:17).
      B. The king of Salem met Abram with provisions (14:18).
      B'. Abram accepted Salem's blessing with worship (14:19–20).
   A'. Abram refused Sodom's possessions with an oath (14:21–24).

The second half of the narrative provides the main theological impact. The appearance of the king of Sodom and his offer to Abram frames the appearance of the king of Salem and his blessing for Abram. It reminds the reader of God's promise to bless Abram and those who would bless him but to curse all who would dishonor Abram (12:3). It also highlights Abram's closing words, revealing Abram's loyalty and faith in Yahweh, concern for his glory, and loyal generosity to his allies.

Not only does this narrative show the continuing growth of Abram in faith, it immediately reveals Lot's losses. He had left God's presence and his blessed brother to identify with Sodom (14:12) and experience their captivity. Genesis 14 begins to show the deceptive nature of Lot's choice while emphasizing Abram's choice of God's blessing over the immediate (and expected) plunder, identifying with God Most High rather than Sodom.

- ***The Battle Reports Revealed Abram's Faith (14:1–16)***
- ***Abram Declared His Allegiance (14:17–24)***

EXPOSITION

Genesis 14 presents what initially appears to be a digression from the rest of the Abram stories. Abram disappears for the first half of the section while the narrator rehearses a campaign from a coalition of northern kings to exact retribution on a coalition of rebellious vassal kings in the Dead Sea valley. The link to the larger narrative appears quickly in the form of the king of Sodom (v. 2), and numerous additional links tie this narrative closely into what has preceded and what will follow, despite Abram's absence. The raiding party from Mesopotamia and Asia Minor subjugate the nations east of the Jordan before turning their attention to the rebels they came to discipline, showing their formidable power. All of this enhances the impression of

Abram's confidence in Yahweh's blessing (in contrast to Egypt!) as Abram routed the invading kings. It also prepares for the encounter of Abram with the two kings who will test his loyalties and motivations. When Lot was caught up in retribution against his neighbors, Abram exhibited faith, rescuing Lot and his neighbors with their goods, giving public glory to Yahweh, and valuing God's promise over immediate gain that could tarnish God's greatness.

The Battle Reports Revealed Abram's Faith (14:1–16)

When Lot was captured in a war between Sodom and their overlords, Abram exhibited faith and extended blessing, rescuing Lot and all his neighbors with all their goods

The Dead Sea Kings Rebelled Against Their Mesopotamian Overlords (14:1–4)

The five kings in the Dead Sea valley rebelled after twelve years of subjugation to their Mesopotamian overlord.

14:1. Setting the timeframe in the days of "Amraphel king of Shinar," Moses immediately reminds the reader of humanity's initial great civilization and God's judgment (10:10; 11:2), from which Abram came to establish a new homeland and bring blessing to all these peoples (11:27–12:3). Amraphel and his allies are unknown from extrabiblical sources, but their names fit the time and regions from which they come: Shinar refers to Babylon (11:1–9); Ellasar is unknown though Arioch is a name attested at Mari, so it may be northern Mesopotamia; Elam was the state south and east of Babylon in modern southwestern Iran; and Goiim simply means "peoples" (*HALOT* s.v. "גּוֹי" 183), but the name of the king, Tidal, likely was Hittite, possibly leading a group of peoples from Asia Minor (Kitchen 2003, 320). The coalition, then, was a broadly powerful group from the north and east. The narrative will underscore their dominance with their recorded victories.

14:2–3. These kings fought against five kings of the Dead Sea valley (v. 3). Again, the historical names and precise geographic locations of the southern kings have been lost with time, but their general placement may best fit the southeastern end of the Dead Sea, due to the larger concentration of bitumen pits there (Wenham 1987, 310) and the itinerary the invaders follow (vv. 5–7). The king of Sodom appears first and is the most prominent because of his interaction with Abram later. He draws attention to the impending trouble for Abram's nephew (13:12), as well as prejudicing the reader with his character and expected judgment (13:10, 13). Adding to the reader's expectation of judgement for Sodom and their allies, the names of the kings of Sodom and Gomorrah are possibly compounded with "evil" (Bera, from רע) and "wicked" (Birsha, from רשע; Wenham 1987, 309). These five kings banded together against the foreign aggressors in the "Valley of Siddim," which is explained as "the Salt Sea" or the Dead Sea.

14:4. The four kings subjugated the five kings for twelve years. The five kings now rebelled in the thirteenth year, bringing the wrath of the Mesopotamian master and his allies. The driving force of the northern coalition, and one to whom tribute was due, was Chedorlaomer. Amraphel had been listed first in verse 1 (alphabetically), possibly to highlight the connection with Shinar and the previously noted themes of powerful despots, God's judgement, and Abram's homeland. Their service to Chedorlaomer was likely tribute, so withholding it would indicate their rebellion.

> *TRANSLATION ANALYSIS 14:4*
> Most translations take the perfect here (עָבְדוּ) as a pluperfect, "had served" (so ESV, NET, etc.), possibly implying that the first three verses are the preparations for redress to the rebellion recorded in verse 4. NJPS, however, translates it more naturally, "Twelve years they served Chedorlaomer," implying that the first three verses

were the initial conquest with a subsequent rebellion. The difference does not affect the historical development but, more subtly, the impression of Abram's valor, who wins his great victory in the third battle account (Wenham 1987, 304). It also better fits the literary format of an individual campaign report (Kitchen 2003, 322).

The Mesopotamian Kings Brought Retribution and Defeat (14:5–12)

The foreign coalition swept down the Transjordan, crushing all opposition in their way before turning and routing the alliance of southern kings and taking Lot.

14:5–7. Chedorlaomer and his allies responded in the next year. Coming down the King's Highway through the Transjordan, the itinerary moves from southern Syria (Ashteroth-karnaim) all the way down to Eilat (possibly the location of El Paran; J. Zorn, "Elath," *ABD* 2:429) at the tip of the Gulf of Aqabah. They defeated the Rephaim, later remembered for their great size (Deut. 3:11); the Zuzim, possibly related to the Rephaim (if they are equated with the Zamzummim, Deut. 2:20); the Emim, also remembered for their great size and related to the Rephaim (Deut. 2:10–11); and the Horites in Seir (later Edom). As they swung north into the Negev, they defeated the Amalekites around Kadesh and the Amorites at Hazazon-tamar.[1]

The report shows the formidable nature of the coalition of kings from the north and east. They are not to be taken lightly. It also removes any possible support for the rebellious kings from their surrounding neighbors as they face retribution. Though the rebels included more kings, the attackers were battle-hardened with six people groups already under their heel. They made short work of the five kings.

14:8–10. Once again listing the kings facing off and reminding the reader of the numbers, the narrator proves the superiority of the invaders. The battle is too short to even describe. They line up for battle, and all we hear is the report of the defenders running headlong into the tar pits or up into the hill country.

In verse 10, the narrator stops to note the presence of pits of "bitumen" (חֵמָר). The text is ambiguous regarding who fell into the pits. Since the king of Sodom shows up soon after in receiving the goods back from Abram (v. 17), either he did not fall into them, he did not die in them, or a new king was already crowned (Currid 2003, 284). Walton (2009a, 80) supposes that the kings were hiding in the pits, but more likely, some of the troops fell in and the rest of the troops fled to the hills, with the king among those that survived (Waltke and Fredricks 2001, 230–31). Either way, they left the towns completely undefended, which the invaders took full advantage of.

TRANSLATION ANALYSIS 14:10

The Hebrew is ambiguous, as most directly reflected by the NASB95: "and the kings of Sodom and Gomorrah fled, and they fell into them. But those who survived fled to the hill country" (cf. NET). The subject of the plural verb "they fell" is most naturally the kings, resulting in the question as to the survival of the king of Sodom. It could indicate that they "threw themselves into them" (NJPS) and so Walton's (2009a, 80) suggestion that they were intentionally hiding. However, the mention of the "kings" fleeing could be understood as metonymies for the armies fleeing, in which case the ESV would imply the men of the army fell in ("some fell into them," see also NKJV, NRSV, RSV) or more explicitly, "some of the men fell into them" (NIV), or even more interpretively, "as the army of the kings of Sodom

1 Probably located at the southern end of the Dead Sea (Ezek. 47:19; 48:28) rather than En Gedi (2 Chron. 20:2); see M. Astour, "Hazazon-Tamar," *ABD* 3:86.

and Gomorrah fled, some fell into the tar pits" (NLT, cf. NCV).

14:11–12. The looting by the enemy of Sodom and Gomorrah in verse 11 explicitly parallels the taking of Lot and his possessions in verse 12, drawing attention to the occasion that would draw Abram into the war (v. 14). In both cases they "took" (וַיִּקְחוּ) the "possessions" (רְכֻשׁ) of Sodom and Gomorrah and Lot and "went their way" (וַיֵּלֵכוּ). The repetition clarifies that Lot was taken as well, emphasized by the final comment that he had settled in Sodom. We (and Abram) may have expected Lot to be away from the danger as a nomad. Lot had been last seen moving toward Sodom (13:12). He was now, however, resident within Sodom and sharing their fate.

The aside regarding Lot's movements also prepares us for Lot's role in Sodom in chapter 19 and shapes the perception of his character. He is weak and enticed by wealth. The ambiguity of Lot's choice of the valley based on the obvious benefit (13:11) despite the narrator's warning of their wickedness (13:13) now begins to clarify. Certainly, he knew their character by now, yet he was living among them. It also contrasts subtly but distinctly with Abram's clear response to the king of Sodom: Abram would not take a shoestring since it could discredit his God (14:22–24).

Abram Rescued All the Captives and Property (14:13–16)

Responding to the capture of Lot, Abram pursued the invaders and rescued Lot with all the property and people of the plain.

14:13. One unknown escapee managed to report the action and the capture of Lot to Abram, who was still encamped near Hebron (cf. 13:18). Abram here is called a "Hebrew," distinguishing him from the Amorites, his allies. It also reminds the reader that he is a foreigner in the land that God had promised him. These allies had a covenant with Abram (lit. "partners of the covenant," *HALOT* s.v. "בַּעַל" 142–44), which bound them to support him. We learn that they are Amorites, a people group the invaders had attacked at Hazazon-tamar, so they may have personal stakes in this reprisal.

Ḫapiru

Numerous scholars have related "Hebrew" here to the *ḫapiru* referenced in the Amarna letters and elsewhere, referring either to bands of outlaws, or foreigners in service to the official government, or in some cases a derogatory title derived from the former (e.g., Wenham 1987, 313; cf. N. Lemche, "Ḫabiru, Ḫapiru" *ABD* 3:6–10). Here, however, it is better seen as the gentilic connected to Eber, Abram's ancestor (10:24–25; 11:14–17), because the form of the Hebrew is appropriate for the gentilic, but not the *ḫapiru*, and Abram does not fit the characteristics of the *ḫapiru* in the literature (Waltke and Fredricks 2001, 231).

14:14–15. While the narrative had suggested a large camp as the source of conflict with Lot (13:6), we now learn how large. Abram's contingent of home-bred personal defense forces numbered 318 at his disposal, suggesting an encampment of up to one thousand (Wenham 1987, 305). While the numbers of the invading force in this case are unknown, it is clearly a formidable foe, based on the victorious campaign to this point. In fact, the prolific use of the title "king" in chapter 14 (twenty-eight times if you count Melchizedek's name; Kuruvilla 2014, 178) only underlines the greatness of the opposition and the greater standing of God's champion, Abram.

Abram's Army

In comparison with the garrisons requested in the later Amarna letters from this area to Egypt, 318 is a large number. Requests for defense of a city and its land ranged from 30–50 (EA 139) to a hundred men (EA 244) to a couple of hundred men (EA 127) in the Amarna period (mid to late fourteenth century BC), hundreds of years after Abram (Moran 1992).

Abram did not hesitate. The picture of Abram here provides an additional contrast to his sojourn in Egypt. Instead of the fear he expressed then, he now appears fearless and without hesitation. Abram displayed the basis for that courage when he returned and declared his loyalties to Yahweh before the kings of Salem and Sodom (14:22–24).

Abram's action was motivated by relationship to Lot. He mustered his force when he heard that Lot, "his kinsman" (lit. "brother," אָח, v. 14) was captured, recalling Abram's concern that they not quarrel (13:8). Previously, the relationship was worth giving up the best portion, but here it was worth risking his life and allies. Again, in contrast with Cain (ch. 4), Abram shows loyalty (love) for his brother. Chedorlaomer's undoing was his opposition to Abram by abusing Lot. He put himself under God's curse (12:3).

Abram pursued the attackers over 120 miles (as the crow flies) to near Dan before engaging them.[2] After the long trek north, he launched a surprise night attack, routing the army and pursuing them to Hobah (which is no longer known) north of Damascus, more than forty additional miles.

14:16. Just as verses 11–12 recorded the taking of the possessions both from Sodom and Lot, so verse 16 carefully records the return of both the possessions of Sodom and Lot with his possessions. Abram routed the vaunted invaders and recovered all the captured people and possessions. The narrative sounds very much like a campaign report up to this point, with no mention of Yahweh. His intervention and blessing on his chosen representative, Abram, is clear, however, both from the preceding promise (12:3) and from what follows. In the declaration of Melchizedek and the response of Abram to both kings, Yahweh will be honored.

Abram Declared His Allegiance (14:17–24)

Faced with the clear choice of blessing from God or goods from Sodom, Abram declared his loyalty and intent to give glory to Yahweh alone.

The appearance and offer of the king of Sodom to Abram frames the final section of the narrative. Melchizedek's blessing, centered between the king of Sodom's appearance and his offer, provides the theological focus for understanding the overall narrative, the offer from Sodom, and Abram's response. God was at work honoring his promise and blessing his chosen (12:1–3).

The appearance of the two kings and their two speeches are recorded chiastically:

A. The king of Sodom met Abram (14:17).
 B. The king of Salem met Abram with a banquet (14:18).
 B'. Abram accepted Salem's blessing with worship (14:19–20).
A'. Abram refused Sodom's possessions with an oath (14:21–24).

Moses inserts the king of Salem here to contrast with and emphasize the king of Sodom's offer. Abram responds to both kings in the final half, showcasing his loyalties, his perspective, and his character.

The King of Sodom Met Abram (14:17)

The king of Sodom met Abram returning from his victory near Jerusalem.

14:17. The king of Sodom headlines the scene, coming to meet Abram. His interaction with Abram will provide the focus of the scene, which will be interrupted by Melchizedek (see v. 18). Geographically, the subsequent appearance of the king of Salem

2 Of course, "Dan" is a later update to the text from the earlier name of Laish (Judg. 18:29).

(Jerusalem) suggests that Abram is returning down the patriarchal highway following the general ridgeline of the central hill country, past Jerusalem, and to his home near Hebron. The king of Sodom had traveled up from Sodom to meet him, and they all intersect in the "Valley of Shaveh," explained in the text as "the King's Valley" (v. 17). They are probably meeting outside Jerusalem, possibly in one of the valleys immediately south or east of the city (or their confluence, M. Astour, "Shaveh, Valley of," *ABD* 5:1168).

The King of Salem Met Abram with a Banquet (14:18)

The king of Salem met Abram with a celebratory banquet after his victory over the invaders.

14:18. The narrative introduces Melchizedek with background information. We must evaluate the king of Sodom and his response to Abram by Melchizedek and his action, as well as Abram's response to the king of Sodom in light of what we learn from Melchizedek and Abram's response to him.

TRANSLATION ANALYSIS 14:18

The *waw* on a non-verb at the beginning of a clause classically introduces both of the first two clauses of verse 18 as disjunctive (WOC, §39.2.3 a, 650). Because it does not change scenes but does introduce a new character, it is best understood here as explanatory or parenthetical (WOC, §39.2.3 c, 651–52). The translations typically do not distinguish these clauses, but NET Bible and ESV show the second as a parenthesis, and NASB95 indicates the second with a disjunctive "now." The initial clause is only set off in NET and NCV by the lack of any conjunction. The Hebrew construction is important to demonstrate the central focus on the king of Sodom rather than Melchizedek. Melchizedek is presented as the backdrop for the interaction of Abram with Sodom (cf. Sailhamer 1990, 123). Els (1998, 203–5) views Melchizedek as the "centre piece" of the narrative because of the chiastic structure but understands a similar message, drawing out the significance of the concluding conversation with the king of Sodom and showing Abram as the instrument of blessing to the nations. Melchizedek draws attention to Abram's faith and Yahweh's role as deliverer.

Even Melchizedek's name contrasts his character and position with the king of Sodom. The name for Sodom's king related in verse 2 was Bera, which was noted as a compound with "evil" (רַע), and his city was labeled as full of the worst kinds of sinners (13:13). Melchizedek, however, as the book of Hebrews notes, is compounded with "righteous" or "right, honesty" (Heb. 7:2; cf. *HALOT* s.v. "צֶדֶק" 1004–05). It can mean "my king is righteous" or "king of righteousness," or it can be a theophoric, "my king is Ṣedeq" or "Milku is righteous," using the names of gods (Wenham 1987, 316).

The first disjunctive clause declares his position (king of Salem, an early name for Jerusalem, Ps. 76:3, cf. *HALOT* s.v. "שָׁלֵם" 1539) and his response to Abram (providing a celebratory meal for the returning victor). In contrast to the king of Sodom who appeared empty handed, the bread and wine provided a royal banquet, not just a meal (bread and water), in celebration of Abram's great victory (Wenham 1987, 316).[3] Bread here may well be a metonymy for "food" and go beyond merely loaves of bread.

3 Of course, early Christian expositors understood this as a reference to the Eucharist and Melchizedek as a Christophany (a misunderstanding of Hebrews), neither of which fits this context. Genesis presents Melchizedek as a neighbor of Abram and a real king-priest who only comes on the scene briefly to draw attention to Yahweh's working and provide the significant contrast to the king of Sodom, showing Abram's faith and loyalty to Yahweh.

The second disjunctive clause establishes Melchizedek's role with relation to Abram. Not only was he king of Salem, but he was priest of God Most High. The blessing he offered and the response of Abram in tithing acknowledged his position to mediate blessing to Abram, who is already called and blessed by Yahweh.

Abram Accepted Salem's Blessing with Worship (14:19–20)

Abram received the king of Salem's blessing, which praised God and his intervention, by responding with a tithe in worship.

14:19–20. Most significantly, however, Melchizedek blessed Abram by "God Most High, Creator of heaven and earth" (v. 19 NET). He calls on God Most High to "bless" Abram (see "Blessing" in the Introduction, p. 60), which would convey benefits based on his relationship with his servant. This blessing directly recalls God's promise to Abram to bless all who would bless Abram (12:3). Melchizedek not only called for God's favor on Abram (something Abram clearly has) but assured God's favor on himself. This reminder of God's promise is particularly important for the contrast with the king of Sodom in verses 21–22.

> *TRANSLATION ANALYSIS 14:19*
> ESV translates "Possessor" (קֹנֵה, see also NASB95, NKJV) but gives a footnote, "Or Creator." The Hebrew root can be understood either way, but the typical Canaanite formula for their high God El suggests that Creator is the better translation (Brueggemann 1982a, 137), as in, for example, NET, NIV, NJPS.

Melchizedek also praised "God Most High" for his victory on behalf of Abram in the recent battle, a sentiment that Moses clearly agreed with by his citation. Melchizedek's recognition of God's work on Abram's behalf provides the narrator's theological explanation of the events. God has been at work, and Abram's act of bravado was a testament to the intervention of Yahweh, not to Abram's military might. Apparently, Abram's faith in the sole Creator of all creation was well known so that a neighboring king would know to attribute Abram's victory appropriately. Abram recognized and clarified what may have been ambiguous up to now.

> *TRANSLATION ANALYSIS 14:20*
> To "bless" God (14:20 ESV, NJPS, NLT), a common pronouncement in the Old Testament, makes much better sense of the clear idea of praise when placed in the context of relationship, so it is often translated "praise" (NCV, NET, NIV). Understanding the relationship between God and man changes the force of the term when man responds by benefitting the deity with praise for the benefits received in the relationship (K. Richards, "Bless/Blessing," *ABD* 1:754; cf. Brown, בָּרַךְ, *NIDOTTE* 1:764).

Melchizedek's theological declaration grounds Abram's response of worship and confession of God's working on his behalf. Abram's tithe to Melchizedek legitimates both the claim of Melchizedek and his position to make that claim. Abram, in his response to the king of Sodom, would specify that El Elyon, the "Most High God" is indeed Yahweh (14:22). Abram, then, both acknowledged Yahweh's intervention and declared his loyalty to Yahweh through this otherwise unknown priest-king.

> **Melchizedek**
> Melchizedek assumes a larger-than-life persona through reflection on this passage and Psalm 110 in the intertestamental literature and Hebrews, where he appears as a type of Christ (Heb. 5–7).

The meal provided is the celebration of the victory and an acknowledgement of Abram's status in the community. They had no sense of a eucharist before Christ.

In Genesis, he is briefly mentioned in three verses without any history or follow-up. The brevity of his role in the narrative, together with the clear significance and function of his priesthood in blessing the father of the nation of Israel and the friend of God, contribute to the importance placed on him in later literature and the use of him as a type of Christ. Neither the narrative here nor the use in Hebrews requires anything more than a historical king-priest in service of Yahweh, God Most High, bringing perspective and blessing to God's servant Abram and a significant narrative contrast to the king of Sodom. Cf. Hamilton 1990, 408–10, 414–16. In Hebrews 7:3, the writer explicitly understands Melchizedek to be an illustration of Christ, using ἀφομοιόω ("resembling").

Abram Refused Sodom's Possessions with an Oath (14:21–24)

Abram refused the king of Sodom's reward, responding with an oath honoring Yahweh alone as his benefactor.

14:21. The king of Sodom's response to Abram provides an additional contrast with Melchizedek. While Melchizedek brought out a feast and offered blessing, celebrating God's working through Abram's victory, the king of Sodom's first words were, "Give me," and he offered the very goods to which Abram had actually already won the right by his military victory. The king of Sodom offered Abram no praise, thanksgiving, blessing, or gracious and joyful response to having his townspeople (family?) and goods rescued. The king of Sodom appears to be the conniving, evil, and fully self-absorbed churl, as expected from the description of Sodom (13:13), previewing Abram's suspicion (14:23).

His response also illustrates God's promise to Abram. Where Melchizedek had blessed Abram and honored God, the king of Sodom dishonored both Abram and God by failing to give him credit. He owed Abram the lives and property of his entire town, which he had been unable to protect. Instead of gratitude, however, he attempts to dictate the terms as if he has some authority, placing Abram beneath him. Abram's reaction is understandable, and the reader should expect God's cursing to fall on this king, which will be fulfilled in chapter 19. Ironically, however, Abram will still bless him there through intercession.

14:22–24. Abram's reply exhibits his growth in faith and character, which also anticipates God's response to him in the following chapter. Abram took an oath, rejecting any personal benefit from the proceeds of his victory because of his concern for how the king of Sodom would market that. He clearly knew something of Sodom at this point. Abram immediately swore his oath based on his perception of the king of Sodom. In taking his oath, he used the same name for God that Melchizedek had used in his blessing, but he added Yahweh, clarifying that the God Melchizedek was invoking was the same God Abram was following and expecting the blessing from.

TRANSLATION ANALYSIS 14:22

The timing of the oath is ambiguous here in the Hebrew. The perfect form of the verb often gives past time and can be a perfective nuance, "I have lifted my hand" (ESV, also NASB95, NKJV, NIV, NRSV, RSV), which suggests a previous oath at some undisclosed time that is now in force. Morschauser (2013, 139–41) suggests it was an oath taken at the beginning of his campaign to ensure none of his detachment stoop to looting anything, no matter how insignificant. However, the verb can also carry an "instantaneous perfective" nuance, representing "a situation occurring at the very instant the expression is being uttered" (WOC, §30.5.1 d, 488). Here it may be an immediate reaction with an oath, "I raise my hand" (NET, also NCV, NJPS, NLT). It may even be a reapplication of a previous oath, considering his desire to give Yahweh full credit.

Abram's oath excludes even the smallest piece of apparel. His concern, justified by the king of Sodom's offer, is less that Sodom is promoted as it is that Yahweh's working is diminished. The verb Abram used here (הֶעֱשַׁרְתִּי) comes from the same root as the tithe he gave to Melchizedek (מַעֲשֵׂר). The allusion back to Melchizedek's blessing and his response draws attention to the praise of Yahweh, God Most High, and Abram's expectation of blessing from Yahweh, which spoil from Sodom could not satisfy. If Sodom claimed credit, it would discredit the working of Yahweh, diminish the blessing received, and of course diminish the glory of God. The sentiment of his oath, then, proclaims his faith in the promise of God (12:2). God must be honored for his faithfulness.

At the same time, Abram's generosity and justice showed in his treatment of his allies. He stood for their rights to share in the spoil, as any good ancient Near Eastern victor should. His appropriate defense of their rights also underlined his own right, which he was giving up for the exaltation of his God. The king of Sodom had been routed in battle and would not profit from Abram's victory, even though Abram would generously give all the people their freedom, along with their property, to return to Sodom.

THEOLOGICAL FOCUS

Loyal faith shows in loving my brother or sister, even at personal expense; honoring God with necessary praise and sacrificial worship; and guarding God's glory, trusting him for his promised outcomes.

God provides numerous opportunities to test the faith of his servant, whether with personal security, comfort, possessions, or power. We do not always see God directly involved, but he is clearly and appropriately credited in the outcomes of faithful actions (14:20), as well as anticipated faithful actions (14:22–23). The faithful servant, then, must act according to his responsibilities in God's world whether he has clear direction or merely clearly appropriate principles guiding him. He must love his brother, sister, and his neighbor, trusting God for the outcomes. He must also resist temptations to secure his own future from the allures of the world, rejecting anything attached to the system opposed to God.

Yahweh, the creator of the universe (14:19), is the "source for life, buoyancy, and joy in the trials of the day" (Brueggemann 1982a, 137). He is the means to successfully navigate the pain, frustration, or fears that assail the believer. God works through faithful servants who act consistent with his character (4:7). God honors their faith and will bring about his greatest good (as Joseph would discover, even though not all actions may be immediately successful or "victorious;" ch. 37–50, especially 50:20). Yahweh, then, is the deliverer of individuals (Lot) and nations (the five kings). Melchizedek clearly acknowledged Abram's victory as God's working (14:20), emphasized in the narrative by the overwhelming odds against Abram (14:5–12). Consequently, Abram pursued God's promise and blessing, which was much greater than used household goods and travel-weary animals. Abram was looking for Yahweh to bless him and make him a great nation in the land (12:2–3; 13:14–17), to Yahweh's exclusive glory.

Faith, then, acts under testing but does not presume to take what only God can give. In fact, faith does not cling to what is immediate but willingly waits for what God chooses to give, when he chooses to give it. It does not presume that the natural and just reward of righteous action is the best or only reward that God will provide. Faith recognizes that true loyalty cannot compromise God's glory, nor exalt another at God's expense.

The actions of loyal faith include honoring appropriate relationships and showing love to one's brother at personal expense, even when the brother is acting out of self-interest and not walking by faith. Faith puts God first and lives in loyalty to him as absolute sovereign. The covenant Abram had with Yahweh was lived out by fully loyal intentions and actions. All honor and appropriate sacrifice and gifts in worship must go to the sovereign and not to the servant or to any mercenaries along the way. Faith also shows in generous and just dealings with all relationships. Abram's standing for the rights of his allies is instructive. He rightly honored those who stood with him in his defense of Lot, showing God's honor.

Abram's actions illustrate that loyalty in loving God appears in loving people (rescuing Lot, honoring his allies), aligning with God's servants (accepting Melchizedek's blessing), and refusing to align with those opposed to God's kingdom (refusing to accommodate the king of Sodom's self-promotion). In contrast, Lot illustrates compromise with the wicked for personal gain, which, ironically, leads to greater conflict and loss. Unfortunately, Lot would not learn the lesson and would lose everything.

PREACHING AND TEACHING STRATEGIES

Exegetical and Theological Synthesis

For this historical narrative to function for the church, we begin with the repetition of "king." Noteworthy mentions are "Shinar" (14:1), "Sodom" (v. 2), and "Gomorrah" (v. 2). Powerful armies go to war, with the winning side defeating "all the country of the Amalekites, and also the Amorites" (v. 7). Start with that display of regal power and you can see how this narrative moves toward God's divine provision for his people. God's people have always been outgunned in the world from a purely human perspective, but the story in Genesis so far emphasizes God's blessing and promises. We do not thrive in this broken world on human strength alone but because of God's powerful will.

As far as the fallen aspect of humanity is concerned, Lot is the prime example of what happens to us when our choices are based on something other than the worship of God. Lot chose to live "as far as Sodom. Now the men of Sodom were wicked, great sinners against the Lord" (13:12b–13). You knew he was in trouble! Many of your listeners will know the rest of the story already and will readily agree with your observation. Lot-like listeners can expect to be defeated by the enemies of the world, the flesh, and the devil. Abram, on the other hand, is a picture of strength. I find it interesting that "he led forth his trained men, born in his house, 318 of them" (14:14). Abram certainly knew that his faith journey meant he needed to be ready for combat. Our fight for faith in a badly broken world is no less dangerous, which means our readiness is no less important. The blessing of Melchizedek on Abram and God provides the encouragement for God's people to live for him with confidence.

We dare not miss the emphasis on loyalty to God that underscores all of this. I must do all these things as an expression of my loyalty to God, and I must measure them all by who gets the credit (v. 20).

Preaching Idea

Faith in God empowers you to love your brothers and sisters at great personal cost for God's sole glory.

Contemporary Connections

What does it mean?

Because of the mention of so many names, kings, and places, it is important to explain how the show of force contributes to the characterization of Abram and, to some degree, Lot. All these powerful kings and confederations should have easily defeated non-king Abram and "his trained men, born in his house" (v. 14). But Abram defeats Lot's captors with an effective nighttime military maneuver (v. 15).

Then, we need to interpret the significance of Melchizedek's title (v. 18, "king of Salem"), actions (v. 18 "brought out bread and wine"), and double blessing of Abram and God ("Blessed be Abram by God . . . and blessed be God" in v. 19).

Melchizedek is very special in redemptive history, and you may want to include how the New Testament authors describe his significance to the church with respect to our Savior (e.g., Heb. 5–7, for instance). The blessing on Abram is solid and secure because of Melchizedek's kingship/priesthood. He is a priest to "God Most High," who is "Yahweh" himself (Gen. 14:22).

Finally, Abram's loyal faith withstands the test provided by the king of Sodom (vv. 21–24). Abram doesn't take the bait but sticks with his oath to the Lord (v. 22). Abram will not allow anyone to get the credit that only God deserves. God's people know deep down that every good gift comes from the Lord. And the world around Abram—the king of Salem—knew that God performed a powerful miracle for Abram. It was good for God's glory!

Is it true?

You may have to help your people believe in the truthfulness of the history presented in this chapter. As I said above, there is no way Abram should have been able to divide his small army at night and defeat the coalition that captured Lot. But we know from verse 20 and Melchizedek's blessing that it was "God Most High, who has delivered [Abram's] enemies into [his] hand!" For some of the historical questions that have been raised here, Wenham (1987, 318–20) explains the historically appropriate and accurate nature of the details, such as the names, itinerary, glosses, terms, and legal phraseology, even if you cannot prove objectively that the events happened. Kitchen (2003, 319–23) similarly sets the details in the historical and cultural context, showing that it fits nicely in the early second millennium BC.

Now what?

The impressive display of geopolitical powers in this chapter provides an accurate assessment of the kinds of spiritual battles that rage in heaven and on earth. God's people are always underpowered in the fight for faith and the glory of God. Yet, the blessing of God means his people will always accomplish his will in his world. Lot's choice in chapter 13 and his plight in chapter 14 continue to show what happens when we walk by sight and not by faith. Without faith it is impossible to please God, and without God's pleasure we cannot thrive in his world. Even if experienced for a lifetime, any supposed success apart from a vibrant relationship with God is short-lived in view of eternity. But that success cannot satisfy like loving God can; that success cannot secure eternal bliss at the judgment. Abram's actions show faith at work as he rescues his brother, despite the risk to his own life.

Every one of our listeners needs to see their relationship with God in Melchizedek's blessing. No power above, on, or beneath the earth can prevent God's people from accomplishing his will for his glory on earth or prevent them from reaching their final destination and the restoration of all things. For the New Testament believer, prosperity and victory may not be physical wealth and dominance over other competition, but it may be peace through persecution and joy in pain.

Creativity in Presentation

Our homiletical idea is: Faith in God empowers you to love your brothers and sisters at great personal cost for God's sole glory. That angle means the sermon will focus on how Abram's faith drove his reaction to hearing the news about Lot's lot. This narrative is not about a good moral person but about a worshipper who is living within the blessing of God. That kind of person does the impossible, because it is God at work so that God looks good.

- This first move in the sermon can focus on what the blessing of God does for those who believe (14:1–15). It's a great time to remind everyone that God is ultimately concerned about his name. I can't imagine how God's reputation in that region grew! Imagine how many "likes" on social media such a report would earn! Whatever you can do to show the force of the kingdoms of this world will help your listeners know how much they are outgunned from a human perspective. You might also tell a story of someone whose faith gave them great courage to step out and love a neighbor at great cost. If Abram acts only based on family loyalty, that's something that some cultures will understand; if his bravery is faith-based, we've got something very different.

- A second move in the sermon could highlight Melchizedek's blessing, especially the source of it (14:17–20). His significance as the king of Salem, his meal, and his blessing all point our attention to "God Most High." We simply do not understand such verbal blessings (and cursings, for that matter). You might help your listeners by pointing to the biblical view of blessing and cursing as effective when sanctioned and enacted by God alone (Prov. 3:33; 26:2).
- Finally, it's by faith we all share in Abram's blessing. Like Abram, God blesses us with every spiritual blessing in the heavenly places (see Eph. 1:3). Don't miss the reason, however. Abram declares his absolute loyalty to Yahweh, turning down any physical advantage that would deprive God of the glory (Gen. 14:21–24).

DISCUSSION QUESTIONS

1. Chapter 14 opens with a detailed description of ancient history. Discuss what makes this approach helpful in conveying theology but also what makes it difficult.
2. Discuss the bigger picture as Sodom keeps getting mentioned in chapters 13–14, culminating in its destruction in chapters 18–19. Our chapter 14 narrative is not the last time Lot will need rescuing! What role does Sodom play in the larger Abraham narratives? Why does it keep showing up in Abraham's life?
3. I'm not sure we can ever state and restate the blessing of God too much in Genesis, so here's another opportunity to give your listeners a quiz on its meaning.
4. What is the significance of Abram tithing to Melchizedek (v. 20)?
5. When God does great things in your life, how many of your friends and neighbors know about it to celebrate with you? When you accomplish something significant, how will they know it was God at work?

Genesis 15:1–21

EXEGETICAL IDEA

Acknowledging Abram's righteousness by faith, Yahweh assured Abram of security and reward, including innumerable descendants, and confirmed through covenant his promise of descendants and land, clarifying their extended painful waiting with subsequent justice for all.

THEOLOGICAL FOCUS

Based on his righteous and just control over history and nations, and his servants' faith, Yahweh secures his promises for his righteous people, despite struggle, through his covenant.

PREACHING IDEA

God said it, I believe it, he guarantees it, and I have to accept the suffering part.

PREACHING POINTERS

While Genesis 15:6 gets the most press—certainly warranted—the prophetic vision that opens the chapter is enough to let you know that this pericope will preach: "Fear not, Abram, I am your shield; your reward shall be very great" (v. 1). Like your listeners, Abram has been repeatedly faced with the decision: "Will I believe God or not?" So much depends on what Abram believes about God. For instance, if Abram doesn't think much of God's abilities, then God being his shield doesn't amount to much. That is like my son when he was very young saying that he would protect *me*.

The original audience was greatly encouraged to hear God make this promise, to see Abram ask for clarification without being chastised for asking, to hear the omniscient narrator announce Abram's faith and reception of righteousness, and to witness God's elaborate covenant ceremony that gave Abram assurance. Many of those details explain the Christian's faith journey. In fact, just like us, his faith is not yet mature and complete. He has and will continue to stumble. Yet God considered him righteous! So much boils down to whether or not we believe God each day as we walk with him. One reason that faith is necessary is because the promise remains in the distance (cf. v. 13, and Israel's sojourner status matches ours). Besides that, by the time God announced this promise to Abram, only God could do it. Despite all the oppression of living in exile, God will keep his promise to those who trust and obey.

PROMISE AND FAITH: GOD'S GUARANTEE (15:1–21)

LITERARY STRUCTURE AND THEMES

Against the background of Abram's victory over the four-king coalition and declaration of loyalty to Yahweh before the kings of Salem and Sodom (Gen. 14), God formalized his promises through covenant with Abram (ch. 15).[1] The narrative proceeds in two parallel scenes framing a narrative aside on God's evaluation of Abram that links the two. The first scene focuses largely on the promise of an heir. The second scene focuses largely on the promise of land for the heirs to inherit.

A. Yahweh promised innumerable heirs (15:1–5).
   1. Yahweh promised security and reward (15:1).
   2. Abram requested assurance (15:2–3).
   3. Yahweh clarified and certified his promise (15:4–5).

B. Abram was righteous by faith (15:6).

A'. Yahweh promised a future inheritance (15:7–21).
   1'. Yahweh reiterated his land promise (15:7).
   2'. Abram requested assurance (15:8).
   3'. Yahweh clarified and formalized his promise (15:9–21).

Between scenes, Moses interjects an evaluation of Abram that prepares for the formal covenant. Based on Abram's consistent confidence in Yahweh's word up to this point, Yahweh considered him righteous (15:6). This comment founds God's imputation of righteousness in faith rather than actions, and it provides significant background for the covenant. God guaranteed his promise to righteous Abram, in contrast to the current inhabitants, and with significance for the future inhabitants of the land.

The two scenes further specify, integrate, and formalize the promise of land and descendants through a covenant ceremony. Yahweh continued to build and develop his promises from chapter 12, as Abram grew in faith. These two intertwined promises would form the coalescing basis for the expectation of Israel as a nation in the land of promise throughout the Old Testament and God's purpose to bring blessing to all the families of the earth (12:3), leading to the prophetic hope of the new covenant (e.g., Ezek. 36–37).

- ***Yahweh Promised Innumerable Heirs (15:1–5)***
- ***Abram Was Righteous by Faith (15:6)***
- ***Yahweh Promised Abram a Future Inheritance (15:7–21)***

EXPOSITION

The Abram stories build on the promise from Yahweh to make Abram a great nation (12:2) residing in a promised place (12:7) so that they can be the channel to bring blessing to all the families of the earth (12:3). Those promises to Abram in chapter 12 are reiterated, expanded, formalized, and guaranteed progressively through Abram's narratives (13:15–17; 15:4–5, 7, 13–21; 17:2–8, 16, 19; 18:18–19; 22:16–18) and beyond (26:4; 28:14;

1 A covenant can simply be defined as "a formal agreement involving two or more parties" (Knoppers 1996, 696). That agreement defines the expectations for the relationship between them.

35:11–12). Genesis 15 presents a key passage, both in the structure of the Abram narratives (see the Introduction, Narrative Structure of Genesis, p. 68, and the Introduction to the Abraham Narratives, p. 236) and in the progression of the promise, enacting the formal covenant. In the overall *toledot* structure, Genesis 15 and 17 form the center of the chiasm, emphasizing the covenant (formally enacting and establishing the sign of the covenant, respectively) and the certainty of the promises to those in appropriate relationship with Yahweh. In Genesis 15, in a prophetic vision, Yahweh assured Abram of security and reward, including innumerable direct descendants. He also acknowledged Abram's righteousness by faith and clarified the prolonged and painful time and extent of the promise to accomplish justice and grant the land to Abram's heirs, confirming it through formal covenant.

Yahweh Promised Innumerable Heirs (15:1–5)

Yahweh promised and clarified security and reward for Abram.

Yahweh Promised Security and Reward (15:1)

In a prophetic vision, Yahweh assured Abram of security and reward.

15:1. The initial "After these things" acknowledges some time lapse but, more significantly, relates God's revelation to Abram with what has just taken place. Genesis 15 draws heavily from the imagery of Genesis 14 to emphasize the correlation between the covenant and the faith of Abram.[2] Moses affirms Abram's righteousness because of his faith (v. 6), on display in the previous narrative, as the centerpiece of this section, highlighting God's expectation for those in relation with him.

"The word of the Lord came to" Abram, (הָיָה דְבַר־יְהוָה אֶל) introducing Yahweh's revelation to Abram, using a unique expression in the Pentateuch[3] that introduces prophetic revelation over one hundred times in the rest of the Old Testament (e.g., 1 Sam. 15:10; 2 Sam. 7:4; Isa. 38:4; Jer. 1:2; Ezek. 1:3). The implication of Abram's prophetic status (confirmed in Gen. 20:7), strengthened by his "vision" (מַחֲזֶה, only four times in the OT: Num. 24:4, 16; Ezek. 13:7), draws attention to his direct audience with Yahweh and legitimates the prophecy that Abram will receive (Gen. 15:13–16).

Yahweh's assurance to Abram would continue to clarify Abram's expectations from Yahweh's promises. God's encouragement to "fear not" may be directed at his reaction to theophany (Mathews 2005, 163), a reflection on the response of the kings he had just defeated (Sarna 1989, 112), or a concern for God's promise of offspring (Sailhamer 1990, 128). Considering God's assurance, however, it may be a complex concern both for safety ("shield," v. 1) and for the specific out working of the promises (heir).

God's pledge included both his protection and reward. The image of a "shield" (מָגֵן), a common metaphor for protection (e.g., Deut. 33:29; Pss. 3:4; 7:11), also recalls

2 Sarna (1989, 112) lists a dozen parallels between chapters 14 and 15, and Zucker (2018) shows both the unity of 13–15 and the linkages between 13–14 and 15 as discreet but connected units. Parallels Sarna lists include key terms (e.g., Heb. root *mgn* [מגן], 14:20; 15:1; "covenant" [בְּרִית], 14:13; 15:18), word associations (e.g., Damascus, 14:15; 15:2; Salem, 14:18; and peace, 15:15), and key ideas (e.g., warfare in 14 and "fear not" as God's address, 15:1; reward and possessions of Abram and his descendants, 15:1, 14 [with use of "possessions," רְכוּשׁ 15:14 and in 14:11, 12, 16, 21]).

3 It also occurs in verse 4 with the unexpressed verb, the only other use of "the word of the Lord" in the Pentateuch.

Melchizedek's proclamation that God Most High had delivered (מִגֵּן, from the same root) Abram's adversaries into his hand (Gen. 14:20). The wordplay on the verbal meaning "give" also looks ahead to what will follow (Rendsburg 1992, 268). Yahweh would continue to protect and deliver Abram. In fact, he would provide a very great "reward" (שָׂכָר, v. 1). Abram had refused his legitimate claim to the spoils of war, trusting in God to prosper him (14:22–24; cf. 12:2), and God assured him that his reward would be very great.[4]

TRANSLATION ANALYSIS 15:1
The vision is cryptic, allowing for different translations depending on what the translator supplies. If the clause parallels the previous clause, Yahweh is also the reward, emphasizing the source of that reward, "I am . . ., your very great reward" (NIV, cf. NKJV). If the clause provides additional explanation, the focus is on the extent of the reward, "your reward shall be very great" (ESV, NASB95, NJPS).

Abram Requested Assurance (15:2–3)

Abram asked Yahweh what to expect for the promised heir since he had none.

15:2–3. Abram responded with concern not for prosperity, but for an heir. God's promise had indicated he would become a "great nation" (12:2), "as the dust of the earth" for number (13:16) inhabiting this land (13:15). Yet, as Abram lamented, he was "childless" (15:2) and in danger of the promise going unfulfilled. Wenham (1987, 328) notes that Abram's childlessness not only goes against the promise but the expectation of Genesis (cf. 1:28; 9:1; 26:24; 35:11). Abram questioned the reward ("what will you give me," 15:2) since he felt as if he was going to die childless. Yet his lament does not come from lack of faith (v. 6).

TRANSLATION ANALYSIS 15:2a
Even his address to God may indicate his faith. "Sovereign LORD" (NIV, אֲדֹנָי יֱהוִה) may be a better translation than "Lord GOD" (ESV, and most translations) based on Ugaritic parallels and Abram's previous recognition of Yahweh as the sovereign creator (14:22; Eissfeldt, אָדוֹן, *TDOT* 1:62–72; Wenham, 1987, 327).

TRANSLATION ANALYSIS 15:2b
The Hebrew participle (הוֹלֵךְ) translated "continue," with the idea of "live," can mean "pass away, die" (cf. Ps. 39:14, *HALOT* s.v. "הלך" 246–49), as translated by the NJPS (cf. ESV footnote). Considering Abram's age and stated concern for providing an heir, the latter seems preferable.

If Yahweh would not provide an heir, Abram felt the need to appoint an heir from his servants. Unfortunately, the text here is problematic. It seems that Abram is contemplating making Eliezer, who is from Damascus, his heir apparent, but God allays his fears so that he does not carry out the plan (Sarna 1989, 113). Verse 3 summarizes the concern: Abram wants a direct offspring for an heir, which is God's plan, albeit delayed until it can only be God's doing.

Eliezer

In Abram's world it was possible to adopt a slave as one's heir when there was no natural son. That adopted son would serve them for life, care for their burial, mourn them at death, and then inherit from them. If a son was born after the adoption, the adopted heir would no longer be the "chief heir" (Gordon 1940, 2).

4 Van Dam notes that God does not pay wages (as this term is often used with people as the source), but he gives gifts and rewards obedience (Van Dam, שָׂכָר, *NIDOTTE* 3:1245).

TRANSLATION ANALYSIS 15:2c
"The heir" (ESV, וּבֶן־מֶשֶׁק) uses a term that does not occur anywhere else in the Old Testament (מֶשֶׁק) and is uncertain. *HALOT* simply labels it "unexplained" (s.v. "מֶשֶׁק" 652). BDB conjectures "acquisition, possession" based on context and (uncertain) use of the similar מִמְשַׁק in Zephaniah 2:9 with the idea of "he who is to acquire, the heir of" (s.v. "מֶשֶׁק" 606), which is then the consistent English translation. The idea is clearly dealing with an heir (Gen. 15:3), but specifically what is expressed is difficult. For the various possibilities, see Hamilton (1990, 420–22) and Sarna (1989, 382–83). As Mathews (2005, 165) concludes, "at least we can say that the present form of the text possesses a wordplay between *mešeq* ('heir') and *dammeśeq* ('Damascus') which plays up that the inheritance will go to an alien (cf. Jer 49:1)."

Yahweh Clarified and Certified His Promise (15:4–5)
Yahweh affirmed that the heir would be from his body and become innumerable.

15:4. Yahweh affirmed Abram's appeal with a second word from the creator. Dismissing Eliezer without direct reference (lit. "this one"), Yahweh declared Abram would have his own son, from his own body. The initial concern was the source of the heir. Abram would be the source, physically. Therefore, the great nation was promised from an old man that appeared to have no prospect of any descendants.

TRANSLATION ANALYSIS 15:4
The Hebrew uses a term that refers to the inner part of the body or "that part of the body through which people come into existence" and can refer to males or females (HALOT s.v. "מֵעָה" 609–10). So, the various translations try to clarify, such as "your very own son" (ESV), "your own flesh and blood" (NIV), "one who will come forth from your own body" (NASB95), or "your very own issue" (NRSV, NJPS).

15:5. Yahweh addressed the second concern with a visual aid. Yahweh had already used dust as a simile for the number. Now he took Abram outside and used the stars of the heavens to describe his anticipated outcome. Reminiscent of the creative command in Genesis 1, Yahweh declared the future existence of Abram's seed, like the stars of the heavens—without number. The Creator of heaven and earth (14:19, 22), who spoke the stars into being, declared by his word (15:1, 4) the future existence of Abram's innumerable descendants (15:5).

Abram Was Righteous by Faith (15:6)
God counted Abram righteous based on his faith.

15:6. Ironically, Moses does not give Abram's immediate reaction, per se. Rather he provides an editorial comment on Abram's ongoing response to Yahweh up to and including this vision. Abram had not just finally believed, but he had been showing faith in Yahweh since he left Ur (12:1; 15:7) as evidenced by his cross country trek, sojourn in Canaan, and deliverance of Lot, as well as declared by his consistent worship (12:7, 8; 13:4, 18; 14:20) and pronouncements (12:8; 13:4; 15:22). Abram continues what he has been demonstrating. He "kept believing" Yahweh (Rogland 2008, 241). He consistently trusted in Yahweh, taking him at his word and acting on it. Yahweh, then, considered him "righteous" (צְדָקָה), laying the groundwork for the covenant.

TRANSLATION ANALYSIS 15:6a
Several English translations begin verse 6 with "and," giving the impression that Abram's response of faith is in sequence or as a result of the vision he has experienced (e.g., ESV, NKJV, NLT, NRSV). Even more suggestive is NASB95 with "then." The Hebrew text, however, indicates this is not sequential. Rather than the normal narrative sequence of the *waw* on a preterit, indicating continuing

sequence, verse 6 begins with a *waw* on a perfect, indicating disjunction or background information (WOC, §32.3e, 541), which they translate, "Now he trusted YHWH and he counted *it* to him as righteousness" (as a parenthetical idea, WOC, §16.4f, 305). The construction presents a summary statement of Abram's faith (Ross 1988, 310), a typical or frequentative use of how Abram has responded (Longacre 1994, 56–66, 95) or, more specifically, a "habitual-iterative past" that should be translated "he *kept believing* Yahweh" (Rogland 2008, 241, emphasis his). *GKC* calls it "a longer or constant continuance in a past state" (§112 ss).

The assessment that Abram believed Yahweh declares that Abram considered God's word to be reliable—he trusted him (*hiphil* from אמן). When it is used with the *bet* preposition, as here, it includes action, responding to the message "with trust or obedience" (Moberly, *NIDOTTE* 1:431). Abram had displayed that action (mostly!) for the previous three chapters.

Yahweh had just challenged Abram to count the stars, and in view of Abram's faith, Yahweh has "counted" it to him as righteousness (15:6). In other words, he assigned or credited righteousness to Abram (Hartley, חָשַׁב, *NIDOTTE* 2:305). God's crediting Abram with righteousness presents an additional key theological concept. "Righteousness" (צְדָקָה) typically "indicates right behavior or status in relation to some standard of behavior" (Reimer, צָדַק, *NIDOTTE* 3:750). Here, however, the focus is not on the actions that his faith has produced but on the faith itself. He is acquitted by "the divine judge" based on his faith, which does then lead to right action (Wenham 1987, 330).

TRANSLATION ANALYSIS 15:6b

While some translations clarify that Yahweh counted Abram's faith as righteousness by repeating "Lord" (e.g., NET, NLT, NRSV) or clarify with word order that Yahweh is the subject, the Hebrew text does not express the subject and is not clear who considered it the righteousness of whom. The Hebrew could assert that Abram considered Yahweh as "righteous" (or "just," one traditional Jewish interpretation). Alternately, many rabbis understood the term translated "righteousness" to indicate "merit," which made Abram worthy of God's reward (Sarna 1989, 113). The broader context favors the traditional Christian view (Hamilton 1990, 424–25). The ESV, then, is appropriately ambiguous, though the New Testament (quoting the passive in the LXX) rightly understands Yahweh as the subject crediting Abram with righteousness (e.g., Rom. 4:9; James 2:23).

Abram's questions here, then, were not construed as "unbelief" (15:2–3, 8). But his attempts to complete the promise in his own culturally attuned means (ch. 16), his incredulity and reliance on his own plan (17:17–18), and his ongoing struggle to fully trust God's protection (20:1–13) suggest his faith is not fully formed. Kuruvilla (2014, 196–97) appropriately calls it "immature faith." Yet God, who looks at the heart, considers this growing faith as righteousness.

God's evaluation of Abram provides the basis for the covenant (the formal agreement on their relationship) that God is about enact with Abram. Relationship with God, and his promise of the land, requires righteousness by faith (cf. 6:9). Genesis 15:6, then, provides the connection with the second scene. It both concludes the first scene with a summary of Abram's faith and resulting position before Yahweh as righteous judge, but also provides the necessary backstory to Yahweh formalizing his covenant with Abram.

Yahweh Promised Abram a Future Inheritance (15:7–21)

Yahweh clarified the outworking of Abram's reward in the land for his heirs.

Yahweh Reiterated His Land Promise (15:7)

Reminding Abram of his working so far, Yahweh reiterated his promise of the land inheritance he had led Abram there for.

15:7. Paralleling verse 1, the second scene opens with a divine speech.[5] Whether this continues the initial vision (v. 1), broken only by the aside of Abram's righteousness, or whether this is a new vision is ambiguous. Time has passed. Verse 5 was at night, but this will be before the (next?) evening (the birds would only come in daylight hours, v. 10, and the sun begins to set in v. 11). God, then, approached Abram with his continued assurance by way of reminder.

As in verse 1, Yahweh declared his role in Abram's life. In verse 1 Yahweh was Abram's protector who would greatly reward him. Now he reminded Abram that he was the promise-maker who had brought Abram to this point. Of course, Yahweh's declaration raised the issue that Abram would continue to press. God had assured Abram of posterity, but now Abram asked for assurance on the inheritance of the land. Yahweh's statement reminded Abram of Yahweh's purposeful working in Abram's long and difficult journey to find the fulfillment of the promise, which would only be initially realized after hundreds of years of his descendants in servitude and affliction (v. 13).

Yahweh's review, however, would also remind Israel of his role in their lives, bringing them out of Egypt (Exod. 20:2; Deut. 5:6).[6] After the exodus, Yahweh would not only remind Israel of his working in the exodus, but he would remind them through these verbal parallels of his promises to Abram and that he had been at work long before their exodus. His goal and his guiding hand had been behind the scenes for centuries, even when they had no sense of his presence.

Abram Requested Assurance (15:8)

Abram requested assurance for the promised inheritance.

15:8. Abram's response showed his concern. He seemed to recognize not only that he did not have the land but that he could not really inhabit the whole land without the large number of descendants promised. It must be future—distant future. How would he know this would happen if it was so far away? Without the editorial assurance of verse 6, we might assume that Abram is doubting God's promise. With that context, however, Abram is not presented as testing God in unbelief but as looking for assurance and possibly clarification. He needed more details![7]

God responded with assurance of the promise in a formal covenant. He added details and explanation that delineated the promise more precisely and explained the outworking more clearly. The promise would not be immediate. It would be certain.

Yahweh Clarified and Formalized His Promise (15:9–21)

Yahweh promised possession of the land for Abram's descendants after a dark, oppressive sojourn in a foreign land, assuring the promise, including the extent of the land, with a formal covenant.

In the final section of the second scene, Yahweh provides both a ritual visual aid to formalize his promise and accompanying explanation to set expectations. It flows in three parts. First, Yahweh instructed Abram to prepare for the ceremony (vv. 9–11) followed by the timing for inhabiting the inheritance

---

5 The parallels between the two scenes enhance the natural tie between the promise of heir and innumerable descendants (scene 1) with the promise of the land (scene 2), the timing of the promise (including how his descendants will become the large nation to take the land), and the extent of the land promise.

6 As has often been noticed, the phrase "I am the LORD who brought you out from" (15:7) is nearly identical with "I am the LORD your God, who brought you out of" (Exod. 20:2; Deut. 5:6).

7 Hamilton (1990a, 430) notes the use of *bammah* (בַּמָּה, "how," ESV, or "by what," NET) in "contexts where further supporting data is desired, see Exod. 33:16; Mal. 1:2, 6, 7; 2:17; 3:7–8."

(vv. 12–16) and the extent of that inheritance (vv. 17–21). The parallels in the final two subsections draw attention to the unity and certainty of the promise.

15:9–11. Yahweh responded to Abram's question by commanding Abram to prepare for a covenant ceremony to articulate and guarantee God's promise (v. 18). The animals required were mostly used in sacrificial service[8] and are all clean, but the issue here is covenant ceremony rather than sacrifice. The additional stipulation that the three animals be three years old is of uncertain significance, as is much of the symbolism of the ceremony.

While the recorded command only refers to bringing animals to Yahweh, Abram's response shows that he understood much more was involved, including the preparation of those animals appropriately for the ceremony. Each of the animals was divided in two, but the two birds were merely killed and all of them arranged as a pathway. The literal Hebrew expression "cut (כָּרַת, 15:18) a covenant" may come from this sort of ceremony. For the ceremony itself, see Exposition on verses 17–18 below.

After arranging the pieces, the text records that Abram had to drive off the "birds of prey" (הָעַיִט, v. 11). Sarna (1989, 115) identifies these as the "carrion-eating falcon," which was representative of the Egyptian god Horus, who was also identified in Egypt with the living king. Given the symbolic nature of the ceremony and what follows, this may foreshadow the danger of the nation in Egypt and their deliverance (Ross 2008, 112; Sarna 1989, 115), implying that the pieces of the animals represented Israel (Wenham 1982; Wenham 1987, 332).[9]

15:12–16. Falling into a deep sleep at dark and overcome with dark fear, Abram received an oracle from Yahweh promising possession of the land to his descendants only after a long and oppressive sojourn in a foreign land.

This oracle and the following vision of the actual ceremony (vv. 17–21) are structured with significant and intentional parallels to draw out the connection between the ceremony and the promise that it certified. Both sections follow the same structure, beginning with reference to the setting sun (vv. 12–13// vv. 17–18).[10] Each section then concludes with a divine promise regarding the future land that the descendants of Abram would possess (vv. 13–16//vv. 18–21).

15:12. The setting sun ties this oracle (vv. 12–16) to the following ceremony and explanation (v. 17–21) by pointing to the parallel structure (see Excursus above), their logical connection, and the symbolic significance. The importance of the sacrificial animals in verses 9–11, then, becomes clearer, representing Israel under attack but with the presence of God in their midst.

8 The "heifer" is only mentioned in the Torah for the unsolved murder ceremony and Samuel's sacrifice (עֶגְלָה, Deut. 21:1–9; 1 Sam. 16:2), and the "young pigeon" (גוֹזָל) is only mentioned in Deut. 32:11, outside of this passage. Wenham (1987, 331) supposes that it approximates the "young pigeon" (בן־יונה) used commonly in sacrifices.

9 Many OT rituals (sacrifice, covenant, ritual holiness and cleansing, worship and the arrangement of the tabernacle or temple, etc.) are brimming with symbolism, teaching the nation about the nature of God and the boundaries and expectations of relationship with him. Here Yahweh used the ritual to include both prophetic instruction and symbolic imagery of their future dangerous sojourn in Egypt. Our challenge as modern westerners includes determining and understanding what is symbolic and what that symbolism stood for in the mind of the original audience. For a helpful discussion, see Mary Douglas (1999, 2000, 2002).

10 After a clause marking the setting sun, a disjunctive describes the deep sleep (v. 12) or darkness (v. 17) that envelopes Abram. Then a *hinneh* clause in each sets the stage for the concluding divine oracle.

<table>
<tr><th colspan="2">Genesis 15:12–21</th></tr>
<tr>
<td>12 וַיְהִי הַשֶּׁמֶשׁ לָבוֹא

וְתַרְדֵּמָה נָפְלָה עַל־אַבְרָם
וְהִנֵּה אֵימָה חֲשֵׁכָה גְדֹלָה נֹפֶלֶת עָלָיו׃

13 וַיֹּאמֶר לְאַבְרָם
יָדֹעַ תֵּדַע
כִּי־גֵר יִהְיֶה זַרְעֲךָ בְּאֶרֶץ לֹא לָהֶם
וַעֲבָדוּם
וְעִנּוּ אֹתָם אַרְבַּע מֵאוֹת שָׁנָה׃
14 וְגַם אֶת־הַגּוֹי אֲשֶׁר יַעֲבֹדוּ דָּן אָנֹכִי
וְאַחֲרֵי־כֵן יֵצְאוּ בִּרְכֻשׁ גָּדוֹל׃
15 וְאַתָּה תָּבוֹא אֶל־אֲבֹתֶיךָ בְּשָׁלוֹם
תִּקָּבֵר בְּשֵׂיבָה טוֹבָה׃
16 וְדוֹר רְבִיעִי יָשׁוּבוּ הֵנָּה
כִּי לֹא־שָׁלֵם עֲוֹן הָאֱמֹרִי עַד־הֵנָּה׃</td>
<td>17 וַיְהִי
הַשֶּׁמֶשׁ בָּאָה
וַעֲלָטָה הָיָה
וְהִנֵּה תַנּוּר עָשָׁן וְלַפִּיד אֵשׁ
אֲשֶׁר עָבַר בֵּין הַגְּזָרִים הָאֵלֶּה׃
18 בַּיּוֹם הַהוּא כָּרַת יְהוָה אֶת־אַבְרָם בְּרִית לֵאמֹר
לְזַרְעֲךָ נָתַתִּי אֶת־הָאָרֶץ הַזֹּאת מִנְּהַר מִצְרַיִם עַד־הַנָּהָר הַגָּדֹל
נְהַר־פְּרָת׃ 19 אֶת־הַקֵּינִי וְאֶת־הַקְּנִזִּי וְאֵת הַקַּדְמֹנִי׃ 20 וְאֶת־הַחִתִּי
וְאֶת־הַפְּרִזִּי וְאֶת־הָרְפָאִים׃ 21 וְאֶת־הָאֱמֹרִי וְאֶת־הַכְּנַעֲנִי וְאֶת־
הַגִּרְגָּשִׁי וְאֶת־הַיְבוּסִי׃</td>
</tr>
</table>

Notice the parallels:

1. The introduction is nearly identical, with the sun going down.
2. The next clause is disjunctive (background), describing a deep sleep on Abram (v. 12b) parallel to the darkness of the vision (v. 17c).
3. Each is followed by a formal parallel with a deictic *hinneh* clause, pointing to the fearful great darkness overwhelming Abram (v. 12c) and the vision of the smoke and fire moving between the pieces (v. 17d).
4. Then God speaks in each section:
    a. Reference is made to land (not theirs, v. 13; and then given to them, v. 18).
    b. Both include relations with foreign nations.
    c. Both relate their entry into and promise of this land.
    d. The first oracle precedes and leads into the second oracle.

As occurs consistently through these narratives, significant background information is provided with disjunctive sequence. Here, Abram is overcome by a "deep sleep" (תַּרְדֵּמָה). In its limited Old Testament uses, this often describes God's imposition on people for his purposes, both figuratively and literally (Gen. 2:21; 1 Sam. 26:12; Isa. 29:10). In this case it continues the medium for God's revelation to Abram of the future of his descendants.

In his deep sleep, a "dreadful and great darkness" fell on Abram (v. 12). The experience is ambiguous. It could reflect the meeting with God in theophany (Wenham 1987, 331–32), or it could prefigure the coming dangers to promise in the delay, the oppression of his descendants, or the dangers to his progeny from the iniquity of the Canaanites (Stigers 1976, 155, suggests all of these). While theophany certainly produces similar feelings and images, the terms usually result from Yahweh's presence in warfare or judgment ("terror" or "dreadful" in the ESV, see Exod. 15:16; 23:27; Josh. 2:9; and "darkness," Isa. 8:22; Ps. 82:5). Here the following verses focus on the oppression of his descendants, which suggests the connection with both the "great terror" (NET Bible) and the birds of prey in the previous verse (Ross 1988, 311). The generation hearing this from Moses would identify deeply with these images as they reflected on their time in Egyptian captivity.

15:13–14. The oracle that Abram received responded to how he would "know" (אֵדַע, v. 8) that he would possess the land. Yahweh answered he could "know for certain" (יָדֹעַ תֵּדַע, v. 13), which would be certified in the ensuing ceremony (vv. 17–21), but what followed immediately was unexpected. His descendants would not receive it soon, but they would "sojourn" (live as "strangers," *HALOT* s.v. "גֵּר" 201) in a foreign land and be "afflicted for four hundred years" (v. 13) before coming back to inherit the land.[11]

Yahweh's timeframe aids Abram's expectations and was crucial for Israel to read later. Their long and painful sojourn was not only expected but part of God's greater plan. As they would see in the Joseph stories, it was intended by God for good. God anticipated their struggle, both in its length, intensity, and end point, so Israel's exodus was already planned in God's mind long before they cried out (Exod. 2:23–24).

It also declared God's justice for their oppression. He does not plan and sanction evil, but he will justly judge and hold all parties accountable. Israel will be vindicated and rewarded, like Abram's experience in Egypt (Gen. 12:10–20). If God would deliver and care for Abram, who acted foolishly, how much more would he deliver and care for Abram's offspring of promise, oppressed through no fault of their own?

15:15–16. At the same time, God assured Abram that he himself would be cared for. The assurance that Abram would "go to [his] fathers in peace" (v. 15) declared that none of the horrors he had seen anticipating the slavery of his descendants would affect him in his lifetime (cf. 2 Kings 22:20; 2 Chron. 34:28). Instead, God's blessing on him (Gen. 12:2) would be evident even in his long life (Deut. 6:2; 1 Kings 3:14; Pss. 21:4; 91:16).

God's assurance that the descendants of Abram would return to possess the land in verse 16 again provides a rationale for the timeframe, which allows for both God's justice and his grace. While God was clearly announcing that he would judge the iniquity of the Amorites, he was also providing grace.[12] The judgment would not fall until it was fully necessary. An announcement of judgment allows opportunity for repentance (Jonah 4:2)! As we will note below, it also declares a condition for those occupying the land. They cannot persist in their iniquity and remain in this land. God has specific plans that will be accomplished—to bring blessing to all the families of the earth (Gen. 12:1–3).

At the same time, God implied a reason for Israel to be in another land during this time of

11 The prediction of four hundred years appears to conflict both with the four generations of verse 16 and the 430 years of Exod. 12:40–41. Kitchen's (2003, 355) solution solves the latter problem by viewing the four hundred years as a round number looking forward and the 430 years as the more precise elapsed time for the events. Kitchen (2003, 356) cites Shamshi-Adad I of Assyria (from about the same time period) who used a cognate word to the Hebrew translated "generation" in verse 16 (דּוֹר) in a very similar way so that the "generation" (or "lifetime," Hamilton, דּוֹר, *NIDOTTE* 1:930–31) is between seventy-five and one hundred years in that document as well. Mathews (2005, 174–75) supports the correlation of the "generation" to approximately one hundred years from the OT context.

12 "Amorites" can occasionally refer to the whole population of Canaan by metonymy (cf. Amos 2:10) or, more often, a specific people group in the land (Gen. 15:21; G. Long, "Canaanites, Amorites, and Israel," *NIDOTTE* 4:457–60).

grace, which will be fleshed out later. The sin of their neighbors has already been noted (13:13) and the dangers documented (ch. 14, culminating in chs. 18–19). Israel needs to grow into a great nation (Exod. 1:7) while being protected from the evils and false worship of these peoples so that God can bless them and use them for his purposes (Deut. 7). The dangers of assimilation and intermarriage (Gen. 38) and subsequent idolatry will become a recurring theme throughout Israel's history (Deut. 30:15–20; Josh. 23:13; Judg. 2:1–3; 1 Kings 9:1–9). While Egypt will not keep them from idolatry (Josh. 24:14), it will isolate them and allow them to grow into a nation, prepared for Yahweh's purpose even while he graciously allows time for Canaanite repentance.

15:17–21. After dark, God confirmed his covenant symbolically, promising Abram's descendants the entire land currently inhabited by ten people groups. Parallel to the previous oracle (vv. 12–16) and within the same vision, Yahweh visualized the covenant for Abram and explained the promise, fleshing out the specific land that Abram's descendants would inherit. The parallels emphasize the connection between the covenant promise of the land with the timing and terrifying preparation for the promise from the previous oracle. The certainty of God's gift and future hope will only come through the terrifying oppression, but it will come. God will certainly give them this land.

15:17. The ceremony is unexplained and somewhat uncertain, but the main point is clear. The text explains that God was verifying his promise to Abram by way of a formal covenant ceremony (v. 18). Because of the structural parallels with what immediately preceded, we expect the symbolism to relate as well.

The "fire pot" (תַּנּוּר) typically refers to an oven (for bread) or a furnace (for pottery or metallurgy), though this one is portable (Cornelius, תַּנּוּר, *NIDOTTE* 4:312–13). It does appear as a symbol for God's divine judgment (Isa. 31:9; Mal. 4:1 [HB 3:19]) but also for God's presence in theophany (with a different Hebrew term, כִּבְשָׁן, Exod. 19:18). The smoke (עָשָׁן) occasionally adorns God's presence (Exod. 19:18; Ps. 18:9; Isa. 4:5; 6:4). The "torch" (לַפִּיד) can also refer to "lightning," which accompanies the theophany at Sinai (Exod. 20:18). The flame (אֵשׁ) is the fourth element that also appears in the theophany at Sinai (Exod. 19:18). Because Israel is hearing this on coming out of Egypt, the correlation with the theophany on Sinai is significant. They would have made those connections, especially since the vision is all about their sojourn in Egypt and the exodus into Canaan. In addition, of course, are the pillar of cloud and fire that accompany Israel (Exod. 13:21–22), supporting Wenham's (1987, 332–33) correlation with theophany. While the specific imagery is unique and unexplained in Scripture, the multiple correlations with theophany emphasize God alone enacting his covenant while Abram watches in his vision.[13]

The details of the ceremony itself are also uncertain. Some have viewed this as divine self-imprecation.[14] Rather than imprecation, however, the ceremony formed a seal of God's

13 Shetter dissents, pointing out that there are two images, which fits a bilateral covenant better, and that the Land Grant Treaty does have implied conditions even when they are not always stated, which accords with the implications here that are fleshed out later in the Abraham stories (Shetter 2019, especially 166–72). While there are certainly conditions implied, they do not affect the ultimate outcome of the land given to the nation (the promise). They rather impact who will experience the benefits.

14 The only possible biblical analogy (Jer. 34:18–19) records a self-imprecation with a similar ceremony. Hasel (1981, 63–64, 70) points out that the differences are so significant that Jer. 34 should not be related to Gen. 15. In Jeremiah, the officials of Judah had made a covenant with Yahweh by cutting a calf in two and passing between the parts. By

promise (Hauan 1986, 341–46), as declared by Yahweh (Gen. 15:18). Wenham (1987, 332–33) suggests it symbolized Yahweh walking among his people, with the pieces representing Israel or its priestly leaders. Regardless of the details, God clearly personally guaranteed the disposition of the land (vv. 18–21) to Abram's descendants.

Abrahamic Covenant

The Abrahamic Covenant is generally related to a Royal Land Grant Treaty and often declared to be unconditional (Weinfeld 1993, 222–61, esp. 236–51). Similar sorts of grants were given by kings and appear as treaties in Hittite documents as well as later neo-Assyrian documents. The pattern of the Abrahamic covenant is closer to the older Hittite documents (Weinfeld 1993, 236), reflecting the gift of the king to one who has shown loyalty to him. In 17:1–2 and 22:16–18, however, the covenant appears to have conditions attached. Both the specific genre of the Land Grant as a distinct and clear form and the unconditionality of any covenant have been challenged, both from the ancient Near Eastern materials and from the biblical covenants (Knoppers 1996). In both cases conditions are implied even when they are not directly stated (Shetter 2019).

God's guarantee, however, does not absolve Abram or Israel of responsibility. Loyalty to the king is expected, and disloyalty will bring consequences. In this text, God is dispossessing the Canaanites who have been wicked (v. 16), and Abram is given the promise after being declared righteous (v. 6). While the fourth generation is promised to return to get the land (v. 16), they would not go in because of their sin (Num. 22:28–35). Similarly, Israel would be told that they must keep the law for blessing (as expressions of their loyalty, Deut. 6:4–5), including remaining in the land, but ongoing disobedience would forfeit the land and they would go into captivity (Lev. 26; Deut. 28). Clearly, while the promise of the land would be fulfilled (it is "irrevocable," Rom. 11:29), the ones who would participate in the promise would necessarily be loyal subjects.

15:18–21. Yahweh, then, made a covenant with Abram, promising his descendants the land that they would eventually possess from the "river of Egypt" to the "Euphrates" (v. 18). The boundaries are somewhat ambiguous, though, in any case, Israel never fully possessed the geographical boundaries.

The River of Egypt

The "river of Egypt" (15:18) may refer to the eastern-most branch of the Nile (Waltke and Fredricks 2001, 245), the Wadi el-'Arish (Mathews 2005, 176), or possibly Nahal Bezor (M.Görg, "Egypt, River of," *ABD* 2:378). Similarly, "the great river, the river Euphrates" (v. 18) is usually understood to correctly be identified with the Euphrates, but Kaiser (1981, 304) dissents, positing the *Nahr el-Kebir* on the border of Lebanon and Syria.

After giving a general geographic outline of the land, Yahweh identified ten people groups that Israel would dispossess. The list of ten nations represents all the inhabitants of the land, though the lists of nations vary.[15] The list of

Yahweh's response, it appears they invoked a curse on themselves that if they were to break the covenant, they would forfeit their lives like the calf. A similar sort of curse is invoked in the "Treaty Between Ashurnirari V of Assyria and Mati'ilu of Arpad" (*ANET*, 532). Yahweh was calling them to pay the price for their breach of covenant by announcing their impending doom. Self-imprecation, however, does not fit God's eternal character. Elsewhere he has sworn on his life ("as I live," e.g., Num. 14:21, 28; Deut. 32:40), not the threat of death, which is impossible for him. It may also be noted that in both Jeremiah and the similar case of Mati'ilu the subject takes the oath, not the sovereign.

15 The lists vary in number and composition, though six is the most common number, e.g., Exod. 23:28 (three nations); Exod. 13:5 (five nations); Exod. 3:8, 17 and many others (six nations); Deut. 7:1 (seven nations); some

nations, or ethnographic boundaries, seems to fit the actual occupation of the land better than the geographic boundaries, prompting Waltke to suggest that the geographic boundaries are an idealization to show the greatness of the future nation (Waltke and Fredricks 2001, 245).

This narrative, then, has reached a key turning point in the Abraham stories. The initial promise has become much clearer, including both his progeny (innumerable multitude coming from his body) and the boundaries of the land promised and peoples to be dispossessed. While clarifying the promise, Yahweh formalized it with a covenant, certifying the claim of Abram's descendants and asserting his requirement that permanent residents must be loyal to him alone.

THEOLOGICAL FOCUS

Based on his righteous and just control over history and nations, and his servants' faith, Yahweh secures his promises for his righteous people, despite struggle, through his covenant.

Yahweh displays his care, confirming his consistent presence and certain fulfillment of his promised blessing to his follower. God may allow a time without clear affirmation, but he also gives significant and opportune reminders, clarifying expectations, certifying his promise, and showing his control over history and humanity to his trusting servant. With Christ, God has provided even greater access to his presence and opportunity to gain insight into the working of his program. In the progress of revelation, God has given gracious, caring, and concerned clarification to the concerns of his people. As Israel would have understood far more of the implications of his revelation to Abram, so the modern believer is able to benefit even more greatly from his revelation through the ages.

At the same time, God presented his full and just control of his creatures and their history as the creator of the universe. He declared coming events, from the number of Abram's personal physical descendants and the boundaries of their future home to his just response to evil, showing his sovereignty over all nations. He revealed his gracious and long-suffering nature that would wait until justice was required. Yet he declared that he would judge when needed.

By developing his promises over time and with greater detail, Yahweh shows his consistency to his word and his control of history. He demonstrates that he rewards loyalty and faith on those who follow him in faith (17:1–2; 22:16–18), even when that faith is not yet fully formed in maturity. Appraising Abram's response to God's initial command with the resultant promise (12:1–3), the affirmation of Abram's faith and consequent credit in God's eyes even before the official covenant set the benchmark for God's people who would enjoy the relationship of covenant with Yahweh. Anyone walking with God, enjoying his protection and presence, as affirmed in the initial verse (15:1) and visualized in the ceremony, must believe him in faith that acts. Yet he or she must realize that God would indeed also respond with appropriate justice for failing to seek Yahweh (Exod. 33:1–3; 34:10–16; Amos 5:4–17; cf. Hauan 1986).

When God declared judgment would come in four hundred years (Gen. 15:1; 20:7), the implication for the nations included his compassion even for the wicked and their opportunity to repent (Jer. 18:7–10). Their hope was expressed by Abram, consistently and publicly acknowledging God's character (Gen. 12:8; 13:4). As noted, however, God's justice will come.

Humankind, then, appears here as deserving God's judgment but experiencing his patience as he crafts a response that will take time to develop and accomplish his plan of blessing all families. God is neither hurried nor unintentional in his response, but neither is he tardy, regardless of

---

would include Gen. 10:15–18 (twelve nations); cf. P. E. Satterthwaite and D. W. Baker, "Nations of Canaan," *DOTP*, 596–605.

how we may feel in our limited perspective. He will bring about his goal in his time and according to his purposes, even through painful waiting. That goal, however, will necessarily be developed through succeeding covenants to show the conditions for the occupants of the land, the means to bring blessing, and the expectations of that blessing (Mosaic Covenant). It will require the expected kingship to lead his nation as God's representative (Davidic Covenant), and it must bring about and culminate in the needed heart change, with the clear revelation of the father and the ultimate and faithful high priest, king, and redeemer, Jesus Christ bringing all previous covenants to their culmination (New Covenant).

He will bring that goal about for those who are righteous before him by faith. The pivotal statement on Abram's faith provides a paradigmatic statement of God's assessment of faith as the basis for a righteous standing before him. It is with the righteous that God enacts covenant (e.g., Noah, 6:9, 18). Here that righteousness is acknowledged to be by faith. That faith, however, is faith that leads to right action which was and would continue to be displayed, even if not yet fully formed.

PREACHING AND TEACHING STRATEGIES

Exegetical and Theological Synthesis

God's pledge to Abram in verse 1 ("your shield . . . your reward") sets the stage for our response of faith, just as it did for Abram. God promises protection and reward; God promised, and Abram immediately took the conversation to the obstacles he was facing (v. 2, "childless"). You have got to admit that Abram's circumstances ("no offspring" in v. 3) and "the word of the Lord" (vv. 4–5) about Abram's offspring being as numerous as the stars are incompatible. In every sense, believing in God's unbelievable promises is miraculous. Abram leads the way for our own faith journey. This doctrine, often referred to as imputation, is critical for the Christian life. Faith alone is what God requires of his children. Faith alone leads to God declaring us right according to his standard of living.

Abram's response to God's instructions about arranging for a covenant ceremony is telling: his faith in God equals obedience to God. His zeal is seen in verse 11 ("Abram drove [the birds of prey] away"). Our fallenness will make such faith a fight throughout our lives, especially since the assurance God gave Abram included the need for patient endurance (v. 13, "afflicted for four hundred years"). God has designed redemptive history to include our suffering; in this sense we follow our Savior's experiences on earth leading up to the cross and the new covenant in his blood.

Finally, within the covenant ceremony that God carried out, verse 16 teaches us about God's overall plan for history ("for the iniquity of the Amorites is not yet complete"). I don't like the thought of ongoing pain and persecution, but the promises of God stand within the context of all that. Most of your listeners will confess that they trusted God more during times of trouble than in times of enjoyment. We know that our trials in this life contribute to our Christian maturity like nothing else. You will help your listeners continue to trust God for their deliverance, now and into eternity. The other side: God's justice will prevail, but not one minute before it is absolutely necessary. He is concerned for the wicked and for gracious justice. That may frustrate us when we want to see justice in our world right now, but it also will encourage us when we realize we are sinners saved by grace.

Preaching Idea

God said it, I believe it, he guarantees it, and I have to accept the suffering part.

Contemporary Connections

What does it mean?

Genesis 15 requires sufficient time explaining the opening promise of God to protect and reward Abram and all those God considers like him. There are differences to what that meant for Abram and Israel in the land versus our listeners today. Spiritual protection, for instance, does not always mean no physical or emotional trauma in this life. It does mean that God has defeated the archenemy of our souls and provides the power for wise living in the world. Reward is not always tangible or what we desire.

As stated above, verse 6 is crucial for an understanding of how any human being can enjoy fellowship with their Creator. This is a transaction that needs explaining: God makes a promise; a human being believes God, which shows over time in his response in life; God assigns a righteous status to that believer. Why is faith the key? Faith takes God at his word; faith assumes great risk because of the lack of certainty that requires faith (versus a sight kind of certainty). Believing puts the person in a relationship with God where he can direct and guide. The declaration of a right standing is matched by doing right by God. The default setting of the human heart exerts a gravitational pull away from faith alone toward some form of merit to earn such a right standing.

This narrative is instructive partly because there is nothing Abram could do, humanly speaking, to achieve the results God promised. While you do not want to get lost in all the details of the intricate covenant ceremony, you will want to address the significance of God sealing the deal by himself.

Is it true?

It is possible that many of your listeners will question the truthfulness of God's promised protection and reward due to their struggles. This is the time to highlight the place of affliction within the promise and the time frame of fulfillment (v. 13). We may not see the full picture in this life. First Peter 2:11 is a fitting way to remind your listeners that they are considered "sojourners and exiles" too. Ultimate salvation or experiences of the promises of God were never said to be without pain. God has been up-front with us about how patience, endurance, and hope are instrumental in our salvation. As has been said for centuries, there is no crown without the cross.

As stated above, the whole transaction of faith equaling righteous standing is unbelievable. You may want to spend time making sure your listeners understand that believing is the only thing a fallen human being can do in response to incredible promises. And, of course, genuine faith will always work itself out in loyalty to God's ways. Eternal life is beyond our ability to manufacture.

One good thing about preaching through Genesis is that Exodus is next. You might allude to the exodus story briefly to show that God's prophecy about Israel's plight in Egypt also came true just as he said (Gen. 15:14 "afterward they shall come out with great possessions").

Now what?

The promises of God and believing those promises is as relevant as it gets! Everything about the Christian life is miraculous from start to finish (realizing, of course, there is no finish!). Every day is an opportunity to trust in the promises of God or to trust in what temptation is promising. The righteous standing that God credited to your listeners' account the moment they believed the gospel is something that is worked out every day. It is one way to frame one's walk with God. Faith leads to righteousness; unbelief leads to unrighteousness. So, in one sense, if you want to attack disobedience, you must first attack foundational unbelief because every act of disobedience is first and foremost an act of unbelief.

And I cannot think of anything more relevant than letting your listeners know that the promises of God are always being worked out in a badly broken world where suffering is real but temporary. And God is with us through the struggle. The apostle Paul refers to our troubles as "light momentary affliction" that "is preparing for us an eternal weight of glory beyond all comparison" (2 Cor. 4:17).

Creativity in Presentation

A suggested preaching idea for this chapter is: God said it, I believe it, he guarantees it, and I have to accept the suffering part.

You might flesh this out with the following sequence of thought:

> Begin with God's promise contained in the prophetic vision (vv. 1, 4–5, 18–21); include both aspects of protection and reward.
>
> Then highlight Abram's response of faith and the righteous standing announced (v. 6; which also includes his questions for clarification in vv. 2–3, 8; faith does at times have its doubts and concerns, and God honors that). Make the promise as unbelievable as it is by thinking of a modern-day parallel promise (saying to an elderly retiree who is barely able to live on a low fixed income: "You will earn millions of dollars.). Highlight that our faith is not without questions or entertained doubts, but God has always awarded genuine faith that is not yet fully mature. Spend time helping your listeners feel how absurd the transaction is of granting righteousness for faith alone. The more everyone feels how unnatural that is, the more the grace of God will shine. This is especially important in a time when most everyone in society believes in the inherent goodness of the human heart (see the research by Mercadante in *Belief without Borders*, especially chapter 26, Human Nature, on pages 126–154).
>
> Finally, devote time to God's covenant ceremony with all its assurance, plus the forecast of affliction (vv. 7, 9–17). The scene is filled with opportunities to use the senses to help your listeners feel the covenant process. God alone, not Abram, completes the covenant, guaranteeing its fulfillment in history. God's covenant with Abram becomes the foundation for other agreements God makes with his people throughout redemptive history, culminating in the new covenant sealed with the sacrifice of Christ.

On the other hand, following the flow of the narrative you could structure it based on the progression of promise.

- God presents "outlandish" promises that contradict our experience or ability to verify them (vv. 1–5).
- Our faith in him, however, seals our righteousness before him (v. 6).
- Therefore, he guarantees our future hope, though it may be through painful waiting (vv. 7–21).

DISCUSSION QUESTIONS

1. Describe the kind of "shield" and "reward" God promises for Christians today.
2. What kinds of circumstances cause Christians to doubt God's promises?
3. How does the prophecy of temporary affliction in verse 13 help offset our bouts with doubt?
4. What should we expect from God's presence amid our trials?
5. How do Abram's questions encourage us to respond to God when we feel uncertainty with God's Word?
6. How does God's declaration of his judgment coming for the Canaanites four hundred years ahead of time impact how you evaluate and feel about God's justice when it does come?

Genesis 16:1–16

EXEGETICAL IDEA

When Sarai pursued God's promise in the flesh from unbelief, breeding pain, conflict, and alienation, Yahweh rescued Hagar with promised blessing, rewarding her faith with a son and giving Abram and Sarai a lesson in faith to God's glory.

THEOLOGICAL FOCUS

Teaching faith and endurance for blessing through the pain of unbelief, God honors any who trust him, mitigating loss from faithlessness, fulfilling his promises, and lifting the humble to the praise of his glory.

PREACHING IDEA

It pays to patiently wait for the Lord's blessing rather than working out our own "blessing."

PREACHING POINTERS

Chapter 16 provides another opportunity for us to see how our sinful tendencies surface during lapses of faith. There is comfort knowing that we struggle in our faith journey just like God's finest did way back then. This time it is Sarai that finds herself in a most difficult situation for an Old Testament matriarch: she's barren. But she is resourceful and devises a plan to "obtain children by" Hagar, her Egyptian servant (16:1–2). We know that "ten years" had passed before we read those two fateful verbs again: "took" and "gave . . . to . . . her husband" (v. 3). "And Abram listened to the voice of Sarai" (v. 2); he didn't learn Adam's lesson back in Genesis 3:17.

The narrative shows how sin destroys relationships: Hagar turned on Sarai (v. 4), Sarai turned on Abram (v. 5), Abram abdicated any responsibility to do good by Hagar (v. 6), and Sarai "dealt harshly with" Hagar (v. 6). This is what happens whenever God's people take matters into their own hands. But in verses 7–14 what the angel of the Lord does and says to Hagar demonstrates God's mercy and intention to bless all who believe. His instructions to Hagar show how difficult obedience can be and how obeying goes against all our instincts (v. 9). Of all the people in the story, Hagar is the good example of a faith that works itself out in obedience. Even though the prophecy about Ishmael isn't all roses (v. 12), the narrative shows us that our God hears us and sees us when we're in pain (vv. 11, 13).

FAITH AND FAITHLESS: LEARNING IN GOD'S CLASSROOM (16:1–16)

LITERARY STRUCTURE AND THEMES

Following the pivotal declaration of Abram's faith, dramatic ceremony, and expanded covenant promises, the reader might expect the story to flow smoothly into the initial fulfillment and outworking. Instead, we find our heroes back in a dark valley and realize Abram's faith is not yet as formed as we expected. The crisis in Sarai's life spewed pain into her world, and Abram was powerless to address it.

The narrative, bounded by notes on Sarai's infertility and Abram's age, records Hagar's transition from personal servant to blessed mother of Abram's son with promise. At the end of the narrative, Abram has a son from his own body (15:4) and deep division and strife in his household. With the promise of innumerable offspring expected through Ishmael (16:10) and the repetition about Hagar bearing a son to Abram (three times in 16:15–16), it seems the promise is moving toward fulfillment, yet Sarai is left out and Abram has division and conflict instead of peace and blessing.

A. Sarai had borne Abram no children (16:1).
  B. Sarai's subversive scheming produced conflict and pain (16:2–6).
  B'. God's intervention provided promise and hope (16:7–14).
A'. Hagar bore aged Abram Ishmael (16:15–16).

The narrative follows two main movements with an introduction and conclusion. The initial verse provides the necessary background and problem of the narrative with the infertility of Sarai and the introduction to her personal servant, Hagar. The first movement focuses on Sarai attempting to salvage her honor as the patriarchal mother through her servant. She accomplished her ambition but added conflict, losing her place, her dignity, and her surrogate son, when Hagar fled (vv. 2–6). The second movement concentrates on Hagar, describing God's intervention by pursuing her (vv. 7–14). With God's promise reminiscent of his promise to Abram, Hagar acknowledged God's care. The narrative ends with Sarai absent and Hagar presented as the mother of Abram's son (vv. 15–16).

The structure emphasizes the painful consequences for Sarai's scheming. Yet, the narrative again demonstrates God's gracious intervention to establish his blessing to Abram and deliver the oppressed, rewarding Hagar's faith in contrast to Sarai's manipulations. Sarai found that her self-reliance, rather than trusting God, led to pain and complications, rather than fulfilling her expected outcome. God used foolish choices to teach his chosen couple another valuable lesson in walking by faith, though those choices would continue to bring struggle and ongoing lessons.

- ***Sarai Had Borne Abram No Children (16:1)***
- ***Sarai's Subversive Scheming Produced Conflict and Pain (16:2–6)***
- ***God's Intervention Provided Promise and Hope (16:7–14)***
- ***Hagar Bore Ishmael to Aged Abram (16:15–16)***

EXPOSITION

The frame of the section contrasts the role of Hagar as Sarai's Egyptian servant and Sarai's barrenness (v. 1, with Abram absent) with Hagar as the mother of Abram's son (vv. 15–16, and Sarai absent). The two intervening movements contrast the manipulation of Sarai to gain a child in unbelieving accusation of God (vv. 2–6) with the faith of Hagar in God's promise, celebrating God's care for her (vv. 7–14). The contrast in the frame highlights the differing outcomes for the response of faith (Hagar is the blessed mother of Abram's son) or unbelieving manipulation (Sarai has no child and languishes in the background). Pursuing God's promise in the flesh from unbelief, Sarai only bred pain and conflict, abusing and alienating Hagar, but Yahweh rescued Hagar with promised blessing, rewarding her faith with a son and giving passive Abram a lesson to God's glory.

Sarai Had Borne Abram No Children (16:1)

While Sarai had borne Abram no children, she had an Egyptian servant (16:1).

16:1. The initial verse grounds the story, as indicated by the initial disjunctive clauses, though the statements raise questions. On the heels of the elaborate ceremony and promises to Abram of a child from his own body, the narrative reminds the reader of the obstacles. The redundancy of Sarai's barrenness (cf. 11:30) seems initially to anticipate the greatness of the promise (ch. 15). The notice of the Egyptian servant reminds the reader, however, of a previous lapse of faith (12:10–20), and the two notes anticipate foreboding and uncertainties. The concluding *inclusio* (15:15–16) will clarify the implied censure for Sarai's faithlessness.

Sarai's Subversive Scheming Produced Conflict and Pain (16:2–6)

Blaming God for her barrenness, Sarai's demand for redress produced the desired child, resulting in conflict, pain, and loss rather than her expected status.

Act one of the narrative flows in two parallel scenes (Wenham 1994, 3):

A. Sarai complained to Abram about God's injustice, scheming for redress (v. 2a).
 B. Abram acquiesced to her proposal, accepting Hagar as his wife (v. 2b).
  C. Sarai acted without regard for Hagar who conceived and disdained Sarai (vv. 2–4).
A'. Sarai complained to Abram about Hagar's injustice, blaming Abram (v. 5).
 B'. Abram acquiesced to her proposal (v. 6a).
  C'. Sarai abused Hagar, who fled (v. 6b).

The parallel development of these two scenes highlights the painful consequences of Sarai's unbelief and resulting actions: Sarai maneuvered for a son and the assumed prestige but instead received contempt from her servant. Abram listened to his wife, compromising his faith, ceding his authority, and giving pain and frustration instead of blessing to Sarai and Hagar. Hagar moved from pawn to proud, to abused, and then to homeless.

16:2–4. Sarai addressed Abram, blaming her childlessness on Yahweh but offering her own solution. While childbearing was clearly the provenance of the gods in the ancient world and barrenness was their judgment (Walton 2009a, 67–68), Sarai's comment and scheme does not merely verbalize the obvious. Following the promises to Abram (12:2, 7; 13:15–16; 15:5, 13–16, 18), she asserts Yahweh's direct opposition to her. Rather than trust, she will present a culturally approved option that would both accomplish God's promise and maintain her status. Such a solution was common in her world. She could, therefore, assert that the children of this union would be hers, it would seem to fall within the parameters of what God has promised so far, and it would mitigate her apparent disfavor (Steinberg 1994, 50).

Surrogates

In Sarai's world, it was culturally acceptable for a barren wife to use a maidservant as a surrogate for her children, and they would be considered hers. The main wife had the rights over the child, and such a contingency could be built into the marriage contract to keep the girl from being replaced in her position as wife (Walton 2009a, 87). This common practice appears again in the actions of Leah and Rachel (30:1–22).

Unfortunately, however, she does not ask God in faith (e.g., Rachel, 30:6; or Hannah, 1 Sam. 1:10–12), nor go to her husband to ask God (e.g., Isaac for Rebekah, Gen. 25:21) either for the child or for further clarification. In fact, her expressed purpose was not the accomplishing of God's promise in providing seed for Abram according to promise. Rather, her expressed intent was to build up herself (אִבָּנֶה מִמֶּנָּה, lit. "I will be built up from her") revealing her unbelief (16:2). Her plot, then, was not only following social custom to accomplish God's promise but also an impatient attempt to subvert God's will and assure her own place in self-reliance (Drey 2002, 186–88). Rather than faith, much like Eve, Sarai believed God was withholding from her, so she attempted to secure her own desire apart from him. Not trusting God's good blessing for her, her ambition and faulty beliefs only brought her pain and conflict.

TRANSLATION ANALYSIS 16:2a

The verb "build" (בנה) was a common metaphor for building a family or having children (HALOT s.v. "בנה" 139), and so it is appropriately translated here as "obtain children" (ESV) or "build a family" (NIV), and so forth. The verb (אִבָּנֶה, 'ibbaneh) sounds like the Hebrew word for "children" or "sons" (בָּנִים, banim).

Abram passively accepted her proposal and "listened to the voice of Sarai" (16:2). The phrase "listen to the voice of" only occurs one other place in Genesis precisely as it is here: when God noted that Adam had listened to the voice of Eve (3:17). In addition, the next two verbs also occur in Genesis 3. Both Sarai and Eve "took" (לקח) something and "gave" (נתן) it to their husband (3:6; 16:3). These three terms in correlation add to the growing indications of Abram's (and Sarai's) faithless and fleshly attempt to secure their own future apart from God and foreshadow the coming pain that would result. The problem, then, was not that Abram listened to his wife (in fact, God told him to listen to her in 21:12!) but that he joined her in pursuing their goals apart from God and faith. One gets the feeling we have seen this before and it did not end well (12:10–20).

TRANSLATION ANALYSIS 16:2b

To "listen to" (שמע) often included accepting a request or even obedience (e.g., Gen. 22:18; *HALOT* s.v. "שמע" 1570–74), prompting "Abram did what Sarai told him" (NET, cf. NCV, NJPS, NKJV) or "Abram agreed to what Sarai said" (NIV, cf. NLT). Clearly Abram responded according to her expectation but contrary to faith.

For the first time in the Abram stories, Sarai is the focus. In verses 1–3 she is the subject, and she alone speaks. She gave Hagar to Abram. This focus on Sarai and her self-serving manipulation to become the mother of promise (vv. 1–6) contrasts with Hagar, who would trust when confronted with promise (vv. 7–14). The background frame noting their time in Canaan and Abram's age (vv. 3, 16) emphasizes the growing tension with God's promises and their impatience. The choice of "wife" repeated in verse 3 foreshadows Sarai's coming frustration with Hagar's position and the concluding emphasis on Ishmael as Abram's son, without mention of Sarai. Sarai, Abram's wife, gives Hagar to be Abram's wife.[1]

Sarai's plan seemed to happen as scripted, for a few months. When Hagar knew she was pregnant, however, she felt her importance and "looked with contempt" on Sarai (v. 4, וַתֵּקַל).

TRANSLATION ANALYSIS 16:4

The verb used of Hagar's contempt of Sarai is from the same root (קלל) as God's promise that he would curse anyone who "dishonors" Abram (12:3). However, here it is in the *qal* stem and indicates an attitude that would "count [Sarai] as nothing" (or consider her "insignificant" or even "despicable," cf. C. A. Keller, קלל, *TLOT* 1142), whereas 12:3 is in the *piel*, indicating to "designate as contemptible" or "declare cursed" (*HALOT* s.v. "קלל" 1104). "Look with contempt," then, (e.g., ESV, NRSV) or "despise" (e.g., NET, NIV) fit well, but "treat her mistress badly" (NCV) may imply physical mistreatment rather than attitude, which may mislead.

16:5–6. Sarah, recognizing that her scheme had backfired, shifted her blame to Abram, though she must come to him for redress. She labeled her treatment from Hagar "wrong" (חָמָס), which often refers to physical "violence" but here deals with broken "ANE family law" (Swart and Van Dam, חָמָס, *NIDOTTE* 2:178).[2] Hagar had overstepped her boundaries as a servant, even as the mother of Abram's son. Sarai invoked God's judgment on Abram for his role if he did not protect her.

In response, Abram gave Sarai freedom to respond as she saw fit, failing to even mention Hagar's name. Abram appears to be trying to be diplomatic, appease Sarah, and perhaps hope she would be gracious. In being passive, however, he shirked his responsibility, and he failed to be a blessing in his own family (12:2–3).

TRANSLATION ANALYSIS 16:6

The versions are accurate here. He is not instructing her to do the right thing (contra. Mathews 2005, 186). The phrase to "do what is right in your eyes" (16:6) leaves the standard up to the one being addressed, as is clear in 19:8 where the old man told the mob to do what was "right in their eyes" to his two daughters but not to the stranger. On the other hand, it appears to be talionic justice, since literally "her mistress was insignificant in her eyes" (16:4), so she was given to Sarai to do "what is good in your eyes" (v. 6, Kuruvilla 2014, 199, n. 51).

According to Hammurabi, Sarai could make Hagar a slave if she were aspiring to equal status. Hagar's intent is unclear, but Sarai treated her "harshly" (וַתְּעַנֶּהָ). The verb had just been used of Israel's treatment in Egypt (15:13, fulfilled in Exod. 1:11) and in the *piel* can describe anything from humiliation and physical or psychological oppression to violence (Wegner, עָנָה, *NIDOTTE* 3:449–52). The description indicts Sarai. Hagar fled, and the bright promise as God cut his covenant has turned tragic. Sarai lost her confidence in God, her prestige, her hope for a son, and her maid. Abram lost his perspective, an opportunity to lead his family to blessing, and his new wife and son. Hagar lost her security and her place of potential blessing. Apart from God's intervention, disaster was near.

---

1 Hagar is explicitly called a "wife" here (אִשָּׁה) rather than a concubine (פִּלֶגֶשׁ) and is only possibly referred to as a concubine in 25:6. Clearly, Hagar does not have status equal to Sarai and is in fact subjected to her will even after marriage to Abram, with Abram's consent. Hamilton (1990a, 445–46) argues she does have status, however, between that of a concubine and a wife.

2 Similarly, Mabee calls it a complaint before the *paterfamilias*, in which Sarai comes to Abram for legal protection, threatening him that God will judge if Abram does not respond (Mabee 1980, 198, 206).

Nadītu

According to the law of Hammurabi, #146, "If a man marries a *nadītu*, and she gives a slave woman to her husband, and she (the slave) then bears children, after which that slave woman aspires to equal status with her mistress—because she bore children, her mistress will not sell her; (but) she may place upon her the slave-hairlock and reckon her with the slave women" (Roth 2000, 345). *CAD* identifies a *nadītu* as a "woman dedicated to a god," so this would be analogous to Sarai's situation from a different status (s.v. *nadītu A*, n1:63). For the difficulties of relating the Laws of Hammurabi to biblical practice, see Frymer-Kensky (1981, 211–12).

God's Intervention Provided Promise and Hope (16:7–14)

The angel of Yahweh intervened to restore Hagar to Sarai with a promise, mirroring Abram's promise, for her future and her descendants, which she believed.

Act two of this narrative develops chiastically (Wenham 1994, 3):

- A. Geographical note: the angel "found" Hagar (v. 7)
  - B. Dialogue: The angel probed Hagar's purpose and movements, which she answered openly (v. 8)
    - C. Angel: Hagar must return to her place (v. 9)
    - C'. Angel: Hagar is blessed and secure (v. 10)
  - B'. Dialogue: The angel assured her son's future, which she responded to with faith and wonder (vv. 11–13)
- A'. Geographical note: Hagar memorialized God's care for her (v. 14)

This scene, then, centers on God's difficult demand for her submission to her mistress and corresponding promise of sharing in Abram's blessing, which prompted her response of faith and recognition of Yahweh's care for her.

16:7. The angel of Yahweh "found" (וַיִּמְצָאָהּ) Hagar by a spring in the wilderness. The basic idea of "found" as a consistent word pair with "seek" (בָּקַשׁ) "clearly connotes . . . the result of a search" (Grisanti, מָצָא, *NIDOTTE* 2:1061). God anthropomorphically looked for her. Hagar acknowledged and embraced God's gracious pursuit of her, a struggling foreign servant. The fact that it was on the way to Shur, in the western Sinai, implies she was heading back to Egypt, probably the only place she could think of to go. Feeling lost, she had been found and would react in wonder at God's care for her (vv. 13–14).

The Angel of the LORD

The "angel of the LORD" has been identified in various ways, from Christophany to theophany to a commissioned messenger from Yahweh. Since the use of messengers by royalty with all of the rights, privileges, and authority of the master, including first-person dialogue, was common in Abram's (and Moses's) world, it is not necessary to assume a corporeal appearance of Yahweh nor a pre-incarnate Christ (Walton 2009a, 87–88). It does not diminish the care of Yahweh for Hagar, nor the authority of the message for the angel to speak authoritatively for Yahweh.

16:8. The angel addressed Hagar with clear knowledge of her status and origin yet questioned her travel plans. Reminiscent of God's questions to Adam and Eve (3:9) or Cain (4:6, 9), the angel was not uninformed. Rather, he probed her heart. Hagar did not register surprise and, unlike Adam or Cain, she answered openly. She was running away. Without revealing her destination (and perhaps without a clear destination), she acknowledged her broken responsibility and relationship. Yahweh had pursued Hagar and arrested her attention with gentle grace and obvious interest.

16:9–10. In response to her openness, the angel presented three formal statements. He required her return (v. 9), promised her innumerable offspring (v. 10), and declared the future of her developing son (vv. 11–12). Verses 9 and 10 form the center of the section and the center of the four angelic speeches, pairing the incomprehensible requirement to return and submit to the abuse she had already run from with the bright promise of innumerable progeny. The verb he chose requiring she "submit" (ענה in the *hithpael*) echoed Sarai's harsh treatment (ענה in the *piel*, v. 6), requiring that she face her fear and her pain directly and return to Sarai and so to Abram, the chosen source of blessing. The following statement of progeny guaranteed her security despite her experience and her fears.

Again, the angel spoke, replicating God's promise of innumerable offspring to Abram, which she presumably knew (13:16; 15:5). The assurance of multiplication also recalls God's general blessing of multiplying offspring (1:28; 9:1, 7). Despite Sarai's jealousy and Hagar's own struggle with her place, her future was secure, and her baby was safe in God's blessed future. She was now tied to God's work through Abram, the father of her child, which God was promising to honor. The ambiguity of the promise would allow Abram to assume this was the fulfillment of God's word to him as well (17:18), but God would have other plans that would show his power and glory more clearly.

16:11–13. The angel's final oracle moved now to the specific child she was carrying. After finally acknowledging her abuse and declaring God's care for her as the basis for naming the child, he declared the future disposition and relation of the boy to his brothers. Hagar then responded in faith and wonder.

When the angel revealed her baby's sex, he for the first time also revealed that God was responding with specific care from her "affliction," using the noun from the root already used with Sarai's harsh treatment (v. 6) and her required submission (v. 9). Clearly God had judged as Sarai asked, bringing protection and comfort to Hagar rather than Sarai. Because God had "listened" (שָׁמַע, v. 11) to her affliction, he acted on her behalf. His working for her, then, was the basis for the name of Ishmael ("God heard"). This name would memorialize God's intervention, judging on behalf of Hagar and granting his blessing, mitigating Sarai's mistreatment. Abram's conferral of the name would provide an ongoing reminder for him (and Sarai) of their responsibility before Yahweh as well as God's intervention and promise.

> *TRANSLATION ANALYSIS 16:11*
> The Hebrew states literally that "the Lord has listened to your affliction" (v. 11 ESV) but by metonymy, it means that he heard her "cry of distress" (NLT) or "painful groans" (NET). God has, then, "paid heed to [her] suffering" (NJPS). Also, by metonymy, the assertion that God "hears" intends to convey that God also acts based on his attention, or "paid heed."

Verse 12 moves to the future disposition and relations of the boy. The angel called him a "wild donkey of a man." The "wild donkey" (פֶּרֶא) was a solitary animal in uninhabited places (Moore and Brown, פֶּרֶא, *NIDOTTE* 3:672–73). The metaphor describes an independent, uninhibited, and undisciplined person (Wenham 1994, 11) and is explained with pervasive conflict. The angel clarified by declaring that he would live a life of struggle and hostility to all around. The use of "hand" (יָד) figures prominently in this narrative, emphasizing the ongoing conflict. The maid who had been under the abusive hand of Sarai (ESV, "power," v. 6) must return and submit to her (lit. "under her hand," v. 9) and would raise a son whose hand would be against everyone, and theirs against him (v. 12). The conflict of power would be perpetuated.

Ishmael and his clan would settle in the Sinai and probably parts of Arabia ("Havilah to Shur," 25:18; cf. W. W. Müller, "Havilah," *ABD* 3:82), fulfilling the oracle that he would dwell "over against" his brothers (see 25:18

quoting the phrase from 16:12). His dwelling would fit his disposition as he would be on the fringe, opposite them or "against" them geographically and relationally.

TRANSLATION ANALYSIS 16:12
The final clause of verse 12 has numerous translations because of the prepositional phrase "over against" (ESV, וְעַל־פְּנֵי), which can be understood in a variety of ways, including "away from" (NET), "in hostility toward" (NIV), "east of" (NASB95), "in the presence of" (NKJV), and "alongside of" (NJPS). Genesis 25:18 uses the same phrase to describe the geographic settlement of the clan, suggesting a translation such as "opposite, facing" (*HALOT* s.v. "פָּנֶה" 944, §8.b.ii.), though it probably has hostile connotations (*HALOT* s.v. "פָּנֶה" 944, §8.c.iii.). Considering the preceding clauses, it may well indicate an attitude of defiance (Hamilton 1990, 454–55) or on the outskirts (NET, note 39) with a double entendre that is somewhat captured in "against" (ESV).

Hagar responded in grateful faith, recognizing God's care for her and memorializing it both in her characterization of God and her naming of the place (v. 14). Hagar praised Yahweh because he noticed her, resulting in his action toward her. For her, he was El Roi, or "the God who sees me." Her praise clearly is the basis for the following exclamation, though the precise translation is difficult. The ESV effectively shows her surprise that God had allowed her a glimpse of God and cared for her through the angel.

TRANSLATION ANALYSIS 16:13a
The pointing is unusual, leaving some ambiguity as to whether it intends a pronominal suffix, "sees me" (e.g., ESV marg., NET, NIV), or merely a gerund, "of seeing" (e.g., ESV, NASB95, NKJV; cf. *HALOT* s.v. "רֳאִי" 1162–63). The final exclamation in praise of God would favor the pronominal suffix. She may well have intended to characterize him by name, "You are El-roi" (NJPS, NRSV), though the result by translation is the same.

TRANSLATION ANALYSIS 16:13b
Westermann (1995, 247) calls the Hebrew text "incomprehensible", and many translations assume some degree of emendation to the text. RSV and NRSV emend "here" (הֲלֹם) to "God" (אֱלֹהִים) and add "remained alive," producing, "Have I really seen God and remained alive after seeing him?" The other challenges include interpreting the use of "after" (אַחֲרֵי), which can mean "after(ward)," "back," or "behind" (*HALOT* s.v. "אַחַר" 35–36), and whether to take the question as actual or rhetorical. Following Koenen (1988) and without emendation, it makes excellent sense as "Truly here I have seen him who looks after me," where "looks after" understands "sees" as caring for (ESV, cf. NET, NIV), or, if retaining the question, "Have I truly seen the one who sees me?" (NLT, cf. NKJV).

16:14. The spring, then, "was called Beer-lahai-roi" or the "well of the living one who sees me." Both her praise to God and the name of the place memorialize God's gracious care and provision for a runaway slave and her faith to respond and declare his goodness to her world. It also highlights the message of the story within the Abram narratives. People, even chosen and blessed people, may try to assure their own future, but it is God who must intervene and mitigate the cost of sin and self-effort, providing for the marginalized and powerless to bring blessing and a hopeful future as they respond in faith.

Hagar Bore Ishmael to Aged Abram (16:15–16)

Hagar bore Abram a son in his old age, commemorating God's provision in her struggle.

16:15–16. Without comment on Hagar's return, renewed relationships, or possible continued abuse, the narrator moves to Ishmael's birth. Abram continues to be silent in the narrative, and Sarai is absent. The narrative began by noting Sarai's barrenness (16:1). She then schemed to provide the promised heir, which she blamed God for denying her. Ironically, however, the child she engineered was never called hers, even though that was the cultural expectation and her right. Instead, she drove Hagar away and God intervened. Now Hagar, with God's promise equivalent to Abram's for innumerable offspring, is noted three times as the mother of Abram's son. We are not certain that he is not the child of promise (though we might expect he is not from the oracle). We do know, however, that Hagar is blessed, and Abram has a son in his old age.

Sarai's absence suggests the outcome for scheming and self-promotion over trusting God. Blessing comes by faith (ironically experienced by Hagar) and often after extended and painful waiting. Ishmael's naming according to the word of the angel (mentioned twice) reminds of God's intervention, hearing and responding to the abuse she endured. It also records her faith in returning, submitting, and recounting the story (and instructions) to Abram. Abram, to his credit, accepted her word and followed the angel's instructions naming Ishmael, because God had heard.

THEOLOGICAL FOCUS

Teaching faith and endurance for blessing through the pain of unbelief, God honors any who trust him, mitigating loss from faithlessness, fulfilling his promises, and lifting the humble to the praise of his glory.

As with several of the Abraham stories, the narrative begins with human scheming in unbelief, but God intervened spectacularly for his purpose and glory. God showed his care for the abused and marginalized and his faithfulness to his promises. God is faithful despite human, self-focused, faithless scheming. He honors his promise to the benefit of those impacted by sin when they respond in faith and obedience, offering hope and safekeeping, even through suffering and insecurity.

In doing so, Yahweh shows his intimate knowledge of individual circumstances and struggles, his care for the distressed, and their requisite faith. He would bless even a foreign slave who would respond to him in faith. He would also show his justice, answering the challenge of his choice matriarch to judge fairly, though it would cost her the immediate security and position she sought. Yahweh will teach the righteous growing lessons of faith and blessing, which often require patient waiting and endurance, from an unlikely, powerless, and socially suspect source. God does not bless manipulation, but he does reward faith. Sarai was correct that God is responsible for opening wombs and giving children, but his timing and purpose cannot be sidestepped or controlled. Waiting for the fulfillment of promise does not mean it will not happen. Rather, greater promises often seem to require longer waiting and so greater faith. Exploitation and self-promotion due to impatience will only lead to more pain and conflict, and perhaps even more waiting.

Hagar naming God and the well, and God naming Ishmael, all glorify God and his actions. The names appropriately memorialize his gracious intervention through faith and praise. Humanity has the responsibility to acknowledge and publicly praise the faithful interventions of God in his world. He deserves the appropriate acclaim. The praise of humanity provides the needed explanation for the watching world of the actions of their faithful God. Obedience by faith and publicly sharing the outcomes (e.g., Hagar relaying the message and Abram naming the child) also deliver the necessary caution or rebuke to both watching and participating skeptics.

God uses all things for good, bringing hope and promise to Hagar (and Ishmael) out of Sarai's foolish act and Abram's passive acceptance. God's people, however, often experience ongoing struggle and pain because of those foolish and unbelieving responses. Human action in response to felt needs must be in concert with the expressed and solicited direction of Yahweh, rather than in independent and culturally conditioned practices that ignore or attempt to circumvent the poorly or wrongly perceived working of God.

PREACHING AND TEACHING STRATEGIES

Exegetical and Theological Synthesis

The tension in this narrative begins immediately in verse 1 with the narrator's announcement of Sarai's barrenness. This creates what we know to be ten years of waiting on God's promise to Abram (v. 3). Patience is wearing thin and endurance is wearing down, creating the temptation to take matters into our own hands. Here are the ingredients for a crisis of faith. Two lexical connections tie the exegesis with the theology to tell us Sarai failed the test (and so did Abram). First, the end of verse 2 echoes back to Genesis 3:17 and the Lord's statement to Adam after he had sinned: "And Abram [like Adam] listened to the voice of" his wife. Second, like Eve, Sarai "took" and "gave" to her husband (cf. 3:6 with 16:3). What Sarai did was not good in the eyes of the narrator and, therefore, not good in the eyes of the Lord who promised blessing to the couple. He will not choose to bless them for their unbelief.

How many times in our faith journey do we get impatient with God's timing and take matters into our own hands? Then, everything that happens after the self-directed plan succeeds shows instead spiritual failure. The consequences of sin are devastating and certainly not what we hope for. Instead of getting honor from having a child through Hagar, Sarai gets "contempt" (vv. 4–5). All relationships come unglued.

Yet, our gracious God finds the runaway Egyptian servant (v. 7) and will bring her news as refreshing as the desert spring where she is resting. But our obedience must prove our faith for God to administer his blessing. Hagar provides a positive exemplar for us all. And our "God of seeing" (v. 13) graciously allows us a glimpse of his matchless grace in Ishmael's name and explanation (v. 11). What an amazingly powerful God who can bless the likes of Hagar in a peripheral yet significant way.

Preaching Idea

It pays to patiently wait for the Lord's blessing rather than working out our own "blessing."

Contemporary Connections

What does it mean?

For Sarai to be barren all this time makes the fulfillment of the promises of God to Abram seem impossible (15:2, "for I continue childless"). Ten years is a long time to wait for God to make good on his word! It is telling that Sarai credits the Lord with her barrenness, but that knowledge does not extend to honoring him by asking him for direction (16:2, "the Lord has prevented me from bearing children"). By creating verbal links back to Genesis 3 and the fateful decisions of Eve and Adam, the narrator makes it clear Sarai's idea is a bad one that will cause tremendous heartache for all involved. You may want to explain Abram's lack of spiritual discernment (v. 2) and his seemingly heartless response, "do to her as you please" (v. 6).

It is nearly impossible for us in our day and culture to understand the devastation of Hagar's contempt for Sarai and the seriousness of Sarai's cry to Abram, "May the LORD judge between you and me!" (v. 5). But Hagar's reaction to Sarai is the opposite result Sarai wanted from the birth of Ishmael. Instead of being praised, Sarai is scorned by an Egyptian servant-girl. The angel of the Lord's instruction to Hagar to return and submit to Sarai was the worst thing Hagar could imagine. However, her faith-driven obedience is designed for all of us to "go and do likewise."

Is it true?

Some of your listeners may question the truthfulness of Sarai's plan. What's more foreign to American contemporary readers than to hear a wife say to her husband: "Go ahead and have a baby with our housemaid." So, at some point in the sermon/lesson you will want to prove through historical context why that was Sarai's best plan. That will be easier than trying to prove or explain Sarai's reaction to her husband, "May the wrong done to me be on you!" (v. 5). Of course, so much of the end of the narrative relies on the miraculous prophecy of the angel of the Lord concerning Hagar's son, Ishmael. By God's mercy, Hagar becomes the mother of a huge nation herself, but Ishmael was headed for rough days ahead.

Now what?

The relevance of Genesis 16 and the Sarai, Hagar, and Abram narrative is the common situation of God's people needing to learn that patience is truly a virtue. Without it, there can be no faith in God to eventually fulfill his promises to us. Sarai had waited long enough and felt it was time to take matters into her own hands to secure the promises of God to them as a couple. Like us, Sarai cannot anticipate the amount of pain sin can cause. Years ago I heard someone say that sin will take you further than you want to go, keep you longer than you intend to stay, and cost you more than you're willing to pay. Imagine the ongoing emotional toll this must have had on this family! As stated above, Hagar's faith and obedience lead the way for us in our walk with the Lord. All her instincts would scream at her to reject the angel of the Lord's instruction as not being in her best interest. Surely she would be better off back in Egypt. And every one of us needs to be assured that our God hears us in our affliction when we share Hagar's heart. We get to see what Hagar saw so we can also rest comfortably in his care.

Creativity in Presentation

To help your listeners recognize that it pays to patiently wait for the Lord's blessing rather than working out our own blessing, ask your listeners to think about a situation in their life when they said something like this: "The Lord hasn't answered my prayer, so I am going to work my own plan. I can't wait any longer." In his commentary, Genesis, Waltke appropriately labels this faithless or human engineering (cf. pp. 248, 252, 256). It is a possible way to help them assess the plans we make in unbelief. Waiting patiently for the Lord is agonizing at times, especially when time marches on with no indication of God doing something about our situation. The more we can help our listeners feel the weight of waiting, the better they will sense the strong pull to secure the blessing of God in a way that makes sense to us.

- The struggle of waiting: It might also help us all to realize that when we can't wait any longer for God to deliver, we often have resources and socially acceptable avenues to help us succeed (in this case, Sarai and Abram have Hagar, for instance, and the socially acceptable practice of a barren wife obtaining children through a slave girl). This angle can help everyone enter the scene described in verses 1–3 where Sarai announces her plan, and Abram goes along with it.

- The greater pain of faithlessness: then in verses 4–6 we can help everyone see again the terrible consequences of sin. As noted above, all relationships are damaged because of this plan to bring about a good end through ungodly means. It is impossible to restate and overstate what sin is, and the damage it causes by virtue of what sin is, in God's kingdom.

- God's redemption: Finally, verses 7–16 provide confidence that God will keep his promises to those who trust him. He extends such mercy to Hagar, who models faith for us. And the names she gives God also give us comfort as we journey through this badly broken world.

DISCUSSION QUESTIONS

1. Discuss the connections between faith in God and patience, a fruit of the Holy Spirit.

2. Why might a believer, when he or she knows that the Lord is preventing something from happening, still attempt to make the forbidden thing happen?

3. The angel of the Lord asks Hagar to do something extremely difficult. Gain input from a few listeners on times when obedience was very difficult for them. Discuss the common experience of God's ways seeming so backward, so harmful, and how self-preservation instincts make disobedience so attractive.

4. How have you learned lessons in faith from believers who have had less teaching or years in the faith? What does that teach us about walking by faith for a lifetime?

5. As with Hagar, how does God bring comfort to us when we experience injustice?

Genesis 17:1–27

EXEGETICAL IDEA

Yahweh appeared to Abram in his old age to pledge his covenant through Sarah and Isaac, eternally establishing relation with them as Sovereign with expanded promises requiring loyalty from Abram and his descendants, as evidenced by their new names and circumcision.

THEOLOGICAL FOCUS

Yahweh remains faithful to his promise, offering increasing blessing in relationship with him for greater loyalty and faith, and extending grace and hope to his struggling servants, despite deepening human obstacles, to his glory.

PREACHING IDEA

The only right response to Almighty God's promises is unhesitating faithfulness that leads to full benefit.

PREACHING POINTERS

When the original audience read Genesis 17 their faith was bolstered to see God revealing himself to Abram and challenging him to "walk before me and be blameless" (v. 1). All that was so that God might confirm the covenant agreement he made with Abram back in chapter 15, and now Sarah and Isaac too. Listeners with ears to hear will be just as encouraged when they read and believe that what God said to Abram is at work in their lives. The narrative is one of those classic places in the Old Testament where God's work and our response of obedient faith somehow work together in the salvation package. For instance, the former occurs in all God's "I will's" (vv. 6–8), and the latter is spelled out in verse 9 when "God said to Abraham, 'As for you, you shall keep my covenant.'"

More encouragement comes from seeing the faithful as part of Abraham's huge family tree. Those hearing this for the first time must put themselves into this narrative and assess whether or not they are putting their faith to work like Abraham did when he made sure Ishmael and everyone in his household were circumcised.

This is an excellent time for us to urge listeners to evaluate their attitude toward God in every area of their lives. Like Abraham, we must be faithful to the Lord with our motives (loving God and his reputation above all things), time (making sure we serve him as part of the body of Christ), and money (using our money to further his agenda in the world of making disciples). This is the only way to enjoy all the privileges and blessings that come from being in a covenant relationship with our Creator/Redeemer. And this is a foretaste of eternity for all who display a faith that works.

REWARDED LOYALTY: OBEDIENCE THROUGH GROWING OBSTACLES (17:1–27)

LITERARY STRUCTURE AND THEMES

Genesis 17 turns to Abram's (and future descendants') responsibility to be loyal to the covenant promises. God called Abram to loyalty, extending the promise. Then he instructed Abram and all promised offspring to show commitment to the covenant through circumcision. Abram's age at God's appearance and his obedience frames the narrative (17:1a, 22–27), reminding Isreal of the obstacles to the promise. El Shaddai's five speeches[1] expand the promise and center on the requirement to circumcise, forming another elaborate chiasm (largely following McEvenue 1971, 157–58):[2]

A. Yahweh appeared to Abram at ninety-nine (17:1a).
  B. Speech 1: God Almighty required loyalty (17:1b–2).
    C. Abram bowed (17:3a).
      D. Speech 2: God bestowed a new name and promises (17:3b–8).
        E. Speech 3: Circumcision showed loyalty (17:9–14).
      D'. Speech 4: God bestowed a new name and promises (17:15–16).
    C'. Abraham bowed (17:17–18).
  B'. Speech 5: The covenant would go to Isaac (17:19–21).
A'. God left an obedient Abram at ninety-nine (17:22–24).

Genesis 17, then, emphasizes God's faithful commitment to his promises, which would show in his impossible blessing on an old Abram and Sarai of a new child of promise. God would still honor his promise to Ishmael, extending Abram's influence and blessing. It also recognizes the responsibility of anyone in covenant with God to be loyal, requiring all male participants to be marked

1 The five speeches each begin with God "said" to Abram (vv. 1b, 3b, 9a, 15a, 19a).

2 McEvenue (1971, 158–59) also shows that the structure is complex with two parallel panels interlocking with the chiasm:

A Yahweh's intention to make an oath about progeny (17:1–2)
  B Abraham falls on his face (17:3a)
    C Abraham, father of nations (17:4b–6)
      D God will carry out his oath forever (17:7)
        E The sign of the oath (17:9–14)
A' God's intention to bless Sarah with a progeny (17:16)
  B' Abraham falls on his face (etc.) (17:17–18)
    C' Sarah, mother of a son, Isaac (17:19)
      D' God will carry out his oath forever (17:18b[*sic*]–2la)
        E' The sign of the oath (17:23–27)

The parallel panels highlight both Abraham's fulfillment (vv. 23–27) of the command to circumcise (vv. 9–14, keeping covenant in loyalty) and God's continuing promise of an eternal covenant to Abraham's descendants (vv. 7, 19–21). Both aspects of the interlocking structures highlight circumcision as the central focus of the narrative.

with a reminder of their status and relationship. Extending the covenant perpetually, God required circumcision of all generations to benefit from the covenant. Abram's obedience shows his faith, confirming the expectation of promise from Yahweh and providing the paradigm for all succeeding generations.

- ***Yahweh Appeared to Abram at Ninety-Nine (17:1a)***
- ***God Almighty Required Loyalty (17:1b–2)***
- ***Abram Bowed (17:3a)***
- ***God Bestowed a New Name and Promises (17:3b–8)***
- ***Circumcision Showed Loyalty (17:9–14)***
- ***God Bestowed a New Name and Promises (17:15–16)***
- ***Abraham Bowed (17:17–18)***
- ***The Covenant Would Go to Isaac (17:19–21)***
- ***God Left an Obedient Abram at Ninety-Nine (17:22–27)***

EXPOSITION

Chapter 17 parallels chapter 15, expanding and clarifying the promises (see the structure of the Abraham stories above, p. 237, with many points of contact pointed out in Sarna 1989, 123). It also marks a turning point in the Abraham stories. Paralleling 12:1–9, it starts a new stage in Abram's life. In 12:1–3 Yahweh gave Abram two foundational imperatives, providing purposeful responsibility ("go . . . and be a blessing," author's translation) as the basis for his promises (vv. 2–3). Abram's response with immediate obedience, then worked out through chapters 12–15, culminates in God's declaration of Abram's faith (15:6) and results in the covenant (15:7–21).

Twenty-four years later Yahweh again gave Abram two foundational imperatives ("walk before me, and be blameless," 17:1), providing his responsibility for God's extended promises (vv. 2–21). Abraham's immediate obedience (vv. 23–27) began working out his loyalty, growing through chapters 18–22. God's call to covenant loyalty here in 17:1 culminated in his extreme test of Abaham's faith (ch. 22), leading to his affirmation of Abraham's loyalties in 22:12 and ratification of the covenant (22:15–18). Here God extended his promise, specifying his chosen means. Yahweh appeared to Abram in his old age to pledge his covenant through Sarah and Isaac, eternally establishing relation with them as Sovereign, with expanded promises requiring loyalty from Abram and his descendants demonstrated in new names and circumcision, which Abraham immediately did.

Yahweh Appeared to Abram at Ninety-Nine (17:1a)

Yahweh appeared to Abram at ninety-nine.

17:1a. Framing the narrative with another note about Abram's age (17:24), Moses draws attention to both the passage of thirteen years since the earlier events of the previous verse (emphasized by his age in 16:16) and the advanced age of the recipient of the promises twenty-four years previously (12:4). With the passage of time, Abram's age, and no word from God, Abram's skepticism makes sense (vv. 17–18). Assumptions and expectations have been solidifying and God has been silent . . . until now. Now, at this late stage, Yahweh, who would self-identify as El Shaddai, appeared to Abram with even grander promises.

God Almighty Required Loyalty (17:1b–2)

Revealing himself as "El Shaddai," Yahweh demanded covenant loyalty in response to his expanded covenant promise.

17:1b. Yahweh's appearance initiates five speeches to Abram. In this first short introduction, Yahweh characterized himself as God Almighty (El Shaddai), emphasizing his sovereign authority to grant blessing and fertility and introducing his purpose of establishing his covenant promise of future descendants. In order to assure his blessing of covenant fertility, he will require complete loyalty from his vassal. Abram must live up to the examples of Enoch and Noah in his faithful life of integrity before Yahweh. Such loyalty required faith in the power of the one revealing himself as Almighty to carry out the promise at ninety-nine. Such faith was necessary both to experience the benefits of the covenant and to be a blessing through the covenant. Yahweh was both expanding the promises and explaining more clearly Abram's obligation for Yahweh to ratify the extended promises, as well as the responsibility of Abram's descendants (see the Introduction to the Abraham Narratives, p. 236). God would keep his word, but only those living in obedience would fully benefit.

TRANSLATION ANALYSIS 17:1

Some versions simply transliterate the Hebrew, "El Shaddai" (e.g., NJPS), and some follow the traditional interpretation "God Almighty" (e.g., ESV, NASB95, NIV) from the LXX translation in Job (or both, NLT). The derivation of the term "Shaddai" is uncertain, most often linked to either the mountains (Akkadian cognate) or "breasts" (שַׁד). El Shaddai appears only seven times in the MT, mainly referencing God's covenant promises to the patriarchs (and only in Exod. 6:3 and Ezek. 10:5 outside of Genesis). Shaddai alone appears thirty-nine times in the MT, with thirty-one of those in Job. The reference to God as Shaddai consistently occurs in contexts of covenant blessing and fertility (the promises to the patriarchs in Genesis) or judgment and control over life (e.g., Job 5:17; 6:4, 14, etc., Ruth 1:20–21, Isa. 13:6). It emphasizes the sovereign authority of God over life and blessing (Hamilton 1990, 462–63).

God required loyalty from Abram with two imperatives in 17:1: he must "walk before" (הִתְהַלֵּךְ לְפָנַי) God and "be blameless" (וֶהְיֵה תָמִים). To "walk before" God reminds the reader of both Enoch and Noah who "walked with" God, showing their lives of fellowship and intimacy with God (see exegesis at 5:22, p. 159, and sidebar there). God's command here to "walk before" God focuses on the accountability of Abram to be loyal to God. Sarna (1989, 123) emphasizes this point, noting the corresponding Akkadian phrase that was a "technical term for absolute loyalty to a king." It required living in God's presence and reflecting his expectations.

The second phrase is familiar from Moses's characterization of Noah, referring to a life of integrity, genuineness, and piety before the Lord (see Exposition on Gen. 6:9, p. 176; Olivier, תָּמַם, *NIDOTTE* 4:307). It is a high calling and the expectation for all in covenant relation with Yahweh (Deut. 18:13) to enter the presence of Yahweh (Ps. 15:2). In sequence, the two imperatives work together, calling for personal loyalty with the intended consequence that Abram live out righteousness. God called Abram, then, to "walk before" him in loyalty "and be blameless" as the basis for extravagant multiplication and extended fulfillment of covenant promise. God's command implied that Abram still needed to grow in loyalty and integrity (i.e., Egypt and Hagar).

These two commands also remind the reader of Abraham's call (12:1–3) and God's two imperatives calling Abraham to faith and a life of spreading God's blessing. These two imperatives come from the same two Hebrew roots (12:1–2, 17:1 || וֶהְיֵה . . . לֵךְ, וֶהְיֵה . . . הִתְהַלֵּךְ), recalling the earlier commands and structurally initiating the second half of the Abraham narratives (see Introduction to the Abraham Narratives, p. 236). While the specific commands elevate Abraham's responsibility before God, Yahweh will also expand the covenant promises in response.

17:2. God explained his purpose for his call for Abram's loyalty, promising to multiply Abram very greatly (בִּמְאֹד מְאֹד). If Abram would be loyal, God would "confirm" (וְאֶתְּנָה, NET) his covenant promises with Abram. God had already sworn to the possession of the land and promise of descendants (15:12–21) as reassurance to Abram's questioning (15:8), but with implied conditions (see comments, footnote, and sidebar with 15:17, p. 302). Now God expanded the possibilities and promised to greatly multiply Abram, affirming a multitude of nations with kings (17:5–6), with an eternal covenant (vv. 7, 13, 19) for his descendants through Isaac (by Sarai, now Sarah, vv. 7, 15–21) adding everlasting possession of the land (v. 8).

TRANSLATION ANALYSIS 17:2a
As with the volitive sequence in Genesis 12:1–3, the cohortative (וְאֶתְּנָה, "I may make") following the imperatives ("walk . . . be blameless") specifies purpose or result (WOC, §34.6a, 577–78). ESV clearly indicates purpose ("that I may"). "Then I will" indicates more result (NET, NIV). Other versions leave it more to inference and interpretation ("I will," NASB95, NJPS; see also NKJV, NRSV).

TRANSLATION ANALYSIS 17:2b
The verb used here, "make" (נתן, ESV, NIV, NLT), occurs with "covenant" in only two other places in the MT (Gen. 9:12; Num. 25:12). Here it is explained by the following verses, which use "establish" (קוּם, Gen. 17:7, 19, 21). God was not making a new covenant but establishing extended promises for the covenant already given based on Abram's faithfulness. Other translations clarify that distinction with "establish" (NASB95, NJPS) or "confirm" (NET). For detailed exposition of the progressive growth and ratification of the covenant promises throughout the Abraham narratives with implications for what follows, see Chisholm (1992).

Abram Bowed (17:3a)

Abram bowed in reverence.

17:3a. Abram immediately responded to God's appearance and promise, falling prostrate on his face. In the context of God's presence and promise, Abram showed appropriate submission and awe before God (cf. Lev. 9:24; Josh. 5:14; Ezek. 1:28; Dan. 8:17). Despite his struggle with the specifics of the promise (Gen. 17:17), his response to God's command would echo his immediate reaction (vv. 22–27) and bind the narrative together with his obedient faith.

God Bestowed a New Name and Promises (17:3b–8)

Changing Abram's name, God established and extended his covenant with promise of nations and everlasting relationship.

17:3b–6. Honoring Abram's worship, God addressed him a second time, explaining his intent. Beginning with his own obligations ("as for me," NASB95, NIV, NJPS), Yahweh elaborated his covenant with Abram. While Yahweh's "covenant" was initially cut with Abram in chapter 15, the term is only mentioned there one time. Here, where God is elaborating his formal agreement on their relationship, the text will use the term thirteen times (nearly half of the twenty-seven times "covenant" is used in Genesis). Though he will use the term in several different ways, the emphasis is clearly on fleshing out Abraham's relationship with God, with both benefits and responsibilities.

TRANSLATION ANALYSIS 17:4
God's discourse begins with the 1cs pronoun, "As for me" (אֲנִי, NASB95, NIV, NJPS). Numerous translations leave off the somewhat-awkward-to-translate pronoun (e.g., ESV, NCV, NLT). The emphasis on God's responsibility is especially significant, however, since he will begin the next statement with foregrounding the 2cs pronoun, "As for you," and Abraham's responsibility, which most translations include (e.g., ESV, NLT).

God's promises relayed here focus on the progeny coming from Abram, where they will live, and the relationship they will have with him. What previously had been uncountable offspring (13:16; 15:4–5) now becomes "a multitude of nations," emphasized by repetition (17:4–5). Abram's legacy will span national boundaries, including kings. Sandwiched between the two affirmations of Abram's future progeny, Yahweh changed his name.

The name Abram means "exalted father" (meaning the person is eminent) or "he is exalted with regard to the father" (meaning from a distinguished lineage, Verhoef, "Abraham/Abram," *NIDOTTE* 4:351). God changed it to Abraham, which is of uncertain derivation, but it is similar in sound to his declaration that Abram would be "a father of a multitude" of nations (אַב־הֲמוֹן) and may be merely a dialectical variant (Wenham 1994). The name change symbolized "the transformation of character and destiny" and was used for kings in the "inauguration of a new era" (Sarna 1989, 124). More importantly here, it symbolized and solidified the growing relationship between Abram and Yahweh (Walton 2001, 449–50). It would be a constant reminder to Abraham and his world of God's promises to him and God's plan for God's world through Abram.[3] In repeating his intent, God asserted the certainty of his promise.

TRANSLATION ANALYSIS 17:5
In restating the intent of the name change, Yahweh declared, "I have made you the father of a multitude of nations" (17:5 ESV, NASB2020, RSV). A few versions, however, translate his declaration as future, since it has not yet happened ("I will make you" NASB95, NET). Daniel Carver argues that the use of the perfect of *ntn* (נתן) frequently indicated a divine decision that had been made but had yet to be realized (private communication regarding his forthcoming book on the grammar of prophecy). Yahweh *will* do it.

God then expanded even this new promise. Reminding the reader of God's initial blessing to humanity to "be fruitful and multiply" (1:28; 9:1, 7), he repeated and strengthened both terms. In 17:2 he had promised to multiply Abram greatly, and now he promised to make Abraham "exceedingly fruitful" (v. 6). God now guaranteed to Abraham the plan he had offered to Adam and Noah to live out. A new era began with Abraham that marks a significant clarification in God's plan for redemption. God was moving clearly and boldly to accomplish his purpose for all humanity through his choice of one. With both terms he strengthened the promise ("greatly," v. 2, or "exceedingly," v. 6, בִּמְאֹד מְאֹד). The initial opportunity for mankind through Adam, and renewed with Noah, now blossoms into God's potent promise for humanity through the line of Abram.

This assurance would not only extend to a great number of people, but to nations and to kings. Again, we see God moving to accomplish through Abraham his purposes from creation. He had created humankind to rule and represent him (1:26–28). The theme of rule has permeated the initial chapters of Genesis as the given purpose for the designated representatives of Yahweh (chs. 1–2; 5:1–2; 9:5–6) and then as rebellious independent authorities sought self-rule and perpetrated oppression and violence (chs. 3–6, 10–11). God designated Abraham now as the source of kings, which will accomplish God's plan to bring blessing to all the families of the earth (12:3; 18:18; 22:18; 26:4; 28:14), specifically promising kings through Isaac (17:16), Israel (35:18), and Judah (49:10), leading to David, and of course his promised descendant, Jesus. All God's blessing, as we have seen, is expressed and accomplished in terms of relationship with him. He is intervening in human history through Abraham to establish

3 From this point, the old name is only used twice, referring to God's choice of him from Ur (Neh. 9:7) and when the Chronicler identified him as the son of Terah (1 Chron. 1:17).

relationship and opportunity for blessing for all of humanity. He makes that relationship explicit in 17:7–8.

17:7–8. God's purpose is not to make a new covenant, but to establish or confirm the extended promises of the covenant he had already made. The use of "establish" (קוּם) instead of the normal verb "cut" (כָּרַת) a covenant, "suggests the reestablishment of something already in place" (McConville, בְּרִית, *NIDOTTE* 1:748). Yahweh was extending the promises of the covenant and clarifying the responsibilities (Chisholm 1992). Part of the growing promise includes extending the covenant to Abraham's offspring as an "everlasting covenant" (לִבְרִית עוֹלָם, 3x: vv. 7, 13, 19) with Canaan as an "everlasting possession" (לַאֲחֻזַּת עוֹלָם, v. 8).

> *TRANSLATION ANALYSIS 17:8*
> "Everlasting" (עוֹלָם, ESV, among many others) elicits several other translations: "forever" (NLT), "perpetual" (NRSV), or "permanent" (NET). The term, however, does not always require "eternal" as in "unbounded" (Tomasino, עוֹלָם, *NIDOTTE* 3:346) or something that cannot become obsolete (e.g., the priesthood, Exod. 40:15, given to the line of Phineas, Num. 25:13, or the temple sacrifice, Exod. 27:21, none of which continue in the new covenant). The additional "throughout their generations" (Gen. 17:9) strengthens an already enduring promise in the context of the Abrahamic covenant (Hamilton 1990, 465), but the ongoing nature of the land promise (and the Abrahamic covenant) must be debated with regard to its inclusion or continuation in future covenants, especially the new covenant.

Perhaps the most significant additions to the promise are the final clauses in both verse 7, "to be God to you and to your offspring after you," and verse 8, "and I will be their God." Yahweh's purpose for confirming the covenant with Abraham and his offspring was to take them as his people into a new relationship as their sovereign (v. 7).[4] The concluding clause of verse 8 summarizes El Shaddai's intention: that he will be their God, calling them to relationship as his nation, which is the basis for their place in his world, in order to accomplish his purpose of blessing all families (12:3). Blessing is both experienced in relationship with God and transmitted to his world as those in relationship with him represent him and mediate his blessing of relationship with him (Exod. 19:5–6).

To enjoy those benefits in relationship, however, Abraham and his descendants must be loyal to God as well. Therefore, God established circumcision as the sign of the everlasting covenant.

Circumcision Showed Loyalty (17:9–14)

God established circumcision for every male descendant as the ongoing outward reminder of loyalty to the covenant.

17:9. Yahweh's third speech forms the center focus of the chiasm, clarifying his requirement for Abram and all future generations that will claim relationship with him and promise from him. Just as he began verse 4 (speech two) with his responsibility in the relationship ("as for me"), now he begins this new statement with Abram's (and his descendants') responsibility ("As for you," see Translation Analysis 17:4 above. Abram and all future generations must keep God's "covenant" (בְּרִית), referring to the obligations of his covenant. Once the covenant is fully ratified (ch. 22), even the fully expanded promise will be secure, but only those who are committed to Yahweh and obedient by faith will participate. He will spell out his initial requirement for them in the following statement. Every male will be required to bear a mark that will appropriately remind them of the promise and

---

4 לְ with inf. indicating "intention," *HALOT* s.v. "לְ" 510.

their responsibility to the promise giver. Those requirements would be further delineated in the Mosaic covenant.

> *TRANSLATION ANALYSIS 17:9*
> By metonymy, "covenant" stands for the obligations it requires (cf. *HALOT* s.v. "בְּרִית" 159, C.c.), clarified as "covenantal requirement" (NET) or "the terms of the covenant" (NLT).

17:10–13. God spelled out the obligation that he required of them or, as he would elaborate, the specific sign of that covenant.[5] Every male in the community must be circumcised. Circumcision was not unusual in Abraham's world. In fact, most of the nations in Canaan and Egypt already practiced circumcision later in life, though their reasons are unclear and full removal of the foreskin was unusual.[6] God, however, transformed a common cultural practice into a symbol of identification with him and his promise of future descendants and relationship.[7]

When God designated circumcision to be the sign of his covenant, he was calling Abraham and all subsequent heirs of God's promise to declare their faith in that promise. Signs could be used for various purposes, as we have already seen in Genesis.[8] Here, God required a mark that both illustrated the promise (seed) and provided a permanent mark of that relationship (a sign "of the covenant"). To become circumcised marked the faith of the participant. For the parent circumcising their baby, it was the acknowledgement of the ongoing promise of God. For the adult who had not been circumcised, their responsibility to be circumcised marked their faith in the covenant, and failure to be circumcised marked them as outside the covenant of promise, without faith. It reminded them daily of the promise, their responsibility, and the danger of breaking covenant. Anyone not circumcised would be cut off from the community of promise (v. 14). Circumcision, then, was their identification with God as his covenant people, signifying and formalizing his lordship over them, in faith (Hamilton 1990, 471–72).[9]

The sign of circumcision was an ongoing identification for all generations and for every male in the community, whether they were native born, of foreign origin, or even the

5 Again, by metonymy, the rite of circumcision is for the covenant it signifies, but it is not intended to be the substance of the covenant, which encompassed the promises and the responsibilities of the recipients (Mathews 2005, 203).

6 Sasson (1966) notes that it was common in Egypt and Canaan and documented as early as 2800 BC in Egypt and 3200 BC in N. Syria, but it was practiced later in life, possibly as a passage into manhood or as a marriage rite. Israel was alone, however, in fully removing the foreskin (DeRouchie 2004, 187–88, esp. n. 24). It was not practiced in Mesopotamia (so Abram), and it was not practiced by some of the tribes in Canaan ("uncircumcised Philistines," Judg. 15:8, and the Shechemites in Gen. 34).

7 Avalos (2015) equates it to a "slave mark," identifying "the property of the ultimate Hebrew slave owner, Yahweh." While there is some merit to the identification (Lev. 25:39–42), there is more involved, symbolically reminding of the promise and relationship to Yahweh as God (Gen. 17:7–8).

8 The term "sign" (אוֹת) was used several ways in the OT and has already been used as identification (luminaries identifying the seasons, 1:14, and the mark identifying Cain, 4:15) and a reminder (the rainbow reminding God of his promise, 9:8–17). Signs could be evidence or guarantee (Josh. 2:12; Job 21:29), confirmation (1 Sam. 2:34), or even an illustration of God's message (Isa. 8:18). See Kruger, אוֹת, *NIDOTTE* 1:331–33. The purpose here is debated but best functions as a reminder to the man to walk as Abram walked, in integrity and loyalty with God (Wenham 1994).

9 The meaning of circumcision for the participant, then, was multifaceted, both reminding the circumcised of their identity, responsibilities, and dangers, as well as symbolizing the future reality of God's promise (DeRouchie 2004, 184–85).

servants and slaves. Concluding and framing this central instruction, circumcision was to be "an everlasting covenant" (v. 13, see v. 9, "throughout their generations"). On the other hand, neglecting the sign brought stringent punishment.

17:14. Any male who chose not to be circumcised was to be "cut off from his people." The responsibility was clear. Failure to respond in faith was to break covenant (אֶת־בְּרִיתִי הֵפַר). To be cut off from the community was catastrophic. The expression was used in 9:11 of those killed in the flood, as well as of what God would do to the Canaanites (Deut. 12:29; 19:1). The penalty may refer to expulsion from the community, symbolically signifying death (so Mathews 2005, 205). Or it may refer to divine punishment in an untimely death (Wenham 1994, 25, 29). Generally, the sentence is stated as a passive with no clear indication of the agent, but in Leviticus 20:1–6 it is active with God as the agent. The rabbis, then, argued it was to be a divine rather than human punishment (Sarna 1989, 126). In the various uses, it may carry different outcomes for different circumstances, leaving the precise implication here unclear (Ross 1988, 334), but all include loss of covenant and alienation, ultimately from God and any opportunity for life and blessing. On the other hand, all who chose to participate in the promise must live in loyalty before their king. They must willingly accept the mark of that loyalty and reminder of their responsibilities within the promised blessings of the covenant.

God Bestowed a New Name and Promises (17:15–16)

Changing Sarai's name, God extended the covenant promises of nations and kings to Sarah.

17:15–16. Framing the instruction on circumcision, the announcement of Sarai's name change and promise to her of a son leading to nations and kings (vv. 15–16) parallels Abram's name change and promise of nations and kings from him (vv. 3b–8). The requirement to keep covenant by circumcision comes in the context of the extension and clarification of God's promise for both Abraham and Sarah (vv. 9–14). God chose to bless Sarah, who was last seen blaming God for her childlessness, taking her future into her own hands, and mistreating her servant. He graciously extended his promise to her, showing, as Abram's further reaction will clarify, his own sovereign bestowal of favor and blessing apart from the ability of humanity to act. Though no one can fully deserve his generous blessing, full participation in his promised favor will require the response of his beneficiaries in loyal submission and commitment, symbolized here by circumcision (vv. 9–14) and lived out in loyal committed integrity (v. 1).

The name change, as with that of Abraham, was probably a dialectical variant, updating the ending from an archaic feminine. Both names mean "princess" (*HALOT* s.v. "שָׂרָה" 1354), so even though it is not explained, it logically leads to the promise of "kings of peoples" coming from her (v. 16). As with Abraham, the new name highlights Sarah's new future in the promise of God, providing an ongoing testimony to El Shaddai's power and grace to transform barren, aged, and unbelieving Sarai into the matriarch of nations and kings.

Abraham Bowed (17:17–18)

Abraham bowed in skepticism, asking his blessing for Ishmael.

17:17–18. Abraham again bowed before Yahweh (see v. 3), but this time the narrator exposes Abraham's heart, showing his skepticism and explaining his request regarding Ishmael. His inner thoughts betray his posture, which both God and the reader now see. His prostration appears conflicted as he turns God's attention to his previously assumed means of fulfilling God's promise to him—Ishmael.

His thoughts also reveal the significance of God's promise, including waiting these twenty-four years. Abraham's immediate recognition of the impossibility of the promise, both for himself (though he will have more kids!) and for Sarah, also suggests that initially it may not have been so ludicrous to him, even though she was known to be barren (11:30). With the passage of so much time, however, Sarah bearing a child had become inconceivable. The fulfillment of God's promise would now be far more spectacular and obvious to a watching world, given to a ninety-year-old woman.

Abraham, however, was still locked in his physical world, not seeing the perspective of El Shaddai, or El Elyon, Creator of heaven and earth (14:19–20). He did not ask overtly for Ishmael to fulfill the promise, but he brought him to God's attention as if to say, "You have already provided the blessing and may he gain your full favor! May he thrive in your sight!" Was Abraham's laughter unbelief? Perhaps more incredulity, but clearly not hardened unbelief. In fact, God did not rebuke him at all. Abram's faith was still not fully formed, but it was growing, and it would show. When God reaffirmed that it was indeed his intent to bless Sarah with a child, Abram immediately obeyed in faith.

The Covenant Would Go to Isaac (17:19–21)

God reiterated his promise to Sarah and extended his covenant to Isaac, promising to bless Ishmael as well.

17:19–21. God's response was gracious. He gently pulled Abraham out of his this-world-only view and refocused him on God's sovereign authority to give life. He even named the child, making him more real and more relevant to Abraham's reaction. God addressed both Abraham's request and skepticism, but he began with his promise, moved to Abraham's concern, and closed with a renewal of his promise to Sarah. God's repetition of his promise framed his promise to Ishmael with the repeated and emphasized promise to establish his covenant through Isaac. While Ishmael would be blessed, Isaac would clearly be the only child of promise for God's work of bringing blessing to the families of the earth.

Contrary to Abram's carefully worded suggestion, Sarah would have a child. God began his statement with an emphatic redirection. "No, but" (ESV, or "Yes, but" NIV, אֲבָל) redirects Abram's attention back to the promise. No mistake! God meant what he said. Sarah at ninety-one would bear a son, and they would name him "he laughs!" God's naming of Isaac will be used to commemorate both Abraham and Sarah's responses (see also 18:12) as well as the joy that he would bring to an old couple (21:6). This covenant that God was establishing with Abraham would be continued and established with his son, Isaac (emphasized by repetition in 17:21). And again, Yahweh classified the covenant as "everlasting." The perpetual promise of land and seed would be accomplished through Sarah's son in her old age.

God promised continued blessing for Ishmael as well. Responding to Abraham's request, God enhanced the initial promise to Ishmael of innumerable offspring (16:10) to become twelve princes and a great nation. In fact, as with Abraham earlier, God promised he would "make him fruitful [פרה] and multiply [רבה] him greatly" (17:20), extending the initial blessing on humankind to Ishmael as well.[10] Ishmael would be blessed with many offspring (16:10), including twelve leaders and a great nation (17:20). Ishmael would even be circumcised and enjoy the benefits of God's covenant promises to Abraham as part of his household (vv. 23–26). The covenant promises to Abraham, however, would pass on to Isaac, not Ishmael (26:3–4), and then to Jacob

10 Moses will record the fulfillment of this promise in 25:12–16.

(35:11–12) and their descendants for God's ultimate working through the nation of Israel.

God closed his address with the renewed promise to establish the covenant as an "everlasting covenant" with Isaac for his offspring. As noted above ("Literary Structure and Themes," p. 321, including footnote 2), the interlocking structure of the parallel panels draws attention to this fulfillment. The repetition (stated twice here) emphasizes the certainty of his word. The waiting was coming to an end. It would happen in about a year. Abraham and Sarah would conceive their own child very soon, inaugurating the next phase of God's eternal covenant promise.

God Left an Obedient Abram at Ninety-Nine (17:22–27)

When God left, Abraham at ninety-nine immediately obeyed, fully circumcising all males in his house.

17:22. Abraham's audience with El Shaddai ended with God's five statements. He had established his covenant terms, providing the initial conditions he expected from his trusting vassal and his descendants for the land and national heritage. He left his reaffirmed and extended covenant promises to Abraham, Sarah, and the yet-to-be-conceived Isaac.

17:23–27. In the concluding scene, Abraham's compliance framed his old age. Abraham acted in faith on "that very day" (17:23, בְּעֶצֶם הַיּוֹם הַזֶּה) that God appeared to him, circumcising all males "as God had said to him" (v. 23, 26). Abraham was ninety-nine and Ishmael was thirteen when they obeyed (vv. 24–25). Abraham showed no hesitation or lingering doubt that God Almighty was not accounting for his age. He immediately complied with God's command and followed through with the considerable number of men and boys in his camp.

Ethically, God had commanded complete loyalty in attentive, submissive, obedient living (v. 1) and specified how that would look in this covenant with circumcision (vv. 9–14, esp. note v. 9: "as for you, you shall keep my covenant," spelled out in the next few verses). Abraham concluded the scene with a show of exactly what God had called for (vv. 23–27). The interlocking structure of the narrative emphasizes Abram's obedience to God's command by faith: in the chiasm, the command to loyalty (v. 1) undergirds the closing complete obedience (vv. 23–27); in the parallel development ("Literary Structure and Themes" above, p. 321, including footnote 2), the first panel ends with the command to circumcise, and the second panel ends with Abraham carrying out the command exactly. The initial covenant ceremony (ch. 15) was precipitated by Abram's faith (15:6). Now God's confirmation of his covenant proceeded with Abram's faith in obedience, demonstrating his integrity and growing in his response to the radical assurances and obligations of his God. It will all culminate in his greatest test and act of faith (ch. 22).

THEOLOGICAL FOCUS

Yahweh remains faithful to his promise despite deepening human obstacles, offering increasing blessing in relationship with him for greater loyalty and faith and extending grace and hope to his struggling servants, to his glory.

In response to faith, God extends blessing and promise beyond human ability, showing his power and faithfully carrying out his word. His long silence and Abram's advanced age reinforced God's sovereign power as the sole means to accomplish his guarantees. Even when the difficulty escalates, God demands full loyalty to participate in the benefits. God's orchestration of events and timing provides opportunity for the believer to grow in faith and to make progressively deeper commitments through testing, demonstrating that faith. As with Abraham, every believer must learn that "God's word overrides present circumstance" (Brueggemann 1991, 57).

At the same time, God graciously provides reassurances. For Abraham, he gave direct revelation to ground Abraham's perspective and provide clear reminders, to keep his and future generations' focus on the promises. Now we see the revelation and reminders that God has promised and would fulfill. Even when the believer struggles with the promise, God gently corrects misplaced expectation. He graciously provides more hope and blessing. He even uses and blesses those who have openly doubted and struggled with the promise, trying to accomplish it on their own, as God did through Sarah.

As God declared his sovereign control and power to bring life out of even an old man and a dead womb, he also clarified the necessity of loyalty to him for participation in the promise. Loyalty requires both the personal choice to bow, and to pass the legacy to the next generation (circumcision). It is a moral stance for daily living, in humble and ongoing relationship with God. In fact, the basis of the blessing in the covenant is always relationship with Yahweh as sovereign king and God. The use of the covenant in its ancient context placed Yahweh in the position of sovereign over the future nation, which would be clarified in the Mosaic covenant. His repeated statement that he would be their God revealed his foundational desire to have that relationship and grant the blessing that goes with it. That relationship and necessary response continue in the New Covenant. Now God's rule is embodied in Christ to whom all allegiance is required.

From the human perspective, then, we must necessarily bow and live out our faith in loyal obedience and integrity. Given the human penchant for lapses or outright selfish rebellion, it is encouraging to see God's grace to Abraham in his misguided assumptions (and emerging faith), as well as to Sarah in her obvious self-absorption and self-protection. God acts unexpectedly for all who respond. Yet, each has multiple opportunities to recalibrate and recommit to the hope of God's promise. Abraham models the exemplary, unhesitating obedience, living out the required faith despite obvious reasons to doubt.

God's choice of his servant, extravagant promises that extended waiting makes human accomplishment impossible, as well as the responsibility of humanity to respond in loyalty to experience his blessing, all lead to God's greater glory and humankind's greater good. Yahweh is restoring the relationship lost in the garden and demonstrating to his images the need and privilege of waiting and depending on him for their benefit. As faith grows and responds more deeply, the opportunity for blessing also grows in relationship with God, for the purpose of extending that relationship and its blessing to all the nations of the earth.

PREACHING AND TEACHING STRATEGIES

Exegetical and Theological Synthesis

Let us begin our journey of sermon/lesson preparation with Abraham being ninety-nine years old when the Lord appears to him. Everything about our Christian experience from start to finish is a miracle from God that requires faith on our part. It is quite a stretch that the Lord would announce to a ninety-nine-year-old man that he would become "the father of a multitude of nations" (17:5). Abraham's reaction in verse 17 shows how hard it is for human beings to believe God's promises. Every Sunday, however, we give our listeners of all ages an opportunity to worship "God Almighty" as we flesh out the implications of his great name (v. 1).

While we do not claim the land promises in verses 7–8 and 19, we do share the ultimate benefit of being able to walk with God in this life with all the spiritual blessings that accompany forgiveness of sins and the Spirit's empowerment for living life the way God designed it to be lived (character traits of the Spirit). Those of us with that hope add loyalty to God and his commands to the equation. As verse

14 makes clear, God will not tolerate anyone breaking his covenant through disbelief/disobedience. Genuine faith will show itself in genuine faithfulness. All those with ears to hear follow Abraham's example of complete, faith-driven obedience to God, necessary to receive and enjoy these unbelievable promises.

We should not forget what characters God is dealing with in the case of Abraham, Sarah, Isaac, and us. Considering what we know of Abraham and Sarah, for instance, they have not always been the best examples of faith and faithfulness. God's grace is truly amazing that he would choose to redeem the likes of us!

Preaching Idea

The only right response to Almighty God's promises is unhesitating faithfulness that leads to full benefit.

Contemporary Connections

What does it mean?

It is always good to spend time carefully defining the implications of God revealing himself: "I am God Almighty" (17:1). Everything about our relationship revolves around his character and power. In this case, he has both the authority and the ability to make these promises come true. He is the Source of the kind of life he was creating in and through Abraham, Sarah, Isaac, and everyone who believes.

The same goes for explaining the details of God's command to "walk before [him] and be blameless" (v. 1). Our Christian walk of faith is wrapped up in these commands, especially the last part, where God commands us to be a person of faithfulness and integrity in their overall commitment to him. You may want to explain how your listeners find their way into these promises. By faith, they are a part of Abraham's family tree.

If you spend any time on the details of the circumcision God required of Abraham, you will want to also spend time explaining that circumcision in God's eyes is not "outward and physical" but "inwardly, and . . . a matter of the heart, by the Spirit" (Rom. 2:28–29) and that your hearers "were circumcised with a circumcision made without hands, by putting off the body of the flesh, by the circumcision of Christ" (Col. 2:11). This is a way to show how faith leads to the faithfulness portrayed by Abraham.

Is it true?

Do not assume that all your listeners will believe that God is "God Almighty." You may want to take some time building an argument for the God of Scripture to occupy this role all by himself. Other gods compete with him, as Keller suggests in *Counterfeit Gods* (you can see this especially in the Introduction on pages ix–xxiv, but throughout the excellent book).

Anyone skeptical of the size of Abraham's current faith-family might benefit from some stats from the U.S. Center for World Missions or some other mission agency. Truly, the gospel of Christ is moving all over the world.

Now what?

The relevance of Genesis 17 includes at least the following:

- the need for a miracle for God to create LifePlus in us (or, better, that our entire Christian life, from justification to glorification, is the result of God's gracious miraculous work);
- the command to enjoy intimate fellowship with him and his ways to the point of blamelessness (again, virtually every part of our Christian existence is contained in the instruction in v. 1);
- our eternal inheritance, enjoyed in part now and in full at the judgment;
- our participation in new covenant blessings through a Spirit-given

circumcision (making the link but noting differences and similarities between the two covenants);

- and the responsibility that we Christians have in responding to God's gracious invitation with wholehearted loyalty and obedience (see v. 9's statement: "As for you, you shall keep my covenant").

Creativity in Presentation

As you can see from the "Now what?" section above, we have followed the way in which chapter 17 unfolds to declare that the only right response to Almighty God's promises is unhesitating faithfulness that leads to full benefit. But let me begin by stating that one of the most important aspects of this message is the ability to help our listeners move from God's covenant with Abraham to his new covenant with Christ-followers.

- You could begin with the obvious absurdity of all this taking place when Abraham is ninety-nine.

- Follow the narrative, which begins with God revealing himself uniquely and powerfully: "I am God Almighty." Everything about our relationship with him by faith begins with the foundation of his character and greatness as our Creator and Redeemer.

- Then, move on to the life-giving command to enjoy moving through life, step by step, with him. That, of course, means a certain kind of morality or lifestyle or ethic ("be blameless," v. 1).

- Then you have that wonderful "that" clause, which allows you to flex your theological muscles and declare your stance on the connection between fulfilling the commands in verse 1 and being in covenant with God (v. 2). Christians have obligations to God now to enjoy life with him to the fullest. God's ability to work in my life is somehow connected to my loyalty and obedience. Grace is not opposed to effort, but to earning. We don't earn favor with God, but favor with God is not possible outside of this covenant agreement, which includes human responses of faith and obedience. Several minutes need to be devoted to the concept of God's covenant and its implications for the believer. This may be repetition from earlier chapters, so you will need to decide how much time to give it now if you are preaching through Genesis, pericope by pericope.

- Finally, you may want to make a connection between this covenant and the new covenant promises in the Old Testament and the New Testament. Of special interest will be the ability of Christians by the Spirit to keep their end of the agreement and reach their eternal inheritance when God creates all things new.

A pathway to this preaching and teaching could be:

- What God requires us to do in relationship with him.
- What God promises to do for us as we are faithful to him.
- Our struggle to believe and obey.

You can also follow the shape of the passage more closely:

- God's call to loyalty (17:1–14)

- The tensions of faith (17:15–21)
- The response of loyalty (17:22–27)

DISCUSSION QUESTIONS

1. Why did God decide to record redemptive history in Scripture with these miraculous events involving barrenness? What does this say about God and about our salvation that he provides?
2. Why does God wait until it is humanly impossible to fulfill some promises? How can we keep his almighty power in mind when we feel that his promise is impossible?
3. Discuss the progression from chapters 12, 15, and 17 to get a fuller sense of the relationship God calls us into (the promise expands, along with expectations and human responses, as faith grows).
4. What is the significance of believing that God is "God Almighty" when it comes to living the Christian life in a badly broken world? What are some areas that we need to hear this characteristic clearly in our world? In a world of pandemics, bitter elections, racial tensions, natural disasters, and human-created disasters, how do we see God as "almighty"?
5. God declared that his covenant with Abraham was so he "may multiply [him] greatly" (17:2). How does this compare to the way many people feel about a relationship with God where he makes demands on their lives? ("Does this mean I have to give up_____?")?
6. What prompts us to remember God's promises and live in submission to his authority?

Genesis 18:1–15

EXEGETICAL IDEA
Yahweh, sharing covenant fellowship in theophany through Abraham's hospitality, confirmed his promise of descendants by confronting Sarah's unbelief; revealing his presence, omniscience, and omnipotence; and challenging them to trust him for his promise.

THEOLOGICAL FOCUS
With deepening relationship and through consciousness of our own inability, Yahweh confronts unbelief in his covenant people, challenging them to trust in his presence and power to accomplish his promise.

PREACHING IDEA
Faith is no laughing matter: how our faith grows each time we learn that nothing is too hard for God!

PREACHING POINTERS
There are times in every parishioner's faith journey where they need to hear the Lord say to them: "Is anything too hard for the Lord?" (v. 14). Abraham and Sarah, both "advanced in years" (v. 11), certainly needed to hear it in light of the Lord's unbelievable prophecy. Our struggles to believe require the same assurance of the Lord's powerful ability to remain faithful to deliver us in a badly broken world.

As we've seen throughout these narratives, Abraham shows us the kind of person to whom God gives his precious promises. His reception of the "three men" (v. 2) was remarkable. Just as remarkable is seeing God spend that kind of quality time with his own. Readers must see themselves in this story, reacting in the same way for the same reasons: lavish hospitality is a fruit of faith.

And, of course, since the human heart doesn't change with respect to its natural response to God's revelation, Sarah's laugh (v. 12) shows that faith indeed is required for our walk with God. Our tendency is to judge God's ability to deliver us in terms of our own capacity. Ridiculous, I know! We can probably all identify with Sarah's fearful attempt to cover her tracks: when she denied her incredulity, the Lord graciously corrected her. He handles our unbelief very well. Thankfully, he takes it within the context of an overall stance of faith.

IMPOSSIBLE PROMISES: NO LAUGHING MATTER (18:1–15)

LITERARY STRUCTURE AND THEMES

Rather than following the annunciation of Isaac with the birth narrative as might be expected, Genesis 18:1–15 repeats the birth announcement, transitioning to unexpected accounts of God's destruction of Sodom, the family of Lot, and the endangering of God's promise before finally reaching Isaac's birth in Genesis 21. Reiterating the promise of a son through Sarah, the narrative emphasizes God's power over the naturally impossible promise, with obvious parallels to chapter 17. It could, then, be included with that preaching portion (cf. Brueggemann 1982, 150).

It also, however, formally begins a new section (18:1–19:38), introducing Sodom's destruction and the birth of the sons of Lot (see the Literary Structure and Themes for the next preaching portion, p. 347). As such, it contrasts God's fellowship and blessing on righteous Abraham with his judgment on the wicked (ch. 19) and illustrates God's basis in relationship for bringing blessing to the nations of the earth through faithful offspring in contrast to the offspring of Lot (18:18–19, cf. 19:30–38). Considering the preaching of the text, the subsection itself provides a forceful statement of God's ability to keep any promise, no matter how impossible it appears to humanity, as he graciously refocuses and corrects unbelief.

After announcing Yahweh's theophanic appearance to Abraham (18:1, cf. 17:1), the first of two movements illustrates the fellowship of the covenant parties through the lavish hospitality of Abraham to his guests (18:2–8). The second movement turns to the reason for the visit. Yahweh graciously challenged Sarah's natural incredulity. Perhaps responding to her accusation (16:2), Yahweh confronted her with his good plan and his supernatural capability to accomplish it (18:9–15). He made her face her heart and see his real and good presence.

A. Yahweh appeared to Abraham (18:1).
B. Abraham offered lavish hospitality (18:2–8).
C. Yahweh confronted Sarah's heart (18:9–15).

Yahweh's sovereign power will form the basis, not only to bring about his promised birth but looking ahead, the promised blessing to all nations (18:18) through righteous offspring (v. 19) in the face of infectious wickedness (19:1–38).

- ***Yahweh Appeared to Abraham (18:1)***
- ***Abraham Offered Lavish Hospitality (18:2–8)***
- ***Yahweh Confronted Sarah's Heart (18:9–15)***

EXPOSITION

Genesis 18 records a second theophany to Abraham in a very short chronological timeframe. While the thrust of this scene reflects chapter 17, with Sarah instead of Abraham, the important message moves the narrative ahead. God moves from urging Abram's ongoing loyalty, to actualizing his growing promises (ch. 17), to engaging and encouraging his called covenantees in their faith (18:1–15). God now refocuses Sarah from her inability to his ability. Simultaneously, he connects tangibly with Abraham, and motivates Abraham to live out his calling in what will follow (18:16–33). Sarah, as well as Abraham,

Israel, and modern children of Abraham, must understand and trust Yahweh's ability to carry out his word not only as a basis for their own confident living based on his promise, but also to be the blessing to the world they were called to be. Yahweh, sharing covenant fellowship in theophany through Abraham's hospitality, confirmed his promise of descendants; confronted Sarah's unbelief; revealed his presence, omniscience, and omnipotence; and challenged them to trust him for his promise.

Yahweh Appeared to Abraham (18:1)

Yahweh appeared unexpectedly to Abraham again in theophany.

18:1. Yahweh again appeared to Abraham (cf. 12:7; 17:1; 26:2, 24; 35:1, 9; 48:3). For the first time a description is given of how he appeared to Abraham: Yahweh came as three men (18:2). The initial statement lets the reader know what Abraham only found out gradually. The inside information points out Abraham's actions and words as more significant than Abraham realized, revealing a generous heart that is not motivated by knowing who he is entertaining. It also piques the reader interest in God's intent in this covert mission.

The Lord appeared to Abraham where he had been living since Lot separated from him (13:18), in Hebron at the Oaks of Mamre. It occurred at the hot midday when Abraham was resting from the morning's work, enjoying the shade of the tent and probably a breeze through the opened curtains, the normal custom. It was unusual to see travelers in the heat of the day, adding to Abraham's surprise.

Abraham Offered Lavish Hospitality (18:2–8)

Abraham's extravagant hospitality hints at covenant fellowship, the source of blessing.

18:2–5. When Abraham looked up, three men surprised him, standing in front of him. He immediately jumped to action, running to meet them and bowing down before them. While this was an appropriate way to greet a stranger in his time, it was also more appropriate than he knew for his as-yet unperceived visitation from God. Abraham was displaying his character in ancient terms. He would be elaborately hospitable.

> *TRANSLATION ANALYSIS 18:2*
> The use of *hinneh* (וְהִנֵּה, often translated "behold," ESV), conveys the surprise of suddenly noticing them (NLT) when he had not seen them coming.

Abraham appears to address the leader of the trio (using the singular for both pronouns, "your"), and the MT suggests that he recognized him as God himself ("My Lord," ESV). More likely, however, as you follow the actions of Abraham, he gradually realized who he was entertaining through the course of the conversation.[1] Abraham requested that the strangers stay and allow him the privilege of serving them with his hospitality. His words, however, cap a sequence that appears to speak much more adequately than he realized to the appearance of Yahweh (Wenham 1994, 46). Not only had he bowed with the polite address of "my lord," but he asked for their favor to stay. "If I have found favor in your sight" (using the singular "your," 18:3) recalls Noah finding grace in Yahweh's eyes (6:8, the only previous use of the phrase). The following meal fleshes out Abraham's request, with fellowship around extravagant hospitality, an appropriate expression of the one Yahweh has called "righteous" and commanded to walk before him in blameless loyalty (15:6; 17:1).

1 The Masoretes may assume he recognized Yahweh or possibly wanted to connect the three men to the appearance of Yahweh in verse 1 for the reader (Ross 2008, 123).

The Three Men

The "three men" (18:2) describes the appearance of Yahweh in theophany (v. 1). The alternation between Abraham's singular (v. 3) and plural (vv. 4–5) address, which continues alternating through the narrative but is not clear in the English, suggests that he recognized a leader among the three. Because Yahweh stayed to talk with Abraham while the "men" headed for Sodom (vv. 22–33) and only two "angels" (19:1) arrived in Sodom, many suggest that the three men consisted of God in human form with two angels or one that represented Yahweh and two other angels. Sailhamer (1990, 144–45) argues, however, that the text is not clear, and the group represents Yahweh. The alternating singular and plural forms help the reader to understand that God is present but not to be identified with any individual form and so preserve the ability of God to "appear" without his form being visible (Exod. 33:23; Deut. 4:15; cf. Frankena 1972, 204). "The demarcation between God and His angel is often blurred," so that at one moment it is the angel speaking and at another it is God himself (Sarna 1989, 383), supporting Wenham's (1994, 51) contention that the confusion that continues into the next scenes intentionally expresses "the difficulty of human comprehension of the divine world." See the sidebar at 16:7, p. 313.

TRANSLATION ANALYSIS 18:3

The MT has pointed the Hebrew *adonai* with the form that was only used of Yahweh (אֲדֹנָי), indicated by "O Lord" (18:3 ESV) or "My Lord" (NASB95). Based on Abraham's actions, it is more often translated "My lord," as if it had been pointed with the common form (אֲדֹנִי, e.g., NET, NIV), "Sir" (NCV), or even the plural "My lords" (אֲדֹנַי, NJPS). All are possible from the consonants, but the context suggests he still perceived them as men and addressed the leader.

Abraham's offer understated his hospitality: a little water to wash, rest in the shade, and a bit of food to refresh them. His extravagant hospitality, however, will go far beyond. All of this is his pleasure since they had "come your servant's way" (18:5 NJPS). His assumption still seems to be that it is a random visit. Though they had stopped already and so presumedly had already decided to stay, their brief reply gives no hint as to their purpose.

TRANSLATION ANALYSIS 18:5

Since "bread" (לֶחֶם) is often used metaphorically for food, literally, "a morsel of bread" (18:5 ESV), is appropriately "a bit of food" (NET) or "something to eat" (NIV).

18:6–8. Their assent initiated a flurry of activity. The preparations show Abraham's concern for excellent hospitality. Abraham hurries, he tells Sarah to hurry, and the young man hurries, even as Abraham runs to the herd. Even his words to Sarah are abbreviated and hurried, "Quick! Three seahs of fine flour! Knead it, and make cakes" (18:6). The amount of food they prepared is enormous. The three seahs of flour (about nineteen quarts), was extravagant![2] An entire calf would feed a huge group in a culture that ate little meat. The meal demonstrated Abraham's wealth as well as his hospitality. The flour was finely ground wheat flour, appropriate for a visiting dignitary or an offering to Yahweh (Lev. 2:1, 4), and the calf was the best tender veal, extremely generous.

Though Abraham did not yet understand the full import of this visit, he may be starting to suspect they are not merely traveling strangers. In the ancient world a shared meal was a very significant, moral obligation to the traveler, codified in the Mosaic covenant (Lev. 19:33–34), and a serious offense when neglected (Deut. 23:3–4). The meal symbolized fellowship and a

2 The size of a seah is uncertain, but Fuller estimates six liters (preexilic, and twelve liters postexilic, אֵיפָה, *NIDOTTE* 1:383)

responsibility of care and protection, being used to seal covenants with people (Gen. 26:28–30) and God (Exod. 24:9–11; cf. King and Stager 2001, 61–63). Here it pictures the relationship that God had established with Abraham, even though Abraham was unaware, adding personal intimacy to the reiterated promise of the impending birth (see Ross 1988, 342–43).

Providing the bread, tender veal, yogurt, and milk, Abraham was an exceptional host, personally standing by to serve in the background while the guests ate. No conversation is recorded until the meal appears to be over.

Yahweh Confronted Sarah's Heart (18:9–15)

Yahweh initiated a confrontation with Sarah's unbelief, reiterating his impossible promise and revealing his presence, omniscience, and omnipotence to redirect her attention to his power to act.

18:9–10. The visitors broke the silence after the meal with an unexpected question regarding Sarah that must have surprised both Abraham and Sarah. While the text places the question in the mouths of all three, it is clearly God's question (Yahweh will explicitly speak for the first time in v. 10). As with God's previous questions, however, he already knew the answer (3:9; 4:6–7, 9–10). He used the question to address Sarah formally without breaking protocols, but also to indicate his presence. He was more than a casual visitor. He not only knew her name, but he used her new God-given name, indicating her role in the promised future. The reference to Sarah would make Abraham (and Sarah!) recall God's promise and begin to recognize their visitor.

When Abraham indicated her presence in the tent, Yahweh formally responded to Abraham but was really talking for Sarah's benefit, as the following dialogue clarifies. He reiterated the promise recently given to Abraham of a son to be born through Sarah within the year (17:16, 19, 21). Here, however, he emphasized the miraculous nature with the promise of another special visitation.[3]

TRANSLATION ANALYSIS 18:10a

The phrase used here and in 18:14, "about this time next year" (ESV, translating כָּעֵת חַיָּה), only occurs twice here and twice in 1 Kings 4:16–17 with Elisha's similar promise of a child to the Shunammite the following year. Literally, the phrase is "according to the time of life" (NKJV). Because of the clear reference to the following year in 17:21 and a similar Akkadian phrase (cited by Wenham 1994, 47–48), many versions mirror the ESV (NCV, NIV, NLT). Relating the "time of life" to the springtime, RSV translates "in the spring" (Mathews 2005, 218). NRSV may relate it to the gestational cycle, "in due season." Though the exact reference is not certain, the general intent is clear.

Sarah finally entered the scene. She had been listening, but the narrative makes clear that the visitor could not see her. She was behind him. He asked his question, however, not because he did not know, as we discover, but to confront her heart.

TRANSLATION ANALYSIS 18:10b

The narrator adds that "Sarah was listening at the tent door behind him" (18:10 ESV). The modern reader may imagine a closed "door," at least assuming she is behind the tent curtain. However, the term used for "door" (פֶּתַח, so ESV and others), refers to an "entrance" or "opening" (*HALOT* s.v. "פֶּתַח" 988–89) rather than the door itself and so is better translated "entrance" (e.g., NIV). That curtain in the heat of the day may well have been open so that, had the angel been

3 Yahweh's promise to "return" the next year does not require another physical appearance but the fulfillment of the promise, as noted in 21:1.

facing the tent, Sarah would have been clearly visible.

18:11–12. The narrative inserts a note explaining the reaction of Sarah (v. 11). The reader is already aware of their advanced ages. In fact, Abraham's age was repeated twice in chapter 17. Of course, the reader may wonder, with the extended ages of their ancestors (11:10–26) and the patriarchs themselves, how late they could bear children. Moses makes it clear that Sarah is beyond menopause. By explaining, the narrative lends sympathy to Sarah's reaction. As a result of her clear physical condition, she "laughed to herself" (v. 12). The narrative even reports her thoughts: she was worn out, Abraham was old, and she did not expect to have the pleasure of relations with him, much less a child! We sympathize. What woman, who has longed for a child and seen her possibility disappear with menopause years earlier, would let herself believe such an impossible promise?

TRANSLATION ANALYSIS 18:11

Literally, "The way of women had ceased to be with Sarah" (18:11 ESV) certainly indicates that she was "past the age of childbearing," (NASB95, NIV). The phrase itself refers to the monthly period (31:35), so the NJPS is more direct, "Sarah had stopped having the periods of women." Similarly, NET paraphrases, "Sarah had long since passed menopause."

18:13–15. Not only did this stranger know her special new name from God, however, but he knew her thoughts and paraphrased them to Abraham, without seeing her. Sarah had focused on Abraham's age and her physical incapacity (v. 12). God, however, in his paraphrase went to the heart of her problem. Abraham was certainly old (ch. 17), but her concern was with her own inability to have a child, based on her age after menopause. The stranger's explanation of her natural reaction adds to his supernatural insight as he knows her thoughts without even seeing her face (Sternberg 1987, 91). It also shows God's grace in gently calling out the natural but misplaced focus of Sarah in the face of Yahweh's promise.

Since the narrative does not say, commentators have debated whether Abraham had told Sarah about the promise and her name change in chapter 17. God's reiteration of the promise (18:10) suggests she might not have heard it. Was she dumbfounded, much like Abraham had been just recently? Or had Abraham dutifully related the promise, which she was struggling to believe, so that Yahweh's visit was at least partly necessitated by her unbelief? Yahweh's rebuke of her unbelief, with the pointed reference to his ability, suggests the latter (Hamilton 1990, 13). The use of Sarah's new name without reaction from Sarah corroborates that. Yahweh was addressing a heart issue that was hindering her response of faith to God.

Yahweh's rebuke of Sarah was gentle, nonetheless. He did not expose all her thoughts, including her thoughts about Abraham. Rather, he turned the attention to the ability of Yahweh to keep his promise. One even wonders if it might not have been orchestrated for both Sarah and Abraham to hear. Of course, the question was rhetorical. Certainly, no promise is too hard for Yahweh to keep. In fact, the question itself causes the doubter to recognize the improper focus of their doubts. Doubt is built on personal inability. Doubt assumes that God has no other resource than my abilities, opportunities, or perspectives afford him. Doubt fails to account for the supernatural. If God's brief conversation with Sarah through Abraham did anything, it pinpointed a different and necessary supernatural perspective for faith.

God then reiterated the promise, nearly word for word (cf. 17:21). It would happen at the appointed time, and Sarah would have a son. The reiteration of the promise provides yet another clue that God was not merely explaining to Sarah what Abraham had forgotten to relay. Rather, Yahweh was reassuring his struggling matriarch (and patriarch) that he would indeed complete his promise, even though he had allowed them to wait until any human possibility was totally (and obviously) past. There would be no question for anyone that this child was a supernatural fulfillment of promise. Those knowing sympathetic glances when people heard their new names would turn to joyful praise of the only God who could produce such life.

Sarah, realizing her predicament with this supernatural stranger, spoke up finally, denying her laugh. From the narrator's description, she had not laughed out loud, and so she probably felt justified in declaring she had, in fact, not laughed. Anyone who had been watching her would know that. It seems she is not yet connecting this with a theophany of Yahweh. She thinks she can hide her inner reaction. The simple denial by Yahweh that indeed she had cut to the heart and ended the conversation. God confronted her with her own unbelief so that she must reckon with her own heart and God's full perception of it. She must know that he knew. She had persisted in her unbelief because she could not get past her physical capacity. Her private thoughts were open to him. She could not bow in belief until she recognized the Lord of her heart and body.

Unexpectedly, the name of Isaac did not come up at all in chapter 18. Even though the verbal root for his name occurs four times in the brief narrative, reference to Isaac's name is left simply as an allusion. Coming immediately after chapter 17, however, it is a powerful allusion. When Isaac was born, "he will laugh" would encompass both the initial struggle to believe as well as the joy of relief and anticipation when the child finally arrived. The promise that was not a laughing matter became the excellent medicine of a joyful heart in boundless laughter (21:6).

The effects of Yahweh's mission will show in the following narratives. Abraham would respond with initial insight but struggle in his area of previous compromise. Sarah would have her son, understand the significance of her promise, and be remembered as believing Yahweh (Heb. 11:11). Isaac's birth would demonstrate that nothing is too hard for Yahweh.

THEOLOGICAL FOCUS

With deepening relationship and through conscious inability, Yahweh confronts unbelief in his covenant people, challenging them to trust in his presence and power to accomplish his promise.

God graciously confronts unbelief with both gentle and clear rebuke. He brilliantly sets up his correction of Sarah during his attendance at the sumptuous meal by demonstrating their relationship, the foundation for his blessing that includes the promised descendants. The very presence of God provides the basis for promise and assurance in that promise. Yahweh again shows his creative confrontation, bringing his servants to see both their need and their misdirected viewpoint by revealing his presence, his complete understanding of the human heart, and his ability to accomplish his will. He challenges one's inability with his ability and provides the needed evidence that will expose unbelief, even to oneself. Such faith is necessary to the full participation in the promise, bringing blessing to all the families of the earth.

Hospitality consistently provides a positive expression of the righteous (contrast to the city of Sodom), showing the generous character of the righteous (cf. 1 Tim. 3:2). The point initially is less Abraham's hospitality and more the gracious intersection of the divine with Abraham in sharing that hospitality. Abraham giving his best to Yahweh is expected, even though he initially did not realize who it was. His initial unawareness enhances his generosity. The focus, beginning with the initial declaration (Gen. 18:1a), highlights Yahweh eating with his chosen friend, enjoying relationship, and giving blessing even in the presence of struggling unbelief. God's gracious condescension to humanity to spur on faith and accomplish his purpose provides another paradigm of his loyal love and faithfulness behind the necessary righteousness and justice he must show in the following judgment (v. 19).

God had just called Abraham to walk in loyalty, including radical obedient faith in circumcising his ninety-nine-year-old body. God now challenged Sarah's unbelief, showing that faith, which precedes loyalty, must be based on the clear evaluation of one's belief structure in light of God's presence and power, viewing life from his transcendent viewpoint. While Sarah mimicked Abraham's initial reaction, Yahweh's response is different. It seems that her greater knowledge (knowing the promise already and considering the obstacles) has warranted his gentle rebuke. God expects more when there is greater understanding. He elicits her reactions twice with his initial statement of promise and then his challenge to her laughter. He would redirect unbelief and certify his complete knowledge of the human heart. Understanding both is necessary for growing faith.

The human condition sees the physical and the immediate. We have limited perspective. We are bound by our circumstances. God's grace, however, reveals his presence and his power in and for our lives. God has interrupted our circumstances with his outlandish promises. We struggle because we can only see our world. We assume that God can only work through our abilities. The needed remedy is not to dismiss the barriers to God's work as irrelevant. The remedy is to view God as all sufficient through his revelation to us. He both knows fully my condition and has absolute control over that condition to accomplish whatever he wills. He is not limited to any of my disabilities. In fact, his power is fully demonstrated only in our weakness (2 Cor. 12:9). Without his gracious revelation, however, we are unable to see the appropriate response. Unless we know him, we cannot trust him. His presence guarantees his response, our blessing, and our growing faith through knowing him. How much more, as New Covenant believers, with the indwelling Holy Spirit, do we realize and benefit from the presence of God. And how much more, with the coming of Christ, do we know God and his loyal love and care in our lives!

PREACHING AND TEACHING STRATEGIES

Exegetical and Theological Synthesis

You might begin to think about your sermon/lesson preparation with God's gracious appearance to Abraham in the form of three men meeting him at his tent in the middle of the day. Abraham's hospitality was a fruit of faith. You can see Abraham's righteousness in the way he responds to strangers. The narrator doesn't tell us that Abraham knew his three visitors. Had he known the identity of the visitors, I could reason my way to his eagerness to please and accommodate. The fact that he doesn't know makes his actions noteworthy (e.g., "he ran from the tent door to meet them and bowed himself to the earth," v. 2). He makes it clear that he is their "servant" (vv. 3, 5). What a wonderful picture of the relationship we have with our Lord.

God graciously asks about Sarah's whereabouts since the message certainly affects her. Verse 11 makes it clear that there was no way under heaven that this promise, that Sarah would have a son, could come true. Throughout the Old Testament story, barrenness plays an important role, and a miracle of redemptive history continues each time. I always like to encourage my listeners to answer questions such as in verse 13: "The Lord said to Abraham, 'Why did Sarah laugh and say, "Shall I indeed bear a child, now that I am old?"'" Answer: "Because that's ridiculous at our age, that's why!" That way everyone is ready for the assurance of God's power: "Is anything too hard for the Lord?" (v. 14). And this time, everyone in the house answers, "No, of course not!" There's no sense denying it. Sometimes it's best for us to confess and pray with the character in Mark 9:24, "I believe; help my unbelief."

Preaching Idea
Promise is no laughing matter: how our faith grows each time we learn that nothing is too hard for God.

Contemporary Connections

What does it mean?
You may want to explain again the significance of these theophanies. As stated above, this is the second time our Lord appeared to Abraham.

Hospitality in our American culture is much different from the kind experienced in the ancient Near Eastern world. Listeners will benefit from hearing how Abraham excelled in this assignment. I keep referring to it as a fruit of faith because this shows Abraham's righteousness in action.

Some listeners may find it hard to believe that Sarah could get caught in unbelief and not pay for it. Our God graciously deals with us within the context of his covenant loyalty, defined often as his steadfast love.

Is it true?
As we've talked about before, it's possible that some listeners will struggle with the sheer size of this miracle. It's best not to find a modern parallel of a couple told by a medical specialist that they could never have children, only to find themselves pregnant. Better to agree with the narrator that "The way of women had ceased to be with Sarah" (v. 11). There's no way God could redeem any one of us unless he was able to create life from non-life. Is it true that there is nothing too hard for the Lord? Answer with a resounding, "Yes!" This is truly a first-class miracle—completely impossible apart from divine intervention. It is not a second-class miracle—unlikely and perfect timing that makes it appear to be a miracle but with a fully natural explanation. God was not behind the scenes merely manipulating the timing. He was fully enacting the humanly impossible.

Now what?
I can't think of anything more relevant than the Lord graciously revealing himself and challenging our tendency toward unbelief in his mighty power. But relevance begins with the kind of person God reveals himself to. Abraham is a special person because of his faith in God and his character. God reveals himself, and we should respond accordingly by living out our faith in him in all things. Abraham is a man of faith and therefore faithful to the Lord in what I consider to be a small thing: hospitality. Of course, it was a huge thing back then and still is in some parts of the world. Abraham leads the way for us to follow his example. We should consistently believe God. There are times when we do not know what God is doing, but we need to show the world what it looks like to serve him.

Everyone who has responded to the call of God is transformed little by little into this kind of person. It's a good time for us to assess our spiritual development. We never know what God is doing or how our righteous responses are serving him and his kingdom. And Sarah, of course, shows us how easy it is for us to forget the kind of power our Lord has at his disposal.

Creativity in Presentation
Frame the presentation around the homiletical idea: Faith is no laughing matter: how our faith grows each time we learn that nothing is too hard for God. I could easily hear a sermon refrain repeated at strategic times: "Is anything too hard for the Lord?" Some congregations will be eager to respond with a resounding: "No!" You can see how easy it would be for this sermon to bolster their faith as they believe the truths stated in the homiletical idea. Provide or solicit personal illustrations of experiences where extreme faith was on display in the Christian life. That should include the times when you or they laughed, just as Sarah did, in unbelief.

Consider this possible sermon structure:

- The promise is given to a certain kind of character (vv. 1–8). (Abraham teaches us through one of those "go and do likewise" sections. In this case his over-the-top hospitality shows his faith at work. This is Abraham keeping his end of the covenant. Allow his attitudes and actions to drive those in your listeners with respect to their own daily lives.)
- Disbelief is our natural response to God's unbelievable promises (vv. 9–13, 15). (Here it is Sarah who teaches us with a "go and do otherwise" response. The whole section keys on Sarah and her response, so this is a time to acknowledge our need to fight for faith and against unbelief.)
- God's character is the theological basis for our faith in God's promises (v. 14). (I prefer separating this verse/concept and dealing with it at or near the end of the sermon. If you attempt to use it as a refrain as I stated above, your listeners will have heard it many times. If not, here is where you challenge them to believe, to answer with an unhesitating, "No!")

"You've got to be kidding me!" is a way to modernize and explain Sarah's laugh. Match that emotion with a positive emotion that signifies full faith. Help them exchange the laugh of incredulity with the approving "Yes!" smile and nod of faith.

DISCUSSION QUESTIONS

1. Think of a time in your life when God waited until the situation was humanly impossible before he came to your rescue. What did you learn then, what do you see now, and how do you keep those lessons fresh?

2. What is it about faith in God that created Abraham's unique brand of hospitality?

3. Why is it easy to answer the question in verse 14 correctly on a quiz but difficult to live that answer out under the pressure of life?

4. Verse 15 shows Sarah denying that she laughed at the promises. She was called out on it. Ask how many of your listeners have been brutally honest with God about their feelings about his promises. When is it easy to be honest, and when is it hard to be honest with God? Why?

5. Why is it so hard to acknowledge to God how we really feel when we say we know that he knows our hearts?

6. What are ways we can show God's character in our lives in our responses to the people around us with acts of service to his glory?

Genesis 18:16–19:38

EXEGETICAL IDEA

God chose Abraham to be a blessing, teaching righteousness and justice, interceding for his world in the face of God's paradigmatic judgment, justly condemning the wicked, and graciously delivering Lot and his family despite their costly infection by the world.

THEOLOGICAL FOCUS

God teaches humanity his character and expectations of righteousness and justice through his loyal followers and his actions, justly judging the wicked and graciously delivering the righteous, despite serious compromise and loss.

PREACHING IDEA

Make sure we are "the righteous" ones not swept away by the judgment of God and able to bring blessing to others.

PREACHING POINTERS

One of the most exciting things about preaching through Genesis is the opportunity to communicate the justice of God in a way that will elicit worship in church. That is especially true in a climate when more and more listeners are breathing the air where modern sensibilities are offended by such doctrine. In this pericope, the original audience comes face to face with the justice and judgment of God. Critical, however, is seeing that God's pronouncement of impending judgment on wicked citizens occurs within the context of God's previous promises made to righteous-by-faith Abraham. The move from those readers to our listeners is straightforward: the patience of God will run out at some point. As the Judge of all the earth he will certainly judge rightly (separating the righteous from the wicked), he will tolerate much wickedness to exist ("For the sake of ten I will not destroy it," 18:32), and judgment will fall on the wicked.

Abraham's intercession frames the story and becomes crucial to the point. The Christian needs to see the privilege he has both in declaring God's character (his justice and righteousness) and interceding for the wicked and the righteous among them. We are called to bless our world. We cannot do that if we become like it. We can only do it by living out God's character and teaching his goodness to our world.

Two other things to consider as we think about moving from the original audience to our listeners: (1) Lot's wife shows a different level of wickedness and also experiences a different judgment; and (2) the situation that occurs after the destruction of Sodom and Gomorrah between Lot and his two daughters shows the ongoing effects of sin's spread—more incentive for us and our listeners to be righteous by faith and obedience.

JUSTICE AND GRACE: LIVING BRIGHTLY IN A DARK WORLD (18:16–19:38)

LITERARY STRUCTURE AND THEMES

The literary unity of Genesis 18–19 includes parallels between chapters 18 and 19 and a complex chiastic structure tying the whole unit together (cf. Wenham 1994, 40–41, 44):[1]

- A. Abraham would have a son in his old age (18:1–15).
  - B. Abraham accompanied his guests (18:16).
    - C. God revealed his plan to Abraham (18:17–21).
      - D. Abraham pled for Sodom (18:22–33).
        - E. Lot took in the angels (19:1–3).
          - F. Lot failed to placate the crowd (19:4–11).
            - G. The angels announced judgment (19:12–13).
          - F'. Lot failed to convince his sons-in-law (19:14).
        - E'. The angels took Lot out (19:15–16).
      - D'. Lot pled for Zoar (19:17–22).
    - C'. God carried out his plan of judgment (19:23–26).
  - B'. Abraham surveyed the destruction (19:27–29).
- A'. Lot had two sons in his old age (19:30–38).

The many repeated words and motifs not only unify the passage and connect the scenes but draw out numerous theological connections and implications. The pericope focuses on the justice of God. The judge of all the earth does indeed do what is right, going far beyond the expectations of even his saints.

The heart of the narrative (18:16–19:29) begins with the clear theological basis for Yahweh's desire to bring blessing to the nations through people who live out his righteousness and justice (18:19). He then revealed to Abraham that he would evaluate Sodom and Gomorrah for immediate justice. The following narrative validates Abraham's rhetorical query, expecting the judge of all the earth to do justice (18:25). The angelic entrance into Sodom drives the narrative toward its pivot exposing the grave nature of Sodom's sin (19:1–11) and bringing God's judgment yet hope for Lot and his family (19:12–13).

The angelic confirmation of certain destruction, the focus of the chiasm, verifies God's evaluation and his just response, culminating in the fiery cataclysm. The narrative then presses toward the climax when judgment falls, yet it details God's grace that would deliver a hesitant Lot and his corrupted daughters, and even spare a little village for Lot's sake. God balanced justice with Abraham's petition and revealed his character of mercy and longsuffering.

The concluding outworking for Lot (19:30–38), siring his own grandsons in a cave, graphically reveals how infection with the world damages even the righteous believer and his family. It frames the narrative with God's contrasting promise of his chosen line that will bring blessing through those that will wait for him in faith (18:1–15). Instead, the wealthy Lot

1 Parallels highlight the two hospitality scenes (18:1–8//19:1–3) and the intercession scenes (18:23–32//19:18–22), drawing out the contrasts between Abraham and Lot (cf. Wenham 1994, 44).

(13:5–6), fixated on appearances (13:10–11), had neglected the heart issues (13:13) to his ultimate loss, including even his family. His legacy would be two people groups that would oppose God's people and promise. It starkly juxtaposes one who walks before God in integrity (17:1; see 18:22) and one corrupted by the world.

- ***Abraham Accompanied His Guests (18:16)***
- ***God Revealed His Plan to Abraham (18:17–21)***
- ***Abraham Pled for Sodom (18:22–33)***
- ***Lot Took in the Angels (19:1–3)***
- ***Lot Failed to Placate the Crowd (19:4–11)***
- ***The Angels Announced Judgment (19:12–13)***
- ***Lot Failed to Convince His Sons-in-law (19:14)***
- ***The Angels Took Lot Out (19:15–16)***
- ***Lot Pled for Zoar (19:17–22)***
- ***God Carried Out His Plan of Judgment (19:23–26)***
- ***Abraham Surveyed the Destruction (19:27–29)***
- ***Lot Had Two Sons in His Old Age (19:30–38)***

EXPOSITION

Abraham's hospitality and interaction with Yahweh and Yahweh's reiterated promise of the coming son through Sarah in their old age provide the backdrop to God's judgment. Abraham was chosen to bring blessing to all families of the earth. That purpose is gaining clarity as we see the opportunity and expectation God is providing. Abraham must teach justice and righteousness (18:19), and he will intercede, being a blessing. Though Lot showed hospitality, he lacked justice and righteousness and did not pass it along to his daughters or sons-in-law, much less his neighbors. Lot was not a blessing. Lot may be saved, but he lost nearly everything, and even his daughters and grandsons would testify to his corruption. In many ways Lot is merely a foil for the righteous life and expectation of Abraham. God chose Abraham to be a blessing, teaching righteousness and justice and interceding for his world in the face of God's paradigmatic judgment, which justly condemned the wicked and graciously delivered Lot and his family despite their costly infection by the world.

Abraham Accompanied His Guests (18:16)

Abraham accompanied his guests as they look toward Sodom.

18:16. When the men left, they pointedly looked down (שׁקף) toward Sodom. Abraham will similarly look down (שׁקף, 19:28) toward Sodom, showing his concern to see the outcome of his petition. The focus is on Abraham's responsibility and what God will do. Abraham, the consummate host, accompanied Yahweh with his representatives as the men started out on their journey. The imagery of Abraham walking with the men (הלך) is particularly apt, recalling Enoch and Noah, who walked with God (וַיִּתְהַלֵּךְ, 5:22–24; 6:9) and God's command for Abraham to "walk before me and be blameless" (הִתְהַלֵּךְ לְפָנַי, 17:1). Abraham, acting in righteousness, will not only walk out with them but will present himself "before Yahweh" (לִפְנֵי יְהוָה, 18:22; cf. 19:27, אֲשֶׁר־עָמַד שָׁם אֶת־פְּנֵי יְהוָה).

God Revealed His Plan to Abraham (18:17–21)

Reflecting on Abraham's future and purpose, Yahweh revealed to Abraham his mission to evaluate the evil of Sodom and Gomorrah.

18:17–19. Yahweh's reflection on his purposes, also background to the narrative, was not addressed to Abraham. Rather, Yahweh's thoughts show the reader Yahweh's plan and anticipate his purpose for talking with Abraham. Yahweh would declare his coming judgment to Abraham, giving him entry to God's personal council as prophet (Jer. 23:18; Amos 3:7; cf. Gen. 20:7) and friend (2 Chron. 20:7).

TRANSLATION ANALYSIS 18:17

As with the remark concerning Abraham accompanying them, the clause is introduced with a waw-disjunctive. The significance of the syntax here is to place the words of Yahweh as background and indicate that they were not directed to Abraham until 18:20. Rather, as the NJPS translates, it is a parenthetical remark or previous musing of Yahweh: "Now the LORD had said, 'Shall I hide from Abraham what I am about to do?'" Most English translations make it ambiguous at best as to whether Abraham heard this remark.

Yahweh had chosen Abraham and would reveal his purposes to him because the nation that comes from him would be the means for blessing all nations. God intended for Abraham to raise up a family to become a nation who would "keep the way of the LORD" (18:19). They were to be a nation that walks with God. Abraham's purpose, then, grounds God's desired outcome. He wants to bless humanity (12:3) by building a worshipping nation that is in relationship with him (17:7–8) and exhibiting his character (keeping his "way") by practicing righteousness and justice (18:19). The outcome is the fulfillment of the initial promise and goal of offering blessing to all the nations (v. 18). As the nations see the character of Yahweh in the people of Yahweh, they will find access to blessing and the means to relationship with him to share in that blessing. The need for a people doing righteousness and justice grows in a land crying out to heaven against the grave sin of its inhabitants.

TRANSLATION ANALYSIS 18:19

God had "chosen him" (18:19 lit. "known him," יְדַעְתִּיו) for his purpose. While "chosen" is an appropriate translation of the intent here (or "singled him out," NJPS, NLT), the use of the verb "know" will tie the narrative together (18:21; 19:5, 8, 33, 35) and mark out Abraham in his unique role before Yahweh, implying intimacy (Fretheim, יָדַע *NIDOTTE* 2:411). A similar expression will be used of Moses (Exod. 33:12, 17; cf. Deut. 34:10) and Jeremiah (Jer. 1:5; see also David, 2 Sam. 7:20; 1 Chron. 17:18). In God's use of this for Israel, it clearly requires responsibility (Amos 3:2; Hos. 13:5), as God will similarly lay out his expectations for Abraham.

"Righteousness" (צְדָקָה) generally refers to acting in accordance with a standard (Reimer, צדק, *NIDOTTE* 3:746), here based in Yahweh's character (18:19 "to keep the way of the LORD," וְשָׁמְרוּ דֶּרֶךְ יְהוָה).[2] "Justice" (מִשְׁפָּט) describes appropriate functioning, especially of government, so that the governance (of all sorts) reflects the "rightness rooted in God's character" (Culver, *TWOT* 949). Justice and righteousness together consistently refer to a good administration reflecting Yahweh (2 Sam. 8:15; 1 Kings 10:9; Ps. 33:5; Isa. 9:6; 33:5; Jer. 9:23), a nation that keeps his ways (Isa. 58:2), or an individual that lives by his laws (Ezek. 18:5, 19, 21, 27). Reflecting God's purpose for Abraham (and his offspring), Jeremiah called Israel to swear by Yahweh in truth, justice, and righteousness, so that the nations would find blessing in him (Jer. 4:2).

Here, God identified the future nation living out his standard as the basis for fulfilling his promise to Abraham since God cannot bless either the individual, nation, or all of humanity without that standard of righteousness and justice. The contingency of the promise is becoming clearer as God progressively reveals his expectations. God will certainly keep his promise, but it will require people living out his ways and teaching them to their world. The

2 So, Moses declares that keeping the law of Yahweh will be "righteousness" (צְדָקָה) for Israel (Deut. 6:25).

ones who will enjoy and see the fulfillment of the promises will be those who live and teach the way of the Lord.

18:20–21. Speaking to Abraham, the Lord declared his plan to personally verify the degree of sin in Sodom and Gomorrah. He had heard the cries of the oppressed, indicating very grievous sin. The cohortative in verse 21 indicates God's resolve to go personally ("I will," ESV, or "I must," NRSV). Far from indicating God does not know, the anthropomorphism emphasizes God's justice, demonstrating to Abraham and to future generations that his judgment is warranted.[3] If it is not, he will "know." Ironically, the attempt of the men of Sodom to "know" the strangers (19:5) would verify God's knowledge of their evil.

> *TRANSLATION ANALYSIS 18:20*
> The degree of sin is intensified both by the verbs "great" (רָבָּה) and "grave" (lit. "heavy," כָבְדָה); the use of the emphatic particle (כִּי), often translated "so" (e.g., NIV, NJPS), though not translated in the ESV; and the adverb with the second phrase "very" (מְאֹד, e.g., ESV) or "exceedingly" (e.g., NASB95).

God had mused that he must reveal to Abraham his purpose to verify Sodom's sin for destruction because of his choice to bring blessing to all nations through him (18:18). Abraham must teach his children and house to keep the way of the Lord, so Abraham must see God's justice in action and have opportunity to understand God's righteous response. As with his previous conversation with Sarah, God was prompting and testing Abraham. Abraham, called to be a blessing, responded appropriately with intercession.

Abraham Pled for Sodom (18:22–33)

Abraham pled for Sodom and Gomorrah based on God's justice and the presence of righteous people.

18:22–26. The "men" left for Sodom, and Abraham was left standing before Yahweh. It may be that one of the men stayed behind, representing Yahweh himself (Mathews 2005, 226–27). or it may be that all three left, one to go to Gomorrah while two went to Sodom (Sailhamer 1990, 150–51). Clearly, however, Abraham was left with an audience directly with Yahweh, and he did not hesitate. He took his new knowledge and boldly approached Yahweh with his concern, both for God's reputation and for the people in Sodom. He would be a blessing by interceding for the righteous and the wicked.

Abraham initially expressed concern that God would judge the whole plain without differentiating the righteous from the wicked. His request, however, was not just to spare the righteous, but that God would spare Sodom if he found fifty righteous. He did not address the possibility of God simply sparing the righteous. Rather, he pled for the wicked as well, asking for mercy. He may have felt that the presence of fifty righteous (or ten, when he concluded), would have a redeeming quality capable of turning the wicked to repentance (being a blessing!). Sadly, the large contingent with Lot that had lived with Abraham for years (13:5–6) had not impacted Sodom. In fact, it had been quite the opposite.

Abraham sharpened his argument, affirming God's justice that would certainly not put the righteous to death for the sins of the wicked without differentiation (v. 25). God's very character was on the line. His concluding question forms the theme of the section: "Shall not the Judge of all the earth do what is just (מִשְׁפָּט)?" (v. 25). The clear and obvious answer is,

3 The indictment of Sodom and Gomorrah presupposes a moral law to which God holds all humanity responsible (Sarna 1989, 132). Here, the outcry refers to the cries of the oppressed and social violence. See exposition on 19:5 below. On the anthropomorphism, see Chisholm (2007).

"Of course!" The very thing that Abraham was to teach his children and household to do, "righteousness and justice" (מִשְׁפָּט), the hallmark of Yahweh, would be denied if Yahweh destroyed the righteous with the wicked.

TRANSLATION ANALYSIS 18:25

The typical translation "Far be it from you" (חָלִלָה לְּךָ, *v.* 25 ESV) reflects the noun from the root that often describes profaning God's name or his holy things in Leviticus (e.g., 18:21; 19:8). Brueggemann (1982a, 171) notes that the impression in English is misleading. Such a response was not merely a matter of human equity, but it would jeopardize his holiness.

God's answer was direct and affirmed Abraham's request. He would spare "the whole place" (v. 26) for the sake of fifty righteous. God is gracious as well as just.

18:27–29. Recognizing the position he was in, Abraham continued. A man of "dust" (עָפָר, Gen. 2:7) stood before his Creator and questioned God's justice and intent. His boldness underlined his own righteous character, concerned for God's reputation and the wicked, asking for the sake of forty-five. When God agreed, he quickly dropped the number again, to forty, and God again agreed.

18:30–33. From there, Abraham became more apologetic, realizing his tenuous footing but pushing on. With three more requests, he dropped the threshold to ten righteous and God agreed. At that point, the conversation ended.[4] Though the reason Abraham ended his query with ten is not given, the exchange has focused the reader's expectations on how God will demonstrate his justice and mercy against the obvious evil at hand. God must reveal his holy character as he judges, to show his righteousness, justice, and mercy for the wicked and the righteous.

Lot Took in the Angels (19:1–3)

Lot urged the two angels who had arrived in Sodom to stay in his home.

19:1–3. The men who left for Sodom after lunch with Abraham arrived before dark. The trip from Mamre to Sodom, all in the late afternoon, at least twenty miles,[5] prompted the obvious explanation that they were "angels" (19:1, הַמַּלְאָכִים) appearing as men (v. 5). Reminding the reader of Abraham in the beginning of chapter 18, Lot sees them approach from his seat in the gate. Since the gate was the traditional place for public assembly, business, justice, and the normal busy traffic of the day, it appears he was well entrenched in the Sodomite society (cf. King and Stager 2001, 234–36). He likely has risen to a position of importance, implied by his later rebuke from the townsmen (v. 9).

As with Abraham, he also offered the expected hospitality. Surprisingly, the angels declined, but he insisted and they consented. Perhaps their demur was to be able to better gauge the nature of the town, from which no one else had reached out to them. Or perhaps they were testing Lot's character.

---

4 The reason for stopping is not given, but the suggestions have been numerous. Perhaps Abraham thought that ten was "the minimum effective social entity" (Sarna 1989, 134). Or perhaps God ended the conversation by hinting at his impatience with his use of "destroy" (שחת) in vv. 31–32, finally terminating the conversation and leaving (v. 33; Wenham 1994, 53). Perhaps Abraham had now learned he could trust the merciful justice of Yahweh (Mathews 2005, 230). Perhaps ten was the smallest community after which they need to be saved individually (Waltke and Fredricks 2001, 271). Abraham counted on Lot, his family, and their spouses all being righteous (Stigers 1976, 172–73), or it was a merely literary device that should not be taken literally (Brueggemann 1982a, 172).

5 If the location of Sodom is on the northern edge of the Dead Sea, it was nearly twenty miles, but if it was at the southern end of the Dead Sea as we suggested earlier, the trip would be closer to forty miles.

The obvious similarities between Abraham and Lot in their offers of hospitality also point out some dissimilarity. Lot also bowed to meet them and offered them refreshment and lodging. When they agreed, "he made them a feast and baked unleavened bread" (v. 3). Lot's response, however, lacks both the detailed excitement and bustle of Abraham's preparations, noting only Lot working on the meal and only the freshly baked bread. There is no similar extravagance like Abraham's tender young calf. Lot's "feast" (מִשְׁתֶּה, v. 3) does not live up to Abraham's precedent, though he was quite wealthy (13:5–6).

Lot Failed to Placate the Crowd (19:4–11)

Lot attempted to dissuade the men of Sodom from their evil, who rejected his warning and offer.

19:4–5. "Before they lay down" (v. 4) suggests that they had barely finished dinner before the townsmen had gathered. Moses emphasizes the complete and hurried participation of the men of the town: all ages, "all the people," and "to the last man" (NET). Not only was Lot alone in providing hospitality, but he would also be alone in protecting their welfare. While he does not live up to Abraham's generosity, he does provide a clear contrast to the mob of Sodom coming in mass to abuse the men.

> *TRANSLATION ANALYSIS 19:4*
> The ESV's "to the last man" (cf. NJPS, NRSV) paraphrases the Hebrew here (מִקָּצֶה), which is an abbreviation for the common expression "from one end to the other" (*HALOT* s.v. "קָצֶה" 1120–21). It can be rendered "from every part of the city" (NET, NIV) or "from every quarter" (NASB95, NKJV), though the sense of the ESV follows.

The men of Sodom announced their intentions. They wanted to "know" (וְנֵדְעָה, v. 5) the strangers. The verb "know" (ידע) can be translated various ways.[6] Lot's offer of his daughters, however, who had "not known any man" (v. 8), clearly refers to their virginity, and Walton (2009a, 93) notes that whenever this verb uses a personal direct object in Hebrew it is always sexual. In this context, and in conjunction with the similar passage in Judges 19, sexual intimacy is the objective. While it is true that the term itself does not denote "abuse" (Hamilton 1995, 34), the context makes it clear that a meaning of "sexual intercourse" here would lead to abuse. The townsmen were not expecting consent, as their treatment of Lot attests. Their demand, then, validated God's knowledge of their evil (18:21). In fact, the repetition of the verb "know" (ידע) suggests a subtle play on words. God's validated knowledge justified their judgment and precluded them from knowing him (Doyle 1998).

Torah was clear for Israel. Same-sex practices required the death penalty (Lev. 18:22; 20:13) and were specifically related to the practices of the residents of the land before Israel (Lev. 18:24–30). From a Mosaic viewpoint, Sodom stood condemned. Even the contemporaneous laws around Sodom and Canaan condemned this outrage. While same-sex practices were accepted for consenting adults across the ancient world, rape was commonly condemned (Wenham 1991). The actions of these men were not acceptable even in their time in their broader culture. Their sin, however, was not limited to rape.

6 Morschauser (2003) has proposed that the issue was one of protecting the city from spies trying to breach the city defenses through infiltration and subterfuge. The offer of Lot's daughters was to provide hostages to be sure the men left town the next day as expected. While the proposal removes the modern social objections to the traditional interpretation of the passage, it fails to account for significant details in the story, including the immediate context and use of the verb "to know."

Ezekiel 16:49 decries their pride, refusing to use their prosperity to help the poor and needy. The incident in Genesis 19 becomes emblematic for a much more pervasive overturning of social morality.

19:6–9. Lot, however, stood out from the Sodomites and stood up to them. He was clearly not willing to go along with their abuse. His condemnation of their demands that it would be acting "wickedly" (תָּרֵעוּ, v. 7) falls in line with the broader culture but is soundly rebuffed by the men themselves. Here they declare that, whatever status he may have acquired in Sodom, he is still a "sojourner" (v. 9) and has no authority to judge them (וַיִּשְׁפֹּט שָׁפוֹט, reminding the reader that they would be judged by God's standard).[7] While he was offering hospitality and so protection to the strangers, he himself required protection because the men of the city did not consider him to be part of their community. Lot was powerless to carry out his responsibilities as host.

Hospitality was a duty for Israel rooted in their response to Yahweh as their God (Lev. 19:33–34). Their responsibility was not unique, however. Hospitality was a hallowed obligation across the ancient world. The host was responsible for the care and safety of his guests while they were with him or, as Lot notes, under his roof (19:8; Hamilton 1995, 36; King and Stager 2001, 61–63). Lot's ethical duty to his guests drove him to a dilemma, which he solved with the abhorrent sacrifice of his daughters as substitutes for the men.

While Lot may not have been as wicked as the Sodomites, from the reader's perspective, both ancient and modern, he does not seem far behind them. His infection from his world had left him deeply compromised. He had moved from identification with Abraham ("we are kinsmen," lit. "brothers," 13:8, אַחִים), to settling in the valley and moving toward Sodom (13:13), to living in the city (14:12), to a leading role sitting in the gate (19:1) and identifying with them (v. 7, "my brothers," אַחַי). He did still call wickedness wicked (v. 7), but he was willing to sacrifice his own daughters, and though he would leave, he would need to be nearly dragged away (v. 16).

The men of Sodom refused both his correction and his offer. He was not one of them, and they threatened to abuse him even worse than they had planned for the strangers. He was on the cusp of destruction himself.

19:10–11. Ironically, the angels he was trying to protect rescued him. They revealed their supernatural nature by plucking him from the fire and blinding the mob. The only other use of "blindness" (סַנְוֵרִים) occurs in 2 Kings 6:18 when Elisha asked the Lord to blind the Arameans. They similarly experienced confusion so that they were able to follow Elisha but did not know who he was or where they were.[8]

The Angels Announced Judgment (19:12–13)

The angels warned Lot of impending judgment, urging him to remove all his family to safety.

19:12–13. The warning from the angels was direct and pointed. Lot must remove all his family from the city because the men were there to destroy it. Recalling Yahweh's conversation with Abraham, they stated their intent to "destroy" (שׁחת, v. 13 [2x]; see 18:28 [2x], 31, 32; 19:14, 29) this "place" (מָקוֹם, vv. 12, 13; see 18:24, 26, 33; 19:14, 27). This call for destruction also joins numerous other terms and motifs clearly alluding

7 The sojourner was "anyone outside the kin group or solidarity unit and, therefore, defenseless" and had to be protected by someone in the community as an act of hospitality (King and Stager 2001, 61).

8 Speiser (1964, 139–40) suggests it was a blinding light (a loanword from Akkadian) producing something "like desert or snow blindness" rather than total blindness.

to the flood narrative (6:11, 12, 13, 17; 9:11, 15). The numerous, intentional parallels drive home the point that God's judgment on Sodom and its allies was paradigmatic of his judgment on any that scorn God's righteousness and justice and refuse to listen to rebuke, as well as his grace to rescue the righteous (2 Peter 2:4–10).[9] God was again returning the consequences of human destruction of his world back on humanity, demonstrating his righteous judgment.

These verses focus the narrative, centering the chiasm. The angels have validated the "outcry" to Yahweh (Gen. 19:13; see also 18:21, first half of the chiasm), and judgment is decreed. Only Lot was willing to stand against the evil. They would now bring the threatened destruction, yet Abraham's petition stands in the background. The announcement of judgment logically concluded the mob scene: there were not ten righteous. Yet the angels extended grace beyond Abraham's request. God would not destroy the righteous with the wicked in his judgment. The judge of all the earth would indeed do what is just, warning Lot to gather all he could to flee the coming catastrophe.

Lot Failed to Convince His Sons-in-law (19:14)

Lot warned his sons-in-law of the coming judgment, who rejected his warning.

19:14. Lot's only attempt to save his family was his brief warning to his future sons-in-law, repeating the angelic warning of coming destruction. Consistent with the rest of the townsmen, they thought he was joking. The use of "jesting" (*piel* participle from צחק) here, the same root used of Abraham's (17:17) and Sarah's laughter (18:12, 13) and Isaac's name (17:3), reminds the reader again of God's promise to bring blessing to this world, requiring the knowledge of him and his justice.

TRANSLATION ANALYSIS 19:14

The Hebrew participle (לֹקְחֵי בְנֹתָיו) can be understood either as "his sons-in-law, who were to marry his daughters" (ESV, cf. NIV, RSV) or "who had married his daughters" (NJPS, NKJV). Whether Lot had other daughters (or sons, v. 12) is left uncertain.

The Angels Took Lot Out (19:15–16)

The two angels compelled Lot and his family to leave their home and Sodom.

19:15–16. The angels had arrived in the evening, but now, as dawn was approaching, they pressed Lot to leave. Both the timeframe and statement of Lot's hesitance reflect the battle going on inside Lot. After a full night of conflict, in the face of divine intervention, Lot's reluctance underlines the hold that Sodom had on him and his family. Knowing and believing the calamitous judgment to fall, he still found it difficult to release his world, so that the angels had to compel Lot and his family to leave the city.

The angelic warning that he and his family would be "swept away" recalls Abraham's prayer that Yahweh not "sweep away" the righteous with the wicked (ספה, 19:15, 17; see 18:23, 24). The angel affirmed both Yahweh's righteousness in delivering the righteous, as well as Lot's responsibility to separate himself from the wicked to escape the judgment. Yet Lot is not pictured as wholly virtuous.

Measuring Lot by the standard God gave Abraham of keeping the way of the Lord produces a mixed impression. He stood against the overt wickedness, but he clung to the amenities and advantages of it. Lot was not delivered, then, because of his response to Yahweh, but because Yahweh was "merciful to him" (v. 16), expressing God's "compassion" or "pity" (Tsevat, חֶמְלָה, *TDOT* 4:471). His deliverance by God's grace

9 Parallels with the flood story include thematic parallels, verbal similarities and repetitions, and the overall chiastic structure (Wenham 1994, 42–43). See the following exegesis.

points to his righteousness (2 Peter 2:7) through Abraham's intercession (Gen. 19:29).

Lot Pled for Zoar (19:17–22)

Lot pled for Zoar based on God's grace and his own fears.

19:17. Again reminding the reader of Abraham's concern, the angel urged Lot to flee to safety. They must not look back or dawdle in the plain so that they might not be "swept away" with the wicked. Lot's obvious hesitation could bring his destruction. Rather, he must find safety in the hills nearby. Yahweh's clear verdict was judgment for the whole valley.

19:18–20. Lot, however, was concerned that he could not escape in time (לֹא אוּכַל, v. 19). Was he worried about being able to drag his family away soon enough? Acknowledging God's "favor" (חֵן, reminding the reader of God's evaluation of Noah, 9:8) and "great kindness" toward him (Gen. 19:19), Lot pled for asylum in the little village nearby. Abraham, living out his purpose to bring blessing and showing concern for his world, had prayed to preserve the wicked based on God's justice and grace toward them, for their benefit and because of the presence of the righteous. Lot prayed to preserve the place based on God's grace toward him and for his benefit, to allow his presence because it was small, not considering the death of the wicked.

19:21–22. Lot's motivation and concern contrasted dramatically with Abraham. His self-focus showed concern only for his own life. No wonder there were not even ten righteous in Sodom, yet God was overwhelmingly gracious. God granted his request, urging Lot to hurry so that the appointed judgment could fall. God's concession revealed that Lot's concern for escape was misplaced. The angel could not (לֹא אוּכַל, v. 22; cf. v. 19) destroy the valley until Lot was safe. Significantly, however, he saved the entire village for the sake of one. The character of God was on display in saving the small remnant, reflecting and exceeding Abraham's intercession (Kuruvilla 2014, 231–32).

God Carried Out His Plan of Judgment (19:23–26)

God destroyed Sodom and Gomorrah as he had warned, sparing Lot and Zoar.

19:23–26. After Lot was safe in Zoar, Yahweh brought the promised destruction. Again reminiscent of the flood, Yahweh "rained" destruction on the wicked (מטר, 19:24; cf. 7:4). The miraculous destruction may well have included some of the natural sulfur and bitumen at hand (Walton 2009a, 93), but it was clearly a supernatural event. Contrary to the angelic prohibition, Lot's wife looked back and shared in the destructive consequences for the plain. It may be that she turned back to the city (possibly Luke's understanding, Luke 17:31–32) or lingered in the plain while Lot and his daughters went into Zoar (Gen. 19:17).

Abraham Surveyed the Destruction (19:27–29)

Abraham went out to look toward Sodom and its destruction in which God had remembered him, saving Lot.

19:27–29. Framing the narrative (cf. 18:16), Abraham again walked out to look toward Sodom, this time to see the results of his intercession. Numerous reminders of that initial scene validate God's righteous justice in judging the wicked, showcasing his grace to Lot and his daughters because of Abraham's intercession. Though Abraham did not yet know the results, God did what Abraham had not envisioned. Yahweh's just salvation of the righteous (and even some wicked) endorsed Abraham's role in blessing his world. It would be up to his descendants to continue Yahweh's redemptive purpose, bringing blessing to their world by keeping and teaching the way of the Lord (18:18–19).

Again reminding the reader of the flood, God "remembered Abraham" (19:29). Whereas in Genesis 8:1 Yahweh delivered the object of his covenant promise, here he delivered one because of the intercession of his covenant partner. He acted according to his character, extending the benefits of Abraham's relation with God to Lot. Abraham had appropriately used his privilege with Yahweh to the benefit of his world.

Lot Had Two Sons in His Old Age (19:30–38)

Lot had two sons in his old age by his daughters, according to the way of all the earth.

19:30. Lot belatedly followed the angel's instructions, moving to a cave in the hills. He did not move from obedience, however, but moved out of unidentified fear. It is worth noting that he did not return to Abraham, where he might have experienced blessing. Instead, he settled in a cave in isolation. As a result, his daughters reveal the depth of the impact of Sodom. Reminiscent of the aftermath of the flood, the children of the one delivered are in the tent with their drunk, naked father. The shameful actions of the children were memorialized, not by a curse from an indignant, knowing father, but by producing two nations from a pathetically unknowing father.

19:31–33. Lot's oldest daughter plotted to keep their line alive, despairing of ever finding husbands. Her words declare more than she intends. She was certain they could never have a family "after the manner of all the earth" (v. 31). She would certainly show the way of all the earth in her actions, in contrast to Yahweh's concern that Abraham teach his offspring and household "to keep the way of the LORD" (18:19). The actions produced the desired offspring, but they did not produce blessing. And while Lot was not implicated directly in the plot since he did not "know" (v. 35), neither was he exonerated. Instead, he appears as a pathetically ignorant accomplice. God "knew" (18:21) what he did not know—the corrosive cost of sin to his own family.

19:34–35. The firstborn instigated the younger daughter's reproduction of her success. Lot was equally ignorant, and the girls were equally successful. Lot had moved from the place of blessing and hope in the household of Abraham to alone in a cave, fathering his own illegitimate grandchildren. His daughters were removed from Sodom, but Sodom was not removed from them. The two girls that he had offered as bribes to the men of Sodom, to violate without their consent to try to preserve his warped sense of duty to the angels, showed their complicity in the sins of Sodom as they violate him without his consent to preserve their warped sense of heritage.

19:36–38. The outcome of the sordid affair in the cave would be two nations. The names of the two sons would reflect the shameless character of the girls and their seamy means of guaranteeing their legacy. Both would be neighbors of the nation of Israel and would come into conflict from Israel's initial entry into the land.

The framing of the larger unit with 18:1–15 and 19:30–38 draws out the contrasts between the progenitors and their responses to God's intervention in their lives. Abraham's clear and direct concern for God's reputation and his neighbors, righteous and wicked, throws Lot's selfishness into sharp relief. The reader sees the depth of compromise the world can elicit from the righteous (2 Peter 2:7) and the catastrophic effects on his children and legacy. Abraham's promise of a great nation from a supernatural child and his responsibility to teach God's ways form a devastating contrast to Lot's line built from incest and children living far from God's righteousness and justice. The story of Lot highlights the character and standing of Abraham before God as the forefather of the nation God would use to bring blessing to the families of the earth (Coats 1985, 120–27).

THEOLOGICAL FOCUS

God teaches humanity his character and expectations of righteousness and justice through his loyal followers and his actions, justly judging the wicked and graciously delivering the righteous, despite serious compromise and loss.

As with the flood narrative, the destruction of Sodom and Gomorrah places God's character and, specifically, God's justice on display. He announces the theme in his soliloquy before Abraham. The teaching and keeping of his ways of righteousness and justice must necessarily precede blessing for all peoples whom God desires to ultimately bless. Blessing requires a relationship with the source of blessing. Abraham epitomizes that, while Lot barely qualifies. Yahweh will reveal his justice as he judges outrageous evil even while graciously delivering the righteous. God's justice will challenge and encourage the righteous follower in his mission and warn him of compromise.

In his justice, Yahweh demonstrates that he is "merciful and gracious, slow to anger and abounding in steadfast love and faithfulness" (Exod. 34:6). He delivers hesitant and double-minded people, even saving the deeply compromised (Lot's daughters) at the behest of the righteous, and the guilty (Zoar) at the request of the compromised. He continues to provide his compassionate grace for generations (the descendants of Lot, Deut. 2:9, 19). Yahweh's pity (חֶמְלָה, v. 16), grace (חֵן, v. 19), and loyal love (חֶסֶד, v. 19) shine brightly amid the devastation. In answer to Abraham's question, Yahweh will certainly deliver the righteous before he judges the wicked (2 Peter 2:9).

Lot's need for grace also serves to highlight the fragile nature of humanity. His infatuation with the world and its benefits cost him dearly. Clearly Abraham's expectations (and the responsibilities of the righteous) are not met, perhaps anticipating at least ten righteous in Lot's entourage or even many more had Lot influenced his community. However, the impact was reversed, stressing the need for the righteous to be wary of their world and take seriously the dangers of valuing immediate comforts over God's call. The way of the Lord may not be popular nor attractive to the eyes (Gen. 13:10), but it is the way of life and lasting blessing. The way of the world is the way of judgment and death. Ironically, it was in conjunction with Abraham and the way of the Lord that Lot experienced his greatest prosperity, illustrating the uncertainty and transitory nature of material gain.

To impact one's world and offer blessing to humanity, God's people must live out his righteousness and justice (18:18–19), using their relationship with Yahweh to his world's benefit. Leaving that path reaps awful consequences and squanders the opportunity. Living in that way leverages God's grace to the believer and his world. God responds to the prayer of the righteous, to accomplish God's purposes. For the coming nation of Israel and the righteous to follow, the destruction of Sodom highlights the need to bring blessing to the nations, beginning with intercession and extending relationship with Yahweh through living and teaching the way of the Lord (righteousness and justice) rather than lawlessness and destruction. The way of all the world will only lead to destruction.

PREACHING AND TEACHING STRATEGIES

Exegetical and Theological Synthesis

Begin with the description of Abraham in Genesis 18:18–19 so that your hearers can see their place within Abraham's faith family. If we are participating in the blessing, we must also be participating in the character development that separates Abraham and us from the wicked in our world.

There is no doubting the fact that God cannot tolerate sin; he does judge it and will judge it completely in the end (v. 20). Fallen humanity has indeed fallen! You may have noticed that the general public does not believe it is God's prerogative to judge his creatures. Human beings will often allow him to be loving but not just, if being just means carrying out justice by punishing those who offend his laws.

Of course, Abraham knows what your listeners know: it is not fair for God to punish those who have not broken the law ("Far be that from you!" in v. 25). The question at the end of 18:25 requires the answer, "Yes, certainly the Judge of all the earth will do right!" Abraham's response displays great love for the lost in our world as he tests God's patience with his formulaic questions.

This provides a look into God's patience with wickedness in his world. You and I might not calculate mercy the way he did and does! Before going much further, we are already in a great position to urge all listeners toward righteousness to escape God's impending judgment; we are also ready to provide an urgent call to ongoing disciple-making in our locales.

Finally, chapter 19 shows that it is possible for the righteous to have no impact on their surroundings, despite having influence (cf. 19:1 and Lot "sitting in the gate of Sodom"). Genesis 19:14 and the response of "his [future] sons-in-law" is a very sad commentary and breaks any Christian dad's heart. But so is the fact that Lot "lingered" (v. 16), his wife "looked back" (v. 26), and his daughters do the unthinkable (v. 32). Can you see how difficult it will be—or better, impossible—for God's blessing to be experienced in such a spiritual state?

Preaching Idea

Make sure we are "the righteous" ones, not swept away by the judgment of God and able to bring blessing to others.

Contemporary Connections

What does it mean?

If you are not preaching through Genesis, you may have to explain the covenant language in 18:18–19. God has made promises to Abraham, given him commands, and prophesied great blessing on and through him to the nations. You may want to help your listeners understand that God does not announce his plans to "go down to see whether they have done" all this wickedness (18:21) because his knowledge is limited. God verifies this to help readers understand his justice in harsh judgment.

You might explain the significance of Abraham's barrage of questions to God following God's announcement of judgment: Abraham is a fitting conduit of blessing; look at how he cares for his world. And God's repeated answer, "I will not," highlights his mercy and grace in what is largely a judgment context.

In this age in which we minister, you may want to explain the sexual activity in Sodom (cf. 19:5). At the time of our writing this commentary, our own country is seeing a wide range of readings of such Scripture within the church. Although Lot has been secularized by his fellow citizens, he still begs, "do not act so wickedly" (19:7).

I frankly do not know how you can explain Lot's plan that involves his two daughters. It is a sign of his times or culture (hospitality at all costs!); it is also a sign of his own carnality or worldliness; it is even more a signal that in a badly broken world it seems that God's people often are choosing between the lesser of two evils than between good and bad options.

Finally, Lot's wife was so close to escaping with the righteous, but she did not. It would have been easier for all of us to understand her spiritual condition if she opted to stay behind. She and her two daughters loved the city way too much.

Is it true?

By now, if you are preaching through Genesis, your listeners should be used to God's seemingly excessive judgment—I am thinking of the flood. And here we are again with God raining fire and brimstone down upon an entire city and all their inhabitants, who are labeled wicked.

Our listeners may struggle to believe in the justice of God when all they ever hear and relate to best is his love. Great love is matched with great anger when what is loved greatly is threatened with destruction. Is it true that humankind can sin greatly against God? Is it true that God will only allow sin to go so far?

You might also consider the veracity of God's great mercy as the number of righteous continues to fall according to Abraham's hypothetical scenario. It is helpful to think about the world in which we live in the context of hearing that God would allow great wickedness to remain for the sake of a handful of righteous ones. Abraham and those like him experience the blessing of God; Lot and all Lotites, not so much! Finally, the truthfulness of complete destruction (19:25, "all the inhabitants . . . and what grew on the ground") will one day result in the complete restoration or recreation of all things in a new heaven and earth.

Now what?

Every listener needs to: (1) find themselves within the covenant God made with Abraham (18:19–19); (2) believe that God judges sin, sometimes now and certainly in the future; (3) see themselves as a kind of Lot living in the world with opportunities to let people know what God's salvation is like; (4) be just as merciful toward the lost as Abraham was as he pled with God to spare the wicked twin cities; (5) guard against being as negatively influenced by the world as Lot and his family were; and (6) thank God for his mercy that allows us to escape the judgment caused by our sinfulness.

Creativity in Presentation

Let me begin by posing a couple of questions that arise from this tragic narrative. First, although the New Testament calls Lot righteous, what kind of righteous life do you suppose afforded him the opportunity and position to be "sitting in the gate of Sodom" (19:1) when the two angels arrive in Sodom at nighttime? At the time of this writing, our country is still waiting for the final decision on a presidential election. Think about how difficult it must be for a truth-telling Christian politician to enter an arena where the rules of communication assume the bending of or avoidance of truth or constant personal attacks on the opposing candidate. Here we find Lot as the only righteous person, along with his wife and two daughters, that escape from the doomed cities. The narrative urges us all to make sure we are the righteous ones that escape the judgment of God. Second, you might consider spending some time asking your listeners about the kind of influence they are having on their families, neighborhoods, gyms, and workplaces. Would there be any evidence that you are a conduit for the blessing of God? Here is how you could structure a teaching time:

- The kind of person that is not swept away in judgment (18:16–19; 19:1–3, 15–22).
- Why God acts in judgment (18:20–21; 19:4–14, 26).
- How worldliness keeps the serpent's seed active in this world (19:30–38).

The statistics keep telling us year after year that the morality in the church creeps closer and closer to the morality in the world. This contrast between Abraham and the blessing and Lot and the curse provides a wonderful opportunity for the church to distinguish itself in the world. Lot is certainly a "go and do otherwise" example of how to live in a wicked world.

If you prefer to follow the flow of the text in your exposition, you could structure it something like:

- The righteous are privileged to teach God's justice and intercede for their world (18:16–33).

- God will judge justly, showing unexpected grace and answering the prayer of the righteous (19:1–29).
- Those infected with the world, even though righteous, will lose greatly (19:30–38).

DISCUSSION QUESTIONS

1. What effective ways have you discovered for training your family or circle of influence to keep the ways of the Lord?
2. Discuss the moral dilemmas that could result from a Christian holding influential political office and how one could stand firm in righteousness.
3. What characteristics of our God would allow him to allow wickedness to remain in a city like Sodom if, perchance, there were ten righteous inhabitants to be found?
4. Where are you tempted to compromise in your interaction with your world?
5. How can you identify areas of compromise in your life so that you can repent and live by faith?
6. How are you currently interceding for your community and your world?

Genesis 20:1–18

EXEGETICAL IDEA

When Abraham lied about Sarah, precipitating her abduction, God intervened to preserve his promise, endangering Abimelech and revealing Abraham's status and responsibility to intercede for the innocent Abimelech to bring blessing instead of cursing.

THEOLOGICAL FOCUS

The failings of God's people may endanger God's redemptive plan and threaten cursing on God's world, but God faithfully works to accomplish his good purposes, developing his servants in their faith to bring blessing.

PREACHING IDEA

Praise God for times when our unbelief is overturned by the faithfulness of God and we are back on track to bring blessing.

PREACHING POINTERS

One of the goals of these homiletical sections is to continue to explore how meaning is made in the narrative. In this case first readers and current readers have a hard time comprehending that Abraham would lie again, saying about "Sarah, his wife, 'She is my sister'" (v. 2). Not this again! Yes. This is another "go and do otherwise" narrative, at least from the perspective of Abraham's actions. Many listeners are familiar with the concept of a besetting sin. Whether the cause is rationalizing it, downgrading it, or simply enjoying it too much, the besetting sin repeats itself in the Christian life along with its damaging effect.

As you can see, though, in the Theological Focus, Abraham is not the main character of this narrative; God is. So, while we are all appalled at Abraham's fear and lack of faith, our own faith is also bolstered as we watch our God continue to make sure his promises remain. If we spend just a moment with Abraham's actions, we are reminded again how it is possible for one intended to be a conduit of blessing to end up becoming a curse-causer. Poor Abimelech does not know what hit him in this narrative when he hears in a dream, "Behold, you are a dead man because of the woman" (v. 3). Certainly, our God will not "kill an innocent people" (v. 4). Unfortunately, because of what God tells us in his word about birth-sin, none are innocent. If we move back to God for a moment, listeners may gain confidence in God's faithfulness as they hear God tell Abimelech, "it was I who kept you from sinning against me. Therefore I did not let you touch her" (v. 6).

FAITH OR CONSEQUENCES: RESPONSIBILITY IN GOD'S WORLD (20:1–18)

LITERARY STRUCTURE AND THEMES

Abraham moved into the Negev and endangered his promised son through his lie regarding Sarah (20:1–2). His lie frames the narrative with his prayer to save Abimelech from God's judgment (20:17–18). Two dialogues form the heart of the narrative. First, God confronted Abimelech, intervening to save his promise to Sarah and to spare Abimelech's life and lineage because of his innocence (20:3–7). Then Abimelech confronted Abraham for endangering him demonstrating his innocence (20:8–16).

- A. Abraham lied to Abimelech, endangering the promise (20:1–2).
  - B. God confronted Abimelech (20:3–7).
  - B'. Abimelech confronted Abraham (20:8–16).
- A'. Abraham prayed for Abimelech, bringing healing (20:17–18).

The main impact of the narrative revolves around the characterization of Abraham and Yahweh. Abraham is much more complex than recognized up to this point. He is not fully formed in his faith and maturity yet, misjudging his neighbors, responding with a clear lack of faith, and initiating cursing on those neighbors. God's justice, however, is enhanced as he intervenes not only to save Sarah and the integrity of his promised descendant, but to offer Abimelech an opportunity to prove his innocence and find blessing despite Abraham's foolish lie. In both, Abraham's responsibility showed starkly against the background of conflicting characterization. The lying sojourner was a prophet of God who lamely provided excuses for his lie and must pray for healing and blessing on a Canaanite king and his nation, who acted with greater integrity than he.

STRUCTURE OF ABRAHAM AND ABIMELECH

Wenham sees a much more intricate chiasm in this passage following the shifts from narrative to dialog, though he acknowledges that the outer two levels are not as tightly connected (Wenham 1994, 68):

A	Abraham settles in Gerar (20:1)	Narrative
B	Abraham's instructions to Sarah (20:2a)	Dialogue
C	Abimelek "takes" Sarah (20:2b)	Narrative
D	God warns Abimelek (20:3–7)	Dialogue
E	Abimelek warns his servants (20:8)	Narrative
D'	Abimelek rebukes Abraham (20:9–13)	Dialogue
C'	Abimelek returns Sarah (20:14)	Narrative
B'	Abimelek speaks to Abraham and Sarah (20:15–16)	Dialogue
A'	Abraham prays for Abimelek and his household (20:17–18)	Narrative

The chiasm focuses on Abimelech's warning to his servants, which emphasizes the international consequences of the actions of Abraham. It not only impacts Abimelech, but his whole nation (vv. 4, 7, 9).

- ***Abraham Lied to Abimelech, Endangering the Promise (20:1–2)***
- ***God Confronted Abimelech (20:3–7)***
- ***Abimelech Confronted Abraham (20:8–16)***
- ***Abraham Prayed for Abimelech, Bringing Healing (20:17–18)***

EXPOSITION

After Lot's tragic story, the narrative refocuses on Abraham, heading south and west into the Negev. The brief interlude before the promised birth of Isaac seems out of place at first glance, until the reader notices connections with the stories up to this point. It begs to be compared with 12:10–20 and the first story in which Sarah is endangered, in Egypt. In addition, it shares numerous key words and themes with the immediately preceding story of Abraham's intercession for Sodom and God's judgment on the cities of the plain. Previously Abraham prayed proactively for the innocent and that the wicked might live despite their guilt. Now he endangers the innocent and must pray that the righteous may not die despite their innocence.

In addition, this story sets the stage for what will follow. God must protect Sarah for the birth of the promised child. Abraham must learn to be a blessing instead of a cursing, suggesting a need for further evidence of growth, which will be accomplished in the offering of Isaac. All these connections bear theologically on God's purposes. He is preparing to accomplish his covenant through a flawed subject whom he is crafting into a faithful servant. Abraham's lie about Sarah precipitated her abduction and God's intervention to preserve his promise, endangering Abimelech and revealing Abraham's status and responsibility to intercede for the innocent Abimelech and bring blessing instead of cursing. Abraham would learn to intercede and to teach his family and household to walk in the way of the Lord (18:19).

Abraham Lied to Abimelech, Endangering the Promise (20:1–2)

Abraham sojourned in Gerar and again claimed Sarah as his sister, allowing Abimelech to abduct her for a wife and endangering his promised child with Sarah.

20:1. Leaving Mamre, Abraham headed south into the Negev. He moved toward Egypt (Shur was possibly the string of Egyptian forts on their eastern frontier) before sojourning in Gerar, back in the northern Negev. Though the reason is not given, Abraham's move removed him from his allies (14:13), and he again became an unprotected alien or sojourner in foreign territory, reminding of his sojourn in Egypt (cf. 12:10).

20:2. In contrast to 12:11–13, in which Abram laid out his concern and requested Sarai go along with the deception, here he simply lies without recorded consultation or rationale. Sarah seems to have agreed, at least according to Abimelech (20:5). But the lack of discussion corroborates Abraham's claim that it was an established pattern they have used previously (v. 13). As a result, however, Abimelech takes her into his harem, much as Pharaoh had done (12:15).

The current narrative relates the abduction much more briefly than in Egypt, without mentioning her beauty (emphasized in the earlier narrative of Abraham's deception, the response of the Egyptians, and the report of the princes, 12:11, 14, 15). Of course, she is now twenty-four years older. The reason for taking an eighty-nine-year-old woman as a wife may rather have been related to establishing an economic alliance with a wealthy and powerful nomad (Sarna 1989, 141). The statement is short and precise. Abimelech "took" her (וַיִּקַּח). His intent was clear, as the narrative shows. Sarah's abduction was without consent, and Abraham did not intervene.

God Confronted Abimelech (20:3–7)

God intervened, acknowledging Abimelech's claim to innocence but demanding her return or Abimelech and all that were his would die.

20:3. Whereas the crisis is related much more briefly than the Egyptian episode, God's confrontation of Abimelech's sin and the impending judgment include much more detail. God intervened to secure his promise, emphasized by the chiastic structure of the scene. God warned Abimelech directly in a dream of his imminent death because he had abducted a married woman. The ensuing conversations emphasize the innocence of Abimelech and his people, in contrast to the generally expected guilt of the Canaanites (13:13; 15:16; 18:19–20; 19:13; cf. 20:11).

Structure of Abimelech's Dream

Alexander (1997a, 39) has noted the tight chiastic structure of the dream sequence:

A v. 3 Behold you are a dead man
B v. 3 You have taken a man's wife
C v. 4 Abimelech has not approached her
D v. 4 Abimelech claims to be innocent
E v. 5 In the integrity of my heart
F v. 6 God said to him in a dream
E' v. 6 In the integrity of my heart
D' v. 6 God kept him from sinning
C' v. 6 I did not let you touch her
B' v. 7 Restore the man's wife
A' v. 7 You shall live; if not you shall die

The chiasm focuses attention on the direct message from God to a pagan king (rarely given to a pagan, cf. Mathews 2005, 249–50). God's direct intervention emphasizes the extent to which God goes to protect his promise to Abraham. It also underlines the point of the preceding passage that the judge of all the earth will do what is right. He will not destroy the innocent and in fact intervenes to protect the innocent pagan endangered by the foolish righteous.

TRANSLATION ANALYSIS 20:3

The particle *hinneh* plus the participle (הִנְּךָ מֵת) has the "nuance of vivid immediacy" (WOC, 675, §40.2.1) as in NRSV, "You are about to die." Other translations express the immediacy as an accomplished fact: "you are a dead man" (ESV), or "You are as good as dead" (NIV).

20:4–5. The narrator clarified that Abimelech had not violated Sarah (v. 4), though we will only learn later that it was God's intervention protecting her (v. 6), possibly through the very disease that threatened his life (v. 17). Abimelech protested his innocence vigorously, with terms reminiscent of the previous narrative. Reflecting Abraham in chapter 18, Abimelech asked God if he would "kill an innocent people" (v. 4). The term translated "innocent" (צַדִּיק) is the term used seven times in Abraham's prayer before Yahweh in 18:23–28, where God would certainly not destroy the "righteous" with the wicked. Clemency is demanded by the previous narrative.

Abimelech also realized the threat to his entire "nation" (גּוֹי) or population. Ironically, God had declared in 18:18 that it was through Abraham that all the nations (גּוֹיִם) of the earth would be blessed, if his children and household would "keep the way of the Lord by doing righteousness and justice" (18:19). Abraham is neither doing righteousness (צְדָקָה, related to the claim of Abimelech to be an "innocent" or "righteous" people in v. 4) nor justice by bringing judgment on an innocent Abimelech and his kingdom. The Canaanites are more righteous than Abraham, who will be revealed to be Yahweh's prophet (v. 7). God's chosen servant and prophet must realize the impact of his life to do good or evil to his world.

Abimelech defends abducting Sarah on the grounds that both Abraham and Sarah had claimed they were not married. He maintained the "integrity of [his] heart," which God confirmed (v. 6), and the innocence, "guiltlessness," or "purity," (*HALOT* s.v. "נִקָּי(וֹ)ן" 720–21) of his hands (action). In another irony, "integrity" (תֹּם) is from the same root as God's command to Abraham in 17:1 to be "blameless" (תָמִים). Abimelech was doing what God had commanded Abraham to do but was not doing in this episode. The piling up of terms for Abimelech's defense both highlight his impassioned claim of blamelessness and Abraham's costly lie, contrary to Abraham's purpose as God's source of blessing.

TRANSLATION ANALYSIS 20:5
"Heart" (לֵבָב) refers to the inner person, will, or character (Bowling, 1071, *TWOT* 466–67). The combination with integrity refers to a "clear conscience" (NET) or "guilelessness" (*HALOT* s.v. "תֹּם" 516).

20:6–7. God's response affirmed Abimelech's innocence of intent in taking her. He also declared that Abimelech's innocence of any sin against God, as Abimelech claimed (innocence of his hands), was only because of God's intervention. Was the dream itself the immediate intervention stopping the act of adultery? Or had God waited before revealing Abraham's ruse, intervening with disease or plague to prohibit Abimelech's purpose? Perhaps the latter, since the royal household seemed to know that they needed healing (20:17–18; Wenham 1994, 71). Either way, God was clear. Adultery was not merely a sin against the husband or the wife, but against God, as God would clearly establish (Exod. 20:14; Lev. 20:10; Deut. 5:18; 22:13–27).

In the flow of the narrative, this lapse of Abraham's faith also endangered the promise of God. The child was to be born within the year. Whose would it be? The narrator is clearly affirming from the claim of Abimelech, the narrator, and God himself that Sarah was not molested and so any child she would have would be Abraham's and not Abimelech's. Abimelech would go to great expense to make his innocence public as well (Gen. 20:16). Abraham's lie cost Abimelech dearly and threatened to cost Abraham and Sarah the very promise of hope for which they had waited twenty-five years.

God's demand on Abimelech, however, also revealed the dissonance between Abraham's action and his position before Yahweh. As prophet, he had the opportunity to have an audience with the Almighty and offer blessing to the nations. The prayer he had offered in chapter 18 God would now command to bring healing to Abimelech and his household. Of course, it would also clearly impress on Abraham his responsibility to those around him to reflect the character of Yahweh and be that blessing (18:18–19), along with the consequences of failing in his responsibility and their effect on his own promises and the good of his world.

Despite God's affirmation of Abimelech's innocence up to that point, he demanded the return of Sarah and reiterated the consequence of failing to comply. Abimelech and his household would certainly die. In effect God was testing Abimelech's claimed innocence and Abraham's willingness to live out his purpose with the same obligation. It would be up to Abraham to resolve both ironies by his prophetic prayer. From Abimelech's viewpoint, he would be in the hands of the aggrieved party and must await Abraham's mercy, which may be reflected in the tone and value of Abimelech's response to both Abraham and Sarah.

> *TRANSLATION ANALYSIS 20:7*
> The construction affirming Abimelech's judgment mirrors the judgment of eating the forbidden fruit in Eden (2:17). The cognate infinitive absolute emphasized the certainty of their death (מוֹת תָּמוּת) and is appropriately translated by most as "you shall surely die" (e.g., ESV).

Here God also affirmed Abraham's role, which was illustrated already in his audience with Yahweh in chapter 18. In Abimelech's view, the prophet had audience with God through his seat in the divine council. He could then bring up matters and advocate for the earthly concerns (Walton 2009a, 94–95). The prophet in Israel similarly functioned as an advocate, having direct audience with God, illustrated by Moses (Exod. 32) and Samuel (1 Sam. 7), among many. Abimelech apparently lacked any previous knowledge of Yahweh. God did not appear to him as Yahweh, and there was no reference to Yahweh on his lips. He did, however, fear God and responded immediately to his intervention.[1] God revealed Abimelech's only hope of relief and life through reconciling with Abraham, even though the offense had resulted from Abraham's lie. The lesson was needed for both parties.

Abimelech Confronted Abraham (20:8–16)

Abimelech confronted Abraham and Sarah, demonstrating his innocence by humbly declaring his predicament, prompting Abraham's explanation, and making generous restitution.

20:8. Abimelech's immediate response of publicly declaring God's nocturnal revelation not only upheld his innocence but demonstrated the general fear of God, which Abraham had doubted (20:11). This transition gives background against which to evaluate Abraham's defense, which moved from lame to self-incriminating. It also suggests that Abimelech called Abraham to defend his actions in front of the royal court (v. 9), increasing the pressure on Abraham for a favorable answer.

20:9–10. Abimelech's query placed responsibility with Abraham: "what have you done to us?" (v. 9). The reader may recognize Pharaoh's demand (12:18) and even the echo of God's question to Eve (3:13), which was strengthened when Abraham suggested it resulted from God causing them to wander into unknown territory (20:13). Here, the rebuke from a pagan king to a prophet of Yahweh deepens Abraham's culpability.

Even though Abimelech seemed to suggest he may share blame by inquiring about his own preliminary sin ("how have I sinned," v. 9), his diplomatic language still placed the onus on Abraham: "that you have brought on me and my kingdom this great sin?" (v. 9). He recognized that the judgment extended to his whole kingdom (cf. the imminent death for "you and all who are yours," v. 7). Even though he had not committed the "great sin" of adultery, he and his kingdom were in jeopardy.[2]

1 Petersen (1973, 41) considers the fear of God the major theme of the narrative. While it is significant, the bigger issue is the integrity of the promise of Yahweh, closely connected to the role of the patriarch in bringing blessing and cursing to the nations.

2 Adultery was called "the great sin" both in Egypt (Rabinowitz 1959) and in Canaan (Moran 1959), bringing the death penalty.

Abraham had broken cultural norms where he had assumed there were none. Abraham had done what "ought not to be done" (v. 9). Abimelech pressed Abraham for an explanation, wondering what he had seen to do such a thing.

20:11–13. Rather than simply confess, Abraham's explanation began with faulty assumptions and became shakier as he proceeded. His assumption that there was no fear of God appears immediately after his experience with God's evaluation of and judgment on Sodom. His logical conclusion, considering God's statement years earlier that "the iniquity of the Amorites is not yet complete" (15:16), unwisely lumped all peoples together. His assumptions, however, were unfounded and wrong. Why he might expect them to kill him for his eighty-nine-year-old wife is left unexplained. With significant irony, his assumption that there was a lack of the fear of God revealed his own lack of fearing Yahweh.

Abraham's defense that it was not a complete lie only made him look conniving, and to add that it was planned and practiced (was it only in 12:10–20?) sealed the negative impression against him. The effect gives empathy to Abimelech and raises significant questions regarding God's chosen prophet and conduit of blessing. He completely avoided the rationale of her beauty, which was the presenting issue previously, implying that this had become a habitual lie that had lost its (faithless and inadequate) reason for being, but which he had not really stopped to evaluate, even after a strong rebuke from the Pharaoh years before. Clearly his faith was flawed still, and it would need to be proven in following the way of the Lord to expect God to accomplish his purposes through him (12:2–3; 18:18–19).

20:14–16. Abimelech's response included not only restoring Sarah to Abraham but gifts that would appease the god and curry favor with this powerful prophet.[3] In contrast to the Pharaoh's reaction, Abimelech allowed him to remain in the land, though his presence provided an uneasy peace (21:22–26). He also gave Abraham an exorbitant sum of money[4] to testify to her purity and his innocence. Abimelech's reference to Sarah's "brother" reflects the lie and may be sincere acceptance of Abraham's story (Sailhamer 1990, 162), or it may be intended to sarcastically dig at Abraham's lie (Sarna 1989, 144). Though unclear, the reader recognizes the added irony.

TRANSLATION ANALYSIS 20:16

Literally, the Hebrew states, "It is for you a covering of the eyes to all who are with you, and with all. And you are found to be right" (v. 16). The exact meaning is uncertain, but most translations take this to express a public exoneration of Sarah (cf. Wenham 1994, 74), though NCV understands it to include restitution for a harmed reputation ("to make up for any wrong that people may think about you. I want everyone to know that you are innocent").

The difference between Pharaoh's and Abimelech's responses may well have been the message from God revealing the stature Abraham had with God and so his ability to bring blessing or cursing. Abimelech treated Abraham extremely well even after learning the truth, qualifying him for blessing (12:3).

3 While these gifts were a direct response to God's intervention and he needed Abraham's good will, Hamilton (1995, 69) also cites a Middle Assyrian law requiring restitution from a man who takes a woman on a trip and later finds out that she was already married, without reference to infidelity. Abimelech, then, was already guilty even though he had not committed adultery, according to this law, and would be required to make restitution.

4 Walton (2009a, 95) cites a Ugaritic poem in which one thousand shekels of silver is part of the bride price for a goddess. It was about twenty-five pounds and represented about hundred years' wages for an average worker.

Abraham Prayed for Abimelech, Bringing Healing (20:17–18)

When Abraham prayed, God healed Abimelech and his household so that they could live and bear children.

20:17–18. "Abraham prayed to God, and God healed Abimelech" (v. 17). The brevity of the two clauses belies the drama surrounding the event. Clearly Abimelech was experiencing some disease or plague, which was "healed" (רפא) by God in response to Abraham's prayer. There is no indication how the ladies knew that they could again bear children, but that seems to be in addition to the threat of death (v. 7). The re-opening of the wombs reminds the reader of the threat this had posed to the promise of God to Abraham and Sarah. In the next two verses, God also opens Sarah's womb to conceive and bear Isaac. In talionic justice, the threat that Abimelech posed to God's promised child became the consequence he faced for his action, had he failed to act in faith and submission to God's command. With added irony, Abraham must pray for the opening of the wombs of Canaanites before God opened the womb of Sarah. Surely, he had prayed many times for his wife, but only after his blessing this nation would he experience God's blessing, and his own great nation would begin.

In the structure of the Abraham stories, the endangering of the promised child by Abraham's lie occurs both immediately after the initial promise of the seed in chapter 12 and immediately before the fulfillment of the promise in chapter 21, twenty-five years apart. Initially, Abraham's lapse in faith was easily explained as the failings of a new follower of Yahweh. The effect, however, was to demonstrate the danger of Abraham effecting a curse on the nations by his actions. Now Abraham's lie is revealed to be habitual. Such actions are inexcusable for a righteous prophet commanded to be fully loyal (15:6; 17:1; 18:18–19). But here it also demonstrates the opportunity for Abraham to be either a blessing or a cursing on the nations.

Called to Be a Blessing

Abraham has been called to be a blessing (his responsibility; 12:2), which will be accomplished through a life of faith lived in loyalty to God and walking in the way of Yahweh (blameless and righteous: 17:1; 18:18–19). "The patriarch does not convey blessing or cursing by his mere presence or wish: the nations are not passive recipients only. Neither do the nations appropriate blessing or cursing for themselves without the patriarch's participation. Rather, both parties bear a degree of responsibility. The patriarch may act in a manner that endangers the nations (i.e., his deception), or in a manner that offers blessing (as when he lives among them as Yahweh's blessed). The patriarch presents the nations with the opportunity to choose whether they will stand in a relationship of blessing or cursing, depending on their treatment of Yahweh's holy one" (Biddle 1990, 610).

In addition, the second endangering occurred within the timeframe of the year between the renewed and specific promise to Sarah (18:10–14) and its outworking (21:1–2). The "From there" (מִשָּׁם, 20:1) indicates that this is chronologically after the promise in chapter 18 and so within the timeframe of the possible conception of the child, making it crucial that the narrative emphasizes (and Abimelech asserts publicly) that he never had relations with her during that time. In both cases, Abraham foolishly and faithlessly jeopardized the promise. God also faithfully intervened in both cases but provided significant rebuke through the pagan kings to Abraham, with the final event providing a much stronger and pointed message. Abraham had responsibility within his covenant, which he must fulfill to fully realize the benefits. God would accomplish his plan, but Abraham would suffer if he failed to live in faith, walking before God blamelessly (17:1). His world would not be able to realize the benefits of his mediation of blessing through seeing his character and the opportunity to walk with Yahweh. God, therefore, will continue to intervene to accomplish his purpose, offering blessing to all the nations of the world.

THEOLOGICAL FOCUS

The failings of God's people may endanger God's redemptive plan and threaten cursing on God's world, but God faithfully works to accomplish his good purposes, developing his servants in their faith to bring blessing.

The narrative focuses on a failure of faith of the righteous man of God, chosen by God to accomplish his purpose and bring blessing to the world. His unbelief endangered God's promise and plan and exposed his own shortcomings. God's choice of his servant is not because of his perfections, "but *in spite of* his human imperfections" (Cotter 2003, 134, emphasis original). The narrative teaches, however, not only about failure, but about the faithful character of God to assure that his promise and purpose continue and to teach his followers necessary lessons of faith and responsibility.

God shows his faithfulness, defending the integrity of his promise, even when his chosen images disappoint. His defense of his purposes, however, does not run roughshod over those who have no knowledge of him. He gives justice to the innocent but not-necessarily-pure pagan who is in over his head. God is both just and good. He offered Abimelech the opportunity to prove his intentions and respond in submission to God, with a clear explanation of consequences, even when God's servant endangered him. He is not the bully that many misjudge in the Old Testament. He is holy and just, and he is gracious and good as well.

God also uses failure in the lives of his servants. God turned Abraham's lie into a teaching moment for Abraham, neither rejecting him nor excusing him but allowing him to respond to the conflict, own up to his duplicity, and bring blessing out of cursing by acting in faith. He also offered blessing and hope through him to a pagan king who probably did not know about Yahweh previously. God turns even faithless and sinful actions into opportunities for good and redemption.

God's servant, on the other hand, has responsibility to reflect the character of God as his image and be the conduit of blessing to his world. Faithless action endangers both God's promise through him and brings the possibility of cursing in his world rather than the blessing God provides, apart from the intervention of God. God can certainly intervene, and does, bringing both discipline and corrective action to his servant as well as opportunity to his world. The servant, however, experiences loss, in this case reputation and relationship with his world.

The representative of the Lord does not have the ability nor responsibility to decide the spiritual condition of those around him. He does have the responsibility to pray for them and reflect the character of God to them. He also can impact their world with his life, in both words and actions. Integrity, justice, and righteousness provide the key foundation for pointing to God and his blessing.

Even the righteous servant of the Lord who has walked with God for decades is seen again to be vulnerable and flawed (remember Noah). The fear of man can preempt the fear of God in even the seasoned believer. In addition, habitual sins can continue unseen in a believer until some crisis drives them to the surface. They must be recognized and ruthlessly rooted out.

God, however, does not go back on his promise nor on his plan. He continues providing opportunities for his servant to grow in faith and integrity, learning about the way of the Lord and redeeming failure to allow blessing despite weaknesses. His expectation after failing includes confession and restoration, responding in integrity with God's grace to those damaged by his sin.

PREACHING AND TEACHING STRATEGIES

Exegetical and Theological Synthesis

Begin by seeing the promise endangered by our sinful tendencies (Abraham's lie about Sarah in light of 17:19 and God's promise about Sarah's son, Isaac). That puts Abraham's actions in the context of the covenant. Abraham's fear of those who supposedly had no fear of God outstripped his own fear of God in that moment. Abraham is an example for us to avoid and reminds us of what happens when we do not believe God will take care of us and be faithful to his promises. God's actions show that not only is he faithful to carry out the promise despite our lapses into unbelief, but he is also just. God acknowledges "the integrity" of Abimelech's heart (v. 5). The sheer power of our God to prevent sin from severely complicating or even damaging the promise is on display. I am glad that kind of God controls his kingdom, especially since my own spiritual integrity at times, like Abraham, leaves much to be desired. God will not lose any piece of the promise in Abraham's life or ours. He will finish what he started.

Abimelech's question, "What have you done to us?" (v. 9), haunts any reader who remembers that they are intended to be conduits of blessing within their sphere of influence. Some might even find hope in knowing that there is some fear of God in places where we least expect it (v. 11). The tendency of many conservative evangelicals is to think the worst in non-Christians.

Finally, the power of our status as a kingdom of priests is on display as we watch the effectiveness of Abraham's prayer—of all people, Abraham—to heal Abimelech and his entire household. God was not fooling around when his promise was in jeopardy! And he is just as serious about making sure his children learn valuable lessons in life so that greater usefulness and fruitfulness might result, all for his eternal glory.

Preaching Idea

Praise God for times when our unbelief is overturned by the faithfulness of God, and we are back on track to bring blessing.

Contemporary Connections

What does it mean?

Abraham's lie needs to be interpreted in the context of the covenant. As a covenant-breaker, he no longer functions as a conduit for blessing in the world. The narrative clearly shows Abraham and Sarah's actions compromising God's plan for his people. Not until the end of the chapter do we see just how powerful God's representative is in the world. We do function as a kingdom of priests (1 Peter 2:5, "a spiritual house, to be a holy priesthood," and v. 9, "a royal priesthood") for the purpose of proclaiming the excellencies of our God in the world. Our character and integrity are part of that proclamation as we identify with Christ.

Most listeners will need help understanding the kind of "integrity of heart" that Abimelech had (Gen. 20:5, 6). Abimelech confesses this about himself, and God verifies the claim. Many churchgoers will struggle seeing the non-Christians as having any fear of God. Abimelech's integrity, while short of being justified by faith, has a form of cultural morality in the sense that he was not breaking any laws of his land.

This narrative also calls on us to explain the control of God in his world. Theological terms such as "sovereignty" (his control of his own) and "providence" (his care for his own) provide stability for the faithful in the badly broken world.

Is it true?

This probably goes without saying, but this is Abraham's second recorded lie of the same kind! What is wrong with him? What is wrong with us? Whether from this narrative in Genesis 20 or from 1 John (for instance, 1:5–10, but throughout the book), the relationship between the Christian and sin needs to be addressed so that everyone relates to sin's addictive qualities. It is true that Abraham struggles to believe God's promises; it is true that I do too.

I can imagine some listeners wondering whether God really does control the details of his world. How many read, "I . . . kept you from sinning against me" (Gen. 20:6) and do not stop for a moment to confess that God can and does do this, not only to those outside the covenant but to those inside it as well. The key, of course, is to recognize but not normalize this act of God. He did not stop Abraham from sinning in this narrative. Anyone who can believe God restrains sin like that has good reason to worship him during the sermon!

Finally, your listeners will benefit from your theological explanation as to why Abraham's prayer was necessary for Abimelech's healing. See comments above concerning our responsibility as priests in the world (p. 371). In addition, God teaches Abraham a clear lesson about faith and faithfulness. We have the privilege of reading this humbling turn of events in Abraham's life to remind us that God may expose our sins to teach us our responsibilities to represent him well in his world.

Now what?

Nothing is more relevant than seeing one of God's finest struggle with faith. Nothing is more relevant than seeing that struggle followed up with God's sovereign control and providential care for the covenant and covenant-keepers so both continue to function in the world. Every day is a new experience of the sovereignty and providence of God. I (Randal) am currently writing near the end of 2020, the year now infamous for the arrival and stubborn lingering of COVID-19. Never before have I heard Christians talk about trusting in God's ability to care for his own, whether they contract the disease or not and whether they survive it or not. If God's plan for healing of all things in heaven and earth were left up to us, it would indeed fail; it is not left up to us. The faithful who allow God to build their faith by his Spirit's power will continue to have a small part to play in the restoration of all things, all the while the greater prophet than Abraham (v. 7) prays for us until he returns to rule.

Creativity in Presentation

It is often a fruitful exercise to have our listeners think of times in their lives where God's providential care for them was clear. Hindsight is 20/20, and we need that desperately. We need to remember times when God mercifully stepped in and preserved our relationship with him, keeping us from sinning like we were intending. Ask your listeners to think of times when they knew he was preserving them from danger.

Then, can they think of the opposite, those times when God allows our sin to take place so that exposure, repentance, and growth can take place? That reflection gets everyone thinking about our tendency toward unbelief and God's steady hand guiding us forward to glorification. Our preaching idea, praise for times when our unbelief is overturned by the faithfulness of God and we are back on track to bring blessing, shows that this narrative should result in the praise of God. It should also result in reaffirmation of our part as conduits of God's blessing in his world.

A preaching structure for chapter 20 could be as follows:

- Begin with the potential for our unbelief or lapses in faith to jeopardize or at least interrupt the blessing (considering Abraham's lie, vv. 1–2).
- Second, allow everyone to see how God steps in to ensure that the blessing can continue (God coming to Abimelech in a dream and explaining his options, vv. 3–16).

- Finally, in verses 7 and 17–18 you can help all your listeners see their part to play in this wonderful kingdom of priests God is building and using until he returns.

Your listeners should be able to leave the corporate worship service praising God for the way he guides his people through this world, through all the ups and downs of faith. They should also leave with a firm resolve to avoid Abraham's example of unbelief and to look for ways to extend God's blessing to those around them.

DISCUSSION QUESTIONS

1. Discuss the habitual nature of sin and what keeps God's people from despair in the fight for spirituality and maturity. Ask if anyone has a difficult time continuing to rely on 1 John 1:9 ("If we confess our sin").
2. What interaction have you had with a non-Christian that could be potential for either curse or blessing?
3. What are common reactions to God being sovereign over the details in one's life?
4. Have you seen any evidence of a non-Christian displaying integrity of heart? How does that help you view them and pray for them?
5. Above, you may have noticed that a reference to 1 Peter was provided. Ask for ways in which Christians shine brightly in a dark world and function as a holy priesthood.
6. How has God pointed out blind spots in your life in the past? How do you show openness to God to show you your blind spots? Are you asking him? Are you willing to hear it from other believers near you?

Genesis 21:1–34

EXEGETICAL IDEA

God began fulfilling his covenant promises to Abraham by providing and protecting a son through Sarah, delivering and blessing Ishmael, extending blessing to Abimelech, and giving Abraham a foothold in the land through the faith and faithful action of his servants, to the praise of his name among the nations.

THEOLOGICAL FOCUS

God faithfully honors his promises, blessing believing responses to his word in difficult conditions, to his praise among the nations.

PREACHING IDEA

God will be faithful to his promise to bless, and we will be faith-filled to be a blessing.

PREACHING POINTERS

The narrative confronts its initial audience and its modern audience alike with the faithfulness of God to fulfill his promises to us. No one can miss the emphasis on the impossibility of this fulfillment: "a son in his old age. . . . Abraham was a hundred years old when his son Isaac was born to him" (21:2, 5, 7). We should all laugh with Sarah! But Hagar the Egyptian's son soon interrupts the celebration of the promise fulfilled. God makes it clear, contrary to Abraham's feelings, that his inheritance is not for the "children of the slave" (Gal. 4:30–31). Human effort cannot secure the blessing of God; it is only by faith in his miraculous promises that God works personally in and for us.

The mercy of God is on display in the way he promised to make another nation from Ishmael. We see Abraham's obedience, and he functions as an example of faith in action. The middle of the chapter shows an even greater display of God's mercy (vv. 15–21) as God rescues Hagar and her son and restates his promises in response to the boy's prayer.

This chapter closes as chapter 20 began, reminding us of the kind of influence God's people are to have in the world as they function as conduits of his blessing. It is also a great comfort to know that God can redeem even poor testimonies when his people respond humbly to him. Abraham gets off to a poor spiritual start, but through God's intervention and Abraham's humble cooperation, God accomplishes his will.

LAUGHING LAST: PROMISES SECURED (21:1–34)

LITERARY STRUCTURE AND THEMES

Genesis 21 presents three movements that work together to demonstrate the specific fulfillment of God's promises that he has repeatedly affirmed to Abraham—the birth of Isaac, the sending away and delivering of Ishmael, and Abraham's covenant with Abimelech. Interlocking with the structure in chapter 20, the narrative develops chiastically:

A. Abraham sojourned in Gerar (20:1).
  B. Abimelech secured healing with Abraham's intercession (20:2–18).
    C. God gave Isaac as promised (21:1–7).
      D. God aided Sarah, assuring Isaac's future (21:8–13).
      D'. God aided Hagar, assuring Ishmael's future (21:14–19).
    C'. God blessed Ishmael as promised (21:20–21).
  B'. Abimelech secured a covenant with Abraham's blessing (21:22–32).
A'. Abraham sojourned with the Philistines, calling on the name of the Lord (21:33–34).

The central sections of the narrative (21:1–21) emphasize the working of God to fulfill his promises, both to Sarah and Hagar through the two sons. God faithfully demonstrated his sovereign power, both by producing the child of promise through Sarah at ninety and Abraham at one hundred, as well as protecting Ishmael (and Hagar) for his promised future, sovereignly delivering them in the desert. The final scene returns to Abraham's uneasy sojourn in Abimelech's territory, providing the background to Abraham's first acquisition in the land and formalizing God's promise to bless those who would bless him. God's covenant with Abraham, then, moves toward fulfillment with promises of seed (Isaac rather than Ishmael), land (the well at Beersheba), and blessing on the nations (Abimelech and future Ishmaelites) as Abraham publicly exalts his eternal God.

- ***God Gave Isaac as Promised (21:1–7)***
- ***God Aided Sarah, Assuring Isaac's Future (21:8–13)***
- ***God Aided Hagar, Assuring Ishmael's Future (21:14–19)***
- ***God Blessed Ishmael as Promised (21:20–21)***
- ***Abimelech Secured a Covenant with Abraham's Blessing (21:22–32)***
- ***Abraham Sojourned with the Philistines, Calling on the Name of the Lord (21:33–34)***

EXPOSITION

As the Abraham narratives move toward their climax, the reader may expect the birth of Isaac to announce that climax, suggested by the repeated "as [God] had said," looking back at the continuous repeating of the promise of a son up to this point (12:2; 13:16; 15:4–5; 17:3–8, 16–19, 21; 18:10, 14, 18). However, the fulfillment notice is short (seven verses), and the longer account of the conflict with Ishmael (fourteen verses) and the concluding treaty with Abimelech that reflects the earlier account in chapter 20 (another thirteen verses) shift the focus. The promise of the son is only part of the larger covenant promises to Abraham, which also move toward fulfillment in the rest of the chapter. Yet all of this prepares for the real climax in chapter 22, fully demonstrating Abraham's loyalty and ratifying the covenant promises through the sacrifice of Isaac. Here, God began fulfilling his covenant promises to Abraham, providing and protecting a son through Sarah, delivering and blessing Ishmael, extending blessing to Abimelech, and giving Abraham a foothold in the land through the faith and faithful action of his servants, to the praise of his name among the nations.

God Gave Isaac as Promised (21:1–7)

God fulfilled his promise to Abraham and Sarah, giving Isaac, to Sarah's overflowing joy (21:1–7).

21:1–2. Following the notice of the opening the wombs of Abimelech's household (20:17–18), Yahweh "visited" Sarah (21:1), specifically fulfilling the promise spoken to Abraham and Sarah a year earlier (18:10, 14). The figure of speech connects the blessing of God with a special acknowledgment of his attention and presence in intervention, drawing further attention to the connection between the presence of Yahweh and his blessing.

> *TRANSLATION ANALYSIS 21:1*
> The verb translated "visited" (21:1 ESV) and variously in other translations (e.g., "was gracious," NIV; "kept his word," NLT; "took note of," NASB95; "dealt with," NRSV; "cared for," NCV) has a broad range of meaning. When God is the subject, however, it most often indicates God's intervention to accomplish his promise to benefit his people (e.g., Israel's deliverance from Egypt, Gen. 50:24–25; Exod. 4:31; 13:19; cf. Jer. 29:10; or general blessing, Ps. 65:10), or, more frequently, to bring judgment (Exod. 32:34; and often in the prophets, e.g., Isa. 13:11). Williams suggests the basic idea when God is the subject is "attend" or "take note of" someone or something for blessing or judgment (Williams, פָּקַד, *NIDOTTE* 3:659). The idea of God attentively bringing blessing resonates throughout this passage.

Moses highlighted the significance of this event in the program of God.[1] God was miraculously fulfilling his promise (18:10, 14; Abraham was old, stated here and repeated in verse 7, framing the birth announcement and specified as one hundred in 21:5), which was acknowledged twice in verse 1, at the exact time he had specified (v. 2).

21:3–5. Abraham obeyed Yahweh, naming the child Isaac ("he laughs," 17:19) and circumcising him on the eighth day (17:12), just "as God had commanded him" (21:4). Again, Moses emphasizes that the child was from Sarah as promised (17:16; 18:10, 14). The time stamp on Abraham's age tracks the progress of the promise, beginning with Abraham at seventy-five (12:4). God had moved the promise from unlikely to impossible. Now the impossible was a public spectacle of joy.

The time stamp also reminds of the previous birth. After ten years, Abraham and Sarah had taken matters into their own hands with Hagar (16:16). The statement of his age at the birth of each son ties the two together for the reader, foreshadowing the coming conflict (21:8–21). Abraham's previously struggling faith had produced fruit that would be bitter, even though God would redeem it for good with the fulfillment of his perfect plan.

21:6–7. Sarah at this point saw the joy. What had been a cause for incredulous laughter (17:17) or disbelief (18:12) was now a cause for rejoicing and perhaps a hint of embarrassment. Using the same root for laughter memorialized in Isaac's naming (צחק), Sarah proclaimed her amazement in poetic verse. Who would have believed that a one-hundred-year-old Abraham would get a birth announcement that his ninety-year-old wife would be nursing a son? It was truly a miracle that would bring public glory to their God as their world rejoiced.

1 The grammar (*waw* disjunctive beginning the clause) sets the initial clause apart from the narrative flow and emphasizes this information as foundational to the following narrative.

TRANSLATION ANALYSIS 21:6
While most versions translate verse 6 as laughter without any hint of embarrassment, the same root will be used in verse 9, which seems to include more than innocent laughter (see below). Alter (1996, 97) suggests double entendre, with "Laughter has God made me, whoever hears will laugh at me." He notes the ambiguity of the preposition and that the noun can also mean "mockery," stating "All who hear it may laugh, rejoice, with Sarah, but the hint that they might also laugh at her is evident in her language." Tal (2015, 128) supports the double entendre with Ezek. 23:32.

TRANSLATION ANALYSIS 21:7
While it is possible that Sarah was wishing for more children, the plural "children" (בָּנִים) more likely reflects the plural of generalization (JM, §136j), referring to Isaac. Thus, "Sarah would nurse children" (ESV) can be understood as "Sarah would nurse a baby" (NLT).

God Aided Sarah, Assuring Isaac's Future (21:8–13)

God resolved Sarah's distress, assuring Isaac's status and Ishmael's future by sending away Ishmael.

21:8–11. The day of weaning the child was a significant milestone. It may have been about age three[2] and, with high infant mortality, was a time for celebration of the next phase of the life. The focus of the account, however, was Sarah's perception and the conflict it produced. Without naming him, we read that Sarah saw Ishmael "laughing" (מְצַחֵק). What he was doing is not clear in the text and is widely debated. While the term in the *piel* generally has negative connotations such as mocking (see Translation Analysis), the real problem is not mere jealousy. Sarah points out the competition Ishmael presents to be the heir to Abraham. She may have been focused on the physical inheritance, but God would redirect Abraham's attention to the necessary concern of carrying on his name without confusion (v. 12), so the heir of the promise and the covenant fulfillment, which he had already guaranteed, was Isaac (17:7–8, 17–21).

TRANSLATION ANALYSIS 21:9
The innocuous translation "laughing" (ESV) or "playing" (NRSV, NJPS) suggests that Ishmael was merely enjoying the party. The LXX and Vulgate add "with Isaac, her son" (μετὰ Ἰσαὰκ τοῦ υἱοῦ ἑαυτῆς), which could be taken innocently or not (cf. NRSV, RSV). While an innocent understanding is possible, the term in the *piel* (only occurring seven times in the OT) has negative connotations, including "making fun of" (NLT) or "mocking" (NASB95, NET, NIV; cf. especially Gen. 39:14, 17; and possibly 19:14). The latter seems to be closer to the intent.

Ishmael as Abraham's Heir
Abraham's acceptance of Ishmael as his heir (ch. 16; 17:18), according to contemporary law, gave inheritance rights to Ishmael that would not be easily dismissed. One brother trying to disinherit another legitimate brother from another wife could result in his own disinheritance (Frymer-Kensky 1981, 212). Though the rights of the firstborn may be clearly given to the son of the first wife, complete disinheritance would require divorce and freeing from slavery (Walton 2009a, 95). The later son, then, could be declared "firstborn" since it was "a juridical relationship which may be entered into by contract as well as by birth" (Frymer-Kensky 1981, 214).

Sarah's solution was to expel the boy and his mother (which granted both freedom and divorce). Her focus was clearly demeaning. She did not name the boy, nor did she name Hagar, but referred to her as "this slave woman" (21:10,

2 Sarna (1989, 146) cites both Egyptian and Assyrian documents supporting an age of about three for the weaning, as well as 2 Macc. 7:27 for the Second Temple Jewish practice of about the same.

twice), a term recognizing both her status as a slave and as the mother of the child through Abraham (Schultz, אָמָה, *NIDOTTE* 1:419–20). Clearly, Abraham loved Ishmael as a father should, with an attachment that Sarah was dismissing or ignoring, driving his angry reaction. It was her son against the slave woman's son, completely discounting Abraham's stake in this. According to the laws of Lipit-Ishtar, their freedom would come at the expense of their share of the inheritance (Sarna 1989, 147). Between Sarah's animosity and Abraham's reaction to her request, God's response presents something of a surprise.

> *TRANSLATION ANALYSIS 21:11*
> Abraham's reaction (וַיֵּרַע הַדָּבָר מְאֹד) is translated in various ways, from "very displeasing" (ESV, cf. NET, NKJV) to "distressed greatly" (NASB95, NIV) or "troubled . . . very much" (NCV). Wenham (1994, 83) notes the "explosive" nature of the description of his anger, where without the strengthened "very" displeased, men erupt in anger (Num. 11:10; 1 Sam. 18:8) and God takes lives (Gen. 38:10; 2 Sam. 11:7).

21:12–13. From Abraham's perspective, God's command for Hagar to return to Sarah (and Abraham, 16:9) would need to be countermanded by God to send her away (Alexander 1997a, 107). God directly addressed Abraham's concern, with some significant modifications. God redirected Abraham's "displeasure," shifting the focus from the relationship ("his son," בְּנוֹ, v. 11) to the youth himself ("the boy," הַנַּעַר, v. 12, cf. Reis 2000, 100). The term God used for "boy" can refer to an unmarried male of any age (from before birth, Judg. 13:5, to a thirty-year-old, Gen 41:12; Hamilton, נַעַר, *NIDOTTE* 3:125). Here, the boy was fourteen at the birth of Isaac and now is about seventeen. The troubling aspect of relationship may be put into the perspective of the ability of the young man to make a way for himself under God's protective supervision. God's response directed attention to his capability and promise to make a nation of Ishmael (Gen. 21:13) but may well have indicated care for the boy as well (Hamilton, נַעַר, *NIDOTTE* 3:125), putting Abraham's mind at ease. God also acknowledged the concern Abraham (should have?) felt for Hagar, implicit in his promise.

While God agreed with Sarah's conclusion (lit. "listen to her voice," v. 12, contrasting Abraham's poor decision in 16:2), he shifted that concern from the inheritance to the carrying on of Abraham's name and so the covenant promises. In doing so, God avoided naming either Ishmael or Hagar. They would fade from the narrative of the promise and plan of God's redemptive purpose, but not without God's care or blessing to fulfill his promise to Abraham and Hagar to be a great nation (17:20; 21:18). The "offspring" (זֶרַע) of promise (cf. 12:7; 13:15–16; 15:5, 13, 18; 16:10; 17:7–10, 12, 19) was to be through Isaac, without confusion, even though Ishmael was also his offspring (21:13). Ishmael would, then, have his promise fulfilled but not the covenant promise of God's greater purpose, bringing blessing to all the nations of the earth. The narrative has shifted attention from the fulfilling of the promise to have a child to the greater promise of a great nation to bring blessing to all the families of the earth. The birth was certainly a significant milestone in the narrative, but for the greater purpose to which the narrative will continue to drive.

God Aided Hagar, Assuring Ishmael's Future (21:14–19)

At the end of their resources and facing certain death, God intervened in the wilderness, rescuing Hagar and Ishmael in their distress, assuring Ishmael's future promise.

21:14. With God's promise of care, what was deeply disturbing to Abraham (and many since then) became bearable through faith in God's provision. Abraham gave Hagar basic provisions and sent her away into the care of Yahweh.

Whether he communicated Yahweh's promise of care to her, however, is not clear. The term used to "send her away" (שׁלח) is less harsh than Sarah's "cast out" (גרשׁ, v. 10), but it also indicates divorce (Deut. 24:1). She left and appears to have gotten lost, running immediately into life-threatening trouble.

TRANSLATION ANALYSIS 21:14

The grammar of verse 14 has caused some confusion in translation, suggesting to some that the narrative was out of place and reflected a much younger child that Hagar could carry along with the provisions (e.g., von Rad 1972, 233), as in the ESV translation, "putting it on her shoulder, along with the child." However, "the child" is likely held to the end of the clause to indicate Abraham's hesitance, waiting until the last moment to send him away. He was still the object of "gave," fitting the context of an older youth being put in her charge (Wenham 1994, 77, 84). The translation of the NASB95 and others, then, is warranted: "putting them on her shoulder, and gave her the boy."

21:15–16. Desperate, lost, and out of water in the wilderness, she left Ishmael in the shade of a bush and sat down far enough away that she would not have to watch him die or, more likely, hear his moans and cries. While she weeps, there is no indication she cried out to Yahweh, even though he had intervened in her life previously, causing her to acknowledge that God was looking after her (16:7–14). Perhaps that explains God's response.

TRANSLATION ANALYSIS 21:15

The verb can be used to throw or "cast" (שׁלך, NRSV, RSV), but here is more likely "left" (NJPS) and not "shoved" (NET), which would indicate abandonment out of her desperation (Cogan 1968).

21:17–19. While Hagar could not hear him, the narrative unexpectedly declares that "God heard the voice of the boy" (v. 17) rather than Hagar's voice, even though the boy had not been mentioned as crying out. Ishmael was carrying on the faith of Abraham, crying out to Yahweh for salvation, and God heard and responded. Hagar wept while the boy prayed.[3] The angel's query regarding her trouble and pointed reference to "the boy" suggests she should have cried out to God, but God was graciously delivering them. The repeated reminder that God heard (v. 17, וַיִּשְׁמַע אֱלֹהִים) pointed to Ishmael's name (יִשְׁמָעֵאל), God's promise, and the lesson she should have learned seventeen years before, which formed the basis for faith (and her expected prayer) that God would care for them now (16:11–12).

The angel then reiterated God's promise, which he had twice given to Abraham, that Ishmael would be a great nation (17:20; 21:13). Their lives were not in doubt, regardless of how she felt. He then opened her eyes, and she saw what had been there all along, hidden from her view. God provided water, life, and blessing.

God Blessed Ishmael as Promised (21:20–21)

God fulfilled his promise to Abraham and Hagar, blessing Ishmael with his presence to thrive in the wilderness.

21:20–21. Continuing the connection between the presence of God and blessing throughout Genesis, the conclusion to the narrative summarizes God honoring his promise to make Ishmael a great nation by declaring his presence with Ishmael and living out his prophecy

3 When God is the subject of the verb "hear" (שׁמע, in the *qal*) with the direct object of "voice" (קול), the construction consistently indicates prayer and not merely weeping: Gen. 21:17; 30:6; Num. 20:16; Deut. 1:34, 45; 5:28; 26:7; Josh. 10:14; Judg. 13:9; 2 Sam. 22:7; 1 Kings 17:22; Pss. 5:4; 6:9; 18:7; 27:7; 28:2, 6; 31:23; 55:18; 64:2; 116:1; 119:149; 130:2; Jer. 30:5; Lam. 3:56; Jonah 2:3.

to Hagar (16:12). As a result of God's presence, Ishmael thrived in the wilderness as an archer and would establish a new nation with the wife Hagar provided from Egypt.

The conflict generated by the birth of Isaac demonstrated the working of God to honor his word, removing obstacles to his overarching purpose and blessing another nation through Abraham and his promise to Ishmael. This narrative, which may seem anticlimactic to the anticipation of Isaac's birth, draws attention to the nature of the covenant and the larger intent of God to accomplish his promised redemption, removing all obstacles and using Abraham to bring blessing, which will be the point of the final movement.

Abimelech Secured a Covenant with Abraham's Blessing (21:22–32)

At Abimelech's request, Abraham made a covenant with him, securing Abimelech's progeny and Abraham's welfare in the land.

The narrative returns to Abimelech and Abraham's sojourn in his territory. While it may seem out of place, allowing the birth of Isaac and conflict with Ishmael to intervene with the initial interaction with Abimelech, it was carefully constructed, underscoring the importance of the narrative (see the overall structure above, p. 375). The structure demonstrates the coherence of the entire narrative with the greater purpose of the overall covenant promises of God to Abraham as they are working out in his life practically. The Abraham and Abimelech stories frame the birth and conflict narrative, providing a larger context for Abraham's impact in his world for blessing and cursing as God works to accomplish his covenant promises. While Abraham had not yet fully arrived in his faith (ch. 20), God was accomplishing his greater purposes, yet he would also refine and demonstrate Abraham's growing faith in chapter 22.

The Number Seven

The account itself has been carefully edited around the number seven. Not only does the number seven show up three times, but both Abraham's and Abimelech's names appear seven times, and the word "swear" uses the same consonants in Hebrew (occurring three times), concluding with the naming of Beersheba, containing the ambiguous reference to either oath or seven (Sarna 1989, 148). The thoughtful crafting suggests its importance to the larger narrative, which Steinmann (2019, 213) ties to the first acquisition of property for Abraham in the promised land. The repetition suggests completion, possibly reflecting an inflection point in Abraham's growth before his testing. Abraham treated a foreign king in righteousness and justice, sharing blessing, and showing faith without fear.[4]

21:22–24. Moses tied the treaty with Abimelech into the immediately preceding narratives with a time stamp, "at that time," and with the repetition of the notice of God's presence ("God is with you," v. 22), reflecting his blessing on Ishmael (v. 20). God's presence showed in the tangible illustrations of fertility (crowned now with Isaac's birth, cf. 20:17–18) and his great wealth, as well as his access to water (21:25–30; cf. v. 19). Considering this obvious working of God, Abimelech wanted a guarantee of Abraham's good will (truthfulness and kindness) with him and his progeny.

Along with his commanding officer, Phicol, Abimelech called for an oath to guarantee the relationship, which would result in a covenant. Specifically, he requested immediate action

4 Thank you to Daniel Carver for pointing out this significant event before the test of chapter 22. Notice the similar faith in his response to the enemy kings and king of Sodom in Genesis 14, just before God's evaluation of his faith and covenant ceremony (ch. 15).

("Now swear to me right here," v. 23 NET, וְעַתָּה).[5] After their previous interaction, and seeing God's favor on him, Abimelech wanted Abraham to make a covenant guarantee that he would not break,[6] not merely for himself but for ongoing generations of his posterity. He has seen both God's power and Abraham's close relationship with him, so he requested a covenant sworn in God's name.

> *TRANSLATION ANALYSIS 21:23*
> Using both "descendants" (נִין) and "posterity" (נֶכֶד), Abimelech indicates ongoing future generations, not merely his immediate children (cf. Hamilton, נֶכֶד, *NIDOTTE* 3:102), or even "forever" (Sarna 1989, 149)!

He did not merely ask Abraham to keep his word, but he asked for him to "deal kindly" (חֶסֶד, v. 23) with him as he had done with Abraham. This common term for covenant loyalty also describes his claim as one who had "blessed" Abraham (12:3) and so was eligible for God's blessing. After Abimelech's lengthy request, Abraham tersely emphasized his personal responsibility,[7] agreeing to the terms. His confrontive complaint that followed, however, indicates that he was not entirely satisfied with Abimelech's treatment of him, requiring further negotiation before a covenant could be concluded.

21:25–26. Specifically, Abraham had not been treated well by Abimelech's servants. The grammar indicates that he was or had been making consistent complaints or reproofs to Abimelech. It was not merely a single or minor grievance. In fact, the reproof referred to Abimelech's servants taking his well by force (Domeris, גָּזַל, *NIDOTTE* 1:844). Water rights in an arid region were crucial and would have been assumed with Abimelech's previous offer to live wherever he wished (20:15).

> *TRANSLATION ANALYSIS 21:25*
> The clause initial waw on the perfect is not the normal narrative sequence. As in Genesis 15:6 (see Translation Analysis 15:6a), this use may be a frequentative or habitual-iterative use, showing a continual or repetitive reproach.

Abimelech protested ignorance, claiming he had not heard of it previously. Whether he convinced Abraham, it seems to have prompted Abraham's additional insurance.

21:27–32. Reminiscent of Abimelech's previous apology (20:14), Abraham gave "sheep and oxen" (without the servants, 21:27) to Abimelech as part of the covenant ceremony. Unexpectedly, however, he also set aside seven ewe lambs. These seven lambs appear to be in addition to the animals that were part of the covenant (Wenham 1994, 93), explaining why Abimelech was uncertain as to their function. Abraham clarified that they were security on his rights to the well he had dug there. Not only would they agree to mutual covenant fidelity, but Abraham would secure the water rights to his well for the future. With the making of the covenant, Abimelech agreed to the water rights and possibly the tract of land (Steinmann 2019, 215). The name of the well and place commemorated the covenant as the "well of the oath," Beersheba (though it could also be interpreted as the "well of the seven"). Satisfied, Abimelech and his commander "returned to the land of the

5 The clause initial expression draws added attention and emphasis. It could be translated "under these conditions" (*HALOT* s.v. "עַתָּה" 902, 3.b)).

6 Abimelech is not merely concerned about telling a lie but breaking the covenant (Hamilton 1995, 88; Sarna 1989, 148–49).

7 Abraham used the long form of the first-person pronoun, reduplicating the subject of the verb. He is clearly emphasizing his personal response and responsibility.

Philistines" (v. 32), suggesting they were on the edge of Abimelech's territory. Abraham had finally fully blessed Abimelech in faith.

The Philistines

The mention of Philistines hundreds of years before the earliest attested reference to them outside of the Old Testament, in the twelfth century BC, presents a challenge to the historicity of Genesis. Here it is possible that the name is used anachronistically for the area, updating a place name with the common later description for the place the later Philistines would live (Walton 2009a, 96). It is also very possible that the term refers to non-Canaanite peoples connected to the Aegean and so precursors to the later ethnically related Philistines (Kitchen 2003, 339–41).

Abraham Sojourned with the Philistines, Calling on the Name of the Lord (21:33–34)

Abraham put down roots and called on the name of the Lord, sojourning in the land of the Philistines many days.

21:33–34. Abraham showed his intent to stay in this area for an extended period by planting a tree.[8] At the same time he again proclaimed Yahweh's character (see Exposition on 4:25, and 12:8). The implication that, as his prophet, he proclaimed Yahweh beyond merely private worship is strengthened by the inclusion of another epithet for Yahweh.[9] Yahweh is eternal. Concluding the scene and the larger context of the fulfillment of the promises to this point, the acknowledgement of the eternity of God grounds his faithfulness to his promises and ongoing purpose in his eternal existence, connecting

Well at gate to ancient Beersheba. Photo by Tami Heim

the covenant fulfilment for Abraham with his eternal redemptive purpose (3:15).

Completing the larger narrative with the final *inclusio*, Abraham "sojourned (וַיָּגָר) many days in the land of the Philistines" (21:34; cf. 20:1, וַיָּגָר). Abraham's sojourn on the edge of the promised land brought him to the initial fulfillment of God's promise. He had his own child through Sarah and assurance of Isaac's future. He possessed an initial toehold in the land with a well and perhaps the tract of land with it. And he was blessing the nations, represented by Abimelech and Ishmael. God's covenant promises were finally taking shape as God had sworn.

THEOLOGICAL FOCUS

God faithfully honors his promises, blessing believing responses to his word in difficult conditions to his praise among the nations.

God's faithfulness to his promises shines clearly through Genesis 21. His plan finally sees some initial fulfillment, with promises of land, seed, and blessing all bearing fruit, along

8 Planting a tree was of uncertain significance, possibly relating to the covenant ceremony (Kitchen 2003, 324) or his worship (Sarna 1989, 149). Placed where it is, at the end of the scene and in connection with his recognition of Yahweh's faithfulness to promise, it may also indicate appreciation of the initial foothold in the land with the possession of the water rights and immediate tract of land, showing he will stay and enjoy the benefits for a period of time (Ross 2008, 138–39).

9 The phrase must refer to an attribute rather than a proper name because a proper name cannot be in construct with a noun (Sarna 1989, 150).

with the assurance of Ishmael's future. As God's promises blossom, the presence of God figures prominently in the blessing, visiting Sarah and residing with Ishmael and Abraham. As we have noted through Genesis, God's presence engenders blessing as the believer walks in relationship with him. God created humanity as his images to reveal his glory among his creation, and he continues to demonstrate that intent, working through his chosen servants to accomplish his plans and draw humanity to true worship. Abraham closes the scenes with his public worship of the eternal God who has been at work from the beginning.

As God honors his promises, he also builds the faith of his chosen servants and redirects their attention to the more important issues. Sarah sees the precise fulfillment of promise and the movement from disbelief to exultant joy in the public and miraculous working of God. Abraham must refocus from his priorities to God's priorities yet trust God's faithful working to accomplish all his promises for the benefit of all people, regardless of the ability to see how it can be accomplished. Hagar must learn to trust the God who consistently works for her good and does not forget her in her crises, honoring the prayer of faith of the child. The one who comes to him for blessing through his servant does not leave disappointed as God's servant deals in truth and covenant loyalty, offering the opportunity for God's world to see blessing through the proclamation of true worship to the eternal God.

So, God honors the faith of all, from the established prophet and his struggling wife to the child and even to the pagan king. Any who call on the Lord receive his attention and action for their good and his glory. People, however, must respond in faith to the degree of insight they are given, rather than fear or anger at the challenges to the expectations they hold.

God does expect obedience and faithful action. He requires his old prophet to act according to his will and instructions when it would be personally difficult because of previous and fleshly failures to which he was attached. He expects the recipient of his grace to respond in appropriate faith and pursuit of him. He requires the person of faith to live in integrity and righteousness in his world, providing blessing to those around him, even in the face of resistance and injustice. They must respond in worship as God acts and declare the character of their eternal God to their world who needs to see the source of blessing.

God does expect his world to see his working and respond in faith rather than fear. If he honors the cry of the child and the pagan, how much more does he honor the faith and response or prayer of his seasoned saint?

PREACHING AND TEACHING STRATEGIES

Exegetical and Theological Synthesis

There is enough brokenness in our world and in our lives to make God's promises to bless us seem very unlikely. So, when Sarah finally conceives in her old age, not to mention Abraham's old age, our tendency to doubt gives way to increasing confidence in God. We see the same faithfulness and reliability of our God in the way he treats Hagar and her son. We desperately need to believe the promises of God, especially during those times when there is no evidence of fulfillment.

If there was any doubt in our minds about God's character, his mercy shines brightly in his dealings with Hagar and her son. They too experience God's faithfulness in answer to prayers. And when God tells Abraham to listen to his wife's seemingly harsh treatment of Hagar and her son, we are instructed in how the kingdom of God operates: based on faith in God's power, not in human effort.

Through it all, Abraham, of course, is learning and growing in his own faith. He leads the way in showing how conduits of God's blessing in the world must be first and foremost people of faith. Only then can God's blessing be evident and appealing to a cursed world. For a foreign king and his commander to say to Abraham, "God is with you in all that you do" (21:22), there must have been some tangible evidence in Abraham's life of successful living, of God's blessing. The chapter ends with Abraham leading the way to worship despite being "many days in the land of the Philistines" (v. 34). There's great encouragement to know that we can walk with God in this world! In fact, that blessing is only found in walking with God. It is his presence that brings the blessing. Our lives should show the presence of God so that even the pagans around us see that God is with us.

Preaching Idea

God will be faithful to his promise to bless, and we will be faith-filled to be a blessing.

Contemporary Connections

What does it mean?

Some listeners will benefit from hearing your explanation about the miraculous fulfillment of God's promise to Sarah (21:2, 7). Our entire Christian experience, start to finish, is the result of God creating a miracle, not to mention his ability to continue to work his plan in the lives of badly flawed people against impossible odds. Our God receives great glory when his strength, not our abilities, accomplishes his kingdom work.

Beginning at verse 9 you will want to explain Sarah's reaction toward Hagar and Ishmael and why God sided (at least in principle!) with Sarah. The promise was through Abraham and Isaac, not Ishmael; the inheritance was Isaac's, not Ishmael's. However, God clearly extends mercy and a blessing to Ishmael (vv. 12–13).

Congregants may wonder about the significance of Abraham's treaty with Abimelech. Here is another opportunity to remind listeners of the covenant, including God's people being a conduit of blessing in the world. The strength of God's blessing on Abraham caused a foreign king to ask for an agreement that would benefit the king. Three times in the narrative, the fact that God is with someone explains the prosperous life and, more importantly, the clear fulfillment of God's promises (cf. vv. 1, 20, 22).

Is it true?

This larger section of Scripture that began in chapter 20 and ends at the end of chapter 21 shows two sides of Abraham. Some listeners struggle with their own spiritual Jekyll-and-Hyde self. They have good spiritual days walking with the Lord and bad spiritual days walking in the darkness of sin. In the beginning of the larger section, 20:2, Abraham lies again about his relationship to Sarah. He represents all of us who battle with reoccurring sins that are difficult to shake. The rest of the narrative shows Abraham doing very well spiritually. He shows great compassion for Ishmael; he succeeds with his relationship with Abimelech, the same king he lied to earlier. Abraham proves that God works with us in all our weaknesses and builds faith in us along the way. Perhaps this is one reason that the working of God must be clearly his work and not ours, by showing our inability apart from him.

Now what?

Nothing is more relevant than God's people experiencing their own covenant renewal service surrounding the faithfulness of God to fulfill his promises. Too often God seems to delay his blessing. The longer we wait the easier it is to forget the rock-solid character of our God. He can be trusted! The conflict between Isaac and Ishmael shows us the special status we have and the spiritual inheritance we enjoy in Christ. Many of our listeners enter church on Sunday experiencing alienation similar to Hagar and Ishmael's. What a comfort to see God hearing "the voice of the boy where he" was (v. 17). The scenes involving Abraham's treaty with Abimelech continue to show us the kind of witness God can give us in the world, with both our responsibility for the impact of our actions and the opportunity to image God.

Creativity in Presentation

If you follow the narrative flow in chapter 21 you can structure a sermon along the lines of:

- The Lord keeps his miraculous promises to his children (vv. 1–7; this section also includes Abraham's obedient response).
- The Lord guards his promises from foolish self-effort while extending grace to those caught in the crosshairs (vv. 8–21; this section includes the mercy of God extended to the oppressed and outcasts; look at all the fallout God addresses!). God's promises cannot be fulfilled through human ingenuity (in this case, both faithless and foolish efforts on the part of his own people!).
- The Lord extends his life-giving relationship through his people to his world (vv. 22–34; the section also includes Abraham's worship-filled response).

Our homiletical idea for this section is: God will be faithful to his promise to bless. Will you be faith-filled to be a blessing? If you are looking for potential lenses from which to view this narrative, you can teach from the perspectives of main characters: Abraham, Hagar, and Abimelech. For the New Testament application of the story, see Galatians 4:28, where Paul refers to Christians as "children of promise," like Isaac was.

Another interesting angle on this narrative is tracing the dominant emotions. You can begin with the celebration and laughter resulting from fulfilled promise. Move to the other kind of laughing occurring against Isaac. Then, there is the displeasure Abraham faces, the utter despair of Hagar and her son, and, finally, solemnity of oath and worship ceremonies. The gut-wrenching episode is a strong warning about how our unwise, fleshly decisions, even when they are attempts at accomplishing God's will, cause great damage to the kingdom. But God can clean up even tangled messes to accomplish his purpose and honor his name.

DISCUSSION QUESTIONS

1. Think of all the major moments in Old Testament redemptive history when a miracle birth occurs after barrenness. What implications do you see from divine promises or divinely empowered men being brought about through supernatural births?

2. Discuss why Ishmael and Isaac both couldn't reside in Abraham's house moving forward in redemptive history.

3. Discuss ways in which neighbors and coworkers are able to see that God is with us.

4. How and when do we honor God when we see God working in our lives (Abraham and Sarah's great party or Abraham's public worship and proclamation)?

5. How have you seen God pick up the pieces after you have acted foolishly or ignorantly, and how have you responded to him, either in gratitude or in renewed faith?

6. Because God often allows our weakness to showcase his power, what reminders can we place for ourselves to look back at this story, and others like it, for encouragement when we can only seem to see the impossibility of our circumstances?

Genesis 22:1–19 (20–24)

EXEGETICAL IDEA

Abraham passed God's extreme test in faith, offering his beloved son of promise and receiving God's ratification of the extended promises of his covenant as God's loyal vassal, guaranteeing blessing to all nations.

THEOLOGICAL FOCUS

A believer's faithful obedience, choosing loyalty to God over every competitor, allows God's greatest blessing in his life and his world.

PREACHING IDEA

God blesses his people and all nations through the tested obedient faith of his servants.

PREACHING POINTERS

First readers of this "test" narrative watch in horror as God asks Abraham to do the unthinkable. It is the ultimate test of faith, and readers have been watching his faith grow as he gets up there in years. As you begin to transition to your listeners, begin by noting that this is another of those "go and do likewise" stories. Abraham is now functioning as a positive exemplar. His unhesitating obedience sets the stage for all future sons and daughters of Abraham to take their own place in redemptive history.

On his part, God ratifies his covenant promises to Abraham in response to or in conjunction with Abraham's obedience. This is nothing new since all along in Genesis we have seen God be faithful to those who are also faithful to him. God creates this kind of faith in his children; his children exhibit this loyal faith just like Abraham did. Early and later readers should all be made aware of what makes this test so radical. God called Abraham to give up his most loved person, the son he had waited for twenty-five years for. God asked Abraham to choose God over all that he valued most.

Does all faith in all ages look like this? By definition, the answer is "yes." God tests Abraham's faith because ultimately faith, like the fear of the Lord, obeys. God's tailor-made test examined whether or not Abraham would believe God or his own reasoning ("God is asking me to do something that destroys his promise?"). Well, you know how the story goes: Abraham passes the test; God delivers just in the nick of time and ratifies his covenant promises to Abraham so the blessing might continue.

COMPLETE LOYALTY: EXPRESSING EXTREME WORSHIP (22:1–19 [HB 20–24])

LITERARY STRUCTURE AND THEMES

The binding of Isaac (Jewish title) or sacrifice of Isaac (Christian title) forms the concluding bookend of the main Abraham stories (paralleling 12:1–9, see Introduction to the Abraham Narratives, p. 236). This scene climaxes and ratifies the covenant promises, revealing the growth in Abraham's faith and setting the future expectation for the promised nation. The narrative, then, completes the trajectory of all that has preceded it, explicitly and implicitly drawing the characters and narratives together into a cohesive whole and tying up the loose ends.[1]

The simple storyline belies an intricate structure of repeated terms, themes, and discourse, all presenting complex and substantial theological implications. Moses presents the crisis, rising tension, climax, and resolution chiastically.[2] The purpose for the test (22:1a) resolves with the final pronouncement of the angel of Yahweh (vv. 15–19); the command to sacrifice Isaac (vv. 1b–2) culminates in Abraham's intent and was fulfilled with a surrogate (vv. 11–14); the preparations and journey of Abraham (vv. 3–4) culminate in the preparations of the altar and binding Isaac (vv. 9–10); and the tensions and gaps in the dialogue with the servants (vv. 5–6) are matched by the tensions and gaps in the dialog with Isaac (vv. 7–8), stressing the faith of Abraham and both ending with "they went both of them together" (וַיֵּלְכוּ שְׁנֵיהֶם יַחְדָּו, vv. 6, 8).

A. God tested Abraham (22:1a).
 B. God required Isaac in sacrifice (22:1b–2).
  C. Abraham took Isaac as God said (22:3–4).
   D. Abraham prepared for expectant worship (22:5–6).
   D'. Abraham anticipated God's provision (22:7–8).
  C'. Abraham bound Isaac for sacrifice (22:9–10)
 B'. God substituted a ram (22:11–14).
A'. God ratified his promise to Abraham (22:15–19 [20–24]).[3]

The structure centers around the faith of Abraham, though it is not yet clear his intent (22:5–6::7–8). The outer frame sets the narrative in the context of testing and the results of Abraham passing the test, with the second angelic speech (vv. 15–18) as the climactic conclusion and culmination of the test (v. 1a). All but the outer frame have clear verbal parallels with their counterparts in the chiasm:

1 Not everyone agrees with this assessment. Many see it as a later addition that presents a different picture of God than in Gen. 12–21, which has already concluded with the natural culmination of the birth of Isaac (Ska 2013). As we shall see, however, not only was the birth of Isaac anticlimactic, but the testing was a significant conclusion to the narrative, both structurally (closing the promise from ch. 12) and theologically (underlining the requirement of absolute loyalty in obedient faith, completing the command in 17:1 and ratifying the covenant initially broached in 12:1–3).

2 The details of the structure, including whether it is chiasm, parallel panels, or a combination, are assembled in differing ways, due to the complexity, but the coherence and general flow are clear (cf. Mathews 2005, 287–88).

3 This structure is similar to Ska (1988) and Wenham (1994, 100–101).

1a	Introduction: God tested Abraham.
1b–2	God commanded Abraham to sacrifice Isaac. v. 1: "and said to him, "Abraham!" And he said, "Here I am." וַיֹּאמֶר אֵלָיו אַבְרָהָם וַיֹּאמֶר הִנֵּנִי v. 2: "'Take your son, your only son'" קַח־נָא אֶת־בִּנְךָ אֶת־יְחִידְךָ
3–4	Abraham immediately prepared for the sacrifice, taking Isaac. v. 3: "and went to the place of which God had told him." וַיֵּלֶךְ אֶל־הַמָּקוֹם אֲשֶׁר־אָמַר־לוֹ הָאֱלֹהִים׃ v. 4: "and saw the place from afar." וַיַּרְא אֶת־הַמָּקוֹם מֵרָחֹק
5–6	Expecting to return with Isaac, Abraham took the supplies for the sacrifice. v. 6: "So they went both of them together." וַיֵּלְכוּ שְׁנֵיהֶם יַחְדָּו׃
7–8	Answering Isaac, Abraham anticipated God's provision for the sacrifice. v. 8: "So they went both of them together." וַיֵּלְכוּ שְׁנֵיהֶם יַחְדָּו
9–10	With Isaac, Abraham prepared the altar for the sacrifice, binding Isaac. v. 9: "When they came to the place of which God had told him" וַיָּבֹאוּ אֶל־הַמָּקוֹם אֲשֶׁר אָמַר־לוֹ הָאֱלֹהִים
11–14	For Abraham, intending to sacrifice Isaac, v. 11: "and said, 'Abraham, Abraham!' And he said, 'Here I am.'" וַיֹּאמֶר אַבְרָהָם אַבְרָהָם וַיֹּאמֶר הִנֵּנִי v. 12: "'you have not withheld your son, your only son'" וְלֹא חָשַׂכְתָּ אֶת־בִּנְךָ אֶת־יְחִידְךָ, God provided a ram.
15–19	Conclusion: God ratified his covenant promises to his loyal servant Abraham, who returned with Isaac to Beersheba.

For similar understanding, see Ska (1988) and Wenham (1994, 100–101).

The Abraham stories, presenting God's covenant with Abraham, initiate and concentrate the promises around a descendant who would become a great nation to bless all humanity. The consistently narrowing focus leads to the birth of Isaac in chapter 21. Shockingly, God then jeopardized his miraculous provision (22:1). At issue is both the integrity and honoring of God's clear and specific promise, as well as Abraham's unquestioning loyalty to God.

With the resolution (22:15–18), showing both the faithful provision of Yahweh and the unquestioning loyalty of Abraham, the covenant that God has been developing with Abraham finally comes to completion. Yahweh expands the promises to their greatest extent and confirms them with a personal oath, including the vast expansion of the nation, victory over enemies, and blessing to all the nations of the earth because Abraham passed the test, putting God before all other loyalties.

- ***God Tested Abraham (22:1a)***
- ***God Required Isaac in Sacrifice (22:1b–2)***
- ***Abraham Took Isaac as God Said (22:3–4)***
- ***Abraham Prepared for Expectant Worship (22:5–6)***
- ***Abraham Anticipated God's Provision (22:7–8)***
- ***Abraham Bound Isaac for Sacrifice (22:9–10)***
- ***God Substituted a Ram (22:11–14)***
- ***God Ratified His Promise to Abraham (22:15–19 [20–24])***

EXPOSITION

While this narrative reflects all the Abraham stories, the parallels are particularly close with the initial call of Abraham (12:1–9; see vv. 1b–2 below) and the Ishmael narratives (16:1–16, and especially 21:8–21). In both cases, the close reminders of the previous events add tension to the narrative. The parallels to Abraham's initial call directly question that initial promise (and all subsequent clarification). On the other hand, they also demonstrate the growth of Abraham in faith. The parallels with the expulsion of Ishmael increase the concern that God will indeed expect this unthinkable requirement.

Sacrifice of Isaac and the Expulsion of Ishmael

Parallels between the sacrifice of Isaac and the expulsion of Ishmael include specific phrasing and parallel ideas in the birth and naming of the two boys (16:15; 21:2–3); God's instruction threatening the boys (21:12; 22:2); Abraham's response (21:14; 22:3, 6); the accompaniment of a parent to the place of potential death and preparations (21:15; 22:10); intervention through an angel (21:17; 22:11); specific verbal parallels of "lifting up," "fear," "listen," "God," "hand," "boy," and "voice" (21:16–18; 22:12, 18); God's provision to save from death (21:19; 22:13); and a promise of numerous offspring (21:18; 22:17) (Cotter 2003, 147–51; Leviant 1999). Cotter also notes other parallels including mention of specific geography, naming of the places, and even identical death notices for the two men (25:15; 35:29). The parallel promises of great nations from both fortifies the advantage of close relation to Abraham for Ishmael (12:2–3; 17:5–6, 20; 21:13), but also the greater promise and hope for Isaac (22:17–18).

The parallels with chapter 21 appear to invalidate the necessity of removing the threat of Ishmael and the pain it produced. They also increase Abraham's burden, highlighting his second loss of a son, stressed in God's description of Isaac (22:2). Finally, they increase the concern that God will indeed expect this unthinkable requirement. For the reader, the numerous parallels and allusions to the previous narratives arrest their attention and draw them into the story. They will agonize with Abraham, who passed God's extreme test in faith, offering his beloved son of promise and receiving God's ratification of the extended promises of his covenant as God's loyal vassal, to extend blessing to all nations.

God Tested Abraham (22:1a)

After all his working in Abraham's life, God tested Abraham.

22:1a. Though the initial clause, "After these things," draws attention to what precedes, it does not specify which events, allowing the ambiguity to draw on several facets from the previous chapter. The birth of Isaac provided the obvious prerequisite for God's request, but the conflict and expulsion of Ishmael raised the stakes. The covenant with

Abimelech reminds the reader of Abraham's struggles in trusting God ("she is my sister," 20:2) and his breakthrough in faith, readying him for testing. It also suggests the lapse of some time. While emphasizing the fulfilling of God's promises, expectations and tensions grow with the request. How much time has elapsed is unclear, but Isaac's task carrying the wood up the mountain suggests that he was certainly an older boy, perhaps even a teenager (adding another comparison to Ishmael in chapter 21).

In conjunction with God's description of Isaac, the backward glance puts the reader on alert for the comparisons that will escalate the tension from the notice that God "tested" (נִסָּה) Abraham. The "test"[4] warns the reader and mitigates the shock of God's extreme request. The reader also realizes, then, that Abraham did not know it was a test. Rather, God was providing a powerful opportunity for Abraham to demonstrate his absolute loyalty to his master. This test, however, will reveal as much about God as about Abraham.

Testing God

God objects to people testing him or proving whether he was telling the truth or is really going to act, because such testing rejects his authority, promise, or previous revelation (Exod. 17:7; Num. 14:22; Pss. 78:41, 56; 95:8; 106:14). God, however, regularly tests his people to reveal their loyalty and faith and to promote greater faith, commitment, and obedience (Exod. 15:25; 16:4; 20:20; Deut. 8:2, 16; 13:4; Judg. 3:1, 4; 2 Chron. 32:31). Here, the goal is clearly to expose the heart of loyalty as justification for the promise (see Exposition below, v. 12, "now I know," cf. Deut. 8:2; 13:4; Judg. 3:4; 2 Chron. 32:31).

God Required Isaac in Sacrifice (22:1b–2)

God commanded Abraham to sacrifice Isaac, his beloved child of promise.

22:1b–2. Even with the warning, God's radical request jolts the reader. The dissonance occurs on several levels. The entire narrative from 12:2 has largely focused on the promise of a great nation through a descendant, which has been progressively defined until he was finally supernaturally given in 21:1–2 and protected as the sole heir in 21:12–14. It seems as if the question was finally settled, only to be completely upended. Now he must pass the test with the promise at stake, yet passing the test threatens the promise as well (Coats 1973, 393)!

God dramatically builds up the paternal attachment to the boy in his request: "your son—your only son, whom you love, Isaac" (NET). It is the very son of promise, Abraham's son, his only son, to whom he is deeply attached. While Isaac was not his only physical descendant, the sending away of Ishmael made him the only heir. He is effectively the only son (reminding of the painful loss in ch. 21). The problem is that this is the son Abraham loves. This tests true worship versus idolatry (Tribble in Moyers 1996, 227). Who will Abraham truly love more? As we will note, this phrase is missing in the climax when God declares Abraham's loyalty, demonstrating the core of the question (22:12, 16).

TRANSLATION ANALYSIS 22:2a

A very minor translation variant impacts the hearing of the words from God. Some translations place the relative clause "whom you love" after the proper name "Isaac" (e.g., ESV, NKJV, NLT, NRSV), as opposed to the Hebrew order, which places "Isaac" last (cf. NASB95,

4 The disjunctive initiates the new section, drawing attention to crucial information unknown to Abraham but necessary for the reader, who knows that such an act is an abomination to Yahweh (Lev. 20:2–5; Deut. 18:10). As we shall see, this raises tensions for the reader and exposes the extreme stakes of loyalty to God. It also heightens Abraham's faith who does not know it is a test.

> NET, NIV). The Hebrew text saves the specific name to the end as the capstone, building to the naming of the child of promise with the name that recalls both the absurdity of the promise and the supernatural birth.

Saving Isaac's name until last, God left no doubt in his request. He was asking Abraham to return the unexpected, impossible, supernatural gift that God had built up for twenty-five years and on whom Abraham had set his joy and hopes. The culminating declaration, "Isaac," fused the promise, Abraham and Sarah's initial skepticism and struggle, the resulting joy, and even the conflict with Ishmael and confirmation that this was the child of promise. This boy is the one God will ask for.

And on yet another level God's test seems inconceivable. It is unimaginably difficult, completely unexpected, and contrary to the (subsequently) revealed character of God. Though Abraham lived long before God's clearly declared hatred of child sacrifice (Lev. 20:2–5; Deut. 18:10), the reader would know God's character and passions, that he would never do such a thing (Jer. 32:35). Even in Abraham's world, the use of child sacrifice was typically soon after birth and limited to fertility, protection, or extreme circumstances (Green 1975, 156–59; Walton 2009a, 97–98). This was startling and contrary to reason.

Because God had yet to reveal his hatred of human sacrifice, and even though it would necessarily conflict with the revealed value of his images and protection of them (Gen. 9:5–6), God's request defined the ultimate test of Abraham's loyalty to him. Would Abraham choose loyalty to God over reason, affection, ambition, or even God's own previous promise and his love for Isaac? Ironically, the extreme test provided the basis for the final ratification of the promise to use Abraham's descendants to bring God's blessing and his end to the cosmic battle begun in Genesis 3 that brought about the need for sacrifice and death.

The phrasing of the command only adds to the tension. In effect the imperative here becomes a "polite request" (Cotter 2003, 153). Hamilton (1995, 101) has noted that this particle only occurs "five times in the entire OT when God speaks to a person. Each time God asks the individual to do something staggering, something that defies rational explanation or understanding. Here then is an inkling at least that God is fully aware of the magnitude of his test for Abraham." It also may provide Abraham the expectation that the choice is his to freely make, without guilt if he does not (Sarna 1989, 151). But such an implication only makes the obedience that much more radical (Ross 2008, 141).

> *TRANSLATION ANALYSIS 22:2b*
> God's command to "take" (קַח) Isaac included the enclitic particle (נָא), which "soften[ed] the harshness of the bare verbal form" (Harman, "Particles," NIDOTTE 4:1033). Most English translations leave it untranslated, so it is not clear in the text. Wenham, however, translates it "Please take" (Wenham 1994, 97; cf. Hamilton 1995, 97). Waltke follows Lambdin, however, in taking this after the response of Abraham (הִנֵּנִי), to show logical consequence, meaning, "since you are ready to obey me, take your son" (Lambdin 1971, 170–71; Waltke and Fredricks 2001, 304–5; WOC, §34.7a;).

Abraham was to take Isaac and go. The command to "go" (וְלֶךְ־לְךָ) mirrors the command in 12:1 to "go" (לֶךְ־לְךָ) to a place that God would show him (12:1 ,אֲשֶׁר אַרְאֶךָּ; cf. 22:2, "of which I will tell you," אֲשֶׁר אֹמַר אֵלֶיךָ). The comparison not only highlights the tension of the threat to the long-awaited promise, but it also demonstrates the growth of Abraham. The shift from faith in a promise to faith despite the apparent recall of the promise, without any recorded protest, speaks loudly as "the exemplar of steadfast, disinterested loyalty to God" (Sarna 1967, 163; cf. Lawlor 1980, 32–33).

God directed him to the land of Moriah, a name that will only show up again in 2 Chronicles 3:1 to refer to the temple mount where Solomon will build the temple to Yahweh. While the exact identification of the two places of the same name has been disputed, the number of ambiguities in the text allows at least a tentative identification.[5] Abraham's act of faith and God's provision for the future nation would parallel God's provision for all those who would come to him in faith, like their forefather Abraham, to the temple.

Abraham Took Isaac as God Said (22:3–4)

Abraham immediately prepared for the sacrifice, taking Isaac as God had said.

22:3–4. Abraham responded immediately to God's request. Just as with his expulsion of Ishmael, also clearly distasteful, he began "early in the morning" (v. 3, cf. 21:14). The narrative wastes no time describing the preparations, leaving many questions to the imagination. Where was Sarah, and did she know? What was he telling Isaac? Why did he take the two servants? Why does it mention the woodcutting after the party is gathered and ready to go? The terseness of his response, however, indicates complete and uncompromising obedience to God's request.

In two verses, the narrative briefly moves the reader the course of three days from Abraham's camp in Beersheba to within sight of one of the designated hills of Moriah, the place that God was pointing him toward. Though the narrator does not linger on them, those three days of travel with Isaac add to the test of Abraham's resolution and faith in God, as the reader asks the questions that we might expect the old man to be crying out in his silence. Three days also moves the response to the test from impulsive obedience to considered, reflective, sober resolve, an "undoubting act of free will" (Sarna 1989, 152).

Abraham Prepared for Expectant Worship (22:5–6)

Expecting to return with Isaac, Abraham took the supplies for the sacrifice.

22:5. The brief instructions to the servants in verse 5 add to the pathos as the trip continues (v. 6). Abraham speaks, only to provide meager instructions that continue to raise questions. Certainly, he gives no inclination of his dreadful task to the servants, though the reader can imagine any number of possible implications. He asserts that they would both return (plural subjects for "go," "worship," and "come again"). Is he intentionally lying to conceal from Isaac the awful reality of the next few hours (Sarna 1989, 152)? Is he contemplating disobedience and simply not giving Isaac up in sacrifice? Is he resolute in faith and confident in God's provision (v. 8)? Or is there some mixture of emotions and tension in Abraham, vacillating between all of these as he struggles with a terrible obedience (Wenham 1994, 107–8)? The reader does not know . . . yet.

22:6. Much like verse 3, Abraham moves resolutely and efficiently. For the first time we hear Abraham take "the fire and the knife" as he laid the wood on Isaac, soon to be laying Isaac on the

5 The identification with the future site of the temple is questioned because the distance would not necessarily take three days, the name is presented slightly differently, there was plenty of wood around Jerusalem, traveling straight there would make it hard to see from a distance, and we might have expected the designation "Salem" as in chapter 14 (e.g., Walton 2009a, 96–97). Chronicles does not make any reference to Genesis, drawing out any parallel, which we might expect. Despite the paucity of information in Gen. 22, these and other questions can be answered (Moberly 1992, 47–48; Waltke and Fredricks 2001, 304–5). The identification as the same place remains a likely possibility.

wood (v. 9). The anguish of the moment is underlined by the phrase, repeated in verse 8, that "they went both of them together." The image overwhelms the imagination with the agony of what will follow.

Abraham Anticipated God's Provision (22:7–8)

Responding to Isaac's question about the supplies, Abraham anticipated God's provision for the sacrifice.

22:7–8. Recalling verses 5–6, Isaac noted the tools and supplies just enumerated and simply asked about what was missing. In fact, the many missing elements of the story have been begging for address, and yet Abraham's answer is hardly satisfactory to the reader. It is another enigmatic statement that at this point can be taken as a statement of certain faith, a statement of evasion, or an honest expectation of Isaac's sacrifice. Abraham simply asserts that "God will see to the sheep for His burnt offering, my son" (NJPS, v. 8). The NJPS effectively presents the word play of "see" (ראה), meaning to "provide" (ESV, and many translations), which will foreshadow Abraham "seeing" the ram substitute (v. 13) and tie together God's provision with Abraham's faith.

The wording in the Hebrew, however, also allows for opposing intentions. The final "my son" can be taken as words of address (as in most English translations) or it can be taken in apposition to "burnt offering," specifying what that burnt offering would be: Abraham's son (Cotter 2003, 155)! The initial reader would see the ambiguity and rising drama, while the modern English reader may simply assume only expectant faith.

It will not be until we see Abraham's extreme loyalty acted out that we can return to these statements and actions leading up to the actual sacrifice and wonder at the resolute confidence prefiguring God's intervention or breathe a sigh of relief that the struggle in Abraham coalesced in the act of steadfast faith. Considering the outcome, "his complete certainty of God, together with complete openness as to detail, makes this a model reply to an agonizing question. God's method was his own affair; it would take them both by surprise" (Kidner 1967, 154). Even if he spoke more than he felt, when it came time to choose, Abraham was willing to release his dearest possession to Yahweh in complete surrender and absolute loyalty to his sovereign benefactor.

These statements of faith and tension provide the central focus of the narrative. In the overall structure these two parallel scenes, with the implements, the statements of hope that would all be fulfilled in God's great plan, and the image of the two of them walking together (repeated in v. 8) toward God's climactic promise for their future, provide the questions to be answered. We wonder at both Abraham's response, which will turn out to be faith, and God's provision, which will not only be the sacrifice for his obedient worshipper but the climactic promise to his obedient vassal, leading to the transformation of humanity. These two scenes highlight both the responsibility of the vassal and the promise of provision from the suzerain in the sealing of the covenant that has been the central focus of the Abraham stories.

Abraham Bound Isaac for Sacrifice (22:9–10)

With Isaac, Abraham prepared an altar for the sacrifice, binding Isaac.

22:9–10. Just as Abraham had set about the task of leaving early in the morning to go to the place (הַמָּקוֹם, v. 3) of which God had told him, then seeing that place (הַמָּקוֹם, v. 4) from afar, they now arrived at that place (הַמָּקוֹם, v. 9). At the place of God's choosing, Abraham did God's bidding without hesitation: building the altar, laying the wood, and binding Isaac. Three days after God's command, Abraham stood with knife in hand over his son.

As a young man, old enough to carry the wood up the mountain, perhaps even a middle to later teen, Isaac would certainly have been able to resist or run from his father, who was well over one hundred. Perhaps that is the reason for the binding of Isaac, yet he could have resisted. So perhaps the binding itself is testimony to the submission of Isaac, who remained still to allow Abraham to tie the knots. The evidence of faith, then, shines through both worshippers before Yahweh (Wenham 1994, 109).

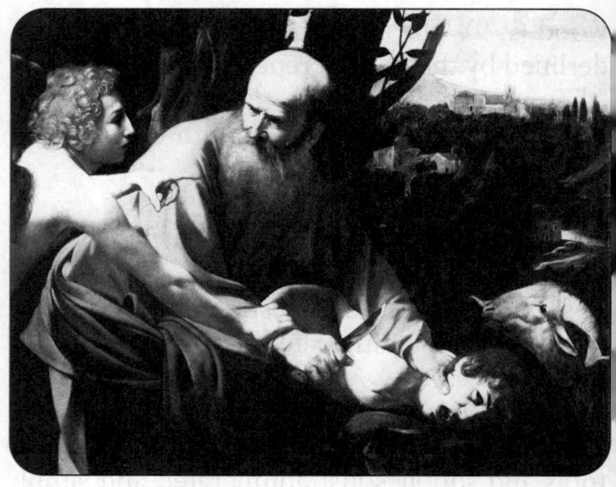
Sacrifice of Isaac. Painting by Caravaggio

God Substituted a Ram (22:11–14)

For Abraham, intending to sacrifice Isaac, God provided a ram.

22:11–12. Abraham fully intended to carry out God's command in 22:2. With Isaac prepared and knife poised, God stopped him with his urgent call from heaven (v. 11). Here Yahweh declared for Abraham and all future generations to know that Abraham had passed the test, fully trusting God.[6] He was willing to entrust Isaac to Yahweh in sacrifice with full expectation that God would deal with the dilemma that God himself had created (Mathews 2005, 285).

The angel's words are as significant as they are confusing to the modern reader. Did God not know if Abraham feared him? The anthropomorphism sounds strange, almost sacrilegious with our modern expectations of God's omniscience. It is not a matter of God discovering new facts, however. Rather, he is declaring the outcome of the testing (v. 1), demonstrating Abraham's full right to God's promise as a loyal vassal.

God's objective in testing was to determine, to "know," what was in the heart (v. 12; cf. Deut. 8:2; 13:4; Judg. 3:4; 2 Chron. 32:31). Specifically, the desired outcome was obedience (cf. Deut. 8:2; Judg. 3:4), which was the outward sign of loyalty, or loving God with the whole heart (Deut. 13:4). Yahweh was the sovereign king of Israel, and their responsibility was loyalty to him (Deut. 6:4–5), which showed in obedience (Wright 2001). The idea is clear, specifically defined as one who "fear[s] God" (Gen. 22:12). To fear God is simply to honor God in worship "characterized by obedience" (Van Pelt and Kaiser, יָרֵא, *NIDOTTE* 2:530). Abraham had been commanded to be loyal (17:1, see above) and now showed fidelity to his king with his radical obedience, passing the test.

For some, God's demand becomes a cruel instigation of an extreme and profane act if God already knew the answer (1 Sam. 16:7; Ps. 139:1–4; Jer. 17:10), even if God had no intention of allowing Abraham to carry it out. The point of the narrative, however, opposes such a derogatory understanding (cf. Moberly 1992, 43–46). In language Abraham and, later, Israel would resonate with, God was declaring to Abraham and all future generations the security of the promise from Yahweh, the great king, to his loyal servant (Chisholm 2007, 11–16). God evaluated Abraham's faithful action of obedience and declared him loyal and,

6 The text tells us that the angel of the Lord speaks (vv. 11, 15), but he clearly is speaking for Yahweh (v. 13, "me"; v. 16, "By myself I have sworn, declares the LORD").

so, worthy of the full promise (Gen. 22:12), resulting in the certainty of innumerable offspring living in victory and bringing blessing to all the nations of the earth (vv. 16–18). In highly figurative and emotionally charged language, God alone guaranteed the complete and now certain promises (Heb. 6:13–18).

Abrahamic Covenant Through the Abraham Narratives

The Abrahamic covenant is often understood as an unconditional, unilateral covenant in the form of a land grant from a king to his loyal subject (see Exposition above on ch. 15, p. 293, Weinfeld 1970). Chisholm (1992; 2007, 11–16) argues that there are conditions for the full ratification of the covenant that Abraham met here, leading to God's oath (22:16–18). Shetter (2019) develops the argument with ANE background support from land grant treaties much more fully. See the Introduction to the Abraham Narratives for the progression of the promises and expectations of the Abrahamic covenant through the Abraham narratives.

22:13–14. As soon as the angel had stopped him, Abraham noticed a ram caught in the thicket, which he offered as a burnt offering in the place of Isaac. Abraham's statement of faith (v. 8) becomes reality as God "sees to" him seeing Isaac's substitute. Abraham then uses the faithful response of God to see to his sacrifice, as the name for the place: "The LORD will provide" (ESV) or, as NJPS translates, "Adonai-yireh, whence the present saying, 'On the mount of the LORD there is vision.'" The NJPS translation again captures the connection between the seeing (Abraham saw the ram) that led to the substitute and God's seeing to (provision for) his worship.

God Ratified His Promise to Abraham (22:15–24)

By personal oath, God summarized and ratified his promises to his loyal servant.

22:15–16. The angel moved the focus from Abraham and his obedience to the consequent ratification of the covenant with his second address. With the declaration of Abraham's fidelity to Yahweh and worthiness to the promise (v. 12), after Abraham's appropriate sacrifice (v. 13), Yahweh declared his commitment to the enhanced, full promises of the covenant with a personal oath (vv. 16–18). The conditionality of God's promise ("because you have done this," v. 16) reveals again the "dynamic relationship" that "granted the dignity of the causality to Abraham, His responsible covenantal partner" (Chisholm 2007, 15).

In both verse 12 and again here in verse 16, God referenced Abraham not withholding his son, his only son. He repeated his initial address to Abraham (v. 2) but notably removed "whom you love." Abraham had passed the test by showing his love of Yahweh over Isaac (Tribble, in Moyers 1996, 227). God honors obedient faith, putting him first.[7]

22:17–18. While the land promise to the future nation was already established (15:8, 13–21), this ratification confirmed the clarifications and enhancements since Genesis 15. Yahweh now swore to the ongoing nature of the covenant, including the ongoing promise of the land (17:2–21), especially re-emphasizing Abraham's innumerable progeny (22:17), their power over their enemies (v. 17), and God's blessing through them to all the nations of the earth (v. 18). He closed by reiterating the role of Abraham's obedience (v. 18b). All future generations must

7 Tribble notes that the issue is really idolatry. It is a matter of faith. Will Abraham put his son or God first (Moyers 1996, 227)? It reminds of Jesus's words to the disciples, "If anyone comes to me and does not hate his own father and mother and wife and children and brothers and sisters, yes, and even his own life, he cannot be my disciple" (Luke 14:26).

understand God's expectation for his covenant partners to live in faith. God will accomplish his purpose, benefiting loyal servants.

The oath, then, brings together all the threads of the covenant that had gone before. Although the enhanced promises since cutting the covenant remained unchanged, the summary of the promise emphasized the climactic nature of this ratification. For the first time, God added the infinitive ("I will *surely* bless you," בָּרֵךְ אֲבָרֶכְךָ, v. 17, emphasis added), adding emphasis and putting this blessing beyond all previous promises. Similarly, he emphasized the extravagant multiplication of Abraham's offspring ("I will *greatly* multiply your offspring," וְהַרְבָּה אַרְבֶּה, NET, v. 17, emphasis added), illustrated with the first use of "as the sand that is on the seashore" in parallel to the stars for numbers. God guaranteed innumerable future offspring.

TRANSLATION ANALYSIS 22:17a
The cognate infinitive absolute typically adds certainty (WOC, §35.3.1b). This supports the ESV translation, "I will surely multiply." Occasionally, however, the infinitive can emphasize the meaning of the verb (WOC, §35.3.1c), which fits this use because the following illustrations emphasize the extent of the multiplication, "as the stars " and "as the sand," leading to the NET, "greatly multiply" (cf. NASB95, NLT). Some translations avoid the debate by leaving out any impact completely (cf. NIV, NRSV).

For the first time, God also declared the power of Abraham's future offspring over their enemies, possessing their gates (or taking over their cities, v. 17). This statement of supremacy reflects the initial cursing on any who would dishonor Abraham (12:3). If they are enemies of his blessed nation, they will be occupied, especially realized in the conquest (e.g., emphasis on the cities, Deut. 2:34–37; 3:4–12; 6:10–15; 19:1). Also reflecting that initial blessing on all who bless Abraham, the "nations" (cf. 18:18; rather than the "families," cf. 12:3), emphasizing the international impact of Abraham's coming descendants, will experience blessing through Abraham's "offspring" (זֶרַע; cf. 26:4; previously blessing was directed through Abraham, 12:3; 18:18).

TRANSLATION ANALYSIS 22:17b
While most English translations take the 3ms pronominal suffix on "enemies" as a collective (like the antecedent, "seed") and translate it "their" (e.g., NASB95, NIV, NCV, NRSV), the ESV translates it "his," adding the plural in a footnote. The implication suggests a shift of focus from the multitudes in v. 17a to a singular focus on perhaps a single royal messianic seed (cf. Ps. 72:17b; Alexander 1997b). The ambiguity of both allows at least a biblical theological preparation for a later typological messianic understanding (Alexander 2012).

TRANSLATION ANALYSIS 22:18
The Hebrew for "be blessed" (וְהִתְבָּרְכוּ) occurs in the *hithpael* stem rather than the *niphal* (as in 12:3; 18:18). In 12:3 we argued for a passive sense of the *niphal*. Here, however, some translations take the *hithpael* in its more usual reflexive sense, "shall bless themselves" (NJPS, cf. NET, RSV). Rather than seeing them as necessary equivalents, they may present slight but important nuances. Consistent with usage outside of Genesis, Lee (2012, 294) argues the estimative-declarative indirect reflexive sense in which the subject recognizes or considers themselves to be blessed: "all nations of the earth shall regard or declare themselves as blessed on account of your offspring." The blessing is not just occurring but recognized as coming through the descendant(s) of Abraham.

Beginning with his choice of Abraham, God had called him to go and be a blessing (12:1–3). God then acknowledged Abraham's obedient faith in 15:6, leading to the initial cutting of the covenant and affirming the initial promise of the land to the promised nation. God then challenged Abraham to complete loyalty, to "walk before" him and "be blameless" (17:1). Now God has acknowledged Abraham's loyalty in his obedience, leading to this climactic promise, which he twice tied to the unquestioning obedience of Abraham (22:15, 18). In verse 15, Yahweh focused on the action of offering his only son back to Yahweh. In verse 18 he focused on Abraham listening to his voice. In pointed contrast to Adam listening to his wife's voice (3:17) instead of God's (3:11), and Abraham listening to Sarah's (16:2) rather than trusting Yahweh, Abraham obeyed God's voice.

Abraham passed his test with flying colors, clearly showing his righteousness (15:6; cf. James 2:21; Maxwell 2007) and was greatly rewarded. As Israel will later be reminded on many occasions, the outworking of the promises for them as a nation results from Abraham's obedience (Gen. 26:3–5) and will be experienced by their analogous loyal obedience (Deut. 30:11–20), passing their tests as well (ch. 8).[8] Unfortunately, Israel often failed the testing from God and experienced God's discipline rather than God's blessing.

22:19. The return trip is merely noted, closing the narrative and leaving many questions unanswered. Even Isaac disappears from the narrative as Abraham and the young men go home. The tension is settled, and the son is no longer the focus. The focus of the narrative was not concerned with those questions, such as Sarah's knowledge or reaction. Rather, the necessary focus was on the promise and the needed statement of faith as the foundation for God's blessing and promise. Abraham, with his nearly silent march to obedience, pictured the ideal and faithful servant of Yahweh. His unmatched faith through an unimaginable test led to God's faithful working, as Abraham trusted God to resolve apparent conflicts between his promise and his command, responding in appropriate worship.

22:20–24. The following genealogy reflects the opening genealogy in the overall structure (11:27–32; see the overview in the Introduction to the Abraham Narratives, p. 236). It functions in the ongoing narrative to introduce Rebekah (22:23), the future bride of Isaac and means to accomplish the extravagant promise of Yahweh (ch. 24).

THEOLOGICAL FOCUS

A believer's faithful obedience, choosing loyalty to God over every competitor, allows God's greatest blessing in his life and his world.

While our modern expectations may try to make God out to be a monster, the narrative gives no sense of that. The warning that this is only a test alerts the reader that God has no intention of allowing human sacrifice and, in fact, he would not. Rather, he has appropriately arranged an extreme test for his vassal to demonstrate for all generations the radical nature of Abraham's loyalty and the appropriate gift to Abraham of his covenant grant of land and future national prominence. God's gift provided the means to bring blessing to all nations through them. The test, however, also provides an initial picture of God's dealings with his people, in which he may allow or orchestrate hardship, suffering, or uncertainty or give difficult instructions. God is interested in revealing the degree of his people's loyalty and faith (Exod. 15:25; 16:4; Deut. 13:4) and teaching them greater faith, commitment, and obedience (Deut. 8:2–3, 16).

God's goal in testing is not pain, frustration, and damage to his people, but good (Deut. 8:16). He desires to bring blessing and fulfill

8 Moberly (1988, 305) notes the connection of both testing (נסה) and fear of God (יִרְאָה) in Exod. 20:20 as well, concluding that "Abraham supremely exemplifies the meaning of living by torah. He demonstrates individually the quality of response to God that should characterize Israel as a whole."

promise (Gen. 22:15–18; cf. Deut. 8). He does not promise, however, that he will return or maintain any loyalty that he requires his people to give up for him. Isaac was necessarily spared, but the good of God's blessing and presence provides far more than any loss a loyal follower may release to him. Isaac, then, represents the most valuable asset a believer has, even the very promise of God. Nothing can take God's supremacy in my life (Matt. 6:24; Luke 14:26).

The necessary response, then, for God's servants is to trust God amid struggle (James 1:2–4). We must live in obedience, expecting God to provide because he sees and will see to whatever we need. The faith that shows in obedience expects God to provide and lives according to his revealed will, even when it feels like it will bring more pain and loss. Faith recognizes that God does not take all he deserves, but he requires and accepts loyalty from his subjects and their substitutionary sacrifices that he himself provides, ultimately of course in Christ. That loyalty does not allow anything to take his place in our lives.

God also shows his sovereign faithfulness to his declared promises and plan. Though humanity cannot see the future, God will accomplish his purposes and remain true to his word, even when it appears to be impossible to both receive his pledge and keep his expectation. Lingering uncertainty and delay may intensify testing but does not diminish God's trustworthy character to the person of faith. Rather, delayed fulfillment increases the evidence of faith and the reliability of God as the good benefactor.

God uses the outcomes of testing and faith for the benefit of the one tested. The faith of Abraham is not a testimony to his superhuman character but to the working of God to grow his faith through their ongoing and progressive relationship over time. The passage of time is crucial to reveal growth and to provide the environment in which that faith can grow. Clearly Abraham has progressed from his sojourn in Egypt and the multiple episodes of "she is my sister" (12:10–20; 20:1–18). The time was not merely for the sake of showing the sovereign sufficiency of God to a barren couple past the years of bearing. Rather, God was working in their lives to produce the fruit of that relationship as well.

God also used the time to reveal his character to his world. He demonstrates his goodness, faithfulness, and righteousness as the redeemer of humanity through his salvation history. He shows his constancy and power through what is humanly impossible. The test added tension, but God kept all his promises, providing even the sacrifice for Abraham so that the entire benefit for Abraham is from beginning to end from God himself.

PREACHING AND TEACHING STRATEGIES

Exegetical and Theological Synthesis

We begin to synthesize the exegesis and theology with how Abraham's test becomes a model for all believers. It is the nature of God and his relationship with us that testing is a part of saving faith. Whether in this Old Testament narrative or in a New Testament letter like James's, the testing of one's faith is a necessary component of salvation. Genuine Christ-followers are tested and pass those tests. From a human perspective, faith is tested, and all are judged by works at the judgment; from God's perspective, he tests the loyalty of his subjects but also provides for them. Our sinful selves struggle to obey in times like those. Abraham's obedience is exemplary: immediate and single-minded, with no visible signs of doubt or hesitation.

We need to place our confident trust in the way God reveals himself as able to see to our needs (cf. 22:8, "God will see to the sheep," my translation of the Hebrew). God tested Abraham, Abraham passed the test, and God saw to it to provide his own sacrifice. It is always that way for God's people. That does not mean all trying times for believers will end happily ever after in this world. It does mean that God blesses those who fear him like Abraham did. All genuine faith has the seeds of such radical obedience. All through redemptive history God proves that he will accomplish his purpose to bring glory to himself by redeeming some from every tribe and tongue. The spread of God's blessing starts with one man, Abraham, one nation, Israel, and then on to the church worldwide. Fidelity to the covenant, as portrayed by Abraham in this narrative, is non-negotiable.

Preaching Idea

God blesses his people and all nations through the tested, obedient faith of his servants.

Contemporary Connections

What does it mean?

The entire narrative means that a person's faith must move beyond profession or confession and show itself through obedience. This explains, for instance, why both end-time judgments, the great white throne and judgment seat of Christ, are judgments of works, not only a profession of faith. Both judgments assess works because the works are the fruit, the proof, of genuine faith. It is important that God's people know what the narrative means for their own faith. All our listeners must find themselves with the faith portrayed in Abraham's life. The narrative means all of us can grow in our loyalty to our King so that we continue to be faithful in our walk with him.

If someone asked, "Why did God devise that test for Abraham?", the exegetical/theological discussion showed God asking Abraham to trust him with something that seemed to destroy the very promise of God. God was asking Abraham to do the most illogical thing with respect to receiving what God had already promised. That is incredible faith! God was asking Abraham to give up his most beloved possession (a relationship, promise, future, etc.) in loyalty to his King. That is incredible loyalty; that is the essence of faith!

This section presents the opportunity to help someone note the difference between God testing Abraham versus God putting Abraham to the test in the sense of tempting him. While God tests the genuineness of the faith of his children, he does not tempt his children to sin against him. That's the tempter's job.

Is it true?

One of the burdens to communicating this narrative to postmodern listeners is the fact that God's plan to test Abraham like this offends our sensibilities. Older generations listening might not even think like this, but the current generations do. Is it true that our loving God would devise such a cruel test for Abraham? The answer is "yes." It will be difficult—maybe impossible—to prove this. In some ways this could function in the "What does it mean?" section above. There is no way around this: in his infinite wisdom God does what we cannot understand. He causes Abraham intense emotional trauma, all for the purpose of testing his fidelity to God. The danger is for our listeners to believe that the God they believe in could not possibly do that to one of his own, even though the narrative says he did. Is God's revelation true or not? Again, the answer is "yes," even though the fight for such faith is difficult.

Now what?

All the faith-filled are tested in some way, shape, or form. That is the norm. All the faithful habitually, consistently, but not perfectly, pass such tests. Scripture is clear, for instance in the book of James, that the testing of our faith does something that is a necessary part of the Christian's journey. Think of this contrast: we read this testing narrative with an emotional gasp; James 1 teaches us to "count it all joy." Our listeners need to hear from Genesis 22 how this test functions as part of God's overall plan to bless us so we can be a blessing to the world. In that way, the tests God brings our way are instrumental in our disciple-making efforts.

Creativity in Presentation

Our homiletical idea is: God blesses his people and all nations through the tested, obedient faith of his servants. I am not sure if you could concoct a test to equal the one God put Abraham through. However, the closer you could come to that, the better for helping everyone feel the emotional pain that God's instruction caused. Then the question, "Would your faith work like Abraham's did?", would have much force. Of course, you and I know that our listeners are at different stages in their spiritual development. God administered this test to Abraham when he was up there in years with respect to his walk with God. Different levels of faith require different levels of testing, and God is the perfect proctor. Consider the following breakdown of this chapter:

- What a test is (vv. 1–2). This segment could define the tests God puts his children through. This includes differentiating between testing and tempting, including the different goals of both actions and the different initiators of each. It is critical to show that faith, by definition, must be tested. God-given faith contains the seeds of loyal obedience.

- How people of faith respond to God's test (vv. 3–10). Here is the place to highlight how the narrative paints Abraham's loyalty to God's radical demand. It is a "go and do likewise" narrative. Everyone in the house should leave bound and determined to follow Abraham's example of faith. Especially important is Abraham's example of believing God even though everything inside of him may have screamed, "This is crazy!"

- What passing the test does (vv. 15–24). The text makes it clear that there is some kind of causal connection (vv. 16, 18, "because you have") between Abraham's obedience and God's ratifying the promise. There is no way for God's plan to advance if Abraham is not loyal to God and his agenda for his world. However, when God has loyal subjects on board, he can continue to show his glory in the world through the lives of his citizens. You and I probably have listeners who believe God should bless them even though they are not loyal to him. This narrative corrects such notions.

- Finally, the narrative does tell us why genuine believers pass the test (vv. 11–14). I suggest saving this for last only because it is a fitting way to end the sermon/lesson so that worship can occur. First, the angel of the Lord articulates the reason for Abraham's loyal obedience: "for now I know that you fear God" (v. 12). Second, each reading of this story creates a new fascination with our God, who provides a sacrifice that spares Isaac's life (v. 13, "behind him was a ram"). Third, with each test through life we learn the lesson of that place named "The LORD will provide" (v. 14).

DISCUSSION QUESTIONS

1. What temptation was inherent in Abraham's test?

2. What is your equivalent "only son . . . whom you love" that would be the most difficult thing to sacrifice to the Lord?

3. Think of your worst occurrences of disobedience/disloyalty to the Lord. Can you locate your "Isaac" in that situation?

4. What does the angel mean by the "fear" of the Lord, and how does it show in your life?

5. Can you articulate the connection between genuine saving faith and the fear of the Lord?

6. How do the results of complete loyalty compensate for what you willingly give up to put God first? How has God provided and blessed you in the past for obedience?

Genesis 23:1–20

EXEGETICAL IDEA

When Sarah died, Abraham negotiated and purchased a heritable tomb in the land of Canaan for her burial, in faith securing a portent of God's promise and impetus for his descendants to follow his anticipation of God's fidelity, despite the immediate cost.

THEOLOGICAL FOCUS

The righteous respond to death with faith, looking beyond this world to follow God's unfailing promises and prepare future generations to embrace God's ultimate plan and working, regardless of cost.

PREACHING IDEA

The faithful trust God and provide a foundation for a legacy of faith for future generations of the faithful.

PREACHING POINTERS

One way to begin the move from the original audience to current listeners is with the opening reference in verses 2 and 19 to "the land of Canaan." That location translates into our Christian experience. Listeners are currently exercising their faith in the promises of God in this world. Our ultimate home and full realization of the promise exist in the future new heaven and earth. Abraham continues to function for us because his faith, which drives his purchase, continues to inform our faith and the prospect of God's favor. For anyone wanting some kind of New Testament validation of our likeness to Abraham's situation, they might benefit from the description of Abraham saying, "I am a sojourner and foreigner among you" (v. 4). We Christians are also considered "elect exiles" (1 Peter 1:1). One day this will not be the case, but now we strive to be faithful to God until he returns.

As noted in many of our homiletical discussions, this narrative is one of those "go and do likewise" exemplars. Abraham's faith, his reputation (cf. v. 6, "you are a prince of God among us"), and his wise dealings during the entire transaction are exemplary; all of this leads the way for us. This is all being accomplished among outsiders of the covenant (cf. vv. 3, 5, 7, "Hittites"). Abraham's faith in the promise of God meant that he purchased property for his family long into the future. This is the kind of faith in the promises of God that allows Christians to flourish in their walk with God, even though they are exiles. First, we believe strongly in the promises of God now, and that faith translates into faithfulness to God. Like Abraham, we will not turn back into slavery to sin. And like Abraham, our faith and obedience will ensure that our families and future generations continue to experience the blessing of God as they follow our example.

LOOKING AHEAD: FAITH AND PREPARATION (23:1–20)

LITERARY STRUCTURE AND THEMES

As we have noted in the Introduction to the Abraham Narratives (p. 236), Genesis 11:27–22:24 provides the main body of the stories. Genesis 23:1–25:11 appends three vignettes in which Abraham anticipated possession of the land and provision for his descendants, key themes of the larger narrative. In chapter 23, Abraham needed a burial place for Sarah, but his concern was a possession as a foothold for the promised descendants. Moses frames the chapter with a reminder that Sarah died "in the land of Canaan" (23:1–2) and was buried "in the land of Canaan" (23:19–20), the promised possession (17:8; אֲחֻזָּה) of the future nation. The frame, then, connects the purchase to the promise, foregrounding Abraham's purpose and faith in the promise. The dialogue in between occurs in three movements (23:3–6, 7–11, 12–15) detailing the negotiations for a "burying place" (23:4, 9, 20; אֲחֻזַּת־קָבֶר) followed by the transaction (23:16–18).

A. Sarah died in the land of Canaan (23:1–2).
- B. Abraham negotiated a burial place (23:3–15).
  1. Abraham inquired about a burial place (23:3–6).
  2. Abraham requested Ephron's cave (23:7–11).
  3. Abraham asked the price (23:12–15).
- B'. Abraham paid full price for the land (23:16–18).

A'. Abraham buried Sarah in the land of Canaan (23:19–20).

Abraham established an ongoing homeland for his descendants (25:9; 49:30; 50:13). God would provide the land in his time, so Abraham focused his progeny on God's promised inheritance.

- ***Sarah Died in the Land of Canaan (23:1–2)***
- ***Abraham Negotiated a Burial Place (23:3–15)***
- ***Abraham Paid Full Price (23:16–18)***
- ***Abraham Buried Sarah in the Land of Canaan (23:19–20)***

EXPOSITION

The narrative focuses on the purchase of the field and its cave, stressing Abraham's insistence on a permanent possession for his descendants that could not be legally challenged. He paid the full asking price in front of witnesses, and he declared his commitment to the promise with his burial of Sarah. While her death is instrumental in the story, the real interest is possession of a heritable tomb in Canaan, a harbinger of the promise. The final verse crystallizes the issue, summarizing the transaction, deeding the property to Abraham as a possession in Canaan (cf. 17:8, 18:19). The significance of this transaction lies in Abraham's faith in and preparation for his descendants to live for God's promise. When Sarah died, Abraham negotiated and purchased a heritable tomb in the land of Canaan for her burial, in faith securing a portent of God's promise and impetus for his descendants to follow his anticipation of God's fidelity, despite the immediate cost and God's seeming absence.

Sarah Died in the Land of Canaan (23:1–2)

Sarah died at 127 in Hebron, in the land of Canaan.

23:1. The narrative does not indicate how long after Abraham offered Isaac that Sarah died. Rashi, a medieval rabbi, speculated that she died after hearing the story of Isaac being offered, leading to the placement of the story here (Cotter 2003, 161). Her death, while prompting the action, is incidental to the main point. The point of the story follows with the comment of the location of her death.

23:2. Sarah died at Kiriath-Arba, or Hebron. There is no explanation why they are not in Beersheba (22:19). The seemingly unimportant note, "in the land of Canaan," frames the narrative (cf. 23:19) and indicates the significance. Abraham has a choice to make. Now that she has died, will he try to bury her in the homeland (going back to Haran), or will he establish a new homeland for his descendants to be gathered to their fathers? His immediate response after mourning her will be to obtain permanent possession of a burial property, alluding to God's promise of Canaan as his permanent possession (17:8).

> *TRANSLATION ANALYSIS 23:2*
> Some have suggested that Abraham was still at Beersheba while Sarah was at Hebron, following the translation, "Abram came to mourn" (e.g., NKJV, Sailhamer 1990, 172). The verb is naturally translated "went in," however, noting his public mourning for his wife (e.g., ESV, NRSV).

Abraham Negotiated a Burial Place (23:3–15)

Abraham secured a permanent family tomb from the Hittites.

Abraham Inquired About a Burial Place (23:3–6)

Abraham asked to purchase a burying place, which the Hittites offered freely.

23:3–4. Abraham rose from his mourning and made his request to his resident Hittite neighbors. Abraham began with his social status, which is both important for understanding the challenges to his goal as well as recognizing the connection to God's promise to him. As a "sojourner and foreigner" among them (v. 4), he was without land rights. He could neither use burial grounds without permission, possess any land, nor (normally) pass it along as an inheritance (Sarna 1989, 156–57). Israel's own law forbade selling one's inheritance beyond a short-term lease until the year of Jubilee (Lev. 25:23; Num. 36:7). In Leviticus 25:23 Moses used the same two terms to show why. The Israelites did not really own their own land. It was Yahweh's. They were "strangers and sojourners" with Yahweh. These two terms together identify Abraham as "a citizen who does not have full civic rights, a resident alien" (*HALOT* s.v. "תּוֹשָׁב" 1712–13). The "foreigner" (תּוֹשָׁב) had less rights than the "sojourner" (גֵּר), who was dependent on the citizens. The foreigner was not allowed to participate in the festivals in Israel, being even less assimilated than the sojourner (Konkel, תּוֹשָׁב, *NIDOTTE* 4:284).

> **The Hittites**
> The presence of the Hittites in Hebron has been puzzling because the Hittite kingdom was in Asia Minor until they were overrun by the Sea Peoples in about 1200 BC. There is no clear evidence of them settling this far south, especially at the time of Abraham. Hamilton has argued, however, that these are a group originally from Anatolia that settled here (Hamilton 1995, 126–28), but because they have Semitic names and Genesis 10:15 relates Heth to the line of Canaan (the Hebrew has "sons of Heth," which is translated "Hittites"), an unrelated group with a similar name may be more likely (Mathews 2005, 316–17).

By drawing attention to his status, Abraham acknowledged his dependence on their generosity and the significance of his request. He desired "property" (Gen. 23:4, אֲחֻזָּה), which indicated a permanent possession to be passed down as an inheritance, rather than merely temporary use. The last time the term was used (and first time in Genesis) it described God's promise of the land of Canaan to Abraham and his offspring forever (17:8). It becomes a symbol of their expectation of God's fulfilled promise. It is not explicit, but it is likely that Abraham had the promise in mind as he bargained.

TRANSLATION ANALYSIS 23:4b

The combination of "property . . . for a burying place" (ESV) reflects two Hebrew words that certainly denote a "burial site" (NASB95, NJPS) but, more clearly, "ownership of a burial site" (NET), as the combination describes "an inheritable sepulcher" (Sarna 1989, 158; cf. Westbrook 1971, 33).

His intent in asking them to "give" (23:4) him property was not to get something free of charge. He was asking to purchase it. So, the rest of the patriarchs and their wives would be buried there as well (49:29–31; 50:13–14). His purpose was to bury Sarah, but he was not asking for a borrowed grave that would revert to its owner or be used in conjunction with another family.

TRANSLATION ANALYSIS 23:4a

The Hebrew verb here "give" (נתן) is properly translated "sell" (NCV, NIV, NJPS, NLT; HALOT s.v. "נתן" 733–35), as the following narrative makes clear.

23:5–6. The Hittites' response ignored the specific request and offered Abraham a choice of any of the graves to use without cost. They made no mention of property, but they did acknowledge his status among them in much different terms than Abraham used. In their very polite response, they use "my lord" (ESV, NLT, NKJV) or "sir" (NET, NIV) and address him as a "prince of God" (v. 6). The rhetoric goes beyond mere courtesy and may suggest manipulation (Sternberg 1991, 55). Or it may fit with the history of the previous chapters (and the ultimate response later), suggesting respect and recognition of God's blessing on him and those who bless him (cf. 21:22).

TRANSLATION ANALYSIS 23:6

The Hebrew can be translated directly as "prince of God" (ESV) or, taking "god" as a modifier, it can be understood as "mighty prince" (NET, NIV, NRSV). Trying to communicate the sense of their complement, NJPS translates it "elect of God," and NCV understands "great leader." The honor may well recognize the blessing of God on him and through him, much as Abimelech noted (21:22).

Their offer, however, still avoided the idea of a possession. Their generous offer of any tomb he liked implies only borrowing and not ownership.[1] The pronouns make it clear. She is Abraham's dead, but the graves were theirs: "your dead," "our tombs," "his tomb," "your dead" (23:6). Abraham graciously but firmly pressed the matter.

1 Of course, the motives of the Hittites are not expressed and are difficult to be sure about. Sternberg suggests several options, including "politeness, politics and profits" (Sternberg 1991, 34). Granting the murky motives, the dialogue is even more clouded since we also recognize that we do not have enough information on the bargaining protocols in Abraham's time to be dogmatic on any implications or connotations of the use of terms and expectations from the parties. It could be very much normal polite bargaining, or it may be a breach of protocol for Abraham to ask for and press the matter of ownership. Regardless, ownership is clearly his goal, and the outcome indicates God's working on his behalf as well.

Abraham Requested Ephron's Cave (23:7–11)

Abraham asked to purchase the cave of Machpelah from Ephron the Hittite, which Ephron offered with the field as a gift.

23:7–9. With their generous reply, Abraham rose and bowed to them, showing his deference and acknowledging their authority here. He is the resident alien asking for land from the rightful landowners and citizens of Hebron. Abraham apparently already had in mind what he believed would be the best option. With their generous offer and permission to bury, Abraham took them at their word, ignored the possible implication of a temporary site, and pressed the matter of ownership.[2] With Ephron sitting nearby (v. 10), Abraham specified Ephron's cave and asked them to intercede for him to be able to purchase it, describing its location.

> *TRANSLATION ANALYSIS 23:7*
> The Hittites are termed the "people of the land," recognizing their status as the free citizenry (cf. Vaux 1965, 1:70–72). The translation, "local people" (NET), still lacks the idea of their control over the land for the modern reader, though it is understood in the context. In contrast, Reviv (1977, 190–91) argues this denotes the council of the elders, along with all who enter the gate.

Abraham offers full price, preempting any subsequent question of fairness or his right to the land.[3] Again, he specified that it would be "property for a burying place" (v. 9; see v. 4). He asks for the transaction to be in the Hittite presence to verify the deed, assuring it is authorized and transparent.

23:10–11. The reader only now realizes that Ephron has been seated there all along and heard the dialogue. He responded in the hearing of not only the Hittites but everyone going through the gate. The sale would be a very public affair. Ephron continued the polite discourse. He appeared to refuse the payment and give it to Abraham freely. He repeated the offer of the leaders from verse 6. Abraham may bury his dead there without charge.

While Ephron ignored Abraham's request for a possession, he included the field in the transaction, which may suggest he is angling for more than he states or perhaps trying to put the idea out of reach (Sternberg 1991, 42–43). Or is this the normal bartering in the ancient world? Is this a genuine offer of a gift? Or yet is this a manipulative offer that will maintain ownership so that the field and cave can be retrieved later? The addition of the field adds considerable value to the offer (as seen later), but it also raises the stakes of possession. Given that Ephron also avoided Abraham's clear request for property (vv. 4, 7), it is less likely that the offer is to be taken at face value (or it is extraordinarily generous) and more likely that he is either angling for a large price or wanting to keep the rights after Abraham is done with the burial. While we cannot know for sure, Abraham capitalized on his inclusion of the field with the cave (v. 13). Abraham would also make clear that he would not accept a gift.

Abraham Asked the Price (23:12–15)

Abraham requested to give the price for the field, which Ephron named.

23:12–13. Abraham again bowed down to the local citizenry (see v. 7). He would now make

2 Sailhamer (1990, 172) suggests that Abraham is responding to 14:23, in which he voiced the concern that no one be able to claim making Abraham rich so that he would not accept a Canaanite gift. Perhaps more likely, he is concerned that it is his land as a possession, not their land or grave that he is merely using without any claim to ownership.

3 "The phrase 'at full price' has legal force and appears in ancient Near Eastern commercial documents in one form or another in several Semitic languages over an extended period of time" (Sarna 1989, 159).

his final request, which was formally directed to Ephron but was very public before all the assembled local audience (repeated in v. 13). In effect, and perhaps calling his bluff, Abraham requested that Ephron accept full price for the field (whatever Ephron deemed appropriate) so that he could bury Sarah.

23:14–15. Ephron finally responded with a price. In naming the price, he appears to minimize any reluctance from Abraham, considering their relationship and the task at hand, and assume the price is fully reasonable. The price he named, four hundred shekels of silver, is difficult to evaluate.[4] If we compare it with other land purchases later in the Old Testament, it appears to be exorbitant (Hamilton 1995, 135). In 2 Samuel 24:24, David bought the threshing floor of Araunah for fifty shekels of silver. In Jeremiah 32:9, Jeremiah bought a field from his cousin (of course while under siege) for seventeen shekels of silver, and Omri bought the entire hill of Samaria for two talents of silver (1 Kings 16:24).[5] However, the weight[6] of the shekel at that time in history is uncertain, and the size and value of the field is unknown.

Abraham Paid Full Price (23:16–18)

Abraham paid full price, securing possession of the field, the cave, and the trees, in front of the witnesses.

23:16. Without comment, Abraham paid the full price named by Ephron. Moses includes two significant notes. The price was witnessed by the Hittites and would be deeded to him in their presence (v. 18), and Abraham paid it according to the current weight of the shekel among the merchants.[7] Abraham does everything fully by the book to have the claim beyond dispute, so that it would not be able to revert to Ephron or his heirs later.

23:17–18. The cave, the field, and all the trees are deeded to Abraham in legal terms, before the public witnesses of the Hittites and everyone going through the gate. It was now Abraham's "possession" (מִקְנָה), denoting a thing purchased. The term Abraham had originally used, looking for "an inheritable sepulcher" (v. 4, Translation Analysis 23:4b; see v. 9) will finalize the narrative in verse 20, recognizing Abraham's success in providing a heritable tract that will prefigure the full promise of Yahweh to the nation.

> *TRANSLATION ANALYSIS 23:17*
> "Made over" (וַיָּקָם, ESV) or "secured" (NET) is appropriately translated "deeded" (NASB95, NIV) as legal terminology "meaning 'to transfer property obligated to someone' (e.g., Lev 25:30; 27:19)" (Mathews 2005, 321).

Abraham Buried Sarah in the Land of Canaan (23:19–20)

With the burying place secured, Abraham buried Sarah in the cave of Machpelah in the land of Canaan.

23:19. The burial of Sarah, while not the focus of the narrative, is still crucial here because it legitimates Abraham's intentions. He was not merely after landholdings but had a legitimate need. On the other hand, it also provided the

---

4 Walton (2009a, 100) estimates it at about seven and a half pounds.

5 A talent was three thousand shekels by the Late Bronze Age (five hundred years or so later, cf. Exod. 38:25–26; Powell, "Weights and Measures," *ABD* 6:905).

6 Since coinage was not yet being used, the silver was to be weighed out according to whatever the standard measure would be, as noted in v. 16.

7 Walton notes contemporary documents using the phrase to conform "to the standard for silver that was used in overland trade" (Walton, Matthews, and Chavalas 1997, 54).

impetus for Abraham to look ahead and plan for the needs and future direction of his family. Abraham used this opportunity to demonstrate his faith in the promise. Sarah would not be buried in the old homeland but was buried "in the land of Canaan" (23:2, 19). Her burial would be the first in a series of public statements by the patriarchs of their faith in the promise of God that this land was gifted by the true landowner, Yahweh, to their family. All three patriarchs would be buried here, with three of their wives. Jacob required Joseph to swear to return his body to the land and bury him with the patriarchs (47:29–31; see 49:29–32) because the land was promised by Yahweh (48:3–4).

23:20. The final verse makes the point of the narrative clear. While Sarah's death occasioned Abraham's reflection on the life and future of the nation that God had promised, the narrative in the Abraham stories points to possession of the land. Abraham recognized the need to remain in the land of promise to show his faith and to direct his future descendants to this land as the new homeland in which they would all be gathered to their fathers. The "property" (אֲחֻזָּה) materialized God's promise of an eternal "possession" (17:8 ,אֲחֻזָּה) and looked ahead to the final realization of that promise.

THEOLOGICAL FOCUS

The righteous respond to death with faith, looking beyond this world to follow God's unfailing promises and prepare future generations to embrace God's ultimate plan and working, regardless of cost.

Though God is formally absent, his promise and Abraham's concern for his promise are central. In stark contrast to testing that directly challenges the loyalties or faith of the righteous (e.g., the sacrifice of Isaac), he or she is often left to act without clear direction. The tension with the promise provides the test. In Abraham's case, he knew the land was promised but not to be realized for a long period (15:13–16). Faith must consider how to best respond while waiting for complete fulfillment. The person of faith must pursue the intent of God's revealed will (stay in the land and establish a new homeland), trusting God to provide the means until he fully fulfills his will.

God had challenged Abraham to "command his children and his household after him to keep the way of the Lord by doing righteousness and justice, so that the Lord may bring to Abraham what he has promised him" (18:19). Here the issue was the homeland, and Abraham illustrates how the righteous prepare for future generations to also realize the promise and live in faithfulness to the expectations of their God. Teaching the way of the Lord goes beyond ethical behavior to honoring and fulfilling all expectations of the master. The believer must put God's priorities and responsibilities over personal and cultural expectations and lay the groundwork for future generations to do the same. In every generation, the faithful servant of Yahweh must actively pass their faith on to future generations and establish patterns and set precedence that will encourage them to live out their faith in the promises and working of God as well (Deut. 6:7–11).

The greeting of the Hittites to Abraham, "prince of God" (Gen. 23:4), shows the obvious (and ironic, noting his status) working of God in his life (12:2), as well as the ongoing tension with the fulfilled promise. As with most of life, though God may only obliquely be recognized in the moment, he is fully present in the background, influencing the necessary dealings, both in the specific actions of living (the negotiations for the land) and in prompting appropriate concerns for faithful living (an ongoing "possession" or heritable tomb, 23:4, 9, 20). The difference with acting in the flesh or in faith relates to living fully in line with the promise or revealed will of God, without conflicting with the intent or means of the promise. In fact, faith must act in accord with the promise at precisely the time when God seems most distant. Abraham's purchase did not (nor could it) preempt or fulfill God's promise (as only one small plot) but could and did provide an indication of the ongoing expectation of the promise. It gave a symbolic foreshadowing and enduring reminder to each following generation, though perhaps costly. In fact, faith is often costly with little tangible return in this world, but the faithful leave a legacy for succeeding generations to follow for a promise that is eternal.

Death provides opportunity to reflect on God's promises and exercise faith in God who transcends death to maintain his promise to thousands of generations (Exod. 34:7). Righteous actions reflect that faith. When confronted with death, the righteous expect the outworking of God's promises, whether it will be seen in this life or the next, in future generations or in eternity (Heb. 11:10, 13–16). Such a declaration may be verbal, but it is also and often more powerfully done by expectant action. Abraham would not leave this promised land, even in death, nor would his descendants be required to. Death is the final test of faith in the eternal promise from the Giver of life. Both the person dying and those left behind must face the shrouded transition that will expose the depth of their confidence in the promise of God and for the New Testament believer, the hope of the resurrection in Christ.

The faithful actions of the people of God draw attention to God's working: his character and faithfulness, their faith in his promise, and the need to be in appropriate relation with him. They must clearly declare their hope in him (Gen. 12:8; 13:4) and teach it (18:19), but they must also live it. The onlooking world sees the reality of faith in the life of God's people. The legacy of the righteous, and so the working of Yahweh, continues amidst all those touched by them.

PREACHING AND TEACHING STRATEGIES

Exegetical and Theological Synthesis

Note the bookend references to the land of Canaan in 23:2 and 19. These anchor meaning in the promises of God and present Abraham as the consummate believer in those promises. We and our listeners follow Abraham's example of trusting in God's promises to us while we inhabit this world as resident aliens. For this to happen, God must continue to provide circumstances for our faith to flourish. In the case of Abraham, God's inheritance in Canaan came at a price that he was more than able to pay. Abraham knows that one day God's people—his family—will inherit the land. Abraham's legal purchase makes this his permanent possession and is a picture of great things to come.

It is helpful also to point out that Abraham not only receives a burial site but an additional "field with the cave . . . and all the trees that were in the field" (v. 17). All of this takes place publicly "in the presence of the Hittites" (v. 18). This chapter shows Abraham's strong faith. It also shows to what degree God blessed Abraham. Our listeners benefit from knowing that this relationship is theirs by faith too. Just as Abraham ends up with the best burial site, plus extra, believers have spiritual blessings in their own walk with God. Abraham's exemplary actions securing the land—the skillful way he negotiates with outsiders—teaches all of us to believe like he did and be faithful to God in everything we do. Wouldn't you like your neighbors to think of you as "a prince of God among" them? Better yet, wouldn't that reputation add to God's reputation in his world? Finally, Abraham leads the way for us to make sure our lives help prepare future generations to be ready to follow in his steps, believing that God's promises are worth believing in.

Preaching Idea

The faithful trust God and provide a foundation for a legacy of faith for future generations of the faithful.

Contemporary Connections

What does it mean?

The land of Canaan functions as the historical/geopolitical entity that points to our spiritual inheritance. Our listeners may have difficulty moving from the land to their current life of faith. God promised Canaan as a place where worship and witness could continue to spread his glory over all the world. Abraham's decision to bury Sarah in Canaan means that his faith in the promises of God was rock-solid. He is focused on securing a permanent homeland because of God's promise, and this solidifies the opportunity for future family members to reside in it. The Hittites' reply to Abraham's request means that they recognize the blessing of God on Abraham. Abraham negotiated a price even though the land was offered as a gift. God's wisdom led him not to take what appeared to be too good to be true. I could see a Christian thinking: "Wow! This is great! God is giving this cave for nothing." Abraham was not buying that sweet deal because he wanted that land for himself and his future family.

Is it true?

If someone asked, "Is it true that God always blesses his children the same way he did Abraham?", our answer is "yes" and "no." The "yes" part centers on the faithfulness of God, who will make sure we have everything we need in this world to accomplish his will. That does not mean that everything will always work out the way we want it to. There will be tests and trouble in this world. However, God's faithfulness means that God will make sure we accomplish what he has gifted us to do for him. The "no" part, of course, means that God will not always arrange things to work out as we planned or desired.

Now what?

Relevance is achieved in this chapter as soon as we place people of faith into this narrative. We need to see ourselves functioning faithfully and wisely as aliens and exiles. "This world is not my home," wrote Albert E. Brumley in his old song of the same title, "I'm just a a-passin' through, our treasures are laid up, somewhere beyond the blue. . . . I can't feel at home in this world anymore." But in this world, God continues to bless his faithful so that they flourish for the sake of his reputation. Abraham's forward-looking faith is a great example for all of us who feel the alien status and long for the new creation to come.

Creativity in Presentation

I quoted an old song above, and this narrative lends itself to worship centered on our spiritual inheritance. Listeners will struggle with the big deal over where Sarah was buried unless they see the connection between Canaan and their own faith in the promises of God now. Like Abraham, there is no turning back. Like Abraham, our faith also includes living in such a way that our future families can experience the promises, too, as they place their faith in God. We experience some of our inheritance now while we wait for the redemption of our bodies. The inheritance is secure, and our listeners should be seeing signs of it in the way in which they trust the Lord and faithfully follow him. We live a certain way in the world to show that we are redeemed. In other words, the faithful trust God and provide a foundation for a legacy of faith for future generations of the faithful.

It is helpful to ask the following questions for your listeners:

- Why does Abraham ask for a cemetery plot in Canaan? It is a sign of his faith in the promise of God, including the blessing of family and land. We enjoy a spiritual inheritance as solid as his tract of land.

- But then there is the matter of why Abraham gets what he wants and needs since he is "a sojourner and foreigner" (v. 4). The answer in the narrative is Abraham's reputation or status in the land of the Hittites: "you are a prince of God among us" (v. 6), they say. That is an incredible testimony. We mentioned earlier how good it would be if that were our neighbor's assessment of us. All the dialogue Abraham engages in is an example of the blessing of God in terms of his wisdom to assess the situation.

- Finally, it is important to begin to show various ways in which our Christian experience can follow this narrative toward a mature faith. The following items might help: spiritual inheritance now, our future inheritance at the return of Christ, forward-looking faith that creates the proper perspective now on all things earthly, testimony among the outsiders that displays the blessing of God, and wisdom in all our dealings with outsiders.

Anyone wanting to follow the narrative could take the following route:

- Critical moments in our lives create a juncture where we can put our faith to work, following the promise of God, both for ourselves and as a standard for those who will follow (vv. 1–2).

- Our response needs to focus on the issues of faith in God's promise and not be distracted by attractive but temporary solutions that bypass the core of the promise. This is the means to set up those who follow us in their expectation of faith (vv. 3–16). This is where the wisdom of God informs our dealings in this world, especially among the outsiders.

- Our desired outcome is to provide ongoing testimony to our faith and a monument to God's working that will continue to challenge future generations to walk in faith in God's future promises (vv. 17–20).

DISCUSSION QUESTIONS

1. What did the "land of Canaan" (vv. 2, 19) signify for Abraham?

2. What is the significance of Abraham referring to himself as "a sojourner and foreigner among you" (v. 4)?

3. What might the Hittites have seen in Abraham to refer to him as "a prince of God among" them (v. 6)?

4. How does our faith in God's promises show in tangible ways in our lives?

5. How does our faith walk encourage future generations to follow in faith?

6. What monuments to our faith are we establishing that will continue to challenge future generations to follow in faith as well?

Genesis 24:1–25:11

EXEGETICAL IDEA

Abraham secured Isaac's promised future by sending his godly servant to find Yahweh's choice of a wife for Isaac, Rebekah, and by protecting Isaac's status, sending his other sons away with gifts.

THEOLOGICAL FOCUS

God's faithful servants walk confidently in God's loyal love, expecting his faithful working to accomplish his promises, taking each necessary step to pursue his priorities and prepare for his intended future, according to the light given.

PREACHING IDEA

The faithful trust their Father's blessing as they follow him each step on the way.

PREACHING POINTERS

To read the narrative of Abraham making arrangements with his servant to locate a suitable wife for Isaac is to gain confidence in the Lord's sovereign control in the lives of his faithful. Abraham makes it clear that the promises of God must go forward; a wife from the old life will not do, but a wife there must be. Everything about this plan is so important that a serious oath is taken.

Abraham's servant shares Abraham's faith, as can be seen in the servant's prayer. Twice the servant refers to God's steadfast love for Abraham. God's loyal love will have to answer this prayer very specifically—and he does. When the servant speaks to Laban about Abraham, he reminds us about the kind of kingdom we inhabit by faith: truly we are blessed with every spiritual blessing.

It is very encouraging to listeners to see themselves in this same redemptive history and with the challenge to follow the example of Abraham's servant. Add to that the encouragement of watching God provide the perfect wife for Isaac, someone who matches Abraham's character. Rebekah's family announces this in their blessing on her as she departs with the servant. The promise will continue. Abraham made sure of that at the end of his life as readers enter chapter 25: he is generous to all his children, but the promise would go through Isaac. God showed his steadfast love to Abraham, and he continues to show that to his own today.

FAITHFUL FOLLOWING: PLANNING A GODLY FUTURE (24:1–25:11)

LITERARY STRUCTURE AND THEMES

This preaching unit includes both the servant finding a wife for Isaac, Abraham's final disposition to his sons, and his death.[1] These narratives combine with the burial of Sarah to show Abraham's pursuit of God's agenda, and God's provision for the continuation of God's promises. The initial section (24:1–67) forms a cohesive pattern, highlighted by the servant recounting God's working (vv. 33–49). His commentary rehearses the initial narrative (vv. 1–32), building to the climactic fulfillment of his quest and the family's choice to approve God's working. Their response and his return with Rebekah to comfort Isaac mirrors the two quest reports (vv. 50–67). Abraham's final disposition of his estate to secure Isaac's future concludes his life (25:1–11).

I. Abraham secured a wife for Isaac (24:1–67).
   A. Yahweh had blessed Abraham (24:1).
      B. Abraham commissioned his servant (24:2–9).
         C. Abraham's servant succeeded in faith (24:10–32).
   A'. The servant recounted Abraham's blessing (24:33–36).
      B'. The servant recounted his commission (24:37–41).
         C'. The servant recounted his success (24:42–49).
         C''. The family acknowledged God's leading (24:50–61).
      B''. The servant returned with Rebekah (24:62–66).
   A''. Isaac was comforted (24:67).
II. Abraham secured a future for Isaac (25:1–11).

In the main narrative, the parallel A and A' emphasize the unmistakable working of God through the servant's exemplary faith and loyalty to Abraham and Abraham's God. The final concluding resolution (A'') resolves Abraham's concern with God's faithful provision of a bride for his son. In the B sections, Abraham's commission of faith looks ahead to the outworking in Rebeca's return. The climactic C sections of success and public acknowledgement of God's intervention validate Abraham's (and the servant's) faith. God's promises will certainly flower through God's superintending as his people respond in faith. The final short report details Abraham's final concerns to safeguard his son's inheritance and the fulfillment of God's promise.

- ***Abraham Secured a Wife for Isaac (24:1–67)***
- ***Abraham Secured a Future for Isaac (25:1–11)***

EXPOSITION

After detailing Abraham's faithful concern to keep his family in Canaan, the land of

---

1 See the Introduction to the Abraham Narratives (p. 236) for the larger structure and some preaching options, such as using the short summary of Abraham's final disposition and his death to conclude and summarize a series on the Abraham narratives.

promise (Gen. 23), the attention of Abraham, and the narrative, turns to the family that would be there. His son had no wife and needed a suitable woman to produce the great line of promise. In Genesis 24, then, Abraham pursued a divinely appointed wife for Isaac to continue the promised line in Canaan. The extended narrative makes sure the reader sees the clear intervention of God and the appropriate outcome of Abraham's faith. God's choice would move his program forward. Finally, in Genesis 25:1–11, Abraham prevented confusion or competition to his heir by sending his other sons east with gifts before he died. In both sections, Abraham showed his faith in and concern for the smooth outworking of God's promise by directing his family in loyalty to and dependence on his Lord (18:19). Abraham secured Isaac's promised future by sending his godly servant to find Yahweh's choice of a wife for Isaac, Rebekah, bringing comfort to Isaac, and by protecting Isaac's status, sending his other sons away with gifts.

Abraham Secured a Wife for Isaac (24:1–67)

Abraham, blessed by God, commissioned his servant, who brought back God's clearly chosen wife for Isaac.

Commissioning his most senior and trusted servant, Abraham initiated the procuring of an appropriate wife for Isaac. Shunning the Canaanites and their coming judgment (15:16), Abraham sent the servant to the home country but forbade him from allowing Isaac to go back. Abraham was focused on Yahweh's promise and necessary provision. His servant found that provision to be clearer and greater than he had dared to ask, returning with God's clear provision for his master's son.

Yahweh Had Blessed Abraham (24:1)

Yahweh had blessed Abraham in all things, conspicuously revealed in his age.

24:1. Yahweh's promised blessing on Abraham (12:2) was clearly showing in Abraham's aging years (24:1, "in all things.")[2] Beyond his long life (25:7), the servant would enumerate Abraham's great wealth (24:35). However, the promised "great nation" (12:2; cf. 13:16; 15:40; 17:2; 18:18; 22:17) was still only a single, unmarried son. The blessing of descendants, apparently stalled at one, was on his mind.

Framing the narrative with Abraham "old, well advanced in years" (24:1) suggests a deathbed scene (cf. Josh. 13:1; 23:1; 1 Kings 1:1; Wenham 1994, 152). Given the chronology of the narrative, however, Abraham is only 140 on his way to 175 (25:7, 20), indicating rather that this final scene of Abraham's life provides his "last will and testament" and final glimpse of his mature faith (Kuruvilla 2014, 280). Abraham, and the reader, must look ahead to the outworking of God's purposes in faith, expectantly working for God's intended outcome.

Abraham Commissioned His Servant (24:2–9)

Abraham commissioned his servant to get God's chosen wife for Isaac.

24:2–4. Abraham called on his most senior and trusted servant. By not naming the servant, the narrative focuses attention on the mission, the promise, and the faithfulness of Yahweh to provide for Isaac, even though he is absent. The servant's faith, service, and anonymity become the exemplar for any follower in the service of God.

Abraham required the servant to swear with a ritual oath that he would not take a

2 God had certainly "blessed" Abraham in all things, empowering him and filling him with life to accomplish his purpose (see Introduction, "Blessing," p. 60), especially in his relationship with Yahweh, before whom he had walked in loyalty (24:40).

wife for Isaac from the Canaanites, but only a suitable wife from the family line. The ritual (placing the hand "under" the "thigh," the "area of genitals, touched during uttering an oath," *HALOT* s.v. "יָרֵךְ" 439) is not clearly understood but is graphically appropriate for the focus on the promise of the seed.[3]

The oath was made to Yahweh, "the God of Heaven and God of the earth" (24:3). It certainly echoes the blessing of Melchizedek and Abraham's response to the king of Sodom (14:19, 22). The significance, however, comes from the creation account and the implications of God's initial blessing on humankind. The creator of the universe blessed his creation, and particularly humanity, with fertility and fecundity (1:22, 28). He is the promise-giver (24:7). He empowers the flesh to accomplish the promise (18:10–14). He will see the promise through to completion, including arranging for future generations (24:7).

This wife, however, must not be from the Canaanites. Without explanation here, even the initial reader knew of their coming judgment and loss of the land (15:16, 18–20), as well as the later prohibition of marriage to maintain purity of worship (Exod. 34:12–16; Deut. 7:3–4). Abraham's family stock would initially, at least, keep the line from melting into the local population.

24:5. The servant's requested clarification for Isaac's future suggests a concern that Abraham might not be alive to arrange details for a marriage when he returned (Sarna 1989, 162). In fact, the opening words declaring Abraham's age (v. 1) hint that he may have considered this a final preparation for the future of his estate.[4] With seemingly limited time, Abraham must prepare for Isaac to continue the promise.[5] Apart from his age, the servant's request reveals the tension between the danger of an unsuitable wife and the danger of leaving the land of promise. God must provide.

24:6–9. Abraham's servant, and so Isaac, must carefully balance the demands of fidelity to the promise (land and seed) and to the God of the promise (purity and so being a blessing). Abraham framed his confidence in God's provision with his concern that Isaac must not return to Haran (vv. 6, 8c). Abraham's reference to Yahweh as God of heaven and sending his angel alluded to his interventions with both Hagar (21:17–20) and his own sacrifice (22:11–14) and will provide significant parallels with the similar journey of Jacob to find a wife. The God of heaven sees and provides. This will be the theme of the narrative. God will in fact answer above and beyond either Abraham's (24:4) or the servant's request (vv. 12–14), so there will be no need to remove Isaac from the land.

Abraham's Servant Succeeded in Faith (24:10–32)

Abraham's servant, trusting God's clear intervention, found God's choice for Isaac.

24:10–14. Demonstrating God's great blessing on Abraham, the servant took ten camels and loaded them with good gifts for the bride-to-be and her family. The month-long trip is

3 Walton (2009a, 100) knows of no parallels in the ancient world. Freedman (1976) suggests that by grasping the sign of the covenant, they were invoking the presence of Yahweh to seal the oath.

4 Being "old, well advanced in years" (זָקֵן בָּא בַּיָּמִים) only occurs in three other passages. It occurs twice in Josh. 13:1, twice in Josh. 23:1–2, and once in 1 Kings 1:1. Of those, Josh. 23 and 1 Kings 1 are clearly the final instructions of Joshua and David before dying.

5 Wenham, among others, argues that Abraham was dead when the servant returned, but that the following narrative (25:1–11) is out of order chronologically. This also supposes that the large ages of the patriarchs should be understood figuratively (Wenham 1994, 151, cf. xxviii–xxx, 158). However, see Mathews (2005, 340).

glossed over as the servant prepared and arrived in the same verse.[6] Stopping at the well outside the city, the servant suggested an opportunity to determine the will of God in the matter.[7] A woman who would offer to water ten camels, providing up to twenty-five gallons each, would rival Abraham himself in hospitality, and the unexpected and outrageous offer would surely mark out God's choice from any coincidental candidates.[8]

Camels

While evidence for the domestication of camels did not become common until much later, Kitchen (2003, 338–39) has rehearsed the evidence that they were used marginally in the patriarchal period, and the sparse use of the camel in Genesis (and the Pentateuch) fits the evidence, being used only for long distance caravans and mentioned last in the wealth of the patriarchs (12:16; 24:10–64; 30:43; 31:17, 34; 32:7, 15).

Above all, however, the servant placed his full dependence on Yahweh to show his "steadfast love" (חֶסֶד) to Abraham. Yahweh had made covenant promises, informing Abraham's faith and grounding the servant's appeal to Yahweh to be loyal to those promises (24:12, 14; cf. Baer and Gordon, חֶסֶד, *NIDOTTE* 2:211–18). The answer to his request would be God's response to Abraham, not only to the servant (v. 14).

24:15–20. Before the servant had finished his prayer, the narrator informs the reader that the answer was coming with Rebekah's arrival, freeing the reader to observe the reactions of the servant and marvel that God was answering above and beyond his request. Rebekah had the qualifications (v. 15). She was family, beautiful, and available (v. 16). She responded to his request with deference, and she not only offered to water his camels, but added "until they have finished drinking" (v. 19). Her energy and enthusiasm for a burdensome task was impressive, quickly emptying her jar and running back and forth (v. 20), rivaling Abraham's hospitality with her vigor (cf. 18:2–8; Sternberg 1987, 138).

24:21–28. The servant's expressed patience to confirm God's working highlights his character and confirms for the reader the faithful working of Yahweh, as well (v. 21). Rebekah's completion of the monumental task prompted rich gifts (suggesting bride price) even before confirming her identity.[9] In response to his query, she provided more than required, confirming her connection to Abraham's brother (cf. 22:20, 23) and offering extravagant hospitality to care for the camels as well.

The servant's response again validated his piety. He immediately bowed and publicly worshipped with praise for God's steadfast love (חֶסֶד) and faithfulness (אֱמֶת) to Abraham (vv. 26–27).[10]

6 The distance of nearly 550 miles from Hebron to Haran could be covered at only about 17–23 miles per day (Beitzel, "Travel and Communication," *ABD* 6:646–47), for a travel time between twenty-four and thirty-two days. If he was farther south in the Negev (the servant would find Isaac at Beer-lahai-roi on the return) it would be longer.

7 "It should be noted that the servant does not ask for a miraculous divine intervention or for a revelation that would designate Isaac's bride-to-be. He prays, rather, that the rational criteria of suitability that he himself determines might be in accordance with God's will and be effective" (Sarna 1989, 164).

8 "The criteria that the servant establishes are aspects of nobility of character. The ideal wife must be hospitable to strangers, kind to animals, and willing to give of herself to others" (Sarna 1989, 164).

9 A ten-shekel bracelet would represent a year's wage for an average worker (Walton, Matthews, and Chavalas 1997, 56).

10 What he "said" (v. 27) appears to be vocal, since Laban later refers to Yahweh as the source of blessing (v. 31), and Laban was not, exclusively at least, a Yahweh worshipper (31:30). Without a vocal statement (or some unrecorded statement) Laban would not know which god to connect the blessing with (Hamilton 1995, 152–53). Later we see that the servant's initial prayer for direction was silent (24:45).

His clearly answered prayer, with the confirmation of Rebekah's appropriate lineage and character, overwhelmed the servant with God's clear resolution to his quest, even as Rebekah ran to report the events to her "mother's household" (v. 28).[11]

TRANSLATION ANALYSIS 24:26

The ESV may be misleading, translating that he "bowed his head and worshiped" (see also NET, NRSV). The initial verb (וַיִּקֹּד) always occurs with the secondary verb (וַיִּשְׁתַּחוּ), and together they reflect the physical act of prostration before God or a king (*HALOT* s.v. "קדד" 1065; cf. Fretheim, קָדַד, *NIDOTTE* 3:868). Therefore, it is more likely that he "bowed low in homage" (NJPS). The physical posture and vocal words made an open display of his worship and praise to Yahweh (so also v. 48).

24:29–32. Introducing Laban, the narrator describes him running to the man as soon as he saw the gifts and heard the report. His haste is reported both before and after seeing the gifts, revealing his character and rush to cash in on the opportunity (vv. 29b & 30b; Mathews 2005, 338; cf. Alter 1996, 117). He extended the formal invitation, having prepared for the servant and his retinue. His reference to Yahweh may reflect an attempt to ingratiate the servant (see note on v. 27 above).

The Servant Recounted Abraham's Blessing (24:33–36)

The servant recounted God's blessing on Abraham, emphasizing his wealth.

24:33. After the servants and animals are cared for, a meal was offered to the servant. The servant, however, was on a mission and would not be distracted. He refused food until he could explain his business. The seeming break with the etiquette of hospitality underlined the urgency of his mission. It also showed the responsibility of the servant to pursue his master's concerns before his own.

Recounting his mission from the beginning to this point, he reiterated large portions of the narrator's words. The recorded repetition functions to convince the family both of God's leading and the divine design of this marriage (made in heaven), but also to confirm for the reader "in our minds that God is indeed in control, answers prayer, and fulfills his promises" (Wenham 1994, 146). The servant's account included strategic omissions and additions, shaping his message to his audience for his desired outcome and further validating his commission.

24:34–36. Possibly playing into the greed evidenced by Laban and certainly emphasizing the attractive "catch" that his master's son would be as a new in-law, the servant clarified the blessing of Yahweh on Abraham (24:1) in terms of herds, bank account, and servants. All would go to the son of aged Abraham.

The Servant Recounted His Commission (24:37–41)

The servant recounted his commission to find a wife for the heir.

24:37–38. In recounting his oath, the servant appealed to their shared identity but left out the specific identification of Yahweh (perhaps not confident of their religious

11 The description here of "her mother's household," along with her largely absent father, has suggested that his lone appearance in v. 50 is a corruption or a gloss and that Bethuel was actually dead (e.g., Speiser 1964, v. 28, 180–81, cf. v. 50, 181–82). Alternatively, a matrilineal society and the prominence of the brother in such negotiations (as well as the narrator introducing Laban's later role with Jacob) may account for the largely absent Bethuel (Hamilton 1995, 157). Sarna (1989, 168) references "numerous ancient Near Eastern texts" detailing this sort of authority for a mother and son.

loyalties). Rather, he related the ideal desire of Abraham's general request to find a woman from his "country" and "kindred" (מוֹלֶדֶת, v. 4) which he identified more clearly as his "father's house" and "clan" (מִשְׁפָּחָה, v. 38, also v. 40). Indeed, Yahweh had answered much more specifically than Abraham had dared to ask, and the servant clarified the outcome as Abraham's deepest desire.

24:39–41. He rehearsed his concern that whomever he found not return with him (making her choice implicit rather than explicit), but he omitted Abraham's refusal to allow Isaac to travel to Haran. In both cases he avoided raising unnecessary obstacles. Rather, he used it as an opportunity to assure the continued leading of Yahweh for his master and his master's family.

Summarizing Abraham's loyal service to Yahweh, he omitted the specific purpose of leaving Haran for a land that Yahweh was bequeathing to his descendants, avoiding the permanence of Rebekah's possible move. Rather, he powerfully emphasized Abraham's appropriate expectation of Yahweh's intervention, who had obviously blessed Abraham so far and would "prosper" the search for a wife (צלח, v. 40). Again focusing attention much more specifically on the present family than Abraham's words (though undoubtedly his desire, "my clan and . . . my father's house," v. 40), the servant strongly implied that only their willingness to let her go hindered his divinely ordained success (v. 41). While that would annul his obligation (again omitting the possible hesitance of the girl herself), he now argued forcefully for Yahweh's guidance to this family and this girl.

Living Loyally

God's call to Abraham to live loyally to him (17:1, "walk before me," see exposition there) was now a fitting summary statement of Abraham's life. He had lived in loyalty. As such, it also firmly grounded Abraham's (and the servant's) appropriate expectation of Yahweh's provision of his promised heir's wife.

The Servant Recounted His Success (24:42–49)

The servant recounted his arrival with God's clear intervention, asking for Rebekah, God's clear choice for Isaac.

24:42–44. The servant recounted his petition on arriving, the crux of his certainty, and the basis of his request from the family, which God clearly answered. This spectacularly and eagerly hospitable woman must be the one selected by Yahweh. God had prospered him with an answer (v. 42) and had appointed an appropriate wife (v. 44).

24:45–47. Impressed by Yahweh's answer to his inaudible prayer ("in my heart," v. 45) before he had finished asking, the servant summarized Rebekah's clear fulfillment. Her heritage sealed his certainty. The servant's report frontloaded Nahor, highlighting Rebekah's descent from the brother of Abraham (11:27). It is only now that he related putting the ring on her nose and bracelets on her arms.[12]

24:48. The servant's immediate response of worship not only showed his piety and gratitude to Yahweh for working, but his report of it emphasized his conclusion before Rebekah's family. He was convinced that Yahweh, God of Abraham, had followed through in faithfulness (אֱמֶת, 24:27,

12 It is possible that he only began taking out the jewelry as he was asking about her heritage (24:22–23) and then placed them on her after hearing her lineage, or it is possible that he delayed relating his gift giving until after he reported her answer, to appear less forward. Certainly, her matching up to his devised test and Abraham's desired lineage would impact his audience and confirm God's clear provision of the appointed bride (v. 44).

49) with his promise to Abraham, leading him by the "right" (אֱמֶת) way to this girl (Mathews 2005, 341). He rested his case that God had exercised his loyal love to Abraham and that Rebekah's husband was chosen by God himself.

24:49. The recounting of his mission, journey, and outcomes had been designed to lead his audience to follow along and agree with his conclusion. God's working was indisputable (van Wolde 1995, 239–42). Now he called on the family to acknowledge God's working, submit to his will, and exercise the same "steadfast love and faithfulness" (חֶסֶד וֶאֱמֶת) to their relative, Abraham, that Yahweh had (vv. 12, 14, 27, 48). He asked for an immediate decision because it was obviously God's will, and they must simply choose to submit (and prosper) or resist it. His next steps would depend on their choice.

The reader should hear the servant's account, comparing it to the events, and reach the same conclusion. The servant was faithful and loyal, both to Abraham and to Yahweh. He responded righteously at each step. But the outcome was God's clear working. The final concern would be the agreement of the girl to go (cf. 24:5).

The Family Acknowledged God's Leading (24:50–61)

The family acknowledged God's clear leading, and Rebekah agreed to go.

24:50–51. Laban and Bethuel answered.[13] Fully convinced by the testimony of the servant, it was God's decision. They could have no response.[14] They offered Rebekah to him according to God's decree, to take back as Isaac's wife.

24:52–53. At their agreement, the servant again bowed in worship to Yahweh. His faith consistently showed in his public, vocal, and frequent praise to Yahweh, acknowledging his answers to prayer and his faithful loyalty to his promise. After appropriate praise to Yahweh, he brought out the gifts for the family and for Rebekah, his bride price.

Bride Money

The gifts for the family appear to be the "bride-money," given by the groom to the bride's family at betrothal, legalizing the marriage (Matthews, "Family Relationships," *DOTP* 295). The purpose and disposition of the money is debated, whether it remains with the father, is (largely) given to the bride as dowry, or is kept in case she becomes destitute (cf. Hamilton, "Marriage: Old Testament and Ancient Near East," *ABD* 4:562–63; Wakely, מֹהַר, *NIDOTTE* 2:860; Walton, Matthews, and Chavalas 1997, 102; Wenham 1994, 149–50).

24:54–58. With the matter settled, they feasted and slept. The servant then surprised his hosts the next day with his request to immediately turn around to head back to Canaan. With God's clear answer, he was ready to complete his task, but the family was not. The servant cited God's clear leading, so the family deferred to Rebekah, who very simply agreed.

24:59–61. With Rebekah's acquiescence, the family packed her up with her nurse and a blessing and sent her to follow the Lord's leading. The blessing echoed God's blessing on Isaac after Abraham offered him to the Lord on Moriah (22:17–18). By citing the blessing, Moses draws his reader's attention to the human instrument through whom the promise to Isaac would be fulfilled and the final evidence for the reader that God was superintending each step

13 This is the first appearance of Bethuel in the narrative, see note on v. 28 above.

14 "Bad or good" expresses a merism, two opposite extremes that includes everything in between. There was nothing they could say of any sort.

of the completion of his covenant promises. She was not only hospitable, but courageous and willing to trust Yahweh's direction. She was a second-generation Abraham.[15]

This statement completed the servant's quest for a wife under God's direction. The final obstacle had been successfully navigated, laying to rest the servant's wise concern (24:5). God's will was clear and God's promise assured.

The Servant Returned with Rebekah (24:62–66)

Abraham's servant returned with a wife for the waiting Isaac.

24:62–65. Without comment on the return, Moses turns to the consummation of the quest. Surprisingly, Isaac was in Beer-lahai-roi, the site of God's care for Hagar, named to commemorate God seeing Hagar and meeting her needs ("the well of the living one who sees me," 16:14). God was again seeing and meeting the needs of his promise-bearer. What he was doing in the field is uncertain. What is clear, however, is that he saw them and recognized his servant's caravan at about the same time as Rebekah saw him and realized his intent to meet them (24:64–65). Seeing her husband-to-be, she veiled herself until the wedding night.

TRANSLATION ANALYSIS 24:63

"The interpretation is uncertain" for the main verb since this is the only appearance of this word in the Old Testament (HALOT s.v. "שׂוח" 1311–12). The versions similarly present a variety of ideas, such as "gossip" (LXX, ἀδολεσχέω), "meditate" (Vulgate, *ad meditandum*), or "pray" (Targum, *ləṣallāʾāh*, listed in *HALOT*). Similarly, the English versions suggest "meditate" (ESV, NASB95, NKJV), "think" (NCV), "relax" (NET), "walk" (NJPS, NRSV), or even a combination of "walking and meditating" (NLT). The idea of walking is suggested by Rebekah's question in verse 65, where she sees him and notes he is "walking in the field to meet us."

24:66. The brief note concerning the servant's report is only surprising in that he reports to Isaac, and Abraham does not appear. Again, some suppose from this that Abraham has died (e.g., Alter 1996, 122). However, the movement of the narrative is intentional, from Abraham to Isaac, and the realization of the promise must now be vested fully in the new family being initiated with Isaac taking Rebekah. He is (and will be) the master now (v. 65).

Isaac Was Comforted (24:67)

Abraham's blessing has now come to Isaac as he finds comfort and promise in God's choice for him.

24:67. The brief conclusion not only confirms Isaac's replacement of Abraham in God's plan but similarly Sarah's replacement by Rebekah. Isaac finds comfort, and Yahweh has provided for the continuing of his oath. The blessing of Abraham, through Abraham's descendants, will continue as guaranteed. Abraham's (and the servant's) faith is rewarded. Rather than a Canaanite, Isaac has a "female Abraham" (Wenham 1994, 138), and the line will be in good hands.

Abraham Secured a Future for Isaac (25:1–11)

Abraham protected Isaac's inheritance and status as heir of the promise, sending away his

15 Van Wolde (1995, 233–39) draws attention to the parallels in this narrative between God taking Abraham from his father's house (v. 7) and the servant taking Rebekah from her father's house (vv. 48, 51, 61; לקח). And again, as Abraham went (12:1, 4), so Rebekah also chose to go (24:8, 58; הלך). These parallels show both God's active intervention and human responsibility in their choices.

other sons with gifts before he died, and Isaac received God's blessing.

Abraham Protected Isaac's Inheritance (25:1–6)
While Abraham took another wife, he sent all his other sons away with gifts, protecting the promised inheritance to Isaac.

25:1–5. The final notes in the life of Abraham deal with the disposition of his estate to his other sons and continues to show his blessing (fathering many nations, 17:4). While no hint of other children had been given up to this point, the narrative is not all chronological (as noted several times), so these could well have been born while Sarah was alive. The narrative names Keturah as Abraham's wife.[16] Her name comes from the root קטר used in the *piel*, "to make a sacrifice, go up in smoke," and in the *puel* for "completely filled with fragrance, completely filled with incense" (*HALOT* s.v. "קטר" 1094); some of the names of her sons are connected to the Arabian spice trade (Steinmann 2019, 242–43). Otherwise, her sons are largely unknown.

TRANSLATION ANALYSIS 25:1
The Hebrew is not clear, so some assume that Keturah was taken previously and now reported ("had taken," e.g., NET, NIV) while others maintain a straightforward chronology ("took another wife," ESV, NASB95, NRSV). Either is possible.

25:6. The narrative emphasizes Abraham's preparation for the promise to be carried out as God intended. He gave all the other sons gifts and sent them eastward. None could be his heir for the promises of God. Isaac's claim to the blessing would be unchallenged.

Abraham Was Gathered to His People (25:7–11)
With Abraham buried in the tomb he had prepared in the land of promise by his sons and at a good old age, God blessed Isaac.

25:7–10. Abraham's blessing extended to his unusually long and full life. The burial with Sarah in the cave of Machpelah recalls the narrative in chapter 23 and Abraham's conscious preparations for future generations to maintain faith in the promise and stay in the land. That concern continued when he forbade Isaac from leaving to find a wife. His faith remained true to the end, as a monument to future generations of faith and God's faithfulness. Abraham entered eternity[17] content in God's working.

25:11. The Abraham narratives end with the blessing passing to Isaac. The child of promise will only briefly be the main actor as the next set of narratives, bearing his name, will focus attention on his sons and God's faithful investment to prepare Jacob for blessing.

THEOLOGICAL FOCUS

God's faithful servants walk confidently in God's loyal love, expecting his faithful working to accomplish his promises, taking each necessary step to pursue his priorities and prepare for his intended future, according to the light given.

While the servant is the main actor, God is the clear hero of this narrative. Abraham pointed to Yahweh as the one who would lead and provide. The narrator validates God's response to the servant's prayer, and the

16 Here Keturah is called another "wife" (אִשָּׁה), but in verse 6 she seems to be viewed as a concubine, as she is called in 1 Chron. 1:22. Abraham, then, was removing any threat, as he had with Ishmael (21:8–21), showing "unusual generosity" (Walton 2009a, 103).

17 To be "gathered to his people" points to an expectation of life after death in the Torah (Hamilton 1995, 168; Sarna 1989, 174).

servant explained Yahweh's clear leading and providing and honored Yahweh with praise for his intervention. Laban and Bethuel acknowledged God's clear direction in choosing Rebekah, and Rebekah agreed. While God's intervention was not a direct theophany, his arrangement of circumstances left no doubt in anyone's mind. In fact, God seldom works in the open but through timing and circumstances, often seen most clearly after the fact. This becomes more apparent the farther we go through Genesis. God's direct appearances recede, though his involvement is no less expected (50:20).

The God who had already blessed abundantly continued to bless the faith and faithful actions of his servants. He was empowering them to accomplish his will by choreographing their actions and opening their eyes to his working. He was at work in their hearts to not only accomplish his will, but to accomplish their ultimate good. He did not override their will but worked with their will to reveal his best outcome, which they willingly embraced. He used Rebekah's outstanding hospitality to accomplish the servant's request without violating either her intent or the servant's desires, all the time working through submitted and committed followers (Abraham and the unnamed servant).

Yahweh's intervention reveals his character throughout the narrative. He acts with loyal love and faithfulness to his covenant promises. God acts on behalf of his loyal subjects. God accomplishes his purposes according to his word, through faithful people as they walk in faith before him.

The narrative provides several models of faith and appropriate service for the believer to emulate. Abraham implicitly trusted God's care and direction, while at the same time pursuing the provision for Isaac to the best of his ability. He showed both faith and faithful pursuit of God and his promise with as much insight as he had. He was willing to step out in faith and do what appeared best to him while trusting God to accomplish his plan in whatever way he desired (Prov. 16:1, 9).

From a human perspective, the unnamed servant was clearly in charge of the situation and pursued his master's agenda with intent and vigor, but he was also fully and consciously dependent on the working of God—he was a man of prayer. He did not take anything for granted but followed God's lead while still taking the initiative and expecting God to work. He refused to be distracted by his own needs or cultural expectations. Rather, he maintained God's priorities in loyalty to his master and to God. "Abraham's servant is a man who prays before he acts, praises when his prayers are answered, and lives ever conscious that the affairs of men are controlled by the hand of God" (Wenham 1994, 154). We might simply add the servant's appropriate and necessary public praise that the whole affair was the working of God from start to finish. Even the lack of a name for him provides a model of selfless service to the King for God's glory and the furtherance of God's purposes without personal agenda or distraction. "He must increase, but I must decrease" (John 3:30).

Rebekah (and her family) acknowledged God's leading and willingly submitted to the clear intervention of God despite her meager knowledge of the future or the situation. Her selfless and energetic hospitality was matched by her faith and unhesitating trust in God's clear direction, submitting to the clear but new, unexpected, and humanly uncertain future.

All three of these characters provide lessons in faith and appropriate responses to God and his work. All three demonstrate pursuit of God with lives, dreams, and decisions, while allowing God to reveal the next steps as he saw fit. God used all three to advance his kingdom purposes, and he blessed all three for their faith.

PREACHING AND TEACHING STRATEGIES

Exegetical and Theological Synthesis

As is the case in narratives like this, the theology shines through the characters and their actions. The narrator lets us know that "the LORD had blessed Abraham in all things" (24:1). That is the general description of all God's faithful servants. Abraham and Rebekah both function in the familiar "go and do likewise" mode. Abraham knows Isaac needs a certain kind of wife if the promise is to go forward. He makes his servant take a serious oath to carry out the mission exactly according to the promise-plan. The servant's recounting of what Abraham said to him also shows great confidence in what the Lord would do (24:40). Abraham ends his life still experiencing the blessing of God, passed on to all his children while reserving the special place for Isaac. The blessing is directly transferred to Isaac (25:11).

The narrator makes Abraham's servant even more of an exemplar. His initial reaction to the plan allows us to see how important it is that God's people do not revert to the old land and old ways (24:5–9). His prayer is a model for any of God's people whenever they are accomplishing a task for his glory (vv. 12–14). His prayer teaches us that God is bound by his character ("show steadfast love," v. 14). From God's perspective, this is the only way to realize Abraham's success to the end. From our perspective, each of the three characters lead the way to faithfulness to God, our part of the covenant. The servant's speech to Rebekah's family highlights the Lord's leading each step of the way. And Rebekah is exactly what Isaac needed in every way (24:16–20).

Preaching Idea

The faithful trust their Father's blessing as they follow him each step on the way.

Contemporary Connections

What does it mean?

Listeners may need to be taught why the Canaanite women were off limits to Isaac. God's promises are for a holy people who are separate from the nations around them, who have not been redeemed. You might explain how the servant's faith in Abraham's God led to a very specific prayer, down to the very words the woman would say to him. The servant knew that such a response would speak volumes about the woman's character. Since the Lord's sovereignty and providence are not overt in this narrative, it might also help to explain that the detailed interaction between the servant and Rebekah are a sign of God at work keeping his covenant promises.

Genesis 24:26 makes clear that the details show God "has not forsaken his steadfast love and his faithfulness." That does not always mean things work out exactly as we plan. It does mean that we can count on God to fulfill his plan for us, whether through perceived blessing or pain in this life. The person who seeks the Lord's will in their life can be assured that the Lord will carry it out. Of course, Abraham, his servant, and Rebekah lead the way to what faithfulness looks like as God's will is unveiled before our eyes each day.

Is it true?

Just for a moment I would take listeners back to the various miracles that God performed for Rebekah to be located and for her to agree to go back with this stranger. Is it true that our God sends his angels before his own when it comes to being faithful to his plan? It must be true too that Abraham, a man of faith, can also consider the remote possibility that the plan might not work exactly like planned (24:8, "But if the woman is not willing to follow you"). I tried to put myself in the servant's shoes as he faced this weighty responsibility. Even before he finishes his prayer, he sees the young woman described in verse

16 ("very attractive in appearance"). He doesn't know what the narrator tells us about her moral status. Could this be truly happening? Could it be any better than this: very beautiful, eligible, and hospitable-to-the-max? Is it true that God gives us exactly what he needs for his glory and what we need to succeed for him? Yes, it is.

Now what?

The narrative is relevant with respect to (1) our blessed condition; (2) remaining faithful to the Lord's plan (all three main characters' examples); (3) gaining encouragement from the steadfast love of the Lord on display; (4) the privilege of being a part of God's grand plan for the ages; (5) the opportunity to experience the satisfaction of being successful in the part we play; and (6) gaining stability in life, knowing that God will lead us in his will and we can trust him as it unfolds each day.

Creativity in Presentation

Our preaching idea for the section is: the faithful trust their Father's blessing as they follow him each step on the way. Notice the combination of God's faithfulness to us and our faithfulness to him. The Christian life is both. Many of our listeners can look back on their lives and see God's specific leading. This is an excellent time to mine your favorite robust theology books for detailed descriptions of the providence of God. While you may be able to search for illustrations from history, effective stories reside in your congregations.

As you work through the narrative, you may want to structure your sermon according to the three faithful characters.

- Abraham can cover 24:1–9; 25:1–11.
- Abraham's servant occurs in 24:10–14, 26–27, 32–49, 52–56.
- Rebekah appears in 24:18–20, 24–25, 28, 58, 61. Because of the length and details of the narrative, you will want to pick your spots carefully and determine what parts of the details carry the theology.
- Along with the three main characters providing structure, frame their faithfulness within God's steadfast love repeated in 24:12, 14, and 49. That is what keeps the blessing intact throughout our ups and downs of faith.

Similarly, but following the flow of the passage and focusing on the faith requests and God's provision:

- Abraham's faith request (24:1–9).
- The servant's faith request (24:10–14).
- God's miraculous provision (24:15–67).
- Abraham's faithfulness to the promise (25:1–11).

God's selection of Rebekah says a lot about his promise to bless his people who trust him. If there is any doubt in our minds about our own blessed condition, confidence comes from seeing God bless Isaac after Abraham's death (25:11). People of faith find themselves in this long line of faithful, though not perfect, covenant-keepers. Our God never fails to show his steadfast love to us, including providentially working out the details so his plan is a success.

DISCUSSION QUESTIONS

1. Take some time to rehearse all the ways you have experienced God's blessing. Are you able to articulate how the blessing of God remains, especially through the painful times?

2. In what ways has God led you in your personal life? In what ways has he led you to accomplish his will?

3. What would keep you from praying as specifically as Abraham's servant (24:12–14)? Are those sound theological reasons?

4. Why was being aggressively hospitable so important in the ANE and as a sign of Rebekah being a worthy wife for Isaac?

5. Define the providence of God. How might you worship the Lord after reading such a magnificent display of his providence?

6. When can you see coincidence as the intervention of God rather than the result of chance?

THE FAMILY HISTORY OF ISHMAEL (GENESIS 25:12–18)

This short *toledot* gives the genealogy of Ishmael, and in doing so shows the fulfillment of God's promises to Abraham and Hagar regarding Ishmael. Beginning by highlighting the connection to Abraham through Hagar, it draws the attention of the reader back to those promises. To Abraham, God had promised Ishmael would be a nation (21:13) and to Hagar a "great nation" (21:18). According to the genealogy, he produced twelve sons that were the heads of twelve tribes (25:13–16). He lived 137 years, adding to the impression of God's blessing.

God had also declared to Hagar that he would "dwell over against all of his kinsmen" (16:12), which he does in 25:18, repeating "over against all his kinsmen" with the verb "fall" or "settle" (נָפַל) instead of "dwell" (יִשְׁכֹּן). Moses draws out the fulfillment of God's word to his patriarch and Hagar, emphasizing the blessing to Abraham and his offspring. He is also paralleling the following introduction to Isaac's *toledot* to prefigure the fulfillment of his promises to Abraham's greater heir (cf. Exposition on 25:19, p. 434).

Though most preaching schedules will not allow enough time to include this passage, if you had the space, this passage could be combined with the *toledot* of Esau (ch. 36) to show God's faithfulness to his promises and his heart to bless the nations through Abraham. Ishmael was specifically promised blessing because he was Abraham's son (21:13), and Esau was promised independence (27:40) and clearly received God's blessing (33:9–10; 36:6–8). The preacher would need to go back to both founding histories in the birth oracles for the two boys, their subsequent promises, and the outworking in these genealogies to show God's hand at work. These two sets of narratives and genealogies help the reader to see that God was (and is) not merely interested in the one nation that he chose, but the nations for which he chose the one nation (12:3; 18:18; 22:18; 26:4; 28:14).

INTRODUCTION TO THE JACOB NARRATIVES (GENESIS 25:19–35:29)

The Jacob narratives closely follow the Abraham stories structurally as well as thematically, clarifying the promises of the Abrahamic covenant with Isaac (26:3–4) and Jacob (28:13–14; 35:11–12). The Abraham stories focus on the developing faith of Abraham in loyalty to Yahweh (particularly highlighted in chapters 12, 15, 17, 22) as he received the growing promise, declaring his responsibility to inculcate God's ways by doing righteousness and justice (18:19). As expected, Isaac and then Jacob receive those promises, but righteousness and justice seem to be increasingly absent. As each character in each generation experiences the consequences of their lack of righteousness and justice, usually in deception and selfish manipulation, the narrative develops the means for obtaining and passing on God's blessing. Blessing cannot be obtained by personal struggle or maneuvering but must be granted graciously by God to his submissive servant in relationship with him—not apart from him.[1] Perhaps more significantly, only in that submissive relationship, practicing justice and righteousness, can blessing be passed on to the needy world.

LITERARY STRUCTURE AND THEOLOGICAL THEMES

The structure of the Jacob narratives mimics the structure of the Abrahamic narratives, developing the plot tensions and promises chiastically and concluding with a similar focus on the passing patriarchs, their wives, and the next generation of their sons. Again, the Abrahamic covenant promises dominate as they move through and drive the narrative progress. In this series of stories, however, the covenant promises are envisioned as "blessing" and mixed with the inheritance rights, which is the express goal of Jacob and Esau.

God's choice and blessing of Jacob as the heir of the promise frame the stories. Even though he was the divinely promised heir of the covenant promises, Jacob's attempts to guarantee his place of blessing dominate the first half of the narratives, from his purchase of the birthright to his manipulation of the rods in the birthing of Laban's flocks. As such, this leads to a secondary but pervasive theme of conflict.[2] Jacob struggles with Esau, Isaac (who also clashes with the Philistines), Laban, his sons (who fight with Shechem), and ultimately with God. As he realized (and declared) with his growing family (30:3) and his herds (31:9), God had given the blessing, not his manipulations.[3]

1 Mathews (2005, 370–71) sees the change in Jacob's character as the focus, but Kuruvilla (2014, 283), for example, recognizes the "driving force" in these narratives as Jacob recognizing how to "experience the divine blessing." Putting these together, the Jacob stories focus on how God's chosen servant will acquire and experience the blessing of God's promise, becoming fit to pass on blessing to God's world.

2 Mathews (2005, 371) calls it "the constitutive motif for the Jacob narrative."

3 The stories turn on the explicit comment that "God remembered Rachel" and provided a son (30:22). It is the final son in Paddan-Aram who will be the key figure in the following stories, before the family returns to establish the promise of God in the land.

Unfortunately, however, it would take divine intervention, initiating a battle with Jacob, before he would give up his struggle and cling to God for blessing (32:26). Even so it was a considerable time before he finally fulfilled his promised vow in full worship (35:7, 14), to receive the complete blessing. Only then, with Jacob's unreserved, exclusive worship, would God restate the Abrahamic covenant promises in their final and full state for Israel (as God reminds Jacob, 35:11–12), bringing to completion God's pronouncement of his promises to the patriarchs. The epilogue, mirroring the Abraham stories, brings the growth of the family to a conclusion and prepares for the ensuing stories, with the interfamily conflicts that will endanger their ability to bring God's blessing to the nations and showcase God's gracious and sovereign working.

Toledot 8: God passed his promise of blessing through Isaac to Jacob, refining Jacob's character and concluding his covenant promises (25:19–35:29).[4]

A. God would fulfill his covenant promises to Abraham through Isaac's line, by prayer, with his unexpected choice of the younger Jacob (25:19–34).

B. Isaac's fearful deception endangered God's promised blessing and threatened his neighbors with judgment but his faith brought blessing (26:1–34).

C. Jacob, taking the blessing by deception, feared Esau, and fled to Haran for a wife (27:1–28:9).

D. God, with his angels, confronted Jacob's fear with promise and blessing, prompting Jacob to vow exclusive worship (28:10–22).

E. Arriving in Haran, Jacob received two wives through Laban's deception (29:1–30).

F. Amid conflict within the family, God blessed Jacob with children (29:31–30:24).

F' Amid conflict in the extended family, God blessed Jacob with flocks (30:25–43).

E' Leaving Haran, Jacob fled with his family, deceiving Laban (31:1–55).

D' God, with his angels, confronted Jacob's fear through conflict, promising blessing with Jacob's submission (32:1–32).

C' Jacob, giving blessing, reconciled with Esau when he returned from Haran (33:1–20).

B' Jacob's sons used deception to destroy their Canaanite neighbors, avenging the rape of Dinah (34:1–31).

A' Jacob fulfilled his vow to Yahweh in purified worship, who renewed and extended his covenant promises to Jacob (35:1–18).

Epilogue to the* toledot*: Jacob strengthened ties to the homeland, siring the progenitors of the nation.

1' Jacob buried Rachel with a special marker, adding a foothold in the land (19–20).

2' Reuben's affair with Bilhah would redirect the promised blessing (21–22a).

3' The twelve sons of Jacob mainly born in Paddan-Aram, showing God's promised fruitfulness, would advance God's purposes despite their conflicts (22b–26).

4' When Isaac died, Jacob and Esau buried him in Hebron, further establishing the homeland (27–29).

---

4 The structure generally follows Gary Rendsburg (2014, 53–69), with some private communication and influence from K. Lawson Younger.

The outer frame of promise (oracle of choice, 25:19–34, and covenant promise, 35:1–18) orients the narrative to Israel's future in the land as a great and dominant nation. The flow of the narrative appears to be intent on preempting God's promises through the deceptions and passions of Isaac (26:1–34), Jacob (27:1–28:9), and his sons (34:1–31). God's interventions, however (26:24; 28:10–22; 32:1–32; 35:1–5), offered blessing to the nations (26:26–31; 28:14; 33:11) and fulfillment of his promises. The narrative revolves around God's fulfillment of his promised security and fertility for Jacob during his sojourn in Haran (29:1–31:55).

The epilogue parallels the Abraham stories' epilogue. Jacob also declared his place in the land, burying his wife (35:19–20). In contrast to Isaac, the expected heir forfeited his position (35:21–22a; cf. 49:3–4). Rather than being competition and sent away, the sons of Jacob are named to become the future tribes of the nation (35:22b–26). Finally, Jacob and Esau buried Isaac in Abraham's family tomb, further establishing the homeland (35:27–29).

God's plan for humanity remains on display in this section, but his grace and pursuit of his purposes in the brokenness of human failings takes center stage. The consistently barren matriarchs, and the naming dialogue of the wives of Jacob showcase God's sovereign control over the promise (cf. Sailhamer 1990, 182). He chooses, orchestrates, and then he must mold his chosen instrument into the shape and condition needed to accomplish his plan. Though at times it appears that the ultimate purpose may be slipping away, God continues to work and change hearts. Esau did an otherwise inexplicable about-face, and Jacob made progress as he chose to worship Yahweh alone.

God's work in human lives comes with clear talionic justice as Jacob and Laban (and Isaac and Rebekah) face the consequences of their own actions. At the same time, God shows his authority and the folly of trusting anything else, including blatant idolatry. The nation of Israel would have clearly seen many implications for their own sojourn out of the land with God's presence protecting and providing even amid their service and struggle in Egypt.

Jacob, Israel, and every person desiring God's blessing must learn to cling to God in worship and give up attempts to secure one's own future. It can only be "an unexpected gift. Promise requires an end to grasping and certitude and an embrace of precariousness. It is only God who gives life. Any pretense that the future is secured by rights or claims of the family is a deception (cf. Matt. 3:9)" (Brueggemann 1982a, 214).

While the Abraham stories focus on God's growing promise and Abraham's journey of growing faith, the Jacob stories focus on how God's chosen servant will acquire and experience the blessing of God's promise, becoming fit to pass on blessing to God's world. God's direct interventions diminish as God moves more into the background with Jacob, but his working is no less significant, though more often recognized in retrospect. God's prominence will fade even more significantly in the Joseph stories.

COVENANT GROWTH, CLARIFICATION, AND IMPACT

As promised, God specifically extended the covenant promises to Isaac (26:2–5) and then to Jacob (25:23; 28:13–15; 35:11–12). There are several things to notice, however, as we look at the progress of the covenant promises. All the promises were reiterated to all the patriarchs. The responsibility, however, expected to guarantee the fulfillment of the promises was fully met by Abraham. There are no conditions given or implied after Abraham's obedience in the offering of Isaac, and that obedience was specifically mentioned to Isaac as the ground for the promise to him (26:5). Finally, the concluding reiteration of the promise to Jacob at Bethel (35:11–12) focuses exclusively on the land and the descendants. The purpose of blessing to all nations is certainly still expected (28:14) and implied in Jacob's blessing to Esau (33:11). Jacob's flight to Paddan-Aram and drama of fertility, however, highlight God's promise of the land and future as a great nation with kings in that land, emphasized in the final reiteration to Jacob (35:11–12).

	Promise initiated and reiterated (Gen. 12–13)	**Covenant cut (Gen. 15)**	**Promise extended (Gen. 17–18)**	**Covenant ratified (Gen. 22)**	**Promise transmitted (Gen. 26)**	**Promise transmitted (Gen. 28)**	**Promise concluded (Gen. 35)**
Land promise	Given to Abram and his descendants (12:7; 13:15) delineated (12:1, 7; 13:14, 17)	Delineated geographically and ethnographically (15:18–21) with timing (15:13, 16, 18)	Named ("Canaan") as everlasting possession (17:8)	No mention	"all these lands" to Isaac and offspring (26:3–4)	"the land on which you lie" (28:13)	Land given to Abraham and Isaac (35:12)
Seed promise	Great nation (12:2), innumerable as dust (13:16)	Innumerable as the stars (15:5)	Multiply greatly (17:2), multitude of nations (17:4, 5), nations and kings (17: 6; 16)	Multiply like the stars and sand (22:17)	"As the stars of the heaven" (26:4)	"dust of the earth" (28:14)	"a nation and a company of nations . . . and kings" (35:11)
Blessing promise	"In you all the families of the earth shall be blessed" (12:3)	No mention	Yahweh will be God to you and to your offspring (17:7, 8) All "nations of the earth" blessed in Abraham (18:18)	"In your offspring shall all the nations of the earth be blessed" (22:18)	"I will be with you and bless you" (26:3); "In your offspring all the nations of the earth shall be blessed" (26:4)	"in you and your offspring shall all the families of the earth be blessed" (28:14)	
Covenant progress and formal oath	Promises made (12:2, 3, 7)	Formal covenant cut (15:18): land and descendants (15:6, 16).	Condition (sign) given for relationship (17:9–14); everlasting covenant (17:6, 13) to Isaac (17:19, 21)	Formal oath: multiplied offspring, power over enemies, and blessing to all nations (22:16–18).	Promise made	Promise of fulfillment	

Condition expected	Obedience (12:1–2)	Faith credited as righteousness (15:6, 16)	Loyalty/obedience (17:1, 9–14), righteousness and justice (18:19)	Because of loyalty (22:12); "because you have obeyed my voice" (22:18)	Promise stated, "because Abraham obeyed" (26:5)	None given, God's fulfillment guaranteed	None: promise stated

PREACHING SUGGESTIONS (25:19–35:29)

As with the Abraham narratives, these can be preached as a standalone series. An introductory message could set the stage of humanity's need and God's intervention with the Abrahamic Covenant promises. The issue of the heart and the need for real change would help prepare for the unexpected working in and through a scoundrel (Jacob) who needed to be rehabilitated to be useful in God's program. Blessing would also need to be explained with some reference to the context of Genesis that has provided such a rich background.

While we see the incredible value of preaching through this series in its entirety, to be able to teach the full perspective on God's preparations for his nation, we also see value in a more limited series that can give the congregation the broad picture of Scripture. This series could be done effectively with an introduction to the Jacob stories and the initial pericope (25:19–34), the precipitating conflict between the sons (26:34–28:9), and Jacob's dream (28:10–22). The sojourn in Haran could be put together into a single message (29:1–31:55), before his return and wrestling match, which would work very well together with his meeting of Esau (32:1–33:20), culminating with his final visit to Bethel (35:1–29). A more condensed version could include the combined fraternal conflict and quest for blessing (25:19–34; 26:34–28:9), God's encounters leaving and returning (28:10–22; 32:1–33:20), and God's final blessing at Bethel (35:1–29).

Genesis 25:19–34

EXEGETICAL IDEA

God revealed his plan to fulfill his covenant promises to Abraham through Isaac's line, responding to prayer, with his unexpected choice of the younger Jacob despite his obvious flaws, and rejecting Esau who despised his birthright.

THEOLOGICAL FOCUS

God's sovereign work, realized through prayer, will be accomplished through flawed faith, rejecting one who despises his promise.

PREACHING IDEA

"It's not for sale!": What Esau should have said and how faith feels about the blessing of God.

PREACHING POINTERS

When the Lord graciously allows Rebekah to conceive twins, their struggles within the womb culminate in the reversal of cultural norms seen so often in redemptive history (the prophecy in v. 23). God often chooses the unlikely for carrying out his work to remind us that it is his work, not ours alone. Another unexpected—or maybe better, unwanted—element is that God's plan for his people includes what appear to be long delays. According to verse 26 it took twenty years for the couple to conceive. That is a long time for a child of God to wait for the promises of God to come true! That is a long time to keep praying to God. That is a lot of patient waiting in hope.

Finally, God presents to us two sons representing two nations that could not be more different. God chose the younger, Jacob, to be the conduit of blessing. Jacob is far from perfect, but the Lord will see to it that he is being perfected along the way. Esau's profane nature is on display in the way he treats his birthright (see v. 34's summary statement: "Thus Esau despised his birthright"), what should be his most prized possession because all the promises of God and his plan are wrapped up in that gift. Jacob, on the other hand, wants that birthright for himself more than anything. Readers find themselves in the story: some, like Esau, treasuring the temporal things of this world, and others, like Jacob, with a new nature desiring the best God can give.

USEFULNESS: VALUING GOD'S GIFTS (25:19–34)

LITERARY STRUCTURE AND THEMES

The new *toledot* begins with three brief notes introducing the characters and conflicts that will carry the message of the section. The Abraham narratives presented Abraham's growth as the exemplar of learning to walk with God by faith. Now, with God's sworn promises, the Jacob stories will show how God shaped his chosen vessel, Jacob, to be able to gain real blessing in true worship, to provide that blessing to God's world (12:3). Jacob pursues blessing, but he will need to learn what real blessing is and the responsibility of being the channel of God's blessing that goes with the promised blessing.[1] This section will initiate the conflicts and begin to uncover the flaws in the characters that will threaten God's redemptive purposes.

I. Title: the family history of Isaac (25:19).

II. God's sovereignly chose the younger twin (25:20–26).[2]

   A. "Isaac was forty years old when he took Rebekah . . . to be his wife" (25:20).

      B. "Isaac prayed . . . because [Rebekah] was barren" (25:21a).

         C. "Rebekah . . . conceived. The children struggled" (25:21b–22).

            D. "[Rebekah] went to inquire of the LORD" (25:22).

            D'. "The LORD said . . . Two nations . . . the older shall serve the younger" (25:23).

         C'. "When her days to give birth were completed, behold, there were twins" (25:24).

      B'. Jacob and Esau described at birth (25:25–26a).

   A'. "Isaac was sixty years old when she bore them" (25:26b).

III. Conflict extended to the family (25:27–28).

IV. Esau despised his birthright (25:29–34).

   A. "Jacob was cooking stew" (25:29a).

      B. "Esau came in from the field . . . exhausted" (25:29b).

         C. "Esau said . . . 'Let me eat . . . I am exhausted' (25:30).

            D. "Jacob said, 'Sell me your birthright now'" (25:31).

               E. "Esau said, 'I am about to die; of what use is a birthright to me?'" (25:32).

            D'. "Jacob said, 'Swear to me now.' So he swore" (25:33).

         C'. "Jacob gave, . . . and he ate and drank" (25:34aα)

      B'. Esau "went his way." (25:34aβ).

   A'. "Esau despised his birthright" (25:34b). (Fokkelman 2004, 94–97)

The title (25:19) moves the narrative from Abraham, through Isaac, to Jacob. As the Terah *toledot* focused on his sons, especially God's choosing and working with Abraham, the Isaac *toledot* will focus on God's choosing and working with Jacob. The first note (vv. 20–26)

1 As empowerment to accomplish God's purposes, Jacob will need to learn that blessing only comes in relationship with Yahweh. See Introduction, "Blessing," p. 60.

2 The structure here follows Fokkelman (2004, 86–94), who recognizes that the structure is not completely "compelling" because of fuzzy divisions and appositions but still shows the heart of the narrative with the oracle central.

sets the miraculous birth of the third patriarch against a backdrop of immediate prenatal conflict with his sibling rival. The chiastic structure centers attention on the oracle from Yahweh, declaring his choice of the younger over the elder for his promise and future dominion. The predicted conflict would continue from conception through future nationhood until the people from the older served the people from the younger. Their resulting births provide cryptic insight into the future for both children.

The second note (vv. 27–28) characterizes the two boys as they develop into men and extends the conflict to the family dynamics of ongoing favoritism that will plague the family for the remainder of Genesis. The narrative extends that characterization in the final vignette (vv. 29–34), revealing the values of the two men and their approach to the promise. Both men expose serious character flaws. This final chiastic structure highlights Esau's disdain for his birthright, both at the center and in the narrator's concluding evaluation. God's choice was warranted, even though Jacob would require remedial attention.

Through this narrative sequence, Moses juxtaposes God's sovereign choice for his redemptive plan and the choices of his human subjects, showing their motivations, makeup, and values, which confirm both God's choice and the challenge ahead to use Jacob for his purposes. God's working does not vitiate human choice and responsibility but works with the human will to bring about his good purposes, as Joseph will state (50:20; cf. Sailhamer 1990, 182).

- ***The Family History of Isaac (25:19)***
- ***God's Sovereignly Chose the Younger Twin (25:20–26)***
- ***Conflict Extended to the Family (25:27–28)***
- ***Esau Despised His Birthright (25:29–34)***

EXPOSITION

The initial section, and particularly the initial vignette, parallels the beginning of the Abraham stories in numerous ways, including matriarchal barrenness (25:21; cf. 11:30), the age of the patriarch (25:20; cf. 12:4), and an oracle with a promise/prediction of future descendants (25:23; cf. 12:1–3).[3] The final *toledot* will similarly open with an oracle in the form of two dreams (37:7, 9). All three patriarchal *toledots* open with programmatic oracles for the narratives that follow (to Abram, 12:1–3; Rebekah, 25:23; and Joseph 37:7, 9).

This introductory section (25:19–34) looks ahead to the following narratives to provide the themes and issues that will direct the story line, including the character and roles of the boys, the favoritism of the parents, and, most significantly, the acquisition of the blessing. The plan and choice of Yahweh will interface with the machinations of the human characters to finally realize God's desired outcome. God revealed his plan to fulfill his covenant promises to Abraham through Isaac's line, responding to prayer with his unexpected choice of the younger Jacob despite his obvious flaws and rejecting Esau, who despised his birthright.

The Family History of Isaac (25:19)

The family history of Isaac will carry the promise to Abraham forward.

25:19. The introduction to the new *toledot* in Genesis parallels the brief note on the descendants of Ishmael (25:12–18). Contrasting the other *toledot* formulae, these two include the father of the featured family head. Abraham and his promises form the backdrop to both men and their expectations. The blessing on Ishmael (16:11–12; 17:20), recalled by reference to Abraham and Hagar, bears fruit in the *toledot* of Ishmael. The blessing on Isaac as the heir of promise similarly recalls Yahweh's covenant

3 For an extended listing of the specific parallels and implications, see Wenham (1994, 172–73).

promises to Abraham. These promises draw attention to the hope of blessing and the future great nation (22:17–18). This promise and blessing from God that will be passed along to the chosen descendants forms the implicit and necessary background to the conflict that will be introduced with the sons of Isaac.

God's Sovereignly Chose the Younger Twin (25:20–26)

God miraculously gave twins to Rebekah and unexpectedly chose the younger brother to accomplish his covenantal plan of blessing through the ensuing conflict.

The chiastic initial vignette focuses the reader's attention on the oracle, which will be key to all that follows (Literary Structure and Themes above). Rather than focus on the barrenness, which had been foundational to the ongoing struggle and conflict in the Abraham stories, here the focus revolves around the conflict for ascendancy and blessing, which will ultimately go to Jacob. Merely acquiring blessing, however, does not accomplish God's purpose. Rather, the program of God, including blessing all nations, requires transforming Jacob's self-serving ambition to submissive worship (ch. 35).

25:20. Isaac's age curiously introduces the section, with no explanation until verse 26, framing the section with the time of waiting for the births. The extended rehearsal of Rebekah's pedigree draws attention to the servant finding Rebekah as wife for Isaac and the final blessing with which she left to marry (24:60). Mirroring the promise to Abraham (22:17), she would become the mother of "ten thousands" (24:60), yet she was barren for twenty years. The narrative does not dwell on that here but drops it in at the end (v. 26b), almost as an afterthought. Here the focus is on the unsettling answer to Isaac's prayer, felt in the battle of two nations in the confined space of Rebekah's womb. Rather than the drama of the barrenness and the fulfillment of promise, the narrative focuses on the conflict between the sons, their values, and the question of how God will prepare this family to bring about his good ends for all people.

25:21a. To his credit, Isaac avoided Abraham's folly, choosing to "plead" (JPS, עתר) for his wife rather than attempt his own answer, because she was "barren" (עֲקָרָה). The only three uses of the term "barren" in Genesis unite Sarah (11:30), Rebekah (25:21), and Rachel (29:31). In each case, the difficulty highlights the needed divine intervention and the miraculous birth of a child for Yahweh's purpose. The promise can only be fulfilled by God's direct intervention. The pleading of Isaac underlines this reality (Fokkelman 2004, 87–88, 92).

> *TRANSLATION ANALYSIS 25:21*
> The verb typically translated "pray" (עתר) here may have a more specific and intense use in Genesis and Exodus (Albertz, עתר, TLOT, 962) and is appropriately translated "plead" (NJPS, NKJV, NLT; cf. Exod. 8:4, 5, 24, 25, 26; 9:28; 10:17, 18).

25:21b–22b. God's answer initially appears immediate. "Isaac prayed [וַיֶּעְתַּר] . . . And the Lord granted his prayer [וַיֵּעָתֶר]." The focus on the answer draws attention to God's working, rather than the twenty years of waiting and the necessary faith involved (v. 26). The obvious working of God stands in tension with the struggle of Rebekah to make sense of her difficult pregnancy, the struggle of the boys in her, and the ongoing struggle for the future of two nations. How they will fit together will teach the readers of all generations something of the work of God, accomplishing his good purposes through and despite the foolish actions of flawed human subjects, while at the same time redeeming them and working on their character.

The children in Rebekah's womb are in a free-for-all. The term used for "struggle" (רצץ) denotes the crushing of oppression (Deut. 28:33;

Judg. 10:8; Amos 4:1) or the effect of a millstone on Abimelech's head (Judg. 9:53). Speiser (1964, 193) translates it "clashed", and Wenham (1994, 171) suggests "smashed" to show the intensity. Extreme "kicking and shoving" expresses the idea (*HALOT* s.v. "רצץ" 1285–86). The battle elicits an anguished reaction from Rebekah.

Rebekah's cry is difficult and abbreviated. She may be despairing of life itself (Wenham 1994, 175) or doubting the future for the children and the possible outcomes for her family (Mathews 2005, 387). Clearly stressed by the commotion, she desperately wanted to understand what was happening to her. We might not expect God's promise or blessing to bring such turmoil, even to the point of despairing of life itself. We might expect, rather, some assurance of health, especially with the precarious nature of childbirth for mother and child (cf. Rachel; 35:16–19).

TRANSLATION ANALYSIS 25:22

The Hebrew text cryptically asserts, "If so, why this, I . . . ?", appearing to break off her thought in mid-sentence (Hamilton 1995, 173). The translations have wrestled with the implications: "If it is thus, why is this happening to me?" (ESV); "If it is so, why then am I this way?" (NASB95); or more forcefully, "If it is going to be like this, I'm not so sure I want to be pregnant!" (NET); "If it is to be this way, why do I live?" (NRSV); or "If so, why do I exist?" (NJPS).

25:22c–23. In her distress, Rebekah inquired of Yahweh.[4] In the key oracle, setting the stage for the Jacob stories, Yahweh revealed that the conflict within her portended ongoing future national conflict between the descendants of the two children. The descendants of the younger would be stronger and dominate the nation from the elder. While the oracle did not directly answer her concerns, it implied more than is clearly stated. Her concern for the children and the pregnancy can rest in God's overarching plan and promised future.

Because the promises to Abraham have already been the focus of the previous narratives (11:27–25:11) and clearly provided a backdrop to these narratives (25:19), the oracle declaring the future nations and the dominance of the younger provides the fulfillment of those promises to Abraham (of "nations," 17:16) and the blessing on Rebekah (24:60). That also implies Yahweh's choice of the younger son for the promise and outworking of his plan to bring blessing to all peoples (22:17–18) as confirmed by Isaac (27:29, 40) and understood by Paul (Rom. 9:12). This prenatal struggle anticipates both the aggressive attitude of the boys and their posterity, and the working of God to accomplish his purpose.

This oracle, the focus of the chiastic structure, provides the initial key to understanding the narratives that will follow. As with Abraham's painful choices, it does not absolve any of the characters of responsibility, but it rather guarantees God's protective working for his outcome. Considering the promises to Abraham and God's purpose to bring blessing to all the nations of the earth, now through Jacob, it anticipates God's remedial work in Jacob's life to prepare him for his role.

25:24–26a. Moses describes the birth of the twins by the appearance of Esau and the action of Jacob, both of which lead to reflections on their naming. The text connects the firstborn's reddish color and hairy appearance to his naming as Esau, even though "red" (אַדְמוֹנִי) is more closely related to his nickname, "Edom"

4 The phrase "to go to inquire of Yahweh" (הלך + דרשׁ + יהוה) generally refers to going to a prophet (e.g., 1 Sam. 9:9; 2 Kings 1:2, 3; 8:8; 22:13; 2 Chron. 34:21). Perhaps she asked Abraham (20:7), her husband, Isaac, went to a sacred place, or she went directly to Yahweh herself (Hamilton 1995, 177), but whatever the mechanism, she clearly heard the oracle from Yahweh. Whether Isaac was aware of this will impact our understanding of chapter 27.

(only noted in v. 30), and "hairy" (שֵׂעָר) is much closer in sound to "Seir," where Esau and his descendants will later live (32:4).[5] These descriptions draw the reader's attention to the resulting nation of Edom and Israel's interaction with them when Israel left Egypt and tie it together with the impact of the oracle (Ross 2008, 155).

Jacob's name, however, is related to his action of holding Esau's heel (עָקֵב) when he emerged. Clearly Jacob's name sounds like "heel" and is typically related as the heel-grabber or supplanter (trying to take Esau's place and get ahead, 27:36). However, as often noted, Jacob was a common name in that time and was a shortened form of a theophoric ("may God protect"), which would have been common knowledge (*HALOT* s.v. "יַעֲקֹב" 422; cf. Frankena 1972, 265).[6] Rebekah's appropriate choice and the implications of protection (especially considering her stated concerns) result in a play on that name in Esau's words, because of Jacob's action as a newborn and Esau's later connection to his "supplanting" and "deception" as a young adult (the sort of derogatory word play some of us may have experienced in adolescence!).

25:26b. We now learn that Rebekah's barrenness had lasted twenty years. The note on Isaac's age frames the narrative and is a tacit reminder again of the promise and Yahweh's necessary and sole working to accomplish it. Just as Abraham bore his son in his old age, so Isaac bore his son of promise at an older age. Fokkelman (2004, 92–93) also notes a subtle implication in the summary. Typically, the *toledot* introductions will give the reader the line that the family head bears. Here, however, it is not Isaac who bears the sons, but Rebekah, emphasizing Isaac's reduced role and Yahweh's responsibility for the outcome.

Conflict Extended to the Family (25:27–28)

The boys diverged profoundly, polarizing the family between the tastes of Isaac and the affection of Rebekah.

25:27–28. While the births of the two boys provide a visual that will characterize them as the narrative progresses, the narrative will also portray them by their occupations and temperament. Esau was the mountain-man outdoorsman, living on the fringe of society. Jacob was the traditional pastoralist, appearing more "civilized" (*HALOT* s.v. "תָּם" 1742–43). Clearly, he valued "the things that made life good" (Ross 2008, 157).

> *TRANSLATION ANALYSIS 25:27*
>
> The translation of the adjective for Jacob is difficult because it generally refers to moral integrity (e.g., Job 1:8), but that does not appear to be the intent here, since Jacob does not show an upright character, and it would not provide a fitting contrast with Esau (Hamilton 1995, 181). The idea of "complete" (from the verbal root, *HALOT* s.v. "תָּמַם" 1752–54) provides the rationale for commonly translating the adjective as "quiet" (Wenham 1994, 177). It may also

5 Two of the consonants of "hairy" also occur in Esau, but the origins of the name Esau and its meaning are unknown. Interpreters are divided on whether red here (only used of David elsewhere, 1 Sam. 16:12; 17:42) refers to their hair color or complexion. For the importance of the reddish color and name "Edom" in this narrative, see v. 30 below. The explanations for names in the OT often provide word plays (or puns) on the name, to relate them to the circumstances or occasion of the birth in the life of the parents, rather than specifically describing the literal meaning of the name.

6 Malul (1996, 211–12) argues that this narrative and chapter 27 record an elaborate word play on the root used in Jacob's name representing three homonyms, "to supplant" (from "heel"), "to cheat," and "to protect." Most likely, Rebekah would have been thinking of God's protection, though Esau would later turn it to his advantage with his "sounds like" a cheater.

provide "a suggestion of 'sound' or 'solid', the level-headed quality that made Jacob, at his best, toughly dependable, and at his worst a formidably cool opponent" (Kidner 1967, 162), which may lead to one who is "bent on one purpose" (Fokkelman 2004, 91). In contrast to Esau, however, it may simply be "sophisticated and refined," "detail-oriented" (Walton 2001, 550), or well-rounded, "well-cultured," and so "civilized" (Waltke and Fredricks 2001, 362). The full implications are not clear.

These traits endeared them to different parents, however, with Isaac valuing his palate and the benefits of Esau's skills. Rebekah preferred Jacob, though it does not explicitly state why, though it may be because he is the one God chose, remembering her oracle. Both the preferences of the parents and the character of the sons will impact the following narratives, providing conflicts that will need to be resolved for the progress of the promises.

TRANSLATION ANALYSIS 25:28
While the Old Testament uses the verb "love" in a variety of ways, every use for parental love in the Old Testament refers to preferential love, motivated by some external factor (Els, אָהַב, NIDOTTE 1:293). Here the point is less affection and more the desire to further the favored child's well-being and future, leading to both parents committing self-incriminating acts on behalf of their favorites.

Esau Despised His Birthright (25:29–34)

Taking advantage of Esau's vulnerability and values, Jacob enticed Esau, who despised his birthright, selling it to Jacob.

Another chiastic structure (see above, p. 433) centers around Esau spurning his birthright in favor of his immediate appetites (v. 32) from which Moses concluded that "Esau despised his birthright" (v. 34b). The structure emphasizes the point for the reader, drawing attention to their values and the concern of the subsequent story. This section validates God's choice of Jacob and exposes the need for remedial work that he will require to be useful for the promised blessing.

25:29. The frame of the narrative begins by fleshing out the characterization of Jacob. The "civilized" man (v. 27) preparing stew reveals his callous pursuit of Esau's birthright behind a refined veneer. The counterpart of the frame (v. 34b) suggests that Jacob was the hunter baiting his trap, Esau was the prey, and Esau's own defective values betrayed him.

Esau, returning from a hunting trip, was worn out from his hunt. He was "exhausted" (ESV) or "famished" (NIV), which he also notes (v. 30) as the basis for his imminently imagined death (v. 32). A little stew, however, perked him right up (v. 34)!

TRANSLATION ANALYSIS 25:29
"Exhausted" (ESV, עָיֵף) can reflect being worn out from physical exertion (Deut. 25:18; 2 Sam. 17:29; so also NKJV, "weary"), famished with hunger (Judg. 8:4–5; so NET, "starving," cf. NLT; or NASB95, NIV, "famished"), or parched from thirst (Job 22:7; Prov. 25:25; all of which are experienced during a long hunt for wild game), so it can be remediated by rest (Isa. 28:12), food (Judg. 8:5), or drink (Isa. 29:8). Jacob's stew, then, would satisfy both hunger and thirst and possibly revive a weary body as well.

25:30. The text is silent on whether Esau was unsuccessful in the hunt or whether he was merely too tired to take the time to cook his game. Either possibility reveals his impetuous and misguided priorities. His exaggerated reactions lead to his real loss. Here, he politely, if somewhat coarsely, requests a swallow of the red stuff. He simply refers to the stew by its color, repeating, "some of the red stuff—yes, this red stuff—because I'm starving!" (NET; lit., "from the red, this red, because I am famished!").

TRANSLATION ANALYSIS 25:30a
Esau's request to "eat" (הַלְעִיטֵנִי נָא) translates a *hapax legomenon*, which probably indicates more of a ravenous and uncouth "swallow" (NASB95; cf. O'Connell, לָעַט, *NIDOTTE* 2:807) or "gulp" (NJPS), indicating his "boorish manners" (Sarna 1989, 182). The particle (נָא) often translated "please" (NASB2020, NKJV) may simply add emphasis (*HALOT* s.v. "נָא" 656–57).

TRANSLATION ANALYSIS 25:30b
Alternatively, the two uses of "red" (הָאָדֹם) could be understood as two different words, the adjective "red" and the noun, used only here, for "pottage" or "stew" (Brueggemann 1982a, 218; reflected in ESV, NIV, NLT "red stew"; cf. RSV). In this case, the word play on the color adds to the impact of the naming. If it is his brutish repetition of "red," implying "red stuff" (NASB95, NJPS, NRSV), the report focuses more on his inarticulate and desperate state of mind.

The popular etymology here comes as a surprise. Why is the note added that "therefore his name was called Edom"? "Edom" uses the same consonants and sounds like the word used here for "red" (אָדֹם), so that is obvious, but why is it significant at this point? This name, of course, will be passed along to his descendants, the Edomites. Fokkelman (2004, 96) notes the connection with Esau's appearance (v. 25), suggesting that it is a statement of the nature of Esau: "Jacob outwits his 'red' brother with his own nature." In his words, his actions, and even (symbolically) his appearance, Esau shows his profane nature, living down to the primal instincts implied in his resulting nickname. He craves what is temporal and immediate. He does not value what is truly valuable and eternal.

25:31–33. Jacob appears prepared for Esau. His demand suggests premeditation. The center section frames Esau's rejection of his birthright by Jacob's repeated demand to sell it to him "now." The "birthright" is at the core of this narrative, and Jacob ruthlessly pursued it.

TRANSLATION ANALYSIS 25:31
Lit. "today" (NKJV, "as of this day," כַיּוֹם). By implication, then, "first" (NIV, NRSV, NJPS).

The "birthright" (בְּכֹרָה) will later be codified as the double portion for every first-born Israelite son (Deut. 21:17), compared to the single portion of all other sons (cf. Tsevat, בְּכֹרָה, *TDOT* 2:125–27). The full implications for Esau are unclear, as is what he sold. Did he sell all that he would have received or merely the extra portion (Walton 2001, 550)? The additional need to acquire Isaac's blessing (ch. 27) indicates he did not sell his "rank and position" (M. Tsevat, בְּכֹרָה, *TDOT* 2:126). Indeed, God's promises to Abraham become the focus in chapter 26 and the object of the struggle in the next round of Jacob versus Esau (27:27–29). Jacob, then, would use further intrigue to gain his goal his way.

The Birthright

The birthright was established in Israel by law (Deut. 21:15–17) and could not be given to a different son. In the ancient Near East at the time of Jacob, however, it was something that could be sold between brothers, as attested in Old Babylonia and Nuzi (M. Tsevat, בְּכֹרָה, *TDOT* 2:126). Such a sale, however, only reflected tangible property (the double portion). Jacob's demand, then, was not contrary to custom.

This narrative, then, does more to show the misplaced values and perspectives of the men than it does to determine their possessions, much less their future. God had already declared the future for Jacob. Jacob showed here his value for the tangible properties and the "good life," as well as his callous willingness to take advantage of his brother's weakness and folly. If he knew of the oracle to Rebekah, which seems likely, he did not trust Yahweh to accomplish it without his help (like his grandmother, Sarah, 16:2?). He would not wait ("today," vv. 31, 33). Rather he would resort to manipulation to accomplish the promise of God, and he would pay dearly, learning similar lessons to those of Sarah and Abraham with his efforts at self-realization rather than faith.

Esau, on the other hand, over-valued his physical desires and under-valued his place in God's promise (Heb. 12:16–17). The drama revealed his core values and his rejection of his role as primary heir. The rapid report of his silent response to the meal ("he ate and drank and rose and went his way" Gen. 25:34) belied his stated concern of dying from hunger. Esau only valued the immediate and tangible. In his need, he would not wait. Rather, he swore to Jacob and sold his birthright.

25:34. The narrative ends as quickly as it has progressed. For the first time we hear that it was lentils. The hunter sold his birthright for a bowl of vegan stew. Jacob gave; Esau ate, drank, rose, and left. There is no backward glance, no remorse, no thought. Esau does not acknowledge or recognize his folly. The final statement seals his image and his fate: "Esau despised his birthright." In despising his birthright, he disdained God and his promise. While he had sold what would be tangible assets, they were not yet concrete. Indeed, his position and all that went with it, including Abraham's legacy and Yahweh's promise, was of little consequence to him. A narrator in the Hebrew Bible seldom directly states the point, but here he does. Esau's disregard of his position, and so God's promise and God himself, showed he was profane and unworthy of God's good gifts.

TRANSLATION ANALYSIS 25:34
To "despise" (בזה) denotes thinking "lightly of" or treating something "with contempt" (Grisanti, בזה, NIDOTTE 1:628). In treating it flippantly, he depreciated God, his promise, and his own role in that promise. Though he would later regret it, his choice was irreversible, (27:36; cf. Görg, בזה, *TDOT* 2:63; Malul 1996).

While Esau did not value his birthright, Jacob did. Jacob understood the importance and mercilessly drove his quarry into his trap. Esau was oblivious to all but his hunger, while Jacob prized the promise. Yet he also fell short. Neither man showed the character and values required for God to fulfill his promise (cf. 18:19). "Morally speaking there are only losers" (Fokkelman 2004, 97). Yet God's promise still holds hope for the woefully inadequate. "If God could use him [Jacob], may he now graciously use us" (Wenham 1994, 181).

THEOLOGICAL FOCUS

God's sovereign work, realized through prayer, will be accomplished through flawed faith, rejecting one who despises his promise.

God continues to sovereignly move his plan forward, even as he moves into the background. The initial statement of barrenness and Isaac's pleading (which we finally hear extends the better part of twenty years) reinforces the sole responsibility of the promise through the working of Yahweh. He alone gives life and blessing. That realization highlights the tension between experience and promise of blessing for God's people and the recognition of necessary human dependence on God (in contrast to Jacob later).

Though he chose the younger Jacob, and though the elder Esau showed his unworthiness, it would still be a battle to reform Jacob's character and prepare him for God's use. God's choice was initially vindicated when the profane Esau rejected his position in favor of his appetite. At least Jacob valued what was valuable. God's responsibility for the outcomes of his promise and redemptive purposes seem to be challenged by Jacob's character, however, despite his appropriate value on the birthright. It will remain to be seen how God will produce his desired blessing despite resulting conflicts and personal ambitions. In fact, God often chooses and uses the less likely and deeply flawed, from a human viewpoint, to show his nature and power (1 Cor. 1:27–31).

God's sovereign choice and working remained in the background in the second main vignette. Instead, we see the character of the two men, especially regarding the promise and their values. Esau values the temporary and immediate, while Jacob values the future and the promise of a better life, exercising faith in the promise and hope of God. His faith, however, was not grounded in God's sovereign working to accomplish his plan but framed in his own ability to manipulate his situation to bring about his desired goals. Both sets of values will lead to loss. Not valuing the eternal cannot obtain it, since it is rejected. Valuing the eternal for selfish reasons and attempting to attain it in fleshly ways will lead to conflict and loss as well. God's images must learn to trust God for his promise rather than try to take what they want at the expense of those around them.

In this intersection between God's sovereign choice and the freedom of his subjects to pursue their own agendas, this introduction sets up the following narratives for God to show his sovereign control, even through foolish and unbelieving human choices, which he will use to accomplish his eternal ends, either by direct intervention (31:24; 32:24–29) or by the school of hard knocks (chs. 29, 34). Yahweh will need to move Jacob from a mercenary worshipper (28:20–22) to a committed true worshipper (35:1–15) whom he could use to bring blessing to the nations (47:10; 48:15–16).

Still, the seeds of conflict that would characterize Jacob's life and relationship with Esau (as well as Laban and the Canaanites) would be some of the tools that Yahweh would use to accomplish his ends. Jacob would have to learn that he could not gain blessing through his manipulative self-interest but rather through God's working on his behalf (e.g., see Exposition on 33:10, p. 544). God seldom intervenes in Jacob's personal conflicts, often allowing him to sow the seeds and reap the consequences of the divisions and relational briar patches. However, God will use even those to accomplish his ends and shape Jacob. God will work to shape each of his chosen subjects to accomplish his purposes for his glory, now, in Christ, transforming us into the image of his son (Rom. 8:29; 1 Cor. 15:49)

PREACHING AND TEACHING STRATEGIES

Exegetical and Theological Synthesis

Beginning in verse 19 we find ourselves in the line of blessing from Abraham to Isaac and now to Jacob. The descriptions of each son are amoral: Esau, "a man of the field," and Jacob, "a quiet man, dwelling in tents" (v. 27). The narrator creates tension in verse 28 as the parents are split in their affections for the twins. The cook, Jacob, gets the upper hand on the hunter, Esau, through the "red stew" (v. 30). While the description of their inclinations is amoral, their spiritual nature surfaces when it comes to Jacob's desire for Esau's birthright.

Now, in a sense, God's choice of the younger (v. 23) is justified. Esau doesn't value the birthright, and he symbolizes all who do not value the gift of God, encompassing such things as the blessing of God, the promises and plan of God, and the whole life he provides to all who trust him. The summary statement from the narrator says it all about Esau's heart: "Thus Esau despised his birthright" (v. 34). Whatever Jacob's character is at that moment, and despite his scheming, one thing is certain: the birthright means a great deal to him. He may not have the pureist of motives or full understanding of the theological implications of the birthright—Jacob is far from perfect—but God is used to this by now and fully capable of grooming the new heir. The twins' attitude toward the should-be-coveted, ancient family birthright draws our listeners toward Jacob, urging us to believe in God's promises, live life accordingly, and take our part in faithfully passing on all the blessings of God that accompany them.

Preaching Idea

"It's not for sale!": What Esau should have said and how faith feels about the blessing of God.

Contemporary Connections

What does it mean?

You might begin by explaining the significance of God's prophecy about the two nations in verse 23, especially the part about "the older shall serve the younger." This clearly signifies that our listeners need to identify themselves with the younger, with Jacob. At the very least, the position of the younger in this case points to the blessing of God in this life and the next, to freedom versus servitude.

Another concept needing explanation is the "birthright." Beyond the evidence from ancient history about its value, in redemptive history the birthright signifies all the promised blessings of God for his people. So, when the narrator says that "Esau despised his birthright" (v. 34), this is a devastating commentary on his spiritual condition. All the description of the twins highlights their differences. Those differences culminate in Jacob's cunning plan to get the prized possession. While his methods reveal spiritual immaturity at best, and possibly blatant unbelief, the fact that he valued the prime place in God's plan speaks volumes to the church. Hebrews 12 reads Esau's attitude and action toward the birthright as the perfect warning for God's people.

Is it true?

Our listeners may benefit from some proof or evidence that the ancient birthright was extremely valuable. Brief minutes in the exegesis during the sermon will discuss the historical and sociological aspects of the birthright in terms of land and monetary value and all that goes along with that. The more we can raise the value of the birthright in our listeners' eyes, the worse Esau looks. Bad for Esau, of course, but good for communicating theology. Despising the birthright is certainly a "go and do otherwise" exemplar, and we will certainly follow Jacob, as he was God's choice for the one to be blessed by God and function as the conduit of blessing in the world. Help your congregants see that, beyond the historical/sociological advantages of the birthright, Esau rejects and Jacob accepts the promises of God and his part to play in the plan of God, wrapped up in a theology of birthright and, later in the narrative, blessing.

Now what?

As noted above, relevance occurs in the line of blessing, and believers find themselves in this storyline. The stern warning in Hebrews 12 uses Esau as a negative example for the church. Placed within the context of all the other warnings in that ancient sermon/letter, the narrative of the twins in our text provides our listeners with an opportunity to assess their own relationship with God and his promises. We all want to make sure that we respond to the narrative knowing that the promises and plan of God in the world is most valuable. Our Lord would later teach his followers that "the kingdom of heaven is like treasure hidden in a field" or "fine pearls," valuable enough that someone would sell everything they owned to possess it (cf. Matt. 13:44–45).

Creativity in Presentation

Two illustrations may help your listeners relate to the twins and their respective attitudes toward the ancient birthright. First, family members have often faced the loss of a parent or grandparent and inevitably were caught in a bidding war for valuables left behind. Children do not always feel the same about heirlooms. Second, anyone who has seen *Antiques Roadshow* knows what it is like to see ugly lamps worth thousands of dollars. Only the professional appraiser knows just how valuable the lamp is. The point of the pictures is simply to help listeners come to see how foolish Esau's trade was: red stew for real blessing. Despising the birthright is the ultimate statement about one's thoughts toward God and his kingdom program, not to mention where we fit in it. In gladly parting with the birthright, he had no thoughts about his part to play in the unfolding drama of redemption.

At the beginning of the narrative, however, the listed generations show God's promise to bless progressing through the ages. The two nations divide our listeners with respect to their leaders: Esau and Jacob. We do not want to be Esau; we prefer to be "the stronger" of the two (Gen. 25:23). For us to align with Jacob, God's chosen one, we will need to guard against loving the physical and temporal more than the spiritual and eternal. We must urge our listeners to love God and desire his blessing more than life itself. According to Hebrews 12:15–17, each Sunday we are in danger of failing to obtain the grace of God (v. 15). We continually warn that none of us can afford to be "unholy like Esau, who sold his birthright for a single meal" (v. 16). Our only option, then, is the heel-grabber, Jacob, who treasures the blessing of God and is, by faith, transformed little by little into the holy seed.

You might consider the following structure for the message:

- God chooses the less likely for his purpose to show that it is not accomplished by human effort alone (25:19–28).
- His choice of servant is matched by an attitude that treasures his promises and plan (25:29–34).

DISCUSSION QUESTIONS

1. How is patient waiting for the promises of God a part of saving faith?
2. What does the reoccurring reversal of societal norms—"the older shall serve the younger"—say about God's kingdom, promises, and plans?
3. What are the theological implications of the strong language, "Esau despised his birthright"?
4. How does patient waiting work together with persistent prayer for God's promises?
5. What are you committed to consistently praying for even if you do not see an answer for twenty years?
6. How do those close to you see your faith in your pursuits?

Genesis 26:1–33

EXEGETICAL IDEA
When Isaac received the covenant promises from Yahweh, his fear and deception brought conflict despite initial obedience, endangering God's purpose of blessing the nations, but his subsequent worship and faith in God's reassurance brought peace and blessing for the nations.

THEOLOGICAL FOCUS
The servant of God must respond to the presence and promise of God with faith, in true worship, to bring blessing and peace to his world, rather than fearfully, creating conflict and loss.

PREACHING IDEA
It takes faith, not fear, to both receive God's blessing and be a blessing to others.

PREACHING POINTERS
One way to transition from the original audience to current audiences is to focus on the Lord's commands to his chosen conduit of blessing, Isaac. Begin with the negative command in verse 2, "Do not go down to Egypt," and continue to the positive side of that same command: "dwell in the land of which I shall tell you. Sojourn in this land" (vv. 2–3). The famine provided the pull or push to return to Egypt, but the promises of God are enjoyed alongside the challenges related to trusting him for life. The promises of his presence, blessing, and being a conduit of universal blessing continue to drive our faith journey. And we cannot miss that all of this is explained by Abraham's obedience (v. 5), which is to be passed down to Isaac and on down the line.

However, readers are caught off guard as another "go and do otherwise" series of scenes occur as fear takes center stage instead of faith (vv. 6–11). As the saying goes, the apple didn't fall far from the tree. Yet, the blessing of God causes Isaac to be a most successful farmer (vv. 12–16). Isaac is still the conduit of blessing, warts and all. There is a great deal of comfort knowing the promises of God are not dependent only on our fickle faith. However, there is just as great a warning from watching all the conflict that occurs from Isaac's lack of faith (vv. 17–22).

When the Lord appears to Isaac a second time, his first command is "Fear not" (v. 24), especially appropriate after Isaac's reaction recorded in verse 7. Isaac is now in a position to be a blessing to others. He leads the way to genuine worship and trust and a testimony of the powerful presence of God (see especially v. 28). Fellowship replaces friction as the narrative closes.

FEARFUL FAITH: COMPROMISED BLESSING (26:1–33)

LITERARY STRUCTURE AND THEMES

Genesis 26 invests God's promises to Abraham in Isaac, with the expectations and responsibilities that go with them. The initial returns from God's investment, however, suggest it is misplaced when Isaac lies, jeopardizing the Philistines and his own ability to prosper in the land of promise. When he chooses to respond in faith and true worship, peace and prosperity follow.

The narrative unfolds chiastically: Isaac's visit to Abimelech at Gerar because of famine (26:1) frames the narrative with Abimelech's return visit to Isaac at Beersheba because of Isaac's prosperity (26:26–33). Within that outer frame, Yahweh appeared to Isaac with an extended reiteration of his promises to Abraham following Isaac's move (26:2–5) and immediately before Abimelech's visit (26:23–25). The center of the narrative draws attention to Isaac's ongoing conflict with the Philistines as he mimicked Abraham's wife-sister lie (26:7–11) and as God blessed him with water and crops, but without peace (26:12–22). The flow emphasizes the conflict and endangerment of Isaac's fear reversed by his worship and honesty with Abimelech after God's intervention, mitigating the conflict and impact on his neighbors.

Concurrent with the chiastic structure, the narrative develops in two parallel panels:[1]

- A. Isaac moved to Gerar (26:1).
  - B. Yahweh blessed an obedient Isaac (26:2–6).
    - C. Isaac's deception brought conflict and rebuke (26:7–16).
      - D. God's blessing only increased conflict (26:17–22).
- A'. Isaac moved to Beersheba (26:23).
  - B'. Yahweh blessed a worshipful Isaac (26:24–25).
    - C'. Isaac's confident confrontation brought peace (26:26–31).
      - D'. God's blessing commemorated peace (26:32–33).

The parallel panels emphasize the two appearances of Yahweh, with Isaac's responses and the differing outcomes. In the first panel, Isaac obeyed God's encouragement to stay in the land, despite the famine, with the promise of protection and provision. Isaac's initial obedience did not include full confidence in God's protection, however, adding conflict and jeopardizing the promise of blessing to the nations through his lie, ending in alienation. In the second panel, Isaac responded to God's reiterated promise by identifying with Yahweh in public worship, following up with a much more forthright response to Abimelech, which led to peace with the Philistines. In both cases, God did all he had promised, blessing and protecting Isaac. In both cases the Philistines recognized both the threat and the opportunity in their treatment of Isaac. And in both cases, the Philistine king directed Isaac to his responsibility to be the conduit of blessing, amid the possibility of cursing by his actions.

1 Wenham notes the basic parallels of "promises" (vv. 1–6//vv. 23–25), "Isaac and Abimelek" (vv. 7–17// vv. 26–31), and "wells" (vv. 18–22//vv. 32–32) though the text offers more specific parallels (Wenham 1994, 185).

The text provides much more specific parallel development			
1	v. 1	וַיֵּלֶךְ יִצְחָק אֶל־אֲבִימֶלֶךְ... גְּרָרָה	Isaac went to Gerar.
2	vv. 2–6	וַיֵּרָא אֵלָיו יְהוָה וְאֶהְיֶה עִמְּךָ וַאֲבָרְכֶךָּ וְהִרְבֵּיתִי אֶת־זַרְעֲךָ אַבְרָהָם	Yahweh appeared to Isaac, calling him to stay in the land and promising him protection and blessing, land, descendants, and that all nations would be blessed in his descendants. Isaac obeyed.
3	vv. 7–16	וַיֹּאמֶר אֲבִימֶלֶךְ אֶל־יִצְחָק לֵךְ מֵעִמָּנוּ	But Isaac's lie produced conflict, intensified by God's blessing, until Abimelech sent Isaac away.
4	vv. 17–22	חפר used five times–the only uses of Isaac's servants digging other than v. 32.	Isaac moved to the valley, but conflict followed him over God's blessing of water until God made room.
1'	v. 23	וַיַּעַל מִשָּׁם בְּאֵר שָׁבַע	Isaac moved to Beersheba.
2'	vv. 24–25	וַיֵּרָא אֵלָיו יְהוָה כִּי־אִתְּךָ אָנֹכִי וּבֵרַכְתִּיךָ וְהִרְבֵּיתִי אֶת־זַרְעֲךָ אַבְרָהָם	Yahweh appeared to Isaac, reminding him of his protection, blessing, and promised offspring. Isaac worshipped.
3'	vv. 26–31	וְאַתֶּם שְׂנֵאתֶם אֹתִי וַתְּשַׁלְּחוּנִי מֵאִתְּכֶם וַיְשַׁלְּחֵם יִצְחָק וַיֵּלְכוּ מֵאִתּוֹ בְּשָׁלוֹם	Abimelech came to Isaac even though he had sent Isaac away (reference to vv. 7–16). After a covenant, Isaac sent him away in peace.
4'	vv. 32–33	Isaac's servants again dug (חפר)	They dug and found water (cf. v. 25).

- ***Isaac Moved to Gerar (26:1)***
- ***Yahweh Blessed an Obedient Isaac (26:2–6)***
- ***Isaac's Deception Brought Conflict and Rebuke (26:7–16)***
- ***God's Blessing Only Increased Conflict (26:17–22)***
- ***Isaac Moved to Beersheba (26:23)***
- ***Yahweh Blessed a Worshipful Isaac (26:24–25)***
- ***Isaac's Confident Confrontation Brought Peace (26:26–31)***
- ***God's Blessing Commemorated Peace (26:32–33)***

EXPOSITION

After the introduction of the *toledot* to the conflict between Jacob and Esau over the birthright, with the guiding oracle that the promises to Abraham would go to the younger, the reader is surprised by what seems like a digression with Isaac's sojourn in Gerar. Without mention of either Jacob or Esau, the chapter reiterates God's covenant promises to Isaac and details Isaac's conflicts with the Philistines over his lie and his prosperity. Within the larger structure of the Jacob stories, however, this narrative performs a significant role.

In the flow of the book, the parallels with the Abraham stories cement the role of Isaac as Abraham's heir and "invite the reader to reflect on the similarities and the differences between the careers of Abraham and of Isaac" (Wenham 1994, 187).[2] God will keep his promise and continue to do for succeeding generations what he promised to Abraham (Sailhamer 1990, 185). As he does, the reader sees Isaac respond in similar struggling fear—and growing faith. Just within the Jacob stories, this interlude between Jacob's choice and the initial conflict over birthright and their extended conflict over blessing, balances out the interlude in chapter 34 between the reconciliation of the brothers and Jacob's final blessing (Fishbane 1975, 24; see Introduction to the Jacob Narratives, p. 427).[3] Within both the patriarchal narratives and Jacob stories, this chapter clearly presents intentional composition and narrative purpose.

In the immediate context, it functions to refocus on the extent of God's promised blessing, reinforcing the heritage that frames the battle for the rights of the firstborn and blessing between the sons. Isaac is formally given the blessing from God, setting up his role in bestowing blessing on the sons in chapter 27. It also ironically shows Isaac as a deceiver who will get his reckoning in chapter 27, much as Jacob will later (Cotter 2003, 192). When Isaac received the covenant promises from Yahweh, his fear and deception brought conflict despite initial obedience, endangering God's purpose of blessing the nations, but his subsequent worship and faith in God's reassurance brought peace and blessing for the nations.

Isaac Moved to Gerar (26:1)

Because of another famine, Isaac moved to Gerar on his way to Egypt.

26:1. With another famine in the land, Isaac headed for Egypt (26:2). He specifically went "to Gerar to Abimelech king of the Philistines," suggesting more than merely a coincidental passing through.[4] The famine in the land reminds the reader of Abraham (12:10), which Moses makes explicit. The reference to Abimelech, king of the Philistines at Gerar, also suggests Abraham's treaty with a former Abimelech of Gerar (21:22–34).[5] Isaac's father had a covenant with Abimelech's predecessor, making this a natural stop on the way out of the land. Isaac would follow in his father's footsteps in too many ways, unfortunately.

---

2 In addition to the parallels between the beginning section (25:19–34) and the beginning of the Abraham narratives, Wenham (1994, 187) shows parallels between Gen. 26 and 12:10–14:20 (famine and the wife/sister story; wealth prompting quarreling among herdsmen; separation; divine promise of descendants; altar built, patriarch encamps; good relations established with foreigners; patriarch blessed by a foreign king). Wenham also shows parallels between ch. 26 and 20:1–21:31 (the wife/sister story; disputes about wells; Abimelech and Phicol; "The LORD has been with you;" making of an oath; treaty; well of Beersheba named).

3 While Fishbane shows thematic parallels (Fishbane 1979, 43–60), Rendsburg adds numerous lexical parallels between ch. 26 and ch. 34 (Rendsburg 2014, 56–58).

4 For discussion of the Philistines and the relation to the later Philistines in the monarchy, see sidebar at 21:32, p. 382.

5 That this is not the same Abimelech follows from the timeline of the narratives. It is likely out of order chronologically since having twins with them would have made the wife/sister ruse more difficult, and Isaac is not yet wealthy (before the inheritance from Abraham, Gen. 25:5), so it may have been between marriage and children, thus between forty and sixty years following Abraham's treaty (Wenham 1994, 187). If this is not out of order chronologically, it may be closer to eighty or ninety years following the treaty, with the twins grown and less conspicuously attached. Either way, a new generation is in leadership. The names for both Abimelech and Phicol (v. 26; cf. 21:22) would likely be dynastic or royal names (cf. Jost, "Abimelech," *DOTP* 6; Kidner 1967, 164–65, and especially n. 15).

Yahweh Blessed an Obedient Isaac (26:2–6)

When Yahweh appeared to Isaac, commanding him to remain in the land and blessing him with his covenant promises, Isaac obeyed.

26:2–5. Genesis does not record Abraham orally passing on the covenant promises and blessings as we see both Isaac and Jacob do (27:27–29; 28:3–4; 48:15–16; 49:2–27). Rather, Yahweh himself promoted the Abrahamic promises to Isaac. As recipient of the promises, and in terminology reminiscent of Abraham's call, Yahweh called Isaac to remain in the land of promise ("of which I shall tell you;" v. 2; cf. 12:1). He further specified that he should remain as an outsider, living on the hospitality of his indigenous hosts during a famine in "this land" (v. 3). Initially, Yahweh promised what he would show him, but then he specified the land of Gerar where Isaac had come.[6] This command, in conjunction with the following blessing and promise, required Isaac to choose faith over his immediate experience. If he would trust God and stay during a famine, God promised protection and provision ("I will be with you and will bless you," v. 2). Staying and trusting will turn out to be two different things.

TRANSLATION ANALYSIS 26:2
The verb in verse 2 (שׁכן) suggests staying or settling there rather than moving on to Egypt, so "settle down" (NET), "settle" (NRSV), "stay" (NJPS), or, though less clear, "live" (NCV, NIV, NKJV).

TRANSLATION ANALYSIS 26:3
"Sojourn" (גּוּר) reflects a less permanent living (cf. Exposition, 12:10, p. 258), subsisting as an outsider on the hospitality of the host country.

Just as God had promised blessing to Abraham (12:2; 22:17), so now God would bless Isaac. As God had promised Abraham the land, so now God specified that Isaac's blessing would include his covenant promises to Abraham (22:15–18; 26:3). As we have seen in the Abrahamic stories, the promises grew from the initial call (12:1–3) through the final oath (22:16–18; cf. the Introduction to the Abraham Narratives Summary, p. 236). The promise now given to Isaac closely mirrors God's oath to Abraham after Abraham's offering of Isaac (22:16–18).

Yahweh would multiply Isaac's descendants "like the stars of the heavens" (26:4; see 22:17), and they would have "all these lands" (26:4).[7] These narratives focusing on Jacob will trace the movement of this promise to the next generation and how the oracle will not only find fulfillment in him, but how he will come to be the appropriate recipient of the promise. The final promise of the Abrahamic covenant, that God would use his descendants to bring blessing to all nations, both flows naturally from the promise and directly reflects the oath (22:18). It also provides tension, both for this story and for the rest of the Jacob stories. Isaac will be rebuked by Abimelech for posing a threat to their well-being, and Jacob will pose a threat to possible blessing for both Esau and Laban.

---

6 When Yahweh promises "all these lands" (אֶת־כָּל־הָאֲרָצֹת הָאֵל) to Isaac, the plural appears to indicate the Philistine land, as well as the other Canaanite populations previously mentioned (15:19–21). "This" land, then, would likely indicate Gerar, the land of the Philistines. We have previously seen it used of Abraham in Egypt and Gerar (12:10; 20:1; 21:23) and of Lot in Sodom (19:9).

7 The possession of the land, while a common theme in the Abrahamic covenant promises, was not specifically stated that way in the oath (22:16–18). Rather, to Abraham, God swore to give his descendants "the gate of their enemies" (22:17). Either would likely imply the other, and the reference to the oath specifies that the full promise goes to Isaac. It also demonstrates that the oracle to Rebekah (25:23) indicates that Jacob will be the recipient of these promises as well, further tying together the narratives.

God predicated his blessing on the obedience of Abraham, as he had the oath (26:5; cf. 22:16). Abraham's obedience is described in terms of the law, later prescribed for the nation of Israel (Deut. 11:1). Abraham, living before the law, kept the law by faith (he was loyal, cf. Gen. 17:1; 22:12, loving God with his whole heart, Deut. 6:5), providing an example of the ideal servant who kept the law from the heart (Deut. 30:6) and showed the connection between law and faith (Kidner 1967, 163; Sailhamer 1990, 186–87). The recitation of the obedience of Abraham here provides the expectation that the servant of God, including Isaac, would live in just that way. Isaac must imitate the Abraham of Genesis 22, not the Abraham of chapter 12 (or even ch. 20). He, too, however, would have to learn that lesson.

26:6. So Isaac did stay in Gerar, obeying God's command to "sojourn in this land" (v. 3). Ironically, Abraham's obedience (ch. 22) followed struggles much like Isaac will experience in his initial response to God's promise (and which the many parallels reveal). Isaac stayed but would also be rebuked by a pagan king for his lack of faith.

Isaac's Deception Brought Conflict and Rebuke (26:7–16)

Isaac's fearful deception drew Abimelech's rebuke and initial protection but then rejection because of his untrustworthy power.

26:7–11. Despite Yahweh's assurance of his presence and blessing (including promises of future offspring and control over these lands), Isaac feared for his life because of his beautiful wife. Reprising Abraham's two foolish lies, Isaac also endangered his wife.[8] In distinction from Abraham's experience, however, Rebekah was not taken, and Abimelech discovered the ruse accidentally before Rebekah was harmed.

Abimelech noticed Isaac "laughing with" (v. 8) Rebekah and recognized she must be his wife. Obviously, there was more going on than a little humor! Abimelech was incredulous. His question reflects both the previous Abimelech (20:9) and Pharaoh (12:18) in their response to Abraham (as well as God to Eve and Cain, 3:13; 4:10). Like the previous Abimelech, Isaac endangered Abimelech's people with "guilt" (26:10; Abraham had brought on Abimelech and his kingdom "a great sin," cf. Exposition of 20:9, p. 367). He was not concerned about the moral stigma, but he was concerned for the real consequences that may result (Hamilton 1995, 197). Reflecting God's judgment declared to the earlier Abimelech (20:7), this Abimelech declared the same judgment on anyone who would dare to violate her in his kingdom (26:11). Ironically, Abimelech's concern for his people contrasts Isaac's concern for only his own skin. Isaac was not even appropriately concerned for his wife, let alone the nations around him to whom he was to be a blessing (Wenham 1994, 190–91).

TRANSLATION ANALYSIS 26:8
The verb translated "laughing with" (צָחַק) is the verb from which Isaac got his name and generally means "laugh" but could also be used to refer, as here, to sexual acts (cf. 39:17; Exod. 32:6; Allen, צָחַק, *NIDOTTE* 3:796–97). "Caressing" (NASB95, NET, NIV, NLT), or "fondling"

8 While many commentators have questioned the historicity of Isaac's imitative lie, the narrative shows numerous divergences and clearly intends the reader to view this as a similar but distinct event, building on the experience and consequences of Abraham. The uncertainties of Abraham and Isaac's world contributed to their struggle of faith in trusting God and made this repeated faithlessness more understandable and likely. Certainly, children learn more than the positive qualities from their parents, and in fact the deceptions will only grow for the next two generations in Jacob and his sons.

(NJPS, NRSV, RSV) are appropriately suggestive translations. Whatever he was doing showed Abimelech she was his wife.

Abimelech's response suggests several implications. First, either he was concerned that someone may still be base enough to violate Rebekah and cause his kingdom to be under God's wrath, or perhaps he was providing assurance to Isaac that they were safe. Second, it suggests familiarity with the previous narrative (from his predecessor) since his wording and concern closely imitates that expressed previously. The covenant made between the former Abimelech and Abraham specifically forbade this sort of deceit (21:23). While this was not Abraham's deceit, it will appear that the former treaty impacted this story, since Isaac specifically came to Abimelech, implying relationship (26:1), and he would later accuse Abimelech of breaking it (see v. 27, Exposition below).

Finally, a pagan king again shows greater integrity than God's choice servant and highlights the problem unbelief causes for the believer. Not only does he not offer hope and blessing to those in his world, but he also becomes the source of possible cursing and destruction. An additional implication will follow. Without the character that engendered trust by his pagan neighbors, God's blessing in his life gave him power that they perceived as danger rather than good (cf. v. 29).

26:12–16. If the hundredfold harvest of grain was not clear enough, Moses clarified that "the Lord blessed him" (v. 12).[9] God's blessing in this case included the crops, livestock, and servants, leading to envy and alarm from the Philistines. They tried running him off by stopping up the wells dug by Abraham, the water supply for his flocks, but it did not work. Abraham had been living in the land for many years with such blessing (and with a covenant with the previous Abimelech, including water rights, 21:22–34), but the reason for the negative reaction here may well be the deceit that Abimelech realized had brought them to the brink of catastrophe. If Isaac could not be trusted, his greatness posed a threat rather than the source of the blessing envisioned by God's promise (26:4). He would realize his need for assurances from Isaac of peace without harm, taking the form of a covenant (vv. 28–29).

TRANSLATION ANALYSIS 26:15
The Hebrew allows differing interpretations on the timing. It can be read as a pluperfect in line with the clear pluperfect of Abraham having dug the wells, so that they had previously stopped up the wells dug by Abraham (e.g., ESV, NKJV, NRSV). The following events support this translation since other wells had been stopped up previously (26:18). It can also be read as a simple past, so that it records their response to Isaac's prosperity by stopping up the previously dug wells (e.g., NET, NIV, NJPS), presumably to thwart Isaac and run him off. The grammar seems to support the latter more naturally, with "all the wells" frontloading the topic in the Hebrew, interrupted by a relative clause ("which the servants of his father had dug"), then followed by the main clause, "they stopped up," and the pronoun "them" resuming the frontloaded "wells." The immediate context also argues for the latter since they are jealous (immediately preceding), and Abimelech asks him to leave (immediately after). He had need of water for his large herds, and they apparently did not have as much need, so they stopped up the wells. It did not work, however, so Abimelech had to step in.

9 If we take Jesus's parables as applicable in this much earlier agricultural context, reaping a hundredfold would have been a maxed-out harvest and probably extravagant, even if you were not in or coming out of a famine (cf. Matt. 13:8; Mark 4:8; Luke 8:8). Here it appears miraculous.

God's Blessing Only Increased Conflict (26:17–22)

While Isaac left Gerar and God continued to bless with wells, the conflict continued until distance and abundance allowed for an uneasy peace.

26:17–22. Isaac moved out as ordered to the valley nearby, and the conflict followed him. As he re-dug the wells of Abraham, which the Philistines had stopped up, his naming of them with Abraham's names recalls the parallels with Abraham and his treaty with Abimelech of Gerar for water rights (21:30). Isaac claimed rights to those wells, but when they also found a valuable spring, conflict erupted again, so he peacefully moved on, digging another well. More conflict moved him farther away. Finally, when the herdsmen of Gerar left them alone, he commemorated the Lord's blessing and the opportunity to live in peace and be fruitful with the naming of that well. Rather than assert his rights, he continued to move and provided blessing by leaving behind wells, rather than damaging conflict.

Isaac Moved to Beersheba (26:23)

Isaac moved to Beersheba, initiating a new era in his life.

26:23. Without coercion, after God provided peace ("room for us," v. 22) and with the expectation to prosper in the land, Isaac moved to Beersheba. Since this was one of the traditional patriarchal bases (21:31–33; 22:19), it may be that the famine was past, and Isaac was returning home. The appearance of Yahweh (26:24) immediately after this significant move frames the previous narrative, drawing it to a close even as it marks a new beginning for Isaac. In the structure of the chapter, it begins a new panel that will show growth in Isaac as he responds more fully to God's revelation.

Yahweh Blessed a Worshipful Isaac (26:24–25)

When Yahweh appeared to Isaac, summarizing his presence and blessing for Isaac, Isaac worshipped in public loyalty and settled down.

26:24. Yahweh appeared a second time to Isaac after moving to Beersheba. With the threat of famine past and Isaac returning to his normal life, Yahweh reiterated the promises he made in Gerar. He did not need to repeat the command to remain in the land (26:2), but otherwise the oracle summarized the main contours of the previous promise. He reminded Isaac of his relationship with his father, Abraham. God referenced Isaac's admission of fear (vv. 7, 9), assuring Isaac of his presence and protection, as he had clearly shown in the sojourn in and near Gerar. Yahweh continued his intent to bless Isaac, graciously coaching him for his upcoming encounter.

With Isaac back in familiar surroundings, Yahweh focused on the promise of multiplied descendants, which will be an ongoing concern in the Jacob stories (chs. 29–30).[10] As with the initial oracle (v. 5), he declared the ongoing promise was for the sake of Abraham (cf. 22:16). Up to this point, Abraham's faith and loyalty were on display in the continuing working of God in Abraham's line. Isaac, by implication, had a heritage to live up to. Isaac's legacy was already providing mixed reviews. God will accomplish his plan, but the line will require remedial work.

26:25. Isaac's immediate response to Yahweh was appropriate public worship as he built an altar to Yahweh, publicly declaring his loyalty

10 If this is indeed out of order chronologically, this would be of special concern to Isaac and Rebekah, since she was barren, and he prayed up to twenty years for those children (25:20–21; cf. 25:26).

and Yahweh's character (see Exposition on 12:8, p. 251) and settling down. Establishing the place of worship and his camp mark the initial evidence of his response of faith to Yahweh's promise of presence and blessing, following in Abraham's footsteps (cf. 12:7, 8; 13:4, 18). It also previews a more beneficial outcome for his pagan neighbors.

In the first panel, Isaac responded to God's command with obedience (26:6), but he did not internalize the implications of Yahweh's presence and promise of blessing (v. 7). Rather, he fearfully attempted to assure his own life and prosperity through deceit. He had to learn the hard way that he could trust God for his security. Now he expressed his faith in public, loyal worship. When Abimelech appeared again, Isaac would demonstrate faith rather than fear in his response, and both Isaac and Abimelech reaped the benefit of God's promise of blessing. Further evidencing his decision to settle down and setting up the next scene, his servants dug a well.

Isaac's Confident Confrontation Brought Peace (26:26–31)

In faith Isaac confronted Abimelech's breach of covenant, graciously renewing the covenant and sending Abimelech away in peace.

26:26–29. Recalling Genesis 21:22–34 and Abimelech's covenant with Abraham, Abimelech came from Gerar with Phicol and Ahuzzath to request a covenant of peace with Isaac. Up until this point in the narrative, we have only seen Isaac in a very passive, initially deceitful and then conciliatory role. In the parallel section of the first panel, he initially lied, breaking the covenant Abraham had made with Abimelech (21:23). Then when questioned, he responded to Abimelech, tactfully expressing his fear (26:9). Otherwise, he avoided conflict. He left Gerar when asked (v. 16), then later moved rather than assert his rights for water (v. 22), even though his servants had reopened Abraham's wells, and he was the heir of Abraham's covenant and water rights. In each case he responded in deference to Abimelech, possibly as the lesser party but possibly in humility. Now his response changed, challenging Abimelech's narrative yet graciously giving peace. Rather than fear and deception, he offered honesty, fellowship, and grace.

Isaac's challenge accused Abimelech of previously hating him. The literary parallels with the previous covenant between Abraham and Abimelech add to the implication that Isaac was considering that covenant as being broken. If Isaac had broken the covenant with his deception (see 26:11 above and discussion there), he was now calling out Abimelech's subsequent breach of covenant and the relationship.

TRANSLATION ANALYSIS 26:27

The verb "hate" (שָׂנֵא) can reference everything from intense feelings of loathing for enemies (2 Sam. 13:15; Ps. 25:19) to merely wanting to avoid something (Prov. 25:17). It is the common antithesis to "love" (אָהַב), and in this context, while it could refer to an enemy (NCV, "You were my enemy"), it was more a statement of his lack of loyalty to Isaac (perhaps "you have been hostile to me," NJPS, see also NIV), choosing his detractors over Isaac and fearing his possible misuse of his wealth (Gen. 26:16), despite the previous covenant their forefathers had established. The alliance of kings with a covenant was spoken of in terms of "love" (Els, אָהַב, *NIDOTTE* 1:278, 296), and the opposite was enemies or "haters" (Els, אָהַב, *NIDOTTE* 1:285). In other words, Abimelech chose to break the covenant and send him away rather than work out the conflicts in justice. He acted more like an enemy than a covenant partner.

As formerly with Abraham, Abimelech noted God's presence with Isaac and blessing on him (vv. 28–29; cf. 21:22). The blessing that the narrator foreshadowed (25:11) and God promised (26:3, 24) and had given (v. 12) was evident to all. Instead of struggling with the ongoing opposition and conflict, Isaac had prospered (vv. 12–14). He continued to prosper so that even the greater distance between them made Abimelech concerned that Isaac could still harm them (v. 29; cf. 21:23). Abimelech's words are conciliatory, if disingenuous, and rather than address the breach of covenant, he asserts that they did not "touch" him and only did him "good," sending him away in "peace" (26:29). His focus was on Yahweh's blessing on Isaac, which carried far more weight with him than his previous concerns. Time and increasing prosperity had made it obvious that not only could he not avoid it, but he needed to be in good relations with Isaac, affirming by his intuition the promise of God that through Isaac the nations would be blessed. He had already stated, from Isaac's deception, that he recognized the curse of God on those who would "touch" Isaac, doing him harm (v. 11; cf. 12:3). We will never know what else was said, but Isaac graciously established a renewed covenant with the Philistines.

26:30–31. Isaac celebrated his covenant with Abimelech with a meal and consummated it with an oath (cf. 21:31). Both the meal and the oath were part of the covenant ceremony (cf. 31:51–54), customarily done in the ancient world in conjunction with covenants (Mendenhall and Herion, "Covenant," *ABD* 1:1194). The relationship between the two men and their communities was again formalized in "peace" (26:31).

God's Blessing Commemorated Peace (26:32–33)

Discovering water illustrated God's blessing and commemorated the covenant of peace at Beersheba.

26:32–33. That very day, the servants reported the successful discovery of water in the well being dug, framing the treaty (see 26:25). God's blessing was evident in the digging of the wells (reflecting the parallel panel in vv. 17–22), underlining the peaceful negotiations with his neighbors, not just the expansion of open space and extra resources (v. 22). Isaac was now moving toward his purpose of being a blessing. He commemorated the treaty, again renaming the well with the same name Abraham used following a similar event in the same place (cf. 21:31; 26:18).[11]

Initially, Isaac had obeyed Yahweh's command, staying in the land, but his fear, which led to his deception, caused conflict with the Philistines and endangered them before Yahweh. It ultimately led to the parting of ways and apparent dissolution of Abraham's covenant. In contrast, after Yahweh's second appearance and promise of blessing and protection, Isaac fully worshipped, responding to Abimelech in honest and gracious negotiation. The outcome was peace amid God's blessing, allowing Isaac to be a blessing to the nations near him and God's character to be proclaimed.

As preparation for the rest of the Jacob stories, this narrative provides Abraham's example of faith and obedience referenced in both of Yahweh's promises to Isaac, but also it shows the outcome of Isaac's growing faith. The reader knows what Jacob also should know (chs. 25, 27) but will have to learn. Faith and not deception leads to blessing and a fulfilling of God's purposes. Faith allows God's image to be a blessing. But God will be faithful to accomplish his promise and to lead his servant to the appropriate response of worship.

11 "Shibah" (שִׁבְעָה) uses the same consonants as the Hebrew for "oath" (שְׁבֻעָה) but is pointed as a variant of "seven" (שֶׁבַע). Seven was part of the initial covenant with Abraham (seven animals, 21:29–30), suggesting again that the previous treaty is in the background of this narrative and showing Isaac's intent to rename Abraham's wells with their original names (Sarna 1989, 188).

THEOLOGICAL FOCUS

The servant of God must respond to the presence and promise of God with faith in true worship to bring blessing and peace to his world, rather than fearfully, creating conflict and loss.

God consistently uses stressful times (like a famine) to grab our attention and redirect our focus. In this case, God used the opportunity to both remind of his promises as the basis for future decisions for living, but also to teach his representative a lesson in living by faith. God shows he is faithful to fulfill his promises. Here he will bless Isaac and keep his covenant with Abraham. In fact, as God often does, he will use weak and flawed vessels to show his glory. And he will bless and continue to work in those flawed vessels, even when they do not choose faith consistently. But Yahweh also reveals the responsibilities that follow from the choice to represent him and be his conduit of blessing.

God's struggling servant, then, will also experience the consequences of his unbelief. He will suffer, and others will suffer. Those around him who need God's blessing and whom God desires to bless will not be able to see it or feel safe to pursue it when God's servant is not walking in faith. God can still work (as he did in Abimelech's world), but the believer will not be the means to accomplish God's intended purpose until he chooses faith. The onlooker also has responsibility in recognizing God's chosen and choosing to pursue and engage God's blessing (Biddle 1990, 610).

God's promised presence with his servant does not entail a stress-free nor temptation-free environment. In fact, the very definition of faith expects that one must make decisions and live consistently with God's character and expectations without seeing ahead of time how God will accomplish his desired ends. The servant of God must fear him more than any perceived consequences of living by God's expectations (26:5). He must live out the character of God, not because it is the law, but because he is loyal to his king by faith, as Abraham and Isaac both learned.

When the servant of God falls prey to fear, he or she loses the possibility of revealing God's character and instead opens the door to conflict and subjects those nearby to the threat of cursing. The response of faith and living out God's gracious character in relationships, however, allows God's blessing to follow into his world through them. The world can then see his character and recognize the benefits of true worship. Contrary to the expectation of fear, faith and integrity can lead to peace and reconciliation, which fear, hiding, and deceit cannot produce. Fear and deceit will lead instead to conflict and loss of relationship.

God can bless (not just materially—see Introduction on "blessing," p. 60) through the obedient servant in ways that he cannot do when his servants are fearful. While the immediate outcome may not be certain, God's promise of presence and blessing secures the ultimate outcome. Isaac's greatest blessing was not the water or the flocks, herds, and servants, but God's presence. God's oversight in relationship, observed by Abimelech, establishes blessing and attracts the world to the working of God.

PREACHING AND TEACHING STRATEGIES

Exegetical and Theological Synthesis

Our exegetical analysis leads to preaching and teaching through two veins. One is watching the character of Isaac exercise his faith (or, at least, partial faith) among the Philistines. In the first part of the narrative Isaac will reveal partial faith—he obeys with respect to staying in Gerar but chooses fear over faith at the first test that threatens his life. The second vein is the commands, promises, and projections the Lord gives to Isaac. The Lord will speak to Isaac twice in this chapter; Isaac will respond twice, thankfully showing improvement in his faith the second time around.

Much of the chapter is devoted to God's people being a conduit of blessing in the world. In this case and in the first episode, Isaac potentially brings guilt upon Abimelech and his people (v. 10). That is the opposite of bringing blessing (v. 4b). It is a sad commentary when the Philistines rebuke the people of God. There is no opportunity for blessing the Philistines; instead, there is suspicion and friction (note the envy in vv. 14–15 caused by Isaac's prosperity in their land). This is a clear example of how faith and witness go together in the Christian life. As we have seen throughout Genesis, the Lord will fulfill his promises to his chosen ones. He will also command faith and obedience. Moreover, he will, inevitably, continue to create such faith and obedience in his children who, like Abraham, Isaac, and Jacob, struggle with powerful urges toward unbelief and disobedience.

Preaching Idea

It takes faith, not fear, to both receive God's blessing and be a blessing to others.

Contemporary Connections

What does it mean?

One of the first things that needs to be explained in this passage is the fact of God's people living among the Philistines, the context for being a conduit of blessing. Both Testaments teach us how to represent God among unbelievers (e.g., 1 Peter 2:12). There can never be too much repetition and restatement concerning the nature of God's promises. Promises such as "I will be with you and will bless you" sound too familiar to our listeners. They form some of those church words everyone has heard but seldom know the meaning or significance of. This sermon provides an opportunity to explain the powerful working of God in Christians, so they can perform all God gives them to do in this life, including being a blessing to others.

If it has been some time since you taught the last "lie" episode, you may want to review the cultural background and the morality that causes Isaac to fear for his life because of his beautiful wife, Rebekah. That is so foreign to us. The same goes for helping listeners learn the importance of two people making "a covenant" (vv. 28–29). It should go without saying that wells in that day and geographic locations were of utmost importance for survival (vv. 15, 18–22, 25, 32).

Is it true?

As the biblical author argues for the blessing of God on Isaac's life, our listeners need to hear us prove that this is possible for them in their circumstances. You may want to nuance this so that your listeners do not expect God to always make them rich, healthy, and favored in the world. This is especially helpful when their circumstances prove to be anything but blessing. It is important to teach our hearers that the blessing of God on his people—the power of God on them to accomplish his will in the world—always takes place in a badly broken world. Trouble does not erase the blessing of God. Much of the upcoming Joseph narrative in Genesis will show this to be true; in his case, the blessing of God looks much different, depending on whether you consider him as the purchased slave or the people's sovereign. Some listeners will need help seeing that they are conduits of God's blessing in their circle of influence. They may not realize that they represent God in their context by showing his power and character in action.

Now what?

Our listeners are learning that Isaac's trip to Gerar mirrors their own existence in the world where they are to function as God's representatives, the conduits of blessing. Whether redemptive history finds us among the Philistines, in exile, or among the nations, from the beginning God ordained that his people spread his blessing all over the globe. Those around us should see the blessing of God on our lives.

They should see attitudes and actions that are godly, often much different from what they're used to seeing. They should also see a certain kind of effective living, even if times are tough.

So much of our ability to do that depends on whether we believe and trust God. Unbelief, such as that displayed by Isaac, makes it virtually impossible for God to use us for his glory in the world. Thankfully, God allows us to see Isaac responding much better the second time in the narrative, providing a picture of the development of faith that should be taking place in all our lives. God does not give up on us when we fail but keeps working in and through us so that we represent him well in the church and in the world.

Creativity in Presentation

Genesis 26 provides another opportunity for God's people to enter a narrative where they struggle to believe the promises of God. At best, partial faith exists on the part of the main character. This is a time to help our listeners recognize their own current challenges of faith in the faithfulness of God. Our preaching idea is: It takes faith, not fear, to both receive God's blessing and be a blessing to others.

A suggested path might be:

- The condition or context of blessing includes a test of faith (vv. 1–5). This includes the famine, the command, and promises of God to Isaac.
- The threat to the blessing and being a blessing (vv. 6–22). Isaac's fear overrides his faith in God, and it ruins his opportunity to be a blessing to Abimelech. This also includes the obvious blessing of God on Isaac's life (v. 12), but the inability of Isaac to be a conduit of blessing as friction develops between him and the Philistines.
- Finally, the posture of faith and worship necessary to receive and be a blessing (vv. 23–33).

One of the ways to illustrate the concept of being a conduit for blessing is to gather reports from your congregants of how their best opportunities for witness came about, such as times when they put into practice loving their neighbor. Sadly, many of us have heard horror stories of how God's reputation was badly tarnished due to a church leader living poorly (the old, "So and so was a deacon in his church, yet he lived worse than the worse pagan. I don't need that kind of church" story).

DISCUSSION QUESTIONS

1. Discuss the difference between living the life of faith as a second- or third-generation Christian versus being the first person of faith in one's family. What are the pros and cons of each scenario? Think of verse 5 and Abraham's obedience, yet Isaac repeating the sin of his father.

2. Allow everyone to list their circle of influence among the "Philistines" in their world. Are they aware of their unique opportunities to be a conduit of God's blessing?

3. Discuss the possible connections between our greatest fears in life and the idols we are most tempted to worship.

4. How do you see God's blessing in your life as a new covenant believer?

5. How can you help the next generation (your children or disciples) to learn from your lessons of faith and imitate your victories, not just your defeats?

6. How can you help your world to see God's blessing in terms of thriving in life in his presence rather than merely physical benefits?

Genesis 26:34–28:9

EXEGETICAL IDEA

Isaac's blind and self-centered leadership in attempting to subvert God's revealed will by advancing his disqualified son, though thwarted by deception, precipitated foolish responses and unnecessary conflict leading to sin and division, before conveying the appropriate Abrahamic blessing to his divinely chosen son.

THEOLOGICAL FOCUS

Poor leadership by God's chosen leaders produces dysfunction and conflict and engenders foolish choices by those under their lead, creating greater pain, even when rectified by God's providence.

PREACHING IDEA

God's people learn from this messed-up family to lead the way to be a blessing in their world.

PREACHING POINTERS

Forty-year-old Esau's action of taking wives forms the outer rim or bookends of this preaching portion and the first potential preaching point: he continues to function as a "go and do otherwise" character who does not share values associated with the promises and blessing of God. However, Isaac, Rebekah, and Jacob quickly join Esau and show God's chosen vessels to be a complete mess. They are all poor examples! Yet, this is God's chosen family, and he will continue to work his plan through Jacob.

God will accomplish his plan, and that includes directing the affairs of those with little or no faith. Esau's father, Isaac, had spiritual sight that matched his physical sight, as he intended to bless Esau. Isaac appears to value his favorite meal more than the plan of God. And then the parade of bad examples continues in this family as Rebekah and Jacob devise a plan to secure the blessing. Jacob's only concern is that their actions might bring a curse on himself "and not a blessing" (27:12). When Isaac delivers the blessing, its contents barely resemble the blessing promised to Abraham, another sign that Isaac's faith is immature at best. If any of our congregants questioned all the fuss about this family blessing, they learn from the father and son's reaction about what just happened. Both react with extreme emotion. And the anti-blessing or curse Esau receives makes it clear: to be blessed is far better. If Esau gets his way, another Cain-like murder will occur in Genesis due to the hatred Jacob's ruse created. Despite all her scheming, Rebekah does know how important it is that the son of promise marry in such a way that the promise and blessing might continue. Imagine a God powerful enough to move his purposes along with such ungodly means!

LEADING BLIND: HUNTING FOR BLESSING (26:34–28:9)

LITERARY STRUCTURE AND THEMES

Esau's choice of wives (26:34–35; 28:6–9) marks off the literary unit, forming an *inclusio* that frames the giving of the blessing with Esau's spiritual and cultural folly. The entire section flows chiastically, centering on the giving of the blessing to Jacob (27:18–29) and the "anti-blessing" to Esau (27:30–40; Fokkelman 2004, 98):

A. Esau married Canaanites (26:34–35).
  B. Isaac spurned spiritual expectations (27:1–4).
    C. Rebekah plotted for Jacob's blessing (27:5–17).
      D. Jacob receiving the blessing (27:18–29).
      D'. Esau received an anti-blessing (27:30–40).
    C'. Rebekah plotted for Jacob's life (27:41–45).
  B'. Isaac embraced God's will (27:46–28:5).
A'. Esau married again (28:6–9).

This narrative revolves around "blessing" (used seven times as a noun [בְּרָכָה] and twenty-one times as a verb [ברך]), which will focus on leadership of the family and so the Abrahamic covenant. The section fulfills the initial intent of Yahweh's oracle to Rebekah (25:23), passing the Abrahamic covenant promise and blessing to Jacob with its leadership responsibilities. It also highlights the dysfunction in the family and the consequences of pursuing God's blessing apart from trusting God's promise or asking for his intervention.

The structure focuses attention on Isaac's failing leadership and its outcomes (Smith 2001). At the center of the chiasm, Isaac blindly not only gives the right blessing to Jacob, but also the appropriate outcomes for profane living to Esau. Isaac's blindness and appetites form the background and motivate the poor choices by all the characters, leading to pervasive conflict and threats to God's plan.

Though God is absent from the narrative, he is invoked, and his will is accomplished through the devious working of Rebekah and Jacob. None of the characters act in righteousness and justice (18:19), generating conflict, separation, and uncertainty for the outcome. Yet, God's promise remains in the forefront, with the assurance of the accomplishment of his purposes. The pursuit of blessing, the central theme, shows the working of God even through foolish and destructive means. The foolish means, however emphasize the devastating consequences of those foolish fleshly manipulations.

- ***Esau Married Canaanites (26:34–35)***
- ***Isaac Spurned Expectations (27:1–4)***
- ***Rebekah Plotted for Jacob's Blessing (27:5–17)***
- ***Jacob Received the Blessing (27:18–29)***
- ***Esau Received an Anti-blessing (27:30–40)***
- ***Rebekah Plotted for Jacob's Life (27:41–45)***
- ***Isaac Embraced God's Will (27:46–28:5)***
- ***Esau Married Again (28:6–9)***

EXPOSITION

While Isaac bears the promise of Yahweh and experiences his blessing, Esau shows he is oblivious to spiritual values and his heritage, building on his previous disregard for the birthright (25:34), by marrying the Hittite women. Isaac's attempt to bless Esau and his intended disregard for Jacob after the oracle to Rebekah are disturbing. The entire narrative seems to be contrary to expectation as the chosen mother of the patriarchs and child of promise team up in deception and intrigue in a high stakes plot to steal what God had already promised. Yet the focus on Isaac's physical senses rather than faith in his old age (in contrast to Abraham) provides important perspective for the expectations and outcomes of the intrigue. As Esau's role model, Isaac led with his appetites and relied on his failing senses rather than faith. Much anguish for both Isaac and Esau follows from their own profane choices.

The pain Rebekah and Jacob experience likewise resulted from their own folly. Both act in self-interest and without love or righteousness. So, in many ways all deserve their experience, and none deserve the blessing that God will ultimately give. The outworking will give temporary and uneasy relief as Jacob escapes Esau's revenge, but the family is fractured. Isaac's blind and self-centered leadership, attempting to subvert God's revealed will by advancing his disqualified son though thwarted by deception, precipitated foolish responses and unnecessary conflict, leading to sin and division before conveying the appropriate Abrahamic blessing to his divinely chosen son.

Esau Married Canaanites (26:34–35)

Esau spurned cultural, spiritual, and family norms, marrying Hittite women.

26:34–35. The note on Esau's age at his marriage immediately recalls Isaac's age at his marriage (25:20). Isaac could not marry a local woman (24:3), but only one at Abraham's direction, under the guidance of Yahweh, through the extended family (24:7). In contrast, Esau spurned the cultural norm of arranged or parentally sanctioned marriage (cf. 21:21; 24; 28:1; 34:4–6; 38:6; etc.), as well as the spiritual expectations of remaining separate from the Canaanites and their influences (15:16; 24:3; cf. Deut. 7:3–4) and the expectation of marrying within the extended clan (Gen. 24:4, 7; 27:46; 28:1–2; cf. Sarna 1989, 189). Rather, he chose two[1] local Hittite women.[2] The line was in danger of merging with the Canaanites. Given Esau's attitude toward the birthright (25:34), his choice is not surprising, but it is noteworthy that Isaac had not made any arrangements by the time the boys were forty, nor do we know if he raised an objection. Isaac appears completely passive, abdicating his responsibility.

Moses notes that Esau's choice "made life bitter" (26:35) for both parents. Without explanation, we only know the ongoing irritation. Esau failed to honor his parents, making what follows even more surprising.

Isaac Spurned Expectations (27:1–4)

Isaac spurned cultural and spiritual expectations, preparing to solely bless Esau.

27:1–4. The narrative focuses on Isaac's senses, frontloading his old age and failing eyesight. While chapter 26 concluded with Isaac responding to Yahweh in public worship and faith, in his old age he regressed to his senses rather than growing in faith and obedience to God's revealed will. His characterization as growing blind seems to provide a metaphor for

1 Polygamy has a clearly negative connotation, putting Esau in the same category as Lamech (4:19–24).

2 The names are different from those listed in the genealogy in 36:2–5. Mathews (2005, 416) suggests that they can be reconciled by either or both understanding more than one person with the same name or more than one name for the same person (including the possibility of a name change).

his spiritual condition as well. He would focus on his appetites rather than his responsibilities as the covenant bearer and conduit of blessing to his family and his world (vv. 3–5). Ironically, his blindness would allow others to remedy his spiritual oversights (cf. Sternberg 1987, 350), albeit by intrigue, bringing greater conflict.

Previously, Esau had despised and sold his birthright, giving away the extra portion or tangible inheritance (25:29–34). Now both Isaac and Esau assume that he can extend blessing to Esau. Rather than viewing this as a violation of Esau's previous oath or "sale" to Jacob (Ross 2008, 164), Westbrook argues that the blessing is focused on leadership or formal head of household (Westbrook 1991, 136–38) as a distinct gift, consistent with the blessing of Jacob to Judah (leadership) in 49:8 and Joseph's sons (double portion, giving one each to Ephraim and Manasseh) in 48:15–20. In Isaac's plan, then, Esau would be "lord over your brothers" (27:29), contrary to the oracle (25:23).

Though there is no record that Abraham formally blessed his sons, he was careful to pray and care for each appropriately, promoting God's choice of Isaac (17:18, 20; 21:11, 13; 25:6). Here, however, Isaac called Esau to what he billed as his deathbed blessing but which he was setting up as a blessing for Esau only. In his attempt to secretly bless only Esau, he would ironically remove blessing from Esau (27:37).

Whereas Abraham had ordered his final disposition according to the command and promises of God with foresight and planning, providing order and harmony in the family, Isaac was circumventing God's explicit plan (25:23). He ignored Esau's rejection of spiritual norms and his birthright, offering blessing to Esau with no intended instructions or blessing for Jacob (cf. 48:15–16, 20; 49:3–27). Though he was not certain of the length of his remaining life, he would make his disposition in secret (Rebekah must eavesdrop to know, and Jacob is in the dark). In contrast to Abraham's deathbed scene (24:1–9 and Jacob later, 48:15–20; 49:2–27), instead of faith pursuing God's promise, Isaac was focused on his appetites and affinity with Esau for the sort of food he loved (Wenham 1994, 215). His blessing would communicate that value (sustaining him "with grain and wine," 27:37, cf. vv. 26–29) rather than his promises and faith, dealing with survival and prosperity rather than the Abrahamic covenant promises. As Esau despised his birthright by selling it for food, Isaac also seems to sell the blessing for food, showing their kindred spirits.

Rebekah Plotted for Jacob's Blessing (27:5–17)

Rebekah plotted with Jacob to thwart Isaac and obtain the blessing.

27:5–10. While the blessing should have been a public celebration, Rebekah overheard the secretive scheming and hatched her own plot. She would take the opportunity of Esau's absence in pursuit of Isaac's appetites to intervene. She reported Isaac's words to Jacob, with a few adjustments.

Rebekah's summary of Isaac's instructions to Esau left out his reasoning (old age and uncertainty) and added the divine ground for the blessing, "before the LORD" (27:7). In leaving out his age and uncertain future, Rebekah "trivializes" his request and "underscores that he merely desires a delicacy" (Han 2015, 8). She did not seem to doubt his fragile life (v. 10), but rather focused on the connection between his palate and his pronouncement, though perhaps she suspected his vitality, since the text indicates he would live for decades (35:27–29).

Her addition, however, drew attention to the significance of the act, even though Isaac had not said it.[3] This was not just any blessing

3 In light of Rebekah's oracle and the conflict this would entail, Isaac may have been attempting to ignore or downplay the implications of his actions for himself, Esau, or both—consciously or unconsciously.

that a father might give. This blessing had implications for God's redemptive purpose for humanity, as already expressed through the Abrahamic covenant and God's oracle to Rebekah. Though the one pronouncing blessing may have his own agenda, blessing in the biblical world (and this one especially!) is only effective as an act of God, drawing even more serious attention to the act and so to the attempted circumvention of Isaac's will. If the blessing is really from God, then would the deception be effective, since presumably they would know that God was not deceived? Or are they feeling justified (after all they had the oracle, 25:23)? Or do they not really think of God's view (see discussion, 27:1–4 above)?

27:11–13. Instead of concern for God's view or his intervention, Jacob's only concern is that he be discovered and so bring upon himself a curse instead of a blessing. His view of cursing and blessing here appear more magical than biblical, assuming the discretion of the father to pronounce and the effectiveness of such a pronouncement (not necessarily the case, cf. Prov. 26:2). In his objection, however, he surfaced another issue. He was dishonoring or "mocking" his father (Gen. 27:12) in deceiving him and subjecting himself to the danger of curse rather than blessing (Deut. 5:16). Instead, his mother volunteered to accept the consequences of the deception, not realizing she would lose Jacob. Indeed, both would lose the moral high ground.

27:14–17. Rebekah, the driver behind the deception, was prepared for every contingency. She made the "delicious food, such as his father loved" (v. 14; see vv. 4, 7, 9, 14, 17). The repetition of the delicious food that Isaac loved reinforces Isaac's focus on his personal desires and appetites, rather than faith and promise. He saw only himself, not the responsibility or legacy that his role before Yahweh entailed. Rebekah knew her husband, and his blindness left him open to her deception.

Rebekah covered Jacob's smooth skin with goat's skins to deceive her husband. She used Esau's best clothes, which would be instrumental in the deception (v. 27), and she quieted Jacob's nerves, even adding bread to top off the meal. All was done quickly, as noted by Isaac (v. 20), yet just in time (v. 30).

Jacob Received the Blessing (27:18–29)

Jacob deceived Isaac, receiving the blessing.

27:18–20. Jacob's initial approach to Isaac raised Isaac's suspicions because of the speed of his return. Jacob's reply to Isaac attributed his success to Yahweh, deepening his lie, but also suggesting his broader disregard for or perhaps ignorance of Yahweh and any real fear of the Lord. For Jacob to understand his blessing and responsibility, he would need to know and fear Yahweh. Yahweh will initiate that knowledge with Jacob's dream (28:12–15), wrestling match (32:22–32), and final appearance to Jacob (35:9–13).

27:21–25. Trying to convince his aged father of his identity, Jacob reduced his initial verbosity to a single word ("I" in the Hebrew, אָנִי, v. 24) perhaps realizing Isaac was not as inept as he believed. Isaac's hearing heightened his suspicion, so he asked for the touch test. Rebekah's planning paid off when his touch failed him. He was not able to distinguish between the goat skins and Esau's hairy hands. He was convinced and would bless Jacob.[4] With one final question as to

4 The final clause that "he blessed him" does not constitute a separate blessing from what he would pronounce in vv. 27–29 but was the conclusion of the deception, so that he decided he would bless him (functioning as "telic" after not recognizing the deception, WOC, §33.3.1.a, #6). He would still ask the question (v. 24) and smell his garments (v. 27), as he was still wrestling with the incongruities, but the ruse had succeeded.

his identity, he called for the meal that he might confer the blessing. While the meal may have been a standard part of such a ritual blessing and festive occasion, it is more significant here for the character and intent of Isaac than as a symbol of fellowship, abundance, and goodness before Yahweh. His characterization continues to highlight his appetites rather than his faith.

27:26–27. Feeling and tasting nothing amiss to support his auditory suspicions, he called for one more test as he prepared to bless. His smell of Esau's clothing provided the final security that he could pronounce his chosen blessing. He equated the smell of Esau's sweat from hard work with the field that God had blessed. Believing his taste, touch, and smell over his hearing, with his eyes failing, his attempt to circumvent Yahweh and thwart his revelation to Rebekah would ironically confirm that oracle.

27:28–29. Isaac's initial blessing was for provision for his son from the best products of the ground, from grain and wine, to the needed moisture from the heavens in the form of dew that would allow for the productivity of the land during a dry season when there was little to no rainfall (cf. Deut. 33:28; 2 Sam. 1:21; 1 Kings 17:1; Zech. 8:12; where dew is prominent in blessing and its absence in cursing; cf. Frick, "Palestine, Climate of," *ABD* 5:119–26; Futato, טַל, *NIDOTTE* 2:363–64). Rather than leading with the Abrahamic covenant and promises of the land and descendants to be a blessing, God's consistent focus for the family and line of Abraham, as we might expect (cf. Gen. 12:1–3; 13:14–17; 17:2–4; 22:16–18; 26:3–4), he focused on fertility and dominion over the rest of the family, in seeming opposition to the oracle (25:23). His blessing correlates with his physical concerns at the expense of God's redemptive concerns.

Finally, specifically, the Abrahamic promise of cursing or blessing for the nations depending on their response to Abraham's descendants forms the final statement of Isaac's blessing and desire for the prosperity and supremacy of Esau. Isaac intended to give Esau the authority of Abraham's descendants over all their enemies (22:18; 24:60) and over family members promised to Jacob (25:23). Isaac's desire for Esau appears to have focused only on the tangible aspects of God's promises through Abraham, missing God's intent for his people to know and walk with him as their ultimate blessing and the resulting opportunity to bless their world. Instead, Isaac guaranteed supremacy and ongoing tangible prosperity. This impression is confirmed by Isaac's summary of his blessing to Esau later (27:37).

TRANSLATION ANALYSIS 27:29
Rather than suggesting there were other children of Rebekah, the use of "brothers" and "your mother's sons" (27:29) can commonly refer to relatives and their descendants. More specifically, it performs the legal function of declaring him the head of household (Westbrook 1991, 137–38).

Esau Received an Anti-blessing (27:30–40)

Esau pled for blessing, receiving only an anti-blessing from Isaac.

27:30–33. Jacob's exit from deceiving Isaac and receiving his blessing just evaded Esau's return from his successful hunting trip. When he brought the meal to Isaac, one can only imagine the surprise and consternation as Isaac blindly groped for words to make sense of this. His question and Esau's reply remind directly of Isaac puzzling over Jacob's ruse. This time, however, he is deeply shaken as the pieces fall into place. Even as he is voicing his question, he understands what has happened.

While there is no explanation given for the violent reaction of Isaac, his words suggest the cause. He had blessed "him" (Jacob, as he now realized), and it must happen: "Yes, and he shall be blessed" (v. 33). Isaac emphatically certified his blessing, without explanation. He had consciously or unconsciously attempted to frustrate the express will of Yahweh, and he had been thwarted. He must have known of the oracle, and perhaps his blindness finally cleared enough to see his folly of opposing Yahweh.[5] The necessary certainty of the blessing is sometimes attributed to the nature of patriarchal blessing, which cannot be rescinded.[6] However, blessing is ultimately from Yahweh, and, apart from his intent, blessing does not happen, particularly regarding his revealed will! If this was the moment when Isaac recognized that Yahweh had used Jacob's deception to accomplish his intent, it explains both his violent reaction and his emphatic statement. He corrected his rebellious plan with his subsequent blessing on Jacob (28:3–4), even though he still expressed frustration with his younger son's deceit (27:35).

TRANSLATION ANALYSIS 27:33

Isaac emphasized his conclusion, both by using the adverb גַּם, and by putting the passive participle ("blessed," 27:33) ahead of the verb in the clause. The emphasis may be better captured by more dramatic translations: "He will indeed be blessed" (NET, see also NIV, NKJV) or "now he must remain blessed" (NJPS).

27:34–38. Esau's reaction was equally violent, though for a different reason, as his later plan would indicate. The description of his reaction mirrors that of Isaac, emphasizing the similarities of Isaac and his favorite son, Esau. The apparent contrast with his earlier rejection of his birthright (25:34) reflects the impact of chapter 26 and both the prosperity and authority of being the head of the family (cf. Mathews 2005, 420). Esau will later come to terms with God's intent (33:4), but his initial reaction was murderous. His bitter cry was for blessing, which, judging from the blessing that Isaac gave, was more concerned with his individual prosperity and future dominance than with any spiritual desire for the covenantal promises and relationship with Yahweh. Unfortunately, however, Jacob did not seem to have any better motivation. It would be some time before Jacob saw the value and opportunity of walking with God.

Isaac's summary stoked the sibling rivalry, declaring "your brother came deceitfully" and took "your blessing" (27:35), leading to Esau's bitter reflection on Jacob's name. Isaac's summary of his blessing on Jacob shows that Isaac had intended to make Esau master over Jacob, making Esau lord over all relatives and providing for his sustenance, specifically threatening God's promise to Rebekah (25:23). Esau's pitiful response adds to the impression that he was profane, begging for anything, without taking any responsibility. He charged Jacob with getting ahead of him two times but failed to acknowledge his own role, despising the birthright and selling it for a bowl of stew.

5 So Kidner (1967, 167) and Ross (2008, 165). It is difficult to imagine Isaac did not know the oracle to Rebekah, especially since Jacob was her favorite and she was advocating for him. Considering chapter 26, he knew the Abrahamic covenant promises, though he does not expressly include the land and descendants until 28:3–4. Rather, he appears to have wanted to "bend the oracle" and bless Esau rather than Jacob, but he was thwarted (Fokkelman 2004, 111).

6 Hamilton (1995, 226), for example, argues from the essence of an oracle and Isaac's blessing "in Yahweh's presence" (v. 7), though Rebekah's assertion is not found in Isaac's speech. Thiselton (1974, 294) argues that there was no culturally appropriate means to reverse a blessing given appropriately, though a couple of pages later he shows that the earliest view of the OT supports God as the ultimate giver and withholder of blessing. While the motivation is not recorded and the presumed basis in Yahweh's authority is likely, his deep reaction suggests that it may be more than being fooled by Jacob and Rebekah. He may have realized his own opposition to God's direct and revealed will. He would shortly and willingly fully acknowledge Jacob as the recipient of the divine promises through Abraham (28:3–4), without further hesitation. God had willed it, and he acceded (Kidner 1967, 167).

TRANSLATION ANALYSIS 27:36
Esau used a play on words, since the root from which Jacob's name was derived, 'qv (עקב), can be used as a verb to mean "supplant" or "replace," as well as the noun "heel," which he was holding in the naming scene (25:26; see discussion there, p. 437). In view of the context, the idea of deception by extension becomes synonymous with supplanting (cf. Jer. 9:3 [4]; Carpenter and Grisanti, עקב, *NIDOTTE* 3:504–5). The ESV translates it "cheated" (cf. NCV, NIV, NLT), while others use the more direct and literal "supplanted" (NASB95; NKJV, NRSV). On the other hand, NET uses the imagery of grasping the heal to render "He has tripped me up."

The dialogue graphically portrays the conflict that Jacob's deception caused. While he obtained his blessing and accomplished the stated will of God, his (and Rebekah's) actions tore the family apart. Esau is revealed as another Cain, hating his brother, but Jacob is not walking in righteousness and justice either. It would be two decades before there was reconciliation (33:1–17), and Rebekah would disappear from the narrative without being able to carry out her plan to restore Jacob in "a few days" (or "a while," יָמִים אֲחָדִים, ESV, 27:44).

27:39–40. Isaac responded to Esau's pleading with an "anti-blessing" (Fokkelman 2004, 98). Whereas Jacob was to be sustained with the "dew of heaven and the fatness of the earth" (27:28), Isaac used the same phrases to describe Esau's deprivation "away from the fatness of the earth" and "away from the dew of heaven" (v. 39). He would live by the sword, and he would be the servant to his brother. The only respite comes as eventual relief when he would finally be able to break the yoke and gain freedom.

TRANSLATION ANALYSIS 27:39
The same phrases provide ambiguity and so differing translations. The problem is in the use of the preposition (מִן). It can be partitive, as in 27:28, denoting "some of," or it can be privative, denoting "separation from" [WOC, 213–14, §§ 11.2.11.e (1–2)]. Both passages, then, can be translated as partitive and giving the same blessing to both sons (NJPS, "See, your abode shall enjoy the fat of the earth and the dew of heaven above"; see NKJV), but the immediately preceding disclaimer from Isaac that he was not able to bless him (v. 37), the differing word order of the prepositional phrases with the verbs in verses 28 and 39, and the immediately following statement that Esau would have to live by his sword (v. 39) argue for the contrasting intent. With verse 39 intending privation as translated in the ESV (and many others), the obviously intended play on words adds to the poignancy of the "anti-blessing" describing what Esau could not have.

That this blessing was speaking of the future nations and not individually follows from the oracle to Rebekah (25:23). Historically, their home would be in Seir, or Edom (36:8, 16), which was much less fertile than Canaan, and Edom would be dominated by Israel from the time of David (2 Sam. 8:11–14) until their successful revolt from Judah under Jehoram (2 Kings 8:20–22), with ongoing conflict for long after (Obadiah, probably written at the beginning of the exile).

Ironically, in the personal realm, Jacob and his sons would bow to Esau as they repair the relationship and restore blessing and the family (Gen. 33:3). But in the international realm, Mathews (2005, 436) notes that Edom will only finally thrive under the rule of David among the nations called by Yahweh's name (Amos 9:12).

Esau's reaction to the news continues the mixed feelings from the reader. While he was clearly not deserving of the blessing due to his previous actions, the deceitful way it was stolen garners some sympathy for him. His extreme reaction here, along with his plot against Jacob, will remove what little capital he may have gained.

Rebekah Plotted for Jacob's Life (27:41–45)

Rebekah plotted with Jacob to thwart Esau's revenge.

27:41. Esau's reaction to the news and the anti-blessing put him in the category of Cain and other brother-haters. In the larger context of Genesis, humanity sports a long line of those that attempt to kill their brothers. Beginning with Cain's paradigmatic conversation with Yahweh (4:6–7), such hatred and plotting require repentance and the risk of judgment. Esau assumed he would be able to destroy Jacob soon when Isaac died, but ironically, the text indicates Isaac would live as much as eighty more years, dying long after they had reconciled (ch. 33; 35:27–29).

27:42–45. Rebekah's sources provided the plot so that she could head it off. Again, she rose to the occasion with a plan to save Jacob. Now the narrative emphasizes the conflict in the family between "her older son" and "her younger son" (v. 42) as she worked to give space to allow for resolution. She expected Esau's temper would quickly cool and she could restore calm (v. 44). Either she would not have a chance, or his anger continued. She sent Jacob to Laban in Haran, but he would never get the promised return call (v. 45). She stated her fear of losing "you both" in one day (v. 45), which may refer to Jacob and Isaac, since Esau planned to kill Jacob when Isaac died. Or perhaps she intended her two sons, assuming vengeance on Esau after he killed Jacob.

Isaac Embraced God's Will (27:46–28:5)

At Rebekah's urging, Isaac embraced God's will, blessing Jacob and sending him to find a suitable wife.

27:46. For the first time, Isaac and Rebekah are together in the narrative. In contrast to Isaac's intent to bless Esau contrary to expectations (27:1–4), Rebekah spurred Isaac to bless Jacob, consistent with cultural and spiritual norms. While she was clear in her plan for Jacob, her message to Isaac was much more diplomatic. She approached him with a common concern, drawing the reader back to the beginning of the narrative. She did not suggest her goal (save Jacob) or even the solution, but she used the bitterness caused by Esau's marriages to influence Isaac toward her plan, sending Jacob to the family back in Haran for a wife. Tying the narrative together, then, the reader remembers Esau's unfit status, now both because of his plotting to kill his brother (27:41) and also his disdain for his parents and the promise (26:34–35).

28:1–2. Isaac appears to have come to grips with the turn of events, complying with Rebekah's urging without objection, and now states a very different purpose for Jacob and his future from his earlier attempt to bless Esau. It is as if he finally recognized God's will and submitted. Calling Jacob, he gave him the unreserved Abrahamic blessing, beginning with instructions to go to "the house of Bethuel" to take a wife from one of the daughters of Laban (v. 2) rather than a Canaanite. He now reflects Abraham's concerns to remain separate from the Canaanites, contrasting his previous indifference to Esau's marriages. He will need a wife to become a company of peoples (v. 3)!

28:3–5. Isaac's blessing draws directly from the Abrahamic covenant (stated in v. 4), beginning with his invocation of "God Almighty" (El Shaddai), used previously in God's self-introduction as he expanded the covenant (17:1) and later in God's appearance to Jacob in 35:11 (cf. 43:14 and 48:3 in Jacob's reflection on God's promise). Isaac now focused on fulfilling the national and land promises to Abraham, finally acknowledging Jacob as the heir to the covenant. Isaac's blessing awaited Yahweh's ratification of Isaac's scoundrel son (28:13–15).

Esau Married Again (28:6–9)

Esau confirmed his spiritual dullness, marrying a daughter of Ishmael.

28:6–9. Esau finally realized that his marriages had been troublesome to Isaac. He did not appear to care about his mother's feelings (only Isaac is mentioned, v. 8), apparently previously oblivious to Isaac's feelings (26:35). The note that "Jacob had obeyed his father and his mother" (v. 7) directly contrasts Esau in his marriages. Esau's response was to take an additional wife, choosing a closer cousin but again revealing his spiritual insensitivity. Ishmael was not in the line of promise but something of a kindred spirit as the one not chosen. "While Esau took the point, his attempt to do the approved thing was, like most religious efforts of the natural man, superficial and ill-judged. To take a third wife, even though an Ishmaelite was better than a Hittite, was hardly the way back to blessing" (Kidner 1967, 168). Esau was understandably not the choice of God, but it remains to be seen how Jacob would be useful as that choice.

Esau's marriage accounts, framing the narrative, emphasize his unsuitability for the blessing and future of the covenant. For the larger context, God's choice of Jacob remains enigmatic. It raises the question of how to obtain and experience the promise of blessing. Jacob seems to have obtained it by trickery, yet he would experience dramatic penalties as a result (see 47:9, "few and evil . . . days," in his own words). In comparison with Abraham's faith and obedience, Jacob falls far short. Yet, God would work to redeem his choice. He would demonstrate for later sons of Abraham the benefits of faith rather than fleshly pursuits, as well as his faithfulness to his covenant promises to Abraham despite the unworthy actions of all involved.

THEOLOGICAL FOCUS

Poor leadership by God's chosen leaders produces dysfunction and conflict and engenders foolish choices by those under their lead, creating greater pain, even when rectified by God's providence.

Though absent from the narrative, God works faithfully behind the scenes to guarantee his purpose and promises in the face of human disinterest and attempts to thwart him and selfish pursuits. He rests sovereignly behind the scenes as the only character to be trusted for righteousness and justice. He will not be frustrated. Though the characters will not immediately recognize their responsibility to and benefit from living by faith, he will deal graciously and appropriately with all. Though God does not require faith and faithfulness to accomplish his purposes, human attempts to frustrate them or even to bring them about through deceit and scheming incur pain, conflict, and frustration.

God, however, continues to bestow his favor, which is clearly not the result of human merit (cf. Mathews 2005, 422). Rather, his grace is the ultimate ground of his eternal plan of redemption. He does not choose based on past performance and will even work with people who will still act in dishonorable ways. He does, however, pass over the one who despises the promise.

He also allows consequences for ignoring his will, attempting to subvert his will, and even attempting to accomplish his will apart from his righteousness. Human folly, deception, and pursuit of one's flesh cause damage and conflict and cannot always be remediated. God's grace will still prevail, while humanity experiences loss.

In God's world, blessing cannot really be stolen or sold—it is a gift of God by faith. Humanity has no ability to influence God's blessing. It cannot be controlled, manipulated, or purchased (cf. Sailhamer 1990, 193). It is much more significant than merely prosperity or power, as we have seen already, and leads to the accomplishment of God's redemptive purposes. As God's enabling to accomplish his plan (see Introduction, p. 60), blessing is grounded in relationship with God and found in walking with him. Conspicuous in its absence in this narrative, that relationship, or disregard for it, provides the reason for the struggle both in bestowing and in receiving blessing. Yahweh will confront Jacob with this lesson during his escape from the land (28:10–17).

Abdication of godly and faithful leadership for personal gain or fleshly pursuits instigates conflict and attempts to remediate the inappropriate outcomes that only intensify the pain and frustration. Since blessing cannot be sold or given illegitimately as it is only finally validated by God as the giver, fighting against God's desires will only bring greater pain and damage. Spiritual blessing and fulfillment of God's promise, then, can only come from God and may run counter to one's own insight, expectations, or physical senses. "Reliance on the senses to discern spiritual choices not only proves fallible but can also foul up one's life unduly" (Ross 2008, 166).

Apart from blessing, "Isaac pronounces over Esau the appropriate destiny of the 'profane person': the freedom to live unblessed (39) and untamed (40)" (Kidner 1967, 168). Of course, the end of freedom from submission and rejection of God's ways will be pain and conflict. Weeping cannot reverse it, and opposition to God's choice can only open the rebellious one up to God's cursing. Restoration to blessing can only come through restoration to God and his chosen instrument of blessing (ch. 33). Of course, that instrument of blessing is Christ and his followers have opportunity to mediate that blessing, which offers thriving in life with God, both in this world and the next.

PREACHING AND TEACHING STRATEGIES

Exegetical and Theological Synthesis

These ancient scenes from Israel's history convey theology through real characters, and I mean "characters" in a pejorative sense. In order of appearance, like in modern movie credits, Esau, Isaac, Rebekah, and Jacob all display signs of spiritual shallowness, at best. In Esau's case, it's worse. Our sovereign God can work his plan to perfection with imperfect characters; it has always been that way from day one.

Our listeners continue to evaluate their own spiritual sensitivities through the lens of these characters. For instance, the observation about the literary structure teaches us that we cannot be like Esau. God receives glory in the world as his people clearly separate themselves from idol worship. The characterization of Isaac shows a man in need of spiritual growth ("he could not see" in 27:1 and "delicious food, such as I love" in 27:4). Left alone, he intends to bless the boy who already despised the birthright for food. As noted above, the actions of Rebekah and Jacob continue to display fallen humanity among the people of God even though, in a sense, Isaac's poor spiritual eyesight created this mess. And yet, God in his grace and power will continue to make sure his covenant promises come true for a people he will transform.

Along the way, we invite our listeners into this narrative. We offer them an opportunity to confirm that their attitudes toward the promises of God are different from these characters. They can confirm their faith and righteousness in their circumstances and vow to live to the glory of God. Those with a sphere of influence will allow others to thrive, instead of creating the kind of chaos Isaac did in his family.

Preaching Idea

God's people learn from this messed-up family to lead the way to be a blessing in their world.

Contemporary Connections

What does it mean?

The narrator assumes we know the significance of placing marriage-to-foreigner scenes at the beginning and end of the pericope. We now know that Esau's decision to marry like that confirms his unfitness to be the blessing-bearer.

The same is true near the end of chapter 28 where Esau expresses his hatred for his brother, including the intent to murder him, just like Cain did.

It is near impossible for us postmodern westerners to understand anything about the importance of the blessing being passed down in a family. This blessing from Isaac, however, has a special place in redemptive history because it is connected to the promises of God throughout Scripture, from the promise of a descendant to crush the snake and culminating with the Son of David and the new covenant. From the start, this blessing was attached to a certain kind of person that God creates to represent him and become a conduit for that blessing to others. Our listeners may be puzzled by Esau's question and Isaac's answer: "Have you but one blessing, my father?" (27:38), followed by what amounts to an anti-blessing. God is the one in charge of this blessing (empowering his people to accomplish his purpose through relationship with God).

Is it true?

Our listeners do need to know how important biblical separation from the world is. That's the reason why Esau's action of taking wives from the Hittites, for instance, begins the narrative. Twice the narrator tells us that these wives made life miserable for Rebekah. Could those women really have been such a pain? It is true that idol worshippers threaten the very shalom of God in his world.

Like what we wrote above, this blessing within Isaac's family was a huge deal to God. Jacob realizes it, even if his motives are not as godly as they will be later. God's reputation is on the line as he entrusts his people with his plan. Sadly, Isaac's poor example shows how important it is for all of God's people to live a life of faith in their context. We have the privilege of helping others experience the blessing of God, but to do that we must walk with God ourselves. And, if anyone wondered whether it was true that God could carry out his perfect plan with grossly imperfect people, the answer of this narrative is a resounding, "Yes!"

Now what?

I always want to yell out the answer, "Yes. Of course this narrative is relevant!" Here's how. Every Sunday people gather, and by their attendance, they place themselves in the situation of being addressed as God's people. That posture also assumes that they are not like Esau in the story. So, what we have before us are some Isaacs, Rebekahs, and Jacobs. They have some spiritual sensitivities about them—they love God and neighbor—but they struggle with their carnality. Sound familiar? Sounds like me. But they cannot stay like those characters and experience and extend the blessing of God around them. So, we urge our listeners to learn from the negative examples. Many exert some leadership influence in their families, church, and business. They need to be reminded of the opportunities they have to extend the blessing of God through their own walk with God. The narrative has shown them what kind of damage someone like Isaac can create.

Creativity in Presentation

One of the best things you could do for your listeners is help them see the huge mess this family is in. If nothing else, many of us will take comfort in the fact that God is working his plan amid all this; he does not discard Jacob, for instance, for his part in Rebekah's scheme. It cannot turn us into "Are we to continue in sin that grace may abound" (Rom. 6:1) kind of people. But it can turn us into a people who express their gratitude for God's incredible mercy. So, do not minimize the spiritual disfunction in this holy family.

The preaching idea captures this: God's people learn from this messed up family to trust and obey him to be a blessing to the world. In keeping with the narrative:

- You could arrange the sermon in terms of each major character's part in the storyline. Each of them has their spiritual flaws, some worse than others. Allow your listeners to commit themselves to trusting God better in their circumstances.

- The second major part of the message could surround the concept of the blessing and anti-blessing. If you are preaching a series in Genesis, this will be familiar by now but still needs to be stated clearly lest it become too familiar. Everyone in the house of God should choose blessing over anti-blessing, "fatness" over "away from fatness" (27:28, 39).

- Finally, as noted above, I recommend the final minutes be devoted to our wonderful, sovereign God who continues to work out his perfect plan with imperfect people. However, while God will work his plan, his plan also involves showing his people that there are consequences to our unspiritual thinking and acting. God's holy family is anything but holy in this narrative and will suffer severe consequences in their harmony. Part of our faith means avoiding this kind of chaotic, immature faith that destroys rather than blesses. Worship occurs as people gladly submit to his molding process and become better equipped as blessing bearers in his world. And, by the way, any Esaus in the house have a wonderful opportunity to receive the blessing instead of anti-blessing.

DISCUSSION QUESTIONS

1. What was the major problem with God's people intermarrying? Why was that so destructive to God's plan?

2. Since the author of Genesis expects his readers to read carefully, discuss some of the ways the story is crafted to describe the spiritual condition of the characters.

3. How does our working definition of "blessing" compare with what we are seeing the sons want in this passage? How does that inform our typical desire for blessing?

4. How does "cursing" in Genesis contrast with this idea of "blessing?"

5. Where might you need to trust God more or live in obedience more fully so that you leave a legacy of leading others to walk with God, not struggle in their faith?

6. What in your life might blind you to God's best purposes and direction in your life?

Genesis 28:10–22

EXEGETICAL IDEA

Appearing to Jacob as he fled, God granted him the Abrahamic promises of the land, innumerable offspring, and blessing to all people, with necessary personal protection and provision, prompting Jacob to consecrate the place as a worship center with vows of personal devotion.

THEOLOGICAL FOCUS

Never out of God's purview nor separated from his promises, God's people must recognize their role through committed devotion for his glory.

PREACHING IDEA

The dream of God's powerful presence comes true as we awake to worship him.

PREACHING POINTERS

Once again, the original audience hears theology through the adventures of Jacob. He is now the carrier of the promises of God and is on his way to secure a wife (see 27:46b–28:2). On this trip Jacob encounters the Lord in a spectacular dream. In that dream the original audience and our audiences experience their own review of God's promises to his people. One of the most comforting and stabilizing of all the promises of God is found in verse 15, "Behold, I am with you and will keep you wherever you go." Each generation of God's children hears him speak to them and has an opportunity to affirm that they believe God's promise. In this way God's people on earth are always at that "awesome . . . place" and "house of God" and "gate of heaven" (v. 17). Christians have been and continue to be encouraged by Jacob's dream throughout their own faith journeys. Early and later readers follow Jacob's example and respond to God's promises with their own: "then the Lord shall be my God. . . . And of all that you give me I will give a full tenth to you" (vv. 21–22).

JACOB'S DREAM: AWED BY GOD (28:10–22)

LITERARY STRUCTURE AND THEMES

As we consistently see in Genesis, the structure is carefully crafted and complex. Here it flows in two parallel scenes (28:10–15; 16–22), each including Jacob's immediate perception of the place and his activity with the stones (vv. 10–12; 16–19)[1] followed by promise or vow (God addressed Jacob in a dream, vv. 13–15, and Jacob responded to God's promise, vv. 20–22).[2] The parallels highlight the direct response of Jacob to the theophany, both in his actions and in his vow.

I. God startled Jacob with his presence and promise (28:10–15).
   A. God interrupted Jacob's random stop (28:10–12).
   B. God revealed his presence and promise (28:13–15).

II. Jacob worshipped in awe (28:16–22).
   A. Jacob awoke in awe (28:16–19).
   B. Jacob vowed devoted worship (28:20–22).

At the same time, however, other repetitions of terms and themes tie the whole narrative together in chiastic structures centered on God's covenant promises to Jacob and Jacob's response. These chiastic structures emphasize the core of Yahweh's promise in the ongoing covenant and purpose of Yahweh, while Jacob's focus was on his personal provision and protection, overlooking the covenant promises and implications for him but promising worship in return. Jacob initially responded appropriately with fear and worship (though with likely mixed motives), promising future loyalty. This vow, obligating his return and worship (and requiring reminders, 31:3, 12–13; 35:1), leads the reader to the climax with theophany, renewed promise, changing character, and his worship in Genesis 35:1–15.

The overall chiasm focuses the reader on the Abrahamic covenant promises. The final chiasm in Jacob's vow shows his attention to the implications of the promises for his personal necessities and security, passing over the long-range covenant promises (see Exposition, p. 481). The structure is adapted from Terino (1988, 52–55).

1. Randomly stopping for the night on his way toward Haran, Jacob took random stones and laid down (28:10–11).
   2. Jacob dreamed of a stairway to heaven with angels of God (28:12).
      3. In his dream, Yahweh identified himself (28:13a–c).
         4. Yahweh promised the *land* to Jacob (28:13dα).
            5. Yahweh promised the land to Jacob and to his descendants (28:13dβ).

1 Fokkelman (2004, 71) documented six parallel terms between vv. 11–12 and vv. 16–19, including the "place" (מָקוֹם, used 3x in verse 11 and repeated 3x in vv. 16–19). The verb "take" (לקח, vv. 11, 18), "stone" (אֶבֶן, vv. 11, 18), "put" (שִׂים, vv. 11, 18), "at its head" / "top" (רֹאשׁ ,מְרַאֲשֹׁות, vv. 11, 12, 18), and forms of "stand" (מַצֵּבָה ,נצב, vv. 12, [13], 18) are all repeated in the same order. See exposition at v. 18, p. 480.

2 Again, key terms show the parallels between Yahweh's promise and Jacob's vow, including Yahweh's immediate promises to be "with" him (עִם, v. 15; עִמָּד, v. 20) and "keep" him (שׁמר, vv. 15, 20) in the way he was going (הלך, vv. 15, 20) and that he would return (שׁוּב, vv. 15, 21). See the exposition at vv. 20–21, p. 481, for some implications.

6. Yahweh promised innumerable descendants spreading through the land (28:14a–b).
5' Yahweh promised blessing for all the families of the earth in Jacob and in his descendants (28:14c).
4' Yahweh promised to bring Jacob back to the land (28:15).
3' Jacob acknowledged the presence of Yahweh in that place (28:16).
2' Jacob identified the place as the house of God, the gateway of heaven (28:17).
1' Jacob rose early and dedicated a standing stone for the holy place, "Bethel" (28:18–19).
4" Jacob's vow was based on God's promise of protection and provision (28:20–21).
a. "If God will be with me" (28:20a–b).
b. "in this way that I go" (28:20c–d).
c. "and will give me bread to eat and clothing to wear" (28:20e).
b' "so that I come again to my father's house in peace" (28:21a).
a' "then the LORD shall be my God" (28:21b).
1" Jacob promised his personal worship at his newly consecrated shrine (28:22).

- ***God Startled Jacob with His Presence and Promise (28:10–15)***
- ***Jacob Worshipped in Awe (28:16–22)***

EXPOSITION

Genesis 28:10–22 forms the transition from the Jacob-Esau conflict to the Jacob-Laban conflict and sets the parameters for the rest of the Jacob narratives. Within the land, Jacob struggled with Esau for the blessing. God interrupted Jacob's flight with confirmation of the blessing offered by Isaac (28:3–4). His promises mirror his promises to Abraham (especially 12:1–3 and 13:14–17). More to Jacob's concerns, Yahweh assured Jacob of his presence and protection, which will underlie the following narratives and provide a means to evaluate Jacob's actions and responses to the coming challenges. He would now have the promise fully and directly from Yahweh but would be out of the land, struggling with Laban, and under threat when he might return. When he did return, he again encountered angels and God, and he finally clung to God for blessing (ch. 32) before he encountered Esau and recognized that God had been at work (ch. 33).

This narrative, then, sets the stage for all that will follow, providing the benchmark from which to evaluate Jacob's reactions and measure his growth in faith. God's intervention secured Jacob's future and required Jacob's response and growth to warrant God's work through him. Jacob's initial reaction would require Jacob's follow-through and would ground his responsibility for God's further action. Appearing to Jacob as he fled, God granted him the Abrahamic promises of the land, innumerable offspring, and blessing to all people, with necessary personal protection and provision, prompting Jacob to consecrate the place as a worship center with vows of personal devotion.

God Startled Jacob with His Presence and Promise (28:10–15)

On Jacob's flight to Haran, at a random stop for the night, Yahweh revealed his presence in a dream, granting to him the Abrahamic promises of the land, uncountable offspring, and blessing through him to all families of the earth, with necessary personal provision and protection.

The unit flows in two sections, introducing the account with Jacob's flight to Haran and randomly stopping for the night when he ran out of daylight, fell asleep, and encountered God in a dream (vv. 10–12). In his dream, Yahweh gave Jacob the assurance of his presence and the Abrahamic promises (vv. 13–15), which Isaac had asked him (as El Shaddai) to give him (v. 3). The complex structure focuses on the Abrahamic promises and the implications for Jacob. The structure emphasizes, as we will see below, that Jacob's fear and worship are directly

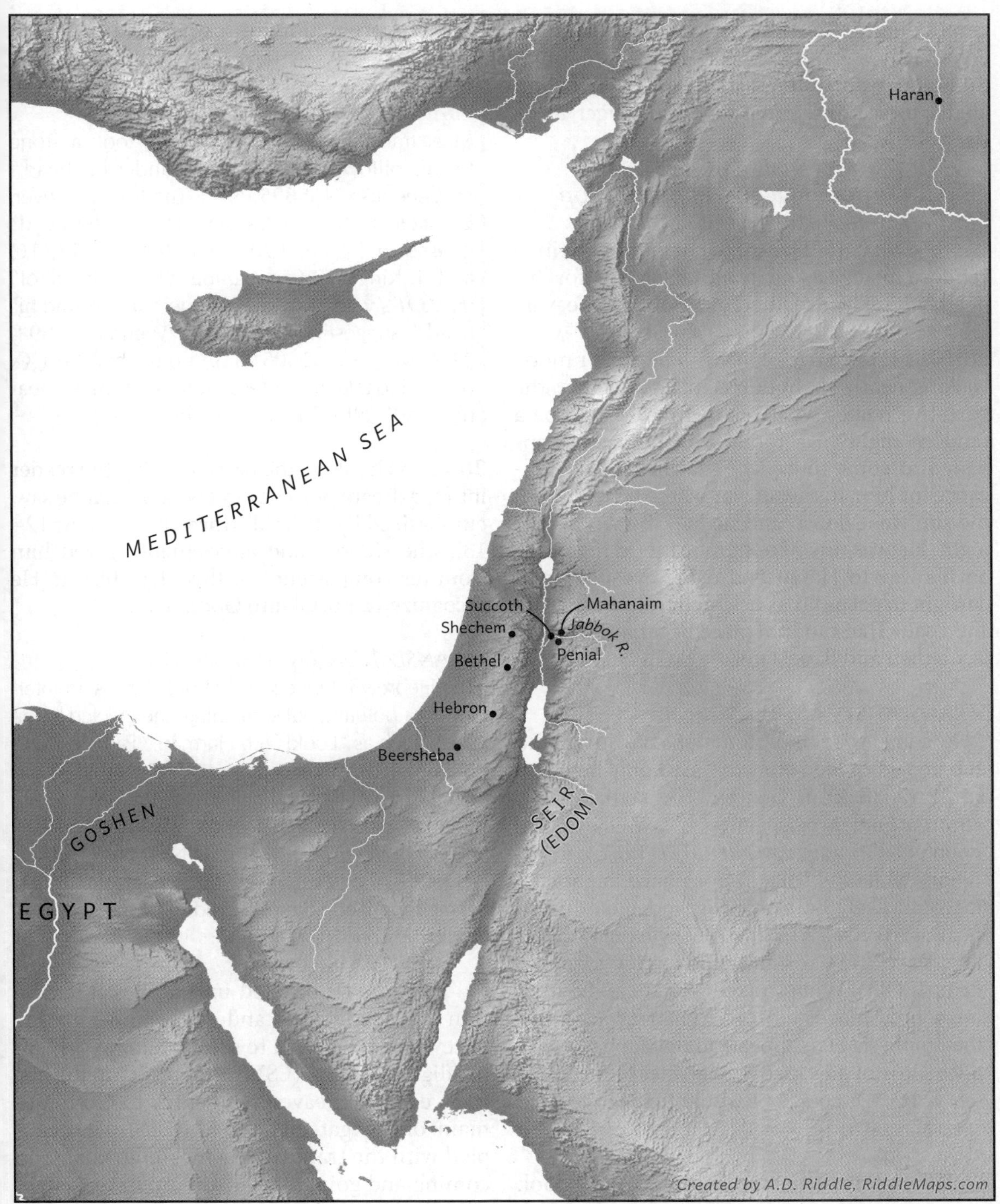

Map of Journeys of Jacob. By A.D. Riddle, used by permission

responding to Yahweh's revelation, though Jacob's focus was not the heart of God's message. Sometimes our immediate needs override our ability to see an eternal, or even longer term, perspective!

God Interrupted Jacob's Random Stop (28:10–12)

On his way to Haran, Jacob stopped in a random place, using random stones for his head, where he dreamed of a portal to heaven.

28:10–11. On a trip of nearly a month or more, walking nearly six hundred miles to Haran, the narrative relates what seemed to Jacob to be a random night in a random place. Jacob happened to come to a place that held no significance for him. Rather, it was where he was when the sun went down, and he had to stop for the night. He was nowhere significant (in his view), on his way to Haran and using every hour of daylight to get as far as he could from Beersheba and Esau. That random place became critical to Jacob then and Israel later.

> *TRANSLATION ANALYSIS 28:11a*
> "He came" does not communicate in English the impact of the verb (פגע), used only here and in 32:1 (HB 2) in Genesis. The verb suggests "from a human perspective, . . . a chance encounter" (Grisanti, פָּגַע, *NIDOTTE* 3:575). In addition, while the "place" does have the article, it would likely be a "specific indefinite identification" (WOC, §13.2b, 236), yielding "a certain place" (ESV) or any "good place to set up camp" (NLT). While "place" (מָקוֹם) can be used for a holy place (*HALOT* s.v. "מָקוֹם" 627, 6.), the emphasis here appears to be Jacob's lack of awareness of any special character to the place (cf. v. 16). Of course, it would turn out to be a special, holy place.

When forced to stop by nightfall, he took from the stones of the place for his head. Perhaps using the stone(s) as a support or better, as protection for his head, he lay down to sleep.

> *TRANSLATION ANALYSIS 28:11b*
> Most translations assume that he took a stone for his pillow (e.g., "he put it under his head," ESV, see also NASB95, NIV). The text, however, is not clear. The term translated "under his head" is used in 1 Sam. 19:13, 16; 26:7, 11–12, 16, and 1 Kings 19:6, meaning "at the head of" (*HALOT* s.v. "מְרַאֲשׁוֹת" 631) or perhaps "round his head," suggesting protection (Wenham 1994, 221). Mathews (2005, 449) notes that the LXX seemed to take this interpretation, so then, "near his head" (NET) or "at his head" (NKJV).

28:12. As he slept, the narrator takes the reader into the dream of Jacob, and we see what he saw, emphasized by "behold" (three times in vv. 12–13). The wonder and amazement moved him from his complacency in this place to fear. He recognized a portal into God's realm.

> *TRANSLATION ANALYSIS 28:12a*
> The Hebrew interjection "behold" (הִנֵּה) is an interruption, pointing out something unexpected being seen, such as "Look!" (cf. Harman, "Particles," *NIDOTTE* 4:1032; Vetter, הִנֵּה, *TLOT* 379–80;). It is difficult to translate into English with the same sense, so it is typically either "behold" (ESV, NASB2020, NKJV) or simply left out (e.g., NET, NIV). The interjection, however, gives the impact of surprise, something like, "there, a ladder! oh, angels! and look, the Lord Himself!" (Ross 1985a, 228).

Jacob had stumbled into a busy intersection between heaven and earth. In his dream, his eyes were opened to see a "stairway" (NIV) or "flight of steps" (ESV, note) bridging the gap from earth to heaven. The entry to God's domain, or the "gate of heaven" (v. 17), was occupied with the traffic of the messengers of God coming and going. Jacob's dream is consistent with the perception that the work of the angels or messengers was patrolling of the earth (cf.

Job 1:6; 2:1; Zech. 1:8–17), carrying out God's bidding (Gen. 19:1–22; 24:7, 40; Ps. 103:20), and reporting on their work (cf. Gen. 18:21). Here, the angels are revealed as a show of force since nothing else is stated about them. This vision, along with Yahweh's promise (28:15), provided a visual aid to back up Yahweh's promise, indicating security for Jacob (cf. Exod. 23:20; 32:34; 33:2; Pss. 34:8; 91:11) and encouragement, at least when he realized the implications (Gen. 31:7; 48:16).[3] Of course, he (and all subsequent readers) needed to realize that God's presence was not limited to a specific place, but God is always present and at work, though we seldom see him.

TRANSLATION ANALYSIS 28:12b

The Hebrew term traditionally translated "ladder" (סֻלָּם, cf. ESV text, NASB95, NKJV) appears only here in the Hebrew Bible. The cognate term in Akkadian, *simmiltu* with metathesis of the consonants (Moscati 1964, 63), indicates a "ladder, stair," can refer to a stairway in a house or temple, and is used of the "stairs of heaven" leading to heaven's door (*CAD* S:273–74). *HALOT* suggests "stepped ramp, flight of steps" (s.v. "סֻלָּם" 757–58), and so, "stairway" (NET, NIV, NLT).

God Revealed His Presence and Promises (28:13–15)

In Jacob's dream, God revealed his presence, granting Jacob the Abrahamic promises of the land and uncountable offspring to bring blessing to all families, implying his protection and provision to accomplish it.

28:13. "And look, Yahweh himself!" (author's translation) The dream now moves from the visual impression and the portal to God's revelation to Jacob. Yahweh was standing over the stairway, preparing to address Jacob. He identified himself as the God of Abraham and Isaac, reminding Jacob of Isaac's blessing and his passing on the "blessing of Abraham" (28:3–4). Yahweh's words to Jacob mirror his promise to Abraham near this spot (13:15–17; cf. 13:3). Whereas Abraham had looked in all directions with the promise that "all the land that you see I will give to you and to your offspring forever" (13:15), now for Isaac the same promise is made that the "land on which you lie" would be given to him and his offspring (28:13). Of course, as Jacob was leaving the land of promise with a death threat behind, this was a crucial moment, guaranteeing a future for him back in the land with children from the wife that he had yet to find. God was directly affirming what Isaac had asked for in asking God to give Jacob the blessing of Abraham (v. 4).

TRANSLATION ANALYSIS 28:13

Translations vary on whether Yahweh was standing "above it" (ESV, NASB95, NIV) or "beside him" (ESV note, NJPS, NRSV). The prepositional phrase can support either translation (or even "beside it"). Grammatically, the stairway is the nearest antecedent to the pronoun, and the imagery is still being seen through the eyes of Jacob. To refer to Jacob in the third person here would break the flow. In addition, heaven is God's realm, and so he is expected there; the parallels with Jacob's actions, anointing the top of the stone in verse 18, and the idea of the angels reporting back to Yahweh all support the traditional translation, "over it" (Ross 1985a, 236, n. 21; Wenham 1994, 222). Either way, Yahweh is not distant, speaking directly to Jacob.

28:14. Continuing the echo from God's promise to Abraham, Isaac's seed would be like the dust of the earth (which he was lying in, 13:16).

3 While the comparison has been often made with the ziggurat of ancient Mesopotamia, the ziggurat was not for the angels, but for the gods to come down for worship (Walton 2009a, 106), and here, the "stairway" does not provide communication between God and humanity (Sarna 1989, 198). Rather, it shows the presence of the holy, and God spoke directly.

While Abraham had been instructed to look in all directions of the compass (13:14), Isaac's seed would spread in all directions of the compass. That spread was intended to accomplish the covenant purpose to bless all the families of the earth through his descendants, now quoting most closely Genesis 12:3 (cf. 18:17; 22:18).

Yahweh, then, extended the full promise of Abraham to Jacob, including the possession of the land and fruitful progeny, leading to blessing for all peoples. Using the wording of his initial promissory statements to Abraham (12:1–3; 13:15–17) suggests a similar expectation for Jacob's response (follow in faith as Abraham did, 15:6) and for God's protection and shaping of Jacob through what will follow (e.g., 12:10–20; 20:1–18; and the general testing of Abraham, leading to the final test in ch. 22). While Jacob is starting with greater privilege from his heritage, the narrative has revealed a deeper deficit in his character.

28:15. What was clear by implication, both from the vision and the promise, Yahweh now specified. He would maintain his presence with Jacob and assure the promises. Jacob would return safely to the land with a clear title and innumerable descendants, bringing blessing to all families. As with the promises to Abraham, it would be considerable time (twenty years) before he would return (31:38) and realize peace with his brother (ch. 33). He would have many children, but that would also include barrenness (30:1–2) and necessitate God's clear working to provide the children (29:31; 30:17, 22). In the process, Jacob would have to learn to trust God instead of his own plots and cling to God for blessing instead of trying to wrest it for himself (32:26).

It appears surprising that God has not censured Jacob's intrigue and deception up to this point, though perhaps Jacob was conscious of the tension in his reaction of fear to the dream (28:16–19). What he had been attempting to ensure by deception and ruthless manipulation, God gave freely. When he would begin to realize his inability to assure his own prosperity, God would provide, protect, and direct him (31:4–13, 42). Jacob would have to learn in the school of hard knocks, however. God's presence, as Israel would learn in their wilderness wandering, brought discipline when needed to rehabilitate a less-than-righteous character to accomplish his purpose (Deut. 8:5–6).

To do all that he promised would include the covenant promises, and not merely the immediate needs of survival and return, even in peace. God's promise that he would not leave until such a time as they are completed, then (Gen. 28:25), cannot mean God would leave when Jacob returned, nor even at some later undefined point. Rather, it is an unreserved promise of God's presence for Jacob, since the blessing cannot be completed until many generations in the future, eventually leading to Christ. It was a promise that God would fully accomplish his plan, but if Jacob had understood the character of God and the purpose promised, he would also have understood the necessary building of his character to accomplish the purpose of Yahweh.

Jacob Worshipped in Awe (28:16–22)

Jacob recognized the fearful presence of Yahweh in that unassuming place, indicating a gateway to heaven, which he consecrated the next morning, vowing his devotion when God fulfilled his promises.

Jacob immediately responded in fear, recognizing the encounter with the divine in what he had thought was a random place (vv. 16–17), dedicating a shrine the next morning (vv. 18–19). With his dedication, Jacob vowed his worship when Yahweh fulfilled his promise (vv. 20–22). Again chiastic, Jacob's vow directly responded only to God's promise of presence and protection (v. 15):

1. "If God will be with me" (28:20a–b)
   2. "in this way that I go" (28:20c–d)
      3. "and will give me bread to eat and clothing to wear" (28:20e)

2' "so that I come again to my father's house in peace" (28:21a)
1' "then the LORD shall be my God" (28:21b)

Jacob appears to be solely concerned with his immediate welfare, passing over the covenant promises for his more pressing concerns (vv. 13–14). The final verse will return to his immediate surroundings and the impression of the presence of God in what he had thought was a nowhere place, resuming the themes of verses 10–11 and 18–19 in his actual promise of worship to Yahweh.

Jacob Awoke in Awe (28:16–19)
Waking, Jacob recognized the fearful presence of Yahweh in this holy gateway to heaven, which he consecrated the next morning as a worship center.

Jacob's reaction here follows in two stages, with the immediate verbal description by Jacob as he awoke in a fright (vv. 16–17) and his dedication of the place when he arose the next morning (vv. 18–19). All is preparatory to his vow, recognizing the work and promise of God in a memorial that Jacob promised to enshrine with his gifts when God brought him back safely (v. 22).

28:16. When he awoke, he immediately recognized the dissonance between his perceptions and God's revelation (v. 16), prompting his reaction of fear as the reality penetrated his thinking (v. 17). The discord between Jacob's new insight based on his dream and his previous perception (or lack thereof) that this was a random and unmarked place (v. 11) reveals the difficulty of seeing the working of God in this world for God's limited images. Apart from God's intervention and revelation, humankind has no access to the spiritual world and no means to perceive God's activity. Jacob's observation underlines the necessity of revelation, which God was providing, and faith, which was Jacob's necessary and required response. It also suggests the ongoing challenge of faith, since the ongoing activity of God is no more visible than Jacob had experienced the night before, but no less real than the promise declared for his life moving forward.

28:17. The realization of God's presence produces fear when the holy intersects with the unholy. God's people must realize that there is very real danger for the unholy in the presence of a holy God (Exod. 32:33–34; 33:3). Jacob expressed his fear, the natural and necessary response to his encounter, connecting it with the geographical place. While his reaction was appropriate, it may reflect another misunderstanding that he had merely stumbled upon a sacred place and that the revelation was more concerned with the place than God's purpose for him.

Instead, the flow of Genesis shows that the place is incidental to the working of God in arresting Jacob's attention and transferring the promise and God's purposes to the chosen instrument. The timing and place were significant because Jacob was leaving the land. God reflected his ongoing plan to choose and use his people for his redemptive work. As he moved his choice to the next generation, he would make it clear that Jacob's absence from the land was not an absence from God's presence or promise.

It is not merely giving an etiology for the naming of a sacred place, then. Jacob recognized the presence of God and expressed it as his culture would expect. He commemorated the event as God's place, God's house, and so it would be Bethel ("house of God," 28:19; see also v. 17). He had seen heaven opened and the presence of God's messengers doing God's bidding, so this must be a portal or gateway to heaven. More to the point, however, God was revealing his presence and protection to Jacob and for Jacob in his travels, not just in this place (his stated goal, v. 15). God's revelation was not intended to establish a cultic site but to found Jacob's future and to continue the promise of a representative nation to channel his blessing to his world (vv. 13–14).

28:18–19. Jacob, when he rose the next morning, formalized his response, both with a monument (vv. 18–19) and a vow for future service (vv. 20–22). Jacob was not wrong to consecrate a new shrine and declare his (potential!) worship of Yahweh here. Where Abram had built altars (12:7, 8; 13:18) and called on the name of the Lord (12:8) in response to the promises, Jacob dedicated a shrine symbolized by the standing stone and made his vow. His response, however, falls short of Abraham's clear and public identification with Yahweh.

The wording of these verses draws attention directly back to the dream he had witnessed. Where the "place" (מָקוֹם) was emphasized (used three times) in verse 11, "place" is repeated three times in verses 16–19. The verb "take" (לקח), "stone" (אֶבֶן), "put" (שׂים), "at its head" / "top" (ראשׁ, מְרַאֲשֹׁות), and forms of "stand" (נצב, מַצֵּבָה) are repeated in the same order in verses 11–13 and verses 18–19, showing their connection (Fokkelman 2004, 71). The narrative shows that Jacob's actions mirror the dream and appropriately commemorate what he saw. The standing stone or "pillar" (מַצֵּבָה) commemorated the intersection of earth and heaven, with his pouring of oil on the top,[4] consecrating the stone as symbolically recognizing the holy place of God (Fokkelman 2004, 72–74).

TRANSLATION ANALYSIS 28:18

The "sacred stone" (NET) or "pillar" (ESV, מַצֵּבָה), was later forbidden (Lev. 26:1; Deut. 16:22) for Israel, and they were to destroy those they found in the land because of their connection to Canaanite idolatry (Exod. 23:24; 24:13; Deut. 7:5; 12:3). Here, however, there had not yet been a prohibition, and it did not represent idolatry but God's intersection with Jacob's life. It did not symbolize a deity but the place (Gen. 28:17, 19). The place is "Bethel" (v. 19), yet the stone is "Bethel" (v. 22), standing for the whole place by metonymy. Other pillars were also used to commemorate events appropriately without the censure of pagan worship (31:45, 51–52; 35:20; Exod. 24:4).

The repetition of "place" (three times in v. 11 and three times in vv. 16–19) culminates with the naming of the "place" Bethel (v. 19). What had been a random place of no account or interest to Jacob except to find a brief refuge in sleep from his flight to Haran he now recognized as significant for God's presence, the "house of God" (vv. 17, 19, 22). It would be commemorated as a worship center (35:7; Judg. 20:18, 26; 1 Sam. 7:16; 10:3) and even later as a false center of worship to Yahweh (1 Kings 12:29).

We now are told, however, that this "nowhere" place for Jacob had been a center of cultic activity all along, and it had a name. It was a Canaanite city. It was also near Abraham's initial entry into the land (12:8), to which he returned (13:3), and where he had received the previous promises (13:15–17).[5] It was an appropriate place for Yahweh to interrupt Jacob's flight, but the previous cultic activity was irrelevant to Yahweh's revelation. Yahweh was showing his sovereign control in what Jacob thought was a random part of his self-directed course of life. Jacob was beginning to feel the impact of the birth oracle, as God began to assert his intent and design on his self-centered and headstrong selection.

---

4 The outpouring of oil on the top of the stone was a common symbol used throughout the OT that could represent consecration, as done with the anointing of oil of the priests and sacred objects (Lev. 8:12; 21:10; 40:9). It could also be poured as part of the sacrificial system when mixed with the offering (Lev. 2:6, 15). Here, it could be either or both, but his vow suggests that consecration is a major focus. As we will see there, the standing stone represents the whole place as a sanctuary to Yahweh.

5 Of course, the previous calling of the place "Bethel" assumed, by the narrator, this later naming for the sake of the reader's understanding.

Jacob Vowed Devoted Worship (28:20–22)
Jacob vowed he would worship at this newly consecrated place of worship when God fulfilled his promises.

28:20–21. Jacob extended his response with a vow to provide future worship (vv. 20–22). Yahweh's promise presupposed a long and arduous journey with many dangers ahead that Yahweh would provide for and protect through, so the vow was appropriate as a culmination of Yahweh's work in Jacob's life (done often throughout the OT and referenced often by David, e.g., Ps. 22:26; 56:13). However, the comparison with Abraham, together with Jacob's record to date, does leave the impression that Jacob was self-absorbed, not fully understanding the authority of Yahweh or the opportunity to rest in his promise (illustrated by his ensuing conflicts with Laban). In fact, he would have to be reminded (more than once) to fulfill his vow (Gen. 31:13; 35:1).

Jacob's vow directly reflects the wording of Yahweh's immediate promises to be "with" him (עִמָּד, v. 20; cf. עִם, v. 15) and "keep" him (שׁמר, vv. 15, 20) in the way he was going (הלך, vv. 15, 20). He then spelled out the implications of those promises and of his needs (bread and clothing)[6] before returning to God's promise and the consequence—that he would return (שׁוב, vv. 15, 21), which Jacob again specified as "in peace." Jacob clearly resonated with the promise, as it related to his immediate concerns. In contrast to Abraham, however, he did not respond to the greater covenant promises. It is as if they were of little consequence to him considering his present distress and mission. He was concerned with survival, both now and on his return. He did not yet have Abraham's desire for future progeny (15:2), nor was he conscious of being a blessing throughout his conflict with Laban, until perhaps his return (33:11, see Exposition there, p. 544). Rather, Jacob was focused on his immediate needs with self-serving manipulation. His specification of the promise appears to be his attempt to assure the favors he wanted and expected (Cartledge 1992, 169–70).

Jacob's promised response begins with a promise to acknowledge Yahweh as his God. Jacob, then, vowed his response if God would be with him, protect him, and provide his needs so that he returned in peace to his father's house. He vowed then that he would acknowledge God as his patron deity, establish the place as a place of worship, and offer his tithe to Yahweh. The second two flow from the recognition of God's role in his life.

TRANSLATION ANALYSIS 28:21b–22
The translations have consistently begun the apodosis in 28:21b. Verse 21b, however, continues with the same verbal form and subject (Yahweh) as the two previous verbs in verses 20 through 21a (*waw* on a perfect). The construction changes in verse 22, where each of the final two clauses begins with a disjunctive (*waw* on a non-verb at the beginning of the clause) with the succeeding imperfect form suggesting the shift to apodosis (cf. Fokkelman 2004, 75–79). The apodosis provides what the one presenting the vow will do. Verse 21b can be taken either way. Rashi (a medieval rabbi, cited by Wenham 1994, 225) considered this clause as the final condition, "and if the Lord is my God." Theologically, it fits God's perspective of choosing and pursuing Jacob better than Jacob choosing God (Hamilton 1995, 248), as well as the wider context of God's choice of Israel as his people (cf. Exod. 6:7; 1 Sam. 12:22; Jer. 7:23; cf. Jer. 24:4–7; 31:33). Certainly, God has already chosen him (Gen. 17:7; Ross 1985a, 233, n. 31). Jacob, however, has not shown an astute theological perspective, and in his mind, he is still in control (as the following narrative suggests) and may well assume that he can choose his own god and so put God under obligation to keep his word. Since these are Jacob's words, we think the traditional understanding more likely.

6 These two commodities may be functioning here as a hendiadys for "all that I need" (Cartledge 1992, 170).

While from God's perspective, he was clearly choosing Jacob, Jacob had yet to learn that sovereign oversight. His offer to truly worship God as his god continued Jacob's attempts to guarantee his own future. This understanding is confirmed by Jacob's fulfillment of his vow in chapter 35. When God reminded him (again) of his vow and responsibility to return to Bethel (35:1), he finally went, requiring his household to remove all foreign gods, making Yahweh his "patron deity" (35:2–4; Cartledge 1992, 174).

28:22. Jacob continued his vow by specifying his promise of worship. He would make this intersection of heaven and earth a place of worship, and he would show his loyal worship with a tithe of all that God had given him. His statement that the stone, set up as a pillar, would "be God's house" sounds difficult to modern ears. Was he thinking God would inhabit the stone?[7] If we compare this with verses 17 and 19 above, however, we can see that he considered the place to be a temple site ("house of God") because he could now see that God was there and it was a portal to heaven itself. The stone, then, is merely a marker, which he consecrated to memorialize the event and mark the place by metonymy. The repeated ceremony in 35:14 supports this conclusion, where he clearly calls the name of the place (again) Bethel (35:15).

Given Jacob's history of attempting to guarantee his own future, he again appears to be manipulating God here, attempting to motivate Yahweh to fulfill his word. Spelling out the implications of God "keeping" him (28:15) by providing bread and clothing (v. 20) and bringing him back (v. 15) "in peace" (v. 21) suggests he wanted to be sure he got all that he expected (Cartledge 1992, 149–50). Regardless of Jacob's true motives or view of God's promise, God had already guaranteed his promises.

While God cannot be manipulated by a human's paltry gifts, such a vow was entirely appropriate for a worshipper's response to God's promise as a gift of thanksgiving (1 Sam. 1:11; Ps. 76:12; Isa. 19:21). The heart motivation, however, is open only to God. Jacob's motivations may be debated, but his obligations are now clear. Jacob, in his response to God's revelation, was now binding himself to establish the sanctuary and to personally worship Yahweh. Yahweh would hold him accountable (31:13; 35:1; cf. Num. 30:3; Deut. 23:22–24), and he must pay his vow in worship and submission, even if under some duress (Gen. 35:1–4, 7, 14–15 because of his brush with disaster at Shechem, ch. 34). Fear and worship, appropriate and necessary responses to God's presence and promise, must be offered to honor him, regardless of initial motivations.

THEOLOGICAL FOCUS

Never out of God's purview nor separated from his promises, God's people must recognize their role through committed devotion for his glory.

God's revelation to Jacob shocked him when he thought he was "alone and nowhere" (Cotter 2003, 210). God's people are never out of his sight, regardless of their perceptions of being hidden and sidetracked. His presence in every situation merely underscores his gracious imminence, caring for our present and future apart from our ability or responsibility.

With Jacob's scheming seemingly put on hold while he ran for his life, God interrupted him, declaring his presence apart from Jacob's pursuit of him. When his people despair or attempt to control their future, God may interrupt their struggle with a reminder or reaffirmation of his plan and the implicit demand to bow. Yahweh, as sovereign, carries out his plan, sometimes despite and apart from his chosen saint's plots or problems. We are surprised that

7 Alternately, Sarna (1989, 200–201) cites an inscription from Sfire on a stone called an "abode of the gods" and suggests that it symbolizes God's presence which monitors the terms of a treaty or vow. While possible, the focus of the text is on the place being "Bethel" or God's house (vv. 17, 19; contr. v. 11).

God gives us an audience when we seem least likely to deserve it yet need it most.

God has always granted access without being sought and without merit In the New Covenant, that access is full and available to all in Christ at any time (Heb. 4:14–16; 10:19–22). His promise to the undeserving (all of us) shows his grace and sovereign redemptive purposes. In those purposes, he faithfully keeps promises, here to Abraham, Isaac, and Rebekah. God works even when his human instruments interfere or inhibit his righteous actions, distorting his character. Consequently, he may intervene, putting his representatives into places where they must learn his character, his faithfulness, and respond in submission and worship.

God's promise has always, of necessity, prompted response. Prayer appropriately responds to promise, whether in thanksgiving, petition, or vows (so the psalms). God's presence and revelation necessarily drives faith to worship, turning "no place" into a place of fear and blessing. That worship always comes at personal cost, requiring the worshippers to respond in costly expressions of gratitude and service. They must declare the greatness of the one worshipped, treasuring that relationship. Ironically, God can even use selfishly motivated worship to accomplish his plan.

Humanity, then, is not only always within God's view but always subject to his working and completely dependent on his revelation to know that working. We are fully dependent on his grace, not only for the eternal but for the immediate. It does, however, often take extraordinary insight to recognize. In fact, it may need to come unexpectedly and apart from human intent, to recognize that God's blessing comes by his gracious gift and cannot be wrested from him. Unfortunately, Jacob, with most of humanity, needs to continue learning that lesson the hard way.

Finally, humankind's focus on gaining "blessing" may overlook God's best or most significant gifts in lieu of immediate needs or desires. The felt needs of security and sustenance may overshadow the eternal opportunities and working of God to accomplish his redemptive plan (or even the presence of God with us), even though they presuppose God's immediate supervision. God's grace, however, will accomplish his work despite human frailty and misconception.

PREACHING AND TEACHING STRATEGIES

Exegetical and Theological Synthesis

Sermon seeds begin with the context of Jacob's position as carrier of the blessing and promises of God to the nations. He is both recipient and conduit. By faith in Christ, many of our congregants live their lives within the blessing of God. They, like Jacob, believe the promises of God and live their lives according to a similar vow of worship, "the Lord shall be my God. . . . And of all that you give me I will give a full tenth to you" (28:21–22). The sermon arrives there by following the narrative sequence. God graciously reveals himself to his children throughout their faith journey, especially at critical moments. He graciously reminds us of his promises, lest we forget.

Whenever one of God's children gets to the place where they feel all alone, let the ladder-dream remind them of God's promise: "I am with you and will keep you wherever you go" (28:15). The entire promise reminds us of God's faithfulness and grants us great courage to continue to walk with him in this badly broken world. Unlike Jacob, God's people now say, "Surely the LORD is in this place, and I know it!" (28:16). The final part of the narrative provides an important lesson: all who believe the promises of God must worship. We, however, also need to be careful to check our motives.

Preaching Idea

The dream of God's powerful presence comes true as we awaken to worship him.

Contemporary Connections

What does it mean?

Some of our listeners may struggle with God revealing himself to someone in a dream. God graciously allowed Jacob to hear that what he heard from his father (28:3–4) would indeed come true. God would make it happen. God makes it very clear in this dream that he would guarantee the completion of what he had promised (vv. 13–15). You can explain the concept, "I . . . will keep you wherever you go" (v. 15). In our new covenant context, we have a similar promise: God will complete the salvation process he began in all who believe.

Jacob's response to the dream (vv. 18–22) contains two concepts that require explanation. First is the confession, "the LORD shall be my God." Jacob vows his allegiance to the Lord as the one he will worship. The Lord will be Jacob's sole source of sustenance, satisfaction, security, and significance. Second, Jacob promises to tithe to the Lord. Honoring the Lord as God includes honoring him with the bounty he supplies. Many of our listeners struggle with the idea of giving the Lord his "full tenth" and will benefit from your explanation of its significance.

Is it true?

The biblical author assumes the validity of God's promises, but our listeners may not always accept them as reality for them. During their own dark nights of the soul, they will especially need to know that the promises of God are true. You might take a moment to review all the ways God has proven himself faithful through the earlier chapters of Genesis. Do we really believe that what God said to Jacob is true of us? While you may not be able to "prove" this to be true, you can press the issue of faith. This will help your listeners confirm that they trust in the Lord for their faith journey. Urge them to believe that the Lord is with them in a powerful way (Heb. 13:5–6).

Now what?

Genesis 28:10–22 is an example of a narrative where God states ideas about himself but does not apply them to the reader. Readers are responsible to apply the theology, and we are responsible to help them see what difference Jacob's encounter with God in this dream makes in their faith journey. Help your listeners see what parts of the promises belong to them by virtue of their relationship with God through faith in Christ and the power of the Spirit. No matter what circumstances your listeners are going through, God's promise, "I am with you and will keep you" (v. 15), gives them courage to keep walking with him in faithful trust and obedience. They are never alone; God knows their needs and acts accordingly to fulfill his promises to save them.

Creativity in Presentation

Our preaching idea for this section affirms that the dream of God's powerful presence does come true as we awaken to worship him. The sermon could follow the broad structure of the narrative:

- Begin by setting the context of the Christian life being lived in between the promises of God and the completion of those promises. That is always the way it is for pilgrims and strangers in this land. We are not home yet but are walking with God toward our final destination. While we walk with him, it is always by faith in his promises. God graciously reveals himself to us just at the right time. In those times when it seems we are journeying all alone, God provides a dose of reality.

- The second section of the sermon develops from the revelation of God to Jacob in the dream. Here God provides another look at his covenant promises. Its content is a stabilizing force for those with ears to hear: God's presence and power to keep us in faith till we arrive home. In this way, both the "house of God" and "the gate of heaven" (vv. 17, 19) are accurate titles for any place God's people find themselves.

- The final section of the sermon centers on the believer's response to the revelation of God: worship. Jacob's vow describes the Christian life as one of worshipping God. We all say with Jacob that the Lord is our God, and we will give him a full tenth of all he has given us. Whether Jacob's motives were pure in his vow, God would hold him to it, and it would become a crucial instrument for his growth and return to Yahweh.

Some creative elements are:

- Help listeners feel the hardness of the rock and the darkness of the night (v. 11). This will help them feel the need for God's gracious revelation in the dream.

- We are writing nearing the second-year mark of having to trust God in a world where the coronavirus has seriously disrupted everything. This has made it easy to help our listeners express their faith and, hopefully, their gratitude for the Lord's promises in verse 15.

- Challenge listeners' worship of God, including their response of giving of their resources. Provide them with a list of potential counterfeit gods or American idols that vie for our allegiance. Ask your listeners about their giving habits. Even though church gets a bad rap with all things related to money, this revelation does specify a tenth, a tithe. Sadly, many listeners will want you to legitimize a lesser percentage; if anything, you will be able to justify a greater percentage from Scripture but not less. Consider how the early church dealt with their money and goods in the early chapters of Acts.

DISCUSSION QUESTIONS

1. Discuss the times in your life when God revealed himself to you in reassuring ways. Do those times mirror Jacob's in the sense of the revelation coming at a strategic time?

2. Discuss the perception of dreams in our culture in comparison to other cultures where Christians are more comfortable with and expect God to communicate with them. How were dreams viewed and experienced differently in the Old Testament than in modern western culture?

3. Discuss the dangers of believing in God's ability to communicate with his people in dreams. This is helpful for both charismatic and noncharismatic churches.

4. Discuss all the implications of the reality that God is with us for our faith journey.

5. Discuss the biggest hindrances to God's people giving him a tithe. What proportion of our income does God deserve, and how do we decide what is appropriate?

6. Given God's current presence and promises in our lives as new covenant believers, how should we respond to him today? How will our devotion show?

Genesis 29:1–30

EXEGETICAL IDEA
Jacob's arrival in Haran revealed God's provision for Jacob's progeny and necessary lessons in deception and self-will, even as Jacob's pursuit of his own agenda ended in frustration and fitting consequences.

THEOLOGICAL FOCUS
Even when he is not obvious, God delivers on his promises, teaching his self-willed images the consequences of their folly and their need to walk with him for blessing.

PREACHING IDEA
We are all sons and daughters learning to endure the discipline of God to bring his blessing to the world.

PREACHING POINTERS
If you're preaching through this section of Genesis, by now your listeners know what kind of person Jacob is. He's God's chosen blessing-bearer, but Jacob has shown himself to be anything but godly. God has some work to do in him, in us, to accomplish his purposes in the world.

Enter the character of Laban. This explains why God would put Jacob through this long ordeal with his soon to be father-in-law. Jacob is about to come face-to-face with someone who plays by his own rules. God is about to refine Jacob's character through another character who does to him what Jacob did to his own father in order to secure the blessing. Jacob's patience will be tested through Laban's deception.

More importantly, instead of being served (one element of Isaac's blessing), Jacob ends up serving Laban. And all of this is God's way of training his chosen one to receive God's blessing so that he can be a blessing in the world. God is teaching Jacob how much he needs God's guidance and transforming power. Jacob's lack of wisdom and arrogance simply will not do. The way God disciplines and molds Jacob is a picture of what God is doing to each of his own children.

BLESSING: LEARNING GOD'S BEST (29:1–30)

LITERARY STRUCTURE AND THEMES

The narrative moves directly from Bethel to Haran, passing over the long journey. It relates in two main movements Jacob's arrival, meeting Rachel and Laban (vv. 1–14), and his negotiations for and marriage to both Rachel and Leah through Laban's deceit (vv. 15–30). The straightforward structure, however, provides numerous subtle indications of the complex development of both the purposes and promises of God and the outfoxing of the fox as God begins to refine Jacob's character.

I. Jacob was taken with Rachel at Haran (29:1–14).
  A. Jacob arrived an outsider in Haran (29:1–8).
  B. Jacob met Rachel (29:9–12).
  C. Jacob met Laban (29:13–14).
II. Jacob was taken by Laban (29:15–30).
  C'. Jacob bargained with Laban for Rachel (29:15–20).
  B'. Jacob received Leah (29:21–24).
  A'. Jacob, the outsider, served additional years for Rachel (29:25–30).

This short narrative, then, begins working out God's promises to be with Jacob and keep him (28:15). As with Rebekah's appearance (24:15), God was clearly at work when Rachel showed up on cue. However, the implications of his promises to Jacob will need to be nuanced when we see the bait and switch that Laban pulled, obligating Jacob to a wife he did not want. Is that what Jacob (or we) expected when he heard God was with him? Reminders of Jacob's deception provide additional opportunities to consider both God's refining and the outcomes of one's actions.

Jacob's outsider status, which obscured the customs and Laban's deception from Jacob, frame the account, providing cues to compare with Abraham's servant (Gen. 24) and showing the need to depend on God's help rather than proud self-reliance. Additional comparisons with the narrative of finding a wife for Isaac show both subtle characterizations of Jacob and God's provision despite Jacob's personal shortcomings. God will pursue Jacob's best interests, particularly focused on his character and submission to God though not always his comfort or pleasure (31:5, 42), and God will not override evil but use it for good.

- ***Jacob Was Taken with Rachel at Haran (29:1–14)***
- ***Jacob Was Taken by Laban (29:15–30)***

EXPOSITION

Genesis 29 optimistically begins the central portion of the Jacob stories and the conflict with Laban. As the reader recalls the search for Isaac's wife, Rachel's appearance at the appropriate time at the well, running off to tell her father, and Laban running to meet Jacob mix a happy ending (God's promised provision, 28:15, and Jacob's desired shalom, 28:21) with hints of trouble brewing (Jacob's focus, Rachel's silence, and Laban's expectations). The dark turn of events jolts the reader as Laban deceives Jacob, and the narrative ends with another seven years of service for the bride Jacob had already worked for. Suddenly the promise that

Jacob would be master with nations bowing to him (25:23; 27:29) as God accompanies him and protects him (28:15) seems turned on its head, and the reader struggles with the implications, even while recognizing the talionic justice of Laban's deceit (29:25–26).

In the structure of the Jacob narratives, the central section (29:1–31:54 [E–E' in the Introduction to the Jacob Narratives, p. 427]) will highlight Jacob's acknowledgment of God's intervention in his life and begin the journey back to Canaan where he will face Esau, fulfill his vow, and move into relationship with Yahweh, characterized by a new name. The immediate narrative initiates the conflict that must be resolved, though it will intensify first. It also extends the characterization of Jacob and reveals, in surprising ways, God's involvement in human events.

God, in the Jacob stories, has become much less visible and seemingly less accessible, as the narrative focuses more on the attempts of the characters to realize their own agendas. Of course, Jacob appears far less interested in seeking God and his input than Abraham. Yet, it reveals God's oversight, as he breaks into their world at crucial times (28:12–15) while remaining increasingly out of obvious view (29:1–30). Jacob's arrival in Haran revealed God's provision for Jacob's progeny and necessary lessons in deception and self-will, even as Jacob's pursuit of his own agenda ended in frustration and fitting consequences.

Jacob Was Taken with Rachel at Haran (29:1–14)

Jacob arrived in Haran, revealing both God's provision and Jacob's oblivion to God's working, local customs, and possible dangers as he encountered the shepherds, Rachel, and Laban.

Jacob Arrived an Outsider in Haran (29:1–8)

Jacob arrived in Haran, revealing both God's provision and Jacob's oblivion to God's working and local customs as he met the shepherds.

29:1. Jacob "went on his journey" and "came to the land of people of the east" summarizes the month-long trip to Haran. Unexpectedly, his journey to Haran (27:43; 28:10) or "Paddan-Aram" (28:2, 5, 7) and the house of Bethuel (28:2, 5) or Laban (27:43; 28:2, 5) is now characterized as the "people of the east."[1] The movement here subtly suggests danger (movement east has been consistently negative in Gen. 3:2; 4:16; 11:2; 13:11; 25:6) and that he does not know his precise location (Waltke and Fredricks 2001, 85, 400). The latter sets the stage for the ignorance of local customs that will mark the story.

> *TRANSLATION ANALYSIS 29:1*
> Literally, "Jacob picked up his feet," used only here in the Old Testament, has uncertain significance. It may emphasize the journey, summarizing it in a brief phrase (Speiser 1964, 222). Sarna (1989, 201), citing the rabbinic literature, suggests it was easier now for Jacob, he had more confidence, or "he had to force himself to leave." Regardless, this brief note propels the narrative to the significant interactions he will have and the important outcomes in Haran.

As with the search for a wife for Isaac, the narrative time focuses on the interaction with the shepherds, Rachel, and Laban. Parallels and distinctions from Abraham's servant's success characterize Jacob, Rachel, and Laban, setting the stage for the following negotiation and marriage scene.

29:2–3. As with Jacob's dream, when Jacob arrived, the reader sees the scene through Jacob's

1 The phrase is not used elsewhere in the Pentateuch. Elsewhere in the OT, it refers to the nearer neighbors to the east, of the Midianites or Amalekites (Judg. 6:3, 33; 7:12; 8:10), or those farther east from Mesopotamia (Ezek. 24:4, 10).

eyes ("Look, a well in the field! And look there, three flocks of sheep!" [author's translation]), calling attention to his surprise (use of "behold" [וְהִנֵּה], used twice in this verse) and reinforcing his uncertainty as to his location. What Jacob observed (the large stone, v. 2) is followed by the narrator's explanation (v. 3), which Jacob would only learn through the shepherds (v. 8). The clarification emphasizes the size and challenge of moving the stone, highlighting Jacob's feat of doing it by himself, but also exposes Jacob's unfamiliarity with the local culture and their customs. They would wait until there were enough to move it (because of the large size), ensuring both equitable access to the local demands[2] and protection against outsiders taking their valuable resources without appropriate compensation (Sarna 1989, 202).

29:4–6. In chapter 24, the servant had immediately stopped and asked Yahweh for success in his mission to find a wife (24:12). Jacob, after Yahweh's explicit promise of his presence and provision (28:13–15), which must include the wife (numerous offspring!), does not mention Yahweh nor hear from him for the next fourteen years (31:3). Instead, he appears presumptuous of God-given success. He engaged the shepherds in conversation, showing both his uncertainty of his location and unfamiliarity with the customs yet brash and self-confident, telling them what they should be doing (29:7).

Jacob's arrival outside of Haran, meeting shepherds that knew Laban, and the immediate approach of the daughter of Laban come as no surprise but indicate the presence of Yahweh granting his mission success (24:12, 26–27, 48, 50; cf. 28:15) even though Jacob failed to acknowledge him. On the other hand, Jacob's question and his answer from the shepherds regarding Laban's well-being reflect Jacob's vow and concern for his own welfare. Both question and answer use the Hebrew for "peace" (*shalom*, שָׁלוֹם, v. 6), echoing his conditional vow to return in "peace" (28:21) and heightening the reader's expectation of God's working, yet setting the ironic stage for the next twenty years of conflict.

29:7–8. Rather than acknowledging an answer to his quest in the appearance of Rachel, as pointed out by the shepherds ("Look, Rachel, his daughter" v. 6, author's translation), Jacob questioned their practice as if they were lazy ("Look, the day is still high!" v. 7, author's translation). Their explanation reinforced Jacob's outsider status ("We cannot," suggesting something like, "You are not from around here, are you!?"). While there is no recorded response to his following actions, disregarding their custom, Jacob is characterized as both uninformed and unconcerned with the local practice. Laban will use his ignorance and indifference against him.

Jacob Met Rachel (29:9–12)

Jacob met Rachel and watered her flock to impress her father.

29:9–12. Rachel's timely appearance echoes the similar timing of Rebekah (24:15), and again billboards God's intervention. Jacob's response, however, suggests again oblivion to God and his focus on himself and desire to ensure his outcomes. Though we are tempted to assume Jacob was immediately taken with Rachel's beauty, the narrator does not mention her beauty until it explains Jacob's request for her in marriage (29:17). Here the focus is on her family connection. In verse 6, she was "Laban's daughter." Now she came with "her father's sheep" (v. 9), and "Jacob saw Rachel the daughter of Laban his mother's brother, and the sheep of Laban his mother's brother…and watered the flock of Laban his mother's brother" (relationship repeated three times, v. 10). Then in verse 12, he tells Rachel his

2 Walton cites ancient herding contracts that ensured the fair distribution of the limited resources (Walton 2009a, 108).

relation as "her father's kinsman, . . .Rebekah's son." Jacob's focus was clearly on the relation to Laban, implying his desire to ingratiate himself to Laban (Sternberg 1987, 538, n. 15). Rebekah did not respond in the narrative except to go with the news directly to Laban.

Ironically, rather than Rachel showing her appropriateness for the line by serving Jacob (contrast Rebekah, ch. 24), Jacob shows his disregard for the local custom (and his prodigious strength) by rolling the stone away alone and watering Laban's sheep (contr. 27:29). Rather than bowing for his expected response to Yahweh's leading and worshipping Yahweh (like Abraham's servant, 24:26–27), Jacob bent his shoulder to impress the one who would use him for his own advantage. He gave no indication that he was conscious of or concerned for Yahweh and his will.

Jacob Met Laban (29:13–14)

Jacob met Laban, cooling Laban's initial enthusiasm after telling his story.

29:13–14. Again paralleling Abraham's servant's arrival in Haran, Laban ran to meet Jacob as soon as he heard (cf. 24:29–30).[3] The identical wording reminds the reader of Laban's apparent greed years earlier (see Exposition on 24:29–32, p. 417), making his show of hospitality suspect, though Jacob was unaware. The final statement that "Jacob told Laban all these things" (v. 13) in its ambiguity adds drama to the interaction. The reader is tempted to see Laban's initial excitement turning to sarcasm or worse. What "all these things" included is not clear, but Rebekah's parallel report to her mother's household (24:28, 30) suggests that Jacob's report would have revealed both mission and affluence (or lack).

Sheep grazing near Haran. Photo by K. Lawson Younger

Laban likely now knew that Jacob was without assets and looking for a wife. That would be enough to suggest to Laban that all was not well with Jacob at home, and he may be more easily taken advantage of.

Laban's response was also more ambiguous than we may hear. Jacob probably assumed something like, "Of course, you are my flesh and blood, so I will be happy to meet your needs!" (29:14). On the other hand, the introductory adverb "surely" (אַךְ, understood as emphasizing) could be understood as antithetic, "however," leading to a suggestion of disappointment like, "'oh well, yet you are my flesh and blood'" (Fokkelman 2004, 126). Though Jacob would not necessarily hear disappointment, the reader would be forewarned.[4] The reader's previous experience with Laban (24:29–31) has already predisposed them to expect a level of self-service and underlying agenda. The ambiguity foreshadows the coming storms and Laban's duplicity.

Jacob Was Taken by Laban (29:15–30)

When Laban deceived Jacob, giving him Leah for Jacob's seven years of service, Jacob felt the

---

3 "As soon as Laban heard" (וַיְהִי כִשְׁמֹעַ לָבָן) echoes 24:30, "As soon as he . . . heard" (וַיְהִי . . . וּכְשָׁמְעוֹ), and his response to both was to run to meet the potential benefactor (וַיָּרָץ, 24:29; 29:13).

4 Daube and Yaron (1956, 256) have suggested another option, that this was a formal declaration of kinship ties and therefore obligations, which he would later repudiate. Hamilton (1995, 256) similarly sees here the beginnings of a covenant relationship in which Laban will be primary and Jacob a "junior partner."

consequences of deception, serving an additional seven years to realize his dream of marrying Rachel.

Jacob Bargained with Laban for Rachel (29:15–20)

With Laban's prompting, Jacob pledged and served seven years for Rachel's hand in marriage.

29:15. After a month, Laban again spoke. In contrast to the servant wanting to return with the wife speedily (24:54–56), Jacob was in no hurry and had made no movement toward accomplishing his aim, even though we will learn that he was quite taken with Rachel (29:18). Laban, however, appears much less tolerant of his contented guest. While Jacob may be serving Laban (possibly implied in Laban's question), Laban wanted to clarify the relationship and expectations and, of course, benefit.

The precise intent of Laban's question is debated, but the outworking of the conversation is clear. Rather than generously supporting Jacob as a family member and helping him start a new branch of the family tree (as Jacob requested, 30:25–30), Laban used Jacob and attempted to cheat him, even beyond the marriage of Leah first (31:6–7, 38–42), by making him a laborer (Waltke and Fredricks 2001, 404). His "offer" to pay Jacob was a ploy, under cover of generosity, to use Jacob for his own gain. By issuing such a contract he would "exclude Jacob from the family holdings" and protect his family estate yet gain his services and benefit for the family should he succeed (Morrison 1983, 160).

TRANSLATION ANALYSIS 29:15

Daube and Yaron (1956, 61–62) proposed that Laban began with two questions, "'Art thou not my brother? Why then shouldest thou serve me for nought?'", which resulted in disavowing the relationship and degrading his status to a "hireling." Even if he is not repudiating the family tie, the outcome is still to place Jacob under obligation as an employee (Hamilton 1995, 258) and degrade the ties to merely economic (Waltke and Fredricks 2001, 404).

Herding Contracts

Herding contracts are well known from Nuzi and other locations throughout the second millennium BC and into the first. While the herdsman was a professional and independent, they were often bound to the owner of the herds by debts from having to repay the losses to the flocks under their watch (as Jacob stated, 31:38–40). The contracts would be issued shortly after shearing for the coming year, when all the herds were still gathered near the home base. The herdsman would agree to work for a year for a percentage of the flock and/or other considerations but would agree to be responsible for the losses incurred, other than acts of the gods. Jacob's request would change the expected outcome by entangling a marriage agreement with the contract (see Sidebar, The Marriage Agreement, p. 492). Laban's purpose, especially as we see it working out through the changing contracts (see 30:25–36; 31:7, 41), seems to be to keep Jacob dependent on him through debt and unable to leave so that Laban would not be responsible to fulfill the marriage agreement (give the dowry) yet would continue to prosper. See Morrison (1983) for a helpful summary of the implications of both the herding contracts and marriage agreements and their interaction in this narrative (cf. Postgate 1975). The outcome of recognizing the background here is a greater appreciation for the ongoing protection of Yahweh for Jacob despite his oblivion to Yahweh's presence and his attempts to manipulate the situation for his own gain (31:5, 7, 12–13, 42).

Ironically, Isaac's blessing that Jacob received by deceit echoed in Laban's words, as Jacob would choose to "serve" (עבד) Laban (describing his work for Laban eleven times in 29:15–31:55), rather than his expectation of being served by the peoples (27:29). The "wages" (מַשְׂכֻּרְת) he would name would be subject to Laban's control and frequent revision (29:25; 31:7, 41). Laban, then, "degrades the uncle-nephew relationship into a lord-servant relationship" (Fokkelman 2004, 127).

29:16–17. The backstory begins to come into focus as we learn that Laban had two daughters, not just one. As in Isaac's family, there was an older (גָּדוֹל) and a younger (קָטָן, cf. ch. 27 where "older" is use three times and "younger" is used twice) and Rachel, the younger, was the gorgeous one ("form and appearance," 29:17), while Leah just had nice eyes! As the main object of Jacob's attention, Rachel is solely described by her appearance and that only here, as Jacob made his bid for her hand. In Jacob's eyes, she is merely the object of his infatuation.

TRANSLATION ANALYSIS 29:17
The term translated "weak" (ESV, but footnote, "soft," רַךְ, see also NASB95, NIV) has been translated in a variety of ways. Are they "weak" or "tender" (NET), without "sparkle" (NLT), "delicate" (NKJV), or "lovely" (NRSV)? The idea is not clear because the term is not used anywhere else of eyes, nor in this way. Used of the heart, it is timid or "fainthearted" (Deut. 20:8), of adults it can be soft or "tender" (Deut. 28:54, 56), and of children, "frail" (Gen. 33:13). It comes from a root usually meaning "tender, gentle" or "soft" (*HALOT* s.v. "רכך" 1230). It is clearly in contrast with the beauty of Rachel and may be giving her main detriment, perhaps lacking luster (Sarna 1989, 204), or her main attraction, "the biblical equivalent of being said to have 'a nice personality'" (Alter 1996, 153; Cotter 2003, 222).

The Marriage Agreement

The marriage agreement in the ancient world typically included a bride price paid by the groom to the father, here covered by the working agreement, and a dowry given by the father to his daughter as her share in the family estate and sometimes constituted by some of the bride-price (Van Seters 1969, 392). The whole agreement could be formalized in a contract recording the transaction. The dowry would go to the groom with the bride at the marriage. Jacob, however, only received the two maidservants. Since the dowry was not mentioned here, it would become a source of contention for the women (31:15–16), not resolved until the final parting (31:50, see comments there, p. 521; Morrison 1983, 163).

29:18–19. In contrast with the servant of Abraham, Jacob looked solely at the outside and did not ask for Yahweh's help, direction, or approval (cf. 24:12–14). Rachel has no other characterization in the narrative (other than being a shepherdess), and her beauty is described only as the prelude to Jacob's love for her (repeated three times, 29:18, 20, 30), rather than complementing her actions (contr. Rebekah, 24:16, characterized also with her actions and Yahweh's approval; Alter 1981, 56). Leah cannot compete with her appearance but will be the fertile one (cf. 28:3) and the object of God's initial compassion (29:31).

Since it was customary for the groom to pay a bride price and Jacob had nothing, he offered seven years of work. Contemporary documents put the average bride price at thirty to forty shekels, and Jacob's expected wage would be about a shekel per month (Walton 2009a, 109). He was therefore offering a very substantial amount at about double the expected price. Perhaps he was taking no chances at being turned down, but his eagerness reminds of Esau's desperation to eat something, which Jacob had exploited and which Laban will imitate (Kidner 1967, 171).

Laban's reply remains ambiguous. He did not name Rachel, and his agreement was not a ringing endorsement of Jacob. Instead, he seems to be agreeing to the best offer he has had, and possibly leaving wiggle room for his later deception. Considering the herding contracts (sidebar above, he sees an opening to keep Jacob obligated for seven years (which he will be able to extend) and from which he will benefit greatly (30:27–28). Though his motives are not yet clear, the reader's suspicions are growing.

His concluding "stay with me" (29:19) reminds of Rebekah's plan (27:44) and may have been encouraging to Jacob. Yet it may also suggest that he was less than sympathetic with Jacob's drain on the family resources. Jacob can stay since he will be giving an exorbitant price in service. Again, the readers' inside knowledge provides nuances that Jacob would not have heard, highlighting Jacob's negligence in failing to consult Yahweh, but also cultivating sympathy for Jacob when he is the one deceived.

29:20. Jacob was deeply smitten, so that the seven years felt like "a few days," reminding the reader again of Rebekah's instructions. She had told Jacob to stay with Laban "a while" (27:44) or, literally, "a few days" (יָמִים אֲחָדִים), the same phrase used here. While Jacob may have forgotten his troubles, the careful reader sees connections to his deception of Esau, adding to the implication of repayment in Laban's ruse.

Jacob Received Leah (29:21–24)

When Jacob demanded the fulfillment of his marriage contract, Laban deceived him, giving him Leah with her servant.

29:21. Seven years passed, again without comment, as the narrator moves to the climactic scene. Seven years before, Jacob was happy to take advantage of Laban and Laban was anxious to put his nephew to work, but now the tables were turned. Jacob must be the one to initiate, and his demand irrupts abruptly in the narrative. Without formalities or pleasantries, he demanded his rights. Jacob has been watching the clock while Laban has been content to keep the status quo. Jacob's intention is clear. He was ready to have his full marital rights and privileges with the girl of his dreams. He had kept his bargain, and he wanted payment. Jacob, however, did not name Rachel, playing into Laban's deception.

TRANSLATION ANALYSIS 29:21

The imperative is not softened with a polite particle *-na* ("please"), and Jacob supported his demand with both his claim of fulfilling the commitment and his expected payment. Jacob appears impatient and indignant.

29:22–24. Without a word, Laban prepared for the celebration—and substituted the prize. Rachel and Leah are not given a voice. It is the work of Laban to deceive Jacob, though Leah was of course complicit. Jacob had specifically asked to go into his wife, and the fulfillment is merely noted. Technically, Jacob got what he asked for. Verse 24 notes Laban's gift of a servant to Leah, delaying the surprise and preparing for later narratives.

Jacob, the Outsider, Served Additional Years for Rachel (29:26–30)

When Jacob awakened to the deception, Laban cited custom, requiring an additional seven years for Rachel, which Jacob served.

29:25. It was not until morning that Jacob awakened to the ruse. Revealing the deception through Jacob's eyes, we feel his astonishment at Leah lying beside him. The wine from the feast, coupled with the darkness and her veil, had blinded his ability to detect the deception.[5] Eyes opened with the morning light, Jacob felt

5 Explained as the result of "being both in drink and in the dark" as early as Josephus (*Antiquities* I, 301, Josephus and Whiston 1988, 49).

the shock. You can imagine Jacob shouting from the tent as he rushed to confront Laban.

The Marriage Ceremony

The marriage ceremony in Israel and in Mesopotamia was a legal and cultural act rooted in theological underpinnings that regulated the legitimacy of the marriage. In Mesopotamia it included a contract between the families involved, a feast at the appropriate time that could last seven days to two weeks, and the consummation of the marriage after the festive meal on the first day, often within the compound of the wife's parents. The woman may continue to live with her parents for several months (intending her to become pregnant). She would then leave her family for full allegiance to her new family and their gods (van der Toorn and Denning-Bolle 1994, 59–76).

Jacob's accusation, however, condemned himself. Laban had "deceived" (from the root *rmh*, רמה) Jacob, the one who had come "deceitfully" (from the same root *rmh*, רמה) to get Esau's blessing (27:35). The one who used the darkness of Isaac's sight to betray his senses and steal the desired blessing from the beloved child feels the bitter pain as the delight of his eyes is replaced in his darkness.[6] Without justifying Laban's action, Jacob's complaint against Laban for the deception condemned his own use of deception against his father and demonstrated the talionic justice of his experience (cf. Frisch 2003, 279–85).[7] The con had been conned. Laban's response would embed the point in Jacob.

29:26–27. Laban defended his deception with custom, of which Jacob had not been conscious. Jacob should have known that the younger cannot be given precedence over the firstborn (הַבְּכִירָה)! Yet Jacob himself had claimed to be the firstborn (בְּכֹר, 27:19) in his deception, to take precedence (and blessing) contrary to custom. Jacob was still the outsider and paid a heavy price.

Laban's solution was simple and totally self-serving. In one stroke he married both daughters for the cost of a single wedding, indentured his son-in-law for an additional seven years, and guaranteed his own ongoing exceptional profit (30:27). Laban's proposal to Jacob gave Jacob little choice: he could have both women, saving face and custom as well as getting what he wanted. He could honor Leah after his blind wedding night and get his beloved Rachel (29:18, 20, 30). Jacob simply needed to give Leah her time as the new bride, then he could take Rachel as well, for the small price of another seven years. Jacob was caught.

29:28–30. Jacob had no choice if he wanted Rachel, so he complied without comment. Again, Laban gave a servant to Rachel for her wedding, laying the narrative groundwork for the later stories. The tragic note of Jacob's love for Rachel over Leah not only flows expectedly from the plot but provides necessary background for what will follow.

Again, Jacob served seven years. This time there was no comment that it was only a few days. While the narrative time is not fully clear, it appears most likely that the following narrative regarding the births of the children occurs during this time. It is logical that Jacob's request to leave and the renegotiation of the working

6 Jagendorf (1984, 190) notes numerous parallels, including the irony that "sensual knowledge," in both cases, "turned out to be the opposite of true knowledge."

7 While Laban had violated the terms of the contract as Jacob understood it, Laban's answer was that custom superseded the contract. Of course, Laban's original wording in the contract had suggested his slippery intentions, since he had not named Rachel (29:19). Nor had he revealed this custom to Jacob at any time in the seven preceding years, delaying the confrontation. Laban, rather, progressively revealed his intent for greatest personal benefit.

arrangement (30:25–34) happen at the end of the second seven years or relatively soon after.

God had been at work with Jacob and would use his wives to fulfill the promise yet expose the consequences of deception. Without seeking Yahweh's direction in faith, Jacob relied on appearances and his ingenuity, paying a heavy price for his ignorance and self-reliance. In fact, the consequences of his favoritism would continue in Jacob's life and family, even as he had experienced it from his parents.

THEOLOGICAL FOCUS

Even when he is not obvious, God delivers on his promises, teaching his self-willed images the consequences of their folly and their need to walk with him for blessing.

Though generally God is not obvious in life, as in this narrative, he is always at work, even if only seen in retrospect. Jacob would later realize his intervention, though it is doubtful he was thinking of that during the second seven years of service. The presence and activity of God shows in coincidences and unexpected benefits, as well as the appropriate outcomes of our actions.

We can expect God to keep his promises, but we should also realize that when we presume on his promise and walk by sight rather than by faith, failing to consciously seek his participation and input, we may face outcomes that we regret. We will need to learn the blessing of dependence and pursuit of God in true worship, rather than dependence on self in self-worship. Even when blessing is promised, it must be pursued in relationship with God as we walk with him in loyal dependence. Of course, we also must allow God to determine the form that his promised answers will take. We may assume we know what he will do, or we may demand a particular outcome, but God will allow our responses and his bigger picture to shape the outcomes that will eventually both accomplish his greater goals and keep his promised blessings.

God uses the consequences of human tendencies to operate by sight and self-interest to teach lessons on faith and dependence, as well as shaping our values to reflect his eternal purposes and values. Jacob may not exhibit those qualities yet, but the lessons are beginning as the reader recognizes the discipline of a good Father. From the human perspective, we can be sure our sins will find us out. The reader sees the appropriate consequences. Later, Jacob would realize the working of God in all his life (48:15) and God's deliverance from all evil (48:16), even though he had experienced numerous effects of his and others' sins.

The significance of these lessons must be connected to Jacob's pursuit of blessing (27:18–29). We dare not act as if God does not care what we have done and will ignore it only to provide blessing as we envision it. Blessing is only found in walking with God, as we have often seen. God's blessing will empower us to accomplish his purpose for us, not fulfill our desires. Like Jacob, however, we must learn God's essential gracious presence through painful lessons, and sometimes only in retrospect. While God fulfills his promises, the fullness of the blessing only necessarily follows the pursuit of God and his agenda, rather than a personal agenda.

PREACHING AND TEACHING STRATEGIES

Exegetical and Theological Synthesis

When God's chosen person arrives "to the land of the people of the east" (29:1), we can expect trouble ahead. Jacob is portrayed as someone who is ignorant of the culture of that land. His arrogance or self-centeredness shows in the way he barges ahead of shepherding traditions to encounter Laban's daughter, Rachel (v. 10). Verse 15 also shows us a man in need of transformation by describing Jacob as Laban's servant. Jacob is not yet experiencing what was promised to him: the blessing of being served. Maybe more importantly, Jacob is about to be tested because he asks to marry Laban's younger daughter, not the older, less attractive one (v. 18). It was all because of Jacob's ignorance and lack of guidance from the Lord.

In this way, the narrator invites us to take our place in the narrative. We are all little Jacobs in our faith journey who require much molding from our Lord so that we can serve him well in the world. Of course, our Lord is going to use Jacob's brashness and self-confidence to continue molding him into a proper servant. That molding process is always painful, and Jacob feels the pain when, the morning after the honeymoon, he awakes to find he married the wrong daughter (v. 25). So, Jacob is characterized as needing transformation to function well as God's representative and conduit of blessing. And because of our own selfish tendencies and foolishness, we provide our Lord with tons of opportunities to stretch us and mold us. Like Jacob, God is bringing all of us through trials and tests designed to make us more Christlike and better suited to experience God's blessing and bring it to the world around us.

Preaching Idea

We are all sons and daughters, learning to appreciate the discipline of God to bring his blessing to the world.

Contemporary Connections

What does it mean?

The biblical writer assumes readers will note the ominous description of Jacob's arrival "to the land of the people of the east" (v. 1). Help your listeners see that this spells trouble for Jacob. The narrator does explain the custom or traditions involved in well etiquette (v. 3) to tell us what Jacob does not know. The whole scene at the well and the dialogue with Laban requires our listeners to learn the customs of the ancient world that influence how Jacob will acquire first one wife, then two (see v. 26).

While we may not know everything there is to know about Jacob's psyche, we will want our listeners to enter the happy tears (v. 11) that resulted from him learning that Rachel is a relative (three times we read "his mother's brother" in v. 10). Without our help, our listeners may also miss the irony of Jacob being deceived by Laban, just as Jacob had deceived his own father to get the birthright and blessing. Our listener's curiosity will no doubt want some explanation as to how Jacob could be so blind as to not know that he consummated the marriage to Leah, not Rachel!

Is it true?

In a way subtle to the modern reader, the author is proving that Jacob needs major spiritual renovation. In the previous chapter, the Lord revealed himself to Jacob and promised, "Behold, I am with you and will keep you wherever you go" (28:15). Well, Jacob arrives "to the land of the people of the east" (29:1) and to his uncle, Laban. Nothing in this narrative looks like the Lord is keeping his promise to Jacob. If it is true that the Lord is with Jacob, then what is he doing, allowing Jacob to be deceived in this way? Some of our listeners may need to be convinced that God disciplines all his children to build practical righteousness in them. This helps prove why suffering is an instrumental part of our faith journey. Our listeners will often ask why the Lord has allowed trauma into their lives.

Now what?

There is only narrative description in this passage; there is no prescription. In this sense, the story yields application as Jacob's situation in some ways mirrors that of every Christian worshipper. Jacob showed himself anything but worthy of receiving and extending God's blessing in the way he dealt with his father and brother. In the spirit of our day, we might say, "Well, at least Jacob was a better choice than Esau!" God allows the deceiver to be deceived for the purpose of transforming his character. He must learn that blessing only comes on God's terms, in submission to him. It will not be until Genesis 32 when we see God changing Jacob's name after the famous all-night wrestling match, that Jacob finally begins to learn to cling to God. Our chapter sees God behind the scenes, beginning to work on Jacob's character to make him a more suitable representative of God.

Creativity in Presentation

As you prepare to teach on Jacob's encounter with "the people of the east" and his uncle, Laban, begin to think of how the Lord has disciplined you along your faith journey. This would also be an appropriate time for someone else to share how the Lord has molded their character along the way. Our congregations are filled with people who have suffered hardships and realized that the hardship was building righteousness in them. Ask the question, "Have you grown more in your faith through difficulties or times of delight?" and watch their reaction.

Your exegesis of the story will show how Jacob's tendency to deceive comes back to haunt him, but all for the purpose of building righteousness in him and us. As stated above, we are all sons and daughters, learning to appreciate the discipline of God to bring his blessing to the world. The writer of Hebrews 12 teaches us not to regard God's disciple lightly or to grow weary of it; every child must endure such discipline in order to share in God's holiness (vv. 5, 7, 10).

If you desire to preach or teach the story without retelling it as it is presented in chapter 29, consider the following structure:

- Why we need the discipline of the Lord.
- How the Lord disciplines us in our difficulties.
- Why the Lord's discipline does not destroy us.

In the first point, we have an opportunity to see Jacob's character and our own in need of renovation. The second point shows how the Lord uses our choices and others to form the discipline that is tailor-made for us. The final point interprets Jacob's circumstances in the broader context of the covenant the Lord has made with him. God continues to be faithful to his people because he said he would. Plus, God's ability to reform us along the way results in our ability to represent him well in the world.

DISCUSSION QUESTIONS

1. Discuss times when you know the Lord was disciplining you through hardship.
2. Discuss why times of trouble can build righteousness and holiness in God's people. What is it about the nature of trouble that builds our trust?
3. Discuss why arrogance and self-focus is so destructive to God's plan for us.
4. What practical steps can I take to cultivate dependence on God for decisions and important moments in life like Abraham's servant, rather than in self-reliance like Jacob?
5. How do I need to learn to react to hardship and struggle to be able to see God's working and maximize my benefit?
6. Look back over your life and write down times in which you could not see God at work but that in looking back you can see how God was with you and accomplishing his purpose. Share one of these with a friend.

Genesis 29:31–30:43

EXEGETICAL IDEA

God humbled Rachel and Jacob and graciously provided children and flocks to his hurting, imperfect servants, fulfilling his promises and answering their desperate cries even as they experienced the consequences of their self-interest and foolish manipulations through conflict and broken relationships.

THEOLOGICAL FOCUS

God graciously fulfills his promises, helping the hurting, humbling the proud, and providing protection and provision for his chosen servants while allowing them to experience the consequences of their folly.

PREACHING IDEA

We receive hope and help from watching God keep his promise to a most dysfunctional family.

PREACHING POINTERS

The narrative portrays the faithfulness of God to bless Jacob despite the utter dysfunction of his family life. The original audience has a front row seat to watch the Lord spring into action to build Jacob's family tree, a big part of the promise. God first responds to unloved Leah (29:31–35), then uses Rachel's servant (30:1–8), Leah's servant (30:9–13), and bizarre bargaining for Jacob (30:14–20)—and finally remembers Rachel (30:22–24). God is gracious to both Leah and Rachel in the middle of ancient Near Eastern family dynamics. God promised Jacob a huge family and God delivered, regardless of all the conflict (28:14). The Lord sees Leah and the Lord remembers Rachel, but there is no record yet in the narrative of Jacob interacting with the Lord on any of these family matters. Jacob does take initiative in 30:25–43 with respect to returning to his own country. What is clear through these pastoral scenes is that the Lord is causing Jacob to prosper: "Thus the man increased greatly" (v. 43).

What is amazing to readers is how the Lord grants his grace to Jacob and his family despite all the ungodly actions and motives of all members! And, again, we learn of God's intention not only to grant blessing but also to extend it through the ones he blesses (v. 30, "and the Lord has blessed you wherever I turned"). Finally, all readers should realize how much damage is done when God's people act selfishly instead of gladly submitting to his will in their lives.

JACOB'S BLESSING: HOPE IN THE TRENCHES (29:31–30:43)

LITERARY STRUCTURE AND THEMES

The two units that make up this preaching portion constitute the parallel center sections of the Jacob stories and provide the turning point of the narrative (see Introduction to the Jacob Narratives, p. 427). Up until this narrative, Jacob had been running from Esau and seemed content away from the conflict. Beginning in 30:25, however, Jacob turned his attention back to Canaan, though he would spend another six years providing for his household. Previously, Jacob had been maneuvering to gain his own prosperity. Now he began to acknowledge God's intervention and provision for him (30:2, 30; cf. 31:5–9, 12–13; 33:5, 11). Previously, God had promised to be with Jacob and bring him back (28:15). Now, after growing his family and flocks, God would call him back to Canaan to fulfill his vow (31:3, 11–13).

A. Sister-wife wars: God grew the family (29:31–30:24).
   1. God saw, giving children to unloved Leah (29:31–35).
   2. Rachel saw her barrenness, gaining children through Bilhah (30:1–8).
   2'. Leah saw her own inability, gaining children through Zilpah before God again added children (30:9–21).
   1'. God remembered Rachel (30:22–24).

B. Labor wars: God grew the herds (30:25–43).
   1. Jacob negotiated his wage (30:25–36).
   2. God intervened, growing the herds (30:37–43).

These two narrative portraits describe God's provision of children for Jacob through the struggle of his sister-wives (29:31–30:24) and God's provision of property for Jacob through his struggle with Laban (30:25–43). God worked despite and through human plotting, struggle, and superstition. At the same time, these narratives expose the characters' motives and their faulty understanding of God and his role in their lives, even though they were chosen for his purposes. The first section frames Leah and Rachel's struggle with each other for love and children respectively, with God's intervention and control as he opens (and closes) wombs (29:31; 30:32). The second section frames Jacob's struggle with Laban for flocks with God's (previous) blessing for Laban through Jacob (30:27–30) and his (current) provision for Jacob through Laban (30:43).

- ***Sister-Wife Wars: God Grew the Family (29:31–30:24)***
- ***Labor Wars: God Grew the Herds (30:25–43)***

EXPOSITION

Chronologically, the first section occurs during Jacob's second seven years of service to Laban for Rachel's hand in marriage, during which time twelve children are born to the two sisters and their maids (29:31–30:24). The second section adds another six years of service, in which Jacob grew wealthy at Laban's expense (30:25–43). The two narratives both deal with blessing to Jacob in the sense of enrichment and the fulfilling of God's promise (28:13–15), forming the center of the Jacob stories (see Introduction to the Jacob Narratives, p. 427).

The children are self-consciously and repeatedly stated to be God's provision. Jacob's prosperous flocks recall God's intervention, in retrospect, as Jacob recognizes God's working (31:5–9) and the sisters acknowledge it (30:16). In both cases the conflict among the characters spurs unexpected fertility until the curtain withdraws to reveal God faithfully at work amid the struggles. Throughout the narrative, God humbled Rachel and Jacob and provided children and flocks to his hurting, imperfect servants, fulfilling his promises and answering their desperate cries even as they experienced the consequences of their self-interest and foolish manipulations in conflict and broken relationships.

Sister-Wife Wars: God Grew the Family (29:31–30:24)

God graciously gave children to the two warring sisters, comforting the afflicted and answering the desperate, despite their self-interest, foolish manipulation of custom, and superstition.

The first three sections each begin when the main character of the section assessed the conflict, leading to the controlling action of the section. The center two sections emphasize the response of the women, showing their sister war first, before moving toward dependence on Yahweh. God's interventions frame the passage (cf. Mathews 2005, 478).

1. God "saw" (ראה) Leah's unloved state and intervened with children, while Rachel was barren (29:31–35).
2. Rachel "saw" (ראה) her barrenness, demanding her way and using Sarah's trick of surrogate mothering through her maid (30:1–9).

2'. Leah "saw" (ראה) that she stopped having children, so she imitated Rachel, giving her maid to Jacob and generating two more sons before God "listened to" (שמע) Leah, producing three more children (30:9–21).

1'. God "remembered" (זכר) Rachel and "listened to" (שמע) her (30:22–24).

Initially, then, Yahweh intervened compassionately, providing some relief for Leah's affliction (29:32). This intervention, however, does not seem to impact Jacob, but it certainly impacted Rachel, leading her to enlist her surrogate to gain some ground. Leah continued the competition, however, with her own maid. It is only when the women pray that God grants more children to Leah (30:17) and Rachel (v. 22). Sadly, Jacob is not seen interceding for his wives, even though he knew it was God's prerogative to grant children (v. 2; contr. Isaac, 25:21).

God Saw, Giving Children to Unloved Leah (29:31–35)

Because of Jacob's neglect of Leah, God intervened, giving her sons while Rachel remained barren.

29:31. Yahweh sees injustice and Yahweh acts. When God "sees" (*qal* of ראה), it may express his evaluation of the situation (1:4, 10, 12, 18), but when the text says he "sees" evil or injustice or deep need, he not only evaluates the need, but he responds, whether in judgment (6:5, 12; 11:5; 18:21), salvation (7:1; 16:13), or provision (22:8, 14). Here the narrator indicates the direct correlation between Yahweh's evaluation of Leah's status with Jacob and his provision of children for her. Leah was "unloved" (שְׂנוּאָה, NASB95). God's compassionate response to Leah's struggle was to give her children. Only in this passage does God explicitly open wombs, and he does it both here for Leah and, at the close, for Rachel (30:22).[1] Rachel's barrenness was also attributed

1 Obviously, in other places God specifically gave children to barren women—twice in Genesis already, in Sarah and Rebekah. He also closes wombs (20:18). The expression of "opening a womb" only occurs here, however, tying together the narrative and the place of the women before God as he hears their cry (29:33; 30:22).

to God (30:1–2). God was specifically working through childbearing.

TRANSLATION ANALYSIS 29:31
"Hated" provides misleading connotations to most English readers. The Hebrew term translated "hated" (ESV, שְׂנוּאָה) can mean a strong animosity, whether dealing with individuals (37:4; 2 Sam. 13:15) or nationalities as enemies (Exod. 1:10). It can also refer to something to avoid (Prov. 11:15), an aversion (Prov. 19:7), or an aggravation (Prov. 25:17; cf. Konkel, שָׂנֵא, *NIDOTTE* 3:1275). In the context of multiple wives, however, it reflects the choice of one as favored, and the demotion of the other to a lower status (without basis), a legal issue, so that the demoted is "unloved" (cf. Deut. 21:15–17, Wells 2011, 105–15). Usually the first wife (Leah) and the one with children (Leah again) would claim the favored status. Here she was immediately demoted just one week into the marriage without reason and despite her fertility she was unable to recover the favored position (Gen. 29:32–34, Wells 2011, 115–22). For her claim to "affliction" see verse 32 below.

29:32. When Yahweh saw that Leah was unloved, he opened her womb, and she gave birth to her first son, naming him Reuben ("see a son") with the explanation that God had "seen" her "affliction" (עֳנִי). Her complaint does not require that she was abused, though it recalls God's response to Hagar when he "listened to [her] affliction" (17:20). It may simply describe her "misery" (NIV) or "troubles" (NCV), deeply desiring to be loved by her husband and feeling the injustice of her demotion. Yahweh would bless her with a large role in fulfilling his promise to build his nation, with Leah producing half of the patriarchs as well as one daughter, more children than all the other wives together. Whether she ever experienced Jacob's love is not clear, but she clearly never was reinstated as favored wife. By the end of the narrative, the tensions had eased a bit (29:15), so that Jacob fathered three more children with her. Jacob buried her with the patriarchs and matriarchs in the cave of Machpelah (49:31). God was gracious to her in her pain, as the next birth would underline, providing some measure of comfort.

Names in the Old Testament

The explanations for names in the Old Testament often provide word plays (or puns) on the name to relate them to the circumstances or occasion of the birth or in the life of the parents, rather than specifically describing the literal meaning of the name (as, for example, Esau's pun on Jacob's name, 27:36). In this case Leah plays on the verb "see" but adds that it is her affliction that Yahweh saw, evening the score with her sister by providing the coveted son. These sons that will be born will each have descriptions of the significance of their birth in the life of their mother, documenting the women's struggle and shifting perspectives.

29:33–35. God gave Leah a second son, whom she named Simeon, stating "the Lord has heard that I am unloved" (v. 33 NASB95). The meaning of the name is uncertain, but Leah plays on the consonants, with the first three giving the root "hear" (שמע), again recalling for the reader Hagar and Ishmael (16:11; 17:20; 21:17).[2] Rachel prematurely claims the same favor (30:6), but God would also hear her cry (30:17).

With the birth of her third son, her explanation moved from God's favor to her desire for Jacob's love. Two sons have not produced the desired change in his heart, but perhaps now, with three sons, he will be "attached" to her (29:34). "Levi" sounds like the Hebrew verb that she uses in explaining her desire for Jacob to "be attached" or "joined" to her (cf. Brooke, לָוָה, *NIDOTTE* 2:767). Unfortunately, as the remaining

2 As Leah recognized, when God "hears" God acts on behalf of the one he listened to (see discussion and note on Gen. 16:11, p. 314).

narrative shows, the three sons did not heal the relationship, but her focus changed.

With her fourth son, she shifted her perspective to praise for all Yahweh had done. She named her fourth son Judah, stating she would "praise the Lord" (v. 35). In this case, the name Judah means "May Yah be praised."[3] It seems she is moving to a healthier emotional and spiritual place. She may be finding her hope in Yahweh, rather than Jacob (Ross 2008, 177). If so, it is short-lived or shallow.

These names may also suggest more struggle with Rachel than is sometimes assumed. Leah, exulting in God's working on her behalf, would imprint extra pain on Rachel, who was without children. Even the praise of God (Judah) would be a painful and frustrating reminder to Rachel, which may contribute to her harsh words for Jacob (Sherwood 1990, 156). At this point, Leah stops bearing children.

Rachel Saw Her Barrenness, Gaining Children Through Bilhah (30:1–8)

Desperate for children, Rachel offered her servant Bilhah as a surrogate, producing two sons and personal vindication.

30:1–2. God had observed Leah's unloved state and intervened. Rachel recognized that she was not bearing children but did not see that Leah now had children as a gift from God. Rather, Rachel envied her sister. Leah had children without love. Rachel had love without children. Rachel shows only her desperate fight for herself, threatening Jacob with her imminent death without "sons" (lit., בָּנִים). Tragically, she would die with the fulfilled desire of a second son (35:16–19). Her words remind the reader of the repeated conflict between siblings throughout Genesis (brothers up to now), as she is jealous of "her sister" (אֲחוֹת). She does not threaten her sister as Cain or Esau but threatened her own death. Rather than go to Yahweh, Leah's focus in her pain, Rachel turned on her husband. Jacob angrily (but rightly) deflected to God as the one to give or withhold children, yet there is no record of him going to God for his wives, in contrast to his father (25:21). The focus clearly shows the sole agency of God in having children, a theme from the beginning, but emphasized beginning with Abram and Sarai. Children are God's blessing, but as such they provide opportunity to show faith and see God's work and purpose. The family was melting down in self-pity even as they identified the necessary role of Yahweh, yet they did not entreat him.

30:3–8. Rachel's solution also reminds the reader of Hagar—Sarah's foolish gift to Abraham. Repeating Sarah's faithless action (see comments and sidebar for 16:2–4, p. 310), Rachel used the same words to her husband: "Go in (בּא) to her . . . that even I may have children through her" (30:3, lit. "be built up from her," אִבָּנֶה מִמֶּנָּה, cf. 16:2). The narrator's clear negative evaluation of both the request and the lack of faith behind it follows in both situations. Unfortunately, like Abraham, Jacob merely complied and fathered two children with Rachel's maid, Bilhah. In contrast to Hagar, God would use even their foolish self-interest to build his promised family.

Rachel, as surrogate mother, named the first son Dan because she felt vindicated. With her play on the Hebrew verb "to judge," she claimed God had heard her voice. Though she may have prayed, the narrator ironically only confirms that God heard her in verse 22, when he gave her Joseph. Rachel was accomplishing her dreams by culturally approved means, apart from Yahweh. She waged her battle for first wife on her own, with only a self-applied veneer of divine approval.

TRANSLATION ANALYSIS 30:6

Rachel's choice comes from the Hebrew verb "judge" (דִּין; ESV, NKJV, NRSV), which certainly

3 Or perhaps, "May God be praised" (Millard 1974).

refers to judicial activity. In the human realm, it often describes the defense of the weak and oppressed (e.g., Ps. 72:4) leading to a fair adjudication of their cases and, with God as the subject, may result in judgment (Gen. 15:14) or deliverance (Deut. 32:36). Here it shows the result of a positive judgment, in the sense of "vindication," by giving children (NASB95, NET, NIV, NLT).

Her second son through Bilhah highlights her struggle with her "sister" (אָחוֹת) by naming him Naphtali, which sounds like the twisting of a wrestling match (see *HALOT s.v.* פתל 990). Her explanation (lit. "wrestlings of God," נַפְתּוּלֵי אֱלֹהִים) emphasized the greatness of the struggle. Such a holy struggle in her view becomes, in the reader's view, a toxic tangle that will continue to tear apart the family and nation. Significantly, she does not use the name "Yahweh" until God works on her behalf personally (30:24). It is as if, after working on Leah's behalf, Yahweh is distanced from the struggle while the women battle through their surrogate maids.

TRANSLATION ANALYSIS 30:8
Rachel's use of "God" (אֱלֹהִים) has generally been translated as an intensifying epithet, such as "mighty wrestlings" (30:8 ESV, NASB95, NRSV), "a desperate struggle" (NET), or "a great struggle" (NIV). Thomas argues that if we leave the relationship to God out of the expression, we are missing the point (Thomas 1953, 215–18). The use of the divine name raises something "to a pre-eminent degree" by bringing it into relationship with God (p. 215), leading to something like "divine struggles" (Wenham 1994, 245) or perhaps "fateful contest" (NJPS).

Leah Saw Her Own Inability, Gaining Children Through Zilpah Before God Again Added Children (30:9–21)

Initially, Leah countered in kind with Zilpah, producing two more sons, but, taking advantage of Rachel's superstition, God intervened with two sons and a daughter.

30:9–13. God had considered the situation ("saw") and stepped in on Leah's behalf (29:31). Rachel had realized ("saw") her barrenness and offered her surrogate (30:1). Now Leah had stopped bearing, and she also realized ("saw") it. Fighting maidservant with maidservant in their epic battle, she too imitated Sarah, giving Zilpah to Jacob, who complied passively. Leah named the first son Gad, simply meaning "luck" or "fortune." In her words, with no mention of Yahweh, "Good fortune has come" (v. 11). Similarly, Asher (אָשֵׁר), her second, sounds like "happy" or "fortunate," because she was considered happy (v. 15, אשׁר). Her claims, however, ring hollow, with the continuing struggle and the statement in verse 17 that "God listened to Leah." While putting on a happy front, she was crying out to God. Her heart's desire remained the love of her husband (v. 20).

30:14–15. A change of pace in the narrative describes Reuben, the oldest, finding mandrakes in the field at the time of the wheat harvest. The wheat harvest (mid-April to mid-May) was significant to the narrative because Jacob, who would be tending the flocks, would have been close at hand, rather than some distance away with the flocks (Morrison 1983, 158). Rachel wanted the mandrakes, presumably because they were widely believed to be an aphrodisiac (cf. Song 7:13). Not satisfied with her two surrogate children, Rachel was trying to have her own. In fact, she was also controlling the bed that Jacob would sleep in, bartering him for mandrakes. Leah's angry retort showcases the struggle and declares what Rachel may have forgotten. Rachel was depriving Leah of her husband.[4] The barter restored some order.

4 This statement may also explain why she stopped bearing children (Sarna 1989, 207; Wenham 1994, 244).

Photo of Autumn Mandrake. By Uzi Paz Pikiwiki Israel

Mandrakes

The power of the mandrake to "arouse passion, to intoxicate, to create sons" was legendary and became a symbol of love in ancient Egypt (Bosse-Griffiths 1983, 69).

30:16–18. God again graciously intervened, expressed by the anthropomorphic "God listened to Leah" (v. 17; see 29:33 above). Leah named her fifth son Issachar, honoring God's intervention yet mistakenly crediting her own use of her maid as a surrogate (Issachar includes the consonants of "wage" [שָׂכָר] with debated meaning). As her final son's name will show, Jacob's attention was still her elusive desire.

30:19–21. With the birth of her final son, Zebulun, Leah both honored God and craved Jacob's honor.[5] As the mother of six sons, Leah was still competing with her sister, who had none of her own.

She finally bore a daughter, naming her Dinah (from the same root as Dan, "judge") but without explanation. The birth of Dinah is stated as an aside from the main line of the narrative. It was a necessary note because it introduces the sister that will be the focal point of chapter 34 when she is raped. It also notes her birth as "afterward" chronologically, which may refer to after this time of Jacob fulfilling his service (and so, perhaps, after Joseph in 30:22–24). The correlation with the name of Bilhah's first son suggests that the competition continued without resolve.

God Remembered Rachel (30:22–24)

God chose to act on behalf of Rachel, answering her prayer for a son, which she acknowledged, extending her request to another.

30:22. God did not leave Rachel childless. After the births of ten or eleven children in the family, we can imagine that Rachel was getting even more desperate.[6] That God "remembered" her reminds the reader of Noah (8:1) and Abraham (19:29), when God acted on their behalf (see discussion on 8:1a, p. 183).[7] God now chose to intervene graciously in accord with his character and in response to her prayer ("God listened to her"). Rachel may have assumed vindication earlier (v. 6) from "answered" prayer,

5 Punning in two ways on his name, she stated, "God has endowed me with a good endowment," using the Hebrew root *zbd* twice ("to make a gift" or "endow," Grisanti, זָבַד, *NIDOTTE* 1:1066). She also wished that Jacob would "honor" her (Hebrew root *zbl* [זבל], used only here and probably meaning "honor" or "exalt" Smith, זָבַל, *NIDOTTE* 1:1074).

6 This assumes an implied chronology that, when Jacob asked for leave to return to Canaan after the birth of Joseph (30:25), he had just finished his service. It could perhaps have been a bit longer, but it requires that Leah had her first four children in quick succession, and that there were some overlapping pregnancies. Joseph may have been conceived before Dinah was born. In fact, Dinah is not necessarily chronologically between Leah's last sons and the birth of Joseph. Or perhaps Jacob waited until the birth of Joseph, even if it was after he had fulfilled his responsibilities, to ask to return.

7 Wenham (1994, 170) recognizes this as the turning point of the Jacob narratives, much as God remembering Noah was the turning point of the flood account.

but the narrator tells us that this truly was answered prayer when she finally (?) turned to God. The birth of Joseph was divine intervention as Yahweh opened her womb, bringing this section to a close with the bookend from 29:31. God's intervention marks Joseph with purpose, suggesting the role he will play in the succeeding series. God had now finished his intervention for the family of Jacob to produce the patriarchs and complete his promise of children to become like the dust of the earth (28:14).

30:23–24. Rachel understood the significance of Joseph's birth. A woman in the ancient world without children (even with her surrogate sons) was looked down on. She was not only held in contempt by her culture but rejected by the gods and potentially under suspicion of grave sin (van der Toorn and Denning-Bolle 1994, 77–82). Rachel used two word plays in naming Joseph. Her initial statement exulted in her freedom from reproach, crediting God with "taking away" (*'asaph* [אָסַף], sounds like Joseph) her reproach. She also prayed that God would add another son to her (*yoseph*, [יֹסֵף], also sounds like Joseph). By her two puns, she both praised Yahweh for his gracious intervention and prayed for additional blessing, which would tragically include her death.

The birth narratives, then, present God beginning to fulfill the promise he made to Jacob at Bethel with children consciously described as God's intervention by the wives, Jacob, and the narrator. However, he intervened into a context of struggle, self-interest, favoritism, and superstition that often missed the full truth, even when they saw God's intervention. The family was torn by their fears and disappointments, even when faith was nominally present. Into this common human existence, God brought uncommon grace, hope, and life. His grace, however, was most clearly and significantly extended to the women when they turned to him.

Labor Wars: God Grew the Herds (30:25–43)

When Laban tacitly refused to let Jacob go easily, Jacob negotiated what seemed to be a minimal wage to provide for his family, which God used to make Jacob very wealthy.

The narrative section begins with Laban's prosperity at Jacob's expense and ends with Jacob's prosperity at Laban's expense. In both cases, God had intervened, though only the first intervention was explicitly acknowledged by all parties, while God's role in the present was yet to be seen. In the first movement, Jacob negotiated with Laban with obvious concern that he be above reproach. In the following narrative, Laban and his sons would nevertheless distrust him. In contrast, Laban openly took advantage to minimize Jacob's ability to profit. In the second movement, Jacob acted shrewdly to maximize his profits, succeeding dramatically. As with all of Jacob's sojourn in Haran, his triumph over Laban would only later be recognized as God's intervention.

In both sections, the narrative is difficult to follow and may even be intentionally ambiguous, with many exegetical difficulties both in the negotiation and in the outworking of it (e.g., v. 35), so that the broad scene appears clearly, but fog shrouds the details.[8] "The result is a conversation which is a masterpiece of suspicious wriggle in negotiations, full of ambivalence and false bottoms" (Fokkelman 2004, 142). The outworking of the contract(s) (30:37–43) also summarizes six years of Jacob's wrangling, providing additional reason for some confusion.[9]

---

8 "The passage on Jacob outwitting Laban, 30:25–43, has presented exegetes with great difficulties, above all because from Jacob's offer to Laban right up to the very last act it is not clear what is going on" (Westermann 1995, 479).

9 Contracts were renegotiated each year (Morrison 1981, 158), and Jacob charged Laban with changing the terms ten times in the six years (31:7, 41).

Jacob Negotiated His Wage (30:25–36)

When Laban tacitly refused to let Jacob go easily, Jacob negotiated what seemed to be a minimal wage to provide for his family, which Laban tried to reduce even more.

30:25–26. Joseph's birth precipitated Jacob's request to return to Canaan, having fulfilled his responsibilities to Laban. He wanted to go home or, specifically, "my place and my land" (v. 25, lit., אֶל־מְקוֹמִי וּלְאַרְצִי). The reader is not sure if he was claiming God's promise (28:13) or merely referring to his home country. Either way, the reminders that he is not a local have not ended well for Jacob so far.

Jacob's concern had shifted to providing for the very large family he now led. He had completed his responsibilities of the second seven-year contract (30:26). It may also be that even if it had been fully completed somewhat sooner, Jacob was now freed to go after Joseph's birth since "a woman's status in the marriage was not fully attained until she bore a son" (Walton 2009a, 110). Rachel would not be considered secure, and her family may not easily release her to move far away. Whether that was the case here or not, he emphatically claimed completion of his obligation, demanding permission to leave with his family (no polite request!). Jacob had finally fully paid the bride price for both wives and was under no further obligation to Laban. For the second time he asked for his wife/wives (cf. 29:21), putting the reader on alert for Laban's trickery.

30:27–28. Heightening the concern that Jacob would be fleeced again, Laban ignored Jacob's request. Instead, he acknowledged God's blessing on account of Jacob and asked Jacob to name his wages to continue with his suddenly grateful uncle. This is the first time the readers have heard of how Jacob's work had gone and the amazing growth of Laban's flocks. It is not surprising, however, considering God's promise to bless the families of the earth through Jacob (28:14) and the precedent of God's blessing on foreigners connected to his patriarchs (13:5–6; 14:13–24; 21:22–24; 26:28–29). Whether Laban had used divination is uncertain. The outcome, however, was clear, and everyone agreed that Yahweh had blessed him because of Jacob (30:30).

TRANSLATION ANALYSIS 30:27

Some have objected that divination is not known to have been used to determine the reason for past events, but only for predicting future events. Some translations, then, take this as a figure of speech, "I have learned by experience" (NKJV) or "I know" (NCV). Finkelstein has connected the verb to an Akkadian word meaning "to flourish, prosper," leading to the translation, "I have become wealthy" (NLT, cf. ESV footnote; Finkelstein 1968, 34, n. 19). The irony of claiming divination, forbidden by Yahweh, to learn that Yahweh is the source would further characterize Laban for the Israelite reader (Sherwood 1990, 215).

Laban's offer to Jacob of naming his wages reminds the reader of a similar offer when Jacob first arrived (29:15). Laban seems to have the same intent: to keep Jacob in his employ for his advantage and possibly keep from giving Jacob the expected dowry. A herdsman may incur losses that could keep them locked into service for their cattle owners until they could be repaid, to the benefit of the owner (Finkelstein 1968).

Jacob's Contracts and Marriage Arrangements

The narrative will show us that Jacob's contracts were clearly unfavorable (see discussion on 31:38–42) in comparison with other known contracts from ancient Babylon and Nuzi (Morrison 1983, 157–58). For Jacob's desire to leave, in addition to Laban's clear benefit from Jacob's presence, the bigger issue may be the payment of dowry for the brides. When the bride price was fully paid, the groom would receive the dowry as an advance inheritance for the brides, to be passed on to the next generation (Grosz 1981, 161–63). Rachel and Leah decry their lack of dowry or "inheritance left to us" (31:14). Morrison argues that Jacob was asking for the conclusion of the marriage arrangement, including dowry. Laban's stalling would keep them there and delay his need to pay it (Morrison 1983, 161). The stakes, then, are higher, and Laban is craftier than it might sound to our modern western ears.

30:29–30. Jacob responded with a rehearsal of Yahweh's blessing on Laban through his exemplary service. Laban did not balk, even though we might expect Jacob's description to be overstatement (from little to abundance and blessed wherever Jacob turned!). Jacob's concern was now to provide for his own family. The dowry would be only a part of that, since to sell it to pay for "everyday expenses is considered reprehensible" (Grosz 1981, 162). It may be that Jacob is suggesting that after the stellar service he has given, he should be entitled to a nest egg to begin life for the daughters and grandchildren of Laban. The law provided just such a responsibility for Israel when a servant gained his freedom (Deut. 15:12–14). Israel would be reminded that the responsibility of the master was to be generous to the servant "as the Lord your God has blessed you" (which both Laban and Jacob state, Deut. 15:14).

30:31–33. Laban's question again sounds innocent and open, "What shall I give you?" (v. 31). In effect, he ignored Jacob again. Jacob's response was surprising: "Nothing!" He seemed to finally have a good sense of Laban's character. The expected wage of the herdsman would typically be about 20 percent of the new animals born in the herds (Finkelstein 1968, 35). Rather than a specific wage, however, Jacob offered to work for the unusually marked animals in the herds. Typically, the sheep would be white, and the goats would be black. The abnormal animals would make up much less than 20 percent of the new births, so Jacob seems to be offering a great deal for Laban (Walton 2009a, 110). Such a deal would make it obvious that he was not cheating, nor would it be easy for Laban to cheat him.

TRANSLATION ANALYSIS 30:32
The Hebrew text is ambiguous as to who should remove the animals.

30:34–36. Recognizing what appeared to be a very lopsided deal, Laban quickly agreed and took one additional step to minimize Jacob's wages. He removed the uncommonly colored animals and kept them three days' journey from Jacob's herds. The contract agreed on appears to make the beneficiary of the off-colored animals Jacob (v. 32, see Translation Analysis 30:35), but there is ambiguity there, which Laban appears to take advantage of (Sherwood 1990, 221). Not only does Jacob lose those initial animals, but now he will have a difficult time breeding more of the abnormally colored animals. Laban seems to have an early lead in the struggle for wages.

TRANSLATION ANALYSIS 30:35
The subject of the verb "remove" is not expressed as, for example, in the NASB95, NIV, and NKJV. Other versions remove the ambiguity by supplying the subject (e.g., ESV, NET, NLT). To add to the ambiguity here, the infinitive in verse 32 ("removing") is also the form in the Hebrew as the imperative, so that the same ambiguity exists there (so was Jacob saying he or Laban should remove the animals?). The English versions uniformly take verse 32 as Jacob removing them. The ambiguity in the Hebrew of these two verses points to Jacob until verse 36, which clarifies that it was Laban (at least for v. 35). Laban may be taking advantage of that ambiguity in Jacob's original proposition.

God Intervened, Growing the Herds (30:37–43)

Jacob manipulated the breeding of the sheep and goats, gaining great wealth from Laban's herds, by God's gracious intervention.

30:37–40. Jacob's actions over the course of the next six years (cf. 31:38) have generated considerable discussion, both because of the ambiguity in the text of what he did[10] and because of the uncertainty of the significance and motivation. Some things are clear. Jacob peeled the "poplar (לִבְנֶה) and almond and plane" sticks, exposing the "white" (לָבָן) of the sticks (30:37), making a play on Laban's name[11] and so beating him at his own game. The flocks certainly produced excessive numbers of abnormally colored animals. Did this work because of some supposed magic or superstition (Westermann 1995, 483), unknown (until modern times) epigenetics (Backon 2008, 263), or perhaps given by special insight from God in his dream (31:10–12)? Or was it wise breeding methods that maximize the desired recessive traits (Mathews 2005, 502), all ultimately resulting from divine intervention? None of these methods can adequately account for the phenomenal success of Jacob. The statements by Jacob, Rachel, Leah and the voice of God in Jacob's dream, by Jacob's report, all declare that Yahweh intervened and accomplished the unexpected (31:9, 12, 16), regardless of Jacob's efforts and manipulations.

30:41–43. Jacob also selectively bred the stronger of the flocks into his herds and left the weaker animals for Laban. Jacob grew wealthy, and Laban's wealth diminished. Jacob not only increased in sheep and goats, but presumably he traded or sold his increasing herds to gain servants, camels, and donkeys as well. Jacob's wealth reminds the reader of what God had done for Abraham in Egypt (12:16; 13:2; see 24:35) and Isaac in Gerar (26:12–14). When the patriarchs are out of the country, God keeps increasing them as he fulfills his promises to them. The Israelites would find similar success as they leave Egypt (15:14; Exod. 12:35–36).

This final verse provides the point of the passage. The repetition of the unusual verb "increased" (וַיִּפְרֹץ) from 30:30 and 28:14 (God's promise to Jacob, there translated "spread abroad") reminds the reader that Yahweh is blessing (explicit in 30:20 and ch. 31). Just as God intervened to grow Jacob's family despite the conflict, folly, and superstition in the first narrative section (29:31–30:24), so God intervened to grow Jacob's wealth despite conflict, manipulation, possible superstition, and selfish pursuits. God was fulfilling his promise to Jacob to be with him and protect him, bringing him back to prosper and inherit the land so that Jacob could be the means for God to accomplish his bigger purposes of bringing blessing to the families of the earth. Unfortunately, Jacob would still need lessons in being a blessing. His character is beginning to shift, as we see him acknowledging God's work on his behalf, but he has a long way to go to be the patriarch he needs to be for the nation that God will produce.

THEOLOGICAL FOCUS

God graciously fulfills his promises, helping the hurting, humbling the proud, and providing protection and provision for his chosen servants while allowing them to experience the consequences of their folly.

God is mentioned extensively in the first movement and only mentioned regarding past action in the second movement, but the text clearly points to God at work, providing Jacob a family and wealth, protecting him, and responding graciously to all involved despite their foolish, selfish actions or misunderstandings. Yahweh shows his care for the afflicted and disenfranchised with Leah. He also shows grace

10 There are questions, for example, of the intent of exposing the white, whether he put the rods in the water or in front of the water, and what was intended with the way the flocks faced.

11 Both "poplar" (לִבְנֶה) and "white" (לָבָן) sound like Laban's name ("white"). For an extended exposition of the wordplay on "white" throughout this passage, see Fokkelman (2004, 149–50).

with some remedial discipline for the proud as he allows the selfish Rachel to wait and struggle but responds to her prayer, giving her a son despite her spiteful actions, superstitions, and misunderstanding of God.

God faithfully fulfills his promises even to struggling and self-absorbed servants. He gave Jacob children, extensive flocks, herds, servants, and more. God faithfully kept his promises, protecting and providing for Jacob, whether Jacob could see him or not and whether Jacob acknowledged him or not. God blessed the wily Laban with flocks through Jacob and then used them to enrich Jacob and prepare for his return. God even uses folly and fleshly pursuits to accomplish his purposes, illustrated both by the women trying to guarantee children and Jacob trying to manipulate his stock.

At the core of this narrative, we see God as the giver of life and blessing. It is God who opens the womb and closes the womb (whether of woman or beast). It is Yahweh who gives wealth and takes it away. And it is God who chooses "difficult and unpromising material" to work with to produce his plans (Kidner 1967, 172). He does all of this behind the scenes, in a foreign place, through pain and struggle and disappointment. He keeps his promises whether his servants fully trust him, understand him, call on him, or pursue him. Yet he acts most clearly and directly when they turn to him in dependent prayer.

Humanity often misunderstands God's working and assumes that if their plans work according to their scheming then God has blessed their work. Unfortunately, our fleshly scheming only incites more tensions and conflict. Certainly, God can and does work through even fleshly scheming, but the schemer will incur loss. That loss includes both relationship on the horizontal level with our fellow humans and on the vertical level with God, which is at the core of our loss of the fullness of the blessing that he desires for us.

The presence of blessing in the answers of God to prayer or in the fulfilling of his promises does not guarantee the fullness of relationship that would indicate the extent of blessing that is possible. God keeps promises and allows prosperity, but the struggle of self-will robs the joy and relationship that God created humanity for, as Jacob would eloquently express to Pharaoh (47:9). Abraham's walk with God was replaced by Jacob's struggle with God, as the incident at Penial would powerfully illustrate.

PREACHING AND TEACHING STRATEGIES

Exegetical and Theological Synthesis

One way that this narrative speaks to our listeners' faith journey is to observe how it opens with God's life-giving action. God is moved by Leah's plight of being the unloved wife of Jacob and begins the process of expanding Jacob's family as promised. God miraculously gives children to the unloved and loved wives, all in the context of their family feud. Not much, if any, grace is being extended between God's chosen family members, but he extends his grace to keep his promise to Jacob. The largest part of the narrative contains the saga of how eleven of twelve tribes of Israel come into existence.

Jacob appears helpless in the rivalry of the wives and at one point, out of exasperation, cries out, "Am I in the place of God?" (30:2). Readers might wish Jacob portrayed stronger spiritual leadership in his home! By now we know he is a work in progress, as are we all. God's divine provision in the middle of fallen humanity is also on display as he blesses Laban through Jacob (v. 27 "the LORD has blessed me because of you").

We also discover that nothing the enemy of God's people does can prevent God from blessing his chosen ones. We see this in the latter part of the chapter as Laban and Jacob jockey for the best-bred flock. Jacob clearly wins this battle of the shepherds (30:43, "Thus the man increased greatly and had large flocks").

Preaching Idea
God's people receive hope and help as they watch Him keep his promise to a most dysfunctional family.

Contemporary Connections

What does it mean?
The narrator states matter-of-factly that the Lord is responsible for the birth of children (29:31). No explanation is provided. This concept could also require answering the question, "Is it true?" In either case, the biblical author provides an opportunity to explain God's sovereignty in this important detail of life. Most, if not all, unchurched listeners will not believe in the Lord's supernatural intervention.

We cannot assume that all our listeners understand what the narrator did. Non-Hebrew readers and listeners will not be able to see all the wordplay the wives use in naming their children. Most of our listeners will need an explanation of the role the servants of the wives played in building Jacob's family. Bearing children seems to go above and beyond the call of duty. The wives in our congregations might also object to the physical intimacy required on the part of a husband in this situation—you think? Finally, the narrative closes with Jacob's success, which we should explain in terms of the blessing of God according to his promise.

Is it true?
Listeners may not easily accept the supernatural dimensions in this section. Is it true that the Lord is responsible for child-bearing capability, or is this solely physiological? Our listeners may also have to be convinced that the Lord hears them in their difficulties, just as he did Leah (29:31) and Rachel (30:22). Is it true that the blessing of the Lord on Jacob includes his uncanny ability to manipulate the breeding of the sheep and goats? Is it true that Jacob was able to use some kind of magic involving "fresh sticks of poplar and almond and plane trees, and peeled white streaks" (30:37)? Our listeners may need to be convinced that the blessing of God results in their being able to fulfill everything he has for them to do in this world to be a blessing to those around them.

Now what?
Since the narrator is not directly applying any biblical idea in this section, application will come indirectly from concepts about God and his relationship with the main characters in the narrative. Later in Genesis the author uses the words of Joseph to provide reassurance for God's people who go through difficulties like what Jacob was facing in Laban's actions: "As for you, you meant evil against me, but God meant it for good" (50:20). Here in this Jacob narrative, God's people can see the hand of God at work, making good on his promises.

At one point Jacob preaches to his wives, "But the God of my father has been with me. You know that I have served your father with all my strength" (31:5–6). And all while Jacob is being cheated! What an example for us to follow at times when those in authority are not righteous. This should provide spiritual stability amid a badly broken world. As our listeners rehearse this story of Jacob's interaction with his wives, they should have a strong desire to act in ways that reflect the grace of God. Finally, the narrative ends with Jacob flourishing, which should provide confidence in God's ability to allow all his children to accomplish his will in the world.

Creativity in Presentation
Begin by dividing this section into two broad sections:

- The first section involves God's provision of Jacob's growing family through the two wives and their servants. This covers 29:31–30:24.
- The second section involves God's provision of supernatural shepherding

skills to Jacob to ensure that he leaves his uncle, Laban, with tremendous physical blessing: "large flocks, female servants and male servants, and camels and donkeys" (30:43).

Our preaching idea for these two sections is: God's people receive hope and help from watching God keep his promise to a most dysfunctional family. The hope comes from watching God be faithful to Jacob; the help comes from us watching Jacob and his family continue to struggle because of their carnality and selfishness.

While we learn from this most dysfunctional family, we also take heart in knowing that throughout church history, God has continued to keep his promises to his people even though they struggle to be faithful to him. The narrative is not a license to sin and expect God to bless anyway. The narrative is an opportunity to see the grace of God and not presume upon it. A trip down memory lane by you or some of your listeners may provide vivid examples of the blessing of God in hardship. The more you can bring out the spiritual dysfunctions of Jacob, his wives, and his uncle, the better you will be able to show the grace of God in blessing that holy mess.

The danger of such narratives is that God's people will hear this and assume that God intends to bless every one of his children with the same physical blessings as Jacob's. It is better to explain the blessing of God in terms of the ability to be a blessing to others and experience the spiritual blessings of Ephesians 1.

DISCUSSION QUESTIONS

1. What are some attributes of God that are highlighted in this series of scenes in Jacob's life?

2. How does the fact that "the Lord saw that Leah was hated" bolster your own faith journey? What about the part when "God remembered Rachel, and God listened to her"?

3. How do you handle all the superstition involved in the shepherding antics to gain the best flock possible? More precisely, how do you handle the fact that Jacob used it?

4. What does Leah's situation (not being loved) teach you about the need to worship the Lord supremely? Note particularly, "now my husband will honor me, because I have borne him six sons" (30:20).

5. Why might God bring such prosperity when Jacob and his wives all seem to be so oblivious to him, and even pagan in their attitudes?

6. Why do you think God, through Moses, exposed so much of the dysfunction in Jacob, Rachel, and Leah? How does that contribute to the overall message and opportunity for application?

Genesis 31:1–55 (HB 32:1)

EXEGETICAL IDEA
In escalating conflict, God directed Jacob to return to the promised land to fulfill his vow, teaching him God's authority over people and deities to protect, endow, and establish boundaries for his servants, despite their fearful and foolish reactions.

THEOLOGICAL FOCUS
God protects his servants, drawing them to faith and loyalty, keeping their promises, and trusting him to provide and protect even through foolish reactions and conflicts that only he can resolve.

PREACHING IDEA
Look at what God does to secure the blessing for and extend the blessing through his struggling, growing chosen ones!

PREACHING POINTERS
The original audience must have been encouraged to hear the record of how God protected Jacob through the Laban years. If any listeners are doubting God's ability to cause them to flourish in his will and in their relationship with him, their faith will be strengthened by seeing all that God does to bless Jacob despite Laban. God's wonderful promise, "and I will be with you," provides courage for his people just as it did for Jacob (v. 3). What congregant who is facing gross injustices isn't encouraged by overhearing "the angel of God" say to Jacob, "I have seen all that Laban is doing to you" (vv. 11–12)? Modern listeners will join early readers in seeing that God indeed has the desire and capacity to deliver on his wonderful promises to bless his faithful ones.

And what listener wouldn't be encouraged by reading about a helpless god being stolen? The so-called household gods (v. 35) are no match for Yahweh's power. Nothing can stop God from keeping his promises to bless his children so they can be a blessing. Laban's benefiting from Jacob's presence and work shows how the blessing of God extends to others through his faithful ones (v. 38), but it also shows how God ultimately used Laban to provide for Jacob (v. 43).

VOW CALLED: LESSONS IN SECURITY (31:1–55 [HB 32:1])

LITERARY STRUCTURE AND THEMES

Genesis 31 draws the Jacob-Laban stories to a close, exposing God's consistent work in keeping his promises to protect Jacob, provide for him, and bring him back to the land (28:15). This final crisis would head Jacob's family back toward the land and God's plan. Despite Jacob's (and Rachel's) fearful (and foolish) reactions, Yahweh's intervention would resolve the conflicts with Laban and his clan, establishing boundaries. The presenting issue was inheritance and property ownership, but theologically God asserted his authority as the true source of wealth, to give and remove both property and power, overruling both people and gods. He alone reserves the right to judge and give justice, even restraining vengeance. He remains faithful regardless of the faith (or lack thereof) and reactions of his servants, and yet he will hold his servants accountable to fulfill their promises.

The initial conflict between Jacob and Laban (and his sons, 31:1–3) frames the narrative with the final resolution and covenant between Jacob and Laban (and their "brothers," vv. 45–55). The narrative divides easily into Jacob's flight from Haran (vv. 1–21) and Jacob's confrontation with Laban (vv. 22–55 [HB 32:1]). Each pericope begins with a narrative conflict requiring God's intervention (vv. 1–3; 22–25), followed by two blocks of dialogue (Jacob and his wives [vv. 4–13, 14–16] and Laban and Jacob [vv. 26–30, 31–32]). They are divided by the initial resolution of Jacob's flight from Haran (vv. 17–21). The second section builds tension with a second narrative interlude as Laban searches for his gods (vv. 33–35), followed by two additional blocks of dialogue (Jacob and Laban [vv. 36–42, 43–44]). The final scene resolves the conflict with Laban and his clan, establishing Yahweh as the arbiter (vv. 45–55 [HB 32:1]).

1. At God's command, Jacob stole away (31:1–21).
   - a. Narration: God directed Jacob back to Canaan (31:1–3).
     - b. Dialogue: Jacob accused Laban to his wives (31:4–13).
     - c. Dialogue: Jacob's wives agreed (31:14–16).
     - d. Narration (initial resolution): Jacob stole away (31:17–21).
2. God protected Jacob, establishing boundaries (31:22–55 [HB 32:1]).
   - a'. Narration: God protected Jacob from Laban (31:22–25).
     - b'. Dialogue: Laban accused Jacob of theft (31:26–30).
     - c'. Dialogue: Jacob denied wrongdoing (31:31–32).
   - a''. Narration: Laban could not find his gods (31:33–35).
     - b''. Dialogue: Jacob accused Laban of systematic abuse (31:36–42).
     - c''. Dialogue: Laban requested a covenant (31:43–44).
     - d'. Narration (final resolution): Jacob and Laban cut a covenant (31:45–55 [HB 32:1]).

The parallel structure, through the building tension, emphasizes the authority of Yahweh to protect his servant and fulfill his promise over the powerlessness of people and other gods.

- ***At God's Command, Jacob Stole Away (31:1–21)***
- ***God Protected Jacob, Establishing Boundaries (31:22–55 [HB 32:1])***

EXPOSITION

Jacob's flight from Haran in Genesis 31 complements his arrival (29:1–30), framing the account of his prosperity there (29:31–30:43; for the macro structure, see the Introduction to the Jacob Narratives, p. 427). When Jacob arrived, he was the outsider that Laban used to marry off his two daughters and gain wealth. When Jacob left, God had given him wives, children, and wealth, at Laban's expense. By the end of this narrative, Laban was the outsider, and Jacob's security was formalized in a covenant.

In both passages, deception plays a significant role as Jacob must learn difficult lessons of faith to consciously depend on his God rather than his wits. Throughout Jacob's stay, God was at work to accomplish his ends despite human shortcomings. In extricating Jacob from Haran, God would both provide the necessary security and engineer a lasting and amicable parting that resolved the tensions. Yet he held Jacob accountable for his vow, reminding him of his responsibility to Yahweh on his return. In escalating conflict, God directed Jacob to return to the promised land to fulfill his vow, teaching him God's authority over people and deities to protect, endow, and establish boundaries for his servants, despite their fearful and foolish reactions.

At God's Command, Jacob Stole Away (31:1–21)

When Jacob recognized the conflict brewing with Laban and his sons, and at God's direction, he collected his family and possessions and fled Haran and Laban for Canaan (31:1–21).

God Directed Jacob Back to Canaan (31:1–3)

When Jacob recognized the souring attitude of Laban and his sons, God directed him to return to Canaan.

31:1–2. Laban's sons, previously only mentioned as caring for the odd-colored animals to keep Jacob from realizing greater profits (30:35), now express jealousy over his growing wealth.[1] One is tempted to see them as lazy, embracing Laban's strategy to use Jacob for his own gain (30:27–28), doing none of the hard work and realizing all of the profits (Cotter 2003). Their complaint seemed to jar Jacob into realizing that Laban was no longer acting favorably towards him with his growing wealth (30:43). As Jacob would express forcefully, Laban had been trying to cheat him for a long time, but now the pleasant façade was removed.

31:3. At that point God intervened, reminding Jacob of his promised presence and Jacob's vow (28:15, 20–22; cf. 31:13), calling him to return. Reminiscent of God's call to Abraham (12:1; cf. Wenham 1994, 270), it was time for Jacob to fulfill his vow and take his place in God's program. It was Yahweh, not Rebekah, who called Jacob to return, drawing attention to Jacob's response of faith and faithfulness to Yahweh (Bunn 2018, 176). The report of Jacob's dream here prepares for Jacob's claims to his wives in the following scene.

Jacob Accused Laban to His Wives (31:4–13)

Jacob presented his case against Laban for unfair labor practices to Rachel and Leah, with God's command to return to Canaan.

1 The sons' claim that Jacob had taken all their father's wealth may not be as clearly hyperbole as we might expect. Nuzi documents show an expected turnover of the flock in about six and a half years (Morrison 1983, 158).

31:4–5. Jacob called the sister-wives out to the pasture for a conference. A safe distance from listening ears (cf. 27:5), he isolated the two most-impacted and significant members. Omitting the reaction of their brothers, Jacob focused on the attitude and actions of "your father" (repeated four times in vv. 4–13) in contrast to God's care for him ("Elohim" is also repeated four times).

He began with his observations of Laban's changed attitude. In contrast, God was "with" him, a clear allusion to God's promise in his vision at Bethel (28:15). This opening gambit directly escalated the conflict from Jacob versus Laban to Laban ("your father") versus God ("the God of my father").[2] As he would clarify, Jacob was not taking their father's wealth (the accusation of the brothers, 31:1), but God had given it to him.

31:6–9. In contrast, Jacob directed their attention to his unflagging work ethic, serving Laban "with all my strength" (v. 6). In response, twice more he contrasted Laban deliberately cheating him (תלל, v. 7) by repeatedly changing his wages (v. 8), with God protecting him ("did not permit him to harm me," v. 7).[3] God had transferred the flocks to Jacob (v. 9). Jacob appears as merely a bystander in his retelling of the past six years. His manipulation of the sticks and the flocks did not accomplish the transfer of wealth. God was fully responsible for the outcome in his favor, again asserting God was "with" him (v. 7), fulfilling his promise (28:15).

Shepherd's Wages

Wages for a shepherd were typically set each spring at the time of shearing and the renewing of the contract for the following year (Morrison 1983, 158). That would give Laban five natural times to change his wages, and he may have intervened at other times, but since the birthing is once a year, it would be unlikely that he would have occasion other than at the reconsignment after shearing. He may also be including Laban substituting Leah for Rachel and requiring an additional seven years of service. Consequently, the "ten times" is likely figurative for "repeatedly" (Sarna 1989, 214).

TRANSLATION ANALYSIS 31:9

Jacob's conclusion that God had "taken away" Laban's flocks and given them to him is stated curiously. The verb here in the *hiphil* stem (נצל) usually implies an act of rescue (i.e., Judg. 11:26; Prov. 2:12; Amos 3:12). So, Wenham (1994, 271) and Mathews (2005, 513) argue for that sense here, as well as in Genesis 31:16 in the mouth of Rachel and Leah. Sarna (1989, 214), however, notes the use of this term as a common Aramaism for the transfer of property in various ancient documents, which fits very well in the context of Haran without necessarily implying divine rescue of the animals. For an Israelite audience, Moses may have used that Aramaism tongue-in-cheek.

31:10–13. Jacob concluded his appeal with his strongest argument. He had seen a vision of the flock mating, and an angel had explained that the siring of the unusually colored flocks was because God had "seen" (רָאִיתִי) what Laban had done to him. As we noted when Yahweh "saw (וַיַּרְא) that Leah was hated" (29:31), Yahweh's observation includes intervention. The vision of the "striped, spotted, and mottled" goats

2 Wenham (1994, 270) notes that three times Jacob compared Laban's attitude and actions with God's protection and provision (vv. 5, 6–7, 8–9) before concluding with his vision report (vv. 10–13). Actually, the conflict was between God and Laban, not between Jacob and Laban.

3 The specifics of the wage changes, from "spotted" to "striped" (v. 8) and the dream listing all three recessive coloring traits, suggest that the confusing nature of the bargaining (30:28–33) and the outworking (v. 39) may result from telescoping all the haggling into a single conversation.

exclusively mating (31:12), standing for all the animals (sheep and goats), explained the outcome for Jacob. God then reminded Jacob of his vow and called him to return to the land of his kindred.

While Jacob's dream report is significantly longer than the account in verse 3, it ends with the nearly identical call to return to Canaan (only leaving out "of your fathers"). It is not immediately clear if Jacob was adding to the dream to impress his wives or if he was accurately reporting. Since the following narrative substantiates the claims that it was all from God, there is no reason to doubt him here. Jacob may have telescoped multiple dreams into a single report.[4] On the other hand, he may have had the dream (or dreams) earlier and waited until the time was right to implement his plan when Laban was away.[5] Either way, Jacob responded in obedience and used the dream to add incentive to his wives to leave their family, community, and way of life for a new place and the promise of Yahweh.

Jacob's Wives Agreed (31:14–16)

Rachel and Leah affirmed Laban's culpability and agreed to go, in obedience to God.

31:14–16. Jacob's focus on Laban resonated with his two wives. Finally united in their disillusionment against their father after so much struggle and referring to him five times in these three verses, they describe feeling bereft of any expected inheritance (v. 14), sold as a commodity, and treated like a foreigner only to satisfy his appetites (v. 15). They agreed (repeating Jacob's Aramaism from v. 9) that all Laban's wealth had been transferred to Jacob by God as compensation for all they should have received from their father.

Without further insight into their local customs, the complaint of the women is not clear. They seem to be complaining of a missing dowry or perhaps the expectation of their share of the brideprice. Since there was not any actual bride price paid, but only service, they may simply be asserting that their father had indeed cheated Jacob and so them (Wenham 1994, 273). On the other hand, they seem to expect some part of the inheritance, but without a "formal assignment" they would get nothing (see The Bride Price Sidebar), and Laban had indicated no inclination to do so (Westbrook 1991, 158). They then saw Jacob's property as their deserved dowry, provided by God against Laban's intention (Morrison 1983, 161). As such, they acknowledged God's provision for them within God's promise to Jacob, forming the basis for their willingness to go with Jacob, obeying God's command.

The Bride Price

Often the bride price (paid by the groom to the father) would be given to the bride "as an indirect dowry" and a sort of "financial reserve" to care for her if need arose (Walton 2009a, 160–61). Thus, they may be expecting part of the inheritance as a bride price. Certainly, they both got a slave girl, a significant bridal gift, and part of the dowry (Westbrook 1991, 145). Daughters may also expect a gift at marriage that would be their share of the inheritance as dowry (Westbrook

4 Sarna (1989, 214) takes this to show that God had given him the strategy earlier.

5 If the order of events in verses 1 through 3 is intended chronologically and in fairly quick succession, then the command to return from Yahweh may not have been at the time of the mating (v. 10, occurring June to September; Firmage, "Sheep," *ABD* 6:1127) since they left during the shearing (v. 19, typically in the spring; Morrison 1983, 158). Either there was more than one dream, with the acknowledgment of Yahweh's oversight earlier and his command to leave later, or Jacob did not act immediately on the command, so that the chronology is not tight in the narrative. Nevertheless, he does obey, albeit at a time that shows both his response to Yahweh and his fear of Laban.

1991, 157). The only way to receive it, however, if her father does not give it during his life, was when he died and then only if he had made a "formal assignment" (Westbrook 1991, 158).

In going with Jacob, they were willing to trust Yahweh and his promises, leaving their previous lives behind. The chosen family seems to be growing in their recognition of God's working (building on the births in 29:31–30:24). Rachel's subsequent theft, however, reminds of the competition among the worldviews for her loyalties to God and his promise, even as they return with Jacob to pay his vow to worship Yahweh alone (28:21).

Jacob Stole Away (31:17–21)
Jacob took his family and belongings and stole away, with Rachel's stolen gods.

31:17–21. Jacob responded immediately to their agreement. Without waiting for the ladies to change their minds or Laban to catch wind, he loaded his family on camels and put all his animals and possessions on the road to Canaan and Isaac (see Sidebar at 24:10–14 for camels in this era, p. 416). In providing this accounting of "his property," Moses legitimates Jacob's claims (31:9, cf. v. 16), exposing the sons' jealousy (v. 1) and Laban's false claim to ownership of all of it (v. 43).

Verse 19 clarifies why Jacob wanted to leave immediately. Laban was shearing his sheep, providing another evidence of ill feelings. We already know they were pasturing three days away (30:36; the length of time to get the report, 31:22). Sheep shearing was a massive undertaking, requiring huge amounts of labor and time.[6] Laban was fully occupied and unable to immediately follow. It was a celebration, but Jacob had not been invited to the party.

In the rush to leave, Rachel "stole" (גנב) her father's "household gods" (lit. "teraphim" [הַתְּרָפִים], v. 19). Jacob, by leaving secretly, "tricked" Laban (lit. "stole the heart of," also using the same verb as Rachel's theft [גנב]). Being outwitted was probably less significant for Laban, but the actions of both Jacob and Rachel contributed to the confrontation with Laban that would both demonstrate God's power and presence and bring resolution to Jacob's Aramean sojourn, preparing for their return to Canaan. Jacob made his break, crossing the Euphrates and heading for home. For the moment it seemed that Jacob had finally won.

Household Gods

Here, the "teraphim" are consistently translated "household gods" (e.g., ESV, NIV, NRSV), "household idols" (e.g., NET, NJPS, NLT), or just "idols" (NCV). After all, Laban called the "teraphim" his "gods" (אֱלֹהָי, v. 30). The significance of these is widely debated, however. They have been viewed as household deities, with possession signifying "legal title to a given estate" (based on some Nuzi documents; Speiser 1964, 250; cf. Heltzer 1998). Since they are leaving with no intent to return, this has less relevance. Spanier (1992) claims they gave Rachel's children priority. Van der Toorn (1990) has argued that they are better understood as ancestor figurines (not strictly speaking deities) that could be used in divination. Divination is clearly connected to them in the Old Testament (e.g., Ezek. 21:21 [HB 26]; Zech. 10:2), though the specific ritual is uncertain. Prized possessions for whatever reason, they were a significant loss for Laban, and while they may not be intended for personal worship (Walton 2009a, 112), here they contribute to a powerful apologetic for Yahweh's exclusive authority over people, property, and the future.

6 Sarna (1989, 216) notes Mesopotamian records from the eighteenth century BC describing the need for over one thousand men and another requiring three to four hundred men for three days (cf. Frankena 1972, 57).

TRANSLATION ANALYSIS 31:20
The expression "to steal the heart" is used only here in the Old Testament. It is translated "tricked" (ESV, NCV), "deceived" (NASB95, NET, NIV, see *HALOT* s.v. "גנב" 198), or "outwitted" (NLT, RSV). Bringing the figure into English, NKJV translates it "stole away." In the context, it is explained as leaving stealthily, without Laban knowing and so without being able to give a proper farewell (vv. 27–28). The Hebrew idiom with "heart," however, packs more punch than the translations imply. If "heart" here denotes the "seat of feeling and emotions" (*HALOT* s.v. "לֵב" 514, 3.), by metonymy it emphasizes Laban's loss of what "he held most dear" (Cotter 2003, 235). If it refers to his "attention, consideration, reason," then it would intend "to outwit" (*HALOT* s.v. "לֵב" 514, 7., their evaluation, cf. "kept in the dark," NJPS). Perhaps the ambiguity adds impact by double entendre.

God Protected Jacob, Establishing Boundaries (31:22–55 [HB 32:1])

Pursuing Jacob for theft, Laban was warned by God, and, unable to find his stolen gods, he asked for peace, concluding a covenant with Jacob and establishing peace and boundaries between their clans.

Yahweh Protected Jacob from Laban (31:22–25)

When Laban pursued Jacob, God intervened, warning him not to harm Jacob.

31:22–23. Laban heard about Jacob running on the third day, gathered his kinsmen, and gave chase, catching Jacob seven days later. The chronology sounds simple until you look at a map and realize the distance is over three hundred miles. Jacob would not be able to take his family, flocks, and possessions at a pace of thirty miles per day.[7] The numbers, then, may well be figurative, but the likely reason Laban did not catch him sooner is because of having to finish up the shearing and prepare for the trip (Walton 2001, 591).

31:24–25. Before Laban could confront Jacob, however, God intervened, warning Laban. God's prohibition, "Be careful not to say anything to Jacob, either good or bad," may refer to not passing sentence against Jacob (to bring harm to him, cf. v. 29; Sherwood 1990, 315).[8] Rather than merely prohibiting Laban's habit of bait and switch, saying good and doing bad (Steinmann 2019, 299), Yahweh was prohibiting Laban from unjust judgment and so vengeance against him.

Laban Accused Jacob of Theft (31:26–30)

Laban pressed his case against Jacob for stealing away with his gods, admitting God's protection of Jacob.

31:26–28. Laban confronted Jacob with the same question with which Yahweh confronted Eve and Cain (3:13; 4:10) and Pharoah and Abimelech confronted Abraham (12:18; 20:9). In all cases it indicated a deep affront caused by foolish and supposedly hidden actions. In this case, however, the accusation was not fully accurate. Jacob had indeed "stolen his heart" (see footnote on 31:20), stealing away secretly, though Laban's claim to want to merely send off his family with

7 The distance is uncertain. Walton (2001, 591) estimates about three hundred miles and an average pace of about ten miles per day for Jacob, while Sarna (1989, 217) estimates four hundred miles and an average progress from ancient Near Eastern evidence of only about six miles a day for such a large caravan.

8 We have already argued that "knowing good and evil" indicates choosing one's own standards autonomously (see discussion on 2:16–17, p. 106), leading to the idea of judging by declaring "good or evil" (cf. 2 Sam. 14:17; 1 Kings 3:9). Steinmann appropriately notes, however, that Jacob allowed for just claims against him (Gen. 31:32).

a celebration is suspect (cf. 30:27–28 and discussion there, p. 506). Jacob had not, of course, driven off Laban's daughters as "captives of the sword" (31:27). They were clearly in favor and themselves disillusioned with their father's lack of concern for them (v. 15). In fact, Wenham has noted the ironic hypocrisy in claiming that Jacob is both a brigand, raiding Laban's property of (Jacob's own) women and children, and at the same time a fugitive, fleeing Laban (v. 29, cf. v. 27; Wenham 1994, 274–75). Laban's claim to Jacob's lack of courtesy turned ominous, however, when he stated that Jacob had "done foolishly" (v. 28), leading up to what he considered the main complaint.

31:29–30. Laban clarified his insinuation as he described God's intervention in the previously reported dream, preventing his (apparent) intention to harm Jacob and exposing his dishonesty. God's protection had unmasked his hypocrisy and powerless threat. In his frustration, Laban shifted to patronizing sympathy for Jacob's long absence from his home before clarifying his real complaint. He believed Jacob had stolen his "gods" (אֱלֹהִים, see discussion and Sidebar at 31:19). While the shift to "gods" here instead of "teraphim" is appropriate for ancestral images, it also suggests a contrast with Yahweh, Jacob's ancestral God (v. 29), which will become more acute in the following scene. Jacob's God prevented Laban from retaliating for the theft of his "gods," showing who held power. If they were specifically connected to divination, it was in the absence of any ability to gain direction that Yahweh specifically (and ironically) gave him instruction in how he must act, protecting Jacob and his family and denying Laban's complaint.

Jacob Denied Wrongdoing (31:31–32)
Jacob rejected Laban's accusation, questioning Laban's motives.

31:31–32. Jacob explained his fear that Laban would forcibly take Jacob's family from him ("your daughters" would necessarily include their children, v. 31). We now realize, however, that Jacob did not know of Rachel's theft. Whether the theft of teraphim was a capital offense or not, Jacob pronounced the death penalty on whoever was found with them, raising the stakes and endangering his most loved wife. Jacob demanded that Laban produce anything that belonged to him before the witness of the assembled clansmen. Jacob not only maintained his innocence but revealed Laban's claim against all his property (v. 43) to be false. Laban would find nothing he could declare to be stolen.

Laban Could Not Find His Gods (31:33–35)
Laban searched for his gods but could not find them.

31:33–35. In this highly charged scene, Laban began with his most likely suspect, yet farthest from the truth, moving methodically closer to the truth (which the reader knows) but further from his expectations. Searching each tent, he of course found nothing. At this point the reader is finally told of Rachel's strategy, claiming to be in her monthly cycle. Her claim that she was not being disrespectful convinced her father, aided by the cultural discomfort with ritual uncleanness. The Babylonians believed that "a person could contact pollution merely by coming close to [a woman in her period] or by looking at her" (van der Toorn and Denning-Bolle 1994, 51)!

Of course, the "gods" were defiled by proximity to her, and additionally in the minds of the Israelite reader, by being hidden in a camel saddle on which she sat ("reinforcing the author's disapproval," [Lev. 11:4; Deut. 14:7]; Mathews 2005, 526). The "ironic humor" of Laban looking for his presumably powerful gods under an unclean woman (Cotter 2003, 238), is compounded by their hiddenness and inability to help Laban in his dilemma. In contrast, Yahweh had openly and powerfully orchestrated Jacob's wealth, protection, and return to his homeland.

Jacob Accused Laban of Systematic Abuse (31:36–42)

Jacob presented his case against Laban for false accusations and unfair labor practices, claiming God's vindication.

31:36–37. Jacob's pent-up anger overflowed. He "berated Laban" (v. 36), demanding that Laban produce the evidence of the wrong-doing that he had accused Jacob of before the clansmen. Jacob's demand would vindicate him. Laban had clearly found nothing with which to validate his charges, and Jacob would claim not only innocence but establish his own grievances before the witnesses.[9]

TRANSLATION ANALYSIS 31:36

Translated variously, "berated" (from the root ריב, "argued," NET; "took to task," NIV; "contended," NASB95; "rebuked," NKJV; "upbraided," NRSV) can be used in formal accusations requiring formal court proceedings (e.g., Exod. 23:2; Deut. 19:17), though here the trial is called before the witnesses at hand. Jacob was forcefully repudiating the accusations.

31:38–42. Jacob's accusations span his sojourn in Haran, framing them with "these twenty years" (vv. 38, 41). He presented Laban's offenses as systematic, intentional, and oppressive. Contrary to custom and reasonable expectations, his faithful and impeccable service under extreme working conditions had been rewarded by unreasonable demands. Rather than share in the profits of herding for Laban, Jacob contracted for his wives for fourteen years, then set wages for the rest, which Laban consistently changed to his expected advantage. Jacob's lengthy participation in Laban's household had been met by an excessive bride price, and still Laban had actively tried to steal from him what he legitimately earned by changing the wage consistently (see exposition on v. 7 above).

Herding Contracts

Compared to the Old Babylonian herding contracts, Jacob's complaints show he was treated unfairly. The herdsmen were typically exempted from repaying losses if they had not been negligent or from wild animals (cf. Exod. 22:12 [HB 13]), and they were allowed a 15 percent loss rate from the expected birthrate without bearing responsibility (Morrison 1983, 156–57). The owner should have provided the appropriate clothing for him year around, suggesting another serious breach of protocol (Finkelstein 1968, 36).

Laban had concluded his accusations against Jacob by acknowledging that his opportunity (desire?) to harm Jacob had been thwarted by God's intervention (v. 29). Jacob concluded with his interpretation of Laban's threat that, apart from God's intervention, he would be sent away empty. Instead, God, the "Fear of Isaac"[10] had "seen" (רָאָה, v. 42, cf. v. 12) his affliction and hard work and had rebuked Laban, vindicating Jacob. While Jacob had invited Laban to display any stolen goods so that the witnessing kinsmen could render judgment (v. 37), he now declared that God had already rendered the verdict of his innocence and Laban's oppression.[11] Jacob had been fully protected by the presence of Yahweh,

9 Sarna (1989, 220) notes the forensic overtones of Jacob's complaint, as he calls the witnesses to decide "the real thief."

10 "The Fear of Isaac" as a title for Yahweh occurs only here and in v. 53. While it is unusual, it fits the context exceptionally well, describing the God of his fathers (cf. vv. 5, 29, 53) who was with him, with the fear produced in the heart of his enemies who would oppose Israel after the exodus (Exod. 15:16; Deut. 2:25; 11:25; cf. Mathews 2005, 529–30).

11 As with much in the patriarchal narratives, God's oversight while out of the land anticipates Israel coming out of Egypt (Exod. 3:7; Deut. 26.7; cf. Wenham 1994, 278).

as Yahweh had promised, vindicating his innocence and fully providing all that he had, despite Laban's intentions.

Laban Requested a Covenant (31:43–44)
Admitting only helplessness, Laban requested a covenant.

31:43–44. Laban was trapped. He had no gods, he had no evidence, and he had been warned by Yahweh. Without any basis, he weakly complained that all was his. Frustrated, he requested a covenant that would protect him from any future aggression by Jacob and protect his daughters' position with Jacob (vv. 50, 52).

Jacob and Laban Cut a Covenant (31:45–55 [HB 32:1])
Laban and Jacob made a covenant before Yahweh, establishing a nonaggression treaty as equals.

31:45–54. Reminiscent of his vow at Bethel, Jacob erected a standing stone and directed the kinsmen to erect a pile of stones, where they ate a covenant meal together. Both Laban and Jacob named it "(the) heap of witness" (author's translation) in their respective languages, marking the boundary between their respective spheres. With the oath of the covenant, the stones formed a physical reminder of their agreement, while Yahweh would hold them accountable to maintain their oaths. Laban clarified his concern for his daughters being beyond his protection.

The focus on the daughters and their rights as wives suggests that at least the covenant finally completed the marriage agreement (Morrison 1983, 160–63). Walton (2009a, 114) views this as a marriage contract, only to be used when necessary to protect someone's rights. Either way, Laban seems to settle for the best he can get, realizing he no longer has any direct role in their lives and perhaps saving some face.

Laban continued with what may have been his greater concern, that Jacob would not return to do him harm (vv. 51–53). As was his habit, taking credit for what he did not do (or would not do, vv. 27–28; or did not have, v. 43), he claimed to have set up the pile and pillar for the witness (cf. vv. 45–46). He then called on the gods of both families to judge between them, showing the polytheistic background of the family in Haran (cf. Josh. 24:2). Only Jacob is reported as swearing, though it would have been a mutually sworn covenant, perhaps to keep the focus on the responsibility of Jacob and his descendants to convey blessing (cf. Gen. 21:22–32) and Yahweh's sole authority.

TRANSLATION ANALYSIS 31:53
"God" in all three instances is plural (אֱלֹהִים, v. 53). It is generally plural, even when only one God is intended (usually Yahweh), but it is then typically used with a singular verb. In this case, however, the verb is plural (lit. "may they judge," יִשְׁפְּטוּ). Grammatically, then, it should most likely be translated, "May the God of Abraham and the god of Nahor, the gods of their father, judge" (NET, cf. NJPS), rather than the more common translation found in the ESV and many others.

Again, the text mentions the meal (31:46, 54) accompanying the covenant (31:44) provided by Jacob with his sacrifice (31:54). As with Isaac's covenant with Abimelech, the meal formalized the covenant and symbolized their new relationship (26:30).

The Covenant Meal
The covenant meal was a common ANE custom that symbolically expressed the solidarity of the covenant enacted (Mendenhall and Herion, "Covenant," *ABD* 1:1194). "The covenant feast, being sacrificial, was intended to create more than a merely social bond between the parties, who would regard themselves as bound together in the table-fellowship of their divine host" (Kidner 1967, 178). It was incorporated into the Mosaic covenant in a meal between the elders of Israel and Yahweh (Exod. 24:9–11), showing

the new relationship between Israel and Yahweh. In the New Covenant it appears again in the Lord's table, to be celebrated regularly in Christ's church.

31:55 [HB 32:1]. With the covenant enacted, Laban blessed his daughters and grandchildren before returning home. The initial conflict, seen both in the words of his sons and his attitude (vv. 1–2), as well as in the perceptions of his daughters (vv. 14–15), was resolved with a covenant of peace. The master/servant relationship (vv. 6, 41) was replaced with a covenant between equals. God had been at work protecting and providing, despite Jacob's fear and Rachel's folly. Jacob's conditions for his vow had been fulfilled far beyond his desire for food and clothing, with wives, children, many possessions, and a formally enacted peace (cf. 28:20–21). He had yet to meet Esau, but he was fully obligated to return and complete his vow, as God had reminded him.

THEOLOGICAL FOCUS

God protects his servants, drawing them to faith and loyalty, keeping their promises, and trusting him to provide and protect even through foolish reactions and conflicts that only he can resolve.

Yahweh oversees his creation, supplying children and resources, restraining the predatory intentions of people, restoring relationships, and reassuring his fearful servants. He graciously works for the good of his people and his purposes despite mixed and self-centered motives. He does not dictate actions or reactions, but he directs to his intended destination. He judges his creatures justly, repaying Laban's deception with deception (as he did for Jacob, 29:1–30; cf. Fuchs 1988).

The main narrative issue was the rightful title to the material goods, the theft of the gods, and justice. Theologically, the narrative presents Yahweh as the source of wealth, judgement, and justice, including overruling animal genetics, human manipulation, human intent, and ability to bring vengeance or harm. All of this was vetted in public when Yahweh vindicated Jacob before the whole family so that none could mistake it as merely Jacob outwitting Laban.

Within that theological arena, the gods of Laban were absent. In contrast to Jacob's God, Laban's gods are stolen, defiled, lost, silent, and powerless to protect Laban and his sons from his servant Jacob and his God, Yahweh. Only Jacob swears to the covenant, perhaps even here passively showing the right of Yahweh alone to guarantee the future. Yahweh shows his authority over other gods and peoples outside of the land.

Jacob must bow and respond in faith and obedience to Yahweh, the final judge and sovereign giver of all. God summoned Jacob to pay his vow, which would mean that Jacob would finally and necessarily acknowledge Yahweh alone as God, illustrated in this narrative. The necessary response to the sole sovereign king is faith and loyalty, both of which must grow in our walking with God.[12]

At Yahweh's direction, Laban can make no judgment against Jacob. Of course, the source of blessing (or cursing) is only to be found in Yahweh. No agenda apart from his can stand. His purpose and promise will not fail. His stated promise of protection for Jacob declares his ability to oversee his servants anywhere in his creation.

Yahweh will continue to uphold his promise to Abraham. He will bless those who bless him and his family and curse the one who curses. Laban reaps the benefits of his opposition to Jacob with his loss of his property and family. Yet Jacob has also had to learn that his fear and foolish actions are not without consequences. God does not always act as quickly as we might expect or desire, giving Jacob a twenty-year lesson in serving, but he will remain faithful to

12 Cf. Bunn (2018, esp. 182), who sees Jacob's response of faith as the main issue of the narrative.

his promises, even when his chosen servant is unfaithful or faltering in faith.

At the same time, he expects his images to live in righteousness and justice (18:19) and, of course, faith, not fear (28:15; 31:3, 12–13; cf. 31:31). God will hold them accountable for their actions. They can walk in honesty and open faithfulness even during conflict. God uses conflict to show humanity their dependence. Jacob did respond in obedience and showed faith, though he tried to minimize his danger because of his fear of Laban. He must learn that his schemes and trickery do not save. Only Yahweh can ultimately bring the desired peace and freedom that Jacob and God's people of all ages desperately need. Each of these theological lessons only deepens as we see God more clearly in Christ and our responsibilities as his representatives in his world. God has not changed and we must bow in faith, living out his character in justice and righteousness (1 Peter 2:9–12).

PREACHING AND TEACHING STRATEGIES

Exegetical and Theological Synthesis

The preacher or teacher can begin preparation by highlighting all the places in this lengthy narrative that describe God's preserving actions that allow Jacob to experience the blessing (31:3, 5, 7, 9, 11, 16, 24, 29, 42). The repeated references to God's actions on behalf of Jacob teach us that our best human efforts alone are not enough to secure the blessing of God in this world. This is a classic example of fallen humanity meeting divine provision.

Add to this the amount of effort Laban exerted to thwart Jacob's rise to prominence and independence and we can see that the enemy is active but not able to stop the Lord from accomplishing his will for his chosen one. One of the greatest oppositions to Jacob's success was Rachel's decision to take her father's "household gods" (v. 34). The narrative doesn't tell us her motive. All we know is that she took them without Jacob knowing (v. 32). For some reason, Rachel's actions have no repercussions. Jacob's own faith is affirmed at the end of the narrative and the covenant-making process. He calls on the Lord in verse 49. The Lord faithfully brought Jacob this far. Our listeners take courage seeing God's faithfulness through it all.

Preaching Idea

Look at what God does to secure the blessing for and extend the blessing through his struggling, growing chosen ones!

Contemporary Connections

What does it mean?

In verse 7 Jacob states, "But God did not permit him to harm me." This allows preachers to explain the sovereignty and providence of God. God protects Jacob's success or, to put it negatively, does not allow Laban to thwart Jacob's success. It is important to notice, however, that Laban created great grief for Jacob. The Lord's protection did not equal smooth sailing for Jacob (v. 7, "your father has cheated me. . . . But God did not permit him to harm me"). The same protection occurs in verse 24 when the Lord speaks to Laban in a dream.

The implications of Rachel's decision to steal his father's gods is another matter that can be cleared up. Evidently Rachel is not convinced that the Lord is the only god to rely on. Other gods vie for our affections in this world and promise what only the Lord can deliver. Readers may miss the subtle way in which the household gods are portrayed as powerless: they are stolen, hidden, defiled, and offer no help at all to Laban.

Is it true?

Some listeners will have difficulty believing that the Lord protected Jacob by not permitting Laban to harm him (v. 7). The biblical author is not proving that this is true but simply stating it as a reality. Early readers would readily accept this as true; our readers and listeners may not. It is important that the Lord's protection of Jacob is couched in the context of how the Lord has been dealing with the patriarchs throughout the Genesis story. In other words, Scripture has been portraying God like this all along. All throughout the narrative God has been faithfully keeping his promises to bless his chosen ones. Others may not accept the fact that God spoke directly to Laban "in a dream by night" (v. 24). Finally, some of our listeners may need convincing that "the God of Abraham and the Fear of Isaac" (v. 42) is the true God, while "the household gods" (v. 34) of Laban are counterfeit, helpless deities.

Now what?

When it comes to applying Scripture like this Jacob narrative, let's begin with making a link between the blessing of God on Jacob and God's blessing on all of us who believe. We may have to move from primarily tangible, physical blessings, such as family size and acreage, to "spiritual blessing[s] in the heavenly places" (Eph. 1:3). And we should probably be crystal clear and point out that God's blessing on Jacob did not erase years of abuse at the hands of his uncle. With that said, our listeners should be encouraged to see God's faithfulness and know that he will continue to be faithful to them in their faith journey until it is completed. Reading all that God did on behalf of Jacob provides tremendous stability when Laban takes the form of the world, the flesh, and the devil.

Creativity in Presentation

Many of your listeners will be able to look back over their faith journey and see God at work. The 20/20 vision that hindsight provides also gives tremendous encouragement to our faith. It shows us the faithfulness of God firsthand. We can then proclaim, "Look at what God does to secure the blessing for and extend the blessing through his struggling, growing chosen ones!"

- You might begin your teaching and preaching with God's foundational promise: "and I will be with you" (31:3, 5, 42, 49, 50, 53). As noted above, the narrative rehearses all that God did to bless Jacob in the context of Laban's injustices. Include all those details in this section so that everyone knows the power of God to bless his chosen ones.
- The second section can be somewhat shorter but includes the opposition Laban presented to Jacob. Instead of God's people seeing God erase all difficulty from Jacob's life, the opposite is true: often bane, not the absence of pain, is the context of God's blessing. Those newer to the faith benefit from hearing this reality early in their Christian experience.
- Finally, verses 43 to the end of the chapter highlight God's sole ability to provide true shalom in this world. This is on display in the covenant-building that takes place at Laban's request (v. 44). All the witness language culminates in, "God is witness between you and me" (vv. 50, 53). Jacob and all of us who profess faith in Christ must live our lives faithfully; it is the only right response to such a faithful God.

DISCUSSION QUESTIONS

1. Rehearse the times when God clearly protected you from some danger. This will help solidify God's providential care on display in this chapter.

2. Discuss what makes it difficult in our society's thinking to accept God's miraculous handling of biological genetics (cf. v. 8, "then all the flock bore spotted . . . then all the flock bore striped").

3. Create a list of competing loyalties and discuss the pull of today's counterfeit gods on our loyalties.

4. What has God done recently in your life that you need to publicly praise him for? Spend some time praising God for being on our side (v. 42, "If the God of my father, the God of Abraham and the Fear of Isaac, had not been on my side, surely").

5. Review the fact that God's plan for his people often involves years of pain, even though he is faithfully bringing about his blessing. Why and how does God use that pain?

6. When God is clearly working, why are we still tempted so strongly to try to work some things out on our own?

Genesis 32:1–32 (HB 32:2–33)

EXEGETICAL IDEA

God's presence, verified by his angels, guaranteed Jacob's security and future blessing, despite Esau's threat and Jacob's self-reliance, ironically, by incapacitating him so that he might cling to Yahweh and receive blessing, commemorated by a new name.

THEOLOGICAL FOCUS

God's presence guarantees the security and blessing of his servants who turn to him in prayer, requiring humble dependence, graciously fostered through confrontation with their inability to secure it on their own.

PREACHING IDEA

God's training camp is where his children receive his blessing in his presence through trials, prayer, and humble dependence.

PREACHING POINTERS

The original audience learns theology that functions for the church through following Jacob's experiences as he journeys back to the promised land. His character functions both as a "go and do likewise" and a "go and do otherwise" exemplar. The pathway to transition for listeners occurs through encouraging them not to follow Jacob's example of fear and distress. Readers can see that Jacob only trusts God to a point, but that faith does not overcome his fears with respect to Esau's reaction. That explains why Jacob prepares for Esau's attack.

We can also encourage listeners to emulate Jacob as he prays to the Lord. His prayer is packed with instructions on how to address the Lord. The prayer also shows Jacob confessing his unworthiness to be on the receiving end of God's love and faithfulness. Jacob is honest with God about his fear of his brother, Esau. And, for his own sake, Jacob reminds God of the promise God made him.

One of the highlights of the section is Jacob wrestling with God at night. Jacob's bout shows his tenacity in desiring to receive God's blessing. His experience results in the kind of dependence that every true child of God must grow into. God changes Jacob's name to Israel, the meaning of which marks every true Christian because of Christ's work. God fought for his own and continues to fight in the person of Christ. And by faith we, like Jacob, cling to Christ and receive the blessing, the result of our wrestling with God.

BLESSED DISABILITY: LIMPING INTO TRUST (32:1–32 [HB 32:2–33])[1]

LITERARY STRUCTURE AND THEMES

Jacob was back, almost to the land of promise. Having been delivered from Laban, he now faced Esau and the unknown threat remaining from Esau's vow to kill him twenty years previously. This short narrative is long on unanswered questions. It begins with Jacob's encounter with "God's camp" of angels (vv. 1–2) and concludes with Jacob wrestling with "God" (vv. 24–32). Sandwiched between, Jacob reached out to Esau only to be terrified by what he heard, leading to his defensive maneuvering, urgent prayer, and ingratiating diplomacy. At the center of the flow of the narrative, Jacob prayed for God to fulfill his promises by protecting Jacob and his family yet sending extravagant gifts to his estranged brother. The narrative climaxes with God's answer to his prayer in the most unexpected way as God tackled him and reduced him to dependent and blessed humility.

A. Angels met Jacob (32:1–2).
  B. Jacob divided his camp (32:3–8).
    C. Jacob implored Yahweh for help (32:9–12).
    C'. Jacob sent Esau extravagant gifts (32:13–21).
  B'. Jacob divided his family (32:22–23).
A'. God met Jacob with a blessed disability (32:24–32).

By framing Jacob's reactions with God's presence in the angels and the night attack, the narrative emphasizes God's protection and imminent intervention on Jacob's behalf even as he waited to encounter Esau. The centered tension between Jacob's prayer and his fearful response to Esau's threat is resolved unexpectedly with his divine confrontation. Jacob's fear finds hope in his disabling nocturnal battle by clinging to God and his blessing.

- ***Angels Met Jacob (32:1–2)***
- ***Jacob Divided His Camp (32:3–8)***
- ***Jacob Implored Yahweh for Help (32:9–12)***
- ***Jacob Sent Esau Extravagant Gifts (32:13–21)***
- ***Jacob Divided His family (32:22–23)***
- ***God Met Jacob with Blessed Disability (32:24–32)***

EXPOSITION

In the larger flow of the Jacob stories, this passage mirrors many facets of Genesis 28:10–22 (cf. the Introduction to the Jacob Narratives, p. 427). Numerous verbal connections, in addition to the main themes of Jacob meeting angels, God unexpectedly confronting him at night to give him blessing, and rehearsing Yahweh's promises, remind the reader of the first confrontation in 28:13–15.

The differences stand out clearly against the common background. Here God is initially hidden, appearing as an antagonist to confront Jacob's fear rather than as Jacob's sovereign, calling him to loyalty. In both passages Jacob

1 The commentary will follow the English versification. The Hebrew is one verse off beginning with 31:55 (32:1 in the Hebrew) through the end of v. 32.

receives blessing. Formerly, he had received the Abrahamic promises. Now his struggle for blessing is memorialized in his name change, with the realization that he must be fully dependent on Yahweh for that blessing.

As Jacob reenters the land, he must reckon with his brother. The encounter with the angels seemed to prompt his initiation of contact with Esau, whom he could have easily skirted (at least initially). However, the report of Esau's welcoming party precipitated Jacob's response, both of self-preservation and of calling on God's promises. God's surprising answer provided precisely what he needed to prepare him to meet Esau the next day. God's presence, verified by his angels, guaranteed Jacob's security and future blessing despite Esau's threat and Jacob's self-reliance. Ironically, his security required incapacitating him so that he might cling to Yahweh and receive blessing, commemorated by a new name.

Angels Met Jacob (32:1–2)

Angels met Jacob as he returned, whom he recognized as "God's camp," and named the place Mahanaim.

32:1–2. The entire narrative is filled with unanswered gaps or questions. How and when did he see the angels? Why does it say that they met him? Does his naming intend two camps (cf. Translation Analysis 32:3), and, if so, which two is he thinking of? The questions will only grow and climax with the identity of the assailant in verse 24. The very ambiguity, however, will help point to the message for Jacob and the reader. In the darkness and uncertainty, Jacob will have to cling to God as his only hope, learning that God is present, in control, and working in his life.

As Jacob neared the land of promise, the narrative draws numerous connections with Jacob's dream of Yahweh and his angels in chapter 28.[2] Surprised by the angels of God, Jacob declared that it was "God's camp" (32:2). As at Bethel, he commemorated the significance with the same naming formula, calling it Mahanaim. Conscious of the former encounter, Jacob's reminder to Yahweh of his promise at Bethel (v. 12) situates all that follows in light of God's plan and oversight. It also contrasts Jacob's stated reliance on Yahweh with his fear and efforts to appease Esau. Yahweh showed Jacob that he was present and in charge.

TRANSLATION ANALYSIS 32:2

"God's camp" (מַחֲנֵה אֱלֹהִים) is translated as "God's army" by the RSV. The word, which will be used six times in this chapter, can certainly refer to the army by metonymy as the people from the camp (e.g., Josh. 11:4; Judg. 4:15). Here the reference seems to be to the angels (32:1) rather than their camp per se, and the connotation of God's army and so his protection is appropriate.

TRANSLATION ANALYSIS 32:3

On "two camps," see ESV footnote. Mahanaim (מַחֲנָיִם) is a dual in Hebrew. Though Sarna (1989, 223) notes that in place names it does not necessarily carry that force, here it clearly intends at least a play on the "camps" of Jacob and on the frequently referenced "gift" (מִנְחָה) Jacob would send, which includes the same consonants as "camp" (מַחֲנֶה). The impact on the reader is to

2 The many shared verbal features require that we read this passage in light of the encounter at Bethel (cf. Cotter 2003, 240–41): Verse 1 shares the initial verb with 28:10 ("went," הָלַךְ) and the second verb with 28:11 ("met," וַיִּפְגְּעוּ), which is only used one other time in Genesis (23:8) though it shows up forty-six times in the OT. Both texts refer to the "place" (six times in 28:11, 16, 17, 19; here in 32:3; מָקוֹם). In addition, "the angels of God" (מַלְאֲכֵי אֱלֹהִים) appears only here and in 28:12 in the entire OT (though the singular "angel of God" occurs often). Finally, the formula of his naming of the place ("So he called the name of that place Mahanaim," 32:3) is the same as his naming of Bethel ("He called the name of that place Bethel," 28:19).

recall the sight of God's angels in contrast to Jacob's attempt to curry favor.

The "two camps" may refer to both God's and Jacob's camps (v. 2), suggesting he was acknowledging God's presence with him. With the memory of the promise and the reminder of God's presence and his army of angels, Jacob had all he needed to rest in God's care and safe passage, expectation of the land, and innumerable offspring to bring blessing to all the families of the world. Instead, he would panic when confronted with the possibility of attack.

Jacob Divided His Camp (32:3–8)

When Jacob sent messengers to Esau, he was terrified to hear that Esau was coming to meet him with four hundred men, so he divided his camp for protection.

32:3–5. It may have been the vision of the angels and the expectation of God's answered promises that prompted Jacob to initiate the contact with Esau as he was drawing closer. Or perhaps he simply wanted to head off trouble rather than wait for trouble to find him. Whatever his motive, he announced his return to Esau. Explaining his long absence with Laban (his previously intended destination, 28:1–5), he cleverly hinted at his resulting prosperity without detailing his net worth, by using the singular for each category as a collective (Sarna 1989, 224). He specified his purpose with conciliatory language, placing himself in a subservient position, in ironic contrast to both his birth oracle (25:23) and Isaac's blessing on him (27:29).[3] He requested "favor" or "grace" (חֵן), entailing forgiveness (see 32:20), to provide the peace that Jacob had asked from God as the condition to his vow (28:21).

32:7–8. The response he received terrified him. Without a message from Esau, he fully got the message about Esau coming to meet him with four hundred men. Once again, the ambiguity is striking. To "go" (הלך) to "meet" (קרא) someone can be either friendly (Aaron meeting Moses, Exod. 4:27) or hostile (Saul meeting the Philistines, 1 Sam. 23:28). Four hundred men could be a war party (David going to destroy Nabal, 1 Sam. 25:13), but could it be a welcoming party? It was certainly impressive (Abraham had only taken 318 from his own household after the coalition of kings, Gen. 14:14). Yet Esau had allowed the messengers to return and report. While the reader does not have access to any more information, Jacob had the messengers to question, so his concern that Esau intended harm is plausible.

Jacob assumed the worst and prepared for defense, or at least for a way for some to be able to get away should Esau attack. Moses gives us a glimpse of his thinking (32:8), which both confirms his terror already stated emphatically (v. 7) and shows him putting his efforts into saving as many of his family, servants, and animals as possible. Jacob's plotting and planning has not stopped, but perhaps he was thinking of others as well as himself.

Jacob Implored Yahweh for Help (32:9–12)

Fearfully, Jacob implored Yahweh to keep his promises, protecting him with his family.

32:9–10. In what seems to be a new development in Jacob's life, even though he was in crisis mode, he went to God with his problem. Centered in his response to the news of Esau's approach, Jacob's prayer presents a model for petition. He began with his address to God reflecting his previous acknowledging of God as

3 Cotter (2003, 241–42) concludes that Jacob intended to undo the effect of the oracles in order to find favor in Esau's sight because he repeated "my lord" (לַאדֹנִי), going beyond mere convention. While he cannot undo the oracles themselves, he does portray deceptive humility and deference to perhaps distance himself from the perception previously created.

the faithful God of his father and grandfather (cf. 31:42). Perhaps more to the point of this prayer, he recalled how God had introduced himself to Jacob at Bethel (28:13). Jacob was recalling and reminding Yahweh of both the dream and promise (32:12; cf. 28:14), including the covenant promises made to the patriarchs to which he was heir. He then reminded God of his promise to him when he called Jacob to return home. He appropriately interpreted God's promise to "be with [him]" (31:3) as doing "good" to him.

He also rightly confessed his unworthiness for God's acts of "steadfast love" and "faithfulness" (32:10) that God had already done for him. The two terms he used here present significant terms for Yahweh's reliable maintenance of his covenant relationships. He acts in loyalty or "steadfast love" (חֶסֶד) toward his chosen covenant recipients by keeping promises and delivering them from calamity (cf. Baer and Gordon, חֶסֶד, *NIDOTTE* 2:211–18). God's consistency is emphasized with the second term, "faithfulness" (אֱמֶת), which emphasizes God's trustworthy or reliable response (Moberly, אָמַן, *NIDOTTE* 1:427–33). While these terms relate to what God had already done for Jacob, they also form a significant recognition of God's character and hope for what he will continue to do.

Ironically, in his confession of his unworthiness Jacob used a verb that means "be small, insignificant" (used only here in the Pentateuch, *HALOT* s.v. "קטן" 1092), which is the verbal form of "younger" (קָטָן), used of Jacob twice in his deception of Esau, the older son (27:15, 42). In the pressure of the moment, he appears to be acutely conscious of his previous deception that had initiated this mess, as well as God's grace to work despite his unsavory and foolish past. Specifically, he pointed to the fulfillment of God's promise to be with him, providing a great start on the promise to make his offspring like the dust of the earth (28:14) and going above and beyond Jacob's audacious condition in his vow that God provide his food and clothing (28:20). Where he had gone out with only a staff, Jacob was now two large camps!

32:11–12. Based on his recognition of God's promises, faithful working, and his own undeserving status, Jacob petitioned God to deliver him from Esau. He admitted his fear, but his concern was focused not just on himself. Again, he showed his distress for his wives and children. He was afraid for his entire line, the very promise itself.

Feeling the tension between his fear of Esau and God's promise, he reminded God that he had promised Jacob the certainty of good. God's good plan had included descendants like the sand of the sea from the beginning.[4] That promise was in jeopardy if Jacob was right about the reason for Esau bringing his four hundred men.

> *TRANSLATION ANALYSIS 32:13*
> The certainty of the promise is added with the cognate infinitive absolute (הֵיטֵב אֵיטִיב), usually translated "surely" (ESV, NIV) or "certainly" (NET), though left out in some translations (NCV, NJPS, RSV).

God's promise to Jacob framed his petition, showing his dependence on Yahweh. While it is difficult to judge his heart, the manipulative bargaining that was present in his vow (28:20–22)

4 At Bethel, God had made a promise to greatly multiply Jacob's offspring, but the simile he used was "like the dust of the earth" (28:14). Here Jacob used the simile God had used with Abraham in 22:17 when God had ratified the Abrahamic covenant. Clearly both figures relate to Jacob's offspring, but he seems to realize the continuity of the promise and strengthen his claim by correctly conflating his promise with the larger context of the promise to Abraham and Isaac. He has seen the bigger picture that God was offering him but which will make demands on him that he will subsequently ignore for a time.

seems less apparent. Jacob was calling for God's fulfillment. As is often the case, however, his faith was mixed with his drive to ensure the outcome he desperately desired. He would do all he could to assure that outcome.

Jacob Sent Esau Extravagant Gifts (32:13–21)

Jacob sent servants ahead with extravagant gifts to appease Esau.

32:13–21. Jacob's prayer is framed with his attempts to control his situation. "He basically lived by the principle that God helps those who help themselves" (Curtis 1987, 132). He had already divided his camp as a defensive measure, but now he decides to try diplomacy. He arranged an extravagant gift to be delivered at intervals, designed to sway Esau's heart with the goods that Jacob knew Esau would desire and, at least in theory, had lost with the birthright. The sheer volume and number of droves were bound to impress his brother and occupy not only time, but some of his forces to secure them before meeting Jacob.

Jacob's Gift to Esau

Walton (2009a, 115) notes an Assyrian tribute list showing that Jacob's gift to Esau was "larger than many towns would have been able to pay in tribute to conquering kings even at later dates." It was truly an extravagant gift, but also showed the degree of wealth that God had given to Jacob in only six years of working for Laban. Jacob was not sending all he had!

While some have argued that Jacob was simply being wise, presenting an appropriate peace offering to an estranged and offended brother (Kidner 1967, 179; Mathews 2005, 553), his expression of fear and the struggle to follow suggest that he was still trying to control the outcome himself. Fokkelman (2004, 207) notes that a gift cannot resolve a broken relationship and can only be helpful "if given with the right intention, altruistically." In fear, Jacob tried to purchase Esau's good will with an extravagant gift. Every incident up to this point of a patriarch acting in fear and trying to preserve his life through his own means has ended in conflict (12:11–13; 20:11–13; 26:7; 31:31), leading the reader to expect a troubling end. Despite his model prayer, Jacob's over-the-top approach and admitted fear showed his struggle with trusting God's promise. He attempted to assure his desired outcome rather than trusting God and responding in a tempered and reasonable manner. While he had asked for help, he had not asked how he should respond.

To illustrate the point, the narrative describes the flocks of goats, sheep, camels, cows, and donkeys, providing an elaborate gift of mostly females that would produce milk and young, adding ongoing value to Esau's holdings. The 550 animals (plus young camels) were arranged in droves that would impress Esau by the continuing waves of animals. Each was accompanied by a message to be delivered and just barely digested before the next wave approached. The recurring point was that Jacob was subservient to Esau and currying favor with his gifts. The "gift" (מִנְחָה) can refer to a present of friendship or respect (2 Kings 20:12; Isa. 39:1) but can also refer to tribute (2 Sam. 8:2, 6). The ambiguity would suit Jacob, attempting to ingratiate himself to Esau, who would have to decipher the intent (Sarna 1989, 225), and perhaps delay any aggression.

The Hebrew word for "gift" (מִנְחָה) here shares the same consonants with the Hebrew word for "camp," in a slightly different order (מַחֲנֶה) and uses the two consonants of "favor" (חֵן). The repetition of the gift reminds the reader of the angelic camp and God's protection. Jacob's efforts appear in tension with God's revelation, motivated by his fear rather than God's presence (Ross 2008, 188).

Jacob's thoughts reveal his heart. While he was calling on God for help, he was hedging his bets by trying to impact Esau's outlook.

With an extended wordplay on the word for "face" (which will continue into the next pericope), we hear his intentions. Jacob was hoping to "appease" Esau, or literally "wipe his face," wiping the anger away (cf. Prov. 16:14; Averbeck, כָּפַר, *NIDOTTE* 2:696), so that when he saw "his face," Esau would "lift [Jacob's] face" (lit., יִשָּׂא פָנָי) or "accept" him (Gen. 32:20). Jacob worked to gain Esau's forgiveness (cf. Job 10:15; 11:15). Only a "face-to-face" with God, however (32:30), could solve his anticipation of Esau's face. Then he could say that seeing Esau was "like seeing the face of God" (33:10). He would finally realize that it was God who had been at work and not his own attempt to buy Esau off. Then he would be able to give blessing (see Exposition on 33:10, p. 544).

Jacob Divided His Family (32:22–23)

Jacob divided his family from his camp, sending everyone across the Jabbok.

32:22–23. Jacob's sleepless night continued with additional planning. Dividing his family from the rest of the camp, he sent them all over the Jabbok. Jacob's actions are unexplained, and they were traveling south over the Jabbok, which would be heading toward the oncoming Esau. On the one hand, he seems to be deeply concerned for his family, so he may have been putting the rest of the camp out as a distraction to allow his family space to escape if needed. He himself, however, would not be with them for the night. Remaining behind, he had placed himself farthest from danger (he thinks), again showing his terror (Geller 1982, 43).

These verses transition to the wrestling match, beginning with the crossing of the Jabbok that will not be completed until the newly humbled Israel limps into the new day (32:31). However, they also provide a parallel to Jacob's division of his camp (vv. 7–8). In each case, after sending the messengers ahead, he reacted with fear, leading to his prayer (vv. 9–12) and encounter with God (vv. 24–32). Jacob initiated the prayer, but God initiated the struggle, in answer to the prayer and in preparation for his encounter with Esau.

God Met Jacob with Blessed Disability (32:24–32)

Fighting a shadowy assailant alone, Jacob felt God's supernatural touch and implored God's blessing, receiving a new name with a limp and named the place Peniel.

32:24. As soon as Jacob was alone, he was ambushed by a "man" for the remainder of the night. This encounter interrupts the narrative flow, forestalling the much-anticipated meeting with Esau and making it anticlimactic. The entire battle is only four sentences in verses 24–25 because the real import is the following dialogue. The identity of the assailant is not immediately clear, either to the reader or to Jacob, which provided incentive for Jacob to fight for his life. Was it Esau? One of Esau's men? Someone else?

Jacob had been obsessing over how to gain favor with Esau. He was deathly afraid of a confrontation in which he would be attacked and killed. This adversary presented the very worst of Jacob's fears and would not let up. Jacob's prodigious strength (cf. 29:10 and comment there, p. 489) was evenly matched. This unnamed foe also matched Jacob's tenacity. The battle continued until dawn approached.

The verb translated "wrestled" (אבק) only occurs here in the Old Testament, and it makes a wordplay on Jacob's name (יַעֲקֹב) and on the Jabbok (יַבֹּק), all of which share two of their three consonants. This wrestling match has Jacob's (old) name written all over it. Jacob, the Jabbok, and his wrestling match will forever be linked because here his name would change, and he would begin to leave that identity behind.

32:25. As dawn approached, and "the man saw that he did not prevail against Jacob," he incapacitated Jacob's hip. Clearly, the man could have won any time he wished, but he had to expose Jacob's self-will and break him, causing the reader to ponder the explanation of the name Israel in verse 28. God was intending to get Jacob's attention and teach him dependence on God for his security. The identity of the man only slowly dawned on Jacob, and he would identify him as "God" (v. 30).

> *TRANSLATION ANALYSIS 32:25*
> ESV says he "touched" Jacob's hip socket and put it out of joint. Other translations say he "struck" it (NET, NRSV). The verb (נגע) can be used (with the בְּ preposition, as here) of everything from merely touching (Gen. 3:3) to extreme violence (Josh. 9:19). There is no indication that it was either vicious or gentle except that the hip was incapacitated. Either way, it was clearly supernatural and indicated that the man was not intending to kill Jacob. The extent of the injury is also unclear as Jacob could walk the next morning, but with a limp.

In the flow of the narrative, this wrestling match separates Jacob's elaborate preparations to meet Esau and their meeting in chapter 33. It forms the answer to Jacob's prayer in a most unexpected way. God intervened in Jacob's world to turn his attention away from his conflict with Esau and how to fix it and toward his conflict with God and how he needed to respond. If he was right with God, he would be right with Esau (the opposite of how we might think). God confronted Jacob with his worst nightmare, only to reveal his presence amid Jacob's struggle by inflicting a healing disability on him. The dawning realization moved Jacob to an action totally out of character for him, but it was all he could do. He struggled to cling on to win a blessing.

32:26–28. The man requested to be released. Jacob now held on for a blessing. He had realized that this foe was no enemy and was able to impart more than painful injury. When he understood this identity is not clear, but the supernatural touch provided the final confirmation. Grasping that blessing was near, and perhaps that his grip was only as strong as the man allowed, he requested God's favor.

The man's reply must have been unnerving because it exposed Jacob's character. In context with his struggle with Esau, Esau's accusation must have been reverberating in his mind (27:36). He had been obsessing with his conflict with Esau. Terrified and guilty, he was trying to solve it with extravagant gifts. Esau's anger was expressed in Jacob's name. He was the cheat (27:35–36). To say it out loud with this man whom he had perhaps initially mistaken for Esau brought him face to face with his heart. Whether Jacob saw it or not, the reader certainly would. He had been struggling his entire life for what he wanted. In fact, the man's reply was clearly appropriate yet so unexpected.

Jacob would have a new identity as Israel. Jacob's renaming asserted "the assailant's authority to impart a new life and a new status (cf. 2 Kings 23:34; 24:17)" (Ross 1985b, 345). The expected meaning for "Israel" is "God fights" (Hamilton 1995, 334), but the explanation for the name was that Jacob had fought "with God and with men, and [had] prevailed" (Gen 32:28). The intended irony allowed Jacob (and the reader) to begin to see the truth. When he lost, he won. When he lost the wrestling match, recognized his inability, and had to cling and pray for blessing, he received it, a needed lesson for all his descendants. The promise of blessing God had conveyed in the parallel passage at Bethel (28:10–17) was not for Jacob to accomplish on his own but was and must be truly a gift from God.

> *TRANSLATION ANALYSIS 32:28*
> The meaning and explanation of the name "Israel" have been extensively debated. The Hebrew root (שׂרה) occurs only here and in Hosea 12:3–4 [HB 4–5], with the meaning to "strive" (ESV, NASB95), "struggle" (NIV, NKJV), "wrestle" (NCV), or "fight" (NET, NLT). Other possibilities

have been proposed (e.g., Coote 1972), but the traditional translation and explanation fit well with the text and context (Ross 1985b, 346–48). Popular etymologies of names in the Old Testament generally do not follow a strict translation of the name but use a play on the name for the meaning in the context. See Exposition on 25:26 (p. 437) and 27:36 (p. 464).

He had been in conflict from before birth. He had come out on top, but as he had already begun to realize, it was not the result of his cunning or hard work. It was only because God was with him and was keeping his promise, made even before he was born. In fact, he had certainly fought with men (Laban and Esau), but he was really fighting with God, who was making a claim on his life. He now was able to gain blessing (and win), but only because he tenaciously held on for blessing. This vivid nocturnal battle became a defining moment. "Jacob's struggle with God is meant to epitomize the whole of the Jacob narratives" (Sailhamer 1990, 210).

32:29–30. When Jacob asked for the man's name, he demurred but gave Jacob the blessing. In fact, more than blessing, he renamed Jacob Israel.[5] Jacob was in God's favor and had a new beginning with his character.[6] More importantly, he had seen God at work in his life in a dramatic way, and he now had the answer to his prayer. He was Israel. He had prevailed. His life was delivered. He had also realized that his struggle was with none other than God himself. The ambiguity of the assailant and the struggle in the darkness matches the ambiguity in Abraham's theophany and angelic visitation (cf. 18:2, 22; 19:1, 5 and Exposition there, pp. 340, 352–53; cf. Hos. 12:4).

Jacob's Assailant

The identity of Jacob's assailant and the interpretation of the account have been the matter of extensive discussion (cf. Ross 1985b, 339–41). Jacob believed that he had encountered God. The narrator's description of a "man" matches previous descriptions of angelic visitations (e.g., chs.18–19; and cf. Josh. 5:13–15; Judg. 13). In Genesis 18, there is similar ambiguity between the "men," who are clearly angelic messengers, and God, who spoke to Abraham (vv. 17–22, cf. 19:1). Later, Manoah saw a "man" who was "the angel of the Lord" (Judg. 13, esp. vv. 3, 6, 8–10), and he also believed he had seen God (v. 22). Hosea 12:3–4 (HB 4–5) clarifies that Jacob met an angel, and God spoke (cf. Excursus 24, "Jacob's Struggle with the Angel," in Sarna 1989, 403–4). The earliest readers also appear to have identified an angel here, with God's authority (Including Targum Onqelos, Targum Neofiti, the Peshitta, and likely the Samaritan Pentateuch; Wessner 2000, 175–76). Regardless of how we identify the assailant, whether an angel with God's authority or a theophany of God himself, God has confronted Jacob. The ambiguity serves

5 It may be simply intended that the naming was the blessing (Sarna 1989, 227). Or perhaps it intends to imply the reiteration of the covenant blessing (28:13–15; cf. 28:3–4). Clearly in 35:9–12 the "blessing," naming, and Abrahamic covenant promises are all a package conferred to Jacob. Here, however, the ambiguity again serves the ends of the narrator, drawing attention both to the change in Jacob as Israel and to the conferral of "blessing" (the event rather than the content), which will play a significant role in the culmination of this narrative in Genesis 33. God had blessed Jacob, one of the major motifs of the larger context, who will be able to bless others.

6 Mathews (2005, 559–61) argues that Jacob's life changed dramatically here and was forever different. The record of his life, however, suggests that he is not yet a fully changed man (Cotter 2003, 248). Certainly, there is a new beginning here that would put him on a new trajectory, but he would still be cagey with Esau (ch. 33) and go to Shechem instead of Bethel and experience much more pain (ch. 34) before he finally went to Bethel and fulfilled his vow (ch. 35). In contrast to Cotter's evaluation, however, there does appear to be real growth and change by the end of his life (chs. 48–49).

the narrative by drawing attention to the struggle that Jacob has been engaged in his entire life and the message for him, and the reader, that God in his grace gives victory, renewal, and blessing, but only as one submits and clings to God.

As a result, and as at Bethel, Jacob commemorated the event, naming the place Peniel, "face of God," because he said, "I have seen God face to face, and yet my life has been delivered" (Gen. 32:30). He recognized that God had directly intervened. He saw in the wrestling a direct encounter with God, and yet he walked away. More than that, however, he not only did not perish from the encounter, but he limped away with the realization that God had answered his prayer. He had prayed to be "delivered" (v. 11, נצל), and now his life was "delivered" (נצל). He would certainly be delivered from Esau. Jacob would connect those dots fully the next day.

32:31–32. The sun rose as he limped triumphantly to meet his family and his impending conflict, a new and delivered man. "The crippling and the naming show that God's ends were still the same: He would have all of Jacob's will to win, to attain and obtain, yet purged of self-sufficiency and redirected to the proper object of man's love, God himself" (Kidner 1967, 180). The dietary note provides confirmatory reminder to the original reader of Jacob's nocturnal struggle and the lesson learned at Peniel. It also celebrates the victorious outcome of Israel's disability (Geller 1982, 46–47). It was a physical event (Ross 1985b, 343), reminding Israel that they must remain "Israel" in submission to Yahweh to find victory and blessing.

THEOLOGICAL FOCUS

God's presence guarantees the security and blessing of his servants who turn to him in prayer, requiring humble dependence, graciously fostered through confrontation with their inability to secure it on their own.

God reveals his presence explicitly, surreptitiously, and always surprisingly. The angels were unexpected, though Jacob recognized the clear connection to God's previous revelation and promises. And yet when Jacob turned to God in fearful prayer, Yahweh graciously answered with a graphic, startling, and mysterious response that confronted Jacob's fear. It was in wrestling with his fear and discovering his inability that Jacob saw the presence of God and found security. God had been there and, in fact, was present in the struggle, though not immediately visible.

Struggle and fear, then, are not indications that God is far. Rather, God can use struggle to bring us to a realization of his working, and we must trust him to be present even when we are in the dark. We must also realize that we cannot coerce God to do our will, nor can we accomplish his promise in our strength. Rather, we must submit to him. We must recognize our weakness and inability. We must depend on him alone for promise, blessing, and life.[7] On the other hand, with relief, we realize that God's working "is not thwarted by human stupidity and deceit" (Curtis 1987, 131, n. 15)!

When our fears conflict with God's promises or character, struggle is not the answer. Victory requires clinging to him, giving up attempting to gain in our own strength what only he can give. Sometimes we need reminders to submit and cling to God rather than struggle for ourselves. The very disability that Jacob carried away from his encounter with God was an ongoing reminder that only in our weakness can we really see the strength of God (2 Cor. 12:9–10).

7 Curtis (1987, 131) notes a consistent theme of Genesis, that "man's efforts fail while the work that God does succeeds." Perhaps even more pointedly, blessing and thriving in life can only come from God and cannot be accomplished by any pursuits apart from him.

With the angels and the mysterious man, through his presence God demonstrated again his loyal love toward his chosen servant. Jacob's prayer of dependence on God's loyal love and faithfulness appropriately recognized the consistent working of God as the source of his security. His prayer appropriately offered praise for past faithfulness, as well as his petition for what he needed. God's past work on our behalf is intended to give us hope for the future and confidence in God's care (Ps. 52, especially vv. 8–9 [HB 10–11]). We must acknowledge his working and offer praise. It is both to our benefit as well as to those who hear that praise.

We also appropriately petition God when we acknowledge our fear and lay it before God. We need to confess not only the working of God but the struggle of our own hearts to trust him. God honored Jacob's confession, though his method of confronting Jacob's fear may not be what we would prefer. Occasionally God may take his people into exposure therapy to show them his presence even in their fears.

Finally, we find blessing in clinging to God in faith, asking for his work, rather than in the struggle to defeat our fears and control our lives. Blessing may come in painful reminders of our inability, but it also comes with hope for the change of character and destiny that can only be accomplished by the working of God for his ultimate and eternal purposes. In fact, blessing is only really found in that relationship with God, through his empowering and providing to accomplish his purpose in our lives. God can only enable us by disabling us.

PREACHING AND TEACHING STRATEGIES

Exegetical and Theological Synthesis

I begin the process of preparing the sermon or teaching by highlighting how God's Word portrays Jacob's faith in the Lord. Clearly Jacob's faith needs work since he has forgotten his privileged position with respect to his brother (32:5). The same goes for his being "greatly afraid and distressed" (v. 7; vv. 13–20 provide detail on how Jacob's fear of Esau played out with respect to maneuvering for the best chance of his family's survival).

Jacob would see that God changed Esau's heart; God would continue to be faithful to Jacob. At the beginning and end of Jacob's prayer, he reminded God of his promise to do good; Jacob would see God make good on that promise and deliver him from Esau. These are those "go and do otherwise" sections. Yet Jacob's faith is present and active as he prays to God. His prayer for deliverance includes many admirable elements, one of which is the double reference to God's promise to do Jacob good (vv. 9–12). Our listeners experience many times when this prayer is appropriate for them.

While literal, physical wrestling matches may be impossible for us, we can teach how Jacob's experience mirrors some aspects of every Christian's life. The wrestling is different, but the desire for God's blessing and the learning to depend on God and clinging to God in faith are appropriate for all his children. In this sense, God transforms all his children so that they reflect Israel's new name. This is the only way in which Christians can represent God in his world and experience life where he makes all things new.

Preaching Idea

God's training camp is where his children receive his blessing in his presence through trials, prayer, and humble dependence.

Contemporary Connections

What does it mean?

The biblical writer assumes his readers will know that Jacob's meeting with "the angels of God" and naming the place "God's camp" mean that God met Jacob at a strategic time in his life. In the context of a once-strained relationship, Jacob is now soon to meet Esau. Jacob can only imagine that this reunion will threaten his life and his family's lives. God's meeting with Jacob, including the form of the man who wrestles with Jacob all evening, shows God's desire and ability to continue to transform his choice servant.

In verses 13–21 Jacob functions as a negative role model for Christians. If he displays trust in the Lord, it is minimal when compared to the amount of planning he does to protect himself, his family, and entourage. Jacob admitted to God in prayer that he was afraid of Esau (v. 11). Jacob needed more faith and less fear in this critical moment.

Our listeners will need to learn the significance of God ambushing Jacob that night prior to meeting Esau. From a human perspective, Jacob will be in no physical shape to meet Esau the next day; he will be running on fumes. However, the encounter with God was changing Jacob into a proper worshipper: someone who was learning to rely on God for success in life, instead of on his own ingenuity. He was maturing through these trials. From the very beginning, Jacob has shown that he values God's blessing, and the wrestling match shows that nothing has changed. He has yet to fulfill his vow and return to Bethel to worship. But more time and more pressure would move him in that direction.

Is it true?

If the biblical author is arguing anything in this narrative, he is defending God's character. Once again Jacob finds himself in a situation that threatens the promise of God. Two times in one prayer Jacob reminds God—as if God needed reminding—that God promised to do good to Jacob. Only time will tell whether God will be faithful; that depends largely on how things go with the encounter with Esau. Faith-filled readers will see God wrestling with Jacob through the night as another example of God fulfilling his promise to Jacob, despite the surprising way he does it. God wrestles with this person who desperately wants God's blessing, and God graciously engages that person in a way that sovereignly creates a new person (think of the change of name and the meaning of that new name). When difficult circumstances ambush them, our listeners may not readily accept this idea that God is being faithful. As they put themselves into this narrative, they see God at work and see themselves putting their own limited faith in action. They can see a growth pattern developing as God slowly changes them into the kind of servant that can reflect God's glory in the church and in the world.

Now what?

One of the difficulties of applying biblical narratives like this one is that the biblical writer does not provide his own application. He is presenting an idea that implies a relevant application. Some of these ideas overlap with the question, "Is it true?" Our listeners need to believe that God is powerfully present with them as they embark on their faith journey. This explains why they can succeed in their walk with God in a badly broken world where threats to faith exist. They all live and breathe in God's camp.

That is one reason why our prayers are effective: God hears his children when they pray to him. And speaking of prayer, we can learn from Jacob's pleading with God. Our listeners see a man struggling with fear but praying. To quote the character in Mark 9:24, "I believe; help my unbelief." Since we see how the narrative ends, we are encouraged to keep strengthening our faith, which includes putting our fears to rest. We should see ourselves losing our confidence in self and gaining confidence in God's ability to make us succeed in doing his will, whatever that may be for each individual Christian. In this way we are all following Jacob's example of being in God's training camp and experiencing the transformation that results.

Creativity in Presentation

We want our listener to understand that God's training camp is where his children receive his blessing in his presence through trials, prayer, and humble dependence. One way to illustrate this main idea is to highlight a key moment in your life or in someone else's life where God surprised them with his powerful presence. In verses 1 and 24, God surprises Jacob. God strategically revealed himself to Jacob prior to meeting Esau and reentering his home country. Often God's surprise revelation of himself comes at a time when we are about to experience something important for him. Much is at stake for the kingdom, and God makes sure his will gets done with his servants.

Another illustration is those times in our lives when God has humbled us through physical ailments, accidents, or significant disappointments and loss. Many Christians can look back at their lives and see circumstances God used to humble them (to make them less dependent on their abilities and more dependent on him).

The sermon and lesson can be structured like this:

- The assurance of God's powerful presence guarantees the blessing (vv. 1–2). Help listeners believe that they live in God's camp.
- There are threats to that promised blessing (vv. 3–6). Their spiritual lives are filled with landmines that threaten faith and make us doubt God's ability to keep his promises to do good.
- There are wrong reactions to those threats (vv. 7–8, 13–21; notice that I am assuming that Jacob's planning to meet Esau is not simply wisdom in action, but more fear than faith). There is a reason why Jesus repeated the command, "Do not be afraid," more than any other instruction (in the ESV, for instance, you'll find some variation of this almost twenty times in the Gospels).
- The proper reaction to those threats is prayer (vv. 9–12). Jacob's prayer is a model for any Christian who needs deliverance when facing dire straits.
- The encounter with God makes us fit for blessing and service (vv. 22–32). As noted above, each Christian finds themselves in Jacob's line, having "prevailed" with God and men. Self-sufficiency slowly but surely decreases, and our dependency on God increases (in this sense we are consciously clinging to God in faith as we move through life and face the trials he allows our way). Jacob's name change fits us all, and we say after such encounters that we're never the same.

You might ask your listeners whether they are enrolled in "God's Camp."

Homiletical Option: Combining Chapters 32–33 into One Sermon

Our preaching idea from chapter 32 is: God's training camp is where his children receive his blessing through trials, prayer, and humble dependence.

Chapter 33's idea is: Trust the Lord to fulfill his promise to bless you and make you a blessing.

A combined preaching idea for both chapters could be: welcome to God's training camp, where his children learn to trust him through trials in order to be blessed and be a blessing.

A possible sermon structure could be:

- Introduction: those times in the Christian life when we need assurance of God's powerful presence.
- The assurance of God's powerful presence that guarantees blessing (32:1–2).

- The threats to that promised blessing (32:3–6; 33:1).

- The wrong reaction to those threats: fearful planning (32:7–8, 13–21; 33:2–16).

- The right reaction to those threats: faith-filled prayer and worship (32:9–12; 33:17–20).

- The encounter with God that makes us fit for blessing and service (32:22–32).

Remember that, because of God's favor on Jacob, he can confer a blessing on Esau. This is what the Lord prophesied to Abraham and through Isaac. The final chapter shows Jacob worrying at the start but worshipping at the end, a wonderful route that teaches all of us who walk with God in this faith journey.

Another option may be to go straight through the passage:

- God's presence assures his people and reminds of his promises (32:1–2).

- God confronts his people in their fears with his presence and their need to cling (32:3–32).

- God shows his presence in their world by resolving conflicts, calming fears, and fulfilling his promises so that they can bless their world and worship him (33:1–20).

DISCUSSION QUESTIONS

1. Ask participants to share times when they know God met them unexpectedly. Include how such encounters changed their lives.

2. In Jacob's prayer, notice the combination of unworthiness (v. 10) and yet the request for deliverance (v. 11). Explain why both can occur in the Christian's life.

3. Discuss the meaning and significance of God's "deeds of steadfast love and . . . faithfulness" (v. 10). How does God's character stabilize our faith?

4. When is your response to trials and fears wisdom and necessary responsibility, and when does it cross the line into fear and failure to trust God?

5. How can you consciously refocus on your trials through the promises and reminders of God's presence and working in your life, rather than through your inabilities or fears?

6. What are your greatest fears that you need to submit to the work of God in your life?

Genesis 33:1–20

EXEGETICAL IDEA

Meeting Esau relieved Jacob's fears and revealed God's work in Esau bringing reconciliation and prompting Jacob to extend blessing and part in peace with public worship.

THEOLOGICAL FOCUS

God's working in hearts provides hope for reconciliation, blessing, and opportunity to extend blessing to others, exposes false hope in manipulation of relationships and circumstances, and leads to appropriate public worship.

PREACHING IDEA

Trust the Lord to fulfill his promise to bless you and make you a blessing—easier said than done in difficult relationships.

PREACHING POINTERS

Readers of Jacob's encounter with Esau are anxious to know how the meeting will go for Jacob. More specifically, listeners will be encouraged to see how the Lord fulfilled his promises to bless Jacob and make him a blessing when the situation with his brother was so tense. As the scenes proceed, the Lord clearly has been working in Jacob's and Esau's lives. With respect to Jacob's faith journey, the narrative shows his desire and capacity to bless his brother. Jacob can present Esau with an extravagant gift because the Lord has given Jacob so much.

The way Jacob reacts to Esau shows that he is not sure whether the Lord will protect him from his brother's rage (Jacob bows down to Esau, instead of the other way around, according to Isaac's oracle). There is no guarantee that God will give healing and peace in all difficult relationships. One way the Lord carries out his promise to Jacob is to change Esau's heart and allow reconciliation to take place. Jacob's worship at his arrival in Shechem shows his heart for the Lord. God had revealed his faithfulness to Jacob in this encounter with Esau, and now Jacob will move toward greater faithfulness to the Lord.

RECONCILIATION: GOD'S WORK IN HUMAN HEARTS (33:1–20)

LITERARY STRUCTURE AND THEMES

Genesis 33 concludes the narrative that began in chapter 32 of Jacob and Esau's meeting, interrupted by God's intervention. It presents a series of surprising comparisons between Jacob and Esau, drawing together many of the themes from chapter 32 with themes and tensions left unaddressed from the birth oracle and the fracturing of their family twenty years previously, all culminating in their meeting. The pericope begins with a narrative introduction when Jacob sees Esau approaching, makes final preparations, and the two brothers meet. The reunion includes three panes of dialogue between the brothers, concluding with a final narrative as the brothers go their own ways (cf. Mathews 2005, 563).

A. Narrative introduction: Jacob fearfully met magnanimous Esau (33:1–4).
B. Dialogue: God's working allowed reconciliation and blessing (33:5–16).
   1. Jacob displayed God's grace (33:5–7).
   2. Jacob gave blessing (33:8–11).
   1'. Jacob requested grace (33:12–15).
C. Narrative conclusion: Jacob separated from Esau in peace (33:16–20).

Fokkelman (2004, 225–28) has shown that verses 8–11 chiastically develop the focus of the narrative, coalescing key terms in the center (v. 10c–d) to highlight God's working in Jacob's response to Esau and Esau's forgiveness (see discussion vv. 8–11). God was fulfilling his promise, bringing Jacob back to the land in peace and blessing, while Jacob offered blessing and returned worship to God. Unfortunately, Jacob did not yet fully keep his vow, threatening difficult days ahead.

- ***Jacob Fearfully Met Magnanimous Esau (33:1–4)***
- ***God's Working Allowed Reconciliation and Blessing (33:5–15)***
- ***Jacob Separated from Esau in Peace (33:16–20)***

EXPOSITION

In the overall structure of the Jacob stories, this reconciliation of the brothers and its relational restoration (ch. 33) partially resolves Jacob's deception of Isaac with his resulting estrangement from Esau and Esau's threatened fratricide (27:1–28:9; see Introduction to the Jacob Narratives, p. 427). Of the many points of contact between the two narratives,[1] the key reversal links the "blessing" (בְּרָכָה) that Jacob stole (esp. 27:35) with his "gift" (בְּרָכָה, 33:11) to Esau, related specifically to the working of God in Esau's and Jacob's lives. Other reversals and ironies abound, such as the reversal of Isaac's blessing when Jacob bowed to his brother (33:3) rather than Esau bowing to him (27:29), and while Jacob would have "plenty" (רֹב, 27:28), it is Esau who has "enough" (רָב, 33:9; Rendsburg 2014, 60).

These reversals, ironies, and contrasts do not restore to Esau what he lost, but rather

1 Cf. Rendsburg (2014, 59–62), who lists seventeen connections between the two narratives, showing their relationship in the overall structure.

reveal the working of God in Jacob to recognize responsibility and opportunity to restore relationship and give generous blessing from an abundance of God's grace. It worked out the lesson from Jacob's encounter with God, receiving and extending blessing and reversing the recurring theme in Genesis of sibling conflict and fratricide. Instead, they initiated healing, and Jacob fulfilled God's purpose of blessing to his world (28:14). Meeting Esau relieved Jacob's fears and revealed God's work in Esau bringing reconciliation and prompting Jacob to extend blessing and part in peace with public worship.

Jacob Fearfully Met Magnanimous Esau (33:1–4)

When Esau appeared, Jacob divided his entourage, bowing before Esau who unexpectedly welcomed him with a warm embrace.

33:1–2. As God's nocturnal intervention faded and Jacob limped into the sunrise (32:31), the narrative time abruptly moved to Jacob's alarm at Esau approaching with his four hundred men (וְהִנֵּה, 33:1). Across the Jabbok, Jacob had caught his family before Esau appeared, which the reader now sees through Jacob's eyes.

Jacob's response sounds familiar as he divided his family, putting the least favored in front, with "Rachel and Joseph last of all" (v. 2). The favoritism and focus on Joseph prefigure the coming Joseph stories. What is not expected, however, is Jacob's personal response that follows.

33:3–4. Up until this, Jacob had been putting everything between himself and the perceived danger. Now, however, we see a new Jacob taking the lead and prostrating himself before Esau. Repeated prostration was a common response of a vassal to their king, showing Jacob's humility before Esau.[2] Ironically, this is directly contrary to the blessing of Isaac, in which his brothers would bow to Jacob (27:29, though it was intended for Esau!), as well as the oracle in which "the older shall serve the younger" (25:23).[3] Yet, Jacob continued to call Esau his "lord" and himself Esau's "servant" (33:5, 8, 13–15; cf. 32:4–5, 18–20). Jacob's motivation is not yet clear, though one wonders if he is not trying to manipulate Esau.

> *TRANSLATION ANALYSIS 33:3*
> The emphasis might be missed in the English, but the repeated use of "face" (noted at 32:20, p. 531) includes the preposition "before" (lit. "to the face of," לִפְנֵי), which is used seven times between chapters 32 and 33. Previously he had sent messengers (32:4) and gifts (32:17, 18, 21) before him, specifically to appease Esau. Now he goes "before them." In addition, the verb "went" or "crossed over" (עָבַר, NKJV) has been used seven times already in chapter 32 in the sending of the droves in front of him and taking his family across the river. Surprisingly, Jacob went before (cf. Geller 1982, 43).

In pointed contrast, Esau responded with completely unanticipated generosity and warmth. Rather than the expected sword, Esau offered genuine affection, signaling grace and forgiveness. Several repeated terms recall the initial offense of Jacob, hinting at Jacob's "kiss" (cf. 27:26–27) and the role of his "neck" (cf. 27:16) in the deception (Mathews 2005, 567). The text does not indicate the reason for Esau's change of heart from his initial vow to kill Jacob (27:41). It seems to connect with God's work in Jacob's life the night before, and it clearly was not forced or begrudging when he met Jacob (unlike Abimelech or Laban [20:3–78; 31:24]; Mathews

2 According to Moran, speaking of the common occurrence in the Amarna letters from about the fourteenth century BC, considerably later than Jacob, "the sevenfold prostration is given to the king alone" and intends "over and over" rather than a specific number (Moran 1992, 313, n. 1; xxix–xxx, n. 85).

3 The oracle clearly looks ahead nationally rather than individually ("two nations").

2005, 567). We do not know if Esau already had the change of heart (perhaps God's intervention as Esau approached, as with Laban) or if the actions and gift of Jacob influenced his response. All we see is the outcome, and the reader is as surprised as Jacob, who wept with Esau.

God's Working Allowed Reconciliation and Blessing (33:5–15)

The two brothers met, resolving the tensions through God's working in both, as Esau extended forgiveness and Jacob extended blessing, parting amicably.

Jacob Displayed God's Grace (33:5–7)

At Esau's query, Jacob displayed God's grace, which was responsible for his large family.

33:5. A contrast of perspectives follows the contrast of reactions. We now view the scene through Esau's eyes. He had not seen Jacob for twenty years and appeared amazed at the change. He wondered aloud who all these people were and how they might be related to Jacob. Jacob's response provides a second indication of a changing heart. Though it may be self-serving to avoid his purpose for leaving in finding a wife, and possibly avoiding the term "blessing" in God's provision (Westermann 1995, 525), he fully gave the credit for his burgeoning family to God's grace, describing himself as Esau's servant.[4]

> *TRANSLATION ANALYSIS 33:5*
> The initial two clauses of verse 5 repeat the initial two clauses of verse 1, with Esau as subject instead of Jacob. The repetition draws attention to the contrast between the brothers presented consistently through the narrative. Here Esau's curiosity contrasts with Jacob's fear. Esau was not looking for revenge.

33:6–7. Each family group approached Esau in order from less favored to more favored, reinforced by the naming. The concubines or their children are not named. Leah is named but not her sons, but both Rachel and Joseph are named. Unexpectedly, Joseph is named first before even Rachel. Again, Moses seems to be preparing the reader for the favoritism that will follow in the Joseph stories. All bow before Esau, imitating Jacob's obeisance. While the drama shows Jacob's projected humility, it also indicates his family's recognized vulnerability before Esau and his army. Jacob and his family are fully at Esau's mercy, which Jacob has, and will again, ask for (an emphasis of the story).

Jacob Gave Blessing (33:8–11)

At Esau's query, Jacob explained his gift, acknowledging God's work and convincing Esau to receive blessing.

Fokkelman (2004, 225–27) has shown that these verses form the "core of the story," not only coalescing most of the key terms here ("before," "favor," "camp," "bow down," "blessing") but focusing on Jacob's culminating recognition of God's working in verse 10b.[5] Structurally, as well as logically, they are the fulcrum of the narrative.

a. Esau asked the purpose of the gifts, which Jacob described for finding favor with Esau (33:8).
  b. Esau, addressing Jacob as brother, politely refused because he had much already ("enough," 33:9).
    c. Jacob seeks favor in Esau's sight (33:10a).
      d. Jacob again offered his "gift" (33:10b).
        e. Jacob described seeing Esau's face as seeing the face of God and being accepted (33:10c–d).

4 Westermann (1995, 525) notes that Jacob's choice of "graciously given" rather than "blessed" also includes the idea of forgiveness absent in "blessing," which indicates something of Jacob's heart.

5 The structure is slightly adapted from Fokkelman (2004, 225–27).

d′. Jacob requested Esau take his "blessing" (33:11aα–β).
c′. God was gracious to Jacob (33:11aγ).
b′. Jacob insisted because he had it all ("enough," 33:11aδ).
a′. Jacob convinced Esau to accept them (33:11b–c).

This chiasm highlights helpful observations and implications for the narrative and the resulting theology. In both c and c′, and in the center focus, Jacob connected Esau's response to God's response and saw God's working in and through Esau. Jacob finally saw his gift as something more than merely a manipulative tribute to curry favor. He saw it as a blessing to give to Esau, possible because God had already been gracious, and he had "enough" (v. 11).

33:8. The contrast between the two in the overall narrative continued as Esau wanted to know Jacob's intent in sending the "company" (הַמַּחֲנֶה) to meet him. Esau's unusual description of Jacob's gift was the term repeated six times in chapter 32 (seven if you count Mahanaim) for the two camps of angels and Jacob dividing his own retinue into two camps. It is as if Esau was punning on the extravagant numbers of the gift to ask about the "army" that Jacob had sent to him (see Translation Analysis 32:2, p. 528, and Exposition on 32:14, p. 531). Jacob would pick that up and shift the focus in 33:11. Here, however, Jacob repeated his desire for Esau's favor.

33:9. Esau pointedly refused the gift. It may have been culturally appropriate to initially refuse and not appear eager, or Esau may be feeling like Jacob was trying to buy his acceptance (Steinmann 2019, 315). Either way, Esau's statement that he had "enough" (רָב) recalled Isaac's blessing on Jacob that he would have "plenty" (רֹב) of grain and wine (27:28). It was as if he was showing Jacob that, despite Jacob's deceit, he was prospering.[6] The effect seems to have heightened Jacob's guilt and perhaps shifted his focus.

33:10–11. Jacob urged Esau to take his "present" (מִנְחָה), if he had found "favor" (v. 10, repeating his request for grace, v. 8, חֵן) in Esau's sight, reflecting his initial offer to Esau (32:14, 19, 21, 22). Drawing on the imagery of his terrified initial reaction, in which he wanted to appease Esau (lit. "wipe" the anger from Esau's face, 32:20) so that when he saw "his face" he would experience forgiveness (or lit. "lifting of his face"), Jacob now realized that God had been at work. When he saw Esau's face, it was "like seeing the face of God" (33:10).[7]

In seeing the forgiveness in Esau's heart (as Jacob had asked, 32:11), Jacob connected God's working in Esau with his own experience the previous night, when Jacob saw God "face to face" (32:30). It was not his gift that had accomplished appeasement (32:20), but rather much better. God had worked reconciliation. Esau was restored as a brother. Esau had "accepted" him (וַתִּרְצֵנִי).

TRANSLATION ANALYSIS 33:10

The expression Jacob used simply means to "be favourable [sic] to someone" or "well disposed" (HALOT s.v. I "רצה" 1280–81), but much as his expression for his desire to "appease" Esau (32:20) would be used theologically, this term for acceptance would also commonly be used in the rest of the Old Testament of God's acceptance of people (e.g., Deut. 33:11; 2 Sam. 24:23), implying favor and acceptance of sacrifices or service (Lev. 1:3; Isa. 42:1).

6 Sarna (1989, 230) sees this as Esau's "concession of the birthright," though that is not clear.

7 "Jacob realized that Esau, like God, had already given him favor (חֵן) and received him with favor (רָצָה), independent of the gift (v. 10). Jacob could now offer the gift, not to obtain favor, but in gratitude for God's favor (חָנַן, vv. 5, 11), made visible in the face of Esau" (Fretheim, חָנַן, *NIDOTTE* 2:204).

It is unlikely Jacob had a slip of the tongue, showing his guilty conscience in an attempt to return the blessing (Fishbane 1979, 52; even though the term "blessing" can also mean "gift"). More likely, he had a moment of clarity as he realized God's blessing on him and his opportunity to give blessing (rather than cursing and conflict). He stated, "Please accept my blessing (בִּרְכָתִי)!" (33:11). He does not ask Esau to accept his blessing back, nor was he able to give back the blessing.[8] God had given it to him specifically through oracle (25:23), Isaac's blessing (27:27–29; 28:3–4), and fully in theophany (28:13–15). However, God had also called him to be a blessing to all the nations (28:14). Jacob extended blessing specifically "because God has dealt graciously with me and because I have enough" (33:11), so that he can give to Esau "my blessing." It may not be a restoration of Esau's blessing, but it was an attempt to make amends for his wrongdoing, not to purchase his favor but to show gratitude for that favor (Steinmann 2019, 315).

In an ironic twist, Esau had "enough" (רָב, v. 9) recalling the blessing on Jacob, but Jacob had "enough" (כֹּל, v. 11) and wanted to give. Jacob shifted terms from Esau's claim, literally meaning "all" or "everything" (*HALOT* s.v. "כֹּל" 474–75). The shift cannot be accidental. Jacob had been fully blessed by Yahweh (cf. 32:26, 29). Now as God's servant, he offered Esau blessing. This is not to suggest that Jacob's motives were pure. Jacob would show ongoing tension with his calling, but though Esau could not have the Abrahamic blessing of leadership, Jacob could bless him, adding to what God had already been doing in his life, both tangibly and intangibly. When he insisted, Esau accepted it.

Rather than tit for tat or restoration of what was lost, it was the recognition of responsibility and opportunity to restore relationship and give generously from an abundance of God's grace. It moves the focus from self-interest and self-enrichment at all costs to responsibility to a brother and restoration at significant personal cost. The theme of fractured brother relationships and fratricide, linking chapter 27 with chapter 4, is now reversing to provide a hint of the redemption expected from the working of God in human hearts and the ability to bless another rather than hoard blessing for oneself. Reception of blessing from God requires a sharing of that blessing with my world, as it changes me.

Jacob Requested Grace (33:12–15)

At Esau's offers of help, Jacob demurred, entreating his grace.

33:12–15. Still, Jacob was not ready to accept Esau's offers of help.[9] Jacob declined Esau's escort, citing his necessarily slow pace (forgetting, of course, his flight from Laban). Though Jacob seems to be changing, he does not appear to trust Esau, nor is he willing to tell him that Seir is not his destination. With Esau's offer to leave help for the trip, Jacob simply asked for his favor (again) to be left alone.

Perhaps from politeness or perhaps the old Jacob is lingering beneath the surface, but he says he will follow Esau to Seir. It seems doubtful that Esau fully understood the implications that they were going their own ways, and Jacob would not

8 Scholars are divided on this, arguing he was returning the stolen blessing (e.g., Westermann 1995, 526), not intending to return the stolen blessing (e.g., Mathews 2005, 570), or perhaps to give part of it to Esau to appear to give back what he had taken (Ross 2008, 193). Curtis (1987, 135), however, observes that the transformation is real, even though it is not yet complete.

9 Esau now suggested two motivations for the large company of men. First, he could provide an escort and probably protection. Second, he could provide help with the herding and care for the animals and people. We cannot know if Esau had either of these in mind when he initially brought the force with him, but whether in the twenty years of Jacob's absence or immediately before their meeting, God had worked miraculously in his heart.

show up at Seir.[10] Rather, change comes slowly with growing pains, and Jacob shows difficulty in fully trusting God.

Jacob Separated from Esau in Peace (33:16–20)

Esau returned to Seir, but Jacob travelled to Succoth and finally to Shechem, settling down and offering public worship to God.

33:16–17. Whether Esau understood Jacob's intent or not, he returned that day south to Seir with no future conflict recorded with Jacob. Jacob headed the other direction, going northwest toward the Jordan (apparently recrossing the Jabbok) and his promised return to the land of Canaan. Stopping before the Jordan, he spent some time in Succoth, a place he named for the temporary shelters he built. How much time they spent here is difficult to say, but in the next chapter the children have grown up considerably from the six- to twelve-year-olds implied by the timeline so far.

33:18–20. Finally, the narrative closes with a transition to the ensuing story. Jacob crossed the Jordan and made his way to Shechem, where he purchased land and established his home. Two important observations conclude the implications of this story. First, and most obviously, he established public worship with an altar that he named El-Elohe-Israel, or God, the God of Israel. Certainly, he was worshipping Yahweh and acknowledging the new relationship God had called him to with his name change. He was outwardly moving toward his vow to make Yahweh his God (28:20–22). He may be expecting this to fulfill his vow, since he was back in the land and Yahweh was stated to be his God. But God would have other ideas because he had not yet fulfilled his promise.

Instead of keeping his vow, however, there is no mention of his promised tithe, nor is he back at Bethel, his promised destination, a little over twenty miles to the south. Whether he felt that he was keeping his vow is not clear, but God would need to prompt him to make the final short trip south, with a little motivation from the tragic events at Shechem (35:1). The astute reader sees trouble brewing for Jacob, a work in progress, because God will not relent in his protection or purpose, holding his chosen one accountable.

THEOLOGICAL FOCUS

God's working in hearts provides hope for reconciliation and blessing, exposing false hope in manipulation of relationships and circumstances and leading to appropriate public worship.

God's working in this narrative clearly shows in the reactions of both Esau and Jacob. God faithfully kept his promise of protection to Jacob, showing a much more significant level of work in the life of Esau than anticipated by Jacob or the reader and providing a much deeper sense of "peace" than even Jacob anticipated (28:21). Esau's response reminds the reader that God's working is usually out of public view, is always occurring whether we expect it or not, and is generally much more significant than we expect (Eph. 3:20). Just because he does not choose an individual for a specific assignment, and we recognize that person to be unfit or profane, does not mean God will not work in their life or cannot accomplish great things in them.

Esau appears in this narrative as a transformed character from the boor who despised his birthright (25:29–34) and plotted murder (27:41). Rather, he is gracious, thoughtful, generous, satisfied, and willing to allow Jacob space.

10 Westermann (1995, 526–27) argues that Esau knew Jacob was not to be taken literally but was just being polite (similarly, cf. Steinmann 2019, 316). Verses 14 and 15, however, are difficult to read that way (Hamilton 1995, 347, esp. n. 32).

Jacob's conclusion is justified. God had been at work, and it showed both in his possessions and, more importantly, in his reactions, especially his grace and forgiveness. His genuine joy at seeing Jacob, as well as his obvious power and satisfaction with his possessions, speak loudly to God's renovations. God was not only radically transforming Jacob, but Esau. He showed his ability to work in anyone's life.

Looking at this from a human perspective, scheming is seen for what it is—futile. We are unable to control our own lives, much less anyone else's. Only God changes hearts, even though people make choices and can reject God's working. We can trust him to work. That work allows new avenues for blessing.

Jacob also accurately understood the implications of God's working in his own life. While he was fearful and still trying to manipulate things, he showed courage and leadership, and he willingly offered generous blessing to his estranged brother whom he had wronged. He appropriately asked for forgiveness and grace with an equally appropriate gift of blessing to show his own transforming heart. God's blessing is not meant to hoard, but to share, and God's purpose for Jacob can be seen in Jacob's response to Esau in extending blessing. God blesses so that he might be seen through extending that blessing (12:2).

One of the implications of God's redemptive plan throughout the book of Genesis is to reverse the fratricidal impulse of sin (ch. 4). Abraham's life suggested that reversal as he prayed for his "brother" Lot, sealing his deliverance (19:29). Now we see God working to reverse that impulse in Esau, foreshadowing an even more dramatic working in Joseph and his brothers (50:18–21). From the beginning, the heart has been the problem that needed God's special work (see comments on 8:21, p. 193). Here we see a glimpse of what God can do in people, even though we do not know any of the circumstances. Again, it reminds us that God is at work in many ways that we are not privy to and may only catch occasional glances of in divinely ordained encounters.

Finally, we end the narrative with Jacob's appropriate response of public worship, necessitated by God's work. Not only must the blessed one praise God for the blessing and acknowledge his sole place as God, but he must do it publicly. Yet the disquieting realization that Jacob was not fully keeping his vow suggests that more work needed to be done. God had clearly reminded him of his need to keep it, and perhaps he expected this was close enough. However, as we shall see, God does expect fulfillment of all vows made. He also does not stop short of the full transformation of his chosen servants. Jacob had clearly made significant growth but was not yet fully Israel. As with all of us, that growth must continue until glory, yet we bear responsibility to fully conform to the expectations of the King whom we serve.

PREACHING AND TEACHING STRATEGIES

Exegetical and Theological Synthesis

After receiving the blessing and realizing God's presence in the previous scene (ch. 32), Jacob now sees Esau coming toward him with a huge army of men. It is time to see whether God will protect Jacob in this encounter, as he promised. Jacob still has work to do on his faith since he, not Esau, is the one who bows down (cf. 27:29). If this is not just customary courtesy, Jacob has forgotten his place in God's plan. However, how encouraging to see God at work in both men's lives as they finally meet and embrace (33:4)!

We should learn from this encounter to expect God to work miracles in us and around us for his glory. There is no doubt that the Lord can move the hearts of anyone to accomplish his purposes. In an act that directly fulfills the covenant God made to Abraham, Jacob extends a blessing to Esau. We see this in the way God graciously deals with Jacob (v. 11; also 28:14). In this way the Lord has graciously, miraculously reversed the terrible tendency in Genesis for family members to destroy one another (cf. ch. 4 and Cain and Abel!).

The narrative portrays the faithfulness of God as Jacob finally ends up in Canaan (Shechem). Jacob leads the way at the end of the narrative by building an altar for the purpose of worshipping his God (33:20). Like all of us, Jacob is a work in progress, and the Lord will keep his promise to mature us as we trust him on our faith journey.

Preaching Idea

Trust the Lord to fulfill his promise to bless you and make you a blessing—easier said than done in difficult relationships.

Contemporary Connections

What does it mean?

One connection you might make for your listeners is between Jacob's nighttime wrestling match with the God-Man and Jacob's encounter with his brother Esau. Jacob receives a blessing in that first encounter, but that blessing does not eliminate the need for Jacob to confront his brother, Esau, who had vowed to kill him. Jacob prepares for an attack, and you will have to help your listeners decide whether this is wisdom in action or a lack of faith in God. Remind your listeners that building an altar (33:20) means preparation for the worship of Yahweh.

Another connection with the previous narrative is the repetition of seeing the "face of God" (33:10 and 32:30). In 32:30, seeing God's face resulted in Jacob receiving the blessing (v. 29 "And there he blessed him"). In 33:10 Jacob realizes that he is being treated well because God had been at work in Esau's life ("and you have accepted me"). In both cases, it acknowledges God's intervention.

Is it true?

Let your listeners know that the Lord is showing his faithfulness to Jacob in preserving his life from Esau's hatred. The narrative assumes this but does not state this. God has done a miracle to heal this relationship between brothers.

Now what?

The biblical author is assuming our listeners will see the application of this narrative. The author does not directly apply the meaning of Jacob's encounter with Esau. You will make it clear that this scene that begins with great stress and ends in peace is the result of God's faithfulness to his promises to bless his people and make them a blessing. God did a miracle in changing both men's hearts. Jacob could not scheme his way to relational peace; God had to do it. Jacob continues to struggle to trust the Lord completely; we do well to admit our own struggle, even though most of our listeners have experienced his faithfulness. Thankfully, God continues to work patiently in us as we struggle to walk with him by faith!

Creativity in Presentation

In this narrative we also must learn to trust the Lord to fulfill his promise to bless you and make you a blessing—easier said than done in difficult relationships.

- The sermon/lesson could begin with worry ("behold, Esau was coming" v. 1) and end with worship (the altar in v. 20).

- In the middle, God is faithful and wonderfully patches the relationship between the brothers. Because of the Lord's working, Jacob did "find favor" (a repeated phrase). Because of the Lord's favor on Jacob's life, he can confer a blessing on Esau. This is what the Lord prophesied to Abraham and through Isaac. Our listeners may be able to provide adequate testimony of God's faithfulness to them, which in turn led to opportunities to bless others.

Another optional structure presents the stages we sometimes experience while learning to trust and see God at work:

- Worry and staging to control the outcome (33:1–3)
- Wrestling through the situation on our own (33:4–8)
- Recognizing the working of God already present (33:9–11)
- Continued hesitance to fully trust (33:12–17)
- Worship to a faithful God despite our shortcomings (33:18–20)

DISCUSSION QUESTIONS

1. Discuss whether Jacob's plan of action in the opening verses displays godly wisdom or a lack of faith in the promise of God to protect him and his family. What makes the difference?
2. How have you seen God clearly show up in unexpected ways in your life that could not be explained any other way?
3. Why is it still difficult to fully trust God, even after we see him work, and acknowledge it to be his presence?
4. What areas might we still need to consciously turn over to God in prayer, giving them to him to work for us?
5. How can we reconcile and extend blessing to those that may be at odds with us, even when we think it justified?
6. Are we consistently asking God to work in our difficult relationships to bring healing, reconciliation, and shalom? How can we appropriately trust God for that and work toward those ends?

Genesis 34:1–31

EXEGETICAL IDEA

When Shechem raped Dinah, Jacob abdicated leadership to his sons, who deceptively risked their blessing and threatened assimilation for vengeance and profit, killing and plundering an entire Canaanite city instead of doing righteousness and justice and extending blessing from Yahweh.

THEOLOGICAL FOCUS

God's people must respond to evil in faith, according to God's character, by doing righteousness and justice to experience and extend blessing to their world rather than cursing from self-interest or vengeance.

PREACHING IDEA

Overcoming "evil with good" is the only way to be a blessing in God's world.

PREACHING POINTERS

The original audience would have been appalled to read what Shechem did to Dinah (v. 2). Even the tenderness recorded by the narrator in verse 3 would not be enough. The transition to modern listeners begins with this unfolding plot of Shechem trying to marry Dinah after what he had done to her. What a test for Jacob's family! According to Jacob's mission, they have a job to do in the world: bring God's blessing by the way they live and reveal Yahweh (see Gen. 28:14). In Genesis 18:19 the Lord had said, "For I have chosen him, that he may command his children and his household after him to keep the way of the LORD by doing righteousness and justice, so that the LORD may bring to Abraham what he has promised him."

Jacob's sons are furious because they recognize the injustice; all the while, their father is silent (34:5, 7). And early readers recognize the spiritual danger in Shechem's father's request: "Make marriages with us" (vv. 9–10). Will anyone trust the Lord in this narrative? Evidently not, as Jacob's sons act the way he used to ("deceitfully" in v. 13). So much for doing righteousness and justice.

The Hivites fall for it and suffer because of it. And so does God's plan for his people, at least temporarily, because of Jacob's inactivity. The narrative concludes with the question, "Should he treat our sister like a prostitute?" (v. 31). The answer is, "No." Preachers might conclude with another question, "Should God's people act in the place of God and act vengefully?" The answer is also, "No."

SHECHEM'S FALL: THE CURSE OF VENGEANCE (34:1–31)

LITERARY STRUCTURE AND THEMES

The story of Dinah's rape and the resulting sack of Shechem comes as an unsettling departure from the expected storyline, with especially difficult application for the New Testament believer.[1] Jacob, previously showing spiritual promise, hardly appears and then does so unfavorably. The family has grown significantly, and the sons are developing the disturbing characteristics of their father, from deception to murder and plunder. The many significant connections to the immediate context do not clearly provide the thematic and theological links for the reader. Instead, we must see much of the significance in the macrostructure of the Jacob stories and as preparation for the Joseph stories to come.

The narrative itself develops in four balanced panels. The presenting conflict, centered around Shechem's rape of Dinah and desire to marry her and described briefly in the first four verses, precipitates the reactions of Jacob and his sons. The center dialogue presents Hamor and Shechem negotiating an acceptable marriage proposal and broader treaty with her deceptive brothers, which they then pitch to the townsmen so that they can fulfill the required circumcision for every male. With their compliance, the brothers murder and pillage the town, rescuing Dinah and exposing Jacob's fear and their folly. Abraham's descendants do not practice righteousness and justice (18:19) and bring cursing rather than blessing (28:14).

A. Shechem raped Dinah, infuriating her brothers (34:1–7).
  1. Shechem raped Dinah, wanting to marry her (34:1–4).
  2. Jacob kept silent (34:5–6).
  3. Jacob's sons were furious (34:7).
B. Jacob's sons offered to intermarry (34:8–17).
  4. Hamor offered wealth for Dinah (34:8–12).
  5. Jacob's sons required circumcision (34:13–17).
B'. Hamor and Shechem secured agreement (34:18–24).
  5'. Hamor and Shechem agreed to circumcision (34:18–19).
  4'. The townsmen agreed for wealth (34:20–24).
A'. Jacob's sons raped[2] Shechem (34:25–31).
  3'. Simeon and Levi murdered all the men, rescuing Dinah (34:25–29).
  2'. Jacob rebuked Simeon and Levi (34:30).
  1'. Simeon and Levi defended Dinah (34:31).

Jacob only appears twice, bracketing the narrative in silence, failing to address the rape at the beginning and, in fear of reprisals, rebuking his sons at the end. In both cases he is marginalized by his sons and sadly missing the needed

1 Earl (2011, 48) declares, "Genesis 34 fails to find Christian significance because it inherently reflects the 'oldness' of the old covenant and does not provide a narrative that lends itself to development in contexts other than this" but see Ber's (2016) helpful response.

2 Several scholars have noted the parallel between the rape of Shechem and the rape of Dinah (Bechtel 1994, 34, Bechtel disputes that Dinah was raped, but views the brothers' actions as a "rape;" cf. Wenham 1994, 308).

righteous leadership of the clan. God's choice seems to be going badly.

The center narrative dialogues focus on the offers of prosperity from Hamor and Shechem, competing with God's previous promises to Jacob and his descendants. Where will their security and prosperity come from? The clan was missing God's intended purpose. They were scheming rather than clinging to Yahweh and bringing cursing rather than blessing.

The sons reduced the hope of the covenant and their promises to a bargaining chip, ostensibly for their own prosperity but actually to wreak their own vengeance and guarantee their own security, benefit, and ill-defined honor. The horrors of the narrative, with their ambiguities and mixed signals, highlight the dangers for the nascent nation in the land and the seemingly precarious nature of God's purposes. God appears absent, and his stars have lost their luster.

In the flow of the stories, then, God's expected intervention has not (yet) shown up, and his chosen heir has moved into the shadows of potential pagan assimilation. Even if the physical assimilation was a ruse, the moral assimilation appears dangerously near. As with the threats God's people would repeatedly face, rather than fulfilling his vow, living up to his new name, and moving into God's glorious promises, the patriarch endangered his family and his future. God's redemptive plan truly cannot be dependent on his weak images.

- ***Shechem Raped Dinah, Infuriating Her Brothers (34:1–7)***
- ***Jacob's Sons Offered to Intermarry (34:8–17)***
- ***Hamor and Shechem Secured Citywide Agreement (34:18–24)***
- ***Jacob's Sons Raped Shechem (34:25–31)***

EXPOSITION

The narrative must be placed in its canonical setting to capture the intent of the stark realities. Within the covenant promises, God's purpose of blessing for all peoples (12:3; 18:18; 22:18; 26:4; 28:18), the stipulation that those who bless Abraham and his descendants will be blessed and the one who curses them will be cursed, forms an important foundation (12:3; 27:29). That blessing for all will only come as the descendants of Abraham "keep the way of the LORD by doing righteousness and justice" (18:19). Jacob and his sons' actions and their consequences will be evaluated by this standard, which for the nation of Israel reading this must accord with the Torah (thus the several allusions and references to God's standard, vv. 7, 14, 31).

Within the Jacob narratives, we must also evaluate the numerous connections to Genesis 26 (Isaac's fearful introduction of Rebekah to Abimelech as his sister) and their implications (see Introduction to the Jacob Narratives, p. 427). In both cases, deception revolves around the endangering of and (potential) molesting of a woman in the clan by a Canaanite, resulting in negotiations for peace and prosperity. The outcomes are very different, and the responses of the patriarch are key to those outcomes. In the first, God is active, but in the second, God seems absent. The lessons of faith learned in the first are absent in the second. Instead, when Shechem raped Dinah, Jacob abdicated leadership to his sons, who deceptively risked their blessing and threatened assimilation for vengeance and profit, killing and plundering an entire Canaanite city instead of doing righteousness and justice and extending blessing from Yahweh.

Shechem Raped Dinah, Infuriating Her Brothers (34:1–7)

When Shechem raped Dinah and tried to legitimize his love with marriage, Jacob's silence abdicated the lead to his angry sons.

Shechem Raped Dinah, Wanting to Marry (34:1–4)

Shechem raped but loved Dinah, seeking her hand.

34:1–2. The crisis begins with Dinah visiting the local young ladies.[3] The description foregrounds two observations that will color the impressions of the account. First, the only other time the phrase "women of the land" (lit. "daughters of the land," NASB95, בְּנוֹת הָאָרֶץ) occurs in the Old Testament is in 27:46 and Rebekah's disgust with Esau's wives. It now raises concern for the family and the specter of intermarriage with the Canaanites (cf. 24:3; 26:34–35; 27:46; 28:1).

Second, Jacob's reactions must be evaluated through the reminder that Dinah was "the daughter of Leah," one of the few places anyone's lineage is traced through their mother.[4] Jacob's silence (34:5) and his concern (v. 30) will now be viewed through his history of neglect toward Leah. It also colors the responses of Simeon and Levi, her full brothers (vv. 25–26, 31).

With four verbs in quick succession, Shechem violated Dinah. Reminiscent of Genesis 3:6, Shechem "saw" (ראה) Dinah and "seized" (lit. "took," לקח) her, then "lay with her and humiliated her" (34:2). The act is clear. That it was forced (rape) rather than seduction seems apparent.

TRANSLATION ANALYSIS 34:2

The outcome ("humiliated," II ענה) elsewhere in the piel can be translated "oppress" or "humiliate" (HALOT s.v. II "ענה" 852–54). Some argue, then, that the verbs technically do not require "rape," and Shechem evidenced real affection for her (e.g., Bechtel 1994, 23–31; Joseph 2016; van Wolde 2002). Some translations keep the intent ambiguous ("humiliated her," ESV; "humbled her," RSV). However, the cascade of terms, the evaluations later, and the general usage of the final term all point to the clear intent of rape (Noble 1996, 178–79; Shemesh 2007, 2–21), reflected in numerous translations ("sexually assaulted her," NET; "raped her," NIV, NLT; "lay with her by force," NASB95, NJPS, NRSV; "violated her," NKJV). In fact, as Shemesh (2007, 5) notes, the final verb is never used of normal sexual relations in the Old Testament, and elsewhere always involves force and distress, whether related to sexual activity or not (cf. Wegner, עָנָה, *NIDOTTE* 3:450).

34:3–4. Following the rape, Shechem's attraction only grew for Dinah. Her description as the daughter of Jacob reminds the reader that she was Jacob's responsibility and highlights the different worlds and expectations of the two families. Shechem is privileged in his world, but he will have to negotiate for her. He was hooked, and he began sweet-talking her and asked his father to negotiate her hand in marriage, the appropriate avenue for a young man in love. In his request, Shechem calls her a "girl" (יַלְדָּה, v. 4), a term used only three times in the Old Testament and suggesting her young age and his disrespect.

TRANSLATION ANALYSIS 34:3

Literally "he spoke to the heart of the girl" (וַיְדַבֵּר עַל־לֵב הַנַּעֲרָ), which is variously translated as "spoke tenderly" (ESV, NASB95, NIV), "spoke romantically" (NET), or "spoke kindly" (NCV, NKJV). It can be used of calming fears (50:21), repairing relationships (Judg. 19:3), and winning loyalty (Hos. 2:14), all of which was needed if he was to make her his wife.

---

3 Some have argued Dinah's actions were inappropriate. Sarna (1989, 233), for example, states it was not normal and could be "promiscuous" for a young woman to leave the safety of her father's compound and wander in the town (cf. Wenham 1994, 317). Others defend her (Parry 2002, 13–16). Even assuming it was ill advised, given the outcome, it adds further warning to the dangers of living in the Canaanite world and makes the reader wonder why Jacob had allowed her to do so. Yet any impropriety is not stressed in the text, which emphasizes her being "defiled" (vv. 5, 13, 27) and Shechem's responsibility (vv. 2, 5, 7, 13, 27).

4 Steinmann (2019, 320) finds only seven times, and this is the only place in the Pentateuch.

TRANSLATION ANALYSIS 34:4

Wenham (1994, 311) suggests the term יַלְדָּה not only denotes her young age, but disparages her. In conversation with her family, he will call her the more respectful "young woman" (הַנַּעֲרָ, v. 12). Some translations in verse 4 include the implied age, translating it "young girl" (NASB95, NET, NLT). Others seem to make it less obvious, translating "young woman" (NKJV) or "maiden" (RSV). The significance here is both Dinah's age (increasing the concern of the rape) and the character of Shechem, who to her family appears (more) respectful and conciliatory than in his conversation with his father.

Jacob Kept Silent (34:5–6)

Jacob heard but kept silent before Hamor, waiting for his sons.

34:5–6. Jacob heard that Shechem had "defiled" (טִמֵּא) Dinah (v. 5). The term, used extensively in Leviticus for ceremonial uncleanness, here reflects the cultural shame for the crime against the family's honor. For the Israelite reader, however, this freighted judgment against Shechem becomes the rationale for the deceit (v. 13) and plunder (v. 27) of Shechem, lending a façade of legitimacy to the actions of the sons.

We are not told how Jacob heard, only that he "held his peace" (v. 5) until his sons could come in. This last clause connects his silence with Hamor's attempt to negotiate a marriage. There would be no negotiating without the brothers. His silence starkly contrasts with the reaction of the brothers in verse 7. Was he waiting for them to give backup before making a stand for righteousness? At this point we don't know, but he will disappear from the narrative until after all the action (v. 30). On the one hand, waiting for his sons was appropriate, since the brothers were often included in the negotiations for marriage (Sarna 1989, 168). On the other, his continued silence suggests indifference to the daughter of his less-loved wife and his missing leadership, stressed in verse 30. Hamor had to wait, and Jacob missed the opportunity to lead his family in justice and righteousness (18:19).

Jacob's Sons Were Furious (34:7)

Jacob's sons reacted with grief and fury.

34:7. In glaring contrast, Jacob's sons were deeply grieved and angry when they heard.[5] Their fury appropriately recognized that Shechem "had done an outrageous thing in Israel." Occurring only seven times in the Old Testament, the "outrageous thing in Israel" requires a drastic response to a deeply disturbing breach of Yahweh's law.[6] This evaluation reflects the attitude of the sons but states the narrator's evaluation, suggesting the view of later Israel. As such it highlights the theological and moral tension between a heinous act and appropriate response. No one will come out of this story with the moral high ground. The narrative recognizes that the clan would become a nation, relating to the recently given name for Jacob. The statement, then, also stresses again the world of difference between the growing clan and the powerful but pagan Hivite leaders.

The evaluation also demonstrates the serious nature of the threat and ironically shows the appropriate grief and anger of the sons and

5 It is "undecidable" whether they heard in the field and came in immediately, or they came in and heard when they returned, since the clauses can be understood either way (citing the rabbinic discussion, Sternberg 1987, 452).

6 The stated or applied responses when used in the OT include death for an unfaithful woman, Deut. 22:21; death for the violator of holy war, Josh. 7:15; civil war against the gang rape in Gibeah, Judg. 20:6, 10; God's curse on the exiles in Babylon for their sin, Jer. 29:23; and Tamar's rebuke and warning for Amnon, 2 Sam. 13:12. These highlight the future perspective, looking ahead to the national identity, applying the outrage from the mouths of the brothers to the burgeoning nation Moses was addressing.

the inappropriate reticence of Jacob, who is neither standing for justice nor clinging to God. Rather, he stays in the shadows even though she is his daughter (and his responsibility, stated for the fourth time in only seven verses: vv. 1, 3, 5, 7, cf. 19). That such a thing should not be done indicates that justice must be done. Jacob, however, refused to do it.

Jacob's Sons Offered to Intermarry (34:8–17)

The families negotiated for her hand, with Hamor offering prosperity, but Jacob's sons, deceptively risking their blessing, require circumcision for the community.

Hamor Offered Wealth for Dinah (34:8–12)

Hamor and Shechem offered property and opportunity for wealth for Dinah's hand.

34:8. The father of the would-be groom began the negotiations with both Jacob and his sons.[7] Hamor completely ignored the rape, which the whole family had already strongly reacted against, and instead stressed Shechem's love for Dinah. In verse 4 Shechem's soul "was drawn" (lit. "clung," דבק) to Dinah, and now in Hamor's report, his soul "longs" for her. Perhaps thinking that Shechem's evident love would smooth things over, he then requested her hand for his son in marriage.

TRANSLATION ANALYSIS 34:8

The intent seems to be to indicate deep attachment or "love" for someone (HALOT s.v. "חשק" 362), so Shechem "is in love with" (NET), "deeply in love with" (NCV, NLT), or "has his heart set on" (NIV) Dinah.

34:9–10. To sweeten the deal, Hamor proposed not merely a single wedding, but an intermingling of the tribes so that they all would become one big family (see v. 16). They would exchange their daughters and dwell together, opening the entire area around Shechem for their settlement, trade, and acquisition of property. The irony of the previous use of "Israel" now deepens. Jacob had previously pursued blessing with his own manipulations, but in his encounter, God had given him the new name Israel with the intent that he cling to Yahweh and let him fight for Jacob (see notes on 32:28, p. 533). God had already promised Jacob the land for himself and his descendants, as well as prosperity (28:13–14; Exod. 3:8, 17). Hamor's offer pointedly used the verbal form ("get property," וְהֵאָחֲזוּ) of the noun God had used in his offer to Abraham (Gen. 17:8; Wenham 1994, 312). Who would they trust? Jacob's silence through all of this is deafening.

Shechem

Sarna (1989, 233) cites Egyptian, Akkadian, and Amarna texts to show that Shechem at this time controlled the entire central hill country from Jerusalem to Megiddo ("about 1,000 square miles") and was a significant and prosperous city. Hamor, as "leader" (34:2), then wielded significant authority, ruling a city "governed by its urban institutions" rather than a king, to make this offer (Reviv 1977, 193).

Hamor's proposal brings into full view the danger of assimilation into the Canaanites, melting into their surroundings, and losing their identity as the chosen people of God. The wording of Hamor closely mirrors the prohibition Moses gave to Israel (Deut. 7:3). The danger was real, not just of losing their identity but losing their exclusive worship of Yahweh (Deut. 7:4, see the vow of Jacob which he has yet to fulfill, Gen. 28:21).

---

7 He refers to Dinah as "your (pl.) daughter," which at the same time recognizes Jacob's fatherhood and includes the sons in the deal, possibly thinking of the clan, which fits with the offer of intermarriage (vv. 9, 16, and esp. 17). Shechem addressed both "her father" and "her brothers" (v. 11).

Hamor's Offer

The Hebrew text of Genesis 34:9 (Hamor's offer) directly follows the Hebrew text of Deuteronomy 7:3, so that Hamor's offer directly proposes what Moses later prohibited. Moses intends the reader to make the connection of this offer and the danger of violating God's purpose for the nation and remaining separate from the Canaanites. The brothers affirm his words directly in Genesis 34:16. It also implies that the bigger issue is not only assimilation but idolatry (Deut. 7:4, "for they would turn away your sons from following me, to serve other gods.")

Genesis 34:9	Deuteronomy 7:3
וְהִתְחַתְּנוּ אֹתָנוּ בְּנֹתֵיכֶם תִּתְּנוּ־לָנוּ וְאֶת־בְּנֹתֵינוּ תִּקְחוּ לָכֶם	וְלֹא תִתְחַתֵּן בָּם בִּתְּךָ לֹא־תִתֵּן לִבְנוֹ וּבִתּוֹ לֹא־תִקַּח לִבְנֶךָ
Make marriages with us. Give your daughters to us and take our daughters for yourselves.	You shall not intermarry with them, giving your daughters to their sons or taking their daughters for your sons.

34:11–12. Shechem, waiting in the background, makes his own appeal. While Hamor was thinking big picture as the "prince of the land" (v. 2), with profit for himself and his people (v. 23), Shechem focused on his desire for Dinah. Without mentioning his violation of her or any repentant heart, Shechem asked for "favor," offering to pay "whatever" they would ask[8] (v. 11)! He then doubled down, offering as great a bride price as they might require! While he appears serious, he offered financial gain rather than repentance and never acknowledged his offense.

Jacob's Sons Required Circumcision (34:13–17)

Jacob's sons countered deceptively, requiring circumcision for the entire town.

34:13. Jacob's sons responded, reminding the reader of Jacob's deceit in taking Esau's blessing (27:35). The sons are living like their father, but the heads-up from the narrator that they were being deceitful provides an evaluation of their actions as well. Their deceit goes far beyond Jacob's, leading to murder and the clear condemnation of their violation of Israel's later code (Exod. 22:16–17 [HB 15–16]; Deut 22:28–28; Mathews 2005, 601).

Their excuse, of course, was the rape that "defiled" their sister Dinah. Shechem's crime needed to be addressed, but their means would be excessive in the extreme. The next generation of Jacobs furnished a clear look at the direction the clan was headed without divine intervention, preparing the reader for the murderous internal strife beginning the Joseph narratives.

In contrast to the incensed response of Dinah's brothers, the one who should have addressed it in negotiation with Shechem's father remained silent. Her father does not speak for her. The consistent notices of their father-daughter relationship remind the reader of Jacob's favoritism and his silence. The hallmark of his dealings with his wives and children tragically bears fruit in his indifference toward the only daughter of his least-loved wife.

34:14–17. Addressing Shechem, Dinah's brothers refused without his circumcision, claiming it would be a "disgrace" (v. 14). They then expanded the demand to every male. On that condition they would not only give up Dinah but agreed to intermarry, citing Hamor's proposal in verses 10–11a. The sons, then,

8 Some have assumed that the offer of payment admits culpability (Wagner 2013, 156–57), but the text makes no indication of any admission and certainly no indication of the degree of wrongfulness.

drew out the implication. They would become "one people," underlining the danger to Israel and God's purposes. Making it more significant and shocking for Israel, they were using their unique status under the Abrahamic covenant and risking their blessing before Yahweh, given to Jacob as the expression of his choice of the family (17:9–14; 28:13–15). Rather than uphold Yahweh's promise to them for the land, they offered, in deception at least, to assimilate with the very ones Yahweh had promised to drive out because they were unfit (15:16, 18–21; Exod. 23:28; 33:2; 34:11; Deut. 7:1; 20:17; Josh. 3:10).

The sons were not proposing that the Shechemites all become Yahweh worshippers. They were using the common understanding of circumcision as a rite of manhood or transition to marriage as a ploy, but their interest was not spiritual. "The Canaanites were not joining the offspring of Abraham; rather, the descendants of Abraham were joining with the Canaanites" (Sailhamer 1990, 215). Although their offer was a ploy, they revealed their misunderstanding or cavalier attitude toward their circumcision and appeared willing to barter their identity to gain their agenda. The offer risked mistaking ritual conformity with the necessary unity in true worship and worldview and risked their blessing from Yahweh for their own self-interest.

What the reader does not yet know, however, is that Hamor and Shechem seem to be holding all the cards. What will come as a surprise to the reader, but not to the brothers, is that Dinah was back at Shechem's house. Simeon and Levi would rescue her later (Gen. 34:26), but they hint at the need for force to rescue her here. If the townsmen do not agree, they will "take" her and go. Shechem had begun the crisis when he "seized" Dinah (v. 2, לקח), but they would end it by taking her back (לקח).

Of course, Dinah's removal would appear to require force, and they were greatly outnumbered. It is easy to see why they resorted to deception and even force. That, however, discounts the promise of Yahweh (28:15) and the lessons he had taught Jacob (and the family), whether it was protection from Laban (ch. 31) or Esau (chs. 32–33).

Hamor and Shechem Secured Citywide Agreement (34:18–24)

Agreeing, Hamor and Shechem pitched the requirement to the men of the town as an opportunity to plunder Jacob's clan, and they agreed.

Hamor and Shechem Agreed to Circumcision (34:18–19)

Hamor and Shechem agreed, acting on it immediately.

34:18–19. Hamor and Shechem were quick to agree. As we see in their pitch to the Shechemites, Hamor seems motivated by more than true love. Shechem, however, does seem truly smitten. He "delighted" in "Jacob's daughter" (v. 19). The story highlights both Shechem's infatuation and Dinah's missing father.

The note ends with a preview of the next scene. Shechem had some pull with his neighbors. The prince was the most respected in the house of the leader of the land, so his word and his desire would carry weight.

The Townsmen Agreed for Wealth (34:20–24)

Hamor and Shechem pitched the requirement to the townsmen, emphasizing their acquisition of all the property of Jacob's clan, and they all agreed.

34:20–23. Hamor and Shechem together brought the opportunity to the men of the town. They naturally went to the gate, but it was not just the elders. They had to have the agreement of all the "free and permanent residents" ("men of the city") to seal the deal for land acquisition (Reviv 1977, 192).

They began with the argument that there was no economic downside. The land was spacious, and they were already at peace together, so there would be no loss for them. In fact, there would be more options for spouses for their sons and daughters. The only downside was the temporary, physical act of circumcision. They countered that painful requirement with the upside of financial gain. They would fully assimilate all the assets of Jacob's clan.

Here, their line seems to deviate from what they had pitched Jacob's sons. They had expressed the openness of the country and opportunity for trade to the family, emphasizing what the Jacobites would gain through trade and acquisition of property (v. 10). For the Shechemites, however, they envision all that the Jacobites have becoming theirs, from their livestock and animals to their personal property. They would plunder the new family coming in.

34:24. They convinced "all who went out of the gate" (repeating it). Every male would be circumcised. Certainly, Jacob's sons must neutralize any ability of the townspeople to fight back or retaliate if they were to take back Dinah by force, unless, of course, God intervened.

> *TRANSLATION ANALYSIS 34:24*
> Schmutzer has argued that rather than the "town council" (NLT), all "who assembled at the city gate" (NET), or even "able-bodied" (HCSB, NEB), "all who go out of the gate" would be specifically the "battle-ready warriors," repeated to emphasize the vulnerability of the city to attack (Schmutzer 2007, 50; cf. Speiser 1956). The specific need for the sons here, as we see in what follows, was to disable their ability to fight back.

Jacob's Sons Raped Shechem (34:25–31)

Jacob's sons raped Shechem, defending Dinah's honor, while they all missed Yahweh's way of righteousness and justice, extending only cursing.

Simeon and Levi Rescued Dinah, Murdering All the Men (34:25–29)

When the men of Shechem were in pain, Simeon and Levi murdered them all, rescuing Dinah while the rest of the sons plundered the town.

34:25–29. For the first time, two of the sons are singled out—Dinah's (full) brothers. Leah, mother of Dinah, had six sons. Reuben was oldest, then Simeon, Levi, and Judah (29:31–35). After giving her maid as a wife to Jacob, she had two more sons, Issachar and Zebulun, before bearing Dinah (30:17–21). Simeon and Levi take up the offense with a vengeance. While the other brothers do not participate, perhaps highlighting their excess (Mathews 2005, 590), the two men take up their swords and slaughter the men of the town.

> **When Did This Occur?**
> The chronology of this narrative is not obvious. Simeon and Levi are clearly fully grown, though they were no more than eleven and twelve when they left Haran. Dinah was a woman, even though young, though she was probably less than six when they left. They spent some time in Succoth and then here in Shechem, so they may be very familiar with these people and already have established relationships. Jacob seems to have no interest in going the last twenty miles to Bethel to complete his vow.

For Israel reading this account, their response should be evaluated by Torah. Primarily, the laws on rape would apply. The closest parallel is Deuteronomy 22:28–29 and Exodus 22:16–17. If a man rapes (or seduces) a woman who is not betrothed, he must pay a large bride price, marry her, and he may not divorce her. Exodus adds that the father may refuse to give her to him, but he must still pay the large bride price.[9] The death penalty would only apply if she was betrothed (Deut. 22:23–27) or married (Deut. 22:22). Presumably Dinah was not betrothed, though it is not stated. While a large fine may be appropriate, such an act would not have indicated the death penalty.

Rape Laws

Extrabiblical laws appear to generally agree with the biblical laws that rape of a betrothed or married woman would bring death, but sex with an unmarried and unattached virgin (whether rape or consensual) would require payment and marriage with no penalty of death (Wagner 2013, 151–55). Sarna (1989, 235) cites one Middle Assyrian law presenting a very similar picture to Exodus 22:15–16, where the offender pays compensation, and the father can decide if he will allow the marriage. Neither Hamor nor Shechem appear to take the offense too seriously or expect repercussions beyond payment of a hefty price (they assume they are all "at peace" [Gen. 34:21] and the village "felt secure" [v. 25]).

Simeon and Levi's crime of personal vengeance in executing Shechem was compounded by putting Hamor to death (contra. Deut. 24:16) and then the entire male population. Further exacerbating the crimes of the two sons, the rest of the sons finished by pillaging and enslaving the town. The plunder of the city was justified in their minds because Dinah had been defiled (Gen. 34:27). They took everything, from the property to the people. "Ironically, the defilement of one woman, Dinah, led to the painful capture of many women and children" (Ross 2008, 197). The structure, with their parallel "rape" of the town, reinforces the conclusion that the Israelites here are no better than the Hivites.

Their heinous acts shredded Yahweh's purpose for his chosen family. Instead of blessing, they inflicted cursing and destruction (cf. 12:3; 18:18; 22:18; 26:4; 28:14). Instead of keeping "the way of the Lord by doing righteousness and justice" (18:19), they deceived, murdered, and plundered the land, transgressing his ways and perverting his character.

Jacob Rebuked Simeon and Levi (34:30)

Missing Yahweh's way of righteousness, justice, and extending blessing, Jacob rebuked Simeon and Levi because of the family vulnerability.

34:30. Jacob finally responded, rebuking the two sons who had murdered the men of the city. Surprisingly, his concern was not for their murders or plundering of the city because he wanted to pursue righteousness and justice (18:19)! Rather than desiring to bring blessing through appropriate justice (28:14), he expressed vulnerability to retaliation from the surrounding country. While his pragmatism was astute (they were certainly in a danger that they had not considered, 35:5), his moral compass was missing, and it was as if he did not expect God's protection (was it lack of faith or realization of their flaunting the righteousness of Yahweh?). In fact, the reader may wonder if God would continue to protect them, with such grievous offenses.

The reactions of Jacob frame the narrative. His silence in the face of the offense against his daughter haunts the reader with the tragic favoritism that will blossom in the Joseph stories. Not only did he not stand up for his daughter, but he failed to resolve her heartbreak with justice and righteousness as the head of the family, leaving the opening for his sons to carry out their vendetta against the population and bringing cursing to the nation near them.

---

9 Mathews (2005, 590) notes that it does not specifically address the alien raping an Israelite. The law assumes that the marriage would be acceptable, since the Canaanites were not intended to be living among the Israelites. However, see the sidebar, "Rape Laws."

Neither avenging nor appeasing bring justice or show God's character (Kidner 1967, 195).

Simeon and Levi Defended Dinah's Honor (34:31)

Missing Yahweh's honor, Simeon and Levi defended Dinah's honor.

34:31. Jacob's response left the brothers feeling self-righteous as the sole defenders of their sister's honor. Concluding the narrative with Simeon and Levi's question could be taken as approval of their actions (Hyman 2000). Certainly, the need for justice and the tension with the under-reaction of their father hangs heavily over the story. Shechem had merely offered money for Dinah "*without acknowledging that he had previously abused her*" (Noble 1996, 194, emphasis his). Their anger was understandable, though their extreme personal vengeance was reprehensible (cf. 49:5–7). The tensions point to the folly of both parties and the dangers for the nation in the land when they are not keeping their responsibilities before Yahweh.

They have been living back in the land for a significant period so that the sons are grown. Jacob has given every indication that he was content staying there, and his concerns may have been simply pragmatic, recognizing the need to live at peace with his neighbors (Brueggemann 1982a, 279). However, he had a heritage he did not satisfy, promises he did not recall, and a vow that he had yet to fulfill. Though he had made no move to satisfy that vow, this event would propel him to Bethel, with God's reminder (35:1).

While God is absent from the narrative, the placement of the story, right after God's deliverance from both Laban and Esau and immediately prior to God's command, provides context for Jacob's expected response to the promises of God. The absence of any mention of God reflects his vacancy in the thoughts and responses of the characters. The context, however, situates Israel's necessary perspective.

The reflection of the themes and structure with the story of Isaac in Gerar highlights the needed response of the patriarch in faith and righteousness to the leader of the land in an appropriate covenant. In Genesis 26, Abimelech was very fearful that one of his would violate Rebekah and bring guilt on the community (v. 10). In contrast, Hamor ignored the problem, and Jacob was silent. Isaac's growth from fear to faith and honest approach resulted in blessing, both for Isaac and for the local inhabitants, as well as security through the covenant (see ch. 26). Here, Jacob's fear left his family with ill-gotten material goods and insecurity, and the local inhabitants murdered and plundered. No one experienced blessing.

The message of the passage (and all of Genesis) was for Israel. Here it shows more clearly with the repetition of loaded terms like "defiled," "outrageous thing in Israel," focus on circumcision as a family distinctive, intermarriage, and allusions to later law (Walton and Moberly 2003, 200). Israel, and God's people in all times, must heed the warnings and recognize the tensions of living in a messy world, with its opportunity to trust in a faithful God, keep his way, and bring blessing. They must live in the world but must not and cannot become part of the world (Ber 2016).

THEOLOGICAL FOCUS

God's people must respond to evil in faith, according to God's character, by doing righteousness and justice to experience and extend blessing to their world, rather than cursing from self-interest or vengeance.

God's silence loudly decries the actions and protests the outcomes. The structural ties to chapter 26 remind the reader that God has given blessing and promised his presence, guaranteeing his appropriate response to those who bless or curse the chosen family. They must learn to trust him and live in light of his promises, rather than fear. The mention of the new name, Israel, similarly reminds of God's promise to fight on their behalf. They must cling.

At the same time, God's grace will shine through the darkness. Yahweh will keep his word. He is faithful. Jacob and his sons all stand guilty and faithless, but the covenant promises will come true. "God works through and often in spite of the limited self-serving plans of man" (Sailhamer 1990, 214).

God holds the patriarch responsible for leading his family "to keep the way of the Lord by doing righteousness and justice" so that they may experience the promises of God (18:19). God puts people in place to lead and show his character and proper reactions in life. They must live in faith and demonstrate his appropriate responses to the evil in our world, trusting God to work through them. They must depend on his word to them.

The narrative presents negative actions and responses, mixed with some appropriate reactions, without (yet) showing God's intervention. The foolish and self-serving deception, murder, looting, and self-righteous defense misses the standard of justice, as much as silence and overlooking of grievous evil or fear before human power. These negative examples from God's representatives display human tendencies and only imply the corresponding godly expectations of honesty, justice, accountability, and trust in Yahweh, both for personal protection but also for resolving grievous evil and providing the promised prosperity.

The dangers of the people of God in a world of unbelievers with a very different worldview and standards comes through clearly. The temptation to use the good promises of God as a bargaining chip only exacerbates the faulty thinking that ultimately relies on one's own devices, rather than those promises and the working of God on behalf of his people. They are continually at risk of assimilation, either blending into their culture or becoming like their culture as they choose human logic and motivations, rather than God's standards.

Rather than assimilate, the people of God must stand for justice and righteousness by living out the way of the Lord. They must find their blessing and prosperity in God, rather than in their own manipulations and pursuits. True blessing follows from faith, not fear or retaliation, from dependence, not self-reliance.

The relationship and privilege of the people of God in walking with God begins with true worship. The immediate context (33:20) anticipates a different outcome. That privilege, expressed in an exclusive heart response to God, defines the boundaries of appropriate human relationships as well. If you love God, you will love your neighbor. The relationship with God cannot be profaned or misused with impunity in personal agendas. Mistaking conformity to ritual with true worship and necessary agreement in worldview risks the basis and reality of that relationship and all the benefits and expectations attached to it.

PREACHING AND TEACHING STRATEGIES

Exegetical and Theological Synthesis

This ancient text is rooted in an ancient world where powerful men (34:19) have a habit of taking what they want (cf. also Gen. 6:2). Shechem's humiliation of Dinah sets off a chain reaction that tests the ability of God's people to function in his world as his representatives. Led by Jacob's inactivity, they all fail the test. The narrative functions as another "go and do otherwise" instruction for God's people. To quote earlier exegesis: "Abraham's descendants do not practice righteousness and justice (18:19) and bring cursing rather than blessing (28:14)" (p. 348 and p. 477). The narrative portrays the tendencies of fallen humanity to act unjustly, especially in the face of injustice.

Along with that is the tendency to disbelieve in the promises of God. At the end of our story Jacob states the likely scenario, "if they gather themselves against me and attack me, I shall be destroyed" (v. 30). Never mind that the Lord had promised otherwise. Our listeners can only see God's divine provision in this chapter if they see Jacob and his sons within the larger context of God continuing to transform his people so that his plan comes true. God will have to work extra hard to repair the damage done to his reputation because of the disbelief of his chosen vessels. The grace of God is truly amazing in that he chooses to work with such flawed representatives. Our listeners should easily worship such a gracious God. His faithfulness should also lead us all to our own faithfulness as we learn from Jacob's lack of spiritual leadership.

Preaching Idea

Overcoming "evil with good" (cf. Romans 12:21) is the only way to be a blessing in God's world.

Contemporary Connections

What does it mean?

Certainly, the stigma of rape exists in our society, but listeners may need explanations about the use of "humiliated" (v. 2), "an outrageous thing" (v. 7), "defiled" (v. 13), and "treat . . . like a prostitute" (v. 31). The author assumes the original readers understand this cultural angle. This will help our listeners understand the extreme retaliation of Jacob's sons.

Spend time explaining the spiritual danger of the request: "Make marriages with us" (v. 9). Intermarrying would lead to idolatry, which in turn would result in Israel breaking the covenant with the Lord. Since some chapters have passed in our study of Genesis, it will be helpful to also explain the significance of circumcision with respect to the Israelites and their covenant agreement with the Lord. Circumcision was required for all Israelites, so the condition made sense if they were truly to "become one people" (v. 16).

Is it true?

Our listeners may need to be convinced from the immediate context that the sons' retaliation or revenge in this chapter is not what God wants from his representatives. It is true that their actions cannot lead to extending God's blessing to their neighboring people-groups. The opposite was true: their actions brought a curse-like destruction on the Hivites.

Now what?

The biblical writer is not applying his theological focus to his readers. We will have to help our listeners realize that the actions of Jacob's sons are not in line with God's purposes for his people. Instead of conveying blessing to those around them, they deliver curse-like, unrighteous vengeance. Jacob's own inactivity and silence (v. 5) provides a double "go and do otherwise" angle on application. The biblical author implies through their actions that God's people should not represent him that poorly on earth. This implies that God has more work to do to transform his people, and his people have more work to do to respond in faith in the face of injustice. Only faith allows his people to "overcome evil with good" (Rom. 12:21).

Creativity in Presentation

Overcoming evil with good is the only way to be a blessing in God's world. It is as true now as it was then. The sermon can be structured as:

- God desires us to extend his blessings in the world. Here is an opportunity to quickly review the immediate context and God's plan to use his people. See Genesis 18:19 and 28:14. This sets Jacob's sons' actions against the backdrop of God's assignment for his people.

- There is a temptation to overcome evil with evil. The section covers the way Jacob's sons went about getting revenge on the Hivites. It would be helpful to illustrate this from more contemporary situations in which you or one of your listeners has experienced similar temptation to take matters into their own hands. This section also includes Jacob's inactivity and lack of leadership. The whole section functions as a "go and do otherwise" example. This is a fitting time to explore what it is about fallen humanity that creates a default setting of wanting to get revenge.

DISCUSSION QUESTIONS

1. Discuss what it means to be a blessing in the world.

2. When is anger appropriate, and how should a believer respond to injustice, oppression, and personal injury?

3. How can we show righteousness and justice when we have been deeply injured, assaulted, or offended?

4. Discuss ways in which a Christian brings the opposite of blessing in their neighborhood or workplace.

5. Is silence ever an appropriate response to evil? If so, when, and if not, why not?

Genesis 35:1–29

EXEGETICAL IDEA
At God's prompting, Jacob purified his camp and traveled to Bethel to fulfill his vow, where he worshipped, received God's extended covenant promises and challenge for God's future program, and continued in the land, burying the past with its human failures and struggles and erecting monuments to God's faithful working.

THEOLOGICAL FOCUS
God moves his servant to faithful service and worship, putting away self-effort and fruitless struggle, centering on God's faithfulness, and trusting God's promise for future blessing and fulfillment of God's good purposes.

PREACHING IDEA
Worship, purify, and trust: three responses to God's promised blessing in a curse-contaminated world.

PREACHING POINTERS
God's command to Jacob in 35:1 provides ancient and postmodern audiences with an opportunity to learn or review one of the most basic aspects of the life of faith: true worship of Yahweh alone. God graciously nudges Jacob to fulfill the vow he promised earlier about going to Bethel. A vital part of worshipping the Lord is putting away the foreign gods (v. 2), anything that competes with God for supremacy in our lives.

Jacob's instruction to his own household and those traveling with him signifies the need for all of God's people to continually allow the Spirit of God to transform them into righteous pilgrims. True worship includes being changed into a person that reflects God's holiness. As we've seen so many times before in Genesis, God continues to protect his children so they can experience his blessing (v. 5).

Experiencing the blessing, however, is always in the context of suffering the results of the curse. The narrative shows this by recording multiple deaths of significant people (vv. 8, 19, 29). And there is still the presence of sin (v. 22 on Reuben's immorality and Israel's hearing but doing nothing). However, God also reinforces his promise to bless Jacob. The blessing includes a name change, which teaches us about the importance of growing into the kind of person who represents God well in his world. Another name-changing event occurs around the death of Rachel as she gave birth to Benjamin (v. 18). There is hope for God's children in the future even though they are badly flawed and live in a badly broken world.

BURYING THE PAST: ANTICIPATE THE PROMISE (35:1–29)

LITERARY STRUCTURE AND THEMES

Genesis 35 brackets the *toledot* of Isaac with 25:19–34 and adds the appendix, closing the narrative and preparing for the sequel (see Introduction to the Jacob Narratives, p. 427). Jacob's fulfilled vow with Yahweh's renewed and extended Abrahamic promises to him (35:1–18) draws the initial phase of God's oracle to Rebekah (25:19–34) to a close, also reflecting the promises to Abraham (esp. 17:1–8). The concluding accounts of Rachel's death and burial (35:19–20), Reuben's foolish relationship with Bilhah (vv. 21–22a), the sons of Jacob (vv. 22b–26), and Isaac's death and burial (vv. 27–29) all parallel the end of the Abraham stories, with the death of Sarah (23:1–20), the wife for Isaac (24:1–67), Abraham's additional sons (25:1–6), and Abraham's death and burial (25:7–11).[1]

Jacob's burial of the foreign gods (35:4), Deborah (v. 8), Rachel (vv. 19–20), and Isaac (vv. 27–29) unify the various strands as one era comes to an end and a new era dawns, with God's promise of enduring, fruitful blessing. The repetition and detailing of Jacob's itinerary emphasize his return to the land, successfully completing his quest. These all reflect God's faithfulness, underlined by God's reiterated promise of the land to him and his descendants, who are listed. The parallel development ties these elements together.

A. God directed Jacob to Bethel (35:1–4).
  B. Jacob worshipped at Bethel (35:5–7).
    C. Deborah died (35:8).
A'. God reaffirmed his covenant promises (35:9–13).
  B'. Jacob worshipped at Bethel (35:14–15).
    C'. Rachel died (35:16–18).

Appendix to the *toledot*:
1'. Jacob buried Rachel (35:19–20).
2'. Reuben lay with Bilhah (35:21–22a).
3'. Jacob had twelve sons (35:22b–26).
4'. Jacob and Esau buried Isaac (35:27–29).

The concluding narrative for the *toledot* of Isaac (35:1–18) presents two parallel sections, each beginning with God's oracle to Jacob, to which Jacob responded in obedience and worship, then culminating in the death of a beloved woman, showing the completion of an era and its expectation. While concluding one phase of God's working, it extends the promise of continued, greater working. It also highlights obedience and purity as prerequisite for blessing, hope in the face of great loss, and the necessary response of worship and commemoration of God's acts and promises.

- ***God Renewed His Promise (35:1–18)***
- ***Appendix to the Isaac* Toledot *(35:19–29)***

1 While these appear to be, as Cotter (2003, 258) suggests, "a conglomeration of odds and ends . . . in order to finish off earlier stories," we will argue that they are cohesive with a larger purpose.

EXPOSITION

This multifaceted pericope ties together many themes from previous narratives, both drawing the Jacob stories to a conclusion but also tying it back into the Abraham narratives and capping off the promises of the covenant with Abraham.[2] As we noted above, it also previews the future for the promise, preparing for the coming conflict of the sons and the beginning of the nation, with the challenge of being Israel, rather than Jacob.

God used the pressure of Jacob's fear of reprisal from his sons' actions to move Jacob on to Bethel. God's reappearance was not a surprise but the expectation of his promise. At God's prompting, Jacob purified his camp and traveled to Bethel to fulfill his vow, where he worshipped, received God's extended covenant promises and challenge for God's future program, and continued in the land, burying the past with its human failures and struggles and erecting monuments to God's faithful working.

God Renewed His Promise (35:1–18)

When Jacob responded to God's direction to fulfill his vow at Bethel with purification and exclusive worship, God expanded his promises to Jacob, calling for commitment and offering hope that transcended immediate loss and the current generation.

Genesis 35:1–18 develops in two panels: God's command, Jacob's worship, and Deborah's death (35:1–8), correspond with God's reiteration of his promises, Jacob's worship, and Rachel's death (35:9–18). The first section (35:1–8) also develops in three parallel sections, using nearly identical terms with God's command for Jacob to go to Bethel (vv. 1–2), Jacob's instructions that they go to Bethel (vv. 3–4), and the actual trip to Bethel (vv. 5–7; Terino 1988, 59–60). Hamilton (1995, 378–79) notes the parallels between the burial of the gods under the "terebinth" (v. 4, תַּחַת הָאֵלָה) near Shechem and Jacob's burial of Deborah under an "oak" (v. 8, תַּחַת הָאַלּוֹן) below Bethel. These similarities suggest the burying of the past and the former life that was not submitted to God in faith (see Exposition, 35:8).[3] At the same time, there are parallels with Rachel's burial, suggesting a larger pattern as well (see Exposition, 35:16–18).

Jacob Buries the Past

Terino (1988, 59–60) shows the clear step parallelism through verse 7 (with our additions in []):

A. 'Arise' (Elohim)
  B. 'Go to Bethel'
    C. 'Make an altar'
      D. ('When you fled from Esau')
        E. 'Put away foreign gods' (Jacob) THEN
a 'Let us arise'
  b 'go to Bethel'
    c 'make an altar'
      d in the day of my distress
        e so they gave Jacob foreign gods [which Jacob buried under the terebinth near Shechem]

---

2 Numerous commentators have noticed the varied collection of elements in the narrative and have assumed varying degrees of intrusion, especially from the account of Deborah's death. Westerman (1995, 552) calls it "beyond comprehension" that she is with Jacob and only fits because of the geographic location. Olejede (2016) argues for its significance in the context, and we shall see both theological and structural reasons for the various narrative pieces. Wenham (1994, 322) also notes the various narrative pieces at the end and shows parallels with the Abraham stories.

3 It was certainly the end of an era, with new expectations in the context of the twelve sons (Mathews 2005, 611; Ross 2008, 201). The next generation will be the next set of stories, which we often think of in terms of Joseph but which present the whole fourth generation as underlined by Jacob's blessing (ch. 49), with Judah and Joseph most prominent.

A' As they journeyed
B' Jacob came to Luz (Bethel)
C' There he built an altar
D' when he fled from his brother
[E' Jacob buried Deborah under an oak below Bethel]

God Directed Jacob to Bethel (35:1–4)

At God's direction, Jacob prepared for his journey to Bethel to fulfill his vow, purifying his camp.

35:1. With the question from Simeon and Levi hanging (34:31), God spoke to Jacob. Jacob must go to Bethel and fulfill the vow he made to God when he had fled Esau, the clear implication of the command (cf. 31:13). Long after he had arrived from Paddan-Aram, Jacob had not yet returned to Bethel with exclusive worship to Yahweh and his tithe of all he had received (28:20–22). God had waited for this deep crisis to call Jacob to obedience. While he had set up an altar at Shechem (33:20), he clearly still had foreign gods in the camp, and he had stopped short of Bethel. God's command was clear and specific. He was to move there and set up an altar to worship God, commemorating God's intervention and promise when he had fled Esau.

35:2–4. In stark contrast to his lack of leadership at Shechem, Jacob responded immediately, with his instructions to his household and all who were with him, directly mirroring God's command. The reference to "all who were with him" (v. 2, repeated in v. 6) seems to acknowledge the Shechemites whom the sons had captured. It implies that the gods that were among them would include not only any the family might have, but also the booty from the town (34:28–29) and the gods that Rachel had stolen from her father (31:19).

Jacob's expressed purpose for moving and establishing a new worship center appropriately focused on God's intervention and faithful provision rather than his flight (35:1). Purity was necessary for such an undertaking (cf. Exod. 19:10) and was expressed both spiritually with the removal of the idols and physically, including a change of clothing. Jacob not only understood God's message, but he took it to heart, fully addressing the implications. Jacob required and received all the foreign gods, along with the earrings,[4] which he "hid" (וַיִּטְמֹן) or buried under the large tree there.[5]

Jacob Worshipped at Bethel (35:5–7)

Jacob traveled with God's protection to Bethel where he built an altar, naming it El Bethel in honor of God's first appearance to him.

35:5. When they set out for Bethel, God blocked any retaliation, putting his fear in their neighbors. The reasonable nature of Jacob's fear is underlined by God preventing the Canaanites from pursuing "the sons of Jacob." That also reminds the reader of the murderous actions from which they needed purification, along with the foreign deities.

TRANSLATION ANALYSIS 35:5

The "terror from God" (ESV, NLT, NRSV, חִתַּת אֱלֹהִים) translates a construct that can also be understood as "afraid of God" (NET, NKJV), "terror of God" (NIV), or alternatively, understanding "god" to indicate a superlative, thus "great terror" (NASB95). Given God's promise to Israel to send his terror before them (though

4 The earrings in question likely were adorning the images, not the people, making them also "holy" and so an abomination to God (cf. Deut. 7:25–26; Hallo 1983, 16; Hurowitz 2000).

5 Burying was an acceptable way to dispose of images in his culture (Hallo 1983, 16–17; Walton 2009a, 118), though later God would require burning (Deut. 7:5, 25; 12:3; see also Exod. 32:20; 1 Chron. 14:12).

a different Hebrew word, Exod. 23:27; Deut. 2:25; cf. 11:25) and his actions on their behalf (Exod. 15:16; Josh. 2:9), the "terror from God" fits well and would be a natural understanding for Israel reading this, but the outcome is comparable for each different understanding: it was divine and undeserved intervention (Kidner 1967, 186).

35:6–7. When they arrived at Luz, Moses reminds the reader that it is the same as Bethel and that it is "in the land of Canaan" (v. 6). Both are important to connect this place with the vow and God's command, as well as the reminder that being back in the land of Canaan, Jacob has completed his odyssey. His quest is finally done with the completion of his vow.

It is here, then, that he built the altar God had called for, again naming the place El-Bethel ("God of Bethel"), with a focus on God, who had revealed himself to Jacob there. So far, the attention is on Jacob's actions in fulfilling God's commission. He finally finished his search for a wife and the initial prosperity of family with his re-entry to the land, return to Bethel, and completion of his vow. The only element of the vow not yet stated is the promised tithe to Yahweh. Perhaps the reader should assume the sacrifice on the altar would include his payment of the tithe since there is no sanctuary to Yahweh where he could present a gift (Mathews 2005, 623; Walton 2001, 631). The indicators that this is the passing of an era and the completion of Jacob's quest support that suggestion, though the text is silent. One more indicator remains.

Deborah Died (35:8)

Deborah died and Jacob buried her, naming the place Allon-bacuth.

35:8. Moses's inclusion of Deborah's death and burial at this juncture seems intrusive.[6] As suggested above, however, the placement here parallels the burial of the images (v. 4) as well as Rachel's death and burial (vv. 16–18). While Deborah has not been named until now, her death provides oblique reference to God's working, justice, and purpose. It reveals God's working, fulfilling Rebekah's desire to find a wife for Jacob and restore him safely (27:44–45) by mentioning her name at this juncture since her memory implicitly invokes Rebekah, and Jacob is finally back in the land in peace. Yet Rebekah's manipulations did not accomplish it (ch. 33), and her name is glaringly omitted. Rebekah's omission suggests, since she will not show up again in the narrative, that she had died while Jacob was away and experienced a tragic but appropriate justice for her scheming. Finally, the passing of the previous generation helps bring the *toledot* of Isaac to a conclusion, reflecting the new chapter in God's purpose in his oracle to Jacob, with the implication of burying the past.

God Reaffirmed His Covenant Promises (35:9–13)

God appeared to Jacob at Bethel, renaming him Israel and reaffirming the Abrahamic covenant promises of descendants and land.

35:9–10. With Jacob's trek complete, God exposed more of his plan, the core of this pericope. Apparently responding to Jacob's worship, "God appeared to Jacob again" (v. 9). The note reminds the reader of both God's first appearance to Jacob at Bethel and his return from Paddan-Aram (v. 6, "to Luz . . . which is in the land of Canaan"). God reiterated Jacob's name change (v. 10) and extended his promise (vv. 11–12) before

6 Von Rad (1972, 338) suggests it was merely a known tradition related to Bethel, so it was attached here.

leaving him (v. 13). God had done what he promised (28:15) and, with Jacob's obedience, expanded his expected future.

Blessing Jacob (cf. 32:27–29), God indicated a change was needed.[7] Recognizing that Jacob was his name, God declared that he should no longer be known by that name. Rather, he should be known as Israel. God's statement that his name was Jacob is surprising; after all, God had already changed it (32:27–28)! Yet, since the change at Peniel, "Israel" has generally not been used, while "Jacob" has been used twenty-six times.[8] It seems Jacob is not using nor requiring others to use the new name. Ironically, "Israel" is not consistently used after this either.[9]

On the one hand, God's point seems to be less what Jacob was called, but rather how Jacob acted, declaring Jacob's need to discard the character associated with "Jacob" (manipulation and self-sufficiency in wrestling with God and man), replacing it with clinging to God, the intent of "Israel" (see Exposition on 32:28, p. 533).[10] God, then, was calling Jacob to live out the implications of his now fulfilled vow, of bowing before Yahweh alone and living in light of the faithful work of God on his behalf. Such a message would be significant for a listening nation as they make and renew covenant with Yahweh, moving into Canaan and setting up their theocracy in a hostile world. Not only would the nation struggle with it, however, but Jacob would struggle with his response as the coming narratives will show, bringing his change of heart with great pain and difficulty.

God's reminder of Jacob's name change, however, also relates to what follows. God's self-identification as El-Shaddai and his extended promises to Jacob for him and his offspring draw the closest parallels to Yahweh's appearance to Abram when he called Abram to loyal service. There he extended his covenant promises to Abram and his offspring and changed his name to Abraham (17:1–14), establishing the sign of circumcision for their perpetual reminder. God's reference to Jacob's name change here points the reader's attention to the Abrahamic narrative and the implications of the comparison.

---

7 When God blesses, he provides the means or enabling to accomplish his purpose through the one he blesses. Here he points to the source (clinging to God, see ch. 32 and exposition of vv. 26–28, p. 533) and to the promise that he would then fulfill as his people walk before him in faith.

8 The exceptions are two editorial comments and naming a worship center: in 32:32 Moses comments that the nation Israel would not eat the sinew, in 33:20 Jacob named his new altar in Shechem El-Elohe-Israel, and in 34:7 her brothers were enraged at Dinah's rape because an outrageous thing had been done "in Israel" (see on 34:7, p. 554). The references to "Israel" focus on the coming (and listening) nation, rather than the individual.

9 In the rest of ch. 35, Jacob is used eight more times and Israel is only used twice in the account of Reuben's sin (vv. 21–22, see below, p. 574). In Genesis 36–50, Jacob is used thirty-three times and Israel only thirty-one times. In contrast, "Abram" is only used two times after his name change in the OT, and both are used appropriately, referring to him before it was changed (Neh. 9:7; 1 Chron. 1:27). The implication may include the struggle of clinging to God alone in faith, though sometimes it may simply be stylistic.

10 "Name" (שֵׁם) here is taken in the "intensified" or figurative sense of "standing, reputation" (*HALOT* s.v. "שֵׁם" 1549, I, D. 2.) or, better, with that implication by double entendre. Cf. Hamilton 1995, 381. Nataf argues similarly that Jacob would have a dual identity, referencing his more "passive approach" in his childhood with his more "confrontational approach" of his later years, symbolized by his wrestling with God (Nataf 2012, 245). The name used, then, may be loosely tied to character qualities displayed, though the usage is not clearly consistent.

Covenant Promises Continued								
Genesis 35:9–13 most closely aligns with 17:1–23 of all the covenant promissory passages (see chart below):								
	35:9–13	12:1–3, 7	15:18–21	17:1–23	22:16–18	26:2–5, 24	28:3–4	28:12–15
God "appeared" to	9	7		1		2, 24		
"No longer shall your name be called . . . your name shall be"	10			5				
"I am El Shaddai"	11			1			3	
"Be fruitful"	11			6			3	
"and multiply"	11			2	17	4, 24	3	
"nation"	11	2		6 (pl)				
"And a company of nations"	11			4, 5			(3)	
"And kings shall come from" you	11			6, 16				
Land promise	12	7	18–21	8	(17)	3–4	4	13
"God went up from him" (וַיַּעַל אֱלֹהִים מֵעָל)	13			22				
"God had spoken to him" (וְדִבֶּר אִתּוֹ אֱלֹהִים)	13			3, 22, 23				

A comparison of the specific terms repeated throughout the promise passages shows clear and expected parallels, but the most parallels, both of specific terms and of total elements of promise, is between chapters 17 and 35. For the land and the descendants promises, God's promise to Abraham in 17:1–21 provides the most expansive promise, repeated to Jacob. Several parallels are unique to these passages as noted in the Covenant Promises Continued sidebar, but the name change is specifically significant, not only because of the parallel but because it is a duplication and unexpected for Jacob, but the terminology specifically reflects the change for Abram to Abraham.

Genesis	**ESV**
35:9–13	9God **appeared** to Jacob again, when he came from Paddan-Aram, and blessed him. 10And God said to him, "Your name is Jacob; **no longer shall your name be called Jacob, but Israel shall be your name."** So he called his name Israel. 11**And God said to him, "I am God Almighty: be fruitful and multiply. A nation and a company of nations shall come from you, and kings shall come from your own body.** 12**The land that I gave to Abraham and Isaac I will give to you, and I will give the land to your offspring after you."** 13**Then God went up from him in the place where he had spoken with him.**
12:1–3, 7	1Now the LORD said to Abram, "Go from your country and your kindred and your father's house to the land that I will show you. 2And **I will make of you a great nation**, and I will bless you and make your name great, so that you will be a blessing. 3I will bless those who bless you, and him who dishonors you I will curse, and in you all the families of the earth shall be blessed." . . . 7Then the LORD **appeared** to Abram and said, **"To your offspring I will give this land."** So he built there an altar to the LORD, who had **appeared** to him.

Genesis	ESV
15:18–21	[18]On that day the LORD made a covenant with Abram, saying, "**To your offspring I give this land**, from the river of Egypt to the great river, the river Euphrates,[19]the land of the Kenites, the Kenizzites, the Kadmonites,[20]the Hittites, the Perizzites, the Rephaim, [21]the Amorites, the Canaanites, the Gir- gashites and the Jebusites."
17:1–8, 22–23	[1]When Abram was ninety-nine years old the LORD **appeared** to Abram and said to him, "**I am God** **Almighty**; walk before me, and be blameless, [2]that I may make my covenant between me and you, and may **multiply** you greatly." [3]Then Abram fell on his face. And God **said to him,** [4]"Behold, my covenant is with you, and you shall be the father of a multitude of nations. [5]**No longer shall your name be** **called Abram, but your name shall be Abraham,** for I have made you the **father of a multitude of** **nations.** [6]**I will make you exceedingly fruitful, and I will make you into nations, and kings shall** **come from you.**
	[7]And I will establish my covenant between me and you and your offspring after you throughout their generations for an everlasting covenant, to be God to you and to your offspring after you. [8]**And I will** **give to you and to your offspring after you the land of your sojournings, all the land of Canaan,** **for an everlasting possession,** and I will be their God." … [22]When he had finished **talking with him, God went up from Abraham.** [23]Then Abraham took Ishmael his son and all those born in his house or bought with his money, every male among the men of Abraham's house, and he circumcised the flesh of their foreskins that very day, as God **had said to him**.
22:16–18	[16]and said, "By myself I have sworn, declares the LORD, because you have done this and have not with- held your son, your only son, [17]I will surely bless you, and I will surely **multiply** your offspring as the stars of heaven and as the sand that is on the seashore. And your offspring shall possess the gate of his enemies, [18]and in your offspring shall all the nations of the earth be blessed, because you have obeyed my voice."
26:2–5, 24	[2]And the LORD **appeared** to him and said, "Do not go down to Egypt; dwell in the land of which I shall tell you. [3]Sojourn in this land, and I will be with you and will bless you, **for to you and to your** **offspring I will give all these lands,** and I will establish the oath that I swore to Abraham your father. [4]I will **multiply** your offspring as the stars of heaven **and will give to your offspring all these lands.** And in your offspring all the nations of the earth shall be blessed, [5]because Abraham obeyed my voice and kept my charge, my commandments, my statutes, and my laws." … [24]And the LORD **appeared** to him the same night and said, "I am the God of Abraham your father. Fear not, for I am with you and will bless you and **multiply** your offspring for my servant Abraham's sake."
28:3–4	[3]**God Almighty** bless you and **make you fruitful and multiply** you, that you may become a **company** **of peoples.** [4]May he give the blessing of Abraham to you and to your offspring with you, that you may take possession of the **land** of your sojournings that God gave to Abraham!"
28:12–15	[12]And he dreamed, and behold, there was a ladder set up on the earth, and the top of it reached to heaven. And behold, the angels of God were ascending and descending on it! [13]And behold, the LORD stood above it and said, "I am the LORD, the God of Abraham your father and the God of Isaac. The **land on which you lie I will give to you and to your offspring.** [14]Your offspring shall be like the dust of the earth, and you shall spread abroad to the west and to the east and to the north and to the south, and in you and your offspring shall all the families of the earth be blessed. [15]Behold, I am with you and will keep you wherever you go, and will bring you back to this land. For I will not leave you until I have done what I have promised you."

God's blessing both pointed to Jacob's need to trust Yahweh and live in loyalty, and it climaxed the covenant promises God began with Abraham. In both contexts God called his chosen patriarch to loyal service and ongoing reliance for the resulting progeny. After Abraham, the promises would be necessarily remembered with the sign of circumcision. After Jacob, the promises would also be recalled with the name "Israel," with which they would forever be identified and reminded of their needed submission to and reliance on their God. This was God's final expression of the covenant promises to the patriarchs, bookending the covenant from Abraham to Jacob. Every statement after this recalls his covenant with Abraham, Isaac, and Jacob.

35:11–12. God identified himself as El Shaddai for the third time in the patriarchal narratives (17:1; 28:3). The God who extended the blessing to Abram when he changed his name to Abraham, and whom Isaac called on to extend those promises to Jacob, tied together the promises, leaving no doubt Jacob was the recipient of the ongoing promise of blessing through Abraham to be established in the land. It is as appropriate here, as with Abraham. The One with sovereign authority over life and blessing (Hamilton 1995, 462–63; cf. Translation Analysis 17:1b, p. 322) has guaranteed the future. His command of blessing, mirroring the initial command of blessing to humanity (1:28) and indicating the means for finally fulfilling God's desired blessing to humanity (12:3), introduced his promise of Jacob becoming a nation, a "company of nations," (35:11), and producing kings.

Abram had been promised a multitude of nations, which might be understood to include the descendants of Ishmael and Esau (17:6). Isaac had asked for Jacob to be a "company of peoples" (28:3), possibly referring simply to the tribes (*HALOT* s.v. "עַם" 838), but now God points to a "company of nations," suggesting even bigger growth. Again, mirroring the promise to Abraham (17:6), and Sarah (17:16), God promised kings from Jacob. The significance of this assurance follows the impact of the genealogies of Genesis, which move from the initial royal decree for humanity (1:28) and the expected destroyer of the snake (3:15) to a culminating promise of royalty in the line of Judah to destroy his enemies (49:8–12).

TRANSLATION ANALYSIS 35:11

The common "company of nations" (ESV, NET; or "community of nations," NIV; "assembly of nations," NJPS) is explained as "many nations" (NCV, NLT). Hamilton (1995, 381), citing Greenberg (*Ezekiel*, Anchor Bible Commentary on Ezek. 3:2 [1983, 63]), supposes it to simply refer to the "tribes" of Israel, though Lee (2009) effectively discounts that possibility, arguing instead for an eschatological fulfillment in the church (see Gal. 3:6–14). Most naturally, God's pronouncement points to a great inclusion of nations, however it will be worked out.

God concluded by bestowing the land promise to Jacob and his descendants after him, specifically recalling his gift to Abraham (12:7; 13:14–17; 15:18–21; 17:8) and Isaac (26:3–4), which would now go to Jacob's descendants (28:4). The clear assumption here includes the full description of the extent of the land (cf. 13:17; 15:18–21) and the everlasting possession (cf. 13:15; 17:8). This final statement pulls together the completed package of the Abrahamic covenant promises to the nation of Israel as it will develop from the twelve sons in the ensuing years.

This theological climax of the Jacob narratives[11] both looks back to the initiation of the

11 Each of the patriarchal narratives climaxes theologically in the final movement of the *toledot*, with Abraham's sacrifice of Isaac (22:1–19), this final statement of promise in response to Jacob's worship, and Joseph's final reconciliation with his brothers (49:29–50:21).

promises and looks ahead to the outworking of them through the descendants of Jacob. It forms a hinge to the future working of God, calling Jacob (and Israel) to faith and to live out that faith before their promise-keeping, promise-extending God who would complete his plan and bring blessing to all the nations of the earth, the purpose given to Abraham (12:3; 18:18; 22:18), Isaac (26:4), and Jacob (28:14). God would now turn to developing that future nation by working in this fractured family to bring blessing in their world (Joseph stories, chs. 37–50) and produce descendants who can carry forward God's purposes (49:1–27).

35:13. Concluding his oracle and clinching the allusion to his appearance to Abraham, "God went up from him."[12] This final clause appears only here and in 17:22 in the entire Old Testament to speak of God leaving after conversing with anyone. The tie to the Abrahamic promise is unmistakable. God's covenant promises to Abraham, Isaac, and Jacob are complete, only awaiting the progressive outworking through the history of the nascent nation.

Jacob Worshipped at Bethel (35:14–15)

Jacob set up and anointed a standing stone, reaffirming the name Bethel that reflected his first response to God at Bethel.

35:14–15. Jacob's response echoes his initial response at Bethel: setting up a stone pillar, pouring oil on it, and naming the place (again) "Bethel" (see 28:18–19). The nearly identical action confirms this account as the conclusion to the first Bethel account and fulfillment of the vow. Additionally, as we noted in the Exposition of 28:16–19 (p. 478), "place" is repeated three times, emphasizing the surprising uniqueness of the place where he encountered God's presence. Here the threefold repetition identifies this as the same place. Jacob had again encountered Yahweh, driving him to worship and calling him to commitment.

Rachel Died (35:16–18)

Rachel died bearing a son, naming him Ben-oni, whom Jacob renamed Benjamin.

35:16–18. Concluding the Jacob stories, the birth of Benjamin reflects both the beginning of the Jacob stories (birth of Jacob and Esau, 25:19–34, with the promise of God's choice of Jacob) and looks ahead to the coming narratives with the birth of the final son (cf. 35:22b–26). Rachel's death in childbirth tragically validates her prayer for another son (30:24; see 30:1) and adds one final marker to the conclusion of the era of Jacob's search for a wife and family.

Benjamin's naming and renaming appropriately concludes a section with several instances of naming and renaming that draw attention to sorrow for what was lost (Allon-bacuth, 35:8) and moving from the past in anticipation of what will yet come (Jacob to Israel, Luz to Bethel). The pain and frustration of the curse of sin with pain and death in childbirth (3:16) as Rachel named him Ben-oni ("son of my sorrow," v. 18) gives way to the promise of new life and hope of future generations and the eventual destruction of the snake and evil (3:15). His new name, Benjamin ("son of my right hand," 35:18), marks the transition, indicating Jacob's "good fortune" or "wealth" (Sailhamer 1990, 219).

TRANSLATION ANALYSIS 35:18

Other possible translations include "mourning" (HALOT s.v. "אוֹנִי" 23), or possibly "son of my wickedness" (for stealing the household deities; Hamilton 1995, 385) or "son of my vigor" (for

12 Cf. sidebar on the parallels with God's oracle to Abraham in Genesis 17. Both oracles begin with God "appearing" to the patriarch (17:1, וַיֵּרָא יְהוָה; 35:9, וַיֵּרָא אֱלֹהִים), and both oracles end when God "went up from" the patriarch (17:22, וַיַּעַל אֱלֹהִים מֵעַל; 35:13, וַיַּעַל מֵעָלָיו אֱלֹהִים).

draining her vigor; Hamilton 1995, 383, n. 8). The traditional translation fits the context.

Appendix to the Isaac Toledot *(35:19–29)*

Jacob strengthened ties to the homeland, siring the progenitors of the nation.

Jacob Buried Rachel (35:19–20)

Jacob buried Rachel and something of his past, with a special marker, adding a foothold in the land.

35:19–20. As the Terah *toledot* (Abraham stories) concluded with the death and burial of Sarah (23:1–20), so the Isaac *toledot* (Jacob stories) concludes with the death and burial of Rachel. She does not die near the family tomb, so her burial is marked with an enduring standing stone marker. Jacob's greatest love was left behind. Yet Israel's ties to the land grow with each worship center and special event marker placed in the land.

Reuben Lay with Bilhah (35:21–22a)

Israel moved to Migdal Eder[13] where Reuben had an affair with Bilhah, redirecting the promised blessing.

35:21–22a. As Jacob continued through the land, the narrative briefly relates Reuben's affair with Bilhah. While no explanation has been given, it is possible that he was trying to establish his leadership of the clan before Jacob died, perhaps he wanted to pre-empt Rachel's maid from taking the favored wife status from his own mother, Leah, or perhaps both were involved (Wenham 1994, 327). Jacob heard of it but did nothing yet. He would pass over Reuben when he blessed the sons and deny him the birthright and leadership in the coming nation (49:3–4).

Possibly as well, this is the reason for the only use of "Israel" in this section. The impact of the affair is really on the future of the nation and the outworking of the tribes through the blessings of Jacob on the sons. Jacob continued to show weakness toward his sons, with no immediate response, but would declare the consequences that would impact the affairs of the developing tribes. Jacob's weakness and the less-than-stellar character of the sons will have major implications for the following stories of the sons and God's working in them to produce the nation that he can use to accomplish these promises reiterated to Abraham, Isaac, and Jacob.

Jacob Had Twelve Sons (35:22b–26)

The twelve sons of Jacob, mainly born in Paddan-Aram, showing God's promised fruitfulness, would advance God's purposes despite their conflicts.

35:22b–26. The twelve sons of Jacob are listed according to their birth order to the wives of Jacob in order of Jacob's taking of those wives (Leah, Rachel, Bilhah, then Zilpah).[14] The past is specifically recalled with reference to Paddan-Aram, even though the last was just born. The promise for descendants has borne fruit, anticipating the coming narrative and the fracturing of the family along the lines of the mothers and their families. The main competition will be between the sons of Leah and the sons of Rachel. In all, God will continue to work his redemptive promises.

Jacob and Esau Buried Isaac (35:27–29)

When Isaac died, Jacob and Esau buried him in Hebron, further establishing the homeland.

---

13 This is more likely a place name (NET, NIV, JPS) rather than a description of a location ("tower of Eder," ESV).

14 The order is the same as that in Exod. 1:2–4 (except, of course, Joseph is omitted from Exodus since he is already in Egypt). In Gen. 46:8–25, however, they are listed according to the mothers, with Leah first and her maid, then Rachel and her maid. In 49:3–27 the order is closer to the birth order, but Zebulun and Dan are out of order.

35:27–29. Finally, the self-described old and fragile patriarch of the family (27:2), Isaac, died, nearly eighty years after Jacob's theft of the blessing (25:26; 26:34; 27:46; 35:28).[15] His death and burial in the tomb Abraham purchased for Sarah marks the end of the narrative and further establishes Canaan as the homeland for the beginning nation. Jacob and Esau bury him together without comment. The relationship appears to be healed, or at least functioning. The torch is passed to the family of Jacob, and the narrative anticipates the outworking of the promise.

This epilogue closely parallels the epilogue to the Abraham stories (23:1–25:11), dealing with the same general themes (burial of the wife in the land, wife for the son, future for the promised line in the land, and the end of one patriarch's life as the doorway to the next stage in God's program). Here, however, the differences point to challenges to the promise as Rachel dies in labor and is buried outside of the family tomb, Reuben pre-empts any blessing by his affair with Bilhah, and the fracturing of the family will fall along the lines of the favored wife and her sons, so even the unremarkable burial of Isaac by both Jacob and Esau suggests that the healing of one generation of conflict will be simply replaced by another, with even greater strains to be healed for God's plan to unfold in his desired way. His redemptive purposes cannot be the natural outcome of superior human instruments but must be the divine working through weak vessels to put away the failings of the past and accomplish the bright future promise of blessing to all the nations of the earth.

THEOLOGICAL FOCUS

God moves his servant to faithful service and worship, putting away self-effort and fruitless struggle, centering on God's faithfulness, and trusting God's promise for future blessing and fulfillment of God's good purposes.

God's grace, purposes, and expectations are front and center in this section. God uses the uncertainties and struggles of human brokenness to spur his servant on to pursue God and complete what was promised during previous duress. Though Jacob's response to God's prompting was good, he would have saved his family significant pain and perhaps brought blessing instead of cursing to the Canaanites had he fulfilled his vow initially. God, however, was gracious and faithful, continuing to pursue his distracted servant and protect him from his own folly.

God's purposes continued despite Jacob's delayed pursuit of him. God used the obedience and worship of Jacob as the opportunity to move his program ahead, clarifying and expanding his promise of the nations and kings coming from Jacob and his descendants. God's program would not be deterred, and the anticipation is held in tension with the brokenness of the human instruments, including Jacob and his son Reuben. That program meant land, nations, and kings for Jacob, extending to Israel in the land but finally to all nations in Christ and the ultimate blessing of enjoying relationship with God, where all nations would live before Yahweh as his people in loyal service.

At the same time, God expressed his expectations for Jacob as he reminded him of his new name, Israel, the lessons learned at Peniel, and Jacob's need to rely on God and leave his fleshly pursuits of his own agenda behind. God's servant must rely on God's working and pursue God's purposes in God's way. The reminders of the past serve to reinforce both God's faithfulness and human failure when attempted with human strength and scheming.

Jacob's response to God's prompting showed the necessity for pure, exclusive obedience and worship, as well as public acknowledgement of God's working in his life. The public display of the worship center and renaming focused

15 See Wenham, (1994, xxiii–xxx) on the problem of the long lifespans of the patriarchs.

attention on Yahweh in exclusive distinction from the foreign gods, expressly removed from his camp and contrasted in the Canaanite center of Luz (Judg. 1:23). Purity was needed for God's presence and protection and for acceptable worship and fulfilling of his vow. While this is the first recognition of the exclusive nature of Yahweh worship, it illustrates an important early understanding of God's claim to sole loyalty and status as the only deity.

In addition to the constant reminders to put away the past and look to the promise of the future in God's covenant, the numerous burials remind the reader of the transitory nature of the human instruments in contrast to God's eternal rule and ongoing promise. The frail and failing human servants will pass away as generations come and go, but God's promise and purposes will move forward with each successive generation. This life will include great loss as sin maintains its hold. However, with each new birth come new hope, expectations, and obstacles. Through it all, God will remain constant and carry out his good will. The promise does not fade but only grows as God reveals more of his intent to bring an end to sin and death and to bring blessing to all the nations of the earth.

PREACHING AND TEACHING STRATEGIES

Exegetical and Theological Synthesis

As you can see from this narrative, our Lord continues to show his faithfulness to his promises to bless his people. He does so by the way he instructed Jacob to complete his vow to return to Bethel and set up a worship center there. And Jacob leads the way toward faithfulness by responding well to God's instruction, plus realizing the need for him and all who were with him to be spiritually clean as they worshipped God alone.

Our listeners continue to receive encouragement from these Genesis narratives as the Lord continues to restate his promises to bless his children and their children. God's plan has not changed, and he continues to work out his plan among children who are slowly but surely being changed into his image so that they represent him well in the world. The two name changes in the chapter (35:10, 18) provide direction for spiritual growth and hope that God's purposes will be achieved through a being-transformed people.

As significant people pass from this earth's scene, the blessing of God continues to move along the family tree and branches of faith. This, plus the sinfulness of Reuben and Israel's passivity to his immorality, remind us that we experience the blessing in the context of the curse. For now, God's people experience what is often a very frustrating mixture. It's no wonder hope plays such an important role in our salvation (cf. Rom. 5:1–5).

Preaching Idea

Worship, purify, and trust: three responses to God's promised blessing in a curse-contaminated world.

Contemporary Connections

What does it mean?

Many of our listeners will benefit from an explanation of the theological significance of altar-building (vv. 1, 7, 14). Jacob/Israel's actions show a person who worships God alone as the one to whom he looks for every aspect of his life, such as security, supply, significance, and satisfaction. When things go well, we know God is the source of blessing; when things go poorly, we know God will watch out for his own children.

In conjunction with such worship, we can also explain the significance of putting all other foreign gods away and cleaning ourselves up as acts of consecration and holiness, including repentance from sin and replacing sin with righteousness. None of these can exist with genuine saving faith in the Lord.

As was noted in the exegetical section, listeners may be confused by the one-verse inclusion of Reuben's immorality. It is a vivid reminder of how any of God's people, at any time, can move away from faith and follow their sinful hearts (v. 22, "While Israel lived in that land [of promise]"). In this case, Reuben, Israel's firstborn, commits one of the most, if not the most, disrespectful act in that culture. Finally, as significant characters from Israel's life pass away, hope lies in God continuing to keep his promises to his children.

Is it true?

Throughout the Genesis narrative, our listeners are learning of God's desire to bless his people. Some may need to be convinced that this is true for them in their circumstances. It is important to highlight that God's blessing for Jacob/Israel does not eliminate all heartache. The death of his favorite wife, Rachel, in verses 18–19 is an example of this. We have an opportunity to explain the blessing of God so that traumatic, troubling circumstances do not stop that blessing from being experienced. That means the blessing of God, rather than nations and landmass, involves the stabilizing presence of God and the transforming power of God.

Now what?

If we have done our job adequately in explaining the restated blessing of God in this chapter, then our listeners may begin to realize that this is the most important thing in this life and in eternity. This, in turn, means that nothing is more important than following Israel's lead in worshipping and being sanctified in one's personal life and family. Ultimately, we are calling on our listeners to believe that what God promised is true for them based on their faith. But to experience the promises of God, a faith that works must be on display.

Creativity in Presentation

The homiletical idea—worship, purify, and trust: three responses to god's promised blessing in a curse-contaminated world—presents a sermon or lesson focused on encouraging our listeners to put into practice these three foundational actions. Using this angle, each of the three actions represents three major points in the sermon/lesson.

The goal is to make sure we show our listeners that they are part of this story and their faith journey is found in Jacob's story. For instance, imagine urging your listeners to be able to say with Jacob that they worship "the God who answers [them] in the day of [their distress] and [who] has been with [them] wherever [they] have gone" (v. 3). Some will doubt this because of their current struggles; you will be able to reassure them but also challenge them in their walk with God. In other words, it is possible that their lives do not reflect Jacob's worship, purification, and trust. If not, it is time to turn and return to God.

Another way of structuring the message is:

- Preparing for worshipping God (vv. 1–7).
- Believing our new identity and promised blessing (vv. 9–15).
- Embracing the hope in God's continuing plan (vv. 8, 16–29).

Remember that this chapter is filled with the mixture of blessing and curse, the latter seen in the recorded deaths. Jacob is in the promised land, worshipping the Lord as he should. He is also faced, as all of us are, with the fact that history is marching onward. Death continues to be the unwelcome intruder into this life and, not to mention, the constant companion of unwanted sinfulness in those of us who believe. Through it all, this sermon allows us to celebrate the small part each of us can play in contributing to God's plan to bless his people and to bring that blessing to the entire world.

DISCUSSION QUESTIONS

1. Discuss the various ways individuals and families in your group worship and sacrifice to their Lord.
2. The action, "purify yourselves" (v. 2), is an excellent time for small groups to practice confessing their sins to each other. Not all will be comfortable doing this aloud, but you can encourage silent confession of sin.
3. Purity requires removal of idols and sinful beliefs and practices. What needs to be buried with Christ in your life to walk in newness of life? What will you do to leave it behind and trust God for transformation as you follow him?
4. Ask for examples of people in your church who have made significant changes in their lives because of their relationship with God.
5. How can you focus my heart on the promise of God and the expectation for his blessing while you walk through this pain-filled world?

Genesis 36:1–37:1

EXEGETICAL IDEA

From his Canaanite wives Esau produced a large family with powerful clans, which he moved to Seir, establishing a national identity and fulfilling God's word, while Jacob sojourned in Canaan waiting for God's promise.

THEOLOGICAL FOCUS

God can always be trusted to keep his word, even to profane people, but his purposes in his chosen servants are often only realized over extended time through testing and trials.

PREACHING IDEA

God will do what he says, moving his people out into his promised rule, but we may have to wait, enduring testing, to experience his best.

PREACHING POINTERS

While few preaching venues will allow the time to devote to this section, it provides fertile ground for reflection and instruction for the people of God. Though few modern western listeners enjoy a genealogy, reflection on the implications of this genealogy in the context of God's promises to his people shows God's working. He works not only in Israel's life, but also in the lives of the nations around them. He keeps the promises not only to Abraham, Isaac, and Jacob, but also to their other offspring. In fact, here we see the promises to Esau bearing fruit while Jacob seems to be in a waiting state. Our chapter, then, focuses on Esau's family tree (36:1).

The fact that Esau takes "wives from the Canaanites" is a bad sign (v. 2). This means that "the sons of Esau who were born to him in the land of Canaan" (v. 5) will be Jacob's neighboring nations. You can see that God's blessing is on Esau's family along with Jacob's family, so much so that they must separate in the land (vv. 7–8). You may want to do some cross-referencing to find more about the Edomites, "the sons of Esau (that is, Edom)" (v. 19). Esau's family tree includes numerous kings and kingdoms (v. 31). And this is all before Israel had any king. Later in redemptive history, the fact that all the nations have kings drives Israel's request for a king, to be like them. We learn from 37:1 that "Jacob lived in the land of his father's sojournings, in the land of Canaan." The two brothers may have reconciled, but we must wonder how these families will get along as neighbors.

WHERE'S THE BLESSING? WAITING FOR GOD'S BEST (36:1–37:1)

LITERARY STRUCTURE AND THEMES

Before following the promise through the descendants of Jacob, Genesis 36 includes two connected *toledot* sections listing the descendants of Esau in Canaan and then in Edom (36:1–8, 9–43). The overall structure moves from the sons to the clans and kings, both for Esau and his predecessors in Seir, which he overthrew (Deut. 2:12, 22). The final verse of the section contrasts Jacob dwelling in Canaan.

A. *Toledot* of Esau: Esau grew and moved from Canaan to Seir (36:1–8).
B. *Toledot* of Esau in Seir: Esau produced kings (36:9–43).
C. Jacob sojourned in Canaan (37:1).

The chapter shows the geographical movement of Esau from Canaan to the hill country of Seir and his growth in wealth and power outside of the promised land. The genealogy emphasizes the national implications (repeating "Edom," "chiefs," "kings," "clans," and regions). The notice on kingship (before Israel, v. 31) reflects the previously noted promise of kings to Jacob (35:11) and the expectation of rule in Joseph (37:5–10). Yet in this section, Jacob was dwelling in the land of promise but without any property rights or national fulfillment.[1] The section connects the nation of Israel to their Edomite neighbors as they later enter the land.

- ***Toledot of Esau: Esau Grew and Moved from Canaan to Seir (36:1–8)***
- ***Toledot of Esau in Seir: Esau Produced Kings (36:9–43)***
- ***Jacob Sojourned in Canaan (37:1)***

EXPOSITION

Transitioning from the Jacob stories to the stories of his sons, the *toledots* of Esau uniquely recounts two related *toledot* sections, first giving Esau's immediate family in Canaan, and then showing Esau's growth and power after his move to the hill country of Seir. Theologically, it shows God's blessing materially on Esau's family, as the descendant of Abraham and with a promised national identity (cf. 21:13; 25:23; The Family History of Ishmael, 25:12–18), and the outworking of the oracles, both to Rebekah that he would develop into a nation (25:23) and from Isaac that he would live by the sword and serve his brother (though he does not serve Jacob yet, he leaves the land promised to Jacob, 27:39–40). For Israel, it is both hopeful (God has blessed Esau, who did not have the promise; how much more will he bless Israel with the promised land and nationhood?) and sobering. God's warning to Abraham of a long Egyptian sojourn resonates in the background. Israel must wait in faith in God's promise and his perfect, but often delayed, fulfillment. From his Canaanite wives Esau produced a large family with powerful clans, which he moved to Seir,

1 The point is made narratively even though, chronologically, the genealogy goes far beyond the time of Jacob. The contrast shows the prospering of Esau and growth of his clans while Israel appears to be languishing, and the reader knows they will be in Egypt for hundreds of years, including bondage.

establishing a national identity, while Jacob sojourned in Canaan.[2]

Toledot *of Esau: Esau Grew and Moved from Canaan to Seir (36:1–8)*

After marrying Canaanite wives and thriving in Canaan, Esau moved to the hill country of Seir.

36:1. Just as the *toledot* of Ishmael, Abraham's oldest son, followed the Abraham stories (25:12–18) in preparation for the *toledot* of God's chosen, Isaac (the Jacob stories), so the *toledot* of Esau, Isaac's oldest, follows the Jacob stories in preparation for the *toledot* of God's chosen, Jacob. This initial section details Esau's wives and sons, as well as their move from Canaan to the hill country of Seir. It emphasizes, though, the national importance of this with the repeated "Esau . . . is Edom" (36:1, 8), as God keeps his promise to Abraham and Sarah (17:4, 6, 16) and to Rebekah (25:23) to produce nations (and kings!) from them. Esau will become a nation in a land given by Yahweh (Deut. 2:5) and will have extensive contact with the nation of Israel, from its birth (Num. 20:14) to long after the exile (Mal. 1:4).

36:2–5. The account of Esau's children focuses on their Canaanite identity from his wives and their birth in Canaan. By reminding the reader of the Canaanite heritage of Esau's wives, the narrative highlights Esau's disregard for his parents and his profane nature and pursuits. The first time "Edom" was used (25:30), the point was similar as Esau despised his birthright and showed his profane nature. Now, with "Edom" repeated (36:1, 5), his character is similarly on display in the outworking of his family. Though the question of the names and ancestry of Esau's wives is uncertain,[3] the point here clearly shows, in contrast to Jacob, that Esau both married and had his family in Canaan before leaving the land of promise. His prosperity would not be because of his personal piety. Rather, God blessed him, much as he did Ishmael (17:20).

36:6–8. The wording here reminds the reader of Abraham's conflict with Lot (13:6),[4] though there is no mention of strife here.[5] As in Lot's case, Esau chose the expedient and seemingly productive choice away from the redemptive plan of God to the family. He certainly did prosper in the short term, and as noted, God blessed him with land and a nation (Deut. 2:5). The implication of the reflection of Lot's choice seems to also hint at Esau's motivations (supported by his response to Isaac, Gen. 27:34–36).

---

2 For help on the many exegetical, linguistic, and historical challenges in this chapter, see one of the more extensive commentaries such as Wenham (Word Biblical Commentary), Hamilton (New International Commentary on the Old Testament), or Mathews (New American Commentary). We will focus on the broad overview and main theological points since few will likely devote a separate message to this chapter, though the message will resonate with many.

3 Given the disparity between this passage, 26:34–35, and 28:9, and the lack of information available, it is impossible to say whether these are three of more wives, whether some had multiple names, or some other solution exists. As Cyrus Gordon (1960, 126, n. 30) famously quipped, unraveling these ladies is "as futile as an attempt to unscramble an omelette."

4 In both cases (and only here for Esau and Jacob) the text talks of two families whose "possessions were too great for them to dwell together" and that "the land . . . could not support them."

5 The resolution of this narrative with Esau already in Seir in ch. 33 is uncertain with the limited information. Rabbinic interpretation suggested he was nomadic until after Jacob returned (Sarna 1989, 249), perhaps a final separation after the death of Isaac (Hamilton 1995, 392), stereotypical language for clans splitting up (Wenham 1994, 337), or something else.

Toledot *of Esau in Seir: Esau Produced Kings (36:9–43)*

Esau became great as his family grew into clans, conquered territory, and produced kings.

36:9. The *toledot* relates both the line of Esau with the clans and kings that will come from him as well as the Horites that predated Esau in Edom with their clans. Esau both conquered them with the sword (cf. 27:40; Deut. 2:12, 22) and intermarried with them.[6] The genealogies look into Israel's future, when they will be interacting with the Edomites as nations, and specifically draw attention to the prior kings in Edom before Israel had kings (Gen. 36:31, obviously edited much later), also alluding to the struggles they would have as nations (25:23). That struggle is underlined by repeating that Esau is the father of the Edomites (36:9, 43) and tying in with the initial *toledot* with the third repetition identifying Esau as Edom (v. 19).

36:10–19. The genealogy reiterates the wives and sons from 36:2–5 and adds the grandsons to the sons of Adah and Basemath, giving a total of five sons and ten grandsons. Those sons and grandsons all become "chiefs" (אַלֻּפִים), or heads of clans (cf. Hamilton 1995, 396). Edom is growing as a nation as the tribes grow, indicated by the structural terminology. The point is again emphasized by reminding the reader that the sons of Esau are referring to the nation Edom (v. 19) and their leaders.

36:20–30. Moses makes clear that the hill country of Seir was already inhabited. The Horites were in possession of the land, so the movement of Esau required the use of his sword (27:40; Deut. 2:12, 22). He was not merely looking for unoccupied land for his family. This also adds some context to Jacob's fear at the report of Esau coming with four hundred men (Gen. 32:7). To underline the point, the Horites were not merely a family but were already well established since before Abraham (14:6). Their "chiefs" (or better, "clans," Hamilton 1995, 396) were listed, showing their broad habitation of the land. The list also reveals the growth and strength of Esau and helps explain Edom's rise to prominence by absorbing peoples already there.

36:31–43. Edom's national prosperity, power, and structure, with their kings[7] and clans, predated the rise of the monarchy in Israel.[8] Their rise contrasts with the promise to Jacob (35:11) as the culmination of promises to Abraham and Sarah (17:6, 16) in tension with the hundreds of years before they even have a land, much less kings (15:13, 16, 18–21). The final four verses list the geographical spread of the clans, showing the growing nation of Edom that Israel will encounter on their exit from Egypt and that will be neighbors and often at odds with Israel throughout their history, with numerous wars (cf. 1 Sam. 14:47; 2 Sam. 8:13–14; 2 Kings 8:20–21) and rancor (Obadiah).

6 The inclusion of the Horites here suggests their intermarriage with Esau, as perhaps the noting of Oholibamah (36:25, cf. v. 2, though perhaps they are being distinguished). The comparison with Deut. 2:12, 22 suggests both conquest and intermarriage, with Deuteronomy perhaps simplifying the history (Wenham 1994, 338; cf. Mathews 2005, 647; Sarna 1989, 251).

7 "Kings" here does not require "the existence of a national, unified kingdom of Edom. The various individuals cited were simply localized tribal chieftains, as were also 'the king of Edom' with whom Moses dealt" (Sarna 1989, 409; see his "Excursus 28: the Edomite King List," pp. 408–10).

8 The precise dating of the genealogy and so the insertion into the book of Genesis cannot be determined. While the note about the kings of Israel was certainly after Israel had kings, the main contours of the rest of the genealogy could have been earlier (see Mathews 2005, 635). That Genesis was edited after Moses is clear in many places, yet we still view the initial corpus as Mosaic (see Authorship of Genesis, p. 54), including at least the main contours of Esau's line and their migration to Seir.

Jacob Sojourned in Canaan (37:1)

In contrast to Esau's growth and power, Jacob continued in the land of promise as a sojourner.

37:1. The final verse of the section seems as if it should be part of the following *toledot*, but it would be the only *toledot* that did not begin with the *toledot* formula. While it provides the transition to Jacob's descendants, it also provides a significant point for the narrative, contrasting the burgeoning nation of Edom from Esau (36:1–8, see structure above, p. 581) with the sojourn of the patriarchs of promise in the land without realizing the outworking of that promise.[9] God had indicated that Israel would rule over Edom (25:23; 27:29), yet Edom became large and powerful while Israel would languish in Egypt. Esau took territory, and Jacob had only a field. In fact, it would be more than four hundred years before the nation of Israel had a land (15:13).

God's purposes required ongoing faith and were not realized in their lifetimes. While God's promises are sure, they are not immediate. The realities of faith are the assurances of things hoped for but not yet realized, or it would not be faith. God was at work building that faith and showing his faithfulness through barren women and periods of waiting. Jacob must live and wait "in the land of his father's sojournings" (37:1).

Genesis will now turn back to the line of promise, showing God's working in the family of Jacob to produce Israel. The recalcitrant sons will have to be tamed before they can bring blessing to the families of the earth, by knowing Yahweh and producing kings to lead to his ultimate redemption.

THEOLOGICAL FOCUS

God can always be trusted to keep his word, even to profane people, but his purposes in his chosen servants are often only realized over extended time through testing and trials.

Several theological points can be made here. God's faithfulness in keeping his promise long before to Abraham materialized in Esau's national prosperity (25:23). He graciously honored his word even for a profane son, though that son does show some working of God in his life (ch. 33). Together with the Ishmael genealogy, this genealogy helps to tie up the threads of Abraham's offspring and God's working. It foreshadows Edom's future conflicts with Israel, promised long before (25:23) and realized throughout Israel's history. God's word is true. God will accomplish his promised plan and fulfill his word.

The final verse, however, shows another role for this genealogy in the history and consciousness of Israel. At the time that Esau is burgeoning and conquering lands, Jacob is sojourning and then going to Egypt, where the nation will be enslaved. The implications are significant. God has promised Israel tangible greatness and success as a nation (12:2; 13:16; 15:5; 26:4; 28:14; 35:11). That promise, however, must be held in tension with God's anticipation of their protracted time in Egypt with slavery that Israel would experience while Edom was thriving before experiencing God's promise (15:13–14). Israel and all of God's people need to learn that achieving success in personal pursuits often comes more quickly than attaining the outworking of God's great promises. "The promised spiritual blessing demanded patience and faith" (Ross 2008, 205). In addition, that time of waiting provides opportunity for testing, which produces needed maturing growth (James 1:2–3). The writer to the Hebrews highlights that patience in his discussion on faith (Heb. 11), not merely for Abraham but for many Old Testament saints as well as his own audience.

9 This understanding also recognizes the impact of the larger context on this passage.

PREACHING AND TEACHING STRATEGIES

Exegetical and Theological Synthesis

Our chapter forms a transition in the narrative. Before returning to Jacob, the blessed line, chapter 36 contains a long list of "the generations of Esau (that is, Edom)" (v. 1). Readers can see that God is keeping his promises to Esau. However, Esau's family are Edomites (v. 9). Note Esau's decision to leave the land of promise and go to "Seir" (v. 8). This contrasts with Jacob remaining "in the land of Canaan" (37:1). Waltke and Fredricks (2001, 488) state: "It functions to show the geographical and spiritual divide between the brothers." Long before Israel has a king, kings were reigning "in the land of Edom" (36:31). It will be some time before Jacob's family tree experiences kingship in the land. You will want to alert your listeners to the *inclusio* in 36:5 and 37:1 ("in the land of Canaan"). Esau moved just east, so that Esau's family and Jacob's family would be neighbors (cf. Seir in 36:8 and "Canaan" in 37:1). Since "Esau took his wives from the Canaanites" (36:2), we can expect that the relationship poses a threat to the family of promise. While Jacob waits for God to deliver on his promises, he will do so in a land full of temptation to worship other gods.

Preaching Idea

God will do what he says, moving his people out into his promised rule, but we may have to wait and endure testing to experience his best.

Contemporary Connections

What does it mean?

We have seen this sequence before in Genesis: the nonelect line of Esau occurs after the report of the death of his father (35:28–29) but before the elect line of Jacob's story continues. The same sequence occurred with Ishmael following Abraham's death in chapter 25 but before the story of the elect line of Isaac continues. Throughout Genesis God has presented a contrast between the two lines, and we urge our listeners to identify with the line of promise. In chapter 36 we continue to call our listeners to assess their faith in God's promises and whether their lifestyle matches their faith.

Is it true?

Chapter 36 presents resounding evidence for the blessing of God on Esau, just as God promised. God is extremely gracious to Esau and his family, even though he did not value God's blessing and birthright. Some of our listeners may have trouble believing that God would bless Esau this much. But if God keeps his promises to the nonelect, surely he will keep his promises to those he loves!

Now what?

We urge our listeners not to identify with Esau ("go and do otherwise"). He and his family leave the land of promise for greener pastures. God's people by faith remain faithful to him, knowing that one day they will reign with God when his kingdom comes in full. That faith will be tested in waiting as God prepares his people to accomplish his purposes.

Creativity in Presentation

Should the preacher or teacher decide to specifically relate the lessons of this section, we want to communicate that God will do what he says, moving his people out into his promised rule, but we may have to wait and endure testing to experience his best. We would suggest a possible combination with the Ishmael genealogy along these lines:

- God keeps his word, even to profane characters (25:12–8; 36:1–43).
- God's best, however, often requires ongoing faith, waiting for God's timing

while enduring testing and refining (37:1).

You might also consider the following sermon structure:

- Remember the lifestyle of our nonelect neighbors (36:1–8).
- Remember their tremendous influence in the world (36:9–43).
- Remember our place as representatives of the King (37:1; 1 Peter 2:9–10).

DISCUSSION QUESTIONS

1. Why does God often wait so long before he brings his promises to fruition? What benefits should the worshipper expect?
2. Why does God often seem to bless people who are not following him fully and sometimes appear profane?
3. How should we relate to those who appear to thrive while far from God?
4. What does God call us to do and how should we live when we feel that we are in a waiting period in our lives?

INTRODUCTION TO THE FOURTH-GENERATION NARRATIVES (GENESIS 37:2–50:26)

Throughout the primeval narratives, humanity continuously turned away from God, pursuing their own autonomy and security in rebellion and receiving God's judgments. Humankind's evil heart (6:5; 8:21) resisted God's gracious plan of redemption at every stage. God's purposes would not be thwarted, however. He would choose a conduit for his blessing and a means to reveal his nature and bring redemption to human hearts. The Abraham stories present the call of Abraham and God's building promises to him in covenant as he grew in his faith and loyalty to his King. God's blessing would be realized and disseminated through Abraham and his descendants (12:3; 18:18; 22:18; 26:4; 28:14). In the Jacob stories, God passed those promises to Isaac (26:3–4) and then to Jacob (28:13–14; 35:11–12), clarifying their future. The Jacob narratives focus on how they could obtain and pass on his blessing through the promises to their world as they learned to walk in submissive, loyal relationship, practicing his justice and righteousness. Unexpectedly, however, the fourth generation from Abraham seemed to move even farther from God, taking the family conflicts to a new low.

Not only do the covenant promises appear to be in jeopardy, but the very existence of the family appears compromised. God, however, even as he moved farther into the background, dramatically intervened not only in circumstances but in changing hearts. He transformed the evil, brother-killing sons, unworthy of promise, to brother-loving men, exemplified in Judah, who would be exalted to leadership. The family would experience reconciliation, and their world would be blessed through the faithful actions of Jacob, Joseph, and Judah. Jacob then projected the Abrahamic covenant promises into Israel's future with his oracles and his expectation of their fulfillment in the land of promise.

LITERARY STRUCTURE AND THEOLOGICAL THEMES

The Abraham stories focus on the developing faith of Abraham in loyalty to Yahweh as he received the growing promise, declaring his responsibility to inculcate God's ways by doing righteousness and justice. The Jacob stories, then, teach the reader that blessing can only be experienced and shared in submissive relationship with God, living out his character of justice and righteousness. Now the fourth-generation stories move to the outworking of those lessons in blessing. God has redemptive purposes that he will accomplish according to his plan, even in the face of great human evil. He will both move in hearts to rehabilitate them and prepare them to receive and convey his blessing. He will also offer the future promise of blessing for all who will follow him in faith and loyal obedience. He will accomplish his purposes through his budding nation, and he offers a vision for all who will follow him to experience.

The family history of Jacob traces the movement of the budding nation through Jacob's sons, from Canaan to Egypt. It details the working of God to preserve his people and prepare them for their role in his divine purposes, even while he uses them to bring blessing to all the families of the earth. Ironically, however, God steps into the background of the narrative, directing from the shadows rather than the bright lights as in the Abraham stories or the intermittent interventions of the Jacob stories. The clear promises from the patriarchs will be carried out through coincidence and intrigue in the final narratives. God's people must acknowledge his role in the end (45:5–9; 50:20), but the fog of life will cloud their perceptions in the process.[10] If the *toledot* of Jacob were isolated, God's working would come as an unanticipated and debatable surprise. As the sequel to the Abraham and Jacob stories, however, the hiddenness of Yahweh is the surprise, making the stories much more relatable to future generations. His oversight rewards expectations, with the intrigue adding interest and challenging those expectations until the bigger picture emerges with far greater impact than could have been realized without the human plotting.

It is easy to view these as the Joseph stories, since he is central to large portions of the narrative, but the *toledot* portrays all the brothers and their future tribal expectations, especially the leadership of the family. The focus, then, will be on Joseph and Judah, with cameos from Reuben, who loses leadership. We can, perhaps, call these the "fourth-generation" stories as a better indicator of their significance, rather than "Joseph stories," since they will lead to the future prospects for all of the tribes (48:14–49:27; Cotter 2003, 263–64).

Toledot 11: God passed his promise of blessing through Jacob to his sons, blessing their world, refining their character, and giving the birthright to Joseph and leadership to Judah (37:2–50:26).[11]

A. Announcing God's choice of him, Joseph alienated his brothers who sold him to Egypt and deceived Jacob (37:2–36).

B. God judged Judah's evil sons, blessing Tamar, and exposing Judah's character, initiating heart change in Judah (38:1–30).

C. God blessed Joseph with his presence and success, despite his unjust accusation and unexpected imprisonment (39:1–23).

D. God raised Joseph to power in Egypt to save lives (40:1–41:57).

E. Joseph's brothers traveled to Egypt twice to save their families, bringing them to repentance and unity (42:1–43:34).

F. Joseph tested his brothers, revealing Judah's changed heart (44:1–34).

F' Joseph revealed his heart to his brothers, declaring God's work and prompting restoration for the family (45:1–28).

E' With God's promise, Jacob took all his family to Egypt to save them, expressing blessing to pharaoh (46:1–47:12).

D' Joseph saved lives, enriching the Pharaoh, and prospering the family of Israel (47:13–31).

10 The narrative itself concludes with the final oversight of Yahweh as the controlling influence, even though he is seldom mentioned throughout (45:5–9; 50:20). The clear intent, then, is to show his sovereign oversight of circumstances to bring about his greater good. Longacre (1989, 41) calls this the "foregrounded macrostructure" of the narrative.

11 As with the Abraham and Jacob narratives, the structure generally follows Gary Rendsburg (2014, 79–97), with some private communication and influence from K. Lawson Younger, and personal adjustments.

C' Based on God's presence and care, Jacob blessed Joseph with the birthright, elevating Joseph's sons (48:1–22).

B' Jacob blessed his sons, elevating Judah to leadership and prospering Joseph with God's abundance (49:1–28).

A' Jacob and Joseph demonstrated their faith, with Jacob requesting burial in Canaan, and Joseph reconciling fully with his brothers (49:29–50:21).

Epilogue to the* Toledot*:

3" God blessed Joseph in Egypt with great grandchildren (50:22–23).

4" Joseph, dying, requested in faith to be buried in Canaan (50:24–26).

The theme of brother conflict, prevalent since chapter 4 frames these fourth-generation stories. They begin with conflict and the threat of fratricide (37:2–36) and end with repentance from real heart change and reconciliation (49:29–50:21). That heart change is exemplified in Judah who had already sold his brother, married a Canaanite, and raised evil sons, only to be confronted with his unrighteousness (38:1–30) and grow to love his brother (44:1–34). He rose to leadership with God's future ruler coming from his lineage (49:8–12). Jacob's blessing not only brings Judah's transformation to a climax, but culminates the entire book, drawing out the themes of blessing, rule, and God's redemptive plan as he describes the concluding hope of the Abrahamic Covenant. Salvation will come from Yahweh (49:18).

The core of the fourth-generation stories is not just the resolution of the conflict in the family, but the working of God to bring blessing to the family and all the families of the earth. In the next inner frame of the chiasm, God's presence directly blessed Joseph in his righteous service, even amidst injustice (39:1–23), and Jacob blessed Joseph, elevating Joseph's sons with the blessing of the birthright (48:1–22). Moving toward the center in the macrostructure, God's blessing on Joseph led to his exaltation as promised to save lives (40:1–41:57) which he did spectacularly (47:13–31). Within that framework, God used the famine and Joseph's faithfulness to save his clan (42:1–43:34; 46:1–47:12), revealing the heart change and accompanying reconciliation at the center of the narratives (44:1–34; 45:1–28).

The epilogue concludes the *toledot* and Genesis simply, recording Joseph's grandchildren and his request to be buried in Canaan. The family is not in the land, and this is the end of the single-family lineage. Now there are twelve sons, soon to be tribes, and they are in Egypt, so the burial of the wife to mark their commitment to the land needs no parallel. Without a single family to trace, and with the blessings pronounced, there is no need for a marriage of the heirs of the clans (cf. the Introduction to the Abraham Narratives and Introduction to the Jacob Narratives). Instead, Joseph's grandchildren symbolize the growth of the nation and his request to be buried in Canaan finalizes their confidence in the promise and the future return of the nation according to promise (48:4, 21).

The greater hiddenness of God in these stories moves the patriarchal narratives closer to the experience of most of God's people throughout history. Even though he was not directly evident, God was clearly at work, exposed by the narrator and retrospect. His sovereign rule came through even more strongly as he mysteriously used natural disaster and even the evil plans of wicked men to ultimately accomplish his good purposes. The necessity of and evident working of God to bring about heart change provides both encouragement for the wayward, and appropriate concern for the consequences of living without loyalty to the ultimate king. Faith should be strengthened with the consistent accomplishment of God's purposes, bringing about his promises and looking ahead to his ultimate redemption of humanity.

COVENANT GROWTH, CLARIFICATION, AND IMPACT

These stories do not mention the Abrahamic Covenant until Jacob headed for Egypt (46:3) where God alluded to his promise to Abraham, Isaac, and Jacob to make them a great nation. Now, however, God anticipated their initial growth in Egypt (46:3), but he would bring Jacob (46:4; and the nation, 48:21; 50:25) back to the land of promise. In chapter 48, Jacob then expressed his confidence in that covenant as he passed on the blessing to Joseph of the double portion by elevating Joseph's two sons to receive an equal share in the inheritance in the new land with his other sons. Then in chapter 49, Jacob pronounced his "blessings" on the twelve sons, describing the future that God would enable as they chose to follow him. Jacob's blessing expanded the covenant promises, empowering the tribes to experience God's blessing in ways that they could extend Yahweh's rule on earth and share his blessing with their world as they followed him in loyalty. Yahweh's rule would be focused through Judah's line (49:8–12), providing the final hint in Genesis of the coming king to accomplish the redemptive purpose of God in his response to human evil, beginning after the fall (3:15).

PREACHING SUGGESTIONS

As with any of the sets of narratives in Genesis, these stories could easily be used as a standalone series. Again, an introductory message (or two) could set the stage of humanity's need and God's intervention with the Abrahamic Covenant promises, passed down through the generations. The issue of the heart and the need for real change should be included especially for this series in which it finds expression and resolution in the behind-the-scenes working of God. Blessing would also need to be explained with some reference to the context of Genesis that has provided such a rich background.

If the schedule requires a shortened series for the fourth-generation stories, we suggest beginning with Joseph's choice and sale (37:2–36). A summary of God's blessing in his painful trials (39:1–23) could be combined with his rise to power (40:1–41:57) to show God's working through struggle. The brothers' arrival and testing (42:1–43:34) could be briefly summarized with the focus on Judah's changed heart (as representative of the brothers, 44:1–34) and Joseph's shocking revelation (45:1–28), or these could be two messages focused on what God was doing in the brothers and what he was doing in Joseph. The outworking and blessing of the family, Pharaoh, Egypt, and the nations could be included in a quick overview focusing on the outworking of the promise of blessing to all (46:1–49:28). Finally, the concluding climax of reconciliation with the working of God to bring good in human history regardless of motives and actions necessarily concludes the narratives (49:29–50:21).

Genesis 37:2–36

EXEGETICAL IDEA

Joseph's favored status and future role in God's program deepen his brothers' animosity, supplying their excuse to eliminate him by selling him into slavery and covering it up, devastating Jacob yet advancing God's plan for his chosen family.

THEOLOGICAL FOCUS

Though human failings and even God's favor may induce desperate evil actions that cause grievous human suffering, God will quietly orchestrate circumstances to accomplish his purposes.

PREACHING IDEA

Make no doubt about it: no forms of evil in or around us can stop God's purpose for us.

PREACHING POINTERS

This is not the first time the original audience becomes engrossed in redemptive history featuring an unlikely pathway to God keeping his covenant promises to royal families (the families God chooses to receive and extend His blessing). No one expects Joseph to ascend to power the way he does! The boy Joseph is featured and favored but gets into immediate trouble that threatens his life. Sibling rivalry once again threatens the promise. And, as God's people have seen before, this promising youngster has a lot of growing up to do. He is chosen by God to lead his people, but God will mature him along the way. Because of the dreams, readers know what is in store for Joseph and his brothers.

Our audience can be assured that their God will also keep his promises to them despite the ups and downs experienced through life. Some of the bumps are self-caused, as in Joseph's case; it is no wonder his brothers loathe him! Other bumps are caused by others, as is also Joseph's case. Either way, God will not abandon his own. It may feel like God's people are "wandering" about through life (v. 15), but everything is moving according to God's plan. That is true even when God's plan includes our pain.

If not for the prophecy of Genesis 15:13, first readers and modern readers might think all is lost as they read the end of chapter 37: "They took Joseph to Egypt" (v. 28). Joseph's dream will come true after all; he will rule over his family, and God's purposes will be established. It was true then and is just as true now.

FAVORITISM AND FRATRICIDE: GOD'S HIDDEN WORK AMID DESPERATE EVIL (37:2–36)

LITERARY STRUCTURE AND THEMES

The initial narrative of these "fourth-generation" stories (see Introduction to the Fourth-Generation Narratives above, p. 587) highlights the chosen young Joseph tormenting his brothers with his favored status, from his father and his God, and reaping the consequences of his imprudence. Joseph's alienation of his brothers and their retaliation by selling him into slavery, resulting in his descent into Egypt, are resolved in the final narrative of the *toledot* when Joseph reconciled finally with his brothers and asserted that ultimately God was working out his good plan despite their evil intentions (50:20). The hidden working of God at the beginning of the *toledot* progressively moves more clearly into the light until Joseph's climactic statement expresses what the perceptive reader was recognizing.

The initial pericope (37:2–36) divides into two sections, using Joseph's coat and dreams to symbolize the main conflict and progress of the story. Joseph's special coat frames the story, billboarding Jacob's favoritism (vv. 2–4) and underlining the brothers' callous attitudes, which bring Jacob inconsolable pain (vv. 29–35). In the center, Joseph's dreams goad the brothers to deeper hatred and jealousy (vv. 5–11), ultimately selling him into slavery (vv. 12–28). At the same time, the supernatural expectation of the dreams ironically influences the reader's perceptions on numerous coincidences. Without the chance encounter with the unnamed stranger guiding Joseph to his possible demise and the timely merchants' arrival to save him from the pit with the dubiously better prospects of slavery, or the unfortunate (!) absence of Reuben at the wrong time, Joseph would not have been in Egypt, surprisingly purchased by an officer of Pharaoh.

I. God's chosen family was treacherously divided (37:2–11).
   A. God's promise would continue through Jacob's family (37:2a).
   B. Jacob stoked his sons' rivalry (37:2b–4).
   C. Joseph further alienated his brothers (37:5–11).
II. Joseph's brothers sold him, devastating Jacob, yet in God's providence (37:12–36).
   A. Joseph's brothers chose selling him over murder (37:12–28).
   B. Joseph's brothers devastated Jacob (37:29–35).
   C. God's warning began to take shape (37:36).

The tragedies of favoritism and fratricide, whether overtly or implicitly, oppose the divine appointment of Joseph to authority and add intrigue to the Abrahamic covenant promises to the patriarchs. The initial story of the continuing family history pits the degenerating character of the family members against the clear promises of Yahweh, raising tensions and requiring divine intervention, both to rehabilitate the family for God's purposes and to accomplish the promises themselves.

- ***God's Chosen Family Was Treacherously Divided (37:2–11)***
- ***Joseph's Brothers Sold Him, Devastating Jacob Yet in God's Providence (37:12–36)***

EXPOSITION

The Jacob stories concluded with Jacob back in the land in peace and Jacob and Esau burying Isaac with their conflicts apparently mended. The transitional chapter 36 showed God's blessing on Esau with his growth and territory as a nation (cf. Deut. 2:5). But Jacob was living in the land of promise without yet inheriting that land (Gen. 37:1). For the reader, Jacob's life in the land prepares for the final *toledot*, which will relate their tensions and reasons for leaving the land, as foretold to Abraham (15:13–16) and guided by God's providence.

The narrative opens with deepening conflicts and mounting obstacles to El Shaddai's promises, focused partly around two dreams, paralleling Yahweh's initial call to Abraham in the *toledot* of Terah (12:1–3) and his opening oracle to Rebekah in the *toledot* of Isaac (25:23). As with each of those previous narratives, the opening oracle will prove controlling for the remainder of the narrative, raising expectations that will only be realized through the twists and turns of this superbly told story. Joseph's favored status and future role in God's program deepen his brothers' animosity, supplying their excuse to eliminate him by selling him into slavery and covering it up, devastating Jacob yet advancing God's plan for his chosen family.

God's Chosen Family Was Treacherously Divided (37:2–11)

The family history of Jacob begins with favoritism, creating deep animosity between his sons, symbolized by Joseph's special coat and catalyzed by Joseph's dreams, foreshadowing his future role.

God's Promise Would Continue Through Jacob's Family (37:2a)

The family history of Jacob will detail God's working in and through his sons, Abraham's great-grandsons.

37:2a. The eleventh and final *toledot* section, the "generations" or "family history" (NCV) of Jacob, will detail the outworking of the promises to the patriarchs through the great-grandsons of Abraham. It culminates in the oracles of Jacob describing the future of the tribes that would come from these sons (48:13–49:28). The covenant promises to the patriarchs drive the narrative and inform the ambiguities.

> *TRANSLATION ANALYSIS 37:2a*
> For the various translations and intent of *toledot* (תֹּלְדוֹת), see the Introduction, "Structure of Genesis," p. 65.

Jacob Stoked His Sons' Rivalry (37:2b–4)

Jacob's preferential love for Joseph, embodied in Joseph's coat, fueled his remaining sons' hatred and strife.

37:2b–4. A young man of seventeen, Joseph was shepherding with his brothers and possibly in an apprenticeship or subordinate role to them. The conflict for the plot begins immediately with the first of three aggravating factors. Joseph brought a "bad report" of his brothers (דִּבָּתָם רָעָה, v. 2b) to his father. His report clearly put his brothers in a negative light, whether he "maligned" them (Hamilton 1995, 406) or fulfilled his responsibility to his father (Ross 1988, 598).[1] Either way, it added to their ill will toward Joseph.

---

1 The term "report" (דִּבָּה) only occurs nine times in the OT, and elsewhere the report itself is false (including the report of the spies in Num. 13:32; 14:36, 37). Here, however, the addition of the adjective and the character of the brothers, as well as the later character of Joseph, suggest he may have simply been bringing bad news of what they had done, which was not a popular thing to do and certainly put them in a bad light. Conversely, Joseph's delight in telling his dreams and obliviousness to their attitudes in the following narrative suggest that at least he took full advantage of it or even "slanted" it "to damage the victim" (Waltke and Fredricks 2001, 499).

TRANSLATION ANALYSIS 37:2b

The term for "boy" (נַעַר) can refer to a male from infancy up to at least thirty (Gen. 41:12) that is yet unmarried (Hamilton, נַעַר, *NIDOTTE* 3:125), leading to the common translation of "boy," "lad," "youth," or the like (ESV, NKJV, NASB95, respectively). It can also, however, refer to a servant (18:7), suggesting that Joseph is here called a "boy" to indicate a supporting role to his brothers, leading to the translation "helper" (NJPS, NRSV) or "He worked for" (NLT), intensifying the tension with his report against them. The disjunctive (וְהוּא) draws attention to this status as important background to his "bad report," which would be unexpected if merely a "youth" was intended, since his age was already established.

The favoritism that Jacob had displayed to his wives bore obviously rotten fruit in his public treatment of Joseph over his other sons. The robe he made for Joseph heralded Joseph's status, which may have included the inheritance rights of the firstborn (Ross 2008, 208) and added to the offense of his elevated status in his later dreams.[2] Predictably, the brothers hated him and could not speak civilly or peaceably (לְשָׁלֹם) to him. While the narrative will relate the actions of the brothers toward Joseph, escalating from their words to their murderous intent to selling him into slavery, their heart is emphasized initially, as their hatred (שׂנא) grows (37:4, 5, 8).

TRANSLATION ANALYSIS 37:3

The special coat (כְּתֹנֶת פַּסִּים) Jacob gave to Joseph has been translated traditionally as a "robe of many colors" (ESV), "ornate robe" (NIV), a "long robe with sleeves" (NRSV), or a "special robe with long sleeves" (NCV). The modifying noun is used only here and in 2 Samuel 13:18–19 of Tamar's robe. The meaning was not clear in the earliest translations, with numerous suggestions being made. For a discussion of the options, see Hamilton (1995, 408–9). Based on the use of the term in Aramaic and possible Hebrew connections, Steinmann (2019, 350) plausibly supports the long sleeves as best.

Joseph Further Alienated His Brothers (37:5–11)

Joseph's grandiose dreams, foreshadowing God's purpose, alienated his brothers.

37:5–8. The final straw(s) for the brothers came as a pair of dreams. Joseph's initial dream simply referred to his brothers, symbolized by sheaves of grain, bowing to him, another sheaf. While the significance of the grain would not be understood for many years until the future famine in Egypt, ironically, the obvious intent did not require any interpreter. They immediately assumed his aspirations to "rule" over them (מָשׁוֹל תִּמְשֹׁל בָּנוּ, v. 8, ultimately fulfilled in Egypt where they bowed before him (42:6; 43:26, 28; cf. 44:14), and he was "ruler over all the land of Egypt" (45:8, 26; וּמֹשֵׁל בְּכָל־אֶרֶץ מִצְרָיִם). Their hatred grew, not only for the dream he told them but for "his words" (דְּבָרָיו, 37:8) or the way he told them. Joseph may have been justified in his reports to his father, though that is ambiguous, but he appears foolish (at best naive and at worst narcissistic) in his reporting of his dreams to his brothers and later his father.[3]

2 The significance of the robe, beyond the obvious favoritism, is not certain, though it could indicate birthright. Jacob gave the double portion of the firstborn to Joseph when he elevated the two sons of Joseph to equal status with the other sons, so that they also gained an allotment of the land of promise as full tribes with the other ten (Gen. 48:5, 15–16; cf. discussion on Jacob's purchase of Esau's birthright, 25:31–34, p. 439). He gave the leadership, however, to Judah (49:8–12).

3 The narrator's play on Joseph's name in "they hated him even more" (וַיּוֹסִפוּ עוֹד שְׂנֹא אֹתוֹ, vv. 5, 8), using the verb "add" (ESV, "even more," וַיּוֹסִפוּ, which looks and sounds like "Joseph," יוֹסֵף), seems to point at him with a negative evaluation. They were getting too much "Joseph!"

37:9–11. Joseph's second dream included his parents.[4] Later, Joseph would note that Pharaoh's repeated dream indicated both the certainty and the near fulfillment of the events (41:32). Wenham (1994, 351) suggests that the setting of one on earth and the other in heaven adds to this certainty. Joseph's zeal, repeating the dream not only to his brothers but also to his father, garnered Jacob's rebuke (37:10), adding to the impression that Joseph's character also needs transformation. While he will show great wisdom later in a narrative with numerous wisdom themes (Ross 2008, 208), he does not begin with insight into his brothers or even his father. Rather, he appears oblivious and entirely self-absorbed (Sarna 1989, 256). The attitude of Joseph's brothers moved here from anger to jealousy (וַיְקַנְאוּ־בוֹ, v. 11), pointing to a deep-seated rage (Prov 6:34; 27:4) and inspiring the subsequent conspiracy.

The dreams form a somewhat ambiguous beginning to the narrative. Contrary to Abraham's direct encounter with God, Rebekah's inquiry of God, or even Jacob's revelations from God, God does not directly speak here. The ambiguity is important for the working of the narrative and the lack of insight for the characters. The brothers appear to take the dreams as Joseph's pride of place. In their immediate context they could simply be Joseph's narcissistic imagination. Jacob's pause to ponder them, however (Gen. 37:11), suggests deeper implications. Joseph must deal with the uncertainty and seems to cling to God's oversight (39:9). Based on the parallels with the *toledots* of Terah (Abraham stories, 12:1–3) and Isaac (Jacob stories, 25:23), readers recognize them as revelatory, as well as programmatic for the following narrative, adding tensions and drama to the plot. While the main idea is obvious to everyone, the outworking will follow a tortuous, divinely directed path.

The first movement of this narrative sets the stage for the conflict to blossom into murder. The emphasis of this passage is not on the meaning of the dreams, though they provide important anticipation, but on the response of the brothers (Becking 1991). The two main catalysts, Joseph's coat and dreams, emphasized by his brothers' hatred (37:4, 5, 8) and jealousy (v. 11), form the symbols of their response to him in the final movement of the narrative. The dreams, anticipating and visualizing Joseph's rise to power, catalyze their response of intended murder (vv. 12–28). His coat and their abuse of it embodies their cold hatred (vv. 29–35).

Joseph's Brothers Sold Him, Devastating Jacob Yet in God's Providence (37:12–36)

Attempting to eliminate Joseph and his dreams, his brothers sold him into slavery and covered their crime with his coat, devastating Jacob with grief yet moving Abraham's descendants closer to God's appointed plan.

Joseph's Brothers Chose Selling Him over Murder (37:12–28)

When given the opportunity, Joseph's brothers attempted to destroy Joseph and his dreams with slavery, a preferable option to murder.

37:12–17. Joseph's actions (and Jacob's desires) leave a lot of unanswered questions. How could they be so oblivious that Jacob would send Joseph (and he would go) at least fifty miles away to check on his seething brothers while wearing the offending coat? Why were they up at Shechem when in the recent past they were afraid of being ambushed and killed by nearby locals after massacring the town? Who was this unnamed informant who wanted to help

4 It has been often noted that Joseph's mother had already died with the birth of Benjamin (35:19). The sun and moon here may be generally figurative (Coats 1976, 14) or symbolize the whole ancestral line, without strictly intending his mother and father, or it may refer to Bilhah as a surrogate or stepmother (Walton 2009a, 122).

Joseph, knew his brothers, and knew where to find them? The ambiguity serves to heighten the tension, focus on the immediate conflict, and hint at divine providence.

Joseph's mission reminds the reader of his first two offences against his brothers, adding an ominous tension. Not only was he to report on them again (cf. v. 2), but he was to seek their "peace" (שְׁלוֹם) when they could not speak to him in "peace" (לְשָׁלֹם, v. 4). He even wore the offensive coat (v. 23, see v. 4). The last we had heard of Shechem, a few years previously, Jacob was running for his life (34:30; 35:5).

At Shechem, apparently Joseph was recognized by an unnamed man. Ironically, if he had not found Joseph "wandering in the field" (37:15, תֹעֶה בַּשָּׂדֶה), known the brothers, and overheard their conversation, Joseph would not have found his brothers and been sold into slavery. The coincidences that lead to God's appointed ends suggest his unseen working, even when it seems to lead to tragedy in the short term.

37:18–24. When the brothers recognized Joseph coming from a distance, his dreams motivated their revenge (vv. 19–20). Possibly because of his coat (v. 23), there was enough time for them to plot his murder and for Reuben to hear of it later and talk them out of murder but into abandoning him to die. Reuben's intervention saved Joseph's life, though it did not finally accomplish Reuben's plan.

The expressed motivation for killing him was to remove any possibility of him realizing his dreams (vv. 19–20). Ironically, it was their very plotting that would realize the dreams. Again, questions arise. Why did Reuben want to spare Joseph? Was it to regain favor with his father after his affair (35:22, cf. 49:4)? While he gained an immediate stay on Joseph's execution, Reuben's attempted leadership failed, perhaps partly because he avoided the real issue of their threat against Joseph. He proposed abandoning him in a "pit" (בּוֹר) or dry cistern and so avoid the direct violation of the prohibition given to all humanity through Noah of shedding his blood (cf. 9:6). Apparently, however, the brothers still believed the objective was to let him die without being the direct agent, as Judah expressed in his argument to sell Joseph (37:26–27). Reuben's plan to deliver Joseph spared his life but did not restore him because Reuben was coincidentally absent at the wrong time and was not able to help Joseph escape.

TRANSLATION ANALYSIS 37:19

"Dreamer" is literally "lord of the dreams" (בַּעַל הַחֲלֹמוֹת). The expression "lord of" is typically used to indicate someone's "manner, his character or his occupation" (*HALOT* s.v. "בַּעַל" 143, A. 6.), such as "allies" ("lords of the covenant," 14:13), or "archers" ("lords of arrows," 49:23). The phrase itself is normally translated simply as "dreamer" (ESV and most translations), which in the context may adequately convey their intent (Kidner 1967, 193). Hamilton (1995, 417), however, appropriately notes their sarcasm, leading to his "master dreamer" translation (cf. "master of dreams," NET). His translation may imply stronger implications than initially intended, though as he notes, it foreshadows what will be entirely appropriate later in Pharaoh's court.

Cisterns

In the hill country where there was no consistent water supply, cisterns had been the technological innovation that allowed communities to thrive. It was necessary to carve large bottle shaped pits out of the soft stone, line them with plaster, and fill them with water from the rains to maintain both the people and the livestock over the dry months. The note that it was dry was important since they had a very narrow neck and there was no way out without help. Even a "dry" cistern could have significant muck at the bottom (cf. Jer. 38:6).

37:25–28. Further exposing their callous indifference to Joseph, the brothers immediately sat down to eat just as a caravan of traders happened

Cistern near Michmash Pass, Israel.

by.[5] Judah saw an opportunity to both get rid of Joseph and absolve them of the guilt of murder (perhaps prompted by Reuben's argument). His motive seems to be split between profit (v. 26) and some conscious recognition of responsibility to a brother (v. 27), or perhaps concern for the consequences of actively spilling his blood (v. 26). The crime, however, is hardly better. "Stealing" a "brother" and "selling" him (cf. 40:15, where Joseph claims he was "stolen") was forbidden in the law (Exod. 21:16; Deut. 24:7), as well as similarly in Hammurabi's law code, and punishable by death (Hamilton 1995, 421). Even in the surrounding culture, this was a serious offense! They may have assumed that he would die in slavery or simply disappear in Egypt (Gen. 42:13). While Judah, then, pads his wallet and salves his conscience, he also unwittingly contributes to God's greater plan, putting Joseph on the caravan to Egypt for twenty shekels of silver.

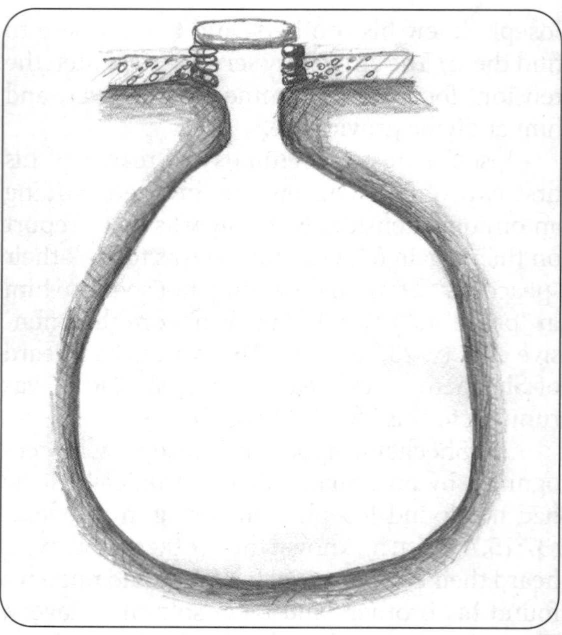

A well was dug down to a water source, but a cistern was a pear-shaped pit cut into the bedrock and plastered to hold water. Channels were cut or dug in the ground to collect the rainwater. It would often dry up in the dry season but there could still be significant sediment at the bottom.

The Price of Joseph

The price of Joseph fits the time frame indicated in the patriarchal narratives closely. Earlier, the price was closer to ten shekels (Third Dynasty of Ur, twenty-first century BC), and later rose to thirty shekels (fifteenth–thirteenth centuries BC in Nuzi and Ugarit), but in the eighteenth century BC, the average price was about twenty shekels (Kitchen 2003, 344–45).

5 The traders are initially called Ishmaelites (v. 25). Then the Midianites pass (v. 28), but they sell him to the Ishmaelites (v. 28). Verse 36 in the MT lists "Medanites" as the ones selling him to Potiphar (LXX and other versions read "Midianites" here, the difference only being the letter *yod* in the Hebrew [י]), yet 39:1 calls them "Ishmaelites." Ethnic Midianites were descendants of Abraham through Keturah, as were Medanites (25:2–3), cousins to ethnic Ishmaelites. Scholars have suggested different traditions that were poorly merged (von Rad 1972, 353) or, assuming the unity of the text, two (or three) different groups were among the passing traders, who were working together (Walton 2009a, 124). A third solution views the name "Ishmaelites" "as an epithet for 'nomadic traders' rather than in an ethnic sense" (Sarna 1989, 260; also Ross 2008, 207; cf. Revell 2001). Longacre (1986) arrives at the same conclusion via discourse analysis. Regardless of the specific solution, Judges 8:24 supports the use of "Ishmaelites" and "Midianites" to refer to the same group.

Joseph's Brothers Devastated Jacob (37:29–35)

Highlighting their callous hearts, Joseph's brothers deceived Jacob with Joseph's coat, producing inconsolable grief.

37:29–31. Apparently tending the animals or on some other errand, Reuben returned to rescue Joseph and found him gone. He expressed grief, but the answer to his query was to carry out their plan to deceive Jacob (v. 20). In an eerily familiar routine, they used a slaughtered goat and a garment to deceive their father. The parallel with Jacob's deception of Isaac has grown in scale and consequences, yet similarly, it would accomplish God's will even through evil actions. The perpetrators would face their own consequences and needed transformation.

37:32–35. Jacob's immediate reaction, jumping to the intended conclusion without any prompting, adds to the pathos of the scene. His deep mourning for Joseph intensifies the later demands of Joseph and his brothers' reaction before him in Egypt (44:27–31). It also deepens the perception of the tragic favoritism expressed in the family in the opening scene (37:3–4), especially compared to his lack of response to Dinah's rape (34:5–17, 30).

God's Warning Began to Take Shape (37:36)

God's warning to Abraham of his descendants in Egypt began to take shape as Joseph was sold to a ranking official in Pharaoh's court.

37:36. The note of Joseph's sale to Potiphar prepares for the continuing narrative (Gen. 39), but it also contrasts with the expectations of the brothers. He was not sold into anonymity or oblivion. The tracking of his movements enhances the growing expectation of Yahweh's work and purpose. He safely arrived in Egypt (see v. 28b) and was placed in a prominent household. The outworking of the plan, however, will have to wait for a foundational update on the other high-profile son, Judah.

THEOLOGICAL FOCUS

Though human failings and even God's favor may induce desperate evil actions that cause grievous human suffering, God will quietly orchestrate circumstances to accomplish his purposes.

The Abrahamic covenant primarily provides the theological context for the fourth-generation stories, but the character requirements of God's program underlie those expectations. Questions such as how God will use these miscreants to bring blessing to all the families of the earth (12:3) point us to the clear conflict with Yahweh's explicit notice that these descendants must learn and practice "righteousness and justice" to bring about his promise (18:19). The extreme violations of justice and righteousness beg for God's intervention (ch. 4). God's promise to Abraham that his descendants would reside in Egypt for four hundred years as prelude to the promised fulfillment (15:13) adds intrigue and expectation to the nefarious way that Joseph gets to Egypt, as well as the anticipation of what will happen there.[6]

The initiation of the *toledot* with Joseph's two dreams adds the prospect of great things for him as decreed by God and colors both the tragedies of his sale and the circumstances leading up to that sale. As we have noted, God's obscurity makes the narrative feel much more relatable to human experience, yet the careful ambiguity of the text and clear coincidences prepare rigorously for Joseph's conclusion that all of this has

6 Though God does not explicitly say "Egypt" to Abram, Israel coming out of Egypt would have immediately made the connection and seen the implication.

been orchestrated by God (45:5–9; 50:20). God's work seldom shows clearly until seen in retrospect.

On the other hand, the unrestrained hatred for one's brother has been a repeated motif since Abel's murder, but as with Lamech (4:23–24), it becomes more brazen with time. Without clear answers, the story asks familiar questions about the suffering of the innocent and the frustrations of evil acting with impunity. Answers are sometimes understood in time and sometimes only in eternity.

We also see competing agendas, not necessarily virtuous but combining to bring about a better result (Joseph lives and goes to Egypt), which in the moment reeks of evil yet avoids the catastrophic murder of God's chosen future leader. The way that they accomplish a greater good is unclear, but the still unverified expectation, carefully cultivated since Adam, is that God will somehow bring about his desired end. The God who makes all things good stands behind the promise. Faith looks ahead.

The result of such implications is to recognize the opacity of much of God's work and find his fingerprints in coincidence and unexplained, unexpected outcomes. That is not to say that evil should not be opposed or mourned. Nor does it mitigate the painful outworking of favoritism and strife in families. The evil and pain are very real and must be addressed. Sin arising in human weakness ripens into destructive behaviors and painful consequences. Evil simply requires self-centered pursuits and a focus on immediate, personal concerns. Righteousness and justice can only come through integrity with God's working.

Yet God will also be able to and will deal with failings, even intentional evil. His program will accomplish mitigating work in the lives of his chosen men and women, even as he has already done in the lives of the patriarchs. The initial dreams, as ambiguous as they may appear, offer hope through the eyes of faith in the outworking of God's program, despite rebellion and calamity.

PREACHING AND TEACHING STRATEGIES

Exegetical and Theological Synthesis

This section of Scripture speaks to our listeners through the life of Joseph, the one through whom God would carry out his promises. Joseph's first action ("brought a bad report of [his brothers] to their father" in 37:2) starts the conflict and immediately signals trouble ahead for the promise. Add Israel's favoritism of Joseph and Joseph's dreams, and readers know he is headed for major trouble.

The attitude of his brothers mirrors Genesis 4, and they intend to repeat Cain's murder. Only Reuben saves Joseph's life; Judah contributes to Joseph's "deliverance," stating, "for he is our brother, our own flesh" (37:27). With Judah's recommendation, Joseph is on his way to Egypt, just as God prophesied in Genesis 15:13.

Read in isolation, the story could seem hopeless; read in context, readers see God's powerful hand at work, guiding Joseph to his destiny of leading God's people. The chapter ends by letting readers know where Joseph lands upon arrival in Egypt. He is sold as a slave to "an officer of Pharoah, the captain of the guard" (37:36). At this point, Joseph is only closer to leadership and certainly not in authority over his family, not unless they somehow end up in Egypt. Stay tuned. What we know for sure is that pain and suffering are sometimes part of God's plan for his people. It is not the sign that God has abandoned his own; just the opposite: the cross always goes before the crown.

Preaching Idea

Make no doubt about it: no forms of evil in or around us can stop God's purpose for us.

Contemporary Connections

What does it mean?

Readers may need an explanation as to why God often chooses the unlikely son to accomplish his goals. In the case of Jacob's family, the oldest is not selected, but the seventeen-year-old is. God accomplishes his work in a way that is different from the world's methods. Some postmodern readers may be put off by the way dreams function in this story, but in some places in the world believers often receive guidance from the Lord through dreams. The dream interprets part of the blessing on Joseph's life. The narrative also teaches that the Lord chooses and uses people who need to mature in their faith. The Lord doesn't choose the perfect ones—there are none! He chooses and transforms them along the way.

The random stranger (37:15) and Joseph's brothers Reuben and Judah show that our Lord controls the details of our lives. There are no pure coincidences in God's kingdom. If readers could count the number of factors that brought Joseph to Egypt, they would gain an appreciation for God's sovereignty and providence. For instance, of all places to land in Egypt, Joseph lands in Potiphar's house, "an officer of Pharaoh, the captain of the guard" (v. 36). God was positioning Joseph to take charge, bringing the dream to life.

Is it true?

This is a narrative that makes readers shake their heads with disbelief. Is it true that God could keep his promises through Joseph when he is in such bad shape? Is it true that God controls all the moving parts of this narrative to position Joseph in Egypt? Many of our readers will know the rest of the story. They know Jacob and his sons all end up in Egypt, only to find that Joseph is in command. They know the dreams come true. But in the middle of the narrative, such as in our chapter 37, the author assumes the sovereignty and providence of God. Any reader that needs to be convinced must wait for the rest of the story to unfold.

Now what?

The "So what?" of this narrative is implied through God's ability to move Joseph into the position of power through his and his brothers' sins. The author assumes his readers will see God remaining faithful to his promises to Abraham, Isaac, and Jacob. I cannot think of anything more relevant than God's people being able to trust in the faithfulness of God in the middle of their suffering. There is no humanly possible explanation for Joseph's subsequent success in Egypt. Only God can receive the credit for working his plan to perfection through the imperfections of all major characters. Even when it feels that evil is winning the war, this narrative preaches the opposite.

Creativity in Presentation

Our homiletical idea for this section is: Make no doubt about it: no forms of evil in or around us can stop God's purpose. A commonly experienced illustration may help provide a foundation for the sermon. Many Christians testify to experiencing a surgical procedure for one problem, only to discover another, more deadly condition lurking. Had it not been for the first unpleasant surgery, the second, more deadly disease would not have been discovered.

One way to structure the sermon is through the dream motif:

- The dream as a picture of God's blessing ("Joseph had a dream," 37:5).
- Opposition to the dream ("Here comes this dreamer," 37:19, or "we will see what will become of his dreams," 37:20).
- God's ability to make the dream come true.

This angle depends on our ability to stay focused on the similarities between Joseph's situation and that of our hearers. In the first point, the narrative exposes Joseph's immaturity, Jacob's continued battle with favoritism, and the vengeful attitudes of his sons ("they hated him even more," v. 5). Concerning the second point, you might highlight how impossible this situation was for Joseph. From a human perspective he is as good as dead and, of course, his dream dies with him. And yet in the third point we can highlight how God guided Joseph all the way to Potiphar's house in Egypt. As stated above, list all the variables that had to take place for Joseph to survive this ordeal. List all that God did to remain faithful to himself and his plan.

Another variation focuses on God's veiled working:

- Joseph's entitlement overshadows God's program (37:2–11). God's purpose and plan may be clear and expected, but we may not see it because of the folly of God's people.

- The brother's retaliation frustrates expectations (37:12–35). To make matters worse, human agents, both inside and outside of God's chosen people, may team up to bury any human hope for God's good outcomes.

- God's program shows hope (37:36). But if we look carefully and wait for God's intervention, we will see that God's plans are still viable, even if we feel like they are on life support.

DISCUSSION QUESTIONS

1. How do the main characters all contribute to the tension in the opening scenes?

2. Discuss how Joseph's dream related to God's promised blessing.

3. Review some of the "coincidences" in your history that take on new meaning, as you look back on your lives from the angle of God's providential care and sovereignty.

4. How might you know if a coincidence is merely that, or if it is God working behind the scenes?

5. Why might God allow us to feel the pain of the sin of others without clear insight into how he *might* bring about good?

Genesis 38:1–30

EXEGETICAL IDEA
God prepared the line of Judah for his promise, judging evil and blessing Tamar's righteous actions, granting her children to prepare for greater blessing while exposing Judah's heart to initiate heart change.

THEOLOGICAL FOCUS
God achieves his promises and program both directly by judging sin and indirectly by rewarding the righteous acts of all who value his promises and standards and disciplining his people who stray.

PREACHING IDEA
Neither blatant sin nor borderline righteousness will keep God from fulfilling his promises for the sake of his reputation.

PREACHING POINTERS
While the original audience is left wondering what will happen to the main character, Joseph, they learn about the character of his brother, Judah. Our audience will once again find themselves in this narrative through the examples of Judah and his daughter-in-law Tamar. Judah and his sons provide several "go and do otherwise" examples. Although Judah is clearly in the line of the Messiah, his actions help all listeners by urging us to reflect God's character and remain faithful to him.

Tamar, on the other hand, is more in tune with God's plan and purposes. She is a widow that suffers from Judah's injustice and takes matters into her own hands. While, from our cultural perspective, it is difficult to applaud her methods, she does emerge as the more righteous one. Original and contemporary audiences all get a glimpse of God's judgment as he shows his displeasure with Judah's sons.

If listeners have been traveling with us through this Genesis journey, the way God's promise is carried in Judah's family is another example of God working his plan through unlikely events. He will not be thwarted with respect to fulfilling his promise to bless a people and to bless the nations through that people. His people are not always godly, but God is always working his plan to perfection through imperfect people.

JUDAH'S BACKSTORY: HOW TAMAR SALVAGED THE PROMISE (38:1–30)

LITERARY STRUCTURE AND THEMES

Genesis 38 initially appears to be a digression from the Joseph stories. The expansion of Judah's line, however, will develop both the immediate plot and characterization of Judah for his role in the clan, as well as the bigger purpose of the fourth-generation stories as they set up the future nation of Israel (see Introduction to the Fourth-Generation Narratives above, p. 587).[1] The narrative itself develops in six scenes which work chiastically to draw attention to Judah's line and character (Kim 2012).

A. Judah fathered three Canaanite sons (38:1–5).
  B. Judah quietly withheld Tamar's right (38:6–11).
    C. Tamar shrewdly gained her right with Judah's ID (38:12–19).
    C'. Judah was unsuspecting and without his ID (38:20–23).
  B'. Judah was exposed and declared Tamar righteous (38:24–26).
A'. Judah fathered two additional sons (38:27–30).

Judah's line provides the framework for the chapter, with Judah fathering sons from his Canaanite wife (vv. 1–5) and through Tamar unwittingly replacing the two God had killed (vv. 27–30). The core of the narrative extends Judah's negative characterization and reveals his moment of truth. Beginning with Er's divine capital punishment, Judah's secondborn treated his sister-in-law as a prostitute (vv. 6–11). Tamar then convinced Judah she was a prostitute to gain her rightful children (vv. 12–19). Judah's actions indicated something of the source of his sons' character flaws, exposing the incompatibility of the line with God's promises. Judah heightened his culpability, self-righteously claiming to do his duty (vv. 20–23) until he was uncovered. Declaring his Canaanite daughter-in-law more righteous than he, he had ironically given her what he had previously denied her (vv. 24–26).

The story begins with the descent of Judah (39:1, ירד), mingling the chosen line with the Canaanites. It stands in direct contrast with the following account of Joseph's descent (39:1, ירד) to Egypt, where God would preserve the chosen people from the Canaanite influence (Ross 2008, 214). It ends with a "righteous" Canaanite "prostitute" exposing Judah's heart. God worked in unexpected ways.

This narrative provides the backdrop and impetus for the change in Judah's character, which will be seen in the following accounts. Judah began the story by marrying a Canaanite and providing his oldest son with a (presumably) Canaanite wife before God took the lives of the two older sons for their evil. He showed his hypocrisy before he publicly recognized his own folly. The movement conveys God's work, both explicitly and implicitly, to bring both accountability and justice as he prepares his chosen family for their future responsibilities, foreshadowed in the genealogical frame.

1 Judah's genealogy and character formation are both crucial for the national formation since Judah will receive the blessing of leadership while Joseph will receive the double portion of the firstborn (cf. Wünch 2012).

- ***Judah Fathered Three Canaanite Sons (38:1–5)***
- ***Judah Quietly Withheld Tamar's Right (38:6–11)***
- ***Tamar Shrewdly Gained Her Right with Judah's ID (38:12–19)***
- ***Judah Was Unsuspecting and Without His ID (38:20–23)***
- ***Judah Was Exposed and Declared Tamar Righteous (38:24–26)***
- ***Judah Fathered Two Additional Sons (38:27–30)***

EXPOSITION

Judah's backstory fills the time between Joseph's sale and the brothers' arrival in Egypt, revealing some of the activities of the family left in Canaan, suggesting the passage of that time and creating suspense (Wenham 1994, 363). The formal outcome of the narrative with Judah's line prepares for the broader expectation of the Abrahamic promise of descendants to bring blessing to all nations and the (Davidic) monarchy to Israel (49:10; cf. Ruth 4:18–22; 1 Chron. 2:4–15).[2] The ethos of the narrative, however, shows the immediate danger for the family becoming Canaanized, both in their identity, as Judah married a Canaanite, and their morality, as God judged both Er and Onan for evil and Judah self-righteously oppressed and accused his daughter-in-law. Even as the line grows toward the promised nation, the promise of blessing to all nations through a righteous people (Gen. 18:18–19) appears to be in jeopardy.

The contextual links for the narrative highlight the moral tensions as once again the perpetrator of deception, Judah, who deceived his father, became the deceived with similar instruments (a garment and a goat), driving him to publicly acknowledge his culpability as he experienced talionic justice. At the same time, his moral bankruptcy, which mirrored in his two evil sons, pictured in his proposition of a prostitute, and coupled with his self-righteous pronouncement upon Tamar, will be emphasized by Joseph's integrity in the face of his much more intense temptation with Potiphar's wife in the next episode (Mathews 2005, 704).[3] The impact of his confession will only become apparent when the narrative reveals his change of heart with his father and brothers, which must occur soon after his lessons from Tamar (chs. 43–44).

Judah Fathered Three Canaanite Sons (38:1–5)

Taking a Canaanite wife, Judah fathered three sons.

38:1–5. The specific timing of the narrative is not clear, but "at that time" (v. 1) puts it in the general time frame of the preceding events. It is possible to fit the events into the time between Joseph's sale and the brothers' arrival in Egypt, culminating with the birth of the twins in the same year that the family all went down to Egypt (cf. 45:6; 46:12; Cassuto 1973, 32–40). If Cassuto is right, the significance of the timing becomes apparent as we consider Judah's character and transformation. The minimum of twenty years for the events of this chapter would fill the approximate twenty-two years of Joseph's absence before the brothers recognize him in Egypt, with Judah's self-revelation coming shortly before the famine. The strong contrast in Judah's actions, the placement in the text, and the short turnaround for him chronologically suggest that this event provided a catalyst for his change

2 Sarna (1989, 264) notes the numerous names of people and places that also situate the line of Judah with the later territory of Judah, as well as the Davidic line.

3 Numerous connections with the previous and following accounts have been well documented by various commentators, including themes, catchwords and catchphrases, and specific contrasts and comparisons (e.g., Cotter 2003, 278; Hamilton 1995, 431).

of heart and help to explain his actions toward Jacob, Benjamin, and Joseph (Steinmann 2019, 365–66).[4] Judah's makeover required God's exquisitely timed work, preparing his plan for his emerging nation.

In contrast to Joseph, who was "brought down" to Egypt (twice in 39:1, from ירד), Judah "went down" from his brothers (v. 1, from ירד) and married a Canaanite, the specific fear of Abraham (24:3) and frustration of Jacob and Rebekah (26:35; 27:46; cf. Deut. 7:3). With the family fracturing in Canaan, Judah fathered three children in Chezib, which ironically comes from a root meaning "lie" or "deceive" (*HALOT* s.v. "כזב" 467–68), a key theme in the narrative. The children born there would be judged "wicked" in the eyes of Yahweh (Er and Onan, Gen. 38:7, 10) or assumed to be so in Judah's judgment (Shelah, v. 11, though Judah may have been placing the blame on Tamar). Judah's legacy began with three sons and serious questions regarding their fitness to carry on the Abrahamic promise. After God's remedial work, it would end with three sons and indications that the family was moving back onto the right trajectory.

Judah Quietly Withheld Tamar's Right (38:6–11)

When God judged his two oldest sons with death, Judah, fearing for Shelah, withheld him from Tamar, exiling her to her father's house to wait for her right.

38:6–7. Without comment, the narrative fast-forwards from the sons' births to the marriage of the oldest son, Er. Judah arranged his marriage to a local Canaanite.[5] The irony here is that they are fully merging with the locals. Not only did they marry outside the clan, but Judah's sons were now acting like the Canaanites (following in the steps of their mother?), threatening the promise to Abraham, and, as becomes clear, were outclassed morally by Tamar.

With added irony, Er's name, possibly meaning "protected" or "watchful" (*HALOT* s.v. II "עֵר" 876), spells "wicked" in reverse (רַע), the cause of God's judgment on him (v. 7). The text does not express his specific sin, but God put him to death. God's judgment reveals the very real danger of God's chosen line as they mix with the Canaanites and God's intervention to maintain the future of his chosen people. This section will bring the only explicit mention of Yahweh in the pericope, though God's working will be evident throughout, as with Joseph, in the unexplained and unexpected.

38:8–10. According to the current customs broadly across the ancient world and codified later in the Torah (Deut. 25:5–10), Judah required his second-born to take Tamar as his wife to "perform the duty of a brother-in-law to her and raise up offspring for [his] brother" (v. 8). The common custom provided a means both to maintain the line and inheritance rights of the dead husband and to provide for the care of the widow, who would be fully dependent

4 In fact, Clifford (2004) goes so far as to argue that Judah was the first to see God bringing good out of evil as a result of this experience (38:26) and became the catalyst for Joseph understanding God's role. Kruschwitz (2012) argues that this narrative provides a paradigm that allows the reader to more fully understand the plot and implications of the Joseph narratives to follow. Recognizing God at work here allows the reader to see more clearly the working of God, even before Joseph declares it to his brothers, and to understand the implications more fully when he does (45:5–9).

5 The text does not state her ethnicity. Mathews (2005, 715) argues that Tamar was most likely Israelite since ethnicity is not mentioned, in contrast to Judah's wife. It may be just as likely that the silence implies she was Canaanite (Steinmann 2019, 361), since Judah was clearly not concerned with family protocols. Either way, she would be willing to impersonate a Canaanite prostitute for her righteous cause.

on others for her livelihood. Onan refused to fulfill his duty, though he used her for his own pleasure, ejaculating on the ground (v. 9). The narrator's insight into his motivation, knowing "the child would not be considered his" (v. 9), likely indicates his desire to gain the title of the deceased's inheritance rights now that the firstborn was dead (Westbrook 1991, 76).[6]

Levirate Marriage

Levirate marriage was commonly practiced across the ancient world, with laws known from both the Hittite and Assyrian cultures (see Walton 2009a, 125–26, where he quotes the relevant Middle Assyrian and Hittite laws). Not only would the brother be required to fulfill the responsibility, but, if necessary, the father-in-law would be responsible to fulfill it (Hittite Law 193, cited by Walton 2009a, 126). It was to be practiced, not merely to care for the widow, preserve a "financial investment" in her, maintain a family alliance between two families, or preserve the dead man's memory, but more importantly to maintain a successor to the estate of the dead man and the resulting property rights (Westbrook 1991, 71–77).

Onan's intent to rob his sister-in-law of children added to the gravity of his wickedness, drawing God's judgment of death on him as well. His callous habit, then, was essentially incest, because he was not fulfilling his responsibility but only using Tamar (Sarna 1989, 267), bringing the death penalty (cf. Lev. 20:10). As such, he used Tamar as a common prostitute for his own gratification. Rather than bringing blessing on the nations of the earth, Judah's line was bringing cursing. God's judgment, clarified by the narrator, justly dealt with Judah's sons and protected his plan for his people and the nations.

TRANSLATION ANALYSIS 38:9
"Whenever" (ESV, NET, NIV, etc.) better expresses the Hebrew (וְהָיָה אִם־בָּא) than "when" (NASB95, NCV, NKJV, RSV), which could be understood as a single event.

38:11. Because the youngest son was not yet old enough to marry, Judah sent Tamar back to her father's house until he grew up. The narrator, however, again reveals the motivations behind the actions. While no grief or mourning for his sons was recorded (in contrast to Jacob for Joseph), Judah was concerned for the life of his youngest. Though he may have recognized God's judgment (and so considered Shelah to be endangered for his evil), his banishing of Tamar to her father's house suggests he blamed her (Mathews 2005, 716). Judah, fearing the loss of his last son, risked the lineage of Abraham, his blessing, and God's purpose for the line. At the same time, however, he violated his responsibilities as father-in-law.

Judah was not willing to care for Tamar and relegated her to an impossible existence. She would be in her father's house but without options, as the betrothed to Shelah, Judah's youngest (cf. Cotter 2003, 283). Judah had no intention of fulfilling that obligation to her. Ironically, he seemed to believe his line would die out if Shelah married her, yet because he betrothed her to Shelah, it would die out if he did not (O'Callaghan 1981, 79). One might expect God to intervene with Judah as he had with Er and Onan, but he did not. God appeared silent, much as he seems to be at crucial times in the Joseph stories (Kruschwitz

6 Westbrook explains Onan's actions as more than meanness toward Tamar. If he gave her children, he would lose the right to the inheritance of the firstborn, but if he refused to perform the levirate, Judah could give her to Shelah instead, keeping Onan from the share of the firstborn. He had to pretend to take her and make sure she stayed barren to inherit the share himself.

2012, 399). The moral descent of Judah and his sons from God's purpose for Abraham's family endangered their existence and the promise of progeny and purpose for the line of Abraham through Judah.

Tamar Shrewdly Gained Her Right with Judah's ID (38:12–19)

After Judah's wife died, recognizing Judah's duplicity, Tamar deceived Judah into thinking she was a prostitute, providing her right and leaving behind his ID.

38:12–14. The moral descent of the family seems to hit bottom as Judah's unnamed wife died, and he was lured into an unwitting relationship with his daughter-in-law. Again, significant time passed, marking a new scene and a new stage of life for both Judah and Tamar. Judah was now a widower, and Tamar recognized that he had no intention of fulfilling his promise to her, remedying her widowhood and childlessness and maintaining his own family line. With his formal mourning over, Judah headed for a cultural time of celebration at the sheepshearing, when there would be feasting, drinking, and, commonly, prostitution (Walton 2009a, 126).

His plans were anonymously relayed to Tamar. Removing her widow's garments, she put on a "veil" that covered her face (v. 14). Taking a seat near the entrance to Enaim, she was conspicuously identifiable to him as a prostitute when he passed on his way to the shearing. Moses clarified her motivation, that she was attempting to gain what was promised to her because she realized that Judah had no intention of giving her what was rightfully hers through Shelah. She risked her reputation and life because she valued children and, indirectly at least, the promise of Abraham.

38:15–19. Judah saw her and assumed she was a prostitute.[7] While Onan had wickedly treated her as a prostitute, Tamar tricked Judah into treating her as a prostitute. As with Onan, Judah used her for his own pleasure. In contrast to Onan, Judah unwittingly fulfilled her rightful expectation that he had conspired to keep from her. The text clearly declares his ignorance of her identity, absolving him of intentional incest and so the death penalty (Lev. 20:12) and explaining his self-righteous reaction to her pregnancy.

Tamar shows her careful planning by requiring his identification as a pledge. Ironically, Judah would again use the term with his father when he pledged his own life in lieu of Benjamin's life in Genesis 43, showing the change in his character and drawing attention to the role of this passage in his transformation. In this case, a goat is the promised payment, again drawing attention to Judah's deception of his own father (and the escalating family flaw going back to Abraham's and Isaac's deceptions and Jacob's deception of Isaac). In the last three cases, a garment plays a central role in the deception, as well as the sight (or lack) of the one deceived. The result is a building sense of talionic justice in which God will use circumstances to repay the perpetrator and teach an important lesson.

The pledge Tamar required amounted to clear identification, which Alter (1981, 9) calls "a kind of ancient Near Eastern equivalent of all of a person's major credit cards." While he would not be subjected to identity theft, it was more damning when he was exposed in his hypocrisy and abuse of his daughter-in-law. As the center of the narrative, the scene relates the low point of Judah's character and presents

7 Mathews (2005, 718) notes the irony here. Because Middle Assyrian law forbade a woman from wearing a veil unless she was married (citing MAL §40, *ANET* 183), "The irony of the veil was that it not only hid her identity but it also could have signaled that she had been given in pledge to another, namely, Shelah."

an initially mixed evaluation of Tamar.[8] She was willing to risk everything for the hope of obtaining her desired child, even stooping to impersonating a prostitute to trick Judah into giving her what she rightfully deserved.

Identity Sealed

The "signet" (38:18) was a seal, giving his identity and conveying his authority and name to whatever it was applied to or, as here, his "legal obligation" to fulfill the pledge (Hallo 1985, 24). While it could have been either a cylinder seal or a stamp seal, the request for the cord suggests the cylinder, which had a hole in it to attach it with a cord around one's neck. The staff would likewise represent his identity and authority in his role within the family and clan, likely with a carved top (cf. Amar and Sukenik 2021; Walton 2009a, 127).

Cylinder seal from the third dynasty of Ur (approximately 21st century BC). The seal was drilled and could be worn on a cord.

As with Abimelech before both Abraham and Isaac (chs. 19; 26), the foreigner had greater

Cylinder seal impression

righteousness in the understanding of appropriate behavior before God than the heir of the promise. In each case they would be blessed in their response. For Tamar, she was blessed with sons, a gift of God (cf. 29:31–30:24), and celebrated throughout history (Ruth 4:12; Matt. 1:3), from the only occasion Judah would have relations her (Gen. 38:26). With her mission accomplished as far as she could control it, Tamar returned to her outward show of widowhood. Her actions expose her sole intent to recover what rightfully belonged to her.

Though the narrative does not directly mention Yahweh at this point, the circumstances reveal his working behind the scenes. As with the anonymous man directing Jacob in

8 The initial Israelite reader may have had a mixed response here until Judah cleared her, since the role of the father-in-law as the levirate husband was not included in the later biblical law (Deut. 25:5–10) even though it was part of Judah's society, judging from the Middle Assyrian law (see sidebar "Levirate Marriage," p. 608).

chapter 37, an anonymous report told Tamar of Judah's intent. Her plan went without a hitch, even though many things could have derailed it. The strongest declaration of God's intervention, however, comes with the simple statement that Judah "went in to her, and she conceived by him" (v. 19). God blessed with children and withheld them as he saw fit (29:31–30:24). His promise would continue through Judah, through one God chose that valued the gift. Judah would have to acknowledge her righteousness.

Judah Was Unsuspecting and Without His ID (38:20–23)

With Judah's friend unable to find the prostitute and recover Judah's ID, Judah assumed he had done his duty.

38:20–23. Judah sent his friend back to retrieve his pledge from the "prostitute," but he was unable to find her. While Judah's motivation is specifically stated—he wanted his identification back—when Hirah could not find her, Judah's consolation was that he had tried to keep his bargain by sending the goat. His response is pointed "unwitting irony," since he had no intention of keeping his responsibility to his daughter-in-law but tried to keep it with a Canaanite prostitute and, in so doing, fulfilled his social responsibility with Tamar (Cotter 2003, 286).

Judah's perception of her as a "prostitute" (זֹנָה, 38:15) shifts for the reader when Hirah searched for her as a "cult prostitute" (קְדֵשָׁה, v. 21). While it may be that Hirah was simply being more culturally sensitive and appropriate in his search (Bird 1989a, 126) or using the Canaanite viewpoint (Sarna 1989, 269), when he returned to Judah, he repeated his description of her as a "cult prostitute" (v. 22). Judah's initial, cruder description (v. 15) implies his base motivations and reinforces the reader's impression of Judah's sordid character, in contrast to Hirah's more culturally acceptable description.

Judah Was Exposed and Declared Tamar Righteous (38:24–26)

Discovering Tamar's pregnancy and self-righteously judging her with death, Judah was exposed by his ID, revealing her righteous response to his duplicity.

38:24. Another time marker sets the stage for the developing story. In three months, Tamar's pregnancy became obvious. The disturbing news jarred Judah, raising his self-righteous anger. The report identified Tamar as having "been immoral" (ESV) or "turned to prostitution" (NET), resulting in pregnancy. The verb used here repeats the root (זנה) from Judah's initial perception of Tamar (v. 15), ostensibly emphasizing the heinous nature of her act since she was betrothed to Shelah, yet reinforcing Judah's mistakenly base view of her and his resulting culpability. The repetition of "daughter-in-law" (38:11, 16, 24) and "father-in-law" (38:13, 25) reinforces the irony, continually reminding the reader of their relationship and the elephant in the room. Judah had forced her into this position, and she was desperately trying to preserve what was rightfully hers.

> *TRANSLATION ANALYSIS 38:24*
> Bird argues that the verb does not refer specifically to prostitution but to fornication in general and so is not a direct wordplay on her ruse (Bird 1989b, 75–94), supporting the more general "been immoral" of the ESV (see HALOT, s.v. "זנה" 275, 1. "commit fornication"). The root, however, is the same, and the implication would be clear in the Hebrew without requiring the specific meaning of the verb, which Bird (1989a, 124) recognizes, noting the intended irony.

In tragic contrast to the second scene, in which God brought a just sentence of death for evil, Judah leveled his harsh, unjust sentence. Because she was betrothed to Shelah, her perceived offense carried the death penalty in later biblical law as well (Deut. 22:21).

In biblical law, however, burning was reserved for only the most serious high-profile offenses (Lev. 20:14; 21:9).[9] Of course, the accomplice in the adultery should also bear the same penalty, setting up Judah for his reversal.

38:25–26. The execution of Judah's judgment only revealed Tamar's courage and forethought more clearly. Only when Judah brought the public accusation and punishment did she reveal his complicity, slyly asking him to identify the father of the children by the pledge she had secured. Again recalling the deception of Jacob by Judah, she used the same verbiage to ask Judah to identify (הַכֶּר־נָא, "please identify") the seal, cord, and staff as Judah used for Jacob to identify Joseph's coat.[10] Whether she knew the act of Judah previously or whether it was God's intervention, Judah recognized the pledge. The words he had used to deceive unmasked him as the perpetrator, in an effective talionic intervention (cf. Alter 1981, 10). By 42:21, the whole family recognized the implications. God was at work. Judah received appropriate repayment for his deception of his father and duplicity toward his daughter-in-law.

Judah's immediate response absolved Tamar, declaring her to be "in the right" (NCV, NJPS) suggesting both her moral standing ("righteous," ESV) and her more appropriate actions (cf. *HALOT*, s.v. צדק 1003). While later biblical law would not include the father-in-law in levirate marriage to remedy her widowhood and childlessness, contemporary laws did include the father-in-law as a possible source of offspring to resolve her barrenness (see sidebar, "Levirate Marriage," p. 608). Judah specifically connected her act with rectifying his injustice to her by not giving Shelah as her husband (38:26, see also vv. 11, 14), verifying her motivation. Since she was being led out to be executed, her missive to Judah would have been at least somewhat public. Judah's acknowledgment spared her life and reputation while accepting the indictment on himself.[11]

TRANSLATION ANALYSIS 38:26

Judah's response is generally understood as a comparative evaluation that he bears greater responsibility than she does so that she displays greater moral virtue ("more righteous than I," ESV, NIV; or "more in the right than I," NRSV, NJPS; cf. Reimer, צָדַק, *NIDOTTE* 3:747–48). However, given contemporary law, he was likely declaring her innocent, "She is in the right, *not* I" (citing this as an example of "comparison of exclusion," WOC, 265; cf. Clifford 2004, 530). Wenham (1994, 369) argues that "righteous" here (צְדָקָה) denotes "innocent," but Clifford (2004, 531) notes the context is not formally judicial as much as it recognizes the larger right of the woman and design of God, so she has "carried out the divine purpose of propagating Judah's family." She was, then, "righteous." Tamar was absolved, and her life was spared.

The pledge would likely have been visible to those involved, so his confession was somewhat forced and not necessarily indicative of full repentance, but the final statement indicates a changing expectation for Judah. At least he did not continue to take advantage of her. Any further evaluation will have to wait for more information in the narrative.

---

9 Similar ancient Near Eastern laws at the time of Jacob also reserved burning for egregious offenses (Hamilton 1995, 449), though Sarna (1989, 269) suggests it may have been common Canaanite practice.

10 Numerous commentators draw attention to the parallel scenes with the same three verbs in order, "sent" (שׁלח), "identify" (נכר), and "recognized" (נכר), which Cassuto (1973, 30–31) calls an "internal nexus" showing the integral connection of this chapter to the context.

11 As O'Callaghan (1981, 79) aptly notes, Judah and Tamar are contrasted with outward righteousness (Judah) and an evil heart vs. an appearance of evil (Tamar) who is vindicated with pure motives.

Judah Fathered Two Additional Sons (38:27–30)

Tamar provided Judah two additional sons in an unusual birth alluding to God's intervention.

38:27–30. With the final time marker, Moses marks the birth, recalling Jacob and Esau (25:24) with the identical announcement: "there were twins in her womb" (וְהִנֵּה תְאוֹמִים בְּבִטְנָהּ, 38:27). As with Jacob and Esau, they appeared to struggle in the womb, and the second to appear would be the child of promise (Matt. 1:3). The allusion confirms God's intervention and use of Tamar for his promise despite her background and Judah's abuse of her. God provided the descendants that would replace the firstborn line and inheritance rights, preserving her name in the line of promise (Ruth 4:12; 1 Chron. 2:4; Matt. 1:3).

THEOLOGICAL FOCUS

God achieves his promises and program both directly by judging sin and indirectly by rewarding the righteous acts of all who value his promises and standards and disciplining his people who stray.

While God's working was obvious in the initial stage of the narrative, he moved behind the scenes for the remainder, showing his hand only in the outworking of Tamar's plan, providing opportunity and children. At the beginning, and for the first time on record, God individually judged evil with death, underlining the dangers of the culture to his chosen people and their future. Though Moses made it clear for the reader, it is uncertain how clear God's judgment was for Judah and his family. At least for the reader, the possible consequences of sin must be recognized, producing appropriate fear of God. The outworking of Judah's Canaanite marriage and his failed leadership of his sons also forms the appropriate background to Moses's command to teach God's instructions to one's children (Deut. 6:2, 7–9) and Judah's tragic failure to follow God's instruction to Abraham to command his children "to keep the way of the Lord by doing righteousness and justice" to experience the promises to Abraham (Gen. 18:19).

Judah himself did not fully realize the implications of God's judgment, as we can see in his response. Spurning his responsibility to Tamar, he feared the loss of his son more than Yahweh's promise to have children and maintain his line for the blessings of Abraham's offspring. Humanity commonly fears the wrong things, being more concerned with the immediate and obvious to us, rather than the much more significant but less obvious promise and expectation of our King. Our resulting foolish actions bring greater pain to ourselves and those around us and necessitate God's remedial response to refine our hearts and make us useable for his greater purposes and planned work. But the good news is that he does redeem sinners. Judah was a sinner,[12] yet Judah recognized his fault (38:26), became the leader of his family (chs. 43–44), and received the royal promise over his brothers, including Joseph (49:8–12).

Alternatively, Tamar was willing to risk everything to maintain her rightful place in the line and plan of Yahweh through Judah. How much of God's plan and promises she understood is not clear, but her actions aligned with faith in the promise and the overarching purposes of Yahweh to bring his blessing through the descendants of Abraham. Clearly, she understood Judah's deceit and her right to further his line and the memory and inheritance of her dead husband. God would use her risk far more than she could expect or ever understand. He would right the wrong and defend the cause of the oppressed.

12 To quote Clifford (2004, 524), "He sinned in marrying a Canaanite, in visiting a prostitute, and in peremptorily ordering the burning of his daughter-in-law. He sinned by failing to ensure that the levirate law was observed to benefit his daughter-in-law Tamar" (cf. Curtis 1991, 252–56).

God, then, also worked through the actions of a powerless and wronged woman who had no clear guarantees but was willing to work for what was rightfully hers. On the one hand, it raises the question of the role of self-effort and manipulation in achieving God's purposes. On the other, it shows that God can use righteous actions that may appear wrong and be wrong in another context. In both questions the reader must factor in her degree of understanding of truth and God's view of the heart. He honored a Canaanite acting as a prostitute above his chosen heir to the promise who self-righteously oppressed the powerless. Honoring Tamar with children, God certified her "right," in the words of Judah (38:26) to her role in what would become the line of God's monarch, Christ.

As we see consistently throughout the narratives of Abraham and his descendants, humanity does not naturally move toward righteousness, honoring God. Rather, we all struggle with our fallenness (depravity) in the flesh. Even those chosen and blessed by God naturally move toward the pagan culture around them. Our wellbeing and God's plan of redemption require God's constant intervention and consistent use of the least expected and blessing on the outcast and lowly. He must continually be working to rehabilitate the perspective and character of his chosen instruments to accomplish his greater redemption of his fallen images.

PREACHING AND TEACHING STRATEGIES

Exegetical and Theological Synthesis

Begin sermon and teaching preparation by noting the contrasting characters of Joseph and Judah. Judah and his family do not meet God's requirements for being a conduit of blessing. The narrative makes this clear with Judah's attachment to "the daughter of a certain Canaanite" (38:2). The offspring of that union are also described as "wicked in the sight of the Lord" resulting in "the Lord [putting] him to death" (v. 7). The same is said of the other brother (v. 10). Then there is Judah's injustice toward his daughter-in-law, Tamar, and his own immorality (vv. 11, 15–16). Finally, Judah's un-God-like character shines through with his self-righteous response to the news about Tamar's pregnancy (v. 24).

Tamar knew enough of Judah's character to know he would take the bait. God knew that this kind of family could not accomplish his will for his world. Left alone, only curse, not blessing, would result. And yet, Judah is going to factor prominently in God's plan; a reset was necessary. The method God used made it clear that Judah was experiencing justice because of his past deception (the goat and the garment in 37:31 and 38:14, 17). God was not discarding Judah, but he was going to use Tamar and her deception to continue the line of blessing (v. 18, "and she conceived by him").

Judah's assessment of Tamar is theologically loaded: "She is more righteous than I" (v. 26). In God's plan, Tamar and her secondborn twin find their way into the line of blessing (cf. Ruth 4:12; Matt. 1:3). All our listeners should quickly assess whether their character lines up with Judah's or Tamar's, especially when they see God's reaction to the former. God will mercifully transform his own so that they are fit to work his plan. That includes training our children and grandchildren in the ways of God. That also includes our constant, glad submission to his Spirit so that we are conduits of blessing and not curse.

Preaching Idea

Neither blatant sin nor borderline righteousness will keep God from fulfilling his promises for the sake of his reputation.

Contemporary Connections

What does it mean?

Let your listeners know that, in the larger context, this break from the Joseph story is designed to contrast his character with that of his brother Judah and prepare for the role of Judah. Both are separated from their brothers, but for different reasons. Inform them that the narrator's description of Judah's two sons, "wicked" (vv. 7, 10), clearly shows that they cannot be in the line of blessing. Their wickedness will be contrasted with Tamar's degree of righteousness. The narrative makes it clear that Judah is deceived in the same way he deceived his own father. The lives of the patriarchs include deception an embarrassing amount of times! It is important to show the significance of Tamar and Perez for the plan of God. It is God's way of honoring Tamar's effort to keep the line of blessing going for the glory of God.

The narrative means something by contrasting not only Joseph and Judah, but also Judah and Tamar. In Tamar's case, for instance, if she is a Canaanite, God teaches us that one's history or pedigree is not important. The main thing is whether a person trusts in his plan. Our listeners can see themselves and their character in this narrative, including the graciousness of God allowing them to adjust as needed before leaving worship.

Is it true?

One of the things our listeners may not readily believe is that God would honor Tamar's deception. They will need to see her in contrast to Judah. Judah should be ashamed of himself and his sons for their character. Judah should never have placed Tamar in that position. It may be difficult to believe that Tamar finds her way into the line of blessing with such a deceptive method. But let's remember how Jacob arrived at the blessing. And then, it is also true that Judah ends up where he should have been all along, the father of the sons according to Levirate marriage laws of the day. While you might not say to your listeners, "Go and do likewise," you are able to point out that, in comparison to Judah, his assessment of her is accurate: "She is more righteous than I" (v. 26). For listeners who like things black-and-white, this narrative shows how God works his plan despite messy morality. We know from places like Ruth 4:12 and Matthew 1:3 that Judah, Tamar, and Perez find themselves in *the* line of blessing.

Now what?

This narrative can be applied by helping our congregants assess their own fitness for being conduits of God's blessing. All readers learn what Judah and his sons are like; we see what this does to the powerless, such as Tamar. We see what injustice does: it results in more curse than blessing. We learn how God judges sin—look at what he did to Judah's sons; look at how he administered appropriate judgment on Judah after what he had done to his own father. We see this and say, "That is not the way I want to relate to God!" No, better to find ourselves in Tamar's character, even though we may struggle with her method. Finally, there is comfort in knowing that, as each of us struggle to walk with God in this badly broken world, God graciously transforms us into characters who can function as conduits of blessing in his world.

Creativity in Presentation

A fitting illustration for this section is to find an example of brothers that are complete opposites. This will help explain the contrast between the characters of Joseph (the chapter before and chapters after) and Judah. This can help you set the immediate context for this chapter where Judah appears out of nowhere to interrupt what is happening with Joseph. Both Joseph and Judah will play important, though different, roles as the narrative moves forward. The character study contributes to the larger story, which shows God working his plan to bless his people and make them a blessing to the nations.

Neither blatant sin nor borderline righteousness will keep God from fulfilling his promises for the sake of his reputation. Judah is caught in blatant sin; you might label Tamar's action as borderline righteousness. Consider the development of the narrative to create a sermon structure:

- The Lord's plan is in jeopardy due to severe ungodliness. This is a time for all listeners to assess their faith journey with respect to their fight for faith and righteousness. Judah is a poor example of faith, to say the least. He is a critical part of God's plan, but his character needs a major adjustment.
- The Lord makes it clear that he will judge sin and protect his plan. This is a strong deterrent to unbelief and sin. The Lord will not allow his name to be dragged through the mud.
- He also makes it clear that his plan to bless his people will move forward through those who are righteous. Who qualifies as righteous in God's eyes may surprise us. A Canaanite? Yet Tamar presents a delightful example of someone who values the Lord's plan and purposes. She provides tremendous courage to all who suffer injustice; she provides hope as well, as listeners see God honor her creative and risky plan to get back what was taken from her.

Everyone listening to the sermon/lesson can find themselves in this narrative. They will be able to evaluate their lifestyles and their faith that drives them. They will also be able to immediately adjust, for God's glory and their good.

DISCUSSION QUESTIONS

1. Spend a moment tracing Judah's character throughout the Genesis narratives to see the critical position he holds before and after chapter 38. How does chapter 38 fit into the overall story?
2. Many non-Christians and some professing Christians will struggle with God's severe judgment on the two sons. How might you explain his actions?
3. So much application in this chapter hinges on how much of Tamar's actions are the "go and do likewise" variety. Spend some time arguing both sides.
4. How important is Judah's assessment of Tamar in verse 26 ("She is more righteous than I")?
5. Much of the narrative here works with heart issues that are only seen (sometimes dimly) in actions. How do we evaluate our own hearts and open ourselves to God's evaluation of us?
6. What are our valued possessions or relationships that we might attempt to preserve, rather than submit everything to God's righteous standard (Judah trying to save Shelah)?

Genesis 39:1–23

EXEGETICAL IDEA

Yahweh's presence brought Joseph spectacular success both in Potiphar's service as his personal attendant and in prison after being falsely accused when he righteously resisted Potiphar's wife's advances.

THEOLOGICAL FOCUS

While God's presence provides success, righteous living in the face of temptation may include suffering and loss to accomplish God's purposes within his faithful care.

PREACHING IDEA

Success, severe setback, temptation: expect it all with heavy doses of God's powerful presence and loyal love for the faithful.

PREACHING POINTERS

The original audience sees that things are not going well for Joseph, and they have no idea how the Lord is going to fulfill his promises to bless him so he can be a blessing to the nations. Nothing about the opening verse is promising. That is, until we read: "The Lord was with Joseph, and he became a successful man" (v. 2). Very quickly readers begin to see some hope as his master sees God's blessing on Joseph, gives him almost total control over his affairs, and experiences the blessing of God "on all that he had, in house and field" (vv. 3–6). Listeners are encouraged as they learn that the same Lord is with them in a powerful way as they walk with him each day. Their success may vary, depending on what the Lord has gifted them to do, but they will be able to accomplish his will in their sphere of influence.

But, just as quickly, everything appears to come unglued due to a tragic injustice done to Joseph by Potiphar's wife. God puts Joseph to the test, and he passes it with flying colors (v. 9). But God does not spare Joseph from tremendous heartache. Listeners must see that the life of faith, the powerful presence of God, and the ability to perform his will also include hardship. Great comfort comes with belief that, as the Lord did to Joseph, he will also continue to show "his steadfast love and . . . favor" (v. 21). For listeners who value God's kingdom, great encouragement comes from knowing that the Lord's presence guarantees our success in accomplishing his will. This is especially important when we face circumstances like Joseph's, those times when we have no idea of how things will work together for good.

YAHWEH'S BLESSING: PAINFUL RIGHTEOUSNESS AND UNEXPECTED OUTCOMES (39:1–23)

LITERARY STRUCTURE AND THEMES

God's judgment on evil and his exposure of Judah's corruption contrasts brilliantly with his presence with Joseph and blessing on all Joseph did, especially underlining Joseph's righteous response to testing. Following God's preservation of Judah's line through near disastrous corruption, God's presence and blessing frames Joseph's initial events in Egypt, recalling his dreams (ch. 37). Expectations for prosperity and prominence, however, will only haltingly be realized. Startling reversal interrupts Joseph's meteoric rise while affirming God's presence and grace.

God's presence and blessing provide the necessary perspective for the reader, anticipating resolution for Joseph's circumstances and displaying Joseph's character, in contrast to Judah. While it sets up the narratives to follow, the surprising twists teach valuable lessons to the people of God: the deceptive evil and opposition of this world presents tensions and risks in following God. The life of faith is neither predictable nor safe.

A. Yahweh blessed Joseph in Potiphar's house (39:1–6a).
  B. Joseph steadfastly resisted temptation (39:6b–12).
    C. Potiphar's wife falsely accused Joseph to the servants (39:13–15).
    C'. Potiphar's wife slandered Joseph to Potiphar (39:16–18).
  B'. Potiphar imprisoned Joseph (39:19–20).
A'. Yahweh blessed Joseph in prison (39:21–23).

Yahweh's presence and resulting blessing on the patriarchs (21:22; 26:3, 24; 28:15; 31:3) returns to prominence.[1] The frame of Yahweh's presence and blessing complements Joseph's strong moral character and response to Potiphar's wife yet contrasts the startling outcome. On the one hand, Joseph is a model of wisdom, fearing God and turning away from evil (cf. Prov. 1:7; 3:3–4; 5:3; 6:26; Wenham 1994, 377–78), anticipating the righteous sufferer (e.g., Job). Yet, with only hints at the reasons for Joseph's imprisonment within the plan of God, as suggested by Joseph's dreams (39:20), Joseph is left to continue to live faithfully in an ever-darkening life. The reader will sympathize with the tensions between expectations and experience.

The point of the story in the larger framework is less about Joseph individually and more about God's working for his purposes. Or, as Sailhamer (1990, 234) notes, "this is not a story of the success of Joseph; rather it is a story of God's faithfulness to his promises." The narrative focuses, in Joseph's case, on blessing all nations through the descendants of Abraham, Isaac, and Jacob (22:18; 26:4; 28:14). When Potiphar blessed Joseph (promoting him), he was blessed

1 God's presence was consistently obvious to those around the patriarchs, as here with Joseph. Abimelech saw it with Abraham (21:22), as did the later Abimelech with Isaac (26:28). Laban (30:27), Jacob (31:5), Rachel, and Leah (31:16) all saw the outworking of God's presence with Jacob, which God openly declared to Laban (31: 24).

in all that he had (39:5), with no concern for any of it (v. 6). When the keeper of the prison blessed Joseph with responsibility, everything Joseph did succeeded (v. 23) so that the keeper did not have to pay attention to anything in Joseph's charge. The narrative declares God's working and the main characters recognize it, benefitting from God's work through a faithful servant, Joseph.

- ***Yahweh Blessed Joseph in Potiphar's House (39:1–6a)***
- ***Joseph Steadfastly Resisted Temptation (39:6b–12)***
- ***Potiphar's Wife Falsely Accused Joseph to the Servants (39:13–15)***
- ***Potiphar's Wife Falsely Accused Joseph to Potiphar (39:16–18)***
- ***Potiphar Imprisoned Joseph (39:19–20)***
- ***Yahweh Blessed Joseph in Prison (39:21–23)***

EXPOSITION

Joseph's temptation contrasts directly with Judah's sordid treatment of Tamar after her disgrace with his evil sons, adding characterization and tension for the still-to-be-determined family blessing of rule and the dynastic trajectory of Genesis.[2] Tamar also compares with Joseph and contrasts with Potiphar's wife. Both Tamar and Joseph merit favor and blessing from God, implying God's judgment on Potiphar's wife, though for the moment she succeeds.

Setting the stage for Joseph's expected rise to power (fulfilling his dreams), which Joseph would later summarize as divine intervention (45:5–8; 50:17–21), this narrative forms the "theological entrance piece to the Joseph story" (Westermann 2002, 62). As such, it explicitly foregrounds God's working, in anticipation of Joseph's summary. As such it challenges simple explanations of blessing and God's working and intervention in human affairs. It also adds to the existing tensions surrounding God's promise and human experience. As the background for Joseph's concluding conviction that God works good through evil human actions (50:20), Yahweh's intervention, sometimes obvious and sometimes absent, requires thoughtful reflection. Throughout, Yahweh's presence brought Joseph spectacular success, both in Potiphar's service as his personal attendant and in prison after being falsely accused when he righteously resisted Potiphar's wife's advances.

Yahweh Blessed Joseph in Potiphar's House (39:1–6a)

Yahweh was with Joseph in Egypt under Potiphar, giving success in all he did then blessing Potiphar's house when he advanced Joseph.

39:1. Verse 1 introduces the narrative, resuming where chapter 37 left off. The narrator reiterates Joseph's forcible removal to Egypt at the hands of the Ishmaelites (cf. 37:36).[3] The repeated description of Potiphar prepares the reader for what follows, with the focus on Joseph. The scene has shifted to Egypt. Potiphar was an Egyptian officer of Pharaoh, anticipating Joseph's rise in Egypt.

39:2–3. The initial declaration of God's presence with Joseph explains his overall success (v. 2, מַצְלִיחַ), introductory for the full Joseph stories. Here, however, it is repeated specifically in his service to Potiphar (v. 3), setting the stage for the immediate narrative. The initial impression for the reader returns to chapter 37, raising expectations of fulfilling his dreams (vv. 5–9).

2 The initial dynastic role of humanity in God's economy (Gen. 1) with the promise of the "seed" of the woman to crush evil (3:15), followed by the royal genealogies of Gen. 4, 5, and the promise of kings from Abraham (17:6), Sarah (17:16), and Jacob (35:11) all will culminate in Judah's blessing (49:10). Here, though the reader would know the coming promise to Judah, Joseph has the dreams of ruling and the character of a king, bringing tension to the expectations.

3 For the Ishmaelites as an alternative designation for the Midianites, see 37:25–28 and the footnote there, 600, n.5.

It also contrasts directly with chapter 38, since the notice of Yahweh's judgment on the sons of Judah (vv. 7, 10) provide the only other uses of "Yahweh" in the entire *toledot* other than 48:18 in Jacob's blessing.[4] This contrast with Judah's sons and the confirmation of Yahweh's presence foreshadows Joseph's reaction to Potiphar's wife. It also raises expectations of blessing on Joseph for righteous choices that appear disappointed in his imprisonment.

The introductory and final scenes frame the narrative, describing the unique and significant favor of Yahweh on Joseph and those that would favor him.[5] The frame sets expectations for fulfilling Joseph's dreams but also adjusts the reader's view of Joseph's conflict and resulting imprisonment. The repeated phrases in Joseph's imprisonment confirm that Joseph's consequences are not accidental nor outside of Yahweh's purview but within his providential presence (Ross 2008, 217). Painful outcomes for righteous actions, however unexpected, portray success in God's economy because they will further his larger purposes to accomplish his covenant promises to bless all the families of the earth.

39:4–6a. Observing Joseph's tangible success, Potiphar promoted him as his personal attendant, overseeing all his affairs. The progression of events is significant here. Potiphar observed that God gave Joseph success (v. 2) in "all that he did" (v. 3), giving Potiphar such a favorable impression of Joseph that he promoted him to the top of the serving ranks (v. 4).[6] "From the time" Potiphar promoted Joseph (blessing Joseph), Yahweh "blessed the Egyptian's house for Joseph's sake" (v. 5). The narrative then specifies Yahweh's blessing was on all that Potiphar had in the house and the field.[7] Yahweh was keeping his promise to bless the nations through a righteous descendant of Abraham, Isaac, and Jacob, illustrating the role of the nation (cf. 18:19) and how they might benefit those around them as they followed Yahweh (cf. Steinmann 2019, 369). Consequently, Potiphar could release everything into Joseph's care with no concern for anything except "the food that he ate" (39:6).

TRANSLATION ANALYSIS 39:4

The Hebrew verb שׁרת describes personal service and, in royal contexts particularly, refers to personal attendants (Fretheim, שׁרת, *NIDOTTE* 4:256). "Attended him," then (ESV, NRSV), does not adequately clarify the implication of "personal attendant" (NET, NJPS, NLT) or "personal servant" (NASB95, NCV).

TRANSLATION ANALYSIS 39:6a

While the translations consistently take this literally (though the NLT specifies "what kind of food to eat"), commentators have seen this as a euphemism for his wife (Mathews 2005, 732–33), reference to the Egyptian practice of eating apart from foreigners (cf. 42:32; Steinmann 2019, 369), or merely his private affairs (Wenham 1994, 374).

---

4 "The preference for this proper name of the God of Israel, as opposed to the generic ʾelohim, is determined by an underlying intent to emphasize that the unfolding events in the odyssey of Joseph are key elements in God's plan for the people of Israel" (Sarna 1989, 271).

5 These verses share most of their vocabulary, including several identical or nearly identical clauses with the direct parallel in location (Joseph was in the house of his Egyptian master, v. 2, and he was in the house of confinement, v. 20). See verses 21–23.

6 "All" (כֹּל) is repeated five times in four verses, emphasizing both Yahweh's comprehensive work on Joseph's behalf and Potiphar's resulting complete trust of Joseph.

7 Here God's blessing on Potiphar clearly includes prosperity and smooth household processes, as well as probably relationships in the household—all things that an overseer would be expected to manage. It also implies the impact of God's working through his people in his world, even among those that may not acknowledge him.

While the alternatives are possible, the traditional translation makes good sense, emphasizing the control Joseph exercised over nearly all the affairs of Potiphar, except his most private affairs, and his level of trust, motivating Joseph's response to Potiphar's wife. Potiphar's only concerns were minimal at home (what he wanted to eat).

Joseph Steadfastly Resisted Temptation (39:6b–12)

When Potiphar's wife propositioned Joseph, he steadfastly resisted her persistent advances until she tried to force him so that he fled, leaving his coat behind.

39:6b–9. A personal note about Joseph begins a new scene. Joseph is described with the same terms as Rachel (29:17): attractive (יְפֵה) in both "form" (תֹאַר, 39:6b) and appearance (מַרְאֶה). Joseph is the only man with this description in the Hebrew Bible, and Rachel is the only other person described with both terms, drawing attention to possible resemblance (another reason that Jacob was so attached to him; Steinmann 2019, 370). Joseph certainly got Potiphar's wife's attention.

TRANSLATION ANALYSIS 39:6b

The first description, "handsome in form" (יְפֵה־תֹאַר), most likely describes his physique (so "well built," NET, NIV, NJPS, cf. Youngblood, תֹּאַר, *TWOT* 964) rather than appearance (seeming redundancy in "handsome and good-looking," NRSV). The second expression clearly describes his appearance (וִיפֵה מַרְאֶה, ESV), denoting "good looking" (NET) or "handsome" (NCV, NIV, NJPS).

Though she may have said much more, her proposition to Joseph appears brusque. As his master's wife, it comes across more like an order than an enticement. Joseph's refusal, in contrast, lays out his principled rationale with careful logic, displaying his character for all to see.[8] He began with his responsibilities to his master, rehearsing nearly verbatim the description of Potiphar's trust from verse 6. Joseph felt the weight of his full responsibility for everything, and his master had no concerns for any of it. It was a trust. In fact, the only thing Potiphar had withheld from Joseph was his wife! Here Joseph departs from the previous description, which had not mentioned any restriction and only Potiphar's necessary concern with his food.[9] Joseph's reflection on the sole restriction adds to the weight of his decisive motivation. He calls it a "great wickedness" (הָרָעָה הַגְּדֹלָה, v. 9 directly offending God!

Joseph's response recalls Abimelech's response to Abraham (20:9). As noted there (p. 368, n. 2), adultery was called "the great sin" in Egypt (as well as Canaan), bringing the death penalty (Rabinowitz 1959; cf. Moran 1959). It was widely recognized as an offense to the gods, and Joseph did not appeal here to Yahweh, but to the Egyptian community's basic moral compass using the general name for god (or the gods, using Elohim).[10] Joseph

---

8 Jewish tradition views Joseph as a righteous man, but one who struggled with this temptation greatly. His response to Potiphar's wife is understood as too detailed and involved to merely characterize his own righteousness, but he must be talking himself into refusing (Bakon 2013, 171–72). His extensive response, however, functions to display Joseph's character and expose his rationale for refusing in terms that show both his responsibility and his foundational commitment to God. Moses leaves no doubt that his imprisonment is fully undeserved.

9 This progression is one reason some would tie the note on Potiphar's meals with his wife (Mathews 2005, 732–33). It is better, however, to recognize Joseph's conscious boundaries in his service, especially as he lays the foundation for his culminating responsibility.

10 Galpaz-Feller (2004) argues that the penalties in the ancient societies were similar to the biblical law, but the perception of adultery was still very different. In Mesopotamia the law protected the husband and compensated

recognized the heinous nature of this offense, even if she was not concerned with offending her husband.

39:10–12. Though her answer to Joseph was not recorded, she continually pressed him ("day after day," v. 10). It seems that her tactic changed since Joseph would not listen to her, either to "lie beside her or to be with her" (v. 10). Her initial proposition clearly called for intercourse (שִׁכְבָה עִמִּי, see *HALOT* s.v. "שׁכב" 1487, 2.d), v. 7), but now she seems to try to entice him by lying beside her (לִשְׁכַּב אֶצְלָהּ) or being "with her" (לִהְיוֹת עִמָּהּ). "If Joseph could not be stormed he might be coaxed" (Kidner 1967, 202).

TRANSLATION ANALYSIS 39:10

Sarna (1989, 273) notes two possibilities here. The second clause could be parallel to the first clause, both merely depicting physical proximity (citing medieval rabbinics) and so less directly immoral or indicating the final goal, moving from proximity to intercourse, providing "successive states of intimacy" (clearly intercourse in 2 Sam. 13:20; cf. Mathews 2005, 735).

Joseph's character shone when they were alone. That she "caught" him by his garment indicates forceful seizure, such as taking prisoners (v. 12; see Josh. 8:23; 1 Sam. 15:8), capturing a city (Deut. 20:19; Josh. 8:8), or rape (Deut. 22:28). Holding on tightly to Joseph, she repeated her initial order to "lie" with her (Gen. 39:12). Joseph escaped, leaving his garment in her hand.

The Seductress of Proverbs 7

It is hard to miss the similar situation of Proverbs 7:13, when the seductress seizes the "young man lacking sense" (v. 7) and propositions him, leading to his death (vv. 22–23). It is as if Joseph had been reading the sage advice to keep "far from her" (Prov. 6:8). He epitomizes wisdom in many ways, illustrating the expected success. He provides a good illustration of how God works (Josh. 1:8; cf. Gen. 24:56).

TRANSLATION ANALYSIS 39:13

The "garment" (בֶּגֶד) she seized, which he left, has been understood as an "outer garment" (NET; also indicated by "cloak," NIV, NLT; or "coat," NCV) or either "mid-calf shorts" or "a tunic, a long T-shirt" that would have had to have been more forcibly removed (Wenham 1994, 376). The general nature of the term, however, does not allow clear specification (see *HALOT* s.v. "בֶּגֶד" 108; so merely "garment" ESV, NASB95, NJPS), though the outer garment makes good sense of Joseph slipping out of it relatively easily.

Potiphar's Wife Falsely Accused Joseph to the Servants (39:13–15)

Potiphar's wife accused Joseph to her servants of attempted rape, presenting his garment as evidence.

39:13–15. Potiphar's wife immediately schemed to slander Joseph. Whether she felt she needed to get ahead of any possible accusation against her or she merely wanted to retaliate for his rejection of her advances (or both),[11] she used his garment against him for a second time. Her clever story to the servants maximized their commonalities and sympathies, accusing Joseph of attempting what she had tried to force on him. In her report, he

---

him financially. In Egypt it maintained social cohesion rather than dealing with a moral issue before the gods. They would take care of the moral issue in the afterlife.

11 Cf. Sternberg (1987, 423–28) and Alter (1981, 108–13), who provide insightful readings of this scene. In v. 13 Sternberg recognizes the motivation of seeing the danger to herself of Joseph's "egress in undress" and how that could be perceived by observant servants (p. 424). Partly to protect herself, she took the offensive.

attempted rape and left his garment when she screamed.[12]

Her story pitted "us" (the servants and her) against "them" ("he," her husband, and "the Hebrew" man) who were putting them down ("laugh at us"; v. 14). She used both Joseph's different ethnicity and his place in the authority structure against him. She twisted the events to support her story, since no one other than Joseph could dispute her account. Her report of crying out provided the necessary (and generally assumed) alibi for an attempted rape (cf. Deut. 22:25–27). If there is no possible witness, the less powerful is assumed innocent. Of course, neither is there any corroboration of her testimony or second witness to convict him.

Her accusation to the servants is matched, at the center of the narrative, with her accusation to her husband. For him, her story subtly changes to play to Joseph's responsibilities and concerns, also hinting at her agenda. The two tales work together to show her manipulation of the situation and detail the injustice against Joseph. She used both the servants and Potiphar, slandering Joseph with his life on the line.

Potiphar's Wife Falsely Accused Joseph to Potiphar (39:16–18)

When Joseph's master returned, Potiphar's wife accused Joseph of sporting with her with his garment as evidence.

39:16–18. The story Potiphar heard differed in small though significant details from the "same story" (כַּדְּבָרִים הָאֵלֶּה, v. 17) she told the servants. While she still laid the fault at Potiphar's feet,[13] she did not directly accuse Joseph of attempted rape, but rather of "laughing" at her or sporting with her (לְצַחֶק בִּי, v. 17). Here, in contrast with the same term used with the servants (v. 14), her complaint solely focused on advances toward her (heightening the implications of unwanted and inappropriate advances). Joseph was not a "Hebrew man" (lit. transl., אִישׁ עִבְרִי), emphasizing the ethnic disparity to the servants (v. 14), but a "Hebrew slave" (NET, הָעֶבֶד הָעִבְרִי, v. 17), emphasizing his lowly status and Potiphar's responsibility in elevating him. Joseph's garment was still strategically placed beside her to support her story, as if he had left it there after voluntarily removing it in his advances against her.

> *TRANSLATION ANALYSIS 39:17*
> The difficulty of translating the idea of "laugh at me" (ESV) in a way to capture the appropriate inuendo for this context is illustrated by a quick survey of the many ways it is expressed: "humiliate" (NET); "make sport of" (NASB95, NIV); "fool around with" (NLT); "mock" (NKJV); "insult" (NRSV); "shame" (NCV); "dally with" (NJPS). The term could connote sexual advances (cf. 26:8 and Exposition there, p. 449), though mocking would be another clear option and would at least express demeaning behavior. "Make sport" may be as effectively ambiguous as any term.

Potiphar Imprisoned Joseph (39:19–20)

Enraged, his master put Joseph in prison.

12 Technically, in Egypt rape was not a separate crime and in fact was only a crime if the woman was married (Renate 2015, 231). We emphasize the crime, speaking from a modern perspective, as rape.

13 Sternberg (1987, 426) shows her adjusted report to Potiphar by shifting the way she used the intent of Joseph to "laugh at me" (see Translation Analysis) shrouding her accusation against Potiphar so that it could be taken innocently but would still hint at the point. Her accusation includes several ambiguities designed to maximize impact. To "come in" to her could be either simply to approach her or have intercourse with her (cf. Alter 1981, 110; Sternberg 1987, 426).

39:19–20. Verse 19 reports what Potiphar heard. The only thing noted was the action of his "servant," showing "his special slave" had "betrayed the position of trust to which he [had] been raised" (Sternberg 1987, 427). Potiphar's immediate anger reacted to the report of Joseph's treatment of his wife, also suggesting that his response was appropriate to the reported crime. Since he did not have Joseph executed immediately, the report fell short of the capital offense of attempted rape.[14] Because Potiphar's wife avoided directly accusing Joseph of attempted rape, she may have intended to leave the door open to continue seducing him while showing him her power (Sarna 1989, 275–76). Regardless of the human reason, "the hidden hand of God preserves the young man's life once again" (Mathews 2005, 737). Joseph's consignment to prison effectively ended any further pursuit from Potiphar's wife. Potiphar put Joseph into the prison used for the king's prisoners, which he himself had authority over and where he could presumably keep an eye on Joseph (see 40:3).

Yahweh Blessed Joseph in Prison (39:21–23)

Yahweh was with Joseph in prison, granting Joseph success so that the warden put everything into Joseph's oversight.

39:21–23. Reflecting with clear repetition the opening scene of God's presence and blessing in Joseph's life with Potiphar, the concluding scene confirms God's continued presence with and success for Joseph in prison. As if to answer the objection that Joseph's false accusation and unjust imprisonment must mean God was somehow judging Joseph or had abandoned him, the narrative adds that Yahweh not only was with him, but "showed him steadfast love" (חֶסֶד, v. 21). The term often expresses God's "faithfulness, goodness, [or] graciousness" toward people (*HALOT* s.v. II "חֶסֶד" 336–37), indicating a "deep and enduring commitment," helping when one is unable to help himself (Baer and Gordon, חֶסֶד, *NIDOTTE* 2:212). The obvious conflict with the circumstances and the way Joseph felt about being imprisoned without cause (40:14–15) provides both hope for the reader for Joseph's future and a pause to consider one's expectation from God's presence and resulting success. God had not abandoned Joseph nor was he outside of his continued care.

While the initial scene clearly declared God's blessing on all that Potiphar had (39:6), which we viewed as fulfillment of his promise to the patriarchs, the same is not said of the prison. God's blessing provided the means for Potiphar and his household to recognize the extraordinary opportunity of relating to Joseph's God in contrast to their normal existence. God's working in the prison will allow Joseph to move to the next stage of God's purpose through his interaction with the Pharaoh's servants.

God was still at work and his program was still on track. Joseph's dreams, the elephant in the prison, are still within God's purview. In fact, though hidden from Joseph's view, the wider context allows the reader to recognize, in retrospect, the necessity of the prison stint for God's larger purposes, to bring about the eventual result.

14 Potiphar may well not have believed her report fully, between the ambiguities and the character of Joseph (and his probable disputing the charges), as numerous commentators have noted (e.g., Wenham 1994, 377). Wells (2015) argues that the penalty typically stated in the law throughout the ancient world, and similarly in the OT, was the maximum possible, but that lesser penalties were often allowed. The lesser penalty would be up to the discretion of the aggrieved husband, for whatever reasons he may have, whether doubts as to the veracity, pity on the offender, or any other consideration.

Comparison Between Opening and Closing Scenes of Genesis 39	
39:2–6	**39:20–23**
39:2—"The LORD was with Joseph" 39:3—"His master saw that the LORD was with him" 39:(2), 3—"the LORD caused all that he did to succeed" 39:4—"So Joseph found favor in his sight" 39:4–6—Potiphar put Joseph in charge of everything 39:6—"and because of him he had no concern about anything but the food he ate."	39:21—"The LORD was with Joseph" 39:23—"the keeper of the prison paid no attention . . . because the LORD was with him." 39:23—"And whatever he did, the LORD made it succeed" 39:21—"and gave him favor in the sight of the keeper of the prison." 39:22—the keeper of the prison put Joseph in charge of everything 39:23—"The keeper of the prison paid no attention to anything that was in Joseph's charge"

The two sections provide clear direct verbal and thematic parallels. They are clearly intended to frame the narrative, showing the working of God, which was obvious to all. As a result, the house of Potiphar and the prison house are compared, including Potiphar and the keeper of the prison. In both cases, all things were entrusted into Joseph's care with obvious and complete success from Yahweh. Neither master had any concern with what they had given over to Joseph. God's obvious blessing on Potiphar's house provides a clear distinction between the two. The frame highlights Joseph's right standing before God, the injustice of his accusations, and the clear knowledge, oversight, and working of God through evil and injustice. In fact it will help the reader to see God using even injustice to accomplish his goal.

THEOLOGICAL FOCUS

While God's presence provides success, righteous living in the face of temptation may include suffering and loss to accomplish God's purposes within his faithful care.

God's presence, clearly declared by the narrator and recognized by onlookers, both fulfills and challenges expectations. He brings success to the righteous yet at times allows pain, frustration, and injustice to the same righteous servant. His blessing on those connected to his chosen ones fulfills his promise, bringing good to others. God's goodness, evident to the watching world, tangibly impacts those who will appreciate and benefit from God's working.

God's unexpected failure to intervene in the false accusations against Joseph, however, challenges a common view that God will protect his people from calamity when they are righteous. The notice of Yahweh's presence and work enclosing the narrative, coupled with Joseph's declared motivation and steadfast endurance in his resistance, redirect the attention of the reader to a bigger purpose of God to explain the incongruity. The larger context gives the theological implication of God's working even through evil actions of evil people, accomplishing greater good though it may not bring comfort in the moment to the righteous sufferer. The story, then, does not imply obvious success and prosperity as a universal truth self-evident for all time, but it does show how God can and does work. It also supports the thesis we have been developing that God's blessing (with the outcome of "success") is intended to empower his people to accomplish his intended purposes for them. That blessing requires opportunities to test and refine faith and grow character, and that success may be measured in God's long-range view, rather than immediately felt benefits. The tensions help to temper expectations as we recognize that our experience must be judged in the light of the longer view of God's ultimate purposes.

From the human standpoint, integrity matters, even if it is not immediately rewarded. Integrity allows God's continued presence and blessing, leading to the world's recognition of it. The continued presence of Yahweh with Joseph in prison confirmed Joseph's innocence and God's pleasure, even amid frustration and waiting. While Joseph would one day understand and declare the lesson to his brothers, the righteous may not know the eventual good, certainly in the short term and perhaps even in the longer term. Though the righteous may be squarely in God's program and current work, they may not always feel like it (James 1:2–4)! They dare not decide that their righteousness does not matter or that God has abandoned them based on discomfort or prolonged hardship. Nor can they conclude that God does not see when the wicked succeed.

These tensions require balance. We cannot view prosperity or the world's view of success as the goal or as the only outcome for the righteous (replacing God with my pleasure). While God's plan will prevail, the righteous may only see glimpses of his final goal. Faith lives in light of an eternal perspective. I must subordinate my immediate expectations and comfort to God's will, risking my current comfort serving God's future goals. "At the same time, it is true that life is confidently settled (vv. 1–6, 21–23) and that life must be lived at great risk (vv. 7–20)" (Brueggemann 1982a, 319).

With this in mind, we must also notice the theology of temptation that the narrative illustrates. Righteousness requires a clear view of accountability, both to human authority and to God. Both realms present consequences and necessary responsibilities. Standing up clearly for responsibility and integrity is appropriate, but it may be necessary to run from inevitable compromise, physically removing oneself from both temptation and assault. To remain can bring no good outcome, even when running can bring suffering. There may be no easy solution in the present. Rather, we must wait for justice in God's time.

PREACHING AND TEACHING STRATEGIES

Exegetical and Theological Synthesis

Our sermon preparation begins with a twofold exegetical foundation:

(1) Pay attention to the narrative details that state that the Lord was with Joseph and caused him to succeed. This is critical to the sermon because Joseph's situation up to this point was a nightmare, nothing like the dream he rehearsed to his family. No matter how bad things looked for Joseph, the Lord's powerful presence resulted in overall success. While we cannot say that God will replicate Joseph's kind of success in the lives of every listener, we can say that God's presence will guarantee that his children accomplish his will. God's children succeed when they trust him and display his righteousness, and God can accomplish what he wants for them in the moment. In moments of great trial such as Joseph's, we have no idea of how things will go, but we know God goes with us. In those cases, success means enduring faithfully in the middle of the trial, waiting patiently on the Lord to deliver, whatever form that may take.

(2) Pay attention to the details highlighting Joseph's integrity and stating how his integrity fits with God's powerful presence, which produces success. Joseph was the kind of person that

walked with God. As noted, Joseph contrasts Judah. Joseph instructs all of God's people by the way he stated succumbing to sexual temptation in terms of committing "great wickedness and sin against God" (39:9). Although his righteousness is not immediately rewarded, the Lord continues to walk with Joseph and grant him success. This will help our listeners' faith not crumble every time the Lord allows testing in their lives. They will see that putting faith under pressure at times is also God's plan for his children. God allows the injustice perpetrated by Potiphar's wife and Potiphar (who believes his wife's report); that does not mean he is absent and inactive in keeping his promises to us.

Remind your listeners how the narrative begins and ends with the refrain of the Lord being with Joseph and the Lord making him successful. As long as we define success in terms of our ability to accomplish God's will, we will not expect absolute success according to our thinking. An example of this thinking would be severe disappointment resulting from being passed over for a promotion at work: "Where was God's presence, and why didn't he make me succeed like Joseph?"

Preaching Idea

Success, severe setbacks, temptation: expect it all with heavy doses of God's powerful presence and loyal love for the faithful.

Contemporary Connections

What does it mean?

If you provide the broader context for your listeners, you will want to teach them that Joseph's journey to Egypt and Potiphar's house means that Joseph is getting closer to having his dream come true. From God's perspective, he is moving Joseph into a position where he will be able to confer blessing on that entire region (thus fulfilling the Abrahamic covenant). From Joseph's perspective, his faith and faithfulness are being tested to the max, especially his morality. Explain how Joseph's decision to "flee fornication" (cf. 1 Corinthians 6:18 KJV) means that God has the right man in place to extend his blessing, to his people and beyond.

The theological statements concerning the Lord's presence and accompanying success need very little explanation. But this does not mean that your listeners will experience the same kind of success in their lives. Success must be defined in terms of accomplishing God's will through his supernatural provision. And Joseph succeeds, even though he is pummeled by slanderous accusations.

Finally, this is a great opportunity to help everyone learn of God's "steadfast love" in verse 21. All through Joseph's adventure, the "LORD showed him" covenant loyalty or loyal love. Along with covenant loyalty is "favor." In a nutshell, the keeper of the prison liked Joseph, and that led to success.

Is it true?

I can envision some of our listeners needing us to prove that success can really result from such righteous living. I can hear some arguing that such righteousness will be squashed. Help them see that God's steadfast love occurred in the hardship; it didn't prevent any hardship. So, yes, there may be momentary loss, and "momentary" could mean a lifetime. But success in the eyes of the Lord is measured in terms of faithfulness to him. Joseph's kind of success may or may not happen to us, but the Lord will make sure we are able to succeed for him when we are faithful to him.

This narrative assumes that the Lord is controlling all of Joseph's movements. Our listeners may not believe that the same God is also watching over every facet of their lives, especially the ones where they are vulnerable and powerless, just like Joseph was. Joseph's situation highlights the reality of God's people at times being on the receiving end of ungodly treatment. It can appear that evil wins the day, but this narrative shows God's powerful work in and through evil to accomplish his will.

Now what?
Wouldn't it be great if all our listeners left church with full confidence in God's ability to extend his covenant loyalty to them in their situations? Wouldn't it be great if they all believed that the Lord was with them where they are, especially those that are in dire straits? It is clear from this narrative that the Lord will make sure that his people will accomplish exactly what he wants them to do in the world. Nothing can stop such success. Put positively, look at how the Lord used the evil designs of Joseph's own brothers, plus the lying of Potiphar's wife, to carry out his will for Joseph. And let's remember that Joseph is teaching us through his example of integrity. His practical righteousness is a part of this equation: God is working in the life of someone who is intensely loyal to him.

Creativity in Presentation
Joseph teaches us that with success, severe disappointment, and temptation, we should expect it all with heavy doses of God's powerful presence and loyal love. One way to make a contemporary connection is to share one of your worst moments, the time when things looked the worst for you. You might ask others to provide some examples that you could share with their permission or get someone to share their story during the service.

- The opening move of the sermon can develop around the thought that, despite appearances and feeling, Joseph's terrible situation was bringing him closer to his dreams and rise to power. Some may decide to keep the tension alive until the end of the sermon. In this way our listeners can journey with Joseph through all the emotions he felt through thirteen long years of waiting for God to do something. They will see how easy it is for a child of God to get disillusioned in times of great trial. This reflects the unexpected context for success. This first major point provides great comfort for anyone going through difficult situations that they didn't ask for or create through their own poor choices. In this first section, you can combine Joseph's situation in verse 1 and verses 6b–20. In that lengthy section, the sub-statements could revolve around the nature of temptation and Joseph's response to temptation (especially his important statement in v. 9: "How can I do this great wickedness and sin against God?").

- The second major move of the sermon can center on the narrator's explanation of Joseph's success. You could use something as simple as "But the Lord," or how the Lord keeps his promises. Subunits include the Lord's powerful presence (vv. 2, 21, 23), the blessing of the Lord extended to others (v. 5), the Lord's steadfast love (v. 21), and the Lord granting success (vv. 3, 23).

- Finally, you will want to urge your listeners to place their confidence in God. You've shown them what God did for Joseph, and now it's their turn to leave the sanctuary and enter a badly broken world that needs to see the lives of faithful Christ-followers.

DISCUSSION QUESTIONS

1. Discuss the meaning of "steadfast love."
2. Carefully define "success" from the theology of this narrative. Explain why it doesn't always mean "success" according to society's standards.
3. Discuss the potential impact Christians can have when others can see the Lord's favor on them.
4. What would it look like to react in faith when painful or frustrating things happen to you?
5. How can you prepare my heart to react in integrity and righteousness when you are faced with unexpected temptation?
6. What testing or temptations are you facing that you need to run from or stand firm in, showing complete loyalty to Christ?

Genesis 40:1–41:57

EXEGETICAL IDEA

God clarified Joseph's perspective and provided for his world by moving Joseph to prominence in Egypt, beginning with his dream interpretation for Pharaoh's officials, and culminating in his interpretation and advice for Pharaoh.

THEOLOGICAL FOCUS

Working behind the scenes, God orchestrates events to use his people to accomplish his blessing in his world in his time, while growing their faith and perspective in his service.

PREACHING IDEA

Even when you feel forgotten by God, he is working his purposes and accomplishing his will.

PREACHING POINTERS

For any listeners whose experiences seem to contradict what God has promised them, this segment of the Joseph story is a welcomed tonic. Chapter 39 ended with the hope-filled "And whatever he did, the Lord made it succeed" (v. 23). But at the beginning of chapter 40, Joseph is still in prison unjustly. God is continuing to give success by arranging to have two dreamy prisoners assigned to Joseph's prison. Both original and contemporary audiences see what's happening: God is moving Joseph into position so he can accomplish God's will to experience and extend his blessing to the world.

The vehicle of success in Joseph's case is his God-given ability to interpret dreams. And this ability gets him that much closer to realizing his own dream. The fact that Joseph is forgotten (40:23) only delays Joseph's rise to prominence because in chapter 41 Pharaoh dreams too. We already know who is able to interpret the dream. The cupbearer who forgot about Joseph now "remember[s]" his offenses before Pharaoh and tells him about Joseph's abilities (vv. 9–13). Amazing series of circumstances, don't you think?

Numerous times in the narrative Joseph testifies that his God gets the credit for his interpretative skills (41:16, 25, 28, 32) and even Pharaoh buys this explanation (41:38, 39). In the end, Joseph names his two sons, and listeners can receive hope as they accomplish God's will in a badly broken world. Like Joseph, they too can be an instrument for carrying out God's desire to bless the nations.

JOSEPH'S RISE: GOD'S SURPRISING WORK (40:1–41:57)

LITERARY STRUCTURE AND THEMES

Genesis 40–41 completes Joseph's rise to prominence from the pit, preparing Joseph to realize his dreams of rule. His testing with Potiphar's wife (ch. 39) seemed to leave him farther from ruling, except for the reassuring refrain that Yahweh was with him. The first half of the story, in the prison, initially appears to be *déjà vu*. The optimism of God's presence and Joseph's success (39:23), coupled with his spectacular encounter with and accuracy in interpreting the dreams of the two royal officials, offered Joseph hope that was dashed when the chief cupbearer forgot him. Finally, with the dreams of Pharaoh, the reader (and Joseph!) begins to see more clearly the working of God to orchestrate Joseph's life to accomplish Yahweh's purposes. The structure flows in two parallel sections that build from chapter 39, providing Joseph's needed credentials (ch. 40) for a providential appointment with Pharaoh that advanced Joseph to his calling (ch. 41).

A. Only God reveals dreams and personal affairs (40:1–8).
  B. God revealed the officials' future through Joseph, who pled for his life (40:9–19).
    C. Joseph was forgotten (40:20–23).
A'. Egyptian wisdom could not reveal dreams (41:1–13).
  B'. God revealed Pharaoh's future through Joseph, who pled for the nation (41:14–36).
    C'. Joseph was elevated to rule (41:37–57).

Joseph's rise to prominence continued God's working in history to accomplish God's goals, setting up the fulfillment of Joseph's dreams (37:5–11) and, more significantly, the next stage in the stated plans of God to Abraham. Not only would Joseph bring blessing to the earth, but the family would go to Egypt, fulfilling God's promise to Abraham (15:13–14), preserving the nation from assimilation (ch. 38) while growing them into a great nation (12:2; 46:3), and graciously delaying judgment on the Amorites (15:16). All of this was on God's timetable, not Joseph's, which allowed time for Joseph to grow in his faith and perspective.

The testimony to God's power also provides immediate and written testimony to God's sovereignty in polemic against the gods of Egypt and Pharaoh, also called Horus, "the falcon-god incarnate"[1] and mediator for the gods. Neither Pharaoh nor the wise men in his kingdom knew the dream's meaning or had the wisdom to preserve his kingdom from the coming disaster, which was fully controlled by Yahweh. Yet God showed his grace to Pharaoh, Egypt, and his world through Joseph.

- ***Only God Reveals Dreams and Personal Affairs (40:1–8)***
- ***God Revealed the Officials' Future Through Joseph, Who Pled for His Life (40:9–19)***
- ***Joseph Was Forgotten (40:20–23)***
- ***Egyptian Wisdom Could Not Reveal Dreams (41:1–13)***

1 Redford, "Pharaoh," *ABD* 5:288. The Pharaoh became the "Son of Re" at coronation, transforming him into the "divine king" (Hoffmeier 1997, 90).

- ***God Revealed Pharaoh's Future Through Joseph, Who Pled for the Nation (41:14–36)***
- ***Joseph Was Elevated to Rule (41:37–57)***

EXPOSITION

The fourth-generation stories of the sons of Jacob, beginning with Joseph's sale (ch. 37), describe God's working in Judah's life (ch. 38) before detailing his work in Joseph's drawn-out and painful rise to prominence (chs. 39–41). Joseph had already shown exceptional integrity with Potiphar's wife, only to end up in prison. Now, Moses will pass over most of the thirteen years of slavery and imprisonment (cf. 37:2; 41:46) to focus attention on the initially disappointing contact with the two royal officials and the surprise invitation to the world stage.

Adding to the account of Joseph's integrity and fidelity to Yahweh in the face of great temptation, Joseph's prison stay only enhanced his outspoken loyalty and honor to Yahweh. He testified to God's unique power and transcendent control over dreams and affairs—personal, national, and global—providing the needed basis for his opportunity to represent Yahweh to Pharaoh. God clarified Joseph's perspective and provided for his world by moving Joseph to prominence in Egypt, beginning with his dream interpretation for Pharaoh's officials, and culminating in his interpretation and advice for Pharaoh.

Only God Reveals Dreams and Personal Affairs (40:1–8)

When Pharaoh's disgraced officials landed in prison with Joseph and both dreamed disturbing dreams, Joseph established God's authority over dreams and personal affairs.

40:1–4. "Some time after this" (v. 1) two royal officials earned the Pharaoh's anger, glossing over years of Joseph's life in prison. With no way to know precisely the timing for all these events, the text tells us that it was about eleven years from Joseph's sale (37:2) to the dreams of the two officials, two years before Joseph's release (41:1, 46). The initiating circumstance may have been Pharaoh's illness (Walton 2009a, 128). The two offending officials both had responsibility for Pharaoh's meals, suggesting a connection to a possible sickness he suffered and interpreted as a threat to his life, especially if it happened at a particular celebration, such as his birthday or, perhaps better, the anniversary of his coronation.

TRANSLATION ANALYSIS 40:1

"Committed an offense" (ESV) effectively renders the verb used by Moses, often describing "sin" (חטא) against God (39:9) but here describing a serious offense against Pharaoh that could cost them their lives. The translation "offended" (NET, NIV, NLT, etc.) commonly connotes more of a breach of etiquette than a significant threat against someone. Here, the use of the term previously applied to Joseph in his protest to Potiphar's wife may be intended to remind the reader of Joseph's integrity, in contrast to their actions, and prepare for his subsequent rise.

TRANSLATION ANALYSIS 40:4

Sarna (1989, 277) notes that the "some time" (lit. "days," יָמִים) in custody (v. 4) can refer to an indefinite time, or it can refer to "a year" in Hebrew, indicating not only that they were judged at his birthday (v. 20) but that the original offense may have occurred at that time the previous year. Hoffmeier (1997, 89–91) argues that the celebration is not his biological birthday but is the anniversary of his coronation, which would include divine kingship and the title "Son of Re." The birthday celebration is not known from ancient Egypt, but the divine kingship and celebration of coronation is widely attested. It was his "divine birthday," an even more serious occasion.

The two men were both ranking officials in charge of their areas ("officers" [סָרִיס], "chief cupbearer" [שַׂר הַמַּשְׁקִים] and "chief baker" [שַׂר

הָאוֹפִים], 40:2)[2] and so were put into custody in the "house of the captain of the guard" (שַׂר הַטַּבָּחִים, v. 3), where Joseph was imprisoned. The "captain of the guard" could still be Potiphar (cf. 37:36; 39:1), though it is not certain with the unknown time passing. He is both the one to put them in Joseph's care (40:4) and described as Joseph's master (41:12). They were in temporary "custody" (מִשְׁמָר, 40:3), waiting for their case to be adjudicated (Sarna 1989, cf. Lev. 24:12 and Num. 15:34). They would be understandably anxious at their dreams, emphasized by the reminder of their imprisonment in connection with the dreams (v. 5, Wenham 1994, 382).

40:5–8. The dreams here, and throughout these stories, represent the historical occasion well. Their practice and expectation, however, relied on the right books and knowledgeable people to explain the dreams. Adding to their anxiety, then, the two officials had dreams that they assumed were significant, but they had no access to the royal interpreters and resources for determining their meaning (v. 8).

Dreams

Dreams were an ongoing interest in the ancient world, with a common belief that the gods communicated with people, especially kings, via dreams. Both Egypt and Mesopotamia had guilds of professionals (here "magicians," חַרְטֹם, 41:8) that studied the books written about dream interpretation, including the signs and symbols used and their possible meanings (Walton 2009a, 128). Egypt practiced interpreting dreams long before Joseph, but the Chester Beatty "Dream Book" dates from about the time of Joseph (Twelfth Dynasty, or ca. 1991–1786 BC) and details possible scenarios one might see himself doing in dreams and whether it is good or bad, with the expected meaning (Ritner, "Dream Oracles" §1.33, CoS, 52–54). The explanation of dream imagery centered on "a variety of principles, including wordplay (paronomasia), contemporary symbolism, and contraries" (or contrary to expectations, Ritner, "Dream Books," *OEAE* 1:410–11).

Joseph added sensitivity, tact, and humility to his growing resume of character qualities. Seeing their obvious distress, he inquired. Hearing their concerns, he offered help without being either arrogant or demeaning. His response, however, challenged their worldview and expectations. He asserted God's exclusive claim to dreams and their interpretation. As a result, with neither education nor dream books, he offered his services. His subsequent stunningly accurate account would validate both his theology and his standing with God as interpreter.

God Revealed the Officials' Future Through Joseph, Who Pled for His Life (40:9–19)

When they relayed their dreams, Joseph related the impending restoration of the cupbearer and execution of the baker, imploring the cupbearer to help redress Joseph's injustice.

40:9–15. While the chief cupbearer's job description included confidant and advisor to the king, it also included tasting and serving the king's wine. His necessarily close and trusted role shows in the following chapter, making Joseph's aid to him particularly useful in God's program. His dream, compressing his role, included the time-warped cultivation, production, and service of wine to the king. The three branches, joined by a variety of threefold repetition, led to Joseph's interpretation.[3]

---

2 "Officers" (סָרִיס), will later in history indicate "eunuchs" but at this time were high ranking court officials without clear indication of any sexual status (Johnston, סָרִיס, *NIDOTTE* 3:288–89).

3 Hamilton (1995, 479) notes three verbs for the growth of the plant, "Pharaoh" and "cup" repeated three times, along with three statements of his own activities. The literary repetitions in the dream gave Joseph's interpretation the ring of truth.

Joseph's interpretation flowed immediately from the description, without any prayer or waiting for God, showing God's presence with him, Joseph's faith in God, and Joseph's understanding. In three days, Pharaoh would lift his head, restoring him to his position. Joseph's additional request was immediate as well. He asked the cupbearer to show him "kindness" (חֶסֶד, v. 14) by advocating for him in his position before Pharaoh to redress the injustice done, both in his initial kidnapping (v. 15a) into slavery and subsequent false accusation and imprisonment (v. 15b).

TRANSLATION ANALYSIS 40:13

The literal translation, to "lift your head" (ESV, NASB95, NIV), belies a more debated idiomatic meaning. Wenham (1994, 383) takes it to mean "deal kindly with", but Sarna and Hamilton more plausibly cite an Akkadian cognate phrase to argue for "summon" (Sarna 1989, 278; Hamilton 1995, 479–80). The use of the phrase in 40:20 supports their conclusion when both were summoned with opposite results. Other translations include "reinstate you" (NET), "lift you up" (NLT, by metonymy), "free you" (NCV), or "pardon you" (NJPS, cf. Speiser 1964, 305). In pointed irony, Joseph will begin with the same phrase for the baker, but his head will be lifted fully off (see v. 19 below). Because of this word play in the Hebrew, the literal translation is helpful, allowing the reader to see the irony, even if missing the precise nuance of the idiom, "to lift the head" (Marcus 1990).

TRANSLATION ANALYSIS 40:15

Joseph claimed he was "stolen" (ESV, NKJV, גנב), which would amount to being "kidnapped" (NASB95, NET, NJPS). His claim is not quite accurate, skipping the sale from his brothers and seeming to put the responsibility on the traders. The penalty for kidnapping into slavery was death, for both the kidnapper and anyone possessing a kidnapped person, under the law (Exod. 21:16; Deut. 24:7) and in the ancient world (Hamilton 1995, 421, where he cites Hammurabi). It is unnecessary to assume he was trying to protect his brothers as much as he was simply speaking emotionally, relating his feelings from his perspective.

Ironically, Yahweh had already extended to him "kindness" (חֶסֶד, 39:21) after both offenses, which Joseph would eventually recognize, and which would far surpass his strategy to be released from the prison through the cupbearer. However, he was not yet able to fully see God's kindness to him in the incarceration. Rather, Joseph expressed his frustrations for the offenses against him and his current place in the "pit" (בּוֹר, 40:15).[4] He certainly was growing in his reliance on God and assurance of God using him. He had no doubts about his interpretation. Yet he was still languishing in his heart, harboring resentment toward the evil done to him, and looking for a way out on his own. He needed refocusing in his perspective and strengthening in his faith to find release from the bitterness and peace in the storm.

40:16–19. Reassured by the positive interpretation, the baker also shared his story. The cupbearer's three branches are matched by three baskets for the baker. Unlike the cupbearer serving Pharaoh in his dream, however, the baker was passively carrying the baskets.

4 Joseph's reference to the prison as the "pit" (בּוֹר) is repeated in 41:14 by the narrator, recalling the cistern Joseph's brothers put him in (בּוֹר, used three times in 37:28–29). Both Joseph and Moses draw the parallel, reminding the reader that Joseph was looking for and finally found freedom from his initial injustice, but also that it was the initial evil of the brothers, selling him into slavery, that led eventually (thirteen years later) to his audience before Pharaoh and his rise to power, accomplishing God's blessing (41:52) and leading to Joseph's conclusion of God's superintendence (45:5, 7–8; 50:20).

Instead of giving Pharaoh the baked goods, he was allowing the birds to steal from the top.

Joseph's interpretation came just as easily and immediately as with the cupbearer. Using the same initial phrasing as his interpretation for the cupbearer, Joseph related that in three days, the baker's head would also be lifted, but instead of the building anticipation of restoration from the play on the first interpretation, it would be lifted off and he would be impaled! In both cases, Pharaoh would decide their fate in three days, one for restoration and the other for execution.

TRANSLATION ANALYSIS 40:19

In checking the versions there seem to be different ideas of what is happening. The ESV says "Pharaoh will lift up your head—from you!—and hang you on a tree," giving the contradictory conception of decapitation followed by hanging by the neck (see also NASB95, NKJV, RSV). Still others say he will "impale you on a pole" after decapitation, which at least makes clear the second clause (e.g., NET, NIV, NJPS). Finally, NLT implies that impaling is the cause of death, rather than the desecration of the body: "Pharaoh will lift you up and impale your body on a pole." The final "from off you" in the Hebrew (מֵעָלֶיךָ) is missing in two MSS and the Vulgate, and since this is not the normal Hebrew phrase for decapitation, Sarna (1989, 279–80) suggests it may be execution by impalement rather than decapitation (cf. Hamilton 1995, 482). On the other hand, the phrase in the MT may not require literal decapitation, but execution followed by exposure (Mathews 2005, 751). Walton (2001, 673) notes that executions were not generally by "hanging" (impalement) in the ancient world, but impalement was often used to dishonor the body publicly and "prevent his spirit from resting in the afterlife" (Wenham 1994, 384).

Joseph Was Forgotten (40:20–23)

Though both Joseph's interpretations occurred as stated, the cupbearer forgot Joseph.

40:20–23. The three days of Joseph's interpretations fit the royal calendar, as Pharaoh had his celebration and took care of lingering business. Pharaoh made a feast for his servants and demonstrated his authority and justice. Using the precise phrases from Joseph's interpretation, he summoned ("lifted up the head," v. 20) of each man, putting the cupbearer back into service and the baker to death, including impalement, "as Joseph had interpreted to them" (v. 22). Joseph was vindicated, his theology was proven, and God was honored. However, as if to emphasize Joseph's imminent disappointment, "the chief cupbearer did not remember Joseph, but forgot him" (v. 23).

Up to this point in Genesis, the verb "remember" (זכר) has been used only of God's faithfulness to his word (Noah and his covenant with Noah, 8:1, 9:15, 16; his word to Abraham regarding Lot, 19:29; and Rachel's children, 30:22). God had already shown Joseph his faithfulness, but Joseph was languishing in prison. He saw a way out, but the cupbearer did not remember. Joseph's bid to derive his own freedom from God's working through him failed, ironically keeping him in place for God's faithfulness to prevail. God had a bigger plan and a much grander entrance onto the world stage, two years later, that would finally help Joseph see God's goodness, blessing, and bigger picture. In fact, it is the poor memory of the cupbearer that underlines the necessary and gracious intervention of God (Mathews 2005, 744).

Egyptian Wisdom Could Not Reveal Dreams (41:1–13)

When Pharaoh dreamed two dreams, and his wise men could not satisfy him, the cupbearer remembered Joseph.

41:1–7. Two full years later, at the anniversary of Pharaoh's coronation and with Joseph still languishing, Pharaoh dreamed. While the two dreams of the officials were characterized by three things, Pharaoh had two dreams characterized by sevens.[5] The number seven occurs twenty-eight times in the chapter, emphasizing the certain timing of God's plan. In contrast to the two officials in their dreams, Pharaoh was merely an onlooker in both dreams. The initial narrating of the dreams occurs simply. Seven fat cows came out of the Nile and were eaten by seven thin cows that followed them out. Then seven full ears of grain were swallowed up by seven thin ears. Pharaoh saw it so vividly (six uses of *hinneh*, הִנֵּה) that he had to wake up to realize it was a dream, leaving him troubled in his spirit.

41:8–13. Pharaoh called his professionals in to interpret the dream, but they could not. Rather than not having any idea, they likely were unable to satisfy Pharaoh that they were right in their take on the dream (Hamilton 1995, 488–89). It also seems clear that he saw them as a single dream, while they were interpreting two dreams ("them," אוֹתָם, v. 8), possibly leading to his distrust of their ideas and his acceptance of Joseph's interpretation (Sternberg 1987, 398–400).

> *TRANSLATION ANALYSIS 41:8*
> In most translations, Pharaoh tells his "dreams" (plural, as in the SP, e.g., ESV, NET, NRSV, NJPS), but the MT has the singular "dream" (RSV). Pharaoh seems to be thinking of them as a single dream or message (vv. 15, 17–24).

With providential timing, the cupbearer remembered his "offenses" (v. 9). Reminded of his own dream in prison, he related to Pharaoh Joseph's amazing accuracy in telling them the meaning, which then happened "as he interpreted to us" (v. 13). The two instances of Joseph's ability with their widely divergent results verified Joseph's gift. The purpose of the initial vignette in Joseph's life now begins to take shape as it validated God's working through Joseph to provide an audience with Pharaoh. In the cupbearer's memory, the reader recognizes both Joseph's wisdom and God's sovereign oversight of Joseph's life (Sailhamer 1990, 240).

> *TRANSLATION ANALYSIS 41:9*
> The term the cupbearer uses is cognate to the verb used of the offenses he and the baker committed to put them in prison (see comments on 40:1). He is either referring to the whole situation that brought him into contact with Joseph, or he is referring to forgetting his responsibility to champion Joseph's cause and help him out of prison, so appropriately translated as "offenses" (ESV, NASB95), "failures" (NET, NLT), "faults" (NKJV, NRSV), or similar. Either referent reminds him of Joseph's spectacular success, considering Pharaoh's need and the possibility to find favor with the king.

God Revealed Pharaoh's Future Through Joseph, Who Pled for the Nation (41:14–36)

When Pharaoh relayed his dreams, Joseph asserted God's control over dreams and history, declaring that God would bring both seven years of abundance and seven years of famine, and he encouraged Pharaoh to appoint wise leadership that would prepare appropriately for the shortages.

41:14–16. Pharaoh lost no time. His attendants "quickly" brought Joseph (from the root often translated "run," רוץ), after making him presentable with a shave and a change of clothing.[6] The quick succession of the verbs in one- and

5 Significant revelations to kings in the ancient world were often recorded as coming through pairs of dreams. For a list, see Walton (2009a, 129–30).

6 Joseph was being transformed for the presence of Pharaoh. Men from Canaan would normally be bearded, but men in Egypt would generally shave not only their faces, but their whole heads. The purpose was cleanliness in a hot climate, but the cultural difference was significant. Joseph's first impression on the Pharaoh would

two-word clauses adds to the impression of the rush in the Hebrew.

Pharaoh came right to the point. He had had a dream that "no one" (אַיִן, v. 15) could interpret, but he had heard Joseph could do it. Joseph's response to Pharaoh sounds innocuous to a modern westerner, but it was dramatic for Pharaoh. By declaring his inability and claiming the only source to be God (אֱלֹהִים), Joseph was rejecting both their understanding of dream interpretation as a skill to develop through learning and personal wisdom (something humans could learn and control—so Pharaoh had called the "magicians" and "wise men," v. 8) and claiming his God was the source of the knowledge Pharaoh needed, not their gods.

TRANSLATION ANALYSIS 41:16

As noted in the ESV footnote, the SP (and the LXX) does not include the first-person pronoun, so that the clause is, "Without God it is not possible to give Pharaoh an answer about his welfare." The difference is only in the vowel pointing (the consonants are the same) and the implications are the same, but the variant reduces the emphasis on Joseph's inability, instead emphasizing God's exclusive right.

Joseph claimed God would "answer Pharaoh with shalom" (lit. transl., אֱלֹהִים יַעֲנֶה אֶת־שְׁלוֹם פַּרְעֹה, v. 16). The intent of the clause is ambiguous. According to the ESV, NASB95, and others, he offered Pharaoh a "favorable answer" from God, giving Pharaoh what he was seeking (Mathews 2005, 759). On the other hand, "shalom" could speak to Pharaoh's obvious anxiety and Joseph's certainty that God was providing Pharaoh hope of future well-being ("God will speak concerning the welfare of Pharaoh," NET; "God will see to Pharaoh's welfare," NJPS; cf. Steinmann 2019, 382). The general use of "shalom" favors the latter. Perhaps even more pointed, the Pharaoh's responsibility in his role to his gods was to maintain cosmic order (Hoffmeier 1997, 151), which shalom would appropriately approximate. Only Joseph's God could accomplish this for Pharaoh. Pharaoh was clearly interested, despite the gentle theological polemic.[7]

41:17–24. Pharaoh recounted his dream to Joseph, with a few minor adjustments and two personal observations. In describing the cows, he followed the wording of the dream closely, but he switched the order of the descriptors. With the ears of grain, he substituted a synonym ("full" for "fat," v. 22, cf. v. 5) and summarized "good" for "plump, full" (v. 24, cf. v. 7).[8] He did, however, add some commentary to the description of the cows. First, when he saw the ugly, scrawny cows, he exclaimed that he had not seen anything so bad in all the land of Egypt (v. 19), and after they ate the fat cows, he noted that they were just as scrawny after eating the fat cows as they had been before. This observation, not in the original telling of the dream, would be significant for Joseph's interpretation.

Pharaoh seems to be wrestling with the implications of the dream. Brueggemann (1982a, 327) draws attention to the Egyptian view in which "the Nile River is not only a geographical referent. It is also an expression of the imperial power of fertility. It is administration of

be important. He would be so assimilated that his brothers would not recognize him, perhaps thinking he was Egyptian himself.

7 In his communication with Pharaoh, Joseph did not use the personal name of Yahweh but the generic "God" (הָאֱלֹהִים), which in this context would be expected to be Joseph's God, not the Egyptian gods. However, Joseph did not feel the need to clarify.

8 Sternberg (1987, 399–400) concludes that Pharaoh is blurring the distinctions between the two parts because he has understood them as a single dream. The implication is that Joseph has both satisfied Pharaoh's expectations and correctly understood the dream, even with Pharaoh's possible misunderstanding.

the Nile which permits the king to generate and guarantee life." His wonder at the ugliest and scrawniest cows he had ever seen that were unchanged by consuming the providence of the Nile shows his perception of the threat in his dreams. For Pharaoh, he would recognize a future fully out of his control and in Joseph's God's control.

41:25–32. Joseph's response to Pharaoh again centered on God's agency, intent to show Pharaoh his coming actions and the certainty of their imminence. Three times Joseph asserted that the dreams were communicating what God would do (vv. 25, 28, 32). It was God's working, which could not be influenced by the king, and it was God revealing it. God controlled the prosperity and shortages of Egypt, not Pharaoh (Brueggemann 1982a, 330–31). Pharaoh merely received the information, with the responsibility to prepare for what God graciously revealed.

Joseph stated what Pharaoh had already realized. The dreams had a single point. God was using an Egyptian worldview to make his point to the Pharaoh. Twice he emphasized that the dreams communicated the same intent (vv. 25, 26). The sevens were years, which indicated the "plenty" (שָׂבָע, a word play with "seven," שֶׁבַע, possibly emphasizing the abundance) would be followed immediately by seven more years of famine.[9] Commenting on Pharaoh's observation, the years of abundance would not be remembered after the severe famine.

The two forms of Pharaoh's dream indicated that the prediction was certain and would happen quickly. Joseph's interpretation, in the larger context, also reminds the reader of Joseph's two dreams. Joseph's own future was certain, had always been, and at this point was imminent. Of course, it would not have seemed quick for Joseph, over thirteen years after his own dreams. The obvious immediate intent was a warning to Pharaoh and an opportunity to prepare. Joseph was quick to follow up, merging the implications of both images.

41:33–36. Joseph dared to give Pharaoh advice considering God's revelation. In a passionate response that focused on Egypt's needs before the coming disaster, without self-promotion, Joseph argued for the type of leader Pharaoh needed to find and the program he needed to implement. The reader immediately can see Joseph's name over that job description, and Pharaoh followed the signs. Ironically, Pharaoh had already called on "all" the wisest (חָכָם) in Egypt to help (41:8), and they had failed. The "discerning and wise man" (חָכָם, v. 33) Joseph called for was not among Pharaoh's counselors but was a lowly Hebrew servant from the prison (v. 12).

Joseph argued for a single overseer superintending others that would manage to collect the abundance for seven years in preparation to feed the populace during the seven years of famine. His concern was the survival of Egypt. His response to Pharaoh was far from his appearance of braggadocio with his initial dreams and what his family took as self-promotion. To his credit, Pharaoh was able to see God's hand on Joseph. The reader can also see God's working in Joseph as he was being transformed.

TRANSLATION ANALYSIS 41:34

The Hebrew verb translated "take one-fifth" (וְחִמֵּשׁ) occurs only here in the *piel*. The *qal* passive participle refers to preparations for war (Exod. 13:18; Josh. 1:14; 4:12; perhaps groups

9 As is often noted, long periods of drought and famine were well known in Egypt, when the Nile would fail for an extended period. Seven-year famines are recorded in several texts across the ancient world. Hamilton (1995, 497) lists records of seven-year famines from Egypt, Ugarit, Gilgamesh, and Atrahasis.

of fifty or in five parts, *HALOT* s.v. I "חמשׁ" 331). Some, then, understand the injunction here to "organize the land of Egypt" (NJPS, cf. Sarna 1989, 285). The root commonly appears in the noun "five" (חָמֵשׁ), and other numbers become similar verbal forms in the *piel*, leading to "take one-fifth" (ESV and many translations). Hamilton (1995, 498, n. 4) argues persuasively that the idea of five should be reflected in the translation, whether as understood here or dividing into districts. Given the following work of Joseph in collecting a tax of one-fifth, it is natural to see that in his appeal to Pharaoh.

Joseph Was Elevated to Rule (41:37–57)

When Pharaoh put Joseph in charge, Joseph recognized God's working, wisely using his opportunity to bless his world in crisis, as God had forewarned.

41:37–45. Pharaoh immediately saw the wisdom in Joseph's proposal and the disparity with his own advisors. He saw "the Spirit of God" in Joseph. He recognized that the source of the interpretation, and presumably the advice that followed, was God himself and not Joseph, a tribute to Joseph's humble and persistent honoring of God. He also acknowledged Joseph's connection with God as the source of discernment and wisdom needed for his administration. There were no others in his league (v. 39).

TRANSLATION ANALYSIS 41:38

The Hebrew could also be translated "the spirit of the gods" (רוּחַ אֱלֹהִים, ESV fn, cf. NASB95). The text allows either translation, and Pharaoh's worldview would suggest the latter. The phrase is used in Genesis 1:2 of God's spirit hovering over the waters before creation (see Exposition there, p. 82) and is used of God working in individuals to build the tabernacle (Exod. 31:3; 35:31), utter prophecy (Num. 34:2; 1 Sam. 10:10; 2 Chron. 15:1), and perform feats of battle (1 Sam. 11:6). The equivalent Aramaic was used of Daniel by Belshazzar (and his queen) because he had "an excellent spirit, knowledge, and understanding to interpret dreams, explain riddles, and solve problems" (Dan. 5:12; see also 5:11, 14). To what extent Pharaoh recognized Yahweh is not stated, but he would have realized at least a divine authority in Joseph's words.

As such, Pharaoh raised Joseph from the pit to second in command. The title has been debated, as several possible jobs could fit the description here, and the job description does not clearly fit what is known about the vizier.[10] A foreigner (and even a Semite) could hold such a high office in ancient Egypt (Hoffmeier 1997, 93–95; Sarna 1989, 288). Joseph had authority over all of Pharaoh's house, his people, and all the kingdom. Only Pharaoh himself was greater.

TRANSLATION ANALYSIS 41:40

The meaning of the verse is clear, but the specific use of the Egyptian idiom is obscure. The Hebrew says that at Joseph's command everyone shall "kiss" (יִשַּׁק). Kitchen (1957) proposed the common Egyptian use of "'kiss the earth,' meaning 'to render homage or allegiance,'" so NASB95 ("do homage").

The narrative, then, details the typical installment procedures as Pharaoh gave him authority to carry out policy and decisions in Pharaoh's name (his signet) and dressed him to play the part. He would ride in the second chariot with his own attendants, making sure everyone recognized his authority and enforced his privilege. Joseph could control any action of any person in the realm of Egypt

10 The vizier was second to the king but was tasked with making sure justice prevailed and managing the land (Warburton, "Officials," *OEAE* 579).

(Gen. 41:44), and Pharaoh provided the trappings of his new rank, with a new name[11] and wife of privilege.[12] So Joseph exercised his newfound freedom and began to realize the implications of his initial dreams in personally attending the affairs of the nation in preparation for the coming cataclysm.

TRANSLATION ANALYSIS 41:43
The command issued before his chariot is uncertain, occurring only here in the Old Testament. "Bow the knee," the common translation (ESV, NKJV, NRSV), assumes it is an "Egyptian imperative of a Semitic loan-word" (Kitchen, "Abrech," *NBD* 9, citing Vergote, *Joseph en Egypte*, 135–41, 151). The other option is "Attention!" or "Make way!" (NIV). Whatever the specific meaning, from the context, the runner clearly calls everyone to acknowledge the authority and power of Joseph as second in the land.

41:46–49. Joseph went out over Egypt a vastly changed thirty-year-old from the seventeen-year-old youth with dreams of ruling. He carried out his stated plan, storing the grain in the cities close at hand to the grain. It was so plentiful they stopped keeping track of how much they had. Moses's word choice, "like the sand of the sea," (v. 49), reminds the reader of God's promise for the nation (22:17). The parallel terminology illustrated God keeping his word in seemingly impossible ways, showing his faithfulness to Joseph and implying the fulfillment of his other promises as well.

41:50–52. During Joseph's urgent preparations for the coming famine, God was also at work in Joseph's life. As Joseph's new family began to grow, Joseph commemorated God's lessons to him in the naming of his sons. With his firstborn, Manasseh, in a word play on "forget" (from *nashah*, נשה), Joseph acknowledged how God had worked in his heart, bringing release ("made me forget") from his "hardship" (or "troubles," *HALOT* s.v. I "עָמָל" 845) and "all my father's house" (v. 51), together meaning "my suffering in my parental home."[13]

While the implications of this are not yet evident, they will become clearer soon. He certainly had not forgotten the events of his troubles nor his father's house, but he had found release from the overwhelming impact of them on his life. He had found freedom "from the emotional bondage and trauma" (Hamilton 1995, 512).[14] We will see the implications when he sees his brothers. God was working so that forgiveness was becoming possible for him.

His second son he named Ephraim, playing on the Hebrew for being "fruitful" (from פרה), saying, "God has made me fruitful in the land of my affliction" (v. 52). Not only was Joseph beginning to heal, but he could see God's working in new ways. While God had been with him all along, and he had seen "success" (39:2, 3, 23),

11 The meaning of Joseph's new name is uncertain. Kitchen suggests it stands for "*ḏd-n.f 'Ip-'nḫ* '(Joseph), who is called *'Ip̄'ankḫ*. *ḏd-n.f* would be the well-known construction introducing a second name, the name itself being *'Ip'ankh*, a common name in the Middle Kingdom and Hyksos periods, *i.e.* in the patriarchal and Joseph's age" (Kitchen, "Zaphenath-Paneah," *NBD* 1262).

12 His new wife came from the powerful family at On, or Heliopolis, the center of the sun worship (Re and Atum). "Each pharaoh from the 5th Dynasty onward (25th century BC) was styled 'son of *Rē*', and the priestly corporations of On/Heliopolis were equalled in wealth only by that of the god Ptah of Memphis and exceeded only by that of the god *Amūn* of Thebes, during *c.* 1600–1100 BC" (Kitchen, "On," *NBD* 847–48).

13 Noting the second son's naming deals with his affliction in Egypt, Sarna argues forcefully that both clauses relate a single idea (hendiadys), together meaning "my suffering in my parental home" (Sarna 1989, 289).

14 Steinmann (2019, 390) suggests the idea of "forget" here is "to cease actively thinking about something." Simon (2003, 19) calls it "emotional forgetting (a preliminary to forgiveness)" since he clearly did not forget the information and provides the necessary backdrop for his actions when the brothers arrive.

he characterized it wholly as "suffering." Along with inexplicable pain and frustration, he could now begin to see the end game of his thirteen years of pain, trouble, and disappointment. His fruitfulness could not have been possible without the connections and placement his suffering provided.

41:53–54. The coming of the famine "as Joseph had said" (v. 54) not only validated further his claims, but it also provided the means to accomplish the next stage in God's plans. God had provided for Egypt through Joseph. They had the resources to withstand the coming famine with Joseph's wise management, and Pharaoh continued to give control to Joseph to care for his people.

41:55–57. Joseph opened the storehouses and provided, not only for Egypt, but for "all the earth," "because the famine was severe over all the earth" (v. 57). God's plan and Joseph's work benefitted all the families of the earth. More specifically, it would benefit one family that needed to make the move to Egypt to fulfill God's word and prepare for the next stage in God's plan to bless all the families of the earth.

THEOLOGICAL FOCUS

Working behind the scenes, God orchestrates events to use his people to accomplish his blessing in his world in his time, while growing their faith and perspective in his service.

God most often works behind the scenes, through his people. Without direct divine appearances, Joseph declared God's intention, clearly backed up by the dreams. God alone gives interpretations (40:8), but more importantly, God works in human affairs, revealing that work to Pharaoh to provide salvation for his world (41:25, 38, 32). God used his chosen, Joseph, as the mediator to bring blessing to his world in the form of life through famine. He elevated Joseph in the appropriate time to fulfill Joseph's own dreams, accomplishing his purpose.

At the same time, God showed his power in contrast to the gods of Egypt, presaging the miracles of the exodus. The magicians and wise men of Egypt were unable to interpret the dreams of Pharaoh. Pharaoh showed he was not divine and lacked understanding, much less power to affect the outcome of the coming abundance or famine. The mighty Nile, the source of Egypt's life, both gave life and denied life. It flows at God's command, not Pharaoh's. God would do as he pleased, and Pharaoh could not oppose it. He could only accept God's offer of wisdom through Joseph to mitigate the disaster and preserve lives, passively acknowledging God's sovereignty. God's will is certain.

God had clearly chosen a means to bring about his blessing in his world. He was (and is) moving his plan forward, but he has also revealed that plan and the players in his program that would accomplish his will. The outcome was for the benefit of all humanity, but the means was limited to the chosen conduit. "Ultimately, the outsiders become beneficiaries of the promises through a right relationship with the chosen family (e.g., 12:3; 18:18; 22:18; cf. 49:10)" (Mathews 2005, 740). Under the New Covenant, this truth takes on heightened meaning as we not only see a long period of waiting without clear understanding of how it will resolve, but greater promises and stronger indications of the working of God, even if the pathway is shrouded. We must stand and live in faith, waiting for God to reveal his program and place his king finally in place.

Even in the middle of God's plan, with God's presence and blessing and experiencing God's grace and success, one may feel abandoned and alone, wondering how to find relief from the pain of that life. As with Joseph, we may not understand God's loyal love already on us (39:21) and look for that kindness from sources that cannot ultimately give it (40:14). Since we cannot see the future (shown in multiple ways here), we can never define our own good. We want to choose what we get, how we get it, when we get it, and what it will look like in the end. Instead, we must trust that God not only has the future but each step already in mind and will give the wisdom needed to accomplish his good blessing. God will then faithfully accomplish his work in his timing and graciously reveal his best, occasionally allowing us to glimpse his blessing and find healing from our pain. That is not to say we cannot have ambition, but it is to say that we need to submit our ambition fully to him at each step. Faith requires time, growth, and patient endurance, looking for God's work and learning to trust his hand. My comfort is not a wrong ambition, but it cannot be my highest ambition. Testing must produce the faith and maturity that can come no other way, which leads us to the need for wisdom amid testing (James 1:2–5).

In the process, God calls his people to be faithful, live with integrity, endure hardship patiently, and proclaim the source of all ultimate reality and blessing. We must live in submission to his control, graciously and clearly showing our world the false hope of a pagan worldview and the reality of God's sovereign working. It is the necessary responsibility of the people of God to declare the glory of God so that his world can recognize his working as he accomplishes what only he can do.

PREACHING AND TEACHING STRATEGIES

Exegetical and Theological Synthesis

The opening of chapter 40, "Some time after this," reminds the readers that we are expecting the Lord's powerful presence to result in Joseph being released from prison. One of the important takeaways from this narrative is for us to learn how God accomplishes his will in us during trials, and not just when the trial is over. Ultimately, for Joseph to realize his dream, the Lord must get him closer to Pharaoh. Enter "the cupbearer of the king of Egypt" (v. 1). God moves him into contact with Joseph in prison, where it just so happens that the cupbearer and another important character to the king, "the chief baker" (v. 2), each dream dreams they can't understand. Joseph makes it clear from the start that his God holds the interpretive key, but also says, "Please tell them to me" (v. 8). Joseph, the man of integrity, is linked to his God. He asks to be remembered in hopes of getting out of prison, but the Lord had a different timetable and exit strategy (v. 14).

Readers know Joseph is suffering from injustices at the hands of ungodly men and women. Many of our listeners can relate because they have experienced injustice at home or work. This is one reason why this narrative offers so much hope.

The cupbearer forgot Joseph, but God did not and does not. What is difficult is that sometimes it appears God is in no hurry to alleviate our suffering (41:1 and "After two whole years" on the end of thirteen years!). So, we wait patiently for deliverance; we wait for God to provide the next opportunity to accomplish his will in the world. Faith does that.

God may use our listeners differently than Joseph, but he will always give them a dose of his Spirit (41:38) and place them precisely where he needs them in his kingdom. From there, they can experience and extend the blessing to those around them. In this way all God's children serve the King just as Joseph served the king of Egypt while serving the King of Glory. In this way our listeners find themselves living the life portrayed in the strategic names of Joseph's sons: God will help us forget the troubles and also make us bear fruit in those troubles as we exhibit the kind of spiritual integrity Joseph displayed.

Preaching Idea

Even when you feel forgotten by God, he is working his purposes and accomplishing his will.

Contemporary Connections

What does it mean?

One thing that must be explained so our listeners understand the theology in the section is that Joseph is still in God's hand and headed to a place where he can accomplish his plan for his people and the surrounding world. So, seeing Joseph unjustly in prison intensifies our belief in God's powerful faithfulness to his own plan and purposes in the world. We might not see it this way in our stress-filled moments, but we are beginning to get the big picture as we watch God work his plan in Joseph's life. This prison experience teaches us that God works out his plans for us in a badly broken world. His plan also includes our suffering and our need for patient endurance.

Our listeners and contemporary readers may miss the narrative's emphasis on remembering and forgetting, but you will be sure to highlight this in your exposition. God does not forget us in our suffering. Joseph was forgotten by one character, but not the main character, God! What seems to be a long two years for Joseph does not mean that God forgot him and his promises to his people. It is also important to show how Joseph's dialogue makes it clear that it is his God who receives credit for the ultimate interpretive skills. Finally, help your listeners know the significance of the names Joseph gave to his sons born to him in Egypt. Their names show what God does for his children who rely on him, and they reflect Joseph's integrity.

Is it true?

I can envision some of our listeners being in such dire straits that they say, "Do I really believe that what happened to Joseph can happen to me in my circumstances?" While we can't prove it to them, we can teach and preach this narrative so they see that Joseph's journey is a paradigm for all genuine believers. In Genesis 40–41 the author assumes that God is working behind the scenes throughout Joseph's hardships and roller-coaster existence. Our listeners may need some convincing.

One way to help them is to show how the Lord has been keeping his promises throughout the early chapters of Genesis. You don't need to take a lot of time to recite a long list of unfaithful characters who meet the faithfulness of God time and time again. So far, none of the struggles of faith in the patriarchs is enough to derail God's plan for his people. And even though God takes his sweet ole time, Joseph ends up exalted to power—dream come true. And that is great news for God's children and his world. This is a solid reminder of God's faithfulness in our lives. The more we rehearse this to each other, the more built up is his body.

Now what?

What difference does this narrative make in our lives? I am glad you asked. Every listener needs the assurance that comes from this part of the Joseph story. That is because every one of us inevitably finds ourselves in circumstances that are, to say the least, unpleasant. We say, "Surely this can't be what God has for me!" So, we watch Joseph live with integrity; we watch him wait and hope and even present a possible way out. But we also watch God control the events and circumstances in Joseph's life and in all those who encounter him. And, by the end of the story, Joseph's dream comes true, and he is right where God wants him to be, doing exactly what God called him to do. It does not get any better than that, does it? Watch your listeners leave church with a newfound appreciation for God's sovereign control and faithfulness.

Creativity in Presentation

Joseph helps us see that even when you feel forgotten by God, he is working his purposes and accomplishing his will. You could provide your own example or use another's with permission. Our listeners know what it is like to feel that God is nowhere to be found or that it doesn't look like he is being faithful to his promises. But these are the moments when the faithfulness of God shines brightest, especially in hindsight. What we are hoping is that the hindsight for some creates foresight in all who will, no doubt, face trials in their faith journey. Joseph was not the first or last of God's children to face injustice and be forced to trust in God's faithfulness. The key, of course, is to get everyone in God's house to be able to place themselves in this narrative, following Joseph's example. Joseph is squarely in God's will, despite the hardship; but are all our listeners? Some will need to be challenged to realign themselves with God and his ways; others will need the comfort that comes from seeing how Joseph ends up.

If you follow the narrative, your sermon/lesson might take the following shape:

- God is equipping you to make him look good in the world (ch. 40). These minutes highlight Joseph's integrity (from the last unit) and his ability to tap into the knowledge of God to interpret dreams. Interpretations belong to God, who enabled Joseph. In this sense God equips us all to do what he needs done in our circle of influence. In a general sense, we want all our listeners to be able to answer the question of 41:38: "Yes, I am that person in whom is the Spirit of God."

- God works behind the scenes to bring you to your place of kingdom service (41:1–36). This block repeats and restates the movement of key characters that end up ushering Joseph into Pharaoh's presence, exactly where God wants him. Our listeners may not see this until hindsight provides new perspective. But they can have hope from Joseph's journey and the way God orchestrates the circumstances to use Joseph.

- "God has made me forget all my hardship" and "God has made me fruitful in the land of my affliction" (41:37–57). You might end the sermon/lesson with a theological interpretation of the names of Joseph's two sons. Joseph experiences resolution for this part of his journey and gives appropriate names to his two sons. Our listeners will want to see themselves and their lives reflected in these names.

DISCUSSION QUESTIONS

1. What verses in the New Testament can substantiate our understanding that hardship and affliction are redeemable for all God's children?

2. Joseph evidences the "Spirit of God" with his ability to interpret dreams. What other evidences do Christians show that equip them to do God's will in the world? How can God's wisdom work in our world for God's glory?

3. It's one thing for Egypt's second-in-command to spread the blessing of God to others, but what are some ways the "ordinary Joes and Janes" can do it?

4. Since the testing helps to grow us in maturity (James 1:2–3), how can we balance our desire and ability to remove the testing with resting in God's work and letting him care for the test?

5. What clues help you see God's working while you are experiencing struggle?

6. What are some ways that you can commemorate God's working in your life (such as Joseph naming his sons) so that you and others can be encouraged in the future?

Genesis 42:1–44:34

EXEGETICAL IDEA

Two trips to Egypt with ongoing testing during God's designed famine revealed God's work in Joseph's brothers, bringing them to repentance and unity to save Benjamin through Judah's self-sacrifice.

THEOLOGICAL FOCUS

God uses testing and life circumstances to awaken the consciences of his people and lead them to repentance, prompting them to choose brother-love and self-sacrifice over self-love.

PREACHING IDEA

Our sovereign God, in his perfect timing, transforms us all by testing our faith so we can represent him in the world.

PREACHING POINTERS

The original audience has been watching Joseph's rise to power, albeit with some ups and downs along the way. They know the dreams are coming true. So when chapter 41 concludes with "all the earth [coming] to Egypt to Joseph to buy grain" (v. 57), all that's left is for Joseph's whole family to arrive (chapters 42–44). The first part of the dream comes true in 42:6. Now it is time for Joseph's brothers to come face-to-face with their sins (quite the opposite of their own estimation: "We are honest men" in 42:11, 31, 33, 34).

Joseph crafts the perfect set of circumstances to test their integrity (42:15, "By this you will be tested") and lead them to repentance. Trying to convince his father, Israel, to allow "the boy" to join his brothers, a transformed Judah promises to protect him (43:9). Joseph constructs the visit in a way that highlights how the brothers will treat their youngest brother, Benjamin. Full confession follows in 44:20. This part of the narrative unfolds with Judah leading the way to making sure he and his brothers do not repeat the sins of their past. Their dialogue is replete with confession and genuine guilt for the way in which they treated their brother Joseph. The test works.

TRANSFORMATION: GOD'S HEART WORK (42:1–44:34)

LITERARY STRUCTURE AND THEMES

With Joseph ruling in Egypt, the stage was set to accomplish Joseph's dreams and God's covenant promises to Abraham (15:12–21). This section brings us to the midpoint of the fourth-generation stories, where Joseph's testing of his brothers revealed the working of God in their lives. At the climax, Judah's emotional plea (ch. 44) prompted Joseph's unveiling (ch. 45) and his disclosure of God's working, the theological heart of the fourth-generation series. Chapters 42–45 form a unit describing two parallel trips of the family from Canaan to Egypt and back, with Joseph's testing of his brothers as the main plotline.

For exposition, we have broken this larger section into two sections to be able to focus initially on the working of God in the hearts of the brothers, fostering their repentance (chs. 42–44) and prompting Joseph's response, showing God's working to produce startling forgiveness from his heart (ch. 45). The structure of Joseph's testing of his brothers builds the tensions surrounding their attitude toward Benjamin, their guilt toward Joseph, and their growing awareness of God at work (middle dialogues). In the background (outer frame of each section) lies the broken heart of a father losing sons and struggling to trust God, balanced by an emerging portrait of his sons' hearts melting under the progressive realization of their heinous actions. At the center of each section Joseph increased the pressure, revealing their hearts. The final turning point, where the brothers are interrupted in their return to Canaan with the contrived charge of theft, leads to the climactic interaction between the brothers, led by Judah, and Joseph.[1]

I. Going to Egypt for grain, Jacob's sons were tested by Joseph (42:1–38).
- A. Jacob sent his ten sons to Egypt for grain (42:1–4).
  - B. The men mingled with the crowd going to Egypt (42:5).
    - C. Joseph recognized his brothers and accused them of spying (42:6–16).
      - D. Joseph imprisoned his brothers to test them (42:17).
    - C'. Joseph refined the test, keeping only Simeon (42:18–24).
  - B'. Returning home, the returned silver prompted their growing guilt (42:25–28).
- A'. Jacob refused to allow Benjamin to return to Egypt (42:29–38).

II. Returning to Egypt for more testing, Jacob's sons repented, revealing God's purposes and bringing comfort to Jacob (43:1–45:28).
- A''. Jacob allowed his eleven sons to return to Egypt for grain (43:1–14).
  - B''. The brothers returned to Egypt with gifts (43:15).
    - C''. Joseph isolated the men (43:16).

1 The main contours of the parallels between ch. 42 and chs. 43–45, with the basic chiasm, are noted by Westermann (2002, 118), including the disruption of the second return leading to the "turning point." The details are arranged differently by various authors (cf. Humphreys 1988, 97; Ross 1988, 649; Wenham 1994, 404).

D'. Reassured, they were reunited with Simeon (43:17–25).
C'''. Joseph entertained them generously (43:26–34).
B'''. Joseph dismissed them with a trap (44:1–3).
B''''. Joseph's steward sprung the trap, returning them to Joseph (44:4–13).[2]
C''''. Judah pled for Benjamin, showing transformation (44:14–34).
D''. Joseph was overcome with emotion (45:1–2).
C'''''. Joseph revealed God's sovereign purpose (45:3–15).
B'''''. Israel's sons returned to Canaan with gifts (45:16–24).
A'''. Jacob recognized, with difficulty, Joseph's hand (45:25–28).

Though God's working is not yet foregrounded by Joseph (45:4–8), the reader can see the growing awareness of guilt before God in the reactions of the brothers. The transformation of character is most pronounced in Judah, but all the brothers act in solidarity. Joseph's motives are also only progressively revealed, showing God's work in his heart, though the full transformation will only be unveiled in chapter 45. Even Jacob shows God's work as he grudgingly moves toward trusting El Shaddai for Benjamin. All of this occurs in the crucible of testing, which both reveals what is occurring in the hidden recesses of the heart and confronts each one with the realities and choices he or she must make and the values they must choose. Though Joseph planned the testing, the reader progressively realizes that God was behind it all.

- ***Going to Egypt, Jacob's Sons Were Tested by Joseph (42:1–38)***

- ***Returning to Egypt for More Testing, Jacob's Sons Repented (43:1–44:34)***

EXPOSITION

In the movement of the narrative through the fourth-generation stories, Joseph's dreams and Judah's character will now come into focus as they will combine to exhibit God's superintending of his program, even in the choices and lived tensions of his chosen instruments. While the basic structure follows the geographical flow of their two trips, the themes draw on the whole of the narratives, working to draw together God's work to move forward his covenant with Abraham. Approaching the climax at the center of the *toledot* (chs. 44–45), God's working continues to be backgrounded and only tantalizingly revealed in bits and pieces in the awakening consciences and growing awareness of the characters to God's role. Though they do not fully comprehend nor accurately evaluate it all, the narrator uses them to direct the reader's attention through what he or she knows to a closer recognition of the truth.

The dialogue, as we have come to expect, largely carries the intent of the storyline, with extended retelling of past events that uncovers the movement and subtleties of the plot. The progress and contrasts from the first trip to Egypt (ch. 42) to the second trip (chs. 43–44) highlight the growing tensions and changing character of the men, clarifying God's work and message to the reader. Two trips to Egypt with ongoing testing during God's designed famine revealed God's work in Joseph's brothers, bringing them to repentance and unity to save Benjamin through Judah's self-sacrifice.

2 Cf. Westermann (2002, 118), where he notes that the interruption of the brothers' return to Canaan in 44:4–45:24 forms the "turning point," without which "the structures are parallel." Chapter 45 concludes the parallel, with their return to Canaan and report to Jacob in preparation for the final return to Egypt.

Going to Egypt, Jacob's Sons Were Tested by Joseph (42:1–38)

Jacob sent ten sons to Egypt to buy lifesaving grain, where they unknowingly encountered Joseph, endured his testing that began to reveal God's work in them, and returned home without Simeon to retrieve Benjamin so they could live, which Jacob refused.

The first trip to Egypt by the ten sons of Jacob responds to the need of the famine that "was severe over all the earth" (41:57). Moses frames this pericope with the problem of the famine and the concern to keep Benjamin safe as the favored son. These two factors (one external and one internal) will drive the action and the transformation in the family. The famine shows God bringing pressure to bear on the broken family relations and motivating their move to Egypt. Jacob's prohibition on Benjamin's travel sets the stage for Joseph's test and the revelation (or awakening) of the brother's guilty consciences, opening them up to God's working in their lives. In this section, Reuben, for the final time, awkwardly attempts to take the lead, without earning a reply from Jacob. The stage will be set, however, for the second trip, clarifying the implications for all involved.

Jacob Sent His Ten Sons to Egypt for Grain (42:1–4)

Jacob sent his ten sons to Egypt to buy grain to preserve their lives in the famine God sent, keeping Benjamin home to protect him from harm.

42:1–4. The severe famine "over all the earth" (41:57), orchestrated by God (41:25), had reached Canaan, where Jacob's family faced the real possibility of starvation without grain. Jacob's words, however, reveal both the severity of the situation (it was life or death, 42:2) and his attitude toward his ten sons. His condescending words ("Why do you look at one another?" v. 1) and protection of Benjamin shows that not much had changed in the family dynamics over the past twenty-one years since Joseph was sold into slavery. Ironically, however, Jacob, who sent Joseph to his brothers, landing him in Egypt, now sends the brothers to Joseph, which will land them all in Egypt. Previously, Joseph was at their mercy. Now they are at his (Sarna 1989, 291). In the process, they will relive Joseph's enslavement, for their good.

The Men Mingled with the Crowd Going to Egypt (42:5)

The sons of Israel went to Egypt among the crowd to purchase grain.

42:5. The "sons of Israel" arrived in a crowd from Canaan because of the famine. The fact that they came in such a crowd and bowed before Joseph personally (42:6), in such a vast country of which he was in control, and he recognized them, alerts the reader to God's clandestine control as he moves the players into place for his drama. The choice to call them the "sons of Israel" here (in this unit only used again in 45:21, when they return to bring Jacob back to the land) suggests foreshadowing of the future nation in Egypt or perhaps the tribal implications for the actions of the men (Wenham 1994, 406).

Joseph Recognized His Brothers and Accused Them of Spying (42:6–16)

Recognizing his brothers and remembering his dreams, Joseph maintained his anonymity, accusing them of spying while learning of their family.

42:6–7. The brothers just happened to end up directly before Joseph, bowing to him. He was the "governor" (v. 6, שַׁלִּיט) and was selling the grain.[3] Joseph immediately recognized them

3 Alter (1981, 162–63) connects the two designations to the two dreams in which the sheaves foreshadow his position of provider and the sun, moon, and stars bowing foreshadowed his authority.

(repeated twice), but he spoke to them harshly (cf. 37:4 where they could not speak peacefully to him), keeping them from recognizing him (also repeated in 42:7–8). Did their appearance without Benjamin concern Joseph for his brother (Kuruvilla 2014, 516, n. 16)? His curt introduction questioned their origin.

TRANSLATION ANALYSIS 42:6
The term translated "governor" (שַׁלִּיט) only occurs here and in Ecclesiastes and emphasizes the power of the office (*HALOT* s.v. "שַׁלִּיט" 1524; s.v. "שָׁלַט" 1521–22; H. Austel, s.v. "שָׁלַט" *TWOT* 929). It may well be descriptive of his role as vizier (NJPS), though "governor" (e.g., ESV, NIV) or "ruler" (e.g., NASB95, NET) are appropriate.

TRANSLATION ANALYSIS 42:7
The expression relays the idea of disguising himself from them (*HALOT* s.v. "נכר" 700; cf. 1 Kings 14:5–6, so NASB95) more than merely pretending he did not know them ("treated them like strangers," ESV, NET, NIV, or "acted as if he didn't know them," NCV), though his line of questioning certainly did make it appear he did not know them.

42:8–11. Repeating that Joseph recognized them and clarifying that they did not recognize him, the text reveals that Joseph remembered his dreams. In contrast to the effect of God's working to put away his painful memories of his past (41:51), it seems to come flooding back in. His following accusation of the men leaves the reader wondering about Joseph's motive. Was he plotting revenge (Brueggemann 1982a, 340)? Or were his motives more benign? Sternberg (1987, 286) notes the ambiguity in the text, leading the reader through the changing implications from revenge to testing, teaching, and dream fulfillment and a happier future. The ambiguity helps the reader feel the tensions and be drawn into the drama. Joseph must be tough to discover the truth of their hearts and the well-being of his family.

The note that he remembered the dreams directs the reader's attention back to the dreams, and we realize that his dreams portrayed two different scenarios. In the first, the brothers' sheaves bowed to his (37:7), which appears to have been fulfilled here as they bow when coming to buy grain (see note on 42:6 above). In the second dream, however, it was the sun, moon, and eleven stars that bowed (37:9), which is yet to be fulfilled. They also implied God's future working, which Joseph apparently now recalls. Was this another evidence, allowing him to see all of this painful history as God's clandestine handiwork (Spero 2018, 112)?

The briefly related interview follows Joseph's question regarding their origin with the allegation by Joseph of them spying (three times) to find out where Egypt was vulnerable. Initially, they repeated their mission of buying food, adding that they were all from the same family, and protesting their innocence. The argument of being from one family suggests that they would be foolish to send the entire family as spies and risk the demise of the whole family should they be caught (Wenham 1994, 407).

TRANSLATION ANALYSIS 42:9
To discover the "nakedness" of the land (ESV, and the literal translation, עֶרְוַת) is referencing the weaknesses (NCV, RSV) or vulnerabilities (NET, NLT). Walton (2009a, 132) suggests that Joseph is insinuating they are looking to rob storehouses of food rather than any direct attack.

42:12–16. When he repeated his charge, they elaborated on their family, divulging the existence of Benjamin and the loss of Joseph, though neither is named and their description of the "one [that] is no more" both softens and leaves ambiguous the fate of the twelfth, here deeply ironic in their reply to Joseph. Joseph, seemingly unimpressed, proposed a test to prove the "truth" (אֱמֶת) of their words. He then took an oath that they would be considered spies if their words did not prove true, implying the penalty that comes with spying. Again, the irony significantly impacts the way the reader hears his words. The brothers need to prove their story. Joseph wants to see their integrity—their character (Kruschwitz 2012, 404). His test required one of them to retrieve the unnamed brother from Canaan to prove their veracity, while the rest were left in prison. Presumably they would choose who would go free to gain their freedom. In the process he would see their character.

Joseph's Oath

Joseph's oath "by the life of Pharaoh" (42:15) adds a very Egyptian touch to his harsh questioning. To swear by the life of the god or the king was common and expected here since Pharaoh was a god as well and gave the statement the force of law (Wilson 1948, 130–31). They would be considered spies, with the resulting penalties, if they did not prove their innocence.

Joseph Imprisoned His Brothers to Test Them (42:17)

Joseph imprisoned them to test them by bringing Benjamin to Egypt.

42:17. At the center of this chapter, structurally, Joseph bound his brothers over to "custody" (מִשְׁמָר), the term used four times of the officers of Pharaoh who were in prison with Joseph (40:3, 4, 7; 41:10). Joseph's test of their words was beginning to provide them with a taste of his experience and would get more pointed. It also renews attention on his motivations. It appears now that he was not merely looking for revenge, but that he was probing their reactions to see what was going on in the family. He was concerned for Benjamin and not willing to take their word for it. His ten brothers had shown up without the youngest, whom he knew was also favored. Was Benjamin safe? Their words must be tested.

Joseph Refined the Test, Keeping Only Simeon (42:18–24)

Joseph renegotiated the test, keeping only Simeon, learning of their guilty consciences and Reuben's efforts for Joseph.

42:18–20. On the third day, Joseph changed the terms of his test, ostensibly because he feared God. Within the context of Genesis, the claim to "fear God" requires a higher standard of morality and perhaps compassion (see Exposition on 22:12, p. 394). It calls to mind Abraham's concern that he and Sarah would be abused in Gerar because of Sarah's beauty, since he thought there was "no fear of God" there (20:11). Specifically, here, Joseph acknowledged the need for their families to have food in the famine (42:19). From the reader's perspective, however, Joseph's words suggest his loyalty to Yahweh and so God's working behind the scenes. Joseph at least claimed that his plan was sanctioned by his "god" and so appropriate and moral. It provides another clue that would support Joseph's claim to God's overarching supervision of their history (45:5–9). It also mitigates the question of Joseph's motives, softening his stance toward his brothers and their families. On the other hand, the new conditions even more precisely remind them of their treatment of Joseph. He bound one of them and put him in custody, in what he had called a "pit" (40:15; 41:14), reminiscent of them putting him in a "pit" (37:20, 22, 24, 28, 29).

42:21–22. The men's response to Joseph's mitigation is surprising. Rather than being relieved, they recount their callous guilt from ignoring Joseph's "distress" (צָרָה) and pleas, concluding their current "distress" (צָרָה) was a direct result. They see the connection, the working of God, and perhaps a conviction that the Egyptian was acting with greater integrity than they had (Mathews 2005, 779–80). Now it was Joseph's turn to learn new information as Reuben gave them his "I told you so" speech (v. 22). His conclusion assumed Joseph's death and mirrors the penalty pronounced by God to Noah in 9:5, which would require their own lives.

42:23–24. While the brothers were expressing their guilt and mourning their past cruelty, Joseph was also hearing their remorse for the first time, and it directly led to his deep emotion. The new insight into Joseph's heart shows increasing softness. The reader also realizes for the first time that Joseph's ruse included an interpreter so that the brothers would not realize he understood all that they were saying. Joseph was in control of the events, though his emotions were tender.

Joseph, returning to them, singled out Simeon, the second born, to remain behind. Since Reuben had divulged his attempt to deliver Joseph the first time, Simeon was the next in line of birth and authority. Joseph made a point of binding him in front of them to imprison him (v. 24). How would they respond to a brother in distress this time?

Returning Home, the Silver Prompted Their Growing Guilt (42:25–28)

Returning home, they discovered the silver with the grain, prompting fear and further guilt.

42:25–28. Joseph's orders appear generous, giving them their grain and returning their money, even giving them provisions. Was he reminding them again of their sale of him, by leaving a brother and going home with extra money (Sternberg 1987, 293–94)? Did he hear and remember Judah's comment looking for their own profit from selling him (37:26)? In fact, it seems that the reader is intended to make that connection because the word "silver" (כֶּסֶף) occurs twenty times in Genesis 42–45, the number of pieces for which he was sold (37:28; Sarna 1989, 303). Did they remember Joseph again when they discovered the money in one of the sacks and wondered, "What is this that God has done to us" (v. 28)? Neither the brothers nor the reader know where this twist will lead, but both are convinced that God is at work. They assume God is calling them to account.[4] The brothers were expecting retribution of some sort. The awakened guilt in their consciences, however, suggests to the reader that God is working.

Jacob Refused to Allow Benjamin to Return to Egypt (42:29–38)

Reporting back to Jacob, they lobbied to return, but, discovering the money, Jacob refused to allow Benjamin to go, even with Reuben's assurance.

42:29–34. When they reported to Jacob, they shortened the events, reporting the essential facts. While they were truthful, they downplayed the trauma. They left out their imprisonment for three days and Joseph binding Simeon to put him back in prison. They simply reported that the "lord of the land" required that they "leave one of your brothers with me" (v. 33). Their conclusion that, with Benjamin with them, they could "trade in the land" (v. 34) follows logically, though not specifically reported in the initial account, and they left out the threat of death if they did not come back with Benjamin. All of this appears designed to spare Jacob concern and gain release of Benjamin to return.

42:35–38. Jacob did not respond immediately to their account. Rather, as they unloaded, they discovered the silver in their sacks, alarming all of them. Jacob immediately responded with lament and accusation. Interestingly, at this point he blames them for both Joseph and Simeon. Sternberg (1987, 298) concludes that Jacob saw the silver, remembered the extra money they came home with after Joseph

4 "What is this that God has done to us" (v. 28) echoes God's calling of sinners to account by "put[ting] them in peril (cf. 3:13; 12:18; 26:10; 29:25; Exod 14:11; Jonah 1:10)" (Mathews 2005, 782).

disappeared, and put the pieces together that they had sold both sons for money. Later, after he heard Judah's heart, he would assume (or try to believe) it was merely a mistake (43:12). Though they all assumed it was trouble, they did not know what to make of it.

The Discovery Reports

The narrator reports here that they discovered the money in all their sacks after returning home. However, they told Joseph's steward that they had discovered the money in their sacks that first night on the way home (43:21). While they could have made up the story to try to impress Jacob or mitigate the damage by not admitting they already knew it (Sarna 1989, 296), Alter appropriately notes that when the narrator states something, he is always to be trusted (Alter 1981, 140; cf. Sternberg 1987, chs. 2–3). Rather than assume differing accounts that were poorly put together or attempted deception of their father, the report to the steward should be seen as a summary, telescoping the events, discovering the money initially in one sack on the way home and generalizing since they saw it in all of them at home (Mathews 2005, 769–70).

Reuben attempted for the final time to lead. Offering the lives of two of his four sons if Benjamin was harmed (as if killing grandsons would ease the pain of a father losing his son), he awkwardly attempted to assure Benjamin's safety.[5] Jacob's response only added to the tension. Calling Benjamin his "only one left," even though probably referring to the sons of Rachel, Jacob clearly stated their value to him and his self-focus in contrast to Joseph's consciousness of the others (Cotter 2003, 309–10).

Returning to Egypt for More Testing, Jacob's Sons Repented (43:1–44:34)

Jacob sent eleven of his sons to Egypt a second time to buy lifesaving grain, where they again encountered Joseph, requiring them to unite to save Benjamin through Judah's self-sacrifice.

As noted above, this second trip does not conclude until the end of chapter 45. Though they began to return in this section, their return was interrupted by Joseph's final test, and they all returned to the city to face Joseph and learn the truth. In this section that closely parallels chapter 42, Joseph turned up the pressure again in his testing, exposing God's working in their lives and prompting his own revelation to them in chapter 45. With greater opportunity to abandon Benjamin and greater difficulty to stand up for him, their character would show.

Jacob Allowed His Eleven Sons to Return to Egypt for Grain (43:1–14)

With the specter of starvation and Judah's vow of responsibility, Jacob relented, sending Benjamin with the brothers to Egypt with double money, a gift for the vizier, and a prayer for grace.

43:1–5. The new section begins as the previous one had, with the famine making life difficult. Waiting until they had no choice, having eaten all the grain, Jacob suggested they go back down and buy a little grain, as if it was a trip to the corner grocery. His demeanor was dramatically subdued from his previous sarcastic order to get grain (42:1–2). Judah, again taking the lead, reminded him that they could not go without Benjamin (framing his speech, 43:3, 5).[6]

5 Though it may well have been "hyperbole for dramatic effect" (Mathews 2005, 783), it was a foolish and painful use of hyperbole. Already discredited because of his affair with Bilhah (35:22), Reuben seems to have little pull with his father.

6 The initial narrative did not include Joseph stating they could "not see [his] face" (nor that they could "trade in the land," 42:34). The narrative does not report every word that was said, so it is possible that these were omitted

43:6–7. When Israel[7] complained that they had abused him by mentioning Benjamin, they all seemed to jump in and defend their response, declaring "the man" had specifically questioned them on both their father and other family members. Though these questions were not reported initially, it not only fits, but it makes sense of Judah's account to Joseph that he had questioned them precisely along these lines (44:19–20). They felt the pressure, and Joseph was probing.

43:8–10. Leading, Judah offered to personally vouch for Benjamin's safety. He argued that there was no choice. If they did not go, they would all die ("we and you and also our little ones," v. 8), so the risk was minimal. He could risk one son so that they could all live, or all would die anyway.

Alternately, Judah set himself apart from Reuben, who had offered his own sons' lives for Benjamin. Judah stood responsible himself. While the narrative does not explain all the reasons for their changing characters, it does provide the background, which implies that Judah was dramatically impacted by his personal history (ch. 38). He had lost two sons (vv. 7–10). He had recognized his own unrighteousness (v. 26), and it had not been long since his own unexpected twin sons had been born to him (vv. 27–30). His heart toward Jacob and Benjamin and his responsibilities to the family have dramatically shifted, as the next chapter will show.

43:11–14. Under duress, Israel offered a plan to make as good of an impression as possible. Reminding the reader of his approach to Esau (32:13–21), he put together a gift of the "choice fruits of the land" (43:11). Ironically, the best of the land included the three things the Ishmaelites were taking to Egypt with Joseph ("balm" [צֳרִי], "gum" [נְכֹאת], and "myrrh" [לֹט], 37:25) along with honey, pistachios, and almonds. Amid a famine, this was a desperate attempt (Steinmann 2019, 403–4). Besides trying to convince himself that the returned money was an "oversight" (43:12), Israel offered a prayer for grace from El Shaddai.[8] The use of El Shaddai here appropriately draws on God's covenant promises, specifically since "El Shaddai" had expressed them to him at Bethel (35:11) and renamed him (again) "Israel." At that time, God had specifically promised he would become a company of nations, with kings from his line and the land of Canaan for his offspring (35:11–12). Israel seems less transformed than left with no choice but to let them return and trust God for his promises.

The Brothers Returned to Egypt with Gifts (43:15)

The brothers returned to Egypt with double money and a gift for Joseph.

43:15. The brief statement of their return parallels the initial trip to Egypt, previewing their approach to Joseph. They had the favored son, their double money, and a gift to curry favor. As with Jacob's gift to Esau, it would make no difference since God was at work.

Joseph Isolated the Men (43:16)

Joseph sent them to his house for lunch.

43:16. While both trips to Egypt included two audiences with Joseph, the first audience this

---

in the initial telling of the account. As the account slows, it draws attention to the coming climax (Wenham 1994, 420).

7 On the alternating use of "Israel" and "Jacob," see comments on 35:10 above, p. 569, and nn. 9–10. In chapter 42, where he is fearful and clinging to Benjamin, he is called Jacob. In chapters 43–45, where he must release Benjamin and trust Yahweh, remembering "El Shaddai" and God's promises to him, he is called Israel.

8 "God Almighty," אֵל שַׁדַּי, emphasizes God's authority over life and blessing; cf. Translation Analysis 17:1b, p. 323.

time was merely an appearance. He saw them, noted Benjamin, and sent them to his house for lunch. The paradox was not lost on his brothers.

Reassured, They Were Reunited with Simeon (43:17–25)

Concerned they would be enslaved, they offered to repay the silver but were reassured by the steward and reunited with Simeon to wait for Joseph.

43:17–25. The brothers assumed their move to his home was an effort to enslave them and confiscate their belongings for theft. Though Joseph's reason for returning their money is never revealed, he may simply have intended to see what they would do and add pressure to them. The returned money certainly compounded their problems, with the possible accusation that they were not honest but were in fact thieves (Simon 2003, 23). Would they return to Egypt with that unknown cloud hanging over them, even to rescue Simeon and get grain for their starving families? How long would it take them?

As a result of their concern, they tried to pre-empt any accusation by confessing to the steward and returning the money. His words both reassured the brothers that he had been fully paid and connect the reader's attention to the working of God. Again, ironically, the Egyptian steward wished them "peace" (שָׁלוֹם) and declared the "treasure" from their "God, the God of [their] father" (v. 23). It was as if they were getting an immediate answer to Israel's prayer for mercy when they left. It was "peace" (שָׁלוֹם) they were not able to give to Joseph (37:4) and "peace" (שָׁלוֹם) Jacob had sent Joseph to discover about them (37:14) when Joseph was sold. It will only be through the fire of the coming test that they will gain the peace they so desire.

TRANSLATION ANALYSIS 43:23

The translations consistently focus on the previous payment and seem to miss the point of the brothers thinking they would be accused of stealing it back. In comparing the Aramaic equivalent, however, Muffs (1973, 289, emphasis his) shows that the steward's response was a legal formula stating that they need not worry because their payment had "*already* been received in full and I have absolutely no claims against you."

Joseph's instructions appear intended to make them comfortable and relaxed, necessary for the next stage in the test. Presumably, Joseph scripted the words of the steward. When he brought out Simeon to them, the steward gave them the customary hospitality of water for foot washing and feed for the animals. The brothers prepared their gift for Joseph, hearing they were to eat with him.

Joseph Entertained Them Generously (43:26–34)

Joseph entertained them generously, learning about the family and putting them at ease.

43:26–34. Again, when Joseph arrived, he continued to calm them. This time all eleven brothers bow with their gift, fulfilling the second dream.[9] Joseph's demeanor, dramatically different from the first time, was gracious and gentle, inquiring of the welfare of their father and blessing Benjamin, even calling him "my son" (v. 29). He projected a new image to his brothers. The repeated use of "peace" (שָׁלוֹם, three times in vv. 27–28, translated "welfare" or "well") belies what would follow. His reaction to seeing Benjamin up close again reveals compassion

9 The brothers emphasized their father as "your servant" to Joseph, and Jacob never physically bowed to Joseph in the narrative (Mathews 2005, 790). Jacob's "present" (מִנְחָה, four times in vv. 11, 15, 25, 26), which they are presenting, is often used of tribute to a superior (e.g., Judg. 3:15, 17–18; 2 Sam. 8:2) and showed his submission to Joseph's authority (cf. "present" [מִנְחָה] and bowing to Esau, 32:13–21 [HB 32:14–22]; 33:3, 10).

toward his brothers for the reader, prompting more questions about his motives.

Returning after his tears, he maintained the customary distance of the Egyptians, without indicating any connection with the men. While he raised their curiosity by seating them in order, they do not appear to have thought long enough to be concerned, since they drank and got drunk with Joseph (וַיִּשְׁכְּרוּ, cf. ESV footnote, v. 34). Joseph set up his final test brilliantly.

Joseph Dismissed Them with a Trap (44:1–3)

Joseph sent them away with the silver and his cup planted in the sacks.

44:1–3. Joseph's servant carried out his orders fully, showing Joseph's ongoing plan. He shows both generosity with the grain ("as much as they can carry," v. 1) and again with the returned silver. The cup, presumably visible at their luncheon, would provide the means to probe their hearts more deeply.

Joseph's Steward Sprung the Trap, Returning Them to Joseph (44:4–13)

As soon as they left, the steward overtook them, accused them, searched them, and revealed the cup, so that they all returned to the city.

44:4–5. Joseph's steward exposed the final test. He was, in fact, reenacting the original crime (Sternberg 1987, 303). Would they take the opportunity to be rid of Benjamin? Joseph provided incentive and opportunity to save face and be rid of the final favored son. This test, however, would reveal the working of God in their lives and would reverse the ongoing brotherly conflicts that began in Genesis 4, providing encouraging insight into the working of God to bring healing and reconciliation to the hearts and families torn apart by sin and alienation from God.[10]

Though the report is clearly a summary, it shows that Joseph scripted the steward's approach to the brothers. His accusation of repaying "evil for good" (v. 4) was serious, describing "malicious exploitation of a person's kindness (e.g., 1 Sam 25:21; cf. Prov 17:13)" (Mathews 2005, 798). When David accused Nabal of a similar crime, he was going to exact the death penalty until Abigail intervened (1 Sam. 25:21). Building on the previous day's mystery of knowing their birth order, the steward claimed divination for Joseph.[11] Of course, Joseph would learn a lot through this cup, even if not through traditional divination (Walton 2001, 681). With the previous day's events and Joseph's kindness after his harshness, all of this would have been not only easy to believe but overwhelming when the cup was discovered.

Divination

Divination here refers to several possible means that were used across the ancient world to attempt to determine what could happen in the future. It could include pouring oil on water (or water on oil) and observing the patterns, colors, bubbles, or movements (lecanomancy) or merely observing the movements and reflections of the water (hydromancy), oil (oleomancy), or wine (oenomancy). Little is known from Egypt, while

10 "Brother" (אָח), used fifty times in chs. 42–45, is clearly a theme throughout Genesis (appearing 155 times). The focus on the brothers here, however, after the reconciliation of Jacob and Esau in ch. 33, is only the second resolution of sibling rivalry and conflict and the first with clear resolution in the lives of both parties.

11 While it is true that divination is forbidden in the law and an abomination to Yahweh (Lev. 19:26; Deut. 18:10–12), the narrator does not tell us that Joseph was practicing divination, but only that the steward claimed that Joseph did, certainly for the impression on the brothers. Whether it was true or not is left open. Similarly, in verse 15 Joseph told them a "man like him" (אִישׁ אֲשֶׁר כָּמֹנִי) could certainly practice divination. Even there he did not claim it certainly for himself, though he intended to plant that impression.

extensive texts come from Mesopotamia (Cryer 1994, 145–47; Walton 2001, 681). Divination assumes the constancy of human history as ordered by the gods. If an unusual pattern occurs with a certain event, the repetition of the pattern indicates the gods revealing the same sort of event recurring, presenting the need to record observed correlations.

Divination Text. Near Eastern Antiquities in the Louvre. Photo by Poulpy.

44:6–9. The steward followed Joseph's words precisely, with the desired impact. The brothers were so certain of their innocence they reacted with one voice, vowing death to the offender and slavery for the rest.[12] In their defense, they noted their previous unrequired honesty in returning the first silver, taking the oath to impress the steward with their sincerity ("far be it from," v. 7, is an oath formula, Lehmann 1969, 82–83).

TRANSLATION ANALYSIS 44:7

"Far be it from" uses the verb for profaning (חָלִילָה) and indicated an oath, something like "may it be (my) profanation (in the eyes of God) if I break my oath" (O'Kennedy, חָלַל, NIDOTTE 2:150).

44:10–13. The steward responded agreeably but reduced the penalty to the far lesser sentence of only the guilty party being his servant and the rest allowed to go free.[13] The impact here would continue to tempt the brothers to leave Benjamin while saving face. As with lunch the previous day, the search followed the birth order, certainly driven by Joseph's instructions. Ironically, the silver in each sack is not mentioned, though it must have caused additional consternation.

When the cup was found in Benjamin's sack, the reader now sees the strongest indication that all of them are changing. They all tore their clothes, and "every man" loaded up and returned to the city with the steward (v. 13). They gave no rebuttal nor discussion. There was no indication by any to leave Benjamin and escape. As a unit they all returned to face the charge.

TRANSLATION ANALYSIS 44:13

The Hebrew *אִישׁ*, often translated "man," refers in this case to "each" (NJPS) or "each man" (NET), leading to the sense of "every man" (ESV) or "they all" (NIV), as also twice in verse11.

Judah Pled for Benjamin, Showing Transformation (44:14–34)

Joseph's refusal to accept his brothers' service exposed their transformed hearts, as Judah pled to take Benjamin's place.

12 Their offer is much stiffer than biblical law, and Egyptian law is uncertain (Sarna 1989, 304). They may be using hyperbole to impress the steward with their innocence.

13 Hamilton (1995, 563) notes that in ancient Egypt the parties could propose their own penalties with an oath (as v. 9), and without mitigation by the other party, their offer would stand.

44:14–17. Judah led his brothers into Joseph's house, dramatically falling on their faces.[14] This was not polite deference but desperate pleading. Joseph's response repeated the steward's accusation, with the inference that they could never have gotten away with it. Judah continued to lead, responding to Joseph with resignation, repeating his offer of service from all the brothers (but without the offer of the death penalty to the offender). He acknowledged that they could not "clear" themselves (v. 16).

> *TRANSLATION ANALYSIS 44:16*
> Judah's despair of not being able to "clear ourselves" (נִצְטַדָּק, ESV) or "justify ourselves" (NASB95) repeats a verb only used elsewhere in Genesis when Judah declared Tamar more righteous than him (צָדְקָה מִמֶּנִּי, 38:26). The unusual repetition draws attention to his recognition of their wrongdoing (Kruschwitz 2012, 407).

His statement of their guilt cannot be a confession to Joseph's charge since he knows they are not all guilty, even if he could believe Benjamin would have done it. Rather, by declaring their exposure to God's justice, he used the plural ("servants," עֲבָדֶיךָ, v. 16) for all of them, recognizing this as appropriate retribution for their previous sins against Joseph. They all appear ready to relinquish their freedom, even faced with the false accusation. God has been at work, and they are seeing his fingerprints, even if they are mistaken in how it was working.

Joseph, however, had one more screw to turn, providing yet another opportunity to desert Benjamin for their own safety and profit. He refused their offer with the same oath formula as the brothers had used in verse 7. As emphatically as they asserted their innocence, Joseph rejected their service as innocent parties to the theft. They were free to go "in peace" (לְשָׁלוֹם, v. 17) to their father. Once again, "peace" offers the elusive well-being they have sought for themselves but had been unwilling to give to their brother. They are offered it apart from their brother, and they refuse.

44:18–29. Judah approached Joseph personally. Pleading for an audience, he recounted the events of the past year or so, beginning with their first visit. Judah spoke diplomatically, omitting things that may frustrate this powerful Egyptian but adding new details that would evoke sympathy for their "aged father" (v. 20), referring to their "father" fourteen times (Wenham 1994, 425). Plainly stating their expectation that Joseph was dead, he described the favoritism of their father to Benjamin and attachment to him. That favoritism put them in a difficult position with Joseph's demand to bring him or not return.

In relating Jacob's words, Joseph heard for the first time not only how Jacob had heard of his disappearance, but Judah's (and his brothers') love for Jacob. Judah moved from the difficult decision they were in, to a plea for the well-being of their aged father. He was asking for sympathy for Jacob on the part of this Egyptian, rather than for their own well-being.

44:30–34. Repeating Jacob's melodramatic cry of his impending death, Judah not only accepted it but was willing to give his life in exchange for Benjamin to spare Jacob the trauma. Judah's solution demonstrated love for his father and intent to honor his oath to his father at the expense of his life. He begged to take his brother's place. Judah, as the spokesman for the brothers who had returned in solidarity, showed true

14 Sternberg (1987, 305) notes the shift in the narrative from "the men" (44:1, 3, 4) to "Judah and his brothers" (v. 14), indicating both Judah's leadership and the solidarity of the brothers with Benjamin.

repentance. He had the opportunity to repeat his past sin with ample motivation and personal gain to result, and he chose self-sacrifice and love for his brother and father instead (Alter 1981, 175; Schimmel 1988).

This section has been about the brothers, though we have seen growing and clarifying glimpses into Joseph's heart. While we close here for this preaching unit with the unresolved center of the narrative, the theme of God's work in the lives of the brothers, as particularly expressed in Judah, provides significant opportunities for reflection and encouragement in how God works in hearts over long periods of time and through life choices and circumstances to lead to repentance, as well as how repentance shows and what it requires. The resolution in the following chapter, finishing this section, will provide the other side of the coin as that climactic moment completes the drama of reconciliation. Joseph's response would fully reveal God's work in his heart as well, not only to forgive and restore his relationships but to recognize and foreground God's working, even through evil, to accomplish God's bigger purposes.

THEOLOGICAL FOCUS

God uses testing and life circumstances to awaken the consciences of his people and lead them to repentance, prompting them to choose brother-love and self-sacrifice over self-love.

God's work continues in the background of the narrative. As in most of life, God only appears indirectly. We recognize his working in the inferences and convictions of what appear to us to be coincidence and the pricking of our consciences (the brothers) or worldview (the steward, and Joseph's comment that he fears God). The brothers knew they were being held accountable for their past actions, though they did not fully understand what was happening. This reflects the broader, consistent theology of justice in which God ultimately brings appropriate punishment fitting the crime, even if it is long after the sin (Sailhamer 1990, 253). We see God working consistently in Scripture, and we recognize the same patterns in life, though we also often struggle when he does not do so quickly enough for us.

God's sovereign work shows in accomplishing his grand agenda over time. He had planned and orchestrated their need to go to Egypt (15:13; 41:25), preparing their life circumstance to meet Joseph and recognize their guilt, even as Joseph designed the tests. As Joseph would say in the next chapter, God was working through their evil actions. But he was also working through Joseph's planned testing and contrived crises. Even as the steward suggested with God giving them treasure, God consistently works through human agents to accomplish his purposes (Wenham 1994, 422). That work occurs through "apparently ordinary human deeds and misdeeds" (Cotter 2003, 313–14).

The goal of the testing, from Joseph's perspective, was to expose their hearts and determine the well-being of their father and brother. God, however, used it to bring them to recognition of the consequences of their evil and show true repentance, leading finally to reconciliation. In the process, they would take responsibility, mend relationships, and demonstrate selfless sacrifice for their brother. While Judah stood as the spokesman, the brothers acted in solidarity with him, showing the broad working in each heart. Human agents can contrive tests to determine information, circumstances, and perhaps even motivations, but God works in hearts to bring change. Humanity, however, must respond to his work.

The theme of love for the brother has been consistent in Genesis since Cain and Able (ch. 4). Particularly in the Jacob stories, it has taken center stage again with Jacob and Esau, including their conflicts and their resolution, and now Joseph and his brothers, with their conflicts and resolution. Distance from God shows graphically in hating and deceiving a brother, but the working of God shows in the reconciliation and love for a brother, already seen in Genesis 33 in Jacob's reconciliation with Esau and his words of amazement (v. 10). Here, that love is taken a step farther as God has worked in the ten brothers, with the numerous expressions of guilt and acknowledgement of sin leading to repentance and their show of love for the father who had offended them as well. The righteous love their brother or sister, shown here in Joseph's grace toward his brothers (and more, in his forgiveness in the next passage), but also here in God's working to transform the brothers from trying to kill their brother to giving their lives to save their brother and honor their father. The working of God is showing in the transformation of heart attitudes.

As we see in the brothers, shunning the very sin previously committed when presented with another similar opportunity graphically shows repentance. It includes recognizing the sin, confessing, rejecting the sin, and choosing self-sacrifice instead of using and abusing others. Rather than reengaging in sin, the repentant worshipper exhibits love for God and love for others, even in the very circumstances that previously led to sin. Such actions show God's supernatural work in hearts.

PREACHING AND TEACHING STRATEGIES

Exegetical and Theological Synthesis

This long narrative speaks to timeless aspects of fallen humanity and divine provision by showing how Joseph creates tests for his brothers. His brothers are in desperate need of transformation. God uses Joseph, the dreamer, to disclose the hearts of his brothers. They eventually pass the test as they admit their guilt and evidence changed character by the way they treat their youngest brother, Benjamin.

The testing occurs as Joseph's brothers make two trips to Egypt to secure grain during a severe famine. One brother, Judah, leads the way to showing their transformation of heart as he pledges his own life with respect to Israel's favorite son, Benjamin. Joseph also is being tested throughout the narrative, especially with respect to whether he will be able to forgive his brothers for what they did to him. It would be natural for him to remain bitter and angry all his life. We certainly don't yet know how he feels about God's part in all of this.

We help our congregants place themselves into this storyline: God's children experience the testing of their faith, which is the only pathway to spiritual maturity. Any number of difficult circumstances can bring this about. In many cases, our listeners, like Joseph's brothers, must come to grips with past sins to move forward in their faith journey. And like Joseph, many of us must deal with those who sin against us.

As shown in this narrative, God can arrange circumstances that help us know our sins and grow beyond them. This is how God's plan continues to progress with his children. As we have seen throughout Genesis, God's promise to bless his people and make them a blessing also includes their transformation into a faithful people. In this way, God continues to display his holiness and justice. Through it all, we should not miss the sovereignty of God to rule the details of history and carry out his will for his people. This narrative highlights the staggering number of moving parts that are coordinated for God's glory.

Preaching Idea

Our sovereign God, in his perfect timing, transforms us all by testing our faith so we can represent him in the world.

Contemporary Connections

What does it mean?

Part of explaining the meaning of this narrative involves reminding our listeners how "all the earth [coming] to Egypt to Joseph to buy grain" (41:57) gets readers closer to Joseph's dreams coming true (42:6). God is going to save his people through Joseph's rule in Egypt so "that we may live and not die" (42:2).

Another puzzle to solve for our listeners is what Joseph's testing of his brothers means. Their inaccurate self-promotion, "We are honest men" (42:11), needs to be transformed into true confession (42:21, "In truth we are guilty concerning our brother"). The test turns out to be gut-wrenching for the brothers, culminating in the seeming death sentence on Benjamin because of Joseph's ruse. Everything is designed to reveal the brothers' integrity. God continues to mold his chosen ones into the kind of people that can be a blessing to the world (going all the way back to the covenant the Lord made with Abraham).

We might want to alert our listeners that Joseph's approach with his brothers is not a "go and do likewise" model. Some would say, "He is flat-out mean." We certainly cannot force others to repent. Like many Genesis narratives, God uses all kinds of characters and all kinds of methods to mold his people. And God will grant wisdom to his children so they can evaluate situations for his glory and their good.

Is it true?

It is possible that our listeners need to be convinced that the testing of their faith is always a part of their faith journey (James 1). Otherwise, it will be difficult to move beyond a historical reading (they will hear this narrative as interesting history as you talk to them about the story). We need to move them toward internalizing the story. That can be accomplished simply by helping them see that what is happening with Joseph's brothers is a picture of what happens to every one of God's children at various times in their lives. God has determined to use testing or trials as a way of developing the faith of his children. In this way we are being transformed into a redeemed people who represent him well in the world. This is necessary for a blessed people to extend his blessing.

Now what?

The relevance of this narrative revolves around the faithfulness of our God to carry out his plan for his world. He chooses a people that must be transformed. None of us are fit for service upon his selection; we all must go through fiery trials that shape our character. This always involves God's gracious work that helps us identify our sins, desire to turn from those sins, and replace such sins with his righteousness.

Many of our listeners have heard the phrase, "Live and learn." Through this narrative portrayal of the lives of God's saints, we might help them "Learn and live." In other words, we can show them how God used difficult circumstances to mature them. There is tremendous hope in showing them how God sustained their lives through the miraculous preservation and ascendancy of Joseph.

Joseph's brothers provide an illustration of what genuine repentance looks like. It is not merely saying, "Sorry!" Here is godly sorrow, a genuine recognition and reflection on harm done and offense against God. There is rejection of evil, and there is the sort of change that responds differently under similar circumstances where sin occurs.

Creativity in Presentation

Concerning the big picture of this large section, decide on whether you will treat the two visits to Egypt by Jacob's family as one or two sermon segments. Treating them as one, consider this sermon structure:

- First, we see the plan of God to bless his people and make them a blessing. Because these three chapters are in the middle of a larger Joseph narrative, it may help your listeners to review God's original promise to Abraham and how God is moving Joseph into a prominent position to carry out his promise. God's family must go to Egypt, because that is where the blessing of God is located geographically in the person of Joseph. Plus, Joseph's brothers need to be tested in light of what they had done to Joseph. The justice of God can be highlighted in this section.

- Second, it shows the test God uses to equip his people for kingdom work. The majority of the narrative details how Joseph tests his brothers and, in a sense, turns them into "honest men" (42:11). You will have to decide how many minutes to devote to the details. One way to structure this section is to outline (1) why the test is needed (the spiritual condition of Joseph's brothers is not sufficient for faithfulness in God's kingdom; they are not honest men!); (2) how the test is tailor-made for growth (Here, I'm thinking of Joseph's specification: "unless your youngest brother comes here," 42:15; in this case Joseph's test is directly related to their previous mistreatment of him; have they changed?). And the test continues to grow; each phase builds on the other. As faith grows, the strength of the test must also grow accordingly for faith to be truly tested. This takes place throughout one's lifetime, in contrast to a one-and-done approach (which we probably all would prefer!).
- Third, we see what passing the test looks like. Judah leads the way ("I will be a pledge of his safety," 43:9) in showing true repentance in the form of loving their brother—and their father, for that matter. You can highlight the brothers' confession of guilt and their clear transformation of heart. The brothers are willing and able to put their selfishness aside to honor their father's wishes.

If we follow the shape of the story more fully, we can enhance the tensions and resolution:

- Testing surfaces guilt (42:1–38).
- Continued testing allows reflection and repentance (43:1–44:13).
- Repentance shows in self-sacrificial action (44:14–34).

All of this leads us to the idea that our sovereign God, at one time or another, transforms us all by trouble so we can represent him in the world. While Joseph's brothers provide a vivid example of how trouble transforms us, you may be able to share a personal story about how times of trouble bolster and refine faith and create new levels of righteous character.

DISCUSSION QUESTIONS

1. Discuss the relationship between our sin and the testing God sends our way. How do times of trouble create much-needed humility?
2. What is it about the testing of Joseph's brothers that highlights God's justice?
3. What parts of Joseph's actions toward his brothers did not seem too Christ-like? How do you wrestle with that observation?
4. Does Jesus always promise to give us what we want? What should we expect from him when we face various testings (James 1:1–2)?
5. How does true repentance show in my response to God? To my brothers? Neighbors?
6. How can I identify the trouble I face as testing from God? How might that change my response to trials?

Genesis 45:1–28

EXEGETICAL IDEA
Revealing his identity, Joseph declared God's sovereign oversight of history to accomplish his purposes of preserving life and fulfilling his promises, prompting Joseph's forgiveness and reconciliation of their relationships, and the blessing and restoration for the family in Egypt.

THEOLOGICAL FOCUS
God's sovereign working in human history grounds his faithfulness to his promises and the necessary human responses of forgiveness, reconciliation, and restoration to experience his blessing.

PREACHING IDEA
Trust God's sovereignty and be freed to forgive, reconcile relationships, and experience his blessings.

PREACHING POINTERS
Joseph's actions towards and dialogue with his brothers teaches the original audience and modern listeners. In the opening scene Joseph tells his brothers not to "be distressed or angry with" themselves because they sold him into slavery (v. 5). Clearly God has done a strong work in Joseph's heart for him to arrive at this place. Most of us can think of situations far less extreme than Joseph's when yet it was very hard to extend forgiveness.

At last, all the friction in this family is healed; Joseph stops the intense testing of his brothers, and a reunion is about to take place. In that same verse, Joseph explains his perspective: "for God sent me before you to preserve life" (v. 5). In verses 7 and 8 the announcement of God's sovereignty continues with more detail. This is one of those rare chapters in Genesis that provides a clear doctrine for us to preach. In verses 16–20 Pharaoh announces to Joseph: "the best of all the land of Egypt is yours" (v. 20). Pharaoh's words show that God's promise to Abraham, which we learned about in Genesis 15 is coming true. This is in large part due to Joseph's belief in and faithfulness to God as Joseph's dream finally came true (45:26, "he is ruler over all the land of Egypt").

JOSEPH'S REVEAL: SHOCK AND AWE AT GOD'S WORK (45:1–28)

LITERARY STRUCTURE AND THEMES

Having set the stage with Judah's speech, chapter 45 brings the building tensions to a climax, declaring the theological message and resolving many of the tensions of the fourth-generation stories. After Judah's impassioned plea for Benjamin and their father's well-being, Joseph finally revealed his identity and perspective, as well as his vision for the future of the family. The changing hearts of the brothers had dominated up to this, with only subtle teasers for Joseph's intent. Now Joseph's own transformation is on display, declaring God's oversight of the whole matter and submitting to his sovereign work.

Structurally, the interrupted return to Canaan from the second journey to Egypt brings closure to the unit begun in chapter 42 (chs. 42–44 above for the full complex chiastic structure, p. 649). Chapter 45 begins with a third center in the parallel chiasms, which has shown Joseph adding pressure to his brothers by imprisoning them then taking them to his house in uncertainty. In this third interlude between dual addresses to his brothers, he broke down and dismissed all the Egyptians to finally resolve the tensions. His self-disclosure ended the testing with its revelation of their recent history and guilt, declaring his inspired forgiveness and heartfelt perspective to allay their fear and restore the long-lost relationships. Their report back to Jacob closed the framing of the two trips as Israel's hope to see Joseph alive before he died (45:28) replaced his fear for Benjamin's life (42:4, 38; 43:6, 14).

D''. Joseph was overcome with emotion (45:1–2).

C'''''. Joseph revealed God's sovereign purpose (45:3–15).

B'''''. Israel's sons returned to Canaan with gifts (45:16–24).

A'''. Jacob recognized, with difficulty, Joseph's hand (45:25–28).

Not only does the narrative present the climax of the repentance of the brothers with the forgiveness from Joseph, but it gives one of the clearest statements in Scripture of the overlay of divine sovereignty on the affairs of humanity, even in their responsibility for their evil choices. It showcases God's outworking of his promises to the patriarchs, both in the lives of the chosen family but also in bringing blessing to their world. The themes of saving life and preserving the people of God draw attention to God's redemptive plan from the beginning of history.

- ***Joseph Was Overcome with Emotion (45:1–2)***
- ***Joseph Revealed God's Sovereign Purpose (45:3–15)***
- ***Israel's Sons Returned to Canaan with Gifts (45:16–24)***
- ***Shock to Awe: Jacob Recognized, with Difficulty, Joseph's Hand (45:25–28)***

EXPOSITION

This climax of the fourth-generation stories also brings the patriarchal narratives and the book of Genesis to a head, with the resolution through the following five chapters to work out the implications of God's work in and through his chosen family. Joseph's dreams were fulfilled, showing his connection to the covenant promises: Abraham's promised family would come to Egypt with great favor and security to grow into the promised great nation before returning to their promised inheritance (15:13–16). In the process, God would bring blessing on those who blessed them and to the families of the earth.

This pivotal narrative, then, initiates closure on the patriarchal family conflicts and this stage of God's redemptive plan. In this *toledot,* in which God seems to work less overtly, Joseph billboards God's actions and provides the theological explanation. Revealing his identity, Joseph declared God's sovereign oversight of history to accomplish his purposes of preserving life and fulfilling his promises, permitting Joseph's forgiveness and reconciliation of their relationships and prompting blessing and restoration for the family in Egypt.

Joseph Was Overcome with Emotion (45:1–2)

Overcome with emotion, Joseph dismissed the Egyptians so he could reveal his identity.

45:1–2. The third interlude between the audiences his brothers had with Joseph relates Joseph's reaction to Judah's passionate appeal, removing the Egyptians so that they could be private. With Judah's touching plea to take Benjamin's place, emphasizing his love for his father and desire to honor the old man who loved another wife and another son more, Joseph was convinced. He would reveal his identity and his heart to his brothers in a family-only moment, in both his words and his uncontrolled tears. The Egyptians must go. The "family fracture" was mending, as the "men" would once again be Joseph's "brothers" (Mathews 2005, 807).[1] These central sections of the chiastic progression show the movement of Joseph's testing of his brothers, from imprisoning them (42:17) to taking them home for lunch to relax them for the next test (43:17–25) and finally removing the mask to confront their fears and comfort them with the grand reality (45:1–2).

Joseph's loud weeping, heard by the Egyptians, validated his words. Not only the Egyptians (presumably the dismissed attendants) but the household of Pharaoh heard it, showing Joseph's status in Egypt that the Pharaoh was vitally concerned with his affairs (cf. v. 16). Mainly, however, his emotional response to Judah highlighted his heart and helped to clarify his motives, supporting his following testimony. He was not bent on revenge.

Joseph Revealed God's Sovereign Purpose (45:3–15)

Revealing his identity and his mercy to his brothers, Joseph credited God's sovereign purpose of preserving life so they could renew relationship and move the family to Egypt for the remaining five years of famine.

45:3. As soon as they were alone, Joseph overflowed. In two short clauses he identified himself and his concern. He was Joseph! How was dad (really)? Following Judah's lead, he switched from "your father" (43:27) to "my father" (אָבִי, 45:3), which Judah had used seven times in 44:27–34. Joseph's deepest concern, his father, framed his speech to his brothers (45:3, 9, 13 [2x]). Judah's plea for Benjamin, focused on the welfare of Jacob, had deeply affected Joseph. He was profoundly moved by Judah's stress on the health and well-being of Jacob (44:22, 27–29, 30–31, 34).

TRANSLATION ANALYSIS 45:3

The typical English translation, "Is my father still alive?" (ESV,NET, NCV, NASB2020) is accurate, but since Judah has answered that question

1 Longacre (1989, 146–47) observes the movement in the way the narrator recounts the events, referring to them as "the men" in chs. 43–44 and not as Joseph's brothers until ch. 45, signaling the healing of relationships.

previously (43:7, 27–28) the nuance here may be more whether he was truly doing "well" (NJPS, cf. Kidner 1967, 218, and 45:27).

They panicked. To say "they were dismayed" misses the terror they felt. The verb בהל describes the sudden recognition of impending disaster, such as with the Canaanites after God's demonstration of power in the exodus (Exod. 15:15), soldiers in an ambush (Judg. 20:41), and Saul after the announcement of his coming death (1 Sam. 28:21). "They were terrified at his presence" (NIV)! No wonder they had trouble answering.

45:4–8. Joseph recognized their panic immediately, and with great compassion, he drew them close and reassured them. He repeated his self-identification, reviewing his unspeakable sale, putting all the cards on the table. By reminding them of his enslavement, he was not berating them but reassuring and restoring them.[2] Joseph's balance between human responsibility and hidden divine purpose could bring resolution to their agony (Grossman 2013, 194–95).

His encouragement not to be distressed or angry for their actions flowed from his theological conclusion that God was ultimately in control. When he had concluded this is not clear, but at a time when he could have punished them, he did not express any rancor but called them to forgive themselves. His perspective is beyond impressive—it is supernatural! Joseph, too, had been transformed. Three times he repeated that God had sent him (vv. 5, 7, 8). They had "sold" him (vv. 4, 5) but God had "sent" him "to preserve life" (vv. 5, 7). Their purpose was merely his sale (removal from their lives), but God's purpose was the end result of life (Grossman 2013, 192). They, then, did not send him, God did (v. 8).

Joseph's Forgiveness

Joseph's response of forgiveness and understanding of God's working appears unexpectedly. Had he understood this from the beginning, or was this new for Joseph? The text is not clear. That he had made peace by now is obvious, but whether it was earlier or even through the process of testing them we can't be sure. However, God had been at work in his life from the beginning. He had begun as a self-absorbed teenager, appearing oblivious to his brothers' hatred. Yet his desire to honor God was on display with Potiphar's wife. God was with him (showing Joseph's loyalty) from the beginning in Egypt. He declared God's control and exclusive source of information to the officials and to Pharaoh. Yet he was looking for a way out long before God opened the door, not being at peace in prison (40:14–15). In addition, when he named his sons, he was realizing some peace, though at the time it was not clear if he wanted to forget it all or was coming to terms with it (41:51–52). He had another "Aha!" moment when he remembered the dreams as his brothers bowed before him (42:9), which may have been the final piece to fall into place (Spero 2018, 112). His tears had already shown his heart was not set on revenge, and it appears that his testing was, at least ideally, preparing for something like this moment (42:15).

God's purpose was to "preserve life" (v. 5, 7).[3] The theme of life and death has been growing through the Joseph stories. Initially it was the sibling rivalry and the plot to kill Joseph, redirected to selling him into slavery, which now we see ironically was used by God to save many lives. Then the two sons of Judah died for their evil, leading to the new life from

2 Joseph's main point, marked by "and now" (וְעַתָּה, 45:5, 8; Isaksson 2014, 21) was comfort, not condemnation.

3 Wenham (1994, 428) notes the repetition of "to preserve life" is "a key phrase in the flood story (6:19–20; cf. 7:3; 50:20), implying that Joseph is like Noah, an agent in the divine saving plan."

Tamar's more righteous act (ch. 38). God used the life and death of the officials of Pharaoh to exalt Joseph, show God's oversight of history, and preserve lives in the coming famine (chs. 40–41). Jacob realized their life and death plight, leading to the sons going to Egypt both times (42:2; 43:8). Now both the brothers and the reader hear that all this pales before God's greater purpose of preserving life (45:5), "a remnant on earth" (v. 7). Specifically, he would save the chosen family, the line remaining as a "remnant" (cf. 2 Sam. 14:7). The point is not that only a few of them would survive, but that the line would survive in a dire time in which many may not. Mathews (2005, 813) suggests a double entendre in which the family reflects the "surviving 'remnant' of the world's populations (cf. the Noah imagery, v. 5)." This remnant would be part of a "great deliverance" (Gen. 45:7 NIV), indicating the means through which God would bring a greater salvation.

TRANSLATION ANALYSIS 45:7

The "many survivors" (ESV, NLT, NRSV) can also be translated "great deliverance" (NASB95, NET, NIV) or "extraordinary deliverance" (NJPS; cf. "amazing way," NCV). "Survivor" (פְּלֵיטָה) is used together with "remnant" (שְׁאֵרִית), speaking of God delivering Israel after judgment (2 Kings 19:30f // Isa. 37:31f; Isa. 10:20; 15:9; Ezra 9:14). Here, however, God was not judging Israel, and the alternative idea of "escape, deliverance" (*HALOT* s.v. "פְּלֵיטָה" 2., 932) provides the means of God preserving life, here designated "great" (*HALOT* s.v. "גָּדוֹל" 178–79). Israel here, by implication from the Abrahamic covenant and the flow of Genesis, will be the means of the great deliverance, not merely the result of it.

Understanding the divine purpose of history and Joseph's life, suffering, and rise grounded Joseph's perspective on his pain and forms the basis for his brothers to release their self-recriminations and embrace Joseph. Joseph's point was not to excuse their actions, nor to forget their motives. He would fully acknowledge that it was evil (50:20). Rather, he had seen their remorse and repentance expressed not only in their expressions of guilt, but in their heart change and willing sacrifice of themselves for a brother and for a father who had not deviated in his favoritism and self-centered love of Benjamin. Joseph was free from his prison of anger and vengeance as well as his physical chains, and he offered his brothers freedom from their chains of guilt and fear.

He supported his argument to them by God's obvious working to make Joseph "a father to Pharaoh, and lord of all his house and ruler over all the land of Egypt" (45:8). In concentric levels of influence, Joseph was advisor to Pharaoh himself,[4] master of all his affairs,[5] and had authority over the entire nation (41:40–41). Noting his position and obvious power was not to coerce them but to encourage them with God's working. Joseph's emphasis throughout was not his own achievement but God's working to accomplish God's program. In this address, God was the subject of the action, repeated five times (three times sending Joseph and twice making him ruler of all Egypt). The allusion to his dreams would resonate particularly with the brothers and father (37:5–11). Those dreams had driven all the hatred, and now, guilt. Joseph's accounting, coupled with the dreams, verified God's hand and grounded his forgiveness, his appeal to his brothers for

4 While these roles could refer to specific titles, it is hard to be specific since there are over 1,500 documented titles from just the Middle Kingdom, though they "reflect genuine Egyptian institutions" (Hoffmeier 1996, 93). The idea, however, is clear that he was an advisor, as "father" is occasionally used (*HALOT* s.v. "אָב" 1–2, 4.).

5 "'Lord [ʾādôn] of his entire household' means Joseph had total control of state affairs and treasury (cf. 41:40–44, 55; 42:6)" (Mathews 2005, 814).

their release from guilt, and his appeal to his father to come to Egypt. Five years of serious famine remained (45:6).

45:9–13. Joseph followed his plea to his brothers to see God's work and release their guilt with a message for his father to join him in Egypt. He framed his message to Jacob with a plea to hurry (vv. 9, 13). Time was of the essence, perhaps partly from a concern for his age and health, though he specifically noted the five years of famine that could reduce them to "poverty" if they did not come (v. 11). In Egypt there would be space for all the clan and their livestock near Joseph, where he could care for them.[6] He specifically urged them to share the outworking of the dreams, which was much grander than they had imagined. He was not only ruler of the clan but all of Egypt. They could personally testify that it was Joseph, since he was speaking to them in their own language, not through an interpreter.[7]

45:14–15. This touching scene shows Benjamin and Joseph fully engaged and the brothers beginning to realize what was happening. After Joseph's dramatic address and his gestures of reconciliation toward them, they regained their voice, though their response was not recorded. Joseph had great authority, yet he not only spoke conciliatory words but embraced them and wept over them. Joseph had genuinely forgiven them, though they would not be sure for years to come (50:15). They talked with him, but Benjamin wept on him.

Israel's Sons Returned to Canaan with Gifts (45:16–24)

The sons of Israel followed Pharaoh's orders, taking the generous gifts of Joseph and Pharaoh back to Canaan for the family.

45:16–20. Having heard the commotion (v. 2), Pharaoh now got the full report of Joseph's brothers. He and his servants responded with pleasure (cf. 41:37), and he offered extravagant hospitality, demonstrating his high opinion of Joseph. In Abrahamic covenant terms, Pharaoh blessed the line of Abraham. In many ways Pharaoh was already being blessed, but it would get better (ch. 47). He offered Joseph's family the "best" (טוּב) the land had to offer (they need not bring anything, v. 20!), and they would eat the "fat" (חֵלֶב, v. 18, or best) of the land.

Pharaoh commanded Joseph to send wagons for the weaker members to ride, repeating that the best of the land was at their disposal. Joseph had already offered to provide for them, but Pharaoh went far beyond Joseph, offering them full provision and replacement of goods from the best of Egypt. They were not only Joseph's family; they were Pharaoh's honored guests.[8] As with Joseph and the hearts of the brothers, God's preparation for the future nation is clear in Pharaoh's response. God was not only giving favor to Joseph before Potiphar

---

6 He specifically mentioned the "land of Goshen" (v. 10). The name is known as a Semitic place name in several places in Canaan but is not known in Egypt. It likely refers to the Eastern Delta region of Wadi Tumilat (Walton 2009a, 133).

7 "It is my mouth" refers to his direct speech rather than the façade he had put on with the interpreter (42:23), providing evidence that it was indeed him and not some imposter. They were to report what they had seen and heard to their father to convince him it was true (45:12–13).

8 This does not present any real conflict with Joseph's previous offer, nor his subsequent instructions (cp.Hamilton 1995, 583–84; contra, for example, Speiser 1964, 341). Joseph had authority to offer what he did as "Lord of all Egypt" (v. 9). Pharaoh went generously beyond Joseph's offer, perhaps ratifying it, and Joseph would follow his lead and yet direct their movements to Goshen (46:34), as he had suggested originally, to minimize conflict with Egyptians and provide effectively for the burgeoning family.

(39:2–4), the jailer (39:21–23), and Pharaoh (41:37–38), but the whole family was in God's care as promised to the patriarchs, even though Jacob and the sons may not have seen it until perhaps this time. God was honoring his promises to accomplish his redemptive plan, working in his chosen people and pagan rulers alike.

45:21–24. Pharaoh commanded, "Do this" (v. 17, זֹאת עֲשׂוּ), and they "did so" (v. 21, וַיַּעֲשׂוּ־כֵן). The generosity of Pharaoh, including wagons, ten donkeys with the "best things of Egypt" (NIV, v. 23, מִטּוּב מִצְרָיִם, cf. v. 18), and ten donkeys of provisions, all helped to prove the seeming outrageous claims of the sons when they arrived before Jacob (v. 27). It also provided tangible blessing to the line of Abraham, which God used to preserve his people and accomplish his purposes. God's intent included preserving their lives and preparing his future nation in isolation from the wickedness of the Canaanites (cf. ch. 38) before returning to claim their inheritance and exact God's judgment on those Canaanites (15:13–20).

TRANSLATION ANALYSIS 45:23

The ESV, with its "good things of Egypt," (see also NKJV, NRSV), misses the connection with Pharaoh's generosity (v. 18) by not consistently translating "best" (טוּב, NASB95, NJPS; cf. NLT, "finest"; see *HALOT* s.v. "טוּב" 1.a., 372).

Joseph's gifts helped express his forgiveness. He gave them each a "change of clothes" (שִׂמְלֹת), used earlier in the narrative of Jacob's grief in seeing Joseph's coat when Jacob tore his "garment" (37:34 ,שִׂמְלֹתָיו) and similarly when the brothers tore their "garments" in grief at Benjamin's arrest (שִׂמְלֹתָם, 44:13). The valued gift of clothing, reminding them of the crime symbolized by his coat, offered a fitting gift of reconciliation (Sarna 1989, 311). With his extravagant outlay to Benjamin of five changes of clothing and three hundred shekels of silver, his brothers may well have wondered how to take them, leading to Joseph's final request.

Commentators have understood Joseph's parting cryptic comment to his brothers in varying ways.[9] The verb often translated "quarrel" (ESV and many others) has a basic idea in the *qal* of "tremble" with emotion or fear (*HALOT* s.v. "רגז" 1182–83), leading to the idea of "don't be overcome with fear" (NET) or "do not become troubled" (NKJV). The suggestion of agitation with each other leading to quarreling would naturally flow from their impending confrontation with Jacob and need to explain how Joseph could be alive and ruling in Egypt and their role in it. Given Reuben's "I told you so" speech (42:22), they may have wrestled with responsibility and how to present the truth to Jacob, which he would certainly find out once he talked to Joseph and which Benjamin now knew. On the other hand, given that challenge ahead and the recent history of Joseph's testing, would they begin to second guess the gifts and Joseph's real motives as the distance increased? With Joseph's reassurances and recognition of their guilt and difficulty receiving him, it makes sense to see this as a final encouragement that they need not fear or tremble as they process all that has happened on this trip. It was not another trap (Alter 1996, 271). Joseph was not still looking for a way to get revenge (Steinmann 2019, 417). God was at work and was truly in this move to bring Jacob and his clan to Egypt.

9 The command is ambiguous. Mathews (2005, 819) lists possible views that it could refer to "fraternal strife" related to recrimination and having to confess their previous roles, his attempts to alleviate their fears of his retaliation, a warning against taking "undue risks," and his concern that they might choose to back out, eliminate Benjamin, and continue the cover-up. Cotter suggests they should "not worry about anything" (Cotter 2003, 317).

Shock to Awe: Jacob Recognized, with Difficulty, Joseph's Hand (45:25–28)

Stunned with his sons' story and Joseph's gifts, Jacob is finally convinced that Joseph was truly alive so that he revived, anticipating seeing Joseph again in Egypt.

45:25–28. When they arrived home, their declaration to Jacob was nearly as abrupt as Joseph had been with them. Without explanation, they merely announced Joseph's life and status to the father that had believed him dead for twenty-two years. It is not surprising that "his heart became numb" (v. 26). Following the full explanation and the presentation of all the gifts, his spirit "revived" (וַתְּחִי רוּחַ, v. 47). Apparently, he not only believed the story, once the extravagant caravan finished trailing into camp, but the anticipation of seeing Joseph again energized him and gave him purpose. He would go to Egypt with his clan.

> *TRANSLATION ANALYSIS 45:26*
> "Heart" in the OT (לֵב), along with the organ, can stand for the "inner self," including "feelings and emotions" or the "mind as a whole" or one's "inclination," "courage," "will," "attention," or "conscience" (*HALOT* s.v. "לֵב" 513–15). The verb translated "became numb" (פּוּג, in the *qal*) is glossed by *HALOT* as "turn cold," or "grow weary" and only occurs four times in the Old Testament (916). The common translation, "was stunned" (NASB95, NET, NIV), expresses the same idea. We could say "he grew cold inside," perhaps even indicating that the shock of the announcement and his disbelief left him initially giving up on life. The opposite or reversal of this occurred in verse 27 where his spirit "revived" or "came to life" (וַתְּחִי). Parallel to "heart," "spirit" (רוּחַ), which usually denotes the "life-sustaining function" of humanity (Van Pelt, Kaiser, and Block, רוּחַ, *NIDOTTE* 3:1074), was restored.

The structural frame around the two trips to Egypt (chs. 42–45) adds to the working of God in the family. Jacob was trying to preserve their lives but was afraid to release Benjamin (42:1–2). His fear for Benjamin and the real danger of death drove the tensions in his decisions because he was convinced of Joseph's death (42:29–38; 43:1–14). Quite apart from Jacob's ability to control his world, however, God brought resolution to Jacob as "Israel" finally saw God's working, bringing Joseph back from the dead. It was as abrupt as his realization that God had already been at work in Esau (33:10). The change to "Israel" and the "sons of Israel" (45:21) certainly draws attention to what God would do as the budding nation goes to Egypt for a long sojourn (15:13). However, it also reminds of the significance of moving from the manipulator to the one who learned to cling to Yahweh for his blessing (32:26–28). It "speaks of a new destiny and a new future . . . a new hope and a new expectation" (Hamilton 1995, 587).[10] It is only in the sovereign working of God that we can experience his blessing, as he uses even evil to accomplish his purposes in and through us.

THEOLOGICAL FOCUS

God's sovereign working in human history grounds his faithfulness to his promises and the necessary human responses of forgiveness, reconciliation, and restoration to experience his blessing.

God and his work finally take center stage in this narrative, not because God obviously irrupts in human history, but because Joseph understands and proclaims his sovereign working behind the scenes, as most of human history experiences it. Though evil people do evil things, God works through those very things, as well as through righteous people acting faithfully, to accomplish his goals, one of the clearest examples of Romans 8:28–29, including the

10 Cp. Longacre (1989, 147–48), who argues the use of "Israel" is in "passages where his office and dignity are in view."

transformation of his chosen servants! "God's will makes use of all human action but is domesticated or limited by no human choice" (Brueggemann 1982a, 347).

God's covenant promises will be accomplished along with every expectation that God has expressed in the process. Joseph's life has shown God's oversight of time, place, occupation, relationships, and all the incidentals of human choices. God's control, however, does not deny human responsibility, nor does it counter the consequences of those evil actions. We will experience the appropriate consequences for both righteous acts of faith as well as acts of rebellion. It does, however, mandate release of personal vengeance to him as the sovereign judge (forgiveness, Deut. 32:35; Rom. 12:19) and allow restoration of broken relationships with appropriate repentance and submission to his authority.

It also means, then, that for much of history and our experience of life, we must live in faith in that sovereign working, since it may be years before humanity sees the outcomes, if we see them at all. Since we do not see the hand of God directly, much like Joseph's dreams, we must recognize the fulfilling of his promises and attribute them to the appropriate cause, God. "Only in retrospect can man see what God has been doing" (Wenham 1994, 432). Life, then, is an act of faith, but it is faith in the prior revelation of God and his goodness and faithfulness when we only see the darkness. As with Joseph, we may occasionally see the clues that remind us of the promise, though God will be faithful whether we recognize them or not.

Our love of the sibling, parent, or neighbor, then, is also conditioned by our belief in the sovereignty of God and his oversight, both in rewarding and judging. Forgiveness flows from confidence in God's just and good dealing with all people. Reconciliation results from allowing God to work in hearts and celebrating those gifts as they are revealed. It does not mean reverting to damaging relationships without testing or proving the change in hearts (chs. 42–44). It does mean seeing God's working and extending grace. It also recognizes that even the response of forgiveness, as with repentance, is God's working in one's life.

Likewise, the same sovereignty allows us to receive and experience forgiveness with real repentance. We can find healing and reconciliation with God and others as we accept God's working in and through even poor or evil choices. Such healing does not negate consequences, either from my choices or from others', but it does restore and renew life and relationships with God's work in all involved. It shows us that God's work is not merely talionic justice, and we must expect to receive full measure for our sins (which we might erroneously deduct from God's justice in the flood, for example, Lindvall 2013, 283). Rather, God extends grace to the repentant, full of undeserved favor.

In all of this, humanity can only cling to God and trust him amid the storms. We certainly must respond in integrity and faithfulness to God, knowing we will stand before him (39:9), but we cannot expect the immediate outcomes to be our desires. Rather, we must trust one with a longer view of history and clearer perspective on his ultimate purposes and redemptive plan.

Finally, we must realize that all of this is part of a much bigger drama than our slice of time and space. Each person plays their own unique role in God's larger drama of redemption, seen both in our experience of his working and in our part in extending his blessing to others. Each one with his or her unique opportunity and responsibility can rest in the ultimate outcome of God's plan, set in place before the foundation of the world and progressively revealed in his word and covenants. Today we have seen much more in Christ and we still wait for his final consummation when we will see the full tapestry that he is weaving through our pain and sorrow.

PREACHING AND TEACHING STRATEGIES

Exegetical and Theological Synthesis

While it is important to the narrative that Joseph finally reveals his true identity to his brothers, more important to theological interpretation is Joseph's revelation of his new perspective on all that they did to him. When Joseph restates his identity, he follows that up with: "And now do not be distressed or angry with yourselves because you sold me here" (v. 5). The sermon quickly expands on the status of Joseph's heart that allows him to respond this way. Clearly, he has forgiven them. We do not know when, but we know it happened at some point during his stay in Egypt.

And then, Joseph follows that up immediately with a strong statement on God's sovereignty: "for God sent me before you to preserve life" (v. 5). Joseph's faith is meant to be emulated by all of us. Being sold into Egypt was no accident; even the evil intentions of his brothers cannot fully explain what happens to God's children. Ultimately, God's will is being done. He is keeping his promises to bless the faithful and make them a blessing. The hardship Joseph went through was the vehicle God used to provide a remarkable deliverance.

The sermon also provides an opportunity to flesh out the implication of Pharaoh's declaration to Joseph. Verses 16–20 describe Pharoah's reaction to hearing what was happening in Joseph's family. Joseph is blessed in every way by Pharaoh: the best of the land, the best food the land offers, and supplies for the journey from Egypt to Canaan and back. What a thought, that Pharaoh blessed a seed of Abraham!

Preaching Idea

Trust God's sovereignty and be freed to forgive, reconcile relationships, and experience his blessings.

Contemporary Connections

What does it mean?

It is important to explain to our listeners the connection between Joseph's belief in God's sovereignty and his statement to his brothers about them not being distressed or angry with themselves over what they did. The earlier section showed Joseph's brothers coming to grips with their guilt. It is easy to imagine them now hating themselves for the rest of their lives or, as many people experience, finding it impossible to forgive themselves. God has clearly done something in Joseph's heart for him to talk to his brothers this way. Joseph can see that God's plan was to move Joseph into a position where he could do the utmost good.

The biblical writer assumes our listeners will see the interplay between God's sovereignty and Joseph's brothers' evil decisions. Both actions are occurring in this narrative; God's action takes priority as the guiding force behind it all so that historical events accomplish his will for his people. This might be an excellent place to provide a robust definition of God's sovereignty. You might also explain the preserving a remnant on earth (v. 7) is God's plan throughout redemptive history. Finally, our listeners may need an explanation of how Pharaoh's response to Joseph's family reunion reflects God's faithfulness to his covenant with Abraham.

Is it true?

We must wonder how many of our listeners actually believe in the sovereignty of God when push comes to shove in their lives. I mean when their faith journey hits the intersection of Main and Trouble Streets, do they have Joseph's calm assurance: "God sent me" (vv. 5, 7, 8)? Many of our listeners will say they believe in God's sovereignty, but that belief is not matched with calm assurance in times of trouble. They need to be convinced by Joseph's experience that history does repeat itself over and over again throughout church history.

Another concept that may be difficult to believe is that Pharoah could bless Joseph and his whole family like he did. In a world where Christians are always outnumbered, the concept of guaranteed blessing is something that we really want to be true. Of course, what God guarantees and what we desire or expect as blessing are not always the same!

Now what?

My own personal experience (Randal), plus listening to scores of parishioners, confirms that Christians often believe in the sovereignty of God, but not in a way that provides peace. That is why we are framing it in terms of "trust," a synonym that connotes the appropriate clinging dependence. A narrative like this one can do wonders for a congregation's faith in the sovereignty of God to grow stronger.

This faith works two ways in this narrative. First, it will be one factor in Joseph's brothers' abilities to completely forgive themselves. They have come to grips with their guilt and are coming face to face with the brother they sold. Distress and anger (v. 5) is a natural reaction. Joseph reasons with them from God's sovereignty. The second way faith in sovereignty works is by being the most important factor in a person not being angry at God or others for personal trauma. Joseph has endured great hardship due to the evil intentions of his brothers, but he is able to remain in relationship with God and restore relationships with others. Of course, it may have taken a large portion of the twenty years of separation to fully understand and respond in that faith.

One final thought about faith: our listener's ability to believe God will be bolstered as they see his power put to work in Pharoah's decision to bless Joseph and his family. God uses Egypt and all their gods to carry out his will to bless his children!

Creativity in Presentation

It is only after God's working in our hearts that we can trust God's sovereignty and be freed to forgive, reconcile relationships, and experience his blessings. First- or secondhand experiences provide illustrations of interpersonal friction that require supernatural forgiveness. This helps recreate chapter 45's part of the larger storyline. You will want to take a few minutes to provide the setting and immediate context of Joseph's reveal and subsequent dialogue.

Major thought-blocks or main points in the sermon can include:

- Belief in God's sovereignty allows forgiveness to take place. For Joseph to say what he says to his brothers in v. 5a, he must have already extended forgiveness to them for what they did to him.

- Belief in God's sovereignty involves admitting his ultimate control over the events in our lives. Some preachers might decide to make this the first point even though this begins to develop in v. 5b. Either way, these are the minutes to develop the doctrine of sovereignty and its implications for one's faith. This section covers verses 5–8 and the three occurrences of the concept of God sending Joseph to Egypt. This is also the time to explain the mysterious connection between God's control and human choices, especially the evil ones that are contrary to God's plan. This is God's way to explain how Joseph's dream came true.

- Belief in God's sovereignty provides assurance of God's ability to bless his children. The rest of the chapter, from verses 9–28, describes how God used Joseph's position of power in Egypt to bless his family. A key element of the blessing is Pharoah's reaction to all that was happening. His announcement, "I will give you the best of the land of Egypt" (v. 18), reassures our listeners of God's faithfulness to carry out his promises to the faithful.

DISCUSSION QUESTIONS

1. Discuss various thoughts about the nature of God's sovereignty. One issue might be how much control God has. When you hear "God's sovereignty," what comes to mind?

2. Discuss some reasons why God's sovereignty might be opposed by some Christians. What is offensive about the doctrine?

3. What is the potential tension involved in trying to hold together God's sovereignty and human responsibility?

4. Discuss the connection between belief in God's sovereignty and one's ability to forgive another person. What hinders your ability to forgive offenses against you? What hinders your ability to forgive yourself?

5. What does it mean to forgive? Do you let them off the hook so that they get away completely without consequence, and is that fair?

6. How can you reconcile God's sovereignty and God's good purposes for me with extended periods of suffering, trauma, evil, or hardship? How can that be reconciled with "blessing" or God's desire that you "thrive" in life?

Genesis 46:1–47:31

EXEGETICAL IDEA

God honored Israel's worshipful obedience, richly blessing his family through Pharaoh, increasing them, and blessing Pharaoh and all Egypt for honoring his chosen family.

THEOLOGICAL FOCUS

God moves his plan forward, going with his worshippers into difficult times to accomplish his purpose: blessing his faithful people, those who bless them, and his world.

PREACHING IDEA

God's faithful resist their fears by resting in his presence to experience God's blessing and extend his blessing to others.

PREACHING POINTERS

One of the most exciting features of this narrative section is the way in which it shows God's people experiencing many of the promises of the covenant he made with Abraham. God is showing himself faithful to his covenant; his people are being blessed and extending the blessing to others even though the process has been filled with troubling circumstances. Original and current audiences gain confidence in God's ability to fulfill his promises to them in a badly broken world.

Just think about all that God has put Joseph through en route to ruling in Egypt. Just think about all the emotional agony Israel has experienced concerning Joseph. Just think about all the years that have gone by with all those ups and downs. The narrative begins with Israel worshipping at Beersheba (46:1) and God speaking to him about not being afraid to go to Egypt, where God would make Israel a great nation and accompany him (46:3–4). When Joseph's father and brothers are reunited in Egypt and presented to Pharaoh, they hear evidence of the blessing: "Settle your father and your brothers in the best of the land" (47:6, 11). Then, the narrator makes it clear: "Jacob blessed Pharaoh" (47:7, 10). And then, from verses 13–31 Joseph continues to bless everyone, especially the Egyptians, as he works his wise plan for saving lives through the terrible famine. God is faithful and his faithful can count on experiencing what he promises: "they . . . were fruitful and multiplied greatly" (47:27).

BLESSED WITH GOD'S PRESENCE: LIVING AND GIVING GOD'S BEST (46:1–47:31)

LITERARY STRUCTURE AND THEMES

As Israel moved toward Egypt to meet Joseph, he stopped to worship. God met him with promise of his presence, blessing, and return to the land for his people. God's promise frames the section theologically with the concluding focus on their prosperity and growth in Egypt and Joseph's oath that he would bury Israel in Canaan. (46:1–27; 47:27–31).[1] The center of the narrative reveals the results of God's presence and blessing, providing Israel's material needs (46:28–47:12) so that they greatly increased (47:27), in marked contrast to Egypt and Canaan (vv. 13–26). The Egyptian population was profoundly grateful for life (v. 25), magnifying the extravagant provision for God's people. Pharaoh, who blessed Abraham's descendants with the best of Egypt, was blessed by Jacob (twice, vv. 7, 10) and enriched by Joseph (vv. 13–26).

1. Israel went to Egypt with God's blessing and promise of return to Canaan (46:1–27).
   1a. At Israel's worship, God promised his presence and return to Canaan (46:1–7).
      1b. Jacob took his entire clan to Egypt (46:8–27).
2. Joseph introduced his family to Pharaoh, whom Jacob blessed (46:28–47:12).
   2a. Joseph prepared the way to Goshen (46:28–34).
      2b. Joseph presented his brothers to Pharaoh (47:1–6).
      2b'. Joseph presented his father to Pharaoh (47:7–10).
   2a'. Joseph settled his clan in Goshen (47:11–12).
2'. Joseph gathered all Egypt's resources for Pharaoh to save the people (47:13–26).
   2'a. Egypt and Canaan were starving (47:13).
      2'b. Joseph gathered all Egypt's resources for Pharaoh (47:14–25).
   2'a '. Joseph saved lives in exchange for land (47:26).
1'. God blessed Israel in Goshen, and Joseph promised to bury him in Canaan (47:27–31).
   1'b'. Israel settled in Goshen with God's blessing (47:27).
   1'a'. Joseph promised to bury Israel in Canaan, and Israel worshipped (47:28–31).

Following the rhetorical and emotional climax of Joseph's revelation, the narrative works out the implications and expectations, showing how God will preserve life, use Joseph in his position, and bring blessing to the chosen clan, to Pharaoh, and to the families of the earth. These implications include, then, not only the expectations set up in the fourth-generation stories, such as Joseph's dreams, but also the development and outworking of the Abrahamic covenant promises and the progression

1 In addition to framing the current narrative, Gen. 47:27–31 previews the subsequent section and Jacob's blessing on Ephraim and Manasseh, a common structural device in Genesis (see Exposition below, especially 47:28, p. 688, and Wenham 1994, 437–38).

of the redemptive plan of God initiated with the fall. Initially focusing on the preservation and growth of the clan into a "great nation" (46:3; see 12:2; 17:20; 18:18) before returning to the land (46:4; see 15:13–14, 18–21), this section graphically shows God's blessing on his people amid a distressed world, even while blessing all families by preserving life, especially those who bless his people.

- ***Israel Went to Egypt with God's Blessing and Promise of Return to Canaan (46:1–27)***
- ***Joseph Introduced His Family to Pharaoh, Whom Jacob Blessed (46:28–47:12)***
- ***Joseph Gathered All Egypt's Resources for Pharaoh to Save the People (47:13–26)***
- ***God Blessed Israel in Goshen, and Joseph Promised to Bury Him in Canaan (47:27–31)***

EXPOSITION

In the larger structure of the *toledot*, this narrative works out the expectations of chapters 40–43 (see Introduction to the Fourth-Generation Narratives, p. 587). Pharaoh had raised Joseph to power to save lives (40:1–41:57; cf. 41:36) by collecting the surplus grain. When the famine came, it was up to Joseph to provide relief (41:53–57). The outworking of his strategy, recorded in 47:13–31, gave life to the Egyptians and enrichment to Pharaoh and exposed the magnitude of God's blessing to his own people. The initial two trips to Egypt by the brothers to save their lives (42:1–43:34) climaxed in the entire clan traveling to Egypt to save their lives and make them into a great nation with God's presence and blessing (46:1–47:12). This section, then, develops God's tangible enriching and empowering of his people as he preserved them from the immediate threat (45:4–8) and prepared them for his future purpose (15:13–16). God honored Israel's worshipful obedience, richly blessing his family through Pharaoh, increasing them, and blessing Pharaoh and all Egypt for honoring his chosen family.

Israel Went to Egypt with God's Blessing and Promise of Return to Canaan (46:1–27)

Israel took his whole clan to Egypt, prompted by God's promised presence for blessing and eventual return to Canaan.

God's appearance at the beginning of this narrative provided crucial confirmation, both for Israel and, later, for the nation, of God's intentions and assurance of his presence and restoration of the nation to the land. For the Israelites, hearing this as they came out of Egypt after their long bondage, going to Egypt may have appeared as a huge mistake. The blessing that follows confirms God's presence, and Joseph's oath, framing the passage, eases Jacob's concern with dying in Egypt, considering God's promise to Abraham (47:27–31). The current narrative, then, highlights God's work in his people and his world as he prepares for the next stage of his redemptive plan.

At Israel's Worship, God Promised Israel His Presence and Return to Canaan (46:1–7)

Responding to Israel's worship, God promised his presence, bringing blessing and Israel's eventual return to Canaan, and encouraging their move to Egypt.

46:1–4. Having declared his intent to go to Egypt and see Joseph (45:28), Israel set out.[2] At his last stop in Canaan, the ancestral home

2 The narrator calls him Israel here, appropriate to foreshadow the movement of the emerging nation to Egypt. God, however, will call him Jacob in the theophany. Hamilton (1995, 590) suggests he is indicating Jacob's "fretful, apprehensive, suffering" nature. It may simply be a reminder that he needs to cling to Yahweh through this move that will show God's intervention and blessing (cf. 32:26–28).

in Beersheba, Jacob seemed to be feeling some doubts about going. While the narrative does not state why he stopped here to offer sacrifices, God's reassurance suggests it was his fear of going to Egypt (46:3). Beersheba was the primary residence of Isaac in the narratives (26:33), and he specifically stopped to offer sacrifices (וַיִּזְבַּח זְבָחִים) to "the God of his father, Isaac" (46:1). Since God specifically introduced himself with the same terms, his message appears to be a direct response to Jacob's concerns: going to Egypt and fulfilling the Abrahamic covenant promises passed from Abraham to Isaac (26:3–4) and then to Jacob (28:13–15; 35:11–12). Would God make him a "great nation" (12:2; 18:18; cf. 28:14; 35:11)? It may well be, then, that Jacob was not merely worshipping in general, but looking for confirmation from God (Averbeck, זָבַח, *NIDOTTE* 1:1068) and God's blessing on his move out of the promised land.

God's revelation contrasted both Abraham, who went to Egypt during famine without confirmation from Yahweh but out of fear, endangering the promise (12:10–20), and Isaac, whom Yahweh specifically forbade to go to Egypt during famine, to fulfill the Abrahamic promises (26:2–5). Jacob may have been thinking of both of those events, though approaching "the God of his father Isaac" (46:1) specifically suggests the latter. Perhaps he was also aware of God's warning to Abraham that his descendants would be in Egypt four hundred years with affliction (15:13). God's response here indicates it was his plan and not merely the result of sin or foolish choice to go there. While their presence there allowed later affliction, it was necessary to accomplish God's greater purpose, incubating his nation until the best time for their birth as an independent theocracy.

God's encouragement included both the obvious national promise of greatness, but also the necessary return to the land to possess it and the personal promise of a peaceful death in the presence of Joseph.[3] God's promise of return to the land indicates the future nation, since "there" (שָׁם, 46:3) they would become a great nation (Wenham 1994, 441–42). Not only would Jacob come back to be buried, but the nation embodied in him would return to possess God's promised land. In the meantime, God would be with them, assuring their success in God's purposes (28:15; 39:3, 21, 23). God was confirming that his promises to the patriarchs would be fully honored, and Jacob could take this adventure in his old age in peace.

46:5–7. Using Pharaoh's provision for him, they left for Egypt. Detailing the "all that he had" (46:1), Jacob took all his extended family, his livestock, and his possessions.[4] Even though Pharaoh had generously made it unnecessary (45:20), they were wealthy, and the presence of their animals and goods would serve to reduce possible tensions in Egypt and support their later request to merely sojourn in the land (47:4).

Jacob Took His Entire Clan to Egypt (46:8–27)

Jacob took his entire clan, listed by matriarch, totaling seventy, anticipating God's purposes.

46:8–15. After a brief introduction, Jacob's named descendants are organized by Jacob's wives and concubines. They are listed for Leah, her servant Zilpah, Rachel, and her servant Bilhah, and they include almost exclusively the male descendants and their sons. Each segment then ends with the name of the mother and the

3 To close the eyes, here, relates the practice of closing the eyes after death, if needed, by the firstborn son or near relative (Sarna 1989, 313).

4 "All his offspring" (וְכָל־זַרְעוֹ) repeated twice and described (vv. 6–7), then fully enumerated in verses 8–27, continues the emphasis on innumerable offspring (זֶרַע) to each of the patriarchs (13:16; 15:5; 22:17; 26:4; 28:14).

number of the offspring. The first segment does include Dinah (v. 15), who had figured prominently in the narrative. It also includes the sons of Perez, who could not have been born since Perez could only be a small child, perhaps born the year they went down to Egypt (see Exposition, 38:1–5, p. 606).[5] Including Dinah, he lists thirty-three descendants from Leah.

46:16–18. The descendants from Zilpah number sixteen, or half of the number of Leah's sons.

46:19–22. Rachel is mentioned twice (beginning and ending) and featured as "Jacob's wife," the only one so designated, showing her prominence. Joseph and his sons are included here along with ten sons for Benjamin,[6] bringing the total for Rachel to fourteen.

46:23–25. Bilhah bore seven, half of her mistress's children, as with Zilpah.

46:26–27. The conclusion presents two numbers: those who came with Jacob and those who belonged to him who ended up in Egypt. The number of the enumerated descendants is seventy, and four of those did not come with Jacob (the two sons of Judah who died in Canaan and the two sons of Joseph who were born in Egypt). The number seventy, which the genealogy presents as the key here in the narrative (the final word of the section), also accords with the number of the nations (sons of Noah) listed in Genesis 10. It may simply indicate "totality," showing that "all Israel entered Egypt" (Sarna 1989, 317), or that Israel is representative of the nations (Mathews 2005, 836). Framing the descendants of Jacob as "seventy," however, and listing them as a segmented genealogy as in Genesis 10, provides an image of the spread of humanity. Just as all humanity spread from seventy (ch. 10), the small beginning of Israel in Egypt will become great, like the dust of the earth (13:6; 28:14), the stars of the sky (15:5; 22:17; 26:4), or the sand of the seashore (22:17), foreshadowing God's blessing: "Your fathers went down to Egypt seventy persons, and now the Lord your God has made you as numerous as the stars of heaven" (Deut. 10:22).

Joseph Introduced His Family to Pharaoh, Whom Jacob Blessed (46:28–47:12)

Joseph introduced his family to Pharaoh, convincing him to settle them in Goshen to provide for them, so Jacob blessed Pharaoh.

The clan settling in the region of Goshen frames their audience with Pharaoh. Initially, Joseph directed them to Goshen and explained how to approach Pharaoh to gain his approval to stay (46:28–34). The section concludes with Joseph successfully settling them and providing for them in Goshen (47:11–12). In the center, Joseph presented representatives of his brothers to Pharaoh to explain their fealty and request the prime grazing lands (47:1–6). After Pharaoh's gracious provision to them, Joseph presented his father, honored by Pharaoh for his age, who blessed Pharaoh. The narrative not only shows God blessing Israel with his beneficent presence but also declaring blessing to the one who blessed them through the patriarch. The Abrahamic covenant promises were bearing fruit that would show in the following sections.

---

5 As with the sons of Benjamin (46:21, see footnote 6), it appears that Moses included them here to bring the number to seventy (v. 27). See Exposition at 46:27.

6 The ten sons of Benjamin present a problem because the genealogies in Num. 26:38–40 and 1 Chron. 7:6–12; 8:1 present different numbers of sons, with some of the ones in Genesis listed as grandsons later, "presumably included by anticipation (cf. Heb. 7:10)" (Kidner 1967, 221). Moses was self-consciously crafting the genealogy to equal seventy.

Joseph Prepared the Way to Goshen (46:28–34)

Joseph directed the family to Goshen and briefed them on meeting Pharaoh.

46:28–30. In our final view of Judah in Genesis, ironically, the one who orchestrated Joseph's departure from Jacob to Egypt now orchestrated Jacob's arrival to Joseph in Egypt (Sarna 1989, 317). His leadership had become a benefit to the family and with his change of heart would be celebrated in Jacob's blessing (49:8–12). In the hustle of Joseph going to meet his father, "Israel" is used twice (cf. 46:1–2), implying the nation's move to Egypt to begin the long sojourn. The focus here, however, is on the reunion of Joseph with his father as they embraced and Joseph wept. Israel's response was contented fulfillment. Finally, he saw his living son and felt he could die in peace.

TRANSLATION ANALYSIS 46:28

The Hebrew description of Judah's purpose for going is unusual and disputed. The MT preserves the *hiphil* of *yarah* (לְהוֹרֹת), which means to "instruct" or "teach" (*HALOT* s.v. III "ירה" 436–37) but normally would have a direct object. Here it is assumed to then include something like "to get directions" (NIV, NLT) or perhaps "to let Joseph know" ("advise him," REB), which fits the context (Mathews 2005, 841–42). The SP and the Syr both preserve the *niphal* from *ra'ah* (לְהֵרָאוֹת), meaning "to appear, become visible, present oneself" (*HALOT* s.v. "ראה" 1157–61), leading to "to appear before him" (RSV) or "to see Joseph" (NCV). The LXX seems to be translating the *niphal* of *qarah* (συναντῆσαι), meaning "to meet" him (NLT). The sense is clear with the "before him to Goshen" (לְפָנָיו גֹּשְׁנָה) that he is leading or preparing for Jacob and the family's arrival through Joseph. Regardless of the specific meaning, the intent is clear that Judah is given leadership and is easing the transition for the clan to Joseph and Egypt.

46:31–34. Rather than directly addressing his father, Joseph simply and pointedly instructed his brothers on how to approach and respond to Pharaoh to be able to stay in the land of Goshen in the Eastern Delta (v. 34, see footnote on 45:10, p. 671, n. 6).[7] They needed to let Pharaoh know their occupation so that they could live on the edge of Egyptian society, both where they could pasture their livestock and where they would not be a constant irritant to the Egyptians, who did not appreciate shepherds.[8] The narrative, then, focuses on Goshen as the appropriate place for the nation, with the family coming there (46:28–29), instructions for how to stay there (46:34), their request to stay there (47:4), Pharaoh's permission (47:6), and finally the clan thriving in that land, called Rameses (47:11). Joseph had planned this from the beginning (45:10), though Pharaoh, who had promised the "best" (45:18), had to give permission. Establishing their presence in Goshen both prepared for the exodus (cf. Exod. 1:11) and showed God's presence bringing blessing, particularly providing for their needs through the famine.

Joseph Presented His Brothers to Pharaoh (47:1–6)

Joseph presented his brothers to Pharaoh, securing land and employment.

7 Goshen, or the Eastern Delta region, was known to be used by nomadic herdsmen during famine to provide for their herds in Egyptian history (Hamilton 1995, 580).

8 Egyptian literature does not record the prejudice against shepherds, or the "abomination" mentioned here, so we can't know if it was simply the perennial conflict between the nomadic shepherds and the settled society, a threat to the grazing of other animals, or xenophobia (Walton 2009a, 133–34). Joseph also seems to be intent on removing any threat to Pharaoh and his people, allowing a peaceful transition for his family to the margins of Egyptian society.

47:1–2. Following up on Pharaoh's invitation to his family (45:17–18), Joseph reported back to Pharaoh that they had come. His reported speech summarizes what he expected to tell Pharaoh, focusing on their placement in Goshen. While he brought both his brothers and his father, he presented a representative group of his brothers first, as supplicants, then his father, in his revered age, brought Pharaoh blessing.

TRANSLATION ANALYSIS 47:2
The number five can be used as a small round number as well as the cardinal number (Jensen, חָמֵשׁ, *NIDOTTE* 2:190–91), so it could be "a few" (NJPS).

47:3–4. Pharaoh addressed Joseph's brothers precisely as Joseph had expected (45:33). Their response showed their submission to Pharaoh's authority and mirrored what Joseph had told them he would say to the Pharaoh ("shepherds," 46:32) more closely than what he had suggested they say ("keepers of livestock," 46:34), suggesting that the two phrases were effectively synonymous (Sarna 1989, 318). The brothers went on to both explain their presence because of the famine and make a formal request for shelter and sustenance for them and their flocks. They were asking to "sojourn" (v. 4, גור), indicating a foreigner living temporarily in a foreign country by their hospitality and in need of their protection, without the rights of citizenship (Spencer, "Sojourner," *ABD* 6:103–4).

47:5–6. Pharaoh responded to Joseph, who would carry out the order, giving blessing to Joseph's family in the form of shelter from the famine. He repeated his promise of the "best part of the land" for them (45:18), then specified his permission for Goshen as the destination. Perhaps with Joseph's judgment and success in mind, he also asked for Joseph to put any "able men" (אַנְשֵׁי־חַיִל) among them over his own livestock (also indicating he understood their occupation).[9] Reminiscent of Joseph in Potiphar's house or in the prison (39:2–4, 21–23), the king's response again demonstrated the presence of God with Jacob and his family, giving them favor in his eyes.

Joseph Presented His Father to Pharaoh (47:7–10)

Joseph presented his father to Pharaoh, who blessed Pharaoh.

47:7–10. When Joseph presented Jacob before Pharaoh, the script flipped. The powerful king found himself the one receiving blessing and favor. Jacob blessed Pharaoh twice, framing his audience with the monarch (vv. 7, 10). Jacob's blessing certainly may have been formulaic, but the impact in the narrative reminds the reader not only of God's purpose to bring blessing to all the families of the earth through them, but that the one who blessed them would be blessed (12:3). Pharaoh provided his best for the chosen family, and he in turn would experience Yahweh's blessing. That blessing is worked out tangibly in the following section.

TRANSLATION ANALYSIS 47:7, 10
While "bless" (ברך) can be used merely as a greeting (so "Jacob greeted Pharaoh" and "Jacob bade Pharaoh farewell," NJPS), the implications of offering blessing as a descendant of Abraham in Genesis and within the context of God's promise to the nations becomes paramount, so Jacob "blessed" Pharaoh, shown immediately in the results of Joseph's reforms (ESV, NET, NCV, cf. McKenzie 1983; Stein 2009).

Framed by Jacob's blessing on Pharaoh, Pharaoh inquired about Jacob's age

9 Sarna (1989, 319) points to Egyptian texts recording vast herds for Rameses III, who employed thousands of foreigners to care for them, also suggesting legal protections not normal for alien sojourners.

(apparently showing respect rather than a faux pas in ancient Egypt!). Jacob's declared age of 130 was twenty years longer than the ideal of 110 in Egypt (Wilson, "The Instruction of the Vizier Ptah-Hotep," *ANET*, 414, cf. n. 33), yet he considered it short and marked by pain. He certainly had experienced significant grief, even though much of it was self-imposed, from his deceit with Esau and Isaac to his family favoritism and conflict throughout, even apart from the past twenty years of agony over Joseph. At the same time, even though his life was shorter than his fathers (175 for Abraham, 25:7, and 180 for Isaac, 35:28), his long life expressed God's blessing (Deut. 6:2; 32:47).

> *TRANSLATION ANALYSIS 47:9*
> "Evil" (ESV, NKJV, RSV) translates Hebrew *raʿ* (רַע), which can refer to moral evil but can also refer to things that are "disagreeable, harmful, bad" or generally things that are "detrimental to life or its fullness" (Baker, רָעַע, *NIDOTTE* 3:1154), so better translated "difficult" (NIV), "painful" (NET), "unpleasant" (NASB95), or "hard" (NJPS, NRSV).

Joseph Settled His Clan in Goshen (47:11–12)

Joseph settled his clan in Goshen, providing for their needs.

47:11–12. Completing the frame around this section, Joseph carried out Pharaoh's orders, settling the clan in Goshen, here specified as Rameses,[10] specifically drawing attention to the later experience of Israel in Egypt (Exod. 1:11) and fulfilling God's prophecy to Abraham (Gen. 15:13). It was the "best of the land" as Pharaoh had stipulated (47:11), and Joseph provided all they needed for food, since the famine would continue another five years. This provision from the crown, including property (אֲחֻזָּה), stands in direct contrast to what follows, and with 47:27 will frame the deepening need and struggle of the Egyptians with the provision and fruitfulness of Israel. God's presence was obvious as he cared for his people.

> *TRANSLATION ANALYSIS 47:11*
> Though the English "possession" (ESV) may not convey it clearly, the Hebrew (אֲחֻזָּה) specifically refers to "property" (NIV) or land "holdings" (NJPS, cf. *HALOT* s.v. "אֲחֻזָּה" 32).

Joseph Gathered All Egypt's Resources for Pharaoh to Save the People (47:13–26)

Joseph obtained all the possessions and land of Egypt to keep the Egyptians alive, with an ongoing tax for Pharaoh.

Once again, the narrative uses a framing pattern. Here, the severe famine and lack of food throughout Egypt and Canaan drives the narrative (47:13). The main part of the narrative will work out Joseph's provision of food for the population in exchange for their silver (v. 14), cattle (vv. 15–17), and land (vv. 18–22). Joseph provides ongoing provision for them with the stipulation of a 20 percent tax on the harvests, to their gratitude (vv. 23–25). The concluding verse, completing the frame, summarizes the outcome of the famine, enshrining the deliverance of the population from famine with a continuing tax for the crown, except from the priests (v. 26). Mathews (2005, 855) notes the alternation in each movement of the center section between narrative and dialogue, emphasizing the generosity of Joseph and appreciation from the population for delivering them.

Egypt and Canaan Were Starving (47:13)

Egypt and Canaan had no food because of the severe famine.

10 Though it could have been used earlier without current attestation, the name "Rameses" may well be an editorial comment, since no record has yet been found for "Rameses" before the thirteenth century BC (Kitchen 2003, 348).

47:13. In stark contrast to Israel in Goshen, in which Joseph provided "food" (לֶחֶם, 47:12) for every member of the clan "according to the number of their dependents" (v. 12, lit. "for the mouth [or portion] of the children," לְפִי הַטָּף), the lack of "food" (לֶחֶם) begins the new section.[11] While Israel was blessed with plenty, all of Egypt and Canaan "languished." In fact, the threefold repetition of "Egypt and Canaan" (vv. 13, 14, 15) underlines the broad and serious menace to the entire region, while God provided for his people (they could have starved in Canaan! Sarna 1989, 321). God also had provided for the nations through Joseph. It would just cost them more.

Joseph Gathered All Egypt's Resources for Pharaoh (47:14–25)

Joseph gathered all the silver, cattle, and land in Egypt for Pharaoh, even indenturing the population to Pharaoh to save them, with their gratitude.

47:14. Reminding the reader of the brothers coming to buy grain, all the land brought their silver to Joseph for grain. This introductory verse makes two observations. The money was fully exhausted from buying the food, and all of it went into Pharaoh's treasury. The narrative repeatedly emphasizes that Pharaoh was being enriched through Joseph's stewardship of his responsibilities, but Joseph was not skimming any of the profits (vv. 14, 19, 20, 23, 24, 25, 26).

47:15–17. The timing of all these events is not provided, but the money ran out. When it did, the Egyptians came to Joseph. It was certainly not to anyone's benefit if the population starved, so Joseph accepted their livestock for food to keep them alive. They gladly paid for it.

47:18–22. Again the population came to Joseph, and admitting they had no more money or cattle, proposed that he accept their land and service (their "bodies," v. 18) for food to keep them alive. They readily offer to serve Pharaoh for their lives. Joseph agreed and provided for them. As a result, only the priests were exempted and maintained their independence, because Pharaoh already provided an allowance for them.

> *TRANSLATION ANALYSIS 47:21*
> The MT and Syr have "he removed them to the cities" (NASB95, NKJV, see also NJPS, הֶעֱבִיר אֹתוֹ לֶעָרִים), but the SP and LXX record "he made servants of them" (ESV, cf. NET, NIV, etc.., הֶעֱבִיד אתו לַעֲבָדִים). The textual problem involves the interchange of two very similar Hebrew letters, ר (MT) and ד (SP), and the addition of ב (SP), all of which could be a simple scribal error (either direction). Removing them to the cities could have been temporary to feed them more easily (later they are tenant farmers), but the context fits making them servants better, because that is what they proposed (v. 19) and what Joseph did (v. 20), supporting the SP.

47:23–25. Up to this point the Egyptians had initiated the transactions. Now Joseph stepped to the fore. He had already gotten all their money, animals, and land. Now he proposed that he provide seed for sowing in exchange for a 20 percent tax on the harvests. The rest was theirs to provide for their needs (including the "little ones," v. 24, drawing attention again to God's provision for Israel, v. 12). Their response to Joseph was profound gratitude. They pledged their allegiance, requesting to serve Pharaoh for their food (v. 25). God had provided through Joseph and Pharaoh's dreams, not only for his people but for the peoples of Egypt and Canaan.

11 The new section begins with the disjunctive *waw* on "food," foregrounding the contrast with Joseph's provision of food for the brothers in v. 12 and emphasizing God's provision for his people in the strongest contrast to the world.

Joseph Saved Lives in Exchange for Land (47:26)

Joseph secured the land with a permanent statute requiring a 20 percent tax on all the produce of Egypt, excepting the priests.

47:26. A summary statement reports Joseph's new tax code in Egypt, which still held until the writing of the narrative. Pharaoh took a fifth of the produce, except from the priests. The taking of a fifth part reminds the reader of Joseph's suggestion for preparing for the famine (41:34), providing a surplus reserve against the coming famine (41:36). According to the extant records, the region experienced periodic drought and so famines, suggesting that Joseph's plan would provide ongoing security against possible famine in addition to enriching Pharaoh's coffers (cf. Hamilton 1995, 618). The initial dire need was averted to everyone's satisfaction.

Abject Slavery or Tenant Farmers?

Western readers may think of chattel slavery when they read this account and balk at Joseph's methods, seeing him as more of a villain than a hero (Brueggemann 1982a, 356). The text presents the response of the population as grateful and favorable to him and the outcome. Rather than abject slavery, they were much like tenant farmers, a generous proposition in the ancient world (Mathews 2005, 851). Sarna (1989, 322) notes that under Hammurabi, the government share from their administered fields was 50–66 percent, and 20 percent was common interest on loans in Babylon except for produce, which was 33.3 percent. "Joseph's economic policy in Gn. 47:16–19 simply made Egypt in fact what it always was in theory: the land became pharaoh's property and its inhabitants his tenants" (Kitchen, "Joseph," *NBD* 610). The text presents the outcome as God's gracious provision for humanity to provide for them through the famine and keep many people alive (45:5, 7; 50:20), using his chosen people to bless his world (12:3). Servanthood was the accepted ancient means of dealing with debt, more like "tenured employment" as opposed to the self-employed (cf. Exod. 21:5–6; Deut. 15:12–17; Wenham 1994, 449). We may want to remember that they asked for it, viewing Joseph as their savior with gratitude (Gen. 47:25). It was God's purpose for him (45:7; 50:20).

The scene begins with the specter of starvation (47:13) and ends with Joseph's deliverance (v. 26). In the center, the alternating narrative and dialogue shows Joseph as the provider. In each case, the population asked to purchase the food with what they had, and Joseph complied. In the final direct discourse, Joseph offered the people seed for sowing with a 20 percent tax on the yield. The people hailed him as their deliverer.

God Blessed Israel in Goshen, and Joseph Promised to Bury Him in Canaan (47:27–31)

Israel settled in Goshen with God's blessing and Joseph's promise to bury him in Canaan.

The frame of the growth of the clan and Jacob's death and return to the promised land establishes the narrative as key to the development of God's covenant promises to Abraham, Isaac, and Jacob and shows Jacob's growth in faith in the promise. He was committed and willing to wait, even after death. The sojourn in Egypt would mark the nation and prepare them to be the people of God in his promised land when the time was right, and he led them out. They too must wait with faith in God's promise.

Israel Settled in Goshen with God's Blessing (47:27)

Israel settled in Goshen and were fruitful and multiplied greatly.[12]

12 As noted often, the singular verb Israel "settled," referring to the man, is followed by three plurals ("they gained possessions . . . were fruitful and multiplied greatly"), indicating the clan. The ambiguity is intentional, drawing attention to the emerging national identity (Sarna 1989, 323).

47:27. The narrative reiterates that Israel settled in Goshen (47:11, 27) framing the intervening narrative (47:13–26). Neither a clumsy interruption nor intruder into the narrative, the frame functions as a significant contrast to the Egyptians in the working of God for his people in a crisis. When all the Egyptians were selling everything, including their land and themselves, to Pharaoh, Israel (clearly the emerging nation here) was gaining land holdings and prospering (47:11). That they "were fruitful and multiplied greatly" recalls God's blessing on his creatures and humanity (1:22, 28; 8:17; 9:1), declaring the outworking of God's presence and promise (46:3–4; cf. 28:3; 35:11). The seventy (46:8–27) would become a great nation under the direct care of God, even through the coming struggle of captivity (46:3; cf. Exod. 1:12, 20; Deut. 10:22).

> *TRANSLATION ANALYSIS 47:27*
> The verb translated "gained possessions" (*niphal* of אחז) is used in 34:10 by the Shechemites inviting the clan to gain property, so "they acquired property" (NASB95, NIV, NLT). The contrast to the Egyptians, then, is even stronger than may be understood in the ESV. Note the cognate noun, Translation Analysis 47:11, p. 685, framing the Egyptians selling their land.

Joseph Promised to Bury Israel in Canaan, and Israel Worshipped (47:28–31)

Growing old, Israel secured Joseph's promise to bury him in Canaan and bowed in worship.

47:28. Jacob lived in Egypt for as long as Joseph had lived in Canaan before being sold. Up to now the report of the patriarch's age has been given just before his death and burial (Abraham in 25:7–9; Ishmael in 25:17; Isaac in 35:28–29). Here, however, there will be two intervening chapters in which he declares his blessing on the sons of Joseph and his own sons before his death and burial (49:33–50:14). This notice closes the previous narrative and previews what follows. The following scene begins with "after these things" (48:1; lit., NET, וַיְהִי אַחֲרֵי הַדְּבָרִים הָאֵלֶּה), which often begins a new section (Wenham 1994, 438, citing 15:1; 22:1; 40:1; Longacre 1989, 64). In the current section, the notice of Jacob's age and subsequent oath from Joseph provides closure on God's promise (46:4), completing the response to God's blessing with personal worship (47:31).

47:29–31. Realizing his impending death, Israel called Joseph to swear to bury him in Canaan rather than Egypt.[13] The promise of God both to give the land to his descendants (28:13; 35:12) and to return him from Egypt (46:3) inform this act of faith. With Joseph's oath, which he will carry out in 50:4–14, Israel "bowed himself on the head of his bed" (47:31). This section that began with Israel's worship as he sought God's favor for his trip to Egypt ends with his worship at confirmation of God's fulfilled promise. God's intervention and favor toward his chosen people and all nations is appropriately bounded by worship, in entreaty seeking guidance (46:1) and thanksgiving for answered prayer (47:31). Both model an important dependent posture toward the sovereign King of creation who alone gives ultimate blessing and life. It also provides a helpful indication of Israel's growth in faith as he nears his final days.

> *TRANSLATION ANALYSIS 47:31*
> The final clause has both textual problems and contextual problems. Textually, the MT says he bowed on his "bed" (הַמִּטָּה, ESV, NET, etc.), while the LXX and Syriac understand "staff" (הַמַּטֶּה, NIV, see also NCV). Hebrews 11:21 follows the LXX. The difference is the vowel pointing, which was not in the original. Given his age and his health, the MT makes sense (cf. 1 Kings 1:47) and need

---

13 Placing the hand "under the thigh" was an oath practice to solemnize the oath occasion (see Exposition on 24:2, p. 414).

not be emended. Contextually, however, was Israel bowing in worship (NASB95, NCV, NIV) or should it be understood as humility (NLT), perhaps before Joseph, finally fulfilling the dream (Sailhamer 1990, 268) and so translated merely "bowed" (ESV, NET, NJPS)? The very close parallel to 1 Kings 1:47 suggests worship, as David then praised Yahweh for fulfilling his promise of a descendant to sit on David's throne (v. 48). Given the emphasis of the passage on the working of God fulfilling promise and the parallels with the beginning of the section, worship makes better sense, framing the narrative. Joseph's oath confirmed God's previous promise to Israel. Jacob appropriately responded to God's intervention in worship.

THEOLOGICAL FOCUS

God moves his plan forward, going with his worshippers into difficult times to accomplish his purpose: blessing his faithful people, those who bless them, and his world.

God's promise to Jacob at the beginning of the pericope foregrounds his working, even though he then fades into the background. God directs the affairs of his people and provides blessing and protection with his presence, preparing them to accomplish his purposes. He uses them to bring his blessing to his world. That presence and blessing is not always underlined as miraculous but flows from his people's wise and faithful interactions in his world and appears in the promised outcomes, even when initiated or provided through secular means. God can use a pagan pharaoh to accomplish his greater purposes. Of course, as we have seen and as Israel will come to understand, the greatest blessing they offer to their world is the presence of God. God reveals himself and the means to know him and walk with him through his people.

From the human perspective, uncertainty or tensions between expectations and circumstances should drive people to God in worship and petition for wisdom to respond appropriately to the tensions or testing, showing faith in God's overriding authority and control (James 1:5). God's promised presence gives his people the perspective to face those trials and trust him to work out the circumstances. When the outcome matches the promise, faith concludes that God has faithfully worked and must be worshipped (James 1:7). His provision through unexpected or secular sources provides opportunities for his people to bless his world and acknowledge his work (1 Peter 2:9).

Israel's experience provides another illustration that one can be in the center of God's purpose with full confidence in his leading and presence and still face trouble and suffering. God can use all of that to work his good purposes in and through his people. While God had promised suffering to Abraham for his descendants, it was not initially the result of evil actions (as per Joseph's experience). Rather, it was God's intervention in salvation, even though it put them into the place where they would face future evil actions that produce suffering (46:3–4, cf. 15:13). It all turns out to be part of God's plan. God put them into the place where he could fulfill his promises and accomplish his working, despite the coming suffering and pain. As Joseph had already acknowledged, God uses all those things for his divine purposes for the nation, a powerful message for the nation reading this and subsequent generations of sufferer throughout salvation history (Rom. 8:28–29).

During the sojourn in Egypt, God used Joseph and Israel to bring his blessing to Pharaoh and Egypt, demonstrating that God's people must not wait until God's will is fully accomplished to see and work out their purpose of bringing blessing to his world. Rather, they must bless those who bless them, calling on God to work on their behalf and for the good of his world. Such blessing helps God's world to experience his gracious goodness.

Jacob's travel to Egypt and response to Joseph's oath show his growth in faith. Consciously trusting God's word and living in light of his promises allow that growth. God's people need to rest in the promise of God, especially when one cannot or will not be able to see the outcomes personally.

All of this is framed by appropriate worship. Worship necessarily accompanies seeking God's direction and clarity in life, and it is the necessary response for promises kept and indications of God's working moving toward those promises. God's goodness and sovereign oversight undergirds the response of faith to all of life's challenges.

PREACHING AND TEACHING STRATEGIES

Exegetical and Theological Synthesis

The narrative begins to speak to our listeners through Israel's actions. He functions as a "go and do likewise" example by the way he worships God, seeking God's direction. God responds to him with a revelation of his identity, a command to not be afraid to go down to Egypt, and two wonderful promises concerning his reassuring presence. If Israel was looking for confirmation about going to Egypt, God provided it.

The lengthy section from 46:8–27 ends with the number seventy, to highlight the blessing of God on his people while they sojourn in Egypt, preparing for the exodus. One of the fascinating elements of God's sovereign ability to bless his people is the way in which their occupation as shepherds (46:32, 34; 47:3) creates the opportunity for them to "Settle . . . in the best of the land" (47:6, 11). Joseph's directing his family to Goshen ends up being good for them and the Egyptians (46:34). The final section of 47:13–31 highlights Joseph's abilities to bless his own family and all of Egypt. Even though the Egyptians are taxed heavily, they still confess to Joseph: "You have saved our lives . . . we will be servants to Pharaoh" (47:25).

If there was any doubt as to the narrative's meaning, we read it in 47:27–31. God's people take possession of the land of Goshen and, in the language of Genesis 1:22, they "were fruitful and multiplied greatly" (47:27). And God's blessing continues when Israel requests being buried in the promised land, not Egypt (v. 30). Joseph's reply coordinates with God's original promise to Israel when chapter 46 began.

Preaching Idea

God's faithful resist their fears by resting in his presence to experience God's blessing and extend his blessing to others.

Contemporary Connections

What does it mean?

It is important to explain the significance of all the direct references and allusions to the Abrahamic covenant. In addition to that, you may want to direct your listeners' attention to the repetition of the Creator's earliest command to be fruitful and multiply from Genesis 1. This will help your congregants understand that even in Egypt the Lord is continuing to bless his people, and his people are experiencing the outworking of his plan for them to be blessed and be a blessing to the world. Also, when Pharaoh is blessed by Israel, in addition to being literally saved by Joseph, Pharaoh is experiencing the blessing of those who bless God's people.

This narrative continues to provide opportunities to explain the doctrine of the sovereignty of God: his ability to control circumstances and the decisions of his people and pagans so that everything moves toward the accomplishment of his will for his glory. You might also explain the significance of the number seventy at the end of the names of the descendants: the narrator is foreshadowing the blessing of God on his people, who would become a great nation even though they found themselves enslaved in Egypt (cf. 46:8, 27).

Is it true?
The narrative shows that the doctrine of sovereignty mentioned above is true. God really does control circumstances and decisions so that his people accomplish his will in the world. The narrative is proving that God controls both his people and pagans. In these two chapters, numerous examples appear, such as how the fact that Joseph's family were shepherds provided a way for them to possess the very best land Egypt had to offer. It is true, after all, that our listeners can experience God's blessing in what may appear to be the most difficult circumstances (in Israel's case, a severe famine threatens their lives, and they are saved in Egypt because of the skillfulness of Joseph in his position as second in command to Pharaoh).

Now what?
Because all of us are on a faith journey in a badly broken world, facing fears and uncertainties, nothing is more relevant than to see evidence of God's faithfulness to bless Joseph, his family, and even the Egyptians. After all, we have the permanent presence of God! Our listeners read the story with us and should be able to offer their own praise to God. Of course, Israel's example of being a genuine worshipper also leads the way for all of us. Everything in these two chapters begins with Israel's Beersheba worship service. Then, the Lord responds with a wonderful word of instruction and encouragement. Each Sunday, we communicate to some who need not fear but follow God's leading in difficult times, knowing that the Lord will accompany them and fulfill his promises to deliver.

Creativity in Presentation
In this section we learn that God's faithful resist their fears by resting in his presence, to experience God's blessing and extend his blessing to others. We are coming to the end of a long Joseph narrative. It might be helpful to begin the sermon/lesson with the thought of hindsight being 20/20 vision. Looking back over our lives provides important perspective for seeing God at work. That is certainly true of the Joseph story, when we read of his father and brothers finally being united again in Egypt, of all places, a place where Joseph rules. They all end up experiencing the blessing of God and being a part of extending that blessing to Pharaoh and his kingdom. The circuitous route highlights God's sovereign ability to stay faithful to his promises, and this bolsters the faith of our listeners. From this introduction the sermon/lesson can take the following form:

- God's people worship and respond to his instruction and promises (46:1–27). Israel's worship service at Beersheba shows the proper way for us to relate to our God, seeking his guidance. God responds to Israel's worship with instruction and promises that guide our faith journey. The lengthy section of 46:8–27 numbers the family at seventy to provide a look forward to fulfilling part of the Abrahamic covenant with respect to family size.

- God's people experience his blessing even in the middle of difficult circumstances (46:28–47:6, 27–31). This is a fitting time to stress the sovereignty of God. The narrator emphasizes Goshen in 46:28–47:6 and God's people being shepherds. What is "an abomination to the Egyptians" (46:34) results in Joseph's family being allowed to settle "in est of the land" (47:6, 11). I suggest taking the final segment of the narrative (XX) in major point two because of the similar theme of blessing and the link back to Genesis 1 and ahead to Exodus 1. This section also provides hope for God's people returning to the promised land as seen in Israel's burial request.

- God's people extend his blessing to those around them (47:7–26). God intended his people to extend his blessing to others. Jacob blesses Pharaoh (vv. 7, 10). The lengthiest section in the narrative involves a summary of the way Joseph saves all of Egypt during the severe famine. The definitive statement is: "You have saved our lives" (v. 25).

DISCUSSION QUESTIONS

1. Record all the various elements of the blessing of God on Joseph and his family.
2. What is your emotional reaction to reading that Joseph's family ends up in Egypt "in the best of the land" (47:6, 11)?
3. How do Joseph's actions in Egypt, including especially the use of his power, guide Christians in their ability to represent Christ in the world and extend his blessing?
4. Is there anything about Joseph's decision-making that makes you question how he treated the Egyptians during the famine? How could you justify him?
5. How do we seek God's direction and favor when we are facing fear or uncertainty about our future and decisions?
6. Hindsight is the easiest way to see God's presence and work through difficult times. How have we seen God's presence and blessing in our lives in the past that we can recall for uncertain times today or tomorrow?

Genesis 48:1–22

EXEGETICAL IDEA

Reflecting on God's promises and faithful shepherding throughout his life, Jacob blessed Joseph with the birthright, elevating Joseph's sons and passing the covenant promises on to the next generation for the future blessing of the burgeoning nation, through God's ongoing presence and care.

THEOLOGICAL FOCUS

God's promises and faithful care for his people ground their loyalty and faith, passing on their legacy and pursuit of his future blessing to the next generation as God carries out his redemptive plan.

PREACHING IDEA

Trust in God's promise to bless you and to make you a blessing to the next generation of disciple-makers.

PREACHING POINTERS

Our God has been blessing his creation since the beginning of Genesis. In 1:28 we read, "And God blessed them. And God said to them, 'Be fruitful and multiply.'" And now in chapter 48 we read Jacob telling Joseph: "God . . . blessed me, and said to me, 'Behold, I will make you fruitful and multiply you'" (vv. 3–4). The original audience must have been encouraged to see God's continued faithfulness to his people. As we read of Jacob blessing Joseph and his two sons, we receive encouragement from knowing that our Lord wants to bless us and wants us to extend his blessing to others around us.

Jacob's blessing to Joseph includes a rehearsal of God's faithful care. We take great comfort in his words, "the God who has been my shepherd all my life long to this day" (v. 15b). We too must look for God's faithful care in our past to ground our anticipation and preparation for God's working in future generations.

And, of course, the challenge is for us to make sure we are also characterized as those who walk with God (v. 15a). In the blessing of Joseph's younger son, there is a strong reminder to us that the blessing of God does not move according to conventional standards of the day. It is solely based on his grace and mercy. Finally, Israel teaches us that the blessing of God goes along with his powerful, ongoing presence (v. 21, "but God will be with you").

BIRTHRIGHT: PASSING ON GOD'S BLESSING (48:1–22)

LITERARY STRUCTURE AND THEMES

Genesis 48 records Jacob's adoption of Joseph's two sons as his own, transferring God's blessing of fertility to them and prioritizing Ephraim. Jacob recalled his blessing from El Shaddai at Bethel from chapter 35, drawing out the ongoing promises initiated with Abraham to the future generations of his descendants. Consciously passing his blessing along, he elevated Joseph, giving the birthright to Joseph's two sons in adoption, culminating with the portion of land Jacob could bequeath. The narrative flows in three movements as Jacob recalled God's blessings, extended them to his grandsons as adopted heirs, and disposed of his only tangible property.

A. Israel prepared to pass on God's blessing (48:1–11).
B. Israel passed God's blessing to Joseph (48:12–20).
C. Israel bequeathed his property foreshadowing the land promise (48:21–22).

The Abrahamic covenant promises again take center stage as Jacob recalled God's promise to him at Bethel. He highlighted God's faithfulness throughout his life, culminating in his blessed reunion with Joseph and his family. Faith in the promise and submission to God's will take precedence over human responsibilities and custom, and every new generation is enjoined to remain faithful and committed to the outworking of promise. As in Jacob's experience, God's people may not recognize God's blessing until much later, if then, but God will fulfill his promise.

- ***Israel Prepared to Pass On God's Blessing (48:1–11)***
- ***Israel Passed God's Blessing to Joseph (48:12–20)***
- ***Israel Bequeathed His Property, Foreshadowing the Land Promise (48:21–22)***

EXPOSITION

Since the climax of the narrative when Joseph revealed his identity, the conflicts have largely been resolved. God rescued and prospered the family and blessed Pharaoh and the families of the world through Joseph. Attention now turns to preparations for the future of the nation and their extended stay in Egypt (15:13). They must recognize their greater purpose and intended inheritance in Canaan and plan to return. Jacob's focus throughout this passage turns to the still future promise of God for his descendants to become a "company of peoples" and inherit Canaan as an "everlasting possession" (48:4).

In the larger chiastic structure of the fourth-generation stories (see Introduction to the Fourth-Generation Narratives, p. 587), Joseph's elevation through his two sons presents the final resolution of the false accusations and imprisonment from Potiphar's wife, partially resolved by his elevation and blessing before Pharaoh. For the first generation reading the narrative, both narratives would resonate, as Israel coming out of bondage looked forward to the inheritance of the land. Detailing the promise draws the implication to the surface for

Israel's descendants to keep in mind, working toward their restoration to the land and God's fulfilled promise, as Jacob will envision them in the next couple of chapters. This fulfillment brings the fourth-generation stories, the Jacob stories, and the Abraham stories to a conclusion, crowning God's working throughout Genesis and clarifying God's redemptive promise of the seed that would crush evil and bring blessing to the world. The quest for the seed will gain clarity in the following chapter with the promise of enduring rule through Judah.

As Jacob prepared for death, he blessed his heirs, beginning with Joseph. The double portion appropriately fits the expectations set up from Joseph's dreams. Though Joseph was Jacob's favorite and God's choice as a major player in this phase of his plan, the leadership would ironically go to Judah in the next passage, as the two aspects of the family legacy would formally split among Jacob's heirs. Jacob submitted to God's greater plan even in these choices.

Jacob recalled God's faithfulness throughout his life, with God's constant care and protection, fulfilling his promised oversight (28:15) and revealing his ongoing (48:11) and future (48:21) fulfillment of his promise. Reflecting on God's promises and faithful shepherding throughout his life, Jacob blessed Joseph with the birthright, elevating Joseph's sons and passing the covenant promises on to the next generation for the future blessing of the burgeoning nation through God's ongoing presence and care.

Israel Prepared to Pass On God's Blessing (48:1–11)

Nearing death, Jacob recalled God's blessing to him of fruitful descendants and land in Canaan to pass on to the next generation, elevating Ephraim and Manasseh as full heirs.

48:1–2. "After this" (אַחֲרֵי הַדְּבָרִים הָאֵלֶּה) moves the reader to the final events as Jacob was about to die (48:21). The brief report to Joseph and response to Jacob sets the stage for the ensuing drama of Jacob's deathbed scenes, first with Joseph and his sons and then with all the sons, as Jacob focused his attention and the attention of the reader on God's past faithfulness, present blessing, and future working. Without explanation, Joseph took his two sons with him, though we soon learn Jacob's intentions for the boys and realize Jacob may have asked for them to come. The report that he was "ill" (חֹלֶה) and what follows marks his expectation that he was dying (48:21; cf. 27:2), which would follow soon after (49:33), and his intent to orchestrate the focus and future of his heirs.

48:3–4. Jacob may have been dying and nearly blind, but his memory and his spiritual vision were sharp. In preparation to pass on the blessing to his grandsons, Jacob rehearsed God's appearance and blessing to him at Luz (Bethel). Though God had appeared to him twice at Luz (chs. 28, 35), he clearly refers to the second appearance. He invoked El Shaddai, the name God used on that occasion to emphasize his authority over life and blessing (see Exposition on 35:11–12, p. 572), repeating the specific promises made then that were not made earlier of "blessing," fruitful multiplication, and becoming a "company of nations," along with the promise of the land as an "everlasting possession" (48:4). Jacob merged the promises, understanding the necessary continuity with the initial promises to Abraham. God did not specify an "everlasting possession" (אֲחֻזַּת עוֹלָם) to Israel in Genesis 35:11–12. Rather, it is from God's promise to Abraham in Genesis 17:8. These promises formed the necessary foundation for the blessing he would pass along to Joseph through Ephraim and Manasseh, who would multiply greatly (48:16, 19, 20), and his bequeathed land holding for Joseph (v. 22).

TRANSLATION ANALYSIS 48:4

Though the idea is the same, Jacob's reflection on God's promise of being a "company of nations" (לִקְהַל עַמִּים) reflects Isaac's blessing on him in 28:3 (לִקְהַל עַמִּים) more closely than God's statement recorded in 35:11 (וּקְהַל גּוֹיִם). His combining of various accounts of God's promises shows the continuity and prepares for the ongoing implications of God's covenant promises beginning with Abraham.

Jacob did not mention his name change to Israel, less important for the heritage of the tribes. Moses, however, does use the name "Israel" nine times in this section (and Jacob only twice at the beginning), eight times for the person and once referring to the future nation (v. 20). Using "Israel" reflects Jacob's dependence on God and faith in his promises. Jacob also omitted God's promise of kings coming from him, which he would pass along to Judah in the following blessings on the rest of the sons. Rather, in this section Jacob focused on his blessing and expectation of Joseph gaining the birthright or double portion (see Exposition on 25:31–33 when Esau sold his birthright, p. 439). The "rank and position" would go to Judah in chapter 49 (cf. M. Tsevat, בְּכֹרָה, *TDOT* 2:126).

The final clause of the remembered promise leads the reader to the goal of the narrative. God had promised an "everlasting possession" (אֲחֻזַּת עוֹלָם) for Jacob and his seed after him in the land of Canaan. Merging the various eras and promises of the Abrahamic covenant underlines the continuity of Yahweh's promise. Israel is fully aware of his heritage and his appropriate expectations. His choice of the earlier wording pointedly contrasts their current security in Egypt. Through Joseph's faithful service and Pharaoh's generosity, God had provided a possession of land for the family in Egypt (אֲחֻזָּה; 47:11), and of course they "were fruitful and multiplied greatly" (47:27). With a possession in Egypt, there was danger they would become complacent and forget their "everlasting possession" (אֲחֻזַּת עוֹלָם, 48:4) in Canaan. Israel reminded them of the hope and purpose of their existence.

48:5–6. In light of God's promised blessings to him, Jacob declared his intent to take the two sons of Joseph as his own heirs. "In the same way as" or "just as" (NRSV, *HALOT* s.v. "כְּ" 3., 454) Reuben and Simeon (his two eldest) were his, Joseph's two eldest sons would be considered Israel's sons. Israel's concern was the future inheritance rights of the tribes, based on their size, so that Ephraim and Manasseh would inherit their "everlasting possession" in equal shares with the rest of the tribes of Israel. In effect Joseph would get a double portion of the inheritance by getting two tribal allotments through the adoption of his two sons (1 Chron. 5:1–2).

The Adoption of Ephraim and Manasseh

Comparing a Ugaritic text of a father adopting the sons of a slave woman to inherit along with his other children, Jacob's adoption of Ephraim and Manasseh is "almost identical with the Babylonian adoption formulas employed throughout the ancient Near East" (Mendelsohn 1959, 180). Similarly, Wenham (1994, 463) cites a record of a grandfather adopting his grandson. Sarna (1989, 325) recognizes the "legal precision" of the language and actions used by Jacob to formalize the adoption. Though favoring a later-born son was forbidden by later Deuteronomic law (Deut. 21:15–17), such a law was not yet known, and in Jacob's context, choosing the "firstborn" for the double portion was accepted practice and a matter of contract as well as birth (Frymer-Kensky 1981, 214). Jacob not only established Joseph as the firstborn for the double portion, but he also effectively bypassed the question of Joseph for the future conquest by adopting and elevating Joseph's two sons for future inheritance rights.

Israel gave a younger son (Joseph) the birthright, formally because of Reuben's offense (Gen. 49:3–4; 1 Chron. 5:1). Though none are recorded, any further children Joseph had or would have would be his but would inherit under one of the two tribes of Ephraim and Manasseh. In his blessing, Jacob put Ephraim ahead of Manasseh. God's choice of the younger and unexpected heir continued with Ephraim.

48:7. Israel then returned to his memories, recorded immediately after his vision from God at Luz. The untimely death of Rachel had deeply impacted him and left him not only without his favorite wife, but with only two sons from her. He would now remediate that tragedy by adopting Ephraim and Manasseh, perhaps in memory of their grandmother (Hamilton 1995, 630).

48:8–9. With all his talk about adopting the two young men, it may seem odd that Israel did not recognize them when he saw them, until we realize that he had apparently inherited Isaac's poor eyesight (v. 10). Even though his eyesight was limited (though not fully sightless), it may well also be important for identification of the sons to initiate a formal adoption ceremony (Sarna 1989, 327). Israel declared his adoption of the two boys (v. 5) as Joseph's blessing (v. 15), which he specifically gave to them (v. 9) in preparation to bless his naturally born sons (49:2–27). Joseph's double portion, then, was worked out in the future inheritances of the tribes in Canaan when God gave them their promised possession.[1] The blessing to follow would confer on the two boys the promise of abundance required to take their places at the forefront of the tribes.

48:10–11. The image of the aged Israel with limited vision embracing and kissing his grandsons reverberates with the promises of God to Israel, which seemed for so many years to be impossible to him. Life was hard, Joseph was thought dead, his sons had been reprehensible, and he was without the love of his life. Now he was reunited not only with Joseph, but God had blessed him with his grandsons, and he could see more clearly the working of God through his dimming vision. He recognized and declared his divine blessing.

Israel Passed God's Blessing to Joseph (48:12–20)

Israel passed God's blessing on to Joseph, elevating Ephraim and Manasseh and blessing both boys as his own with Abrahamic covenant promises of great fruitfulness.

48:12–13. When we notice the chronology, Israel has been in Egypt now nearly seventeen years (cf. 47:9, 28), and the sons of Joseph were born during the good years. That means that they must be at least twenty years old. They are not children dandling on his knees. When "Joseph removed them from his knees" (48:12), he took them from standing near Israel, at his knees in honor, to present them formally to Israel for blessing (and as we are then told) in the appropriate order for their ages. Joseph himself bowed deeply before Israel, ironically showing his respect for "the patriarch who mediates God's promises" despite the authority he held and dream he had been given (Waltke and Fredricks 2001, 598).

48:14–16. Contrary to expectation, Israel put his right hand on Ephraim and his left hand on Manasseh and "blessed Joseph" (v. 15), clearly showing the connection between his adoption and his blessing for his "firstborn," Joseph. The blessing that followed applied God's promised abundance to the two young men. More than that, however, he directed God's faithful care and oversight, embodying his protective presence to his newly adopted sons. Given Jacob's life, with its many struggles and fears (much of it self-imposed), his descriptions of God's care reveal deep growth in his faith and insight into God's work in his own life and intentions for his descendants.

1 So the counting of the "twelve tribes" of Israel and their inheriting of the land will now require leaving one of the other tribes out, often Levi, who did not get a land inheritance as the priestly tribe.

He began with the reminder of his legacy of loyalty to Yahweh. His fathers had walked before God (see Exposition on 17:1, p. 322), and Israel had benefitted from relationship with God in true worship (esp. 35:1–15). Abraham and Isaac had not been flawless, but they had proved loyal (cf. ch. 22 and Exposition there, p. 387). Though he did not comment on his own loyalty, he aptly described God's care for him in leading and providing for him throughout his life. God had been his "shepherd" (הָרֹעֶה אֹתִי) for his entire life. During many of those days God's guidance was not obvious at all until seen in retrospect. The hindsight of Jacob's long life as a shepherd recognized God's exceptional, unbroken care, whether obvious or unseen in the moment.

In a third parallel line, Israel invoked "the angel who has redeemed me from all evil" (48:16). In light of the parallelism from the first two lines in verse 15 and the prayer with which he blesses the boys, Israel was likely intending God here again but alluding to the many interventions on his behalf, likely at least thinking of Bethel (28:10–22), Mahanaim (32:1), and Peniel (32:22–31), and perhaps especially the wrestling match there at Peniel with the clear intervention in Esau's life seen the next day (33:4–11; esp. v. 10). In remembering the working of God and in calling on God to bless them in light of his legacy and experience, Israel invoked and offered the same legacy and experience for his sons.

TRANSLATION ANALYSIS 48:16a

The lone use of "redeem" (גאל) here in Genesis parallels its use in God's deliverance of Israel from Egypt (Exod. 6:6; 15:13). It recalls the familiar legal instruction of the close relative to rescue or deliver someone who has had to sell his property, family, and even himself into slavery by buying them back (Lev. 25:25–54). By extension, God was redeeming his people whom he had chosen for relationship, not by purchasing their freedom, but by rescuing them from harm (cf. Hubbard, גָּאַל, *NIDOTTE* 1:789–94). Therefore, it is appropriately translated "protected" (NET), "delivered" (NIV), or "saved" (NCV).

His final line clarifies the blessing as he tied their future directly to his name and heritage, deriving their expectations from God's promises to Abraham, Isaac, and Jacob. They would be full heirs of the Abrahamic covenant with the other sons of Jacob. They would be fully Israel in their expected blessing. They would multiply greatly in the land.

TRANSLATION ANALYSIS 48:16b

The verb "multiply" (דגה) appears only here in the Hebrew Bible. It is generally assumed to derive from the common noun for fish (דָּג; *HALOT* s.v. "דגה" 213), leading to "be teeming multitudes" (NJPS).

48:17–20. Suddenly, it seems, Joseph realized that Israel's hands were elevating Ephraim over Manasseh and tried to intervene. Since the right hand was generally the source of greatest power, it was also the source of special blessing (J. Drinkard, "Right, Right Hand," *ABD* 5:724). His immediate "Not this way, my father" (v. 18) assumed Israel was mistaken and probably mixing the boys. Israel, however, was not mistaken and was fully conscious of what he was doing. While he did not explain, he recognized the blessing was unexpected and contrary to custom. The implication from the pattern of God's choice of the younger sons (Isaac, Jacob, Joseph, now Ephraim) is that this was God's choice and not Israel's. Israel was following orders (cf. Mathews 2005, 864).

Without explanation, Israel affirmed that both would be great, but Ephraim at his right hand would be greater. While Manasseh would be a "people" (עָם), Ephraim would be "a multitude of nations" (מְלֹא־הַגּוֹיִם, v. 19). The promise to Manasseh reflects God's covenant promise to Jacob through Isaac that Jacob would become a "company of peoples"

(וְהָיִיתָ לִקְהַל עַמִּים, 28:3) which Israel quoted in 48:4. The promise to Ephraim, that he would be a "multitude of nations," uses the more common noun for "nations" (הַגּוֹיִם), which he had quoted from Genesis 35:11 but which he modified with a new expression here, elsewhere translated "fulness, full amount, measure" (cf. ESV margin, *HALOT* s.v. "מְלֹא" 584–85). The problem, of course, is that Ephraim will not be a multitude of nations in any historical sense. The MT, however, can be understood here as "plentiful enough for nations" (NJPS, see also NCV), and the plural of "nations" (גּוֹיִם) could be understood as intensification, leading to Ephraim being "full of the qualities that nations would entail" (Lee 2009, 470). Manasseh would be great, but Ephraim would be greater.

As we will see in chapter 49, and as Abraham and Isaac did (20:7; Ps. 105:15), Israel in his blessing was functioning as a prophet. Israel blessed the two boys together, envisioning the day when they would so exemplify God's gifts of fertility and fecundity that the whole nation would ask for God to make them like Ephraim and Manasseh. "Israel" (Gen. 48:20), clearly referring to the future nation, shows the national intent of Jacob's blessing and his vision for his descendants.

The Census

Historically, the initial census in Numbers of Israel coming out of Egypt in the MT is 40,500 for Ephraim (1:33) and 32,200 for Manasseh (1:35). At the end of the book, Ephraim was 32,500 (26:37) and Manasseh was 52,700 (26:34). By the time the kingdom divided, the first king of the Northern Kingdom, Jeroboam, was of the tribe of Ephraim (1 Kings 11:26), and the Northern Kingdom was called "Ephraim" (e.g., Isa. 7:2–17). As with the prophecies of the following chapter of Genesis, it is difficult to know what period they are particularly referencing, though the period of the Judges generally fits. But as we shall see in chapter 49, prophecies are statements of what can and may be unless circumstances occur to change God's response (Chisholm 1995).

Israel Bequeathed His Property, Foreshadowing the Land Promise (48:21–22)

Israel bequeathed his only tangible property in Canaan to Joseph, the foretaste of their future inheritance.

48:21–22. Though the Abrahamic covenant promises had been cited for both the fruitful multiplication of Israel's descendants and the everlasting possession of the land, the blessings themselves had focused on the growth of the two clans into large tribes or peoples. Certainly, Ephraim and Manasseh were intended to see their intended inheritance in the land as full tribes, but the land was not expressly mentioned. Israel's attention now shifted to the tangible promise of land.

God had promised to return them to the land of Canaan when he had begun this sojourn (46:4), so Israel now reminded Joseph of that promise. Israel was expressing his great faith in God's promises, that even though he may be about to die, the past faithfulness of God ensured the future completion of all he had pledged. God's presence guaranteed his word. Regardless of how the future nation under bondage in Egypt would feel, it would be God's presence that would lead them out and guarantee their safe and full conquest of the land of the patriarchs (Exod. 3:7–8).

In addition to the burial plot purchased by Abraham, Israel now revealed he had a single parcel of land that he had acquired by warfare (Gen. 48:22). Israel bequeathed it to Joseph so that, when the nation would go, it would be acquired by one of Joseph's sons. The term translated "mountain slope" has been understood in various ways but may well refer to Shechem. Whether he intended Shechem or some other unrecorded conquest, the gift of the land to Joseph completes the blessing on Joseph and firmly established Joseph as the possessor of the birthright, with both the double portion and the only specific land holding that could at this point be given.

TRANSLATION ANALYSIS 48:22

The MT presents a well-discussed problem here. The first could be the common word for "shoulder," "back of the neck," "back," or "ridge" (*HALOT* s.v. I "שְׁכֶם" 1494–95), leading to the translations "mountain slope" (ESV, NET, RSV) or "ridge" (NIV). It could also be the proper name "Shechem" (*HALOT* s.v. II "שְׁכֶם" 1495–96), as in NCV ("land of Shechem"). Commonly, it has been understood metaphorically as "portion," referring to Joseph getting the double portion ("one portion above," NJPS, NKJV, NRSV) and taking it with the following word, the number "one" (אֶחָד). Both "mountain slope" and "portion" are possible but not attested elsewhere. The simplest understanding, then, is the proper name. Since there is no other record of any battles fought or land conquered, however, the problem is the historical referent. Though Simeon and Levi did conquer the town with their swords (34:25–29), Jacob thoroughly denounced them for it (34:30) and cursed their anger, denouncing them in his oracle (49:5–7). He may, however, have simply accepted the outcome that his name was still attached to the excesses of his sons, making it his, regardless of his disgust (cf. Waltke and Fredricks 2001, 601). Significantly, Joseph was reinterred there (Josh. 24:32), suggesting that both the purchased field and the conquered land were there at Shechem.

Israel's reflection on God's past promises to him showed his confidence in God's faithfulness. God's promises to Abraham, Isaac, and Jacob had consistently provided both the ongoing expectation of God's care, borne out by Jacob's experience as he now acknowledged, and God's future provision of a legacy of descendants and land to accomplish his purposes in his world. Jacob's role in that plan was fading, but he would pass the promises on to the next generation, expressing his faith and encouraging future generations to look forward in faith to their future role and placement in God's plan, for his purposes.

THEOLOGICAL FOCUS

God's promises and faithful care for his people ground their loyalty and faith so they can pass on their legacy and pursuit of his future blessing to the next generation, as God carries out his redemptive plan.

Though God is not directly active in this pericope, his promises and working are prominently displayed in the reflections and blessings of Israel. God's promises ground Jacob's evaluation of his experience and God's faithful care for him through his life. God's faithful care for Israel can be clearly seen in retrospect, providing encouragement to continue to trust for what is yet to come. God was consistent and faithful in declaring his promises to Abraham, Isaac, and Jacob. The promises had grown from the initial expressions to Abraham, but only to expand and clarify God's purposes (see Introduction to the Abraham Narratives, p. 236). Israel could see God's faithful moving through history and found encouragement and rationale to trust him for the future and to maintain perspective in the face of current temptations to become complacent. The God who had consistently provided and maintained his word through the past generations could be counted on for future and unknown obstacles to those same promises.

The working of God in Israel's life had not been consistently visible to him through the difficult times, but in retrospect it was finally clear. God had been shepherding him, providing all his needs his entire life. God had been faithful to his word (28:15) and had been with him, protecting him from all harm. His continued presence (past, present, and future) guaranteed his blessing. He was able to bless Israel's descendants and carry on the promise to its completion. This view of God transcends Israel's experience, describing God's consistent care for his people of all ages as he follows through on his promises and accomplishes his program by his presence in all generations.

Israel's experience of seeing God's faithfulness in retrospect also presents a consistent paradigm. God's work often appears distant and difficult to specify in the moment but can be much more clearly understood and celebrated in hindsight. God seems to consistently choose to build faith with testing and seeming absence. He often makes his presence clear only at key and instructive times. Future generations, however, have the record and reports of God's working to encourage faith and loyal response to his ongoing promise and future hope. Every generation needs to teach the future generations the acts of God in their lives and remind them of his past actions (Deut. 6:20–25; Josh. 4:6–7; Ps. 78:4–6; Eph. 6:4; 1 Thess. 2:11–12)

At the same time, God's redemptive plan stays on track. Though we may be surprised or discouraged by the appearance of our lives or seeming absence of God's working, at each critical juncture God's purposes and plans can be seen to be fully in line with his promises and on track for his stated ends. For the limited perspective of God's creatures, we need the retrospective view to give us courage for the future that is fully in his control.

God's people of every generation, then, have responsibility to relate God's past working to future generations and relay the promises within the context of God's past actions and continuing presence. God's new covenant people have even greater promises and greater certainty of his presence to accomplish his program. His past working, however, still grounds our faith in his promise, which together with submission to his will, positions the believer to thrive in his program.

PREACHING AND TEACHING STRATEGIES

Exegetical and Theological Synthesis

There are at least two major ways that a sermon evolves from this narrative. First, the story functions for the church through the act of Jacob blessing his son, Joseph, and his two sons. The Abrahamic blessing extends now to the conferring of these blessings. Our listeners experience their walk with God in this world within the context of this ancient blessing. In this way the legacy is being passed down to generations. God's promises and purposes are still in process.

Second, Jacob's testimony to the faithfulness of God contains theology that continues to speak to God's people in our congregations. The blessing continues the blessing of God that began in the earliest chapters of Genesis and was especially prominent in the life of Abraham. God was keeping his promises. And God's people continued to function as part of God's plan. Jacob receives blessing from the Lord throughout his lifetime and extends God's blessing to others, within his family and out from his family to the world. Fallen humanity, whether in Joseph's day or ours, needs the blessing of God in order to flourish in this badly broken world. We should not miss the fact that this blessing is for those who walk with God. In this way we follow the example of Abraham and Isaac (48:15). We are the ones who can have confidence in God's blessing and powerful presence.

It is impossible to read this narrative and not see God's faithful care for Jacob throughout his life. We, too, can rely on our great Shepherd to watch over us in this world. We, too, can count on our God to deliver us from evil (v. 16, "the angel who has redeemed me from all evil"). However, we cannot guarantee our congregants that they will enjoy a pain-free life. In his sermon on Proverbs 29:25, "Christian Safety," Jonathan Edwards explains the Lord's protection for all his children: "Though they [aren't] safe from those things that are in themselves evil, yet they are safe from the evil of those things" (page 453 in *The Works of Jonathan Edwards* Volume 10, edited by Wilson H. Kimnach, Yale University Press. 1992).

Preaching Idea

Trust in God's promise to bless you and to make you a blessing to the next generation of disciple-makers.

Contemporary Connections

What does it mean?

The significance of this narrative stems from its connection with the Genesis concept of God blessing his people. We have encountered this idea throughout the book, so it is important to alert readers to the faithfulness of God to carry out his promise and plan for his people. For instance, the statement of Jacob to Joseph in 48:4 matches God's first instruction to his newly created human beings in 1:28.

It is important to translate the land promises in this chapter into the spiritual blessings described in Ephesians 1. Some of you may want to explain that the "everlasting possession" (48:4) also includes a physical promised land inheritance for the future nation of Israel. The significance of God's blessing is that it guarantees God's people will flourish in the world with respect to accomplishing his will. By now, our readers may have forgotten the familiar yet odd practice of skipping the firstborn to bless the younger son. You can remind them of how this action signifies God's grace.

Is it true?

Some of our listeners will struggle with the thought that the Lord is blessing them. Circumstances in their lives contradict this. It is important to define the blessing of God as God's supernatural ability to accomplish his will in the world. The blessing of God does not guarantee success according to the standards of this world. God's blessing means the imparting of supernatural ability to accomplish his will for a person's life. That occurs in poverty or prosperity. As noted above, while we cannot promise the kind of safety Jacob experienced throughout his lifetime (v. 16, "the angel who has redeemed me from all evil"), we can promise spiritual protection. Again, to quote Edwards, "Though they [aren't] safe from those things that are in themselves evil, yet they are safe from the evil of those things" (cf. "Christian Safety."

Now what?

The degree to which our listeners understand the spiritual battle they are in determines the degree to which they understand the importance of receiving God's blessing. Part of the inheritance Jacob gave to Joseph included "one mountain slope" that Jacob won in a battle with the Amorites (48:22). This blessing of God is one important factor in the seed of the woman gaining victory over the serpent's seed (3:15). In this badly broken world currently ruled to some degree by the prince of darkness, nothing is more important than the reality of God's powerful presence and blessing. It is the only way to explain any level of success in living the Christian life.

Creativity in Presentation

As you reflect on God's faithfulness in your life, you learn to trust in God's promise to bless you and to make you a blessing to the next generation of disciple-makers. You can structure the sermon thematically:

- First, God's plan for his people. This is where we can explain God's intention to bless his people, including the restated instruction from Genesis 1:28, which is now stated in terms of God's promise to Jacob: "I will make you . . . and I will make of you" (v. 4). This is a wonderful opportunity to make his faithfulness come alive as you encourage listeners to rehearse all the goodness of God to them through the years.

- Second, God's care for his people. This is seen in the content of Jacob's blessing on Joseph. Here we have the concept of God being our "shepherd all my life long to this day" (v. 15) as well as being our redeeming angel who protects us (v. 16).

- Finally, we can urge our listeners to focus attention on their ability and calling to extend the blessing of God to others. In this way we simply follow Jacob's example of blessing Joseph and his two sons. How we speak into the lives of others is a powerful tool God uses to advance his kingdom in his world. While not the only ones who can testify to God's faithfulness, our senior saints have a unique vantage point from which to tell others that this narrative is true. They too know what it's like to pass on the blessing of God in terms of a godly inheritance, not to mention, in many cases, a physical one as well.

Another option could be to walk through the passage:

- vv. 1–11 is recalling God's blessing on the believer—remember what God has done for us.

- vv. 12–20 is passing blessing on to the next generation—we all can pass on God's good blessing as we teach and challenge the next generation to think and live out their faith in the truth of God's goodness and plans to establish his purposes in and through them.

- vv. 21–22 shows that even the tangible blessings we bequeath (or give earlier than in our wills!) can be used by God to encourage faithful service and pursuit of him, as Joseph himself asked to be taken to Canaan and buried there.

DISCUSSION QUESTIONS

1. We have quoted Jonathan Edwards two times above: "Though they [aren't] safe from those things that are in themselves evil, yet they are safe from the evil of those things." Discuss why this understanding is important for making sense of a Christian who experiences tragedy.

2. Share when God's shepherding was experienced.

3. Discuss how people cling to the presence of God in times of great difficulty. How does faith work itself out in such pain?

4. How have you been challenged to walk faithfully and been blessed by a previous generation of believers?

5. What record or reports of God's faithfulness in your spiritual forebears do you point to as motivation and confidence for your future as well?

6. What record or reports of God's faithfulness in your life do you need to consciously pass on to your disciples so that they will also have God's encouragement of his past and future blessing?

Genesis 49:1–28

EXEGETICAL IDEA
Jacob declared God's blessing for the future tribes of Israel as they would loyally follow him: disqualifying the eldest for unrighteousness and injustice, elevating Judah to lead the tribes and nations, prospering Joseph with God's abundance and fulfilled promises, and reminding all that deliverance only comes from Yahweh.

THEOLOGICAL FOCUS
God's people experience his discipline for unrighteousness and injustice but enjoy his blessing as they loyally follow him, leading his work, experiencing his fulfilled promises, and understanding that deliverance only comes from Yahweh.

PREACHING IDEA
God's people believe in and faithfully follow "the Almighty who will bless you with blessings of heaven above" (49:25) while suffering loss for unfaithfulness.

PREACHING POINTERS
We know from the final verse in our preaching portion that the things Jacob tells his sons that "shall happen to" them (v. 1) are the "blessing" (v. 28). God has promised blessing on his people from the beginning of the Genesis narrative. We preach this section to people who profess to know God through faith in Christ. Primarily, this Scripture reminds them of the spiritual blessings they have in Christ and his Spirit, both now and forever. While the details pertaining to each son are not relevant for modern listeners, the idea of blessing is.

More specifically, the non-blessing on the first three sons and extra blessings on Judah (vv. 8–12) and Joseph (vv. 22–26) do provide glimpses into how God continues to work with his people of faith. Concerning the first three boys, this non-blessing shows that unbelief and disobedience have consequences. It is because of our relationship as children of God that he lovingly disciplines us when we sin against him. His discipline is designed to add righteousness.

The blessing on Judah reminds us of our Savior's rule and our obedience of faith, the combination that results in LifePlus now and complete blessings upon his return. The blessed life, mentioned six times, is described in the Joseph section. We may have attendees overhearing our worship, and this text does show that God is the source of blessing (vv. 18, 24–25), a blessing they can receive only by faith and experience now through obedience.

BLESSING: POSSIBILITY AND PURPOSE (49:1–28)

LITERARY STRUCTURE AND THEMES

After blessing and elevating Joseph's sons, Jacob now called the rest of his sons to hear their own blessings. Framing their "blessing" (49:28) as a window into the distant future (v. 1) for the "twelve tribes" (v. 28), Jacob pronounced the roles of the descendants for each son, including selecting the family leader and firstborn, bringing his judgment to bear on the most egregious sins of his sons, and mapping out the experience of the promised blessings of God to his descendants. Jacob functions as a prophet, and the oracles themselves flow from the first wife's sons (Leah) to the preferred wife's sons (Rachel), with the four sons of the two maidservants between. For Leah's sons, Jacob elevated Judah to leadership, drawing attention to the kingship motif from the early chapters of Genesis and the expected path of promised blessing and righteous rule. Joseph dominates the concluding oracles for Rachel's sons, expanding his birthright through God's promised blessings to the patriarchs.

A. Jacob called his sons for blessing (49:1–2).
  B. With the oldest disqualified, Judah would lead (49:3–15).[1]
    C. Bilhah's and Zilpah's sons highlight Yahweh's necessary deliverance (49:16–21).
  B'. Joseph would prosper while Benjamin would win (49:22–27).
A'. Jacob's blessing offers God's best (49:28).

Jacob's address to his sons draws out the working of God in blessing from the beginning of Genesis. Though evil is judged, God's chosen people will experience his favor and positioning to bring blessing to the earth under his rule. Jacob elevated the descendants of those particularly faithful, Judah and Joseph, and removed potential from the line of those particularly unfaithful, Reuben, Simeon, and Levi. These are not individual but national oracles, detailing the future possibilities for the tribes and the nation, recognizing that the future response of those individuals and tribes will also impact the later outworking.

- ***Jacob Called His Sons for Blessing (49:1–2)***
- ***With the Oldest Disqualified, Judah Would Lead (49:3–15)***
- ***Bilhah's and Zilpah's Sons Highlight Yahweh's Necessary Deliverance (49:16–21)***
- ***Joseph Would Prosper While Benjamin Would Win (49:22–27)***
- ***Jacob's Blessing Offered God's Best (49:28)***

EXPOSITION

What has been told as a family story with international implications, suddenly and self-consciously unveils the national story with redemptive implications for all of humanity. Jacob's final words to his sons promote the future of the nascent nation to work out God's promises from the beginning of Genesis through the patriarchal narratives. The expectation of a royal son to crush the head of the serpent and establish God's rule over all nations in his creation is

1 Sarna (1989, 331) has noted the "deliberate chiastic arrangement" of the sons of the wives: "LEAH, Bilhah-Zilpah, Zilpah-Bilhah, RACHEL."

designated through Judah. God's blessing to all families of the earth through the descendants of Abraham, Isaac, and Jacob will not only be led through the line of Judah but exemplified and transmitted in the bounty and relationship with God of the line of Joseph. The trajectory of the nation was set by their prophetic patriarch, depending on the God who created humanity for blessing. Jacob declared God's blessing for the future tribes of Israel as they would loyally follow him: disqualifying the eldest for unrighteousness and injustice, elevating Judah to lead the tribes and nations, prospering Joseph with God's abundance and fulfilled promises, and reminding all that deliverance only comes from Yahweh.

Jacob Called His Sons for Blessing (49:1–2)

Calling his sons to his side, Jacob declared the working of God and their future expectation for his promises.

49:1–2. Jacob called his sons so that he could declare to them the future for coming generations. "In days to come" (v. 1, lit., "in the last days," NKJV) speaks of the future but does not require a view toward the final eschaton. The phrase appears thirteen times in the Old Testament, always in prophetic contexts.[2] While it can refer to the last times and is consciously future-oriented, it may simply refer to future distant days, as here.[3] In the Balaam oracles, they refer to God's judgment on Moab through a king in Israel (Num. 24:14, 17); Moses refers to Israel's future return to Yahweh (Deut. 4:30), as well as his judgment on them when they rebel (Deut. 31:29). Here in Genesis 49, verse 28 clarifies that these "blessings" were all appropriate for the future "twelve tribes of Israel." As we look at the content expressed, they will apply to various times, some of which are not clear, but at least from the conquest of the land (Joshua) to the ultimate future Davidic monarch.

As Jacob began the poetic blessing, he moved their attention from his ancestry ("sons of Jacob") to his new role in dependence on Yahweh who blesses ("listen to Israel your father," v. 2; see 32:28; 35:10). Particularly in God's final appearance to him at Bethel, when God reminded him of his new name change, God's reiterated promises of fruitfulness, nationhood (with kings), and possession of the land provide significant background to these oracles. This perspective and future orientation would be particularly important for the nation, as it would struggle through the next four hundred years of exile and bondage, waiting for the fulfillment of God's promises, especially embodied in Jacob's testament to his sons and their future. They could lay hold of the hope of the promise, but only as they rested in their faithful God, walking with him in loyalty.

With the Oldest Disqualified, Judah Would Lead (49:3–15)

With Reuben, Simeon, and Levi disqualified for flagrant abuses, Judah would lead the tribes, bringing blessing and headship to the nations.

---

2 Gen. 49:1; Num. 24:14; Deut. 4:30; 31:29; Isa. 2:2; Jer. 23:20; 30:24; 48:47; 49:39; Ezek. 38:16; Dan. 10:14; Hos. 3:5; Mic. 4:1.

3 Walton (2009a, 135) objects that this is not prophecy, since it was not given in the name of a deity, but more like a "weather forecaster" identifying his expectations from what he had observed. However, passing on the Abrahamic covenant blessings goes beyond weather forecasting (see Isaac in chs. 27–28), and prophecy in the OT did not guarantee the absolute certainty of an outcome unless God specifically stated it that way (Chisholm 1995). Rather, future actions of people would affect God's response to them (see Jer. 18:1–17; Ezek. 18; 33:10–20) and could bring modification to those expectations (cf. Levi below, p. 710). Jacob's "blessings," which were appropriate for each son (Gen. 49:28), surprisingly will not include cursing, which would also be subject to future actions of those implicated.

Jacob did not fully follow the birth order of his sons, but he did begin with the first ones born. Following those first four, he would include the final two from Leah before the four from the maidservants, then conclude with the sons of Rachel. The impact is chiastic (see fn. 1 above), beginning and ending with the two main wives and their sons that would figure most prominently in the future of the nation. Jacob initially laid out the rationale for giving the leadership of the clans to Judah and then concluded with the blessing that would accrue to Joseph (building on the double portion already given to the two sons in ch. 48). The rest of the sons would be given appropriate blessings (49:28), generally indicated by plays on their names and figurative language, even if many are currently enigmatic.[4]

Reuben Was Demoted (49:3–4)

Reuben lost his position and power because of his untempered lust.

49:3–4. Addressing Reuben, Jacob acknowledged his primacy of birth and position, piling on the descriptors of power, might, strength, and dignity. Jacob emphasized the stunning opportunity that Reuben had squandered in his faithless and self-focused folly, which Jacob forcefully brought home in verse 4. Reuben's "preeminence" (repeated twice in v. 3) would not be his (v. 4) because of his affair with Bilhah (35:22). Reuben had defiled Jacob's bed, dishonoring him, which Jacob forcefully declared to the brothers and future generations after his initial silence (Rendsburg 2021). Reuben would not benefit from his position, which he may have ironically been trying to assure (see Exposition on 35:21–22a, p. 574), because of his reckless, uncontrolled behavior like foaming water. Far from blessing, Reuben received only censure, and his tribe would fade into oblivion in the Transjordan (Num. 32; Josh. 13:15–23), similarly censured by Deborah for indecision and inaction when needed (Judg. 5:15–16). Reuben had not and would not provide leadership, nor benefit from his first-born status.[5]

TRANSLATION ANALYSIS 49:4a

The noun translated "unstable" (ESV, פַּחַז), though used only here, shares a verbal root used twice more in parallel with "worthless" (ESV, רֵיקִים, Judg. 9:4, or perhaps "unprincipled," *HALOT* s.v. "רֵיק" 1228–29) and "treacherous" (ESV, בֹּגְדוֹת, Zeph. 3:4). The idea may be "deception" or "wily" here (de Hoop 1997, 16–26), or perhaps better, the destructive force of uncontrollable waters, so "destructive" (NET) or "turbulent" (NIV), "uncontrollable" (NASB20, see also NCV, NLT; cf. Smith, פָּחַז, *NIDOTTE* 3:609).

Simeon and Levi Were Denied (49:5–7)

Simeon and Levi lost their inheritance through their unbridled, cruel rage.

49:5–7. As with Reuben, Jacob censured Simeon and Levi together for their wanton slaughter of the Shechemites, denying the two tribes a secure inheritance (see ch. 34). Jacob rejected their plans or "council" (49:6) because of their wanton destruction of the population of Shechem. The Hebrew text describes them hamstringing oxen, though the narrative never related that act. In fact, the brothers plundered all the animals in the fields (34:28). This may relate to a separate

4 Sarna (1989, 331) notes the uncertainty of meaning, allusiveness, and double entendre in this poetry and calls chapter 49 "the most difficult segment of the Book of Genesis." At the same time, the general sense of most of the oracles are clear.

5 After God gave Israel the law, a father was not permitted to remove the firstborn privilege from a son of a demoted wife and give it to another son instead without cause (Deut. 21:15–17). Reuben's actions, however, justify his demotion, even in the culture at large and are appropriately brought up here as the reason for Jacob's elevation of Judah and Joseph above Reuben (Wells 2011, 122–25).

incident or describe something otherwise not related during that event, such as later maiming the oxen since they were shepherds (Mathews 2005, 887), showing their "senseless brutality" (Waltke and Fredricks 2001, 606).

TRANSLATION ANALYSIS 49:5a
"Brothers" here probably intends more the idea of their common goal in their revenge than merely their blood relations, so "two of a kind" (NLT) or "a pair" (NJPS; see, Wenham 1994, 473).

TRANSLATION ANALYSIS 49:5b
Though the referent of their act is clear, the terminology is not. Their "swords" (ESV, מְכֵרֹתֵיהֶם) occurs only here in the MT and has been variously understood as "plan" (*HALOT* s.v. "מְכֵרָה" 582), "dwelling place" (NKJV), or "spades" (NEB). If it comes from the root כרת, "knives" (NET) or "circumcision-blade" (Dahood 1961, 54–56; Dahood 1966, 418) fits, referring to their ruse. Sarna (1989, 334), however, labels any translation as "guesswork."

In response, Jacob cursed their fury and effectively denied them a landed inheritance (Fleishman 2001, 155). Rather, they would both be scattered among the tribes. Historically, Simeon began with an inheritance within the inheritance of Judah (Josh. 19:1–9) but then seems to have been absorbed. Levi was not given an inheritance but was indeed scattered when they received the forty-eight Levitical cities among the tribes (Josh. 21). However, the inheritance of Levi was the Lord and his service (Num. 1:47–54; Deut. 10:6–9) because they stood for Yahweh, even putting family members to death in the sin of the golden calf (Exod. 32:25–29; Deut. 33:8–11). What was a curse for their ancestor's rage against Shechem later became blessing in the tribe's zeal for Yahweh. As we can clearly see with Levi, Jacob's blessing (or, in this case, cursing) comes with implied conditions that affect the ultimate outcome (see Translation Analysis 6:6a, p. 165; footnote on 49:1–2, n. 3 above). Since we do not know what all these blessings refer to in each situation, we see some, like Levi, that clearly show the conditions working out, but with others we cannot see the outcomes. Much as the prophets' pronouncements to Israel later depended on their response to God (e.g., Jer. 18:1–11; Ezek. 18), so these oracles depended on the future descendants' response to God, both for the outcome and for the timing of the outcome. Here, though both were in birth order after Reuben, neither son would provide the formal leadership of the nation.

Judah Would Lead (49:8–12)

Judah would lead the tribes with a future of international rule and unparalleled prosperity.

49:8–9. Though Joseph was given the double portion in chapter 48, Judah is now unexpectedly given the leadership in the tribe, confirmed in 1 Chronicles 5:1–2 (see discussion of the splitting of blessing and leadership in the birthright in the Exposition of 25:31–33, p. 439, and 27:1–4, p. 460). In the second-longest blessing, next to Joseph (Gen. 49:22–26), Jacob plays on Judah's name, assigning his brothers praise and obeisance to him. Contrary to expectations from Joseph's dreams and the experience of the previous narrative, and framing Judah's dominance over his enemies (v. 8b), Judah's brothers will praise and bow to him (v. 8a, c).

Joseph's dreams were realized in Joseph's life, leading the reader to expect that the future kings promised to Abraham, Sarah, and Jacob (17:6, 16; 35:11) would be through Joseph. God, however, again was working contrary to expectations. In his redemption of Judah, highlighted from Judah's evil leadership in selling Joseph, through his enlightenment with Tamar, and culminating in his embracing of both Benjamin and his father in self-sacrificing love, God raised him above his brothers for God's purposes. God now divided the double portion of the inheritance from the leadership, giving that future promise of leadership to the descendants of Judah, rather than Joseph. Yahweh would accomplish his redemptive plan unexpectedly, only incrementally revealing his sovereign choices to his people. Looking ahead to the future tribes, this worked out in Judah's priority among the tribes, greater success in the conquest (Josh. 14:6–15:63; Judg. 1:1–20), and more fully in David's rise to power and expansion of the nation through the reigns of David and Solomon (2 Sam. 1–1 Kings 10; cf. Ps. 78:67–68, 70). Westermann (ידה, *TLOT* 503) shows that the brothers' praise (יוֹדוּךָ) responds "to an action or behavior," drawing attention to the connection between the victories of Judah's descendants (Gen. 49:8b) and the future praise and honor from the brothers (v. 8a, c).

Judah's rehabilitation—and particularly his display of loyalty to Jacob and love for his brother Benjamin—in his complete reversal from the beginning of the *toledot*, shows the working of Yahweh in his life and prepares the reader for this stunning revelation. Judah certainly had taken the leadership, and his humility and repentance before Joseph had been instrumental in the healing of the family. His love of brother is the complete reversal of the initial hatred and murder of brothers: by Cain (ch. 4), as threatened by Esau (27:41), and in Joseph's treatment by his brothers (ch. 37). He then took the lead in the migration to Egypt (46:28). Now he would be honored with the future leadership of the nation and the working of God to bring about his redemption and blessing to his world. Joseph and Judah now remain prominent, with important contrasts from Reuben, Simeon, and Levi. The last testament of Jacob forms the culmination of the narrative as it prepares for the future nation of Israel, suggesting the larger message to the nation as they are leaving Israel. God was declaring Israel's place and purpose in his redemptive plans for his world.

Jacob compared Judah's prowess to a lion that took his prey and rested contentedly in its lair without concern for any threats. The lion was commonly used as a metaphor for the king in ancient Mesopotamia to describe the king's fierce power to destroy his enemies (Watanabe 2002, 42–56). The final question not only conveys power, but the sort of power that deters any external aggression—a "potent military deterrence" (Twersky 2019, 319). Balaam used the same imagery for the future king of Israel, with the implications of the Abrahamic covenant that those blessing Israel would be blessed and those cursing him would be cursed (Num 24:9). John later recognized the lion as a Messianic title (Rev. 5:5).

49:10. In verse 10, Jacob turned to the explicit promise of kingship and international rule. Though the implications are clear, the murky details have been extensively discussed, with numerous possibilities, from ancient times. The rule of the tribe of Judah is symbolized by the authority of the "scepter" and "ruler's staff," which would not depart from Judah or from his descendants "until tribute comes to him" (ESV, cf. NJPS). Regardless of the specific translation of this enigmatic phrase, all probable meanings point to a future king from the line of Judah and, later, David, to which the nations would submit, particularly anticipating an eschatological messianic fulfillment.

TRANSLATION ANALYSIS 49:10a

"Feet" stands as a euphemism for the private parts (Hamilton, רֶגֶל, *NIDOTTE* 3:1048) so that "between his feet" would stand for his "descendants" (NLT, see also NCV) by metonymy.

TRANSLATION ANALYSIS 49:10b

The MT has been variously translated and emended from very early times. The phrase is uncertain largely because the term sometimes translated Shiloh (שִׁילֹה, "until Shiloh comes," NASB20, NCV, NKJV) is unique, and its relation to the verb is uncertain (it could also be "until he comes to Shiloh"; see Frolov 2012, 417–22). Though a proper name is easiest with the received Hebrew text, the place where the ark was kept for a time is never spelled the same and no other Messianic event relates to the known place. Early references from Qumran, Targums, and rabbinic literature assume Shiloh is a Messianic title without other biblical support (Sarna 1989, 337). Similarly, some have looked for a meaning of "prince" or "ruler" in the term (von Rad 1972, 425) but without agreement. Revocalizing the consonants allows "until tribute comes to him" (ESV, see also NJPS) or "until he to whom it belongs shall come" (NIV, see also NET, NLT). The former fits the parallelism better with old Jewish support (Steiner 2010, 219–26, who argues it need not be revocalized; Frolov 2012, 417–22). The latter enjoys broad early support from Qumran (4Q252), LXX, Syr., Targums, and perhaps is the basis of Ezekiel's prophecy of the abasement of Israel's king "until he comes, the one to whom judgment belongs" (Kidner 1967, 229; Mathews 2005, 895; Sailhamer 1990, 279–80). In context it would refer to a coming king to whom the rule belonged, extending even to the nations. While none of the proposals are without problems, the last two make excellent sense.

The extension of the messianic rule over "peoples," referring to the nations (עַמִּים, see Deut. 32:8), crowns a theme that has been building from the beginning. The human representative of Yahweh's rule lost his position in God's temple precinct and his ability to thrive in God's life, waiting for a time when a descendant would crush the snake (Gen. 3:15). The following royal genealogies (chs. 4–5) look for the future royal heir(s) who would bring about the promised redemption and restoration of blessing to all the families of the earth. The narrowed genealogical focus to Abraham, Isaac, and Jacob, along with the promise of restored blessing, draws attention to this royal pronouncement and messianic expectation, especially as he is presented with rule extending over nations (cf. Alexander 1993). This clearly anticipates the Davidic rule and the Davidic covenant in which God promised David an ongoing rule that would also extend to the nations (Pss. 2, 72). The extravagant blessing and prosperity that the following description portrays adds to the anticipation of fulfilling God's redemptive purposes through the line of Judah.

49:11–12. Jacob's description of the coming king paints a picture of extravagant prosperity and health. The grapevines are so lush and prevalent that he can use them to tie up his donkey, even though the donkey will undoubtedly destroy the vine, eating the tender shoots and fruit. The wine from the grapes is so abundant that it can be used for wash water,[6] providing possible background for Jesus's first miracle of the water to wine and the prosperity to come under the messianic rule (Ross 2008, 249). All of this recurs in the prophetic descriptions of the Messianic age and that extravagant harvest (Wenham 1994, 479, noting Lev. 26:5; Ps. 72:16; Isa. 25:6; Joel 2:24; Amos 9:13). This sounds very much like a reversal of the curse of Genesis 3 (Alexander 2012, 36).

The references to the king's eyes and teeth probably refer to his health and splendor as a king, again showing the opulence of his reign and blessing of God on him. The future messianic kingdom would be characterized by prosperity and blessing, showing both the outworking of the Abrahamic covenant promises to Israel and the promise of blessing to the nations as they come under the rule of this king in relationship with his God. It presents, then, the culmination of the growing expectation for God's redemption and blessing from the beginning, with the fall of humanity and God's promised restoration (3:15; Alexander 2012).

Zebulun Would Prosper (49:13)

Zebulun would prosper in trade.

6 Alternatively, it could refer to the royal purple, using the grapes as dye for the cloth (Walton 2009a, 136–37).

49:13. The general picture for Zebulun was prosperity through association with Sidon and the shipping trade. The historical outworking and the placement of Zebulun in the listing of the tribes raise questions. According to Genesis 30:19–20, Leah bore Zebulun sixth after Issachar, though here he is listed before Issachar, possibly because of his larger role in Israel's future as a nation (cf. Sarna 1989, 338, where he notes their role with Deborah, Judg. 5:14, 18; Gideon, Judg. 6:35; and David, 1 Chron. 12:33). Historically, Zebulun's inheritance did not extend to either the Mediterranean or the Sea of Galilee (Josh. 19:10–16, listing his allotment before Issachar as well). However, the historical gap can be explained with a possible corridor to the Mediterranean (Steinmann 2019, 459; cf. Sarna 1989, 338), trade routes that gave them access (Mathews 2005, 898), or merely providing labor for the Phoenician shipping industry (Sarna 1989, 338).

Issachar Would Succeed (49:14–15)

Issachar would benefit from working hard.

49:14–15. Issachar's future is also difficult to place historically. Clearly, Issachar is compared to a strong donkey that works hard and finds good reward in his accommodations. The most common translation understands his outcome to be as "forced labor," however, so that Issachar was willing to give up their independence to enjoy a better life with peace (e.g., ESV, NASB20, NIV). Issachar's largely missing place in the conquest may support this understanding (Waltke and Fredricks 2001, 610). Heck, however, effectively argues that in the flow of the blessings, all Jacob's oracles after Reuben, Simeon, and Levi are positive, all the animal imagery is positive for Jacob's sons, and the key terms that conclude the blessing do not require a later, pejorative sense of "forced labor." Rather they can be understood nontechnically as "a laboring worker" (Heck 1986, 394–96). Rather than selling out for peace and submitting to slavery again, perhaps Issachar would be a hard-working clan that would largely remain in the background but earn their wages honestly (Judg. 5:15; 1 Chron. 12:32; Hamilton 1995, 667–68; de Hoop 1999, 158–61).

> *TRANSLATION ANALYSIS 49:14*
> "Sheepfolds" (מִשְׁפְּתָיִם, ESV, NJPS, NRSV) is better understood as "saddlebaskets" (*HALOT* s.v. "מִשְׁפְּתַיִם" 652; cf. NET, NKJV, NLT), which fits this context nicely (see Heck 1986, 390–91, for a helpful review of the translations and evidence). Issachar is pictured as a donkey resting under its load while working.

Bilhah's and Zilpah's Sons Highlight Yahweh's Necessary Deliverance (49:16–21)

While the maids' sons would lead, prosper, and respond when attacked, deliverance will always come from Yahweh.

The four sons of the maids are not placed in birth order.[7] Rather, after Dan, Naphtali (born next according to Gen. 30:7–8) drops to fourth after Gad and Asher, providing a chiastic center to the narrative with the two sons of Bilhah framing the two sons of Zilpah. Jacob's purpose is not clear, though the south to north order of settlement may account for it (Wenham 1994, 469, citing Dillman, *Die Genesis*. Kurzgefasstes Exegetisches Handbuch. 6th ed. Leipzig: Hirzel, 1892).

Bilhah: Dan Would Lead (49:16–18)

Dan would provide aid and leadership with stealthy retaliation.

49:16–17. Jacob gave Dan prominence by placing him seventh and mentioning his name

7 Contra Armerding, who suggests that this may actually express the birth order rather than the report listed according to the mother in Gen. 30 (Armerding 1955, 321).

twice (along with only Judah and Joseph in these oracles). Dan would "judge" (יָדִין, wordplay on "Dan," דָּן) his people, perhaps illustrated by Samson (Judg. 13–16), though rather than a role model, Judges presents Samson as an image of the decline of Israel as they degenerate toward the Canaanites (Webb 1987, 172; Webb and Hughes 2015, 217–32). In Judges, judging would refer to delivering, though Samson only began to do so (13:5). From Jacob's oracle, Dan would likely expect a broader leadership role than is recorded in the later history ("govern," NJPS, NLT, or "rule" NCV; see Schultz, דִּין, *NIDOTTE* 1:939). Their relative obscurity may be the result of their later lack of faith and disobedience (Josh. 19:47; Judg. 1:34–35; 18:1–31).

The image of a snake striking a horse to throw the rider suggests a small and covert but deadly role. The tribe did not appear to ever grow large and did resort to attacking an unsuspecting village to take as its primary residence (Judg. 18), though that is portrayed as rebellious in Judges. Dan then remained on the fringe of the northern part of the kingdom.

49:18. At this point, Jacob interjected a personal prayer for deliverance from Yahweh. Possibly prompted by the vision of Dan's precarious role or, more generally, near the midpoint of the tribes with the opportunities and challenges that lay ahead for them, Jacob recognized the only source of "salvation" for the nation. Rather than spiritual, the implications are more likely deliverance from enemies (Exod. 14:13; 15:2; Judg. 15:18) for the preservation of the nation and the fulfilling of the promises. Appropriate for Dan and his blessing, it is also appropriate for the recognized success of the nation in its future role as God's holy nation and mediator of divine blessing (Exod. 19:5–6). The central role of this prayer (see Literary Structure and Theological Themes above, p. 707) adds the necessary control to the outcomes of the oracles. This prayer provides the core expectation for all future success of the blessing. All blessing is God's doing alone and necessarily follows loyal service.

Zilpah: Gad Would Repay (49:19)

Gad would survive and repay his attackers.

49:19. Counting Gad, Jacob used the consonants of Gad's name in four of the verse's six words to drive home the point ("raid," גְּדוּד *gadud*, sounds like "Gad," גָּד). Gad may be attacked, but he would hold his own. Gad requested and inherited a portion in the Transjordan (Num. 32), which, as a border state, opened them up to frequent warfare from the Ammonites, Moabites, Arameans, and Assyrians, and gave them a reputation as warriors (Deut. 33:20; 1 Chron. 5:18; 12:8; Waltke and Fredricks 2001, 611).

Zilpah: Asher Would Prosper (49:20)

Asher would produce delicacies.

49:20. Asher's inheritance in the rich coastal plain north of Carmel provided opportunities for both agriculture and trade. Jacob envisions a prosperous use of these resources. Their failure to drive out the Canaanites, however, not only left the idolators in the land (Judg. 1:31–32) but left Asher in the minority, living among the Canaanites (Younger 1995, 83). Though perhaps Jacob's blessing may not be envisioning the historical realities of the conquest (Hamilton 1995, 674), the richness of Asher's delicacies may not have always been for the Israelite kings. The positive nature of the opportunity Jacob envisioned requires obedience to realize, as do God's promises of every age.

Bilhah: Naphtali Would Be Fruitful (49:21)

Naphtali would bear fruit in freedom.

49:21. The first clause compares Naphtali with a doe, proverbial as sure-footed, graceful, and fleet (2 Sam. 22:34; Ps. 18:33; Prov. 5:19; Hab. 3:19). "Let loose" (שְׁלֻחָה) suggests their freedom and frequent movement (Waltke and Fredricks

2001, 612), though it could describe one "sent". The second clause is problematic, both in individual terms and overall interpretation of the clause, as the ESV footnote makes clear. The main translations are a doe bearing "beautiful fawns" (ESV, NIV, etc.) or "bears fawns of the fold" (ESV fn), or Naphtali speaking "delightful words" (NASB20, NET, etc.). The latter translation takes "words" (אִמְרֵי) as the common noun. The connection with the "doe" or "hind" (NJPS, RSV) could be relating to the swiftness of the hind "sent" with a message, perhaps of victory (cf. 2 Sam. 22:34; Ps. 18:33; Isa. 35:5–6; Pehlke 1985, 211–14). The former translation has Ugaritic and Akkadian parallels (Gevirtz 1984, 516–17), though only used here in the MT. Though possibly depicting Naphtali as a wild-born doe being domesticated and producing "lambs of the fold," which indicates a negative "political subservience" (Gevirtz 1984, 520), the more likely "beautiful fawns" stresses a positive referent (de Hoop 1999, 176–79). In this reading, Naphtali would be fruitful. Alternatively, Naphtali would be a sure and fleet messenger, perhaps in battle. Either sense is historically obscure, though Deuteronomy 33:23 may favor their fruitfulness.

Joseph Would Prosper While Benjamin Would Win (49:22–27)

Joseph would prevail and prosper with the abundant blessings of El Shaddai, while Benjamin would be victorious.

Jacob presented Rachel's sons in order of birth, bestowing potential achievements on both tribes. Though Joseph's oracle overall is the "most complex, and most obscure" of all the blessings (Caquot, 1980, 43), his future would clearly include broad blessing from God (repeated six times in 49:25–26). Benjamin would be fiercely victorious.

Joseph Would Be Blessed (49:22–26)

Joseph, aided by his promise-keeping God, had thrived though attacked and would prosper with the fullness of God's promises.

49:22. Joseph's tribes would be independent and free, a significant contrast to Joseph's early experience in Egypt. Jacob's initial metaphor for Joseph begins the intrigue of his blessing. Nearly everything about the verse is obscure, from the lexical forms to syntax and grammar. Though there are numerous suggestions for the initial figure, the two most common are a "fruitful bough" (ESV, NRSV, or similarly "fruitful vine," NIV, cf. NCV) or "the foal of a wild donkey" (NLT, cf. ESV margin, NJPS). The fruitful tree interpretation has been common since the Targums, appropriately marking the righteous. Since Jacob's other images in his blessings are consistently from the animal world and the following imagery in verse 23 of archers or hunters fits more clearly, we lean toward the wild donkey interpretation (cf. Hamilton 1995, 683). The final line, then, would be something like "wild colts on a hillside" (NJPS), celebrating the freedom of his growing family.

TRANSLATION ANALYSIS 49:22a

The figure of a fruitful tree derives from the feminine singular participle of the common Hebrew root "be fruitful" (פרה). The form, however, is only here, and the initial term (בֵּן, "son" or "son of," if repointed) is never used with plants, nor is "daughters" (בָּנוֹת), in the final line of the verse. The idea of a "wild ass" (NJPS) or "foal of a wild donkey" (NLT) assumes a feminine from "wild donkey" (פֶּרֶא, cf. 16:12). Both images have additional problems with the final line of the verse, though there are Arabic parallels for "his wild colts beside the wall" (Wenham 1994, 484–85). The image of a fruitful tree or vine is a common depiction of righteous prosperity (Mathews 2005, 904), and the wild donkey provides an image of independent freedom (Waltke and Fredricks 2001, 613).

TRANSLATION ANALYSIS 49:22b

The more traditional "his branches run over the wall" (ESV) posits a unique use of the verb "stride solemnly, walk along" (*HALOT* s.v. "צעד"

1040), as well as the unusual use of "daughters" (בָּנוֹת) for "branches." On the other hand, "ridge" (NLT) or "hillside" (NJPS) are otherwise unattested extrapolations from "wall" (שׁוּר), perhaps imagining a terrace wall.

49:23–24. Though he was attacked, God intervened. As with the first three sons, Jacob began with an historical allusion to the past conflict and God's deliverance. In his image of Joseph's freedom, the pastoral serenity was disrupted by attackers, attempting to destroy Joseph. Instead, however, he was steady, and by God's intervention he was and would be blessed. The translations of verse 24 generally depict Joseph's steady defense empowered by the hands of God. Even though Joseph was never seen actively defending himself, except perhaps against Potiphar's wife, the image is appropriate, given his faith and God's interventions that brought Joseph to the pre-announced rule in the land with great blessing to Joseph, Pharaoh, Israel, and the nations.[8]

TRANSLATION ANALYSIS 49:23

Verse 23 includes three verbs for the attack: "provoke" (*HALOT* s.v. "מרר" 638), which often includes connotations of making something bitter, "shoot arrows" (*HALOT* s.v. II "רבב" 1175), and "be hostile towards" (*HALOT* s.v. "שׂטם" 1316), all heightening the unprovoked and bitter attack and aptly characterizing Joseph's initial years.

Joseph was empowered by "the hands of the Mighty One of Jacob" (v. 24). Highlighting the promise and the presence of God through the narrative, Joseph was the beneficiary of God's sustaining presence (cf. v. 18). The promise of blessing from the beginning, through Abraham, Isaac, and Jacob, now accrued to Joseph as initially demonstrated through God's intervention and preservation, elevating Joseph to rule and then endowing his descendants with the fulness of creation's blessings and fertility (vv. 25–26).

His security was because of "the Shepherd, the Stone of Israel" (v. 24). Jacob recognized Yahweh as Shepherd throughout his life in his blessing on Joseph's sons (48:15) and so appropriately describes his expectation for Joseph as well. God as the "rock" does not use the expected term (צוּר, Deut. 32:15, 18; Isa. 30:29), but "stone" (אֶבֶן, so ESV, NKJV). This term shows up three times in Gensis 28 and again in 35:14, referring to the pillar Jacob set up where God appeared to him at Bethel, which Jacob had called "God's house" (28:22; see also35:14; Wenham 1994, 486). The confluence of "Shepherd" and "Stone of Israel" recalls God's specific work and his promises to keep Jacob by his presence through Jacob's life, which Jacob then applied to Joseph. This whole section draws deeply on the continuity of God's working through the lives of each of the patriarchs, down to Joseph as the blessed son. Judah was given leadership, but Joseph was given the double portion and extended blessing (see ch. 27 and the distinction between the two). These two longest oracles frame the poem with the two aspects of the inheritance normally reserved for the firstborn but passed to Judah and Joseph. Jacob then spectacularly elaborated his blessing on Joseph, which had been provided through the intervention of Yahweh, in the poem working out the core idea of Yahweh's salvation for all of Israel (49:18).

TRANSLATION ANALYSIS 49:24–25

Four times Jacob attributes Joseph's deliverance to God with the preposition min (מִן), piling up five different names for God as secure helper.

8 Suggestions that it was the bows of the attackers that became stiff and unusable (Speiser 1964, 368–69; Wenham 1994, 485–86) are plausible but unnecessary, given the figurative nature of the oracle. God intervened, much as he had done for Abraham, Isaac, and Jacob, even as Joseph remained faithful and unmoved from his loyalty to Yahweh. As Jacob has said, salvation is from Yahweh (v. 18).

Though sometimes translated "from" or "by" (both in v. 24, ESV), it indicates the source or cause of Joseph's deliverance ("because," v. 24, NET in all four cases). In the second case (introducing "the Shepherd") the MT reads "from there" (ESV, מִשָּׁם), but a slight repointing yields "by the name of" (NRSV, TO, מִשֵּׁם) or "because of the name of" (NET), yielding a more coherent line and consistent sense with the other three uses of the preposition (cf. Speiser 1964, 369).

49:25–26. Recalling and poetically emphasizing the divine name specifically related to blessing, El Shaddai, Jacob pronounced "the God (El, אֵל) of your father" as Joseph's helper in the first line (v. 25). In the second line, he added "Almighty" (ESV, lit. "Shaddai," שַׁדַּי) as Joseph's source of blessing (v. 25). The poetic emphasis by dividing the name into two parts not only extends the idea of blessing to God's aid through all troubles but draws out the implications of El Shaddai (God Almighty) as the source of blessing and fertility (see Translation Analysis 17:1b, p. 323). Jacob specified "the heaven above" and "the deep . . . beneath,"[9] which would provide the resources for abundant crops and animals, as well as "the breasts"[10] and "the womb," which provide and sustain the expected cattle and kids of the blessing.

In blessing Joseph, Jacob multiplied names for Yahweh, recapitulating the continuous working of God through the lives of the patriarchs and applying that secure and powerful presence to Joseph's future tribes. The working and reputation of the God of his fathers formed the basis for Joseph's extravagant blessing. Verse 26, then, steps back and summarizes the greatness of the blessings accruing to Joseph. Jacob's blessing outstripped even the apparent bounty showing on the luxuriant green tops of the surrounding mountains. He prayed that such blessings crown Joseph, who was "set apart" by God (v. 26; cf. 37:5–11) with God's regal blessings and natural resources, yet to serve and share that blessing (Swenson 2008, 424).

TRANSLATION ANALYSIS 49:26

The MT presents a difficult text, with the masculine plural participle with the 1cs pronominal suffix from "conceive" (הוֹרַי) translated by ESV as "my parents," though the masculine is very unusual. The LXX, with a slight emendation to the underlying Hebrew, presents a much more coherent text: "the ancient mountains," including the following Hebrew word (הַרְרֵי עַד; NIV; see also NCV, NET, NRSV), nicely parallels the following clause, "than the bounty of the age-old hills" (NIV; cf. Alter 1996, 300). Rendsburg (1980) argues both are intended, with a double entendre providing a Janus parallelism in which one meaning complements the preceding line and the other the following line.

Jacob used "blessing," one of the main themes of Genesis, six times in these two verses (one time as a verb and five times as a noun; the root occurs ninety times in Genesis). Coupled with the many reminders of the character and faithful working of God in the lives of the patriarchs, it summits the oracles and the book of Genesis theologically like the tops of the eternal mountains. What God had instituted in creation for humanity (1:28), renewed after the flood (9:1), and intended to extend to all of humanity through the line of Abraham, Isaac, and Jacob (12:3; 18:18; 22:18; 26:4; 28:14) culminates in Joseph's offspring. As the immediately preceding

9 The "deep beneath" refers to the subterranean waters that supply the springs and rivers to water the land (Grisanti, תְּהוֹם, *NIDOTTE* 4:276). Similarly, the "heaven above" refers to the physical heavens and reflects an ancient world picture of heavens, earth, and under the earth. They would have abundant rain, water from the ground, and fertility in humanity and animals. It is a very tangible blessing.

10 *Shaddaim*, שָׁדַיִם, "breasts" sounds like (and some have related to) Shaddai, the title usually translated "Almighty."

narrative shows, blessing would flow through them (and the nation as a whole) to the peoples around them as they lived out their faith in El Shaddai. In conjunction with the international rule of Judah, the means for God's redemption, terminating evil and restoring blessing, is slowly clarifying in preparation for the nation to grow, exodus Egypt, and take their place on the world stage as the people of God to show the character of their King and draw the nations to true worship of him.

Benjamin Would Win (49:27)

Benjamin would be victorious, sated, and generous.

49:27. The image of a ravenous wolf devouring his prey and dividing the plunder presents a militaristic view of Benjamin. Clearly, he would be victorious, and the history of the nation does reveal a warlike Benjamin, from the Benjaminites following Barak into battle (Judg. 5:14), to the intertribal warfare in which Benjamin opposed the rest of the nation with their seven hundred exceptional slingers (Judg. 20:16; see Judg. 20–21), to Saul and Jonathon leading Israel into battle (1 Sam. 11; 13–14). Benjamin would be able warriors and fiercely victorious, defeating their enemies with plunder left over to share.

Jacob's Blessing Offered God's Best (49:28)

Jacob's blessing directed all the tribes of Israel toward God's potential for them.

49:28. Jacob summarized his blessing for the "tribes of Israel," which he had pronounced as it was appropriate to them. These oracles were intended to prophetically declare the potential for the nation by tribe as they chose to follow God in loyal faith. Blessing only accrues by the working of God in response to his purposes and human loyalty (Num. 23:8; Deut. 23:5; Prov. 26:2). Israel could thrive in relationship with God, experience his good hand in their lives, and so offer God's blessing in relationship with him to their world (Gen. 18:18–19). At the same time, disloyalty to Yahweh and failure to do "righteousness and justice" (18:19) incurs cursing and loss of privilege (Reuben, Simeon, and Levi). These oracles served as warning. Israel must choose to follow Yahweh and live in relationship with him as their God to experience the potential benefits God offered them through the oracles of Jacob and to avoid the deadly consequences of disloyalty.

THEOLOGICAL FOCUS

God's people experience his discipline for unrighteousness and injustice but enjoy his blessing as they loyally follow him, lead his work, and experience his fulfilled promises, understanding that deliverance only comes from Yahweh. Though the covenants have changed, God's people still expect blessing for loyalty (Eph. 1:3–4) and discipline for disobedience (Heb. 12:7–11).

Though the passage records the last testament of Jacob for his sons, God and his working are front and center. Explicitly, God gives the blessings (49:25–26). Implicitly, blessing only occurs at the intervention of Yahweh according to his will and with the appropriate response of his people. Throughout Genesis, blessing for humanity originates in God (1:28; 9:1) within the context of living in righteous faith and integrity before him (6:9; 18:18–19). God declared his purpose to restore blessing to all humanity through Abraham's descendants (12:3), and that blessing is embodied in relationship with him (17:7–8).

Rebellion and disloyalty, however, bring judgment rather than blessing (chs. 6–9; 11). The unrighteous and unjust (e.g., Reuben, Simeon, and Levi) experience judgment and loss while those who turn to Yahweh in faith and righteous living experience added blessing (e.g., Judah and Joseph). Future generations have opportunity but will find fulfillment of that opportunity directed by their response to God. These two examples, however, also show the grace of God for all. The scoundrel Judah, who sold his brother, was transformed by God's working into a leader fit for the promise of God's future redeemer and king as he loved his brother more than himself. Joseph, who followed faithfully through great trials, also reaped incredible blessing, both personally and in his future descendants and God's plans. All humanity can have hope in God's blessing, both now and forever, if they will turn in obedient faith to him.

As we have been arguing throughout Genesis, God, in blessing his people, empowers them to accomplish his will through knowing him and growing in relationship with him to show the world his character and lead them to know him. It is the result of walking with God (Enoch, Noah, Abraham). The necessary reality of blessing, then, is enjoying relationship with Yahweh as our sovereign King and leading our world to know, bow, and enjoy him as well (12:3).

In Jacob's oracles, God is the source of all blessing (49:25–26). Jacob may proclaim the possibilities, but the outcome is up to God's oversight (Num. 23:8; Deut. 23:5; Prov. 26:2). As embodied in these blessings, God shepherds, defends, strengthens, delivers, sustains, multiplies, prospers, and honors. He also dishonors, judges, deprives, and repays.

Humanity, then, bears responsibility. God responds to the actions of his people, both to reverse cursing and to cancel blessing (Ezek. 18; 33:10–16) as well as to carry out blessing and cursing. He offers a vision of what he will do if his people follow him, but they must live in loyalty and righteousness. He also reveals the consequences of rejecting his ways. Blessing (and cursing) are not forgone conclusions that, once pronounced, are fatalistic future realities. Rather, they provide a glimpse into God's desires and the opportunities he offers for those who will walk with him.

For Israel, blessing included tangible and physical benefits as they represented God in concrete ways to his world. Blessing encompassed the concrete realities of the breast and the womb, the choice vine and pleasant land. But it also included the intangible spiritual realities of walking with God and knowing him. It also embodied the intangible reality of being shepherded by Yahweh, the ongoing presence of the stone of Israel. The oracles emphasize the tangible outcomes of the relationship with Yahweh, the promise-keeper to the patriarchs. That relationship and walking with God provide the underlying expectation from the primeval narratives through the patriarchal narratives. Those intangible relational aspects provide the reality and the meaning behind any physical benefits. The physical is merely the illustration of the real significance, the spiritual truths, much like the law would be for the nation as God established them after the exodus. Israel, and God's people of every age, need to walk with him to enjoy his best, looking forward to the ultimate fulfillment of his promises and the final redemption of his universe.

All of this brings to a head the promised reversal of the curse and destruction of evil and sin from the initial episodes of Genesis. God is truly the one who delivers (49:18). God's purposes continue, and his promise indicates a clearer and further step in the process of reversing the pain and frustration of his initial judgments on the first humans. God's working is clear and clearly anticipated in the future working through the nation that would be formed in the crucible of Egyptian oppression and founded in the center of the influential nations of the known world. He formed them to proclaim the excellencies of him who called them out of darkness, to live out his holy character, and to mediate his worship and blessing to his world (Exod. 19:5–6) still to be carried out by the people of God (1 Peter 2:9–10).

PREACHING AND TEACHING STRATEGIES

Exegetical and Theological Synthesis

This text functions for the church by noting that Jacob's prophecy to his sons is the blessing of God on them. The historical blessing speaks to our need for God's blessing to overturn the curse and provide new life. However, before any blessings are announced, non-blessings appear in verses 3–7. This teaches us that obedience is a part of God's covenant agreement with his children. God's people forfeit blessing whenever they respond in unbelief and disobedience. To continue his faithfulness, God disciplines us to build more righteousness in us (Heb. 12:5–11). We know that obedience is the necessary result of genuine faith (Rom. 1:5; 16:26), which includes confession of sin and cleansing (cf. 1 John 1:9). It also includes ongoing repentance and what I (Randal) refer to as "replacement righteousness" (replacing our sin with practical righteousness).

When it comes to the blessings, Judah and Joseph continue to teach us. In Judah's blessing is the promise of our Savior's eternal rule and resulting obedience and service. His kingdom creates a life of blessing where he empowers his faithful to accomplish his will in the world, including opportunities to represent him well so that others may know him. God emphasizes this blessed life in the Joseph section by referring to blessing six times. Finally, tucked away in the prophetic blessing is the clear teaching that God is the source of this life (e.g., Gen. 49:18, 24–25). What God announced in the creation narrative (ch. 1) appears again as the book closes. God graciously will bless his creation for the sake of his reputation!

Preaching Idea

God's people believe in and faithfully follow "the Almighty who will bless you with blessings of heaven above" (49:25) while suffering loss for unfaithfulness.

Contemporary Connections

What does it mean?

Our listeners will need clarification as to the theological implications of the non-blessings, with which this chapter begins, and the blessings of the rest of the chapter. First, the non-blessings: whereas gross disobedience disqualified the first three sons listed, faith in Christ covers our sins so that the blessing remains. Our disobedience, however, requires discipline from our Lord so that righteousness might grow. Sin does have its consequences. Genuine faith includes confession of sin and repentance, a turning from that sin to live the righteous life. This is a result of God's Spirit continuing to use the Word of God to train his children in righteousness. In this way, God continues to complete the work he started in all genuine believers.

Second, all the blessings on the other sons point to the spiritual blessings that God graciously bestows on all his children. All the detailed blessings on each son translate into God's equipping each of his sons and daughters to accomplish his will in the world. Nothing in this world prevents the prophesied blessings on the saints from coming true. As noted above, we can't expect the blessing of God in times of rebellion against God. All God's children enjoy the benefits of being kingdom citizens or children of the King, but the discipline of God is one of those benefits.

It is also helpful to point out how Jacob's blessing on Judah points to our Savior's eternal kingdom ("The scepter shall not depart . . . nor the ruler's staff" in v. 10a) and the accompanying obedience he will receive ("and to him shall be the obedience of the peoples" in v. 10b). Our in-Christ listeners inhabit that kingdom in part now; complete fulfillment of the prophecy awaits the return of Christ and the establishment of the new heavens and new earth.

Is it true?

Of the three questions we ask in this section, this one might be most pressing for our listeners. Do these oracles come true? If so, how do they work? Jacob looks at the future for his sons' descendants. Verse 28 describes the prophecies this way: "This is what their father said to them as he blessed them, blessing each with the blessing suitable to him." So one way to think about the prophecies being true is to teach that they are based on the blessing of God. God determines how life is going to go with the tribes coming from Israel's famous sons. Notice that each blessing is "suitable to him." God, who is true, decides how best to bless each person.

God confers all his blessings as a part of his grace. Since the blessings also contain non-blessings, the gracious blessings of God factor in human response to his grace. When I am in disbelief and disobedience, the Lord disciplines me to build righteousness. In this sense, the blessing of God is conditioned upon faith and faithfulness to him. So, yes, the blessings come true because God continues to remain faithful to his original plan to bless his creatures who he has redeemed. His salvation includes the outworking of new covenant promises, creating a people who have the desire and capacity to love and serve him faithfully in the world.

Now what?

The constancy of our God to continue to bless his redeemed people makes these ancient prophecies relevant. Our listeners find themselves in a long history that begins with Jacob and his sons and moves onward to the present day. In a general sense, the promised physical blessings on Israel's famous sons reflect similar spiritual blessings on God's church. These are the blessings which the apostle Paul writes about in Ephesians 1. They are based on the accomplishments of the Christ-event that our listeners appropriated by faith. The presence of non-blessings in the section alerts us all to the need for faith to work itself out in obedience to God. As you can see from the first three non-blessings, it pays to be godly (see Ps. 1 and the contrasting images of the righteous and wicked).

Creativity in Presentation

God's people believe in and faithfully follow "the Almighty who will bless you with blessings of heaven above" (49:25) while suffering loss for unfaithfulness. This presents the intended worship response and the main idea of the section.

Consider constructing the sermon as follows:

- God intends to bless his people. In this main point, our listeners hear that the prophecies ("that I may tell you what shall happen to you in days to come," v. 1) describe the blessings of God (e.g., vv. 25–26 and v. 28, "This is what their father said to them as he blessed them, blessing each with the blessing suitable to him."). God equips each child of God (both in the Old Testament and New Testament) with the supernatural desire and unique capacity to accomplish God's will in the world.

- God's blessing is contingent upon a faith that works. This second point explores the non-blessing category developed above in the Exposition. The first three non-blessings of the chapter show that human response to God's gracious redemption is a critical part of this relationship. God does not allow unbelief and disobedience to go unpunished; he will create a holy people who experience the temporal and daily benefits of walking with God, LifePlus.

- God's blessing creates a people who represent him well in the world. Point three is the place to summarize the blessings on Jacob's sons and reemphasize their place in carrying out God's will in the world. This section also highlights Judah's prophecy and the links to the Messiah's rule. This section is also the time to stress the ways in which the church continues to receive the spiritual blessings of the new covenant secured by the Christ-event. God's people need to be reminded that blessing, or any good thing in living, comes from the working of God in our lives and our world.

The mission of enlarging God's reputation remains as the gospel goes to the world through the efforts of his faith-filled and faithful people. As we have learned throughout Genesis, God grants a blessing to his people so they can, in turn, bless others.

DISCUSSION QUESTIONS

1. Discuss the ramifications of Christians thinking that the blessing of God is mostly material.

2. Review a theological understanding of the blessing of God. What did it mean for Israel and what does it mean for our listeners?

3. Discuss the link between the prophesy about Judah and Jesus (vv. 8–12). Why is this important?

4. What does it look like to thrive in living? How does that relate to your walk with God?

5. What will choosing to walk in obedience and loyalty to God look like for me today? What do you need to do, not do, dwell on, or not dwell on? How can you love God and your neighbor better?

6. How can you encourage my brother or sister to walk more closely with God today?

Genesis 49:29–50:26

EXEGETICAL IDEA

Because Jacob and Joseph recognized God's good oversight and expected his promises beyond their last days, God could greatly bless them, and Joseph could respond with grace and forgiveness to his brothers' evil.

THEOLOGICAL FOCUS

Faith in God's current and future working to accomplish his good purposes gains God's blessing and shapes the believer's response to death and life.

PREACHING IDEA

Faith in God's faithfulness and powerful sovereignty inevitably shapes the way believers respond to both death and life.

PREACHING POINTERS

Modern listeners, like the original audience, worship by trusting God like Jacob as he neared death. After blessing his sons, he commanded them to bury him back in Canaan—where God's people ultimately belong (49:29–32). The way that the Egyptians responded to Jacob's death teaches us how God's people can be salt and light in their world (50:11, "a grievous mourning"). Jacob fulfilled his calling of blessing others with the blessing he received from the Lord.

Jacob's faith is not the only faith on display in this section. Joseph also shows us how faith in the promises of God leads to godliness in the form of forgiveness. Joseph's brothers relayed a message from their father, "Please forgive," and Joseph responded with genuine tears and faith, refusing to take God's place by being vengeful (50:17, 19). Joseph also provides one of the clearest statements about the sovereign power and purposes of God: "As for you, you meant evil against me, but God meant it for good, to bring it about that many people should be kept alive" (50:20). It is one of those statements of theological reality that provides stability for believers living in a badly broken world where evil can and does happen.

IN GOOD FAITH: SEEING GOD'S GOODNESS IN DEATH AND LIFE (49:29–50:26)

LITERARY STRUCTURE AND THEMES

This final section of Genesis concludes Jacob's deathbed scene begun in 47:29, adding Joseph's final years and wishes to draw the narratives to a close. The final wills of Jacob and Joseph focus the reader on the promises of God, declaring their faith in their inheritance in Canaan (land) for the burgeoning family (descendants) and illustrating their impact in their world of Egypt and Canaan (blessing for the nations). Those two declarations of faith in the face of death frame the fearful concern of the brothers and provide the basis and impetus for Joseph's forgiveness. Joseph understood and expressed a controlling theme of Genesis: God works his good, redemptive plan throughout human history through and despite whatever heart intentions and resulting evil his world sinks to. Faith in God's promises grounds his people's response to evil and suffering with a gracious reliance on God's oversight and ultimate justice (cf. Brueggemann 1982a, 371). Together with the emphasis on faith in the promise and return to the land, God's good purposes close the book of Genesis. This account anticipates God's next intervention for the listening nation, delivering them from Egypt into their inheritance in Canaan.

A. Honoring his faith, Joseph buried Jacob in Canaan with great mourning (49:29–50:14).
  B. Joseph forgave his brothers' evil, recognizing God's good purposes (50:15–21).
A'. Joseph declared his faith, requiring burial in Canaan (50:22–26).

- ***Honoring His Faith, Joseph Buried Jacob in Canaan with Great Mourning (49:29–50:14)***
- ***Joseph Forgave His Brothers' Evil, Recognizing God's Good Purposes (50:15–21)***
- ***Joseph Declared His Faith, Requiring Burial in Canaan (50:22–26)***

EXPOSITION

Genesis proclaims the good character of God from beginning to end. From darkness, desolation, and emptiness, our good Creator made everything "good" (טוֹב, 1:4, 10, 12, 18, 21, 25), bringing order and life into his empty world. In fact, in the beginning everything was "very good" (טוֹב מְאֹד, 1:31). God's goodness in creation continues in history and should be expected in life and anticipated in the future. Joseph could therefore declare that God's intent, frustrating the evil intentions of others, was "good" (לְטֹבָה) and life producing (לְהַחֲיֹת) for many people (50:20).

Throughout Genesis, God showed his goodness, declaring his redemptive purpose (3:15) to work in hearts (8:21) through covenant promises, first to Noah (9:1–17), then to Abraham (12:1–3; 13:14–17; 15:4–21; 17:1–21; 22:16–18), Isaac (17:21; 26:3–4), and Jacob (28:13–14; 35:11–12; 46:3). God's faithfulness to his promises drove the viewpoint and actions of his chosen servants as they anticipated their future fulfillment. Jacob's final testament to his sons (and grandsons, 48:1–49:28) and necessary return to Canaan for burial (46:4; 47:29–30; 49:29–32) sprang from his faith in God's good purpose.

Joseph, likewise, firmly asserted that he be carried back to Canaan for burial according to the promises to their forefathers (50:24), trusting God's good future for his people and his world.

While this pericope climaxes the entire book of Genesis, completing the patriarchal narratives, Jacob stories, and fourth-generation stories, it also anticipates and foreshadows the next great stage of God's redemptive plan, Israel's exodus from Egypt after their four centuries of exile and bondage (15:13–16). Both Jacob and Joseph draw attention to the future of the nation in the land, a major theme of Jacob's testament (49:1–28) and Joseph's expectation (50:24), preparing Israel for their deliverance and formation as a nation in the exodus. Because Jacob and Joseph recognized God's good oversight and expected his promises beyond their last days, God could greatly bless them, and Joseph could respond with grace and forgiveness to his brothers' evil.

Honoring His Faith, Joseph Buried Jacob in Canaan with Great Mourning (49:29–50:14)

After Jacob declared his wishes and died, Joseph, with his family and all Egypt, carried out his instructions, burying him in Machpelah and mourning the passing of God's regal patriarch.

Having adopted his grandsons and pronounced his blessing on each of his future tribes, Jacob commanded that he be buried only in Machpelah with his forefathers and first wife. His focus on the homeland completed his declaration of faith in the promises that had been on display throughout his testament to his sons. The royal mourning and funeral procession befit his place in the world as God's chosen descendant and conduit of God's promised blessing to his world. Jacob's instruction (49:29–33) and its fulfillment (50:4–14) frame the royal preparations and mourning for his burial (50:1–3).

Jacob Required Return (49:29–33)

Jacob commanded he be buried in Machpelah when he died.

49:29–32. Though Jacob had already made Joseph swear to bury him with his fathers rather than in Egypt (47:29–31), he now commanded all his sons to bury him in Canaan. Joseph's oath was appropriate, since Joseph could carry it out from his position. Jacob's command to all the sons made sure they were all in agreement. Jacob had previously provided only the outcome to Joseph, "with my fathers . . . in their burying place" (47:30). Now he described the specific cave, field, location, purchase by Abraham (noted twice, 49:30, 32), and burial of each of the patriarchs with their wives, including his first wife, Leah (v. 31). Jacob's focus on Abraham's purchase and the burial of his forebears exposes his anticipation of the promise, highlighting Abraham's establishment of a new homeland based on that promise (ch. 23 and Exposition there, p. 403). Jacob's faith required him to return to be part of God's future fulfillment of his guarantee in the land that Jacob had just foretold in his blessings on the tribes.

49:33. With Jacob's instructions complete, Jacob died. The stock phrases may suggest greater significance here than merely the end of his life and burial, however. Here the text states that Jacob was gathered to his people (וַיֵּאָסֶף אֶל־עַמָּיו), but he was not actually buried until over two and a half months later in Canaan (50:4–13). Though this could proleptically indicate his burial, physically placing him with his ancestors in the grave, here it suggests more. Since his burial is clearly stated later, "gathered to his people" may provide a glimpse into the expectation of the afterlife, which seldom surfaces in the Old Testament.

Jacob Was Mourned (50:1–3)

Joseph mourned Jacob's death along with all Egypt.

50:1–3. Joseph's emotional response to Jacob's death testifies to his relationship with his father, who had loved him most (37:3). It also sets him apart from his brothers, who would mourn along with the Egyptians (50:8, 10–11). His brothers would call on this relationship in their fear of retaliation later (vv. 16–17).

Joseph used his position to have Jacob embalmed. It was necessary to be able to carry out his oath. They could not safely transport Jacob's body that distance without dealing with the decay. Yet it also accorded Jacob an honor in Egypt that shows less in a Semite being embalmed (others are documented in ancient Egypt at that time, Kitchen 2003, 351–52), but rather in the opportunity for the Egyptians to also weep for him for seventy days, a typical Egyptian practice (K. Kitchen, "Joseph," *NBD* 610).[1] The general Egyptian mourning may be accounted for as mandated by the Pharaoh in honor of Joseph (Hamilton 1995, 692), but the rank of the procession following into Canaan (50:7–9) suggests Jacob's status.

Embalming Jacob

Embalming in Egypt was a process of dehydration to preserve the body for the soul of the deceased to be able to live in the afterlife, according to Egyptian theology (David, "Mummification," *OEAE* 2:440). For the Egyptians, then, it was a primarily religious expression and was carried out by a special cast of mortuary priests. That Joseph had "physicians" (הָרֹפְאִים) embalm Jacob suggests that he was distinguishing the practical need to preserve Jacob for burial in Canaan from the religious expectation of Jacob's need for his body in the afterlife (Kidner 1967, 233–34). Forty days were adequate for the embalming process, though the ritual could take longer with the associated religious rites (Jones, "Embalming," *ABD* 2:493; David, "Mummification," *OEAE* 2:440–41). The seventy days of mourning would have likely included the forty days of embalming.

Jacob's honor, accorded by Pharaoh in his life (47:7–10), was matched by the populace and nobility in his death (50:7). His blessing on Pharaoh and Egypt through Joseph was recognized and honored, probably precipitated by their honor for Joseph. El Shaddai was blessing the nations through the family, and the nations responded with honor for his regal patriarch.

Jacob Was Buried (50:4–14)

Joseph, his family, and Egypt buried Jacob in Machpelah with great mourning.

50:4–6. At the end of the mourning period, Joseph approached Pharaoh through his contacts in the palace (perhaps because of uncleanness or "mourning taboos," Mathews 2005, 402). Joseph summarized his oath to his father, including a detail not recorded in the initial conversation (47:29–30). Joseph recalled that Jacob asked to be buried in the tomb he had "made ready" for himself (50:5 NJPS) in Canaan. Joseph seems to be appealing to the Pharaonic habit of preparing their elaborate tombs well ahead of time and leaving out anything potentially offensive.[2] Pharaoh was amenable, sending Joseph and quite a retinue with him, including elders of Pharaoh's household and, more broadly, of Egypt (v. 7), all under guard of chariots and horsemen (v. 9).

1 Jacob's seventy days of mourning surpassed that for both Aaron and Moses (thirty days, Num. 20:29; Deut. 34:8). The period in Israel is sometimes seven days (1 Sam. 31:13; 1 Chron 10:12; Job 2:13; cf. Gen. 50:10), the same as the period of uncleanness after contacting death (Num. 19:11, 14, 16; 31:19), and occasionally "many days" (2 Sam. 13:37; 14:2; 1 Chron. 7:22).

2 Joseph's concern may have been the close covenantal connection to Canaan and the dim view the Pharaoh would have to Joseph having loyalties outside of Egypt (Michael 2018, 183–86).

TRANSLATION ANALYSIS 50:5

The root translated "made ready" by NJPS (כרה) has four homonyms, according to *HALOT* (s.v. "כרה" 496–97). Either of the first two are typically understood for this passage: I. "hollow out, dig," ("hewed," ESV, NRSV, or "dug," NET, NIV, etc.), or II. "purchase, buy," (Kidner 1967, 234). The NJPS takes this figuratively to indicate his preparation for his burial (NLT, "prepared"), as in 2 Chronicles 16:14 (Sarna 1989, 348). Since we have no record of him doing or saying anything about it, it is hard to be sure. Mathews (2005, 917–18) suggests he carved out his own chamber in the family cave, but it was not recorded.

50:7–11. Their large entourage included the Egyptian dignitaries and the clan of Jacob, finally mentioning the brothers but excluding the children, flocks, and herds. The military escort was likely for protection for all the dignitaries, though Pharaoh may have had concern for his star administrator, since Joseph seemed conscious of that concern (v. 5). Moses called it a "very great company" (v. 9).

The large entourage of Egyptian dignitaries and military escort certainly gave the impression of a high-ranking Egyptian concern. Jacob was getting the royal treatment, and the Canaanites noticed. They likely noticed the escort with the large contingent of Egyptian dress and customs, seeing it as a "grievous mourning by the Egyptians" (v. 11). They renamed the threshing floor Abel-Mizraim in honor of the event.[3] Even in his burial, Jacob was deeply honored by the nations that God had chosen his line to bless, as the party mourned seven additional days.

50:12–14. The pericope ends acknowledging Jacob's sons' completion of his command. Recalling his words and restating Abraham's purchase of the cave for a permanent possession in the land for his descendants ("to possess," לַאֲחֻזַּת), they anticipate God's promise and Jacob's faith in its fulfillment (49:30; see Translation Analysis 23:4b, p. 405, and the Exposition of ch. 23, esp. 23:20, p. 408). Jacob's burial was a testimony to his faith in the promise and the return of the nation to inhabit the land. Joseph and the entire entourage returned to Egypt as Joseph had promised, where they would await God's intervention, centuries later, to fulfill their faith.

Joseph Forgave His Brothers' Evil, Recognizing God's Good Purposes (50:15–21)

When Joseph's brothers, fearing retaliation after Jacob's death, begged forgiveness for their grievous sin, Joseph wept, affirming God's good purposes through their evil and asserting his own good intentions toward them.

The brothers' unfounded fear and Joseph's previously expressed and now certified perspective and forgiveness frame the narrator's window into their hearts. He will draw together the themes of Genesis, the patriarchal narratives, and the fourth-generation stories. God's working had certainly not always been clear, but it could now be clearly understood.

3 The threshing floor and its location remains uncertain. The qualifying phrase, "which is beyond the Jordan" (אֲשֶׁר בְּעֵבֶר הַיַּרְדֵּן), can be used of either side of the Jordan, depending on which side you are speaking from (Deut. 3:8, 20, 25). Some scholars, noting the natural and much more direct route to Hebron from Egypt, expect the threshing floor to be directly between Egypt and the hill country of southern Canaan, such as Tell el-ʿAjjul (Beth ʿEglaim) just south of Gaza and an Egyptian stronghold (Sarna 1989, 349). Others identify it on the eastern side (Wenham 1994, 489), or near the Jordan, possibly near Jericho (Hamilton 1995, 697). If so, the funeral procession would foreshadow the later route of the exodus (Lunn 2008, 174–78) and so encourage Israel, reading the text, with God's good purpose to take them to Canaan, the burden of the entire final pericope. Regardless of the precise location, the purpose of God and the encouragement for the later nation must not be missed.

He was at work for the nation, and he would prosper them, protect them, and use them for blessing to the nations. Such usefulness required his work in the lives of individuals, moving the brothers from hatred and fratricide to repentance and forgiveness. Not only was God moving his plan for redemption forward, but it included a renovation of hearts. God had exposed the need in the beginning, pointing to it with Cain (4:6–7), exposing it in the flood (6:5; 8:21), leading to it in the lives of Abraham, Isaac, and Jacob, and now unwrapping the dramatic change in Joseph and his brothers.

The Brothers Feared (50:15)

Joseph's brothers feared his retaliation.

50:15. The brothers realized their precarious position. With their father dead and Joseph in power, Joseph could drop any pretense and retaliate if he wished. No one could stop him or would care. They saw their vulnerability, but they had completely underestimated their brother. Perhaps they could only project their own hearts and reactions onto him, or perhaps they could simply not trust such grace. They clearly understood their own debauched actions. What they had done was truly "evil." Now they acknowledged and vocalized it. Their concern for their own well-being drove them to express it for the first time to Joseph.

> *TRANSLATION ANALYSIS 50:15*
> Their actions were certainly "evil" (ESV, NKJV), "harm" (NET), and "wrongs" (NASB20, NIV, NJPS). All of these translate *ra'ah* (רָעָה) from the root *r''* (רעע), which at its core relates to "an action or state that is detrimental to life or its fullness" (Baker, רָעַע, *NIDOTTE* 3:1154). It can span the range from heinous moral evil (e.g., Judg. 9:56; Jer. 32:32) to mere abnormalities that are detrimental to life and its enjoyment (e.g., Gen. 40:7; 41:3). Here, of course, it describes their moral evil, which brought pain and harm to Joseph.

Brothers Beg Forgiveness (50:16–17)

Joseph's brothers sent a message, begging forgiveness and bringing Joseph to tears.

50:16–17. They began with a message expressing their wrongdoing. They claimed Jacob had instructed them to tell Joseph to forgive them, banking on his relationship with his father to smooth his reactions to them. In Jacob's reported words, they framed their actions as a "transgression" (פֶּשַׁע), "sin" (חַטָּאת), and "evil" (רָעָה), repeating their description from verse 15. The two additional terms clarify that they are not viewing this as merely painful to him or harmful. Rather, they use two strong terms for infractions against God and men. "Transgression" expresses intentional crimes against persons and property that are particularly offensive and violate trust and expected standards (Carpenter and Grisanti, פֶּשַׁע, *NIDOTTE* 3:706–10). "Sin" can be unintentional, but whether intentional or not, it was a "failing" or "doing wrong" and, later, required sacrifice (Averbeck, חַטָּאת, *NIDOTTE* 2:93). They fully understood the depth of their sin against Joseph, even if they had not expressed their guilt to Joseph up to this point.

Whether Jacob had indeed issued the reported command is debated. Some do not see it clearly referenced in the blessings, so it appears to be a fabrication (Michael 2018, 186–89; Sarna 1989, 349–50), though we suggested the archers attacking Joseph would have included those actions (49:23). On the other hand, if he did know, perhaps he recognized their predicament and issued his command in hopes it would help if Joseph was putting on a front, in light of their close relationship (Steinmann 2019, 471). The ambiguity, however, is significant. Not only do we not know, but Joseph may not know, so we must measure his response against the uncertainties (Brueggemann 1985, 44). In Joseph's kindness we realize that Jacob's instruction did not matter. Their fear was needless.

They appealed to Joseph's loyalty to God as well as his father. Claiming loyalty to God themselves as his servants, they ask Joseph for forgiveness. He would have to answer to God if he were to retaliate. Joseph immediately reacted with tears. Whether he felt immediate frustration, compassion, or disappointment is clarified by his reaction. His following response showed compassion and generosity. Reporting his reaction, Moses highlighted Joseph's character and response of faith in God as coming from his heart and not merely his duty or studied response. He was far more loyal to God than they realized.

The Brothers Bowed . . . Again (50:18)
Joseph's brothers offered themselves to Joseph as servants.

50:18. Once more, only now in person, the brothers show their contrition. Not only do they offer themselves as his servants, but they fall before him, reliving Joseph's dreams and framing the entire narrative (37:5–11). When they had initially fallen before him, fulfilling the dreams, they had not known who he was (42:6; 44:14). Even then, Judah had offered himself as Joseph's servant in place of Benjamin (44:33). Now they all bow with full understanding and all offer themselves as Joseph's servants, hoping for their own lives. Their statement, however, was not a request. They declared themselves to be his servants to do with as he wished. They recognized their hopeless position and threw themselves on his mercy.

Joseph Extended Forgiveness (50:19–21)
Joseph acknowledged God's good working and pledged support, forgiving them.

50:19. Joseph's reaction draws the reader back to the message of the book and frames the entirety with the goodness of God and his working in human hearts. Not only do we end Genesis with the desired repentance after grievous sin, but we see the gracious and supernatural response of forgiveness based on faith in the good, ultimate work of God to establish his redemptive program. We also are reminded of the sole position God occupies in human history as Sovereign and Judge. Joseph knows his place and honors God's elevation of him, representing God well.

Joseph's immediate response sought to set them at ease. He would repeat it because they were clearly terrified. They could release their fear because Joseph knew his role. He was not God and would not play God. God was the one who knew hearts and could judge justly. While Jacob had only recognized his role when confronted with the impossible demand for children (30:2), Joseph understood his limitations when offered the opportunity for revenge when he had the authority, opportunity, and no obvious repercussions. Joseph, however, understood God's role and trusted in God's promises. Such forgiveness and grace could only come through faith in God's control and larger good purposes (cf. Berthoud 2008, 9).

In Genesis 3, God's first images wanted to be gods to themselves and thus brought death. Now Joseph refused to play God. He would remain in his place and allow God to give life. "Joseph will only be God's instrument, never his substitute" (Hamilton 1995, 705). God was at work changing hearts. and reversing the effects of sin (8:21)

50:20–21. He had experienced God's fulfilled promise from his dreams, and perhaps the bowing brothers again reminded him of God's overwhelming control. Once before he had explained to his brothers that God was sovereignly working and had used their actions to accomplish a greater good (45:4–8).

Then, however, he had focused on their deeds without referencing their motives. Now he accepted their evaluation that their actions were indeed "evil" (רָעָה, vv. 15, 17, 20), intentionally (!), but he then declared a much bigger perspective.

Referencing the same outcome that he had declared when he revealed his identity to them, he now also exposed God's intentions in all of this. Joseph's acknowledgement of their evil intentions recalls God's evaluation of humanity before the flood, the only other place in Genesis the root is used with this implication. At that time, Yahweh saw "that every intention of the thoughts of [humanity's] heart was only evil continually" (6:6). Yahweh's observation on humanity's "intention" (מַחְשְׁבֹת) uses the nominal form of the verb that Joseph used in declaring his brothers "intended" (חֲשַׁבְתֶּם) "evil." That evil (רָעָה) also occurs in Yahweh's observation of humanity in Genesis 6:5, where he noticed that their "wickedness" (רָעַת) was great in the earth. Their intentions being "evil" (רַע) continually (from the same root) drives the point home.

Joseph's understanding, then, draws the reader back to the primeval problem of humanity. Only now, finally, we see the working of God to change hearts. They have moved from rooted in evil to repentant. God has overruled their intentions with his intentions, sovereignly bringing about his good from behind the scenes, without being clearly seen until after the fact. The sons of Jacob had intended to destroy one life. God had used that evil action motivated by evil intent to preserve many lives and accomplish his good purpose, declared long before. Part of that plan was now reality. God had preserved many lives, including his chosen people, many Egyptians, and people from "all the earth" (41:54, 57). But his plan would continue to bring life.

50:21. Drawing their attention back to their concerns, he repeated his reassurance not to fear. Joseph explained that not only had God already provided life, but Joseph himself would continue to provide for them and for the next generations. "He comforted them." And he connected deeply.

TRANSLATION ANALYSIS 50:21a

The *Piel* of *nāḥam* (נָחַם), "comfort" (ESV, NKJV), "console" (NET), or "reassure" (NIV, NRSV), comes in a context similar to the laments and prophetic salvation oracles in which the recipients are in distress, needing rescue or intervention to restore life and hope or "make all things new," so that the past is past and they can move on to the promise of a better future (Brueggemann 1985, 50).

TRANSLATION ANALYSIS 50:21b

Repeating a phrase used of Shechem trying to comfort Dinah, Joseph "spoke kindly to them" or, literally, "spoke to their heart" (וַיְדַבֵּר עַל־לִבָּם). More to this point, Ruth 2:13 includes both phrases used here, where Ruth acknowledged that Boaz had "performed an act of inordinate power and kindness which permits a hopeless person to begin a new life" (Brueggemann 1985, 51). Joseph provided his brothers' needed reassurances.

Joseph Declared His Faith, Requiring Burial in Canaan (50:22–26)

After living a blessedly long life, Joseph declared his faith in God's future fulfillment of his promises to the patriarchs, requiring Israel to bury him in Canaan after he died, when God took them back.

Genesis ends with five verses set chiastically, with Joseph's faith in God's covenant promises centered amid a blessed life (Brueggemann 1982a, 378). The final piece of the puzzle grounds Joseph's gracious reaction to his brothers in his faith in God's promises. The God who created all things good and promised a good future will carry out his sovereign good intentions for his world. Wait for it.

1. Joseph lived to 110 in Egypt (50:22).
   2. Joseph welcomed three generations of grandchildren, looking to his future inheritance (50:23).
      3. Joseph declared his faith in God's promise of their future inheritance and fulfilled promises to the patriarchs in the land of Canaan (50:24).
   2'. Joseph required his family to take his bones with them when they returned to Canaan, expressing his faith in their future inheritance (50:25).

3'. Joseph died in Egypt at 110 (50:26).

50:22–23. God had fully blessed Joseph in his sojourn in Egypt with his extended family around him. Joseph's lifespan of 110 years represented the ideal age in Egyptian thinking (Kitchen 2003, 351). Joseph, however, was looking ahead to his home in Canaan. He enjoyed seeing his great-great-grandchildren from Ephraim, further indicating God's blessing, and he adopted the children of Machir, much like Jacob had done for Ephraim and Manasseh. The adoption, indicating some special inheritance rights, draws parallels with Jacob, showing his faith and his preparation for a future fulfillment of God's promise, providing the basis for God's blessing.

The Age of the Patriarchs

The age of the patriarchs is a perennial question since they are all well beyond normal lifespans, recognized by Psalm 90:10 as seventy or perhaps eighty (ironically assigned to Moses in the superscription). Adding to the mystery, scholars have noted that the ages present some mathematical patterns. Gevirtz, citing Meysing ("The Biblical Chronologies of the Patriarchs," Christian News from Israel 14 [1963] 8), notes the pattern of Abraham, Isaac, and Jacob:

Abraham (25:7):	$175=7x5^2$
Isaac (35:28):	$180=5x6^2$
Jacob (47:28):	$147=3x7^2$
He adds Joseph (50:22, 26):	$110=5^2+6^2+7^2$

The first three represent descending prime numbers multiplied by ascending squares, with Joseph as the sum of the squares (Gevirtz 1977, 571). Labuschagne (1989, 126–27), arguing for a possible connection to Yahweh's name (and its number, 17 [7+5+5; 5+6+6; 3+7+7]), concludes that Joseph's 110 years seems to conclude the pattern in another way: $1 \times 5^2 + 6^2 + 7^2$, or it could be understood as the next prime plus the sum of the previous squares, showing Joseph as the "successor." Joseph symbolically concludes the patriarchal narratives (Hamilton 1995, 710).

TRANSLATION ANALYSIS 50:23

Like Jacob had put Ephraim and Manasseh by or between his knees when he adopted them (48:12), the sons of Machir were "born on Joseph's knees" (NJPS, RSV, etc.). The action of placing them on his knees at birth indicated that they were "counted as Joseph's own" (ESV, see also NCV, NLT), possibly for "special inheritance rights" (NET). Similarly, in Genesis 30:3, Rachel said that Bilhah would "bear on my knees" (NJPS), claiming them as her surrogate children.

50:24. At the core of this final scene, Joseph declared his faith in the promise. Specifically referencing God's promise of the land to the three patriarchs, Jacob declared to his family his confidence in God's intervention to return them to the land of promise. God would reward Joseph's faith, and he would be acknowledged by the nation when Moses responded to God's call and they recognized that God had indeed "visited" them (Exod. 4:31), again noted when they kept their corporate vow by taking Joseph with them in the exodus (Exod. 13:19).

TRANSLATION ANALYSIS 50:24a

The term "brothers" (אָח), often refers to other blood relations, like a nephew (13:8; 14:16), cousin (29:15), or general "kinsmen" (16:12; 25:18). There is no need to assume that Joseph's older brothers outlived him.

TRANSLATION ANALYSIS 50:24b

Jacob asserted full confidence in God's future intervention (his use of the cognate infinitive absolute establishing the certainty, "God will assuredly take care of you," NASB20, וֵאלֹהִים פָּקֹד יִפְקֹד אֶתְכֶם). The chosen verb, translated "visit" (פקד, ESV), "come to your aid" (NIV), "take notice of you" (NJPS), and similarly, has a broad range of meaning. In the context of God's action toward his people, it often relates to God paying careful attention to something and acting accordingly, with either blessing or judgment (Williams, פָּקַד, *NIDOTTE* 3:657–63).

The painted anthropoid wooden coffins could become quite elaborate.

50:25–26. Joseph declared his trust in God most forcefully when he required that his family swear to take him with them when God did intervene. He put his exclamation point on his faith with his personal preparations in death. He made sure he would be embalmed and in a transportable coffin.[4] His preparation was not for the afterlife but demonstrated his faith in God's certain promises. He would symbolically be part of the future working of God in his family's future. Even in death he left a legacy of faith in God's working and testimony to future generations to faithfully follow and wait for El Shaddai, their Shepherd (49:24–25).

For Israel coming out of Egypt, the deaths of Jacob and Joseph frame his reaffirmation of the promises and the certainty of the continuity of the clan because of God's superintending grace. They anticipate the return of the nation to the land, where they will flesh out the expectations of Jacob's blessings. We see in bold relief that the anticipated blessings were not for that generation but for future generations. They provide the transparent confidence in God's future work to match his past work. The good that God brought from the evil that the brothers perpetrated would be overshadowed by the good that God would bring from the evil that Pharaoh would perpetrate against the nation. "The fulfillments of well-being and land do not depend on historical indications of success, upon survival of specific human agents, nor upon the political capacity to capture. They depend only on the faithfulness of God. And that is guaranteed by nothing other than the word of the trusted promise-maker" (Brueggemann 1982a, 369).

The good that God promises his people and his world will use even evil intentions, like the satanically inspired crucifixion, to accomplish his greater good purposes to bring

4 This would refer to an anthropoid wooden coffin with a painted face on one end (Kitchen, "Joseph," *NBD* 610).

his ultimate redemption to his world. And still his people wait for the final fulfillment of his promise, trusting his good purposes through the pain and frustration of evil intentions. He will bring his redemption, his seed to crush the head of the snake, and he will not be thwarted (Rom. 16:20; Heb 2:14; Rev. 2:1–3, 10).

THEOLOGICAL FOCUS

Faith in God's current and future working to accomplish his good purposes gains God's blessing and shapes the believer's response to death and life.

Once again, though God is not an active character in the drama, he is the focus. Jacob, Joseph, and even the brothers acknowledge their dependence and necessary trust in God and his promises. They reveal the effects of God's actions in their lives, both in their physical preservation and blessing, as well as their changed character as they reject rebellion and pain, embracing repentance, grace, and restoration. Transformed human hearts show God's work most vividly. God's people show that faith most graphically when facing death or severe evil.

Though they are not always seen in the fog of evil intentions, God's good purposes are always active in human history, even when his images distort his character and plot evil in his world. God's will overrules all other wills, accomplishing his purposes of life and blessing for his creatures. Often hidden in the seeming victory of evil and pain, and then only seen in the long retrospect, God will even use the evil intentions of evil people to accomplish his good designs, captured in Paul's reflection on God's good purposes through all things, transforming hearts into Christlikeness (Rom. 8:28–29).

God, then, is always working to accomplish his redemptive plans. That work will never be thwarted because he is the creator of all things and the necessary sovereign over it all. Rather, he is the beneficent king who can use all things for his glorious ends. That also means he will judge with perfect justice. His images must never mistake their role as images to usurp his role as lawgiver and judge (Lev. 19:18; Deut. 32:35; Rom. 12:17–19).

In painful irony, our limited perspective often cannot see his working until later, bringing agony as evil appears to exert its twisted will. As with Joseph in prison or Israel in Egypt, we must wait for God's time and trust him to reveal his good outcomes, even through the evil actions and intentions we endure. Those who endure in faith will find his blessing. It may not be in long life and prosperity, but it will be in relationship with him and his empowering to serve his world and show his character to his creation.

We must recognize what God has done in the past and reflect on his promise as we wait in faith for the completion of his plans. We must treasure each insight into God's working as we face new and difficult challenges. God uses innocent sufferers to accomplish his great works of salvation, Jesus being the greatest. That does not mean all suffering is innocent or undeserved, but rather, even the most innocent and undeserved is within the scope of God's good intentions.

In clinging to God's word and past work, we also recognize that God works through flawed people, including us. He is gracious, and we must see our evil and call it such, but he, even more than Joseph, forgives and restores after great disappointment and damage. Though Joseph refused to take God's role in judging, he never reflected God's heart better than in his rich forgiveness and gracious care for the perpetrators of evil against him (Exod. 34:6–7). "To leave all the righting of one's wrongs to God (19; cf. Rom. 12:19; 1 Thess. 5:15; 1 Peter 4:19); to see his providence in man's malice (20; cf. on 45:5), and to repay evil not only with forgiveness but also with practical affection (21; cf. Luke 6:27ff.), are attitudes which anticipate the adjective 'Christian' and even 'Christlike'" (Kidner 1967, 235). Jesus gave us the greatest example on the cross, "Father forgive them" (Luke 23:34).

It is that very confidence in God's good plans and sovereign oversight that allows the believer to respond in grace, forgiveness, and love, even to his or her enemies (Matt. 5:44). Without faith, good works are merely philanthropy and altruism. With faith, done in loyalty to the Creator King, they reveal the Father, springing from confidence in his good and final oversight. His plans will make all things right and will bring ultimate good, establishing righteousness, justice, and life—the eternal thriving life his images were created for.

PREACHING AND TEACHING STRATEGIES

Exegetical and Theological Synthesis

Our sermon/lesson preparation begins with the observation of Jacob's faith in action. As he approaches his own death, he commands his sons to bury him in Canaan, not Egypt. This foreshadows the next great act in redemption history—the exodus of God's people from slavery in Egypt. Jacob sees this as a reality and commands accordingly. Our listeners see Jacob's faith and follow in his footsteps as they process the promises of God for their own lives. In the same way, our faith and hope are not yet seen but are real enough to affect our choices in this life. Since we do believe the promises of God, we act accordingly. We do not allow sin to drive our attitudes and actions.

The next step is to acknowledge the theological meaning of Egypt's reaction to the news of Jacob's death. Genesis 50:10–11 includes that "they lamented there with a very great and grievous lamentation. . . . 'This is a grievous mourning by the Egyptians.'" Clearly Egypt has been on the receiving end of great blessing through Joseph and, secondarily, through his father, Jacob. This has been God's design for his people all along: experience his blessing and extend it to others. We will urge our listeners to aim for similar impact in God's world with all we encounter.

Finally, a significant section of the selected pericope involves Joseph's display of godliness in the form of forgiving his brothers. When their father dies, Joseph's brothers fear the worst—that Joseph will finally get revenge for the way they treated him. Joseph, however, displays the incredible transformation that faith brings by giving up any right to vengeance and stating his realization of God's sovereign power to pull off the impossible, turning intended evil into good.

Preaching Idea

Faith in God's faithfulness and powerful sovereignty inevitably shapes the way believers respond to both death and life.

Contemporary Connections

What does it mean?

Jacob's request to be buried back in Canaan requires an explanation. The historical request by itself does not preach; what does is linking his request to his faith in the promises of God. God's people are not destined to remain in Egypt, and Jacob knows it. Although God will wait hundreds of years before redeeming his people, he will redeem them in Exodus at the exodus. Jacob's request means something to the church within the context of God's faithfulness to his covenant agreement and the overall history of redemption of which we are a part. He will fulfill his promise!

The second thing that needs an explanation is all the fuss Egypt made while they lamented Jacob's death. Part of the announcement God made to Abraham, Isaac, and Jacob was that they were to bless others around them. That certainly was true in Jacob's case through the wisdom and blessing of God on Joseph's life in Egypt. Pharoah was on the receiving end of that blessing constantly. He and all Egypt recognized it.

Is it true?

While the biblical author assumes the reality of God's control of history, all our listeners may not feel the same way. As is often the case in Old Testament narratives, the author assumes the validity of God's sovereignty. For instance, Jacob commands his sons to bury him "in the land of Canaan" (49:30). Then, the narrative ends with Joseph following in his father's footsteps: "Joseph made the sons of Israel swear, saying, 'God will surely visit you, and you shall carry up my bones from here'" (50:24–25). Their confidence bolsters our faith to believe that God controls the affairs of his people so they can accomplish his will in the world.

Finally, Joseph's statement in 50:20 is the author's way of defending a concept that all our listeners want to be true: "you meant evil against me, but God meant it for good." The only question that remains is whether we believe it. Seeing this and other working of God in hindsight supports our faith.

Now what?

Again, as is common in many Old Testament narratives, the biblical author is not directly applying a biblical concept. As we have been showing throughout Genesis, the narratives still make a difference for the believer. There is a reason why Genesis is ending the way it does. God gave his word to his people, a word that could not be fulfilled if they remained in Egypt. Part of the "so what?" of these final scenes includes bolstering our faith in God's ability to keep his promises to deliver us in a world that is hostile to his will. Although the land promises in the original blessing reflect spiritual blessings for the saints, they are just as sure and, when believed, provide stability.

Finally, one of the most difficult actions for a Christian is to extend forgiveness when severely wronged. All Christ-followers are challenged to follow Joseph's example of forgiving his brothers—even to enemies (Matt. 5:44–45; 6:14–15). He made it clear that vengeance was God's prerogative alone (Deut. 32:35). The fact that Joseph knew his place in relation to God's place (Gen. 50:19) unlocked the power to forgive a serious debt.

Creativity in Presentation

Faith in God's faithfulness and powerful sovereignty inevitably shapes the way Christians respond to both death and life. It is as true today as it was for Jacob and Joseph. You will want to identify past or current stories of profound faith in God's faithfulness over a long period of time. Many parents will tell of the many years in which they trusted in the faithfulness of God for their children. And their children will tell of how God moved in their lives after their parents went to be with the Lord. You will also want to illustrate Christians who have forgiven others for horrendous offenses. These illustrations will help listeners follow Jacob's and Joseph's examples of faith portrayed in these scenes.

Consider structuring the message this way:

- We are counting on God's faithfulness for future blessings (49:29–33; 50:22–26). In this section of the sermon, Jacob's and Joseph's commands as they neared their respective deaths signaled their faith in God's faithfulness to bless them.

- We are committed to show God's faithfulness in blessing others (50:1–14). The way the Egyptians mourned for Jacob revealed that he was treated like royalty. Such was Joseph's influence on Pharaoh and company as he extended the blessing of God on everything he touched in the kingdom. This is the time for us to urge our listeners to think carefully about the way they interact with non-Christians in their world.

- We are committed to show God's faithfulness in forgiving those who sin against us (50:15–21). This might be the ultimate test of faith and faithfulness. Joseph displayed the transformative work of God by the way he left vengeance to God alone. According to Jesus's teaching, all his followers must do the same, or else they cannot expect God to forgive them for their trespasses against him (Matt. 6:15).

DISCUSSION QUESTIONS

1. The hundreds of years Israel lived in Egypt teach that God is not in a hurry to execute his redemptive plan in history. Discuss how this forces God's people to patiently wait for him in their lives. Discuss how hope is, at times, synonymous with faith (cf. Heb. 11).
2. Discuss why forgiving others of terrible offenses is so difficult.
3. Genesis 50:20 is a key verse in the Old Testament about the sovereignty and providence of God. Discuss what it says about a person's faith if they say they believe in God's sovereignty but do not rest in him and react accordingly. In other words, could Joseph, for instance, have really believed in God's sovereignty and withheld forgiveness?
4. How have you seen God working in your past to bring good out of evil or painful circumstances?
5. What does resting in God's sovereignty mean in your life currently?

REFERENCES

Alexander, T. Desmond. 1993. "Genealogies, Seed and the Compositional Unity of Genesis." *Tyndale Bulletin* 44, no. 2:255–70.

_____. 1997a. *Abraham in the Negev: a Source-Critical Investigation of Genesis 20:1–22:19*. Carlisle, Cumbria: Paternoster.

_____. 1997b. "Further Observations on the Term 'Seed' in Genesis." *Tyndale Bulletin* 48, no. 2:363–67.

_____. 2012. "Messianic Ideology in the Book of Genesis." In *The Lord's Anointed: Interpretation of Old Testament Messianic Texts*, edited by P. E. Satterthwaite, Richard S. Hess, and Gordon Wenham, 19–39. Eugene, OR: Wipf & Stock. Original edition, 1995.

Alexander, T. Desmond, and David W. Baker. 2003. *Dictionary of the Old Testament: Pentateuch*. Downers Grove, IL: InterVarsity Press.

Allen, James P. 1988. *Genesis in Egypt: The Philosophy of Ancient Egyptian Creation Accounts*.Yale Egyptological Studies 2. New Haven, CT: Yale Egyptological Seminar, Dept. of Near Eastern Languages and Civilizations, Graduate School, Yale University.

Alter, Robert. 1981. *The Art of Biblical Narrative*. New York: Basic Books.

_____. 1996. *Genesis*. New York: Norton.

Amar, Zohar, and Naama Sukenik. 2021. "The Signs That Bind: Why Tamar Requested Judah's Signet, Cord, and Staff." *Biblical Archaeology Review* 47, no. 3:62–64.

Armerding, Carl Edwin. 1955. "The Last Words of Jacob: Genesis 49." *Bibliotheca Sacra* 112, no. 448:320–29.

Atwell, James E. 2000. "An Egyptian Source for Genesis 1." *Journal of Theological Studies* 51, no. 2:441–77.

Avalos, Hector. 2015. "Circumcision as a Slave Mark." *Perspectives in Religious Studies* 42, no. 3:259–74.

Averbeck, Richard E. 2004. "Ancient Near Eastern Mythography as It Relates to Historiography in the Hebrew Bible: Genesis 3 and the Cosmic Battle." In *The Future of Biblical Archaeology*, edited by James K. Hoffmeier and Alan Millard, 328–56. Cambridge: Eerdmans.

Awabdy, Mark A. 2010. "Babel, Suspense, and the Introduction to the Terah-Abram Narrative." *Journal for the Study of the Old Testament* 35, no. 1:3–29.

Backon, Joshua. 2008. "Jacob and the Spotted Sheep: The Role of Prenatal Nutrition on Epigenetics of Fur Color." *Jewish Bible Quarterly* 36, no. 4:263–65.

Baden, Joel S. 2010. "The Morpho-Syntax of Genesis 12:1–3: Translation and Interpretation." *The Catholic Biblical Quarterly* 72, no. 2:223–37.

Bakon, Shimon. 2013. "Subtleties in the Story of Joseph and Potiphar's Wife." *Jewish Bible Quarterly* 41, no. 3:171–74.

Bassett, Frederick W. 1971. "Noah's Nakedness and the Curse of Canaan: A Case of Incest?" *Vetus Testamentum* 21, no. 2:232–37.

Bavinck, Herman. 2019. *The Wonderful Works of God*. Glenside, PA: Westminster Seminary Press.

Beale, G. K. 2004. *The Temple and the Church's Mission: A Biblical Theology of the Dwelling Place of God*. New Studies in Biblical Theology. Downers Grove, IL: InterVarsity Press.

_____. 2014. *God Dwells Among Us: Expanding Eden to the Ends of the Earth*. Downers Grove, IL: InterVarsity Press.

Bechtel, Lyn M. 1994. "What If Dinah is Not Raped? (Genesis 34)." *Journal for the Study of the Old Testament* 19, no. 62:19–36.

Becking, Bob. 1991. "'They Hated Him Even More': Literary Technique in Genesis 37:1–11." *Biblische Notizen* 60:40–47.

Ber, Viktor. 2016. "Unredeemable Literature?: Violence, Identity, and Theology in Genesis 34." *Communio Viatorum* 58, no. 3:268–78.

Bergsma, John Sietze, and Scott Hahn. 2005. "Noah's Nakedness and the Curse on Canaan (Genesis 9:20–27)." *Journal of Biblical Literature* 124, no. 1:25–40.

Berlin, Adele. 1983. *Poetics and Interpretation of Biblical Narrative*. Bible and Literature Series 9. Sheffield: Almond Press.

Berthoud, Pierre. 2008. "The Reconciliation of Joseph with His Brothers: Sin, Forgiveness and Providence Genesis 45.1–11 (42.1–45.11) and 50.15–21." *European Journal of Theology* 17, no. 1:5–11.

Biddle, Mark E. 1990. "The 'Endangered Ancestress' and Blessing for the Nations." *Journal of Biblical Literature* 109, no. 4:599–611.

Bird, Phyllis A. 1989a. "The Harlot as Heroine: Narrative Art and Social Presupposition in Three Old Testament Texts." *Semeia* 46:119–39.

_____. 1989b. "'To Play the Harlot': An Inquiry into an Old Testament Metaphor." In *Gender and Difference in Ancient Israel*, edited by Peggy L. Day, 75–94. Minneapolis: Fortress Press.

Bosse-Griffiths, Kate. 1983. "The Fruit of the Mandrake." In *Fontes Atque Pontes: Eine Festgabe für Hellmut Brunner*, edited by Manfred Görg, Ägypten und das Alte Testament 5, 62–74. Wiesbaden: Otto Harrassowitz.

Botterweck, G. J., H. Ringgren, and H.-J. Fabry, eds. 1974–2006. *Theological Dictionary of the Old Testament*. Trans. J. T. Willis et al. 17 vols. Grand Rapids: Eerdmans.

Brown, Francis, Samuel Rolles Driver, and Charles Augustus Briggs. 1977. *Enhanced Brown-Driver-Briggs Hebrew and English Lexicon*. Oxford: Clarendon.

Brueggemann, Walter. 1982. *Genesis: Interpretation, a Bible Commentary for Teaching and Preaching*. Atlanta: John Knox.

_____. 1985. "Genesis 50:15–21: A Theological Exploration." In *Congress Volume: Salamanca, 1983*, edited by J. A. Emerton, 40–53. Leiden: Brill.

_____. 1991. "Genesis 17:1–22." *Interpretation: A Journal of Bible and Theology* 45, no. 1:55–59.

Bunn, Daniel D. 2018. "'Return, and I Will Be with You': Divine Agenda and Genesis 31:1–24." *Journal of Theological Interpretation* 12, no. 2:170–82.

Caquot, A. "Ben Porat (Gen 49:22)." *Semitica* 30 (1980) 43–56.

Cartledge, Tony W. 1992. *Vows in the Hebrew Bible and the Ancient Near East*. Journal for the Study of the Old Testament Supplements 147. Sheffield: JSOT Press.

Cassuto, Umberto. 1973. *Biblical and Oriental Studies*. Publications of the Perry Foundation for Biblical Research in the Hebrew University of Jerusalem. Jerusalem: Magnes.

_____. 1974. *A Commentary on the Book of Genesis, Part Two: From Noah to Abraham*. Translated by Israel Abrahams. Repr., 1961. Jerusalem: Magnes.

_____. 1978. *A Commentary on the Book of Genesis, Part One: From Adam to Noah*. Translated by Israel Abrahams. Repr., 1961. Jerusalem: Magnes.

Chisholm, Robert B., Jr. 1992. "Evidence fom Genesis." In *A Case for Premillennialism: A New Consensus*, edited by Donald K. Campbell and Jeffrey L. Townsend, 35–54. Chicago: Moody.

_____. 1995. "Does God 'Change His Mind'?" *Bibliotheca Sacra* 152, no. 608:387–99.

_____. 2007. "Anatomy of an Anthropomorphism: Does God Discover Facts?" *Bibliotheca Sacra* 164, no. 653:3–20.

Clifford, Richard J. 1994. *Creation Accounts in the Ancient Near East and the Bible*. The Catholic Biblical Quarterly Monograph Series 26. Washington, DC: Catholic Biblical Association.

_____. 2004. "Genesis 38: Its Contribution to the Jacob Story." *The Catholic Biblical Quarterly* 66, no. 4:519–32.

Clines, David J. A. 2001. *Theme of the Pentateuch*. 2nd ed. Journal for the Study of the Old Testament Supplements. Sheffield: Sheffield Academic.

Coats, George W. 1973. "Abraham's Sacrifice of Faith: A Form-Critical Study of Genesis 22." *Interpretation: A Journal of Bible and Theology* 27, no. 4:389–400.

_____. 1976. *From Canaan to Egypt: Structural and Theological Context for the Joseph Story*. The Catholic Biblical Quarterly Monograph Series 4. Washington, DC: Catholic Biblical Association of America.

_____. 1985. "Lot: A Foil in the Abraham Saga." In *Understanding the Word: Essays in Honour of Bernhard W. Anderson*, edited by James T. Butler, Edgar W. Conrad, and Ben Ollenburger, Journal for the Study of the Old Testament Supplements, 113–32. London: JSOT Press.

Cogan, Morton. 1968. "A Technical Term for Exposure." *Journal of Near Eastern Studies* 27, no. 2:133–35.

Collins, C. John. 1995. "The Wayyiqtol as 'Pluperfect': When and Why." *Tyndale Bulletin* 46, no. 1:117–40.

_____. 1997. "A Syntactical Note (Genesis 3:15): Is the Woman's Seed Singular or Plural?" *Tyndale Bulletin* 48, no. 1:139–48.

_____. 2006. *Genesis 1–4: A Linguistic, Literary, and Theological Commentary*. Phillipsburg, NJ: P&R.

Coote, Robert. 1972. "The Meaning of the Name Israel." *The Harvard Theological Review* 65, no. 1:137–42.

Cotter, David W. 2003. *Genesis*. Berit Olam. Collegeville, MN: Liturgical Press.

Cryer, Frederick H. 1994. *Divination in Ancient Israel and its Near Eastern Environment: A Socio-Historical Investigation*. Sheffield: JSOT Press.

Currid, John D. 2003. *A Study Commentary on Genesis. Vol. 1, Genesis 1:1–25:18*. EP Study Commentary. Darlington, UK: Evangelical.

Curtis, Edward M. 1987. "Structure, Style and Context as a Key to Interpreting Jacob's Encounter at Peniel." *Journal of the Evangelical Theological Society* 30, no. 2:129–37.

_____. 1991. "Genesis 38: Its Context(s) and Function." *Criswell Theological Review* 5:247–57.

Dahood, Mitchell J. 1961. "MKRTYHM in Genesis 49,5." *The Catholic Biblical Quarterly* 23, no. 1:54–56.

_____. 1966. "Hebrew-Ugaritic Lexicography IV." *Biblica* 47, no. 3:403–19.

Daube, David, and Reuven Yaron. 1956. "Jacob's Reception by Laban." *Journal of Semitic Studies* 1, no. 1:60–62.

DeRouchie, Jason S. 2004. "Circumcision in the Hebrew Bible and Targums: Theology, Rhetoric, and the Handling of Metaphor." *Bulletin for Biblical Research* 14, no. 2:175–203.

Douglas, Mary. 1999. *Implicit Meanings: Selected Essays in Anthropology*. London: Routledge.

_____. 2000. *Leviticus as Literature*. Oxford: Oxford University Press.

_____. 2002. *Purity and Danger: An Analysis of Concepts of Pollution and Taboo*. Florence: Taylor & Francis Group.

Doyle, Brian. 1998. "The Sin of Sodom: yāḏa', yāḏa', yāḏa'? A Reading of the Mamre-Sodom Narrative in Genesis 18–19." *Theology & Sexuality* 9:84–100.

Drey, Philip R. 2002. "The Role of Hagar in Genesis 16." *Andrews University Seminary Studies* 40, 2:179–195.

Earl, Douglas. 2011. "Toward a Christian Hermeneutic of Old Testament Narrative: Why

Genesis 34 Fails to Find Christian Significance." *The Catholic Biblical Quarterly* 73, no. 1:30–49.

Els, Pieter J. J. S. 1998. "Old Testament Perspectives on Interfaith Dialogue: The Significance of the Abram-Melchizedek Episode of Genesis 14." *Studies in Interreligious Dialogue* 8, no. 2:191–207.

Embry, Bradley. 2011. "The 'Naked Narrative' from Noah to Leviticus: Reassessing Voyeurism in the Account of Noah's Nakedness in Genesis 9.22–24." *Journal for the Study of the Old Testament* 35, no. 4:417–33.

Fensham, F. C. 1977. "Numeral Seventy in the Old Testament and the Family of Jerubbaal, Ahab, Panammuwa and Athirat." *Palestine Exploration Quarterly* 109:113–15.

Finkelstein, J. J. 1968. "An Old Babylonian Herding Contract and Genesis 31:38 f." *Journal of the American Oriental Society* 88, no. 1:30–36.

Fishbane, Michael A. 1975. "Composition and Structure in the Jacob Cycle (Gen 25:19–35:22)." *Journal of Jewish Studies* 26, nos. 1–2:15–38.

_____. 1979. *Text and Texture: Close Readings of Selected Biblical Texts*. New York: Schocken.

Fleishman, Joseph. 2001. "Towards Understanding the Legal Significance of Jacob's Statement: 'I Will Divide Them in Jacob, I Will Scatter Them in Israel' [Gen 49, 7b]." In *Studies in the Book of Genesis: Literature, Redaction and History*, edited by André Wénin, Bibliotheca Ephemeridum Theologicarum Lovaniensium 155, 541–59. Leuven/Sterling, VA: University Press /Uitgeverij Peeters.

Fockner, Sven. 2008. "Reopening the Discussion: Another Contextual Look at the Sons of God." *Journal for the Study of the Old Testament* 32, no. 4:435–56.

Foh, Susan T. 1975. "What is the Woman's Desire?" *The Westminster Theological Journal* 37, no. 3:376–83.

Fokkelman, J. P. 2004. *Narrative Art in Genesis: Specimens of Stylistic and Structural Analysis*. 2nd ed. Eugene, OR: Wipf & Stock.

Frankena, R. 1972. "Some Remarks on the Semitic Background of Chapters 29–31 of the Book of Genesis." In *Witness of Tradition: Papers Read at the Joint British-Dutch Old Testament Conference, Woudschoten, Netherlands, 1970*, 53–64. Leiden: Brill.

Freedman, D. N., ed. 1992. *Anchor Bible Dictionary*. 6 vols. New York: Doubleday.

Freedman, R. David. 1976. "'Put Your Hand Under My Thigh'—The Patriarchal Oath." *Biblical Archaeology Review* 2, no. 2:3–4.

Frisch, Amos. 2003. "'Your Brother Came with Guile': Responses to an Explicit Moral Evaluation in Biblical Narrative." *Prooftexts* 23, no. 3:271–96.

Frolov, Serge. 2012. "Judah Comes to Shiloh: Genesis 49:10bα, One More Time." *Journal of Biblical Literature* 131, no. 3:417–22.

Frymer-Kensky, Tikva Simone. 1981. "Patriarchal Family Relationships and Near Eastern Law." *The Biblical Archaeologist* 44, no. 4:209–14.

Fuchs, Esther. 1988. "'For I Have the Way of Women': Deception, Gender, and Ideology in Biblical Narrative." *Semeia* 42:68–83.

Futato, Mark D. 1998. "Because It Had Rained: A Study of Gen 2:5–7 with Implications for Gen 2:4–25 and Gen 1:1–2:3." *Westminster Theological Journal* 60, no. 1:1–21.

Galpaz-Feller, Pnina. 2004. "Private Lives and Public Censure: Adultery in Ancient Egypt and Biblical Israel." *Near Eastern Archaeology* 67, no. 3:153–61.

Geller, Stephen A. 1982. "The Struggle at the Jabbok: The Uses of Enigma in a Biblical Narrative." *The Journal of the Ancient Near Eastern Society* 14:37–60.

Gentry, Peter J., and Stephen J. Wellum. 2018. *Kingdom Through Covenant: A Biblical-Theological Understanding of the Covenants*. 2nd ed. Wheaton, IL: Crossway.

George, A. R. 2000. *The Epic of Gilgamesh: The Babylonian Epic Poem and Other Texts in Akkadian and Sumerian*. New York: Penguin Books.

Gesenius, Wilhelm, E. Kautzsch, and A. E. Cowley. 1910. *Gesenius' Hebrew Grammar*. 2nd English ed. Oxford: Clarendon.

Gevirtz, Stanley. 1977. "The Life Spans of Joseph and Enoch and the Paralellism: šibʿṯayim-šibîm wĕšibʾāh." *Journal of Biblical Literature* 96, no. 4:570–71.

_____. 1984. "Naphtali in 'The Blessing of Jacob.'" *Journal of Biblical Literature* 103, no. 4:513–21.

Giorgetti, Andrew. 2014. "The 'Mock Building Account' of Genesis 11:1–9: Polemic Against Mesopotamian Royal Ideology." *Vetus Testamentum* 64, no. 1:1–20.

Goldingay, John. 2010. *Genesis for Everyone*. Old Testament for Everyone. Louisville: Westminster John Knox.

Gordon, Cyrus H. 1940. "Biblical Customs and the Nuzu Tablets." *The Biblical Archaeologist* 3, no. 1:1–12.

_____. 1960. *The World of the Old Testament*. 2nd ed. London: Phoenix House.

Green, Alberto R. W. 1975. *The Role of Human Sacrifice in the Ancient Near East*. Missoula, MT: Scholars Press.

Grisanti, Michael A. 2001. "Inspiration, Inerrancy, and the OT Canon: The Place of Textual Updating in an Inerrant View of Scripture." *Journal of the Evangelical Theological Society* 44 (4): 577–598.

Grossman, Jonathan. 2013. "The Story of Joseph's Brothers in Light of the 'Therapeutic Narrative' Theory." *Biblical Interpretation* 21, no. 2:171–95.

Grosz, Katarzyna. 1981. "Dowry and Brideprice in Nuzi." In *Studies on the Civilization and Culture of Nuzi and Hurrians*, edited by Martha A. Morrison and David I. Owen, 161–82. Winona Lake, IN: Eisenbrauns.

Hallo, William W. 1983. "Cult Statue and Divine Image: A Preliminary Study." In *Scripture in Context II: More Essays on the Comparative Method*, edited by William W. Hallo, James C. Moyer and Leo G. Perdue., 1–17. Winona Lake, IN: Eisenbrauns.

_____. 1985. "'As the Seal Upon Thy Heart': Glyptic Roles in the Biblical World." *Bible Review*. 1, no. 1:20–27.

Hallo, William W., and K. Lawson Younger. 2003. *Context of Scripture*. 4 vols. Leiden: Brill.

Hamilton, Victor P. 1990. *The Book of Genesis: Chapters 1–17*. The New International Commentary on the Old Testament. Grand Rapids: Eerdmans.

_____. 1995. *The Book of Genesis. Chapters 18–50*. The New International Commentary on the Old Testament. Grand Rapids: Eerdmans.

Han, Jin H. 2015. "The Role of 'an Audience' in Isaac's Blessing in Genesis 27." *Perspectives in Religious Studies* 42, no. 1:5–10.

Harris, R. Laird, Gleason Leonard Archer, and Bruce K. Waltke, eds. 1980. *Theological Wordbook of the Old Testament*. Chicago: Moody.

Hasel, Gerhard F. 1974. "Polemic Nature of the Genesis Cosmology." *Evangelical Quarterly* 46:81–102.

_____. 1981. "The Meaning of the Animal Rite in Genesis 15." *Journal for the Study of the Old Testament* 6, no. 19:61–78.

Hauan, Michael James. 1986. "The Background and Meaning of Amos 5:17B." *The Harvard Theological Review* 79, no. 4:337–48.

Hauser, A. J. 1980. "Linguistic and Thematic Links Between Genesis 4:1–16 and Genesis 2–3." *Journal of the Evangelical Theological Society* 23:297–305.

Heck, Joel D. 1986. "Issachar: Slave or Freeman? (Gen 49:14–15)." *Journal of the Evangelical Theological Society* 29, no. 4:385–96.

Heiser, Michael S. 2015. *The Unseen Realm: Recovering the Supernatural Worldview of the Bible*. Bellingham, WA: Lexham.

Heltzer, M. 1998. "New Light from Emar on Genesis 31: The Theft of the Teraphim." In *"Und Mose schrieb dieses Lied auf": Studien zum Alten Testament und zum alten Orient: Festschrift für Oswald Loretz zur Vollendung seines 70. Lebensjahres mit Beiträgen von Freunden, Schülern und Kollegen*, edited by Oswald Loretz, Manfried Dietrich and Ingo Kottsieper, Alter Orient und Altes Testament, 357–62. Münster: Ugarit-Verlag.

Helyer, Larry R. 1983. "The Separation of Abram and Lot: Its Significance in the Patriarchal Narratives." *Journal for the Study of the Old Testament* 8, no. 26:77–88.

Hess, Richard S. 1989. "The Genealogies of Genesis 1–11 and Comparative Literature." *Biblica* 70, no. 2:241–54.

_____. 1991. "Lamech in the Genealogies of Genesis." *Bulletin for Biblical Research* 1:21–25.

_____. 2007. *Israelite Religions: An Archaeological and Biblical Survey*. Grand Rapids: Baker Academic.

_____. 2009. *Studies in the Personal Names of Genesis 1–11*. Winona Lake, IN: Eisenbrauns.

Hoffmeier, James K. 1992. "The Wives' Tales of Genesis 12, 20 and 26 and the Covenants at Beer-Sheba." *Tyndale Bulletin* 43, no. 1:81–99.

_____. 1997. *Israel in Egypt: The Evidence for the Authenticity of the Exodus Tradition*. New York: Oxford University Press.

_____. 2007. "What is the Biblical Date for the Exodus?: A Response to Bryant Wood." *Journal of the Evangelical Theological Society* 50, no. 2:225–47.

Hom, Mary Katherine. 2010. "'. . . A Mighty Hunter Before YHWH': Genesis 10:9 and the Moral-Theological Evaluation of Nimrod." *Vetus Testamentum* 60, no. 1:63–68.

Hoop, R. de. 1997. "The Meaning of pḥz* in Classical Hebrew." *Zeitschrift für Althebraistik* 10, no. 1:16–26.

_____. 1999. *Genesis 49 in its Literary and Historical Context*. Oudtestamentische Studiën 39. Leiden: Brill.

Humphreys, W. Lee. 1988. *Joseph and His Family: A Literary Study*. Studies on Personalities of the Old Testament. Columbia: University of South Carolina Press.

Hurowitz, Victor Avigdor. 2000. "Who Lost an Earring? Genesis 35:4 Reconsidered." *The Catholic Biblical Quarterly* 62, no. 1:28–32.

Hyman, Ronald T. 2000. "Final Judgment: The Ambiguous Moral Question That Culminates Genesis 34." *Jewish Bible Quarterly* 28, no. 2:93–101.

Imes, Carmen Joy. 2023. *Being God's Image: Why Creation Still Matters*. Downers Grove, IL: IVP Academic.

Isaksson, Bo. 2014. "Clause Linking Strategies in the Narrative and Instructional Discourse of Joseph's Speech in Gen. 45:3–15." *Journal of Semitic Studies* 59, no. (1):15–45.

Jacobsen, Thorkild. 2003. "Eridu Genesis (1.158)." In *Context of Scripture*, edited by William W. Hallo and K. Lawson Younger, 513–15. Leiden; Boston: Brill.

Jagendorf, Zvi. 1984. "'In the Morning, Behold, it Was Leah': Genesis and the Reversal of Sexual Knowledge." *Prooftexts* 4, no. 2:187–92.

Jenni, Ernst, and Claus Westermann. 1997. *Theological Lexicon of the Old Testament*. Peabody, MA: Hendrickson.

Joseph, Alison L. 2016. "Understanding Genesis 34:2: 'Innâ.'" *Vetus Testamentum* 66, no. 4:663–68.

Josephus, Flavius. 1988. *The Works of Josephus: Complete and Unabridged*. Translated by William Whiston. New updated ed. Peabody, MA: Hendrickson.

Joüon, Paul, and T. Muraoka. 1993. *A Grammar of Biblical Hebrew*. Subsidia Biblica 14. Rome: Editrice Pontificio Istituto Biblico.

Kaiser, Walter C., Jr. 1978. *Toward an Old Testament Theology*. Grand Rapids: Zondervan.

_____. 1981. "The Promised Land: A Biblical-Historical View." *Bibliotheca Sacra* 138, no. 552:302–12.

Kidner, Derek. 1967. *Genesis: An Introduction and Commentary*. Tyndale Old Testament Commentaries. Downers Grove, IL: InterVarsity Press.

Kikawada, Isaac M. 1974. "The Shape of Genesis 11:1–9." In *Rhetorical Criticism: Essays in Honor of James Muilenburg*, edited by James Muilenburg, Jared Judd Jackson and Martin Kessler, Pittsburgh Theological Monograph Series, 18–32. Eugene, OR: Pickwick.

Kikawada, Isaac M., and Arthur Quinn. 1985. *Before Abraham Was: The Unity of Genesis 1–11*. Nashville: Abingdon.

Kim, Dohyung. 2012. "The Structure of Genesis 38: A Thematic Reading." *Vetus Testamentum* 62, no. 4:550–60.

King, Philip J., and Lawrence E. Stager. 2001. *Life in Biblical Israel*. Library of Ancient Israel. Louisville: Westminster John Knox.

Kitchen, Kenneth A. 1957. "The Term nšq in Genesis 41:40." *The Expository Times* 69, no. 1:30–30.

_____. 2003. *On the Reliability of the Old Testament*. Grand Rapids: Eerdmans.

Knoppers, Gary N. 1996. "Ancient Near Eastern Royal Grants and the Davidic Covenant: A Parallel?" *Journal of the American Oriental Society* 116, no. 4:670–97.

Koenen, Klaus. 1988. "Wer Sieht Wen? Zur Textgeschichte Von Genesis Xvi 131." *Vetus Testamentum* 38, no. 4:468–74.

Köhler, Ludwig, and Walter Baumgartner. 2000. *The Hebrew and Aramaic Lexicon of the Old Testament*. Edited by Johann Jakob Stamm. Translated by M. E. J. Richardson. Leiden: Brill.

Kreider, Glenn R. 2014. "The Flood Is as Bad as It Gets: Never Again Will God Destroy the Earth." *Bibliotheca Sacra* 171, no. 684:418–39.

Kruschwitz, Jonathan. 2012. "The Type-Scene Connection between Genesis 38 and the Joseph Story." *Journal for the Study of the Old Testament* 36, no. 4:383–410.

Kuruvilla, Abraham. 2014. *Genesis: A Theological Commentary for Preachers*. Eugene, OR: Resource Publications.

Labuschagne, C. J. 1989. "The Life Spans of the Patriarchs." *Oudtestamentische Studiën* 25:121–27.

Lambdin, Thomas O. 1971. *Introduction to Biblical Hebrew*. New York: Scribner's Sons.

Lawlor, John I. 1980. "The Test of Abraham: Genesis 22:1–19." *Grace Theological Journal* 1, no. 1:19–35.

Lee, Chee-Chiew. 2009. "גוים in Genesis 35:11 and the Abrahamic Promise of Blessings for the Nations." *Journal of the Evangelical Theological Society* 52, no. 3:467–82.

_____. 2012. "Once Again: The Niphal and the Hithpael of ברך in the Abrahamic Blessing for the Nations." *Journal for the Study of the Old Testament* 36, no. 3:279–96.

Lehmann, Manfred R. 1969. "Biblical Oaths." *Zeitschrift für die alttestamentliche Wissenschaft* 81 (1): 74–92. https://doi.org/10.1515/zatw.1969.81.1.74

Leviant, C. 1999. "Parallel Lives: The Trials and Traumas of Isaac and Ishmael." *Bible Review* 15, no. 2:20.

Lichtheim, Miriam. 1973. *Ancient Egyptian Literature: a Book of Readings*. Vol. 1. Berkeley: University of California Press.

Lindvall, Michael. 2013. "Between Text and Sermon: Genesis 45:1–11, 15." *Interpretation* 67, no. 3:281–83.

Longacre, Robert E. 1986. "Who Sold Joseph into Egypt?" In *Interpretation & History: Essays in Honour of Allan A. MacRae*, edited by Allan A. MacRae, R. Laird Harris,

Swee-Hwa Quek, and J. Robert Vannoy, 75–91. Singapore: Christian Life Publishers.

_____. 1989. *Joseph: A Story of Divine Providence, a Text Theoretical and Textlinguistic Analysis of Genesis 37 and 39–48*. Winona Lake, IN: Eisenbrauns.

_____. 1994. "Weqatal Forms in Biblical Hebrew Prose: A Discourse-Modular Approach." In *Biblical Hebrew and Discourse Linguistics*, edited by Robert D. Bergen, 50–98. Dallas: Summer Institute of Linguistics; Winona Lake, IN: Eisenbrauns.

Longman, Tremper, III, John H. Walton, and Stephen O. Moshier. 2018. *The Lost World of the Flood: Mythology, Theology, and the Deluge Debate*. Downers Grove, IL: IVP Academic.

Louw, J. P., and Eugene A. Nida. 1989. *Greek-English Lexicon of the New Testament: Based on Semantic Domains*. 2nd ed. New York: United Bible Societies.

Lowery, Daniel DeWitt. 2013. *Toward a Poetics of Genesis 1–11: Reading Genesis 4:17–22 in its Near Eastern Context*. Bulletin for Biblical Research Supplements 7. Winona Lake, IN: Eisenbrauns.

Lunn, Nicholas P. 2008. "The Last Words of Jacob and Joseph: A Rhetorico-Structural Analysis of Genesis 49:29–33 and 50:24–26." *Tyndale Bulletin* 59, no. 2:161–79.

Mabee, Charles. 1980. "Jacob and Laban." *Vetus Testamentum* 30, no. 2:192–207.

Malul, Meir. 1996. "'Āqēb 'Heel' and 'Āqab 'to Supplant' and the Concept of Succession in the Jacob-Esau Narratives." *Vetus Testamentum* 46, no. 2:190–212.

Marcus, David. 1990. "'Lifting Up the Head': On the Trail of a Word Play in Genesis 40." *Prooftexts* 10, no. 1:17–27.

Mason, Steven D. 2007. "Another Flood? Genesis 9 and Isaiah's Broken Eternal Covenant." *Journal for the Study of the Old Testament* 32, no. 2:177–98.

Mathews, Kenneth A. 1996. *Genesis 1–11:26*. The New American Commentary 1A. Nashville: Broadman & Holman.

_____. 2005. *Genesis 11:27–50:26*. The New American Commentary 1B. Nashville: Broadman & Holman.

Mathewson, Steven D. 2021. *The Art of Preaching Old Testament Narrative*. Grand Rapids: Baker Academic.

Maxwell, David R. 2007. "Justified by Works and Not by Faith Alone: Reconciling Paul and James." *Concordia Journal* 33, no. 4:375–78.

McCarthy, Dennis J. 1981. *Treaty and Covenant: A Study in Form in the Ancient Oriental Documents and in the Old Testament*. Rev. ed. Analecta Biblica 21a. Rome: Biblical Institute.

McCartney, Dan. 2009. *James*. Baker Exegetical Commentary on the New Testament. Grand Rapids: Baker Academic.

McDowell, Catherine L. 2015. *The Image of God in the Garden of Eden: The Creation of Humankind in Genesis 2:5–3:24 in Light of the mis pî pit pî and wpt-r rituals of Mesopotamia and Ancient Egypt*. Siphrut: Literature and Theology of the Hebrew Scriptures 15. Winona Lake, IN: Eisenbrauns.

McEvenue, Sean E. 1971. *The Narrative Style of the Priestly Writer*. Analecta biblica 50. Rome: Biblical Institute Press.

McKenzie, Brian A. 1983. "Jacob's Blessing on Pharaoh: An Interpretation of Gen 46:31–47:26." *The Westminster Theological Journal* 45, no. 2:386–99.

Mendelsohn, Isaac. 1959. "A Ugaritic Parallel to the Adoption of Ephraim and Manasseh." *Israel Exploration Journal* 9, no. 3:180–83.

Michael, Matthew. 2018. "The Dead Trickster and his Shrewd Children?: The Persuasive Use of the Double Quotations of a Dead Patriarch in Genesis 49:29–50:21." *Journal for the Study of the Old Testament* 43, no. 2:179–90.

Millard, A. R. 1974. "Meaning of the Name Judah." *Zeitschrift für die Alttestamentliche Wissenschaft* 86, no. 2:216–18.

Miller, Johnny V., and John M. Soden. 2012. *In the Beginning . . . We Misunderstood: Interpreting Genesis 1 in Its Original Context*. Grand Rapids: Kregel.

Moberly, R. W. L. 1983. *At the Mountain of God: Story and Theology in Exodus 32–34*. Journal for the Study of the Old Testament Supplements. Sheffield: Sheffield Academic.

_____. 1988. "The Earliest Commentary on the Akedah." *Vetus Testamentum* 38, no. 3:302–23.

_____. 1992. *Genesis 12–50*. Sheffield: JSOT Press.

Moran, William L. 1959. "The Scandal of the 'Great Sin' at Ugarit." *Journal of Near Eastern Studies* 18, no. 4:280–81.

_____. 1992. *The Amarna Letters*. English-language ed. Baltimore: Johns Hopkins University Press.

Morenz, Siegfried. 1992. *Egyptian Religion*. Ithaca, NY: Cornell University Press.

Morrison, Martha A. 1981. "Evidence for Herdsmen and Animal Husbandry in the Nuzi Documents." In *Studies on the Civilization and Culture of Nuzi and Hurrians*, edited by Martha A. Morrison and David I. Owen, 257–96. Winona Lake, IN: Eisenbrauns.

_____. 1983. "The Jacob and Laban Narrative in Light of Near Eastern Sources." *The Biblical Archaeologist* 46, no. 3:155–64.

Morschauser, Scott. 2003. "'Hospitality,' Hostiles and Hostages: On the Legal Background to Genesis 19.1–9." *Journal for the Study of the Old Testament* 27, no. 4:461–85.

_____. 2013. "Campaigning on Less than a Shoe-String: An Ancient Egyptian Parallel to Abram's 'Oath' in Genesis 14.22–13." *Journal for the Study of the Old Testament* 38 (2): 127–144.

Moscati, Sabatino. 1964. *An Introduction to the Comparative Grammar of the Semitic Languages: Phonology and Morphology*. Porta Linguarum Orientalium. Neue Serie 6. Wiesbaden: Otto Harrassowitz.

Moyers, Bill. 1996. *Genesis: A Living Conversation*. New York: Doubleday.

Muffs, Yochanan. 1973. "Two Comparative Lexical Studies." *Journal of the Ancient Near Eastern Society* 5, no. 1:2158.

Nataf, Francis. 2012. "What's in a Name?: Ya'akov and/or Yisrael." *Jewish Bible Quarterly* 40, no. 4:241–46.

Noble, Paul R. 1996. "A 'Balanced' Reading of the Rape of Dinah: Some Exegetical and Methodological Observations." *Biblical Interpretation* 4, no. 2:173–204.

O'Callaghan, Martin. 1981. "The Structure and Meaning of Gen 38—Judah and Tamar." *Proceedings of the Irish Biblical Association* 5:72–97.

Odhiambo, Nicholas. 2013. "The Nature of Ham's Sin." *Bibliotheca Sacra* 170, no. 678:154–65.

Olojede, Funlola. 2016. "The 'First Deborah': Genesis 35:8 in the Literary and Theological Context." *Acta Theologica* 36, no. 1:133–51.

Ouro, Roberto. 2002. "The Garden of Eden Account: The Chiastic Structure of Genesis 2–3." *Andrews University Seminary Studies* 40, no. 2:219–43.

Parry, Robin. 2002. "Feminist Hermeneutics and Evangelical Concerns: The Rape of Dinah as a Case Study." *Tyndale Bulletin* 53, no. 1:1–28.

Parunak, H. Van Dyke. 1981. "Oral Typesetting: Some Uses of Biblical Structure." *Biblica* 62, no. 2:153–68.

Pehlke, Helmuth. 1985. "An Exegetical and Theological Study of Genesis 49:1–28." ThD diss., Dallas Theological Seminary.

Peleg, Yitzhak. 2006. "Was the Ancestress of Israel in Danger?: Did Pharaoh Touch (NG') Sarai?" *Zeitschrift für die Alttestamentliche Wissenschaft* 118, no. 2:197–208.

Petersen, David L. 1973. "Thrice-Told Tale: Genre, Theme, and Motif." *Biblical Research* 18:30–43.

Peterson, Ryan S. 2016. *The Imago Dei As Human Identity: A Theological Interpretation*. Journal of Theological Interpretation Supplements. Winona Lake, IN: Eisenbrauns.

Pickering, Jordan. 2014. "Divine Silence: The Significance of Structure in Genesis 12." *Scriptura* 113:1–13.

Postgate, J. N. 1975. "Some Old Babylonian Shepherds and Their Flocks." *Journal of Semitic Studies* 20, no. 1:1–21.

Pritchard, James B. 1969. *Ancient Near Eastern Texts Relating to the Old Testament*. 3rd ed. Princeton: Princeton University Press.

Rabinowitz, Jacob J. 1959. "The "Great Sin" in Ancient Egyptian Marriage Contracts." *Journal of Near Eastern Studies* 18, no. 1:73.

Rad, Gerhard von. 1972. *Genesis: A Commentary*. Translated by John H. Marks. Rev. ed. The Old Testament Library. Philadelphia: Westminster.

Redford, Donald B., ed. 2001. *The Oxford Encyclopedia of Ancient Egypt*. 3 vols. Oxford: Oxford University Press.

Reis, Pamela Tamarkin. 2000. "Hagar Requited." *Journal for the Study of the Old Testament* 25, no. 87:75–109.

Renate, Müller-Wollermann. 2015. "Crime and Punishment in Pharaonic Egypt." *Near Eastern Archaeology* 78, no. 4:228–35.

Rendsburg, Gary A. 1980. "Janus Parallelism in Gen 49:26." *Journal of Biblical Literature* 99, no. 2:291–93.

_____. 1992. "Notes on Genesis XV." *Vetus Testamentum* 42, no. 2:266–72.

_____. 2014. *The Redaction of Genesis*. Winona Lake, IN: Eisenbrauns.

_____. 2021. "Genesis 49:4: The Route of Facile Textual Emendation vs. Appreciation for Literary Brilliance." *Vetus Testamentum* 71, nos. 4–5:673–86.

Revell, E. J. 2001. "Midian and Ishmael in Genesis 37: Synonyms in the Joseph Story." In *The World of the Aramaeans. I. Biblical Studies in Honour of Paul Eugène Dion*, edited by P. M. Michèle Daviau, John William Wevers, Michael Weigl, and Paul-Eugène Dion, Journal for the Study of the Old Testament. Supplement 324, 70–91. Sheffield: Sheffield Academic.

Reviv, Hanoch. 1977. "Early Elements and Late Terminology in the Descriptions of Non-Israelite Cities in the Bible." *Israel Exploration Journal* 27, no. 4:189–96.

Rickett, Dan. 2011. "Rethinking the Place and Purpose of Genesis 13." *Journal for the Study of the Old Testament* 36, no. 1:31–53.

Riemann, Paul A. 1970. "Am I My Brother's Keeper?" *Interpretation* 24, no. 4:482–91.

Rogland, M. 2008. "Abram's Persistent Faith: Hebrew Verb Semantics in Genesis 15:6." *The Westminster TheologicalJjournal* 70, no. 2:239–44.

Ross, Allen P. 1980a. "Studies in the Book of Genesis, Part 1: The Curse of Canaan." *Bibliotheca Sacra* 137, no. 547:223–40.

_____. 1980b. "Studies in the Book of Genesis, Part 2: The Table of Nations in Genesis 10–Its Structure." *Bibliotheca Sacra* 137, no. 548:340–53.

_____. 1981. "Studies in the Book of Genesis, Part 3: The Table of Nations in Genesis 10–Its Content.*Bibliotheca Sacra* 138, no. 549:22–35.

_____. 1981. "Studies in the Book of Genesis, Part 4: The Dispersion of the Nations in Genesis 11:1–19." *Bibliotheca Sacra* 138, no. 550:119–38.

_____. 1985a. "Studies in the Life of Jacob, Part 1: Jacob's Vision: The Founding of Bethel." *Bibliotheca Sacra* 142, no. 567:224–37.

_____. 1985b. "Studies in the Life of Jacob, Part 2: Jacob at the Jabbok, Israel at Peniel." *Bibliotheca Sacra* 142, no. 568:338–54.

_____. 1988. *Creation and Blessing: A Guide to the Study and Exposition of the Book of Genesis*. Grand Rapids: Baker.

_____. 2008. "Genesis." In *Genesis, Exodus*. Vol. 1. *Cornerstone Biblical Commentary*, 20 vols, edited by Philip Wesley Comfort. Carol Stream, IL: Tyndale House.

Roth, Martha. 2000. "The Laws of Hammurabi (2.131)." In *Context of Scripture*, edited by William W. Hallo and K. Lawson Younger. Leiden; Boston: Brill.

Sailhamer, John H. 1990. "Genesis." In *Genesis–Numbers*, vol. 10 *The Expositor's Bible Commentary*, edited by Frank E. Gaebelein, 1–284. Grand Rapids: Zondervan.

Sarna, Nahum M. 1967. *Understanding Genesis*. Heritage of Biblical Israel 1. New York: Jewish Theological Seminary of America.

_____. 1989. *Genesis: The Traditional Hebrew Text with the New JPS Translation*. The JPS Torah Commentary. Philadelphia: Jewish Publication Society.

Sasson, Jack M. 1966. "Circumcision in the Ancient near East." *Journal of Biblical Literature* 85, no. 4:473–76.

_____. 1980. "The 'Tower of Babel' as a Clue to the Redactional Structuring of the Primeval History (Gen. 1–11:9)." In *The Bible World: Essays in Honor of Cyrus H. Gordon*, edited by Cyrus H. Gordon and Gary Rendsburg, 211–19. New York: Ktav.

Schimmel, Sol. 1988. "Joseph and His Brothers: A Paradigm for Repentance." *Judaism* 37, no. 1:60–65.

Schmutzer, A. J. 2007. "'All Those Going Out of the Gate of His City': Have the Translations Got It Yet?" *Bulletin for Biblical Research* 17, no. 1:37–52.

Schwartz, Sarah. 2016. "Narrative Toledot Formulae in Genesis: The Case of Heaven and Earth, Noah and Isaac." *The Journal of Hebrew Scriptures* 16 (2016), 1–36.

Shemesh, Yael. 2007. "Rape Is Rape: The Story of Dinah and Shechem (Genesis 34)." *Zeitschrift für die Alttestamentliche Wissenschaft* 119, no. 1:2–21.

Sherwood, Stephen K. 1990. *Had God Not Been on My Side: An Examination of the Narrative Technique on the Story of Jacob and Laban, Genesis 29,1–32,2*. Europäische Hochschulschriften. Reihe XXIII, Theologie Bd. 400. Frankfurt am Main: Lang.

Shetter, Tony L. 2019. "The Promissory and Obligatory Elements of the Abrahamic Covenant in the Light of Alalah Texts 1 and 456." PhD diss., Dallas Theological Seminary.

Silberman, Lou H. 1983. "Listening to the Text." *Journal of Biblical Literature* 102, no. 1:3–26.

Simon, Uriel. 2003. *Joseph and His Brothers: Perspectives On Jewish Leadership II*. Ramat Gan: Lookstein Center.

Ska, Jean Louis. 1988. "Gn 22:1–19: Essai sur les Niveaux de Lecture." *Biblica* 69, no. 3:324–39.

_____. 2013. "Genesis 22: What Question Should We Ask the Text?" *Biblica* 94, no. 2:257–67.

Smith, Craig A. 2001. "Reinstating Isaac: the Centrality of Abraham's Son in the 'Jacob-Esau' Narrative of Genesis 27." *Biblical Theology Bulletin* 31, no. 4:130–34.

Smith, James K. A. 2019. *On the Road with St. Augustine: A Real-World Spirituality for Restless Hearts*. Grand Rapids: Brazos.

Soden, John M. 2015. "From the Dust: Creating Adam in Historical Context." *Bibliotheca Sacra* 172, no. 685:45–66.

Spanier, Ktziah. 1992. "Rachel's Theft of the Teraphim: Her Struggle for Family Primacy." *Vetus Testamentum* 42, no. 3:404–12.

Speiser, E. A. 1956. "'Coming' and 'Going' at the "City" Gate." *Bulletin of the American Schools of Oriental Research* 144:20–23.

_____. 1964. *Genesis: Introduction, Translation, and Notes*. 2nd ed. The Anchor Bible 1. New York: Doubleday.

Spero, Shubert. 2018. “The Role of Destiny in the Joseph Story.” *Jewish Bible Quarterly* 46, no. 2:109–16.

Stein, Michael Alan. 2009. “Interpreting b-r-kh in Genesis 47.” *Jewish Bible Quarterly* 37, no. 3:175–80.

Steinberg, Naomi. 1994. “Kinship and Gender in Genesis.” *Biblical Research* 39:46–56.

Steiner, Richard C. 2010. “Poetic Forms in the Masoretic Vocalization and Three Difficult Phrases in Jacob’s Blessing: יֶתֶר שְׂאֵת (Gen 49:3), יְצוּעִי עָלָה (49:4), and יָבֹא שִׁילֹה (49:10).” *Journal of Biblical Literature* 129, no. 2:209–35.

Steinmann, Andrew E. 2017. “Gaps in the Genealogies in Genesis 5 and 11?” *Bibliotheca Sacra* 174, no. 694:141–58.

_____. 2019. *Genesis: An Introduction and Commentary*. Tyndale Old Testament Commentaries 1. Downers Grove, IL: IVP Academic.

Sternberg, Meir. 1987. *The Poetics of Biblical Narrative: Ideological Literature and the Drama of Reading*. Indiana Studies in Biblical Literature. Bloomington: Indiana University Press.

_____. 1991. “Double Cave, Double Talk: The Indirections of Biblical Dialogue.” In *Not in Heaven: Coherence and Complexity in Biblical Narrative*, edited by Jason Philip Rosenblatt and Joseph C. Sitterson, Indiana Studies in Biblical Literature, 28–57. Bloomington: Indiana University Press.

Stigers, Harold G. 1976. *A Commentary on Genesis*. Grand Rapids: Zondervan.

Stordalen, Terje. 1992. “Man, Soil, Garden: Basic Plot in Genesis 2–3 Reconsidered.” *Journal for the Study of the Old Testament* 17, no. 53:3–25.

Swenson, Kristin M. 2008. “Crowned with Blessings: The Riches of Double-Meaning in Gen 49,26b.” *Zeitschrift für die Alttestamentliche Wissenschaft* 120, no. 3:422–25.

Tal, Avraham. 2015. *Genesis. Biblia Hebraica Quinta*. Stuttgart: Deutsche Bibelgesellschaft.

Teeter, Emily. 2002. “Animals in Egyptian Literature.” In *A History of the Animal World in the Ancient Near East*, edited by Billie Jean Collins, 251–70. Leiden: Brill.

Terino, Jonathan. 1988. “A Text Linguistic Study of the Jacob Narrative.” *Vox Evangelica* 18:45–62.

Thiselton, Anthony C. 1974. “The Supposed Power of Words in the Biblical Writings.” *The Journal of Theological Studies* 25, no. 2:283–99.

Thomas, David Winton. 1953. “Consideration of Some Unusual Ways of Expressing the Superlative in Hebrew.” *Vetus Testamentum* 3, no. 3:209–24.

Toorn, Karel van der. 1990. “The Nature of the Biblical Teraphim in the Light of the Cuneiform Evidence.” *The Catholic Biblical Quarterly* 52, no.2:203–22.

Toorn, Karel van der, and Sara J. Denning-Bolle. 1994. *From Her Cradle to Her Grave: the Role of Religion in the Life of the Israelite and the Babylonian Woman*. Sheffield: JSOT Press.

Tsumura, David Toshio. 1989. *The Earth and the Waters in Genesis 1 and 2: A Linguistic Investigation*. Sheffield: Sheffield Academic.

_____. 2005. *Creation and Destruction: A Reappraisal of the Chaoskampf Theory in the Old Testament*. Winona Lake, IN: Eisenbrauns.

Turner, Laurence A. 1993. “The Rainbow as the Sign of the Covenant in Genesis ix 11–13.” *Vetus Testamentum* 43, no. 1:119–24.

Twersky, Geula. 2019. “Genesis 49: The Foundation of Israelite Monarchy and Priesthood.” *Journal for the Study of the Old Testament* 43, no. 3:317–33.

VanGemeren, Willem. 1997. *New International Dictionary of Old Testament Theology and Exegesis*. Grand Rapids: Zondervan.

Van Seters, John. 1969. "Jacob's Marriages and Ancient Near East Customs: A Re-Examination." *Harvard Theological Review* 62, no. 4:377–95.

Vaux, Roland de. 1965. *Ancient Israel*. New York: McGraw-Hill.

Wagner, Angela B. 2013. "Considerations on the Politico-Juridical Proceedings of Genesis 34." *Journal for the Study of the Old Testament* 38, no. 2:145–61.

Walsh, Jerome T. 1977. "Genesis 2:4b–3:24: A Synchronic Approach." *Journal of Biblical Literature* 96, no. 2:161–77.

Waltke, Bruce K. 1975. "The Creation Account in Genesis 1:1–3." *Bibliotheca Sacra* 132:25–36, 136–44, 216–28.

_____. 1976. "The Creation Account in Genesis 1:1–3." *Bibliotheca Sacra* 133:28–41.

_____. 1986. "Cain and His Offering." *The Westminster Theological Journal* 48, no. 2:363–72.

Waltke, Bruce K., and Cathi J. Fredricks. 2001. *Genesis: A Commentary*. Grand Rapids: Zondervan.

Waltke, Bruce K., and Michael Patrick O'Connor. 1990. *An Introduction to Biblical Hebrew Syntax*. Winona Lake, IN: Eisenbrauns.

Walton, John H. 2001. *Genesis: From Biblical Text . . . to Contemporary Life*. The NIV Application Commentary. Grand Rapids: Zondervan.

_____. 2009a. "Genesis." In *Zondervan Illustrated Bible Backgrounds Commentary*, edited by John H. Walton. Grand Rapids: Zondervan.

_____. 2009b. *The Lost World of Genesis One: Ancient Cosmology and the Origins Debate*. Downers Grove, IL: IVP Academic.

Walton, John H., Victor H. Matthews, and Mark W. Chavalas. 1997. *The IVP Bible Background Commentary: Genesis–Deuteronomy*. Downers Grove, IL: InterVarsity Press.

Walton, Kevin Anthony, and R. W. L. Moberly. 2003. *Thou Traveller Unknown: the Presence and Absence of God in the Jacob Narrative*. Paternoster Biblical and Theological Monographs. Carlisle: Paternoster.

Watanabe, Chikako E. 2002. *Animal Symbolism in Mesopotamia: A Contextual Approach*. Wiener Offene Orientalistik 1. Wien: Institut für Orientalistik der Universität Vienna.

Webb, Barry G. 1987. *The Book of the Judges: An Integrated Reading*. Sheffield: JSOT Press.

Webb, Barry G., and R. Kent Hughes. 2015. *Judges and Ruth: God in Chaos*. Wheaton, IL: Crossway.

Weinfeld, Moshe. 1970. "The Covenant of Grant in the Old Testament and in the Ancient Near East." *Journal of the American Oriental Society* 90, no. 2:184–203.

_____. 1993. *The Promise of the Land: The Inheritance of the Land of Canaan by the Israelites*. Berkeley: University of California Press.

Wells, Bruce. 2011. "First Wives Club: Divorce, Demotion, and the Fate of Leah in Genesis 29." *Maarav* 18 (1–2): 101–129.

_____. 2015. "Sex Crimes in the Laws of the Hebrew Bible." *Near Eastern Archaeology* 78, no. 4:294–300.

Wenham, Gordon J. 1978. "The Coherence of the Flood Narrative." *Vetus Testamentum* 28, no. 3:336–48.

_____. 1982. "The Symbolism of the Animal Rite in Genesis 15: A Response To G. F. Hasel, JSOT 19 (1981) 61–78." *Journal for the Study of the Old Testament* 7, no. 22:134–37.

_____. 1987. *Genesis 1–15*. Word Biblical Commentary 1. Dallas: Word.

_____. 1991. "The Old Testament Attitude to Homosexuality." *The Expository Times* 102, no. 12:359–63.

_____. 1994. *Genesis. 16–50*. Word Biblical Commentary 2. Dallas: Word.

Wessner, Mark D. 2000. "Toward a Literary Understanding of 'Face to Face' (panim 'el-panim) in Genesis 32:23–32." *Restoration Quarterly* 42, no. 3:169–77.

Westbrook, Raymond. 1971. "Purchase of the Cave of Machpelah." *Israel Law Review* 6, no. 1:29–38.

_____. 1991. *Property and the Family in Biblical Law*. Sheffield: JSOT Press.

Westermann, Claus. 1994. *A Continental Commentary: Genesis 1–11*. Minneapolis: Fortress.

_____. 1995. *A Continental Commentary: Genesis 12–36*. Minneapolis: Fortress.

_____. 2002. *A Continental Commentary: Genesis 37–50*. Minneapolis: Fortress.

Wilder, William N. 2006. "Illumination and Investiture: The Royal Significance of the Tree of Wisdom in Genesis 3." *The Westminster Theological Journal* 68, no. 1:51–69.

Wilkinson, Richard H. 2003. *The Complete Gods and Goddesses of Ancient Egypt*. New York: Thames & Hudson.

Williams, Wilbur Glenn. 2004. *Genesis: A Bible Commentary in the Wesleyan Tradition*. Wesleyan Bible Commentary Series. Indianapolis: Wesleyan Publishing House.

Wilson, John A. 1948. "The Oath in Ancient Egypt." *Journal of Near Eastern Studies* 7, no. 3:129–56.

Wilson, Stephen M. 2017. "Blood Vengeance and the Imago Dei in the Flood Narrative (Genesis 9:6)." *Interpretation* 71, no. 3:263–73.

Wolde, Ellen J. van. 1995. "Telling and Retelling: the Words of the Servant in Genesis 24." In *Synchronic or Diachronic? A Debate on Method in Old Testament Exegesis: Papers Read at the Ninth Joint Meeting of Het Oudtestamentisch Werkgezelschap in Nederland en Belgie and the Society for Old Testament Study, Held at Kampen 1994*, edited by Johannes C. de Moor, 227–244. Leiden: Brill.

_____. 2002. "Does 'innâ Denote Rape?: A Semantic Analysis of a Controversial Word." *Vetus Testamentum* 52, no. 4:528–44.

Wood, Alice. 2008. *Of Wings and Wheels: A Synthetic Study of the Biblical Cherubim*. Beihefte Zur Zeitschrift Für Die Alttestamentliche Wissenschaft. Berlin: de Gruyter.

Wood, Bryant G. 2007. "The Biblical Date for the Exodus is 1446 B.C: A Response to James Hoffmeier." *Journal of the Evangelical Theological Society* 50, no. 2:249–58.

Wright, Rebecca Abts. 2001. "The Impossible Commandment." *Anglican Theological Review* 83, no. 3:579–84.

Wünch, Hans-Georg. 2012. "Genesis 38—Judah's Turning Point: Structural Analysis and Narrative Techniques and Their Meaning for Genesis 38 and Its Placement in the Story of Joseph." *Old Testament Essays* 25, no. 3:777–806.

Younger, K. Lawson, Jr. 1995. "The Configuring of Judicial Preliminaries: Judges 1.1–2.5 and Its Dependence on the Book of Joshua." *Journal for the Study of the Old Testament* 20, no. 68:75–92.

Zucker, David J. 2018. "Abraham, the Years of Frustration: Genesis 13–14 and 15 as a Literary Unit." *Biblical Theology Bulletin* 48, no. 1:3–9.